THE LETTERS OF
T. S. ELIOT
VOLUME 8

# THE LETTERS OF
# T. S. Eliot

EDITED BY

## VALERIE ELIOT

AND

## JOHN HAFFENDEN

## VOLUME 8
## 1936–1938

**ff**

FABER & FABER

First published in 2019
by Faber & Faber Ltd, Bloomsbury House,
74–77 Great Russell Street, London WC1B 3DA

Typeset by Donald Sommerville
Printed in England by T. J. International,
Padstow, Cornwall

A CIP record for this book is available from the British Library

ISBN 978–0–571–31638–0

For letters omitted from this and the previous volumes of T. S. Eliot's correspondence,
please visit www.tseliot.com

2 4 6 8 10 9 7 5 3 1

# CONTENTS

# ILLUSTRATIONS

*Cover:* TSE sailing with his godson Tom Faber (detail), *c.* 1937. Photographer unknown. *Courtesy Estate of T. S. Eliot*

1. TSE reading his poems at the Shakespeare & Company bookshop, Paris, June 1936. Photograph by Gisèle Freund. *Photo Gisèle Freund/IMEC/Fonds MCC*

2. Eliot's handprint, from Charlotte Wolff, *Studies in Hand-Reading*, 1936. *Wellcome Library, London, licensed under CC BY 4.0*

3. TSE seated on the porch in Randolph, New Hampshire, 1936. Photograph by Henry Eliot. *MS (154), 7b, Houghton Library, Harvard University Library, Cambridge, MA*

4. TSE and Emily Hale at Woods Hole, Massachusetts, September 1936. Photographer unidentified. *Courtesy Ella Strong Denison Library, Scripps College, Claremont, CA*

5. Paul Elmer More, 1937. Photographer unknown. *Seeley G. Mudd Manuscript Library, Princeton University, NJ*

6. Elizabeth Bowen, 25 July 1939. Photograph by Bassano Ltd. *© National Portrait Gallery, London, x127602*

7. TSE and the son of Count Michael de la Bédoyère, accompanying the review by G. M. Turnell, 'Eliot, A Great Poet To-day: But Whither Is He Proceeding?', *Catholic Herald*, 10 July 1936, 4. *The British Library, London*

8. Emily Hale with her dog Boerre, 1939. Photographer unidentified. *Courtesy Ella Strong Denison Library, Scripps College, Claremont, CA*

9. Djuna Barnes, 29 November 1939. Photograph by Carl Van Vechten. *Yale Collection of American Literature, Beinecke Rare Book and Manuscript Library, New Haven, Za V375; © Van Vechten Trust*

10. Brother George Every at the Society of the Sacred Mission, Kelham, 1937–8. Photographer unknown. *Borthwick Institute, University of York, Heslington*

11. Djuna Barnes, *Nightwood*, London: Faber & Faber, 1936. *Courtesy James S. Jaffe Rare Books, Salisbury, CT*

# ACKNOWLEDGEMENTS

For help and advice in many capacities, including copyright permissions, the publishers and editors would like to thank the following individuals and institutions. (Sadly, a number of those named below are now deceased, but we wish still to put on record our gratitude to them.) Dr Donald Adamson; Barry Ahearn; Ruth M. (Beth) Alvarez; The American Jewish Archives, Cincinnati, Ohio; Dr Norma Aubertin-Potter; Camilla Bagg; Buona Barnes; Librarian in Charge, Codrington Library, All Souls College, Oxford; BBC Written Archives Centre; Joan Bailey; Ruth Baker; Susan Bank, Secretary to Revd Carl Scovel, Minister, King's Chapel, Boston, Massachusetts; Owen Barfield; Tansy Barton, Special Collections Administrator, Senate House Library, University of London; H. Baugh; Denison Beach; T. O. Beachcroft; Anne Olivier Bell; Mrs W. J. Bender; Joanne Bentley; Robert J. Bertholf, Curator, The Poetry/Rare Books Collection, University Libraries, State University of New York at Buffalo; Bibliothèque Nationale, Paris; Kevin Birmingham; Kenneth Blackwell, Mills Memorial Library, McMaster University; Michael Harry Blechner, McFarlin Library, University of Tulsa; Nathalie Blondel; Mary Boccaccio, McKeldin Library, University of Maryland; Maxwell Bodenheim; John Bodley; William H. Bond; University of Bonn Library; J. M. L. Booker, Archivist, Lloyds Bank; Michael Borrie, Manuscript Collections, British Library; Ann Bowden, Harry Ransom Humanities Research Center, University of Texas at Austin; David Bradshaw; The British Library; Valerie Brokenshire; Jewel Spears Brooker; Robert Brown, Archivist, Faber & Faber Ltd; Sally Brown; Richard Buckle; Penelope Bulloch, Balliol College Library; Dr R. W. Burchfield; Roland Burke Savage, SJ, Clongowes Wood College; Professor P. H. Butter; William R. Cagle and Saundra Taylor, Lilly Library; Herbert Cahoon, The Pierpont Morgan Library; Anne Caiger, Manuscripts Librarian, University of California, Los Angeles; Douglas Campbell; Kathleen Cann, Department of Manuscripts and University Archives, Cambridge University Library; Humphrey Carpenter; Judith Champ, St Mary's College, Oscott; François Chapon, Bibliotheque Littéraire Jacques Doucet; Mrs Charlton; Christopher M. Cherry; Joseph Chiari; Mary Clapinson, Keeper of Western Manuscripts, Bodleian Library; Alexander P. Clark, Firestone

Library, Princeton University; Alan Clodd; Marguerite Cohn; Dorothy Collins; Henri Colliot, Fondation Saint-John Perse; John Constable; Alistair Cooke; Bonnie Costello; Fiona Courage and Karen Watson, Special Collections, The Library, University of Sussex; Joyce Crick; Peter Croft; Arthur Crook; Tanya Crothers; Tony Cuda; Charles T. Cullen, President and Librarian, The Newberry Library; Rexi Culpin; Helen Davies, Librarian, Royal Central School of Speech and Drama; Dr Robin Darwall-Smith, Archivist, University College, Oxford; Roy L. Davids; Carolyn A. Davis, Reader Services Librarian, The George Arents Research Library for Special Collections, Syracuse University Library; Nigel A. L. Davis; Dr A. Deiss, General Secretariat, Swiss Medical Institutions; Giles de la Mare; the Literary Trustees of Walter de la Mare; Rodney G. Dennis; Herbert Dieckmann; Valentine Dobrée; E. R. Dodds; David Doughan, Fawcett Library; Kenneth W. Duckett, Curator, Morris Library, Southern Illinois University; Ellen S. Dunlap, Harry Ransom Humanities Research Center; Jackie DuPont; Peter du Sautoy; Donald D. Eddy, Department of Rare Books, Cornell University Library; Professor Charles W. Eliot; William G. Eliot III; Sarah Ethier, University of Wisconsin-Milwaukee Libraries; Matthew Evans; Sir Richard Faber, KCVO; Toby Faber; Tom Faber; Elizabeth A. Falsey; Patricia Fanshawe; Christopher Farley; David Farmer, Harry Ransom Humanities Research Center (and Warren Roberts, Mary Hirth, Sally Leach, and many other members of staff); Donald Farren, University of Maryland Libraries; Barbara Fehse, Secretary in Manuscripts, University of Virginia Library; Anton Felton, Continuum Ltd; Dominique Fernandez; James Fergusson Books and Manuscripts; Mrs Harry Fine; Mrs Burnham Finney; Christopher Fletcher; Graham Fletcher; Barbara Floyd, Director of the Ward M. Canaday for Special Collections, University of Toledo; Angel Flores; Henri Fluchère; Fondren Library; Jennifer Formichelli; Robert Fraser; Donald Gallup; Special Collections, Isabella Stewart Gardner Museum, Boston, Mass.; K. C. Gay, Lockwood Memorial Library, State University of New York, Buffalo; Herbert Gerwing, University of Victoria; Mrs Ghika; Catherine Gide; M. A. M. Gilbert; Vincent Giroud, Beinecke Rare Book and Manuscript Library; Robert Giroux; Dr Peter Godman; Emile Goichot; Estate of Enid Goldsmith; Adrian M. Goodman; Philip Goodman; Christian Goodwillie, Director and Curator, Special Collections, Burke Library, Hamilton College, Clinton, New York; Lyndall Gordon; Warwick Gould; Gerald Graham; Nicollette Gray; Herbert T. Greene; Ernest G. Griffin; Maurice Haigh-Wood; J. C. Hall; Dr Michael Halls; Sarah Hamilton; Saskia Hamilton; Bonnie Hardwick, Manuscripts Division, The Bancroft Library,

University of California, Berkeley; P. Allen Hargis; Mrs A. J. Harris; Sir Rupert Hart-Davis; Harvard University Archives; Professor E. N. Hartley, Institute Archives, MIT; Michael Hastings; The Library, Haverford College; Lilace Hatayama, Manuscripts Division, University Research Library, University of California; A. Desmond Hawkins; Cathy Henderson, Research Librarian, Harry Ransom Humanities Research Center; Robert Henderson; David Higham Associates Ltd; Roger Highfield; Robert W. Hill, New York Public Library; Aurelia Bolliger Hodgson; Michael Hofmann; Michael Holroyd; Hornbake Library, University of Maryland (Beth Alvarez, Ann L. Hudak); Lélia Howard; Penelope Hughes-Hallett; J. W. Hunt, Royal Military Academy, Sandhurst; Jeremy Hutchinson; Lord Hutchinson; Juliette Huxley; Elizabeth Inglis (Special Collections, The Library, University of Sussex); Carol Jackson, Chipping Campden History Society; Ian Jackson; Robin Jackson, The British Academy; William A. Jackson, Houghton Library; Carolyn Jakeman; P. D. James; Revd Martin Jarrett-Kerr, CR; Dorothy O. Johansen, Reed College, Portland, Oregon; Gregory A. Johnson, Alderman Library, University of Virginia; William Jovanovich; William L. Joyce, Princeton University Library; Michael Kammen; Paul Keegan; Ann M. Kenne, Head of Special Collections Department/University Archivist, University of St Thomas, St Paul, Minnesota; Professor John Kelly; Dr Paul Kelly, National Library of Scotland; Ann Kenne, University of St Thomas; Mary Kiffer, Assistant Secretary, John Simon Guggenheim Memorial Foundation, New York; Modern Archives Centre, King's College, Cambridge; Monique Kuntz, Bibliothèque Municipale, Vichy; Dr L. R. Leavis; Kathy Lee; Major N. Aylward Leete; Mrs Dorothy Milburn Léger; Paul Levy; Lockwood Memorial Library; Kenneth A. Lohf, Librarian for Rare Books and MSS, Butler Library, Columbia University; London Library; Claude Lorentz, Bibliothèque Nationale et Universitaire de Strasbourg; Pat Lowe; Richard Luckett; Richard M. Ludwig, and Howard C. Rice Jr., Princeton University Library; Candida Lycett Green; Charles Madge; Ed Maggs; Jay Martin; Professor R. B. Martin; Lady Marshall; Professor B. K. Matilal; Francis O. Mattson, Berg Collection, New York Public Library; R. Russell Maylone, Special Collections Department, Northwestern University Library; Jim McCue; Mary C. McGreenery, Harvard Alumni Records; Patricia McGuire, Archivist, and Peter Monteith, Assistant Archivist, King's College, Cambridge; Robert Medley; Bernard Meehan, Keeper of Manuscripts, Trinity College Dublin; Nick Melia, Archives Assistant, Borthwick Institute for Archives, University of York; Ed Mendelson; Erik Mesterton; Wim van Mierlo; Prof. Andrew M. Miller; Marvin A. Miller,

Director of Libraries, University of Arkansas; Mrs Edward S. Mills; University Library, Missouri History Museum; Joe Mitchenson; Kate Mole, Librarian/Archivist, The British Academy; Glen E. Morgan; Frank Vigor Morley; J. D. I. Morley; Leslie A. Morris, Houghton Library, Harvard University; Lewis Morris; Tim Munby; Katherine Middleton Murry; Mary Middleton Murry; Richard Murry; Ben Nelson; The Bursar, New College, Oxford; Jeanne T. Newlin, Harvard Theatre Collection; Canon Donald Nicholson; Anne Oakley, Archivist, Cathedral, City and Diocesan Record Office, Canterbury; Karl O'Hanlon; Richard Ollard; Richard D. Olson, Curator of Rare Books and Special Collections, The University Library, Northwestern University; Jessie Orage; Dr James Marshall Osborn; Anne Owen; Martin Page; Stephen Page; Stephen R. Parks, Curator, The James Marshall and Marie-Louise Osborn Collection, Yale University; Alasdair Paterson, University of Exeter Library; Fondation Saint-John Perse; Rob Petre, College Archivist, St Edmund Hall, Oxford; Christopher G. Petter, Archivist Librarian, Special Collections, University of Victoria; Robert Phillips; Sir Charles Pickthorn, Bt; Charles E. Pierce, Jr., Director, The Pierpont Morgan Library; Jean F. Preston, Princeton University Library; Lord Quinton; Mary de Rachewiltz; Craig Raine; Lawrence S. Rainey; Wanda M. Randall; Graham Wallas and Angela Raspin, London School of Economics; William Rathbone; Benedict Read; Special Collections, Reading University; Real Academia de la Historia; Dr R. T. H. Redpath; Joseph Regenstein Library, University of Chicago; Stanley Revell; Howard C. Rice, Jr., Associate Librarian for Rare Books & Special Collections, Princeton University Library; I. A. and Dorothea Richards; Glyn Richards; Canon Pierre Riches; Anne Ridler; Helene Ritzerfeld; Alain Rivière; Professor A. D. Roberts; Sir Adam Roberts; Ruth R. Rogers, Special Collections Librarian, Margaret Clapp Library, Wellesley College; Galleria Nazionale d'Arte Moderna, Rome; Rosenbach Museum & Library, Philadelphia, PA; Anthony Rota; Bertram Rota; Mme Agathe Rouart-Valéry; Carol Z. Rothkopf; A. L. Rowse; Oliver Rowse; Royal Literary Fund; Lord Russell; Mrs N. Ryan; Professor Alfred W. Satterthwaite; Marcia Satterthwaite; Sean Sayers; Schiller-National-museum, Marbach am Neckar; Gerd Schmidt; Laura Schmidt, Archivist, The Marion E. Wade Center, Wheaton College, Illinois; David E. Schoonover, Yale University Library; Susan Schreibman; Rev. Karl Schroeder, SJ.; Ronald Schuchard; Grace Schulman; Mrs Rivers Scott; Timothy and Marian Seldes; Margalit Serra; Miranda Seymour; Christopher Sheppard, Brotherton Collection, Leeds University; Ethel C. Simpson, Trustee, John Gould Fletcher Literary Estate; G. Singh; Samuel

A. Sizer, Curator, Special Collections, University Libraries, University of Arkansas; Wilma R. Slaight, Archivist, Wellesley College; Janet Adam Smith; Theodora Eliot Smith; Susanna Smithson; Virginia L. Smyers, Harvard University Archives; Revd Charles Smyth; Oliver Soden; Natasha Spender; Sir Stephen Spender; Tom Staley; Jayme Stayer; Dom Julian Stead; Alix Strachey; James Strachey; Jenny Stratford; Kendon L. Stubbs, University of Virginia Library; Barbara Sturtevant; University of Sussex Library; Michael Sutton; Henry S. Swabey, SJ.; Dorothy L. Swerdlove, Curator, The Billy Rose Theatre Collection, New York Public Library; Lola L. Szladits, Berg Collection, New York Public Library; Alison Tandy; Allen Tate; Elizabeth Stege Teleky, The Joseph Regenstein Library, University of Chicago; David S. Thatcher, University of Victoria, British Columbia; Alan G. Thomas; Dr Richard Thompson; Willard Thorp; Dr Michael J. Tilby; Kathleen Tillotson; Trinity College, Cambridge; Francois Valéry; Judith Robinson-Valéry; The Paul Valéry Collection, Bibliotheque Nationale, Paris; Julian Vinogradoff; University of Virginia Library; Paolo Vivante; Rebecca Volk, Archivist, Jesuits in Britain Archives; Jeff Walden, BBC Written Archives Centre; Michael J Walsh, Heythrop College; Mrs Antonia Warren; J. Waterlow; Dr George Watson; John Weightman; John Wells, Cambridge University Library; Richard Wendorf; Gretchen Wheen; James White, National Gallery of Ireland; Brooke Whiting, Curator of Rare Books, Department of Special Collections, University Research Library, University of California, Los Angeles; Widener Library, Harvard University; Helen Willard; David G. Williams; Dr Charlotte Williamson; George Williamson; Julia Ross Williamson; Patricia C. Willis, Beinecke Rare Book and Manuscript Library, Yale University; Joan H. Winterkorn; Melanie Wisner; Harriet Harvey Wood; Woodson Research Center, Rice University; Dr Daniel H. Woodward, Huntington Library; C. J. Wright; Yale University Archives; Michael Yeats; E. D. Yeo, Department of Manuscripts, National Library of Scotland.

For permission to quote from unpublished letters and other material, we thank the following estates and individuals. W. H. Auden: by permission of the Estate of W. H. Auden. George Barker © The Estate of George Barker, by permission of Elspeth Barker. Natalie Clifford Barney, by permission of the Estate of Natalie Clifford Barney. Sylvia Beach, by permission of Lesley M. M. Blume © The Estate of Sylvia Beach. Isaiah Berlin © The Trustees of the Isaiah Berlin Literary Trust. John Betjeman © John Betjeman by permission of The Estate of John Betjeman. Ernest Bird: by permission of the trustees of the Estate of Sir Ernest Bird. Ronald Bottrall, by permission

Read. Michael Roberts © The Estate of Michael Roberts, by permission of Sir Adam Roberts and Professor Andrew Dunlop Roberts. William Saroyan © Stanford University. Janet Adam Smith © The Estate of Janet Adam Smith, by permission of Sir Adam and Professor Andrew Dunlop Roberts. Stephen Spender © The Estate of Stephen Spender, by permission of Matthew and Lizzie Spender. Allen Tate © The Estate of Allen Tate, by permission of Helen H. Tate. Dylan Thomas © The Trustees for the copyrights of Dylan Thomas. Willard Thorp, by permission of Princeton University. Mary Trevelyan © Mary Trevelyan, reproduced by permission of the Estate c/o Rodgers, Coleridge & White Ltd. Vernon Watkins by permission of Gwen Watkins © The Estate of Vernon Watkins. Charles Williams © The Estate of Charles Williams. John Dover Wilson © The Estate of John Dover Wilson, by permission of Professor Francis Wilson. Charlotte Wolff with the permission of The Association of Jewish Refugees. W. B. Yeats © W. B. Yeats, from The Collected Letters of W. B. Yeats (unpublished), by permission of Oxford University Press

Special thanks go to Judith Hooper and Clare Reihill, trustees of the Estate of T. S. Eliot, for their generous support, faith and friendship; Matthew Hollis and Lavinia Singer of Faber & Faber Ltd; Nancy Fulford, Project Archivist – T. S. Eliot Collection; Donald Sommerville for expert copy-editing and typesetting; Iman Javadi, Charlie Louth and Stephen Romer for swift, authoritative help with translations; Sara Ayad for resourceful picture research; David Wilson for proof-reading; Douglas Matthews for indexing; Mrs Valerie Eliot's assistant Debbie Whitfield for her commitment and long hard work; and the Institute of English Studies, University of London, for hosting the T. S. Eliot Editorial Project funded by the Arts and Humanities Research Council. John Haffenden is grateful above all to Jemma Walton for her good humour, love and kindness.

*The editors and publishers apologise if any person, institution or estate has been overlooked. They would be grateful to be informed if any copyright notice has been omitted, or if there have been any changes of ownership or location.*

# PREFACE

'I ran into my late wife in Wigmore Street an hour ago, and had to take to my heels,' wrote Eliot in July 1936; 'only people who have been "wanted" know the sort of life I lead.'

This volume of letters tells in detail the story of the decision taken by Maurice Haigh-Wood in the summer of 1938, following medical advice, to commit his sister Vivien Haigh-Wood Eliot to a psychiatric asylum – after she had been found wandering in a distressed state in the streets of London. It publishes the correspondence in which her long-separated husband writes of the dreadful, necessary business, and of his concern for her well-being and security; as well as the available medico-legal documentation. It also reports Eliot's feelings of affection and care for his close American friend Emily Hale.

The period covered by this volume is one of extraordinarily energetic productivity. Inevitably, as his fame increases, Eliot becomes more and more of a public man, albeit with some reluctance. While feeling averse to public speaking, he sustains a deep, inveterate sense of *noblesse oblige*. He gives lectures, readings and radio broadcasts in places ranging from Dublin to Edinburgh and Paris (where he meets up with James Joyce and André Gide). He visits East Coker in Somerset, Little Gidding in Huntingdonshire; journeys to Scotland, Wales, Austria and the USA; and spends three weeks in Portugal – where he is introduced to the remarkable Catholic dictator President Salazar – having been invited to help adjudicate the inaugural Camoëns Prize.

His professional work as editor and publisher is unrelenting. The books he commissions for Faber & Faber range from Michael Roberts's *The Modern Mind* to Elizabeth Bowen's anthology *The Faber Book of Modern Stories*. Among other ventures, he urges the invariably acerbic critic and editor Geoffrey Grigson to include more of the 'red pepper or vitriol of the editor . . . saucing Edith Sitwell etc.' in his Faber-commissioned anthology of *New Verse*.

The letters are humane and engaging, constructive and inventive, and frequently jokey; and they engage with many of the best-known writers of the 1930s: W. H. Auden; George Barker; Djuna Barnes (Eliot fights to publish *Nightwood*); John Betjeman; Basil Bunting; Walter de la Mare;

Lawrence Durrell (on *The Black Book*: 'I think he is better than Henry Miller, unless Miller gets him down . . . and besides Miller is all gummed up in D. H. Lawrence anyway'); Laurie Lee (whose juvenile poems he rejects); Hugh MacDiarmid (whose work he admires); Henry Miller; Norman Nicholson; Anaïs Nin; William Saroyan; Stephen Spender; Vernon Watkins. Moreover, he willingly copes with the onslaught of the reliably bizarre letters of Ezra Pound.

By 1938 Eliot has become such an eminent, esteemed figure that he sits for a formal portrait by Wyndham Lewis – which is infamously rejected by the Royal Academy of Arts. He pays this fine, loyal tribute: 'it seems to me a very good portrait, and one by which I am quite willing that posterity should know me . . . and I certainly have no desire, now, that my portrait should be painted by any painter whose portrait of me would be accepted by the Royal Academy.'

Other letters reveal Eliot's delight in friends such as John Hayward, Virginia Woolf and Polly Tandy (wife of another good friend, Geoffrey Tandy, Assistant Keeper of Botany at the Natural History Museum, and occasional BBC broadcaster), and in his publishing colleagues Geoffrey Faber and the exuberant American Frank Morley, as well as his solicitude for his godchildren – to whom he posts off the verses that will become *Old Possum's Book of Practical Cats* (1939). 'The verses were certainly intended for children, in so far as they were intended to amuse anyone but myself,' he says. 'I don't want, like one or two popular authors whom I can think of, to write children's poems which will appeal primarily to sentimental adults. That kind of verse seems to me definitely unpleasant.'

The letters to his close adult friends exhibit the true quality of his gifts as letter-writer: his kindliness, his playfulness, his mischievousness. These letters show off the hilarious scope of his ability to 'do the police in different voices': the perfect pitch of his ear for mimicry. It was what made him also such a superb parodist and pasticheur, such a great writer of comic verse.

All the while these numerous strands of correspondence are being played out, Eliot struggles to find the time to write his second play, *The Family Reunion* (1939). The exchanges with his trusted advisers about the emerging dramatic shape and meaning of the work include candid contributions from E. Martin Browne, Frank Morley, Ashley Dukes and Enid Faber. Eliot shows that he can take all of their robust criticisms, and he counters with equal frankness.

JOHN HAFFENDEN

2019

# BIOGRAPHICAL COMMENTARY
## 1936–1938

**1936**  JANUARY – TSE is an Ordinary Director of Faber & Faber Ltd, and Editor of the *Criterion*, at a salary of £500 p.a. He serves too as secretary of the Book Committee of the Church Literature Association. 1 JANUARY – writes to his brother (remembering the time when he was working on *ASG*): 'I was of course too much engrossed in the horrors of my private life to notice much outside; and I was suffering from (1) a feeling of guilt in having married a woman I detested, and consequently a feeling that I must put up with anything (2) perpetually being told, in the most plausible way, that I was a clodhopper and a dunce. Gradually, through making friends, I came to find that English people of the sort that I found congenial were prepared to take me quite as an ordinary human being, and that I had merely married into a rather common suburban family with a streak of abnormality which in the case of my wife had reached the point of liking to give people pain. I shall always be grateful to a few people like the Woolfs who unconsciously helped me to regain my balance and self-respect.' His hand is read by the German-Jewish palm-reader Dr Charlotte Wolff. 5 JANUARY – BBC radio broadcast of *Murder in the Cathedral*. 'When the English company gave a performance here in the BBC studios, I was very well satisfied with the result, and felt that the play was in some respects more suited to radio than to the theatre.' 12 JANUARY – has tea with the artist Jessica Dismorr. 20 JANUARY – begins discussion of *Nightwood* with Djuna Barnes's friend Emily Holmes Coleman, who (as he later remarks) 'practically forced the book down my throat, I admit I didn't appreciate it at first; and as for editing it, well [Frank] Morley and I cut out a lot ourselves, and all to the good, I say. It was one of those rare books in which cutting out a lot of stuff perfectly good in itself actually improved the whole.' 22 JANUARY – meets Oliver St John Gogerty at Ottoline Morrell's house in London.

22 JANUARY – travels to Dublin to speak at the inaugural meeting of the English Literary Society of University College. 23 JANUARY – replies to Roland Burke-Savage's talk 'Literature at the Irish Crossroads'. 24 JANUARY – lectures on 'Tradition and the Practice of Poetry'. Visits St Kevin's Cave at Lake Glendalough in County Wicklow (recalled in 'Little Gidding'). 25 JANUARY – visits a memorial exhibition of paintings by the late George Russell (Æ) , at Egan's Gallery, St Stephen's Square, Dublin, in company with C. P. Curran and Denis Devlin. LATE JANUARY – speaks at King's College London Anglican Society. 28 JANUARY – dines with Elizabeth Bowen. 30 JANUARY – speaks on behalf of the Save the Children Fund at Holborn Town Hall: his talk is published as 'Saving the Future: Mission of the Save the Children Fund: Practical Service at Home and Abroad', in *The World's Children: The Official Organ of the Save the Children Fund* 16 (Mar. 1936). Accepts for publication Rayner Heppenstall's *Apology for Dancing*. FIRST WEEK OF FEBRUARY – TSE is bedridden, suffering from bronchial influenza. Writes a (now lost) poem on goats, and sends it to Christina Morley. Publishes a review of *Preface to a Christian Sociology*, by Cyril E. Hudson, in *The Teaching Church Review: A Journal for Students of Religion*. Maria Jolas delivers to F&F Part III of James Joyce's *Work in Progress* (the work will become *Finnegans Wake*, 1939). 2 FEBRUARY – TSE tells his brother, 'I am actually better off than I have any right to expect, as my play [*Murder in the Cathedral*] has been bringing me in five pounds a week since the beginning of November, and will run for another three weeks.' (5,432 copies of *Murder of the Cathedral* have been sold to date.) 21 FEBRUARY – starts work on a new play: *The Family Reunion*. 27 FEBRUARY – F&F publishes *The Faber Book of Modern Verse*, ed. Michael Roberts. 28 FEBRUARY – TSE lunches at the Junior Carlton Club with his brother-in-law Maurice Haigh-Wood. Begins planning Ezra Pound's volume *Polite Essays*. 3 MARCH – goes to Group Theatre production of *The Dog Beneath the Skin* by W. H. Auden and Christopher Isherwood. 'What did irritate me was the chorus . . . [T]hese interruptions of the action become more and more irritating as the play goes on, and one gets tired of having things explained and being preached at. I do think Auden ought to find a different method in his next play.'

5 MARCH – publishes *Essays Ancient and Modern*: 2,500 copies. (The Harcourt, Brace edition will come out on 27 August 1936.) Dines with Professor Elizabeth Manwaring (visiting from Wellesley College). 6 MARCH – writes to Geoffrey Faber about the work that will become *Old Possum's Book of Practical Cats*: 'I am more and more doubtful of my ability to write a successful book of this kind, and I had rather find out early that I can't do it, than waste a lot of time for nothing. And this sort of thing is flatter if it is flat, than serious verse. Nobody wants to make a fool of himself when he might be better employed.' Requests from Dylan Thomas a contribution to the *Criterion*. 9 MARCH – writes to Ezra Pound's literary agent: 'my position is that to deal with Ezra's poetry and literary criticism is as much as can be expected of any one firm, unless we decided to open a special Ezra Department.' Geoffrey Faber's diary: 'Tom Eliot & John Hayward to dine. Went off well.' 10 MARCH – TSE attends a meeting of the London Society for the Study of Religion; dines with Hope Mirrlees and her mother Mappie. MID-MARCH – dines with the All Souls Club, in Regents Park. 'I have taken to the vice of Dining Clubs,' he tells Virginia Woolf. Plays billiards in a London pub with William Empson and Igor Vinogradoff. 18 MARCH – *Murder in the Cathedral*, staged by Halsted Welles and starring Harry Irvine as Becket, is produced by the Popular Price Theatre, at the Manhattan Theatre, New York City, for three weeks. 19 MARCH – TSE publishes 'The Church as Action: Note on a Recent Correspondence', in *New English Weekly*. John Hayward announces in his 'London Letter' (*New York Sun*, 28 Mar. 1936) that 'Burnt Norton' was 'completed only a month or so ago'. TSE publishes 'The Need for Poetic Drama', in the *Listener*. Sylvia Beach calls on TSE at F&F: the firm agrees to issue the outstanding copies of *Our Exagmination Round His Factification for Incamination of Work in Progress* (1929). TSE takes a warm interest in the case of a White Russian emigré, Dr N. M. Iovetz-Tereshchenko (author of *Friendship-Love in Adolescence*, 1936) – 'pleasant modest and pathetic' – who is having difficulty supporting his mother, wife and children. 25 MARCH – TSE talks about his poetry at the Institute of Education, University of London. APRIL – lunches with Dylan Thomas. Meets the Russian art critic and man of letters Wladimir Weidlé. Visits the schoolteacher and author P. S.

Richards in Sussex (they have a mutual friend in Paul Elmer More). 2 APRIL – publishes *Collected Poems 1909–1935* (6,000 copies): the volume includes 'Burnt Norton'. 9 APRIL – publishes 'The Church as Action', in the *New English Weekly*. 15 APRIL – begins campaign, in league with his colleague Frank Morley, to have *Nightwood* accepted by F&F, writing to Geoffrey Faber: 'I believe that this may be our last chance to do something remarkable in the way of imaginative literature.' 16 APRIL – F&F publishes *The Burning Cactus* by Stephen Spender. TSE lunches with Mirrlees and her mother. TSE corresponds with William Saroyan, about his collection of short stories *Inhale and Exhale* (F&F, 1936). 17 APRIL – remarks to Bonamy Dobrée, 'The doctrine that in order to arrive at the love of God one must divest oneself of the love of created beings was thus expressed by St John of the Cross, you know . . . But the doctrine is fundamentally true, I believe . . . I don't think that ordinary human affections are capable of leading us to the love of God, but rather that the love of God is capable of informing, intensifying and elevating our human affections, which otherwise may have little to distinguish them from the "natural" affections of animals. Try looking at it from that end of the glass!' 20 APRIL – dines with the All Souls Club, at the National Liberal Club. 23 APRIL – dines with Aldous Huxley and wife. 30 APRIL – takes tea with Jessica Dismorr. MAY – publishes 'Introduction' to *Poems of Tennyson* (Thomas Nelson & Sons); as 'In Memoriam' in *Essays Ancient and Modern*. 1 MAY – offers to publish *Nightwood*. Turns down Jean Cocteau's *La Machine Infernale* – albeit an 'exceedingly good' play. 12 MAY – invites Louis MacNeice to submit his translation of *Agamemnon*. 13 MAY – talks at Cambridge English Club. 14 MAY – visits Ottoline Morrell at Gower Street, London. Recommends George Barker for a lectureship in English Literature at Durham University. 18 MAY – dines with the All Souls Club at the United University Club. 20 MAY – *Criterion* party: members of the inner circle are invited for supper at 7.00, the remainder for an 'Evening' at 9.00. The gathering includes the American publisher Jane Heap, co-editor of the *Little Review*, 1916–29. 21 MAY – Harcourt, Brace and Co. (New York) publishes *Collected Poems 1909–1935*. 22 MAY – invites Aldous Huxley to edit an anthology of modern short stories. 23 MAY – visits Cambridge, at the invitation of John Maynard Keynes, to attend the final performance at the Arts Theatre of *Murder in the Cathedral*. Meets the don Basil Willey, who will recall: 'Eliot was immaculate, impenetrable, inscrutable: uttering little but looking very handsome, melancholy and wise.' 25 MAY – conducts *viva voce* examination for the Cambridge PhD thesis of Bernard Blackstone, and visits Little Gidding (in the afternoon of the same day) – being driven there by the Revd H. F. Stewart and his wife Jessie. 28 MAY – lunches with Paul Elmer More's brother Louis T. More: 'his devotion and admiration for Paul are most touching' – a 'somewhat pathetic figure, I think'. 29 MAY – tells Heppenstall, 'If you really hope to become a professional novelist I think the outlook is rather unfavourable for the future of your poetry. I mean that while an exception is always possible I think that the verse of a professional novelist must always be a by-product. I don't think that a single individual can divide himself so successfully as to make a major art of two occupations requiring very different attitudes. I am afraid, that is, that if you become a novelist you will stop writing verse.' JUNE Declines an American offer for the film rights of *Murder in the Cathedral*. 'I don't think that the play would make a good film, and if I did arrange to let it be filmed I should surround the permission with so many restrictions that it would not possibly make a successful one. I confess to a strong aversion to films except for the lightest amusement, and I am sure that it would be a mistake for me to allow this play to be handled in that medium.' Recommends MacNeice for an appointment at Bedford College, London: 'He is the only young poet of my acquaintance who has struck me as being a man of education and culture.' 4 JUNE – travels with his colleague Frank Morley to Paris. 8 June. Dines with Stuart Gilbert. 9 JUNE – gives a poetry reading at the bookshop Shakespeare & Co., where he dines with Sylvia Beach and meets André Gide. Discusses *Work in Progress* with James Joyce. 11 JUNE – invites Michael Roberts to write a critical study of T. E. Hulme. Commissions Elizabeth Bowen to edit the *Faber Book of Modern Stories*. 13/14 JUNE – stays with the editor Bruce Richmond and his wife at Netherhampton House, Salisbury. 16 JUNE – attends reception of the Thomas More Society in Lincoln's Inn, London. 19 JUNE – meets Charles Williams for the first time at the production of his play *Thomas Cranmer of Canterbury* (which TSE finds 'surprisingly good'). 20 JUNE – publishes a memorial essay 'G. K. Chesterton', in the *Tablet*. 25–26 JUNE – in Oxford, for a retreat at Cowley. Visits East Coker in Somerset: 'East Coker was delightful, with a sort of Germelshausen effect.' JUNE – reading and collating, with Morley, the two copies of *Nightwood* that Djuna Barnes has left with them. JULY – publishes a story by Dylan Thomas in the *Criterion*. 2 JULY – publishes 'A Note on the Verse of John Milton' in *Essays and Studies by Members of the English Association* XXI, ed. Herbert Read. Dines with the BBC producer George Barnes and his wife. 7 JULY – accepts MacNeice's play *Out of the Picture* for publication by F&F. 9 JULY – declines invitation to become a sponsor of the American Academy of Poets. 'I do not want in the least to discourage you, but experience leads me to believe that unless such undertakings have the constant attention and vigilance of the small number of intelligent people who really care passionately about their aims, they are apt to decline into mere formalism.' 14 JULY – writes to John Dover Wilson, 'I want to keep the winter free of speaking engagements . . . I find that public speaking of any kind is such an effort to me that it upsets completely any consecutive work on which I may be engaged.' Agrees to contribute an essay to *Revelation*, ed. John Baillie and Hugh Martin (for publication by F&F, 1937). MID-JULY – dines in London with Dorothy Bussy and her husband. Visits the Society of the Sacred Mission at Kelham and then what he calls the 'Student Christian Movement hallelujah Camp', at Swanwick in Derbyshire – an experience, he claims, that left him with neuritis. 20 JULY – lunches with Charles Williams and Montgomery Belgion. 21 JULY – lunches with Father Martin D'Arcy, SJ. 28 JULY – 'I am rather shaky at the moment, because I ran into my late wife in Wigmore Street an hour ago, and had to take to my heels: only people who have been "wanted" know the sort of life I lead.' 29 JULY – booked to go to a cocktail party at the home of Julian Huxley and his wife: does not in fact attend, blaming the pain of neuritis. 30 JULY – approached by George Barnes to arrange a series of poetry readings for the BBC. 'I am not going to undergo another voice test,' insists TSE (14 Aug.). 2 AUGUST – visits Fabers for a week in Wales. Faber notes in his diary, 'The Morleys & Tom Eliot arrived about teatime –

bringing Monopoly with them.' 12 AUGUST – TSE dines with Elizabeth Manwaring. 13 AUGUST – publishes a memorial notice, 'Dr Charles Harris', in the *Times*. 13 AUGUST – entertains Basil Bunting to tea. 14 AUGUST – writes to Donagh MacDonagh, 'I shall certainly say nothing to Niall Montgomery, but why his father should be afraid that I should think he was a Jew, and why he should think that that would make any difference to me anyway, is a complete mystery.' 17 AUGUST – recommends Bunting to Bruce Richmond and to other literary editors: he is 'quite a good poet – a much more efficient workman at the job of writing than a great many of those about us'. 18 AUGUST – attends Chandos Group dinner. 19 AUGUST – turns down invitation to become a Vice-President of the Distributist League, in succession to G. K. Chesterton: 'although I have always been sympathetic I have never been closely associated with Distributism, nor have I taken any active part in propagating the doctrine'. 20 AUGUST – dines with Hugh Gordon Porteus and his wife. 22 AUGUST – sails from Southampton for the USA. Stays in Cambridge, Massachusetts, with his sister Ada. The Eliot clan (together with Emily Hale) gather from 7 September at Mount Crescent Hotel, Randolph, New Hampshire, and then TSE stays with Hale at the seaside home of her friend Dorothy Olcott Elsmith, in Woods Hole, Mass. FROM 21 SEPTEMBER – TSE is back in Cambridge, Mass. At the end of the month, he travels to Princeton to visit Paul Elmer More (for the last time): 'I found him completely lucid, and his same delightful and affectionate self, although obviously with very little physical strength.' (24 SEPTEMBER – F&F publishes *The Ascent of F6*: a tragedy in two acts, by Auden and Isherwood.) 29 SEPTEMBER – TSE gives poetry reading at Wellesley College. Lunches with Ted Spencer. 1 OCTOBER – visits Emily Hale at Northampton, Mass., reporting to Jeanette McPherrin on 26 Oct.: 'When I first saw Emily I thought her very much changed, chiefly in the lack of any animation, in a kind of numbness to the external world, a narrowing of her field of awareness, and a tendency (though one has noticed this before) to think about her own shortcomings all the time. In a person who ordinarily gives out so much to others, this is very painful . . . I do not believe that there is anything settled in her depression, and I think that it will pass in the course of the work, and getting to know the better girls, and making friends locally: though of course to go through any such phase must make a mark on anybody.' 2 OCTOBER – after seven weeks away, TSE sails home from the USA. Arriving at Plymouth on 10 Oct., he is met by Morley and his wife, with their children Oliver and Susanna, and they go for a short tour by car before returning to London. 12 OCTOBER – spends evening with John Hayward, in company with William Empson. 16 OCTOBER – F&F publishes *Nightwood*. TSE resigns position as secretary of the Book Committee of the Church Literature Association; but by late October is persuaded to continue in the role. 22 OCTOBER – F&F publishes *Look, Stranger!*, poems by W. H. Auden. 25 OCTOBER – TSE takes tea with Dismorr. 28 OCTOBER – resigns from the Council of the Shakespeare Association. 29 OCTOBER – F&F publishes *The Agamemnon of Aeschylus*, by MacNeice. 30 OCTOBER – *Murder in the Cathedral* transfers from Mercury Theatre to the Duchess Theatre. 13 NOVEMBER – TSE speaks at the English Club, Cambridge, on the French influences on his work: 'my talk . . . seemed to me scrappy and inconclusive.' 17 NOVEMBER – dines with Canon Maynard Smith. 20 NOVEMBER – gives twenty-minute talk for Sixth Forms, 'The Need for Poetic Drama', broadcast on the BBC Schools programme; published in 'The Need for Poetic Drama', *Listener* (25 Nov. 1936), and in *Good Speech* (Apr./June 1937). 21 NOVEMBER – lunches with Geoffrey Faber. 22 NOVEMBER – addresses Shirley Society, Cambridge University – 'they don't even pay one's fare'. Dines with the academic T. R. Henn. 25 NOVEMBER – accepts invitation to become Vice-President of the Chesterton Club. Expresses interest in publishing a collection of poems by e. e. cummings. 26 NOVEMBER – lunches with Belgion. Invites T. O. Beachcroft and his wife to go to the new Ernie Lotinga review called 'Sanctions' at the Shepherds Bush Theatre. 27 NOVEMBER – attends a buffet party thrown by John Hayward. 28 NOVEMBER – dines in Blackheath with Charles Madge and Kathleen Raine. 29 NOVEMBER – addresses students and staff of St Dionis Hall (City of London). 1 DECEMBER – dines at the Fabers', with John Hayward and Sir Roderick Meiklejohn. 3 DECEMBER – dines with the Woolfs at 52 Tavistock Square. 4 DECEMBER – joins in birthday celebrations – a 'terrific jamboree,' as Frank Morley calls it – for the eight-year-old Oliver Morley, in London. 10 DECEMBER –

announcement of the King's abdication. 11 DECEMBER – TSE and Geoffrey Faber visit Cambridge, to talk with Sir Edwyn Hoskyns about divinity books for public schools, and with Sir Will Spens, Master of Corpus Christi, about publishing the Anglo-Saxon Chronicle. Faber's diary: 'Took T.S.E. back to lunch . . . Edward's broadcast [on the Abdication] was received in complete silence, & I think most of the audience felt embarrassed by it. TSE thought it wld. have been in better taste if he had said nothing.' 12 DECEMBER – dines with Viscountess Rhondda and Sarah Gertrude Millin. 13 DECEMBER – attends All Souls Club dinner, with Lord Wolmer. Gives a fifteen-minute 'address' on John Dryden for the Columbia Broadcasting System, at the Studios of the BBC at Savoy Hill; he is introduced by César Saerchinger, Director of the European Service, CBS. 14 DECEMBER – tells Dobrée he is 'Rotten with money' – with royalties from *Murder*. MID-DECEMBER – dines with the Woolfs. SECOND WEEKEND OF DECEMBER – stays with the Mirrlees family in Surrey. 16 DECEMBER – turns down H. E. Bates' story 'Spring Snow'. 18 DECEMBER – dines with the Fabers. 19 DECEMBER – dines with Dobrée and his wife. 21 DECEMBER – *Murder in the Cathedral* broadcast on BBC TV. Approaches the producer John Grierson for a book on documentary and amateur film. 24 DECEMBER – dines with George Barnes. 26 DECEMBER – dines with his friend George Every, SSM. 29 DECEMBER – lunches with Belgion and Beachcroft. 31 DECEMBER – seeks to publish Gavin Douglas's *Aenead*. Spends the New Year holiday with the Morley family.

**1937** JANUARY – publishes Henri Massis, 'Proust: The Twenty Years' Silence' – an extract from *Le Cas Marcel Proust* – translated by Montgomery Belgion, in the *Criterion*. 1 JANUARY – TSE's secretary Brigid O'Donovan leaves F&F to join the staff of the BBC. 4 JANUARY – TSE writes (*aet*. 49): 'I am getting on in years and must begin to conserve my energy if I can.' 5 JANUARY – lunches with John Betjeman. 6 JANUARY – offers his resignation from the Subjects Committee of the Church Union. 9 JANUARY – speaks at the Chelmsford Diocesan Religious Drama Guild, at Brentford, Essex, following a performance of Charles Williams's epiphany play *The Three Kings*: 'it proved extremely effective; and particularly impressive was the enthusiasm and conviction with which the amateur company acted it. One felt that they were happy in having a religious play to do that was really exciting and out of the ordinary.' 11 JANUARY – tells Paul Elmer More, 'I know a little what is the feeling of being alone – I will not say with God, but alone in the presence and under the observation of God – with the feeling of being stripped, as of frippery, of the qualifications that ordinarily most identify one: one's heredity, one's abilities, and one's name.' 12 JANUARY – TSE attends BBC rehearsal of Geoffrey Tandy's reading of selections from the work of George Herbert, Henry Vaughan and Thomas Traherne. 13 JANUARY – records his introduction to the selection of poems by Herbert, broadcast the same evening. MID-JANUARY – takes Mary Hutchinson to E. Martin Browne's production of the York Nativity Play at the Mercury Theatre. 17 JANUARY – enjoys drinks with John Hayward – downs too much whisky. 18 JANUARY – goes to lunch party thrown by Clive Bell, with Raymond Mortimer, Virginia Woolf, Mary Baker (Bell's 'rich American flame'), and the Hon. Virginia Brett. 21 JANUARY – outing to Wapping, for lunch party with T. W. Earp and Frank Morley. At BBC in the evening: broadcast of TSE's selection from poems of Vaughan and Traherne. 24 JANUARY – TSE gives a radio talk on behalf of the North Kensington Community Centre, in 'The Week's "Good Cause" Appeal'. His London Regional Service appeal draws contributions from 160 people, ultimately realising nearly £100. 30 JANUARY – Geoffrey Faber's diary: 'To Cambridge with Tom Eliot & Enid . . . Meeting at Corpus to talk about Anglo-Saxon Chronicle. Dined with the Spens's.' 1 FEBRUARY – Faber diary: 'Dined, & took chair, at a dinner given by several friends to TSE in honour of *Murder in the Cathedral*. Proposed a toast to the modern stage, in v. brief terms.' 5 FEBRUARY – TSE publishes his tribute 'Paul Elmer More', in *Princeton Alumni Bulletin*. 8 FEBRUARY – speaks at the Annual Meeting of the Church Literature Association. 9 FEBRUARY – lunches with Heppenstall. 11 FEBRUARY – F&F publishes *Polite Essays* by Ezra Pound. 12 FEBRUARY – goes drinking in Earls Court with George Barnes and Geoffrey Tandy. 16 FEBRUARY – broadcasts talk 'The Church's Message to the World', in a series on 'Church, Community and State'; the talk is published in the *Listener* on 17 Feb. (repr. as appendix to *The Idea of a Christian Society* 1939): reaffirms the right of the Church 'to affirm, to teach and to apply, true theology'. 17 FEBRUARY – reports to his brother that in January he earned about £100 from *Murder in the Cathedral*. He has been fitted with a new gold tooth. 'I have kind (I mean kind, not ironically) friends who are always wanting to do me (as a lonely single man etc.) a kindness by asking me to the country to visit them for weekends, when I should be much more comfortable (especially in winter) snuggling in my club by myself: and I have to accept some of their invitations in order to give them the pleasure of feeling that they are doing something for me. Otherwise, one is ungrateful and unsociable!' 18 FEBRUARY – publishes essay 'Byron (1788–1824)' in *From Anne to Victoria: Essays by Various Hands*, ed. Dobrée. Publishes essay 'Mr Reckitt, Mr Tomlin, and the Crisis', in *New English Weekly*. 26 FEBRUARY – dines with Geoffrey and Enid Faber, and goes with them to the first night of Auden and Isherwood's play *The Ascent of F6*. 30 FEBRUARY – lunches with John Grierson. 2 MARCH – dines with Elizabeth Bowen. 4 MARCH – publishes his 'Introduction' to *Nightwood* by Djuna Barnes (New York: Harcourt, Brace). Speaks at King's College, Cambridge, on 'Revelation' (using his essay as text), as guest of the chaplain. 8 MARCH – publishes 'A Note by T. S. Eliot' in the programme of the ADC (Amateur Dramatic Society) and Marlowe Society production of Cyril Tourneur's *The Revenger's Tragedy*, directed by George Rylands, at the ADC Theatre, Cambridge. 9 MARCH – accepts for publication by F&F the poetry of Joe Corrie, a Scottish miner. 10 MARCH – speaks on behalf of the Red Cross Society, at Londonderry House. This fund-raising entertainment – called 'Authors' Night' – hosted by Lord and Lady Londonderry, includes addresses of ten to fifteen minutes each by speakers including C. Day Lewis, Canon H. R. L. 'Dick' Sheppard, and Humbert Wolfe. Lord Esher took the chair; Lord Balniel (chair of the Ex-Committee) proposed thanks. (The British Red Cross Society supplied books and magazines to over 2,000 hospitals and kindred institutions throughout the country.) TSE was the last of six speakers. 12 MARCH – TSE lunches with Baron Luigi Franchetti, writer and pianist (and friend of Pound). 19 MARCH – entertains Charles Williams to lunch, in company with Frank Morley. Agrees to serve on the Vic–Wells Completion Fund Committee. 22 MARCH – visits Francis Underhill, Dean of

Rochester, for a weekend. 25 MARCH – invites C. Day Lewis to write a book on Literature and Marxism, with an advance of £150 (Day Lewis declines). 31 MARCH–5 APRIL – TSE travels to Scotland, visiting George Blake and the Neil Gunns (TSE and Frank Morley sleep in a caravan in their back garden), and paying their respects at the grave of Robert Burns. APRIL – publishes Ezra Pound's 'Cantos XLII–XLIV', and his own introduction to *Nightwood*, as a notice of the novel, in *Criterion*. Moves from 9 Grenville Place to Flat 3, 11 Emperor's Gate, S.W.7 – 'I have 79 steps to climb to get to my roost.' 21 APRIL – attends *New English Weekly* party. Dines with W. B. Yeats. 27 APRIL – 'A hard day yesterday: lunched the Archdeacon of Auckland till 4 o'clock (Divinity Books); directly I reached Russell Square ready for a peaceful tea by myself Djuna Barnes arrived in a state of hysterics and smelling salts because Liveright want to collar her royalties: had to get Frank [Morley] up to soothe her, but managed to send her away tranquillised. Then H. Gordon Porteus to dinner, and that's the way the money goes.' F&F publishes *Calamiterror*, poems by George Barker; *The Disappearing Castle*, poems by Charles Madge. 4 MAY – TSE takes tea with Virginia Woolf. 10 MAY – travels to Austria for two weeks' holiday, returning by 24 May. 12 MAY – Coronation of George VI at Westminster Abbey. 20 MAY – F&F publishes *Spain* by W. H. Auden. 26 MAY – TSE is invited by the Bishop of London to serve on the Evangelistic Council. 27 MAY – F&F publishes *The Modern Mind* by Michael Roberts. 29 MAY – spends a weekend at the Society of the Sacred Mission, Kelham, Nottinghamshire. JUNE – F&F publishes *Out of the Picture*, a play by Louis MacNeice. 2 JUNE – TSE dines with Tom Burns, Ann Bowes Lyon, and David Jones. 3 JUNE – F&F publishes introductory essay, 'I by T. S. Eliot', in *Revelation*, ed. John Baillie (1,517 copies). 3 JUNE – F&F publishes *The Fifth Decad of Cantos* by Ezra Pound. 4 JUNE – TSE addresses the Festival for the Friends of Rochester Cathedral on 'Religious Drama: Mediæval and Modern'. 7 JUNE – writes a sceptical F&F reader's report on the diaries of Anaïs Nin. 8 JUNE – *Murder in the Cathedral* opens at the Old Vic, London. 20 JUNE – TSE spends a day and a night with the Tandy family. MID-JUNE – dines with Charles Williams. 'I have not known so happy and easy a time since the dearest of my male friends died two years ago,' says Williams. 21 JUNE – lunches at the Oxford & Cambridge Club with Sir Hugh Walpole, Geoffrey Faber and Frank Morley. 22 JUNE – attends play at Bradfield College – *Oedipus Tyrannus*, performed in Greek – along with Faber and Hayward. 23 JUNE – turns down a masque entitled 'The Influences' by Vernon Watkins. 24 JUNE – delivers Prize Day Address at the Kingswood (Methodist) School), Bath: the speech is reported in the *Kingswood Magazine* (July 1937): *Complete Prose* 5, 29 JUNE – enjoys a day's outing with Alida Monro. 3 JULY – receives hon. D.Litt. from Edinburgh; delivers a lecture on 'Religious Drama: Mediaeval and Modern', which is printed in *University of Edinburgh Journal* (Aut. 1937). 12–16 JULY – visits Oxford, for the World Conference of Churches. 16 JULY – speaks on 'The Ecumenical Nature of the Church' (under the session title 'The Ecumenical Nature of the Church and its Responsibility to the World'): *Complete Prose* 5. FROM 16 JULY – stays for a few days at Chipping Campden, visiting Dr John and Mrs Perkins and Emily Hale. 17 JULY – publishes 'The Church and the World: Problem of Common Social Action', in the *Times*. 19–24 JULY – *Murder in the Cathedral* is performed at Tewkesbury Abbey, as part of the Tewkesbury Festival. 23 JULY – TSE visits Rochester again. 25 JULY – takes tea with Virginia Woolf. 26 JULY – attends a meeting at Liddon House. 3 AUGUST – TSE visits East Coker, where he calls on Sir Matthew Nathan. 6 AUGUST – F&F publishes *Letters from Iceland* by W. H. Auden and Louis MacNeice. 20 AUGUST – publishes 'The Oxford Conference', in *Church Times*. 31 AUGUST – dines with Elizabeth Manwaring. 1 SEPTEMBER – F&F publishes *The Faber Book of Modern Stories*, ed. Elizabeth Bowen. 21 SEPTEMBER – TSE spends an evening with Theodore Spencer, in London. 25/26 SEPTEMBER – spends weekend with the Woolfs in Sussex, where VW remarks, 'Tom in some ways – with his sensitive, shrinking, timid but idiosyncratic nature – is very like myself . . . Tom is liverish looking, tired.' AUTUMN – TSE publishes 'Religious Drama: Medieval and Modern', *University of Edinburgh Journal*: says he looks for 'something less sedative' in contemporary poetic drama. 2–3 OCTOBER – weekends with the Tandys. 5 OCTOBER – meets Frank Morley's parents. 26 OCTOBER – travels to Edinburgh. 27-28 OCTOBER – delivers two lectures on Shakespeare at Edinburgh University:

*Complete Prose* 5. (Writes to Lawrence Durrell, 5 Nov.: 'I am so alarmed at finding that my interpretation of Shakespeare was really concerned with what I myself am interested in doing in the theatre, that I think I had better leave Shakespeare alone for some time to come. If I am writing a play I think I am better concerned with becoming conscious of how to do it than with becoming conscious of what I am trying to do.') 30 OCTOBER – publishes 'An Anglican Platonist: The Conversion of Elmer More' (an unsigned review of *Pages from an Oxford Diary*), in the *TLS*. Publishes in the *Criterion* an essay by Henry Miller, 'Un Etre Etoilque' (a review of Anaïs Nin). 2 NOVEMBER – goes to tea with Ottoline Morrell, with Djuna Barnes. Publishes a retrospective review of *The Lion and the Fox* (1927) by Wyndham Lewis, in *Twentieth Century Verse*. 5 NOVEMBER – visits the Tandys. MID-NOVEMBER – attends funeral of Valentine Dobrée's father; then visits Conrad Aiken for a night at Rye in Sussex. Spends a weekend at Kelham. Reads new play to Martin Browne. 23–28 NOVEMBER – spends Thanksgiving with the Morley family, along with Faber and another F&F colleague, Morley Kennerley. DECEMBER 1937 – publication of *Authors Take Sides on the Spanish War* (by *Left Review*) – TSE's response is printed under 'Neutral?' 9 DECEMBER – lunches with Auden and Faber; dines with Hayward. Goes to see Eugene O'Neill's *Mourning Becomes Electra*, together with Mary Hutchinson. He explains to Virginia Woolf: 'My bosses (Ashley Dukes and Martin Browne) tell me that I ought to see it, because they think it has enough in common with *The Family Reunion* to make it desirable to postpone my play from the spring to the autumn.' 13 DECEMBER – meeting of All Souls Club.

**1938**  F&F publishes Michael Roberts, *T. E. Hulme*; and Denis Saurat, *The End of Fear*, with introduction by Philip Mairet. Martin Browne and Ashley Dukes take *Murder in the Cathedral* to Boston and New York. TSE discusses the possibility of producing a posthumous volume of art studies by his old friend M. S. Prichard (the plan is ultimately unavailing). 2 JANUARY – TSE attends dinner party at the McKnight Kauffers, in honour of John Hayward's birthday. 6 JANUARY – dines with Wyndham Lewis. Refuses Auden an advance on royalties for *On the Frontier*; but F&F does agree to pay an advance for the Far East book (to be written with Christopher Isherwood) – *Journey to a*

*War.* 11 JANUARY – BBC Radio broadcasts an adaptation of *The Waste Land* – a dramatised interpretation, or 'elementary' conversation, as TSE calls it – created by the producer D. G. Bridson: TSE says it 'gave me some mirth, but not much pleasure'. The producer Val Gielgud thought it 'not worth doing' – indeed, 'pretty well meaningless' to the uninitiated. 13 JANUARY – TSE publishes 'A Note on Two Odes of Cowley by T. S. Eliot', in *Seventeenth Century Studies Presented to Sir Herbert Grierson*, ed. John Purves. 14 JANUARY – attends 'Archbishops meeting' (as TSE notes in his appointments diary). MID-JANUARY – lunches with Djuna Barnes. 22 JANUARY – dines with OUP editor Gerard ('Gerry') Hopkins and his wife Mabel, and goes to a pantomime with them. 29 JANUARY – repeat broadcast of *Practical Cats*, read by Tandy: TSE donates his fee of ten guineas to the Society of the Sacred Mission. FROM FEBRUARY – TSE works for many months towards the publication of James Joyce's *Finnegans Wake*. Donates a set of hand-bells to the House of the Sacred Mission, Kelham. 2 FEBRUARY – gives a brief talk at 'a do at the Mansion House on behalf of Southwark Cathedral' (as reported in the *Times*, 3 Feb.): *Complete Prose* 5. 10 FEBRUARY – TSE attends the All Souls Club. Declines invitation to join the Public Relations Committee of the proposed National Theatre: feels he could not play a useful part. 11 FEBRUARY – writes in praise of Dr J. H. Oldham (who is presently to set up the discussion group, The Moot): 'He seems to me as great a man as I know and that is an opinion which has stood the test of five years or more and only become strengthened. There is very little I would not do, I think, if he asked me.' 15 FEBRUARY – completes the first full draft of his second play *The Family Reunion*, and submits it to the director Martin Browne. (Browne responds on 19 Mar. that he and Ashley Dukes consider the play 'weak in plot'; but they are 'enthralled . . . by the skill and wit of the versification'.) Dukes tells *Time* magazine that it is 'a modern play laid in an English country house, but with a substratum of Greek drama'. (TSE tells Dobrée, 18 Feb.: 'I think that I have now found a better medium for dialogue than I had in *Murder* . . . One reason why I am dissatisfied with *Murder* is that there are too many bumps of poetry sticking up like outcrop, and the poetry is not sufficiently integrated into the drama.' TSE remarks to Enid

Faber, 24 February: 'The tragedy [in *The Family Reunion*], as with my Master, Tchehov, is as much for the people who have to go on living, as for those who die.' On 19 Mar. he tells Martin Browne, of *The Family Reunion*: 'The point of Mary, in relation to Harry, was meant to be this. The effect of his married life upon him was one of such horror as to leave him for the time at least in a state that may be called one of being psychologically partially desexed: or rather, it has given him a horror of women as of unclean creatures. The scene with Mary is meant to bring out, as I am aware it fails to, the conflict inside him between this repulsion for Mary as a woman, and the attraction which the normal part of him that is still left, feels towards her personally for the first time. This is the first time since his marriage ("there was no ecstacy") that he has been attracted towards any woman'. 15 FEBRUARY – invites John Hayward to become his literary executor: 'A will is in case I am knocked (as the saying is) arse over teakettle by a Buss, or some other unexpected calamity cuts me down like a flower . . . The functions would be chiefly negative. I have had to write at one time or another a lot of junk in periodicals the greater portion of which ought never to be reprinted . . . F.&F. might be tempted, and your job would be to say no. And I don't want any biography written, or any letters printed that I wrote prior to 1933, or any letters at all of any intimacy to anybody. In fact, I have a mania for posthumous privacy.' 16 FEBRUARY – The Gilbert Miller–Ashley Dukes production of *Murder in the Cathedral*, starring Robert Speaight (who has played the part of Becket in over 600 performances to date), opens at the Ritz Theatre, New York. MID-FEBRUARY – Wyndham Lewis begins work, in his studio at 29A Notting Hill Gate, on a portrait of TSE: it will take up all of TSE's free evenings for at least a fortnight. 17 FEBRUARY – TSE takes Djuna Barnes to visit Hayward, after dining with her at the Queens Restaurant, Sloane Square. 17 FEBRUARY – TSE tells Ezra Pound: 'You ought to have a look at *The Black Book* by Laurence Durrell . . . [It is] better than Henry Miller . . . more serious as a whole than *Tropic of Cancer* . . . and besides Miller is all gummed up in D. H. Lawrence anyway.' 18 FEBRUARY – turns down *The Triple Thinkers*, by Edmund Wilson: 'this book is merely a collection of essays with nothing to hold them together; furthermore, there is too much cold mutton for the

English market.' Donald Brace says that he likes *The Family Reunion*, and will publish it in the USA. TSE negotiates with John Grierson for a book about documentary film. He turns down Henry Miller's work on D. H. Lawrence: 'I find myself merely grasping at something in the dark, and seemingly only pulling off handfuls of cotton-wool. What I really want is more of yourself and less of Lawrence, an author whom I have always found difficult and irritating . . . And for quite other reasons I cannot make much of Anaïs Nin's fragment about Woman.' 21 FEBRUARY – visits Ottoline Morrell (for the final time). 22 FEBRUARY – goes with Mary Hutchinson to see the Michel St Denis production of Chekhov's *Three Sisters*; he is reduced to tears by the performance – 'my only experience, I think, of weeping visibly in a theatre'. 24 FEBRUARY – writes of William Saroyan: 'I have been fearful for some time that Saroyan's fluency might kill his market . . . It would be a pity if anyone so clever as Saroyan should go dead after such a short run, and we don't want him to have a meteoric Damon Runyon career.' TSE commissions a review from Ronald Duncan of a book on India. MARCH – accepts for F&F the poems of F. T. Prince. 1 MARCH – lunches with Charles Williams. 3 MARCH – lunches with Philip Mairet. 4 MARCH – accepts an invitation from Will Spens, Master of Corpus Christi College, to deliver the Boutwood Lectures at Cambridge in 1939: 'two lectures on any subject in political or religious philosophy or in the border-line between these'. 7 MARCH – dines with the Fabers, along with the historian Keith Feiling. 8 MARCH – TSE is disappointed not to be able to secure publishing rights to the poems of Hart Crane. 14 MARCH – attends meeting of All Souls Club. 16 MARCH – accepts invitation to serve on the panel for the inaugural Camoëns Prize – to be adjudicated in Lisbon – for 'the best literary or scientific work on Portugal published abroad by a foreign author during the last two years'. 17 MARCH – goes again to 'Archbps Commission'. Publishes an essay on 'Who Controls Population-Distribution?' in *New English Weekly*. 18 MARCH – meets with Hugh Macdonald. 18 MARCH – F&F publishes Stephen Spender's play *Trial of a Judge*. (On 22 Mar. TSE tells Spender, 'I was very much impressed and moved . . . My chief criticism of the play itself, on the stage, is that I thought there was too much poetry. It seems to me that for the stage one needs a good deal of straightforward simple verse. So much poetry is deadening to one's sensibility, and also doesn't leave any reserve for hammering with particular passages and phrases.' He will later say, on the question in general: 'I should like to retain the older and more respectable term of Dramatic Poetry, not so much in reference to the plays themselves, but to draw the distinction, which is frequently overlooked, between dramatic poetry and other poetry. It is not merely that a play is written in poetry; it must be written in poetry of a particular kind, which we call dramatic.') 21 MARCH – dines with the Woolfs, and then goes to see the stage production of *Trial of a Judge.* 22 MARCH – meets up with John Hayward, John Betjeman and Richard Jennings. 24 MARCH – turns down a proposal to publish the collected poems of John Skelton. 27 MARCH – dines with the McKnight Kauffers, in honour of Hayward. APRIL – publishes 'On a Recent Piece of Criticism' in the little magazine *Purpose* – a response to G. W. Stonier's article 'The Mystery of Ezra Pound' in the previous issue. 7 APRIL – a further broadcast of verses from *Old Possum's Book of Cats.* 18 APRIL – TSE submits Old *Possum's Book of Practical Cats* to F&F. 19 APRIL – All Souls Club. 21 APRIL – goes to lunch at Maurice Reckitt's residence. Lewis's portrait of TSE is rejected by the Hanging Committee of the Royal Academy. TSE writes to Lewis: 'I am glad to think that a portrait of myself should not appear in the exhibition of the Royal Academy, and I certainly have no desire, now, that my portrait should be painted by any painter whose portrait of me would be accepted by the Royal Academy.' 23 APRIL – journeys to Portugal. Reports: 'The English here seem very dull. Actually, the Portuguese are much the nicest people in Lisbon.' Writes later: 'the impressions of respect and admiration for [the President] Dr Salazar, formed by reading, were confirmed by having the privilege of meeting him.' APRIL / MAY – publishes 'Inquiry into the Spirit and Language of Night', in *transition* (Paris). MAY – F&F publishes *The Earth Compels*, by Louis MacNeice. 7 MAY – a further reading of cat poems on the BBC. 16 MAY – returns from Lisbon to London. 17 MAY – All Souls Club. 21 MAY – takes tea with Virginia Woolf. 25 MAY – stays with the Richmonds; lectures on George Herbert in the chapter house of Salisbury Cathedral: *Complete Prose* 5. 26 MAY – declines to become a member of the British

Committee of the Keats–Shelley Memorial at Rome. 27 MAY – 'Martin Browne's at 7.30.' FROM 30 MAY – seeks to get a hearing for the music of a German-Jewish composer and architect named Dr Richard Fuchs: specifically, his setting of 'A Song for Simeon'. 3 JUNE – in the morning, gives Prize Day address at Truro Methodist Boys School, Devon: published as 'On Christianity and a Useful Life', in the school magazine *The Truronian* (Dec. 1938); in the afternoon, he gives the Prize Day address at West Cornwall School for Girls, Penzance: 'How to Read Poetry': both in *Complete Prose 5*. TSE says he regards 'speechday speeches' as 'the least congenial of all public activities. Had I a stronger character I should refuse to do this sort of thing, which ought to be left to those who can utter platitudes confidently.' 6 JUNE – Chandos Club dinner. 8 JUNE – TSE reluctantly turns down the poem 'Mature Art' by C. M. Grieve: 'while I can sometimes urge them to publish a small book of verse which I know will lose money, I cannot ask them to tie up so much capital in anything so monumental as this. I would like to see it published, and I would be willing to give my personal support, for what it is worth, if you approached some other firm.' 9 JUNE – receives hon. Litt.D. from Cambridge, conferred by Lord Baldwin, Chancellor of the University. 13 JUNE – F&F issues a contract for the publication of *The Family Reunion*. TSE hopes to secure an option to publish the poems of William Carlos Williams. 14 JUNE – All Souls Club. 17 JUNE – writes to Henry Swabey (who is seeking Holy Orders): 'to deny that celibacy is the highest ideal (however few people may be fitted to practise it) seems to me to be in a very bad spiritual muddle'. 21 JUNE – lunches with Louis MacNeice and Theodore Spencer. THIRD WEEK OF JUNE – visits the Dobrées for a weekend in Leeds. 22 JUNE – Chandos Club dinner. 24 JUNE – advised that the *Harvard Advocate* wishes to reprint his juvenile poems, TSE answers: 'I should feel no shame in seeing my undergraduate verse for the *Advocate* reappear, so long as each of the poems that you choose is dated.' 25 JUNE – Tandy broadcasts 'Jellicles and Other Cats' (five unpublished poems). 28 JUNE – dines with the Fabers. JULY – F&F publishes Herbert Read's *Poetry and Anarchism*. TSE publishes 'Five Points on Dramatic Writing', *Townsman* 1: 3 (the text taken from a letter to EP). 1 JULY – encourages Stephen Spender to submit his translation of *Danton's Death*, by George Büchner. 1–3 JULY – visits Bristol. 5 JULY – TSE speaks on 'The Future of Verse Drama' at the International Theatre Congress, Stratford-upon-Avon: printed in *Drama*, Oct. 1938: *Complete Prose* 5. (To J. Betjeman, 22 June: 'I cannot help thinking at the moment that if people will ask me to talk about Verse Drama, it is all the less likely to have any future at all, and I don't like international conventions, but I accepted in order to get out of a rather difficult position in connexion with the National Theatre, which I don't want to be concerned with.') FROM 9 JULY – TSE stays for a week with the Perkinses and Emily Hale in Chipping Campden. 14 JULY – Maurice Haigh-Wood notifies TSE that Vivien has been found wandering the streets of London in the early hours and consequently has been taken into police custody: she may have to go to an asylum or 'some home'. 21 JULY – F&F publishes *Guide to Kulchur* by Ezra Pound. 25 JULY – TSE attends 'Domum Dinner' at Winchester College, where he gives a short speech. 27 JULY – turns down a pioneering book on Picasso: 'I candidly do not see how we or any other firm at the present time could sell it.' 29 JULY – commissions *The End of Fear* by Denis Saurat. 3 AUGUST – commissions a new series of Shell Guides: starting off with *Somerset*, by Betjeman and Peter Quennell. 4 AUGUST – TSE publishes his tribute to 'Professor H. H. Joachim', in the *Times* (*Complete Prose* 5): says he owes to Joachim 'not only whatever knowledge of the philosophy of Aristotle I may once have possessed but also whatever command of prose style I still possess.' Prompted by Geoffrey Faber, TSE seeks to commission a book on Martin Niemöller, Lutheran pastor and anti-Nazi theologian – to cover 'the adventurousness of his earlier life, and the present impressiveness of his behaviour and condition'. He turns down a proposal for an anthology of modern French poetry edited by David Gascoyne. 9 AUGUST – writes to Maurice Haigh-Wood: 'In reply to your letter of the 5th instant, so far as my authority is concerned and so far as my authorisation is necessary, I give you my authority to apply for certification of your sister, Mrs T. S. Eliot, if Dr Bernard Hart thinks advisable, or to take any steps leading thereto which he thinks advisable, which may require my authorisation as well as yours.' MID-AUGUST – on doctors' advice, Vivien Eliot is committed to a London asylum called Northumberland House

– 'certified of unsound mind'. 22 AUGUST – TSE goes to production of *Richard III*. 25 AUGUST – is pleased that John Gielgud is interested in being involved with *The Family Reunion*. 26 AUGUST – TSE spends ten days in Wales with the Faber family. EARLY SEPTEMBER – purchases a Norwegian elkhound, a hunting dog named Boerre, for Emily Hale, who takes it with her to Smith College, Northampton, Mass. 'I felt acute relief at getting Emily off. I had felt anxiety for some weeks; as from no point of view that I can admit, would it be desirable for her to be here in time of war. Please God that may not happen; but the position is still so delicate that I shall, on balance, be glad to think of her on the other side of the water while it lasts. And while she has not gained so much as I should wish, yet she is obviously better in health than a year ago.' 1 SEPTEMBER – writes to Royal Literary Fund in support of an application for a grant for Dylan Thomas. 'I consider him one of a very small number of notable poets of his generation whose names will survive the test of time; he has the additional distinction of being the most brilliant (in my opinion) of younger Welsh writers.' 13 SEPTEMBER – recommends Hugh MacDiarmid's poem 'Mature Art' to Macmillan & Co.: 'I should like to say that it seems to me a remarkable work, which well deserves to be published, and I for one shall be very happy if you think favourably of it.' 15 SEPTEMBER – Vivien Eliot escapes from her asylum for twenty-four hours; is detained and returned. 19 SEPTEMBER – goddaughter Anthea Tandy's birthday. TSE dines with the Fabers, along with Ann and Dick Faber, and they all go off to the cinema to see *Spawn of the North*. 23–25 SEPTEMBER – attends a weekend conference in Hampstead: the first meeting of The Moot convened by J. H. Oldham. 26 SEPTEMBER – comments on Geoffrey Grigson's proposal for an anthology of work from the magazine *New Verse*: 'we were somewhat disappointed not to have some-thing in the nature of a longer and more animated manifesto of *New Verse* policy as a preface . . . [W]hat has made *New Verse* so welcome amongst periodicals has been the red pepper or vitriol of the editor, as much as the major part of the verse contributions.' (*New Verse: An Anthology* is to be published by F&F in 1939.) LATE SEPTEMBER – TSE meets up with his old friend the poet Ralph Hodgson, who is visiting London; invites him to draw the illustrations for the forthcoming volume *Old Possum's Book of Practical Cats*. Sadly this does not come to pass – though TSE still dedicates the volume to 'The Man in White Spats'. OCTOBER 'There seems no hope in contemporary politics at all,' writes TSE in his 'Commentary' (*Criterion* 18). 1 OCTOBER – TSE decides to close down the *Criterion*, telling Geoffrey Faber: 'It is impossible to run a one-man show like this for fifteen years without feeling that it is going stale. I have run it without conviction for several years; only I felt that so long as you and Frank [Morley] felt that it was of some advertising value to the firm – or that my chief use to the firm was running the *Criterion* – I couldn't well give it up [. . .] And there are some bitter memories of the early years – before your time! – it was in no mood of enthusiasm, but more nearly of desperation, that I consented to launch the review: certainly the happiest editorial years have been those when the review belonged exclusively to Faber & Faber. For this, as for many things, I am grateful to you. Incidentally, I do not forget that it was on the pretext of the *Criterion* that I was insinuated – with some difficulty – into Faber & Gwyer's.' 3 OCTOBER – writes to congratulate Duff Cooper on his stance in opposition to the Munich Agreement. 7 OCTOBER – spends weekend at the House of the Resurrection, Mirfield, Yorkshire. 18 OCTOBER – dines in London with Ezra Pound, who is staying at the flat of his mother-in-law (who has just died). 18 OCTOBER – seeks to arrange some speaking engagements in the USA for Louis MacNeice for spring 1939. 19 OCTOBER – dines with John Gielgud and Martin Browne: '[Gielgud] chose oysters, guinness, and a tournedos. Oysters for three make quite a hole in a pound note.' MID-OCTOBER – visits on several occasions his aged friend and servant W. L. Janes, who is in hospital. 21 OCTOBER – gives lunch to Spender at the Oxford & Cambridge Club. 23 OCTOBER – spends the weekend in Oxford. 27 OCTOBER – F&F publishes *On the Frontier* by Auden and Isherwood. 3 NOVEMBER – F&F turns down the short stories of Boris Pasternak. TSE turns down an invitation to join the Academic Committee of the Royal Society of Literature: 'It would be embarrassing for me as a publisher, and especially as a publisher of contemporary poetry, to take part in such decisions.' 8 NOVEMBER – dines at Oxford & Cambridge Club with Ralph Hodgson and John Betjeman. 14 NOVEMBER –

visits the economist J. M. Keynes in Cambridge, where he sees the Auden/Isherwood play *On the Frontier* (with Keynes's wife, the ballerina Lydia Lopokova, acting in it) at the Arts Theatre. 15 NOVEMBER – dines with Elizabeth Bowen and her husband Alan Cameron. 16 NOVEMBER – dines with Pound. 17 NOVEMBER – dines with Charles Williams. 18 NOVEMBER – goes with Frank Morley and Stuart Gilbert for drinks at Hayward's new flat in Swan Court; dines with Pound at the Oxford & Cambridge Club. 23 NOVEMBER – decides to give his Boutwood lectures at Cambridge in 1939 on 'The Idea of a Christian State' – 'I am aiming at discussing the contemporary situation in its novelty.' FIRST WEEK OF DECEMBER – goes to *Twelfth Night* – 'pretty bad, I thought,' he tells Virginia Woolf. 1 DECEMBER – looks over *The Book of the Dead*, by Lawrence Durrell, with a view to running an extract in the *Criterion*. 'I have read your prefatory letter from God with a great deal of interest, and frequent admiration. I do feel, of course, that God uses the very characteristic idioms of Lawrence Durrell, but I suppose that He may be expected to speak to each of us in our own language.' 5 DECEMBER – writes to Sidney Dark, 'I am naturally sympathetic with any protest against maltreatment of Jews, whether abroad or in this country.' 10 DECEMBER – spends weekend with Gerry and Mabel Hopkins (Elizabeth Bowen and her husband are also guests). 12 DECEMBER – dines *chez* Faber, along with Lady Rhondda and the author Sarah Gertrude Millin. 13 DECEMBER – attends his 'serious dining club' – All Souls – at Lord Wolmer's home. 15 DECEMBER – enjoys a 'small Christmas dinner' (complete with crackers) with Hope Mirrlees. 17 DECEMBER – the *Harvard Advocate* republishes 'Eight Poems' – 'The Undergraduate Poems of T. S. Eliot': *Harvard Advocate* 125. 18 DECEMBER – dines with the Woolfs: Virginia Woolf remarks that the flaws in TSE's play *The Family Reunion* are to be found in the 'department of humour'. 23 DECEMBER – goes with the Fabers to a pantomime. 25 DECEMBER – spends Christmas Day with John Hayward. 26 DECEMBER – dines with George Every. 29 DECEMBER – dines with Lawrence Durrell and Henry Miller, in Notting Hill. 31 DECEMBER – spends New Year's Eve with the Morley family.

# ABBREVIATIONS AND SOURCES

PUBLISHED WORKS BY T. S. ELIOT

| | |
|---|---|
| *ASG* | *After Strange Gods* (London: Faber & Faber, 1934) |
| *AVP* | *Ara Vos Prec* (London: The Ovid Press, 1920) |
| *CP* | *The Cocktail Party* (London: Faber & Faber, 1950) |
| *CPP* | *The Complete Poems and Plays of T. S. Eliot* (London: Faber & Faber, 1969) |
| *CProse* | *The Complete Prose of T. S. Eliot: The Critical Edition*, general editor Ronald Schuchard; various volumes, ongoing (Baltimore, MD: Johns Hopkins University Press/London: Faber & Faber, 2014–  ) |
| *EE* | *Elizabethan Essays* (London: Faber & Faber, 1934) |
| *FLA* | *For Lancelot Andrewes: Essays on Style and Order* (London: Faber & Gwyer, 1928) |
| *FR* | *The Family Reunion* (London: Faber & Faber, 1939) |
| Gallup | Donald Gallup, *T. S. Eliot: A Bibliography* (London: Faber & Faber, 1969) |
| *HJD* | *Homage to John Dryden: Three Essays on Poetry of the Seventeenth Century* (London: The Hogarth Press, 1924) |
| *IMH* | *Inventions of the March Hare: Poems 1909–1917*, ed. Christopher Ricks (London: Faber & Faber, 1996) |
| *KEPB* | *Knowledge and Experience in the Philosophy of F. H. Bradley* (London: Faber & Faber, 1964; New York: Farrar, Straus & Company, 1964) |
| *L* | *Letters of T. S. Eliot* (London: Faber & Faber, Vol. 1 [rev. edn], 2009; Vol. 2, 2009; Vol. 3, 2012; Vol. 4, 2013; Vol. 5, 2014; Vol. 6, 2017 |
| *MiC* | *Murder in the Cathedral* (London: Faber & Faber, 1935) |

| | |
|---|---|
| OPP | *On Poetry and Poets* (London: Faber & Faber, 1957; New York: Farrar, Straus & Cudahy, 1957) |
| P | *Poems* (London: The Hogarth Press, 1919) |
| P 1909–1925 | *Poems 1909–1925* (London: Faber & Gwyer, 1925) |
| Poems | *The Poems of T. S. Eliot*, ed. Christopher Ricks & Jim McCue (London: Faber & Faber, 2015) |
| POO | *Prufrock and Other Observations* (London: The Egoist Press, 1917) |
| SA | *Sweeney Agonistes: Fragments of an Aristophanic Melodrama* (London: Faber & Faber, 1932) |
| SE | *Selected Essays: 1917–1932* (London: Faber & Faber, 1932; 3rd English edn, London and Boston: Faber & Faber, 1951) |
| SW | *The Sacred Wood: Essays on Poetry and Criticism* (London: Methuen & Co., 1920) |
| TCC | *To Criticise the Critic* (London: Faber & Faber, 1965; New York: Farrar, Straus & Giroux, 1965) |
| TUPUC | *The Use of Poetry and the Use of Criticism: Studies in the Relation of Criticism to Poetry in England* (London: Faber & Faber, 1933) |
| TWL | *The Waste Land* (1922, 1923) |
| TWL: Facs | *The Waste Land: A Facsimile and Transcript of the Original Drafts*, ed. Valerie Eliot (London: Faber & Faber, 1971; New York: Harcourt, Brace Jovanovich, 1971; reissued, with corrections, 2011) |
| VMP | *The Varieties of Metaphysical Poetry*, ed. Ronald Schuchard (London: Faber & Faber, 1993; New York: Harcourt Brace, 1994) |

PERIODICALS AND PUBLISHERS

| | |
|---|---|
| A. | *The Athenaeum* (see also *N&A*) |
| C. | *The Criterion* |
| F&F | Faber & Faber (publishers) |
| F&G | Faber & Gwyer (publishers) |
| MC | *The Monthly Criterion* |
| N. | *The Nation* |
| N&A | *The Nation & The Athenaeum* |
| NC | *New Criterion* |
| NEW | *New English Weekly* |

| NRF | La Nouvelle Revue Française |
|-----|---------------------------|
| NS | New Statesman |
| NS&N | New Statesman and Nation |
| TLS | Times Literary Supplement |

PERSONS

| CA | Conrad Aiken |
|-----|-------------|
| RA | Richard Aldington |
| WHA | W. H. Auden |
| JB | John Betjeman |
| EMB | E. Martin Browne |
| RC-S | Richard Cobden-Sanderson |
| RdlM | Richard de la Mare |
| BD | Bonamy Dobrée |
| EVE | (Esmé) Valerie Eliot |
| HWE | Henry Ware Eliot (TSE's brother) |
| TSE | T. S. Eliot |
| VHE | Vivien (Haigh-Wood) Eliot |
| GCF | Geoffrey (Cust) Faber |
| MHW | Maurice Haigh-Wood |
| EH | Emily Hale |
| JDH | John Davy Hayward |
| MH | Mary Hutchinson |
| AH | Aldous Huxley |
| JJ | James Joyce |
| GWK | G. Wilson Knight |
| DHL | D. H. Lawrence |
| FRL | F. R. Leavis |
| WL | Wyndham Lewis |
| LM | Louis MacNeice |
| FVM | Frank (Vigor) Morley |
| OM | Ottoline Morrell |
| JMM | John Middleton Murry |
| EP | Ezra Pound |
| HR | Herbert Read |
| IAR | I. A. Richards |
| BLR | Bruce Richmond |
| ALR | A. L. Rowse |
| ES | Edith Sitwell |
| SS | Stephen Spender |

| WFS | William Force Stead |
| CW | Charles Williams |
| LW | Leonard Woolf |
| VW | Virginia Woolf |
| WBY | W. B. Yeats |

ARCHIVE COLLECTIONS

| Arkansas | Special Collections, University Libraries, University of Arkansas |
| BBC | BBC Written Archives, Caversham |
| Beinecke | The Beinecke Rare Book and Manuscript Library, Yale University |
| Berg | Henry W. and Albert A. Berg Collection of English and American Literature, the New York Public Library |
| Bodleian | The Bodleian Library, Oxford University |
| BL | The British Library |
| Boston | Mugar Memorial Library, Boston University |
| Boston Athenaeum | Boston Athenaeum, Boston, Massachusetts |
| Brotherton | The Brotherton Collection, Leeds University Library |
| Buffalo | Poetry Collection, Lockwood Memorial Library, State University of New York, Buffalo |
| Butler | Rare Books and Manuscripts Division, Butler Library, Columbia University, New York |
| Chicago | Special Collections Research Centre, University of Chicago Library |
| Cornell | Department of Rare Books, Olin Library, Cornell University |
| Denison | Ella Strong Denison Library, Scripps College, California |
| Edinburgh | Edinburgh University Library |
| Exeter | Exeter University Library |
| Faber | Faber & Faber Archive, London |
| Galleria Nazionale d'Arte Moderna | Galleria Nazionale d'Arte Moderna, Rome |
| Harvard | Harvard University Archives, Pusey Library, Harvard University |
| John Hay | John Hay Library, Brown University, Providence, Rhode Island |

| | |
|---|---|
| Hornbake | Hornbake Library, University of Maryland |
| Houghton | The Houghton Library, Harvard University |
| Keele | The Library, Keele University, Staffordshire |
| King's | Modern Archive Centre, King's College, Cambridge |
| Kresge | Kresge Library, Oakland University, Rochester, Michigan |
| Lambeth | Lambeth Palace Library, London |
| Lilly | Lilly Library, Indiana University, Bloomington, Illinois |
| Magdalene | Old Library, Magdalene College, Cambridge |
| Morgan | Pierpont Morgan Library, New York |
| Morris | Morris Library, Southern Illinois University, Carbondale, Illinois |
| National Gallery of Ireland | National Gallery of Ireland, Dublin |
| National Library of Scotland | National Library of Scotland, Edinburgh |
| National Library of Wales | National Library of Wales, Aberystwyth, Ceredigion |
| Northwestern | Special Collections Department, Northwestern University Library, Evanston, Illinois |
| Pembroke | The Library, Pembroke College, Cambridge |
| Princeton | Department of Rare Books and Special Collections, Firestone Library, Princeton University |
| Reading | Special Collections, Reading University Library |
| Reed | Special Collections and Archives, Reed College Library, Portland, Oregon |
| Royal Literary Fund | Royal Literary Fund Archive, Fleet Street, London |
| San Feliu de Guíxols | Municipal Archive of Sant Feliu de Guíxols, Catalonia |
| Strasbourg | Bibliothèque Nationale et Universitaire de Strasbourg |
| Sussex | Manuscript Collections, University of Sussex Library |
| Syracuse | George Arents Research Library for Special Collections, Syracuse University Library, New York |

# CHRONOLOGY OF *THE CRITERION*

*The Criterion*

Vol. 1. No. 1. 1–103, Oct. 1922; No. 2. 105–201, Jan. 1923;
No. 3. 203–313, Apr. 1923; No. 4. 315–427, July 1923.

Vol. 2. No. 5. 1–113, Oct. 1923; No. 6. 115–229, Feb. 1924;
No. 7 231–369, Apr. 1924; No. 8 371–503, July 1924.

Vol. 3. No. 9. 1–159, Oct. 1924; No. 10. 161–340, Jan. 1925;
No. 11 341–483, Apr. 1925; No. 12. 485–606, July 1925.

*The New Criterion*

Vol. 4. No. 1. 1–220, Jan. 1926; No. 2. 221–415, Apr. 1926;
No. 3. 417–626, June 1926; No. 4. 627–814, Oct. 1926.

Vol. 5. No. 1. 1–186, Jan. 1927.

*The Monthly Criterion*

Vol. 5. No. 2. 187–282, May 1927; No. 3. 283–374, June 1927.

Vol. 6. No. 1. 1–96, July 1927; No. 2. 97–192, Aug. 1927; No. 3.
193–288, Sept. 1927; No. 4. 289–384, Oct. 1927; No. 5. 385–480,
Nov. 1927; No. 6. 481–584, Dec. 1927.

Vol. 7. No. 1. 1–96, Jan. 1928; No. 2. 97–192, Feb. 1928;
No. 3. 193–288, Mar. 1928.

*The Criterion*

Vol. 7. No. 4. 289–464, June 1928.

Vol. 8. No. 30. 1–183, Sept. 1928; No. 31. 185–376, Dec. 1928;
No. 32. 377–573, Apr. 1929; No. 33. 575–772, July 1929.

Vol. 9. No. 34. 1–178, Oct. 1929; No. 35, 181–380, Jan. 1930;
No. 36, 381–585, Apr. 1930; No. 37, 587–787, July 1930.

Vol. 10. No. 38. 1–209, Oct. 1930; No. 39. 211–391, Jan. 1931;
No. 40. 393–592, Apr. 1931; No. 41. 593–792, July 1931.

Vol. 11. No. 42. 1–182, Oct. 1931; No. 43. 183–374, Jan 1932;
No. 44. 375–579, Apr. 1932; No. 45. 581–775, July 1932.

Vol. 12. No. 46. 1–174, Oct. 1932; No. 47. 175–338, Jan. 1933; No. 48. 339–548, Apr. 1933; No. 49. 549–722, July 1933.

Vol. 13. No. 50. 1–178, Oct. 1933; No. 51. 179–352, Jan. 1934; No. 52. 353–536, Apr. 1934; No. 53. 537–716, July 1934.

Vol. 14. No. 54. 1–180, Oct. 1934; No. 55. 181–350, Jan. 1935; No. 56. 351–546, Apr. 1935; No. 57. 547–730, July 1935.

Vol. 15. No. 58. 1–182, Oct. 1935; No. 59. 183–378, Jan. 1936; No. 60. 379–578, Apr. 1938; No. 61, 579–780. July 1936.

Vol. 16. No. 62. 1–204, Oct. 1936; No. 63, 205–404, Jan. 1937; No. 64. 405–584, Apr. 1937; No 65. 585–772, July 1937.

Vol. 17. No. 66. 1–204, Oct. 1937; No. 67. 205–402, Jan. 1938; No. 68. 403–602, Apr. 1938; No. 69. 603–799, July 1938.

Vol. 18. No. 70. 1–178, Oct. 1938; No. 71. 179–413, Jan. 1939.

Ceased publication.

# EDITORIAL NOTES

The source of each letter is indicated at the top right. CC indicates a carbon copy. Where no other source is shown it may be assumed that the original or carbon copy is in the Valerie Eliot collection or at the Faber Archive.

*del.*   deleted

MS   manuscript

n. d.   no date

PC   postcard

*sc.*   *scilicet*: namely

TS   typescript

<   >   indicates a word or words brought in from another part of the letter.

Place of publication is London, unless otherwise stated.

Some obvious typing or manuscript errors, and slips of grammar and spelling, have been silently corrected.

Dates have been standardised.

Some words and figures which were abbreviated have been expanded.

Punctuation has been occasionally adjusted.

Editorial insertions are indicated by square brackets.

Words both italicised and underlined signify double underlining in the original copy.

Where possible a biographical note accompanies the first letter to or from a correspondent. Where appropriate this brief initial note will also refer the reader to the Biographical Register at the end of the text.

Vivienne Eliot liked her husband and friends to spell her name Vivien; but as there is no consistency it is printed as written.

'Not in Gallup' means that the item in question is not recorded in Donald Gallup, *T. S. Eliot: A Bibliography* (1969).

# THE LETTERS
## 1936–1938

For letters omitted from this and the previous volumes of T. S. Eliot's
correspondence, please visit www.tseliot.com

# 1936

TO *Alison Tandy*[1]                                                    TS copy

[1 January 1936]                    Faber & Faber Ltd

Mr Possum wishes that his name was Tristram Shandy,
Or Mahatma Gandhi
Or even Yankee Doodle Dandy
So that he could reply in poetry to the kind invitation of
Miss Alison Tandy:
But as it is, this is only verse
Going from worse to worse.
In the first place, January 5th is a Sunday,
NOT a Saturday or a Monday,
And Saturday is the Four
Of January, neither less nor more.
FURTHERMORE:
Mr Possum has inadvisedly said
That alive or sleeping or dead
And whether well or poorly
He would go to visit Mr & Mrs Morley
As well as Donald Oliver and Susanna Morley[2]
(Though he may regret it sorely)
And their zoo and aviary,
Carrying his breviary,
And whether sad or merry,
On the Fourth of January,[3]
And with a spell of the Dry G(r)in
To see the New Year WELL in.
O Dear will Miss Tandy give another party a little later

---

1 – Alison Tandy (b. 1930), second child of TSE's close friends Geoffrey and Polly Tandy.
2 – Donald, Oliver and Susanna (TSE left out a comma): John Donald Innes Morley, b. 15
Mar. 1926; Hugh Oliver Morley, b. 4 Dec. 1928; Susanna Loveday Morley, b. 12 May 1932.
3 – FVM's birthday.

And Mr Possum would love to come all rolled up in gravy and
Sweet pertater.

P.S. I ADMIRE your Handsome Drawing.

## TO *Geoffrey Faber*[1]
TS Faber Archive

[Undated: ? January 1936]           [Faber & Faber Ltd]

Mr Eliot's Book of Pollicle Dogs & Jellicle Cats (As Recited to Him by the
Man in White Spats) should be completed by Easter 1936. It is possible
that the drawings submitted may be judged unsatisfactory, and if a new
Artist has to be set to work, that will delay publication still further.

T. S. E.[2]

1 – Geoffrey Faber (1889–1961), publisher: see Biographical Register.
2 – The F&F catalogue 'Spring Books Announcements, 1936' (p. 69) carried this notice of
the work – probably written by GCF or FVM:

Mr Eliot's book of
Pollicle Dogs and Jellicle Cats
As Recited to Him by the Man in White Spats

Mr Eliot informs the Publishers that his book of Children's Verses should be
completed by Easter, 1936. If this statement (for which the Publishers accept no
responsibility) proves to be true, the book will certainly be published this year
with the least possible delay.
There is no doubt that Mr Eliot is writing it; for several of the poems, illustrated
by the author, have been in private circulation in the Publishers' various families
for a considerable time, and at least one of them has been recorded on the
gramophone. (*N.B.* – There is only one record in this country, and there is believed
to be another in America. Applications for duplicates will be thrown into the
waste-paper basket.)
Mr Eliot intends to illustrate the book himself; but it is not yet possible to be
sure that reproduction of the illustrations will be within the scope of any existing
process. No announcement can, therefore, be made about the price of this book,
but every endeavour will be made to keep it within reason.

See JDH, 'London Letter', *New York Sun*, 25 Jan. 1936, 71: 'a volume of nonsense verse
"Pollicle Dogs and Jellicle Cats as Recited to Him by the Man in White Spats!" This, I can
tell you, will be a rare treat, not least on account of the illustrations that Eliot proposes to
make for it.'
TSE's secretary to C. S. Kreiter, 25 June 1959: 'And jellicle, by the way is . . . a diminutive
of "Jellylorum" which was the name of a cat of that description which Mr Eliot once owned.'
Donald Morley to TSE, 14 Mar. 1937: 'Dear Uncle Tomithy [*sic*] . . . I still fail to see how
Pollicle DOGS has to do with CATS.'

1 January 1936                    [Faber & Faber Ltd]

Dear Mairet,

I must apologize for my silence, but I had been hoping to write to you with a *Views and Reviews* enclosed. With the distractions of Christmas and finishing up several odd jobs I have not had not [*sic*] time, but I hope to let you have something within a week or ten days.

By the way Bonamy Dobrée is back again in England.[2] His new address is River House, Earls Colne, Essex.

I have been trying to excogitate a note for you about Racine in order to neutralize to some extent the poisonous doctrine that Herbert Read has lately been preaching in your pages.[3]

I should like to know how your guarantee fund is really getting on. What size guarantee do you aim at? I mean how small subscriptions are acceptable?[4]

1 – Philip Mairet (1886–1975), journalist and author; editor of *New English Weekly*: see Biographical Register.

2 – Bonamy Dobrée (1891–1974), scholar, editor and critic: see Biographical Register.

3 – HR had been lauding Surrealism in his 'Views and Reviews' column. Writing for example on David Gascoyne's *A Short Survey of Surrealism* (1935) and André Breton's *Position politique du surréalisme* (1935), he entered this testimony in a way that must have irked TSE: 'The time is past when anyone can seriously dispute the relevance of the facts established by psycho-analysis; what we might call the unconscious basis of all forms of art is an established fact. I believe that the greatest power of art, especially the greatest power of the greatest art – poetry – is derived from the automatic workings of the poet's mind, and that the poet's essential faculties (his sensibility to language and his agility in metaphor-making) are only operative when the rational faculties are suspended and expression becomes instinctive (intuitive or unconscious). Whatever poetry I myself have written was written in that belief' (*NEW* 8: 10 [19 Dec. 1935], 191–2).

4 – *The New English Weekly: A Review of Public Affairs, Literature and the Arts* issued a Statement (n.d.) to those who subscribed to the Guarantee Fund set up early in 1935 (after the death of A. R. Orage); it included these remarks: 'Much of our success is due to the generous support of established writers such as those who have now for some months undertaken the View and Reviews page – T. S. Eliot, Edwin Muir, Bonamy Dobrée and Herbert Read as well as Ezra Pound, J. S. Collis and others; Mr Eliot and Mr Pound having also rendered invaluable service to the Committee in matters of literary policy . . . An independent organ of opinion such as the *New English Weekly* cannot be run without financial support, and when substantial sources of American support were no longer available, this fund was essential to our survival. We believed that a minimum of £800 per annum would be required, but, by rigid economies, it has been found possible to maintain the paper to the date of enclosed Balance Sheet on the Guarantee Fund of £625 actually supplied, with a deficit of £14. 17. 9.'

Mairet answered TSE, 2 Jan.: 'We ran last year on about a loss of £750. Only about £400 is promised for the present year, so far, and we are going on trusting in Providence and reducing expenses. Of course a small subscription would be acceptable, but if you are thinking of this yourself, in view of your generous help already, I trust you will also make

With best wishes for the New Year, to you and Mrs Mairet,

Yours ever,

[T. S. Eliot]

P.S. I wasn't thinking of the younger generation at all. I was thinking about the tiger at Whipsnade.[1]

TO *Henry Miller*[2]                                        TS ?Jay Martin

1 January 1936                    *The Criterion*

Dear Mr Miller,

Excuse my delay in replying to your letter of December 7th.[3] I have no objection to your using my letter to you of 13th June as you wish to do, if you will make certain deletions. At the end of the first paragraph omit the words 'including Mr Herbert Read'. You will no doubt have a letter from Mr Read himself, and it is improper in a published letter to mention other people's opinions than one's own. And in the second paragraph omit the following sentence: 'Without drawing any general comparisons, your own book is a great deal better both in depth of insight and of course in the actual writing than *Lady Chatterley's Lover*.' As I said in my letter of the 16th August the comparison with D. H. Lawrence is irrelevant and not particularly intelligent.

---

any use of the paper that you may wish to.' (He looked forward to receiving a 'Views and Reviews' article from TSE within a week or so.)

1 – In Nov. 1935 TSE had submitted to *NEW* his lyric 'Lines for an Old Man', opening 'The tiger in the tiger-pit / Is not more irritable than I. / The whipping tail is not more still / Than when I smell the enemy / Writhing in the essential blood . . .' TSE's comment in this letter is his matter-of-fact, funny, deflating rejoinder to Mairet's immediate attempt (26 Nov.) to apply to the poem this local metaphorical reading: 'That's a fine devilish poem you sent us for this week! I wonder if – I rather hope that – it was not without point towards these young cubs who've lately been taking presumptuous liberties with Hargrave, with Gill, and with yourself? I've been letting them get a bit too unruly of late, though I do try, on the whole to keep them within bounds.'

2 – Henry Miller (1901–80): American author: see Biographical Register.

3 – Letter not traced.

I was interested in *Max*, but as I told Kahane, I simply could not see what could be done with a manuscript of that length.[1] I look forward to *Black Spring*.[2]

Yours sincerely,
T. S. Eliot

## TO *Henry Eliot*[3]                                                    TS Houghton

1 January 1936                         Faber & Faber Ltd

My dear brother,

I have many arrears, but first of all must thank you for several gifts and kindnesses. First, for the silk dressing gown. My set of pyjamas will last me for a year or two yet, and I only wear cotton: wool are too hot – bed is the one place in my rooms where I can be really warm in cold weather – and too scratchy; and silk are too clammy and slippery. The dressing gown you gave me last year has been invaluable, but it is of no use for travelling or weekend visits, because it takes up the half of a suitcase. I have already an old silk one, but it is shabby, and also I have been desirous of ridding myself, as rapidly as my means permit, of all the clothing that I had before October 1932. So a silk dressing gown it is, with something over for the next weekend at the Morleys.[4]

1–Robert Ferguson, *Henry Miller: A Life* (1991), 244: '*Max*, a fictionalized account of Miller's brief relationship with Rudolf Bachman, an Austrian-Jewish refugee whom he and Nin tried to help in Paris, is one of his four or five best short pieces . . . *Max* . . . provides a fine example of Miller's narrative trick of attempting to present himself to his readers as a heartless monster only to be overruled by the good opinion of other characters in the account.'

2–Ferguson, *Henry Miller*, 246: '*Black Spring* . . . was published in June 1936 by Obelisk . . . A collection of essays too varied to be described as novel [*sic*], it contained some of his wildest surrealist writing.'

3–Henry Ware Eliot (1879–1947), TSE's elder brother: see Biographical Register.

4–HWE to FVM, 5 Dec. 1935: 'Heigh-ho, the holly, and all that. Here we are with the same old problem and asking for your same old assistance. Have been investigating ways & means of delivering 3 pairs woolly pajamas via Santa Claus to Tom. Why woolly pajamas, you will ask, and I can only say that it is the only form of gift that occurs to me that would occur to no one else, hence avoiding possible duplication. The best ones here are imported from England, so it seems foolish to pay the heavy duty to your customs. Besides with your ample opportunity for detective work you can find out whether warm pajamas are acceptable. My theory is that Tom lives in lodging houses (God knows where, I don't) which depend for heat upon fires which you light in the morning and then leap hastily back into bed until they begin to do their work. The adjective woolly as I use it is probably inaccurate, as I do not know the difference between flannel and wool and other things. I have a prejudice of my own in favor of the blouse type or pull-over which has no buttons, but tastes differ, and it

Also, the charming enlargement of mother in the charming frame. I was puzzled at first how it arrived, until I got my secretary to dig the envelope out of her wastepaper basket, and there I recognised Cobden-Sanderson's writing. I am very happy to have this on my mantel at the office; and I am having framed the two Dawes portraits, to hang in my bedroom. I am beginning to have quite a pretty little collection of ancestors; I collect them as some do postage stamps.

I expect to see the Dobrées at the end of next week. I am very grateful to you for all your kindness to him, and I have no doubt that he is also, to judge from one brief but enthusiastic note I received when he was in Tennessee. It is odd about the Cobden-Sandersons, because I had not known that they were going to America. I rarely see them, though I like them well enough, and Richard has a certain convivial charm; Sally is a little too boisterous for my taste.[1] They are very jovial company, but of course have little intellectual interest. I should hardly have thought of commending them to Ada and Sheff, but I think they would go well with the Wolcotts, who are probably not too discriminating.

The Morleys (both) will be over at the end of January, and will certainly look you up, as they also will Ada. She is his first cousin – her father is a don at Cambridge.[2] She went to America with him soon after they were

---

does seem that the prettier and better pajamas are of ye olde button type. So I leave that to you. Also whether to buy 3 pr. med. Quality or 2 pr. extra select grade. Also the very simple problem of What to Do with any fractional sum left over to be liquidated.

'In case gift hereabove suggested is not agreeable, I can think only of a nice leather traveling toiletry case, with all paraphernalia. If Theresa's and my memories serve, Tom had on his visit here some kind of home-made bag of flimsy fabric of the type which is a continual exasperation. This [toiletry case] wouldn't come to as much, probably, as the garments, but the balance could be divided equally in a cash bonus to Tom and comfort for the inner man.

'All this calls for great discretion, infinite tact, diplomacy, acumen, and psychic powers, qualities notably displayed by you last year in a similar difficult situation.

'Incidentally, what are the general conditions as to comfort, heat, food, etc., in whatever place it is that Tom spends his sleeping hours, when not at your house? A brief word-picture . . .

'P.S. Three quid (or is it bob?) enclosed.'

1 – Richard Cobden-Sanderson (1884–1964): printer and publisher; son of the bookbinder and printer, T. J. Cobden Sanderson (1840–1922). He launched his publishing business in 1919 and was publisher of *The Criterion* from its first number in Oct. 1922 until it was taken over by Faber & Gwyer in 1925. He also published three books with introductions by TSE: Paul Valéry, *Le Serpent* (1924), Charlotte Eliot, *Savanarola* (1926), Harold Monro, *Collected Poems* (1933). In addition, he produced books by Edmund Blunden and David Gascoyne, editions of Shelley, and volumes illustrated by Rex Whistler. His wife was Gwladys (Sally) Cobden-Sanderson.

2 – Christina McLeod Morley (b. 1902) was daughter of the Classicist Hugh McLeod Innes

married, and didn't enjoy herself – but then she was parked for a time with Christopher's wife, who I gather is rather tiresome; and Pa Morley, though charming, is an odd creature – but I am sure that she will enjoy it this time. She is very Scotch, but very nice indeed.

I had thought for a moment that I might be coming in the spring, instead of waiting till the autumn, but now it looks less like that. Ashley Dukes,[1] who has been producing *Murder in the C.* successfully at his small theatre here, has wanted to take the English company over. But meanwhile Donald Brace,[2] with the best of intentions, has gone and allowed Elmer Rice to do it for a fortnight in connexion with his scheme (or is it a government scheme) for making work for unemployed hams.[3] This may frost the hopes of the English company. It is a pity, as I shall only get a hundred dollars, less income tax; and if the other company (which is good) could have a run, it might bring me much more than that, as well as improve the chances for the future. But Dukes is to be in New York for a few days towards the end of this month (I will give him your address, in case he has time to look you up, he is a genial fellow) and will explore the possibilities.[4] I had hoped that a successful run of his company might wipe out my solicitors' bill.

When I got your letter of September 12th, I wrote a long reply (though not nearly as long as your letter) and after a few days destroyed it. Perhaps after this lapse of time I can answer it more briefly and temperately. The first page and a third seems to me to contain some excellent and quite justified criticism (I am assuming that you have a carbon copy) but a great deal of the rest of the letter still seems to me very queer. I will take a few points. Of course I cannot remember very clearly my state of mind in 1920 or so, but if I was playing a part, it was primarily to amuse myself. I can only recall such things as the preface to the *Homage to Dryden.* I didn't know that Wells had caricatured it. The habit or mannerism of confessing ignorance is one that I learned from F. H. Bradley. I think that I exploited people's snobbery a bit socially, but although there is much

---

(1862–1944), Fellow of Trinity College, Cambridge; author of *Fellows of Trinity* (1941).

1–Ashley Dukes (1885–1959), theatre manager, playwright, critic, translator, author: see Biographical Register.

2–Donald Brace (1881–1955), publisher; co-founder of Harcourt, Brace: see Biographical Register.

3–Elmer Rice (1892–1967), playwright, socialist, screenwriter, enjoyed considerable Broadway success with plays including *On Trial* (1914), *The Adding Machine* (1923), *Street Scene* (1929; Pulitzer Prize for Drama). He was the first director of the New York office of the Federal Theater Project.

4–Dukes would seek to reassure TSE on 19 Jan. 1936: 'It seems to be generally agreed by critics and theatre people that these performances will not damage the prospects of an eventual season in New York with the London company.'

in *The Sacred Wood* that seems to me adolescent, I can't see that there is much that is affected. I was of course too much engrossed in the horrors of my private life to notice much outside; and I was suffering from (1) a feeling of guilt in having married a woman I detested, and consequently a feeling that I must put up with anything (2) perpetually being told, in the most plausible way, that I was a clodhopper and a dunce. Gradually, through making friends, I came to find that English people of the sort that I found congenial were prepared to take me quite as an ordinary human being, and that I had merely married into a rather common suburban family with a streak of abnormality which in the case of my wife had reached the point of liking to give people pain.[1] I shall always be grateful to a few people like the Woolfs who unconsciously helped me to regain my balance and self-respect.

It seems a little hard that a man's questioning of his own motives should be taken, as you seem to take it, as evidence of their insincerity. I remember quite clearly that when, in 1927, I was received into the Anglican communion, baptised at Finstock and confirmed at Cuddesdon, I made it as secret as possible. It did not occur to me that this might be an item of interest to American journalists, but it did occur to me (and I was right) that it might provide a fresh reason for domestic persecution. I treated it as a private affair. It was subsequently a few words of Irving Babbitt, when he dined with me in passing through London, that provoked the notorious preface to *For Lancelot Andrewes*. He said that I ought to come out into the open; and so I wrote that unlucky preface: but I had no suspicion that it would be so thumbed and quoted as it was. I was merely nettled by Babbitt's suggestion that I was being secretive.[2]

1 – Stephen Spender recalled how VHE's 'reactions' to TSE 'took forms which exposed him to humiliation before strangers. I cite one example, from a later time, just after he had published *Murder in the Cathedral*. A friend of mine who did not know Eliot used to go to the same hairdresser as Vivien Eliot and sometimes found herself sitting side by side with her under the dryer. On one occasion, Vivien Eliot complained bitterly that when she was in the street coming to the hairdressers people in the road persistently stared at her. My friend found this as unaccountable as Mrs Eliot did, until leaving the hairdressers, Mrs Eliot put on her hat. This had stitched on it the rather garish purple and green wrapper of Eliot's play, with the letter print MURDER IN THE CATHEDRAL very prominent round the rim' (*Eliot* [Glasgow, 1975], 130).

2 – TSE had boldly declared in his preface to *For Lancelot Andrewes* (1928) that his 'general point of view' was 'classicist in literature, royalist in politics, and anglo-catholic in religion'.

See too TSE's recollection, in *Irving Babbitt: Man and Teacher*, ed. Frederick Manchester and Odell Shepherd (1941), 103, of having passed an evening with Babbitt on his way through London in mid-Sept. 1928: 'Babbitt in the rôle of guest was at his most charming – having that quality of the perfect guest, of being able to be formal and informal at once, combining the best of both attitudes. He had at command a graciousness, a wit, and even a light humor which most of those who knew him only as a public figure never suspected.

Of course motives are mixed; and therefore it behooves the Christian convert to analyse his own motives for conversion, to confess and reject the bad ones, and lay hold on the good. I believe that this consequence was indicated by my previous interests – my interest in Sanskrit and Pali literature for example, and in the philosophy of Bergson; and that my abortive attempt to make myself into a professor of philosophy was due to a religious preoccupation. But I cannot see that desire for notoriety, or for being on the right side, had anything to do with it. I think that the poems which you mistakenly call 'blasphemous' ('Hippopotamus' and 'Morning Service' point to this end – (incidentally, I have written one blasphemous poem, 'The Hollow Men': that is blasphemy because it is despair, it stands for the lowest point I ever reached in my sordid domestic affairs).

As for the sensation of a person of my antecedents 'going Romish' etc. as you say; please consider that there was no such sensation, not at any rate in England. Most of the churchfolk I know do not even know that I was once a Unitarian, even if they know what a Unitarian is; they don't know what an Eliot is, except to ask what relation I am to the Eliots of Cornwall. And you might remember that even the Eliots have been Unitarians only for four or five generations. As for my address to the Unitarian clergy of Boston, I did not want to address them at all, and I only acceded to repeated invitation. I gave them exactly what I was asked for, and I did not get fair treatment either. As for my failure on that occasion to honour my father and my mother, I cannot attach any meaning to your words.

It follows, that the 'English churchmen' you speak of were not interested in obtaining the services of a celebrated poet who was widely known as a brand plucked from the hotbed of Unitarianism. Most of them do not know to this day that I was a brand etc. They wanted the services of a poet who was an orthodox Anglican, and I was the obvious choice. And it wasn't even 'they', it was the exceptionally enlightened

---

There was nothing of the ogre known to the conventional academic world, to the world of literary journalism, or to the sluggish pupil. Yet to have been once a pupil of Babbitt's was to remain always in that position, and to be grateful always for (in my case) a very much qualified approval.

'The conversation turned upon the direction that Paul More was taking, and anxious though I was to avoid such a painful subject, I found myself obliged to expose and briefly to account for my own position. I imagine that, in view of some of my previous eccentricities in print, this was only a minor shock to him. He took the matter seriously, however, and managed to convince me that it was my duty, in his own words, to "come out into the open." I had not been conscious of skulking, having been more concerned with making up my own mind than with making any public use of it when made. But Babbitt's words gnawed on my conscience, and provoked, for my next volume of essays, a preface that perhaps went to the opposite extreme from that of which I had felt myself accused.'

TSE sent More a proof copy of *FLA* on 28 Sept. 1928.

Bishop of Chichester, who happened to like my poetry, and especially *Ash Wednesday*, that wanted me. Most had never heard of me.

I doubt, at this point, whether as you think a personality is necessarily revealed during the first half of his life. I don't believe that I was there to be known, during that period, as clearly as you think you knew me.

I cannot help still resenting the paragraph on p. 7 beginning 'The step toward the Church . . .' If it is not an accusation of humbug – and humbug in the most serious matter of all – what is?

To continue with p. 7, the words of mine that you quote seem to me simple honest words. Their publicity value was not in my mind when I wrote them, nor is it now.

I can hardly hope to persuade you that I was sincere in praising Dryden's 'flippant phillippic'. (It is not a phillippic anyway). But if I don't know what's poetry, please tell me.

If Cervantes were writing a modern Quixote, he wouldn't make his hero stuff himself with antique literature: he would fill it with what is being written now.

I shall certainly delete nothing from my collected poems.[1] As Pilate, and after him Robert Browning, said, 'what I have written I have written'.[2] It is all part of the progress.

1 – One detail that was deleted was the dedication of *Ash-Wednesday*: 'To my Wife.'
    GCF to I. Alun Jones, 19 Oct. 1934: 'I can tell you . . . that the sales of Eliot's poems are in the neighbourhood of 15,000. Spender and Auden have naturally not reached anything like this figure but they have sold well over two thousand each . . .'
    *Collected Poems* was first advertised with this bantering blurb (almost certainly penned by FVM), in the Faber catalogue *Spring Book Announcements*, 1936, p. 63:
    'It is a chronic malady that Mr Eliot's poems are dissipated through numerous emaciated tomes, and that some have not yet been clothed with the respectability of cloth bindings. *Poems 1909–1925* is the *only* collection so far: but, as the title would suggest, this does not include Mr Eliot's verse subsequent to 1925, or any of his experiments in dramatic form. To our occasional nagging, Mr Eliot has invariably replied that if he did not have to read so many manuscripts he would have more time for writing poetry. To which our reply has always been that after all we make it possible for him to keep body and soul together, and he ought to take the rough with the smooth. He has also observed that he was not ready: that the *Poems 1909–1925* summed up one phase, and that no further collection could be made until another phase had been more clearly defined.
    'What is, however, certain is: this volume contains in the first part all the poems in the previous volume, and in the second everything written subsequently that Mr Eliot wishes to preserve – including *Sweeney Agonistes* and the *Choruses* from *The Rock* – with the exception of *Murder in the Cathedral* and certain nonsense verses which will in due course have a proper book to themselves (see page 69). Here, then, in a definitive form and in a convenient volume, is Mr Eliot's poetical work for a period of 25 years.'
    FVM to C. A. Pearce (Harcourt, Brace & Co.), 15 Oct. 1935: 'Here are two blurbs for Eliot's Poems. You will perceive which is which. One was my own effort, the second was Eliot's corrected version. We are using the corrected version. Do as you like.'
2 – John 19: 22.

As for your suggestion that I have been remiss, according to my own light, in making no attempt to 'convert' members of my own family: it is merely that I have learned enough about human nature not to make such an attempt. 'Conversion' of people who have had no opportunity to hear the Word preached is one thing: conversion of those who have access to it if they want it is another. Among the latter, a man is not converted: he converts himself. Unless he converts himself, he is unconvertable [*sc.* unconvertible]. Don't you suppose that I have Roman friends, waiting readily for me to come to them when I want to convert myself to Rome? But they (you have met D'Arcy) are wise enough to make no overt attempt upon me.

As to 'Bloomsbury', you must know that most of what I believe is anathema to Bloomsbury. I have good friends such as the Woolfs, and I enjoy their company and I like the company of their friends. But I don't belong there. And I have no disciples. And I don't want to resemble the Aga Khan, whom I used to meet years ago at Lady Rothermere's, and who is rather a vulgar person. And I don't believe that one is 'intellectually free' in one place rather than another.

Affectionately,
Tom.

## TO *Henri Massis*[1]                                                            CC

1 janvier 1936                          [Faber & Faber Ltd]

Cher Ami,

Puisque c'est le jour de l'an – que le bilan de mes défauts de l'année passée soit fermé: c'est-à-dire, j'espère que vous pardonnerez mon silence au sujet de Proust. Simplement, j'ai été très affairé ces derniers deux mois; mais simplement aussi, serais-je toujours srave [?ravi] de recevoir de votre plume quel que ce soit. Puis-je toujours attendre l'article sur Proust, qui sera, j'en suis sur, encore un *jugement* digne de l'auteur.

Il est ennuyeux que je ne suis pas parvenu – à cause du change et d'autres événements malencontreux – à revisiter Paris depuis que je vous ai vu il y a deux ans. Comme vous voyez, je suis même devenu à peu prés incapable d'écrire la langue. Toutefois, je garde l'espoir d'une visite au printemps.

1–Henri Massis (1886–1970), right-wing Roman Catholic critic; contributor to *L'Action Française*; co-founder and editor of *La Revue Universelle*.

Encore une idée. Ici-bas, parmi les toutes jeunes gens, le surréalisme, que j'avais cru mort à demi, est devenu subitement presque populaire; c'est une maladie qui commence à faire ses dégâts. Je serais content de mettre la main sur un article là-dessus, qui l'analyserait d'un point de vue que nous trouverions, tous les deux, sympathique.

En exprimant mes meilleurs vœux pour l'année à venir, à vous et à Madame Massis, je reste,

Cordialement votre
[T. S. Eliot][1]

1 – *Translation*: Dear Friend, Since it is New Year's Day – may all the debts I have accrued last year be cancelled: by which I mean, I hope that you will forgive my silence concerning the piece on Proust. The simple fact is, I have been extremely busy these last months; but equally, I would still be delighted to receive from you whatever you have. May I still expect the article on Proust, which will constitute, I am certain, a real *judgement*, worthy of its author ?

It is vexing that I have not been able – because of the change and other inconveniences – to return to Paris since I saw you two years ago. As you can see, I have more or less forgotten how to write the language. I do, however, hope to get there in the spring.

I have another idea. Over here, among the very young, Surrealism – which I took to be half-dead – has suddenly become almost popular; it is an illness that is starting to do harm. I would be glad to get hold of an article on the subject, treating it from a point of view that the two of us would find congenial.

With all best wishes to you and to Mme Massis for the coming year,

Cordially, [T. S. Eliot]

(TSE's use of 'change' in the second paragraph is not clear: he may mean 'exchange rate'.)

2 January 1936 [misdated 1935]      [Faber & Faber Ltd]

Dear Madame Bussy,

I must apologize for the delay in reporting to you about *Véronicana*.² The translation seems to me admirable, although I have not read the original, and the book itself is extremely interesting. I am very glad to have read it, and I quite agree with you that it was worth translating, and that it was worth publishing, but it is obvious at once that the book is one which would have an extremely small sale apart from the people [who] either have read it in French, or who would, as so often happens, merely be impelled, by hearing of a translation, to get hold of the original. I don't believe there are more than a couple of hundred people in the whole of England who would want to buy it and would understand it if they did.

I don't want to be discouraging. Every decent publishing firm produces every season a few books which have no better prospects than this. It would add distinction to any list. The trouble is that my firm has already invested in more good unsaleable books than it can afford to do for the next year. I should very much like you to try someone else because I should like to see the book published. Therefore I am not returning you the manuscript until I hear from you again, as you may have some other firm in mind.

With best wishes for the New Year to Monsieur Bussy and Janey and yourself, and looking forward to seeing you again in the summer.

I am,

Yours very sincerely,

[T. S. Eliot]

1–Dorothy Bussy, née Strachey (1865–1960) – one of the thirteen children of Sir Richard and Jane Strachey; sister of Lytton – was married to the French painter Simon Bussy. Chief translator of André Gide, with whom she was intimate. Her only novel, *Olivia*, was published anonymously by the Hogarth Press (1949).
2–Marcel Jouhandeau, *Véronicana* (1933).

2 January 1936                          Faber & Faber Ltd

My dear John,

Thank you for your kind letter in return for my small gift – and incidentally if your collectionising goes to such absurd lengths – I trust not – but I could provide a copy of the first American edition also. But still more, thank you for your warning. It came not a moment too soon. On returning late tonight from dining with Maurice [*sc.* Michel] St Denis and the Brownes (of that more anon) I found on my table a packet from Fortnum & Mason. I thought instantly of Bulldog Drummond and the packet from Asprey's which contained a large and excessively poisonous spider – you remember.[2] But you know me, John, as one accustomed to laugh at danger; in fact I seek it out whenever I feel in need of a good laugh. So I opened it and found a box of my favourite (and most expensive) cigarettes. You see the meaning. Made reckless by impunity, he dares to make known to me his presence in London by what, from another, would have been a pretty compliment. Some would have feared to smoke the cigarettes, expecting to find them charged with high explosive: but I know my Aillevard better.[3] I have taken his measure; and I tell you, I have never met a worthier adversary. Your true Napoleon of crime,[4] John, never descends to such commonplace devices. Mark even the sly humour indicated by the telegraphic address of the tobacconist: 'Simplicity, London'. He had the audacity, furthermore, to enclose a card in his bold and unmistakeable writing. 'Don de Aillevard'. It would appear that for his present purpose he has assumed Spanish nationality; in that however he was anticipated by Arsène Lupin, who (you remember) posed at one time as Don Luis Perenna, Grande d'Espagne (you remember that Luis Perenna is an anagram of Arsène Lupin? there is no anagram in this case. *A voir?* 'La Pluie d'Etincelles'). No, when the blow falls, it will come in some totally unexpected manner: no one but myself will be prepared for it. Useless to notify Scotland Yard.

1 – John Davy Hayward (1905–65), editor and critic: see Biographical Register.
2 – Sapper (H. C. McNeile), *The Final Count* (Book 4 in the Bulldog Drummond series, 1926).
3 – David Bowen to Haffenden, 5 Aug. 1981: 'J. H. told me that he had concocted the epigraph to Stephen Potter's *The Muse in Chains* [1937]. It is in the form of a piece of French poetry beginning "La Pauvre Muse deschinée . . ." and is signed Jean Aillevard – the transliteration of how a Frenchman might be expected to pronounce "John Hayward". Incidentally this is not mentioned in the biography of Stephen Potter recently published. A pity, as it seems to me a typical jeu d'esprit.'
4 – See 'Macavity: The Mystery Cat', l. 42.

Well, John, if you do not hear of your old friend for some time, say for several years, do not be too concerned. If you read of the remarkable explorations of a Norwegian named Sigerson in Tibet, it may not occur to you that you are receiving news of your friend. I may look in at Mecca, and pay a short visit to the Khalifa at Khartoum. I shall be in touch with the Foreign Office. I may spend some months at Montpellier (which is in the south of France) in a research into the coal-tar derivatives. But you may be sure that I shall never rest until my old adversary is laid by the heels.

Very sincerely yours,<br>Herlock Sholmes.

P.S. I sign in this way, as this letter may be intercepted.

## TO *Jessica Dismorr*[1]                                     TS King's

3 January 1936                    [Faber & Faber Ltd]

Dear Jessie,

Thank you so much.[2] I think I shall be able to come to tea with you on Sunday the 12th, and it will be a pleasure. I should be grateful, however, if you could give me more explicit instructions, as I am not exactly at home in Putney. Your directions start at Putney Hill, but please tell me how to get to Putney Hill. And I am better acquainted with the Underground system than I am with bus routes.

Yours sincerely,<br>[T. S. Eliot]

1–Jessica Dismorr (1885–1939), artist and illustrator, associated with the Vorticist movement; friend of WL, whom she met in 1913: she was a signatory to the Vorticist manifesto published in *Blast*, 1914. In the 1930s she did portraits of poets including Dylan Thomas and William Empson. See Catherine Elizabeth Heathcock, *Jessica Dismorr (1885–1939): Artist, Writer, Vorticist* (Unpub. PhD diss., Department of the History of Art, University of Birmingham, 1999); *Jessica Dismorr and Catherine Giles* (Fine Art Society, 2001).
2–Dismorr (1 Jan.) invited TSE to tea at 35 St John's Road, Putney, S.W.15. Henry Moore was possibly going to be there, if back from holiday.

3 January 1936                        [Faber & Faber Ltd]

Dear Mr Hassall,

De la Mare² and I have both read your poem, about which Ottoline had spoken to me.³ I find it extremely interesting, and from another point of view almost unreadable. I take it, of course, as a kind of literary masque, and am not criticising it from dramatic weaknesses but solely from the point of view of a reader. I think that what is wrong is that there is too much poetry in it, and not enough attention paid to the structure. One cannot afford to be so poetic as this in a poem of this length. One must begin by finding something which it might be misleading to call a plot. What I mean is a framework which will have its points of interest and excitement on a rather lower level than the poetic. I maintain that a long poem ought to be as interesting as a detective story, and this just isn't. It becomes as hard as the excursion, and rather harder, in *Paradise Regained*. If I pick it up and read a page by itself here or there I can get some enjoyment. For instance, the set of couplets on page 42 is a charming little poem in itself. But when one reads several pages continuously, the effect is of a diction very heavily clotted. It seems to me that you need to practise a more pedestrian style and the use of sparer and bonier language for the places where nothing more is required. Otherwise you lose intensity by aiming at intensity everywhere.

If I have not made myself clear please write and tell me so. But I hope you will take what I have said as an expression of interest.

Yours sincerely,
[T. S. Eliot]

---

1 – Christopher Hassall (1912–63), lyricist and biographer, became an actor after graduating from Wadham College, Oxford; and for fifteen years from 1935 he wrote lyrics for Ivor Novello: hits included *The Dancing Years*, 1939 and *King's Rhapsody*, 1949. Other works included *Devil's Dyke with Compliment and Satire* (1936) and *Penthesperson* (Hawthornden Prize, 1938); and award-winning biographies of Edward Marsh (1958) and Rupert Brooke (1964).
2 – TSE's colleague at Faber, Richard de la Mare, son of the poet Walter.
3 – 'Devil's Dyke'. Ottoline = Ottoline Morrell: see Biographical Register.

3 January 1936                    *The Criterion*

Dear Laughlin,

Thank you for your letter of the 10th December, which gave me much pleasure.[2] If the two poems will be beneficial to the magazine, that is the most important matter, only please publish them fairly soon because they will be appearing in a new volume early in the spring.

I feel that I expressed inadequately my satisfaction in the notice you gave me in the *New English Weekly*. As criticism from a literary rather than from a dramatic point of view I think it gave me more pleasure than any other I have had, and its equipment of phraseology suggested that you had profited, as one should profit, from the critical tuition of Ezra.[3]

I am hoping that Fitzgerald will send me his book, because I have regarded him for several years as almost one of the few real starters whom I have come across in that time. As you suggest, too many of the boys nowadays don't take the trouble over their lines that they ought to, and

1–James Laughlin IV (1914–97): poet and publisher: see Biographical Register.
2–Laughlin was grateful for the poems, 'Rannoch, by Glencoe' and 'Cape Ann', that TSE had allowed him to print in *New Democracy*. 'I'll spare you the rhetoric and sentiment, but just let me say that it is a great thing for me to see two poems by "Possum" in my pages.'
3–Laughlin, 'Mr Eliot on Holy Ground', *NEW* 7: 13 (11 July 1935), 250–1. 'However you want to feel about Mr Eliot's "position", *Murder in the Cathedral* proves that he is still a great master of metric and that he knows how to put together a play . . .
'An examination of the psychological angle provides the clue. Aristotle's criteria call for pity and terror to induce the catharsis. But the fall of A'Becket [*sic*] produces neither: he forsees [*sic*] his doom and declines escape though it is offered – hence no terror; he is obviously ready for death and glad to fulfill his faith – and so no pity. And yet the play's action does release emotion within the observer. Of what kind? The same, I think, as is aroused by a Medieval Mystery or Miracle, one of religious exaltation, of completion of faith. It is clear then that Eliot has attempted a fusion of the Classic and Medieval dramatic formulae . . .
'To make his work completely solid Eliot presents through the assassins' after-murder speeches a clear analysis of the historical forces conditioning the event . . .
'Throughout *Murder in the Cathedral* the versification is of a high and even quality. There are few lines which will catch in your memory and stick there, as do so many of those of the *Waste Land*, and the poems in *Prufrock*, but neither is there a faulty line. There is no fixed metre, but there is, in the best sense, a fine free metric. Mr Eliot has been to school and knows his language-tones and sound-lengths as few others do. He can cut a line of sound in time so that it comes off the page to you as a tangible design. His cadences are soft and cool and flowing, but there is never an unnecessary word. The language is highly charged with meaning, but there is no looseness of rhetoric.'

half the time one suspects that they have never even bothered to *listen* to what they write. No, I don't think Fitzgerald is just Yeats by any means.[1]

I saw your Henry Miller *Advocate*, and wondered what would happen.[2] It was a good piece to liven up the *Advocate*, but I don't think it's good Henry Miller. It is merely marking time with the point of view which was completely expressed in *Tropic of Cancer*. I am wondering whether Miller has it in him or not to move on to a new position. If not he will merely become a bore.[3]

How Ezra has been able all these years to reconcile his enthusiasm for fascism with Social Credit principles has been a mystery to his friends.

I hope you will be over again this summer. It is likely that I shall cross for a short time in the autumn. Will that season find you still at Harvard? If not I shall probably look for you in New York.

Yours sincerely,

T. S. Eliot

1 – Laughlin asked whether TSE had seen F. Scott Fitzgerald's new book. 'He is one of the few young ones who really work over their lines . . . Ezra just says "Yeats", but I think he's wrong.'

2 – 'Harvard has been more lively lately. I tried some Henry Miller on the *Advocate*'s gentle public and got the issue banned and burned in consequence.'

3 – See too TSE to Kristian Smidt, 23 Dec. 1958: 'I don't think I have read anything by Henry Miller except the *Tropic of Cancer*. That was a good many years ago and looking back to the time of its publication and my memories of the book I still think it was quite a remarkable book. But I was unable to interest myself in Mr Henry Miller's later work and didn't even know of the existence of *The Rosy Crucifixion*. Anybody who quotes me in general praise of Miller's work is, therefore, misleading the public . . . I am certainly not prepared to defend Mr Miller against the charge of obscenity, although I should think that, from what I remember of the *Tropic of Cancer*, his work in general would be obscene but not pornographic.'

Miller to Anaïs Nin, 14 Dec. 1934: 'Enclosed is a letter from Pound . . . Kahane was elated to know that the famous T. S. Eliot might print Pound's review [of *Tropic of Cancer*] in his fucking magazine. I'm not. *Je m'en fous de tout ça! Je trouvaille. Plus que jamais!*' (*A Literate Passion: Letters of Anaïs Nin and Henry Miller, 1932–1953*, ed. Gunther Stuhlmann [1988], 259).

FROM *Brigid O'Donovan*[1] TO *Hope Mirrlees*[2]          CC

FROM *Brigid O'Donovan*[1] TO *Hope Mirrlees*[2]          CC

6 January 1936                    [Faber & Faber Ltd]

Dear Miss Mirrlees,

Mr Eliot has asked me to send you this copy of *Murder Isn't Easy*. He is sorry that his blurb has been so much and so badly cut down on the dust cover, but the whole thing can be found in the catalogue.[3]

Yours very truly,
Brigid O'Donovan
Secretary.

1 – Brigid O'Donovan, TSE's secretary from Jan. 1935 to Dec. 1936: see Biographical Register.

2 – Hope Mirrlees (1887–1978), British poet, novelist, translator and biographer, became a close friend of TSE; author of notable works including *Paris: A Poem* (1918), *Lud in the Mist* (novel, 1926), and *A Fly in Amber: Being an Extravagant Biography of the Romantic Antiquary Sir Robert Bruce Cotton* (1962). See too *Collected Poems of Hope Mirrlees*, ed. Sandeep Parmar (2011). Writing to Eleanor Hinkley, 14 Jan. 1959, TSE described Mirrlees as 'a very old and dear friend of mine . . . She has a wonderful sense of humour in addition to everything else . . . She is wildly & most amusingly eccentric and unconventional. A brilliant & erudite linguist (Greek, French, Russian, Icelandic) she was Jane Harrison's best pupil at Cambridge.'

3 – TSE's blurb on the dust jacket of *Murder Isn't Easy*: 'Readers of Mr Hull's two previous blood curdlers, *The Murder of My Aunt* and *Keep It Quiet*, will know that they must expect a plot. *Murder Isn't Easy*, like its predecessors, is a cautionary tale for amateur murderers.'

The full blurb – 'the whole thing' – appeared in the F&F catalogue Spring 1936, 10–11: 'Readers of Mr [Richard] Hull's two previous blood-curdlers, *The Murder of My Aunt* and *Keep It Quiet*, will know that they must expect an unusual plot. *Murder Isn't Easy*, like its predecessors, is a cautionary tale for amateur murderers. As *Keep It Quiet* revealed the horrors and the dangers of life in a highly respectable London club, so *Murder Isn't Easy* shows how unpleasant, and indeed dangerous, it can be to be a director of a private limited company. This book will be a new experience to all readers of detective fiction, and will bring particular consolation to those who happen to be directors of private limited companies. The company in question was an advertising agency; by the terms of its formation the three directors were unable to get rid of each other; and they regarded each other with the most cordial dislike. The reader will acquire, besides an acquaintance with business methods of a particular kind, the same dislike for the three directors that they felt for each other; and the conclusion, though unexpected will be welcome.'

TO *William Power*[1]                                          CC

7 January 1936                          [Faber & Faber Ltd]

Dear Mr Power,

I have considered very carefully your letter of January 2nd, and the enclosed draft of a testimonial and proposed address to C. M. Grieve.[2] I am afraid, however, that I cannot see my way to allowing my name to be used in this context. While I have a respect for such of Mr Grieve's poetry as I know, I cannot see any particular appropriateness in my being one of the signatories. I have never had in the past any connection with the P.E.N. Club, and I don't expect to have any connection with it in the future. Furthermore I am not a Scot, and it seems to me most suitable that such documents should be signed by his fellow-countrymen. I sympathize warmly with the desire to obtain financial aid for Mr Grieve, but I am afraid that it is impossible for me to sign the testimonial and address.

With many regrets, and best wishes for the New Year,

I am,
Yours sincerely,
[T. S. Eliot]

1 – William Power (1873–1951), Scottish journalist, author, politician; wrote for the *Glasgow Herald*, 1907–26; edited the *Scots Observer*, 1926–9; and worked from 1929 for Associated Newspapers. President of Scottish P.E.N., 1935–8. Leader of the Scottish National Party, 1940–2. Works include *Roberts Burns and Other Essays and Sketches* (1926); *My Scotland* (1934); and *Should Auld Acquaintance: An Autobiography* (1937).
2 – Power requested TSE to include his name on a circular and address approved by R. B. Cunningham Graham and H. J. C. Grierson, with the purpose of affording aid to the poet Christopher Grieve (Hugh MacDiarmid) – founder of the Scottish Centre of P.E.N. 'Mr Grieve is at present in the Island of Whalsay, in Shetland; he has been very seriously ill and is living very quietly and in a very modest fashion. He has a wife and child, both with him; and they are having rather a trouble. The money we may raise would be of great assistance . . .

'Though this movement emanates from the Scottish P.E.N., it will not, I think, be theirs officially . . .

'I have not forgotten the great kindness and courtesy you showed to a humble visitor from Scotland!'

The address to Grieve included these sentiments: 'Our appreciation of your genius is deepened by the fact that in your spontaneous self-expression you have expressed also the struggle of the Scots soul to regain a fuller and freer sense of the eternal universe of things. You are more than the "typical" Scot; you are the "different" Scot who, by the magic of a genius which is at the same time intimately Scottish and widely European, can raise native elements to a higher, a universal synthesis.'

TO *Edith Perkins*[1]                                    TS Beinecke

7 January 1936                          Faber & Faber Ltd

Dear Mrs Perkins,

I am in arrears, first of all, for a very charming letter,[2] and second, for the surprise that you and Dr Perkins gave me in a beautiful pair of gloves revealed on Christmas morning from a parcel left with me before your departure. I first thought, that I should not be able to wear such gloves without getting them dirty (in London) at once; and I was tempted to take advantage of your suggestion that I might change them. But they fit perfectly; and I do like the colour: and I think that I prefer to keep the gloves that you gave me, even if they soil more quickly, rather than be practical and change them for something darker. If I did, it would still be your present, I know: but I had rather wear the gloves that you bought for me.

I have had from Emily some account of the voyage – supplemented by information from Mrs Hale, whom I ought to write to, if I knew her address: her report of the bedbugs was quite vivid, and she reported, what I should otherwise not have known, that Emily won half a crown at some game of chance – and I trust that you have recovered from it, and are now resting in Brimmer Street. As for myself, you have quite spoiled me: first making me feel so at home in Campden, and then transplanting me to Rosary Gardens. It quite unbalances my world to have you and Dr Perkins on the other side of the water, when you seem to belong so definitely here. I cannot help thinking that you will return and have a garden which will be still more your own, than the one which I remember so clearly.

The present separation seems to me quite temporary. Meanwhile, you will give me happiness whenever you write to me, and give me news of our dear Emily.

Affectionately,
Tom

1 – Edith Perkins (1868–1958), née Milliken: wife of the Revd John Carroll Perkins (1862–1950), Minister of King's Chapel, First Unitarian Church of Boston. Their niece EH had grown up in their care. TSE visited them at Chipping Campden, Glos., for the first time in 1935.
2 – Letter not traced.

TO *Enid Faber*[1]                                          TS Valerie Eliot

7 January 1936                          Faber & Faber Ltd

Dear Enid,

I was very much shocked to hear of your double misfortune: Tom's crash must have been, especially in the circumstances as Geoffrey told me, enough of a shock for you without Dick's accident. So far as one can expect, I should suppose that Tom was the more likely to come out completely undamaged: that is a miracle in itself; but it will be just as miraculous if Dick grows his fingertip again. There is nothing I can do except to express my sympathy with yourself – and hopes for your speedy recovery from the strain – and prayers for the general restoration. I have written to Tom, but without mentioning the cause of his catastrophe – though rhymes for 'stairs' kept coming into my head.

Yours affectionately,
Tom

P.S. Don't answer.


TO *Tom Faber*[2]                                          TS Valerie Eliot

7 January 1936                          Faber & Faber Ltd

Dear Tom,

While lying in bed getting better and better,
I hope you'll have time for perusing this letter,
Inasmuch as my friend, the Man in White Spats,
Asks me to convey
In a personal way
This poem he composed on

---

1 – Enid Faber (1901–95) – daughter of Sir Henry Erle Richards (1861–1922), Fellow of All Souls College and Chichele Professor of International Law and Diplomacy at Oxford University – wife of Geoffrey Faber.

2 – Thomas Erle Faber (1927–2004), physicist and publisher – TSE's first godchild – was to take a double first in physics at Trinity College, Cambridge; thereafter he became a Fellow of Corpus Christi College, Cambridge, 1953–2004; Lecturer in Physics, 1959–93, specialising in super-conductivity, liquid metals and liquid crystals; he wrote *Introduction to the Theory of Liquid Metals* (1972) and *Fluid Dynamics for Physicists* (1995). From 1969 he was a director of Faber & Faber, and served as Chairman of Geoffrey Faber Holdings, 1977–2004. TSE paid tribute to him in his preface to *Old Possum's Book of Practical Cats* (1939).

# THE NAMING OF CATS

The naming of cats is a difficult matter,
    It isn't just one of your holiday games;
You may think at first I'm as mad as a hatter,
    But I tell you, a Cat must have THREE DIFFERENT NAMES.
First of all, there's the name that the servants use daily,
    Such as Peter, Alonzo, or Betty or James,
Such as Victor, or Jonathan, George or Bill Bailey –
    All of them practical everyday names.
There are fancier names if you think they sound sweeter,
    Some for the gentlemen, some for the dames:
Such as Plato, Admetus, Electra, Demeter –
    But all of them practical everyday names.
But, I tell you, a Cat needs a name that's particular,
    A name that's peculiar, and more dignified,
Else how can he keep up his ears perpendicular,
    Or smooth out his whiskers, or tickle his pride?
Of names of this kind, I can give you a quorum,
    Such as Munkustrap, Quaxo, or Capricopat,
Such as Bombalurina, or else Jellylorum –
    Names that never belong to more than one Cat.
But above and beyond, there's still one name left over,
    And that is the name that you never will guess;
The name that no human research can discover –
But BUT B U T
    BUT the *Cat himself knows*, and will never confess.
When you notice a Cat in profound meditation,
    The reason, I tell you, is always the same;
His mind is engaged in intense contemplation
    Of the thought, of the thought, of the thought of his NAME.
    Not his everyday name,
    Not his personal name,
But just his ineffable
    Effanineffable
Deep and inscrutable singular Name.

Now that's what my friend, the Man in White Spats,
Has asked me to tell you, about names of Cats.
I don't know myself, so I will not endorse it,

For what's true in Yorks may be falsehood in Dorset.
He may be quite right and he may be quite wrong,
But for what it is worth, I will pass it along.
For passing the time it may be an expedient,
He remains, as do I, your obliged and obedient
Servant, now and in years to come.
              Your afexnate
                          Uncle Tom[1]


## TO *T. O. Beachcroft*[2]                                           CC

7 January 1936                    [*The Criterion*]

Dear Beachcroft,

I must apologize for fiddling about so long over your story *The Three Priests*, but as I am still full of doubts, and as you say Scott James wants to publish it,[3] I am now returning it. Frankly I don't think it is quite of your best. The first part, describing the arrival of the new vicar at his dilapidated church and vicarage seems to me very good indeed, and is very real, and has the particular merit of making the late vicar seem as real as the new one. So far as I know the ecclesiastical details are perfectly accurate. It is the final part, dealing with the appearance of the third priest and the consequent revelation to Hugh of his own vocation that seems to me unconvincing. I can't say just what I find wrong with it, but it's a terribly difficult type of experience to make real in words, and I don't feel that you have succeeded.

I should be delighted to come and take a glass of sherry with you when it is possible. Unfortunately Saturday is the only possible day this week, and as I am going to *Hansel and Gretel* with the Dobrées and Georgina I am not certain whether I shall be free in time, and Sunday is never a possible day for me.

                          Yours ever,
                          [T. S. Eliot]


1 – 'The Naming of Cats' was sent off too to Alison Tandy, on about the same date.
2 – T. O. Beachcroft (1902–88), author. A graduate of Balliol College, Oxford, he joined the BBC in 1924 but then worked for Unilevers Advertising Service until 1941. He was Chief Overseas Publicity Officer, BBC, 1941–61; General Editor of the British Council series 'Writers and Their Work', 1949–54. Works include *A Young Man in a Hurry* (novel, 1934).
3 – In the *London Mercury*.

TO *Ashley Sampson*[1]

9 January 1936                    [Faber & Faber Ltd]

Dear Mr Sampson,

I have read with interest the typescript of the pamphlet *Function of the Story* enclosed with your letter of January 1st. I am afraid, however, that we cannot see our way to doing anything nowadays with such an essay of such a length. The Criterion Miscellany has been practically abandoned. That is to say, we only make use of this form when we have a pamphlet which we think worth putting forward in view of some special occasion. H. G. Porteus's pamphlet on Chinese Art is accordingly the only one that we have published for several years, and unfortunately yours does not fall in the same category. In general we have found the publication of pamphlets too unprofitable to pursue.[2]

With many regrets,
Yours sincerely,
[T. S. Eliot]

1 – Ashley Sampson (1900–47), Lawrence House School, St Anne's-on-Sea, Lancashire.
2 – See FVM to Francis P. Miller (National Press Building, Washington, DC), 8 May 1936: 'I am very glad to tell you anything I can about pamphlets, but our problems were, I should judge, rather different. When I joined Faber seven years ago, we were faced with the task of starting a new publisher's imprint, to rise out of the ashes of an older one (Faber & Gwyer). We had a first rate editorial department, but very little else; none too much capital, and a few, but not many, valuable authors and titles. We wanted to begin publishing in the Spring 1929, but due to protracted negotiations about the transformation from Faber & Gwyer, we had nothing particularly with which to make our bow. What we wanted to do was to impress upon an apathetic world that ours was going to be an intelligent and lively imprint; and to that end, primarily for the publicity and not for the profit, I suggested pamphlets. There was great merit in the suggestion for us at that particular time. We could get out pamphlets quickly; they were cheap to give away and provided good advertisement; and many wellknown authors, who would have been beyond our reach for their regular books, were pleased to champion various causes in pamphlet form. Because we had a number of very good names on the pamphlets, booksellers backed us up fairly well. Our means of distribution were almost entirely the bookshops, which was what we wanted. We were, as you see, really more concerned with attracting attention and goodwill in the Book Trade than with looking for other means of distribution.
'Now we soon found out that names count more with the Book Trade than anything else; and that topical subjects, even if handled exceptionally well, didn't sell unless the author's name was known; and that of topic subjects anything in the field of economics was apt to come out worst. That was round about 1929 and 1930, and of course at other moments other things may happen. But by and large, a pamphlet by D. H. Lawrence would sell very well, and a pamphlet on economics would be a plug.
'We made our impact, and [it] was stopped when the good was good; that's to say, when we had skimmed the cream of available authors. We had the benefit of being imitated by other publishers, some of whom went on flogging the idea after booksellers were bored

TO *Elizabeth Bowen*[1]                                          TS Texas

10 January 1936                    *The Criterion*

Dear Mrs Cameron,

I am delighted to hear from you again, and to know that you are now
to be settled in London, so that I hope I may see you more frequently.[2]
I should love to come to dinner, but I am simply forced to decline all
invitations for next week for the reason that I have to go to Dublin the
following week to make a speech and give a lecture, and I must devote
myself to the labour of preparation. May I come in for tea, sherry,
or otherwise, one day after my return? that is to say any time after
the 27th.

> With many regrets for the 14th,
> Yours very sincerely,
> T. S. Eliot

P.S. I have heard very high praises of the *House in Paris*,[3] and I hope to
read it.


TO *Hope Mirrlees*                                               CC

10 January 1936                    [*The Criterion*]

My dear Hope,

Thank you very much for your letter.[4] I am looking forward eagerly to
learning whether you consider *Murder Isn't Easy* up to the level of the

---

with it. We never made any dramatic statement that our series was ended, for some time we
may wish to revive or add to it; but having achieved the contacts and made the impression
we wanted, we went on to our more general object of book publishing. There is no more
editorial work about full size books than there is about pamphlets. I didn't regard pamphlets
as being a lasting or lucrative field. I did regard them as having novelty at that time and as
being very convenient for us; for, as I say, we had editorial power to burn, and had a jump in
that way on rivals who, in every other way, were much better off than we were.'
1 – Elizabeth Bowen (1899–1973) – Mrs Alan Cameron – Irish-born novelist; author of *The
Last September* (1929), *The Death of the Heart* (1938), *The Heat of the Day* (1949).
2 – Bowen wrote on 9 Jan. 1936 (misdated 1935) from 2 Clarence Terrace, Regent's Park,
London, to say they had left Oxford and were 'just settling into the house here': would TSE
please come to dinner on Tues., 14 Jan.?
3 – Bowen, *The House in Paris* (1935).
4 – Mirrlees wrote on 7 Jan.: 'How *frightfully* kind of you to send me the new "Aunt"! I
ate my luncheon & then began it *instantly* & in consequence am going about my various
avocations with that little secret sense of *cosy* expectation which – so oddly! nothing gives
in the same degree as the knowledge that at bed-time there awaits one a good MURDER
story. Thank you so so much. By the way I have been longing to tell you the following facts

two previous stories. I am much interested in the information that you have obtained about the author. Points 2, 3, and 4 are quite new to me. As for 1, I should have said after one meeting that he was merely a fat man, but hardly an enormously fat man. As for 5, I deny absolutely that the club depicted in *Keep It Quiet* is the Oxford and Cambridge Club.[1] The gentleman whom we will continue to call Mr Hull is not a member of that club, but of a rival organization, and I must refer you to the text, and point out that no buses run down Pall Mall. More I am not at liberty to say, except that it is possible that in our efforts to remove from the manuscript some very obvious hints as to what club it was, we may have gone too far in the other direction. I shall send you a copy of our Spring catalogue so that you may see my little masterpiece.

I am sorry to hear that a domestic crisis is impending. I should love to come to dinner either before or after or in the middle of a crisis, but for the moment I am refusing invitations without exception (if one makes exceptions it causes complications) until after the 22nd, when I go to Dublin for a few days. I have to prepare a short speech and a long speech for that occasion, and I shan't have time to think about it until Monday, and then I must do my work in the evenings. Never having been to Dublin,

---

about the author which I learned in the summer from Lady Catherine Ashburnham – he (the author) being an old ~~Balliol~~ Baliol [*sic*] friend of her land-agent & cousin, viz:

(1) He is enormously fat.
(2) He is very fond of games & very good at them, considering his weight – squash being one he is particularly good at.
(3) His mother lives in Wales.
(4) By profession he is a chartered accountant. But Lady C suspects her own estate accounts are about the only ones he . . . Charters (?)
(5) The Club depicted in *Keep It Quiet* is *yours* – which is also his, viz. "Oxford & Cambridge".

'However by now you probably know all these facts & many more besides.

'I was much chagrined that your little master-piece should be so mutilated. How on earth did it happen? It seems to be really *really* bad luck & quite maddening. And on the subject of little master-pieces, I cannot tell you how moved & delighted I was by the lovely Christmas-card-book you so *very* kindly sent me. Incidentally, it also gave a fresh & I am *sure right* direction to my stock of theories & problems, by showing *me* (not any one else) what it is I miss in Chinese art & Chinese poems.

'Domestically – I expect soon to be going through a crisis & my cook-to-be is at the moment lying on the knees of the gods. But an old servant & quite a good cook has most angelically come to my rescue – tho' on Friday week she must return to her former husband in Sussex. It would be so kind nice [*sic*] if you could come & have some dinner with me *while* she is here. Would next Tuesday or Wednesday be possible for you? The dates are respectively 14th & 15th.

'Thanking you again *ever* so much / Yours ever / H. M.'

1 – TSE had joined the Oxford & Cambridge Club in 1931.

I am looking forward to it. May I see you as soon as possible after my return? If I don't hear I will write soon after I am back.

Yours ever,

[T. S. E.]

## TO *Bernard W. Bromage*[1] CC

13 January 1936          [*The Criterion*]

Dear Mr Bromage,

I have a book which has been here for some time, but which I have not been able to think of the right person to review. It is *Mussolini's Italy*, by Dr Herman Finer. I understand that the author is a person of definitely socialist sympathies, and I know that the book is considered unfair and misleading by people who sympathize with fascism. Therefore I wanted a reviewer who sympathized with neither one view or the other, but who took a detached and preferably a catholic attitude. If this would interest you, and if you have not already reviewed it elsewhere, I should be very glad to send it to you.[2]

Yours sincerely,

[T. S. Eliot]

## TO *A. Desmond Hawkins*[3] TS Desmond Hawkins

13 January 1936          *The Criterion*

Dear Hawkins,

Thank you for your letter of the 6th, and for commenting at such length on my play.[4] I think, however, that you ought to give the chorus a little

---

1 – Bernard Bromage taught English at the Sir George Monoux School, Walthamstow, London, from 1934, and researched the Occult.

2 – Bromage on Herman Finer, *Mussolini's Italy*: C. 15 (Apr. 1936), 567–9.

3 – A. Desmond Hawkins (1908–99), novelist, critic, broadcaster: see Biographical Register.

4 – 'I heard the [BBC] broadcast [of *MiC*] last night, & write to congratulate you. I have read it previously, of course, but a lot is added by performance. Speaight & the First Knight were excellent; the tempters & the Second Knight were more than good. I regretted the heavy cutting in some places, but the finished effect was splendid in spite of that. Here at last is a substantial actable play, in verse which sacrifices nothing to the laziness of the usual theatre . . .

'The one disaster was those deplorable women. I sometimes think that there is no hope of getting unison speaking that can be heard without pain. Certainly these genteel ex-High School Dames will never do it. As soon as they have to speak with someone else they lapse

more credit. As for the institution that produced them, I disagree strongly with Elsie Fogerty's methods in some respects, but I don't believe that there is anyone else in England that could provide choral work anywhere near so good.[1] As for the girls themselves, they do improve with a variety of coaching, and one must remember that they suffer from the disadvantage of having to speak choruses really written for women twice their age. There are moments, of course, when the voices sound painfully adolescent, like a performance of *Antony and Cleopatra* in a girls' school, but I think when everything is considered they are doing extremely well. Another thing to remember is that unless I am mistaken, my choruses are the first thing of the kind that has ever been attempted, and the sort of work they have done before has been largely the misapplication of poems written for only one voice. The choruses of Swinburne, and still more those of Gilbert Murray, seem to me to have been written without any sense of the difference between one voice and a group of voices. In theory one would write quite differently according to the number of voices one intended to employ. But I think the art of chorus writing as well as, *a fortiori*, that of chorus production, are still in their infancy.

I can, I hope, depend on you for a chronicle for the March number,[2] and I should like very much to know how your domestic affairs are progressing. I think you will find Ernest Bird[3] a very nice man to have to deal with.

Yours ever,
T. S. Eliot

---

into a pseudo-solemnity, specially patented for the delivery of "Beauty-in-Poesy". It was just the same with the Group Theatre – a mournful bellyaching drone that rose & fell like a dancing elephant.

'I know it can't be helped. Is there any class of person who could learn to speak without that neutered moaning? Or is the whole chorus idea a literary ambition, a pleasure of the study, a thing to be read? I wonder if the Greeks ever satisfied themselves with it . . .

'The Knights' apologia came out magnificently & gave the play a necessary balance. I think that scene in some way dominates the whole & saves you from "chronicle".'

1 – Elsie Fogerty trained the chorus for the Canterbury première in 1935 of *MiC*; see also letter of 14 Jan. 1938, below.

2 – Hawkins, 'Fiction Chronicle', C. 15 (Apr. 1936), 479–88.

3 – TSE's solicitor.

## TO *Georges Cattaui*[1]                                        CC

13 January 1936                        [Faber & Faber Ltd]

My dear Cattaui,

I have to thank you for your charming letter of the 23rd December, and to say that I am highly pleased that you should feel disposed to translate *Murder in the Cathedral*. I should be more than contented to have you do so if I may have the privilege of seeing the translation before it goes to press, and of making criticisms if any occur to me, and I should be very glad if your cousin and my friend Pierre de Menasce would do us the favour of looking through it.[2] His have always seemed to me by far the best of any translations of my work into French.

As for the publication, I should be sorry to have you go to all this trouble without being assured of a publisher. If Paulhan or Gallimard, or whoever is concerned, is willing to undertake publication, I suggest that they should write to me proposing the terms of a contract. I should not be exigent in this matter, but merely wish, *pour la bonne règle*, to have a clear agreement. I am assuming that what is envisaged is publication as a small book, as I should think that the play would be too long for a single number of the *N.R.F.*,[3] and it would be a pity to break it up into parts.

1 – Georges Cattaui (1896–1974), Egyptian-born (scion of aristocratic Alexandrian Jews, and a cousin of Jean de Menasce) French diplomat and writer; his works include *T. S. Eliot* (1958), *Constantine Cavafy* (1964), *Proust and his metamorphoses* (1973). TSE was to write to E. R. Curtius, 21 Nov. 1947: 'I received the book by Cattaui [*Trois poètes: Hopkins, Yeats, Eliot* (1947)] and must say that I found what he had to say about myself slightly irritating. There are some personal details which are unnecessary and which don't strike me as in the best taste.'

2 – Jean de Menasce (1902–73), theologian and orientalist (his writings include studies in Judaism, Zionism and Hasidism), was born in Alexandria into an aristocratic Egyptian Jewish family and educated in Alexandria, at Balliol College, Oxford (where he was contemporary with Graham Greene), and at the Sorbonne (Licence ès-Lettres). In Paris, he was associated with the magazines *Commerce* and *L'Esprit*, and he translated several of TSE's poems for French publication: his translation of *TWL* was marked '*revué et approuvée par l'auteur*'. He became a Catholic convert in 1926, was ordained in 1935 a Dominican priest – Father Pierre de Menasce – and went on to be Professor of the History of Religion at the University of Fribourg, 1938–48; Professor and Director of Studies, specialising in Ancient Iranian Religions, at the École Pratique des Hautes Études, Paris. TSE thought him 'the only really first-rate French translator I have ever had' (to Kathleen Raine, 17 May 1944).

3 – Founded in 1909, the *Nouvelle Revue Française* ran for 252 monthly issues from June 1919 to June 1940; editors included Jacques Copeau, Jacques Rivière and Jean Paulhan. See *From the N.R.F.: An Image of the Twentieth Century from the Pages of 'Nouvelle Revue Française'*, ed. Justin O'Brien (1958). See too William Marx, 'Two Modernisms: T. S. Eliot and *La Nouvelle Revue Française*', in *The International Reception of T. S. Eliot*, ed. Elisabeth Däumer and Shyamal Bagchee (2007), 25–33.

I should be also much interested and pleased to see the critical article which you have written.[1]

I wish that you could come over to London and see a performance of the play, as I am sure that you would be impressed by Bobby Speaight's presentation of his rôle, and I think you would find that the chorus has now reached a very finished state. If there is no chance of your coming to London I shall hope to be able to visit Paris in the Spring and see you there.

> With the warmest good wishes,
> Yours ever,
> [T. S. Eliot]

P.S. I cannot think of any particular points at the moment to mention with regard to translation, except that in one place I have used the verb 'evince' in a sense which is quite new in English, and is practically an adoption of the verb '*évincer*'.[2]

## TO *Denis J. Coffey*[3]                                         cc

14 January 1936                         [Faber & Faber Ltd]

Dear Dr Coffey,

Thank you for your kind invitation of the 13th January.[4] It will give me much pleasure to accept your and Mrs Coffey's hospitality. I expect to take the night boat from Liverpool on Wednesday evening, arriving early Thursday morning, the 23rd. I presume that I can get breakfast on the boat before leaving, and I hope that it will not be inconvenient to have me arrive early in the morning.

> With many thanks,
> Yours sincerely,
> [T. S. Eliot]

1 – Cattaui said he had written a long study of TSE's poetry which he was showing to Jean Paulhan (for publication in either *NRF* or *Mesures*), and would be happy to show it to TSE.
2 – Third Knight accuses Thomas Becket of 'Using every means in your power to evince / The King's faithful servants . . .' *Évincer* (French): to oust or supplant.
3 – Dr Denis J. Coffey (1865–1945), first President of University College Dublin, 1908–40. Formerly Professor of Physiology, and Dean of the Catholic University Medical School.
4 – Coffey wrote from, 41 Fitzwilliam Square: 'Mrs Coffey and myself shall be more than delighted if you will stay with us here during your visit.' TSE stayed there on 23–4 Jan.

TO *Val Gielgud*[1]                                              CC

15 January 1936                    [Faber & Faber Ltd]

Dear Mr Gielgud,

Thank you for your letter of the 8th January.[2] The question of broadcast plays needs a good deal of thinking about, but I should be glad to have a talk with you on the subject in time. From the point of view of the author, there is a question which is both economic and aesthetic: can he be persuaded that it is worth his while to spend so much time on a play which is not likely to be produced more than once? So long as there is any possibility of having plays produced on the stage, one is naturally inclined to prefer that mode of expression. It is, I confess, more interesting, and it also holds out the possibility of continual small increments to one's income from amateur societies in all English speaking countries, whereas there is nothing likely to be derived from the broadcast play after the first production.

On the other hand I believe that there is more possibility of adapting poetic drama to the microphone than there is of adapting most other kinds of play, inasmuch as the words are the most important element in it.[3]

Yours sincerely,
[T. S. Eliot]

1 – Val Gielgud (1900–81), pioneer of radio drama, actor, writer (his output included novels, stage plays, radio plays and works of non-fiction), director and broadcaster; Head of Productions at the BBC (radio drama) from 1929; Head of BBC television drama, 1946–52. See too Gielgud's article 'Radio Play: In the Age of Television' (which includes discussion of the BBC adaptation of *MiC*), *Theatre Arts Monthly* 21: 2 (Feb. 1937), 108–12.

2 – 'In the autumn we are hoping to start a new series of plays, all written by outside writers and I need not say that I should be extremely gratified if we could get a play from you.

'I believe radio drama has still many more exciting possibilities than we have yet realized, but we need writers of distinction more than we need anything else.'

3 – *MiC* was broadcast on Sunday, 5 Jan. 1936.

15 January 1936                Faber & Faber Ltd

Dear Father Savage,

Thank you for your letters of the 7th and the 14th.[2] You had no need to apologise for the errors in the duplication of your address, which I attributed primarily to your wish to let me have a copy as early as possible – and in any case, I am the last person to detect mistakes in quoting from my own writings! What you say interests me very much: indeed it is embarrassingly rich in possibilities of development. I am substantially in accord with your views, I think, though I feel that I must defend – or rather condone the faults of my friend Yeats to whom all English-speaking poets owe so much.

Some of the points on which you touch are such as I feel to be inappropriate for a foreigner who does not know the conditions intimately, to comment upon. It seems more fitting for me to consider, not what Irish Literature has to do for Ireland, but what it has to do for Europe and for civilisation in general, taking into account its position in relation to the Catholic Faith on the one hand, and to England (through the English language) on the other. I should say that not two but three roads cross: Catholicism (with belief in one's race), Nationalism (with exaggeration of race, as in fascism), and Communism (with denial of race).

1–Roland Burke Savage, SJ – a student at the time: a Jesuit scholastic pursuing his university studies – invited TSE to participate in the Inaugural Meeting of the English Literary Society of University College, Dublin, on 22 Jan. 1936 (Burke Savage was the Auditor): they would pay a fee of £25 plus expenses. TSE would be expected in the first instance to speak to the Auditor's Paper, 'Literature at the Irish Crossroads' – of which the 'general trend' would be 'an analysis of the "Celtic Renaissance" movement, and some thoughts on the future development of an "English Literature" in Ireland', said Savage – and they would arrange too for TSE to give, on the following day, a lecture on any literary subject of his own choosing.

2–Burke Savage sent a covering note on 7 Jan. 1936, along with a copy of his address for TSE's information. The Inaugural Meeting of the English Literary Society, University College, Dublin, 23 Jan. 1936, was to be chaired by Dr Coffey, President. The 'Auditor's Address' was entitled 'Literature at the Irish Crossroads': see *CProse* 5, 293–9. TSE would propose the 'Resolution', 'That the Auditor deserves the best thanks of the Society for his Address'; and was to be seconded by Professor Daniel Corkery.

On 14 Jan. Savage apologised for having sent TSE 'an unread draft of my paper': 'I gave my receipt to the duplicating people and went on retreat that evening. Consequently it was only a day or two ago I saw a copy of the draft: I was disgusted to see Yeates consistently turning up; also a bad mistake in a quotation from your work where "which" appears instead of "when" and spoils all sense . . . However please pardon these errors!'

I have thought that I might go on from this, to consider at more length the next day, 'The Relations of Contemporary Literatures' – I might find a less cumbrous title. My position between England and America, still more than my connexions with the Continent, gives me some experience. My view is that no one literature is self-subsistent, and that what binds them together is the common mentality due to the Catholic Faith.

If you have any serious criticism, I beg that you will send me a wire at my expense (to be refunded by me) and I will wire an alternative.

I have written to Dr Coffey to accept his kind invitation. It would be imprudent to come by the day boat on Thursday, in case of fog; and I have a committee on Wednesday; so I am taking the night boat from Liverpool on Wednesday. I find that I arrive at Dublin at 6.45 in the morning; so I do not want to put anyone to the inconvenience of meeting me. I suppose that I can get some breakfast on the boat or at the dock, and I shall then find my way to Fitzwilliam Square. I hope that I may see you as early as may be during the day.

Yours very sincerely,<br>T. S. Eliot

## TO *Ottoline Morrell*[1]

TS Texas

15 January 1936                    *The Criterion*

My dear Ottoline,

Thank you for your letter of January 13th enclosing £2 from Stephen Tennant, which I have sent to the bank.[2]

Maynard Keynes sent me a cheque for £5, which I am having the bank add on to the instalment payable at the March quarter. In order to distribute the payments more evenly, I am asking them to pay over this sum of £2 with the instalment of the June quarter.

I have heard nothing from David Cecil. I am not so surprised that Berners has failed to respond.[3] I should hardly expect him to be interested to the extent of giving support.

1 – Lady Ottoline Morrell (1873–1938), hostess and patron: see Biographical Register.
2 – Tennant's contribution to a fund assisting the struggling poet George Barker (for Barker, see Biographical Register).
3 – Gerald Tyrwhitt-Wilson, 14th Baron Berners (1883–1950): composer, novelist, painter and aesthete. See too *The Diaries of A. L. Rowse*, ed. Richard Ollard (2003), 358–9: 'Gerald Berners told me of an early party of Eliot's while he was with his first wife – at which Tom had put soap in the éclairs so that the guests foamed at the mouth. It was, as A. P. Ryan said to me of Tom's cutting his name in a desk at Harvard, the only criminal act recorded of him.'

I think that Barker will have enough to scrape along on for another year, and at any rate he will be getting quite as much as he expects. I am exceedingly grateful to you from all the trouble you have taken, and I would not have you take any more at present. I may have to bestir myself for more subscriptions in another year.

I am anxious to see you again as soon as possible, and should like to come as soon as I return from Dublin. I am going on the 22nd, and meanwhile must prepare two addresses to deliver while there. I am looking forward to the visit with much interest, though I should be still more interested if Yeats were to be there. I shall try to see Desmond Fitzgerald.[1] If there is anyone you would like me to look up I should be glad if you would let me know. I should like to come to tea with you on Monday the 27th or thereafter.

Yours affectionately
Tom

TO *Elizabeth Bowen*                                        TS Texas

15 January 1936                        Faber & Faber Ltd

Dear Mrs Cameron,

That is very kind of you, first to ask me to dinner and second to send me your book.[2] I really was not spelling to have you give me a copy, but as you have inscribed it I shall have all the more pleasure in reading it. And I shall be delighted to dine on Tuesday the 28th. No, I have never been to Dublin before, and I am looking forward with pleasure, curiosity, and apprehension.

With very grateful thanks,
Yours sincerely,
T. S. Eliot

1 – Desmond Fitzgerald (1888–1947): Irish nationalist politician; poet. See *L* 4.
2 – *The House in Paris* (2nd imp., Sept. 1935), inscribed 'T. S. Eliot from Elizabeth Bowen' (TSE Library).

TO *Bonamy Dobrée*[1]                                    TS Brotherton

16 January 1936                          Faber & Faber Ltd

Dear Bumbaby,

Well well. The *Yorkshire Post* rang up this afternoon to say that there was a rumour that you had been made a professor and had we anything to tell them about it.[2] I told Miss O'D. to say that we knew nothing, but would gladly forward any communications addressed to you at this office. They then said that they understood there was something about it in the evening paper, but the weather was too bad to send out for a paper. So I bought a *Standard*. Well, well, we must make the best of a bad job and consider the amenities of Ilkley, and Herbert has discovered a new Yorkshire cheese called Farmdale. Furthermore, this is to be considered as a valuable stepping stone to Q's job;[3] because I have a strong suspicion that when Q disappears (if he ever does) they will play safe and pick somebody who is already a professor. Interested to know how you feel about it.

                                        Yours etc.
                                        T. S. E.


TO *Ezra Pound*[4]                                      TS Beinecke

[Received 18 January 1936[5]]          Faber & Faber Ltd

Ras Ez, Sir,

Goddamb it, I have had a hell of a time lately, what with the jobs they give me to do, reading mss and cleaning latrines and so on, and I aint paid for being chairman of vickers[6] either. But Im getting round to it, though what with that sloth Morley slopin off to New York I suppose there will be more junk to read than ever and what Do you think I going

---

1–Bonamy Dobrée (1891–1974), scholar, editor and critic: see Biographical Register.
2–BD had been appointed Professor of English at Leeds, in succession to F. P. Wilson.
3–Sir Arthur Quiller-Couch (1863–1944) – 'Q' – critic, poet, novelist, editor, was King Edward VII Professor of English Literature, Cambridge, and Fellow of Jesus College. His works include the *Oxford Book of English Verse 1250–1900* (1900), *On the Art of Writing* (1916), and, with John Dover Wilson, volumes in the New Shakespeare series.
4–Ezra Pound (1885–1972), American poet and critic: see Biographical Register.
5–Noted by EP.
6–Vickers was a steel foundry launched in Sheffield in 1828; by the 1930s, as Vickers Armstrongs, it was manufacturing aircraft, armaments, munitions and ships.

to Dublin next wednesday to talk to Grogan[1] and Hogan[2] and Coffey and Rourke and such like Well there will be something from me in the way of correspondence before that so will close yrs amcably[3]

TP.

TO *Mary Hutchinson*[4]                                   TS Texas

19 January 1936                    Faber & Faber Ltd

Dear Mary,

I did write at once to thank you for your charming picture books at Christmas – the Birds especially gave me much pleasure – but I now find that the address should have been 'Ruthin Castle', instead of 'Ruthven Castle' to which I addressed the letter. So if you did not receive it, please do not think me neglectful. I hope that Jack is now completely re-established. I assume that you are back by now. I am leaving in a couple of days for Dublin, where I have to reply to an address by Father Burke Savage S.J. and shall be followed by Dr Grogan and Professor Hogan; and I am wondering if they will fling chairs about when I mention James Joyce.[5]

---

1 – Vincent B. Grogan, Hon. Sec., English Literary Society, University College Dublin.

2 – Professor J. J. Hogan, MA, B.Litt (Oxon).

3 – 'Tradition and the Practice of Poetry': talk given in Dublin, 23 Jan. 1936, printed with introduction and afterword by A. Walton Litz, in *T. S. Eliot: Essays from 'The Southern Review'*, ed. James Olney (1988), 7–25; repr. from *Southern Review* 21: 4 (Aut. 1985), 873–88. See *CProse* 5, 300–10.

4 – Mary Hutchinson (1889–1977), literary hostess and author: see Biographical Register.

5 – TSE's reply to Burke Savage's presentation – 'Literature at the Crossroads' – includes these remarks (p.4): 'There remains one great and lamentably isolated figure. James Joyce seems to me the most universal, the most Irish and the most Catholic writer in English in his generation. The spectacle of anyone educated in the Faith, who has subsequently lapsed from it or revolted from it, must always be a melancholy one; but we must distinguish here between a man and his work. The important thing in Joyce's work is not the author's conscious attitude towards his hereditary faith, but the fact that he has never been able to escape from it. Whatever he thinks of his education, and whatever its particular effect upon his temperament, his work is certainly an unconscious tribute to the kind of education he received – an education without which, I believe, he would not have achieved such eminence. The mind exhibited in the work remains profoundly Catholic and religious. This aspect of his work is perhaps more conspicuous to an observer brought up in, or habituated to the secularised atmosphere of England or America. What is fundamentally sound in it, for those who are mature enough to find it, is Catholic. In an essay published several years ago I developed this point by a rather detailed comparison of a story in the volume "Dubliners" called The Dead, with stories by Katherine Mansfield, D. H. Lawrence, and Thomas Hardy. I am not here concerned with estimates of the native gifts of all these authors; only with the importance of the religious background. It is to this that the superiority of the story of Joyce is primarily due; and it is the inferiority in this respect that leaves the accomplishment of the others so largely a waste of great gifts in error and triviality.'

And I rather dread seeing Mrs Kiernan again. However, except that I can't get the last four lines right, I think I have written rather a nice poem to conclude my Collected Poetical Works; and I hope I may see you before long.[1] Would you care to come to see the *Dog Beneath the Skin*? I suspect that the production is very bad, but one ought to find out for oneself.

Affectionately,
Tom

---

Patricia Hutchins to TSE, 16 Nov. 1953: 'Someone [Felix Hacket] was talking to me about the disapproval of Joyce at University College until fairly recently, and he said, "When T. S. Eliot mentioned in his lecture that Joyce was a Catholic writer, there was complete silence."'

TSE replied to Hutchins, 23 Nov. 1953: 'The incident in question took place at a meeting at University College, Dublin, I think in 1937 [i.e. 1936] – at any rate, several years before the war. It was an unusual occasion which is, no doubt, well known to you. A local scholar – on this occasion, I think, a young Jesuit, whose name I have forgotten – presents a thesis, and a visitor is invited over to present a different, or at least his own, point of view on the same theme. The thesis of the lecturer consisted primarily, to the best of my recollection, of a severe criticism of W. B. Yeats for having made so much use of the pre-Christian mythology of Ireland, instead of drawing on the equally venerable Catholic traditions. My function accordingly was primarily to present my own view of Yeats's employment of pagan mythology. The whole disputation was certainly very fairly conducted, and of course I was given the opportunity to read the first address in order to prepare my rejoinder to it. After that there were a number of other speakers who talked more or less on the same questions.

'I cannot now remember what was said by anybody and I do not know what became of the text of my own address. I therefore cannot remember whether I made a statement to the effect that Joyce was a Catholic writer. I know, however, that I did speak of Joyce, and of course in his praise. I am sure that complete silence is not an exact description of my words [*sic*]. So far as I can remember, the greater part of the audience remained in silence, but there was a considerable demonstration of applause from a group of young people at the back of the room, who were evidently well pleased that the name of Joyce should be mentioned, and his work openly preferred on such an occasion. But the whole proceedings went forward in perfect order.'

The novelist James Hanley to TSE, 31 Jan. 1936: 'I listened with great interest to your speech on the wireless last week from Ireland and need I say how thrilled I was when you spoke of James Joyce as you did, especially after Father Savage's speech. Though I am myself Irish, having a Cork mother & Dublin father I would not care to live in that country ever again; and though I owe something to Catholicism for stimulating my imagination, I am all against the clerical conception of literary ethics. It was so splendid to hear Joyce championed in his own country and by one not Irish.'

Donagh MacDonagh to TSE, 10 Feb. 1936: 'Our leading Catholic paper has an attack on you for your praise of Joyce.'

Burke Savage to EVE, 4 Jan. 1986: 'I was struck by the way your husband [put] me, a young student, at complete ease and I admired his quiet elegance without a trace of pomposity. I appreciated also the gentle way he made allowance for the black and white nature of parts of my paper which even within a few hours I'd disown.'

1 – 'Burnt Norton', published in *Collected Poems 1909–1935* (2 Apr. 1936), announced in F&F's Autumn List 1936: 'The definitive edition to date, with a new long poem.'

# TO *A. G. Hebert*[1]

20 January 1936                    [Faber & Faber Ltd]

Dear Father Gabriel,

You will be sorry to hear that your book is still selling so well at the original price that there is no hope of my committee acceding to your wishes for a cheap edition for another season more.[2] I can't help being very glad that this is so. It is not this that my Committee have asked me to write to you about, but they are interested to know whether you have another book in view, or if not whether you can be persuaded to consider the matter.

We should, of course, very much like to have another book from you in particular, and in general we should like to develop the publishing of books in the same category as Liturgy and that is to say serious and scholarly Anglican works which will be well written, and which ought to be brought to the attention of possible readers outside of the converted. Besides, therefore, suggestions of your own, we should be grateful for suggestions from you for books by other people. In conferences and elsewhere you must sometimes come in contact with men whose intellects impress you, and who have matter in their minds which ought to be made public.

Among other people I have been hoping that some day Charles Smyth will be moved to write on some subject more modern than Cranmer.[3] Brother George I want also, but I have felt that might be left to the ripeness

---

1 – Fr Arthur Gabriel Hebert (1886–1963), liturgist, New Testament scholar, ecumenist: see Biographical Register.

2 – *Liturgy and Society* (F&F, 1935).

3 – Charles Smyth (1903–87): ecclesiastical historian and preacher in the Anglican communion. In 1925 he gained a double first in the History Tripos at Corpus Christi College, Cambridge, winning the Thirlwell Medal and the Gladstone Prize, and was elected to a fellowship of Corpus. He edited the *Cambridge Review* in 1925, and again in 1940–1. He was ordained deacon in 1929, priest in 1930; and in 1946 he was appointed rector of St Margaret's, Westminster, and canon of Westminster Abbey. (On 28 Apr. 1952 TSE remarked that Smyth should be 'moved up to where he so eminently belongs, an episcopal see'.) Smyth's works include *Cranmer and the Reformation under Edward VI* (1926); *The Art of Preaching (747–1939)* (1940); and a biography of Archbishop Cyril Garbett (1959). Smyth to EVE, 21 May 1979: 'Your husband was one of the best and kindest friends that I have ever had. – He was also a friend of our Siamese cat, Angus (long since departed this life), who was ordinarily terrified of men (particularly bishops in gaiters!), but took to your husband at sight. I have a treasured copy of the *Book of Practical Cats*, inscribed to "Charles and Violet Smyth, and Angus", by "OP" . . . He had a great sense of fun.'

of time. Perhaps you are better able to know than he is when the time comes that he has a book in him that ought to come out.[1]

With best wishes,<br>
Yours very sincerely,<br>
[T. S. Eliot]

P.S. Your letter of the 19th has just come. I shall be delighted to see Dr Adams, whom I remember as the most intelligent of the Unitarian clergy whom I met in America. He is, I believe, coming to see me tomorrow afternoon.[2]

I am indeed sorry that I could not come to Haywards Heath. But I am glad to hear that the conference was so successful, and that it is likely to be repeated.[3] I like your suggestion about Maria Leach, although the reason for hastening to visit it is so painful.[4] I shall certainly keep it in mind as a possible place of visit this summer, although I am afraid that my German is too rusty now for me to get all the benefit from it that I should.

---

1 – Hebert, letter dated 'Charles King and Martyr' (31 Jan.): 'Yes, George [Every] will have to write books one of these days. But his time has not come yet. One thing that he has got to do is to improve his English prose style: it is still too crabbed and difficult, though it is improving.'

2 – Hebert, 19 Jan.: 'We have been entertaining here an old acquaintance of yours from America – Dr James L. Adams, a Unitarian, attracted here because he had read my book. A most refreshing and delightful person: he has been discoursing to George and myself about Profs. Babbitt and More. He has long since left Liberalism behind, and I do not know how he can remain a Unitarian much longer . . . I hope *we* get him when he becomes a Catholic.'

3 – Hebert, 19 Jan.: 'The conference at Hayward's Heath was wonderful. I am very sorry that you were not able to come. But you must come next time: for it will have to meet again in some form another time, since the fruitfulness of the liturgical method of approach was so abundantly proved. It took us straight to the underlying theological issues, as they apply to life.'

George Every, SSM, to TSE, 24 Jan.: 'The Bishop of Chichester told me to tell you that we all shed tears when you didn't come to Haywards Heath, but his were the saltest tears. He is delightfully boyish. But the conference was successful.'

4 – Hebert, 19 Jan.: 'It would be a great thing if you could find your way to Maria Laach in the course of this summer. They tell us if we are coming to come soon, for a dissolution of the monasteries is not at all unexpected, when the conflict between the old faith and the new Nordic religion [i.e. Nazism] has got on a bit further. It is the most wonderful place in all Christendom.'

Maria Laach is a Benedictine Abbey (founded 1093) near Andernach in the Eifel region of the Rhineland-Palatinate.

TO *Louis MacNeice*[1]                                           CC

20 January 1936                    [*The Criterion*]

Dear Mr MacNeice,

I am very glad that you are willing to do something with the Longinus, which has been sent to you.[2]

About lecturing in America,[3] there are two kinds of lecturing to be given there. One is at academic institutions, and the second is at ladies' clubs. The second kind of lecturing, which is less honourable, is reputed to be more profitable, but this is rather illusory because it is arranged as a lecturing tour through one of the lecturing agencies in New York, and the agency takes rather more than half of the profits. It is also extremely tiring. I am afraid that neither kind of lecturing is possible in the summer. The colleges and universities are shut from the middle of June to the latter part of September, and the ladies' clubs have all dispersed to seaside resorts. The American lecturing season runs more or less from October until May, but I think the autumn is the best time, while the audiences are still fresh from their summer holidays. I suppose that in your position you have no chance of getting to America at that time of year unless you got leave of absence. In that case I should advise you to try to get a temporary post in an American college or university, or an engagement to give some series of lectures. Such an experience would be amusing and not unprofitable in other ways than the financial emolument. Lecturing to ladies' clubs I don't advise at all. It is only people like Hugh Walpole and Harold Nicolson who can make any money out of it. It occurs to me as just possible that there are summer camps at which people have courses of lectures, and meet to experience intellectual exaltation. There used to be a place called Chatauqua. I don't know anything about this sort of thing myself, but I will try to make enquiries.

Yours sincerely,
[T. S. Eliot]

1 – Louis MacNeice (1907–63), poet and BBC producer: see Biographical Register.
2 – MacNeice on Frank Granger, *Longinus on the Sublime*: C. 15 (July 1936), 697–9.
3 – MacNeice (15 Jan.): 'For various reasons I should rather like to go the U.S.A. this summer in my long vacation and I wondered if there was any chance of doing this profitably, or at least less expensively, by means of giving lectures . . . Is there an organisation to which one applies?'

TO *Geoffrey Curtis*[1]                          TS Houghton

20 January 1936                    *The Criterion*

My dear Curtis,

Thank you very much indeed for your admonitory letter on the 14th.[2] I have some experience of conferences, which frequently consist of more or less the same people arranged in a slightly different order round a different table. They seldom get anywhere unless they have an extremely able chairman, such as Dr J. H. Oldham, who is really remarkable for his conduct of such meetings.[3] Personally, I had rather come to visit you and your community than to attend a conference. Not just yet, because I shudder at the thought of going so far north in January; but taking the hint from your letter, I should think early in April.

Now as to the possibility of providing the community with the *Criterion*, which I have discussed with my Committee.[4] It was held that one of the occupations of a religious community is well known to be the illumination of books, and that therefore we should be within the law in giving your community a subscription at trade rates, that is to say one third off. I do not know whether that is sufficiently 'on the cheap' to be considered. It means literally 20s. a year instead of 30s. I haven't heard of the book you mention.[5] The specifically religious publishers don't ordinarily send their books unless we ask for them, and I hesitate to do that unless I am sure that a book has general appeal to intellectual readers outside of the faithful, and is not a theological work in the narrowest sense. Can you tell me something more about it?

---

1 – The Revd Geoffrey Curtis (1902–81): in 1936 a novice at the College of the Resurrection, Mirfield, Yorkshire; later Vice-Principal, Dorchester Missionary College, Burcote, Abingdon, Oxfordshire.

2 – Curtis advised TSE he was to be invited to a theological conference (27–30 Apr.), 'in which an attempt is going to be made to get eastern orthodox and Anglican theologians & sociologists to absorb one another's ideas'. But he was not sanguine about it. 'So if you are not inclined to come more than once this year to visit us, cut out the conference . . . If you can come here before that date, you'll catch our glorious (in the strict sense) Superior before he leaves for Borneo.'

3 – Joseph ('Joe') Oldham (1874–1969): missionary, adviser and organiser for national and international councils and mission boards: see Biographical Register.

4 – Curtis asked whether Mirfield might 'get the *Criterion* on the cheap a month late. I can't as a novice propose it for the library, and I can't afford it out of my 10/- a month pocket money.'

5 – Curtis recommended for review a book entitled *From Dyad to Triad: A Plea for Duality against Dualism and An Essay Towards the Synthesis of Orthodoxy*, by Father Alexis van der Mensbrugghe (1935). 'It is very important.' Mensbrugghe (1899–1980) was a Benedictine monk who was received into the Orthodox Church in 1929; he was to be consecrated a bishop in 1960.

I have never written as I intended to let you know how happy I have been at your finding that you were called to be permanently where you now are.[1] I remember our conversation very vividly, and you will I am sure have believed in my sincerity when I said that I should be equally happy whichever way your choice led you, so long as it was the real call for you. I am very happy that my unprejudiced prayers have been answered in this way.

Always your friend,

T. S. Eliot

## TO *Emily Holmes Coleman*[2]         cc

20 January 1936        [Faber & Faber Ltd]

Dear Mrs Coleman,

As so much time has elapsed I think that I ought to let you have an interim report on Miss Barnes's book.[3] It was some time before I was able to get to read it, but on doing so I was very much impressed. The excerpts sent me by Edwin Muir when taken by themselves certainly gave me a rather misleading impression. I feel that the book is one to be taken seriously, and whatever happens I should like Miss Barnes to know I am interested in it. What you say in criticism is true.[4] I think that

1–Curtis had been admitted to the noviciate on 17 Nov. 1935 (feast day of St Hugh of Lincoln).

2–Emily Holmes Coleman (1899–1974), novelist and poet: see Biographical Register.

Andrew Field, *Djuna: The Formidable Miss Barnes* (1983, 1985), 199–202: 'Though jealousy and rage were very much a part of Emily's character, generosity was too, and she was, happily, convinced of her own genius as well as Djuna's – *Make it marvellous!!!* she exhorted Djuna as she was finishing writing [*Nightwood*] . . . Difficult Emily Coleman is one of the heroines of this story, because, when Barnes returned from America with her much-rejected manuscript in 1934, Emily turned all of her considerable energy to getting it published in England and – after Edwin Muir had pressed the manuscript on Eliot – literally bearded the poet-editor in his office and made it clear to him that Faber would publish the novel, or else. Barnes would eventually say that Emily had to be given seventy percent of the credit for the novel's making it into print.'

3–Djuna Barnes (1892–1982), American novelist, poet, playwright: see Biographical Register.

4–Coleman had replied on 2 Nov. 1935 to TSE's letter of 29 Oct. 1935: 'for anyone preoccupied with the problems of evil and suffering this [novel] would be a document which points the way to the things we most want to know.

'It is true that the book is a hodge-podge; that it is the writing of a woman inspired, as few people are ever inspired, but unconscious of the design in which, in more ideal circumstances, her book would have been conceived. But I cannot believe that good writing is so frequent that anyone can afford to overlook it, whatever weaknesses accompany it. It

the beginning needs some revision. I should certainly advise strongly the omission of the last chapter, which is not only superfluous, but really an

———

may be that certain problems of our life occupy me intensely, and that is why I saw a relation between them and some of the passages in this manuscript. But they are universal problems, and ones to which practically no attention has been given . . . You seem to be seeking a solution to some of them, both in your poetry and in your criticism. Yet hers is one who has thought deeply about them, in her heart, with the best equipment I know of, that of genius; and all you have said is that her style compares unfavourably with that of Miss Kay Boyle.

'I do not wish to take up too much of your time. Perhaps I had better just send the manuscript. I should think, if one were eager, this book would captivate one to a point of insane joy. You have appreciated the only other modern writer who seems to me to have an equal poetic talent. I refer to the author [George Barker] of "The Documents of a Death".'

Coleman highlighted several 'passages of delight' in the book, commenting: 'Do you not think that to be able to take the most horrible, degrading and frightening things of our life and turn them into art is the gift of the highest writing? She has not ordered it into a philosophy. But there it is for the reader to see and receive light from it with which to co-ordinate his own philosophy . . . If I have not communicated to you what the book is, the excerpts having failed to rouse you (who are among the few living beings capable of being so aroused), the manuscript itself may not do so. That a book like this should be written and no one got to publish it – not even yourself, who are, to my knowledge, the only man in a publishing house who could have the courage to launch it (because it is art – for no other reason) is heart-rending . . . If you could think of it as a spiritual document, and not a novel, it might be easier for you to glance at it . . .

'The "Doctor" seems to me, on the whole, to be a created character; and a most astonishing one: the very depths of degradation made wise. I do not feel that any of Miss Boyle's degraded characters stand for more than a little girl's representation of Paris. Miss Boyle's books seem to me immoral. Miss Barnes has deep intuitions about the nature of evil. Her book is therefore moral: it is life-giving.'

Coleman posted the manuscript to TSE on 4 Nov. 1935, and told Barnes on 5 Nov.: 'If human art can draw blood out of a stone, I will draw interest from Eliot for this book' (cited in Monika Faltejskova, *Djuna Barnes, T. S. Eliot and the Gender Dynamics of Modernism: Tracing 'Nightwood'* [2010], 42). 'Coleman's January 26, 1936 letter to Barnes mentions Eliot's previous negative response and lack of interest in the manuscript: "His first note (re the excerpts) would have frozen Gibraltar. But I being more frantic than Gibraltar was fired to heights of fury by it. I think my reply was a masterpiece. It got him to read it: I don't think myself he half read the extracts." [. . .] This letter confirms that Eliot never read the manuscript until very late 1935 or early 1936, when it was already down to approximately 65,000 words.' (Faltejskova, 75).

TSE would tell Djuna Barnes on 25 July 1945 that Coleman 'practically forced the book down my throat, I admit I didn't appreciate it at first; and as for editing it, well Morley and I cut out a lot ourselves, and all to the good, I say. It was one of those rare books in which cutting out a lot of stuff perfectly good in itself actually improved the whole. What she told you about what she said to me seems to be perfectly true; and she certainly thought you the greatest genius living, which I won't deny either. She was wrong about the title certainly: *Nightwood* is right.'

Coleman was to write in her diary in 1937: 'When all is known, the story of Coleman and Barnes over the ms. of Nightwood in NY in 1935 will become a saga, a unique thing in literature, as indeed it was' (Faltejskova, *Djuna Barnes*, 42).

anticlimax. The Doctor is so central a character, and so vital, that I think the book ends superbly with his last remarks.[1]

Another director has read the book with equal interest, and I shall be talking it over with the Chairman, who has been away. I hope to be able to give a final decision in a very short time. If the decision should be adverse, I continue to be interested in the possibility of getting someone to publish the book.

Yours sincerely
[T. S. Eliot]

## TO *Jack Kahane*[2]                                             CC

21 January 1936                    [*The Criterion*]

Dear Mr Kahane,

I had your letter of January 17th, and discussed it with another director.[3] While Miss Joyce's work is interesting, and we should always be glad to do anything we could out of regard for her father, we are afraid that we are not the suitable publishers for this type of book. The market

1 – Coleman responded, 28 Jan.: 'If you accept the Doctor as the central character, which indeed he seems to be, though that was not her [Barnes's] intention, I think you are right about the book's ending with his remarks. I do not think the part about the dog should be left out of the book entirely. But these matters can be settled with the author.'

2 – Jack Kahane (1887–1939), Manchester-born novelist and publisher, founded in 1929 – with Henry Babou of the Vendôme Press (which published Norah James's *Sleeveless Errand*, a novel that had been prosecuted in England in 1929; and which issued in 1930 JJ's fragment *Haveth Childers Everywhere*) – the Obelisk Press, with the purpose of publishing in Paris books that were either banned or deemed to be unprintable in the UK and USA. Obelisk Press productions ran to novels by Henry Miller including *Tropic of Cancer* (1934), *Black Spring* (1936) and *Tropic of Capricorn* (1939), JJ's *Pomes Penyeach* (1932), and works by DHL, Anaïs Nin, Lawrence Durrell, Cyril Connolly, RA and Frank Harris – thirty-eight works over ten years. Kahane's son was Maurice Girodias, founder of the Olympia Press. See Neil Pearson, *Obelisk: A History of Jack Kahane and the Obelisk Press* (2007); Gary Miers and James Armstrong, *Of Obelisks and Daffodils: The Publishing History of the Obelisk Press (1929–1939)* (2011).

3 – 'Mr James Joyce has asked me to write to you as his present English publisher on the following subject:

'Miss Lucia Joyce has done a series of illuminated initial letters for an alphabet translated by Geoffrey Chaucer from the French of Guillaume de Guillerville who was abbot of Chaâlis. This monastery is now classed a historical monument by the French Government and its curator is M. Louis Gillet, of the Académie Française. M. Gillet has written an introduction to the work, the publication of which seems to me an interesting plan as the Sixth Centenary of Chaucer will occur in a year or two. You are no doubt familiar with Miss Joyce's work as she did the cover design for the Joyce fragment published by the Servire-Press in Holland, of which your firm are the English distributors.

for expensive and beautifully decorated books in this country is now very small, and can only be handled by publishers with active experience of it. It is quite possible that some smaller firm, specializing in fine books, and therefore better able to give such a book the attention it would need, might be in a position to consider the proposal more favourably.

With many regrets,
Yours very truly,
[T. S. Eliot]

## TO *Elizabeth Manwaring*[1]                                             CC

21 January 1936                        Faber & Faber Ltd

Dear Miss Manwaring,

Thank you so much for your letter of the 10th December.[2] I shall be very glad to answer any enquiries that the industrious Mr Gallup cares to make. I must warn him, however, that I am just as likely to be ignorant of the points he raises, since I am as little of a bibliographer of my own work as of anyone else's.

---

'The initials to be satisfactory would have to be reproduced by the pochoir process which is efficiently executed only in France. As we did the Pomes Penyeach, Mr Joyce has asked me to get out a price for the actual colour-work . . .

'I should be very much obliged if you would kindly give this matter your consideration.'

1 – Elizabeth Wheeler Manwaring (1879–1949), Class of 1902 Professor of Rhetoric and Composition at Wellesley College, Massachusetts; author of a pioneering study, *Italian Landscape in Eighteenth Century England: a study chiefly of the influence of Claude Lorrain and Salvator Rosa on English Taste, 1700–1800* (1925).

2 – Manwaring reported, 10 Dec. 1935: 'When I was in New Haven last week, I met a young and impecunious graduate student who has made a collection of your work, including much periodical material, which is extraordinary for its thoroughness. He has also an excellent, and, I should say, practically complete bibliography up to date, which he made for the Librarian, under whom he had last year a course in bibliography. Most of the fifty-cent pieces which he makes in his spare-time work in the Yale library must have gone into his collection, which shames mine. I want to find out from you one point: does the difference in line 7 on page 41 of *The Waste Land* (American first edition) as it appears in different copies, according to him, represent a misprint? "Dead mountain mouth" etc. The *a* in *mountain* is gone in the second printing, and in some of the first edition, I gather. Mr [Donald] Gallup has some other bibliographical queries which he would like to make of you, and I encouraged him to do so, with the thought that I would prepare you for his letter. He is in Mr Tinker's class this year, and is an excellent student. To have a reply from you would make him very happy. He showed me with pride one letter of yours which he had bought, written on some bibliographical point (and non-committal).'

Gallup had written to TSE in mid-1935 and received a reply from him (not traced).

I am a little puzzled by your query, but I should suppose that if you found the word 'mountain' spelt without an 'a' it must be a misprint. I am glad that they did not put a 'g' on the end as well.

I believe that my play is to run until about 25th February, if the audiences continue to be satisfactory, so there is just a possibility, I suppose, of your being able to see it here.[1] If you like I will send you a short cable when I am certain of the date. But there is a possibility that a few extra performances may be given elsewhere after that.

With best wishes for the New Year, and looking forward to seeing you in London,

Yours sincerely,<br>
T. S. Eliot

## TO *Ross E. Pierce*[2]

CC

21 January 1936                          [Faber & Faber Ltd]

Dear Mr Pierce,

I have had no free time whatever, since seeing you, in which to read and consider your poems, either the selected short poems or the long poem.[3] It is now late in the evening, and I have a good deal of business to attend to before going to bed, so I will answer your letter very briefly.

As for the poems which you have already had published in America, I suggest that you should show them to editors along with the others,

---

1 – 'If your play will only keep on three months longer, I shall have the pleasure of seeing it when I arrive in London towards the last of February, as I hope to do, having the semester off.'

2 – Ross E. Pierce (1892–1963) was staying at Hotel Glenshesk, 14 Bedford Place, London W.C.1.

3 – Pierce, from Buffalo, New York, had begged and borrowed from family and friends (inc. $125 from his sister) enough money to sail to London, where he hoped to be able to place certain poems that he had already published in the USA, plus others including an epic poem on the history of civilisation. TSE had granted him a 1½-hr interview on the Friday afternoon – Pierce sent some poems in advance: 'your secretary told me you had read them' – and thereafter Pierce went back to his digs – he had been lodging in dreadful and cold conditions in Angel but had moved to a more comfortable hotel – and passed many hours of the day and the night over the weekend in writing TSE a wearisomely repetitious, unfocused letter about his ambitions. He earnestly petitioned TSE to allow him a further short visit on the Monday to find out what TSE made of his poems, and possibly the part of the epic poem he had left for TSE's adjudication. He had put in for a Guggenheim fellowship, but had been tipped off that he was unlikely to be successful. His greatest desire was to spend a year in England studying and working on a book of criticism. He esteemed the 'sense of values' in TSE's writings.

merely stating where they have been published, and leaving it to each editor to decide whether the previous publication matters. Even if he cannot use the poem for this reason, the previously published poems will help to give him a fair impression of your work.

I will examine the poems you have left for me as soon as I return. There is no reason why you should not submit the same poems to several editors at once, so long as you immediately inform the others, as soon as any editor accepts one.

As for the publication of the long poem (which I have not yet had time to read): I think it as well to let you know at once that the prospects of getting a whole book accepted are very poor. I think that I know as much about the poetry market as anyone, having been intimately concerned with it for some years. The sales to be hoped for from any book of poems by a new poet are very small indeed, a small part of the cost of production. This is the case with English poets in England, and I believe with American poets in America; and it is practically hopeless to bring out a volume by an American poet in England, or an English poet in America, until the poet has achieved some considerable reputation at home. I think therefore that your hope of getting your long poem published is in New York. Nevertheless, I shall read it without that prejudice in mind, at least enough to be able to write to you on Monday evening.

Meanwhile do not work during the night, but go to bed at a reasonable hour; and I hope that you will find your present lodgings warm, and get enough and regular food. An American unused to the English climate should wear warm woolen underwear in winter, and I hope that you have the suitable clothing. If, as I hope, you have a gas fire in your bedroom, I advise drying your pyjamas at night, and your underclothes in the morning, before the fire. In this climate they absorb a great deal of moisture while not being worn.

When I write I shall suggest a time for your coming to see me again.

Yours sincerely,

[T. S. Eliot]

29 January 1936                    [Faber & Faber Ltd]

Dear Madam,

   Mr Eliot has asked me to send you the enclosed novel, *Come Dungeon Dark*, which he has not read himself, but which he has heard is quite amusing.[2] He would very much like to send you a book of your own choosing, and I therefore enclose our Autumn Catalogue. The Spring Catalogue is out, but not many of the books mentioned in it are published yet. Mr Eliot would be very glad if you would pick some book out of the catalogue, or else tell him what kinds of books you like to read.

Yours very truly,
[Brigid O'Donovan]


TO *Rayner Heppenstall*[3]                             TS Texas

30 January 1936           Faber & Faber Ltd

Dear Heppenstall,

   My Committee have decided that we should like very much to publish your book, although it is definitely not of a popular type, and can hardly be expected to pay for itself.[4] I have written to Pinker making the offer of £25 advance on a ten per cent royalty, to be paid on signing the agreement and on certain improvements being made in the manuscript. You need not be disturbed by these conditions, as most of the alterations we have in mind are quite minor matters of style, and the only matter of any importance is that we think that the first chapter could bear a certain amount of rewriting.

---

1 – Lucia Joyce (1907–82), daughter of James Joyce; a professional dancer, she began in 1930 to show signs of mental illness, and was treated for a while by Carl Jung. In the mid-1930s she was diagnosed as schizophrenic; and at the time of this letter was undergoing tests at St Andrew's Hospital, Northampton, England. Later she was permanently institutionalised, initially in Zurich and eventually at St Andrew's Healthcare, Northampton. See Carol Schloss, *Lucia Schloss, Lucia Joyce: To Dance in the Wake* (2003).
2 – Lucia Joyce had sent 'Mr Elliot' a postcard from St Andrew's Hospital, Northampton, 21 Jan. 1936, to ask if she might have a book before she went to the 'theater' for examination.
3 – Rayner Heppenstall (1911–81): novelist, poet, radio producer; author of *Middleton Murry: A Study in Excellent Normality* (1934); *Apology for Dancing* (1936); *The Blaze of Noon* (novel, 1939); *Four Absentees: Dylan Thomas, George Orwell, Eric Gill, J. Middleton Murry* (1960).
4 – Herbert Read had prompted TSE on 29 Jan.: 'Heppenstall is waiting daily & hourly to be put out of his agony. Can you get a word through to him.'

If these proposals are acceptable I will go through the manuscript again to make notes of the places which could bear improvement, and will then write to you. I will do this as quickly as possible, and then I suggest that you should come to lunch with me and talk the matter over.[1]

Meanwhile I have sent your article to the printers with a view to including it in the next *Criterion*.[2]

Yours sincerely,
T. S. Eliot

## TO *Henry Eliot*

TS Houghton

2 February 1936                    Faber & Faber Ltd

Dear Henry,

I hasten to send you a cheque for one hundred and fifty dollars. The money is lying at the First National and I might as well use it for this as for anything; and it still leaves enough there to pay my life insurance next October. I am actually better off than I have any right to expect, as my play has been bringing me in five pounds a week since the beginning of November, and will run for another three weeks. If it could have a successful run in New York, I should make a good deal more. And I have just earned about thirty guineas speaking in Dublin; and got another thirty for the broadcast of the play. I am just about to pay another £25 on account to my solicitors, which will reduce their bill to about £150 – this miserable business will have cost me about £300, most of it unnecessary. I shall be glad when the real estate is sold and off everyone's hands.

I am not surprised by the Christmas card,[3] because I find she has put my name in the telephone book, at her address; and it will take me six months to get it out again. And if any letters are sent to me at that address, I shall never see them. She has a big box of letters to me deposited at Martin's Bank, and it would cost me more than it is worth to get them.

---

1–GCF to FVM, 23 Jan. 1936: '"Apology for Dancing". We have agreed to do this, feeling ourselves a little bit led by the nose by you and Tom, on condition that Tom takes Heppenstall firmly in tow and makes him cut out some of the more flamboyant bits and behave sensibly with regard to capitals and the like. I agree that the book has got some very good stuff in it but it has also got an awful lot of rot.'

Heppenstall replied to TSE's letter, 31 Jan.: 'Pinker says he will produce a document & send it to you . . . In any case, I can say that the arrangement seems all right to me . . . I hope the MS will come for rewriting quickly . . . It sounds bad, all the same. You say "style".'

2–Heppenstall, 'The Frankness of the West', C. 15 (Apr. 1936), 424–39.

3–VHE must have sent a Christmas card to HWE: signed (as she liked to) by VHE and TSE.

I hope that you will be seeing something of the Morleys. I am still in the dark about the play in New York, but I hope to see Ashley Dukes tomorrow night.[1]

Affectionately,

Tom

I am delighted to have the Cranch photographs, & am having them framed.[2]


TO *Susan Hinkley*[3]                                          TS Houghton

2 February 1936                          Faber & Faber Ltd

Dear Aunt Susie,

I have not yet written to thank you for your Christmas card and the enclosed photographs, although the Revd. Charles Chauncy has been framed and hung to flank the Revd. Andrew Eliot (also president of Harvard) over my office mantelpiece, and the commission of Major Thomas Stearns stands on a bookcase in my rooms. Priscilla[4] also is under glass, and on my office mantelpiece. All such things give me much pleasure.

It is still a possibility that I may be in New York when you are in London. Not more than that, because the prospects of my play being produced there are waning. I shall know a little more by tomorrow night,

---

1 – Ashley Dukes was to recall, 'At some time in the near future we had hoped to transfer *Murder in the Cathedral* to America with the English company, playing it from coast to coast without too much consideration of Broadway; but this plan miscarried because a New York production by WPA (Federal Theatre Project) had been authorized just before our success in London with the play. I made an American visit early in 1936 without being able to influence this decision. The WPA production was already well advanced, it could not be stopped except by a legal pressure we were unwilling to use against such an enterprise, and it eventually succeeded on its own merits' (*The Scene is Changed* [1942], 207).

See too Hugh M. Wade to FVM, 4 Apr. 1936: 'MURDER IN THE CATHEDRAL is now playing to capacity houses on an extended run. Eliot may be amused to know that the ticket speculators are now selling select seats for as much as $3 apiece (the top price in the WPA Theater being 55c).'

2 – One was a portrait by Hiram Powers (1805–73) of William Cranch (1769–1855) – the first male Cranch born in America – who was elected in 1801 Chief Justice of the US Circuit Court, Washington, DC: he served for the unpredented term of fifty-four years, and only two of his decisions were reversed on appeal. His son, Christopher Pearse Cranch, gave up the ministry to become a landscape painter, poet and translator. They were ancestors of TSE through his paternal grandmother. TSE did frame the photographs that his brother sent him.

3 – Susan Heywood Hinkley, née Stearns (1860–1948): TSE's maternal aunt.

4 – Priscilla Stearns Talcott (b. 19 Feb. 1934).

when I expect to see Ashley Dukes who arrived, I believe, from America yesterday; but if the play is produced at all, I think that it is more likely to be in the autumn. So I feel pretty certain of being here in the spring when you come; and I hope that the Dobrées will share a box with me on the first night of Aphra Behn.[1] (Mrs Dobrée is as charming as her husband, and is also of French origin, her name was Brooke-Pechell).[2]

I am glad to hear that Eleanor is at work on another play.[3] I have not had time to begin yet on another: I have had to prepare a volume of essays, and my collected poems, for publication in the spring,[4] and have just returned from a most interesting visit to Dublin, where, among other events, I had to be 'interviewed' on the microphone,[5] and have a speech

1 – Eleanor Hinkley's play *Mrs Aphra Behn* (1933, 1935).

2 – Valentine Dobrée (1894–1974) – née Gladys May Mabel Brooke-Pechell, daughter of Sir Augustus Brooke-Pechel, 7th Baronet – was a noted artist, novelist and short-story writer. In addition to *Your Cuckoo Sings by Kind* (Alfred A. Knopf, 1927), she published one further novel, *The Emperor's Tigers* (F&F, 1929); a collection of stories, *To Blush Unseen* (Cresset Press, 1935); and a volume of verse, *This Green Tide* (F&F, 1965). She married BD in 1913. See further *Valentine Dobrée 1894–1974* (University Gallery Leeds, 2000).

3 – Eleanor Holmes Hinkley (1891–1971): TSE's cousin, second daughter of Susan H. Stearns and Holmes Hinkley (1853–91). She studied at Radcliffe College, Cambridge, Mass.: among the advanced courses she took was Professor George Baker's '47 Workshop'. She went on to act with Baker's group as well as to write plays for it (see *Plays of 47 Workshop*, New York: Brentano, 1920). She wrote in all seven one-act and nine full-length plays: they included *A Flitch of Bacon* (1919) and *Mrs Aphra Behn* (1933). *Dear Jane*, a romantic comedy about Jane Austen, was produced by Eva Le Gallienne in 1931 at the Civic Repertory Theater, New York. Other works included *The Parsonage* – a play about Charlotte Brontë and her family. It was through amateur theatricals held at her family home, 1 Berkeley Place, Cambridge, that in 1912 TSE met and fell for Emily Hale (see Biographical Register). TSE called Eleanor, in a letter to Peter du Sautoy (24 Feb. 1951), 'lively and intelligent'.

4 – *Essays Ancient and Modern*, for 5 Mar. 1936; *Collected Poems 1909–1935*, for 2 Apr. 1936.

5 – TSE was interviewed for the radio on Sat. 25 Jan., by Maura Laverty. His remarks included the following: 'I feel that steady application is even more important to an author than is genius. Most well-known writers, you will find, plan their day in a methodical way. There have been exceptions, of course – notably Balzac, whose best work was done during periods of literary frenzy when he would lock himself into his study for days and nights at a time, emerging only when the frenzy had subsided and the work was completed. In spite of such exceptions, I maintain that a regular system in writing is better and more productive than spasmodic eruptions of genius. <This steady, regular application is not possible to poets, however.> In my opinion, a writer should turn to poetry with a fresh eager mind and this is possible only if he treats his poetry as a side-issue and not as a profession. Only in this way will he avoid staleness.' Of his role as editor of the *Criterion*: 'Reading poetry is something like tea-tasting. After reading a certain amount one's palate, to a great extent, loses the powers of sensitive discrimination, and one is likely to find the taste of what has gone before influencing one's critical perception.' Of poets as writers of prose: 'Frankly, I do not see how anyone can write good poetry and not be capable of writing good prose as well. If a writer possesses the gift of poetic expression it naturally follows that his prose

and two essays to write, and to prepare my book of nonsense verse[1] – and then possible visits to France, and Scotland, and Ireland and Wales – and *hope* to be in New England in the autumn.

Affectionately always,
Tom

## TO *James Joyce*[2]    TS National Gallery of Ireland

3 February 1936    Faber & Faber Ltd

My dear Joyce,

Mrs Jolas, who seems a very pleasant person, brought in the manuscript of Part III [of *Work In Progress*] last week.[3] I gave her a receipt for it, but I would also have written to you direct, but that I had to catch the train to go to Dublin directly she left.

I showed the manuscript to our Director of Production, Richard de la Mare, and he felt quite confident that MacLehose, who are quite at the top of their profession as printers, would be able to handle it as it is. Should there be any difficulty they have expert typists of their own to set it right. But I think the simplest thing will be to have them set up a difficult specimen page. The manuscript, however, seems perfectly orderly, although complicated, and I think it will require great care, but not genius, in composition.

----

will benefit. All of the well-known modern Irish poets are masters of prose. James Joyce is a great poet as well as a great prose writer. Yeats's prose, what there is of it, is recognised as excellent. Admittedly, it lacks the progressiveness, the modern quality which distinguishes his poetry, and it savours a little of the nineties, but it is nevertheless splendid prose of its period.' Of his impressions of Ireland: 'If you accept the axiom that what is lovable and admirable in a man is but a reflection of the country that bore him, I think you will find here an eloquent admission of what I think of Ireland.'

1 – *Old Possum's Book of Practical Cats* (Oct. 1939).

2 – James Joyce (1882–1941), Irish novelist, playwright, poet: see Biographical Register.

3 – Maria Jolas (1893–1987): see Profile in vol I of *Letters of Samuel Beckett* (2009).

Sylvia Beach, *Shakespeare and Company* (1960), 148: 'Certainly one of the best things in Joyce's life was the friendship and collaboration of Maria and Eugene Jolas [1894–1952]. From the time they first undertook to publish his work until his death, they rendered him every service and thought no sacrifice too great.

'Eugene Jolas, with his three mother tongues, English, French, and German (he was from Lorraine), and James Joyce, the multi-linguist, set out to revolutionize the English language ... The reinforcement brought by Jolas was a godsend to Joyce, who was feeling rather lonely with his one-man revolution till [Jolas's magazine] *transition* came along.'

Mrs Jolas seemed fairly sure that you would be getting Part II finished within four or five months. She asked me when we wanted to publish the book, and I said that we naturally would like to bring it out as soon as possible after we had the whole manuscript, and that if there was reasonable likelihood of having the complete text within a few months, we should like to start setting up the book at once.

I was very glad to hear from Mrs Jolas that Lucia is making such a remarkable recovery.

I had a pleasant time in your native city, a large part of the population of which seems anxious to erect a monument in your honour, and another part still anxious to forget your existence. I also met people who said that they were friends of yours, and was shown the principle [*sic*] sights, including the Martello Tower.

With kindest regards to Mrs Joyce,<br>
Yours,<br>
T. S. Eliot

## TO *John Cournos*[1]

CC

3 February 1936    [*The Criterion*]

Dear John,

I was glad to get your letter of 22nd January, although sorry to hear that you had been bothered with sinus trouble, which I know is both painful and expensive.[2] I do hope that Alfred was successful, although I feel that your not mentioning it means the contrary.

I shall be delighted to do anything possible to get a better supply of Russian periodicals for the *Criterion*, as I do think this is one of our more valuable and uncommon features.[3] But before I write to Moscow would you please give me a list of all the periodicals you want, together with what is necessary, or what you can provide, in the way of addresses. I will then write to them all at the same time.

---

1–John Cournos (1881–1966): poet, novelist, essayist, translator: see Biographical Register L6.

2–Cournos thanked TSE for writing to F. O. Matthiessen on behalf of his stepson Alfred Satterthwaite.

3–Cournos recommended writing to the proper authorities in Moscow for Russian periodicals. 'I am especially anxious to get *Literaturniy Gazetta*, which is the best source of literary news and criticism.'

My volume of collected poems is in the press, but will probably not be published until some time in March or April.[1] It will be published simultaneously by Harcourt Brace in America, but I shall try to remember to send you a copy when the English edition is out.

With kindest regards to Mrs Cournos and yourself,

Yours ever,

[T. S. E.]

## TO *A. G. Hebert*                                                   cc

3 February 1936                    [Faber & Faber Ltd]

Dear Father Gabriel,

Thank you for your letter written on the Feast of Charles, King and Martyr. I am interested in your notes of the three volumes you have in view. I agree with you definitely that the first two are S.P.C.K. books, but I shall mention all three to my Committee at its next meeting, and write to you again. The third book is certainly a most interesting possibility for us.[2]

I have read with much interest the memorandum of the Dean of Chichester, which you enclosed, and thank you for sending it.[3] It seems to me that I detect your influence here and there. I find several points which I should like an opportunity to discuss with you. One statement rather puzzles me. The memorandum says 'Mass and Communion must be kept together'. Does this suggest that the ordinary 11 o'clock High Mass should be abandoned? It would seem to do so, because elsewhere the principle of fasting Communion is affirmed. It would seem, furthermore, to discourage the hearing of Low Mass by persons who for one reason or another did not intend to communicate. I should be sorry if this was the intention, and I should like to hear more of its justification.[4]

---

1 – Cournos asked to be sent a copy of *CP 1909–1935* – 'with the bill'.

2 – '(i) Some notes of a lecture-course on St Thomas Aquinas about the attributes of God . . . (ii) I have been strongly urged to edit (or co-edit) a volume of essays to be entitled "The Parish Communion". . . . [Q]uite clearly it is not in your line, and is a book for S.P.C.K. . . . (iii) Another idea which is hovering in my mind is a book of studies in the Gospels, based of course on my lectures here – a book that should not be highbrow, but that would try to give a theological exposition of the main issues that are raised in the Gospels.'

3 – Not traced.

4 – Hebert responded, 4 Feb.: '[T]he fullness of the meaning of the High Mass comes out when it is the occasion of a general communion, as it is here at Kelham. In the proposed book we are not going to run down the late non-communicating High Mass, but point out

It was a capital thing, I think, to have Oldham involved in the Conference. It should be good for him, as well as for everyone else. I should certainly be relieved if Oldham decided not to include MacMurray, as I think the latter is likely to become more, rather than less embarrassing to us in the future.[1]

Yours very sincerely,

[T. S. Eliot]

## TO *Ross E. Pierce* CC

4 February 1936                 [Faber & Faber Ltd]

Dear Mr Pierce,

I have your letter of February 3rd.[2] As to the question of the suitability of publication of your long poem in London or in New York, the considerations which I had in view were purely practical ones, based upon considerable experience, and really have no relation to the argument which you have put forward. I tried to make clear that in the present condition of things it is very difficult to sell poetry at all, and the sales of a first volume depend as much on the beginning of a reputation which a man has made for himself by publishing for some time in periodicals, as on the reviews which his book may receive. It is usual for a man's work to be known for several years in this way before a volume is produced, and it is accordingly natural that the first volume of an English poet does better in England, and the first volume of an American poet in America. I

---

its spiritual value; and then say that there is something better, and that we hope more and more churches will find their way to a Sung Mass about 9 with general communion . . . It is in the working class and lower middle class districts that the 9 o'clock Mass seems the ideal solution.'

1 – John Macmurray (1891–1976), Scottish philosopher: see letter of 16 Dec. 1937, below.

2 – 'Last Thursday . . . you said you still thought the poem ought to be brought out in New York first as you will remember I stressed the argument as to why it might be better to bring it out in England or even Western Europe first – a superficial resemblance to Byron's work, satire and history, its popularity on the Continent and the more solid background and better developed sense of human values over here. Then you mentioned Lindsay in connection with the epitome of history part – Book III – and added that though I might not know his work that would not make any difference and then mentioned Auden in the first part . . . On thinking the matter over . . . I have wondered if you meant that Books I and III – the largest part – of the poem seemed to you a possibly independent but less well done work parallel to that of Lindsay and Auden . . . or if you meant it had merely a superficial resemblance to each of the above mentioned authors' work and in itself represented a distinct and well conceived point of view.' He asked to 'have a short half hour' with TSE to discuss 'this vital side' – 'so I will know where I stand as to your position with respect to this point'.

think I said that it was almost impossible nowadays for a writer to have any success in the other country until he had made some name for himself at home. Even with young English poets who have this advantage of some preliminary reputation, the sales of a small first book of verse will hardly cover the cost. To present what is a volume of comparatively large size to an audience of another country would be a certain financial loss which I could not recommend my own firm to incur.

I still think that the best thing you can do for your poetry is to try to get such verse as you can published in periodicals, both here and in New York, during the next year or two, and I still think that you might more easily find a publisher to undertake your long poem in New York than here. It was, however, partly for the reason that I did not wish you to have only my own opinion to depend upon that I suggested your calling on Mr Richard Church,[1] who is as open-minded and enterprising a publisher of verse as any in London.

The parallel with Byron does not seem to me to have any bearing on the immediate problem. In any case you must remember that Byron's poems were all published in London before they were taken up abroad, and that his first and most striking success was in London, and that the poems of his which were most popular at the time, both here and abroad, are not those on which his present reputation rests.

I did not intend to suggest any parallel between your poem as a whole and any work of Lindsay or Auden. I merely draw attention to a certain similarity of metric. This similarity is not a serious matter in itself, and it does not matter whether you had ever read the work of these poets or not. What does matter is the tendency to monotony, which is almost unescapable in a poem of that length unless the author has practised his ear in varieties of versification during many years. The best model to study among long poems by modern poets is the *30 Cantos* by Ezra Pound. You will find, at any rate in the best of those Cantos, a variety of measures and a musical pattern which relieves them from any suggestion of monotony. I shall hardly have time to see you again for several days, and I do not think that you had better delay in seeing Mr Church until you have seen me, as it would hardly affect that situation. It would be wise also if you could have enough of your shorter poems ready to be able to suggest to him as an alternative a smaller book of selected poems.

Yours sincerely,

[T. S. Eliot]

1 – Of J. M. Dent & Sons.

TO *Rayner Heppenstall*                                          TS Texas

4 February 1936                        Faber & Faber Ltd

Dear Heppenstall,

I have now been through your book again, and have made some notes.
I think that the only part which requires any considerable alteration is
Chapter I.[1] It might be as well if we could have a talk about this, and

---

1 – TSE's notes on Chapter 1 include these useful (and universally commendable) comments:
'The only chapter that seems to me to need re-organising is the first. I think it must have
been written first, whereas the first chapter ought to be written last. It has the quite usual
weaknesses of trying to say everything, and of trying to say everything at the beginning. As
for trying to say everything – you will presumably write other books, and will find more
suitable contexts. As for trying to say everything at the beginning – a book like this cannot
ignore the arts of persuasion. Your pouring everything out in the first chapter will merely
make people regard you as an enthusiast of some kind (not necessarily for ballet, or for a
theory), and your business is not to look enthusiastic, but to arouse enthusiasm in others.
The first chapter gives the impression of thrashing about right and left at the contemporary
world. This first chapter ought to be cut down to what the reader will accept easily as he
goes along as having something to do with ballet and the dance. (All that about Football,
for instance, is admirable sense put in the right place.) But a good deal of what you cut out
of the first chapter could be re-instated at the end of the book. The reader ought to start the
book as a book on dancing, and be led on to consider the relations of dancing to other arts,
to society etc., later. It is a mistake to give the impression of belly-aching about the modern
world at the beginning, before you have time to put into the reader's head all the facts and
several ideas which will incline him to feel the same way. All that sort of thing about the
craze for speed etc. just gives the impression of current fretfulness.

'I am very doubtful about your putting your indictment of "abstraction" and that of
"Louder and Funnier" on the same footing. The first goes very deep indeed in diagnosis of
the modern world; the second is something which might perhaps be resolved into a more
fundamental formula or term. In using words like "Louder and Funnier" there is always the
danger of getting people to agree with you who do not understand what you mean, and are
taking what you say rather superficially – just dislike of vulgarity, noises, speed etc.

'My only other radical criticism is that pp. 132–138, the two illustrative prose pieces,
should come out. In this place, and quite without consideration of their merit in themselves,
they will irritate the reader by holding up the flow of the chapter.

'Make Chapter I an INTRODUCTION to what is to come afterwards, not a MANIFESTO.
You should be TALKING TO PEOPLE, not merely talking to yourself to clear up your own
ideas. Put everything that does not seem to have immediate relevance into a final chapter.
Generalisations in general belong to the end, rather than the beginning of a composition,
when they are developed at any length.'

GCF to TSE, 11 Feb. 1936: 'Heppenstall came in with his typescript revised this afternoon.
He has made in the typescript some but [not] all of the alterations which you recommended,
and hoped you might agree that this would be enough. Assuming, however, that you might
not agree, he has effected the rest of the alterations, together with certain consequential
alterations in the body of the book, in a set of typewritten instructions to the printer . . .
I have agreed that this is good enough, and that we will sign the contract since Pinker has
it ready . . .

'I think it must clearly be your task to study the typescript and make up your mind on
this point . . . I take it that we are contemplating publishing the book a little in advance

---

I should be glad if you would have lunch with me on Monday, which is the first I have free. If that suits you will you meet me at the Etoile in Charlotte Street, at 1.15? But if you are in a hurry to get on with the work I could see you for a little while on Friday afternoon, and give you the manuscript and the notes.

Yours sincerely,
T. S. Eliot

## TO *Donald Brace*[1]                                              CC

7 February 1936                    [Faber & Faber Ltd]

Dear Brace,

Thank you for your very satisfactory letter of January 14th.[2] No doubt Morley will have delivered the material and the list of contents of my

---

of the ballet season this summer; and if that is so, we ought, I suppose, to get to work on the typescript pretty soon . . . He is not an unattractive young man, but he certainly looks as though he needed more to eat and his hesitating vagueness is perhaps the result of starvation.'

The draft blurb for *Apology for Dancing* reads: 'Mr Rayner Heppenstall, who is known to readers of the *New English Weekly* as the most brilliant and ruthless journalistic critic of the ballet, has written a book that should be in the library of every *balletomane*. As the title suggests, it is primarily about *dancing*, and about the ballet as a special development of the dance. The author's approach differs from that of every previous critic. He has his own views about the nature and social significance of dancing in general: instead of beginning with the finished and specialised product of the Ballet Russe, he leads up to this as the peculiar expression of the art in our time and civilisation. Mr Heppenstall is an iconoclast, and will irritate (beneficially, we believe) many admirers of ballet; but he will also provide them with a compendious history of this dance form, and a critique of the greatest dancers. He will annoy especially admirers of Isadora Duncan, about whom (comparing her, incidentally, with D. H. Lawrence) one of his most entertaining chapters is written. He does not write only as a philosopher of dancing, and he does not write solely as a spectator in the stalls; he knows what ballet is like, not only from the wings, but in the gymnasium, and in what the tortures of side-practice and centre-practice consist. Finally, he is a trained musician. When the reader agrees with Mr Heppenstall, he will do so enthusiastically, when he disagrees most violently, he will benefit from the provocation.' (The blurb appeared just so on the published volume; but some of the more provocative sentences here were removed in the F&F Autumn catalogue 1936, p. 28).

1–Donald Brace (1881–1955), publisher; co-founder of Harcourt, Brace: see Biographical Register.

2–Brace was delighted that 'all of the material for the collected volume of verse' was on its way. He wrote again on 30 Jan.: 'The Morleys arrived here yesterday . . . Morley gave me the typewritten copy for the final poem in the book, and he tells me that you will be sending us final English proofs by the end of the first week in February. Meanwhile, we are going ahead to set up from the copy we have, but we will read the proofs carefully with the English proofs when they arrive. Morley tells me that in view of the early arrival of the final English

volume of collected verse, together with any explanations necessary. As soon as I get the complete proof of the English edition I will send it to you with not more than 48 hours' delay for correction. It ought to be possible, therefore, to produce the two editions as near simultaneously as need be.

I am relieved to know that you think there should be no difficulty about the copyright of *Ash Wednesday*. I dare say that you have settled that matter by now.[1]

About the Federal Theatre project, I am only sorry now that you have had so much trouble and worry for no results at all.[2] I saw Ashley Dukes on Monday evening, and he had been much impressed by your anxiety to help in every way. He also found Elmer Rice as obliging as possible. Rice resigned suddenly only a day or so before Dukes sailed, and now, I am informed, by a cable from a correspondent, that the production of *Murder in the Cathedral* has been abandoned. Whether this means that all of Rice's selections have been dropped, or merely that as Rice feared, they were unable to get an actor who could take the part of Becket satisfactorily, I don't know, and it doesn't matter. I am very glad that they have dropped it. It is possible that Dukes will take the play over with one or two others in the autumn. In that event I shall probably be coming over myself rather later in the year than I had intended. I hope, by the way, that Morley will succeed in bringing you back with him in March.

The whole muddle is really due to my lack of foresight, in that it never occurred to me that there would be any requests except for a few scattered performances by amateurs in odd places. I am quite satisfied with Dukes's arrangement with you to continue with applications for amateur performances, and hope that it is satisfactory to you also.

---

proofs, it will not be necessary to send proofs of our edition over to you. So I am taking back my promise to send you proofs. I assume this is in accordance with your wishes. It will save you a certain amount of trouble, and I am sure we can produce our edition accurately.'
1 – 'The copyright must originate from the original limited edition, and Putnam's rights would depend upon the arrangement under which they reissued . . . The fact that there are a certain number of poems in this collection which have not previously been published anywhere enables us to print a copyright notice in the volume, and our publication will fully protect such poems. As for "Sweeney Agonistes", there is nothing that can be done now to establish the copyright.'
2 – '[Y]our letter of December 31st, and especially a letter received by the same mail from Mr Dukes, make me suspect that Elmer Rice must have gone direct to Ashley Dukes and concluded arrangements. I was very reluctant to cable you so persistently, but they were pressing me here and I couldn't help it. It is good of you to say that it is nobody's fault, but I am afraid it is really my fault. The Federal Theatre Project is an entirely new thing – one of the activities of the New Deal – and there is therefore no precedent to go by. The scheme is non-profit-making and its purpose is to provide employment and also to make worth while productions in the hope that they may be taken over into the commercial theatre.'

I have not heard much about the production at Yale, but gather that it went off well, though I don't believe there was anyone there who could compare with the original production.[1]

Yours ever sincerely,

[T. S. Eliot]

P.S. Thank you very much also for the letter from Governor Cross.[2]


## TO *John Hayward*                                         MS King's

Friday night [7 February 1936]          [Faber & Faber Ltd]

Dear John,

Here, it looks like *no Go* Sunday night been in bed with flu 2 days and feel no better Head spinning Like t-totem joints racked by hell pangs Chest like nutmeg grater but I suppose I am not so Bad as I feel as I can't find anything about me in The Times must apologise for not being Life of Party[3] will ring up when Out again I hope you have not caught it.

Yours Tom


## TO *Geoffrey Faber*                                    MS Valerie Eliot

Sunday [?9 February 1936]          [no address: blank paper]

Dear Geoffrey,

This is the worst bronchitis I have ever had – what with tearing my tubes out with coughing at night and sleeping all day I feel thoroughly stupified [*sic*]. Then the doctor thought till yesterday that I ought to be out tomorrow – now he says more likely the end of the week: I wish he had thought of that at once.

---

1 – Brace (14 Jan.): 'The production at Yale seems to have been a distinguished success . . . Although they originally asked permission for only one performance, they later requested permission for two more. No admission was charged at the performances, and we collected a fee of $85.'

2 – Wilbur L. Cross, Governor of Connecticut, to Brace, 10 Jan. 1936: 'I put in a whole evening last week in reading *Murder in the Cathedral*. There has never been any treatment of Becket equal to this. It is a most impressive dramatic poem written by a master. You have doubtless observed how well he used an old dramatic form with verse and prose, unsurpassed in beauty.'

3 – TSE had dined *chez* JDH on 5 Feb.; the other guests were David Garnett and Clive Bell.

Flint[1] has no right to be in such a hurry. If he is right, and I dare say he is, he will have to wait a long time anyway before anyone takes notice of him. The best we could do wd be to send his MS to Frank[2] by Germ. pkt *Europa* sailing Feb 12th. The point being that nobody else can cope with the mathematics, real or pseudo.

A profit-making or a non-profit-making society seems equally dreary to my simple mind. Gollancz will be on top in either case, unless you have pogroms, and I'd rather go on grumbling than be bullied by low class anglo saxons.

That's all my brain will do for me at the moment. Not so resilient as it used to be.

Yours<br>T.

I told Miss O'D to offer you 2 tickets I had ordered for the *Dog* [*Beneath the Skin*] for tomorrow night. Otherwise, she can use them herself.

## TO *Geoffrey Curtis*

TS Houghton

14 February 1936                    *The Criterion*

Dear Curtis,

I have been confined to my rooms for the last ten days with bronchial influenza, but my secretary has forwarded me your letter 'with enclosures'. I will return *Simeon* to Bill Stead, who I suppose is still living at Clifton Hampden:[3] I didn't even know that you knew him – at least you know a typical American Southerner. (I should explain that I am a Northerner). These little pamphlets are to be scrapped, I am glad to say: all these bits are being gathered together in my *Collected Poems*, now in proof, of which I shall send you a copy if I don't forget.

But my dear Sir, don't imagine that the 'fear of Hell' is not capital in my theology.[4] It is only balanced by that 'fear of Heaven' so well expressed

---

1 – Frank Stuart ('F.S.') Flint (1885–1960), poet, translator, civil servant: see letter of 23 Feb. 1937, below.
2 – FVM.
3 – Curtis wrote on 12 Feb. that he realised it had been a long time since he had borrowed William Force Stead's copy of TSE's *A Song for Simeon* – it was 'dishonestly appropriated', yet 'not with conscious wilfulness', he felt – and asked TSE to return it to him.
4 – Curtis had just heard from a 'dear brother (Joseph)' who used to be a 'trifler' but had come 'near to death's door' and was 'revitalised spiritually' by reading John Donne. 'I would like to reply to him that there was one real thing in his religion, and that the now so lacking fear of hell: hence an at least incipient repentance. Is it possible you are so keen on "relevant

in one of Newman's Oxford sermons.[1] I sometimes wonder whether I am not being captured by my powerful Calvinist heredity – a more sensible view, however, is that I am merely revolting against my ancestors of the last two hundred years – though it *is* rather dreadful to be descended from a man who had to leave England because he could not get on with a dear person like Laud.[2] But your friend is all away from the mark: I never said that a taste for Donne's sermons indicated wantonness of mind – a man

---

intensity" that the virtue of religious vehemence as such escapes you? I doubt if queerness would upset you though I venture to doubt whether at that stage compassion had outgrown certain "frigidities" (Hopkins "An untruth to nature, to human nature, is frigid.") . . .

'By "trifler" I mean only a superficial catholic without the kind of awe that made the faith seem relevant to Hulme.'

*For Lancelot Andrewes* (1928): 'The sermons of Andrewes are not easy reading. They are only for the reader who can elevate himself to the subject. The most conspicuous qualities of the style are three: ordonnance, or arrangement and structure, precision in the use of words, and relevant intensity. The last remains to be defined. All of them are best elucidated by comparison with a prose which is much more widely known, but to which I believe we must assign a lower place – that of Donne. Donne's sermons, or fragments from Donne's sermons, are certainly known to hundreds who have hardly heard of Andrewes; and they are known precisely for the reasons because of which they are inferior to those of Andrewes . . . Donne is a "personality" in a sense in which Andrewes is not: his sermons, one feels, are a "means of self-expression." He is constantly finding an object which shall be adequate to his feelings; Andrewes is wholly absorbed in the object and therefore responds with the adequate emotion. Andrewes had the *gout pour la vie spirituelle*, which is not native to Donne . . .

'But Donne is not the less valuable, though he is the more dangerous for this reason. Of the two men, it may be said that Andrewes is the more mediaeval, because he is the more pure, and because his bond was with the Church, with tradition. His intellect was satisfied by theology and his sensibility by prayer and liturgy. Donne is the more modern – if we are careful to take this word exactly, without any implication of value, or any suggestion that we must have more sympathy with Donne than with Andrewes. Donne is much less the mystic; he is primarily interested in man. He is much less traditional.'

1 – J. H. Newman, *Parochial and Plain Ser*mons (1834), I: 'If then a man without religion (supposing it possible) were admitted into heaven, doubtless he would sustain a great disappointment . . . Nay, I will venture to say more than this . . . that if we wished to imagine a punishment for an unholy, reprobate soul, we perhaps could not fancy a greater than to *summon it to heaven.* Heaven would be hell to an irreligious man . . . And so heaven itself would be fire to those, who would fain escape across the great gulf from the torments of hell.'

2 – William Laud (1573–1645), Archbishop of Canterbury from 1633; leader of the High Anglican party. In 'Lancelot Andrewes', TSE said that the bishop's prayers 'illustrate the devotion to private prayer . . . and to public ritual which Andrewes bequeathed to William Laud' (*FLA*, 18). Laud was a passionate advocate for the powers and rights of the established Church in harmony with the monarchy. He was opposed to Puritanism and nonconformism, insisting that ecclesiastical uniformity was the necessary correlative of order in the state. His conviction as to the catholicity of the Church of England led to suspicions of popery. TSE said of Richard Hooker, in *VMP*, 164: 'it is no wonder that before he joined the Church of Rome he found the church of Archbishop Laud the most sympathetic, of Laud who took his stand for the liturgy and "the beauty of holiness"'.

who reads texts so vaguely as that is no theologian. Pearsall Smith is the wanton.[1] People who use words like 'highbrow' so loosely will use the word 'queer' loosely too. I don't *think* that religious vehemence puts me off: indeed, it is just the lack of it that worries me (during my convalescence) in reading Prestige's biography of your founder.[2] For me, Gore (and of course Halifax) was not queer enough. The only contemporary queer enough for my taste was Charles de Foucauld. Compare Lawrence of Arabia: the only kind of queerness England produces is what fits in to the programme of the *Evening Standard* and a tablet in St Paul's. We need a *really ascetic* (and from an English point of view, quite *useless*) order. descalzado.[3]

Yours fretfully,
T. S. Eliot

## TO *John Hayward*                                    TS King's

14 February 1936                    *The Criterion*

Dear John,

The shades are closing in on your old friend, and soon, I fear, there will be nothing left but the closing chapter of the Reichenbach Falls.[4] The enclosure[5] speaks only too clearly. You know me too well, John, to suppose that I will ever concede an inch to such rascals. I tell you, my friend, that if a detailed account of this silent contest could be written, it would take its place as the most brilliant bit of thrust-and-parry work in the history of detection. Never have I risen to such a height, and never have I been so hard pressed by an opponent. He cuts deep, and yet I just undercut him. He has powerful friends, I happen to know, in foreign chancelleries, and even here in London: I have only the silent approbation of one whom I can only indicate as my illustrious client. And one word: do not distrust W. F. Had you only known who he was, things might have gone more smoothly.

Your
[unsigned]

---

1 – *Donne's Sermons: Selected Passages, with an Essay* by Logan Pearsall Smith (1919).
2 – The Revd G. L. Prestige, DD, *The Life of George Gore – A Great Englishman* (1935).
3 – *Descalzado* (Sp.): barefoot.
4 – See A. Conan Doyle, 'The Final Problem', in *The Memoirs of Sherlock Holmes* (1893).
5 – Not traced.

TO *Stuart Gilbert*[1]                              TS Mrs Gilbert

18 February 1936                    Faber & Faber Ltd

Dear Gilbert,

I have your letter of the 7th February. By all means use my name if
you think it has any value as an introduction to the Society for Psychical
Research.[2] I don't know them at all, but I dare say there are one or two
active spirits in the Society whom I do know, such as possibly Julian
Huxley.

I look forward to seeing you if you are coming to London.[3] Morley is
in America, and does not expect to be back until the first week in March,
and I am sure he would be very sorry to miss you, so if you can postpone
your visit for a week or two it would be so much the better.

As you may know, Mrs Jolas was over here a few weeks ago, and left
with me Part III of *Work in Progress*.[4] She assured me that Joyce was
almost certain to have Part II complete by the middle of the year, but
if you have any other information I should be glad to know. When you
come I should like to discuss with you your project for a monograph
on the book. I think we ought to consider seriously putting out such a
handbook, and you are the obvious person to do it.

One more private and confidential matter. I have had a few brief notes
from Lucia from her nursing home in Northampton, and have sent her a
book or two. The previous notes were perfectly normal so far as one could
judge from their brevity.[5] But I have another note today in which she asks
me to get permission for her to leave the clinic. The note is very brief,
and otherwise shows no sign of derangement. I had thought at first of

1 – Stuart Gilbert (1883–1969), literary scholar and translator; expert on James Joyce: see
Biographical Register.
2 – Gilbert wished to join 'the subliminal circle of the S.P.R.': 'I have been reading their
"Proceedings" in bulk, lately, and was as interested in them as I have been in anything
since I was studying the occult for my book on *Ulysses* . . . [T]hey accept "references" from
without, if eminent.'
3 – Gilbert was planning to visit London late in Feb., and hoped to see both TSE and FVM.
4 – Gilbert remarked (7 Feb.): 'One of these days *Work in Progress* will, I suppose, be
coming out. I propose to write a short monograph on its themes and methods – something
much shorter and more precise than my book on *Ulysses*. A full-length commentary would
mean some ten years' work and I don't feel up to it! Also, it would probably discourage
potential readers, who would assume that a book which required so much elucidation must
be intolerably obscure.'
5 – Lucia Joyce wrote in an undated letter from St Andrew's Hospital, Northampton, to
thank TSE for the book he had sent her. If he cared to send her another book, she would
like a copy of *Elizabethan Essays*, and she expressed the hope that TSE would soon write
to her father again.

sending it on to her father, but I don't want to distress him unnecessarily. I understood from Mrs Jolas that the physician in Northampton had been doing her immense benefit, and that it was primarily the encouragement which had made it possible for Joyce to resume work. Have you any information on this matter? If not, I will write to Mrs Jolas.[1]

Yours ever sincerely,
T. S. Eliot

## TO *Polly Tandy*[2]                                                      TS BL

18 February 1936                    *The Criterion*

Dear Polly ma'am I am sorry to hear your news indeed I am but after all it is Normal and chicken is the least unpleasant kind and its not so bad as mumps measles or whoopingcough but I hope the bronchitique cold will disappear before the feathers come and shall be glad of news especially good ones wd. Alison like anything in the way of jigsaw puzzles or what as for Miss Milligan[3] that doesnt sound like a very hardworking locum and on Sunday morning too but I know what some of these medical students Are. Now the only way yo do Miss Milligan is not to shuffle the cards properly, if you don't shuffle the cards properly why after a few goes you get it Now. I think more highly of Pierpoint Morgan because that is more a game of skill which I should be glad to contribute but you must shuffle properly that is to say shuffle each pack 3 times then shuffle them together 3 times then deal out ten on the table face up and ten on top of them and so on until all 104 are dealt in to 10 packs then pick up the packs alternately and shuffle together again 6 times and then you have them nicely shuffled and you can play Pierrepont [*sic*] Morgan and after I mean before the next game you shuffle again in the same wise I am quite

---

1 – Gilbert replied on 22 Feb.: 'The problem has solved itself, I imagine, as [Lucia] is due back in Paris in three days' time. I had a letter from her, too – a quite normal letter. She certainly seems much better, and it will be a great relief to Joyce to have her out of the doctors' hands.'

2 – Doris (Polly) Tandy: wife since 1923 of the marine biologist Geoffrey Tandy (1900–69); characterised by Lyndall Gordon as 'a practical, religious, warm-hearted countrywoman who mothered Eliot': a 'homey countrywoman' (*The Imperfect Life of T. S. Eliot* [2012]). The Tandys had three children – Richard, Alison, Anthea – and became very close friends of TSE, who was godfather to Anthea (one of the dedicatees of *Old Possum's Book of Practical Cats*). See David Collard, 'Old Possum and the limbs of satan', http://davidjcollard. blogspot.co.uk/2013/06/old-possum-and-limbs-of-satan.html.

3 – 'Miss Milligan' is a game of patience played with two decks of cards.

well now thank you and was treated kindly by your husband so awaiting further News I remain yours faithfully

Possum

P.S. Best wishes to the licensee.[1]


## TO *Ezra Pound* TS Yale

18 February 1936 AD *The Criterion*

Ras Ez: : allright allright don't be so fiddgetty I think we can make up a slick selection out of all that[2] Ima slammin away at it amongst 1000 unrecernised good deeds and me just recoverin from influendza which is the penalty of living in a good climbate like this instead of yr. perpetual sunlight which is addlin to the brain to say nothing of yr. siroccos and mistrals and flying foxes swoopin about biting the mangooes and the moskeeters now don't you inflamb me to foul language because when it comes to that I never allowed to pipe down to anybody but old ike Carver down to Mosquito Cove I think However we can arrandge a selegtion of essays most improvin and pervocative only theres no Hurry Because the Wale[3] bein in New York and not back till March 9th I got to have sombody to pass the Ball to I mean nothing serious can be accomplished all by One self Heaven knows I am not defending our public but it is all the public there is Ignorant East & West like Strickland you moving among nothing but volatile wops hither & thither like Homeric bats In the Mahabharata you don't know what it is to have to displace strong quiet men with a business sense so will close

TP

---

1 – Mr Widgery, licensee of the Bell pub at Hampton-on-Thames; also, the tall Tandy himself.
2 – EP had written on 10 Feb.: 'OW! Kumm on, yr/ btd/ 3/6 three an sax penny pubk/ dunno wot it wants ANYhow. Whats wrong with the list of contents send on 7 Dec? yrs EZ.'

    The contents of *Polite Essays* (Feb. 1937) – 'Polecat essays', as EP styled the volume to FVM (1 Jan. 1937) – came to comprise, after long hard work by TSE and FVM: 'Harold Monro'; 'Mr Housman at Little Bethel'; 'Hell'; '"We have had no battles"'; 'The Prose Tradition in Verse'; 'Dr Williams' Position'; 'James Joyce et Pécuchet'; 'Mr Eliot's Solid Merit'; '"Abject and Utter Farce"'; 'The Teacher's Mission'; 'A Letter from Dr Rouse to E.P.'; 'Retrospect: Interlude'; 'Prefatio aut cimicium tumulus'; '"Active Anthology"'; 'How To Read'; 'Civilization'; 'Note on Dante' – the last extrapolated from *The Spirit of Romance*.
3 – 'the Wale': 'Whale', nickname for FVM.

TO *H. W. Chrysler*                                        CC

18 February 1936                    [Faber & Faber Ltd]

Dear Sir,

I have your letter of January 29th, and regret to have to say that I am wholly unacquainted with the poetry of Emily Dickinson.[1] Although her influence in America may be considerable, I should imagine that her work was very little known in England.

Yours very truly,
[T. S. Eliot]


TO *Kenneth Allott*[2]                                     CC

18 February 1936                    [Faber & Faber Ltd]

Dear Mr Allott,

I do not wonder that you are beginning to get impatient with me, and it is quite right and proper because I never succeed in getting anything done until things reach a point at which I can be driven to neglect everything else in order to do it. This letter is later than it should have been, as I have been away for ten days with influenza.

Now I have been meditating the poems you sent me. They none of them seem quite so good as I think you might have made them with more time and trouble, and I wonder whether you always stopped to reflect on the meaning of each sentence when completed. I recognise a force and acidity that I like; all of the poems seem to me worth taking more trouble over than you seem to have taken. I return most with a few pencillings, and am keeping the first poem (four pages) to type out and see how it looks. It seems to me the best, and to need about 10 hours more work.

Yours sincerely.
[T. S. Eliot]


1–Chrysler wrote from Toronto, 'I am making a little study of the influence of Emily Dickinson's poetry on the writers of more recent days, and I should be glad to learn your opinion of that influence – its force and direction.' Chrysler's work was for a dissertation leading to the MA degree at Toronto.

2–Kenneth Allott (1912–73), poet and critic, worked as a reviewer for the *Morning Post* and with Geoffrey Grigson on *New Verse*; he later taught English at Liverpool University, 1948–73. Works include the bestselling *Penguin Book of Contemporary Verse* (ed., 1950; rev., 1962), and *The Poems of Matthew Arnold* (1965).

FROM *J. Husein* TO *John Hayward*                    TS King's

19 February 1936                    15 Upper Bedford Pl.
                                    London W.C.1

Dear Mr Hayward,

I take the permission to address you under the authority of Mr J. Isaacs, Prof. A. W. Reed, and Prof. G. B. Harrison of London University, who will vouch for my bona fides. In partail [*sic*] fulfilment of the requirements for the degree of D.Phil. at London University I am preparing a dissertation on the work of Mr T. S. Eliot, the poet and critic, and I am advised that you are most likely person to be able to assist me with information about his relations with certain foreign thinkers, e.g.: Prof. Serge Bolshakoff of the University of Vilna, Prof. Arsenieff of Kieff, Gen. Araki, the R. P. Delobel of Grenoble, Col. de la Roque, M. Léon Blum and others. Also with certain persons of *international activity* in London. I am aware that your time is so valuable, Mr Hayward, but if you could grant me the favour of an interview I should be completely grateful.

                    Believe me, dear Sir,
                    Yours faithfully,
                    J. Husein
                    B.A. (Calcutta)


TO *Frank Morley*[1]                    cc

19 February 1936                    [Faber & Faber Ltd]

Dear Frank,

Official. All that we did about the American rights of the *Faber Book of Modern Verse* was to tell Roberts to find out from each author who, if anybody, held such rights.[2] If Roberts has done his job he has a list to supply to whatever American publisher is interested. I suppose there ought to be an arrangement with Roberts also. You remember that the sum we paid him was on advance of a small royalty. I should think that an American publisher ought to pay the authors just the same rates that we paid. I don't see why he should pay more.


1 – Frank Morley, TSE's colleague at F&F: see Biographical Register.
2 – FVM asked from New York, 5 Feb.: 'Have we obtained U.S.A. permission for the pieces in Faber book of Voise? Ask Goblin [C. W. Stewart] to write Brace about that.'

I am glad to hear that you are enjoying yourselves.[1] I have just crept up after a week in bed with bronchial influenza, and am going through the usual stages of depression. I hope Christina received the poem I sent her, care of Harcourt, Brace, about the goats. I did not keep a copy of it, and I was rather proud of the effort, except the last line, which I think could be improved.[2]

Yours ever,
[Tom]

## TO *Herbert Read*[3]                                                    TS Victoria

19 February 1936                         *The Criterion*

Dear Herbert,

I am now out and about again, and am beginning to get to work doing something for you, and will see what steady application every morning this week will produce. But it's an awful grind. Very many thanks for enclosing the copy of Shelley for me.[4] I don't believe it will irritate me as much as you think. Certainly not as much as your contributions to the N.E.W.[5] But are your publishers going to let us have a review copy or not? I have already had a request from two reviewers! but I should like to consult you about that first. Can you mention anybody who would be likely to produce the right sort of review? I am not sure, by the way, that

1 – 'The licker is hard but not virulent & the pace is hot but not killing & Christina is having a good time.' Christina added to FVM's letter, 'We are having a grand time & seem to rush round from morning till night seeing people. Yesterday we got hold of the Loomises & they took us round to their apartment to see a film they took that day at Pike's Farm – do you remember? Pandora seemed to be the chief actor but there were some good ones of the children fishing too, & you with them in the boat.'
2 – Not traced.
3 – Herbert Read (1893–1968), English poet and literary critic: see Biographical Register.
4 – 'In Defence of Shelley', in *In Defence of Shelley and Other Essays* (1936), 3–86. HR to TSE, 4 Feb. 1936: 'I wanted you to be the first to see it, so that we can get the scolding over before it becomes public property . . . Sympathy is something more important than agreement. For that reason I would like you to tell me if you think I have gone too far in any phrase or expression of feeling.'

See Hugh Gordon Porteus on HR, *In Defence of Shelley and Other Essays*: C. 15 (July 1936), 724–30. '[A]ny criticism of Mr Read, and of his criticism of Shelley – which was itself motivated by some of Mr Eliot's recent criticism of Shelley – must inevitably criticize Mr Eliot, and *his* criticism of Shelley. Mr Read disbelieves, and seeks to refute, Mr Eliot's plain avowal that "a peculiarity in the poetry, not in the reader, lies at the bottom of his dislike of Shelley . . . It seems to me that both Mr Read and Mr Eliot have been a little mischievous about Shelley; that Mr Eliot's mischief is the more reprehensible, as being the cause of Mr Read's.'
5 – HR's recommendations of the theory and practice of Surrealism.

your title for the book is altogether fortunate. At any rate it gave Selincourt the opportunity to make his own stupid observations on Shelley without saying anything about the rest of the book!

Yours ever,

T.

## FROM *Brigid O'Donovan* TO *Olive M. Cook*       cc

19 February 1936       [Faber & Faber Ltd]

Dear Madam,

Mr Eliot has asked me to apologize for the delay in answering your letter of the 14th February, and to say that he has no objection to your publishing Dr Wolff's analysis of his hand. I am returning your typescript of the analysis with this letter.[1]

Yours very truly,

[Brigid O'Donovan]

Secretary

---

1 – Olive M. Cook (Chatto & Windus) announced on 29 Jan.: 'We are shortly publishing a work on hand-reading by Dr Charlotte Wolff in which we should like to include the analysis she had made of your hand. We are sending you the translation of this analysis and we should be most grateful if you would let us know whether it meets with your approval.'

Fearing that the analysis had not reached TSE, Cook sent a further copy on 14 Feb. Wolff (1897–1986), a psychologist and psychotherapist, and a refugee from Nazi Germany (later noted for her studies of lesbianism and bisexuality), had been encouraged by Maria Huxley to come from Paris to London to pursue her studies in the human hand. Her book *Studies in Hand-Reading* contained palm-readings of 37 individuals (with imprints of their left hands) including TSE, Aldous Huxley, Ottoline Morrell, Bernard Shaw, Osbert Sitwell and Virginia Woolf.

(Hermione Lee, *Virginia Woolf* [1996], 667–8: 'Charlotte Wolff was a German-Jewish refugee who had been taken up by the Huxleys. With their help, Dr Wolff became a fashionable reader of palms. (Her clients included Mrs Simpson, and the monkeys at the zoo. Virginia was "done" twice, for two guineas, at the Huxleys' flat, and was told that her life had completely changed at age thirty-five – no (the palmist corrected herself) at age thirty. Leonard, of course, thought this was all the most "disgusting humbug". Virginia was half-convinced . . .')

Wolff's analysis of TSE's palm includes these remarks: 'The hand has the oval shape of the Venus type and the Zone of Instinct is the most strongly developed part of the palm. The many crosses and oblique lines on the Mount of the Moon . . . betray fetishistic traits in Mr Eliot's system of thought. He sets up obstacles in his own path in order to have some refuge from doubt and uncertainty. Thus he has developed a feeling for ritual and regular custom, and a habit of performing like a schoolboy some daily task which in a primitive, childlike way brings him nearer to the reality he finds so difficult to attain.

'T. S. Eliot is a born ecstatic; his imagination is the chief source of both his mental and emotional nourishment. (Note the proximity of the mighty Mounts of Venus and the Moon.)

## TO *Maurice Haigh-Wood*[1]

20 February 1936                    [Faber & Faber Ltd]

Dear Maurice,

I have been thinking about your letter of the 13th.[2] It depends, I suppose, on what one expects the future of Canadian Rails to be. I haven't myself much hope of the future of any Railway Stock; and I suppose the only hope from Canpac would be the taking over by the Canadian National at a price favourable to the holders, which seems unlikely. I should think that there was much more of a future for Nickel; though the present dividend seems to mean a heavy reduction from the *previous* normal payments on Canpac.

I shall be in favour of your suggestion unless you are up against the usual obstacle. For I take it that a purchase of International Nickel Common would require the approval of the beneficiaries.

---

His thought associations are controlled entirely by the creative force of his subconscious self and are never the result of a weighing of cause and effect. (Note the twice broken Head-line.) In his mode of expression T. S. Eliot is an ecstatic poet, while as a man he is confronted by many difficulties and is full of childlike characteristics. He wastes a good deal of energy because he lacks the power of decision in practical life . . . (Observe the fork at the beginning of the Head-line.) This indecision makes him seek refuge in established conservative conventions. He probably finds mysterious, guiding symbols in the ideas of the Church, the Monarchy and the Family . . . His very large, slightly bulbous thumb betrays his urgent desire to realise the ecstatic poetical powers which I identify with his personality. At the same time this thumb indicates a seething, easily provoked temperament which may explode at any moment, especially as the nervous system is so sensitive . . . He has a very finely developed artistic and moral conscience and he lives for the satisfaction he derives from poetical creation. (Observe how the fingers all incline toward Apollo, the Finger of Art.)'

Wolff's analysis of TSE's palm, along with a print and her diagrammatic representation, was published in her book *Studies in Hand-Reading* (1936), 93–4.

OM's diary: 'Xmas Eve [1935] Then she [Dr Charlotte Wolff] talked about T.S.E. . . . & said that he loved . . . vacillating – too [*sic*] & fro – his poetry comes from his instinct not his Intellect – which of course I know – that he is very superstitious – He also has Fears, fears – .'

1 – TSE's brother-in-law: see Biographical Register.

2 – 'The problem of the revenue from the Trust Funds has been bothering me for a long time. There is one transaction which I should very much like to do and which I feel absolutely convinced would prove beneficial both to the revenue and to the capital value of the Trust, and that is to switch out of Canadian Pacific Common into International Nickel Common. The respective prices are $13 and $49¾.

'The 400 Canpacs would thus buy about 100 International Nickel.

'There would of course be an immediate gain, in that Nickels are actually paying a dividend at the present time. So far it is only a very small one at the rate of $1 a share per year, but there is no doubt whatever that their earnings are very much higher than this, and it appears extremely probable that this rate of dividend will increase in the very near future. On the other hand, Canpacs are paying nothing, neither are the Preferred shares of the C.P.R and there is no telling when they will resume dividend payments.'

Sometime, I should be grateful if you would send me a list of the present holdings. I can't lay my hands on mine, and there have been some changes since it was drawn up.

I could lunch on Friday the 28th, or one day the following week, I think any day except Wednesday, and we could talk the matter over then, unless you write in the meantime.[1]

Yours ever
Tom

## TO *Nicolette Leadbitter*

21 February 1936                    [Faber & Faber Ltd]

Dear Mrs Leadbitter,

I must apologize for having kept so long the poems of yours which our friend Mr A. W. G. Randall was kind enough to send me.[2] I don't know how old you are or how long you have been writing, but these poems certainly show considerable facility in some of the regular stanzas. I feel, however, that there is still a great deal in them that is not personal to yourself, but reminiscent of a good deal of your reading of the older poets, and that it will probably be some time before you are able to develop a more personal idiom. It is of course always valuable to practise some of the more difficult forms such as the sonnet, the sestina, or the Spenserian stanza, in as much as innovation should always be based on experience in more conventional forms of writing. If, also, you know any foreign language, as I hope you do, you can gain a great deal from exercises in translation.

Yours sincerely,
[T. S. Eliot]

1 – They had lunch together at the Junior Carlton Club on 28 Feb.
2 – For Randall, see letter of 15 Sept. 1937, below.
  Randall had written on 9 Nov. 1935: 'I have lately received a blank-verse play and a number of poems from a friend of mine, a girl (just married) called Nicolette Leadbitter. She is an admirer of the "Criterion" and of you in particular, and asked me whether I would first look at her poems and say whether I thought them worth submitting. Having done so, I think I can say that the poems are worth considering; I haven't made up my mind about the play, and won't trouble you with it.' He wrote again on 12 Jan. 1936 to urge TSE to write to Mrs Leadbitter.

TO *E. J. Rumens*[1]                                          CC

21 February 1936                    [Faber & Faber Ltd]

Dear Mr Rumens,

I have had the typescript of your friend's stories for such a long time that it is now almost an impertinence to apologize for the delay.[2] They had to wait until I was in bed for a week with influenza before getting read. I now return them to you.

I must say that I think your friend, although she evidently needs a good deal more practice in writing, has a rather attractive and versatile imagination. Some of the stories are a little flat, but there is a good deal of invention of several kinds. I think that she could probably write rather charming fairy stories and childrens' tales among other things. I should judge from her style that she is still quite young, and that therefore her writing ought to gain with increasing experience and maturity.

With the initial sensitiveness, and by saturation rather than imitation of the best models, I think that your friend deserves to be encouraged.

Yours sincerely,
[T. S. Eliot]

TO *John Hayward*                                           TS King's

Friday [21 February 1936]           [No address given]

My dear John,

I write this hurried note on plain paper, as it may fall into the wrong hands.[3] What you say about the Indian student disquiets me;[4] in fact,

---

1 – E. J. Rumens, House of the Sacred Mission, Kelham, Notts.
2 – The friend has not been identified.
3 – JDH, 21 Feb.: 'Thank you very much for the copy of "Burnt Norton", which has impressed me deeply. Perhaps you will read it to me on Sunday evening.' JDH reported in his 'London Letter' in the New York *Sun*, 28 Mar. 1936, that *BN* was 'completed only a month or so ago'.
4 – JDH went on (21 Feb.): 'I go to my loony-bin on Saturday to see the patients act a play! I've had a peculiar letter from an Indian student [J. Husein: see above] who wants to write you up. I've done nothing about it; and shall do nothing until a satisfactory account is given of the "leakage" of F. O. information to Rome. These are anxious times.'
    See too John Carter (Charles Scribner's Sons) to TSE on 22 Feb.: 'We have been approached by an Indian gentleman of the name of J. Husein, a Bachelor of Arts of the University of Calcutta, who suggests that we publish his doctoral thesis: "T. S. Eliot: A Regurgitation". We have not yet seen the manuscript of this work, though the author tells us that it has been approved by you. As we have reason to suspect his bona fides, we should much appreciate

it anticipates what I was going to warn you of. DID he write from a Monomark? All the really sinister Indian Students (and there are many who are *interested* in me) have Monomarks. Enquiries ought to [be] made at Monomark House, in Holborn (one of the few remaining Regency buildings in that district) but I cannot depend upon the Baker Street Irregulars.[1] I am in particular fear of an Indian Student to whom I lent ten shillings (a note, but I did not keep the number) three or four years ago, in order to get rid of him because of a poem entitled alarmingly EXPECTENCY <S I C>[2]. His name is Daulat Ras.[3] He is a quiet inscrutable fellow (see p. 771, Shorter Stories) as most of these Indians are. He is well up in his work, though his Greek is his weak subject. He is steady and methodical. He inhabits, I have learned, the second floor, at St Luke's College, in one of our great University towns.

I tremble for you until Sunday. Fling the shutters together, and *bolt* them securely.[4] Odd to think of Charley Maurras in the dock.[5] Odd to think that after the Reichenbach Falls Bonamy will be the only distinguished living descendant of Dermot Macmorrah King of Leinster. Odd to think that one of my last last acts was to inscribe for you a copy of *Essays Ancient and Modern* – whether you ever receive it depends upon the fidelity of the O'Donovan. If I live for another 4 weeks, my dear John, I shall inscribe for you a copy of *Poems 1909–1936*: but you must not expect that.

Oops[6] yours faithfully<br>Possum

I think it wiser not even to sign this letter in the usual way. I believe you will be able to identify the author.

---

your confirmation of this statement.'

1 – Baker Street Irregulars refers to Sherlock Holmes's boy gangs acting as his paid secret agents, featured in *A Study in Scarlet* (1887) and in a chapter of *The Sign of Four* (1890); it refers too to the U.S. literary society founded in 1934 by Christopher Morley (FVM's brother).

2 – Word typed thus, above the word 'expectency', by TSE.

3 – Daulat Ras is a character in the story 'Three Students' (*The Return of Sherlock Holmes*).

4 – Sentence added by hand.

5 – Charles Maurras was convicted of inciting death threats against Léon Blum, France's first Jewish prime minister.

6 – 'Oops' indicates that TSE was suddenly aware that his typing was running off the sheet.

## TO *Rupert Doone*[1]                                                    cc

21 February 1936                    [Faber & Faber Ltd]

Dear Doone,

Thank you for your note of the 17th.[2] I should of course be glad to have a talk with you if you would ring up my secretary and make an appointment. At the same time I have not [*sc.* now] begun work on a new play, and until it is pretty well in shape I cannot have any very distinct ideas about its production.[3] I don't intend to work to a date, and as I have no notion when it will be finished I had rather leave the question of its production open until the text is available.

I am sorry that I have not yet been able to see *The Dog Beneath the Skin*, but I hope to go within a week. I did have tickets last week, but unfortunately was ill and unable to use them. I hope that it continues to have good houses. Some of the notices have been very pleasing indeed.

Yours sincerely,
[T. S. Eliot]


## TO *Stephen Spender*[4]                                         ts Northwestern

21 February [1936]                    *The Criterion*

Dear Stephen,

I wrote you a letter a few days ago, but did not send it, because it seemed so dull; but I don't believe that this will be any brighter. After an exhausting though pleasant visit to Dublin, where I had to speak four times in four days, twice broadcast and 3 times photographed (once on the steps of University College in the company of Dr Denis J. Coffey, once looking at an exhibition of Pictures by AE,[5] in the company of Mr Con P.

---

1–Rupert Doone (1903–66), dancer, choreographer, producer; founder of the Group Theatre, London: see Biographical Register.
2–'I'm sorry not to have informed you further, after our telephone conversation about The Dog. As you now see Mr Anmer Hall revised his decision about it, except that after King George's death the Ostnia scene followed the censors cuts.
   'I would like very much to talk to you with the idea that you would let me, if it were possible, do your next play it was a disappointment not doing Murder in the Cathedral. I enjoyed Murder much more at Nottinghill Gate than I did in Canterbury it went so much better on a stage I thought. The poetry is grand stuff.'
3–The first mention of the play that would turn out to be *The Family Reunion* (1939).
4–Stephen Spender (1909–95), poet and critic: see Biographical Register.
5–Æ: pseud. of William George Russell (1867–1935), Irish writer, critic, poet and painter.

Curran[1] and Denis Devlin[2] and Mrs Curran, and once at a performance of Murrrderr in the Cathedral by the Students of University College (producer, Liam O'Rieardmanndh otherwise William Redmond),[3] I contracted bronchial influenza and had a very agreeable week in bed, but I am still in the gloomy after stages. I have however decided to refuse all speaking engagements for six months.

I don't know how your proofs are getting on, of the stories, but I hope that Portugal is favourable to your work, though I suspect the diet is constipating; and it is depressing to think that even in that antiquated country there are landladies who believe in re-incarnation.[4] I hope that you will not fall into any community of Christian Scientists. The swami centre is Minorca, where Yeats is engaged in translating the *Upanishads*, unless he is too ill. And how is our Salazar?[5]

I believe that *The Dog beneath the Skin* has been successful;[6] I took tickets but fell ill and released them to the O'Donovan, who did not appear to enjoy herself and complained that the theatre was not heated. I expect to go next week. I have had a letter from Doone, who is 'disappointed' about something.

1 – C. P. (Constantine Peter) Curran (1880–1972), contemporary and friend of JJ at Trinity College, Dublin: lawyer and historian of eighteenth-century Dublin art and architecture; author of *James Joyce Remembered* (1968). Twenty-four years later, when TSE received a fan-letter from Curran, he responded on 4 May 1960: 'It is a particularly pleasant reminder of a very happy visit to Dublin in the far-away days before the war when you took me to the exhibition of A.E.'s paintings and when we went to see St Kevin's cave (to which I later referred in a poem called "Little Gidding" [I, 35–7]) with the Hogans.' (St Kevin's Cave is at Lake Glendalough in County Wicklow: it is still a site of pilgrimage.)

2 – Denis Devlin (1908–59), Irish poet and career diplomat; close friend of Brian Coffey, with whom he published *Poems* (1930). *Collected Poems* was edited by J. C. C. Mays (1989).

3 – Liam Redmond (1913–89), Irish actor noted for stage, TV and film roles. Invited by WBY to join the Abbey Theatre, Dublin, he starred in WBY's *The Death of Cuchulain* (1939).

4 – Spender, who was staying in a rented house in San Pedro, just outside Sintra, Portugal, reported on 8 Jan.: 'Best of all is our landlady, a firm believer in reincarnation: in her last life she was a Syrian slave boy who was rather grossly treated by some Roman legionaries.'

5 – António de Oliveira Salazar (1889–1970), Prime Minister of Portugal, 1932–68. *Salazar: El Hombre y Su Obra* (1935), by António Ferro, was to be published in translation as *Salazar: Portugal and Her Leader* (F&F, 1939).

In Apr. 1936 the *Catholic Herald* was to report – 'Portugal And Its Leader: "Frugality, Orderliness, and Devotion"' – that the humbly-born Dr António de Oliveira Salazar has achieved a 'miracle' in his governance of Portugal: 'England with her Protestant tradition has done well enough, but it does not follow that all Latin countries are either tyrannic dictatorships or dissipated and rapidly disintegrating democracies.

'Portugal is an example of a country with a wholly Catholic culture that has solved its difficulties in a wholly Catholic way.'

6 – SS, 29 Feb.: 'I am glad Dogskin has been such a success. I look forward more though to seeing what Wystan does after this, as it is very difficult to imagine in what direction Dogskin can be leading him.'

Yes this letter is just as dull as the one I didn't send. But it is a communication, in the hope of hearing from you again,

Ever affectionately

Tom

What do you know about the *Tiger of San Pedro?*[1]

## TO *Herbert Read*

25 February 1936 *The Criterion*

My dear Herbert,

Here is the delayed manuscript.[2] So long delayed, indeed, that I feel that nothing I could produce would be brilliant enough to make up for your waiting so long, and I am afraid you will find it disappointingly short, and I am aware that it is capable of considerable elaboration, but to say more would need several more weeks of quite hard work, so I think best to submit it to you as it is, and await the verdict. I imagine that you will find the general position sympathetic, but that you will see great gaps in the argument. I was a little reassured by discussing my views with Saurat the other day, and finding him much more in accord than I expected.[3]

I hope now, if this is over, that we may make some advances toward both supper and the long postponed teaparty. Let me know how Ludo and you are fixed within the next fortnight. I think I have also, of course, a few manuscripts to consult you about.

Have you any news of Wheen?[4] Frank was asking in a letter, and I can tell him nothing.

Yours ever,

Tom

You haven't answered about reviewing yr essays.

---

1 – The Tiger of San Pedro features in a Sherlock Holmes story by A. Conan Doyle, in *His Last Bow*.

2 – HR had asked TSE in May 1935 for a contribution to *Essays and Studies*, and said he was prepared to wait. On 29 Jan. 1936: 'I have now got all the corrected page-proofs from all the other contributors. I can't hold out much longer . . . Feb. 10th will have to be the extreme limit . . .' See TSE, 'A Note on the Verse of John Milton', *Essays and Studies by members of the English Association* (1936), 32–40; repr. as 'Milton I' in *OPP*, and in TSE's *Milton: Two Studies* (1968).

3 – Denis Saurat (1890–1958), Anglo-French scholar; works include *Milton: Man and Thinker* (1925).

4 – Arthur Wheen (1897–1971), librarian and translator, grew up in Sydney, Australia, and came to Europe with the Australian Expeditionary Force in WW1 (he received the Military

80    TSE at forty-seven

Shrove Tuesday [25 February] 1936 *The Criterion*

Dear John,

Excuse me for ringing up so *inopinément*,[1] when I knew you had an Old Drunken Knight in your company[2] – your voice sounded distraught – but I was in two minds – I wasn't sure whether Elizabeth Bowen hadn't asked me because she thought I had overheard her asking you – which I hadn't – and secondly I didn't really want to go, because of having several other dinners in the immediate vicinity. On the other hand – so different are one's reasons from what people think – I was impelled to accept for fear that if I did not, she might ask me to tea, and I have such a horror of that neighbourhood and a real fear of it in the daytime, and now the days are drawing Out. So I will come: partly because I should prefer to go in your company than otherwise.

I am given pleasure by your letter. I am glad that you are a collector, because it makes it easier to give you my odd volumes; and I don't know anyone else who would both 'collect' and read. Yet there is something more personal in my giving you such as the Japanese volume, which is completely useless.[3] And as for collecting, I am sure that you are observant enough to realise that my sympathy is partly due to the fact that I am always engaged with disabilities of one kind or another – some devised by my ancestry, some 'my own idea' – and coping with them by being either more serious or more trivial than is usual. I have more than one kind of nightmare: hence my interest in Orestes.

The party was by no means a failure – the mechanical difficulties only just enough to make it real. Indeed, I thought it went off very well – if it had been mine, I should have been thankful. I thought Mrs Poliakoff very

---

Cross 'for some incredible act of valour in the last war, which provoked a temporary break-down', as TSE noted). A Rhodes Scholar at New College, Oxford, 1920–3, he worked in the Library of the Victoria & Albert Museum, becoming Keeper, 1939–62. He translated novels relating to WW1, winning praise for his translation of Erich Maria Remarque's *All Quiet on the Western Front* (1929); and he wrote one novella, *Two Masters* (1924, 1929). TSE wrote of him: 'He's completely honest, and one of the most silent men I know.' FVM thought his modest friend Wheen 'the best critic I know, bar none' (to Morley Kennerley, 5 July 1933). See *We talked of other things: The life and letters of Arthur Wheen 1897–1971*, ed. Tanya Crothers (2011).

1 – *inopinément* (Fr.): unexpectedly.

2 – The old drunken knight is not identified; but TSE's allusion implies that JDH is the foolish Sir Andrew Aguecheek from *Twelfth Knight*.

3 – Probably the Japanese translation, by Tsuneo Kitamura, of selected essays, with introd. in English by William Empson (Tokyo, 1933).

lovely and hollow-sounding – spoke perfect English but she didn't *smell* quite English, if I may make so bold – and she tired me.[1] <Is Basil Burton quite real, either?[2]> The films were admirable, and all new to me, and all important. And it would have been a bad sign if either less, or more, liquor had been drunk. You were, as usual, the excellent host. I hope you were not too tired – especially after my staying so inexcusably late the night before.

I have fresh worries. An *Indian Student* has just sent me the manuscript of his Anthology of Donne's Sermons. His name is J. Husein. He says Grierson approves of it. And I am being hounded by Mr Ross E. Pierce of Buffalo. And I have got to have Mrs Trouncer[3] to tea. And on Sunday I am to lunch with Mrs Brocklebanke. o o otototoi. And I have been to Major MacGowan's Shrove Tuesday cocktail party. And I am just off to a party at the Mercury Theatre.

Dolefully
T

## TO *Elizabeth Manwaring*                                      TS Wellesley

26 February 1936                          *The Criterion*

Dear Miss Manwaring,

I am happy to learn from your letter that you are now in London. I hope that you will be here for some little time, as I am too much booked up this week to be able to make any suggestion for a meeting. Would you be able, for instance, to lunch with me on Thursday 5th, which is the first day I have to offer? I was much interested, and wholly horrified by the examination paper you sent.[4] I hope I am not too much influenced by the

---

1 – Vera Poliakoff (1911–92), born in St Petersburg, was better known as the actress Vera Lindsay: wife to Basil Burton.
2 – Basil Burton (1906–70), actor; later featured as Third Tempter in the movie of *MiC* (1951).
3 – Margaret Trouncer (1903–82), author.
4 – Manwaring thought TSE might be 'amused' by the examination paper set for her course English Literature 210, which was being given in her absence by a junior colleague. This Midyear Examination, on 'Triumphal March', ran over four sheets of paper:
    1. What are the oakleaves?
    2. How many speakers' voices are heard?
    3. Write a note on the eagles.
    4. On the City.
    5. On the temple.
    6. Who is "he" (l. 10)? Any connection with any other poem by Eliot?

fact that I should be unable to answer most of the questions, and that I was irritated by the examiner's remark about the Sacring Bell,[1] and by his ignorance of crumpet sellers.[2] No, what horrifies me is that your young people should actually be set to study contemporary verse in qualification for the degree of B.A.* They ought to be reading Aristophanes.

Yours sincerely,

T. S. Eliot

* But ~~believe~~ am told that the same thing goes on here.


## TO *Polly Tandy* TS BL

Ash Wednesday [26 February] 1936 *The Criterion*

Sis Tandy I certainly been down in the mouf thinkin about your pore afflicted fambly and its sundry diseases and I hope to goodness you been feelin a little mo peart lately and the Ole Man not so puny I bet he cussin and rarin and spittin terbacker juice up the chimley and you trapsin down to the Bell fo a bucket of beer fo to keep his mouf quiet. An I hope the Pickerninny isa doin her slimmin exercises regular. Ef I don have no news pretty smartly Im goin expect the worsest & Ill be down your parts befo long with a hearse and a couple of hacks and give yo all a real tony funeral. If you needs any sistance to help keep the Ole Man peaceable you

---

7. Write a note on l. 11.

8. Write a note on ll. 32–34, and include in your note a comment on the phrases "dove's wing", "Turtle's breast", "Palmtree at noon", "running water", and "still point of the turning world."

9. Write a note on ll. 43–45.

10. Write a note on ll. 47–50.

11. What is the effect of the last line?

12. Define the 'objective correlative' as described by Mr Eliot and analyze the poem from this point of view.

13. Does this poem aim at achieving a 'unity of consciousness'? If so, point out how, by reference to specific lines, phrases, devices.

1 – The sacring bell is rung when the Host is elevated during Mass.

2 – The examiner offered this gloss – the only annotation given – on ll. 44–45 of the poem ('So we took young Cyril to church. And they rang a bell / And he said right out loud, *crumpets*.'):

'At a solemn moment in the celebration of the Mass a bell is rung. Also on the streets of London itinerant peddlars of crumpets push little carts with an attachment which rings a bell.'

say the word, sister, say the word, and Ill be along with a mighty powerful monkey-wrench I got handy. So I will now design myself

You reliable

Possum.

Lemme have some news right soon.


## TO *Donagh MacDonagh*[1]                    TS Kresge Library

26 February 1936                    *The Criterion*

Dear Mr MacDonagh,

I am writing, so far as your poems are concerned, to acknowledge their arrival, as I have not yet had time to examine them, and primarily to thank you for sending me the two photographs of the production of *Murder in the Cathedral*, which will be a very pleasant reminder of a happy occasion.[2]

I don't think many interesting books of verse have appeared lately, though possibly James Reeves,[3] published by Constable, may have merit. I think the chief interest of the present season will be the anthologies, of which there is a sudden outburst. I think very well of our own, the *Faber Book of Modern Verse*, of which *The Irish Times* should have a copy, and which I hope they will pass on to you. There is also Yeats's anthology to look forward to.

With best wishes,

Yours sincerely,

T. S. Eliot

1–Donagh MacDonagh (1912–68), Irish poet and playwright; barrister and judge (the youngest judge in Ireland on his appointment in 1941). Works include collections of verse: *Variations and Other Poems* (1941), *The Hungry Grass* (1947), *A Warning to Conquerors* (1968); and plays including the acclaimed *Happy as Larry* (1946) and *Lady Spider* (1980).
2–MacDonagh submitted forty-four poems, seven of them reprinted from a privately printed volume, *Twenty Poems* (with Niall Sheridan).

The first production in Ireland of *MiC* was staged by MacDonagh at the University College Dramatic Society, 26 Jan. 1936, with the noted actor Liam Redmond (later his brother-in-law).

F&F would publish MacDonagh's poems in a later year, when TSE wrote this blurb for *The Hungry Grass* (1947): 'Donagh MacDonagh is an Irish poet of established reputation, whose work has until now been known in England only by those poems which have appeared from time to time in English magazines. This is the first collection of his poems to be published in this country. It will lead, we believe, to a valuation of this poet which will give him an assured place among the poets of his generation.'
3–James Reeves (1909–75), school and college teacher, poet, and anthologist and writer for children. *The Natural Need*, his first collection, was published by Constable in 1935.

TO *George Every*[1]                                        TS Sarah Hamilton

26 February 1936                    [Faber & Faber Ltd]

Dear Brother George,

Thank you for your letter of the 23rd.[2] I should be delighted to come down in the summer term, and discuss dramatic subjects with your Entertainments Chapter. I am diffident about the amount of help that I am able to give, and before I come I shall look for guidance from you as to what you want me to talk about, and what matters ought to be discussed.

I am ashamed that I have not yet got round to studying your play sufficiently to be able to report to you.[3] All I can say is that this is not forgetfulness, as it has been on my mind, and you may therefore expect to hear from me some time, as I have the motive of a guilty conscience.

Your friend Harry Smith is, I believe, coming to see me on March 10th.[4]

Sometime I should like to talk to you about Charles Smyth's review of Maritain and Dawson in *Christendom*. I have for a long time had some misgivings myself about Dawson, and if I am wrong, and if Smyth is still more wrong about him, you are probably qualified to set me right. But I also have misgivings about Smyth's misgivings about Maritain, and I think there may be a good deal to be said in defence of the latter. There is a tone of bustling activity about Smyth's review, but he does not, any more than anyone else so far, really produce the goods.

Yours ever,

T. S. Eliot

P.S. Would you be willing to review any book for the June number? If you have nothing in mind there is a book called *The Birth of the Middle Ages* by Moss, which I have heard well spoken of. Would that be in your line or not?[5] Suggestions welcome.

---

1 – George Every, SSM (1909–2003), historian and poet: see Biographical Register.

2 – Every reported that the Prior of Kelham Theological College had asked whether TSE could advise the 'entertainment chapter' on the subject of 'drama in the house in general and the Averham play in particular'.

3 – 'I have not yet quite finished the additions and alterations to "Stalemate", though I think I have got a much better end, which was needed.' See Helen Gardner, *The Composition of 'Four Quartets'* (1978), 62–3, for an account of the first draft of Every's play, called in full 'Stalemate: The King at Little Gidding'. The topic of the play was Charles I's flight to Little Gidding – where an Anglican community had been established by Nicholas Ferrar in 1625 – after his defeat at the battle of Naseby in June 1645.

4 – 'If Harry Smith of the S.C.M., an old-Kelham priest, wants to see you, I hope you will see him . . . I think you will like him. He is very genuine.'

5 – Every on H. St L. B. Moss, *The Birth of the Middle Ages*: C. 15 (July 1936), 705–7.

## TO *Godfrey Childe*[1]

TS Beinecke

26 February 1936                    *The Criterion*

Dear Childe,

In reply to your letter of last Sunday[2] I enclose four specimen pages of manuscript from *Murder in the Cathedral*. There are only 14 pages altogether of these rough notes. That of course represents only a small part of the play, and these notes are only the first drafts of those parts. My practice is to start a passage with a few pencilled pages, and then when I get going I usually continue it on the typewriter, so that I should never have a complete pencilled manuscript of any poem of any length, and I never have any ink manuscripts at all, unless I prepare them especially. In sending you these specimen pages there are two points I want to make.

i. The amount of my manuscript of any sort in existence is very small. The manuscript of some of my early poems, and the typescript of *The Waste Land* with corrections by myself and Ezra Pound belonged to the late John Quinn of New York. Since his death both these are untraceable, and I should think it was as likely as not that they had been destroyed. The typescript manuscripts of *Anabasis* and *The Rock* are in the possession of the Bodleian Library. There are two short poems in ink in the possession of some unknown stockbroker.[3] Besides ~~all this~~ these, the 14 pages of *Murder in the Cathedral* are practically all that exists. I mention this point in order to justify placing a rather higher value on my manuscript than I otherwise should, especially as I have been told that occasionally letters of mine of no importance have been sold at auctions.

ii. If we should agree about the price I do not want to accept any money myself for the manuscript, as I don't like the idea of selling manuscript unless one is in a state of destitution. I should therefore ask the purchaser to make out the cheque in another name for a charitable purpose which I have in mind.

Yours sincerely,<br>T. S. Eliot

1–Godfrey Childe (b. 1901), author of *Short Head: A Tale* (Cobden-Sanderson, 1927).
2–Childe wrote to ask if a friend, a reputable bookdealer, might see TSE's MSS 'on approval': 'It would be of some personal use to me but I dislike very much the idea of being so importunate. It is unfortunate that the revival in trade should coincide with a very serious shortage of fine books and MSS: in one sense it is rather disgusting; in the other, the demands of one's clients force one to suspend – for a moment, I hope – those better instincts of reserve and respect and do a deal.'
3–See FVM to R. J. G. Johnson (Marshgate House, Sheen Road, Richmond, London), 6 Nov. 1933: 'I have just received back from Bumpuses the two MSS. of Mr T. S. Eliot which are now your property; and I am sending them to you with this.'

TSE at forty-seven

27 February 1936                    [Faber & Faber Ltd]

Dear Mrs Stuart Moore,

Thank you very much for your kind note, which coincides curiously with a business matter about which I was on the point of writing to you. I am not quite sure whether I shall be able to come in to tea on Sunday because I have a lunch engagement, and Sunday is a squeeze for me at best, but if I can get away in time I shall certainly be delighted to come.

What I was going to write to you about is this. We have been offered a small book on St John of the Cross which I found very interesting reading.[2]

---

1 – Evelyn Underhill (1875–1941): esteemed spiritual director and writer on mysticism and the spiritual life. Compelled by deep study and the counsel of Baron Friedrich von Hügel, she became an Anglican in 1919 and dedicated her kindly life to religious writing and guidance, notably as a retreat director. She wrote or edited 39 books and over 350 articles and reviews; among her other activities, she was theology editor for *The Spectator* and wrote too for *Time and Tide*. Her works include *Mysticism: A Study of the Nature and Development of Man's Spiritual Consciousness* (1911) and *Worship* (1936). In 1907 she married Hubert Stuart Moore (1869–1951), a barrister. TSE wrote to Sister Mary Xavier, SSJ, 1 Aug. 1962: 'I . . . wish that I could tell you more about the late Mrs Moore, otherwise Evelyn Underhill. I did not know her intimately and knew [her] I think in the first place through her cousin, Francis Underhill, who was my spiritual director and later Bishop of Bath and Wells. I remember her, however, with affection and regret. I do not know whether you would call her a mystic though she was certainly an authority on mysticism. She was a very cosy person to meet and have tea with in her home in [no. 50] Campden Hill Square and was also very fond of her cats. I should not call her a mystic whether qualified by the adjective Anglican or not, but I should call her an authority on mysticism and indeed would accept your phrase for her "deep spirituality". She was, I am sure, an admirable spiritual director herself and I am pretty sure was a great help to many young women . . . I think that any correspondence we had would have been merely to do with social engagements and I never remember having had any long correspondence with her on spiritual or other matters. I remember her not at all as an intimate friend, but as a very highly valued and regretted acquaintance.'

In an unpublished note to *The Times*, 1941, TSE wrote too: 'She gave (with frail health and constant illness) herself to many, in retreats, which she conducted and in the intercourse of daily life – she was always at the disposal of all who called upon her. With a lively and humorous interest in human beings, especially the young. She was at the same time withdrawn and sociable. With shrewdness and simplicity she helped to support the spiritual life of many more than she could in her humility have been aware of aiding.'

See further Donald J. Childs, 'T. S. Eliot and Evelyn Underhill: An Early Mystical Influence', *Durham University Journal* 80 (Dec. 1987), 83–98.

2 – TSE's Report on Dr Geraldine Hodgson, *Concerning St John of the Cross*, 23 Feb. 1936: 'I do not know why Hodder & Stoughton sent us this book . . . The name of the author is familiar to me (Geraldine Hodgson) but I cannot remember why.

'Now that Alison Peers's translation of the works of St John is complete, there is certainly room for a Primer on the subject in English. Dr Hodgson seems well up in the subject. I imagine her to be an Anglican, from some of her references. Among contemporary expounders of St John she mentions Baruzi, and I think Bruno, but there is a Spanish authority of whom she

Before considering the book seriously for publication we need the opinion of an expert on its quality and usefulness, and the opinion of someone who is already familiar with whatever has been published about St John of the Cross in English. I know something of Baruzi, whose book I believe has been translated into English,[1] and I know of one or two other foreign writers. This book is more in the nature of a short primer – really more for Church people interested in devotion than for scholars of mysticism. You would know whether the ground has already been covered. But it struck me that with the completion of Alison Peers's translation there might be a place for such a small introductory study. Would you be willing to read and report upon this book for the usual reader's fee?[2]

Yours very sincerely,
[T. S. Eliot]

TO *Granville Hicks*[3]                                    TS Butler Library

27 February 1936                    Faber & Faber Ltd

Dear Mr Hicks,

I have your letter of the 15th instant,[4] but I am afraid that I cannot tell you very much about John Reed which others could not tell you

---

has failed to make use. She does not give the authority for her quotations from Bellarmine, yet I doubt whether anyone in England since John Donne has read that author at first hand. I presume that the translations from St John are her own.

'The style is mediocre, but the book seems to me good and useful: though it would have to be vetted by an authority, such as Evelyn Underhill. There is no book on St John in English, that I know of. I question however whether Dent, or a religious press, would not be a more appropriate publisher than this firm. Opinions solicited.'

1 – Jean Baruzi (1881–1954), French philosopher and teacher. A copy of *Saint Jean de la Croix et le problème de l'expérience mystique* (1924; 2nd edn rev. 1931), inscribed by the author, is in TSE's library.

2 – Underhill replied, 28 Feb.: 'I would be very interested to do it but the truth is at the moment I am in a perfect jam with work of various kinds which is in arrears, so that I could not promise to do it quickly; but if this does not matter, then send it along.'

3 – Granville Hicks (1901–82), writer, novelist, literary critic and university teacher, a graduate of Harvard, joined the US Communist Party in 1934 and worked as a Marxist literary critic – his output from this time included *The Great Tradition: An Interpretation of American Literature since the Civil War* (1933) – and as editor of the Party periodical *The New Masses*. He resigned from the Communist Party in 1939, following the Nazi–Soviet Pact; and in 1951, in a fierce article published in *Commentary*, denounced Communism as a 'brutal revolutionary totalitarianism'. Later works include *Part of the Truth* (autobiography, 1965) and *Literary Horizons: A Quarter Century of American Fiction* (1970).

4 – 'I am writing a biography of John Reed. You were a classmate of his at Harvard, and, though I gather that your interests lay in different quarters, I assume that you must have

better.[1] I did, indeed, know him slightly, but I am sure that there must be a number of other classmates living who know much more about him than I do. I don't remember that Reed was very much interested in politics or economics at the time, and I am sure that I was not. I think that he was an editor of the *Harvard Monthly*, and I was an editor of the *Harvard Advocate*. I saw very little of him socially. I remember, by the way, that he was in Paris for some time the year after leaving Harvard, in the company of Waldo Peirce,[2] who could probably throw some light on that period.[3]

Yours sincerely,
T. S. Eliot

## TO *John Hayward*

TS King's

27 February [1936]                *The Criterion*

Dear John,

There has been a hitch in the negotiations. John Sparrow,[4] unable to accept Faber's invitation for the 9th, subsequently asked for the 16th, has replied, that he has just been invited by Elizabeth Cameron to meet us on the 5th, and therefore feels that he ought not to present himself (modesty forbidding) in the same company so soon after. Which seems unanswerable. So for the present we are expected at Faber's on the 9th again, and if he cannot get any suitable company, hopes, we will not mind dining alone with himself and the wife. But a definite decision between 9th and 16th is expected tomorrow.

It was impertinent of me to offer any comment on your friends the Burtons – I was merely maundering – and I beg to withdraw anything

---

known him. The very fact that your interests were different from his would make your impressions of him particularly valuable to me, and if you could take the time to write me about him, I should very much appreciate it. I have, of course, a pretty complete record of Reed's activities at Harvard, but I am eager to gather stories about him, and impressions of his character.'

1–John Reed (1887–1920), journalist, poet, political activist, entered Harvard in 1906, graduating in 1910 (whereupon he travelled through England, France and Spain). He is celebrated for his account of the Russian Revolution: *Ten Days that Shook the World* (1919).
2–Waldo Peirce (1884–1970), American artist.
3–See Hicks, *John Reed: The Making of a Revolutionary* (written with John Stuart, 1936).
4–John Sparrow (1906–92) was so precocious as a scholar at Winchester College that at the age of sixteen he published an edition of John Donne's *Devotions upon Emergent Occasions* (1923). A graduate of New College, Oxford, he was called to the Bar at the Middle Temple, 1931. From 1929 he was a Fellow of All Souls, Oxford, of which he became Warden, 1952–77. Works include *Sense and Poetry: Essays on the Place of Meaning in Contemporary Verse* (1934); *Controversial Essays* (1966); *Mark Pattison and the Idea of a University* (1967).

I said. And I dislike people being critical about persons of whom they have only a superficial impression anyway.

Mr J. Husein is closing in. And I am also worried by Mr Sankoh Pantsoh of Jamaica, and Mr Valkhya-Kharikatya of Ceylon. It is difficult to fathom the Providence of these things. *What* does it all mean?

Yours etc.

T. P.

## TO *Herbert Read* TS Victoria

29 February 1936           *The Criterion*

Dear Herbert,

That's a relief (yours of the 26th).[1] If my paper started anything rolling, I should be satisfied; it's time this matter was ventilated some. I don't think that this attitude about Milton has any bearing upon what you have said, or on anything that might correctly be said, about Shelley; though the fact that it hasn't may have to be demonstrated. However *vague* Shelley's vision may be, the visual imagination is still integral to his quality. Certainly he was lacking in appreciation of plastic art, as you make quite clear, and in minute observation of nature. But in a poem like 'The Witch of Atlas', for example, the vision, however phantasmagoric, is essential to the poem – the reader's *eye* is being exercised as much as his ear; and many lines, such as

> By Moeris and the Mareotid Lakes
> Strewn with faint blooms like bridal-chamber floors[2]

give me a positively visual pleasure – no doubt one could find better examples, but I quote from memory. I think that with Shelley you have a peculiar kind of vision, not the absence of it, and that one must not define the 'visual imagination' too narrowly.

---

1 – HR acknowledged receipt of TSE's essay 'A Note on Milton's Verse'. 'It . . . is sure to set up a good argument . . . As you know, I am in complete agreement with you; only, now that I have defended Shelley's lack of visuality, what am I going to say about Milton's? I feel fairly sure that there is a difference . . . I think probably the explanation you suggest is sufficient – that Milton was visually defective and aurally acute because he was physically so; the mental state was a result of the physical state. Whereas in Shelley's case the verbal blur was a reflection of a mental state – that is to say, of a psychosis. The clear distinction between lesions and complexes in psychology must have a correspondence in the kind of mental expression a poet is capable of. What happens when a poet has both a lesion and a complex is more than Freud himself can say.'

2 – Shelley, 'The Witch of Atlas', 471–2.

The psychological approach is still too steep for my feeble steps, but I like your Shelley: it seems to me that you do everything but demonstrate that he is a great poet. I think something might be said in his favour about his *development*: he seems to me to have been (rather circuitously) improving, and though I find Keats ever so much more sympathetic, I have more doubt about Keats's possible future development than about Shelley's.

Grand parties are something I have no capacity for giving myself, but I hope you will be disposed to come to tea quietly soon.[1]

I think either Porteus or Sykes Davies might do.[2] I certainly want someone who would consider the book as a whole, and not pick out one or two essays.

Yours ever,<br>
Tom

It's too late to pass on your information about Wheen to Morley.[3] He sails today I believe, and ought to be visible by Wednesday week.

## TO *John Hayward*

TS King's

2 March [1936]                 Faber & Faber Ltd

Dear John,

I have just received the following message from Fred Porlock, which I think I ought to pass on to you.

| | Brown | will | be | |
|---|---|---|---|---|
| March 5th SHORT | 336.32.6 | 339.20.7 | 340. | 340.11.7 |
| there | dangerous | | | |
| 340.30.5 | 541.37.9 | | | |

---

1 – 'We gave a grand party last night to 56 people; you were wished for, but spared.'
2 – In response to TSE's enquiry about possible reviewers of HR's *In Defence of Shelley*: 'Porteus has been on to me; he wants them for the art aspect, and that might be a pleasant change, for as you anticipated, all the reviewers are concentrating on the Shelley essay. Sykes Davies might deal interestingly with the psychology, such as it is.'
3 – '[Arthur Wheen] is still away, but I gather that it is mainly a precautionary measure. He has been thoroughly examined and no trace of TB was discovered.'

You I know will decypher this with so little difficulty that I have no
need to say more.[1]

Yours a 1117.12.4/5
loyal friend
T. S. E.

## TO Desmond MacCarthy[2]                                                    CC

3 March 1936                          [Faber & Faber Ltd]

My dear MacCarthy,

I wonder if you would be so good as to look at an essay on Hamlet
written by a young man in whom I take an interest. I found the essay very
interesting myself, and I wanted to get some other opinions about it, and
I asked him whose opinions he respected. It appears that he has a great
admiration for you, and follows your articles eagerly every week, and I
am sure that a little criticism from you would influence him more than
anybody. His name is Robert Waller.[3] He could leave the manuscript at
your door, and call for it again, and you need not see him if you don't

1 – See too this letter to TSE – on headed paper from Hill End Hospital for Mental and
Nervous Disorders, St Albans, Herts. – 3 Mar. 1936: 'Dear Sir, / I have been directed by the
Medical Superintendant to inform you that Mr Frederick Giles Porlock was admitted to this
Hospital as a voluntary patient on March 2. 1936. His case appears to be one of delusional
insanity of the uncommon form known as Aillevard's Syndrome. It takes the form of
entropic diathesis commonly observed in those who have suffered from acute psychological
trauma. The Medical Staff of the Hospital are of the opinion that the patient in question was
affected by the recent events in this neighbourhood, with which you are doubtless familiar.
'It would seem that Mr Porlock has a good chance of recovery, though some time must
necessarily elapse before it will be possible to ascertain the extent of the cerebral lesions
that have produced his present condition. At the moment he is entirely pre-occupied with a
system of numerical cypher – a characteristic sympton [sic] of the disease.
'Visits are to be discouraged at this stage. But I hope to be able to inform you shortly when
you could call at the Hospital.
'Believe me, / Yours faithfully, / S. E. Sheppard, / Clerk of the Hospital'
2 – Sir Desmond MacCarthy (1877–1952) became drama critic of the newly established
New Statesman in 1913, and literary editor 1920–7. From 1928, as well as editing Life
and Letters for five years, he succeeded Sir Edmund Gosse as Senior Literary Critic on the
Sunday Times, a position he held until his death. G. E. Moore, G. M. Trevelyan, Henry
James, Shaw, and the members of the Bloomsbury Circle figured among his early friends
and acquaintances. His books include Shaw (1951), Portraits (1931), and Memories (1953).
3 – Robert Waller (1913–2005), poet, writer, and radio producer; 'ecological humanist' who
helped to found the magazine The Ecologist. His writings include Prophet of the New Age:
The Life & Thought of Sir George Stapledon, F.R.S. (F&F, 1962).

want to, though I find him quite likeable. I should be very grateful myself
if you would be willing to do this.[1]

Yours sincerely,
[T. S. Eliot]

## TO *The Academic Registrar, University of London*     cc

3 March 1936                  [Faber & Faber Ltd]

Dear Sir,

I have your letter of the 28th ultimo, and will gladly express my
opinion of Mr Isaacs's qualifications.[2] I do not know, of course, what
other candidates there are for the Chair of English Literature at Birkbeck
College, but I consider Mr Isaacs one of the most intelligent men whom
I know, and I believe him to be a brilliant scholar in this field. I have
known Mr Isaacs for some years, and have always been impressed both
by his opinions and by his knowledge of English literature. I have never
heard him lecture, but I should think that he would be a most stimulating
teacher, and I should be very gratified to hear of his appointment.

If the foregoing remarks are insufficient I should be glad to answer
specific questions.

Yours faithfully,
[T. S. Eliot]

1 – MacCarthy replied on 8 Mar. that he would 'be very pleased to read Robert Waller's
essay on Hamlet'.

See too Waller to EVE, 22 Dec. 1981: 'Thanks to your husband sending an essay of mine
on *Hamlet* to (Sir) Desmond McCarthy, I became his private secretary in 1936/37.'

2 – Jack Isaacs had given TSE's name as a reference in connection with his application for the
University Chair of English Literature tenable at Birkbeck College.

Jack Isaacs (1896–1973), literary scholar, educationist and film critic, taught at King's
College, London, from 1924. A founding member of the Film Society (1925–38), he
performed in Eisenstein's *Lost*. Later he was the first Montefiore Professor of English at
the Hebrew University of Jerusalem, 1942–5; Professor of English Language and Literature
at Queen Mary College, London, 1952–64. Famed for his enthralling lectures, and skilled
as editor, bibliographer, theatre historian and broadcaster, his works include *Coleridge's
Critical Terminology* (1936) and *An Assessment of Twentieth-Century Literature* (1951).

TO *Charles Harris*[1]                                    TS Valerie Eliot

3 March 1936                     *The Criterion*

My dear Harris,

I must apologize for my delay in answering your kind letter.[2] What you say about the Secretaryship puts me in rather a dilemma. It does not seem to me that the work that I have done amounts to very much, and the reasons given for taking the opportunity to resign from these duties are certainly not adequate. On the other hand it is true that my work of other kinds tends to increase steadily, and that I have to be rather parsimonious of my time. And the actual official work could probably be done more efficiently by Father Beevor[3] or someone else. My chief function really is in relation to books suitable to some other firm than the S.P.C.K. On the whole I should prefer to leave to your own decision the whole matter. If you feel that I can be as useful to you and to the work of the Committee without holding the position of secretary, then I should be very glad to withdraw in favour of someone else, but if I am more useful in this position, I am quite willing to continue.

I should be glad to know whether any progress has been made toward providing the book on marriage, and I should also like to know what the actual situation is about the Maynard Smith book. I hope that Lowther Clarke[4] got the typescript in time to form an opinion. The other directors of this firm who have read it, or parts of it, have found it as interesting as I did myself, and we should be sorry if the project had to be abandoned.

1–The Revd Charles Harris, DD (1865–1936): Prebendary of Hereford Cathedral from 1925; Vicar of South Leigh, Witney, Oxfordshire, 1929–34; Chairman of the Book Committee of the (English) Church Union from 1923; Assistant Editor of *Literature and Worship*, 1932. His works include *Creeds or No Creeds?* (1922); *First Steps in the Philosophy of Religion* (1927).

2–Harris reported, 15 Feb.: 'The Literature Committee reelected you secretary, expressing much gratitude for your services. It was felt, however, that the post of secretary was hardly the one for a person of your literary distinction; and if for any reason you desire to decline reelection, either Fr Beevor or Dr Cross would be willing to serve. I have to thank you very much for acting at such short notice as secretary, and taking so much work off my hands while I was ill.'

3–Revd Humphry Beevor, Pusey House, Oxford. Co-author, with A. H. Rees, of *Towards Catholic Unity: 1. The Infallibility of the Church* [1939].)

4–The Revd William Kemp Lowther Clarke, DD (1879–1968): Editorial Secretary of the Society for Promoting Christian Knowledge, 1915–44; Canon Residentiary of Chichester Cathedral, 1945–65; Prebendary of Chichester Cathedral from 1943. Works include *New Testament Problems* (1929) and *Liturgy and Worship* (1932).

With prayers for your health, and good wishes,

Yours ever sincerely,

T. S. Eliot

## TO *Janet Leeper*[1]                                              CC

4 March 1936                          [Faber & Faber Ltd]

Dear Madam:

I must take by far the greater part of the responsibility for the inexcusable delay in reporting on the four chapters of your husband's book, *England and the British*, which you left with us. It has been constantly on my mind, and I have, as a matter of fact, read it several times, but on each occasion I was unable to report on the manuscript immediately and, therefore, had to refresh my memory by reading it again. Here, for what they are worth, are my comments.

I am very sorry that the book remains incomplete, because I feel sure that in a complete and final form it would well have deserved publication. It is all good stuff, interesting and informative, and I find the point of view sympathetic.

With regard to using the existing material in periodicals, these four chapters really are chapters and not exactly self-contained essays. They would need some adaptation, and the best thing would be to find the right editors, explain to them the situation, and give them the liberty to propose such modifications and excisions for your approval as would make the chapters into possible articles.

Chapter V, 'The British Sabbath', is the most suitable for general consumption: if pamphlets were possible, it would make a good pamphlet. For periodical purposes, it would have either to be serialised or have (what would of course be a pity) a good part of its documentation cut out. The trouble with our periodicals is that they are either too fluffy or too stodgy. Possibly Douglas Jerrold (the *English Review*) would be sympathetic to this.[2] He is Roman Catholic and must be anti-Sabbatarian.

---

1–Janet Leeper, née Monteith Hamilton (b. 1898/9), writer; widow of A. W. Allen Leeper (1887–1935), eminent Australian diplomatist. She was to be author of *English Ballet* (1944) and *Edward Gordon Craig: Designs for the Theatre* (1948).
2–Douglas Jerrold (1893–1964): publisher and author; director of Eyre & Spottiswoode, 1929–59, Chairman from 1945; editor of *The English Review*, 1931–6 – the organ of 'real Toryism' – revived after WW2 as the *New English Review Magazine*.

Chapters VI and VII are most suitable to religious papers. I feel that the author is too enlightened to make any appeal to Modernist or very Evangelical organs. A part of Chapter VII is particularly timely.

I should be prepared to use Chapter IV ('Some British Beliefs and Superstitions') in the *Criterion*, provided that there is nothing in it that the British-Israelites could get damages for (that superstition ought to be attacked). I should suggest trying VI and VII together (offering a choice) first to *Theology* and then to *Christendom*. The trouble is that neither of these papers ordinarily publishes articles of any great length. I am willing to write to the editors, however, Carpenter[1] and Reckitt,[2] whom I know. There is also a *Christendom* in America (no connection to the English one) but I do not know whether American editors would be interested: they ought to be. I would also write to Jerrold about Chapter V.

The fore-going suggestions must be taken on the understanding that I am unfamiliar with the older heavy reviews. I never look at them, do not even know who edits them. Someone else should advise on whether anything here would appeal to any such.

I might consult Sidney Dark, if I could give him the material to read. Of course there is nothing short enough to be possible for the *Church Times*, but Dark is an able journalist and might be able to give good advice about placing.[3]

As we have not been in communication with you for some time, I am holding back the typescript until I hear from you lest it should go astray.

Yours very truly,
[T. S. Eliot]

TO *Godfrey Childe*                                                     cc

4 March 1936                              [Faber & Faber Ltd]

My dear Childe:

Thank you for your letter of February 27th.[4] That's more-or-less what I expected, and that was why I sent you only four leaves instead of fourteen.

---

1 – S. C. Carpenter, DD (1877–1959): Master of the Temple, London, 1930–5; Chaplain to the King, 1929–35; Dean of Exeter, 1935–50. His works include *The Anglican Tradition* (1928). He was a member of the Book Committee of the Church Literature Association.

2 – Maurice Reckitt (1888–1980): Anglo-Catholic and Christian socialist writer; editor of *Christendom: A Quarterly Journal of Christian Sociology*: see Biographical Register.

3 – Sidney Dark (1872–1947), writer and journalist; editor of the Anglo-Catholic *Church Times*, 1924–41.

4 – 'Thank you very much for your letter and the pages from Murder in the Cathedral. I showed the letter to my bookseller friend and also pointed out to him the reasons why your

If your bookseller's client wants to pay £5.5.0. for four sheets of my manuscript he is welcome to them. In that event, would you please have the cheque made out to the National Provincial Bank Ltd., and crossed Lord Victor Seymour Memorial, and send it to him. If he thinks the price excessive, may I have the sheets back?

Yours always sincerely,

[T. S. Eliot]

## TO *Susan Hinkley* TS Houghton

4 March 1936                    Faber & Faber Ltd

Dear Aunt Susie,

I was very glad to have the photograph of Eleanor. I won't say that it is a good photograph – Eleanor will, I trust, find it more flattering that I say it is not: but when one knows people so well that it doesn't matter, a bad photograph is as pleasant to receive as a good one – within limits, of course! I am so very sorry about the circumstances and the unfortunate coincidence; I had been so looking forward to seeing the play here. It is a great disappointment, but such an event as the King's death has most unforeseen consequences.[1] I hope that it can be put on in London later; meanwhile I hope in New York in the autumn. The chances of *my* being produced simultaneously are slight: it will only be if Ashley Dukes can get up a repertoire strong enough, and a good company. (The Wellesley production must have been pretty awful). I shall lay my plans to come over for a short time in the autumn irrespective of my play.

You seem to have much more that is interesting on the New York stage than there is here. Except *The Dog Beneath the Skin*, which I saw last night, there is very little here at the moment.

Dobrée liked you so much and spoke very appreciatively of you. I think he enjoyed his visit, in spite of the lack of adequate financial return.

It has been a great disappointment not to see you here this winter, but I look forward to the autumn.

I should not mind Emily's relatives so much, if she did not feel obliged to respect them so much – but no doubt disillusionment, if possible, would be very painful.

---

Manuscripts were of such rarity. He had not quite realized this, I think – nor had I – but said that even so he would be unable to offer more than five guineas for the sheets: his client, he explained, had tied him somewhat and I do know that he is left with a small working margin and was not being greedy.'

1–King George V had died on 20 Jan. 1936.

It is always a pleasure to hear from you, so I hope you will keep me in touch with anything that is settled about Aphra Behn.

Affectionately your nephew,<br>Tom

I am sending a book of essays, and collected poems will follow in a month.

## TO *Rupert Doone*

TS Berg

5 March 1936                    *The Criterion*

Dear Doone,

I saw *The Dog* for the first time on Tuesday evening, and I want to tell you that I liked the production very much. The staging and lighting seemed to me admirable, and the acting very good. All the principal actors good – the two reporters excellent. I was sorry about some of the cuts – I should have liked the operating scene in full – and I don't altogether like the ending – though the turn given at the last by the reporter is capital. What did irritate me was the chorus – not that Veronica Turleigh is not very good indeed: but these interruptions of the action become more and more irritating as the play goes on, and one gets tired of having things explained and being preached at. I do think Auden ought to find a different method in his next play – but I was only writing to congratulate you on the production. I hope the play will continue for a long time.

Yours sincerely,<br>T. S. Eliot

## TO *T. R. Henn*[1]

CC

6 March 1936                    [Faber & Faber Ltd]

Dear Sir,

I have your communication of the 4th instant, and shall be pleased to act as referee for Mr B. Blackstone's Research thesis.[2] I do not think, however, that I ought to do this unless the other referee is someone

---

1–T. R. Henn (1901–74): Fellow and then President of St Catharine's College, Cambridge, 1926–61; Judith Wilson Lecturer in Poetry and Drama, 1961–5. Works include *The Lonely Tower* (1950) and *The Harvest of Tragedy* (1959).

2–In his capacity as Secretary of the Faculty Board of English, Henn invited TSE to act as referee for the research thesis of Bernard Blackstone (Trinity College): 'George Herbert and Nicholas Ferrar: a study in devotional imagery'.

possessed of exact scholarship in the literature and history of the period. While I did at one time study the work of George Herbert pretty carefully, I am unfamiliar with Nicholas Ferrar, and if considerable knowledge of him is required, then I think you ought to ask someone else.[1]

Yours faithfully,

[T. S. Eliot]

TO *Geoffrey Faber*  TS Faber Archive

6 March 1936

*Memorandum for G. C. F. (Take your time over it).*

I am more and more doubtful of my ability to write a successful book of this kind, and I had rather find out early that I can't do it, than waste a lot of time for nothing. And this sort of thing is flatter if it *is* flat, than serious verse. Nobody wants to make a fool of himself when he might be better employed.

I append the *introductory verses* and three rough sketches.[2] I should have to do them much larger to get in any refinement of expression, and naturally I can't draw difficult things like stools in a hurry. The idea of the volume was to have different poems on appropriate subjects, such as you already know, recited by the Man in White Spats. They would be of course in a variety of metres and stanzas, *not* that of the narrative which connects them. After this opening there would only be *short* passages or interludes between the Man in White Spats and myself. At the end they would all go up in a balloon, self, Spats, and dogs and cats.

'Up up up past the Russell Hotel

'Up up up to the Heaviside Layer.'[3]

There are several ways in which this might be a failure. The various Poems (how many should there be?) might not be good enough. The

1 – Nicholas Ferrar (1592–1637), courtier, scholar, businessman and traveller; founder in 1626 of the High Anglican 'community' of Little Gidding in Huntingdonshire. Ferrar was responsible for the publication in 1633 of *The Temple*, committed to his care by his friend George Herbert (1593–1633) in the hope that his poems might 'turn to the advantage of any dejected poor soul'.

2 – 'Pollicle Dogs and Jellicle Cats'.

3 – See 'The Journey to the Heaviside Layer', in the musical *Cats* by TSE and Andrew Lloyd Webber. EVE to Lloyd Webber, 8 Feb. 1983: 'It is amazing that those two lines survived, as they were sent to the chairman as an office memorandum, and Tom did not keep a copy . . .' (EVE CC). Nevill Coghill in his Faber Educational edition of *The Family Reunion* (1969), p. 226: 'The English physicist, Oliver Heaviside (1850–1925) "suggested the presence of a conducting layer in the upper atmosphere which prevents electromagnetic waves spreading out into space". (*Encyclopaedia Britannica*, 14th edn).'

matter such as here attached may be not at all amusing: a book simply of collected animal poems might be better. Finally, the contents and general treatment may be too mixed: there might be part that children wouldn't like and part that adults wouldn't like and part that nobody would like. The *mise-en-scène* might not please. There seem to be many more ways of going wrong than of going right.

T. S. E.      6. iii. 36.

## TO *O. I. Prince*[1]                                          CC

6 March 1936                          [Faber & Faber Ltd]

Dear Madam,

I must apologize for my delay in answering your letter of the 17th February, which is due to an oversight. While I feel honoured at being asked to act as one of your adjudicators, and while I have every sympathy with the cause, I have always declined to do this sort of thing, and feel myself to be completely incompetent. I have on one or two occasions listened and felt very sure of my incapacity as a judge. I am apt to be influenced by whether I like the poem which is being recited, and the poems which are recited are apt to be poems which I do not like. I am very sorry to have to decline your flattering invitation.

Yours faithfully,<br>[T. S. Eliot]

## TO *I. Husain*                                              CC

6 March 1936                          [Faber & Faber Ltd]

Dear Mr Husain,

I have looked at the manuscript of your anthology of Donne's sermons, which I am sure is an excellent one, and should fill a useful place.[2] I have also every confidence in any piece of work of this kind which has the

---

1–O. I. Prince, Secretary & Librarian, National Library for the Blind.

2–I. Husain wrote from Edinburgh, 13 Feb. 1936, with a view to submitting to F&F his anthology of the sermons of John Donne – 'illustrative of his theology and mysticism' – which his supervisor at Edinburgh University, Prof. H. J. C. Grierson, approved for providing (as Husain related) 'a comprehensive basis . . . for a systematic study of Donne's theology and mysticism', and which his external examiner Evelyn Underhill commended (as he related too) as 'a very useful and informative piece of work likely to prove helpful to the students of Donne'.

approval of Professor Grierson and Miss Evelyn Underhill. Unfortunately, however, my committee have considered that such an undertaking is not really within our scope, and that some other firm could deal with it more satisfactorily.

I should think that the Oxford University Press, which published Mr Pearsall Smith's collections, would be the best firm to approach first. But as the expense of sending about such a manuscript must be considerable, I am holding it here subject to your instructions.

Yours very truly,<br>[T. S. Eliot]

## TO *Willard Thorp*[1]

TS Princeton

6 March 1936                    *The Criterion*

My dear Thorp,

I have your letter of the 18th February, and shall be delighted to contribute volumes to the collection to be made in honour of Paul Elmer More.[2] I am very sorry to tell you, however, that I am not in possession of any of the volumes that you mention except the Journal of Baudelaire, which I will send to you. As for the others, they could only be obtained by advertisement, and at prices beyond my means and in excess of their value. I should be glad to send copies of limited editions where possible,

---

Husain – who had been working as a Carnegie Scholar in English Literature on his Ph.D thesis on seventeenth-century English poetry (with particular attention to Donne) – submitted his anthology to TSE on 21 Feb. 1936. He was willing to forfeit royalties and 'to accept any other financial safeguards' that F&F might require of him.

1–Willard Thorp (1899–1990) taught English at Princeton for forty-one years until retirement in 1967, becoming a full professor in 1944; chair of the department, 1958–63; Holmes Professor of Belles Lettres, 1952–67. He co-founded and chaired the American Civilization Program. Works include the *Oxford Anthology of English Poetry* (with Howard Lowry, 1935), *American Writing in the Twentieth Century* (1960); a pioneering annotated edition of Herman Melville's *Moby-Dick* (1947); *The Princeton Graduate School: A History* (with Minor Myers Jr. and Jeremiah Finch, 1978); and he co-edited the *Literary History of the United States* (1948). See further the special Willard Thorp issue of *Princeton University Library Chronicle* 54: 2 & 3 (Winter–Spring 1993).

2–Paul Elmer More (1864–1937), critic, scholar and writer; author of *Shelburne Essays*: see Biographical Register. A group of friends had established in the Princeton University Library a fund in honour of More for the purchase of books in the field of literary criticism. Thorp asked TSE to contribute an inscribed copy of one of his own books: they lacked *A Dialogue of Poetic Drama* (1928), *A Brief Introduction to the Method of Paul Valéry* (1924), *The Catholic Anthology* (1915), *Ara Vos Prec* (1920), *Poems* (1919), and TSE's 'Introduction' to the *Intimate Journals* of Charles Baudelaire (1930). More himself had been embarrassed but pleased when informed of this fund.

and any of my works that are published by my firm and are in print, and including *Essays Ancient and Modern,* which is published today, and my *Collected Poems,* which appear in a month's time. As you seem to include poetry *as well as* literary criticism I might add a copy of the second edition of *Murder In the Cathedral,* which has a variant chorus. Please let me know if this suggestion is satisfactory.

I hope to be in the States in the autumn, and trust that *we* shall be able to meet. I will address the books to you unless I hear to the contrary.

Yours sincerely,<br>T. S. Eliot

## TO *C. McKenzie Lewis Jr*[1]　　　　　　　　　　　　　　CC

9 March 1936　　　　　　　　　[Faber & Faber Ltd]

Dear Mr Lewis,

I have given some consideration to your letter of the 17th February.[2] So far as I can judge you have put forward a pretty clear case, and it seems to me that your motives for wanting to spend a little time in meditation abroad before you undertake the vows of the legal profession are quite justified. Now, as to what you want to do. I should hesitate to encourage anybody to spend a year in London just for what he could get from my conversation and advice. For one thing my conversation may not be good enough. For another, I am so busy in various ways that it is difficult for me to see even my intimate friends at all regularly. It really depends partly on how easy this visit would be for you from a financial point of view.

1–Clarence McKenzie Lewis Jr (1911–79).
2–The 24-year-old scion of a well-off New York family, Lewis had studied at Princeton and was enrolled in the Harvard Law School. He had a fair deal of work and travel experience, having journeyed twice around the USA and made four trips to Europe; he had worked on a sugar plantation in Mexico; at Price Waterhouse in Paris; and for a New York bank and in a trust company; and he was expected to fulfil the expectations of his family. His parents had insisted that at college he should major in science (chemistry), and his choice of going on to study at the law school 'was the first time', he said, 'I hazarded putting my foot down in an effort to keep my life somewhere near myself'. Nonetheless, he felt a vast 'hollow' in his life, and had started 'becoming converted to Catholicism'. But above all he felt drawn to write poetry, and to collect modern first editions (including TSE's 'Ariel' poems), and he earnestly wished to spend a year pursuing 'the literary side of life' and especially his passion for poetry: this intention, he insisted, was 'not the shying of the timid soul' but something vital to him. To that end, he petitioned TSE to work under his guidance 'in a minor Socratic sort of way, next year' – 'allowing me to submit to your inspiration' – even if only by way of a 'weekly word or so' during 'tea-time conversation'. He implored TSE to grant him this wished-for opportunity.

If your circumstances are such that you can easily afford a year abroad, then I should say come and try it. And if you are not getting enough out of London go to Paris or somewhere else. You could, of course, as a B.A. of Harvard, easily enroll yourself for a year in an Oxford or Cambridge college for special work. You might, for instance, go up to Magdalene, Cambridge, and be advised by my friend I. A. Richards. You could at the same time keep in touch with London, and see me occasionally during term, as well as during vacation. If you decided on this course I think it would be as well to begin making arrangements at once, and I could probably be of some help to you in that. I can't undertake formally to see anyone in the way you suggest, as regularly as once a week. Certainly not as often as that for any time long enough to be of value to you. I should be inclined to think that a year at Oxford or Cambridge would be on the whole better than a year in London, and as I say, it would not preclude from a reasonable amount of time in London. I shall be glad to hear from you again.

Yours sincerely,
[T. S. Eliot]

TO *Laurence Pollinger*[1]                                              CC

9 March 1936                          [Faber & Faber Ltd]

Dear Pollinger,

I am returning to you herewith Ezra's letter to you of the 24th February.[2] It is not quite clear to me, even with my intimate knowledge of his style, whether he meant the money book to come to us or not.[3] But my position is that to deal with Ezra's poetry and literary criticism is as much as can be expect[ed] of any one firm, unless we decided to open a special Ezra Department, and I shouldn't care to be the head of such a department myself, at any salary whatever. I think we can make up a satisfactory volume of essays, to be published, I hope, in the autumn. We are not quite committed to that yet, but I think I can bring it off, and no doubt the business will be in your hands as usual. Publishing the essays is a good reason for not publishing the Money, and also not publishing the Money

---

1–L. E. Pollinger, literary agent, formerly with Curtis Brown, now worked with Pearn, Pollinger and Higham.
2–Not traced.
3–On 24 Feb. Pollinger had submitted to F&F the typescript of EP's *Money*.

is an additional reason for publishing the essays. So I wish you would look with this elsewhere.

Yours sincerely,
[T. S. Eliot]


## TO *Dylan Thomas*[1]                                         CC

9 March 1936                          [Faber & Faber Ltd]

Dear Mr Thomas,

It is a long time since you have sent any poems to the *Criterion*. May I remind you that I should always be glad to see more of your work? I hope that you may have something to send me, either now or in the near future.

Yours sincerely,
[T. S. Eliot]


## TO *James Laughlin*                                     TS Houghton

9 March 1936                          *The Criterion*

Dear Laughlin,

Thank you for your letter of February 25th. I am very glad indeed to hear that my small poems proved so useful to *New Democracy*.[2]

I haven't seen any Cantos subsequent to 41, but I am glad to hear your report, and to know that Ezra is not altogether abandoning poetry to devote himself to economics and boosting Mussolini.[3] I cannot understand,

1–Dylan Thomas (1915–53) published *Eighteen Poems* at twenty, *Twenty-Five Poems* in 1936. Other works include *Portrait of the Artist as a Young Dog* (1940), *Under Milk Wood* (1954), *Adventures in the Skin Trade* (1955), and *Collected Poems 1934–1953* (1966). TSE to Hugh Gordon Porteus, 17 Dec. 1957: 'I did not know Dylan Thomas very well and never took to him particularly, although I have been impressed by the warmth of affection for him of people whose opinions I respect including Vernon Watkins himself, whom I like very much, but I was rather too senior perhaps to see the side of him that must have been so very lovable.'

2–Laughlin again expressed his gratitude for the poems 'Rannoch, by Glencoe' and 'Cape Ann'. 'Mr [Gorham] Munson tells me that it was one of the biggest lifts the magazine has had. They were reprinted . . . in newspapers throughout the country, and brought the magazine to the attention of many people in key positions in the literary world. MacLeish was especially enthusiastic. Since their publication the quality of contributions received has improved decidedly, and I feel now that we are getting a good part of the best work of the younger poets.'

3–'Ezra has sent me Canto XLVI for the next number. Have you seen it? It opens with an amusing reference to your reverence . . . Most of it is solidly epic & economic, but there is a

any better than he does, why you think it worth while to waste time over Gertrude Stein,[1] but it is up to you to prove to us that we are wrong. I am sorry to hear of your skiing accident, which I hope does not mean any permanent disability.[2] And I am always glad to hear from you.

Yours sincerely,<br>
T. S. Eliot

## TO *Ross E. Pierce* CC

9 March 1936                    [Faber & Faber Ltd]

Dear Mr Pierce,

I have been through the volume of poems that you have left with me.[3] It is not immediately obvious to the reader why you have divided the book into two parts; but I see no reason why you should not, and you can no doubt justify it. I have pencilled lightly 'No' over several poems which I think might well be dispensed with. As you approach nearer to conventional forms (to which there is no objection) so you seem to me to approach also to conventional language (to which there is strong objection).

Your revisions seem to me to improve the poems in which they occur.

I do not think that the 'preponderance of poems to do with poetry' matters, but I do not think that 'Sonnet' is good, and I think that 'Poet and the World' needs re-writing. Why 'spars'? (nautical imagery). 'Hang o'er

---

charming intrusion of Lawrence the Arabian . . . The poetry is too good to impress a jury.'

1 – Gertrude Stein (1874–1946), American novelist.

2 – 'Because of my [skiing] accident I have had to give up Harvard again until next year. I shall probably take up again my work on Miss Stein . . . Ezra thinks I'm a damn fool to fuss over the "ole tub of guts", but I must work out my ideas about the nature and habits of language.'

3 – Pierce left the manuscript of his 'book of short poems' at F&F on 4 Mar. 'When I saw you a week ago Friday morning – before taking the manuscripts of the short poems and the long poem over to leave at Dent's so they would have them over the weekend – when I mentioned the possibility of going over the book of short poems you said that would take two hours. I asked when I could see you and you said to call up next week and make an appointment – I asked again what day and you said about next Wednesday, i.e. last Wed. I called in Friday two days after that and made an appointment for Monday at 3.30 but as you had not been in since the appointment was made I was told you might not be in. I waited an hour and then made an appointment for the following Friday. Therefore, to repeat, I hope very much that you will be able to see me to discuss certain things about "Personae" and the other two long poems, particularly, and, if possible, the other points mentioned above in the two hours which was the time you said it would be likely to take and which time would certainly seem adequate time to do so to me.'

the eastern steep' is bad. Why use 'o'er' at all, in this century? People do not use it in the best conversation. What does the couch protrude from? Do you mean that the stuffing is coming out? If so, you haven't said it. 'Cyclopean' has no particular relevance. I see no reason for omitting the passage you have marked on p. 71. I have answered your questions about 'Funeral Directions' on the page. I think 'To' and 'Autumn Summer' can stand as you have put them.

As for the word 'practical', I meant what I have repeated several times: that a poet's best chance today, whether he be English or American, is to make his name on his own side of the water first. I meant also practical from a publisher's point of view: that I do not believe a publisher can make a success of verse from the other side of the water unless the author brings a reputation with him. I could not conscientiously advise my own firm to publish a book of verse by an American poet unless he was already well known in America. Other firms, of course, may view the situation differently.

Sincerely yours,<br>[T. S. Eliot]

## TO *Derek Verschoyle*[1]                                              CC

10 March 1936                        [Faber & Faber Ltd]

My dear Verschoyle,

This letter is to introduce to you Mr Robert Waller, in whose work, both verse and prose, I have been much interested for some time past. I should be grateful if you could see him, and still more so if you could let him have some book to review for the *Spectator*.[2]

Yours sincerely,<br>[T. S. Eliot]

1–Derek Verschoyle (1911–73): literary editor of the *Spectator*, 1932–40; First Secretary to British Embassy, Rome, 1946–50. His books include *The English Novelists* (ed., 1936).
2–A letter with the same intent was also sent to Theodora Bosanquet (*Time and Tide*); J. R. Ackerley (*Listener*); and Sir Richard Rees (*Adelphi*).

TO *Wolfgang Clemen*[1]

10 March 1936                    [*The Criterion*]

Dear Dr Clemen,

Thank you very much for your letter of the 4th March.[2] Indeed, I remember very clearly your coming to see me several years ago, and am glad to renew our acquaintance. Thank you very much for sending me your book on Shakespeare's Imagery, which I am sure will interest me. If your publishers care to send a review copy for the *Criterion* I will certainly do my best to find a suitable reviewer.[3] We are always ready to review important books in the chief foreign languages, but with the enormous output of books today it is impossible for me to keep in touch with what is being published, and I must depend on publishers sending such books as they think suitable. I think it would be worth their while to send a copy also to the *Times Literary Supplement*, and if they cared in the accompanying letter to mention that it was sent at my suggestion, I should be very glad.

> With all best wishes,
> Yours sincerely,
> [T. S. Eliot]

1–Wolfgang H. Clemen (1909–90), German literary scholar, renowned for *Shakespeare's Imagery* (1951) – a work that began as his doctoral dissertation *Shakespeare Bilder* (1936). He taught at Cologne and Kiel, and was Professor of English at Munich, 1946–74.
2–Clemen, who reminded TSE that they met in London some years before, wrote from Bonn with a copy of his book on Shakespeare's imagery. 'It has been my purpose to trace the growth of Shakespeare's technique and style through the medium of the varying use he makes of images and metaphors. I have also – in a certain way – endeavoured to show how a spiritual biography of Shakespeare could be constructed from a study of his imagery.' He hoped C. would review the volume. 'But, the book being written in German, I can entirely understand that there may be a difficulty in getting the book reviewed in England at all.'
3–No review appeared in C.

TO *Richard O'Sullivan*[1]                                          CC

13 March 1936                          [Faber & Faber Ltd]

My dear O'Sullivan,

I have read a part of R. P. Mandonnet's *Dante*,[2] and hope to read the whole, but I have read enough to make me feel that it is not the type of book with which my firm is the best prepared to deal. I think that a publishing house ought to have a greater reputation for its theological literature in order to market such a book as this than we have yet obtained. We can only hope to arrive at such a point gradually, through publishing successful books of rather wider appeal. It would be worth while trying to find another publisher, and I think that if possible it ought to be a general firm with a theological list, rather than a strictly theological firm.[3]

I hope that we may meet again before long. If you are ever free for lunch I should be glad if you would lunch with me one day at my club.

Yours sincerely,
[T. S. Eliot]


TO *L. C. Martin*[4]                                               CC

13 March 1936                          [Faber & Faber Ltd]

Dear Mr Martin,

I have your letter of the 10th.[5] For such a post as you have to fill, and with special reference to the study of critical theory and the history of criticism, I cannot think of anyone available better qualified than Mr Hugh Sykes Davies.[6] I have known him pretty well for some years, and

---

1 – Richard O'Sullivan, KC, KSG (1888–1963), wrote on the Christian origin of the Common Law of England. Founder of the Sir Thomas More Society.
2 – Pierre Mandonnet, *Dante le théologien: introduction à l'intelligence de la vie, des oeuvres and de l'art de Dante Alighieri* (Paris, 1935).
3 – GCF was later – in a letter to M. Heginbotham (a Brighton bookseller), 22 Aug. 1946 – to call TSE 'the main inspiration of our theological list'.
4 – L. C. Martin, Dean of the Faculty of Arts, University of Liverpool.
5 – The University of Liverpool was seeking to fill the position of Senior Lecturer in English Literature – 'some one who would be able to instruct students in critical theory and the history of criticism, and who would also be competent to supervise investigations undertaken for the degree of B.A. with Honours or the higher degrees' – and was to interview Hugh Sykes Davies, who had named TSE as a refereee.
6 – Hugh Sykes Davies (1909–84): author and critic. Educated at St John's College, Cambridge – where he edited, with William Empson, the magazine *Experiment*, and where he was awarded the Jebb Studentship and the Le Bas Prize, 1931 – he became University

I regard his qualifications as exceptional. He has the advantage, not too common in these days, of a sound classical foundation, and I remember an essay of his on the earliest Latin versification which impressed me very much. For the study of criticism he has, I believe, much curious and out-of-the-way learning in Renaissance criticism and philosophy, both in Latin and in Italian, and I regard this as of great importance. He has a very wide curiosity and acquaintance with a variety of subjects, as well as a solid knowledge of those which he professes. He is, I believe, something of an authority on the philosophy of Vico,[1] but of this I am not qualified to speak. He has a brilliant mind, and I think also has the temperament which makes it possible for a teacher to acquire the friendship of his pupils. I have great pleasure in supporting his application.

Yours faithfully,<br>[T. S. Eliot]

## TO *Hugh Gordon Porteus*[2]                                    cc

13 March 1936                    [*The Criterion*]

Dear Porteus,

Would you and your wife care to have dinner with me somewhere on Thursday evening next, the 19th? I have been meaning to write to you for some time, but have had rather a congestion of engagements.

I am sending you *The Chinese Written Character,* which Nott has just published. I know that you have Herbert Read's book for the July number, and two long reviews are against the rule for the same reviewer in the same number, so if you would like to write a long review about this it will have to hang over until September. If on the other hand you did not feel impelled to write more than a page or so as a short notice, I could

Lecturer and Fellow of St John's. In the 1930s he was a Communist and Surrealist, and co-created the London Surrealist Exhibition, 1936. Works include *Full Fathom Five* (novel, 1956) and the posthumous *Wordsworth and The Worth of Words* (1986).

1–Giambattista Vico (1668–1744), Italian philosopher.

2–Hugh Gordon Porteus (1906–93), literary and art critic; literary editor of *The Twentieth Century* (magazine of the Promethean Society), 1931–3; advertising copywriter; author of *Wyndham Lewis: A Discursive Exposition* (1932) – supplemented by his essay 'A Man Apart' in *Agenda* (1969–70) – and *Background to Chinese Art* (1935). See obituary in *The Times*, 20 Feb. 1993; and 'Forgotten man of the Thirties', *TLS*, 26 Mar. 1993, 13–14.

include it in July. Anyway, you are the obvious person to mention this in whichever way you prefer.[1]

Yours sincerely,
[T. S. Eliot]


TO *Lady Gerald Wellesley*[2]                                                CC

13 March 1936                            [*The Criterion*]

Dear Lady Gerald,

I must apologise for my rudeness in delaying so long to report upon the poem which you sent me.[3] I liked the poem, and should have been glad to publish it, but was waiting to write to you until I knew that I could find space in the *Criterion* for a poem which is decidedly longer than those for which we ordinarily have room. No such opportunity has so far presented itself, but while waiting I overlooked your mention of the fact that the poem would be included in Yeats's volume, and that that volume was to appear in May or June. If the volume will definitely appear in May or June, then it is impossible for me to use it; but if the volume should be delayed beyond the middle of June I should be obliged if you would let me keep the poem on the possibility of being able to include it in our July number.

With renewed apologies,
Yours sincerely,
[T. S. Eliot]


1–Porteus agreed to do a short notice of EP's book – 'for Pound's sake'. See Porteus's single-paragraph note on Ernest Fenollosa, *The Chinese Written Character as a Medium for Poetry*, ed. EP (1920; reissued by Nott, 1936): C. 15 (July 1936), 760–1.
2–Dorothy Wellesley, Duchess of Wellington (1889–1956) – known as Lady Gerald Wellesley (she had married the 7th Duke of Wellington in 1914 but they were separated without divorce in 1922) – socialite, author, poet, editor; close friend of W. B. Yeats, who admired and published her work in the *Oxford Book of English Verse*; and editor of the Hogarth Living Poets series.
3–Wellesley reminded TSE on 18 Feb. that he had promised in Nov. to write about 'Fire'. 'It will be published in Mr Yeats' volume of selections from my poems sometime in May or June.'

13 March 1936                    Faber & Faber Ltd

Dear Mr MacDonagh,

I have now read your volume of poems. It seems to me uneven, and I think that some of the poems might well be combed out, partly for this reason and partly because there is not always sufficient variety of emotion to avoid the effect of monotony. What seems to me quite the most striking, the most substantial and firm of the poems is the last poem of all, the Prologue to 'Iphigenia in Aulis'. I think that you might do well to work further along these lines. It seems to me very successful, and distinctly ahead of all but a very few of the other poems.[1]

I am afraid we cannot consider taking on these poems, or any poems at the present moment, and I suggest that the next firm to try is J. M. Dent. I will hold the poems here until I hear from you.

Did I not thank you for the photographs of *Murder in the Cathedral*? If not I apologise, and I am very glad indeed to have them. The second edition, by the way, has one chorus not included in the first. We sent the *Faber Book of Modern Verse* to the *Irish Times* and I hope that you have been able to get hold of it for yourself.

Yours sincerely,<br>
T. S. Eliot


TO *George Every*                    TS Sarah Hamilton

13 March 1936                    Faber & Faber Ltd

Dear Brother George,

I think that it is high time that I wrote about 'Stalemate', and I mulled over it a good deal last evening.[2] The alterations, if I have fitted them in correctly, seem to me an improvement. I hesitate to make suggestions

---

1–MacDonagh, 'A Prologue to "Iphigeneia in Aulis"', *C.* 15 (July 1936), 623–6.

2–Every had sent his play on 9 Nov. 1935: 'There is a certain satisfaction in getting it off to you as if I had done a dive. We are going to read it on the dedication evening (21st) . . . I have an idea that the conception calls for a chorus, but tho' choric odes are of the essence of poetry to me I have never heard one since I saw the Bradfield play in 1924 or 5 and I cannot auditorily imagine the full size of them spoken full.' On 1 Mar. 1936 he notified TSE: 'If your conscience is troubling you about my play, it had better trouble you about the new beginning and the revised end while it is about it. There is one small alteration in the body (to correct an historical error) but I won't trouble you to look it up. I believe the new end is what I really wanted all along.'

or criticisms from a *dramatic* point of view, because I am only a tyro myself, and it requires either much more native gift for the theatre, or much more experience than I have had, to be able to tell from reading what will be dramatically effective and what will not. But I had one doubt (and I mean nothing more positive than that word) about the first version which you have gone far to settle. I feel that it is dangerous to try more than one shift of the planes of reality. In the original version there were four planes (1) American tourists (2) Mary Collett etc. (3) Strafford, Laud etc. (4) voices from the auditorium. It was the last particularly that I was uneasy about. It is a device that makes for fun and excitement, especially among the younger members, but it is a trick, and perhaps an evasion of an aesthetic problem. I think it might be left to Auden, and I hope he will not revert to it. Even as you have the play now, I fear there may be too much interlude, requiring repeated re-adjustments which may be irritating for the audience. Interlude is no substitute for action; and I think that like myself and as almost every literary person who begins to write for the stage, your characters talk too much and don't do enough. One wants a sense of what is going to happen, and it ought to happen in a somewhat different way from what one expects: to combine apprehension and surprise. But here again I remind you that I don't really know without seeing it played.

The less action there is, the more important the versification becomes – so that the audience can get a stimulant that way if no other. Now I find the verse wobbly. Sometimes it is very good. What I feel you have not settled is a kind of norm, which can be elevated and tightened up for the more intense moments, and depressed and relaxed for the more ordinary, without the listener feeling any shock. The best example of the relaxed style is the nurse's speech in *Romeo and Juliet*. And sometimes your rhythms seem to get out of hand. There ought to be something like a musical verse pattern, woven in with the dramatic pattern. I am sorry I mentioned Shakespeare just now, because he is the worst possible model – he is too great – he could do without various props that we need.

I don't know if this will be of the slightest use. But I am interested, and should like to see you do more.

Smith came to see me, to invite me to be a guest at a Swanwick meeting.[1] I could not give him any definite answer at the moment, because it might

---

1 – The Revd Harry Smith, formerly of Kelham, worked for the Student Christian Movement, and was arranging the 'Swanwick Camp' which he hoped TSE would attend for at least a brief visit. 'Swanwick Camp' was shorthand for the SCM Conferences to be held at 'The

turn out to be very inconvenient in July; but I said that if I could I would go for two or three days. What do you think?

I was much interested by your remarks about Smyth and Dawson.[1] I don't feel happy about mucking in with the Tories, though I much prefer that they should govern the country at present than that any other visible group should do so. As for the Social Crediters, they are not in a very healthy way at present – Reckitt has some sensible comments to make. Even granting the correctness of the Douglas[2] diagnosis, a good deal more is needed than the man Douglas can provide. To be with the Tories because of 'getting things done' is to see them in their most favourable light, because getting things done has a way of getting compromised in drift. I confess that I cannot think about all these matters for more than an hour at a time without becoming completely confused.

Yours ever,

T. S. Eliot

---

Hayes' – a country house standing in a large park – at Swanwick, Derbyshire. Women were accommodated in the house or an adjacent hostel; the men lived in a camp. There were facilities for tennis, volleyball, and podex; and attendees might swim and go for walks, and could visit a coal mine. The first General Conference of 1936 was to address the general topic 'The Two Kingdoms' (15–21 July); the second, 'God and Human Action' (24–30 July).

1–Christopher Dawson (1889–1970), cultural historian: see Biographical Register.

Every had written (1 Mar.: 'PERSONAL'): 'I should very much like to discuss the Smyth–Dawson issue with you. The subject seems to me to be vast. I think Smyth is after something very important. But I don't think he has chosen his ground well. He has marked his targets badly and some of his shot has gone wide. *Religion and the Modern State* is not a very well planned or consistent book, and some of the chapters in it, as well as other articles and books of Dawson's, do support his thesis. But there are also chapters or passages in the book in which Dawson has braved public obloquy and "mucked in" on the Fascist side, without accepting for a moment the Fascist totalitarian claim. Now we may both think that he was unwise, but we cannot say that this is "holding aloof". I know that Dawson does feel very passionately about European political struggles. About them he is not aloof . . . He is not really interested in English politics (but then I don't think Smyth is either, and that is one of my complaints about Demant and the Douglas creditors – Pre-1832 Toryism, or Social Credit, can be "escapes"). But Dawson's general philosophy of life and of history, as expressed e.g. in *Progress and Religion* and the *Modern Dilemma*, seems to me to recognize the immersion of the church in the muck of the world . . .

'If you "muck in" with the Tories on the basis of a common belief that politics is a way of getting things done, all the Christian Sociologists get terribly shocked. You must have a Christian theory of politics. But can you have a Christian theory of secular politics in a secular polis?'

2–C. H. Douglas (1879–1952), British engineer and economic theorist; proponent of 'social credit', promulgated in the 1930s as a panacea for the Depression.

TO *John Hayward*                                          TS King's

Friday the 13th [March 1936]          Faber & Faber Ltd

Dear John

I have just found that I have been suffering from an attack of
*dédoublement d'idées*, which has taken the form of promising to spend
Sunday and the night at the Morleys' – who have just returned from
America: I mean that I knew I was coming to you, but I did not think
of the two things at the same time. That occasionally happens to me.
I don't like to tell them I can't come after all, because I should not be
able to come for a fortnight: so could I dine with you another night? I am
free on Monday and on Wednesday and on Friday, only Wednesday and
Friday are fish nights – but on Tuesday I am to attend a dinner of those
notable gastronomes, the All Souls Club, at Lord Wolmer's[1] in Regents
Park, and should like to be able to report on it. I hate to put you out, but
it is difficult to put them off for a fortnight when they know I live within
a snail's constitutional of you, and presumably could see you on other
nights Whereas I can only see them at the weekend. If you will let me
come another night, I will appear in the Old School Tie, which Morley
bought in Boston for me: I can only wear it on very private occasions
during the period of national mourning, so dont say anything about it.
Also the collected poems. I am worried about Fred P.; I think someone
has discovered, or wrung out of him by torture, the cypher, and is using
it in his name. But more of that later. I have been persecuted by Mr Pierce
(of Buffalo) and Mr Mazower[2] (of Christ's) this afternoon, and am rather
distraught. Also by thrombosis or phlebitis.

                                        Abashedly,
                                        T.

I shall be at Russell Square in the morning, and may make so bold as to
ring you up.

---

1 – Roundell Cecil Palmer (1887–1971), Viscount Wolmer, 1895–41; Conservative politician
(MP for Aldershot, 1918–40); Minister for Economic Warfare (running the Special
Operations Executive), 1942–5. In 1940, on the death of his father, he became 3rd Earl of
Selborne.
2 – André Mazower: see Mark Mazower, *What You Did Not Tell: A Russian Past and the
Journey Home* (2017).

## TO *Polly Tandy* TS BL

14 March [1936]     Faber & Faber Ltd

Well now Sister this is bad news you have to give me. What with my gd.daughter gettiing heavier and heavier and yr. old man gettiing cussider and cussider and more ornery all the time not bein able to take his licker and terbacker reglar and proper and the licensee frettin and worryin over my health as is right and proper he should, things must be pretty puny down your way and I reckon its about time you got the Rev. Murray to come and pray over him and if the Rev. Murray aint capable of exorcism you let me know and I'll look out somebody what can come and pray very powerful. I am remarkable sorry I aint been able to run down to Mllsex with some spiritual comfort more especially of the Irish sort not a bead a told till it's seven years old as they say in poetry[1] but one thing after another and now I had to spend this Saturday night at the Yorkshire Castle playin French Billiards as they call it with Bill Empson and a Russian fellar of the blond variety[2] and Tomorrow have to Go to Surrey to those Morleys who have recently returned from the U.S.A. full of vulgarity. If that Coon don't improve well I shall come down for the day on today fortnight well provided with fore-fire I mean works this is serious regards to the licensee so with most affectnate wishes whill now close your faithful & obedneint and prudent
                                POSSUM Love to all so will close[3]
Enc.


## TO *W. H. Auden*[4]

17 March 1936     [Faber & Faber Ltd]

Dear Wystan,

    Thank you for sending Act I of *The Infernal Machine*.[5] I shall be interested in this, although I shall have to make enquiries to find out

---

1–The advertising jingle 'Not a drop is sold till it's seven years old' was launched *c.* 1928 by the Dublin distillers John Jameson & Sons.

2–Igor Vinogradoff (1901–87), historian; son of Sir Paul Vinogradoff.

3–TSE inscribed a pre-publication copy of *Collected Poems 1909–1935*: 'To G. and Polly Tandy, comp[limen]ts. of Possum. 31.iii.36.' (Peter Harrington catalogue 128: Christmas 2016) The official publication date of the volume was 2 Apr.

4–W. H. Auden (1907–73), poet, playwright, librettist, translator, essayist, editor: see Biographical Register.

5–WHA wrote in an undated note: 'Dear Tom, (if I may) / A friend of mine is translating Cocteau's *La Machine Infernale*. Here is the first act in case Faber's are interested.'

115

whether there will be any demand for a translation. Also I shall have to get hold of a copy of the text, in order to form an opinion of this translation. I suppose you are just off for Portugal or the Levant, and hope to hear from you from there.

Yours ever,<br>[Tom]

## FROM *Vivien Eliot*[1] TO *Geoffrey Faber*     MS Bodleian

17 March 1936

The Three Arts Club,
19A Marylebone Road,
London N.W.1

Dear Geoffrey,

The Three Arts Club sent an invitation to Tom, and to sixteen other people, to the Private View of their Spring Exhibition. As a letter for Tom, forwarded from The Mercury Theatre to 24 Russell Square was returned to The Mercury Theatre (apart from various other instances of similar kind) I thought it safer to send it to your private address, where, Care of you, I supposed you would certainly see to it that Tom received it.

I dislike this sort of business more than I can say, and why time should be wasted and annoyance caused by needless acts of rudeness and hostility is more than I can understand.

However, I feel obliged to return you this card of invitation, asking you either to see that Tom (T. S. Eliot) receives it, or else that you will give me an explanation. I sent one of these cards to you and Enid, under separate cover, and I had a civil reply from Enid, who said that she would go.

The point of the whole thing is that The Three Arts Club have hung 2 of my sketches, and that The Private View was opened by Mark Gertler.

It seems too unnecessary to point out that Tom is the same man with whom you dined here, more than once. He is the same man who has been your Director for twelve years at least. He is good enough to be a Director of your Firm, a Godfather to your child. Isn't he good enough for you to take the trouble to forward a card of invitation to an Exhibition of Pictures?

Yours sincerely,<br>[Vivien Haigh-Wood Eliot]

1 – Vivien Eliot, née Haigh-Wood (1888–1947), wife of TSE: see Biographical Register.

P.S. I have not seen you or Enid since November 18th. If you see any point in seeing me, now, or at any time, if you like to write to the Club and give me an appointment, I will come to the Office to see you willingly.

## FROM *Geoffrey Faber* TO *Vivien Eliot*          MS Bodleian

[?18 March 1936][1]                    Faber & Faber Ltd

My dear Vivienne,
    I cannot blame you for accusing me of not forwarding your letter to T. S. E. But I am innocent. I handed it to him myself. What happened to it after that is not my responsibility.

                                   Yours sincerely
                                   Geoffrey Faber

## TO *The Editor,* New English Weekly

[Published 19 March 1936, 451]

        'The Church as Action: Note on a Recent Correspondence'
I should like to rectify a small error, for the existence of which I cannot wholly disclaim responsibility. In a recent letter in your columns, Mr Desmond Hawkins said: 'If, as Mr T. S. Eliot's Lambeth essay suggests, the Church has decided to go to earth during a new Dark Age . . .'[2] Mr Barlow, writing a week later, does not mention my name, but he says, apparently following Mr Hawkins: 'If in fact the Church has gone into hiding against the advent of a new dark age . . .' While I was glad to see Mr Barlow using lower case, instead of Mr Hawkins's capitals, I am still apprehensive, because even a trifling or commonplace figure of speech may make mischief. What I wrote, in 1930, is this:–

---

1 – Actually dated 14 March, but presumably in error since it must post-date VHE's letter of 17 March.
2 – A. Desmond Hawkins, in his letter (*NEW* 8: 18 [13 Feb. 1936], 360), held that the Church is 'a disintegrating form' corrupted into bloodlessness: 'What I am trailing my coat for is an agreement among Christians to define and apply what is left of their dogma . . . Whatever the Church may possess it certainly lacks an ordering intelligence among its accredited doctors . . .
    'I hope some of your Christian readers will assist us by isolating for our instruction what is now *vital* and specifically *Christian*. What I want to assess is the kind of impact on society that can be expected from any possible contemporary Christianity. If, as Mr T. S. Eliot's Lambeth essay suggests, the Church has decided to go to earth during a new Dark Age, then the question becomes a private one and need be discussed no further.'

'The world is trying the experiment of attempting to form a civilized but non-Christian mentality. The experiment will fail; but we must be very patient in awaiting its collapse; meanwhile redeeming the time: so that the Faith may be preserved alive through the dark ages before us; to renew and rebuild civilization, and save the world from suicide.'[1]

Obviously, the parallel which the term 'dark ages' suggests, fails when it is closely applied. There is not much likeness between the situation of Christianity in Merovingian times, and its situation today. And within whatever dates we define the 'dark ages', the Church was hardly 'in hiding', or 'gone to earth'. These terms are more aptly applied to the period of the catacombs, to which Mr Eric Gill, in one of his books, drew a prophetic parallel.[2]

Mr Gill's parallel is much better of the two, if one takes as sombre a view as he does. But I did not say that the Church has gone into hiding, or even that it had 'decided' to 'go to earth'; I did not even prophesy that it would go into hiding; I did not recommend that it should go into hiding. The Church is less in hiding than it was during most of the eighteenth century; it is less hidden, I believe, today than it was in 1910, in which year neither I nor Mr Hawkins nor Mr Barlow (had we all arrived at that date at our present state of maturity) would have been likely to be writing letters about it. I think it is a good sign that much more appears to be *expected* of the Church today than in the past. Mr Barlow and Mr Hawkins cannot realize the difference so well as I do; and older men still can realize it more clearly than I. And such animation as is shown in the wrangling about tithes, and a more inquisitive curiosity about the Eccesiastical Commission, should give reason for hope rather than for despondency. In mentioning tithes, it occurs to me to remark that the exhibition of the Church in the role of enemy of the people may as easily serve Fascist ends as Communist.

One difference which I think it is worthwhile to be clear about, and which has not emerged so far from the discussion in these columns, is that this subject, discussed from different points of view, is not quite the same subject. The point of view of a person really 'inside' (by which I mean a regular communicant, not merely a person who has been baptized and confirmed) and that of a person outside must be different. And of those outside there are several kinds: there is the devout non-conformist, there is the person who regards Christianity with mild disapproval as

1 – *Thoughts After Lambeth* (1931). Hawkins, in 'The Church as Action' (letter), *NEW* 8: 26 (9 Apr. 1936), 523, apologised to TSE for the carelessness of his 'slipshod' memory.
2 – For Gill, see letter of 4 Feb. 1937.

an anachronism, and there is the person who regards it with hostility. And there is another type, which appears to be more recent, and more significant: it is the type of person who is not a churchman, nor even a believer, but who looks sometimes wistfully and sometimes angrily towards the Church, appealing to it to *do* something. Of such, within narrow limits, is Mr Pound; and of such, in a wider, more sympathetic and less secular frame of mind, are Mr Hawkins and Mr Barlow.

It makes all the difference, then, whether you regard the Church in the light of its historical vocation, and are concerned primarily with what it is *for*, or whether you merely take it in its visible form today, and ask what it *does*. From the first point of view, all this talk about boy scouts and tea meetings is trifling. Whether boy-scouting is good, or whether it militarizes, is a practical question: after all, something must be done for children, and if you do not approve of scouting you can try to think of something better. In congregations which consist of old ladies, tea meetings are a natural activity; and I do not see why the old ladies (some of them pretty lonely ones) should be deprived of their tea meetings. It is not their fault if they constitute the whole congregation. I think too, that people outside of the Church are apt to think of the Church as the contents of Crockford: as the actual clergy and the actual bench of Bishops. I am not concerned at this point to defend either clergy or bishops, though I think outsiders are sometimes apt to measure them against a romantically high standard of holiness. The point is that if you regard the Church first as the means of providing the Sacraments, and if you regard these Sacraments as essential, then your criticism of the Church's other activities, or of its supineness or of its weakness, will be different from the criticism of those who are not concerned with the Sacraments. I do not mean that your criticism will be less severe – it may be more severe through being better informed. I do not mean that you condone usury, or erastianism, or any of the abuses inside or outside. I should like to ask certain critics of the Church: 'If the Church were cleansed of all the filth you see in it, if it perfected itself so that you would have to admit that none of your criticisms still held good, what then would be your attitude towards it? Would you regard it as a beautiful and most desirable fraud, for the purpose of deluding a part of humanity for the benefit of the whole? Or would you then believe?' If they then 'believed', I should say that they were really believing something else than what the Church asks them to believe, and that they had come inside for the wrong reason – and on a most precarious basis, for they would claim the right to detach themselves again the moment the least sign of weakness or corruption recurred.

TO *Sylvia Beach*[1]

20 March 1936                         Faber & Faber Ltd

Dear Miss Beach,

I have put up to my committee your suggestion about our taking over
from you the stock of *Exagmination*. While it was not thought we should
be likely to sell very many copies, the general feeling was that we should be
glad to undertake a certain responsibility in connection with such a book,
and that we ought, if we can agree with you upon terms, to obtain the
remaining stock from you. The offer which the Chairman has authorized
me to make is £10 for the existing stock, in addition to which we would
pay for the carriage from Paris to London. We should on these terms want
the cover block, and we should ask you to get the French printers to make
at our expense a cancel title page. We cannot do that here because of the
difficulty of obtaining in England the kind of paper on which the book is
printed.

I hope that this suggestion will appeal to you. It was a great pleasure
to see you the other day, and I look forward in the hope of seeing you in
Paris, and of being able to give the reading there.[2]

                              Yours very sincerely,
                              T. S. Eliot


TO *James Joyce*                                            CC

20 March 1936                         [Faber & Faber Ltd]

My dear Joyce,

We are quite ready to start setting up *Work in Progress*. Indeed I find
that this work might have been begun some time ago, and the reason why

---

1 – Sylvia Beach (1887–1962), American expatriate who opened in Nov. 1919 (with Adrienne
Monnier) Shakespeare & Company, a bookshop and lending library, at 8 rue Dupuytren,
Paris, moving two years later to 12 rue de l'Odéon. Her customers included JJ (she published
*Ulysses*), Gide, Maurois, Valéry, EP, Hemingway and Stein. TSE wrote in tribute ('Miss
Sylvia Beach', *The Times*, 13 Oct. 1962): 'I made the acquaintance of Sylvia Beach, and . . .
Adrienne Monnier, on a visit to Paris early in the 1920s, and thereafter saw them frequently
during that decade. Only the scattered survivors of the Franco-Anglo-American world of
Paris of that period, and a few others like myself who made frequent excursions across the
Channel, know how important a part these two women played in the artistic and intellectual
life of those years.' See Beach, *Shakespeare and Company* (1960); *The Letters of Sylvia
Beach*, ed. Keri Walsh (2010); *James Joyce's Letters to Sylvia Beach 1921–1940*, ed. Melissa
Banta and Oscar A. Silverman (1987).
2 – Beach had arranged to call on TSE when she visited London to see *MiC* on Sat. 14 Mar.

nothing has been done is that you have never returned any of the copies of the specimen page which have been sent to you for approval. I enclose another copy, and shall be glad if you could let me know quite soon that you accept it. We are all agreed that this is the best lay-out of those which have been tried. The volume, so far as can be estimated, would run to about 600 pages in this size of type. The larger size would make the book at least 800 pages. It also seemed to us that having more matter on one page, as you do with this type, actually makes it easier to read. I hope you will find it as satisfactory as I do.

I have been glad to get a little news of you from Stewart [*sic*] Gilbert and Sylvia Beach. I hope to get over to Paris for a few days about the end of April, and I trust you will be there then.

With kindest regards to Mrs Joyce and Lucia.

Yours ever,

[T. S. Eliot]

## TO *Herbert Read* TS Victoria

20 March 1936            *The Criterion*

Dear Herbert,

I was sorry to miss you the other day at the club, but I am looking forward to seeing you both next week. It is true that I have always had a high opinion of Hofmannsthal, and that I did at one time entertain the notion of translating one of his plays.[1] I should still like to do it sooner or

---

1–HR wrote, 16 Mar.: 'I seem to remember that you are interested in Hofmannsthal and even contemplated translating one of his plays. About a week ago I met his daughter and her husband, Professor für Sanskrit Heinrich Zimmer of Heidelberg, and they asked me if I thought I could do anything about an English translation of the *Works*. The *Works* in 3 vols. have been sent to me and I feel impelled to do something about it. The main difficulty is a publisher, but Fabers would be ideal if you can persuade them. As for translators, if you would take on one play, I would take on another, and I think we could easily persuade Edwin Muir and Stephen Spender to do others. That would be a somewhat attractive team if we all came up to the scratch, and Hofmannsthal is surely a solid enough classic to merit a publisher's serious consideration.'

TSE had conceived the notion, in Dec. 1929, to translate what he called 'one or two [of the] Jacobean verse plays' of Hugo von Hofmannsthal (1874–1929) 'back into Jacobean': namely, *Die Hochzeit der Sobeide* and *Die Frau im Fenster*. TSE would later write: 'Yeats was very positively Irish and Protestant . . . Hofmannsthal was equally positively Austrian and Catholic – his Christianity was that of a practising Catholic . . . Hofmannsthal is worthy to stand with Yeats and with Claudel as one of the three men who did most, in the same age, to maintain and re-animate verse drama' ('Preface', Hofmannsthal, *Poems and Verse Plays*, ed. and introd. Michael Hamburger [New York, 1961], xi–xii).

later, but I don't feel that I ought to give the necessary time to such a job. It would simply mean deferring any original work of my own for several months. Candidly I don't feel that you have the time for the job either. Anyway, I'd rather you put the same time into your own poetry instead. It seems to me the sort of occupation that we might well take up after we are seventy. That of course is the dilemma about such works of translation, that the most suitable people to do them are also the people who ought not to spend the time on them, and I don't think that a translation by people who might just as well be translating as doing anything else would have any market. We will talk about this, but I am all for postponing it for another 20 or 25 years.

Yours ever,
T.

TO *Sylvia Beach*                                                      TS Princeton

24 March 1936                          Faber & Faber Ltd

Dear Miss Beach,

Thank you very much for your kind letter of the 21st instant.[1] I note that you have taken up with the printers the question of a cover block, and are getting from them an estimate of the costs of reprinting the title page. I suppose that for regularity's sake we ought to know your printer's price before definitely commissioning them to do the work, but meanwhile I send you, in order to save time, the title page with the necessary alterations. It should be pointed out to the printers that there is some alteration on the back of the page as well as on the front.

What we want replaced is only the leaf, not the whole sheet. And the best arrangement seems to us to be that you should have the printers send the title pages, when printed, to you in Paris, and you could then send on the books and the title pages together. We should certainly prefer to have the title pages inserted by our printers here.

---

1 – Beach had hoped for a larger payment from F&F (£10) for the stock of *Our Exagmination* – 'but I quite understand, too, that it is the best you can do in the circumstances, so I shall be glad to accept even so small an amount. It seems to me very desirable that the publishers of Mr Joyce's new work have this textbook on the subject, and I think he would be pleased.

'I will ask the printers in Chartres for the cover block, and for an estimate of the costs of reprinting the title page, if you will be so kind as to return the enclosed sheet with the corrections you wish to make.'

I think that these are the only business points to be dealt with at the moment. I look forward to seeing you again in April, and thank you for your very kind expression of enjoyment of my play.[1]

    With all good wishes,
    Yours very sincerely,
    T. S. Eliot

Miss Weaver has called and left the *Ulysses*, which is a very magnificent gift. I shall prize it accordingly. Thank you.[2]


## TO *Bonamy Dobrée*                                      CC

24 March 1936                    [Faber & Faber Ltd]

My dear Bonamy,

I was glad to get your letter of the 19th, to the points raised in which I shall reply later.[3] My reason for replying at once before I can reply fully is your remark that you are going to Havre, and I wanted to catch you before your departure. I am relieved to hear that Georgina[4] is convalescent. You must have been having a very harassing time with this illness coincident with your taking up your work at Leeds, of which I should like to hear more. You will be glad to hear that I have been hard at work on my Byron essay for you, and that it promises to be a fairly long essay according to my standards. I am actually enjoying it much more than the Milton for Herbert. One does not have to think quite as hard about Byron, and I am

---

1–'It was a very happy moment for me [on 14 Mar.] when you consented to give a reading for Shakespeare and Company. Such a proof of your interest in this place encouraged me a great deal in the struggle to keep it going in these times, and I felt very proud, and touched at your kindness. What an event the reading will be in Paris, and what a treat for your innumerable admirers over here! Is it true that you are working on a new long poem [*BN*], and would you be willing to read from it? We would love to hear even a piece of it . . .

'I can't tell you how much I admire your beautiful "Murder in the Cathedral"; it is by far the loveliest play of our time, and of such great inspiration from beginning to end! I wish I could hear it every night, but I am reading it over and over again. Miss Weaver will tell you how much she enjoyed it too.'

2–Beach had written: 'When I told [Harriet Weaver] I was going to give you a copy of "Ulysses" to replace the two you had stolen she said she wanted you to have an extra copy of her own edition that happened to be left.'

3–See TSE's letter to BD, 17 Apr., below.

4–The Dobrées' daughter Georgina (b. 1930).

getting some fun out of it. I propose to treat Byron as a Scotch rather than an English poet. This point of view, even if wrong, is, I think, a new one.[1]

Yours ever,
[T. S. E.]


## TO *Bruce Richmond*[2]                                                  cc

24 March 1936                                 [Faber & Faber Ltd]

My dear Richmond,

I have interested myself for some time in a White Russian émigré named Iovetz Tereschenko,[3] whose book *Friendship, Love and Adolescence*, has just been published by Allen and Unwin. It seems to me an interesting book that makes some points well worth making, and I feel that it is worth the attention of some psychologist who happens to be unprejudiced against religion, so I am taking the liberty of mentioning it to you, as it is a sort of book which easily gets overlooked.

Yours sincerely,
[T. S. Eliot]


## TO *Algar Thorold*[4]                                                  cc

24 March 1936                                 [*The Criterion*]

My dear Algar,

Thank you for your kind letter of March 21st. It was good also to see your handwriting again restored completely to its old appearance, and I

---

1 – TSE, 'Byron (1788–1824)', in *From Anne to Victoria: Essays by Various Hands*, ed. BD (1937), 601–19; repr., as 'Byron', in *OPP* (1957)

2 – Bruce Richmond (1871–1964), editor of the *TLS*: see Biographical Register.

3 – N. M. Iovetz-Tereshchenko (1895–1954), B.Litt. (Oxon), PhD (London): Russian exile; Orthodox Catholic Christian; university lecturer in psychology: see Biographical Register.

4 – Algar Thorold (1866–1936): editor of the *Dublin Review*. TSE wrote in a memorial note in *C.* (Oct. 1936, 68) that Thorold 'had been a frequent contributor [to the *Criterion*] since very early in our history: his knowledge especially of modern French philosophy and theology was invaluable. Having written very few books – his *Six Masters of Disillusion* [1909] has been out of print for many years – he was not known to a very wide public, and another generation will not be aware that *The Dublin Review*, under his editorship, was one of the most distinguished periodicals of its time. Being half-French by birth, and at the same time thoroughly English, with the culture of the past and the curiosity of the present, he held a position as a man of letters such that we could say of him, that he was the sort of man whom we could ill afford to lose.'

take this as an augury for your health. I look forward to your renewed activity in the matter of Gabriel Marcel.[1] I have not seen his new book, and indeed I owe most of my knowledge about him to yourself.

I am sorry that you had to return my book intempestatively to the London Library, and I am therefore sending you a copy with my best compliments.[2] Now about Pascal and miracles.[3] I am not sure that what I said arising from this point is perfectly orthodox, and I think that perhaps I should have stated it differently. But in any case, I am not accustomed to think of the Incarnation as a miracle in the ordinary sense. What I mean by a miracle is an event which is conceivably capable of repetition, and of being therefore different in kind from the Incarnation, which one might describe as supramiraculous, and having a significance as a unique historical event which sets it quite apart from what I call miraculous. The Incarnation not only happens to be a unique event, but by its nature can only be a unique event. Do you think that the foregoing remarks were worth making?

I am sorry to say that I cannot give any reference to Voltaire.[4] The essay is some years old, and I suppose that Voltaire turned up in some of the reading which I was doing at the moment. You will say that I ought to have made a note of this, and given the reference in my essay, and I shall entirely agree with you.

I hope that you will let me come out and see you again one day after Easter.

Ever yours,<br>
[T. S. Eliot]

1 – Thorold wrote that he hoped soon 'to get down to Gabriel Marcel for you. Have you seen his *Etre et avoir*? [1934] – quite recent & very important.' Gabriel Marcel (1889–1973), French philosopher and existentialist.

2 – 'My dear Tom (I am a survivor of a generation that was in the habit of using Xtian names, as between friends, when a special identity of aims & ideas existed. Since reading your new re-printed essays, wh I have unfortunately to send back almost at once to the London Library, I am convinced that this exists between us. Will you permit, pardon, and reciprocate?)'

3 – 'I think a point shd be elucidated in the "Pascal". About miracles. When you talk on p. 148 [*Essays Ancient and Modern*, 1936] of faith in Christ preceding belief in miracles & particularly modern miracles so that the latter are not the ground of the former, but vice-versa, you have already stated on p. 146 that the believer finds himself by "powerful and concurrent reasons" committed to the Incarnation.

'But surely the Incarnation cannot be conceived as non-miraculous? Julian Huxley wd admit a sort of "emergent variation". Perhaps I don't quite understand what you mean here?'

Blaise Pascal (1623–62), French mathematician and philosopher.

4 – 'Can you give me the reference in Voltaire to his refutation of Pascal?' Voltaire (born François-Marie Arouet; 1694–1778), French writer and philosopher.

26 March 1936                               [Faber & Faber Ltd]

My dear Brace,

At Morley's suggestion I am sending you three copies of my *Essays Ancient and Modern*, which we published on March 4th, for you to consider whether you could do anything with it in America. I must explain that the first five essays appeared in the volume *Lancelot Andrewes*, which was issued by Doubleday Doran. I think, however, that this has gone out of print, and that Doubleday Doran are no longer interested, and I am having that matter looked up.

None of the last five essays has been copyrighted in America by me, but it seems likely that the American publishers of *Pascal's Pensées* in the Everyman edition will have seen to that. I should be surprised if the book *Faith that Illuminates* had been taken in America at all.[1] In any case, as I have only had to make acknowledgements for these essays, and have not had to pay anything to either J. M. Dent or Nelsons, I see no reason why they should cost anything in New York.

If your firm should hear from the Old Colony Trust Company of Boston I hope that it will not be putting you to too much trouble to give them the information they want. The point is that I have not been making any return to Washington of income derived from American royalties on the ground that Income Tax has been paid at source. The Old Colony Trust Company now tell me that this income must be returned although there is nothing payable on it. What they will want to know will be the amounts which you have paid to me as royalties during 1934 and 1935.

Yours very sincerely,

[T. S. Eliot]

1 – TSE 'Religion and Literature', in *Faith that Illuminates*, ed. V. A. Demant (1935), 29–54.

TO *V. A. Demant*[1]

26 March 1936                    [Faber & Faber Ltd]

My dear Demant,

I have shown your letter of the 18th to my Committee and they wish me to express much interest in your outline for Collected Papers.[2] We should very much like to consider the book ourselves, and I should be glad if you would let me have, at your convenience, copies of all the essays you intend to include. It would be useful to know in advance whether you propose to alter any of them, or whether I may take it that you want them to be published very much as they appeared in the periodicals.

As for the preface by myself, I had better say in advance that that would be rather embarrassing. I have frequently declined to write prefaces, and in particular I refused Gabriel Herbert [*sc.* Hebert], who asked me to write a preface to *Liturgy and Society*. I must add at once that it is my opinion, and that of my fellow directors, that such prefaces are of negligible value for selling a book, and that they are indeed more likely to do harm than good. That is to say, they may give the impression that the author and publishers do not think the book strong enough to stand on its own feet, and believe that it needs every possible support.[3]

Wednesday is rather an awkward day for me, as we have a Committee Meeting here which begins at one o'clock and which is variable in its time of ending. If you are in London on Wednesday mornings we could make an appointment to meet, as I am not ordinarily here of a morning. If the morning does not suit you, I could make it a quarter to half past five.

Sincerely yours,

[T. S. Eliot]

1 – The Revd Vigo Auguste Demant (1893–1983), theologian: see Biographical Register.
2 – 'Reckitt and several other friends have urged me to collect some scattered essays and articles for publication in a volume. I wonder what your opinion of this would be . . .' He enclosed a list of nineteen essays – including 'The Doctrine of Creation', 'The Christian Doctrine of Freedom in Relation to secular Totalitarianism', 'Idolatry' – many of which had appeared in *Christendom*. On 14 May he put forward: 'Man and His Problems: Past and Present in the Light of Theology'.
3 – Demant's collection was to be published as *Christian Polity* (1936), with a blurb that was almost certainly composed by TSE: 'The author of this volume is an unorthodox economist and an orthodox theologian, whose originality, independence and forcefulness of thought have gained him a distinguished place in a field that is becoming more and more important.
'In this book he has collected a number of related essays which make both variety and unity. It should be read by all Christians, whether or not they know anything about economics and sociology, who are at all aware of the social implications of their faith; and by all persons interested in the future of society who are willing to hear what a Christian thinker has to say on the subject.'

TO *Ashley Dukes*[1]                                                    CC

26 March 1936                          [Faber & Faber Ltd]

Dear Dukes,

I could not report sooner in reply to your letter of the 12th, as I had to pass on *Babel* or *The Tower to Heaven* for another opinion after I had read it.[2] I should like to say first that we should whenever possible be very glad to co-operate by publishing plays put on at the Mercury Theatre, but this must be subject of course to our opinion on each play as it comes along, and I am obliged to say it seemed to me and to the other director who read it that *Babel* was simply not up to our literary standard. I have no doubt that it will be a good acting play, else you would not have considered it, but for the publishers its literary quality is quite as important as its dramatic quality, and the blank verse of *Babel* seemed to us completely uninspired and commonplace; so I am sorry to have to send the play back.

There is another matter which I have been meaning to mention to you. One of the original members of the chorus at Canterbury was Miss Diane Reeve. She was certainly quite one of the best in every way, and I understand she also was brilliantly successful at Miss Fogerty's school. She is now teaching in Sydney, Australia. She wrote to a friend of mine to say that she was very anxious to perform the play there, and also mentioned another woman with a peculiar name which I forget, who she said was anxious to do the play, and who she thought would not do it at all well. If you should hear from Diana Reeve I hope that you will give her the necessary permission, assuming of course that the financial terms are satisfactory. I do not know what sort of a production she has in mind, whether public or private, but I am sure that she would make a good job of it.

1–Ashley Dukes (1885–1959), theatre manager, playwright, critic, translator, author: see Biographical Register.
2–The Mercury Theatre was to mount a production – as the second play in their Poets' series – of *The Tower to Heaven*, by J. Redwood Anderson, in an abbreviated version by EMB entitled *Babel: A Dramatic Poem*. The play had been published in 1927 by Ernest Benn, but the copyright had now reverted, and Dukes wondered if F&F might be interested in republishing it.

Can you tell me anything about the arrangement with the people in New York who, I understand, have been producing *Murder in the Cathedral* at the Manhattan Theatre?[1]

Yours ever,
[T. S. Eliot]


TO *Paul Elmer More*[2]                                    TS Princeton

27 March 1936                    *The Criterion*

My dear More,

I have been meaning to write to you a proper letter for some time, but I have let so much time elapse that I think I had better dictate this note in the interval, to thank you for your letter of March 6th. It is good to see your handwriting, and I trust that you are recovering completely from your severe illness.

I am very happy that you like the essay on Religion and Literature, and especially the passage on page 93.[3] I think that what appears to another person to be a change of attitude and even a recantation of former views must often appear to the author himself rather as part of a continuous and more or less consistent development. Certainly my attitude in these matters is very different from what it was fifteen years ago, but I tend to

---

1–Dukes replied, 28 Mar.: 'The performances in New York at the Manhattan Theatre are those of the Federal Theatre Project about which I wrote to you from New York in January. They have asked by cable for a week's extension, and this has been arranged.'

*MiC*, staged by Halsted Welles and starring the veteran actor Harry Irvine as Becket, was produced by the Popular Price Theatre, at the Manhattan Theatre (Broadway and 53rd Street, New York City) for three weeks from 18 Mar.

The programme recorded: 'The Federal Theatre starts with the objective of employing theatre people in the profession for which they have been trained.

'The far reaching purpose is to establish theatres so vital to community life that they will continue to function after the Federal program is completed.'

2–Paul Elmer More (1864–1937), critic, scholar and writer; author of *Shelburne Essays*: see Biographical Register.

3–More (6 Mar.) had been thrilled by TSE's essay on 'Religion and Literature' (in *Essays Ancient and Modern*). 'May I say that your thesis, "The greatness of literature, etc", on page 93, seems to me absolutely sound . . . It is not, I venture to say, the thesis you maintained in your earlier critical writing when, in comparing Shakespeare and Dante, you appeared to have clung to the old romantic fallacy that a poem could be appreciated and enjoyed entirely apart from its content of ideas. I hope I am not misunderstanding you in this, since as a matter of fact I am now engaged in writing an essay on How to Read Lycidas, in which I quote you on Shakespeare and Dante and reject your conclusions; now I can supplement this, to me, erroneous judgement with your position in Religion and Literature which I heartily applaud.'

see it myself rather as a readjustment of values through a widening of interests.

I met P. S. Richards for the first time,[1] and spent a very pleasant weekend with him a few days ago at his hotel in Storrington, where he took you a few years ago. I found him a very agreeable companion, as well as a man of intelligence. I spoke to him about the article which he has written about you, and he will send me a copy when it appears in *Christendom*. I look forward to seeing it with a view to using it in the *Criterion*.[2]

This American *Christendom*, by the way, seems to me a badly edited paper in several vital respects. It is far too bulky, and the editor seems to aim at trying to be much too comprehensive and representative, instead of trying to form a small group of serious people with common aims.[3] I don't think anything will be accomplished by such a very blunt weapon as this. It is unfortunate also that they should have taken the name of an English periodical which has a very different character. Do you ever see the English *Christendom*? It has occasionally very good things in it, and two of the ablest young men in the Church, Charles Smyth and Brother George Every S.S.M., are occasional contributors.

I am just sending you my volume of collected poems, which is due to appear next week. Having produced this book so close on the heels of the volume of essays makes me feel for the moment as if I had been preparing for a dignified retirement, or at least postponing further literary work until another janma.[4]

Yours ever sincerely,
T. S. Eliot

---

1 – More had recently read an essay on his own religious philosophy by P. S. Richards which struck him as 'a beautiful piece of work': it was to appear in the 'hole-in-the-corner' American *Christendom* – 'practically buried' – but More hoped it might come out also in the *Criterion*.

2 – P. S. Richards, 'The Religious Philosophy of Paul Elmer More', C. 16 (Jan. 1937), 205–19. See also letter to Richards, 30 May 1936.

3 – The editor of *Christendom* was Dr Charles Clayton Morrison (1874–1966), an American Disciples of Christ minister and Christian socialist who salvaged the *Christian Century* in 1908.

4 – *Janma*: birth (Sanskrit).

27 March 1936                     Faber & Faber Ltd

Dear Sir,

Your circular letter of the 16th instant tempts me to write to ask whether the Academic Assistance Council is at present in a position to consider new cases.[2] I have in mind a Russian scholar, Dr Iovetz Tereshchenko, whose book *Friendship-Love in Adolescence* has just been published by Allen & Unwin, and who is having great difficulty in supporting himself, his mother, his wife, and two children. He obtains enough work in giving extension courses in psychology to maintain him from October to April, but his prospects from the end of this month until next October are of nothing but destitution. If the Council is in the position to consider any aid for such a man, I should be grateful. He would be very glad to supplement his income by giving Russian lessons, but I am not in a position to put him in touch with possible pupils.

                    Yours faithfully,
                    [T. S. Eliot]

1 – Walter Adams, General Secretary, Academic Assistance Council.
2 – Adams had posted out a copy of the appeal by Lord Rutherford of Nelson, President of the Academic Assistance Council, for support for the establishment of a Society for the Protection of Science and Learning. Formed in May 1933, the Academic Assistance Council assisted scholars and scientists who, on grounds of religion, race or opinion, were unable to continue their work in their own countries. It had focused its work on helping the 1,300 university teachers displaced in Germany, but it also assisted refugee scholars from Russia, Portugal and other countries. In cooperation with other organisations, it had assisted in permanently re-establishing 363 of the 700 displaced scholars who had left Germany.

## TO *Geoffrey Grigson*[1]                                  TS Texas

27 March 1936                              Faber & Faber Ltd

My dear Grigson,

I went through your *New Verse Anthology* on its arrival,[2] but it had to be examined by others also, and we were not able to have a full discussion until this last Wednesday. There is nothing wrong with the anthology as an anthology, but circumstances have rather changed since last September, when we first discussed the matter. The present moment seems to us a very bad one for launching any new anthology of contemporary verse. Including Michael Roberts's, there are now three on the market, which have been largely reviewed together, and Yeats's, which will certainly confirm [*sc.* contain] a fair amount of contemporary stuff, may come out at any moment. While there are, of course, several interesting authors in your anthology who are not represented in any of the others, we don't feel inclined to undertake another anthology at the present time. Indeed, it is my private opinion that you would be well advised to defer consideration for another year. By that time you would presumably have new poems to include, and would possibly omit a few of those already included. I do think that such an anthology would have a much better chance of sale a year or two hence than it would now. Coming out later it could be presented much more as an up-to-date appendix to existing anthologies, whereas coming out in the near future it would give the impression of too nearly covering the same ground.[3]

                                          Yours sincerely,
                                          T. S. Eliot


## TO *John Hayward*                                        TS King's

2 April 1936                              Faber & Faber Ltd

My dear John,

Dining the other night with some Bright Young People (of whom more anon) I fell in with a Friend of yours named Primrose (I think)

---

1 – Geoffrey Grigson (1905–85) – poet, author, critic; editor of *New Verse*, 1933–9.
2 – Grigson wrote on 19 Feb.: 'Here is the "New Verse" selection . . . This selection only covers the first three years. If Fabers decided to publish it, I can add a two-page introduction.'
3 – See *New Verse: An Anthology*, ed. Grigson (F&F, 1939). Grigson, 'Recollections of "New Verse"', *TLS*, 25 Apr. 1968.

Harley,[1] who fell into an admiration of you, and in particular of your epistles. Yours of even date is an example. I presume that your reference to the organ is an allusion to that Gilbertian character, Master Bates, who practised every evening upon that instrument. But my mind is a little mazed, because I had this afternoon to interview an elderly Scottish gentleman who has written a book explaining Shakespeare's Sonnets. Do you know why I brought it to you, said he. No, said I. Because your name is Eliot, said he. A good reason, said I, but there must be more behind that than meets the eye (SHORT p. 887, line 32). There is, said he, my mother was an Elliot of Galloway; and I heard you lecture to the Shakespeare Association, and I said, that man is a true El(l)iot – he is obviously hot tempered, obstinate, and determined to disagree with everybody. But, said I, in some confusion, I am afraid that that is a different family – my people come from the West Country. Just so, said he, the El(l)iots are all descended from Michel de Aliot who arrived in England exactly at the right hand of Wm. the Conqueror, and when Wm. stumbled on the beach at Hastings the said Michel remarked 'the land of England is rising to greet you'. Well, said I, I never heard of that before, but if so he certainly deserved something for that wisecrack. Just so, said my new friend, he obtained a number of manors in Northamptonshire, and from there the El(l)iots spread into Devonshire and Galloway. Well well, I said, I never supposed that the family was so widespread or of such antiquity. Just so, he said. You can always recognise an El(l)iot. Why, he said, the other day in Scotland, I had to take a pair of shoes to be repaired; and the cobbler started to argue with me about it. I said, your name must be El(l)iot. Why, said he (I cannot reproduce the Doric) how'd'ye ken? Yes, said he, you can always tell an El(l)iot – they have blue eyes (here I remained silent) and they will always disagree with everything. So now do you think that your firm would reconsider publishing my essay – the fruit of three years concentrated labour – on Shakespeare? Well, said I, we have to do with obdurate people, and I am only one of five, and we none of us gets everything that we want. Well, said he, do you mind the Elliot marching song?[2] Yes said I, it begins

1 – Primrose Harley (1908–78), painter and engraver (her father was a wealthy doctor whose family had given their name to Harley Street, London).
2 – '"The Marching Song of the Pollicle Dogs" was written to the tune of "The Elliots of Minto"' (EVE, 'Apropos of *Practical Cats*', in *Cats: The Book of the Musical* [NY, 1983], 8). See too TSE to Graham Fletcher (EVE's nephew), 25 June 1963: 'No, I haven't written any more Cats. There are a few creatures however which I have not published, one I like is called *Marching Song of the Pollicle Dogs*' (Graham Fletcher).

My name it is little Jock Elliot

And wha maun meddle wi' me?[1]

Ah ye ken it fine, said he, that shows that ye are a true Elliot. I am afraid that I read it somewhere, I said, I don't know the tune. Ah man it's a graun tune, he said, but I can see ye are a true Elliot. Now aboot Shakespeare. Well, I said, here's our coat of arms, I suppose it's the same? Not precisely, says he, but it's something like, and the motto is Per saxa et ignes. That's not our motto, I says, our mottoe is different.[2] That doesn't matter, says he; all El(l)iots are hot tempered, obstinate, and disagree with everybody. Well, said I, for my pot of tea was waiting in the background, I hope we may meet again. That we must, says he, and I hope you lunch or dine with me at the National Club, in Queen Anne's Gate, of which I am a member.

Well now I look forward to seeing you on Sunday evening, and please don't mention Shakespeare.

Yrs etc.

T.P.

1 – Quoted from a supposedly lost Border Ballad, or song, entitled 'Little Jock Elliott' (the story goes that in 1566 John (Jock) Elliot wounded James Hepburn, 4th Earl of Bothwell, who was attempting to arrest him for crimes he had committed as a 'reiver' – a marauder or plunderer – and that in consequence Mary Queen of Scots fell ill with pneumonia after a very long, hectic, exhausting journey across terrible terrain to see Bothwell, her possibly fatally wounded lover.)

The first of the seven stanzas of the ballad closes:

Oh my name it is Little Jock Elliot

And wha daur meddle wi' me?

TSE assumed that chorus in the final lines of 'The Marching Song of the Pollicle Dogs': 'Yet my name it is Little Tom Pollicle, / And WHA MAUN MEDDLE WI' ME?' Arthur Rogers asked TSE, 14 Mar. 1946: 'In the last line why "Wha Maun Meddle Wi' Me"? The original is surely "Daur" and what Scotsman would say Maun for Daur!' TSE to Rogers, 20 Mar. 1946: 'I do not pretend to be an expert in the Northern language and it may be that I have been guilty of a howler of the grossest kind . . . I only know that it was *maun* in a typed copy of the "Ballad of Little Jock Elliot" which somebody showed me years ago. I admit that I was puzzled by this word which is certainly used much further South and *daur* seems to me, on the face of it, much more probable. If I ever reprint my poem I shall certainly get it vetted by one of my Scottish friends. Many thanks for the admonition.' See further *Poems*, ed. Ricks & McCue, 1207.

2 – See TSE's letter to Samuel Eliot (Boston, Mass.), 31 Mar. 1951 – concerning Samuel Eliot's great uncle – 'It was also welcome to have a copy of his bookplate. I notice that the motto is different from ours (*Tace et fac*, I believe a variant made by my grandfather on the *Tace aut Fac* which was used in the sixteenth century); but that you also turn the elephant's nose up, whereas the Eliots in Cornwall turn it down, as if about to eat a peanut' (Houghton).

TO *Ezra Pound*                                                    TS Beinecke

2 April 1936                    Faber & Faber Ltd

Ras Ez: Certainly, I don't know who your friend is, but if he would like
to send the Criterion an article on Andrewes, Id be delighted.[1] It is more
than likely that he knows a lot more about Andrewes than I do, and
certainly more than I did when I wrote that article of mine, because it is a
human weakness to write about things first and learn about them, if at all,
afterwards. Besides, lemme point out that I wrote a LONG TIME AGO,
and that 10 years is a Decade. Tell him to shoot.[2]

Now about your essays they are still with the Big Fellow[3] who is
wrastlin with em, but I must say you dont quite realise that publishers
have a busy life what tho' there be little to show for it on acct. of a large
proportion of time being spent acting as psychiatrists, labour exchange,
school of journalism and authorship, spiritual legal & medical advisers
and soup kitchen; AND you do hide your gems in about as much muck
of disorderly mss. as Possible and a neat ms. is better than rubies.[4] Never
Mind, but I wd. like to see about 30 mo cantoes & trust you still have a
little time left for that from other activities and one or two in the Criterion
from time to time might help to keep yr name green but our flat rate is a
pount a page and no exceptions.

Possibility of my visiting France's green & pleasant land about end of
this month. Dont suppose you can get that far north and I cant afford to
go fur south.

---

1–EP wrote, 27 Mar.: 'Too bad while you were resurrectin Launcelot Andrews [*sic*] you
didn't READ him.

'Dare say this treatin the bloke as a perlite stylist wuz only way to get into the extremely
LOW mental circles which pay the printers, but still/ he seems to have been better man than
you thought / and you cd NOW venture to boost him for his insides as well as his sentence
structure . . . Meet me fledgloing parson Mr Swabey.'

2–See Henry S. Swabey, 'The English Church and Money', C. 16 (July 1937), 619–37.

On Swabey, see A. David Moody, *Ezra Pound: Poet: A Portrait of the Man & his Work*:
II: *The Epic Years 1921–1939* (2014), 205-7. See too Swabey, 'A Page without Which . . .'
(memoir of EP), *Paideuma* 5: 2 (Fall 1976), 329–37.

3–FVM.

4–Cf. *Proverbs* 3: 15: 'She is more precious than rubies: and all the things thou canst desire
are not to be compared unto her.' *Proverbs* 31: 10: 'Who can find a virtuous woman? for
her price is far above rubies.'

Porteus [*sic*] keen about Fenellosa [*sic*].[1] Good job of Knott's.[2] Chandos group becoming rather more interesting lately.[3] Demant most intelligent of the lot, I think.

yrs
Tp

Am writing to Roberts.

## TO *Geoffrey Curtis*

2 April 1936                                  Faber & Faber Ltd

My dear Curtis,

You know that I am a fitful correspondent, with no conscience whatever (apparently) about answering letters; but I am moved to write to you, returning your paper, before Holy Week. I am in accord with all that you say, I think.[4] It would be irrational to take the 'tepidity' which we find offensive as a sign of any invalidity of the Anglican Church; and the more we examine the causes of this weakness the less irreparable it appears to be. And I believe that a fair examination all round should move us more cheerfully to cultivate our own garden, rather than abandon it. I must personally allow for dispositions of my own, also – accidents of biography, and natural intransigence, and a certain sympathy for the Latin mind – which incline me towards an extreme. But I think that the distinction between tepidity, which is the absence of something necessary, and moderation, which implies to me the control of something excessive, might be drawn more drastically. Moderation in the Church means the discipline of the extreme and fanatical members, as well as of the lax, worldly and indulgent. Real moderation in the individual also implies the presence of some ardour to be restrained. My grumble was not exactly

---

1–Norman W. Porteous (1898–2003), Scottish theologian. Ernest Fenollosa (1853–1908), author of *The Chinese Written Character as a Medium for Poetry*.

2–*Sc.* Nott's.

3–The Chandos Group, which took its name from the restaurant where the group first gathered, was founded in 1926, and met in early years to discuss the sociological implications of economic thinking, notably Social Credit; later, under the informal leadership of Maurice Reckitt, the group – whose most regular participants included the journalist Travers Symons, Philip Mairet (editor of *Purpose*), the American psychologist Alan Porter, and the Revd V. A. Demant, Dirctor of Research at the Christian Social Council – discussed aspects of Christian Sociology. See Mairet's account of Chandos in *T. S. Eliot: A Symposium for his Seventieth Birthday*, ed. Neville Braybrooke (1958). 'T. S. E. once lampooned us all in clerihews.'

4–The enclosed paper has not been identified.

against the Church, it was rather an expression of regret that there should not be individual members with more zeal towards the ascetic and the contemplative life. I do not approve of extreme mortification of the flesh – taking heaven by negative physical means – but I like to think that men should sometimes be impelled in this direction, and then 'moderated'. A man like Foucauld,[1] however different he is from any of the Frenchmen one has known, represents somehow a continued potency in the race; he truly operates for the salvation of the world, but of his own race primarily, in practice. If I say that England needs English saints, this is not to be taken as an addiction to the race heresy of our time![2]

I should agree that St John of the Cross illustrates admirably the 'via media' – though the 'via media' is not quite the same thing for a man of his genius, intensity and spiritual stature that it is for ordinary souls. There is danger, I think, in preaching a sort of democracy of moderation, in which all should be drilled to walk at the same pace.

I offer for you my prayers for a good Holy Week and a happy Easter, & ask for yours.

Affectionately,
T. S. Eliot


TO *Michael Roberts*[3]                                               TS Berg

2 April 1936                        Faber & Faber Ltd

Dear Roberts,

More trouble. We have just heard from the agent Pollinger that Pound is complaining about the inclusion of nine of his poems in the anthology instead of five.[4] It appears that he reckons the 'Mauberley' selection as

---

1–Charles de Foucauld (1858–1916), priest, hermit and martyr; beatified in 2005.
2–Curtis had written (1 Mar.) in response to TSE's last letter: 'I thank God for your love of de Foucauld. Yet with regard to all that side of things, I am more and more convinced that ecclesia anglicana is all that George Herbert believed. How interesting in reading Bruno's life to find Saint John of the Cross specially characterised as the saint of the "Via media"!

'We shall yet see in this land Walter Hilton's & Mother Julian's children finding their way into & through the "Cloud of Unknowing" with a security of step such as will prove to the world that Moderation is a positive & evangelical quality such as renders man connatural to the mind of Christ . . . But how this would shock P.E.M. [Paul Elmer More]! Is it true that he has become an Anglican? If so will he of his charity reread the mystics as an act of penance for heresy overcome?'
3–Michael Roberts (1902–48), critic, editor, teacher, poet: see Biographical Register.
4–EP to Pollinger, 10 March (1936): 'Have you a record of the terms for Fabers Modern Verse. ? I thought they were using FIVE poems but find they have included NINE.

'Mauberley is NOT ONE poem; but a series.'

five poems instead of one. I don't know how anyone was to have known that, and I don't quite know what we are going to do about it, but I should be glad if you could let me have any information and quotations bearing on the matter from your correspondence with Pound or with Pollinger. Is there any evidence that he considered the 'Mauberley' to be five poems instead of one?[1]

Yours ever,<br>T. S. Eliot

P.S. I hope you will find the Tate book suitable to go with the Blackmur.[2]

## TO *Sylvia Beach*

TS Princeton

2 April 1936                          Faber & Faber Ltd

Dear Miss Beach,

Thank you for your letter of March 31st enclosing the letter to you from the Imprimerie Durand, which I return herewith.[3] The price of 145 francs seems quite reasonable to us, and we should be glad if you would authorize the printers to proceed.

I will try to let you know within the next ten days definitely about the visit at the end of April.[4] There seems to be a remote possibility of my

---

'My summer files are not in order; as I was traveling about, but I dont remember a concession, though I wont swear that after a LONG and persistent and BORING correspondence I may not have given way, but I can't REMEMBER doing it.'

EP to Roberts ('10 or 11 Sept. anno XIII [1935]'): 'Right you are. Herewith permission granted to use five poems listed in yrs. of 8th inst. in forthcomin' Faber anthology at terms there stated.'

1–Roberts answered on 17 Apr.: 'The five sections from Mauberley have only one entry (E. P. Ode pour l'election . . .) in the table of contents of his selected poems. I think, but I cannot be sure at the moment, that I mentioned the pages and/or the numbers of the sections when I wrote to him & finally obtained his permission. He might equally well count "Near Perigord" as 3 poems, since it is in three sections. I shall be back in about 10 days, & I'll ring you up then.'

EP had written to TSE, 26 Mar.: 'Hope Pol [Pollinger] is suin the FIRM for those extra poems bootlegged by what his name, unless I agreed in a weak *AND FORGOTTEN* moment.'

2–Roberts, 17 Apr.: 'I haven't seen Tate's book yet, but when I saw it announced I thought of asking for it, to review with Blackmur. I have already written a review of Blackmur, which may have been sent to you: if so, disregard it. I was dissatisfied with it.' Roberts on R. P. Blackmur, *The Double Agent*, and Allen Tate, *Reactionary Essays*: *C.* 15 (July 1936), 702–5.

3–The printers Imprimerie Durand of Chartres estimated a cost of 145 francs for printing a new title page for *Our Exagmination*.

4–'We are so happy to think that you are going to read here, and Adrienne Monnier asks, although we do not want, for anything on earth to hurry you in your plans, if you could set a date for the reading soon so that she may begin to make arrangements for it.'

play being produced two or three times in Paris some time in May, and if that should be settled within the next week I should naturally like to make my visit coincide, but it is quite likely that nothing will come of it. I hope you have received the copy of my collected poems which I sent to you.[1]

Yours sincerely,
T. S. Eliot

TO *Donald Brace*                                                                                   CC

2 April 1936                                          [Faber & Faber Ltd]

Dear Brace,

Many thanks for your letter of the 23rd enclosing cuttings of the critics' notices of *Murder in the Cathedral*. I also had a good deal of misgiving about the production and I am delighted to hear from you personally as well as from the newspapers, that it can be pronounced a success. Ashley Dukes appears to be pleased about it. I hope that the success of the production will also send up your sales.[2]

I don't believe that you have been sent a copy of the second edition, which you will observe is altered by the substitution of a chorus for the beginning of Act II. This second edition gives the text as it has been

1–TSE had overlooked the last sentence of Beach's letter of 31 Mar.: 'I was very much excited to see your "Collected Poems" arriving.' She wrote again on 4 Apr.: 'Thank you so much for the copy of "Collected Poems" that you were so kind as to inscribe for me. Among the many Eliot lovers, I don't believe there is one who has followed your writing closer nor love it more than I.' She added in a postscript to the latter letter that she wished to acquire a photograph of him.

2–Brace wrote, 23 Mar.: 'Several of us went last Friday evening to see the first performance of *Murder in the Cathedral* as produced by the Federal Theatre Project. I am enclosing clippings of the notices I have seen, also a program . . . The play was beautifully staged . . . The performance was extraordinarily fine; the Becket was good and many of the minor parts were extraordinarily well done, particularly the male ones. I think you would have been delighted with it. We hear from the theatre that the play is a hit . . . For me, the performance was a moving and beautiful experience, and I do hope the play may have a further career here beyond this limited production.'

F. O. Matthiessen considered the New York production 'one of the great successes of the WPA theatre': 'the Chorus was handled by dividing its line among several individual speakers, and . . . Harry Irvine's interpretation brought more vitality to the title role than the somewhat too ritualistic performance of Robert Speaight' (*The Achievement of T. S. Eliot*, 3rd edn, 1958, 165).

played during the Mercury Theatre run. If you come to a second printing I suppose you will want to use this text.

> Again with many thanks,
> Yours ever sincerely,
> [T. S. Eliot]

## TO *Lionel Gough*[1]                                                    CC

3 April 1936                              [Faber & Faber Ltd]

My dear Mr Gough,

I am writing to ask your opinions and advice about a matter which concerns your profession and mind. It has been represented to us that there is a deficiency of really good books for teaching divinity in public and ordinary secondary schools, and that there would be a market for a really satisfactory series of books covering the needs. I don't suppose that anyone whose religious views are from the usual public school point of view so unorthodox as yours is actually admitted to give instruction in divinity, but I thought you would know something about the way the subject is taught, and the books in use, and might might be interested in giving me a private confidential opinion.

If my enquiry is merely a nuisance, please forgive.

> Yours very sincerely,
> [T. S. Eliot]

## TO *Dylan Thomas*                                                      CC

3 April 1936                              [*The Criterion*]

Dear Thomas,

What I wrote to you about in the letter which was sent to you care of Archer's was simply to enquire whether you might not have some recent poems which you could let me see for the *Criterion*. It is a long time since I have had anything from you and I should think you must have a good deal of new material by now.[2]

> Yours sincerely,
> [T. S. Eliot]

1 – Lionel Gough: a master at Haileybury School.
2 – See Thomas, 'The Orchards' (story), C. 15 (July 1936), 614–22.

4 April 1936                          At Pike's Farm

Dear Geoffrey:

I have now read *Nightwood* and want to go on record. It is much more remarkable than I knew at first glance. You may think that I say it wildly rather than clearly; but I have no doubt TSE can express it better, and I hope he will.

I don't see how anyone who has any appreciation of T.S.E.'s work can fail to see something in *Nightwood*. It can hardly be called a novel, any more than *The Waste Land* a detective story. For long stretches it is a poem, not 'about' lesbians and such, but a pitiful poem of our time, the facing both ways time, time of the half-and-halfs, time broken in half at the impotent present, time with Tiny O'Toole lying dead in its hand, as the Doctor says. We've been turning a lot of stones these past years, but never a Doctor has come out like that one, all moss and eyes.[1] If I have any quarrel at all it is with the beginning, a little slow and cumbered, Felix remaining, though essential, the least essential to me; and at first only the movement of the writing giving any hint of what's to come; and an Elizabethan cloudiness and wind – one soon feels the wind in that door. Norah and Jenny are alive all right, and at the first, Robin doesn't seem alive at all, until the story builds to that amazing Chapter 5, the long poem on night. Chapter 5 is the contemporary counterpart of Carlyle's 'Everlasting Nay'.[2] There are differences: one is that Carlyle seems obsolete to me in that the nineteenth century optimism of the Everlasting Yea is no longer possible; the worse prognostications of the Everlasting Nay having been duly fulfilled, now make our present reality; what was in Carlyle's time only possible, having now become actual. Another difference is that this Teufelsdrock, the Doctor in an upstairs room telling the world how, in this night of darkness which is now present, it is absolutely esperruquanchuzelublevuzerireliced and confounded in its juices down to the very heel, is not dour as Teufelsdrock was, but Rabelaisian and most rich and lived in. The humour of Teufelsdrock was elephantine, a nineteenth century proprietary brand of Scotch. This Doctor is a most beautiful Irish, the very best vivid Celtic, perhaps as things are the only adequate creation to give us that Tiresias picture of time past holding

---

1 – FVM was quoting from *Nightwood*: 'I was doing well enough until you came along and kicked my stone over, and out I came, all moss and eyes.'
2 – In Thomas Carlyle's *Sartor Resartus* (1836, 1838), the 'Everlasting No' stands for the spirit opposed to a belief in God.

time present limp in its hand, unable to beget a future which shall not be imbecile. That later scene where the Doctor ends up drunk in the café is one of the most piteous things I ever saw. And the very end, which at my first glance I thought unbearable, I see now to be right in all detail. Robin too is afterwards seen to be right – the personification of powerful and wilful silence, the sort of thing that doesn't give its own answer.

There are different levels of meaning, but also they are all together in the concourse, as they are in the Pennsylvania Terminus in N.Y., where the doors open without your touching them, because on approaching you have intercepted an invisible beam of light. There are to me throughout the poetic qualities which leave me, again as the Doctor says, sitting up high and fine, with a rosebush in my arse.[1] It is really most extraordinary, the continual spiritedness of the writing which keeps up the continual impact; and a very fine humour, which scarcely cares whether it is caught up or not. (That's a good story, of the man waiting outside a toilet while someone inside had decided to read the *Decline and Fall of the Roman Empire*.[2])

Well, that's maybe no more than an indication that I'm sure *Nightwood* has permanence as literature. I'm sure that it's communicable: more so than anything I've read of comparable aim since *The Waste Land*. It does quite transcend the contemporary comparisons which were in my mind at my first glance. It shows up Henry Miller as meaningless reporting, served up cold. Djuna Barnes has seen farther down the drain, and is a much deeper person. It shows up Kay Boyle as brittle fiction; Barnes is a much larger person; I wish we'd found her, and all her moss and eyes, before we'd found the Boyle.[3]

1 – 'I know,' said the doctor, 'there you were sitting up high and fine, with a rose-bush up your arse.'

2 – 'In the spring [the birds] form a queue by her bedroom window and stand waiting their turn, holding on to their eggs as hard as they can until she gets around to them, strutting up and down on the ledge, the eyes in their feathers a quick shine and sting, whipped with impatience, like a man waiting at a toilet door for someone inside who had decided to read the Decline and Fall of the Roman Empire.'

3 – Kay Boyle (1902–92): American author, editor, teacher, political activist, whose early novels, including *Year Before Last* (1932) and *My Next Bride* (1934), were published by F&F. From 1923 to 1941 she lived primarily in France, marrying in 1932 Laurence Vail (ex-husband of Peggy Guggenheim) and enjoying friendships with artists and writers including Harry and Caresse Crosby (who published in 1929 her first fictions, entitled *Short Stories*, at their Black Sun Press), and Eugene and Maria Jolas; she also contributed to *transition*. See further Robert McAlmon and Kay Boyle, *Being Geniuses Together, 1920–1930* (1968); Jean Mellen, *Kay Boyle: Author of Herself* (1994).

Boyle to McAlmon, 18 Mar. 1939: 'We've heard so much about the conversation anent T. S. Eliot's cultivation that I must tell you we're all on your side – I'm sick of the man's name

Now being certain of all this (though very eager to see TSE translate the recognition of the book and lay it out all neat along the toothbrush) my main point, which is really serious to me, is that if I am right we *must* study to publish it. I think you know very well how my general activity, and general value to the list, depends on feeling that there are some good things in it. If I know of a lump of leaven I will work like a bottlebrush to make all the doughnuts pay for it; but I really can't work on a list with enthusiasm unless there is something which seems to me to have the chance to be literature. I know perfectly the necessity of making money; but I also know that the best stimulus, for me, is not merely that necessity, but the pride of publishing a few books which I really cherish. That pride sustains a host of other effort; and is the only real sustainer. I feel that here is a book that I recognize and am proud of; to do it is to give me energy; to turn it down, for any insufficient reason, would make me apathetic.

I think that Tom and I, if he could spare the time, could edit it. The point is that there is no *reporting* of lesbianism, no details; the conflict is one of souls, not bodies, and if for censors' sake there have to be any individual words cut out, the work itself wouldn't much suffer. As to the markings, I agree with such deletions as have actually been made, but I would leave practically all the passages which are merely sidelined. I think, as I have said, that the beginning could be pruned a little; and Chapter 5 may be a bit too long, but it would need Tom's sounding-board to say just where. I would suggest to Tom that he might use Chapter 5, or part of it, in the *Criterion*.

With such attention I can't see any danger of being jugged. It isn't the kind of book which could be jailed, surely. That scene of Tiny O'Toole (which is marvellous) can be touched, if necessary.

Now, such is my hypnosis, I feel that *in the long run* it would come even (or more) in the ledger. I honestly do: I feel as I felt when I read *The Waste Land*, and when we and the likes of me went preaching about it and spending our money on copies: a bloodless ragged army and all that, and small; but durable: the kind of minority once in a while to publish for. Our *continued* success depends (I believe) on keeping contact with those to whom literature is (shall we say) a mania. My own enthusiasm hangs on that contact, however carefully I conceal the fact in playing round Fleet Street or with the B.P.R.A.

---

and pretensions and think him over-rated from every point-of-view. Ever since he wrote congratulating me on my "great" book – "Year Before Last" – I knew how incompetent a critic he was' (*Kay Boyle: A Twentieth-Century Life in Letters*, ed. Sandra Spanier [2015], 261).

Though occasionally I have had enthusiasms which died on me, I don't recall quite the same feelings, or the same situation, before. I am passing this letter to Tom before sending it because I know he can describe the appreciation of the book more clearly. If he should say I am cockeyed, I wouldn't know what to do! But I don't think he will.[1]

Still sneezing and coughing and shivering, but nearing haleness.

Hurrah.

Frank

## TO *Ezra Pound*

TS Beinecke

7 Aprile 1936 A.D.                    *The Criterion*

To the Worshipful Ez Po:

> Hon. Mayor of Rappaloo in the 2000th year of the Sung Dynasty, a Saloot of 21 Guns and a pinch of Mustard Gaz.
> Zoforth –

Cor blimey nobody'd do any work round this joint if it wasnt for Old Possum. I had to pump a gallon of sherry into Old Whale before I could get him round to editin your prose paralipomena; and the worst is that I had to drink with him, and that's bad because he can't drink Good sherry, he likes it sweet & resinous. Well no doubt he's uttered a bit of libel about me, but I don't mind bein libelled so long as I can get the lads to do a stroke or two of honest work now and again. Why don't you get somebody besides me to do a lick of work now and again? For instance, that Swabey you mention, he might write to *me* for instance.[2] And that Smith you talk about, he seems a likely lad, and Hamilton will be all the better for him: pity he wasnt there with his candles in your time, it might

---

1–TSE to Robert Giroux, 11 Dec. 1956: 'I should never have been able to push *Nightwood* with Faber and Faber but for Frank's support at the time, and he was very instrumental indeed in lopping and pruning that book into publishable size and telling Djuna what ought to be cut out.'

2–EP wrote, 26 Mar.: 'The Egregious Swabey hath with much diligence and rescrousching ferreted oute several and diverse proofs that all Anglicans weren' sons of bitches or bloodsucking lice such as Calvin and Baxter.

'Needeth he a lytl purging, but in the main vurry interestinge paper, 35 payges whereOF I did reade with pleasure and profyte . . .

'Hen. G Swabey, Yew Hedge, Forest Row, Sussex. will you see him? He studyeth in Durham Yonivursity fer the Church (anglican).'

TSE at forty-seven

have altered European history for the better.[1] Well now as to your trying to frisk us by saying that a part of one poem is five poems,[2] I have written to Roberts about that, but it'll take time, because Roberts is climbing in the Andes at the moment, and his correspondence cant be dealt with.[3]

    Richards & Roberts were two merry men,
    They shinned up the Alps like a 3 legged hen.[4]

Well now Podestà[5] I am certainly pleased & touched at your suggestin a visit from me to Rappalloo, and your hospitality as usual is excessive.[6] Ill just sit down and study that subject. I dont like Nice any better'n you do, I caught the hell of a cold there once, and my landlady put me to bed with a hot brick wrapped up in the daily Post Morning Post. Ill have to consult the F. O. to learn whether a visit by me across the frontier would cause international embarrassment or not, and you'd better put the same question to Musso. I can stay here without approvin of anybody, but if I crossed the Alps I might have to resign like poor old Sam. And Paris is glloomy too: my old friends there is all either in gaol now or in the Academie Id rather be in gaol. What Nott? Will ask Mairet.[7] Why Ideogramic?[8] Is that Homeric? Why not Idiographic or idiogrammatic? What book you intended? If you intended a book why didnt you write it?

1 – EP, 26 Mar.: 'JuhHeer yur frien Smiff wot busted up the English Church in Venice, cause the acolyte struck the risibles, has returned an stuck a mass with candles onto my alma mam's campus!! (EP studied at Hamilton College, Clinton, NY – a Presbyterian foundation – 1903–5.)
2 – See pc from EP, 20 Mar. 1936: 'Mauberley is NOT ONE poem; but a series.'
3 – TSE was joking: Roberts was actually in the Val d'Isère, Savoie, France.
4 – See the eighteenth-century nursery rhyme 'Robin and Richard were two pretty men / They lay in bed till the clock struck ten': Poems, ed. Ricks and McCue (2015), 201.
5 – Podestà (Ital.): chief civilian authority.
6 – EP, 4 Apr.: 'Wot we cd/ do IZ there izza Cou/ach in the stew/dio/ and I wd. be pleezed to horspitalitate you for a week/ purrwidin you with food at the Allbugoo were we eat. said stewdio is separate hunk of this aptment. And you needn'y see us more'n you want to. Separate bog/ but not separate bawth.
    'wot I mean you'd be COM/pletely your own timer, need contact only a lunch and dinner.
    'You wd/ have room and terrace to yr/ self, with usual offices. bawth exists/ but not fer yr/ exclusive.'
7 – EP declared, 28 Mar.: 'Mairet is the only english contributor [to C.] I can read with respect.'
8 – EP reported (4 Apr.) that his friend Fox had just sent 'excellent mss' – 'intended for Ideogramic seereezz' – to the N.E.W., which he hoped Mairet would serialise in volume 4. He told TSE too: 'you can consider getting it with augment and few pretty pixchoors into print'. On 28 Apr. 1936 the London publisher Stanley Nott brought out Ta Hio: The Great Leaning, Newly rendered into the American Language by Ezra Pound, the second in the 'Ideogramic Series' ed. EP (the first being The Chinese Written Character as a Medium for Poetry by Ernest Fenollosa).

Shillink pamphlet I dont think: do you realise how much PROFIT there is out of a shilink?[1] You look over the cantooes and see if there aint one punk enough to print in the Criterion at regular rates. What I mean is that I like the idea of your studio fine, but whatya say to making it Locarno? Locarno, that's a good place to meet, desdoesnt commit anybody to anything, nothing said there matters, come to Locarno, so bracing, no restrictions, Sunday bathing and roulette. Well now first of all you dust off your desk and get round to settin your PROSE in order and so for the present grateful thanks and many Easter eggs to set on so will close

Tp

Please give my Regards to yr. Pater.


## TO *Hallie Flanagan*[2]                                         TS Berg

8 April 1936                         *The Criterion*

Dear Mrs Flanagan,

Thank you for your kind letter of the 25th March, and for sending me the cuttings from the New York papers. It is a great satisfaction to me that the production has been so generally appreciated.[3]

I am interested to hear that the *Dance of Death* is also to be produced. I wish that I could have heard the performance at Vassar, especially if it was directed by yourself. The musical score which was provided for the London production did not seem to me very interesting.[4]

Yours sincerely,<br>T. S. Eliot

---

1–EP suggested, 4 Apr.: 'I had thought that the Usura canto, hidden and misprinted in "Prosperity", plus the canto in current Nude Emocracy, might be issued separate. as a booklet at one shillink.'

2–Hallie Flanagan (1890–1969), director and playwright, taught 1927–35 at Vassar College, where she built up the Experimental Theatre. She was National Director of the Federal Theater Project, 1935–42, and ran the Theatre Department at Smith College, 1942–52. See Flanagan, *Dynamo* (1943); Joanne Bentley, *Hallie Flanagan: A Life in the American Theatre* (1988).

3–Flanagan sent cuttings about *MiC* from the New York newspapers. She added: 'The Federal Theatre Project is bringing out the "Dance of Death" in a few weeks, with the music composed for the performance at Vassar last summer. I wish you and Mr Auden could have seen that. There was a touch of Sweeney in it.'

4–The incidental music for the London production of *The Dance of Death* was by the composer and organist Herbert Murrill (1909–52), who was from 1933 Professor of Composition at the Royal Academy of Music.

8 April 1936                          [*The Criterion*]

Dear John,

I have written to the five Russian periodicals and asked them, if they are willing to exchange, to send direct to you.[1] I do hope they will, as you know I set great store by this feature.

I am delighted to hear that the Oxford University Press is publishing your book, and I trust that they will send us a copy for review.[2] About the prefatory note by myself, I am of course pleased and flattered that you should want to have this, but it is an embarrassing position for me. I have on several occasions with the approval of my firm declined to provide prefaces for some of our own as well as other publishers' authors, and I should not be able to give a very convincing excuse if I now break the rule, even for a personal friend. I hope that you will understand. Incidently, I may say that we are not much interested in having such prefaces in books that we publish, as we find that it makes very little difference to the sale, and indeed sometimes gives the impression that we have not enough confidence in the book to produce it without an extra push.

I am sending a copy of my *Collected Poems*, which I am inscribing for you. I hope you will like both the appearance and the contents. As for the nonsense poems, I fear that those are indefinitely postponed.

With warmest good wishes to Helen[3] and yourself,

Yours ever,
[Tom]

---

1–TSE wrote to the periodicals *Oktiabr*; *Literaturnaya Gazetta*; *Novy Mir*; *Literaturny Sovremennik*; *Literaturny Kritik*. Only the last-named responded.

2–Cournos notified TSE on 24 Mar. that his forthcoming book included two of his essays from the *Criterion*. 'Its theme is the intrusion of the machine into art, and it touches on Communism, religion (or irreligion), etc., etc. You know my attitude toward these things, which (for the most part, I believe) coincides with your own. Would you be willing – provided, of course, you find nothing in the book that you violently oppose – to write a Foreword?'

3–Cournos's wife Helen Kestner (1893–1960) wrote under the *nom de plume* Sybil Norton.

TO *The Editor,* The New English Weekly

[Published 9 April 1936, 523]      [Faber & Faber Ltd]

Sir,[1]

I should be better contented with Mr Barlow's letter in your issue of April 2, if it had been written *before* instead of *after* mine; for I fear that by telling him what not to think, I have led him to think it.[2] I do sympathize with Mr Barlow's complaint; and I am not undertaking to defend contemporary ecclesiastics. But even if all his objections are valid, they are still quite irrelevant to one's decision to become a member of the Church or stay outside. This decision, on the other hand, does have a bearing on one's criticism of the Church.

I do not know where Mr Barlow is looking for his 'focal points'. Cathedral precincts are not necessarily such foci. I should have thought that every thoughtful and intelligent layman might be a focal point; and incidentally that Mr Barlow had the native capacity, only needing improvement by study, to become a focal point himself.

The Church, we might remember, consists not only of the living but of the dead. But at what period, I wonder, was the visible Church pure enough for Mr Barlow to have been a member of it? Would the Apostolical Succession be more genuine, the Sacraments more valid, if the visible Church were all that we should like it to be? I shall not be so disrespectful to Mr Barlow's intelligence as to believe that he could be converted by such flimsy reasons as he pretends.

If I understand the quotation from Professor Macmurray ('to apprehend man we need religion') I should say that the reply should be: '*what*

---

1 – Mairet to TSE, 26 Mar.: 'We were very grateful for your note on the Correspondence. But both Barlow and Hawkins are very eager to say some more, and the former has written a very interesting letter. I don't quite like to closure them: and I think a letter from each of them would be worth printing, if you would follow with one more letter after them.'

2 – Barlow wrote, in 'Defining Christianity' (letter), *NEW* 8: 25 (2 Apr. 1936), 503 – apropos 'Mr Eliot's major distinction, between what the Church is for and what it does' – 'My point is not that the Church is "doing something" for children or that it is catering for lonely women – it is rather that the Church is doing nothing but these things. I understand the impropriety of judging the body of the Church by the action of its individual members but as a living Church I should expect that at focal points there would exist men preoccupied with essentially religious activities. Moreover I should expect these focal activities to affect the common social world in much the same way as did the lives and thoughts of the men who built the Christian economy of the early centuries . . . I would go further and say that the reality of any Church may be measured by the certainty with which action follows on religious sensibility.'

religion'? And I doubt whether Professor Macmurray will provide a satisfactory answer.[1]

T. S. Eliot

## TO *Ezra Pound*

TS Beinecke

15 Aprill A.D. 1936                    Faber & Faber Ltd

To the Hon. Pussface,
        Hetman[2] of Rappalloo, Sir:[3]

Doggone it Ole Ez if your lil brown brothers aint gone and put on one o yr. postage stamps the face of Old Ike Carver of Mosquito Cove. Ef it aint ole Ike then I'll lay my best pants its ole Uncle Joe Cabot of Salem. Well what are we cominto? Cant you go and celebrate the 100th anniversary of the foundation of Carnera without borrowin the face of ole Ike Carver? Wont he turn once or twict in his grave, wont he just. Now then old Ez here we was havin a nice correspondence in the N.E.W. and you come bargin in talkin your foreign language and what you picked up about Lancelot Andrewes from the passin conversation of the Hon. Swabe (whom God preserve) what you need is a pint of brown ale and a game of darts to set your head right. So you lay offn it, I says, lay offn it.[4] Now

1 – See the blurb (almost certainly by TSE) for *The Structure of Religious Experience*, by John MacMurray, for publication by F&F in Oct. 1936: 'Science is fundamentally concerned with the use of things, and art with the enjoyment; their purposes are therefore only to be reconciled by a wider purpose embracing the whole of human activity. It is only the religious man who is concerned with using the vision of the artist and the achievement of the scientist for the true benefit of all mankind; and religion that is not so concerned is no religion at all.

'According to this view, developed with Professor MacMurray's customary conviction and simplicity, every scientific advance and the achievement of every artist and every mystic is to be tested, not against a super-natural world, but in the practical world of human society. It is only in this way that religion will be able to continue its high service to mankind, and perhaps even bring into existence a world of peace and well-being.'

2 – Hetman: 'A captain or military commander in Poland and countries formerly united or subject to it; whence subsequently retained as a title among the Cossacks' (*OED*).

3 – Cf. Wallace Stevens, 'Bantams in Pinewoods' (1922): 'Chieftain Iffucan of Azcan in caftan / Of tan with henna hackles, halt!'

4 – EP sent TSE on 3 Apr. a draft of a letter addressed: 'Editor N.E.W. While the letter column is still open to discussion of Mr Eliot's religion, might we ask whether he thinks the Church of England advocates a religion?

'I have a recurrent curiosity as to whether the titular chiefs of that organisation dare face Launcelot Andrews [*sic*]. I am personally sceptic as to their having the courage to face any fact or *any* clear definition of ideas whatsoever, And (while we are still on the subject) I am not even sure that Mr Eliot HAS faced Launcelot Andrewes after so kindly hoisting him up again from the more obscure depths of oblivion.'

EP's letter did not appear in *NEW*.

then Ez this 3s.6d. is a bargain price, in this business; no-body can begin with 3/6. Dont you see the idea is to get rid of as many copies as possible at 7/6 and then put a new wrapper on the book and sell it at 3s.6d. as a classic in the library. So if you will start at 7/6 we shall hope to come to 3/6 eventually. Not if you was WODEHOUSE you couldnt BEGIN lower than 7/6. So make yr mind up to it. Now then I think we are gettin on nicely.[1] Dont you know ALL classics have to start, and they cant be classics at the start, except in the Classic. Ez you will be surprised being so innocent to learn that I have every sympathy with yr fulmination against the English Church, in fact I thought of it some time before but you know I need a lot of pressure in the boiler before I let the old Creole Belle out for her record run from St Louis to Natchez,[2] I dont like to blow up until just as I reach the levee. You dont hate bishops like I do. That bit from the Dante S. of R. [*The Spirit of Romance*] certainly MUST go in: best thing on the subject in this language, in My opinion.[3] All you need is the mellerin influence of a 4-ale bar about once or twice a week, a little good cheese and roast beef and some decent wine. So will offer my company to yr mother-in- law[4] for an evening in the near future, yours etc.

TP

1 – EP had argued to FVM (9 Apr.) that a volume at 3/6d 'wd. sell': 'I dont mean that I care a damn so long as you git axshun. but cert/ think a 3/6 wd. be better in these hard times ... juh GIT meh. TWO 3 and 6 ers much better than a 7/6 er. fer sellin porpoises. Me thinKEE=EE.'

EP acquiesced to this letter, 17 Apr.: 'Wall 7/ and 6 pence she bee/ thaz O.K. by EZ.'

EP's *Polite Essays* (to be published by F&F in Feb. 1937) was marketed at 7/6d.

2 – The *Belle Creole* was a Missouri paddle steamer, built in 1823. See too Susan Clement, '"All Abroad for Natchez, Cairo and St Louis": The source of a draft heading of T. S. Eliot's *Ash-Wednesday* I', *Notes and Queries*, Mar. 1996, 57–9.

3 – See 'Note on Dante', *Polite Essays*, 196–207: from the end of a chapter in *The Spirit of Romance* (1910).

4 – Olivia Shakespear (1864–1938), mother of Dorothy Pound, made an unhappy marriage in 1885 with Henry Hope Shakespear (1849–1923), a solicitor. She published novels including *Love on a Mortal Lease* (1894) and *The Devotees* (1904). Through her cousin, the poet Lionel Johnson (1867–1902), she arranged a meeting with W. B. Yeats, which resulted in a brief affair, 1895–6, and a lifetime's friendship. WBY wrote at least two poems for her, and she was the 'Diana Vernon' of his *Memoirs* (ed. Denis Donoghue, 1972). See *Ezra Pound and Dorothy Shakespear: Their Letters 1909–1914*, ed. Omar S. Pound and A. Walton Litz (1984), 356–7.

15 April 1936                    Faber & Faber Ltd

Dear Geoffrey,

Frank showed me a letter which he had written to you after a second reading of *Nightwood*, and which he said he would hold up until I had had an opportunity to read the book again. I have read it over the holidays, and I am more strongly in favour of the book than ever. I am even reconciled to the somewhat slow opening, which I think needs only minor alterations. On a second reading, I see the book more as a whole – at first I was impressed by brilliant phrases and passages, and chiefly by the figure of the Doctor: now I see the necessity and rightness of the other characters, and I see the book as bigger than any one character in it.

Where I think you went wrong – I may be wrong – is that you probably approached the book down a Kay Boyle avenue. What there is in common is most superficial: the American *déraciné* world of Paris, and the Lesbianism. The Lesbianism of *Nightwood* is an accident – whereas with Kay Boyle it is a *feature* in a showy circus. I mean that I felt, on second reading of *Nightwood*, that what the author was concerned with was the universal malady of living of which Lesbianism is only one species, as ordinary heterosexuality is another. We are not, as with Boyle, looking on at a degraded peep-show, we are forced to share in it. Lesbianism merely happens to be the variety of the dis-ease that Barnes knows the best, so it is through that form that she has to get at something universal (she has obviously a great deal of the male in her composition). One forgets about its physical specifications, so that even the ghastly figure of the Doll becomes a symbol of some deeper horror. What I feel more strongly after the second reading is the undertone of the book, which gives it unity. This writer is somebody to whom something has happened that happens to very few (because we don't want it): she has caught up with her own sorrow, identified it and tapped it on the shoulder ('You are the mysterious Mr X': she deserves her free trip to Blackpool at the expense of the *News-Chronicle*) – it's a sorrow much deeper than personal vicissitudes, of course, because it is the sorrow of life, the worm unkillable by any of the agents of this world.[1] And as for her style, it has what is for me the authentic evidence of power, in that I find myself having to

---

1 – Mark 9: 47–8: 'And if thine eye offend thee, pluck it out: It is better for thee to enter into the kingdom of God with one eye, than having two eyes to be cast into hell fire; Where their worm dieth not, and the fire is not quenched.'

struggle, directly after reading, not to ape it myself: and very few writers exercise that pull.

I regret Kay Boyle. It seems to me that our motives were mixed: i.e. that we thought of her stuff as something that *might* be good and that *might* sell, and we combined the *mights*. It isn't really first rate and it doesn't sell. Kay Boyle (it is very irritating) *mimics* something good so closely as to make her unsaleable. She has an imitative ability and slickness and an outsider's enjoyment of bestiality and cruelty and sordor – but doesn't feel it keenly enough. Djuna Barnes wont sell – not for some time . . . though I think we could get her some good reviews . . .

But what is important to me is that I believe that this may be our last chance to do something remarkable in the way of imaginative literature. As for our literary reputation, remember that people like Joyce and myself may help to keep the temperature level, but we can't send it any higher. There is something an author does *once* (if at all) in his generation that he can't ever do again. We can go on writing stuff that nobody else could write, if you like, but the *Waste Land* and *Ulysses* remain the historic points. From a publishing point of view, there is a tremendous difference between getting a good author first, and rounding him in after his reputation is made; and if Joyce and I, for example, had up to now been published by some other firm, we should no longer be worth getting. To return to the first sentence of this paragraph – that is merely a prediction, for what it is worth: but my feeling is that this book is very likely the last big thing to be done in our time: the rest of which will belong to the callow *epigoni* of the *Faber Book of Modern Verse*.

As for the police, perhaps my opinion is not the most reliable, because I remain a confused innocent in matters of censorship: as you know, I am perpetually being shocked by what doesn't shock other people, and not being shocked by what does shock other people. There are a few words, and a few incidental passages, which might well come out. But fundamentally the book is sound; and the author has, at bottom, what is a religious point of view.[1] And she *has* a point of view, which Henry Miller hasn't.

1–FVM to T. F. Burns (*The Tablet*), 19 Oct. 1936, of *Nightwood*: 'At bottom, the attitude is religious. The bottom is pretty deep, and I don't know anybody who has looked farther down the drain than Djuna . . .'

Well, if we don't publish this book, I am convinced that we are missing something important: and I shall then go on trying until I can get someone else to publish it.[1]

Yours ever,

Tom

1 – TSE's blurb for NIGHTWOOD: 'This book, upon which Miss Barnes has been at work for a long time, is extremely difficult to describe. It is in prose, but will appeal primarily to readers of poetry; it has something of the form of a novel, but the characters suffer rather than act: and as with Dostoevski and George Chapman, one feels that the action is hardly more than the shadow-play of something taking place on another plane of reality. It is concerned with *le misérable au centre de sa misère*, and has nothing to offer to readers whose temperament attaches them to either an easy or a frightened optimism.' (Faber Catalogue: Autumn Books 1936, p. 10)

For the second UK edn (1950) TSE drafted this puff: 'This novel of the life of deracinated Americans and Europeans in Paris in the nineteen-twenties was first published by ourselves in 1936 prior to its appearance in New York. It immediately gained, and has since kept, the enthusiastic admiration of a small number of discerning critics: and no one who has ever read the book can forget the astonishing "Doctor" O'Connor, in his sorrowful degradation and his endless talk of the Night; or the agonised relationship of Norah and Robin. The book has for some time been out of print in this country: we re-publish it in the belief that there is now a much larger public ready for it than there was at the time of its first appearance, and that it will be recognised as a masterpiece of its period, with amazing passages that lift the style into the region of poetry.

'Miss Barnes, who lives in New York, is anything but a prolific writer. She has another work, of a different kind, in preparation; but whatever she does, *Nightwood* will remain unique amongst works of fiction in the twentieth century, though it appeal only to those who do not flinch before the sombre, the sordid and the "nocturnal".'

TSE was later to draft a blurb for Barnes's *The Antiphon: A Tragedy in Verse* (1958), including these remarks: 'We are firmly persuaded that in 1936 when we published Miss Djuna Barnes's novel *Nightwood*, there was no other publishing house, on either side of the Atlantic, which would not have rejected the book out of hand. ~~Some of them had done so.~~ To people of conventional manners *Nightwood* was shocking; to people of conventional taste in fiction it was tedious and incomprehensible. Yet *Nightwood*, though it never captured a wide public, is now recognised by critics of discrimination as a classic of its period.'

TSE to Barnes, 7 Feb. 1957: 'I am sorry that the blurb I wrote for *The Antiphon* fails to meet with your approval. It was well received by my Board and was designed, of course, to arouse curiosity and stimulate demand. However, as you don't like it, I will design something briefer and more conventional.' He wrote by hand on the draft blurb, evidently with amusement and perhaps even pride: 'Rejected indignantly by Miss Barnes but to be preserved.'

Donald Brace told FVM on 20 Oct. 1936 that he and two editorial colleagues at Harcourt, Brace (Pearce, Sloan) had just read and discussed the novel, and wished to pass on their conclusions: 'I understand, I think, Eliot's high estimate of its importance and the impact it has made on you. It is amazing as a literary performance. It has tremendous power; many of the scenes are superb. I should think that you are right in saying that it will appeal primarily to readers of poetry.

'It is not so easy to decide what to do about it. I don't think there would be trouble with censorship, but the three of us agree in finding it distasteful; it made us shudder in various degrees. In our talk this morning, we tried to estimate what we could expect to get from

15 April [1936]                    Hogarth Cottage,
                                   Hampton-on-Thames

My dear John,

Knowing, as you do, the dangerous nature of my activities, you will not be surprised by my change of address. Between ourselves, the recent cases in which I have been of assistance to the Royal Family of Scandinavia, and to the French Republic, have left me in such a position that I could continue to live in the quiet fashion which is most congenial to me, and to concentrate my attention upon my chemical researches. But I could not rest, I could not sit quiet in my chair, if I thought that such a man as ....... were walking the streets of London unchallenged. It is obvious, therefore, that I cannot do better than get away for the few days which remain before the police are able to act.

You had no need to return the cuttings, but I am more than happy to have the instalment of Tottering Towers – happy in a sense – I mean I am glad to know what is going on – the insidious attack of the plutocracy upon

---

American reviewers . . . It is no light thing to turn down a book about which Eliot feels as he does and about which you feel as you do. On the other hand, we have thought about how the book would look in our list and about what sort of critical reception we could expect.

'To put the book on the right track here, it will need some voice of authority to establish its significance and its kinship with such works as THE WASTE LAND and ULYSSES. The publisher can't do that, and I can't think of anyone else here who can do it. Is it possible that Eliot will write an introduction to it? I can see why he might not want to, but if he would, it would make all the difference. It ought, I think, to be an actual introduction or preface, and no opinions we could get from England that we could print on the jacket would serve as well.'

When Brace cabled FVM, 21 Nov. – 'THINK WE SHOULD PUBLISH NIGHTWOOD WOULD LIKE ELIOT INTRODUCTION FIRST EDITION ONLY WHAT TERMS ARE CALLED FOR = BRACE' – FVM cabled back, 24 Nov.: 'NIGHTWOOD HOW ABOUT TEN TO THREETHOUSAND FIFTEEN AFTER SAY FIFTY POUNDS ADVANCE STOP SUGGEST ELIOT SUPPLY SHORT INTRODUCTION FIFTEENHUNDRED WORDS TO FIRST THREETHOUSAND COPIES IS HUNDRED BUCKS FAIR FOR THAT'. Brace accepted (cable, 24 Nov.) both the terms and the fee expected by TSE.

On 4 Dec. FVM forwarded TSE's introduction. 'I have read it and I think it excellent; though the hardest thing in the world to know is whether remarks, geared to appreciation in one place, will communicate themselves to an unknown audience. Eliot says, characteristically enough, that if you feel the preface to be on the short side, or shorter than you expected, you should reduce the fee. But though very compact, it doesn't seem to me short measure.'

Brace to FVM, 14 Dec. 1936: 'Eliot's introduction to NIGHTWOOD is excellent. Of course, I had no arbitrary idea about the length, and it doesn't seem to me that this is too short. It is characteristically generous of Eliot to suggest that if it is shorter than we expected, we should reduce the fee. But of course, it is in no sense short measure, and the fee stands. It will, I feel, accomplish exactly what we hoped it would do in establishing the serious intentions that we all have about the book.'

the aristocracy. You gave us a very pleasant evening, as you always give your guests. I hope that I did not become tipsy – I had a slight headache the next morning: but I shd. be much more distressed to think that I had lingered too long, fatiguing you with reminiscences and bawdy jingles.

You may communicate with me at this address, by addressing your letters to 'White Cargo'[1] c/o the Licensee the Bell, Hampton-on-Thames. And I may rely upon your not revealing my whereabouts to Miss C. B. or Madame de M.

Yours

P.S. I think it is better not to sign my name.

TO *Humphry Beevor*[2]                                           CC

16 April 1936                    [Faber & Faber Ltd]

Dear Father Beevor,

I am very sorry that you could not stay long enough on Saturday for us to have time to discuss Divinity books, but of course Gough did not know that you would be obliged to leave so early. As I have no idea when we shall be able to meet again, the next best thing is to ask you to be so kind as to give me at your leisure any suggestions that occur to you, as well as information. Gough told me that he had said something to you about the scheme. I had originally written to him in a general way as another schoolmaster had suggested to us the need of good books for use in upper forms. It was Gough himself who suggested that the most useful kind of books would be very small books, practically pamphlets, which could be sold for a shilling or two.

What I particularly want to know is what texts and subjects ought to be treated. If one was undertaking a series of such low priced books it would probably be best to announce it as a series, and bring out three or four at the beginning. I have no ideas of my own on this subject of the teaching of Divinity in English schools. If you had any suggestions to make of possible authors or editors of texts, as well as of the texts and subjects themselves in the best order of publication, I should be very grateful.

It is important, I think, that such a series should rouse no suspicion of being the work of any definite party or the expression of extreme views of any kind. The series would get its character from the authors chosen,

1 – TSE claimed that 'White Cargo' was the code name given to him at the Bell Inn.
2 – Revd Humphry Beevor (1903–65), Pusey House, Oxford.

among whom it might be desirable to have a few names widely known and accepted by all shades of opinion. What we have in mind is obviously something which would defeat its own aims if it appeared over the imprint of the C.L.A., or indeed of any religious publisher.

Gough seemed to have some very good ideas about the way in which the book should be produced, and the way of obtaining publicity and authority for the series.

If you are very busy at the moment please don't bother until you have time. When and if you can, I shall be grateful for as much in the way of information and suggestions as you care to let me have.

Yours sincerely,<br>[T. S. Eliot]

## FROM *Geoffrey Faber*                                        MS Valerie Eliot

[?16 April 1936]                          [Faber & Faber Ltd]

Dear ⎰Tom
      ⎱Frank [Morley],

The established rule applies, to the case of Djuna Barnes:– if any director is all out over a book or author, we must do it – him – her. And when *two* directors go all out in the same direction, still more so. And when they go so completely all out –

What distresses me is that I should have so completely failed to see what you both see in *Nightwood*. After reading your two letters I cannot doubt that you are right, and that I am wrong – which is a discomforting, though perhaps salutary state of mind for a publisher, let alone an educated man, to be in.

No, I didn't approach the book down a Kay Boyle avenue. I agree with most of what TSE says about K. B. though I felt in *My Next Bride* that she had got pretty near something real – a few skins down, anyway.[1] But I didn't at all compare K. B. & D. B. in my mind. D. B. seemed quite

---

1 – GCF wrote to a 'Mrs Andrews', enclosing a proof copy of *My Next Bride*, 27 Nov. 1934: 'I don't pretend to be an infallible judge, but when I read this in MS. it seemed to me a wonderful book; and the end of it moved me more than anything I have read for a long time . . .

'In this new book she has come very much nearer to writing a novel which he who runs may read. Actually it's not more difficult to read than Virginia Woolf – if as difficult. Do you think it's a delusion to say that her genius is comparable to that of Virginia Woolf? It seems so to me; and if I'm even partly right there, she ought to begin to take her proper rank with the reading public.'

different. I don't think I questioned the reality of the experience: certainly I never thought of the book as the result of the observation of *The Rock Pool* (Cyril Connolly's effort in the Paris field)[1] by a professional scene-writer. I didn't say to myself 'The Boyle pulls it off, & the Barnes doesn't'.

Be patient with me for exploring my own reactions – you must see that you have presented me with a rather big pill. I feel like Newman when he said of Wiseman's article in the *Dublin Review* that 'coming on top of the misgivings excited in him by the Monophysite history [*sc.* heresy] it was like a dose on top of an alterative & gave him a stomach-ache'.[2]

I thought that D. B. was writing what was real to her; I found a great deal of it quite unintelligible, and boring; I did find the Doctor exciting, & even if I didn't understand what he was talking about I felt myself bobbing like a cork on the torrent of his talk; I disliked what I called the metaphysical treatment of the sexual act (homo or hetero), & my dislike was connected with the nausea which the too-familiar Paris setting has provoked in me (to this extent there is some connection, I suppose, with Kay Boyle); I didn't feel the universal significance, so plain to you both; &, finally, lacking any perception of this, I couldn't imagine that it would sell.

I still fail to see how it can sell. The technical difficulties of 'putting over' a book, which takes the form of a *novel* but will be unreadable by the novel-reading public, are great. If *Nightwood* is in the category of *The Waste Land*, yet there are no ready-made tracks for it to run on – FVM will have to lay them himself. He says he helped to do so for the *Waste Land*, & I don't doubt it; but the *W.L.* was 'poetry', & so there was a railway system for it to rove about upon! *Ulysses* shows, I suppose, that the difficulty isn't insuperable.

As for the police objection, I see the force of what TSE says. Yet you *must* be prepared for trouble. If the book could make *me* feel, at times, a little sick – not by its reportage, of course, but by its use (to speak very clumsily) of bodies as if they were souls – isn't it going to have that effect on a great many common-sensical people? (I'm not, please get this clear, *defending* such an attitude). Then you must bear in mind that Lesbianism is anathema; whether the absence of reportage makes any difference

---

1 – Cyril Connolly, *The Rock Pool* (novel, 1936).

2 – In 1839, after studying the Monophysite heresy – the claim that Christ has only one nature – condemned by the Council of Chalcedon in 451, John Henry Newman was stunned to read an article in the *Dublin Review* by Cardinal Nicholas Wiseman, 'Tracts for the Times: Anglican Claim of Apostolical Succession', that made him realise that he himself was a Monophysite.

I very much doubt. Was there any in the *Well of Loneliness*? It's the fact, conditioning the whole book.

Coming back to myself. I was tired when I read the book, & it may well be that I didn't do either it or myself justice. I must have another go at it. But I think there are 2 other reasons – causes, rather – for my first verdict. One psychological – one, may be, biological. In my scrawl to TSE about the book I said something about my Yorkshire descent – and TSE said dryly that he couldn't understand this preoccupation with race. What I had clumsily in my mind was the realization that there is something in me, *not* individual, & *not* the result of early repressions or what not, which dislikes and disapproves of what I can only call 'making too much of sex'. I can't analyse it very well; & the moment I put it into words they mean something which I don't mean. It seems to me to be a racial instinct or sentiment, & I feel as if it had some kind of a connection with both English puritanism & English license. Both treating sex as an animal thing – either by rejection or acceptance – & refusing to see more in it than it must see. Without in the least defending this as a *right* attitude, I do believe that it makes for racial stability, & I fancy that it's a quality which is essential to the English, & that that's why we are so, apparently, stupid and cruel in our attitude to sexual abnormalities, which are so often peculiarly charged with the Barnes kind of feeling.

I'm the more conscious of this because a good part of me isn't stable in this way. And this is where my own personal <individual> reaction comes in. My own private struggle all my life has been to prevent sex from meaning too much. (Is this the 'malady of living', or the condition which aggravates it? I don't think I quite understand T. S. E.'s phrase. I'm not even sure that I realise the fact!) When sex becomes charged with something more than physical pleasure, it means all kinds of results I want to avoid. It certainly spoils the sensible enjoyment of life, which *pace* TSE seems to me a desirable and practicable state. It isn't as if it spoiled it by a beatific vision of beauty or truth. Its vision is an illusion, known to be such as soon as it has passed, which distorts the whole perspective – rational & emotional – of life. Anyway, whether this is sense or nonsense, that is how what I feel to be the most useful and permanent part of myself looks at it. There's a kind of pulse or rhythm in one's mood about these things – a period in which one 'gets the better' of sex; & a period in which it gets the better of oneself. At the moment, I seem to myself to be in one of the former periods; &, as I get older, these periods seem to last longer, & be more stable. (Perhaps a dangerous illusion!) So I daresay my attitude towards D. B. is different from what it would have been & may again be. At any rate, I have no doubt that *I*, as an individual, & besides any possible 'racial' instinct, am afraid of the D. B. approach. I don't want to have my more or less precarious balance upset.

These half-conscious causes of my antipathy are buttressed by another, which is possibly more rational. I have always an objection which seems to knock out the possibility of any balance – which doesn't seem to admit any stabilizing rhythm. All these Paris books – Connolly's, Boyle's, & Djuna Barnes's (to connect them up in this respect) – seem like that to me. Everybody is progressively, or permanently, mad. The same kind of reason made me detest Evelyn Waugh's books – I couldn't stand the bonelessness. And for the same kind of reason I still retain a certain (almost!) hostility towards the *Waste Land*.

Please understand that all this is merely the exploration of my own feelings, not meant as *criticism*.

To come to the practical question. It's obvious that we must do *Nightwood*. And all I will say is (a) that in editing be careful to make the task of the prosecutor a difficult one! (b) that FVM & TSE will have to prepare the ground with assiduous skill.[1]

I have got to stop – because of the incredible complexity of the household situation here which consists of:

GCF & EEF

Bill Watt

Ann

Dick

Tom

One John Levetus, who came to stay with Dick & fell sick of a fever.

His mother, who came to nurse him, in a jumper which is beginning to get on Enid's nerves

1–TSE, memo to FVM: '*Nightwood* is scheduled for the 15th October. I think that a little work should be done before on getting the right reviewers, so far as they exist. You will no doubt cheque [*sic*] the review list carefully, and see that the book doesn't go to the wrong places. As Edwin Muir is a back[er] of [the] book already I suggest sending him a copy direct. He might review it for the *Spectator*. I suggest also sending a copy to Cyril Connoley [*sic*] direct, with my compliments, if you wish, and the implication that he should review it for the *Statesman*. I can't think of anyone else for the moment, but possibly you could persuade Orlo [Williams] that it is a good book and get him to ask for it from Richmond [at the *TLS*]. You remember that we talked about the book to Orlo sometime ago. Ackerley ought to be willing to give it a break in the *Listener*, but I can't think of any of his lads who could be persuaded to like it. Send a copy to John Hayward, although it will probably be unwise to have a notice in the *Daily Mirror*. Thare are a few other boys who ought to have complimentary copies. E.g. Michael Roberts. T. S. E.'

'Mouse' – a friend of Ann's
& the problem before us is – what to do this p.m!
Bill Watt send his respects to Mr Morley.

Yours<br>GCF

## TO *Sylvia Beach* TS Princeton

16 April 1936            Faber & Faber Ltd

Dear Miss Beach,

The reason why I have not written before to fix a date for coming to Paris is that my colleague, Mr F. V. Morley, and his wife, were tempted to take a few days in Paris at the same time, and did not know when they would be able to come. As their small boy is home from school for the Easter holidays until the 11th of May they are not free until then, but any time after the middle of May is possible for them and for me. As you said that May would do as well as April, would you let me know now what date would suit you in the latter part of May? I think the most convenient period to take, both for myself and for my friends would be a long weekend, say from Thursday to Monday or Friday to Tuesday. Would an evening falling inside such a period be convenient for you?

I return herewith the new title page which your printers have set up for *Exagmination*. You will notice that one small correction has been made at the foot of the page. Otherwise it will do very nicely.

Yours very sincerely,<br>T. S. Eliot

## TO *William Saroyan*[1] CC

16 April 1936            [Faber & Faber Ltd]

Dear Mr Saroyan,

Morley cabled you just before the Easter holidays in response to your enquiry about the date of publication of the book, and I think I ought to let you know just what I have been doing with it. Your New York publishers are people who know their business, and I hope the book will

---

1 – William Saroyan (1908–81), Armenian-American novelist, playwright, screenwriter, essayist: see Biographical Register.

have a still greater success than the previous one. But for the English market we are definitely of the opinion that the book is much too big. For the English market *Inhale and Exhale*[1] is almost of the dimensions of an omnibus volume. We can sell a much smaller book for the same price – you cannot charge more than 8s. 6d. for a volume of new short stories anyway. Anything above that makes it a luxury article, and 7s. 6d. is still better. Actually I think the book gains by being reduced. I don't mean that some of the stories are not good enough, but that the effect of so much material, including a great number of very short pieces, is rather overpowering and confusing, and that a shorter book can make a much better impact. You have almost the material here for two books. I think that the stories I have picked make about three fifths of the American book, or a little over. I don't think I have left out any of the best ones, but Morley is running through it to see whether he agrees with my choice. I didn't myself see any need for rearranging the pieces, as we did in the case of *The Young Man on the Flying Trapeze* [*sic*]. As soon as Morley has approved my selection we will let you have a list of the proposed contents.[2]

1–*Inhale & Exhale* (New York: Random House, 1936). The F&F edn (1936) carried this blurb, possibly by TSE: 'Readers of Mr Saroyan's first collection of stories, *The Daring Young Man on the Flying Trapeze*, have been awaiting a new volume to satisfy the taste they immediately acquired. Mr Saroyan's "short story" is unlike that of any other writer; yet the pieces in this volume, like the last, are so varied that it is difficult to say in just what the Saroyan quality consists, although it is unmistakable. Saroyan never becomes monotonous, and he always has what is called the "light touch". You can read his stories for pure amusement if you like: in this volume there is much gaiety and some delightful farce – but there is always a seriousness underneath, ranging from bitter criticism of society to lyrical beauty.'
2–FVM to Donald Klopfer, Random House, 17 Apr. 1936: 'You and Bill Saroyan will be thinking that we are pretty slow workers. I admit it, but we do work. It was obvious to me on my voyage back that we were going to enjoy Breathing in and Out, but I felt that we would probably do better if the volume weren't so big. Our problem, as you know, isn't the same as with you. The public here is much slower, and though THE DARING YOUNG MAN was very much of a succès d'estime which particularly fascinated all the bright lads of London, I felt that so large a second collection might frighten them. In the long run I will bet you that the market here will be permanent, but the way towards permanence isn't to rush the gates. When I got back I found that the rest of the gang felt this as strongly as I did, and Eliot in particular considered it desirable and assumed the responsibility of editing the volume. In response to a cable from Saroyan, he has written him direct according to the copy attached, and since he wrote I have studied his proposed selection. It is this. Eliot would retain Resurrection of a Life, Five Ripe Pears, The Oranges, The Younger Brother, London, Ah London, Two Days Wasted in Kansas City, International Harvester, The Bridge, A Night of Nothing, The Drinker, The Horses & the Sea, The War, Our Friends the Mice, Raisins, The Barber Whose Uncle Had His Head Bitten Off by a Circus Tiger, Prelude to an American Symphony, My Picture in the Paper, With a Hey Nonny Nonny, I Can't Put Two &

Incidentally, I like some of the travel stuff very much. I very much enjoyed the one about the black Tartars.

With best wishes,

Yours sincerely,

[T. S. Eliot]

## TO *Bernard W. Bromage* CC

17 April 1936                    [Faber & Faber Ltd]

Dear Mr Bromage,

Thank you for your review of the Lambrian [*sc.* Lavrin] book.[1] I have read your article on T. E. Lawrence with much interest, but I think it would be more suitable for some other periodical.[2] I should be sorry if it was not published at all. The *Criterion* will certainly have to have an article on Lawrence sooner or later, but not, I think, an article of such an intimate and personal kind. What I should like to have done would be to bring out the parallel between Lawrence and Charles de Foucauld, which

---

Two Together, Secrets in Alexandria, The Mother, Antranik of Armenia, The International Song of the Machine Gun, The Revolution, Little Miss Universe, Solemn Advice to a Young Man about to Accept Undertaking as a Profession, Two Thousand Four Hundred and Some Odd Dollars for Kindness, An Occurrence at Izzy's, Our Little Brown Brothers the Filipinos, The Japanese Are Coming, A Christmas Carol, A Note on Travel, The Dark Sea, Malenka Manon, The Proletarian at the Trap Drum, The Black Tartars, The Egg, The Little Dog Laughed to See Such Sport, Finlandia, The Armenian and the Armenian. That would make forty stories, and would be, I think, a considerably larger volume than THE DARING YOUNG MAN. We would publish at 7/6 as soon as possible, and would suggest the same terms as before, 10 per cent to 2,500, 12½ per cent to 5,000, and 15 per cent after. I am particularly anxious to keep all I can in hand in order to nurse THE DARING YOUNG MAN. That Young Man's situation is such that in spite of my eagerness, we have not yet been able to get to a second printing. The first printing of 1500 has been reported out of print for the past several months, but has only accumulated [an] order for 15 copies. As you see, this of itself doesn't justify a reprint; what I hope is that the new volume will revive excitement and enable us to hoist the trapeze again.

'Please give my particular best to Bill. And if you care to, do send him a copy of this letter. If he is in San Francisco he will have had Eliot's letter by this time, but he won't know what Eliot's suggestions are. As I say, I have been over them carefully, and for this market I think they are absolutely right. And I want to tell both of you that I have had great pleasure from the careful re-reading; I agree with Eliot in liking The Black Tartars almost best of all, though there are so many good ones that it is invidious to pick.'

1 – Bromage on Janko Lavrin, *Aspects of Modernism*: C. 13 (July 1936), 762–3.

2 – Bromage submitted (31 Mar.) an essay on T. E. Lawrence – 'whom I knew'.

is of course not in Lawrence's favour. In other words, I think that we should smite once and no more.[1]

Yours sincerely,
[T. S. Eliot]

## TO *A. M. Petitjean*[2]                                          cc

17 April 1936                    [Faber & Faber Ltd]

Dear Mr Petitjean,

I must apologize for the length of time for which we have kept your essay on the *Situation of Joyce*, but it is pretty stiff reading in the first place, and any manuscript that is not immediately rejected has to be read by two or three directors. It is a brilliant piece of work, on which I congratulate you. But in the first place it does not seem to us what is wanted as an *introduction* to Joyce's *Work in Progress*. It is not, I mean, a book for the beginner, or even for the person who is acquainted with Joyce's work through *Ulysses*, but not familiar with *Work in Progress*. It is rather a book for people who are already pretty well acquainted with Joyce's later work, and are therefore ready for your very interesting philosophical study on it. I think the public here will hardly be ready for such a book until Joyce's new book has been published and available for several years.

Secondly, I hope you will not mind my saying that while I very much admire your knowledge of English, and only wish that I had an equal command of French, the style of the English version is rather that of a man writing in a dead language than of a man writing a language with which he is colloquially familiar. This makes still more difficult a book which at best requires the closest attention.

1 – Genesis 8: 21: 'And the Lord smelled a sweet savour; and the Lord said in his heart, I will not again curse the ground any more for man's sake; for the imagination of man's heart is evil from his youth; neither will I again smite any more every thing living, as I have done.'
2 – Armand Marcel Petitjean (1903–2003): gifted essayist and philosopher, who contributed articles to the *Nouvelle Revue Française* during the 1930s ('Petitjean is a man of genius . . . perfectly upright and sure,' said Jean Paulhan), but wrecked his reputation by becoming for a while a collaborationist, 1940–3. Writings include *Imagination et réalisation* (1936) and *Le Moderne et son prochain* (1938). See too Petitjean, 'James Joyce et l'Absorption de Monde par le Language', *Cahiers du Sud* (Marseilles), 21: 165 (Oct. 1934), 607–23.

May I add that what you have sent me has given me a very keen interest in your work, and that I should be very glad at any time to see essays of yours with a view to publication in the *Criterion*.

With many regrets,

Yours sincerely,

[T. S. Eliot]

## TO *Antonio de Mendonça*[1]                                    CC

17 April 1936                              [Faber & Faber Ltd]

Dear Mr Mendonça,

I am returning herewith Sir Austen Chamberlain's preface to Senhor Ferro's book,[2] which I have read again, although I quite made up my mind about it after the first reading at your bureau. I am strongly of the opinion that this preface requires a reply from Dr Salazar, and I hope that you or Senhor Ferro will do everything in your power to persuade Dr Salazar to write, however briefly. I am willing to put my point still more forcibly: I should prefer not to have this preface at all without Dr Salazar's reply. I think that you will probably agree with me on this point. Speaking also from the publisher's point of view I think that the preface alone is of very little value, whereas a reply from Dr Salazar should give it a great deal of interest and selling power.

The member of the firm who deals with contracts is, I find, away for a few days' holiday. He will be back on Monday, and I will then have him draw up a new agreement.

Sincerely yours,

[T. S. Eliot]

1–Antonio de Mendonça, Manager of Casa de Portugal (Portuguese Information Bureau), London.
2–António Ferro (1895–1956), Portuguese writer, journalist, politician: see letter of 27 May 1938, below.

17 April 1936                    *The Criterion*

Dear Heppenstall,

I have your article on Léon Bloy,[1] which is of the sort usually called provocative, and not calculated to please all the orthodox, but I am going to use it. This is not, however, you remember, for the July number, because you had an article in the last number. I intend to put this in to the October number.

*God and Mammon* has arrived, and I have read it, and I cannot see any point in reviewing it together with Gill's book.[2] I don't see how it could be done in the space without injustice to one or the other. So I think *God and Mammon* will have to wait. So I should be grateful if you would go ahead with Gill's book by itself, for the July number, which will mean having your copy in by April 29th.[3]

I am ashamed not to have done anything more about Sebastian.[4] I will keep it on my conscience and write to you next week, but if I had done the job sooner we could have talked about it while you were here. As for your book, I'd like to think about that, and discuss your subject with another director before taking it up with you.[5]

Yours ever
T. S. Eliot

1–In 1928 TSE described the 'ecstatic' Léon Bloy (1846–1917), French Catholic novelist, essayist and poet, as 'violent and rhapsodical'.

2–François Mauriac, *God and Mammon: Essays in Order*, new series 1 (1936).

Heppenstall wrote, 12 Apr.: 'Did God and Mammon not come in? It is published now, I think. Or am I to do The Necessity of Belief by itself?'

3–Heppenstall on Eric Gill, *The Necessity of Belief*: C. 15 (July 1936), 718–21.

4–'Sebastian', a poem which Heppenstall hoped might be 'considered for separate publication as a book', had been submitted to TSE on 12 Dec. 1935. Heppenstall, 12 Apr.: 'I would be glad to hear something about Sebastian, soon . . . I imagine the long wait means . . . that you don't like it well enough to have it published. Or is it that you haven't just got the flaws located?'

5–'I'm not sure that I oughtn't to write a book on the Bourgeois [*sic*], before the Church book that you seemed to hold with. Would you tell me what you think? Would there be any sale for a book with the plain title Bourgeois or The Bourgeois Hell or the Burgher Soul . . .?'

My dear Joyce,

We have now made the experiment of having the printers set up the page which you indicated for a test. While it appears to be quite within their powers to print the book from the text as we have it, there is little doubt that the cost would be outrageously expensive, and we have come to your opinion that the text needs clearly typing out first, and this could best be done in Paris in the way originally suggested and conveyed to me by word of mouth by Mrs Jolas. We understand that if we return the manuscript Léon[1] will have it typed under his supervision, provided that we are willing to defray the costs of a typist up to 1,000 francs. This we are quite willing to do. It was not clear to me whether you thought that the whole of the text should be returned for this purpose, or only the more difficult Part III. It would obviously save a great deal of trouble and expense if you could correct and approve the typescript, so that it should be in a definitive form when it reached us.

We do not like to risk this manuscript in the post, as I understand that there is no existing duplicate of what is in our possession. I am proposing to come over to Paris myself in about a month's time, as I have been in communication with Sylvia Beach about giving a reading at her shop, and I think the best thing would be for me to bring the manuscript with me. Meanwhile I should be glad if I might hear from you or from Paul Léon on the matter.

> Yours very sincerely,
> T. S. Eliot

1–Paul Léon, assistant to JJ; see letter to Léon, 7 July 1936, below.

TO *Stephen Spender*                          TS Northwestern

17 April 1936                    Faber & Faber Ltd

Dear Spender,

Thank you so much for your letter of April 2, from Spain.[1] I must apologise for not replying to it sooner, and the reason is that I snatched a few days' holiday before Easter, and have only just got back.

I am delighted to hear that you are pleased with the appearance of *The Burning Cactus*.[2] I rather liked that little device myself, and I will certainly see that it is used on your other books in future, if you would like it to be so. You may be interested to know that the engraving was done by Reynolds Stone,[3] who is getting quite a reputation just now for his work. I believe he has done some rather nice book plates.

And thank you for telling me about those finely printed books of Gili's.[4] I will certainly write and find out more about them, as it may be that there would be a market for them here. I will let you know of any developments.

I have made a note of your new address, and I will see

[incomplete]


TO *Bonamy Dobrée*                       TS Brotherton Library

17 April 1936                    Faber & Faber Ltd

My dear Bonamy,

I didnt write before because I did not know when you were returning from Le Havre, where I hope you had a pleasant holiday; and I trust that Georgina's health is no longer a cause of anxiety. I will read the *oraison funèbre* on Bremond which you sent me (partly to find out why you sent

---

1 – Not traced.

2 – TSE's blurb for *The Burning Cactus* (1936) – which was at one point to have been called 'The Dead Island' – 'This volume contains five stories: The Dead Island, The Burning Cactus, The Third and a Half International, The Strange Death, and By the Lake. The author says of them: "These are neither anecdotes nor incidents. Each story attempts rather to create a legend. A particular situation is revealed and developed in such a way that a comparison of moral interests is achieved." The reader will infer that this is not a mere collection of short stories – the first story is indeed a long story – and that the book is no by-product of Mr Spender's activity, but will occupy an important place in the development of his creative work.'

3 – Reynolds Stone (1909–79): renowned engraver, designer, typographer.

4 – Joan Lluis Gili i Serra (John Louis Gili) (1907–98), bookseller and publisher; born in Barcelona; founder of Dolphin Books, London.

it).[1] But I am sorry that there is no prospect of seeing you until after this term. We had been speaking (Morley, Orlo and myself) of a possible *Criterion* on the 6th of May: would it be impossible for you to come up for that? I might be able to reserve the Russell Square bedroom, though I imagine that Frank will be staying up for the night and using it. Try to come if you possibly can.

The doctrine that in order to arrive at the love of God one must divest oneself of the love of created beings was thus expressed by St John of the Cross, you know: i.e. a man who was writing primarily not for you and me, but for people seriously engaged in pursuing the Way of Contemplation.[2] It is only to be read in relation to that Way: i.e. merely

1–Dobrée had sent on 12 Apr., 'a *discours de Réception à l'Académie Française* on Brémond, which may interest you': 'I think that with your rigidly humanistic view of humanity, viz that progress is illusory, you will at least like "*les idéologues, les mortels ennemis de l'expérience*", and, from the your theological standpoint, "*les nationalistes, ces mortels ennemis des raisons que la raison connait pas*".' He added that he had been reading *Burnt Norton*. 'You once told us to redeem the time; now you suggest that time is irredeemable. When we meet – I am afraid not till after my next term, damn it! – I shall have to ask you what redeeming the time means. For me it has merely a vaguely emotive flavour – a relic of my pseudo-Christian upbringing.'

2–TSE cited St John of the Cross – 'Hence the soul cannot be possessed of the divine union, until it has divested itself of the love of created beings' – as one of his epigraphs in *SA* (*CPP*, 115). The reference is to Gonzague Truc's translation of *The Ascent of Mount Carmel*, by St John of the Cross, Bk 1, ch. 4, section 8 – cited in Truc's edition of *Les Mystiques espagnols: Sainte Térèse – Saint Jean de la Croix* (Paris, 1921) – '*Toutes les délices et toutes les douceurs des créatures ne sont que des peines et des amertumes très grandes, lorsqu'on les compare avec les délices et les douceurs de Dieu. Celui-là donc ne mérite que des tourments, qui s'abandonne aux plaisirs du monde*': 'All the sweetness and all the pleasures which all the things of this world furnish to the will are, in comparison with the sweetness and pleasure which is God, supreme pain, torment, and bitterness. He, therefore, who shall set his heart upon them is, in the eyes of God, worthy of pain, torment, and bitterness, and can never attain to those delights with which the Divine union abounds' (trans. David Lewis [1906], 20–1). Cf. Saint John of the Cross, *Dark Night of the Soul*, trans. Allison Peers (1935, 1976), II: xxi, 171: 'The soul now divests and strips itself of all these worldly vestments and garments, setting its heart upon naught that is in the world and hoping for naught, whether of that which is or that which is to be, but living clad only in the hope of eternal life.' TSE to Josef Pieper, 19 Mar. 1959: 'my first acquaintance with St John of the Cross was made by a small volume of selections translated into French, which was published many years ago in a series of mystical writings, published in Paris. It was not until 1933 that I acquired the translation of Professor Peers. I believe that the quotation from St John of the Cross which I put at the beginning of *Sweeney Agonistes* (fragments written earlier than The Hollow Men) came from that same French book of selections.'

M. C. Bradbrook points out ('The Liturgical Tradition in English Verse: Herbert and Eliot', *Theology* 44 [1942], 19) that Dante's version of the 'hard saying from St John of the Cross' is to be found in *Purgatorio* XVIII, 100–2:

> Ma, quando al mal si torce, o con più cura
> O con men che non dee corre nel bene,
> Contra il fattore adopra sua fattura.

to kill one's human affections will get one nowhere, it would be only to become rather more completely a living corpse than most people are. But the doctrine is fundamentally true, I believe. Or to put your belief in your way, that only through the love of created beings can we approach the love of God, that I do believe to be UNTRUE. Whether we mean by that domestic and friendly affections, or a more comprehensive love of the 'neighbour', of humanity in general. I don't think that ordinary human affections are capable of leading us to the love of God, but rather that the love of God is capable of informing, intensifying and elevating our human affections, which otherwise may have little to distinguish them from the 'natural' affections of animals. Try looking at it from that end of the glass! And as for the dogma of Original Sin, do you really think that that compels us to deny that men have 'a deal of selflessness, generosity, fellow-feeling, caritas'??? Any doctrine which required us to deny ordinary observation could hardly stand. Of course I am not defending the extreme Lutheran view of human wickedness, which is horrifying and which I can't understand anyway. And surely to identify *Original* Sin with particular species of *sin*, with any or all of the 7 deadly, is almost as much of a misunderstanding as to identify the Immaculate Conception with the Virgin Birth. I confess that I have not come across any systematic treatise on the subject, however; I am writing to two theologians to ask them to recommend some.

I don't think I maintain that 'the teaching of classics' leads to Christianity – or that classical scholars are more likely to be Christians than other people. I mean that you can't disentangle the teaching of classics from a tradition of education in Europe that is Christian (though worn pretty

---

Thus the remainder of this letter by TSE is in reply to a letter from BD dated 19 Mar.: 'I have read your book with extreme interest. It is, of course, a good book . . .

'I do not, of course, share your point of view, but I have got, I think, as far as understanding it. Faith apart, I don't think I shall ever share your view, for two reasons. The first is that I don't believe one can ever arrive at the love of God by weaning oneself from the love of created beings: as far as my imperfect experience goes, it [is] only through the love of created beings that one can ever attain the love of God. That is why I like Traherne. The second is that I cannot accept the view that men are born wholly evil: I can't accept original sin. Not that I accept the noble savage, nor the innocent child trailing clouds of glory as he comes: that is where I differ from Traherne. I believe that men have a deal of lust, cruelty, callousness, greed, but I also believe that they have a deal of selflessness, generosity, fellow-feeling, *caritas* . . .

'Your essay on education appeals to me: I agree with your strictures on modern education, & the teaching of English in provincial universities: but I still have hopes of it. Your idea on the teaching of classics as leading to Christianity startles me. Would you recommend Euripides, Lucian, Petronius, Ovid?'

thin at Haileybury etc. I admit). If Christianity is done away with – I mean if it is expressly denied by all except a surviving remnant, then you will find that reasons will have to be found for teaching the classics. And I do not mean teaching them to a few specialists like Chaldaean or Gothic, but making them integral in education. And you will not have any easy time, in a professedly non-Christian society, in trying to find reasons.

yrs perpetually<br>
T.

## TO *Geoffrey Faber* TS Faber Archive

17 April [1936]  Faber & Faber Ltd

Dear Geoffrey,

Frank showed me your letter this afternoon – but I had only a hurried read of it between two interviews – and after five visitors between 3.30 and 6.30 I should be too limp to reply anyway. It's certainly one of the most interesting letters I have ever received – if I may say that I have received it: even if I were feeling more robust at the moment, I couldn't reply without having it in front of me, and I had to give it back. (Incidentally, I *don't* simply mean, by the unkillable worm, the perpetual letch – that's just it, to me the book gets deeper than 'sex'; I mean *la misère de la condition humaine*). But I must say that I *don't* want to press the firm into publishing a book which will land it with fines and damages – though I should be willing to do a short stretch in the 2nd division for it, that might be a rest: and that aspect of the matter must be gone into carefully. I think yr attitude very sporting & handsome. I am sorry that you are so *umgebaut vom Publikum*,[1] and I hope Enid will get some period of rest presently. And when you come back I have a good photograph of Old Ike Carver of Mosquito Cove to show you.

Yours<br>
T.

1 – *umgebaut vom Publikum* (Ger.): 'remodelled by the public'.

# TO *Virginia Woolf*[1]                                    TS Berg

17 April 1936                        Faber & Faber Ltd

My dear Virginia,

Doubly as I did not expect you to thank me for my book at all (I thought there was a tacit understanding amongst distinguished authors on this point) am I rewarded.[2] I should be unable to compose any letter, during a spell of headaches: yours is as brilliant and accomplished as ever. I am glad that the alternative is sleep. My sending the book was a most delicate way of suggesting that you should ask me to tea – perhaps even by myself: that was all the response desired. However, you are better off at Rodmell: the weather can be no more inclement, and the spring will be more forward; and London is full of mysterious troops of French and German pilgrims, all labelled, and chattering in their barbarous languages. I sit in Russell Square, and collect a few mildly amusing anecdotes, and a good many of other people's troubles: one poet has just put out his brother's eye with a fencing foil,[3] and another has just contracted syphilis; and most of them need a little money. At some expense, I have just persuaded Mr Ross E. Pierce, the Epic Poet of Buffalo, to return to Buffalo. Aldous came in to tea this afternoon, and agrees with me that things are going from Bad to

1 – Virginia Woolf (1882–1941), novelist, essayist, diarist, critic: see Biographical Register.
2 – VW wrote on 16 Apr.: 'What a base receiver of treasure I am! – never to have thanked you for your book. But it proves the depth of my trust in your ancient goodness, that I don't think it matters if I thank you or not. I've been cursed with headaches, & so retired here to sleep them off. That's one reason why I didn't write – the other, the chronic, is that I can't summon faith enough in my own judgment to criticise your poems to you; either to praise, blame, or discriminate. I've been lying in an arm chair in front of the fire with your book open, & such a radiance rises from the words that I can't get near them. So the first bee of summer feels for the first flower. I suspect its what the Lit. Sup. Critic would call enchantment, incantation – there must be a critic's word: but I'm too sleepy to find it; and so must merely testify to the fact: I'm held off from understanding by magic. Now you will have had enough. One of these days I hope to begin to understand again, and then I shall cut the book into ribbons with a thousand pocket knives – so I hope. Because I adore this exercise when I'm awake; and want, even now, to go into a thousand questions with you, about your plays in particular. But again, enough.
'We're staying down here, & perhaps attempting a cruise in Scotland: but I'm still awfully cursed with headache, as these lines show, & when my headaches go, as these are going, sleep rushes in, & I am now going to shut my eyes with affectionate thoughts of Mr Eliot & the Yorkshire terrier & the wild duck in Russell Square, – wish he would come to tea – How pleasant to see Mr Eliot – how very nice that would be. (This line was found in the margin of my copy) / Yr. affec. / V.W.' (Previously unpublished)
3 – In Apr. 1935 George Barker (aged twenty-two) had accidentally plucked out the right eye of his younger brother Kit (nineteen) with a fencing foil during a bout of boisterous play: see Robert Fraser, *The Chameleon Poet: A Life of George Barker* (2001), 76–7.

Worse. I have a photograph of Old Joe Cabot of Salem, which I should like to show you. He married my great-aunt Martha, of whom my Aunt Susan has presented me with a Silhouette at the age of fourteen. I write sarcastic letters about Mussolini to Ezra Pound. I have interviewed a Scot who wanted to sell a book, because my name was Eliot; and, said he, all we El(l)iots are alike – hot-tempered, obstinate, and dislike to agree with anybody. (If you go to Scotland, you should visit that sweet town Inverness, where my exciseman Neil Gunn has the loveliest whisky ever tasted).[1] I am supposed to be reading a book by Goebbels. In short, I am passing the time until Mrs Woolf returns to London and asks me to tea.

And remain, yr. devoted
T. S. E.

## TO *The Editor,* The New English Weekly

[Published 23 April 1936, 38]     [Faber & Faber Ltd]

Sir,

Mr Desmond Hawkins's admirable letter in your issue of April 9th leaves me in some doubt as to what the subject of controversy is.[2] I had assumed (though this was not the point on which my contribution turned) that Mr Hawkins and Mr Barlow, like some other critics, complained of the lack of interest of churchmen in social affairs. But I am wholly in agreement with Mr Hawkins in his objection to 'those who frankly use their ordainment as an instrument solely for social welfare and humanistic activities'. That the clergy, both high and low, should take an active

1–TSE to Theodore Spencer, n. d. (1933): 'The whisky gets better the farther north you go, & is superb in Inverness.'

Neil M. Gunn (1891–1973), novelist, worked as an officer of the Customs and Excise before becoming a full-time writer. Gunn to MacDiarmid, 9 July 1938: 'Eliot is really a sincere kind fellow' (*Dear Grieve: Letters to Hugh MacDiarmid (C. M. Grieve)*, ed. John Manson [2011], 219). See further Gunn, *Whisky and Scotland* (1935); *Selected Letters*, ed. J. B. Pick (1987); F. R. Hart, *Neil M. Gunn: A Highland Life* (1981); C. J. L. Stokoe, *A Bibliography of the Works of Neil M. Gunn* (1987).

2–A. Desmond Hawkins, 'The Church as Action', *NEW*, 9 Apr. 1936, 522–23. 'I maintain . . . that the vitality of a Church depends upon its ability to cherish, defend and expound its central dogma, its "revelation" [. . .] I agree that there is a tendency to measure the clergy "against a romantically high standard of holiness," but that seems to me to be only an adolescent failing. What is more important is that the greatest admiration is reserved for those who frankly use their ordainment as an instrument solely for social welfare and humanistic activities. These men, in abandoning their specific theology, are surrendering all that I could value [. . .] I am maintaining that no society is healthy when it abandons its characteristic theology.'

interest in social reforms (and I include reforms more drastic than such as slum-clearance) is most desirable; but they should bring to this activity the results of specifically *theological* study and reflection. A man can be, I admit, a useful parish priest without either the greatest theological capacity or the highest theological attainments; but for such people there ought to be a recognized body of scholars to provide his doctrines for him. In one way we have not enough theology, and in another we have too much.

The present state of the Church, in these matters, is indicated by the publishers' advertisement of a book of some merit by a clergyman advertized as 'left-wing Modernist'. (This advertisement is not on the jacket, but opposite the title page in the book.) The publishers say that their author,

'owing to fortunate financial circumstances for which he can claim no personal credit, is exceptionally indifferent to ecclesiastical opinion, so that the reader may feel entire confidence that, in the chapters which follow, he is being treated with complete candour.'

What an admission! and how significant, whether justified or not! That publishers can recommend a book by a priest on the ground that the author is independent – and for *financial* reasons! – of ecclesiastical discipline, indicates that the conception of the nature of the *Church* has almost disappeared. And indeed, what we are apt to feel when one or another eminent ecclesiastic speaks his mind on some matter of the day, is that we are being given, not the view of *the Church*, but that of an individual whose public position is such that he is able to command half a column in *The Times*. From our Judicial System we expect more than that.

It is possible that if the Church had been represented continuously by men who both understood and fearlessly maintained the right view of the function of the Church, Mr Hawkins might have been continuously a Christian in a Christian ambience. I do not think, however, that that exonerates him from making up his own mind and assuming the full responsibility for it.

T. S. Eliot

24 April 1936                                    Faber & Faber Ltd

*Personal*

My dear Wilson,

I am dropping you this line to tell you how sorry Morley and I were that we could not see our way to publishing your volume of sketches and travels which Brace let us see. It was all interesting to us personally, but I think you will understand our doubts about the pieces that form the first part of the book, which would be partly unintelligible, and partly of little interest to people who are not acquainted with the American scene. The Russian journey was very good reading, but not enough for a book in itself, and we felt furthermore that there was a lack of coherence between the parts of the book, which would operate more strongly here against its success than it would in New York. I am letting you know this directly because I want you to know that we are keen about your work, and anxious to capture the next book you do which could be launched on the London market.[2]

I should always be glad to hear from you, and I hope that I shall some day be able in London to return your hospitality to me. Meanwhile I hope to be in New York for a short time in the autumn, and look forward to seeing you.

Yours ever,

T. S. Eliot

1–Edmund Wilson (1895–1972): critic, social commentator and cultural historian; worked in the 1920s as managing editor of *Vanity Fair*; later as associate editor of *The New Republic* and as a prolific book reviewer. Works include *Axel's Castle: A Study in the Imaginative Literature of 1870–1930* (1931) – which includes a chapter on TSE – *The Triple Thinkers: Ten Essays on Literature* (1938), and *The Wound and the Bow: Seven Studies in Literature* (1941). TSE to Geoffrey Curtis, 20 Oct. 1943: 'Edmund Wilson is a very good critic except that, like most of his generation in America, he has mixed his literary criticism with too much political ideology of a Trotskyite variety and perhaps he is also too psychological, but I have a great respect for him as a writer and like him as a man.'

2–Wilson replied to TSE, 3 May, 'I didn't know that my book has been submitted to Faber.'

FVM to Donald Brace, 23 Apr. 1936: 'Many thanks for the galleys of Edmund Wilson's TRAVELS IN TWO DEMOCRACIES . . . Eliot and I have both read the galleys with a great deal of private interest, and a good deal of anguish. The anguish is that it gives the impression of a number of occasional pieces slung together; a made book rather than a book. In spite of our own interest in Wilson, I am gloomy about the chances here . . . Eliot is also writing direct to Wilson. We very much enjoyed some of the sketches. The scarlet fever part – and the evening with [William] Saroyan in Moscow is excellent comedy.'

24 April 1936                          [Faber & Faber Ltd]

Dear Miss Levertoff,

Thank you for letting me see your poems, which interest me very much.[2] I hope that you will continue to write poetry and that you will let me see more of your work later. You will remember, I am sure, that you have a good many years ahead of you in which you can write poetry; but you may not understand just yet what I mean when I say that you will be very glad in two or three years that I am not publishing any of this. I do not mean that they are bad; they are in fact very interesting for your age. But you will find, I think, in two or three years, if not sooner, that your notions of poetry will change, and then there will be a time when you are rather ashamed of your earlier work because you will be writing something better. And again, several years after that you will go through the same experience about what you have written before. And this is a

1–Denise Levertov (1923–97), British-born poet, critic and political campaigner (she was born in Ilford, Essex, the daughter of Paul Levertoff – a Russian Hasidic Jew-in-exile who became a serving Anglican priest as well as an editor and leftist activist. In 1955 she became a naturalised American citizen; and in her later years she became a Christian and then converted to Roman Catholicism. She taught at Brandeis University, Massachusetts Institute of Technology, and Tufts University, and ultimately as a full professor at Stanford University, 1982–93. Author of several volumes of poetry, including *The Double Image* (1946), *To Stay Alive* (1971), and *The Collected Poems of Denise Levertov* (2013), and non-fiction including *The Poet in the World* (1973) and *The Letters of Denise Levertov and William Carlos Williams* (1998). See Dana Greene, *Denise Levertov: A Poet's Life* (2012); Donna Hollenburg, *A Poet's Revolution: The Life of Denise Levertov* (2013).

On 25 Nov. 1958 TSE was to write in support of Levertov's application for a Guggenheim Fellowship: 'I told Miss Levertov frankly that her poems did not have a particularly strong appeal to myself, but that I should, nevertheless, be glad to put in a word on her behalf on the basis of her achievement, of the opinion of other critics as well qualified as myself and the undoubted ability which is exhibited in what she has written. Her statement of plans seems to me a very honest statement, and I think that if Miss Levertov were given the benefit of a scholarship, the result would certainly be another volume of poems which would deserve respect and probably win admiration.' (John Simon Guggenheim Memorial Foundation)

2–Levertoff wrote (n.d.): 'I wondered if you could publish any of these poems in Criterion.

'I am twelve (last October) & all of them were written in the later part of 1935 except "The Prisoner" & "The Shroud [illegible] folded very straight."

'I think you know my father, Dr Paul Levertoff . . .

'I heard "Murder in the Cathedral", & I enjoyed it; but I think – I hope you don't mind my saying so – that your writing is apt to be rather chilly & impersonal. Of course I can't really judge, for when I open a book of your poems I look at the title & at the whole poem, but can't bring myself to read it. Perhaps I am not old enough. My favorite modern poets are Walter de la Mare & A. E. Housman. I love Elizabethan poetry too.

'If you don't want any of them, could you send me criticisms please?

'Yours sincerely [*sic*], / Denise Levertoff.'

process we all have to put up with, and it is not until we are well over twenty years old that we begin to write something which we don't become quite so sorry about. Meanwhile I hope you will go on writing when you have time, because if you are going to be a good writer there is a great deal you will have to study and learn. I hope that you already know one or more other languages besides English, because a knowledge of other languages is a great help to a poet in writing his own. It is always useful to try short pieces of translation when you come across a poem in a foreign language that you think you understand and like very much, and it is also useful to practise writing poetry in the most regular forms, such as the sonnet. It is very difficult to write a good sonnet, but even if you do not succeed the practice will help you in writing other things.

With all best wishes,
Yours sincerely,
[T. S. Eliot]

## TO *Stephen Spender*

TS Northwestern

24 April 1936                    *The Criterion*

Dear Stephen,

Thank you very much for your letter of the 13th, which reached me at the beginning of this week. I am not at the moment attempting to reply to it, but merely to answer the business questions which you raise.[1] I have brought up your suggestion of a small book on Spanish poetry to the Committee, and they are unanimously of the opinion that it would be practically unsaleable. I know Marià Manent slightly of course, by correspondence, and he has sent me one or two things of his of which I have not been able to make very much, as I do not know any Catalan.[2] But nobody else knows his name, and we know from experience that

---

1 – 'Whilst I was in Spain I managed to learn enough Castilian to read some very remarkable modern Spanish poems, particularly those by Garcia Lorca . . . I write to ask you whether you think Faber would care to publish a small book of say 30,000 words on Modern Spanish Poetry: also to suggest that it should be written by Marià Manent, who is an intelligent critic and who, as you may know, has a remarkable knowledge of modern English poetry . . . If you wished to do this book, since Manent could not see translations of Spanish poetry through the press unassisted, I would be very glad to help him where he needs help.'
2 – Marià Manent (1898–1988), poet (he wrote original poems in modern literary Catalan), critic and journalist, had contributed to *Commonweal* (New York) and *Hispania* (Paris); and he was in charge of the Foreign Letters section of the Barcelona newspaper *La Veu de Catalunya*.

books by unknown foreigners on subjects limited to a small audience anyway are doomed to complete failure. I doubt if we should sell 100 copies, and translations are only just possible when they appear over the name of some well-known English poet.

If you should be interested in any Spanish poetry enough to want to translate it yourself I would always be delighted to try out your translations in the *Criterion*. I wish that there was more of a market for translation because translating is such good practice for a poet in between his bursts of original work. But as I may have told you, the sales of my translation of *Anabase*, over which I took a good deal of trouble, stopped completely after only some hundreds. I am very glad that I did it, both for my own sake and because it brought the poem to the notice of the few people who could make the most use of it, but it certainly did not pay the firm to do it.

I will be writing later in response to your letter as a whole.

Yours affectionately,
Tom

## TO *Tom Faber* CC

24 April 1936                    *The Criterion*

Dear Tom,[1]

This Lion which I have pourtrayed Will hardly make you much afraid And he is much more mild because Of what I put between his jaws[2] And he, I hasten to remark Is called the Lion of St Mark: A Saint of whom you have heard tell Who wrote a book that sold quite well[3] And had considerable fame Before the firm of Faber

1 – Sent to Tom Faber for his ninth birthday, 25 Apr. 1936.
2 – A ten-shilling note, in the drawing.
3 – St Mark was author of the Second Gospel.

came But not to leave you in the dark The reason why I name St Mark And In my feeble fashion try on A portrait of his favourite lion (Were I an artist which I ain't) Is that this literary Saint Is so to speak a kind of neighbour Of Thomas of the house of Faber Because the day that bears his name Is most auspiciously the same As that on which for Thomas' sake We all are willing to partake Of something called a birthday-cake. With wishes for your health and cheer And wealth throughout the coming year And closing with a joyful psalm I sign myself your

Uncle Tom.[1]


TO *Ezra Pound*                                                   TS Northwestern

24 Aprile 1936 A.D.                          *The Criterion*

Now then, Ez, mon agouti, what about a lick of work? Oxf. Press has published Collectit Poems of Robt. Bridges: why don't ole Ez cut em up for the Crittereum? *Test. of Beauty* not included; I wouldn't ask anybody to break his heart readin that. But this would fit in proper to yr. Memoirs of a Dead Life, wot, my Rabit of Rabits, get to it and let me send you complete wks. of R.B. & thereupon develop the luminous principle of reason which we receive from the sky, and make it shine with full glory, for there is nothing that the sage does not pusch to the last degree of perfection (AND HOW HE DO PUSH!!)[2]

yrs explicitly
TP


1–See further *Poems II*, 170–1.
2–EP responded, 27 Apr.: 'I take it all I gotter do is to talk about Britches, not necessarily read the old petrification? So DO be specific/ Rabbit Britches indeed!!! . . .

'Proposed title of the article
Testicles versus Testament
an embalsamation of the Late Robert's Britches.'

On 28 Apr., he changed his mind on the 'corpse' Bridges: 'If the luminous reason of one's criticism iz that one shd/ focus attention on what deserves it, a note by EP/ on Bridges wd/ be a falsification of values . . . I can't think Britsches has enough influence to be worth attacking.'

24 April 1936                    [Faber & Faber Ltd]

Dear Mrs Coleman,

I really believe that we are now getting to a point at which something can be done about *Nightwood*. I should very much like to see you and have a talk with you about the book and about Miss Barnes. Would it be convenient for you to come to tea with me on Tuesday next the 28th at 4.30. If not, I should be grateful if you would kindly ring up my secretary and arrange another appointment.[1]

Yours sincerely,

[T. S. Eliot]

1 – Coleman took tea with TSE on Tues. 28 Apr. Faltejskova, 84: 'She was so much in awe of the poet that the idea of meeting him in person petrified her. She writes in her diary how she went to the British Museum before meeting him to get courage and was so frightened that she miscalculated the time of their meeting and was early. (D, p. 252)

'Coleman recorded in her diary that Eliot liked the novel but would have not guessed that Nightwood had been written by a woman [. . . ] When Coleman disagreed with him, Eliot explained that "he didnt think the Doctor seemed like a woman's creation" (D, p. 253) . . .

'Secondly, Eliot expressed a worry that "the book might be taken up by a censor." (D, p. 253) [. . .] Frank Morley, Eliot's colleague, also attended the meeting. Morley suggested that Faber's offer to publish *Nightwood* depended on how amenable Barnes would be to the changes they would propose [. . .] She wrote about her feelings of unease at this comment: "I got frightened at this, because Djuna cannot be said to eat out of my hand. But I guaranteed that she would be amenable about small omissions." (D, p. 254)'

On another page of her diary, Coleman recorded too: 'E. [TSE] says the English are against Lesbianism particularly. E. and M. [Morley] are like brothers, conspiring.' (D, p. 25; cited in Faltejskova, 85). See too Cheryl J. Plumb, ed., *Nightwood: The Original Version and Related Drafts* (1995), xxii.

Miriam Fuchs, 'The Triadic Association of Emily Holmes Coleman, T. S. Eliot, and Djuna Barnes', *ANQ: A Quarterly Journal of Short Articles, Notes, and Reviews* 12: 4 (Fall 1999), 35, comments further on Coleman's record of her meeting with TSE: 'Impressed by every aspect of the meeting, Coleman describes Eliot as "affable," "attractive," "sensitive to everything," with "deep and very moving" eyes, "a sad face," "not a very good brow," but having "the sweetest smile." . . . Coleman adds that she and Eliot spent the time in good humor and laughter . . . Though taken aback when Eliot tells his associate [FVM] that Barnes "is a tiger eating out of Mrs Coleman's hand," since she knows this to be untrue, she was probably flattered and encouraged that she and Eliot would become better acquainted . . . A short, final paragraph comes as a surprise . . . Coleman writes, at this point completely out of context: "Eliot said he shd think Djuna would not write again – he felt that pressure so great in this; as though she had writen [*sic*] herself out."'

28 April 1936                         Faber & Faber Ltd

My dear More,

Thank you very much for your letter of the 14th.[1] It has always pleased me that you had a special liking for *Sweeney Agonistes*: I think myself that it is the most *original* thing that I have done. It is useless to speculate whether, if circumstances had permitted my finishing that play at the time, it would have been equally good as a whole; the only thing that is certain is that twelve years have made too great a difference in me for me to touch it now. Of course, I find that I am obliged to believe at any point that what I have done most recently is *in some respect* my best work: otherwise the discouragement and lack of confidence which always attend the labour of composition would prevent me from writing at all. (If you feel the same way at all, you may care to know that I would give the whole Shelburne, though unwillingly, for the *Greek Tradition*; and it seems to me that by and large the actual *writing* of your later work is a more masterly style).

I shall be particularly interested in your 'Milton',[2] because I have had this winter to refresh my knowledge to write a short paper on Milton's versification and its influence, for a volume of Studies of the English Association edited by my friend Herbert Read. (I refuse to join that Association, however, because it publishes very bad anthologies which are used in schools, because I cannot subscribe to any of its (unexamined) premises, and because I think that people who band together to forward the teaching of English ought first to have some views about Education and the place of English in it: also I am now pretty well alienated in thought from Read. Some years ago I thought that he had worked through his psychological phase, but it has come back again worse than ever, and he even takes up with surrealists.)

---

1 – More was grateful for *Collected Poems 1909–1935*. 'The two poems that touch me the most are perhaps *Sweeney Agonistes* and the Choruses from *The Rock*.' It had taken him a number of readings to come fully to appreciate 'the suggestions and artifices by which [the] background of tragedy was intimated – the word let slip here and there that showed how beneath the jazz and cold gayety the actors felt the fearful emptiness beneath their life . . . In my estimation you have never done anything better than *Sweeney*, the economy of art in the thing is masterful.'
2 – Elmer More mentioned that he had recently finished an essay on 'How to Read Lycidas' for publication in the *American Review*: he would send it to TSE as soon as it was out.

I liked P. S. Richards immensely, and hope that our acquaintance will continue. When you next come over we must arrange a visit to Storrington with him.[1]

I have lately met an interesting (white) Russian named Wladimir Weidlé, whose book *Les Abeilles d'Aristée* (Desclée DeBrouwer, Paris) I think you would find as interesting as I did (there is a very good chapter on *la poésie pure*, and his views on the *déchéance* of modern art I found on the whole very sympathetic, though I am a little doubtful of the tendency of his views about Hans Christian Andersen and the infantile).[2] He, and also a Russian professor Zander from their Orthodox Theological college in Paris,[3] speak very enthusiastically about the theological work of Father Sergius Bulgakoff, but as nothing appears to be available in any language but Russian, I am waiting to find some English, French or German theologian who can read that language: as I should like to know whether he is worth translating.

Very sincerely,

T. S. Eliot

Do you know any good treatise on Original Sin?


## TO *Dylan Thomas*                                                    CC

28 April 1936                          [Faber & Faber Ltd]

Dear Thomas,

I found *The Orchards* very interesting and will publish it in the *Criterion*.[4] I am not sure whether that will be in the next number or the following, but I have to make up the next number within the next few

---

1 – The schoolteacher and author Philip S. Richards had written to More with news of TSE's recent visit, in company with Montgomery Belgion, to Storrington, the W. Sussex village near the coast where Richards lived. 'I have come to like Richards almost fondly and to have a high estimation of his talent. I hope you have acquired something of the same feeling.'

2 – Wladimir Weidlé (1895–1979), Russian art critic and man of letters, emigrated to France in 1924; author of *Les Abeilles d'Aristée: Essai sur le destin actuel des lettres et des arts* (1936).

3 – Léon Zander (1893–1964), Institut de Théologie Orthodoxe, Paris

4 – C. July 1936.

days, and will let you know. I hope to see you again when you come back to London.[1]

Yours sincerely,
[T. S. Eliot]

TO *Rayner Heppenstall*                                    TS Texas

28 April 1936                          Faber & Faber Ltd

Dear Heppenstall,

I am extremely sorry to hear from Faber of the unfortunate mistake that has occurred in connection with the publication of your book. I don't know quite how this happened, because I thought that I had clearly arranged with the publication department for the production of your book in June. But perhaps I am as responsible as anybody for the error, in as much as it was my business to make the matter clear, as much as it was theirs to understand it. I hope that the difference in time will not be considerable.

I have a letter from James Hanley, the novelist, from which it appears that Herbert Read had been speaking to him about you.[2] Hanley lives in Wales, and would be glad to put you up in his house for a few months, if that plan of life suited you. I don't know very much about Hanley, as I have only met him once. That is to say, I have no idea, one way or another, what sort of people he and his wife would be to live with. But apparently Herbert Read knows Hanley better than I do, and if you are

1–TSE had lunch with Thomas in Apr. 1936. According to Jonathan Fryer, Thomas 'complained to his friend Trevor Hughes that Eliot had treated him like some curiosity from the Welsh valleys, "from pitboy to poet". However, Eliot was too important a person for the young Dylan to protest to his face, and his failure to publish Dylan's first book . . . would be the result of Eliot's lack of certainty about Dylan's talent rather than of any unpleasantness between the two' (*Dylan: The Nine Lives of Dylan Thomas* [1993], 59). See too Paul Ferris, *Dylan Thomas: The Biography* (new edn, 1999), 132: '"I've never seen him human," Thomas wrote to Desmond Hawkins, "only in his office telling me 'And what is more, surrealism is a dead horse'." They also drank in a pub and had lunch. Vernon Watkins, not one of the boozy pals who laughed behind Eliot's back and called him "the Pope", was told that Eliot was "charming, a great man, I think, utterly unaffected"; Thomas said they talked mainly about rheumatism.'

2–James Hanley (1897–1985): British writer of novels, short stories, and plays (for radio, TV and theatre); author of *Drift* (1930), *Boy* (1931; repr. 2007 with an essay by Chris Gostick, 'Extra Material on James Hanley's *Boy*'); *No Directions* (1943), *A Kingdom* (1978).

Hanley offered (24 Apr.) to accommodate Heppenstall at the large house in Wales where he and his wife were living: it would be a quiet life – 'absolute freedom' – in return for minor chores 'as one of the family'. HR said that Heppenstall was genuine, and in real need.

at all interested I should suggest that you have a few words with him about the matter. In case you should get so far as to take the matter up with James Hanley his address is Bryn Derwen, Cynwyd, Corwen, North Wales.

Yours sincerely,<br>T. S. Eliot

## TO *Henry Eliot* TS Houghton

28 April 1936 Faber & Faber Ltd

My dear Henry,

I have to thank you for various cuttings and finally for your letter of the 16th which arrived yesterday. I am glad to know that both volumes reached you safely.[1] They are the last that I am likely to publish for a year or more. I think that there is something to be said for your suspicion of epigraphs: that is, I am aware that they may appear to be there for the wrong reason. The purpose is to give a clue to the tone and mood of the poem, rather than to the literal meaning.[2] The word LOGOS was important in this way, suggesting the current of Greek thought uniting with the Gospels, coming down to the hermits of the Thebaid, to St John of the Cross, and to an item of individual experience in the world today. But the immediate effect on most readers is very likely wrong.

I have not had any report of *Murder* from which I could judge whether I should have liked the production on the whole or not. Your account makes me incline to think that I should not. The four Tempters should certainly be costumed very differently, and the fourth should be a man of the same stature, and as far as possible of the same type, as the Archbishop himself, and should certainly be clad as a priest and tonsured (as he is here); and it is much more important that this part should be competently played than any of the others. On the other hand, the murder itself, as played in London, is not very effective, and had to be considerably simplified from

1–TSE sent copies of *Essays Ancient and Modern* and *Collected Poems 1909–1935*.
2–HWE wrote on 16 Apr.: 'I like Burnt Norton very much, and nearly all of the new poems, though I still retain my objection to epigraphs; they seem to me the last vestige of the Babbitt-baiting, or as one critic calls it, the contumacious period.'

Perhaps it was not by coincidence that, just thirteen days later, TSE was to insist in a memo relating to the production of Rayner Heppenstall's *An Apology for Dancing*: 'ALL the epigraphs' should be cut out – 'In fact, I feel strongly about this: *epigraphs must be discouraged*: no one under 45 should be allowed to use them at all.' TSE was 47.

the historical facts – Thomas was a powerful man, and knocked the murderers about a bit before they got him down.

I am well aware of grave dramatic effects. The play was written, you remember, for production in a peculiar hall on a particular occasion: I had no expectation that it would ever be put on again, and certainly not as an ordinary play. Its success, as an ordinary play, is largely due to accidents which I could not have foreseen and for which I need no credit.

I also thought Irvine's remarks about the difficulty of the Sermon very pretentious.[1] Why should it be so difficult? It is only a sermon: it was timed to give the effect, in eight or nine minutes, of an ordinary sermon which would take at least fifteen.

The choruses were actually intended to be partitioned between the voices, the whole chorus only speaking together at emphatic moments. If one had the whole chorus speak together (or in two parts) the whole time, the effect would be both monotonous and inaudible. This method is, of course, anything but Greek. Elsie Fogerty who ran the chorus here has an extraordinary gift for 'orchestrating' a chorus among a well-chosen range of voices: I don't know what it would be like with a different director.

The 'satire' on the totalitarian state I should hardly expect to convey very much to an audience in a country where the problem does not exist as it does throughout Europe.

You are, of course, as much entitled to an opinion as I am myself, of how much I have identified Becket with myself, or alternatively how much I have identified myself with Becket: it is never easy to say which an author is doing more. But I must protest against the suggestion that I suffer from persecution mania![2] I have seen something of that not uncommon

1 – In the Manhattan Theater production of *MiC*, Harry Irvine was Becket.
   HWE wrote: 'The interlude was well done, though I hardly see why it is so difficult as Irvine makes out in one of his interviews; nor can I take it very seriously when he says that his lines are like reciting Einstein with dramatic fervor, and that the author has no use whatsoever for time or space. That is pure pseudo-scientifico-mystical tosh such as one might expect from an enraptured reviewer but not from so competent an actor.'
2 – 'I could not find unity running through the play until I conceived of it as a sort of *apologia pro vita sua*, through the medium of what is a sort of allegory. In other words, Becket, it seems to me, is a projection of T. S. Eliot; Becket's doubts are his doubts, Becket's hopes are his hopes, Becket's self-justification and final resolution are T. S. Eliot's; and Becket's murder, though its parallel has not occurred, is what the critics, or certain critics whom T S. Eliot dislikes, would like to consummate in a literary way . . . I think you also have, not delusions, but rather, notions, of persecution . . . Anyway, you believe, certainly, I think, that you are persecuted by certain critics for your professed beliefs; and that these critics are malicious rogues, not animated by the dispassionate disapproval of true critics, but by jealousy and some other equally ignoble motive.'

disease in other people, and it has always been my observation that people suffering from persecution mania thought that they were being persecuted. Now, I do not think that I am being persecuted, so I do not see how I can be suffering from notions of persecution. I think that I have received more credit than anyone has a right to expect during his lifetime, and have also had a good deal of good luck: if I have not had a happy life, that is my own doing, and perhaps I should have been no happier in any other conceivable set of circumstances. I may have suffered now and again at the hands of malicious rogues, but I observe this constantly happening to other people too. I have no grievance against Alan Clutton Brock, who wrote the article in *The Times* to which I referred in the passage from Andrewes which you quote – and anyway, *The Times* was slapped by the Archbishop of York for printing it.[1] As for my fears for the Church, for Christianity, and for civilisation, I think that they are shared by a good few people; and I can't see that they have anything to do with my private situation.

Ever affectionately,<br>Tom

1–Clutton Brock, 'Mr Eliot's New Essays', *TLS*, 6 Dec. 1928, 953: 'It is now some years since it was first suggested by an acute critic that Mr Eliot would find it possible to reconcile his principles with his practice only "by an act of violence, by joining the Catholic Church". A drawing near to Anglo-Catholicism is the step his new book announces . . . But it is our view that by accepting a higher spiritual authority based not upon the deepest personal experience (for that we must still turn to the poems), but upon the anterior and exterior authority of revealed religion, he has abdicated from his high position. Specifically he rejects modernism for medievalism . . . Recently he recorded his conviction that Dante's poetry represents a saner attitude towards "the mystery of life" than Shakespeare's. Not a saner, we would say, but simply a different attitude, and to the majority, the great majority, today no longer a vital one.'

Dr William Temple, Archbishop of York, in his address to the Quadrennial Conference of the Student Christian Movement in Liverpool, 'The Dedication of the Mind', 2–7 Jan. 1929, noted: 'We have reached a stage where the pundits of literature regard the acceptance of any specific revelation as a confession of weakness. The review of Mr T. S. Eliot's last volume of essays in *The Times Literary Supplement* is a symptom, perhaps a portent. The reviewer holds that a gulf is now fixed between Mr Eliot and himself because Mr Eliot accepts the Christian revelation. To base himself on that instead of on "the deepest personal experience" is held to be an abdication. Now that argues a definite deification of pride or self-centredness . . . Why should not a man's acceptance of, and response to, a Divine self-revelation in a Person be as deep a personal experience as his response to the Divine Self-Revelation in Nature or in History generally? . . . Our great need is writers of artistic gifts who will seek to make their own the Christian revelation, and then set it before us recreated by the vividness of their experience' (*The Purpose of God in the Life of the World* [1929], 199–200).

TO *A. G. Hebert*                                            CC

28 April 1936                    [Faber & Faber Ltd]

Dear Father Gabriel,

I am writing to ask for your opinion on a suggestion which was made to me by Professor Léon Zander, who called a few days ago. He tells me that practically none of the work of Father Sergius Bulgakoff[1] has been translated from the Russian into any other language, and he wants us to consider undertaking a translation of one of Bulgakoff's chief works, *The Lamb of God*. He believes that a translation in English would be read by other European theologians, and that the book should have a sale abroad as well as here. I have never met Father Bulgakoff myself, and his name is hardly more than a rumour to me. I had a few words about him on Sunday evening with Wladimir Weidlé, whom by the way I like exceedingly, and Weidlé also spoke of Bulgakoff's work in the highest terms. I don't suppose that Russian is one of your languages, but I thought that very likely you would have some personal knowledge of Bulgakoff, or that you could direct me to others who knew about him. I should be grateful for any help you could give me.

By the way, I found Weidlé's *Les Abeilles d'Aristée*[2] very stimulating. I think George ought to have a look at it.

Yours very sincerely,
[T. S. Eliot]


TO *Michael de la Bédoyère*[3]                              CC

28 April 1936                    [Faber & Faber Ltd]

Dear Bédoyère,

I have been slow in replying to your letter of April 20th, because I wanted to think it over at leisure.[4] I should certainly be glad to appear

---

1–Sergius Bulgakov (1871–1944), Russian Orthodox Christian theologian and philosopher.
2–'Bees of Aristée'.
3–Michael de la Bédoyère (1900–73) entered the Society of Jesus and gained first-class honours in philosophy, politics and economics at Campion Hall, Oxford, before a crisis of faith caused him to relinquish his noviciate. By birth a count in the French nobility, he worked as assistant editor to his uncle and father-in-law Algar Thorold on the *Dublin Review* before becoming editor of the *Catholic Herald*, 1934–62. Works include *The Drift of Democracy* (1931), *Christian Crisis* (1940) and a study of Baron von Hügel.
4–De la Bédoyère, *The New Catholic Herald* (London), wrote on a subject that he had talked over with Father Martin D'Arcy: 'Roman Catholic papers have often run a series

in the *Herald*, for any or no fees (that could hardly be a concern in a discussion like this). What you suggest is something that I have often thought of attempting, but usually dismissed because of the extreme difficulty of conveying exactly what one would be trying to say. Obviously, the views of a layman like myself on such matters as the Petrine Claims, the Apostolic Succession,[1] and so forth, would be merely a reflection of what half-a-dozen theologians could put better. The only significant individual contribution that I could make – the only thing that nobody else perhaps could do better – would be something like this: assuming that Anglican and Roman Orders and Sacraments are equally valid, on what grounds did a person brought up altogether outside the Christian Faith elect to become a member of the former community rather than the latter? (Of course there have been other 'converts', such as, I believe, A. E. Taylor, but I doubt whether a philosopher and theologian like Taylor would occupy himself with the almost imponderable considerations that I have in mind).[2] But when I come to consider the expression, for those holding quite a different view, of what is positive in my mind, I find it a very difficult matter indeed. Even if this sort of thing would suit your book, I doubt if I could do it to my own satisfaction in your space. I see great opportunities of misunderstanding. The only way that would satisfy me would be to make my apologia in full – or at anything from five to fifteen thousand words – and try to boil it down: then, if my digest proved indigestible, I could at least publish the fuller account later. But this would

---

of articles entitled "Why I am a Catholic", and we want to be original enough to run one entitled "Why I am not in communion with the Church of Rome", or some such title. Our purpose is absolutely non-controversial but rather to help ourselves over what is definitely a difficulty to ourselves, namely, why a number of people who seem to us to be in agreement with us on all points nevertheless are not in communion with us . . . The series would be summed up by Father D'Arcy himself – again not with the idea of refuting arguments but with the idea of seeing where the difficulty lies and what can be done to meet it. I am sure this is a more helpful approach to the problem of re-union than many which have been suggested in the past . . .

'Frankly we cannot afford to pay anything like the rates which you would have a right to expect, as we are a paper that is only just beginning in its present form.'

1 – The Petrine Claims depend on Catholic doctrine that the Pope, as lineal successor to St Peter, first Bishop of Rome, is supreme head of the universal Church, with priority over all other bishops: see Matthew 16: 18–19: 'And I say also unto thee, That thou art Peter, and upon this rock I will build my church; and the gates of hell shall not prevail against it. And I will give unto thee the keys of the kingdom of heaven: and whatsoever thou shalt bind on earth shall be bound in heaven: and whatsoever thou shalt loose on earth shall be loosed in heaven.'

2 – Alfred Edward Taylor (1869–1945), Professor of Moral Philosophy, Edinburgh University, 1924–41; President of the Aristotelian Society, 1928–9. Publications include *St Thomas Aquinas as a Philosopher* (1924); *Plato, the Man and his Work* (1927).

take a great deal more time than I can at present afford to give. Possibly, when I see other people's statements (to which I look forward) I may come to feel that it is not so difficult as all that; though I should in any case want to submit what I said for the approval of my director and other theologians. But the long and short of it is, that I simply cannot take the time in the immediate future.

Yours very sincerely,
[T. S. Eliot]


## TO *Sherard Vines*[1]                                              CC

29 April 1936                          [Faber & Faber Ltd]

Dear Vines,

I also was sorry that we were unable to meet the other day, and the subject that you want to discuss could be much more satisfactorily dealt with in conversation than by letter.[2] My immediate response to your question is that I simply have no idea whatever. I don't know what the practice of other firms is, but I don't think we have ever found it necessary to advertise when in need of secretarial assistance. We understand that some departments apply to Secretarial Colleges.

I should think that your problem was really a larger one than it first appears to be from the way in which you put it. I suppose that most of your graduates tend to become teachers, but of those who do not want to teach there must be some who would be interested in a variety of occupations besides publishing. Oughtn't there to be some form of organization in all provincial universities for the purpose of getting jobs for their graduates. I hope we can discuss this when you pass through London next.

Yours sincerely,
[T. S. Eliot]


1–Sherard Vines (1890–1974), poet and academic, taught at Keio University, Tokyo, 1923–8; and was G. F. Grant Professor of English at University College, Hull, 1929–52.
2–Vines asked, 24 Apr., '"What shall we do with our girls?" Several of my women graduates ask me how to get secretaryships in publishing houses, & so forth. (I am not trying to push any on to you! – as a matter of fact I have none at all at the moment). I don't know the ropes: do they (a) write round asking for jobs? or (b) advertise for jobs? Or do you advertise vacancies? I should be most grateful if you could possibly tell me what the general procedure is, before the next batch of graduates comes along. I am trying to persuade as many as possible not to become schoolteachers, & should be glad to be in a position to advise them.'

30 April 1936                    [Faber & Faber Ltd]

My dear Bird,

I am interested to know whether anything can be done concerning the pension of a former servant of mine, an old man of eighty-two. I will put the case as he told it to me: his exposition of facts is not always very lucid, and there may be gaps to be filled in by questioning him further.

He was superannuated from the police force (with a good character) early in the century, but for some years after that served as a plain-clothes detective in the G.P.O. I do not suppose that he drew any pension from the Police while in the Post Office: but at any rate since retiring from the latter (I think in 1921) he has been drawing his Police pension, but nothing from the Post Office. His Police pension is £58:5:4d. p.a. plus a cost-of-living allowance (withdrawable at any time) bringing it up to £87:4:0d. p.a. or £7:5:4d a month. He tells me that Police Officers retired from the Metropolitan Force since the war get a pension of £163:5:4d. p.a.

He has also been drawing 10s. a week Old Age Pension. His wife, who had no Old Age Pension, died at the age of 69 early this year.

He now tells me that the suggestion has been made to him, apparently by the Police Inspector who pays his pension monthly, that he is liable to have the Old Age Pension withdrawn, on the ground that he no longer has a wife to support. He feels, and I strongly sympathise with him, that even alone a total income of £113 – what he has been getting – is only enough for subsistence, as he is too old to work.

While it is admitted that the cost of living supplement to his Police Pension could be withdrawn at any time, I assume that it would only be by general application of a ruling, and not arbitrarily in a particular case. I should not be surprised if the Department *reduced* the pension of a retired officer on his becoming a widower (with no children dependent upon him). But it would be flagitious to withdraw it altogether, and oppressive and unfair even to reduce it, considering the larger pensions given to more recently retired officers.

What is now in question, however, according to his account, is the cancellation of his Old Age Pension. Would the authorities be acting within their rights in taking such a step?

1–Of Bird & Bird, TSE's solicitors.

And is there not some benevolent foundation for the provision of free legal advice to the poor? I seem to have read of some such institution.

Yours sincerely,<br>[T. S. Eliot]

## TO *J. Bayard Morris*[1]                                                 CC

1 May 1936                                    [Faber & Faber Ltd]

Dear Mr Morris,

I have now read your translation of the first act of *La Machine Infernale*, and discussed it with my Committee.[2] We have come to the conclusion that we cannot see any possible sale for a translation of a play by Cocteau at the present time, and that we should not be justified in considering publication.

The play itself, of course, is an exceedingly good one, though I have never seen the Paris production. I should encourage you to persist with your translation, as the play certainly ought to be produced in London. It ought to be done by someone like Rupert Doone or Michel St Denis. If the play could be produced successfully, and become a regular part of any such company it would then be time to consider bringing the translation out as a book.

Cocteau's dialogue is extremely difficult to translate, and I felt that here and there you failed to get the English equivalent for a brilliant colloquialism of his style. I dare say that anything like perfection is impossible, but I do think that this act needs a good deal more work done on it, and that a more living English should be aimed at, even if it means taking liberties with the text. And you will find the two long speeches in Act II calling for all your ability and energy. I return the translation of Act I herewith.

Yours sincerely,<br>[T. S. Eliot]

---

1 – J. Bayard Morris taught at Bryanston School, Blandford, Dorset.
2 – Morris had written (n.d.): 're translation of Cocteau's "*Machine Infernale*", – Mr Auden tells me you have the typescript of the first Act.' WHA had written (n.d.): 'A friend of mine is translating Cocteau's *La Machine Infernale*. Here is the first act in case Faber's are interested.'

TO *Emily Holmes Coleman*

1 May 1936                          [Faber & Faber Ltd]

Dear Mrs Coleman,

I am now able to tell you that my firm will be glad to publish *Nightwood*, subject to Miss Barnes's acceptance of such deletions and alterations as we think necessary. I think you may be sure after discussing the matter with Mr Morley and myself the other day that we do not propose to tamper with the text any further than is essential for obvious reasons.

The terms offered are those usual for a first novel: 10 per cent royalty up to 2,000 copies, thereafter 12½ per cent to 4,000, and 15 per cent after that. We should propose to print the book rather well, and to charge probably 10s. 6d.

When I hear from you of Miss Barnes's acceptance I will have a contract prepared, but as I understand from you that she is on the point of sailing for England I think that the contract might as well be held here until her arrival.

Yours sincerely,
[T. S. Eliot]


TO *Ezra Pound*                                             TS Beinecke

4 May 1936                          Faber & Faber Ltd

Now Then, Ez, mon capybara, hydrochaerus,[1] you know zwellz I do that a prince should before all else watch over his own rational and moral motivation, keep his in-coming letters well filed, and retain in order carbon copies of all that he despatches. With this in mind I refer you to the letter to you from the Eg. Sig. Michael Roberts of the 8th Settembre last A.D., and to your reply which lies before me but of which you being a rational and morally motivated prince will have kep a carbon, of the 8th [*sc.* 12th] settembre last A.D., and ask you to explain that when Roberts said FIVE poems and named em, you replied 'Right you are! Herewith permission granted to use five poems listed in yrs. of 8th inst . . . at terms there stated'. Now then bro, its up to you to explain how five poems is nine poems. You roll em. What?[2]

1 – Capybara (*Hydrochoerus hydrochaeris*): a large rodent.
2 – Roberts had written to TSE, 23 Apr. 1936: 'I am very sorry indeed that I cannot find my copy of the letter I sent to Pound on Sept. 8th, but if you will refer to the table of contents of Pound's Selected Poems, entry: "E. P. Ode pour l'election . . ." and then to the page given,

Now then I got to write an epitaph of yr. Essays Ancient & Ancient before the 6th instant, and I dont get paid for that either. This for the autumb catalogue.[1]

---

you will see that there is no separate entry for sections ii iii iv and v. On the other hand, in the body of the text, he certainly put the heading "E. P. Ode pour . . ." *after* the section-number.

'I'll make another attempt to find the missing copy, but meanwhile you might refer Pound to my letter, which he may have kept, and see what he has to say.'

EP to TSE, 6 May: 'Waaaaaaal; my dear ole Ptospherum Carbunkle

'Wot I said was FIVE POEMS/ and wot I probably meant was FIVE <5> poems, and I never said that makes nine.

'But wot I find in mr rabbit's umpolergy IZ NINE poems/ (9),

'and if YEW sez to me that E.P. his ode for his grave stone/ and the portrait of Mr Plarr alias Verog and Mr Mauberly's final medalion of the gal with the golden eyes IS ONE poem, I sez yr/ arsistotleic sense of UNITY is DEEfective . . .

'But unless I said to mr robot hat he cd/ have NINE poems for the price of FIVE, he was a puttin over a fast one . . .

'REFERRING/ thanks to YOUR ass/istance to the epustl of the rev/ Mike Robot of the 8.ix.35 I find CLEARLY listed

    Exile's Letter
    Near Perigord
    H. S. Mauberly. E.P. Ode pour l'election . . . .)
    Propertius XII
    Canto XIII

'Note he does NOT say H. S. Mauberley? Part ONE/ or Numbers I to XII

'He gives Ode pour l'Election.

'A complete poEM, having nowt to do as unit with the tea rose gown.

'Not that in earlier letter Robot lists Mauberley I, II, III, IV, V which is clear and shows intention . . .

'In the revised and reduced list, letter M. Roberts 28.iii.35, the list is also CLEAR

    H.S.M. I, II, III, IV, V
    and Cantos XIII, XVI.

'This I may pint out DIFFERS from the text of his original request. In which figures E. P. Ode pour l'Election . . .

'NO reductions per poem.

'AND you know perfectly damn well. The ODE does NOT form ONE poem with the other poems of the sequence.

'which is condensed double affair/ portrait of select types in purgatory . . .

'Why try it on with an old friend when correctness wd/ forbid your trying it on the lousiest son of a bitch in Parliament whom you hadn't been introduced to?'

EP had originally responded to Roberts, '10 or 11 Sept. anno XIII' (1935): 'Right you are. Herewith permission granted to use five poems in yrs. of 8th inst. in forcomin' Faber anthology as terms there stated.

'I shd be happier to know that W. C. Williams, Bunting Zukofsky and cummings also appeared, with some of the waftier and slushier authors listed in yr/ earlier communiqué.'

1 – *Polite Essays* (published in Feb. 1937) carried this blurb: 'This may be described as a companion volume to *Make It New*, with the important difference that it is priced at 7s. 6d. instead of 12s. 6d. in order to make it accessible to a much larger public. Also, the former volume consisted primarily of erudite studies in the classical literature of several languages: its successor is more concerned with contemporary problems. It contains the essays on

Boy, there's a critic combliaining in the Observer or somewheres about my havin-a musty mystiticm that I caught from you, he says.[1] Now that we have located the smell, what's to be done about it what?

If you shd. be happier to know that Zukovsky and commings appeared I shd. be still more unhappy, which is the law of compensation. As for Zuk. remember that not to remove a nevil man, remove him to effective distance, is weakness on the part of a prince. Without prejudice or responsibility.

No Sir I aint coming to Rapalloo until your lil brown bros. has recovered from the effort of conquering coons and returned to the old barrel-organ and the fruit stand. But the nightingales in Surrey, the tarts in Piccadilly, the monkeys in Regents Park, the vergers of St Mary Abbot's Kensington, are all whispering: Spring, spring, and where's Ez? And as aforestated, theres also Paris, Locarno and Ajaccio as possible points of repere.[2]

Well I forgive you about Robt. B.[3] but I dont know what to do with his works if you dont want em. It was all meant for yr. own good, but never mind, so will close

yrs.

TP.

———

Housman, Binyon and Monro, which appeared in *The Criterion*; studies of the problems of contemporary poetry and modern education, and other matters of literary actuality. But just as Mr Pound cannot deal with questions of literary history without considering their present application, so his considerations of the present are based upon his knowledge and judgments of the past. In this volume, for instance, he has preserved his essential observations upon the poetry of Dante. The two books together are sufficient to justify the reputation enjoyed by Mr Pound among the discerning – of having been the most fructifying influence upon literary criticism of his time.'

1 – Cyril Connolly, in 'Major Poet: The Influence of Mr Eliot' (*Sunday Times*, 3 May 1936, 8) – a review of *CP 1909–1935* – complained that 'the extraordinary freshness' of the earlier poetry 'disappears from the later Eliot. This is largely due to the influence of Pound, who brings . . . two new features into Eliot. They are the introduction of unassimilated quotations into the body of his work, and the more serious introduction of a mystical, but also rather muddy and disingenuous bardic quality into his thought' (repr. in *T. S. Eliot: The Contemporary Reviews*, ed. Jewel Spears Brooker [2004], 358).

2 – *Point de repère* (Fr.): point of reference.

3 – EP's refusal to write a review of the poems of Robert Bridges.

TO *William Empson*[1]                                        CC

5 May 1936                              [*The Criterion*]

My dear Empson,

I ought to have answered your letter before,[2] but you will presumably
have understood from my silence that it was too late to get an article into
the next number of the *Criterion*, as that number is just being made up. I
should like to have an article from you for the October number if that is
soon enough to suit your book.

I am hoping to come to your party on Friday, but cannot promise
definitely.[3]

                                        Yours sincerely,
                                        [T. S. Eliot]


TO *Robert Speaight*[4]                                       CC

5 May 1936                              [Faber & Faber Ltd]

Dear Bobby,

I must apologise for my delay in answering your card of the 22nd.[5] The
reason is that I wanted to make some enquiries about the usual terms for

---

1 – William Empson (1906–84), poet and critic; author of *Seven Types of Ambiguity* (1930),
*Some Versions of Pastoral* (1935), *The Structure of Complex Words* (1951), *Milton's God*
(1961). TSE would later take pains at F&F to publish *The Gathering Storm* (poems, 1940).
See further *Complete Poems*, ed. John Haffenden (2001); Haffenden, *William Empson:
Among the Mandarins* (2005); *Selected Letters of William Empson* (2006).
2 – Empson wrote ('Saturday', n.d.): 'Would you be prepared to consider an article like
"Feelings in Words" called "Statements in Words" for the coming *Criterion*, and if so when
should I send it in? The stuff is done really: the difficulty is to boil it down to the parts that
seem likely not to be nonsense.' See 'Statements in Words', *C.* 16 (Apr. 1937), 452–67.
3 – 'I should be delighted if you could come to a party I am giving on Friday week at 34
Woburn Sq, about 9; meant to be rather a crowd.'
4 – Robert Speaight (1904–77), actor, producer, and author. A graduate of Oxford University,
he developed as an actor through taking parts at the Liverpool Repertory Company, and at
the Old Vic and Haymarket Theatre in London, before creating the part of Becket in TSE's
*MiC* at Canterbury Cathedral in 1935 and later at the Mercury Theatre, London. Over a
period of many years he played the role more than a thousand times, in numerous revivals all
over the world – travel was a passion – and he presently became a Roman Catholic convert.
In addition to his work as an actor, he wrote many books, articles and lectures: monographs
on figures including George Eliot, Ronald Knox, Hilaire Belloc, William Rothenstein, Eric
Gill, Teilhard de Chardin, Georges Bernanos, and François Mauriac, as well as studies of
Shakespeare. See Speaight, *The Property Basket: Recollections of a Divided Life* (1970).
5 – The gramophone company 'His Master's Voice' (HMV) wished to record Speaight
reciting the Sermon from *MiC*, and was offering a royalty of 5% on 85% of gross sales.

gramophone records first, and this has taken longer than I expected. Of course I should be delighted to have the sermon recorded by your voice. Enquiry from an agent elicits the information that 5 per cent on the total gross sales is a reasonable royalty. I will not hold out for that, however, if the H.M.V. people make any difficulty. What I am not clear about is whether you mean that this 5% is 5% on 85% of gross sales offered to me, or to you and me jointly. In the latter case we would naturally go half and half, I suppose, and 2½% on 85% doesn't look like very much profit. However, I won't make trouble, but I am anxious to be clear on this point, and to know whether the proposal is satisfactory to you. One stipulation which is worth making, I think, is that, if the whole sermon can be got on one side of the record, they should not put anything else on the other side, or certainly not without our consent.

I shall hope to see you at the last performance next week, and before you leave for your tour.

Yours ever,<br>[Tom]

## TO *James Joyce*                     TS National Gallery of Ireland

Telegram 7 May 1936

REFERRING MY LETTER SEVENTEENTH APRIL AM COMING PARIS JUNE SIXTH SHALL I BRING MANUSCRIPT = ELIOT

*Joyce replied*:

STATED MY OPINION FIVE MONTHS AGO[1]

## TO *Emily Holmes Coleman*                     CC

7 May 1936                     [Faber & Faber Ltd]

Dear Mrs Coleman,

Thank you very much for your letter of the 2nd instant.[2] I must say that I immediately rose in opposition to the directions of your first

---

1 – The reply is written in an unknown hand on TSE's telegram. The original has not been found.

2 – Coleman reassured TSE that Barnes would accept the contract; and she went on: 'She wants the book called *The Anatomy of Night. Nightwood* was only a provisional title.' See Andrew Field, *Djuna: The Life and Times of Djuna Barnes* (1983, 1985); Miriam Fuchs,

paragraph, and when I was able to discuss the point with Morley I found him entirely in agreement with me. *Nightwood* seems to me a perfect title for the book; *The Anatomy of Night* not only imperfect, but definitely bad. There is a self-conscious literary flavour about the latter title which does the book a great injustice. In fact it is quite contrary to the spirit of the work. It suggests a volume of totally superfluous maundering essays by some ephemeral and insignificant literary hack. I hope you will excuse my speaking so strongly on this point, but I speak as a person who has often had to struggle with the problem of finding suitable titles for books when the author can't think of any. Here we have a perfect title given us, and the author wants to take it away again. I am quite sure that the title of the book should be something brief and mysterious, giving no clue whatever to the contents. The book is a kind of poetry. That is, at least, its appeal will be to people with native sensibility and some training in the appreciation of poetry, and we don't want to put it out for the ordinary novel-reading public, or for all the other people who won't understand it and will dislike it. I hope Miss Barnes will come round to our point of view.

Thank you very much for the rest of your letter. Your portrait of Miss Barnes is a little alarming.[1] Nevertheless I shall await her coming with eagerness as well as trepidation.

The poem of Lionel Johnson's which you typed out for me is certainly one of his finest, but when Barker said that he had discovered it I cannot imagine that he discovered it for himself.[2] It is as a matter of fact one of

<hr />

'Djuna Barnes and T. S. Eliot: Authority, Resistance and Acquiescence', *Tulsa Studies in Women's Literature* 12: 2 (Fall, 1993), 289–313; Phillip Herring, *Djuna: The Life and Work of Djuna Barnes* (1995); *Nightwood: The Original Version and Related Drafts*, ed. Cheryl J. Plumb (1995); Georgette Fleischer, 'Djuna Barnes and T. S. Eliot: The Politics and Poetics of *Nightwood*', *Studies in the Novel* 30: 3 (Fall, 1998), 405–33. See too Faltejskova, *Djuna Barnes*, 74: 'Both Plumb and Herring corrected the misleading view that the final title of the novel, *Nightwood*, originated from Eliot. Plumb explains that the book's title was "changing at various times from 'Bow Down' to 'Anatomy of the Night', to 'Through the Night' and 'Night without Sleep'", and finally to *Nightwood*. Andrew Field credits Eliot with coming up with the title. In fact, Barnes wrote of the title to Coleman on 23 June 1935: "'Nightwood', like that, one word, it makes it sound like night-shade, poison and night and forest, and tough, in the meaty sense, and simple yet singular . . . do you like it?" According to the letter, Barnes, not T. S. Eliot, chose the word "nightwood" as a title. Although, it was due to T. S. Eliot, that the title was chosen for the novel: even if Coleman objected to it, he liked it. In this case, Barnes listened to her editor, not to her friend.'
1–'I neglected to tell you what Miss Barnes is really like – Mae West.'
2–Coleman had started to talk about George Barker during her meeting with TSE at his office. Now she wrote: 'I am so struck with his gifts, which seem to me to be those which are likely to produce real poetry, as against much of what has been written lately; though he

Johnson's best known poems, and you will find allusions to it in that part of Yeats's autobiography in which he talks about Lionel. I think myself it is perhaps the most satisfactory poem as a whole that Johnson wrote. For the rest, I find him rather a poet of superb scattered lines and phrases than of whole poems. I think that both Ezra Pound and the late A. E. Housman, with whom I once had a talk about Johnson at Cambridge, agree with me on this point. I shall expect to hear from you again when you have more definite news of Miss Barnes's coming.[1]

Yours very sincerely,

[T. S. Eliot]

P.S. I enclose the extracts by Edwin Muir as you request.

## TO *W. H. Auden* CC

8 May 1936                          [Faber & Faber Ltd]

My dear Wystan,

*The Ascent of F6* has just come in from Curtis Brown, and I am reading it with interest and thrills.[2] Why I am writing is that something was said to somebody by Curtis Brown about your having a volume of poems ready

---

is so young, in manner and half-baked . . . [He] was here yesterday. He told me some of the tallest stories, for hours. But he showed me a poem, of Lionel Johnson's, which he says he "discovered". At the risk of your having seen it before, I am sending it to you.' The poem was 'The Dark Angel'.

1–Djuna Barnes was interviewed at the Faber offices by TSE and FVM on Weds. 3 June.

Plumb remarks (p. xxii): 'Coleman entered in her diary Barnes's narration of this session with Eliot and Morley. Barnes reported that with respect to Eliot's corrections, she had said, "I'll take anything from you, Mr Eliot." But later in considering the manuscript when they got on to "balls, testicles and pubic hair . . . they were embarrassed and Djuna vigilant." Djuna reported that Eliot had "that wise but lenient look when he corrected her spelling." She questioned, "Who can spell?" Then added, "Eliot, I can tell from your face that you can spell." Later that evening of Eliot's changing "bugger" to "boys", Barnes exclaimed, "Imagine trying to wake Eliot up!" Yet she had liked him.'

Faltejskova notes of the meeting, 85: '[I]t would appear that Eliot rather than Morley was in charge of the textual changes. Morley's role was merely to agree with Eliot and perform whatever Eliot asked him to do. Barnes bitterly remarked about Morley: "She said Morley was 'a great cabin trunk with nothing in it.'" (D, p. 399) The subversive remark Barnes made to Eliot, on the other hand, shows her mocking the authority he had over her text as the chief editor. It implies that rather than agreeing with his corrections, she acknowledged the fact that she was forced to do so in order to get the book published. Coleman writes that Barnes "said when Eliot made one correction, 'I'll take anything from you, Mr Eliot.' 'What did he say?' 'Oh, he perked up like a hound's ear – it may be a rabbit, it may be a porcupine.'" (D, p. 399)'

2–Submitted by Curtis Brown Ltd to FVM, 30 Apr. 1936.

as well. Is this true? Because I don't think that the play and the poems ought to come out on top of each other, and if the poems are ready we ought to plan a campaign. *A priori* I should be in favour of bringing out one volume early in the autumn and another early in the spring. I should like to know the situation and your wishes about it at once, because I must write a preliminary announcement about the play to appear in our advance autumn catalogue.[1] I hope that you will be able to come to the *Criterion* evening on May 20th.

Yours ever,<br>[T. S. Eliot]

## TO *V. A. Demant*                                                    CC

8 May 1936                          [Faber & Faber Ltd]

My dear Demant,

Thank you for your letter of the 4th instant.[2] I must confess that none of the titles you suggest seems to me quite to hit it off. I should prefer to avoid using the word 'essays' in the title, because it inevitably suggests a collection of unrelated articles, and what we want to emphasize is the unity of the book as well as its diversity. But I shall brood over this question at the weekend.

I think, as the essays are collected from various publications, that a short preface by yourself would be in order, simply saying that the essays do belong together, and that they are the fruit, if I may put it somewhat solemnly, of a single persistent and coherent interest. Unless you are aware

---

1–WHA replied, in an undated letter ('Saturday'): 'Yes the *Poems* are coming next week. Publication date for play depends rather on production date, don't you think? I'm coming to town on Tuesday. Could I see you in the afternoon?' (He asked too, 'If you have a spare copy of the collected poems of T.S.E., I should love to have it.')

TSE's blurb for *The Ascent of F6* (published 24 Sept. 1936): 'Some of the critics of *The Dog Beneath the Skin* thought that it was better to read than to see performed; others thought exactly the reverse: from this it is to be inferred that the play ought to be both read and seen. Admirers of *The Dog Beneath the Skin*, to whichever group of critics they belong, will not be disappointed in this new play. It is concerned with the colonial rivalry of those two great powers, Britain and Ostnia, a rivalry which brings about the tragedy of the ace of mountain-climbers, Michael Ransome, in the struggle to ascend the hitherto unconquered mountain giant know as "F6".

'The play is in verse and prose, and has the poetry and the dialogue, the thrills and surprises, that Auden and Isherwood admirers have come to expect.'

2–In his reply (4 May) to TSE's offer on behalf of F&F to publish his book of essays, Demant ventured six possible titles, including 'The Finger of God in the World' and 'The Status of Man'. In the event, they settled for FVM's suggestion, *Christian Polity*.

of definite alterations, however slight, that you need to make in any of the articles to remove traces of their occasional character, I think that the book might as well be set up as it stands. That is for you to decide.

I am sending you an invitation to a *Criterion* Meeting on May 20th, and as that is a Wednesday I hope that you will be able to come.

Yours very sincerely,
[T. S. Eliot]

## TO *Geoffrey Faber*                                    TS Valerie Eliot

10 May 1936                          Faber & Faber Ltd

Dear Geoffrey,

Your letter[1] touches upon such vast subjects that I have wondered where to begin to answer it from, and at times have felt that it was no use trying. Still, such a letter cannot help provoking the recipient (or one of them) to do something about it, if only to see what it looks like on paper.

The most easy-going kind of start seems to be to protest against your identifying England with Yorkshire, a statement likely to arouse many other regular readers of your paper to etc. etc. What I really mean is, that I think your reference to 'race' has something partly right in it, but needing analysis if possible. For one thing, I believe that there are many people of education, intelligence etc. in France and Germany (for instance) who would feel much the same way – certainly about the particular matter of homosexuality; that there are universal as well as individual elements in all these feelings (which are so difficult to describe). 'Race' is, I think, largely a term for the environment to which one has been submitted for several generations. IF the characteristic is peculiarly English, then one must infer from what you say either that (1) other races are all unstable or (2) they have attitudes of their own making for stability. There is another possibility. It may be a greater instability in the English that compels them to protect themselves: in some lights, certainly, the French are the most stable race in Europe, nervously.

But of course I am puzzled to begin with by the occasion which has led to your remarks, and that increases my difficulty. I can't see that 'making too much of sex' applies any more to this book than to any novel the theme of which is erotic experience at any level. Does this book make any more of sex than *Manon Lescaut,* or the *Vita Nuova,* or *Madame*

---

1–Of 16 Apr. 1936, above.

*Bovary*, or *Jude the Obscure*? The only thing that can be said is that the invert is apt to be more concerned with sex than the normal person, I suspect as much because of the essentially unsatisfactory nature of that relation as because of the social taboo against him or her. (I have rather an antipathy to male inverts, and I find them apt to be rather boring people who somehow remain *immature*: I have had no acquaintance with the females). But this book hardly seemed to me to be concerned with sex at all. *Appointment in Samarra*[1] did *almost* make me sick: it was just saved by being a picture of futility, of really dead people, drawn by a man with a Catholic background. And I have come across other books that seemed to me definitely nasty. I did read *Well of Loneliness*, and it was a nasty book: not because it dealt with lesbians, but because it dealt with sex in general in a disgustingly sentimental way, and because of a kind of <small> Satanic pride[2] in the author.

What puzzles me especially, however, is your statement that 'when sex becomes charged with something more than physical pleasure, it means all kinds of results I want to avoid'. If I took this into my mind in what would be literalness for me, I should say that I held just the opposite point of view. But this is improbable, for two reasons. One is, that it seems to me unlikely that you and I should hold directly opposite views on such a fundamental matter; and the other is, that in my experience two people seldom agree closely enough on the meaning of words to be able to disagree exactly about the use of them in propositions. Now *I* should say (using the terms for what they mean for me, and supposing that they have the same meaning for you – but one can sometimes make one's own meaning a little clearer by developing and combining them in statements) that the anxiety to 'keep sex in its place' was a symptom of instability in itself: of an instability which turned to repression, and which therefore led to a static condition, a mere holding tight and waiting for old age. To begin with, I should think that when sex meant merely physical pleasure, it ceased to mean any kind of pleasure; that it had become merely a habit, as the confirmed cigarette smoker (as we know) ceases to get any gustatory or olfactory pleasure from smoking, and the drunkard and the glutton also cease to enjoy the sense of taste and smell. The first and perhaps most universal complication of sex is I think the pleasure of vanity, which can enter in even when there is no reasonable justification for being vain.

---

1 – *Appointment in Samarra* (F&F, 1934): first novel by American John O'Hara (1905–70).
2 – Cf. Raskolnikov in *Crime and Punishment*. See Dostoyevski's notebooks: *Polnoe sobranie sochinenii*, vol. 7 (1911), 149.

Further, there is the moral element: the heightening of pleasure by the sense of either doing something positively good or something positively evil (the pleasure of consciously doing evil can be a very refined and intense one). I will not admit, to begin with, that the enjoyment of wine is a purely physical pleasure. It is easier to show that, than in the case of sex. To begin with, the enjoyment of wine is an acquired and trained taste (of course I should make the same claim for the pleasures of sex, but that is less easily proved). At one stage, and perhaps always, the enjoyment of wine is complicated by one's self-approval for having a taste in wine; but I have no doubt that those who really enjoy wine to the keenest are enjoying a sense of discrimination which is almost a spiritual good.

I quite agree that the exaltation of love (which is only incidentally but necessarily 'physical') is an illusion, in being the illusion of a unity of two *persons* as well as the transient ~~fusing~~ identification of sensation in two bodies. Between any two people (and the more intimate their relations the more important this becomes) there is always an unresolvable element of hostility which may be only further incubated by the dominance of one over the other. A man in love has moments at least when he feels his condition, with resentment, to be one of slavery rather than of self-realisation. (It is I think, a coming to terms between the elements of attraction and repulsion that constitutes permanent affection, but I am not talking about affection). The E. M. Forster etc. tenet of 'personal relations' being the most important thing in life is a sentimental heresy – D. H. Lawrence saw much deeper than that. Lawrence of course did not come either to your conclusions or to mine, but at any rate he was willing to take a risk and make a metaphysical experiment. I don't hold with the Myth of Diotima either – that is merely a statement of the 'illusion'. I've tried to express something of my belief at the end of *Burnt Norton*. I mean that the 'illusion' of love is something to pass forward through, not to dash into and out of again, like a bath. You will have to put up with a little mystical theology – I can't help that, because I can't talk about the subject without bringing it in. The 'illusion' is merely a degree of reality, then, essentially different from hallucination; and love of created beings should lead us to the only love that is wholly satisfactory and final, the love of God – even though for 99% of parsons this is only a stock phrase: it is *cio che per l'universo si squaderna*.[1]

Of course it is impossible to hold this view and attach the same meaning to 'sensible enjoyment of life'. But this is not to deny in any way the

---

1 – *Paradiso*, XXXIII, 87: 'the scattered leaves of all the universe' (Temple Classics).

'sensible enjoyment of life'. (What I object to is pulling down the blinds and huddling round the fire.) This is still an enjoyment, not perhaps of 'life' itself, for life comes before enjoyment, but of as many things and situations and people as possible in the course of living; and it is still enjoyment, even when felt against the awful background of the futility and misery of the existence of man without God. Most people seem to me to get their enjoying of life only by the continuous strain of trying to forget death – not illness, poverty, disgrace or dying, but death; and surround themselves with all sorts of relations, objects and trivial occupations (and the less *obviously* trivial the more dangerous) in the attempt to exorcise the spectre of vanity.

I don't know whether this letter has turned into an Ars Amandi or a Sermon on Death – but the two things quite properly go together, I think. But to return for a moment to the subject or pretext of the letter, you will perhaps see that this attitude of mine lies behind my interest in a book like *Nightwood*. It does seem to me to be concerned with life at a deeper level than 'sex' in the ordinary fussy frigging sense, the level that Lawrence (perhaps because of his mental tangle in his semi-impotence) just fails to reach. Lawrence is so like a man in a great state of excitement who can't get an erection: a sort of sweaty frustration makes him at times pretty nearly nasty, like a man who can do nothing and takes it out by mental images and peeping through keyholes. . . . And of course, because of my feeling about the misery, I have an abiding interest in and sympathy with all the extreme failures of life – the *déclassé*, the degenerate, the *raté*, the man who has got to the bottom, the disreputable (the 'Doctor' stealing the 100 franc note is an admirable touch). Most of them in actual life are individually dull enough, yet as Kipling understood in an intuitive half-conscious way, the failure – whether Mulvaney or Macintosh Jellaluddin[1] – may be much nearer to reality than the man who arranges his life prudently and 'to get the most out of life'. And the pseudo-failure (T. E. Lawrence) seems to me one of the most obnoxious varieties of success.

There seems no particular reason for stopping, except that this has already *dépassé par beaucoup les limites d'une lettre convenable*.[2]

Yours ever

TP

---

1 – *Plain Tales from the Hills*: 'The Three Musketeers' and 'To be Filed for Reference'.
2 – *dépassé par beaucoup les limites d'une lettre convenable*: '[has] exceeded by a long way the limits of a reasonable letter.'

# TO *Various Recipients*

[10 May 1936]

*LETTER A.*

The following letter is to go to: Morley, Read, Flint, Orlo Williams, Belgion, Tandy, J. B. Trend, A. W. G. Randall, Dobrée.

*CRITERION MEETING* [*sic*].
 Your company is requested at 7 p.m. for supper at 24, Russell Square, on Wednesday the 20th [May] instant. R. S. V. P.
 You are reminded that each member is entitled to invite two guests, the guests to present themselves at 9 o'clock. You are asked to advise the Secretary in good time of any guests invited by you who are to be expected.
 It is hoped that members will not consider excessive a charge of 7s. 6d., to cover cost of supper and to help defray expense of entertaining guests.

Yours faithfully,<br>Secretary.

POSTSCRIPTS TO A LETTERS.

To Herbert Read.
 Mr Eliot thinks it might be desirable to ask Bernard Wall, but doesn't know him.[1] He also suggests Heppenstall as a possibility.

To Geoffrey Tandy.
 Mr Eliot wonders whether you would care to ask J. D. Unwin, who he thinks would be a suitable guest.

*LETTER B.*

The following letter to go to: Beachcroft, Hinks, Radcliffe, Sykes-Davies, Desmond Hawkins, W. H. Auden, Spender, Richard Church, Codrington, W. A. Thorpe, D'Arcy, Smyth, Rowse, Porteus, Hamish Miles, A. W. Wheen.

---

1–Bernard Wall (1908–74), Catholic intellectual; co-founder of the *Catholic Worker* newspaper; founder in 1934 of the periodical *The Colosseum*. Works include *Spain of the Spaniards* (1937), *European Notebook* (1939), and *Headlong Into Change* (autobiog., 1969). His review of *Essays Ancient and Modern* – 'T. S. Eliot's Essays' – appeared in the *Catholic Herald*, 24 Apr. 1936, 4.

*CRITERION MEETING.*

The pleasure of your company is requested at a Criterion Evening to be held at 24, Russell Square on Wednesday, the 20th instant, at 9 p.m. *R.S.V.P.*

> Yours faithfully,
> Secretary.

*LETTER C.*

The following letter is to go to: Charles Madge, William Empson, Dylan Thomas, Walter Tomlin, Philip Mairet, V. A. Demant.

Mr Eliot would be very glad if you would come as his guest to a Criterion Evening to be held at 24, Russell Square on Wednesday evening the 20th instant, at 9 o'clock. *R.S.V.P.*

> Yours faithfully,
> Secretary.

## TO *J. McG. Bottkol*[1]                                    TS Houghton

11 May 1936                                             Faber & Faber Ltd

Dear Mr Bottkol,

Thank you for your letter of April 24th. If Eliot House cares to preserve my very rough and illegible notes I can only be flattered by the compliment. I think it would be better, however, if permission to transcribe them, quote from them, or use them in any way were only given <exc. to Dr Spencer, of course!> after obtaining my consent in each case. After all, I don't in the least remember what is in those notes, and they may require a good deal of interpretation.

> Yours very sincerely,
> T. S. Eliot

1–J. McG. Bottkol: librarian of Eliot House, Cambridge, Mass., to which TSE (who had lodged there in 1932–3) had donated in 1934 manuscripts of a chorus from *The Rock* and of the poem 'Usk'. HWE had also been building up the collection with TSE materials.

TO *Phyllis Bottome*[1]                                         CC

11 May 1936                    [*The Criterion*]

Dear Miss Bottome,

I find that I have had for an unpardonably long time a manuscript
of yours about Ezra Pound. I am very dilatory at looking at unsolicited
contributions for the reason that they are almost uniformly useless, and
induce in the bulk depression and misanthropy. Hence your manuscript
was here for some time before I was aware of its existence, and even after
I had read it I did not keep my good intentions of writing to you.

I think it is a lively and interesting and just appreciation, and I should
like to see it published. My first feeling – which makes the delay still
more unjustifiable – is that it would do very much more good if it could
possibly be rammed down the throat of some other editor. I mean that
my association with Pound is very well known, and that the *Criterion* is
one of the few places in which his own work can get published, so that an
article like this would make much more impression if it appeared in a less
expected vehicle. I don't know what influence or connections you have
with periodicals, but I think the matter is worth considering. Meanwhile
I will keep the article here.[2]

                                        Yours sincerely,
                                        [T. S. Eliot]


FROM *Vivien Eliot* TO *Geoffrey Faber*            MS Bodleian

11 May 1936                    [No address given]

Dear Geoffrey,

May I rely on you to let me know at once if Tom is ill? I was very much
alarmed about Christmas time. I asked someone else to do this for me,
someone in the neighbourhood of your Office, but I do not think it was
at all the right quarter, but at that time I did not know where else to ask.


1–Phyllis Bottome (1884–1963), British writer – who was married to the diplomat and
MI6 agent Forbes Dennis, with whom she lived in the 1930s in Munich (where she studied
psychology under Alfred Adler). She was author of several novels including *Private Worlds*
(1934); the anti-Nazi novel *The Mortal Storm* (F&F, 1937) – filmed in 1940, starring James
Stewart – *Danger Signal* (1939), *The Heat of a Child* (1942); three volumes of autobiography;
*From the Life* (F&F, 1944), and *Alfred Adler: Apostle of Freedom* (F&F, 1939). See further
Pam Hirsch, *The Constant Liberal: The Life and Work of Phyllis Bottome* (2010).
2–See the revised version of 'Ezra Pound' in Bottome, *From the Life* (F&F, 1944), 70–82.

I have been quite ill myself since before Easter, with a poisoned foot, and as this does not get any better, I daresay I shall have to make tracks for my 'French Home', if by that time I can get there.

I hope *you* and Enid and the children are all well.

Relying on You to deal straightly with me on the subject of Tom's health.[1]

Yours,

[V. H. E.]

## TO *A. L. Rowse*[2]                                               TS Exeter

12 May 1936                      *The Criterion*

Dear Rowse,

Thank you for your letter of May 4th.[3] As a matter of fact I found that I had more material for the next number than I could use, so I was not put out. In fact, from the way you had spoken of your pamphlet I got the impression that the article was hardly likely to turn up.

It is impossible for me to say definitely whether I can use an article by you on Erasmus in September.[4] If I get all the articles I expect besides contributions I have in hand, I shan't have room for any more material, but it is always possible that someone will fail me. I don't care very much one way or the other about centenaries, and if you had no objection to giving me the article to use in either September or December, whichever

1–GCF replied, 14 May 1936: 'My dear Vivienne, / Tom is perfectly well – I lunched with him a couple of days ago, & he ate a hearty meal!

'So sorry to hear of your poisoned foot – not a thing to treat lightly. We have only been back a few days from Wales, & the children are all at school & seem to be flourishing.'

2–A. L. Rowse (1903–1997), historian; Fellow of All Souls, Oxford: see Biographical Register.

3–Rowse's 'pamphlet' on Keynes had been turned down by Gollancz – 'he says he won't publish it because he doesn't agree with it! Have you ever heard such rot from a publisher! But I believe it's quite genuine – he has gone more or less Communist and can't bear the official Labour Party now' – and since Gollancz did not return the piece until after the expiry of TSE's deadline, ALR had passed it straight on to Macmillan. He hoped TSE was not put out.

4–The Quartercentenary of Erasmus inspired ALR to propose an article on Erasmus 'in a contemporary perspective: his duel with Luther represents to me the present struggle between rational ideas of reform etc. versus the cult of Irrationalism which Luther (like Hitler) stands for. A dichotomy that runs through all German history. Would you not like me to write an article on "Erasmus and the Modern Dilemma" (or some such title)?'

way things turn out, I should be very glad to have it. Centenary or no, an article on Erasmus would be very welcome.

Yours ever,

T. S. E.

## TO *Louis MacNeice*

12 May 1936                         [*The Criterion*]

Dear Mr MacNeice,

Thank you for your letter of May 9th.[1] By all means let me see your *Agamemnon* with a view to publication. I shall be most interested.[2]

Yours sincerely,

[T. S. Eliot]

## TO *Michael Roberts*                                  TS Berg

13 May 1936                         Faber & Faber Ltd

My dear Roberts,

After receiving your letter of the 23rd April I wrote to Pound referring him to your letter of the 8th September last, but I cannot say that I have got very much satisfaction. He says he cannot find your letter, and from the tone of his I infer that a rereading of your letter is not going to make very much difference to his attitude. So I wish you would let me know what we should pay him *pro rata* according to the price already paid. Don't think this is your fault in the least, so don't worry about it. I want to get the matter settled quickly as Pound is beginning to get on my nerves.[3]

Yours ever,

T. S. Eliot

1–LM was having typed his verse translation of *Agamemnon*, and hoped that TSE might be interested to see it. 'Various people, including Wystan Auden, have read it or part of it and Rupert Doone may possibly be going to produce it with the Group Theatre but I think he will find it too discouraging. It is practically line for line so it has that over G. Murray anyway.'

2–LM reported to his friend Anthony Blunt on 24 May that TSE was interested in the work. LM was to meet Rupert Doone and the stage designer Robert Medley on the following day.

3–Roberts responded on 14 May: 'I offered Pound twenty-five guineas for what I believed to be five poems, and I understand that a cheque for that amount was sent to him. He now claims that he agreed to a rate of five guineas per poem and that nine poems are printed. He is therefore claiming an extra twenty guineas.

FROM *Vivien Eliot* TO *Maurice Haigh-Wood*

TS copy: Bodleian

14 May 1936                    [No address given]

My dear Maurice,

You should not have troubled to write such a long letter of explanation about yesterday evening. I was not really taking it as a test case. I was certainly very much disappointed, and so was Mother.

I am very sorry but I am afraid I cannot meet you on Monday at 6.30, but I could meet you at 6.30 at The Three Arts Club on today week, Thursday, 21st May. Do please send me a postcard immediately in reply.

As I have not seen you for so long, or your wife and child, and have never even seen the inside of your home, I propose calling on you on Sunday afternoon, if you will be at home.

As you do not reply on the subject of birthday presents, I take it that the suggestion of a steel Filing Cabinet is not antipathetic to you.

While I am writing to you I may as well tell you what you no doubt already know, and that is that I met Tom again, and everything was perfectly allright. We met in public, and in front of a large audience, so your idea that we might meet again in a 'Night Club' was not fulfilled.[1]

Again, while I am writing, I will add that I get so sick and nauseated by the sentimental fug and slop of England, now that I have to go about the streets so much, that I await eagerly the time when I shall feel able to leave it for good. And, of-course it is mad to have to say such a thing, but the filthy mass emotions are so bad and so warping to facts, that I do add,

---

'I am indeed sorry that I did not send him a formal agreement to sign and return: the list of poems which we finally printed was decided as early as May of last year and must have been clearly understood by Pound.

'Not having his signature to a document, it is clearly useless to argue. The only cheering thing is that he hasn't thought of arguing that he expected twenty-five pounds per poem. He certainly has no letter of mine which could support his present claim, but I agree with you that the sooner the matter is settled, the better.'

1–MH-W responded, 15 May: 'Thursday 21st at 6.30 at the 3 Arts suits me all right, & I will therefore be there at the appointed time.

'I haven't the remotest idea what safes cost, but at the earliest opportunity I will find out & shall then be able to say whether my purse will be adequate for the acquisition of one.

'You certainly credit me with omniscience. I am very interested to hear that you met Tom again. I of course did not know – there is no reason why I should.'

that I never had any children in my life, I thank God, and never wished to, since I was a little girl of about twelve.[1]

Your affectionate sister,
Vivienne Haigh Eliot

## TO *University Council, Durham University* TS Texas

14 May 1936 *The Criterion*

I have known Mr George Barker for several years and have followed his work with the greatest interest.[2] He is one of a very small number of younger poets whose work I consider important: I have been concerned with it both as editor and as publisher. His prose, both imaginative and critical, is also of great interest and merit. I believe that he has a wide knowledge of English poetry and some experience of lecturing; and I am sure that he would not fail to make any subject in which he lectured, interesting and stimulating to his pupils.[3]

T. S. Eliot

## TO *Frederic Hood*[4] cc

14 May 1936 [Faber & Faber Ltd]

Dear Father Hood,
  I have your letter of May 13th.[5] I am afraid that I cannot tell you much more about Iovetz Tereshchenko's book than you will have discovered

---

1–Cf. *TWL* II, 'A Game of Chess', 164: 'What you get married for if you don't want children?'

2–Barker notified TSE on 7 May that he was applying for the post of Lecturer in English Literature at the University of Durham: he asked for a 'letter of recommendation', to be submitted to the University Council by 20 May. 'I should guess from their prospectus that the University is tolerably advanced in its views & that the fact that I have not received my education at Oxford or Cambridge will not necessarily prejudice them against me.'

3–On 10 June, Barker reported that he had not heard from Durham and 'therefore presumed that I have failed as yesterday was the day of the interviewing of successful candidates'.

4–The Revd Canon Frederic Hood (1895–1975), Principal of Pusey House, Oxford, 1934–51; afterwards Priest-in-Charge of St Mary Aldermary in the City of London; Canon Residentiary, Chancellor and Chapter Treasurer of St Paul's Cathedral, London.

5–'The Editor of the Church Quarterly Review has sent me a book for review which I see that the Editor received at your suggestion. It is entitled Friendship-Love in Adolescence by N. M. Iovetz-Tereshchenko. I have read the book through slowly and carefully (and I admit with some labour) and am much interested in it, though quite unconvinced by its thesis. I am rather at a loss to know what to say in reviewing it. I shall be most grateful if you can tell me from the book itself. The work is the product of studies of work done at the University of London while the author was obtaining a degree there. The author is a very pleasant modest and pathetic person who is naturally an exile from Russia. His actual nationality is Serbian, as he spent some time in that country after the revolution, and became naturalized there, but he is anxious to make his permanent domicile in England. He has a wife, a mother, and two children to support, and has been earning a very meagre income by Extension Lectures. I have been very anxious to help him, and hope that you will honestly be able to say something favourable about his book.

Yours sincerely,<br>[T. S. Eliot]

## TO *K. de B. Codrington*[1]                                              cc

15 May 1936                          [Faber & Faber Ltd]

Dear Codrington,

Your first letter was undecipherable, but looked intelligible. Your second letter is typed but unintelligible. You don't have to drink your Manzanilla standing up.[2] There are tables to sit at, although I admit that the locale, being small and subterranean, is not an ideal place of rendez-vous. But if you're not good at either the casual or the formal, tell me what you are good at, and I will do my best. In any case, are you coming to the *Criterion* evening on Wednesday next? I hope so.

Yours ever,<br>[T. S. Eliot]

---

anything about the book or its author which might help me to write something intelligent and constructive.'

1–Kenneth de Burgh Codrington (1899–1986) worked in the India Section, Victoria & Albert Museum; later as a professor of Indian Archaeology. His writings include *An Introduction to the Study of Mediaeval Indian Sculpture* (1929) and *Cricket in the Grass* (reminiscences, 1959).

2–At the bar in South Kensington underground station.

15 May 1936                          [Faber & Faber Ltd]

Dear Mr Stewart,

Thank you so much for your kind letter of May 14th.[2] I shall be delighted if we can really arrange the projected visit to Little Gidding. I am afraid that I cannot spare the time to accept your kind invitation for the 21st and 22nd, especially as I am going to Cambridge for the week-end of the 23rd. But on that occasion I shall be the guest of Maynard Keynes,[3] and must keep myself at his disposal. I should like very much to come again later if we can arrange it.

But what you say about Blackstone rather alarms me. I had been under the impression that my duties were fulfilled by reading his manuscript and sending a report of it. Am I expected to take part in this viva also? In that case I shall have to do a little mugging up myself in order to be able to ask the right questions.

In my report I shall probably confine myself for the most part to his work on George Herbert. When I was asked to assess Blackstone's work for this purpose I said that I did not feel that my knowledge of Ferrar was enough to enable me to criticize this part, and I was told that you would take care of that.

With best wishes to Mrs Stewart and yourself,

I am,

Yours very truly,

[T. S. Eliot]

---

1 – Hugh Fraser Stewart, DD (1863–1948): Fellow of Trinity College, Cambridge. An authority on Pascal, his works include a posthumous bilingual edition of the *Pensées*.
2 – 'There really does seem a chance of making out that long promised visit to Little Gidding; for first there is your play here next week & then there is the oral examination of the man who has written on Herbert & N. Ferrar in which we two are associated.'

Stewart had not yet finished reading Blackstone's thesis but thought it 'on the whole good'. He invited TSE to stay with his family in Cambridge on 21 or 22 May – 'or both'.
3 – John Maynard Keynes (1883–1946), economist and theorist of money; patron of the arts: see Biographical Register.

## TO *W. H. Auden*                                                 CC

15 May 1936                          [Faber & Faber Ltd]

My dear Wystan,

We have just been informed by Curtis Brown that the travel book which you are going to do has been promised to another firm. We were certainly under the impression that we were to have the opportunity of publishing this book, and are rather puzzled as to how this situation could have arisen. You know that like other firms of our standing we like to feel that our regular authors will give us the opportunity to publish the whole of their work. We should always of course be reasonable in this matter, and would not stand in the way of an author's getting from other publishers anything that he could not get from us. As we have published your work from the beginning, and have published everything so far that you have wanted to publish at all, we are particularly sorry not to have been given the opportunity of making you an offer for a book which, in fact, we did understand was going to come our way.

I had not been particularly concerned with this travel book myself, as the suggestion was being dealt with by Morley. Otherwise I should have remembered to discuss it with you when you were here the other day.

It would be a help to me if you could let me know something more about the matter that I could explain to my Committee, as otherwise I am in a rather weak position.[1]

Yours ever,
[T. S. E.]


## TO *H. F. Stewart*                                               CC

Saturday 16 May 1936                 [Faber & Faber Ltd]

Dear Dr Stewart,

I am at fault. I have re-read the instructions, and find that a *viva* is called for. I was misled by associating this occasion with one or two others on which I have reported on dissertations submitted for fellowships. Now unfortunately I have to be in London until noon on Saturday, so I cannot come down on Friday. But I could stay over in Cambridge till Tuesday

---

1–Spencer Curtis Brown to FVM, 26 May 1936: 'Auden has apparently not changed his mind about the travel book. He tells me that he has written to you personally "putting all the blame on to Cape and Curtis Brown." As blame-taking is one of the purposes of an agent I suppose I mustn't complain.'

morning, spending Monday night with you, if that day was possible? And would it then be possible to combine Blackstone with Little Gidding? If Monday does not suit you, I will come down for the night later in the week at your convenience.[1]

I wish you would let me know whether our examination of Blackstone is to be confined to the subject of the thesis, or should search out his general knowledge of English literature? If the former, I think he ought to be questioned about the English mystics, about mystical literature in general, the baroque, the Jesuits. But I have written my report, and I recommend acceptance of the thesis.[2]

Yours sincerely,<br>[T. S. Eliot]

## TO *Robert Waller*                                                    TS BL

20 May 1936                          *The Criterion*

My dear Waller,

I was glad to get your letter of April 27th, and hope that you keep well. I am very glad to hear that you have had some books to review.[3] As a

---

1 – Stewart wrote, in a letter of 17 May that must have crossed with TSE's: 'I fear we cannot escape an oral (or written) examn. of Blackstone . . . but I think the oral is the simpler plan.'
2 – The Blackstone viva ultimately took place in the morning of Mon., 25 May 1936. TSE was driven over to visit Little Gidding that same afternoon, and he spent the night with the Stewarts.

EVE to Ana Olos, 11 Dec. 1990: 'You will be amused to know that a distinguished American scholar wrote to me recently to say that my husband could not have visited Little Gidding on 25th May 1936, as he claimed, because TSE had said in a letter that it was a lovely day, but the scholar had checked the weather report and found it was wet and windy. Fortunately, with the aid of my archive, I was able to prove that TSE was staying with Lord Keynes in Cambridge just beforehand and had gone to Little Gidding on the afternoon of Monday the 25th.' TSE to Hope Mirrlees, 3 July 1956: 'I certainly remember Jessie Stewart, who drove me to Little Gidding . . . I also remember Hugh Stewart with much affection.'

See further Barry Spurr, 'The Genesis of Little Gidding', *Yeats-Eliot Review* 6 (1979), 29–30; Ronald Schuchard, *Eliot's Dark Angel: Intersections of Life and Art* (1999), 175–95.
3 – Waller had been given books to review by the *Adelphi* and the *Spectator*; *Time & Tide* had made 'vague promises'. At the *Listener* J. R. Ackerley had put Waller's name into his pool of reviewers, and had read some of his poetry – 'but [he] thought they were too influenced by the lock jaw style of poetry begun by Stephen Spender a little while ago'. As to his poems, he assured TSE that he was 'honestly going thro' with my determination to interpret my passions philosophically & then describe them in a kind of poetic parable: I haven't properly reached the latter stage yet.' And Desmond MacCarthy had invited him to lunch last week but had to postpone it because his mother was ill. He hoped that TSE would send him books to review.

permanent occupation it is not one to be recommended, but I think that at the present stage a certain amount of miscellaneous reviewing for several papers is something that you may find useful in more than only a financial way. One of the troubles with your writing in the past, I think, has been that you have been accustomed to writing for yourself only, and some experience in writing directly for an audience, and still more an audience which is not exclusively an élite, is very good practice. If you care to look in on me one day before long I shall be very glad to see you, but of course it is safer to ring up first to fix the appointment.

Yours sincerely,
T. S. Eliot

TO *Henri Massis*                                                    TS Valerie Eliot

le 20 mai 1936                          *The Criterion*

Mon cher ami,

Je vous remercie bien de l'envoi de votre beau 'Proust' – analyse funeste et désolante, que l'on est obligé de croire essentiellement correcte. Comme vous avez remarqué vous-même, l'article entier est de beaucoup trop long pour *Le Criterion*; la seconde partie est ce qu'il convient de faire traduire, malheureusement faut-il encore l'abréger – naturellement, le moins possible. Je vous suggérerai préalablement les réductions qui me sembleront possibles sans nuire à la suite de l'argument.[1]

J'ai l'intention de passer plusieurs jours à Paris vers le 6 juin (c'est que j'ai promis à Sylvia Beach de faire une lecture de poésies) et je tiens beaucoup à vous voir. Espérons que ce moment-là vous trouvera toujours à Paris. Je m'intéresserais à faire la connaissance de Thierry Maulnier:[2] je vous suis bien reconnaissant pour vos démarches chez lui au sujet d'un article sur le surréalisme. Dites-lui, s'il vous plaît, qu'un article tomberait bien à mon gré pour le numéro d'octobre, en raison de l'exposition d'art surréaliste qui aura lieu à Londres de le mois de juin. Il serait avantageux d'avoir un article sous la main avant la fin de juillet, pour que la traduction ne soit pas trop pressé.

---

1–Massis, 'Proust: The Twenty Years' Silence' – an extract from a study entitled *Le Cas Marcel Proust* – trans. Montgomery Belgion, C. 16 (Jan. 1937), 269–86.
2–Thierry Maulnier (1909–88): French journalist, essayist, playwright, critic; contributor to *L'Action française*; author of *La crise est dans l'homme* (1932), *Miracle de la Monarchie* (1935), *Mythes socialistes* (1938); he was elected to the Académie française in 1964.

Avec mes meilleurs sentiments à Madame Massis, je reste
toujours votre
T. S. Eliot[1]


## TO *Serge Bolshakoff*[2]                                           CC

22 May 1936                      [Faber & Faber Ltd]

Dear Mr Bolshakoff,

Thank you for your letter of the 20th, and the information contained
therein.[3] If you can get Reckitt, Bernard Wall and Father Murray I shall
be very glad to come to a Committee with you. Christopher Dawson I
am afraid is an impossibility, as I hear from several sources that he is in
very poor health. I could come late in the afternoon of the 28th or 29th of
this month, or if both those dates are impossible I think I could manage
Tuesday 2nd May [*sc.* June]. I hope you will let me know as soon as you
can arrange a quorum.

Yours ever,
[T. S. Eliot]

---

1 – *Translation*: My dear friend, / Thank you very much for sending your fine 'Proust' – a
dire and damning assessment, that one can only believe is essentially correct. As you yourself
remark, the article as a whole is much too long for the *Criterion* ; the second part is what we
should want to translate, and even that will need shortening – as little as possible, naturally.
I shall notify you in advance of any cuts that seem feasible without damaging your argument.

I intend to spend several days in Paris around June 6th (I have promised to do a poetry
reading for Sylvia Beach) and I hope very much to see you. I trust that you will be in Paris
at that time. I should like to meet Thierry Maulnier, and I am most grateful to you for being
in touch with him about the article on Surrealism. Please tell him that, ideally, I should like
to publish his article in the October number, given that the Exhibition of Surrealist Art is to
take place in London this June. It would be helpful to have the article in hand by the end of
July, so the process of translating it is not too hurried.

All good wishes to Mme Massis, I remain / Ever yours [T. S. Eliot]

2 – Serge (Sergius) Bolshakoff (1901–90), Russian-born ecumenist; educated in St Petersburg
and in Tartu, Estonia, he lived for a while in France and then in England, 1928–51, where
he resided for his first ten years at the Anglican Benedictine community of Nashdom, at
Burnham in Berkshire. An oblate rather than a monk, he committed his extraordinary
energies to working towards an Anglican–Orthodox rapprochement; to that end, he set up
what he called an International Academy of Christian Sociologists: a confraternity with the
object of working for Christian unity. His publications include *The Christian Church and
the Soviet Union* (1942) and *The Foreign Missions of the Russian Orthodox Church* (1943).

3 – Not traced.

22 May 1936                          [Faber & Faber Ltd]

My dear Brace,

Morley has shown me your letter of May 7th. I am relieved to find that the errata you found in the proofs were not present in the final production of my book. I must apologise, however, for our having sent you proofs which were not fully corrected.[1]

You do seem however to have found one glaring error in our edition. The text of *Ash Wednesday* that you have is certainly correct. The line should read:

'Against the Word the unstilled world still whirled'.

I shall be glad at least to have this correct in the American if not the London edition.[2]

Yours ever,
[T. S. Eliot]

---

1 – Brace to FVM, 9 Apr. 1936: 'You will remember that we set up the book from copy supplied by Eliot, and that then it was arranged that we would read our proofs by the finally corrected proofs of your edition. This we have tried to do with painstaking care, but I have been disturbed to find a few instances of clear errors uncorrected in your proofs, and these have left me with some doubt of their accuracy in matters which we wouldn't be able to discover. We are following the proofs, of course, except in two or three cases of obviously misspelled words, and I expect it will turn out all right. What a grand, rich collection it is! I am so glad it has been accomplished.'

Then on 7 May 1936: 'I have just received the two copies of your edition, and I find that the errata I found in the finally corrected proofs have been corrected in your book. In other words, the proofs we had were not actually finally corrected. The errata were:

"listlessness" on page 151.

"Veber" for "Ueber" in the German passage on page 83.

Headings of Parts III, IV, and V in the "Notes on 'The Waste Land'" were omitted. These were obvious, of course, and easily corrected. The only point about them was that they cast some doubt on the whole business. There were a few other things of this same sort, but I can't recall them now.

'I wish you would ask Eliot about the next to the last line in the first verse of Part V of "Ash Wednesday", page 100 in your edition. It reads there:

"Against the World the unstilled world still whirled"

'In our edition it reads:

"Against the Word, etc."

'I expect we should regard your edition as correct, but I am still a little uncertain about it.'

TSE wrote in the margin, against the citation 'Against the Word, etc.': 'Correct.'

2 – Ricks and McCue: 'Brace, 4 June: "I am relieved to hear that the line in *Ash-Wednesday* is correct as we have printed it. I couldn't believe that it could be correct as printed in your edition, so I took the liberty, not without a good deal of hesitation, of adopting the reading which happily turns out to be the correct one." The error persisted in British editions, including *Sesame*, *Penguin* and *Sel Poems* (1954).'

TO *Mario Praz*[1]        TS Galleria Nazionale d'Arte Moderna, Roma

22 May 1936                *The Criterion*

My dear Praz,

I was glad to get your letter of the 15th May, after not hearing from you for such a long time. I am rather alarmed by your subject, and I don't see that there is enough to say without spinning it out, but I shall be very glad to be of any use to you that I can. In any case, so far as I know, nobody else has dealt with this subject.[2]

The volumes you need seem to be *Elizabethan Essays*, *Essays Ancient and Modern*, and my *Collected Poems*, which was published last month. I will ask the firm to let you have these.

I certainly owe a good deal to Ezra Pound in connection with my slight knowledge of the early Italian poets. I don't think that I ever corresponded with him on the subject, because my chief association with him was during the period when he lived in London. I owed a good deal to the essay on Dante in his early book *The Spirit of Romance*, which you would do well to look at if you do not know it. I think the book is out of print now, and I can't find my own copy, but possibly you are in communication with Pound, whose address is Via Marsala 12, int. 5, Rapallo. I had read a smattering of some of the others, especially the two Guidos and Cino before I knew Pound, but he certainly sharpened my interest in these people, and you must understand that my knowledge has never been more than what everyone would call smattering.

With all good wishes,

Yours ever,

T. S. Eliot

1–Mario Praz (1896–1982), scholar and critic of English literature: see Biographical Register.

2–Praz had been invited by the *Southern Review* to write a long essay on 'T. S. Eliot and Dante' – they wished for 'the most authoritative and comprehensive on the subject' – and hoped that TSE was 'not alarmed by the idea . . . I need not stress how helpful your assistance would be, in preventing me from going astray, and pointing to me those of your compositions where you have been conscious of a Dante influence. I do not wish you to write the essay, of course, but to give me a few hints, and to ask Faber & Faber to send me those books of yrs which I have not in my library. [He did not have *Elizabethan Essays* and *Essays Ancient and Modern*.] . . . If I may put to you a question: How much did Ezra Pound contribute towards your acquaintance with the Italian poets? Have you had a correspondence with him on the subject? I hope you don't dislike the idea of my essay, w[hi]ch, you may depend on, would not be an arid *Quellenforschung*.'

22 May 1936                           [Faber & Faber Ltd]

Dear Aldous,

I am instructed by my Board of Directors, meeting in committee, to approach you with the question whether you would consider, for an appropriate consideration, editing – which means either choosing, or exercising a veto upon the choice of somebody else, *and* writing an Introduction about – a volume of the best and most representative (from the best point of view – I mean if you did it the material included would have [to] be such as you approved of, whether the public liked it or not) Short Stories? We mean really the BEST, and if you wrote the introduction they would have to be what *you* consider the Best. If you took the whole responsibility, then we should accept the stories you wanted (if we could get the publishers' permission at something below a fantastic price, and if they were – in the popular sense – 'printable'); if you took only the responsibility of writing an introduction, then we should submit any selection of stories to you for your veto. 'Short Story' of course in the widest sense of the term. But not merely readable or slick, they must have some significance in the development of the genre at the present time (if it does develop at the present time): this is not a volume for station bookstalls.[2]

We are not trying to interfere with the legitimate business of Chatto & Windus: but you did introduce Lawrence's Letters, very well, for another publisher. So I suppose you are in a position to introduce other things for other people.

We want a volume which will be a 'document' for some years to come.

Say either No, or that you are willing to treat further with us.

Is there any possibility of your being able to have me as a guest for a week (and when I say guest, I mean either with you or else that you will take the trouble to engage a room for me in the neighbourhood at my expense, with tolerable bedding and food) at the end of July or the beginning of August? The only deterrent on my part is expense, as I have

---

1 – Aldous Huxley (1894–1963), novelist, poet, essayist: see Biographical Register.
2 – Huxley replied from La Gorguette, Sanary, on the Côte d'Azur, on 30 May: 'About the short stories – the trouble is that I am so deeply ignorant on the subject and that, in order to cope with it, I shd have to undertake a great amount of reading for which I have no time. This being so, I had better say no, but thank you very much for asking me.'

to have enough money to go to America for a few weeks during September–October.[1]

With love to Maria,

Yours

[Tom]

A man named Tom Driberg, who is a busybody on *The Daily Express*,[2] rang me up this afternoon to say that he has found that a volume presented by you to me in 1917 has been sold, or offered for sale, for twenty guineas. I was unable to tell him anything further, except that the twenty guineas are not coming into my pocket. *Mais les chiffres sont intéressants.*[3]

## TO *W. H. Auden*                                                                     cc

26 May 1936                        [Faber & Faber Ltd]

Dear Wystan,

I have thought over your letter, but I still don't feel very happy.[4] After all, it seems that Cape only suggested to you to do a novel, and you told them that you would like to do something in the travel line. If you had that in mind, why didn't you suggest it to *us* first? Please don't think that I am merely expressing personal irritation, or a one-sided business view. The sense is only what I believe any agent, acting on your own behalf, would support. We can do much better with your work, for you and

---

1 – Huxley, 30 May: 'How nice of you to suggest coming to stay with us! The end of July wd suit us very well indeed . . .' Huxley recommended the 3rd class sleeper train – 'the price of which is within 10/- of the ordinary 2nd class fare.'

2 – Tom Driberg (1905–76) – journalist, left-wing politican, Member of Parliament, 1942–55, 1959–74), High Anglican, socialite – wrote the 'William Hickey' gossip column in the *Daily Express*, 1933–43. See Francis Wheen, *Tom Driberg: His Life and Indiscretions* (1990); repr. as *The Soul of Indiscretion: Tom Driberg, Poet, Philanderer, Legislator and Outlaw* (2001).

3 – *Mais les chiffres sont intéressants*: (Fr.) 'But the numbers are interesting.'

4 – WHA wrote (n.d.): 'The affair Iceland was this way. Capes have for some time tried to persuade me to do a novel, and I refused, but told them that I would like to do something in the travel line. I did no more about this until I had the Iceland idea, and told Curtis Brown to do something about it.

'Meeting Morley by chance in the street, I mentioned the idea to him, and that I had told Curtis Brown to negotiate. As the original suggestion for this type of book came from Capes, I told Curtis Brown to let them know.

'I'm very sorry if I've caused trouble and annoyance as I am afraid I have. I noticed that Stephen went to them for his critical book, so I thought that perhaps you didn't mind. I'm so sorry. It shant occur again.'

for ourselves, if we have the whole of it to deal with; and an incident of this sort is bound to give rise to rumours of separation etc. The case of Stephen's book was due to some quite positive misunderstanding between Stephen on the one hand and Faber and Morley on the other; so that Stephen thought that he had offered us his book and that we had declined it and encouraged him to take it elsewhere. This is not parallel: if you had let us know that you were interested in doing a sort of travel book, I know that we would have welcomed the idea.

Yours ever,<br>[Tom]

## TO *Kenneth Pickthorn*[1]

CC

27 May 1936                 [Faber & Faber Ltd]

My dear Pickthorn,

I have just been speaking to Montgomery Belgion[2] on the telephone and he tells me that he heard you remark in conversation that you had written to me several weeks ago to suggest my coming down to Cambridge, but had had no reply. I am writing at once to let you know that I never had your invitation. Possibly you sent it to an old address of mine, 68 Clarence Gate Gardens. I have found that the Post Office sometimes fails to forward letters from there.

I should have been very glad to come if I had received your invitation in time. As it is, I have just come back from Cambridge, as Maynard Keynes asked me down for the weekend to see *Murder in the Cathedral*, and also his theatre.[3] I should like to have seen you, but could not get away, and

---

1–Kenneth Pickthorn (1892–1975): historian and politician; Fellow of Corpus Christi College, Cambridge, from 1914; Dean, 1919–29; Tutor, 1927–35; President, 1937–44. From 1950 to 1966 he was Conservative MP for a Midlands constituency; an outspoken parliamentarian, critical of cant, he was made a baronet in 1959, Privy Councillor in 1964. Works include *Some Historical Principles of the Constitution* (1925) and *Early Tudor Government* (2 vols, 1934).

2–Montgomery Belgion (1892–1975), author: see Biographical Register.

3–On Sun. 23 May, Keynes invited the young don Basil Willey (1897–1978) to meet Eliot at lunch; as Willey was to recall in *Cambridge and Other Memories: 1920–1953* (1968), 92–3: 'I had been asked "to meet T. S. Eliot", and Eliot was indeed there; but it was with our host that real contact was made. Eliot was immaculate, impenetrable, inscrutable: uttering little but looking very handsome, melancholy and wise. Keynes, on the other hand, poured forth words with a virtuosity I had never yet heard approached . . .

'I never met J. M. Keynes again . . . But Eliot I did meet once or twice more. One of these meetings was in the rooms of a young don who had recently been my pupil . . . It will

spent Monday with Dr Stewart as I was assisting him in examining a PhD candidate.

I am very sorry about the misadventure. Is there no possibility of your lunching or dining with me one day when you are in London and have nothing better to do?

Yours ever,
[T. S. Eliot]

## TO *Ashley Dukes* CC

27 May 1936                    [Faber & Faber Ltd]

My dear Dukes,

I am enclosing for your advice a letter I have received from 'Klinte's Forlag in Denmark, together with their draft agreements in duplicate, and stamped envelope to return to me.

I should be very grateful if you would let me have your opinion of the desirability of making an engagement with these people, about whom I know nothing. As for the agreement itself, I query the wording of paragraph 2, as being vague and comprehensive enough to include almost any alterations they might choose to make. And I think paragraph 3 needs rewording. In any case, as Faber and Faber are official agents for me everywhere for book rights this would have to be rewritten.[1]

––––––

hardly be believed, but even then I was so ignorant of men and the world as to suppose that a poet, if actually encountered in the flesh, would talk about poetry, and especially his own poetry. In fact, most of the time not devoted to readings from P. G. Wodehouse by our host, was spent in discussing make-up. "Personally", said Eliot, "I always used to prefer green; it's so much more striking and cadaverous, don't you agree?" I very soon lost my foothold in this torrent of frivolity, and was rather shocked to find Eliot admitting that he had given thought to such trifles. No doubt he was talking nonsense for the very purpose of shocking his juniors, but even this jesting brought him no nearer as a human being; on the contrary it kept others at a distance, and added another layer of thickness to the impenetrable shell within which he chose to live.'

(Carroll F. Terrell, 'Basil Bunting: An Eccentric Biography', in *Basil Bunting: Man and Poet*, ed. Terrell (1981), 45, tells a tale dating back to 1925: 'Bunting saw Eliot at a party wearing an enormous cape lined with red and eyebrows painted green. He responded to Bunting's expression of amazement with these words: "thought the party needed hotting up".')

1 – Dukes replied on 29 May, 'I don't think you should part with the valuable Scandinavian rights of your play, even to a firm of the standing of "Klinte's" Forlag which I know, without a substantial advance royalty.' He suggested they ask for an advance of £50 on account of a royalty of 5% on all dramatic performances and book sales; the translation was to be faithful.

I spent the weekend in Cambridge with Maynard Keynes, and saw the last performance there on Saturday. I was extremely pleased with it. Especially considering how long the company have been performing the play, and the fatigue of crowding Oxford and Cambridge into one week, and unfamiliarity of larger theatres, I think they did remarkably well. Speaight said after the performance that they had never had a more appreciative house. It is a good theatre, I think, and is certainly proving a delightful avocation for Keynes. I hope that you are doing equally well in Dublin.[1]

Yours ever,
[T. S. Eliot]

## TO C. A. *Stonehill* cc

28 May 1936                    [Faber & Faber Ltd]

Dear Mr Stonehill,

I have received your letter of May 26th, and I am extremely sorry that you have been bothered in this way.[2] All I know of the matter is that a young man whom I had previously met, who is connected with the *Daily Express*, rang me up to communicate the news of this sale, which he proposed to mention, or have mentioned, in his paper. I told him that I knew nothing about it. I could not of course ask him to suppress the matter, but I did suggest that he was not to give any implication either that I myself was concerned in the sale, or that the volume had been stolen

1 – EMB informed Dukes that the Dublin receipts promised to balance the accounts, and that he had used Dukes's authority to continue the production for the second week envisaged. Part (probably Part I) of the play had been broadcast by Radio Athlone in the evening of 28 May.

2 – C. A. Stonehill, a dealer in rare books and manuscripts, 26 Museum Street, London, sent TSE a cutting from the 'William Hickey' column [by Tom Driberg] of the *Daily Express*:

'For £20 yesterday Hodgson's [Hodgson & Co.] sold at auction a book catalogued as
    Huxley (A.) *Jonah*. Autograph Presentation Copy to T. S. Eliot, wrappers, 1917.

'This sort of thing is always slightly mysterious. It has happened to me . . . Books have a malignant habit of straying during house-removal. Also, borrowers don't always remember whom they borrowed from. Neither auctioneers not vendors are to blame: it's impossible to trace all antecedents of 2nd hand books that come to one.'

Stonehill, who had purchased the book in question, remarked in his covering letter that he was 'very much disturbed' by the story: 'I do not like the implication that the book has been stolen from you and should like a word from you that I am free to offer the book. Incidentally, I am curious to know just how the book got out of your possession . . . You will realise that it is not a light thing for me to have aspersions cast upon the books in my stock.'

See too TSE to JDH, 4 May 1937, below.

from me. I haven't the slightest reason to suppose that it was stolen, and in any case the book must have disappeared many years ago, as I can't even remember now what it was about. I have always been very careless with my books, and have had a number of removals, and at one time or another have had a good many small volumes presented to me by their authors of which I have not always been careful.

The name of the young man who rang me up was not Hickey, and I don't know who Mr Hickey is.

With many regrets,
Yours sincerely,
[T. S. Eliot]

## TO *James Joyce*                                           CC

28 May 1936                          [Faber & Faber Ltd]

My dear Joyce,

I expect to be in Paris on June 5th for three or four days, and I will let you know as the time approaches and see if you and Mrs Joyce can have a meal with us. Mr and Mrs Morley expect to be coming with me as on the last occasion.[1] I take it from your telegram that my suggestion suits you, and I will therefore bring the manuscript of Part III of *Work in Progress* and give it to you. I hope to find you well, and look forward to seeing you.[2]

Yours ever,
[T. S. Eliot]

---

1–FVM to Donald Brace, 23 Apr. 1936: 'Eliot says he is going to do all the staff work this time. He is very contemptuous about my previous staff work, and says he is going to do so infinitely better. He is already running round the house in a very excited manner, and Christina and he are beginning to talk French all the time, and I can see that the trip is going to be very hard on me unless you will come along.'

2–JJ replied on 3 June: 'I shall be glad to see you again after such a long time but hope that you will do us the pleasure of dining with us instead.

'I am in arrears with my correspondence . . .

'[Paul] Léon will undertake the work of course but he says it is not the same thing now as it would have been in January when the text with insertions and alignments was quite fresh in his mind.' (EVE)

JJ telegrammed on 4 June: 'WROTE YESTERDAY MORNING PLEASE TELEPHONE ME FIRST AFTER ARRIVAL HERE = JOYCE'.

## TO *Sylvia Beach*

28 May 1936                    [Faber & Faber Ltd]

Dear Miss Beach,

Thank you for your letter of May 26th.[1] I only regret that I have nothing to offer that is new and unpublished. I feel that that is what audiences at such readings like to hear, and it would perhaps have been better for your purpose if I could have given the reading before my *Collected Poems* appeared. I must do the best I can with printed matter. I expect to arrive, together with Mr and Mrs Morley, on Friday 5th. I will either telephone or look in during the course of the day. I shall probably return to London on Monday night, so that the best night for dinner would be Saturday or Sunday. But I think that I could manage Friday as well.

I will try to induce the firm to send Monsieur Gillet[2] a review copy.

Yours sincerely,

[T. S. Eliot]


## TO *John Purves*

28 May 1936                    [Faber & Faber Ltd]

Dear Mr Purves,

I must apologize for my delay in answering your enquiry about the possibility of my being able to contribute to the presentation volume for Professor Grierson.[3] I have thought the matter over, and I am sorry that I shall be unable to undertake to write a fresh essay for you. I should like nothing better than to be able to write a paper on Corneille, as this is a project I have had in mind for some time.[4] It is not, however, one that I

---

1–Not traced.
2–Louis Gillet, Curator of the Abbaye de Chaalis; Member of the Académie Française.
3–H. J. C. Grierson (1866–1960): Regius Professor of Rhetoric and English Literature, University of Edinburgh, 1915–35; knighted in 1936; celebrated for his edition of *The Poems of John Donne* (2 vols, 1912) and *Metaphysical Lyrics and Poems of the Seventeenth Century* (1921) – which TSE reviewed in the *TLS*, 21 Oct. 1921. Cairns Craig, in 'The last Romantics: How the scholarship of Herbert Grierson influenced Modernist poetry' (*TLS*, 15 Jan. 2010, 14–15), argues that *TWL* 'is saturated with echoes of Grierson's *Metaphysical Lyrics and Poems*. When Eliot sent a copy of his *Collected Poems* to Grierson, it was inscribed "to whom all English men of letters are indebted".' (Letty Grierson remembers a slightly different wording: 'to whom all poets of today are indebted': noted in the Grierson catalogue issued by James Fergusson Books & Manuscripts 2010.)
4–See too David Gervais, 'T. S. Eliot and Racine: Tragedy and Resignation in *Bérénice*', *Cambridge Quarterly* 36: 1 (2007), 51–70. TSE admired in particular *Polyeucte* (1643).

can undertake at the moment, or for any specific date for publication, and I may not be able to write it for several years. The only suggestion I have to make is this, that I have an old lecture on Cowley, delivered ten years ago, which has never been published, and which I might be able to furbish up suitably to the occasion. If you think that this would be appropriate I will look over the essay carefully with that revision in view.[1]

Yours sincerely,

[T. S. Eliot]

## TO *Rayner Heppenstall*

TS Texas

29 May 1936                          Faber & Faber Ltd

Dear Heppenstall,

I am sorry to be so slow, but I have been thinking seriously about the collection of poems which you called *Ad Cor Altum*.[2] These seem to me, as they did to Herbert Read, an advance on your previous work, and I am inclined to think that they might more suitably appear by themselves than joined to *Sebastian*.[3] But I have still to get another opinion about them, and to write to you again.

I am rather worried by your determination to plunge into a career of novel-writing.[4] If you really hope to become a professional novelist I think the outlook is rather unfavourable for the future of your poetry.

1–'A Note on Two Odes of Cowley by T. S. Eliot', *Seventeenth Century Studies Presented to Sir Herbert Grierson* (1938), 235–42.

2–Heppenstall wrote on 15 May: 'I'm sorry to look as if I'm harping, but I shd be grateful if you cd. decide abt. my poems (Sebastian & Ad Cor Altum) by the end of the month? If not, will you send them back? The position is this. I have 167pp of a novel, working-class Yorkshire in setting, not experimental in form, which James Hanley thinks very well of & wh. I hope to finish in June. I *must* have it out this year, & I can't afford to have the poems unpublished in the meantime, poems being difficult to publish & novels always being effective, it seems, as bait to publishers. Obviously, poems coming from Faber's have an initial survival value, as compared with others . . . But it begins to dawn on me that, if *I'm* to survive, I've got to plan things out for some time ahead. This particular novel will be finished promptly. It's a novel wh. holds nothing to keep it from selling, as well as a good deal that pleases myself. Then I shall go on doing novels after it. It isn't possible for me, as I don't want, to sit abt. legislating on the cosmos.'

3–Heppenstall responded, 30 May: 'I couldn't put Sebastian back in a drawer. Ad Cor Altam would make a very slim volume indeed by itself. My own feeling was for a book titled Sebastian & sub-titled Second Poems, in which, however, Sebastian would be printed as the second half.'

4–Heppenstall, 30 May: 'The rest of your letter terrified me. "A career of novel-writing" & "a professional novelist" haven't come into my head. I don't think I'm prolific enough

I mean that while an exception is always possible I think that the verse of a professional novelist must always be a bye-product [*sc*. by-product]. I don't think that a single individual can divide himself so successfully as to make a major art of two occupations requiring very different attitudes. I am afraid, that is, that if you become a novelist you will stop writing verse. It may be, of course, that the novel is your real form. I wouldn't rule that possibility out.

But about the novel you are doing, is it possible that you will offer it to us, or is it already promised elsewhere? I should like to know, as that would enter into my calculations.

With best wishes, and also to James Hanley,

Yours sincerely,
T. S. Eliot

## TO *Edwin Muir*[1]                                        cc

29 May 1936                    [*The Criterion*]

Dear Muir,

Thank you for your letter of May 18th.[2] I like your poem on Hölderlin very much in the main. That is to say, I am struck by the idea and the imagery, and it is only some minor blemishes, as they appear to me, that I should like to criticize, if you don't mind.

I don't like the adjective 'hot' for Bordeaux. I can't see that making Bordeaux hot contributes anything, and the adjective gives me the impression of only metrical necessity. Then the two lines reading:

'Cruel redemptress from whose side
The living waters start!'

---

for that . . . I expect to write what novels I want to write &, I should think, remain – what I am – a professional mendicant . . . There are, to date, 231 pages of novel. That's the end of Part I.'

*Sebastian* was eventually published by Dent (1937).

1 – Edwin Muir (1887–1959), Scottish poet, novelist, critic, translator: see Biographical Register.

2 – Muir enclosed 'Hölderlin's Journey'. 'You will probably recognise its theme, which is Hölderlin's strange and still unaccounted for journey from Bordeaux to Germany in the summer of 1805. He walked that distance on foot and arrived out of his mind. Nothing is known of the journey, but it has always appealed strongly to my imagination. I wonder if the poem needs some explanation: a note giving the theme? . . . The verse about the Medusa was suggested to me by a portrait of Diotima, showing a beautiful but rather inhuman head. I do not know whether it quite fits in with the rest.'

leave my mind confused. I can't form any clear visual image of this, and such image as does occur seems to me a little inelegant. Then lower down I don't like the adjective 'selfsame', which again appears to be there merely to fill out the line. Surely if a deer's head is carved in stone on each door any reader will assume that all the heads are carved of the same stone, in the absence of any statement to the contrary? I wonder if these criticisms seem to you to have any value?

Yours sincerely,

[T. S. Eliot]

## TO *John Hayward*

TO *John Hayward*                                          TS King's

Friday [29 May 1936]                *The Criterion*

Dear John,

You overwhelm me with consideration.[1] I only hoped that you would preserve the pencil until I saw you again (and perhaps make use of it: there is a reservoir of leads in the behind part) – but to return it to me instanter, carefully encased in an antiseptic toothbrush box (you evidently use much larger toothbrushes than I do; I buy the Infants' or Tom Thumb size for a shilling, two at a time, and thus can afford to renew them more frequently, for I think, a ragged toothbrush is of no more use than none at all, but my dentist says that it doesn't make much difference and one might as well or better eat an apple, but I never remember to buy the apples) that is more than any man could expect from his twin brother in the way of kindness. But the problem is, how to get the box open? without, I mean, breaking the cellophane: presumably you opened it to get out the toothbrush and shut it again with the pencil; but to open it again without damaging the box seems to be, as Janes[2] would say, a thing impossible. Janes was telling me this morning about the merry jests that Mr Bowman, who is now licensee of the Three Tuns in Chancery Lane, used to play upon him when he had a house in the Caledonian Road; and I have had some vestry business, and this afternoon I have had to interview Dr N. M. Iovetz-Tereshchencko and the Revd Vincent

---

1–JDH treated TSE, GCF and FVM to sherry on 20 May, in advance of the *Criterion* meeting.

2–W. L. Janes (1854–1939): ex-policeman who had worked as factotum for TSE since 1924.

Howson[1] and Edouard Roditi[2] and then visit old Jan who has been ill with bronchitis, so perhaps my head is weak and wambling, but my heart is beating in the right place, and so I write to thank you for the pencil and the box and to say that I will bring the box round so that you can show me how to open it and get out the pencil, so will close

yours affectionately,

TP

## TO *Louis MacNeice* CC

30 May 1936 *[The Criterion]*

Dear MacNeice,

Allright, the time for *Agamemnon* is whenever you are satisfied with it yourself; but I look forward to it eagerly.[3] (By the way, I wonder if Dodds would remember me; I think we read Plotinus together with J. A. Smith [*sc.* Stewart], and experimented with crystal-gazing).[4]

I shall be in London until Thursday night, when I go to Paris until the following Tuesday. By all means come in and bring your friend: safest to ring up my secretary first and fix a time.[5]

---

1–The Revd Vincent Howson (d. 1957), St James' Vicarage, Ratcliff, London, was 'Bert' in *The Rock*. Founder-producer of the East End Amateurs, he had been a member of Sir Frank Benson's Shakespearian Company.

2–Edouard Roditi (1910–92), poet, critic, biographer, translator: see Biographical Register L6.

3–LM, 28 May: 'My translation of the Agamemnon is not quite ready. I gave it to my Greek professor, E. R. Dodds, to vet and he is suggesting certain changes. I hope to have it ready in three or four weeks' time.' (*Letters of Louis MacNeice*, ed. Jonathan Allison [2010], 265)

4–See Robert B. Todd, 'An Identification in T. S. Eliot's Letters', *Notes and Queries* 245 (Sept. 2000), 337–8. TSE and E. R. Dodds (1893–1978) – Professor of Greek at Oxford, 1936–60 – had taken a class on Plotinus in Hilary Term 1915 with J. A. Stewart (1846–1933), White's Professor of Moral Philosophy. See Dodds, *Missing Persons: An Autobiography* (1977), 40. Charles King to TSE, 8 Dec. 1936: 'you used to go with Dodds to hear Prof. Stewart on Plotinus, as I did later with Andrews (Rebecca West's husband)'. Blanshard, 'T. S. Eliot at Oxford': 'Recalling how Eliot scattered tag-ends of Greek through his poetry, I asked Dodds whether these represented a solid knowledge of Greek. Yes they did, he replied . . . [I]n a tiny group of four advanced students Eliot could pull his own weight. Once when we were talking about Plato's Dialogues, of which I had read a small number in the original, he remarked that he had read all of them. This meant in Greek.' Dodds told GCF, 6 Dec. 1936, he would be in town from 10 Dec. for four days, and hoped for 'an opportunity . . . to renew my acquaintance with T. S. Eliot'. TSE to H. M. Conacher, 27 Mar. 1953, on neglecting Plotinus 'for a great many years – indeed, since the time when Professor Dodds and I were fellow pupils of Professor Stewart'.

5–'A friend of mine is anxious to meet you. His aunt wants to do a production of *Murder in the Cathedral* in the cathedral at Lahore! I shall probably be in London next week.'

If Bedford College apply to me I shall be delighted to add my testimonial.[1]

And of course I should like to see your own play whenever you are ready to show it; I think we should be keen to publish it.[2]

Yours sincerely,<br>[T. S. Eliot]

TO *Stuart Gilbert*                                    TS Mrs Gilbert

30 May 1936                           *The Criterion*

Dear Gilbert,

I expect to arrive on Friday morning, the 5th, and to come back to London either Monday or Tuesday night. The Morleys are coming with me – if that is too many for dinner could we all dine out together, or we could come in at some other time. On Friday I am asking the Joyces to dine with us, on Saturday I suppose I dine with Sylvia Beach before I give my reading. Would Sunday evening suit you?[3]

Yours ever sincerely,<br>T. S. Eliot

1 – 'I am just applying for a rather absurd job at Bedford College for Women, London – not because I want to teach women but because I should like to live in London. I gave your name to them for purposes of reference. I hope you don't mind?'

2 – 'I have a play of my own which I am writing for the Group theatre. I wonder if you would like to see it also sometime.' On *Station Bell*, see Alec Reid, 'MacNeice in the Theatre', in *Time Was Away: The World of Louis MacNeice*, ed. Terence Brown and Alec Reid (1974), 74–5.

3 – Beach to TSE, 2 June: 'I regret so much that I shall have to ask you to maintain the date of Sunday the 7th to dine with us. Gide has arranged to be in Paris on that particular day to meet you and can only come then. It is usually impossible to get him anywhere as he does not go out and in fact is rarely here. But he has arranged to come up from his country place to join us on Sunday and says he is looking forward with much pleasure to seeing you. You see, as the real head of the "Nouvelle Revue Française" (the "Head Man in that show") and the French writer who has probably taken the greatest interest in English letters, we were anxious that he should be the one to invited to meet you. It is he who had the idea of starting the really fine and efficacious movement among the French writers to enable me to continue "Shakespeare and Company" and who gave a public proof of his interest by offering to inaugurate the readings for the group. I regret that Sunday is not perfectly convenient for you and if we had been able to fix up a dinner on Saturday we would have been glad to do so. Unfortunately, Adrienne Monnier's duties in her shop prevent her from preparing for guests on that day – you know she is not only hostess but chef, and a celebrated one – and I am occupied with the arrangements for the reading and always dine "sur le pouce" at the last moment, so as soon as you wrote that either Saturday or Sunday would suit you we set Sunday as the day and Gide and also Schlumberger accepted. The Gilberts have very kindly consented to postpone their party till Monday, and we hope that will remove the difficulty for you of dining with us on Sunday. They quite understand the situation.'

30 May 1936                          [*The Criterion*]

Dear Richards,

Thank you for your letter. The July number of the *Criterion* is already made up. I should very much like to have your article in the October number, but I am not sure that I shall have the space: I will make space if it can possibly be done; otherwise I hope you would not object to my using it in the December number.[1]

The editor of *Christendom* (N.Y.) called on me the other day, to ask for a contribution. He wants to obtain some circulation in this country, but I

---

See *The Very Rich Hours of Adrienne Monnier*, 136: 'To crown this first cycle of meetings, the great English poet, T. S. Eliot, came to Paris on June 6 to read some poems. The poetry of T. S. Eliot passes, and rightly so, for being obscure. Completely grounded in a very profoundly original sensibility, it is full of incommunicable motifs, slight and overwhelming states of grace that the Zen Buddhists call *satoris*. The poet as he reads knows how to pass his trance on to you; he has a pure voice with a reverberating intonation, well assured in its tranquil torment. His face is handsome and curious: that of an archangel who has too much work to do, and so does only half of it, leaving the rest to the North Wind.'

'T. S. Eliot gave a reading at Shakespeare and Company. On this occasion we had the pleasure of having him to dinner at our place in the company of Gide, Jean Schlumberger, and François Valéry. In the course of this dinner Gide tried to tear apart the spirit of the Orient completely, and in particular certain works that Eliot, Schlumberger, and I myself said that we liked: The *Bhagavad-Gita*, for example, or Milarepa (I have a very amusing letter from him on the subject of Milarepa). Schlumberger let him speak, then he said to him gently: "All the same there is one Oriental work that you have loved very much," and as Gide looked at him with a questioning air he added: "– the Gospels." Following that I tried rather wickedly to prove that Buddha had had a particular attachment to his disciple Ananda and that it was after a disappointment in love caused by him that he had decided to leave the earth' (*idem*, 201).

According to Noel Riley Fitch, *Sylvia Beach and the Lost Generation* (1983), TSE's reading at Shakespeare & Co. included *TWL* and 'early written parts' of *BN*.

François Valéry wrote to TSE ('March' ?1937) that he would always remember TSE's talk and the reading of his poems at Beach's bookshop.

Beach to TSE, 10 June: 'I must thank you again, Dear Mr Eliot, for the very great pleasure you gave us. Mr William Shakespeare himself could not have been more wonderful and our admiration was unbounded.'

On 8 June TSE and the Morleys dined *chez* Gilbert at 7 Rue Jean du Bellay, Paris IV.

FVM to Gilbert, 12 June: 'The trip was from every point of view a magnificent pleasure, and it was you and your kindness which made it so. The highest spot of the whole time was the rendition of AFTER THE BALL WAS OVER. I hope that both of you have forgiven us for keeping you up so late that night.' FVM to Margaret Cuff (Harcourt, Brace & Co.), 12 June: 'We emerged with our lives, and two evenings with various French intellectuals made our last year's dinner with Joyce seem cheerful by comparison. We really did suffer this time, and I wish Mr Brace had been with us. On one of the evenings I was completely surrounded with French people for five hours without being able to talk a word with them.'

1–Richards, 'The Religious Philosophy of Paul Elmer More', C, 16 (Jan. 1937), 205–19.

doubt if he will. Religious periodicals are not very good export articles. I think that his paper is too bulky and too miscellaneous.

If I don't get a copy of their summer number I trust that they will send you a couple of copies, so that you can let me have one.

Louis More had lunch with me a few days ago.[1] He spoke appreciatively of you and I hope you will be able to see him. He is of a much smaller cut than his brother, of course; but his devotion and admiration for Paul are most touching. I expect to be in America for a few weeks in September, and shall make an effort to see More in Princeton.

I'm glad to hear that Merton has done so well.[2] They were head of the river once, but I don't know what they have done in the last twenty years or so.

Yours every sincerely,
[T. S. Eliot]

## TO *Benjamin Gregory*                                                CC

2 June 1936                        [Faber & Faber Ltd]

Dear Dr Gregory,

Thank you for your letter of the 28th May.[3] I have not made any arrangements for filming *Murder in the Cathedral*, and I have declined an offer from New York for the production of the play because the agents asked for film rights as well. I don't think that the play would make a good film, and if I did arrange to let it be filmed I should surround the permission with so many restrictions that it would not possibly make a successful one. I confess to a strong aversion to films except for the lightest amusement, and I am sure that it would be a mistake for me to

1–Louis T. More (1870–1944) – physicist, humanist, critic of the Darwinian theory of evolution; Dean of the Graduate School, University of Cincinnati – was brother of Paul Elmer More. His works include *The Dogma of Evolution* (1925); *Isaac Newton: A Biography* (1934). TSE entertained him to lunch at the Oxford & Cambridge Club on 28 May.

2–Richards wrote on 28 May, 'I drove over to Oxford yesterday afternoon for the last week of viii's week & spent some of the time on Merton barge. An ex-pupil of mine is rowing 4 in their first boat, which made its fifth bump. Another ex-pupil is their Mods. Tutor, so I feel a certain paternal interest in your old College.'

3–The Revd Benjamin Gregory, editor of *The Methodist Times & Leader: The Journal of the New Methodism*, asked, 'Possibly you may know that I am very interested in the production of films, particularly films of a religious and educational character. I am wondering if any arrangement has been made for the filming of your play "Murder in the Cathedral". . .'

allow this play to be handled in that medium. Mr Ashley Dukes, my theatrical manager, agrees with me.

With all best wishes,
Yours very sincerely,
[T. S. Eliot]

## TO *R. B. Onions*                                                     CC

9 June 1936                          [Faber & Faber Ltd]

My dear Sir,

Some little time ago my young friend Mr Louis McNeice [*sic*] asked my permission to give my name as a reference in connexion with his application for a position at Bedford College, permission which I willingly gave. Yesterday, being in Paris, I received a telegram from my secretary asking me to write to you immediately.[1] As I was out all the day, I did not get this wire until the evening, too late to write to you. I was returning to London this morning, and therefore was unable to communicate with you until I reached Newhaven in the afternoon, from which station I telegraphed you.

As for Mr McNeice's scholarship, and his abilities as a teacher, I know nothing of these, and I have no doubt that he can depend upon others to commend him for these attainments. I know from him that he has lately completed a translation of the Agamemnon, which I look forward eagerly to seeing, and which I hope that my firm may be able to publish. I have known Mr McNeice for several years as (in my opinion) one of the very few significant younger poets: at my strong insistence my firm published a volume of his poems, and I look forward to publishing his future work. I have also published (in the *Criterion*) reviews by him, sometimes of works of classical scholarship; and I account him one of my most valuable contributors. He is the only young poet of my acquaintance who has struck me as being a man of education and culture. I find his point of view sympathetic; and when I have met him, he has impressed me as a serious person, not given to any of the vanities or heresies so common among

---

1–R. B. Onions, Professor of Latin, Bedford College, wrote on 7 June: 'Mr F. L. MacNeice is a candidate for the vacant post of lecturer in Latin at Bedford College and has given your name for reference. Will you be so kind as to let us have – if possible by the first post on Wednesday morning . . . any impressions which you think might help us in our choice?'

young men at the present time. From what I know of him, I recommend him warmly for any academic position for which he cares to apply.[1]

> I am,
> My Dear Sir,
> Yours faithfully,
> [T. S. Eliot]

## TO *Michael Roberts*                                      TS Keele

11 June 1936                    Faber & Faber Ltd

My dear Roberts,

I find that I was instructed by my Committee several weeks ago to write to you to ask you whether you would be interested in doing a critical book about T. E. Hulme.[2] I know that he is a difficult man to treat, and

1–Onions answered, 11 June: 'Very many thanks for your letter concerning Mr MacNeice – it arrived in time and was most helpful – and for your telegram from Newhaven. The Selection Committee interviewed Mr MacNeice with 8 others out of a very strong field. The choice was for some while in doubt between him and another candidate but at last fell upon the other. I personally greatly liked what I saw of Mr MacNeice and of his work.'

2–T. E. Hulme (1883–1917): Imagist poet and philosophical critic; killed in action in WW1. See Robert Ferguson, *The Short Sharp Life of T. E. Hulme* (2002). TSE called him in 1926 'the most *fertile* mind of my generation' (*VMP*, 82); and said of his collection *Speculations*, ed. Herbert Read (1924), in C. 2 (Apr. 1924): 'with all its defects – it is an outline of work to be done, and not an accomplished philosophy – it is a book of very great significance . . . In this volume he appears as the forerunner of a new attitude of mind, which should be the twentieth-century mind, if the twentieth century is to have a mind of its own. Hulme is classical, and reactionary, and revolutionary; he is the antipodes of the eclectic, tolerant, and democratic mind of the end of the last century' (231–2).

TSE to Samuel L. Hynes, 23 Mar. 1954: 'I never met T. E. Hulme personally, nor did I have any correspondence with him. He enlisted, I think, at the outbreak of war in 1914, and although I suppose he had the usual spells of leave, I never encountered him. I think Lord Russell's memory must be at fault, as I am pretty confident that my wife never met T. E. Hulme either. She was, I remember, an admirer of his poems, and it is possible that she introduced Lord Russell to them, and not to Hulme himself.

'I cannot remember reading any of Hulme's essays in the *New Age*, and the first of Hulme that I read outside of the poems appended to Pound's *Ripostes*, was the volume entitled *Speculations*. There was also the introduction to a book by George Sorel.'

TSE to Patric Dickinson, 29 Sept. 1955: 'I never met Hulme, and therefore have no personal impressions of the man . . . Hulme's work . . . is fragmentary. It is also tentative and not altogether mature. There are many germinal ideas present in the fragments, but they could not all, if developed, be maintained by the same mind. I regard Hulme as having been a stimulating writer for men of my generation, and a little younger, but I should think that his work was of historical rather than of actual importance.

'The picture you give of Hulme, is that of a rather brutal and aggressive type, such as would have been attracted by one or another form of totaliarianism. I do not know whether

that you will be of course more interested in parts of his work than in others. As a matter of fact I don't believe that his notes on various subjects at various times are perfectly consistent, but this would be worth going into. At any rate we think that it might be very interesting to have a book on Hulme by a critic of a younger generation than his own. How does this strike you?

With best wishes to Mrs Roberts and yourself,

Yours ever,

T. S. Eliot

P.S. The trouble with Pound is not yet cleared up, but I don't see that there is any need to bother you with that.

## TO *Elizabeth Bowen* CC

11 June 1936 [Faber & Faber Ltd]

Dear Mrs Cameron,

I am instructed by my Board of Directors meeting in committee to approach you with the question whether you would consider editing for us a volume of the best short stories of the present time.[1] When I say editing I mean preferably choosing the stories yourself, but if you had no time to undertake such a task, then exercising a veto upon stories to be chosen by someone anonymous, and writing an introduction to the book. We mean seriously the best. If you took the whole responsibility, then we should accept the stories you chose (if we could get permission at reasonable prices); if you took only the responsibility of writing an introduction, then of course the choice would be submitted to you. Or you might be willing to do something in between, merely writing an introduction and

---

this is a true picture or not, but it does seem to me that if you are to give such an impression, it should be more fully substantiated ... The possibility that quite incompatible attitudes may be traced to Hulme, or associated with him, is instanced by your collocation of Mr Pound's fascism and my Anglo-Catholicism, though I cannot see why these two "isms" should be called complementary.'

See further Ronald Schuchard, 'Did Eliot Know Hulme? Final Answer', *Journal of Modern Literature*, 27 (2004), 63–9.

1 – Victoria Glendinning, *Elizabeth Bowen: Portrait of a Writer* (1977), 118: 'Elizabeth was ... involved in the Thirties with literary projects peripheral to her own work. Faber & Faber, in the person of Tom Eliot, asked her to select and edit a collection of modern short stories, which was published in 1937. It turned out to be rather a chore, even though she was able to include work that she admired by people she was fond of (including A. E. Coppard, Frank O'Connor, William Plomer, Peter Quennell, Edward Sackville-West and Stephen Spender; she included her own "The Disinherited" and wrote an introduction).'

doing the whole selection yourself, and co-operating with whoever was responsible for the spade work. We should not expect you to undertake the negotiations with publishers, agents or authors. We should be prepared to take the term 'short story' in the widest sense, especially as we should not want things which were merely highly readable, but things that have some significance in the development of prose in our time. What we have in mind is not, primarily, a volume for station bookstalls, but a volume which might be a companion to our *Faber Book of Modern Verse*.

I confess that I approach you with some diffidence, but I hope that you will at least play with the idea, and then perhaps you will ask me to tea to talk it over.

Yours very sincerely,<br>[T. S. Eliot]

TO *Henrietta Bibas*　　　　　　　　TS Pembroke College, Cambridge

12 June 1936　　　　　　　　Faber & Faber Ltd

Dear Madam,

I have your letter of the 26th, and can explain the point which naturally puzzles you.[1] The play was of course originally designed for production in Canterbury Cathedral, and the opening of Part II, which uses the four introits, was considered suitable for that purpose. The chorus which you heard at the Cambridge performance was substituted for the production at the Mercury Theatre, London, in as much as we presumed that the effect of the original opening would be lost upon the larger part of the audience which could not be expected to be acquainted with Catholic liturgy. The chorus was accordingly substituted also in a second edition, which is not the one in your possession. Possibly at some date it may be desirable to publish a variorum edition of the play, but meanwhile I can

---

1–Henrietta Bibas (Girton College Cambridge), who saw the production staged in Cambridge, appealed to TSE on 26 May 1936: 'Certain divergences in the printed text & acting found me unprepared & somewhat dismayed me, but the greatest shock was the excision of the Dialogue of the Priests at the beginning of Part II. I had read the play in the first edition, & this dialogue had deeply impressed me, conveying as it did in what seemed to me a very noble manner the passing of the three days, December 26–29, & also, in uniquely effective form, the three stages of Thomas' final consummation of sanctity. And, in the "today . . ." lines, it brought together the "in time" & "out of time" themes with grandeur. I cannot conceive why this all-focusing & most important scene should have been done away with. Is it too much to ask you why?'

only express my regret that you were unable to see the performance at Canterbury, in which was used the opening scene that you prefer.

Yours sincerely,

T. S. Eliot

## TO *Sally Cobden-Sanderson*[1]

TS Texas

12 June 1936 Faber & Faber Ltd

Dear Sally,

Can you again help me with the same complete efficiency as before? I want to go to America for about a month; I want to get a passage to arrive there about the beginning of September, and to get back about the 1st October. And I want to arrive via Montreal or Boston, but *not New York*; and I want the cheapest possible CABIN TO MYSELF, as before. Are these things possible???[2]

I should like to come to your party next week, but I dont know whether there will be time: I have to take an old lady out to dinner and the pictures, and I have to fetch her in Bloomsbury.

Yours always, I trust not forgotten

Thomas

## TO *Llewelyn Powys*[3]

CC

16 June 1936 [*The Criterion*]

Dear Mr Powys,

I must apologize for the delay in dealing with your essay on Thomas Shoel. Such delays are by no means unusual, however, unless the author writes to express a special wish for an early decision.[4]

---

1 – Cobden-Sanderson was working for Hutchinson's Agency ('for Domestic Help Male and Female'), Regent Street, London – a firm which also catered for travel arrangements.

2 – Cobden-Sanderson booked him a two-berth cabin on the SS *Alaunia*, sailing on 22 Aug. from Southampton to Montreal. (In the event, he had to share with a married man.) He returned on 2 Oct. on the same ship, with exclusive use of an outside cabin. The round trip cost £40.15s.

3 – Llewellyn Powys (1884–1939), essayist and novelist; younger brother of the the writers John Cowper Powys and T. F. Powys.

4 – Powys (Chydyok, Chaldon Herring, Dorchester, Dorset) had written on 28 Jan. 1936, enclosing his essay on an 'unknown Somerset poet', Thomas Shoel (1752–1823). 'I know it is very simple, but I thought it might please you for this very reason. Would you be kind

236   TSE at forty-seven

I have read the essay several times, and it seems to me more suitable for *The London Mercury*, or for some other paper appearing at more frequent intervals than the *Criterion*. While the essay is very charming the poetry of Thomas Shoel seems to me too slight to deserve that amount of space in a periodical which aims to cover a fairly wide field and which appears only four times a year. With renewed regrets for the delay,

I am,

Yours sincerely,

[T. S. Eliot]

TO *Horace Gregory*[1]       TS Syracuse University Library

18 June 1936       *The Criterion*

My dear Gregory,

I have just received your and Mrs Gregory's letters of June 5th, and am distressed that Ross E. Pierce's unfounded report should have caused you so much anxiety.[2] Pierce did tell me at our first meeting that Mrs

---

enough to return the paper rather promptly if it does not do? My wife, Miss Alyse Gregory, with whom you have corresponded when she was managing editor of the *Dial* – assures me it is a mistake to send the essay to the Criterion!' Shoel (1759–1823), of Montacute (where the Powyses' father had been vicar), was a weaver and composer.

On 12 June Powys asked GCF, 'I do not wish to seem importunate but if you could manage to bring my case before the notice of the Great Cardinal [TSE] *without offence* I shall feel my self very much indebted to you.'

1–Horace Gregory (1898–1982), poet and critic, studied English at the University of Wisconsin before moving to New York City. Poetry includes *Chelsea Rooming House* (1930), *No Retreat* (1933), and *Medusa in Gramercy Park* (1961); prose includes *The House on Jefferson Street* (memoir, 1971) and *Spirit of Time and Place: The Collected Essays of Horace Gregory* (1973). He was awarded a Guggenheim Fellowship in 1951, and won the Bollingen Prize in 1965.

2–Gregory wrote from Bronxville, New York: 'I have just had a telephone conversation with Mr Ross Pierce of Buffalo, New York, in which he asked me to look at his ms again and informed me of his meeting you in London. During the conversation Mr Pierce told me that it was not true that you spoke from soap boxes in London slums. I agreed with him and said: "Of course, it was not true, that's a fantastic story." He then told me that Mrs Gregory told him that you spoke from soap boxes and that he had asked you whether or not you did. I then assured him that he was very much mistaken, that Mrs Gregory told him nothing of the kind. Whenever Mrs Gregory has mentioned your name she has spoken of your kindness and consideration for London's poor and of your fine courtesy – but this is a long distance from describing you as a soap-box orator. And in memory of your hospitality to us in London, she is much upset that there should be remotest possibility of this curious legend being credited to her.' Gregory's Russian-born wife Marya Zaturenska (who was to win a Pulitzer Prize for her second volume of verse, *Cold Morning Sky* [1937]) wrote on the same day to say she was upset by the slander.

Gregory had told him that I spoke from soap boxes in the East End. My first feeling at the time was simply one of embarrassment that I should have been credited with virtues that I do not possess. I wish it was true that I had spoken from soap boxes, or any other platform in the East End or public places elsewhere, as I admire the ability to make this sort of appeal. But I dislike public speaking of all sorts, and do it very badly, and as there are other things which I think I can do better I feel that I am justified in leaving this form of public activity alone. This is first of all to make clear my attitude about soap boxes. Second, I forgot about the remark from that day until receiving your letter, as during the course of two months Pierce gave me a great deal else to think about. Third, even if I had remembered the remark I very quickly saw enough of him to have been able to judge that he might easily be mistaken in any such report.

I appreciate your having preferred not to give Pierce a letter of introduction. Possibly the less said about him the better.[1]

With many regrets on your account and Mrs Gregory's,

Yours very sincerely,
T. S. Eliot

TO *Djuna Barnes*[2]                                                     TS Hornbake

18 June 1936                          Faber & Faber Ltd

My dear Miss Barnes,

I have now had the opportunity of consulting my Committee about the question of reserving the American rights of *Nightwood*. They feel – and I think I made clear at the time that these were my own feelings – that we ought not to be expected to limit our interests to this extent. We not only have taken and are taking a considerable amount of trouble over the book, but we expect that at best we shall not recover the expenses of publication for some considerable time. At the worst it is just possible that the book might be prohibited, in which case we should have a considerable loss. Our publishing the book is certainly not for the purpose of profit, but we do feel that we are entitled to make any minor condition that might help to protect us against loss. I have furthermore in mind, though it is not an argument on the same level, that some at least of the New York publishers

---

1 – Gregory responded on 3 July 1936: 'I want to thank you for your letter about Pierce; it set our minds at rest, for one never enjoys the sensation of being completely misunderstood.'
2 – Djuna Barnes (1892–1982), American novelist, poet, playwright: see Biographical Register.

have already had their opportunity before we saw the book. And you will remember that it is to you and not, as you first thought, to us, that the 75 per cent of the receipts is to go.

I do think I understand your feelings in the matter. Nevertheless I believe that it will be a great advantage to the publishers in New York that it should be published by us here, and I think that we are entitled to that slight tangible recognition of the advantage.

I shall be in London through this month and July, and delighted to see you whenever you come to town. Morley and myself are now engaged in reading and collating the two copies of the text you left with me.[1]

With all best wishes,
Yours very sincerely,
T. S. Eliot

TO *Elena Richmond*[2]                    MS William Rathbone

18 June 1936                    Faber & Faber Ltd

Dear Lady Richmond,

This is the first opportunity I have had to write to tell you what very great pleasure your hospitality gave me.[3] To renew and to extend my acquaintance with Salisbury and its neighbourhood, under such auspices and in such company was a very happy occasion indeed.

East Coker was delightful, with a sort of Germelshausen effect.[4] The landlady of the New Inn has a bedroom which I intend to make use of. She seemed impressed by my enquiry, and asked if I was not a cousin of Colonel Heneage, to which I said no. The only ugliness in the place is a stained glass window in the church, recently erected by some cousin of mine – the most hideous I have seen – the designer, one Leonard Walker, should be infamous.

---

1–Plumb observes, xxiii: 'All in all, the editorial hand was light; certainly because he anticipated potential difficulty with censors, Eliot blurred sexual, particularly homosexual, references and a few points that put religion in an unsavory light. However, meaning was not changed substantially, though the character of the work was adjusted, the language softened.'

2–Elena Richmond (1878–1964), née Rathbone: wife of Bruce Richmond, editor of the *TLS*.

3–TSE had stayed with the Richmonds near Salisbury for the weekend of 13/14 June.

4–*Germelshausen* (1860), a story by Friedrich Gerstäker: see further Helen Gardner, *The Composition of 'Four Quartets'*, 43. This was TSE's first visit to East Coker; he was to return in Aug. 1937.

Please tell Sir Bruce that on my return I found a letter from Canon *Tissington Tatlow*, who is rector of All Hallows, Lombard Street.[1]

And I do hope you will ask me again.

Yours very sincerely,
T. S. Eliot

TO *Michael Roberts* TS Keele

18 June 1936 Faber & Faber Ltd

My dear Roberts,

Thank you for your letter of the 15th.[2] I am glad that you are interested in the suggestion of a book about Hulme. Certainly take a little time to think it over. Meanwhile I suppose that the book you say you have nearly finished[3] is promised to Capes. If not it should be unnecessary to say that we should be delighted to consider it.

I am not sending the poetry to your wife this time as the principal item is probably your own book, and she might find it embarrassing to have to deal with that.

I don't think that I told you how pleased I was with your article about my poems in the *Mercury*.[4] I don't believe that I am able to regard articles and reviews of my own work with sufficient detachment to know whether they are good, but I can surely tell whether there has been understanding of what I was trying to do.

Yours ever,
T. S. Eliot

1–For Tissington Tatlow, see letter of 25 Oct. 1937, below.

2–'The book which you suggest would interest me very much, and I think I appreciate Hulme better than I did three or four years ago when I made some comments on him in the Criterion. But a lifetime is very short, and I have two other books on hand; one of them is nearly finished and the other might be better if it were postponed. May I therefore take ten days or so to think the matter over?'

3–The blurb for *The Modern Mind* (1937) was probably composed by TSE: 'Mr Michael Roberts established himself as the most authoritative critic of contemporary poetry with his *Critique of Poetry*. The present volume might be called *Critique of Philosophy*. It is not concerned by any means solely with contemporary philosophy, since it begins with a discussion of Duns Scotus and the Nominalists – with the origin of the English traditions in philosophy – but Mr Roberts uses the historical method to concentrate his attention in the end upon the contemporary situation. This book, by one of the most rigorous thinkers of the younger generation – who has done as much as anyone to establish values in modern poetry, and who is not only a philosophical poet, but a philosopher – is of importance to all who are interested in the philosophy, the religion, and the social theories of the present time: whether they adhere to the Right, the Centre, or the Left.'

4–'The Poetry of T. S. Eliot', *London Mercury* 34 (May 1936), 38–44.

18 June 1936 *The Criterion*

Mrs Pollytandy 'm,

My conscience is perhaps a kind of a soft conscience but nevertheless the kind that is most painful between the Toes, obliges me to write after some considerable delay, due to my gadding about ma'am, between Paris and Salisbury and Yeovil and tomorrow to Oxford and the next day to Canterbury, to thank you for yr. extreamly civil Letter of the 2nd instant, and glad I was to have yr. packet of news. You were in my mind but this last weekend constantly in visiting yr. noble city of Salisbury (where I lay for two nights at the house of one Richmond, an honest burgess of Liverpool, at Netherhampton. Where I heard Mass and was houselled, and later to evensong at the Minster, then to Tea by one Canon Myers, an elderly bloke with a beard. And also visited Stonehenge, and was mightily pleased to hear that the Druids had no claim upon it whatever, and likewise inspected Old Sarum, the plain of bustards, and the local golf course but had not time to display my skill. Thence to Yeovil, where I lay for one night: a city containing everything one could desire – the *Three Choughs*, which I thought expensive, a conspicuous and convenient public lavatory in the very centre of the town, the worst pictures I have ever seen (but one picture palace only, called the Gaumont) a barmaid with double chin at the *Mermaid* and the most repulsive curate ever I have seen at the Parish Church. By foot to the pretty village of East Coker, the only blemish of which is a memorial stained glass window, the ugliest that ever I saw, Faith Hope & Love with malignant faces, Love a little higher than her villainous sisters by reason of standing upon the family arms incorrectly inscribed, which has been put in only this year by an American cousin. But I made so good an impression upon the landlady of the New Inn, that she asked me, was I not a cousin of Colonel Heneage? To which I replied, No. All of which should be made into a ballet and sung to the tune of 'Three Blind Mice'.

Now is it time I bought Maggy a pair of Sandow dumbbells and a Whiteley exerciser.[1] We've got to turn that fat into Muscle, and make a Lady All-In Wrestler out of her.

---

1 – 'Pumping was a chore Tom liked to do: he said it gave him more regular exercise than he had had since as an undergraduate at Harvard he and his classmate Peters had persuaded themselves to undertake Sandow's instructions' (Frank Morley, 'A Few Recollections of Eliot', in *T. S. Eliot: The Man and His Work*, ed. Allen Tate [1967], 108).

I've been meaning to smoke out Brer Coon for a glass of the inwariable (O and by the Way that Strong's Romsey Stout is prime) but it must be next week. So hoping before long to see you and yr. bantlings in the same condition, I remain, respectfully,

Yr. faithfull<br>Tp.

Regards to the Licensee.[1]

## TO *W. H. Auden* CC

18 June 1936                     [Faber & Faber Ltd]

My dear Wystan,

I hope that this letter will reach you without undue delay. It's a question of the title for your book of poems. Our sales manager, who knows his job, takes grave exception to the title *Poems 1936*. He says that this sort of title always suggests a book of collected poems up to date, that people will expect to find in it everything you have written except plays, and that booksellers will be resentful and impatient. I think he's probably right, and you ought to have no difficulty in finding a good title. Will you put your mind to work and let me have suggestions as soon as you can, because the catalogue is in press?

Yours ever,<br>[TSE]

P.S. Morley thought that he had found a brilliant suggestion with *Vin Audinaire*, but the sales manager doesn't like that either.[2]

1–According to Miles Tandy (Polly's son), in *A Life in Translation: Biography and the Life of Geoffrey Tandy* (1995), p. 35, 'Eliot and the "Ole Man" would often meet at Gordon's Wine Bar in Charing Cross for a glass or two of sherry – "a glass of the inwariable". He often added "Regards to the Licensee" – a reference to Geoffrey.'

2–WHA's mother, Constance R. Auden, acknowledged this letter with a note to TSE dated 19 June: 'Wystan is in Iceland. I am sending on your letter by Tuesday's mail, but there may be some delay. I wish I could think of a title!'

WHA replied by PC from Iceland (though the missive was posted in England on 7 July 1936): 'Morley's suggestion is certainly brilliant but what would St John Irvine [*sc.* Ervine] say? The only titles I can think of are "*It's a way*" or "*The Island*", but if you can think of a better please do. On the analogy of Burnt Norton, I might call it Piddle-in-the-hole. I wish you would come out and join me here. It is very nice except the food.'

Proof copies of *Look, Stranger!* carry the title *Poems 1936*. The blurb (Faber Books Autumn 1936, 48) reads: 'Since the publication of *Poems* in 1930, which immediately marked the author as a leader of a new school of poetry that has since established itself, Mr Auden has published *The Orators* and two plays, but no collection of his non-dramatic verse. This volume is a selection of what the author wishes to preserve of the poems which

18 June 1936                    [*The Criterion*]

My dear Richards,

I should be delighted and should consider it most appropriate if you would review Irving Babbitt's translation of the *Dhammapada* for the *Criterion*. I do not know whether you have seen the book yet, but it is not nearly so formidable as it sounds. It is not a job for an orientalist, at least not for any orientalist that I know in this country, but for a humanist. I think we may take the translation as read. That is, I think we may assume that any translation by Babbitt would be the best in existence, and rather concentrate on his essay on Buddha and the Occident, which takes up the second half of the volume. It really contains a condensed statement also of Babbitt's attitude towards Christianity, and I naturally think that from a Christian point of view there are certain misunderstandings and blind spots; but I leave this to you.[1]

I hope that you have seen, or will be seeing, Louis More, who I believe is in England. He is a somewhat pathetic figure, I think.

Yours ever,<br>[T. S. Eliot]

---

he has written in the last few years, some of which have appeared from time to time in periodicals. As Mr Auden's fame as a dramatist is now such that many people have almost forgotten his achievement in other kinds of verse, this new collection comes at the right moment to round out his reputation.'

1–P. S. Richards on Irving Babbitt, *The Dhammapada* translated from the Pali with an Essay on Buddha and the Occident: C. 16 (Oct. 1936), 123–5. 'It is hard not to escape the conclusion that there is something central in Christianity – and not merely in traditional, historical Christianity, but even in the Christ of the Gospels – which Babbitt altogether failed to understand. The comparison which he institutes between Christ and Buddha, as religious teachers, is illuminating in many ways, but it ignores, as such comparisons mostly do, the one thing which makes Christ, in the last resort, not comparable with any other teacher in human history – the fact, namely, that He never was, and never professed to be, a Seeker.'

FROM *Brigid O'Donovan* TO *John T. MacCurdy*[1]    CC

19 June 1936                    [Faber & Faber Ltd]

Dear Sir,

Mr Eliot has asked me to thank you for your letter of June 7th,[2] and to say that although he has some general knowledge of insanity and hysteria he has never come across any example of this particular form of purification mania, though of course it is familiar in various forms throughout the history of literature, as well as of mental disorders.

Yours very truly,
[Brigid O'Donovan]
Secretary


TO *R. S. Forman*[3]    CC

19 June 1936                    [Faber & Faber Ltd]

Dear Mr Forman,

I have your letter of June 15th, and have nothing but commendation for your project of a restaurant which would pay such attention to cheese, and especially to English cheese.[4] I must confess, however, that I should be very little help to you in the project of launching such a venture. I know nothing of the restaurant business, and I think that the first thing necessary would

1–John T. MacCurdy, Fellow of Corpus Christi College Cambridge; University Lecturer in Psychopathology.
2–'A couple of weeks ago I enjoyed your "Murder in the Cathedral" as given in Cambridge. I may even say that I was moved as well as edified . . . My curiosity is a highly technical one.

'On p. 76 of your book there is a prayer by the Chorus for cleansing. In this you have the women ask to have skin & muscle removed & various organs washed. This is an extraordinary idea but not new to me. I met it once – many years ago – in a paretic who, among many grandiose & ridiculous delusions, had a cure for leprosy. This consisted in removing the leper's bones, washing them & putting them back again.

'It is perhaps not generally known that the insane frequently reproduce ideas once currently accepted but now so obsolete as to be classed as delusional. Hence my question: did you find this prayer in some old record or did you just make it up? The latter would interest me just as much psychologically as the former would psychiatrically, if you grasp the difference.'
3–R. S. Forman, Editorial Department, The Foreign Press Exchange, London.
4–Forman put forward – in response to TSE's newspaper correspondence about cheese (see L.7) – the idea of setting up a specialist restaurant. 'My idea would be to open, preferably in the Strand, a smallish eating house, capable of expansion, where one would cater principally for business men's lunches . . . I should have a section of the menu devoted to cheese cookery, each day having a spécialité dish, notable for its cheese flavouring or cheese sauce.' Would TSE be interested in discussing the idea with him?

be to interest some individual or firm already in that business, and with considerable capital. If even some existing restaurant or chophouse could be interested in the attempt to persuade its customers to eat intelligently in this way that would be most valuable. I was discussing the subject of cheese with a friend over the weekend, and he told me that he would take the matter up with a friend of his who is a director of Trust Houses Ltd. This, however, is of no direct help for London. What would be desirable I think would be if you could get in touch with some important personage in such a firm as J. Lyons and Co., who are perfectly capable of producing good food if and wherever they have any public that demands it.

Yours very truly,

[T. S. Eliot]

## TO *Edwyn Bevan*[1]                                                    CC

19 June 1936                     [Faber & Faber Ltd]

Dear Dr Bevan,

I feel very much honoured by your suggestion that I should become a member of the London Society for the Study of Religion.[2] In principle I should be delighted as well as flattered, but I have got to a point at which I must be very careful about a further multiplication of interests which will only result in my giving imperfect attention to all. It would seem, certainly, that anyone could make the time to attend at least three meetings a year of such an important society, yet even as things are I find that the meetings of committees, etc., have an odd way of coming at the same times. Then I presume also that every member should produce a paper once in a while, and I have to do more of that sort of thing than I want to do as things are. I regret very much what I shall miss, and I hope you will understand that it is conscience rather than torpor that dictates my decision.

With many regrets,

Yours very sincerely,

[T. S. Eliot]

1–Edwyn Bevan (1870–1943), historian of comparative religion; Lecturer in Hellenistic History and Literature, King's College London, 1922–33; author of *Christianity* (1932) and *Christians in a World at War* (1940). Elected FBA, 1942.

2–Bevan wrote (16 June) that the Society met six times a year, and if TSE 'saw a likelihood of attending 3 out of the 6 meetings you could accept the obligations of membership with a good conscience'.

FROM *Vivien Eliot* TO *The Managers, District Bank*

TS copy in Bodleian

21 June 1936                                    The Three Arts Club,
                                                19A Marylebone Road, London

Dear Sirs,

I am allowing it to be supposed, in various quarters, that I have gone to America, with a friend of my husband's, having sailed on June 19th, and having let this flat to a Student of The Royal Academy of Music.[1]

In this way I hope to get a little more time for preparing for the Academy Examinations, although I am hopelessly behindhand.

I have given the entire responsibility for the contents of this flat, solely to Mrs Elizabeth Flint, who has been my maid for more than seven years.

I am therefore asking you to be so very kind as to pay her on my behalf, and from my Account, the sum of 30/-s (thirty shillings) weekly, every Thursday. If this is posted to this address by the early morning post, on Thursdays, she will receive it before she leaves the flat. This sum of money includes her weekly wage, her bus or train fare (£1 3/6d) and 6/6d for her food and cleaning materials. This somewhat mean allowance is all I can afford to give her. She has her own home to attend to and her husband and little boy, therefore she may have to take a holiday soon, in which case she quite clearly understands that she is to give you one week's notice in writing.

At the same time I am arranging with Merrs Allen and Hanburys[2] to send their monthly bill for you to discharge on my behalf, and trust you will not mind again obliging me in these ways.

I posted the fresh Form for Messrs Glyn Mills & Co. to you on Friday, duly signed. I filled in the previous one with the address 24, Russell Square, London, W.C.1, as that is the address given as mine, in WHO'S WHO, and is apparently the only address I have.

I am,

Yours faithfully,

[Vivien Haigh Eliot]

---

1 – '[VHE] gave as her forwarding address 83 Brattle Street, Cambridge, Mass., an apartment block which was the home of Eliot's favourite sister, Marian Cushing Eliot' (Lyndall Gordon, *The Imperfect Life of T. S. Eliot*, [2012], 297).

2 – Allen & Hanbury, dispensing chemist, 7 Vere Street, London W.1, where VHE was befriended by the pharmacist Louise (Louie) Purdon, a spinster.

TO *E. Martin Browne*[1]                                           CC

23 June 1936                    [*The Criterion*]

My dear Martin,

I have signed the two books and they have gone off to you.[2] I enclose
herewith the financial statement.

I hope very much to see you when you are in town next week, as there
was no opportunity to talk on Saturday evening. I shall be going back
from Oxford on Monday morning and so far have no engagements on
either Monday or Tuesday, so if you rang up before I got here my secretary
could arrange with you. Otherwise I suggest that we should have a meal
somewhere on either of those days, and Henzie also if she can come.

I really did think that you and Bobby both gave magnificent
performances, but I'd like to talk about that when we meet.

                                        Yours ever,
                                        [Tom]


TO *M. C. D'Arcy*[3]                                           CC

23 June 1936                    [*The Criterion*]

My dear D'Arcy,

Can I persuade you to review Aldous Huxley's new book for us for
September (*Eyeless in Gaza*)? I don't think there is much of a novel about
it, but there is a great deal of the latest version of the Huxley philosophy.

---

1 – E. (Elliott) Martin Browne (1900–80), theatre director: see Biographical Register.
2 – EMB requested (17 June) signed copies of *Collected Poems* and 'the last book of essays',
because he wanted to give them to his hosts in Canterbury who had looked after him and his
wife at Kent College, Canterbury, during the preparation of Charles Williams's play *Thomas
Cranmer of Canterbury* which he was producing for the first time in the Chapter House,
as part of the Festival of the Friends of Canterbury Cathedral, on 19 June 1936. Robert
Speaight played Cranmer, and EMB himself was Figure Rerum, a skeleton.

  Thomas Beachcroft to EVE, 2 July 1968: 'One occasion that I remember with great
pleasure . . . was the production of Charles Williams' play Thomas Cranmer at Canterbury
Cathedral. This if I remember rightly was the year following the production of Murder
in the Cathedral. Tom had lunch with us in Edwardes Square – and we drove him down
in a small Ford car which I had just acquired – and we met Charles and Mrs Williams at
Canterbury.'

  TSE was to recall: 'I do not remember the stages by which our friendship [i.e. with Charles
Williams] developed . . . I remember being one of a happy party of his friends who motored
down to see the first performance of his *Cranmer* at the Canterbury Festival.'

3 – Martin D'Arcy (1888–1976), Jesuit priest and theologian: see Biographical Register.

I had rather you reviewed it than anybody, and also I think it would be of great interest to Huxley to have your criticism of it.[1]

Will you not be in London again before long? It is a long while since we met.[2]

Yours ever,
[T. S. Eliot]

## TO *Walter Adams*                                                    CC

24 June 1936                          [Faber & Faber Ltd]

Dear Mr Adams,

Thank you very much for your note of the 17th.[3] I am very glad that the Allocation Committee has been able to do something for Dr Tereshchenko. He came to see me on Saturday morning, however, and I find that while his immediate needs are relieved he [is] still in a state of great anxiety, as he seems to need about £150 more to carry him through until the autumn term when he begins earning money again. I report this because of your kind suggestion that you would endeavour to get some further relief for him so that he might be able to take a short holiday. It would seem that his situation is too desperate for him to contemplate taking a holiday. I mean that if funds could be provided they would have to go towards supporting himself and his family for a little longer through the summer. I am really at my wits end to know what further can be done for him in this emergency. Is it possible that the Allocation Committee would reconsider his case?

1 – D'Arcy on Huxley, *Eyeless in Gaza*: C. 16 (Oct. 1936), 116–19.
  See too TSE's report (n.d.) on a book proposal entitled 'Aldous Huxley and the Christian Religion', by the Revd Roger Lloyd: 'This is quite an intelligent and well-reasoned attack on Huxley's point of view, by a provincial clergyman. I do not think, however, that it would make any great impression or sell in large numbers, and it would be rather a pity to spoil the market for someone who could do the job more effectively. An innocent and scrupulous clergyman is not the right man to tackle a dirty fighter like Huxley. He says, "greatness is not explained away by sneering at it"; that is just the reverse of the fault of this essay. The way to deal with Huxley is exactly to sneer at him, and for this purpose there is, I think, a chance for a good pamphlet by some real ruffian – not a gentleman, and preferably not even an Etonian, but, let us say, one who has plumbed life to the very dregs of Carlton House Terrace. I think even Belgion is too polite – in short, I can think of no one except Wyndham Lewis or myself.' (Faber Archive)
2 – D'Arcy expected to be at Farm Street, London, 'after the weekend'.
3 – The Academic Assistance Council had decided to give a 'free grant of £50 ... to Dr Iovetz-Tereshchenko to help him during the summer period while he is not in receipt of an income from his work as a W.E.A. tutor and University Extension lecturer.
  'We have not yet found an opportunity of providing holiday hospitality for him.'

At the same time I want to express my own appreciation of your personal interest and kindness and the trouble you have taken.

Yours sincerely,

[T. S. Eliot]

## TO *Sydney Schiff*[1]                                                    CC

24 June 1936                          [Faber & Faber Ltd]

My dear Sydney,

Thank you for your letter of the 18th.[2] I have indeed heard of the new book of Bernanos, and only through being rather hurried failed to buy a copy when I was in Paris a fortnight ago. I am sending for one. Thank you for reminding me of it.

I hope that you have been or will go this week to see Charles Williams' play at Canterbury. It struck me as surprisingly good, and I thought that Robert Speaight and Martin Browne provided a brilliant performance.

And meanwhile I hope that you are getting on with work of your own. With all good wishes to Violet and yourself,

Ever yours,

[Tom]

1 – Sydney Schiff (1868–1944), British novelist and translator, patron of the arts and friend of WL, JMM, Proust, Osbert Sitwell, published fiction under the name Stephen Hudson. Works include *Richard, Myrtle and I* (1926); and he translated Proust's *Time Regained* (1931). In 1911 he married Violet Beddington (1874–1962), sister of the novelist Ada Leverson (Oscar Wilde's 'Sphinx'). See AH, *Exhumations: correspondence inédite avec Sydney Schiff, 1925–1937*, ed. Robert Clémentine (1976); Richard Davenport-Hines, *A Night at the Majestic: Proust and the Great Modernist Dinner Party of 1922* (2006); Stephen Klaidman, *Sydney and Violet: their life with T. S. Eliot, Proust, Joyce, and the excruciatingly irascible Wyndham Lewis* (2013).

2 – Schiff urged TSE to read *Journal d'un Curé de campagne* by Georges Bernanos – 'one of the most rewarding [works] I have read for years, religious in the best sense'.

TO *John Hayward*                                              TS King's

29 June 1936 St Peter                          *The Criterion*
Double I Class with Common Octave

Dear John,

   Unless I hear from you to the contrary (and I am again available on
the telephone) I shall appear on Thursday evening *chez vous* (as we say
familiarly in my set) complete with button'ole ready for the Faberian
Festivity and Hampstead Gala Gaudy. Much water has flowed etc. but
please stop your cousin F. W. Hayward Inspector of Schools from writing
to me about the fourfold eschatological principle of Dr Albert Schweitzer.[1]
I just cant stand it. Should the mother of quads be churched four times,
according to this principle? I simply don't know. I am too bothered.
What is to be done about Visc. Cecil of Chelwood, Joseph Wood Krutch,
Professor Hotson and André Breton?[2] I don't know. Yet here we are and
I fear we must carry on. Yours etc.


A Thought                    A Thought
for Thursday:                                     for Friday:


A Thought for
Saturday:

                                        Yours distractedly,
                                        T.

1–F. H. Hayward, Inspector of Schools, London County Council, wrote from Chingford,
Essex, 30 May – this letter does not appear to have been a hoax – 'I am struggling manfully
with your *Collected Poems*, and the necessary adjustments are painful & not yet complete.
   'But it is a pleasure to find a poet who has something to say.
   'Reflecting, however, on H. Ross Williamson's pp. 156–8 (Incarnation v. Deification) &
your own very true remark that most men's emotions are so tepid that they think nothing
out "to a conclusion", I would yet raise the question whether you have thought out "to a
conclusion", the eschatalogical principles of the Fourfold Doctor, Dr Albert Schweitzer.'
   F. H. Hayward went on: 'If poetry is, in the future, to be so tremendously allusive &
associational (not simple, sensuous, passionate) I see small hope of a poetically educated
nation. As an educationist, therefore, anxious that masses of men may enjoy poetry, I enjoy
*The Waste Land* more as a *tour de force* than as a portent of the poetry of the future.'
2–André Breton, *What Is Surrealism?* (2nd impression, 1936).

6 July 1936                    *The Criterion*

My dear Barnes,

Thank you for your letter of the 2nd.[2] I was merely talking generally, and had no expectation that you would take my suggestion seriously. My first feeling is that I have not the slightest notion whether I read other people's poetry well or not, because, as I told you, nobody has ever given me the opportunity of trying. In any case, I am afraid I could not manage it during August. I shall be staying with friends in the country during the first week, and shall be extremely busy for the next fortnight, as I am leaving for a short visit to America at the end of the month. I shall be back at the beginning of October, and should like to renew the discussion then, hoping that meanwhile you will have broken the ice by trying out one or two other performers.

I enjoyed dining with you and your wife very much, and hope that I may see you again.

Yours sincerely,
T. S. Eliot

TO *Enid Faber*                    MS Valerie Eliot

Wednesday [postmarked 6 July 1936]     24 Russell Square, W.C.1.

Dear Enid

It's time I wrote a bread & butter letter & I hope it will be acceptable in the present context. I was very happy for a week, as well you know, & my cold did not abate the pleasure, or diminish the benefit.

---

1–Educated at King's College, Cambridge, George Barnes (1904–60) taught at the Royal Naval College, Dartmouth, before becoming Assistant Secretary at Cambridge University Press, 1930–5. In 1935 he joined the BBC Talks Department, becoming Director of Talks in 1941. Head of the Third Programme, 1946–8; Director of TV, 1950–6. From 1956 he was Principal of the University College of North Staffordshire. He was brother-in-law of Mary Hutchinson. Knighted 1953.

2–'Both Anne and I greatly enjoyed seeing you last night, and I was much interested in your suggestion about poets giving broadcast readings of poems which they enjoy.

'Please do not think me importunate if I ask you if you would be willing to give one of these readings for us on the 7th, 10th or 14th of August. The time available – a convenient experimental time – is 11.40 to midnight, but if you think that 18 minutes is too long for one voice, we might introduce another as a foil. I hope that you will consider this suggestion. As I told you last night, I am now going away until July 13; if, on my return, you would like to discuss such a reading, I shall be very pleased if you will lunch with me.'

I rang Ann up this p.m. only to hear from her that she is going home on the first day on which I could propose a visit.

I am very sorry indeed to miss her, but I hope that her being able to go home sooner than expected is, for what it is worth, good.

Affectionately
Tom


## TO *H. F. Stewart*                                        CC

6 July 1936                          [Faber & Faber Ltd]

My dear Stewart,

I have been thinking about your letter of July 1st, and I wonder whether, like a conscientious juryman, I ought not to ask for exemption on the ground of prejudice.[1] I feel that I have already made up my mind that Blackstone is not qualified for a Fellowship of Trinity, so would it not be better if someone else, with no previous acquaintance with him, were invited in my stead? I really feel strong scruples about keeping aloof from further judgement upon the lad.

With all best wishes to Mrs Stewart,

Yours very sincerely,
[T. S. Eliot]


## TO *Charles Williams*[2]                                  CC

6 July 1936                          [Faber & Faber Ltd]

My dear Williams,

I am afraid that next week is going to be impossible for me to lunch, as I shall have to be away for three days.[3] That is, unless Saturday the 18th would suit you. That would do very well for me, but I do not know about Belgion. Otherwise either Monday or Tuesday the 20th or 21st. I hope that one of these three dates is possible.

1–Bernard Blackstone was a candidate for a fellowship at Trinity College, Cambridge; and Stewart invited TSE to write a report on the case (since he had decided the case for a doctorate) by the end of Sept. 'It won't give you much trouble – you know the standard, higher than PhD & challenging comparison with very various performances in other branches of knowledge.'
2–Charles Williams (1886–1945), novelist, poet, playwright, religious and theological writer; historical biographer; member of the Inklings: see Biographical Register.
3–Williams had written, 1 July: 'Belgion suggests that the week after next would be a convenient one for him to lunch. Would it suit you?'

I have been meaning to write to tell you how much I enjoyed and admired your play. I tried to express a little of my appreciation on the occasion, but for myself I never place much confidence in the verbal remarks of my friends at such moments, as they may possibly be no more than politeness. I do really think that you made a great success of it, and I hope that it will be revived in London.[1]

Yours ever,

[T. S. Eliot]

## TO *Elizabeth Bowen*                                                   CC

6 July 1936                        [Faber & Faber Ltd]

Dear Mrs Cameron,

After some delay I am finally writing to put down the conditions on which we agreed about what we will call tentatively *The Faber Book of Modern Stories*.[2] It is understood that you will write an introduction of three to four thousand words, and that incidentally in this introduction

1 – Williams responded on 9 July with thanks for TSE's remarks about his play. 'Politeness is the devil and all I suspect it continuously, but you are one of the few people – the very few people, with whom I should feel almost adequately safe.'

2 – Bowen agreed in principle, in her letter of 15 June, to edit the proposed anthology:
'Points as to which I should like to be clear at the outset are –
(1) As to the length, or bulk, of the proposed book. Eighty thousand words, approximately, exclusive of the preface which would be, I suppose, three to four thousand words? This would mean about sixteen stories – the average length of a short story being taken to be about five thousand words. A hundred thousand words – twenty stories – might be better . . .
(2) I note that the poems in Modern Verse were written, chiefly, since 1910. This should, I take it, apply as far as possible to the stories in the collection I am to make? Should I, however, feel free to make a, considered, exception in the case of any writer whose work seemed to bear the same relation to the present-day short story as the poems of Gerard Manley Hopkins do to the other poems in Modern Verse? Edgar Allen Poe comes to mind in this context. On the whole, though, the short story in English has in its present, in fact in any, form developed so very lately that the question of nineteenth century writers does not arise.
(3) Are the stories to be English *and* American? I take it that you would not wish to include translations of stories by Continental writers? The exclusion of American short stories would narrow down the selection very much – and might, I think myself, be a pity: more than half the most vital as well as the most accomplished short stories written today being American. Their inclusion does, of course, open an almost alarmingly wide field. I see that you have three or four American poets in Modern Verse . . .
'Will you please overlook my very inexpert typing. I have only been at it for about ten days, and still find the machine a complicated affair.'

you can discuss at your discretion, amongst other matters, the work of writers, either contemporary or earlier, whom you have not chosen for inclusion in the book. You will also make a collection of stories yourself. The length of the book should be 100,000 words or more. We say roughly twenty stories, but as the stories you choose may vary considerably in length it is impossible to settle the number in advance. No translations are to be included, but American fiction can, and indeed should, be represented up to a maximum of, say, a fourth of the total, excluding your introduction. You are certainly free to include a story by some author whose work bears the same relation to contemporary authors as that of Gerard Manley Hopkins to contemporary poets – if there is such an author. Poe, whom you mention, seems rather too remote, and too well-known.

You will send in the introduction and a list of the stories you wish to include by October 31st. We agreed in conversation that you would have a supplementary list of about half the number of stories to be included, which would be made use of if for any reason any of the stories on your first list were not available. I think that if any story on your first list can't be obtained, either for reasons of price or any other, we ought to refer again to you to know what story from the supplementary list you prefer to include instead.

While we undertake to do the negotiations with authors, publishers and agents, you have suggested that there may be some authors with whom it would be appropriate and probably more successful for you to negotiate direct. I suggest that you mark on your list the stories with which you propose to deal with [sic] in this way, so there shall be no overlapping. People might be more annoyed than pleased to have an application from us at the same time.

As a rule we do not, with editors of prospective anthologies, make any more formal agreement than this. I suggest that it will be enough if it is understood that at your request we pay the £50 fee due to you on publication to Curtis Brown Ltd. for your account. It would be as well if you would inform Curtis Brown in advance of our arrangement.

I think that this covers all the points that have been raised between us, with the exception of your question about notes. In our *Faber Book of Modern Verse* we have no notes about authors, only the necessary acknowledgements to publishers. I think that when the story has been published in a collection the title of the book in which it is included should be mentioned. Also, in the list of contents I think that we ought to print the date of the author's birth, and of death if he or she is dead.

All that we need now is a note from you acknowledging this letter, and saying that you agree about terms.[1]

Yours very sincerely,
[T. S. Eliot]

## FROM *Vivien Eliot* TO *Theresa & Henry Eliot*

TS copy in Bodleian

6 July 1936                                The Three Arts Club,
                                           19A Marylebone Road,
                                           London, N.W.1

Dear Theresa (and Henry)

I feel that good manners, if no other motive, require me to write to you from time to time, and requires that you should write to me.

I should very much like to hear how you both are (if still living), and I must say that I have a certain curiosity to know if Henry received or did not receive a letter from someone in the City of London whose name he must already know very well. (Name of Broad.) This was sent at my instigation.

Meanwhile, the last of your family I heard from was dear Margaret, who wrote me a very nice letter. She seems in much the same position as myself. Living In A Hotel. As I have done, from one hotel to another for more than a year.

Anyway, I feel a moral obligation to write to you and to say that although I am allowing it to be supposed, by nearly everyone in this country, that I have gone to America with Katherine Spencer, having sailed on June 19th, I am delighted that you, Henry, and any one of the Eliot family (including of-course the Smiths) know that this above address will always find me.[2]

---

1–Bowen responded on 8 July: 'I accept, very gladly, the terms you put out.'

2–See too the draft of a letter from VHE to Mr Broad (Bod. MS Eng lett c. 384, f. 118) from Tiresias/Daisy Miller (MS) – probably from *c*. July 1936 since a letter from Broad & Son (solicitors), dated 23 July 1936, is addressed to 'Mrs V. H. Eliot, c/o Miss Daisy Miller':

Notes for Broad

Better start by *saying* that of-course he understands that I am Mrs T S. Eliot and that I have chosen the incognito of Miller & to allow it to be supposed by as many as possible that I have gone to America with a Miss K. Spencer, on June 19th, for 2 reasons, one to give me more time for the work of the R. A. M. [Royal Academy of Music], & also to get the opportunity of moving certain things away from 68 [Clarence Gate Gardens], and I hope this may be respected. But also to try if possible this experiment to reduce the strain on my brain, & at the same time to see if I could succeed in disappearing so completely & baffling all attempts to trace me as my husband has. And, at the same time I have in my mind such an undying

I do not say much about Tom, because the situation is too fantastic, and because I presume you take no responsibility for your younger brother. But I should enjoy a good talk with you and Henry.

Yours as ever,

V. Haigh Eliot

You cannot now say that you do not know where to find me ........

As Tom has not, apparently, one loyal friend in England, like myself, I am sending his letters to you. (Not all, of-course, there are too many every day, but some I will send.) You know, as you have known me so long, that I never sought friends. And if people seek me, I have come to the point of wondering what they 'want'.

## FROM *C. W. Stewart*[1] TO *T. S. Eliot* TS King's

6 July 1936                 Faber & Faber Ltd

Dear Sir,

The enclosed advertisement, to which I understand that your attention has been already privately drawn, has been under the serious consideration

---

resentment against all those who had any part in this business that I want them to know what it is like to suffer in the same way.

*Tiresias*

At this point I become Daisy Miller.

I am not a friend of Mrs Eliot's because Mrs Eliot's ideas of friendship are so alien to anything she finds that I shd. not like to say I was her friend. She has had very great friends, & she prefers to mourn their loss than to fill the gaps they leave. I am a student of the R.A.M. I have a limited authority to manage certain of her affairs. She made perfectly satisfactory arrangements with her Bankers, but I can ask them on her behalf to . . .

In closing the interview it will be agreed that Mrs Eliot is very much happier out of England than she could be in it.

[This is an autograph letter, stuck hard into a ledger, so the verso of this page is not readable.]

1 – Charles Stewart (1891–1945) joined Faber & Gwyer in 1923 (having learned his trade in the Indian branch of Oxford University Press), at a time when GCF needed 'someone to help me in the day-to-day management of the office and the routine of book production'. Educated at New College, Oxford – where contemporaries including Christopher Morley dubbed him 'Goblin' (he was short-statured and short-sighted), though everyone at F&F always greeted him as 'Stew' – he was a dedicated and loyal colleague. GCF, in 'Charles Stewart: A Personal Tribute' (*The Bookseller*, 19 Apr. 1945, 433), remarked that Stewart had 'a singular power of creating affection': his 'quiet personality . . . held its own with ease and certainty and humour. There was not one member of the board or of the staff who did not love and respect him . . . He never shirked a job of any kind at any time; never complained; never lost his temper; was always ready to laugh at himself; never laughed unkindly, and never said an unkind thing against anybody; yet never let go of common sense and shrewd judgment for the sake of sentiment.'

of the Principal Directors of this Company.[1] While it is true that there is no explicit written prohibition of a Director engaging in an activity of the kind referred to in the advertisement, the Principal Directors are unanimous in regarding it as very undesirable that a mere Ordinary Director should advertise himself in this way. Furthermore they wish you to understand that, in their opinion, the nature of the occupation, in which you have engaged without their previous knowledge or consent, is open to the gravest objections. An Ordinary Director, they point out, who is expected to take part on *equal* terms in the deliberations of the Principal Directors, can scarcely bring the necessary freshness of mind to a Board Meeting, if his nights are spent in the manner sufficiently indicated by the advertisement.[2] A further highly unsatisfactory feature of this surprising disclosure is the evidence which it affords of the use of the connections acquired by you as a Director of this Company for the purposes of private profit.

I am, accordingly, instructed to invite you to make a statement, which should include an account of your profits as a Proprietor of the Club in question and a complete list of the members, for submission to my Board.

I am,
Yours faithfully,
FABER AND FABER LIMITED
C. W. Stewart
Secretary

1–The cutting – a small advertisement from *The Times* – reads: 'GERHARD and his BAND have been engaged to play every night at ELIOT'S CLUB, 28, Charing Cross Road, commencing Monday next, 28th May. – For particulars of Membership apply Secretary.' The Director was the Hon. Mrs Arthur Eliot; the subscription £1. Curiously, VHE joined the club on 23 Mar. 1936, possibly because she too suspected, or avidly hoped, there was a connection with TSE.

2–Article 9 of the terms of association of Faber & Faber Ltd reads: 'The number of Directors, until otherwise determined by the Company in general meeting, shall be not less than three nor more than six, of whom not more than four shall be Principal Directors, and the others Ordinary Directors.' GCF to Unnamed, 18 Mar. 1929 (E1/12, p. 80): 'The Chairman of Faber & Faber Ltd. will be Mr Geoffrey Faber, who is the Chairman of the present Company. Mr C. W. Stewart and Mr Richard de la Mare will be principal directors. Mr Frank Morley, the London representative of the Century Co. of New York, is also joining the Board as a Principal Director. Mr T. S. Eliot, the editor of the Criterion, will also be a director.' GCF was to confirm, in a letter to W. B. Jenkins, Westminster Bank, Tavistock Square, 27 Mar. 1945: 'We have one Ordinary Director, Mr T. S. Eliot.'

TO *Geoffrey Faber*

7 July 1936                                Faber & Faber Ltd
1.30 a.m. on the 8th.

My dear Geoffrey,

I have received this morning a letter from Stewart which has caused me considerable distress of mind. Having been engaged all day, and until 1 o'clock this morning, on business of the firm, I am now in a state of exhaustion, and therefore may not be able to deal with the matter as thoroughly as I should like to do. Still, I cannot let the imputation rest, even for a day; and I am writing to you privately and in confidence, before taking any further steps.

I am assuming that you have cognisance of the content of Stewart's letter; at least, I can hardly understand his having the effrontery to write to me as he did, without consulting you first. If he wrote without your knowledge, I ask your forgiveness for what I am about to say; but otherwise, I must say, Geoffrey, that I think that if such a letter was to be written at all, it should only have been written and signed by the Chairman. It has been said, I do not know when or where or by whom, that a man is entitled to be judged by his peers: in the firm of Faber & Faber Limited that is hardly possible for me; but the person who comes the nearest to being a peer is surely a Chairman. I do not feel that such a letter should have been addressed to me by Stewart: incidentally, he takes advantage of the occasion to provoke me with several cheap sneers. I feel that you, Geoffrey, would have put the accusation (for such in effect, it is) with much more grace and tact, even if just as cheaply.

The problem is exceedingly complex and must be regarded as having different angles and several facets. I will begin at the beginning – I mean, the nominal beginning, for I cannot help feeling that there must be a long history behind this, of intrigue of which I have been innocently unaware. I shall number my paragraphs, for your convenience and to hold your attention.

1. I do not consider it within the competence of three Directors, meeting informally in committee (which I was too busy to attend), to pass resolutions or make any strictures upon the conduct of an absent Director, in an official form. It is usual, of course, for any two or more Directors in informal conversation to make nasty remarks about absent Directors, but that is another matter. The breach to which I object is not a mere matter of bad taste – I am too accustomed to that to take notice of it – but of constitutional practice. Such matters should only be discussed by

Directors meeting in quorum *qua* Board, and a full week's notice should be given by the Secretary (who is by the way very lax in procedure) and the Agenda circulated. Indeed, I think that a matter of such gravity as this should be brought before a General Shareholders' Meeting. I should like Miss Leigh to be present.

2. If there is to be any investigation of the conduct of one director (and I for one should welcome a full investigation), then the activities of *all* directors should be passed in review. There are some directors, whom I will not name, who are obviously maintaining a scale of living (and I only refer to that side of their life which is quite open and regular) far beyond that which would be justified by the salaries they draw according to the books of the firm. I will say no more on this point.

3. I take serious exception to a phrase in Stewart's letter: 'a mere Ordinary Director'. I would point out that in this firm an ordinary director, so-called, is a good deal more extraordinary than a principal director: there are four of the latter, seemingly, and only one of the former. The term 'ordinary director' is therefore a risible misnomer. I suggest that the term 'extraordinary director' should be substituted. Stewart then goes on to say that as an 'ordinary director' I am expected 'to take part on equal terms in the deliberations of the Principal Directors'! There can be, of course, no fundamental equality between two kinds of person one of which is four times as rare as the other (I hope you follow this somewhat subtle reasoning); yet I challenge anyone to say that I have ever shown the slightest arrogance or *hauteur* in my dealings with ordinary Principal Directors. I pride myself on being as democratic as the next man, a good mixer, hail-fellow-well-met, always affable and tolerant. The innuendo is quite baseless.

4. The suggestion is made that it is improper for me to be connected in a business way with a Dance Club (for if there is a Band we may assume that dancing is one of the activities of the Club) – even when that Club has the guarantee of respectability afforded by the name of Eliot. (What sort of impression would the name 'Morley's Club' convey!!!) It is added that I 'can scarcely bring the necessary freshness of mind to a Board Meeting, if my nights are spent . . .' etc. I should like to bring to your attention another possible point of view which is ignored. If the Directors of Faber & Faber Ltd suppose that it is improper for me to be associated with Eliot's Club, what do they suppose the members of Eliot's Club think of my being associated with Faber & Faber? Which is the more sordidly corrupt activity – dancing or publishing? And would not the members of Eliot's Club have the right to object, that if I am to spend my days in Board

Meetings, I can scarcely bring to the Club in the evening the freshness of mind essential if one is to carry on such a venture successfully?

5. I would point out that my emoluments from the publishing house of Faber are not only ridiculously inadequate in consideration of the burden of responsibility that I bear, but are only just sufficient to enable me to dress neatly and modestly and to entertain the innumerable bores at whom I should be able to snap my fingers were I not connected with a publishing house. In a dance club, if any individual fails to behave properly, you chuck him out; in a publishing house, you take him out to lunch. If the firm of Faber & Faber Ltd dislikes the thought of my having to earn a little money elsewhere (and the firm might well blush collectively, even though the Principal Directors, so-called, are unable to blush individually, at the thought of a situation so humiliating for the firm) then it has the remedy in its own hands: to provide me with an income on which I can live. Otherwise, I may find myself tempted to devote the whole of my attention to the legitimate entertainment industry, providing innocent and rhythmical pleasure for people's bodies, instead of conniving at providing so much trash for their minds. Anyway, I am glad to think that Senhor Ferro's next visit to London will be during one of my enforced absences, and that there is not a man among you who has the slightest notion of how to deal with a Portuguese diplomat.

6. Now about the name, 'Eliot's Club'. It does not seem to be realised that I can no more prevent my name being used while I am living, than I can prevent the people of London from erecting statues, memorial busts, or hideous stained-glass windows in my honour after I am dead. This shoulders of the consequences of fame, which afflict anyone bearing on the too-vast orb, Atlantaean, the load Well nigh not to be borne Of thinnest partition. of his fate.[1] Fame and infamy are divided only by the all taking, by deed-poll, could not even prevent the Principal Directors from of the firm, if malice impelled them to go so far, surname of Eliot. They could alter the name Eliot Ltd. (T. S. Eliot, ordinary director, of U.S.A. Origin). Indeed, any organisation wishing to inspire confidence in the public, might easily be tempted to assume a name that is synonym for probity, fastidiousness and impeccable behaviour.

1 – Matthew Arnold, 'Heine's Grave' (1867):
  Bearing on shoulders immense,
  Atlantëan, the load,
  Wellnigh not to be borne,
  Of the too vast orb of her fate.

7. What I think most heartless, in this most irregular inquisition, is that I am compelled to fling open a door revealing a family skeleton. I might cry 'This is unworthy of you, Holmes! I could not have believed that you would have descended to this. You have made inquiries into the history of my unhappy brother'. . . Not that Arthur is my brother, far from it. Poor Arthur! Yet his affairs are no secret; he is known to all the magistrates of London and some in the provinces; and on more than one occasion he has been described from the Bench as 'a very bad case'. There is a strain of eccentricity in his family, deriving from the distaff side, which impels him to found clubs. I think his mother's people came from north of the Trent; anyway, there is something about him which is not English. Need I delve any more deeply into this painful wound?

LATER. 4 a.m. I dropped off into a sound sleep, from pure exhaustion, and now set to work to complete this document which has already caused me so much anguish. This whole affair makes me feel like a lonely Prometheus (the classical allusion will not escape you) chained to a mountain crag, with his liver exposed to the beaks of foul vultures. Yet it would be doing Stewart too much honour to refer to him as a vulture. Morley's friend André Gide once said *il faut avoir un aigle*.[1] He never said *il faut avoir un Stewart*.

8. This is really the last point. I have never had a penny, or the expectation of a penny, or the hope or intention of a penny, out of Eliot's Club. In everything that I have done, I have been completely disinterested, frequently at direct financial loss, with increasing anxieties and dwindling income. I will mention one incident, trivial maybe in itself, but suggestive and typical. Only last week I sacrificed my sense of dignity and reserve, to say nothing of a whole morning, to put myself into the hands of a number of coarse young men in an abandoned Baptist Chapel in the Marylebone Road, for the purpose of making a film which was supposed to be intended

---

1 – André Gide, *Le Prométhée mal enchaînée* (1920): '*Il faut avoir un aigle*': 'It is necessary to have an eagle.'

The joke about 'Morley's friend André Gide' is explained by the fact that FVM had felt uncomfortable throughout an evening in Paris in Gide's presence, to whom he could speak not a word in his own tongue. FVM would later write to TSE, 17 Aug. 1937: 'En France . . . I am quite willing for you to talk to Gide and me never to say him or hear him a word again: and you can have Jack Cahane [*sc.* Kahane] too: and I think Henry Miller and Anais Nin: and I doubt if StJin Perse [*sic*] has really anything to tell me that I dont get better in his English rivals: I mean that the Frenchness of France is just one of those I will make a detour of and an allowance for.'

to persuade people to buy more books.[1] I will pass over the humiliation and the physical discomfort, acute as they were. I performed this act at your request: you were careful, I thought, not to put it into so many words, but a nod is as good as a wink. I submitted myself to be made up, as the phrase is, by a villainous-looking and untidy young man of Jewish origin (I suspect); he was also supposed to un-make me. Later in the day, it was brought to my attention by a person whom I was entertaining at lunch at my own expense in the interests of the firm, that the young man in question had failed to unmake the back of my neck. When I changed my shirt in the evening I found the collar discoloured and probably ruined – 12s.6d. (all I can afford to pay for a shirt out of my modest income) thrown away, so to speak. Need I say more?

I remain, however, in a spirit of Christian charity,

Always your friend and well-wisher,

T. S. Eliot

1–On 1 June Alexander Shaw of the Strand Film Company asked RdlM if he had 'sounded T. S. Eliot on the subject of his appearing in the Book Film': 'The council insisted on [John] Masefield but I think that the modern poets should be represented and I would very much like Mr Eliot to be that representative.' The Strand Film Company to TSE, 7 Sept. 1936: 'There will be a private screening of "Cover to Cover", the documentary about books, writers and publishing, at 11 a.m. on September 16th, at the Carlton Cinema, Haymarket. Produced by Paul Rotha and directed by Alexander Shaw, this was the first film to be televised by the B.B.C.'

EVE to Elizabeth Knights, 8 Sept. 1983: 'Have you heard about the discovery of a twenty-two minute film made by Paul Rotha in 1936 for the National Book League? Consisting of interviews with several writers including Tom, Wystan and Somerset Maugham it has apparently been gathering dust in the vaults of Coutts Bank since 1941 while everyone thought it was lost. The BBC plan to show it on their Book Programme some time this month. It is exciting to know that a little more of Tom has been recovered from oblivion.'

See *Monthly Film Bulletin* [of the British Film Institute] 3: 33 (30 Sept. 1936), 144: 'The brief interviews serve a purpose in bringing us to some extent into touch with prominent literary figures, but the views they express are curtly rounded-off and, for the most part, superficial: they do not find a very exact place in the flow of the film. At some points one gets a certain impression of naïveté of thought.' The other contributors were Somerset Maugham, 'Sapper', Rebecca West, Julian Huxley and A. P. Herbert.

The documentary runs to 21 mins., and TSE appears on screen, speaking directly (and seemingly quite naturally) to the camera for no more than a few seconds. For the record, this is everything he says: 'It is no more use trying to be traditional than it is trying to be original. Nobody invents very much. But there is one thing to be said for contemporary poetry that can't be said in favour of any other, and that is that it is written by our contemporaries.'

Collard, 'Old Possum and the limbs of satan': 'Eliot recommended his friend [Tandy] to the producer Donald Taylor at Strand Films and Geoffrey Tandy is credited as one of the two commentators on The Way to the Sea, the 1936 Strand production which features a verse commentary by Auden and a score by Benjamin Britten (who described Tandy in a diary entry as resembling "a stage bug-hunter").'

TO *Thomas Dawes Eliot*[1]                                    CC

7 July 1936                        [Faber & Faber Ltd]

Dear Tom,

I was glad to hear from you, and should be delighted to see your son and do what I can to entertain him while he is in London. I am very [sorry] to say, however, that during the first week of August I shall be out of town on a visit to some friends in Wales which was arranged some time ago. It is impossible to change the dates now, and I can only hope that he will turn up in London either before or after that period.

I was glad to hear from you that your whole family were able to be present before your father died. I have been sent one or two biographical notices of him which I was very glad to see. He was certainly a very remarkable man, with a life of singular usefulness, and you may all well be proud of him.[2]

Affectionately your cousin,
[T. S. Eliot]


TO *William Saroyan*                                        CC

7 July 1936                        [Faber & Faber Ltd

Dear Mr Saroyan,

I am afraid that I am very late in answering your letter of May 1st.[3] I have finally made a selection, or the rejection, since the larger part of the book is kept, and I hope that you will not be dissatisfied with it.

1–TSE's cousin Thomas Dawes Eliot (1889–1973) was a Professor in the Dept of Sociology and Anthropology, College of Liberal Arts, Northwestern University, Evanston, Wisconsin.
2–Thomas Lamb Eliot (1841–1936), celebrated Unitarian minister of Portland, Oregon, died on 28 Apr. 1936. See 'Sketches of Interesting Personalities: 1. Thomas Lamb Eliot', *The Christian Leader*, 30 Nov. 1935, 1520–1; Earl Morse Wilbur, *Thomas Lamb Eliot 1841–1936* (Portland, Oregon: privately printed, 1937). (Earl Morse Wilbur's wife Dorothea was TSE's first cousin.)
3–Saroyan wrote, in response to TSE's letter of 16 Apr., that he hoped the F&F edition of *Inhale & Exhale* would include the same contents as in the US edition – 'on this theory, that a book is a book, however full it may be of defects'. He agreed, however: 'This book is much too long . . . I believe that I shall be pleased with the book you and [Frank] Morley shall make of what is available.' Nevertheless, he proceeded to detail several suggestions as to his preferred list of contents; and he ended up: 'Please do not make the mistake my American publishers made. The dust jacket, I mean, which is in the lousiest taste. A very simple jacket design or picture would help perhaps: would it be possible for the man [Barnett Freedman] who did the jacket for the book called Early One Morning by de la Mare to do a jacket for Inhale & Exhale: I would suggest either a simple picture of the sea, and land and sky; or a

I have accepted your suggestions as far as possible, and have included the whole of the third section as you wish. I was anxious to keep in 'Little Miss Universe', and have therefore omitted something else instead. And nothing would have induced me to leave out 'Our Little Brown Brothers', which I enjoyed particularly. I will pass on your remarks about the dust jacket to De la Mare when he returns from holiday. I quite agree with you about the jacket of the American edition. I will also discuss with Morley the question of a possible popular edition of the first book.

You say that you would like complimentary copies sent to a dozen British writers or so. Do you care to make any suggestions yourself, or do you wish us to choose the authors? I note what you say about the review copies.

I am afraid that the delay about an advance is entirely my fault, and I am very sorry that it is. We have agreed on an advance of £25, which is better than the $100 that you wanted. I am sorry that you didn't have it when you wanted it, but I imagine that it will still be useful.

I am sorry too that I missed you in London. I can't remember why it was, but I think I was out of town, and you were here a very short time.

With best wishes,
Yours sincerely,
[T. S. Eliot]

---

picture, in the modern manner, of a variety of things of the earth and world, to suggest, in a way, the variety of the book.

'Morley said maybe some day Faber would bring out my first book in a popular edition. I hope this will be done . . .

'Would it be possible for me to have an advance, say, of the equivalent of $100. I know we cannot expect very much more than a sale of 2,000 copies; however, I am broke and in debt and one hundred dollars a month from this date would probably be very useful . . . [I]f possible I should like to have a copy each sent to about a dozen (or even more) significant British writers, with "the compliments of the author". This is to be charged against my account . . .

'I'm sorry I didn't get to say hello to you when I was in London; and I'm glad you enjoyed the one about the black Tartars; I enjoyed writing it, and I still enjoy reading it. As a matter of fact I write today so that a year from today or ten I shall have something worth reading to read. Is that partly what writing is? I figure it is. My first book, for instance, is already the work of a writer who no longer exists; not that bluntly perhaps, but something like that.'

TO *Paul Léon*[1]                    TS National Gallery of Ireland

7 July 1936                         Faber & Faber Ltd

Dear Mr Léon,

I have your letter of the 3rd instant.[2] You will remember that our understanding was that we should contribute to the cost of typing the manuscript up to £10, and I have accordingly sent Joyce a cheque for 576 francs today. I shall look forward to seeing Madame Léon next week if I am here when she comes. Unfortunately I have to be away Wednesday, Thursday and Friday, but if Madame Léon brought the manuscript on one of those days she could ask for Mr Morley or Mr Stewart. I take it that we shall then have the whole of Part I and Part III. I shall be grateful for any news that you can give me about the progress of Part II. I do not know whether Joyce has found conditions more favourable for working than when I saw him a month ago.

I am ordering the pamphlets to be sent to you.[3]

With best wishes to Madame Léon and yourself,

Yours sincerely,

T. S. Eliot

1–Paul Léon, né Paul Léopoldovich (1893–1942?): cultured multilingual Jewish émigré from the Bolshevik revolution who had settled in Paris; he met JJ in 1928, when JJ was forty-seven and Léon thirty-five. He became JJ's unpaid assistant and amanuensis from 1930, and protected his papers even after the Nazis took over Paris. Léon was eventually seized by the German authorities and despatched to a camp where he died in unknown circumstances.

See *The James Joyce–Paul Léon Papers in the National Gallery of Ireland: A Catalogue*, compiled by Catherine Fahy (1992); John Naughton, 'Arm in arm with a literary legend' (interview with Alexis Léon), *Observer*, 13 Jan. 1991.

2–Léon reported on JJ's progress with 'Work in Progress' (*Finnegans Wake*): 'the typing of Parts II & III is progressing with success and I think I will be able to have it sent over to you very soon.

'Part III with which I started because I knew it better is already finished. It has costed [*sic*] Frcs. 376.

'Part I I had to entrust for copy and about half of it is already done. I am taking it up since yesterday with the typist who did Part III, and hope to be through with it in time for Mrs Léon to take it over to London when she goes there on the 12th inst. The first half of it costed Frcs. 200.

'As Mr Joyce had already paid for these two bills you will greatly oblige me if you send a cheque for this amount payable to him.'

3–'I am afraid that the whole brunt of Part I is lying on [JJ] and in order to spare time and expense I would be very thankful if you could have sent over to me 4 copies of the cheap edition of *Anna Livia Plurabelle* and 2 copies of the *Tales Told*. I have been able to use *Haveth Childers* as there are all told but three corrections on it which could be easily done in ink. The corrections on *Anna Livia* are however much greater in number, and I will have to cut out pages and paste them in their order.'

7 July 1936                           [Faber & Faber Ltd]

Dear MacNeice,

I have read your play, and I certainly think that we ought to publish it, but have no time to discuss it in detail at the moment.[1] Nor am I sure unfortunately that you will still be in Birmingham and will get this letter in good time. What I want to say is that unless the play is pretty certain to be produced in the autumn, and I don't even know whether you have discussed the question of production with anybody, I think myself that it would be better if possible to bring out the *Agamemnon* in the autumn, and *The Rising Venus* in the spring. Curiosity about the play will keep and will probably only be increased by having *Agamemnon* first, whereas if it is the other way about the *Agamemnon* may suffer without *The Rising Venus* benefiting. Furthermore, I think that as we are probably publishing Auden's new play in the autumn it would be an advantage to both to have them further spaced. If they appear in the same season they are almost certain to get reviewed together, and this, in my experience is to the advantage of neither book.

This is all very conjectural, and you may disagree completely. If you do agree, the question is whether the *Agamemnon* will be ready in time for the autumn. If not, we must leave matters as they are, as I think it is quite time for a new book from you. If you get this letter will you please let me know whether the *Agamemnon* will be ready before you go away for your holidays, and if so will you let me have a few words about it which I could use in preparing an advertisement for the catalogue?

Yours in haste,

[T. S. Eliot]

1–LM had written on 23 June: 'Here is my new play, The Rising Venus. I shall be very interested to know what you think of it. Auden liked it very much.

'"Agamemnon" progresses; Dodds has made some very helpful suggestions. I hope to have it ready within a month.'

The play was ultimately entitled *Out of the Picture*. (*Letters of Louis MacNeice*, ed. Jonathan Allison [2010], 265–6)

TO *James Joyce*                                    TS Buffalo

7 July 1936                    Faber & Faber Ltd

My dear Joyce,

I have just heard from Léon that you have paid out 576 francs on account of the typing of Part III, and the first half of Part I, and according to our understanding in conversation I am sending you at once our cheque for that amount. Don't bother about receipt stamp.

I have thought frequently about Lucia, and I hope that her health is improving under the present conditions. I should like to have news of your family either direct or indirectly whenever there is anything to report.

                              With best wishes to Mrs Joyce,
                              Yours ever,
                              T. S. Eliot


TO *William Temple*[1]                                    cc

8 July 1936                    [*The Criterion*]

My dear Lord Archbishop,

I have Your Grace's letter of the 4th.[2] I saw Oldham a few days ago, and discussed the suggestion with him. While I feel, of course, that with such urging as Your Grace's, I ought to undertake this piece of work, I was diffident, and am still diffident, of my qualifications for introducing the essays of distinguished theologians on the central point of the Christian Faith. What I said to Oldham was that I should like to have the opportunity of reading the various contributions in their present form (I understand that Christopher Dawson's is not yet written) and would then decide whether I felt myself competent. I assure Your Grace that

---

1–William Temple (1881–1944) – son of Frederick Temple (1821–1902), Archbishop of Canterbury – taught Classics at Oxford; was ordained in 1908; served as Headmaster of Repton School, Derbyshire, 1910–14; and was Bishop of Manchester until translated in 1929 to the Archbishopric of York. In 1942 he was appointed Archbishop of Canterbury. His writings include *Christus Veritas* (1924), *Nature, Man and God* (1934), and *Christianity and Social Order* (1942). In the 1920s he won authority as leader of the movement for international ecumenism – 'this world-wide Christian fellowship,' as he proclaimed it.
2–The Archbishop asked if TSE had heard from J. H. Oldham about 'a project': 'I want to say that I think this project is really important, and that it would be an enormous advantage to it if you see your way to fall in with Oldham's proposal. Please do so if you possibly can; we need *your* help.' See 'I by T. S. Eliot', in *Revelation*, ed. John Baillie and Hugh Martin (F&F, 1937), 1–39.

I will undertake the introduction if, after reading the essays, I feel that it would not be an impertinence on my part.

I am,

Your Grace's obedient servant,

[T. S. Eliot]

TO *Cyril Clemens*[1]                                                                                      CC

8 July 1936                          [Faber & Faber Ltd]

Dear Mr Clemens,

Thank you for your letter of June 6th.[2] I am still regretting that pressure of other business prevented me from carrying out my promise to write something for you about your grandfather, but I felt that I want to refresh my knowledge of his works before doing so, and the necessary time was not to be found. Now you ask me for something on A. E. Housman. I am afraid that I am not the man to contribute conscientiously to such a garland, although I quite approve of its being made. I have never been a very warm admirer of Mr Housman's poetry, and I think that on such an occasion those who contribute should be people who can speak with enthusiasm.

I am afraid that my next visit to America will be such a brief one that it will not carry me further than New England.[3] When I shall be again in St Louis I don't know, but when I do come I shall hope to meet you. My cousin, Mrs Leonard Martin, is, I believe, a neighbour of yours.

*Lancelot Andrewes* has never been translated into French. Nor has anything of mine, except isolated poems and essays published in

1–Cyril Coniston Clemens (1902–99) was born in St Louis, Missouri, and graduated from Washington University. A distant cousin of Samuel Langhorne Clemens, in 1930 he was founder and president of the International Mark Twain Society; founder-editor of the *Mark Twain Quarterly*, 1936–82. Works include biographies of Twain and President Harry Truman.

2–Clemens was arranging 'a garland of tributes . . . in memory of our late member A. E. Housman. We ask you please to send a few lines either in prose or verse.'

3–FVM to Hugh Wade (Harcourt, Brace & Co.), 30 July 1936: 'The great and reverend [*sic*] Mr Eliot will be crossing the ocean at the latter end of August, but I very much doubt if he will get to New York. He is really coming over to have a look at the white mountains and doesn't much want to get caught in traffic.'

periodicals, so I am afraid there is nothing to offer to a French friend who writes in English.

> With all best wishes,
> Yours sincerely
> [T. S. Eliot]

## TO *Nevill Coghill*[1]

9 July 1936                                    [Faber & Faber Ltd]

Dear Mr Coghill,

I must apologise for my delay in answering your kind letter of June 2nd, but I hesitated for a long time before saying no.[2] If I had anything in my mind bursting to be said about poetic drama I might be tempted more easily. But as it is I am finding it necessary to keep my speaking engagements as few as possible. You see, one's ordinary routine work keeps increasing, and it becomes more and more difficult to save the time for my own work. Any speaking engagement means at least a week, and very often two, out of this spare time. So I think as I have a few engagements already for next year I ought to decline. I hope that you will be producing something this summer at Tewkesbury or elsewhere, and that if so I shall be able to see it.

> Yours sincerely,
> [T. S. Eliot]

1–Nevill Coghill (1899–1980), born in Ireland, studied at Exeter College, Oxford, and taught at the Royal Naval College, Dartmouth, before being elected in 1924 to a Research Fellowship at Exeter College and then a full Fellowship. From 1957 he was Merton Professor of English. A passionate member of the Oxford University Dramatic Society, he put on many plays (including *Measure for Measure*, starring Richard Burton, in 1944); and he was friends with C. S. Lewis and J. R. R. Tolkien, as well as with his pupil W. H. Auden. His primary research interest was Chaucer: he translated *The Canterbury Tales* (1956) and *Troilus and Criseyde* (1971), and he wrote *The Poet Chaucer* (1949) and *Geoffrey Chaucer* (1956), as well as *Shakespeare's Professional Skills* (1964). He later edited the Faber Educational editions of *MiC*, *FR* and *CP*.

When Coghill asked FVM, 18 May 1936, 'I enclose a satirical verse-play which I would like you to read with a view to publishing it if it appeals to you. My hopes are that it might make an item in the Criterion Miscellany', TSE wrote on his letter: 'NO. Certainly not. T. S. E.'

2–Coghill wrote from Exeter College, Oxford, to invite TSE to address the Oxford Branch of the English Association (of which Coghill was chair) in June 1937: 'Any matter that you think suitable will satisfy us, though, for myself, I should chiefly like to hear about poetic drama. I saw *Murder in the Cathedral* here with admiration the other day; indeed all who I have spoken to that saw it were greatly moved.'

9 July 1936                              [Faber & Faber Ltd]

Dear Mrs Bullock,

I have been considering your kind and flattering suggestion that I should become one of the sponsors of the Academy of American Poets.[2] I feel very much honoured by the suggestion, and it is therefore due to you to give you the reasons why I do not feel that I can give my name in this way. I have in the past declined one or two similar invitations in this country for similar reasons, so you will see that this is not a particular objection.

It seems to me that the use of a sponsor is simply to add prestige to an undertaking over which he has no control. I do not suggest that I should prefer to have a hand in it, because I should not have time in any case, and it would be unsuitable and inconvenient to have anyone concerned in the direction at such a distance. But giving one's name to an undertaking is in itself accepting responsibility, and I do not think that one ought to take responsibility for anything in which one has no authority. Furthermore, at this distance I should not even know what was going on. While your aims are most laudable, and I wish them all success, even you cannot know that the results will justify your hopes. I do not want in the least to discourage you, but experience leads me to believe that unless such undertakings have the constant attention and vigilance of the small number of intelligent people who really care passionately about their aims, they are apt to decline into mere formalism. A great deal depends, of course, on the people whom you are able to obtain as Chancellors, and until this body is formed one cannot make any prediction about the suitability of their selections.

I have other doubts about attempts to subsidize poets with which I need not trouble you, but on the whole I am inclined to believe that what might be most useful would be a kind of employment bureau which could find suitable jobs for suitable poets, jobs which would leave them the energy – and that is still more important than time – to write poetry.

With all best wishes,
Yours sincerely,
[T. S. Eliot]

1 – Marie (Mrs Hugh) Bullock represented the Academy of American Poets.
2 – Letter not traced.

TO *Henry Eliot*                                    TS Houghton

9 July 1936                      Faber & Faber Ltd

My dear Henry,

I was glad to get your letter, and expect that I shall see Elsa (whom I liked); but there is nothing to be done until I hear from her. I only hope she will know enough to write to this address (you see, V. went and put my name in the telephone book as of 68 Clarence Gate Gardens, and it can't be removed until the new telephone directory comes out in August) but I expect she will see Alida and I will tell Alida to put her right. It depends on when and how long she is here. I have to be out of town for three days next week, and I go to the Fabers in Wales for the first week in August. After that I shall be in town until I sail.

I am sailing for Montreal on the 22nd August, but there is no need to tell everyone in advance; because I want this to be a holiday and a strictly private appearance – it will be the first holiday I have had for some years, as I don't count visits to friends in the country in England as quite the same thing – guests always have obligations.[1] Ada was doubtful whether you and Theresa would be able to come to Randolph,[2] as you will be busy moving, but I shall have some days in Cambridge and will see you there. If you were not moving till October I would come on to New York, but I have no other reason for going there except perhaps to see Paul More, who is very ill at Princeton.

                                        Affectionately,
                                        Tom


TO *Edwin Muir*                                           CC

9 July 1936                      [*The Criterion*]

Dear Muir,

I like your poem, and should like to keep it for publication.[3] It is a great relief to get a poem of this sort once in a while. I have still two queries to

---

1–Miss Evans (F&F) to FVM, 20 Aug. 1936: 'I asked Mr Baker [Accountant at F&F] for 30/- on your account, and went to Jacksons and ordered the Foie Gras, Bath Olivers and Power's Whiskey to be sent to Mr Eliot, SS *Alaunia*. The whole bill came to 24/-, and I have put the receipts and change in the righthand drawer of your desk.'
2–The Eliot family gathered together at the Mount Crescent Hotel, Randolph, New Hampshire.
3–Muir responded on 3 June to TSE's letter of 29 May, enclosing a revised version of 'Hölderlin's Journey': 'Thanks very much for your letter and your criticisms of my Hölderlin

make. In the present version you say 'Its pictured death' at the beginning of the ninth quatrain. But there was the head of a deer on both pillars of the gate, therefore I should think that the living deer should have been gazing on 'their pictured death'. Of course when you say 'Living deer' you may mean one stag or doe, but I think that what the word immediately brings to mind is a herd of deer. The second point is the pronunciation of 'Diotima'. I ordinarily pronounce that name with the accent on the penult. Do you mean it to be pronounced with the accent on the antipenult., and if so is that the way it would be pronounced in German, or do you mean to break the regular rhythm in those places?[1]

I am not sending the poem back. I assume that you have the copy of the revised version.

With best wishes to Mrs Muir and yourself,

Yours ever,

[T. S. Eliot]

TO *Edith Perkins*                                                TS Beinecke

10 July 1936                          *The Criterion*

Dear Mrs Perkins,

I have meant to write you a word of greeting both in time for Easter and for Whitsun, but of course left it until too late on each occasion. But I am

---

poem. They are more than justified, I'm afraid, though I was quite blind to them until you mentioned them. The "hot" Bordeaux, which I see is ridiculous, had quite rich private associations for me when I wrote it; but I see now, of course, that these could not be brought out simply by setting down the word "hot". I have altered the line, and tried to make it inoffensive at least. I have cut out the whole verse about the living waters, which I really think is very bad. The "selfsame stone" arose from a confusion of imagery, which I think I have managed to clear up. If the poem pleases you with these alterations, I shall be very glad; if not, I hope you will feel no further obligations to it . . .

'I have taken up this kind of theme lately, as a means of getting away from the poetry of opinion, into which the younger poets have led me without my noticing it.'

'Hölderlin's Journey', C. 16 (Jan. 1937), 267–8; *Collected Poems*, 67.

1–See 'Hölderlin's Journey':

'On either pillar of the gate
    A deer's head watched within the stone.
The living deer with quiet look
    Seemed to be gazing on

'Its pictured death – and suddenly
    I knew, Diotima was dead,
As if a single thought had sprung
    From the cold and the living head.[']

not so graceless as not to write to thank you for your last letter, enclosing the Story by Emily, which I shall prize among my most carefully preserved papers.[1] Thank you ever so much for letting me have it.

I have thought of you and Dr Perkins often as the spring and summer came in. It may be cheering to you to know that you have missed an especially bad season in this country; indeed, there have been very few occasions when you would have been able to enjoy sitting in the garden. It has been the most consistently cold and grey year that I remember, yet we are told that there has not been enough rain either, though yesterday it pelted cats and dogs. The only really lovely day that I remember was a day at the end of May when I was motored over from Cambridge to Little Gidding. The nightingales were discouraged from singing; and now, in the middle of July, I am sitting huddled before the gas-fire. At the same time you seem to have been perishing of heat in America.

I hope that there will be some warmth left for me, and I look forward very much to seeing you when I come to Cambridge in September.

Yours ever gratefully,<br>Tom

## TO *W. B. Yeats*[2] CC

10 July 1936                [Faber & Faber Ltd]

Dear Yeats,

I have your letter of July 6th, and am sorry that the matter of the *Upanishads* is not yet settled.[3] I am extremely friendly to its publication myself, but the manuscript must be examined by one or two other directors, and is at present in the hands of the Chairman. I hope that we may be able to publish it as well as the other book in preparation which you mentioned in your previous letter. I agree myself that it would be interesting, if not too expensive, to have a short Upanishad in Sanskrit

---

1 – The story is probably an undated piece by Hale entitled 'They flash upon the inward eye' (Smith College Archives); published in *Campden & District Historical & Archæological Society: Notes & Queries* 5: 4 (Spring 2007), 47–8.
2 – William Butler Yeats (1865–1939): Irish poet; Nobel laureate: see Biographical Register.
3 – 'I dont know if you have come to any conclusion yet about the Upanishads, and I dont want to hurry you. I write to make the suggestion that if you accept you might care to have (say) one of the minor Upanishads, or some part of a [*sic*] Upanishad, given in an appendix with the Sanscrit words and the ancient music which accompanies it. I have heard Swami sing a Upanishad to this music and if you think it desirable I will find out if he knows anybody who could record it. He is possibly as incapable of writing music out as Tagore.'

with the music as an appendix, for [*sc*. if] the music is such that it can be scored.[1]

I don't know who would undertake recording an *Upanishad*, but it seems to me something that certainly ought to be done. It is a pity that the Swami is not going to be in London, but I suppose that there are gramophone companies which make records in India.

Anyway, I should be glad if you could find out about the possible scoring for the book, but you need not bother about this until I can give you a definite answer from the firm.

I have eagerly sought any information I could get about your health in the past months, and I hope that you are now making a good recovery. I am sending you a copy of my *Collected Poems*, which I should have sent at the time, except that you were in Majorca, and I thought that you might not want to be bothered with presentations during that period.

> With best wishes to Mrs Yeats,
> Yours ever,
> [T. S. Eliot]

1–This blurb for *The Ten Principal Upanishads: Put into English by W. B. Yeats and Shri Purohit Swami* (1937) appeared in Faber Spring Books 1937, p. 57: 'It is a matter of astonishment and regret that there has been until now no modern translation into English of the Upanishads – that body of literature which is as important for the study of the religion of India as the Old Testament is for Judaism and Christianity. The translations of Max Müller are long since out of date in scholarship, and are written in a style which fails to convey the magnificence of the poetry of the original. Shri Purohit Swami is an Indian scholar well known in England, trained in the ancient tradition of Sanskrit scholarship. He has had throughout the collaboration of Mr Yeats, who explains in his introduction the principles on which they have tried to render in contemporary English speech the beauty and simplicity of the Sanskrit.

'There are many Upanishads – sixty are available in the German translation of Deussen – but much of their content is of interest only to scholars and students of folklore. This selection is made with the purpose of giving the English reader those Upanishads which are both most beautiful as literature and most essential for the understanding of Indian mysticism.'

TO *Caresse Crosby*[1]

10 July 1936                    [Faber & Faber Ltd]

Dear Mrs Crosby,

I should have followed up our conversation by writing to tell you that I have discussed with my Committee both the Grosz drawings[2] and the Joyce Collected Poems, and they are interested to hear more of both projects. When you get back to New York I hope you will be able to let me have further particulars of format, price, etc., of both volumes. The question of the Joyce poems of course involves consideration of the obstacle which I mentioned to you, but I hope that this is not impossible.

> With all best wishes,
> Yours sincerely,
> [T. S. Eliot]


TO *Geoffrey Faber*                              TS memo EVE

12 July 1936

G.C.F.

I think you ought to look at the attached three papers and pass an opinion.[3]

Lionel Gough is a young master (at Haileybury) of whom I think well. I *don't* think that these essays would, as he hopes, 'make a small book'. They were obviously written at various times, and they overlap and both repeat and contradict each other. But I think he has something to say, though he is too indignant: indignatio *non* facit a lot of things besides verses: a man must take *pleasure* in the way in which he says unpleasant

---

1–Caresse Crosby (1892–1970), née Jacob (her parents were wealthy New Yorkers), married in 1922 the poet Harry Crosby, with whom she set up in Paris an imprint called Editions Narcisse, which presently became the Black Sun Press: they published JJ, DHL, Hart Crane, and EP. Following Harry Crosby's suicide in 1929, she proceeded to expand the Black Sun Press – publishing works including Hart Crane's *The Bridge* (1930) and editions of her late husband's writings – before returning to the USA in the mid-1930s. In later years she took initiatives in various fields: she opened the Crosby Gallery of Modern Art, Washington, DC; she launched a quarterly journal, *Portfolio: An Intercontinental Review*; and she was active in the international peace movement, co-founding and supporting both Citizens of the World and Women Against War. Her writings include *Graven Images* (1926) and *The Passionate Years* (memoir, 1953).
2–George Grosz (1893–1959), German-born artist who migrated to the USA in 1933. See Grosz, *Interregnum* (Black Sun Press, 1936): a limited-edition volume of photolithographs.
3–One of the papers seems to have been called 'The Parish Church & the Fifth Form'.

things if he is to say them successfully. I don't see how he could print anything of this sort over his own name, if he is to keep his job: but he is not so well known but that anonymity might not be more effective. It seems to me that he *might* make an effective small book (not so small as all that) though this definitely is not well enough done to give him more than encouragement and advice. He is a layman, and teaches English; but he has had to take the 5th form in divinity. He is a friend of Humphrey Beevor of Pusey House, who is one of the ablest of the young A.C.s'.[1]

T. S. E.

12.vii.36.

1 – GCF replied, in a handwritten memo: 'I have read these papers, & I don't think there's a book in *them*, tho' there may be a book in *him*.

'What he says about Public School religion is perfectly true – it was just as true in my time at Rugby (1903–1908), & I expect it was just as true years before & will be just as true thirty years from now.

'Certainly the *Church* would be wise if it put pressure upon the schools to abandon compulsory services.

'But Gough's constructive ideas seem to me to come to very little. The fault – if fault it is – lies outside the schools. He says it's the parents. But it's more than that – & much more complicated than that: as (a) the indifference of the age generally (b) the active dislike of Anglo-Catholicism in particular. This second point he seems hardly to have realized. A very large number of parents tolerate the existing system *because* there's no room for Anglo-Catholicism in it; they would be deeply suspicious of any alteration which seemed likely to expose the children to proselytizing influences. (I should myself!) And many of them probably feel – & I'm not sure that I don't – that the being forced to go to chapel has the result of making a boy to go through with things which bore him, & fit him to endure a great deal in his after-life with patience for the sake of social continuity.

'These are the criticisms of an irreligious reader!

'But, anyway, and apart from your own very pertinent observations. I think that it would be a mistake for us to publish a book which addressed itself solely to ready-made A.C.'s. I wouldn't have the least objection to publish A.C. apologetic, if it were good enough – indeed, I have often thought of suggesting to you that you might get somebody to write such a book – a direct effort to justify & persuade. But Gough's papers, written exclusively for A.C. readers, aren't our proper meat. I am sometimes a little uneasy to discover from chance remarks of people I meet that F. & F. is thought to have identified itself with Anglo-Catholicism. (Hence, in part, my idea of publishing Loisy.)

'Could Gough write such a book?

'I suppose you haven't any wish to write your own apologia?'

For TSE on Alfred Loisy, see Joanna Rzepa, 'Tradition and Individual Experience: T. S. Eliot's Encounter with Modernist Theology', in *Religion and Myth in T. S. Eliot's Poetry*, ed. Scott Freer and Michael Bell (2016), 101–2: 'As he later recalled, the year that he spent studying at the Sorbonne was the time when "at the Collège de France, Loisy enjoyed his somewhat scandalous distinction." ['A Commentary', C. 13 [1934], 451–2.] Alfred Loisy was a Roman Catholic priest and theologian who advocated the application of modern historical criticism to the Scriptures, and undertook a critique of certain Church doctrines. In 1903, five of his books were placed on the Index of Prohibited Books. After Pope Pius X issued the decree *Lamentabili Sane Exitu* in July 1907, and the encyclical *Pascendi Dominici*

13 July 1936                          [Faber & Faber Ltd]

Dear Mr MacNeice,

I have your letter of the 9th.[1] I hope that you will let us have the *Agamemnon* manuscript before the 28th if possible, as although it should not be difficult to print, the more time we have the better. Meanwhile, do let me have your advance note about it as quickly as possible.[2]

I will bring up the question of price. I think 5s. might be possible.

Yours in haste,<br>[T. S. Eliot]

---

*Gregis* in September 1907, condemning a list of theses considered "modernist" and seen as an attack on the institution of the Church, Loisy refused to conform and to revoke his views. Subsequently, he was excommunicated from the Church, and as a lay intellectual appointed chair of history of religions at Collège de France. Moreover, when Eliot began working for one of the Oxford University Extension centres in 1916 he proposed to run a course on "Tendencies of Contemporary French Thought." In the reading list for the course, he included Alfred Loisy's condemned work *The Gospel and the Church*.'

1–'I am very glad that you think of publishing "The Rising Venus". The Group Theatre think of doing it but I do not know when. They hope however to produce my "Agamemnon" in the autumn, about October, I think. I therefore agree with you that Agamemnon ought to be published first. It would be best, I suppose, if it could come out in time for the Group production?

'I am going away on July 28th and shall be able to let you have Agamemnon before then. In the meantime I will write you a note about it for the catalogue.

'Do you agree that the price of Agamemnon might profitably be lower than in the case of books of original verse?'

2–LM submitted this 'Note on my translation of the Agamemnon of Aeschylus': 'This translation was primarily written for the stage. Of the many English translations already existant none of them seems to me to emerge as a live play. I hope that mine reads like a live play; in working to this end I have been prepared to sacrifice the parts to the whole. I have consciously sacrificed two things in the original: the liturgical flavour of the diction and the metrical complexity of the choruses. I have tried to make this translation vigorous, intelligible, and homogeneous. I have avoided on the whole poetic or archaic diction and any diction or rhythm too reminiscent of familiar English models. The dialogue is an elastic blank verse; the choruses are unrhymed (occasionally they echo the cadences of the original). The translation is, I think, closer to the original than many; I first wrote a very literal version, line for line, sometimes word for word, and afterwards modified it with a view to form, intelligibility, and dramatic effect.'

*The Agamemnon of Aeschylus*, trans. LM, was to be published on 29 Oct. 1936 with this blurb: 'Mr MacNeice is a classical scholar as well as a poet. He is also interested in the theatre, and has a play of his own in preparation. His translation of the *Agamemnon* is in verse, but, unlike most translations, is intended primarily for the stage. While keeping close to the original it employs a modern idiom. It is the first "contemporary" translation of this play to be made by a poet; and its first performance is announced by The Group Theatre for November 1936.'

13 July 1936                              Faber & Faber Ltd

Dear Roberts,

Thank you for your letter of the 9th.[1] Your views on the subject of the Hulme book seem very satisfactory, and we should like to commission you to do it. I don't know quite what you have in mind when you say 240 pages, but I presume you mean 240 typed pages. That would be roughly 60,000 words. We could manage much better if you could make a book of about 80,000 words, which we could sell at 10/6. I think that the sale would probably be as good at 10/6 as it would be at 7/6, and we could manage better terms for you. I shall not be present at the Committee Meeting next Wednesday, but I will have the matter discussed then, and meanwhile I should be glad if you would consider whether a somewhat longer book is not possible.

I am returning two essays which I have had for some time, and which I imagine are being included in your Cape volume. If not I should like to discuss them further.[2]

Yours ever,
T. S. Eliot

1 – 'I presume that the object of the book would be two-fold: firstly an exposition of Hulme's ideas (in *Speculations* and elsewhere) intended to reveal their importance to people who do not already know much about them and their growing influence. Secondly, a critical discussion of the implications of those ideas, treated in such a way that it will appear to be an amplification of what has gone before. That is to say, the book should be "sympathetic" and should aim at being something like the book that Hulme might have written had he had time to tidy up his papers and his ideas and to view them with the detachment which comes with a lapse of twenty years.'

2 – *The Modern Mind*, finally rejected by Cape, was published by F&F in 1937.

TO *Kathleen Raine*[1]          TS Lockwood Memorial Library

13 July 1936                    *The Criterion*

Dear Mrs Madge,

I am interested in your sketch 'The Taurus', and have read it several times,[2] because I feel that if you recast it you could make a great deal more of it than you do. The anecdote itself is a fascinating one, but it seems to me in itself only the material for a story. What one would like, I think, would be to have the situation realised a little more from the point of view of the Pantomime Bull himself. I know that there is danger of meretriciousness if one treats the incident as a kind of Ovidian metamorphosis, but I think that some suggestion of a different personality than the farmer's ordinary one manifesting itself in the disguise would add very much to the effect. The boy's agony of disillusionment is a good point, and I should not like to see that disappear. I think, also, that for such a short story the first two pages of the preamble are much too prolix. One doesn't get any intimation of what is coming, nor does it help what is

---

1 – Kathleen Raine (1908–2003), poet and scholar, read natural sciences and psychology at Girton College, Cambridge, graduating in 1929. Briefly married in 1929 to Hugh Sykes Davies, she then married Charles Madge, though that marriage was almost as short-lived. She was a Research Fellow at Girton College, 1955–61; and Andrew Mellon Lecturer at the National Gallery of Arts in Washington, DC, in 1962. Her early poetry was published by Tambimuttu (founder of *Poetry London*): her first volume was *Stone and Flower* (1943), with illustrations by Barbara Hepworth; and other collections include *The Year One* (1952) and *The Hollow Hill* (1965). Critical works include *Blake and Tradition* (2 vols, 1968–9) – 'It makes all other studies of Blake obsolete,' said C. S. Lewis – *Thomas Taylor the Platonist: Selected Writings* (1969); and *Yeats, The Tarot and the Golden Dawn* (1972); and she published four volumes of autobiography.

TSE to the Assistant to the President, Bryn Mawr College, 3 Feb. 1951: 'I have known Mrs Raine for many years – ever since her first ventures in print; I have frequently seen her socially and informally; and also I know enough about her history, both directly and through mutual friends who know her more intimately than I do, to be able to speak with confidence. She is already recognised as one of the most distinguished poets of her generation – I should be happy if the publishing firm of which I am a director had had the opportunity of publishing her poems. She is fully qualified, by natural talent and by education, to make the most of the benefits which the Fellowship offers, and I know enough of her character to be sure that she will carry out the undertaking conscientiously. Incidentally, her personality is agreeable and sympathetic, and, if she had contact with undergraduates who sought her help in any way, would be most kind and generous.'

2 – Raine submitted her story on 6 June. 'I should like to know your decision as soon as possible, as I think I might be able to market it elsewhere, if you do not find it good enough.'

coming when it arrives. I don't know whether these suggestions will mean anything to you, and I wish that I could put them more effectively.

Yours sincerely,<br>T. S. Eliot

I mean, the first 2pp give it the character of a reflective, mild essay on the minds of yokels, whilst the story itself should inspire pity and terror.

## TO *Philip Mairet*                                         CC

14 July 1936                              [*The Criterion*]

My dear Mairet,

There is another book which I should be very much obliged if you would tackle, not for the next number but for the December *Criterion*, as it will need time. It is a book which has been recommended to me called *La Methode psychoanalytique et la doctrine Freudienne*. It is two volumes, and the man must be pretty good, at least officially, as he has an introduction from Professor Henri Claude, whom I used to know, and who stood in the top rank.[1]

Yours ever,<br>[T. S. Eliot]

1 – The author of the two-vol. work was Roland Dalbiez.

Henri Claude (1869–1945), neurologist and psychiatrist, was Head of the Mental Illness Clinic at St Anne's Hospital, Paris, 1922–39; Professor of Psychiatry at the University of Paris; and was elected a full member of the Académie de Médecine, 1927. He had treated VHE – who greatly appreciated him – at the Sanatorium de la Malmaison, Paris, in 1926.

Mairet accepted on 15 July – 'Though all Freud's earliest medical inspirations were from the French, he failed to inspire French medicos in return. I have often thought I would like to read a masterly French discussion of the theory' – but no review was forthcoming.

TO *Edwin Muir*                                         CC

14 July 1936                        [*The Criterion*]

Dear Muir,

Thank you for your letter of the 10th.[1] That is all right about the deer,
since you defend the singular, and also about Diotima. I will use the poem
as soon as I can.

                                    Yours ever,
                                    [T. S. Eliot]


TO *E. W. F. Tomlin*[2]                        TS Lady Marshall

14 July 1936                        [*The Criterion*]

Dear Tomlin,

I have your letter of the 4th July, and have read your short article once,
but must read it again. My first impression is that it is somewhat too
concentrated and abstract to be successful, and that it needs, as aesthetics so
frequently does, continual immersion in the concrete instance. Meanwhile
I return your earlier essay 'Slaves to the Future', which I imagine you
might want now to revise before you publish it. The objection I raised at
the time, that it was unwise and perhaps unsuitable to criticise a don in
print in this way while you were an undergraduate, no longer exists, and
I should like to do something with this article. Only I feel that Rowse's

---

1–In answer to TSE's letter to Muir of 9 July: 'The first point you mention, about the deer,
troubled me a little too, but I thought afterwards that it was all right. I thought of the deer
as a single deer ("And watched beside a mouldering gate A deer with its rock-crystal eyes".).
In looking at the two sculptured heads it seems to be gazing at its own pictured death: is it
allowable to say it sees its pictured death in the two heads? It seems to me that it is, but I
should like to have your opinion, and would abide by it (I hate to bother you in this way).
I don't know why I made the heads two instead of one, but it seemed to provide a symmetry
and a difference; or seems now, for I am arguing from the result. If you think it can stand,
I should be relieved; but if you think it cannot, then I shall try to work the picture out again.
   'I am rather upset about Diotima. I thought the emphasis came on the "O". I think I must
have got this idea from Hölderlin's own poems, in which Diotima comes in frequently. And
surely the emphasis could not come on the last "I" in the Greek? But of course the English
pronunciation is everything, and I simply do not know what it is. I think that even with
the pronunciation which I did not intend, the verses will still do, though they are not nearly
so good as with the old. But I have had DiOtima so firmly fixed in my head for years now
that I never stopped to think whether there was another way of pronouncing it. At any rate
I hope you think it will do, however pronounced. I am so glad you like the poem.'
2–Walter F. Tomlin (1914–88): writer and administrator: see Biographical Register.

book itself has become a little out of date, and that it is a disadvantage to your article to give it primary place.[1]

I notice that you have nothing to review for the next number of the *Criterion*. Would it interest you to tackle a number of volumes of poetry together as the man I expected to do it is taking a holiday and would hardly be able to get it done by the 29th of July, when I must have the review? It might make an interesting change for once from philosophy. The most important is probably Michael Roberts's, but there are also Frederick Prokosch, Dorothy Wellesley, and a small book of new poems by Marianne Moore. Also there is a translation of Eluard's Surrealist poems, which might give you the opportunity for generalizations about the nature of poetry. Only please let me know at once.[2]

Yours ever,
T. S. Eliot

TO *John Dover Wilson*[3]               TS National Library of Scotland

14 July 1936                    *The Criterion*

My dear Dover Wilson,

I have rather shirked answering your letter of June 23rd, because it is disagreeable to be disobliging.[4] But the fact is that I should very much prefer to postpone coming to Edinburgh until the autumn term of 1937. I mean that I should like very much indeed to come to Edinburgh in this way, but that I want to keep the winter free of speaking engagements so

1–See Tomlin, 'Philosophy and Politics', C. 17 (Jan. 1938), 237–53.
2–Tomlin on Paul Eluard, *Thorns of Thunder*; Michael Roberts, *Poems*; Dorothy Wellesley, *Selected Poems*, sel. and introd. by W. B. Yeats; Marianne Moore, *The Pangolin and other Verse*; Frederic Prokosch, *The Assassins*; Wilfred Rowland Childe, *Selected Poems*; Charles Reznikoff, *Separate Way*; S. F. A. Coles, *With Odysseus*; Geoffrey Winthrop Young, *Collected Poems*; Austin Clarke, *Collected Poems*: C. 16 (Oct. 1936), 133–40.
   Tomlin, *T. S. Eliot*, 76: '[My review] was not as good as I should have wished, partly because I was in a hurry, but also partly because I had not yet learnt – if I was ever to master – the technique of literary criticism. In fact, George Every, then a lay brother at Kelham . . . told me later that Eliot, while praising some individual points, had said that the general impression it gave was of material being put through a machine and coming out the other side more or less as it was before. The simile was so striking and no doubt so apt, that I could not take offence.'
3–John Dover Wilson (1881–1969): literary and textual scholar: see Biographical Register.
4–Dover Wilson wondered if TSE might like to come to Edinburgh in Jan. or Feb. 1937. 'We could arrange a short course of four or five public lectures for you & the University would pay £10 a lecture plus £10 towards expenses . . . I need hardly warn you too that my young people will be after you for their Literary Society.'

that I can get some work done. I find that public speaking of any kind is such an effort to me that it upsets completely any consecutive work on which I may be engaged, and as my last winter was very much broken up for that and other reasons, I am anxious to get something accomplished during the coming winter. I hope that you will not be impatient of my tiresomeness.

With many thanks and hopes,
Yours sincerely,
T. S. Eliot

## TO *L. C. Knights*[1]

 TS L. C. Knights

14 July 1936                    *The Criterion*

Dear Knights,

I should certainly be glad to use your article on Middleton in time, but the supply of Elizabethan criticism is considerably greater than the *Criterion* can consume, and I have two or three things on hand which will have to take precedence.[2] But I could probably use it early next year. Alternatively, if you have another copy and place the article elsewhere meanwhile I shall be glad if you will let me know.

By the way I have just remembered that the copy of the book by Theodore Spencer which I sent to you to make a long review with some other book has a personal inscription in it from him to me, so I shall have to apologise for asking you to take the trouble to return it to me when you have finished with it.[3]

Yours sincerely,
T. S. Eliot

P.S. I think that your criticisms of some of my remarks about Middleton are quite justified. I really was not thoroughly at home in Middleton's

---

1 – L. C. Knights (1906–97), literary critic, held a Research Fellowship at Christ's College, Cambridge, 1930–1, and was a founder-editor of *Scrutiny: A Quarterly Review,* 1932–53. He taught at Manchester University, 1933–47, and was Professor of English Literature at Sheffield, 1947–53; Winterstoke Professor of English at Bristol; King Edward VII Chair of English at Cambridge, 1965–73. Works include *How Many Children had Lady Macbeth?* (1933) and *Drama and Society in the Age of Jonson* (1937). TSE advised Helen Gardner, 20 Oct. 1956, that Knights was 'a former disciple of Leavis, who is, I think, very intelligent'.

2 – Knights (4 June) submitted a note on Middleton, from his forthcoming *Drama and Society in the Age of Jonson*: 'it would only be of use to you if it could be published in the October *Criterion*'.

3 – Spencer, *Death and Elizabethan Tragedy: a study of convention and opinion in the Elizabethan drama* (1936); inscribed 'to T. S. Eliot from *Theodore Spencer* May 1936'.

comedies, although I once prepared a text of *Michaelmas Term*, and I think some of my generalizations are quite superficial.[1]

## TO *Philip Parker*                                      CC

14 July 1936                              [Faber & Faber Ltd]

Dear Sir,

I have your letter of the 9th instant. Your assumptions about my use of classical drama and moralities are correct.[2] I admit that my reference to Christmas Day in the sermon is a statement in excess of the claims made by the Church.[3] It seemed justified for my purpose of the moment, but I am not sure now that it ought not to be modified. I am much obliged to you for finding out a printer's error on page 29.[4]

                                        Yours very truly,
                                        [T. S. Eliot]

## TO *Dean of the Faculty of Arts, Egyptian University*   CC

17 July 1936                              [Faber & Faber Ltd]

Sir,

Mr William Empson has asked me for a letter of recommendation in connexion with his application for a professorship at Cairo. As he tells me

1–Herbert Howarth, *Notes on Some Figures Behind T. S. Eliot* (Boston: Houghton Mifflin, 1964), 145, refers to Baker at Harvard. TSE wrote at the foot of the page: 'Baker, in one course, had me edit a minor play of Middleton ("Michaelmas Term") a profitless task.' (TSE Library)
2–'With regard to Murder in the Cathedral, would it be right to say that you had deliberately attempted a hybrid product by combining some elements of classical drama with the pattern of the Old English morality interlude? The introduction of the Chorus & the use of stichomythia (eg p. 42) are not I believe the common ingredients of church drama. But on the other hand, the personification of the 4 tempters owes its origin, you would probably aver, to allegorical figures like the Vices & Seven Deadly Sins of Old English drama.
'I may say that the combination did not seem to me at all an inharmonious one.'
3–'I am not sure about the reality of a remark by the Archbishop on p. 47 (in his sermon). Has it ever been preached deliberately that Christ was born on the Christmas day which the Church has chosen to celebrate that event? I am under the impression that at a very early date the Church amalgamated the pagan festival with its own commemoration, & recognised the provisional nature of the choice; & has therefore never taught that Dec. 25 was the specific day of Christ's birth, but the commemorative day. But perhaps I have overstated the fact.'
4–'Should not *pretty* privilege read *petty* privilege on p 29?'

that there is no time to lose, I am writing to you direct, instead of giving him this letter to forward.[1]

I have followed Mr Empson's career with interest ever since he left the university. I have no doubt that Mr I. A. Richards, were he in Europe at present, would speak for Mr Empson as warmly as I do. Mr Empson is a literary critic of international reputation already, whose qualifications need no other recommendation than his published works. He is also one of the most interesting younger poets. He is also a person of general likeability and charm, and has already several years experience in teaching abroad, in Japan. I believe that any university would be fortunate to secure a lecturer or professor of such distinction. His intellectual brilliance and superiority are unquestionable.

> I am, Sir,
> Your obedient servant,
> [T. S. Eliot]

Formerly Clark Lecturer at Trinity College, Cambridge, and Charles Eliot Norton Professor of Poetry in Harvard University. Editor of *The Criterion* and Director of Faber & Faber Ltd.


TO *Humphry Beevor*                                      CC

17 July 1936                         [Faber & Faber Ltd]

Dear Father Beevor,

Although I am not much better prepared for the task than when I made my first attempt, I think that it is high time I replied to your circular letter (signed with Lockhart[2] and Reckitt).[3] I will be as brief as I can, and think I had best begin with specific criticisms in connexion with the only part of the machine of which I have been myself a part.

First, *organisation*. I cannot see why the C.L.A.[4] should continue as a separate entity. For one thing there is a discouraging multiplication of subscriptions. It is bad enough to invite separate subscriptions for the

---

1–Empson had written (n.d.): 'I have just heard of an English professorship going in Cairo, which I want to apply for; the thing is decided in Cairo and the application "with testimonials" has to get there by 31st July. I should be very much obliged if you could let me have a testimonial; to be any use it must come quickly. I really am an interested and industrious lecturer, but can hardly expect you to know it; still, I feel you would be willing to put in a word for me . . . I had better ring you up and ask you what you feel about it.'

2–J. G. Lockhart: a Director of the Centenary Press, London.

3–Not traced.

4–Church Literature Association.

C.U.[1] and the C.L.A., but absurdity for us to invite people to subscribe separately to the Tract Committee and the Book Committee. I think that all subscriptions should be to the C.U. alone, and I can see no reason for maintaining the separate existence of the C.L.A. – an existence which, I believe, in spite of overlapping of membership, tends to increase a certain friction between the two committees. I can't exactly put my finger on the friction point, but I feel that it is there.

I do not feel either that we are getting the best value out of either committee. I hardly know enough about the Tract side to be qualified to criticise, but I confess that a good deal of what is put out (including 'The Fiery Cross') merely irritates me. It seems to provide a constant stream of bits of reading matter for old ladies in parishes, a good deal of *bondieuserie* for the devout, invocation of saints etc., extra-liturgical frippery, and nothing for the intelligent unconverted. The Book Committee has not done much better of recent times. This is partly due to Harris's illness, of course, and partly, I think, to a kind of discouragement that has settled upon it. But also I feel that its efforts have been rather dispersed, after producing three important and suitable books. I wish that it could concentrate rather upon united and collective pieces of scholarly theology, and perhaps even leave shorter and more topical books on controversies of the moment to be dealt with by the Tract committee. Harris's encyclopaedia was perhaps too ambitious, and could certainly only be undertaken when the organisation had been overhauled and was running well in good financial trim: but I think the ambition was of the right kind.

Certainly the financial position of the Book Committee ought to be regularised. If the profits made by successful books are to be handed over, and sums doled out in return to be expended, then the C.U. ought to finance larger works which may be expected to pay for themselves only after a number of years. The principle of the financial position of the Committee seems to me very vague.

The E.C.U. was certainly in a stagnant condition when the amalgamation took place. The A.C.C. had a great deal of energy and a remarkable talent for advertisement and staging large shows; and one expected from the amalgamation a renascence that hasn't happened. The present organisation seems a large and powerful machine that doesn't know what to do with itself, and it does not seem to exert the influence in the Church that it ought to. What does the Church Union want to do? Is it merely concerned with protecting Catholic parishes or has it any evangelising

1 – Church Union.

purpose? How much 'irregularity' of a Romanising sort is it prepared to defend? It seems to me that we are now at a point at which it is necessary, not merely to overhaul the organisation of the Union, but to plan the future of the Catholic movement for the next generation. The problem of the rural parishes is, I think, more urgent and difficult than that of the slums, and it won't be dealt with just by a flourish of birettas.

The parish priest is too busy to have time to think for himself: he needs a body of theologians behind him who will do his thinking for him. We need more discipline. We need great precision in theology. Were all the people who talked about Reservation at the Albert Hall (I only have the *Church Times* report) suitable people to present the case? Has the Church Union no responsibility with regard to the prevailing congregationalism?

I wish that the Church Union might consider itself, not merely the defender of a movement within the Anglican Church, but as the exponent of Anglicanism to the outside world. There is a generation of young people growing up outside the Church, which has imbibed from communism the desire for *order*, but which is too intelligent and disillusioned to accept the pretensions of communism, which is unwilling to surrender itself to any political gospel, still less that of fascism, which is willing to listen to the Church if it speaks with conviction and intellectual authority, which is more attracted by dogma than by ritual. The parish priest, who has adapted himself to his existing congregation, cannot appeal to these people. Who will?

Yours sincerely,<br>[T. S. Eliot]

## TO *Will Spens*[1]

CC

17 July 1936                    [Faber & Faber Ltd]

My dear Spens,

I have just returned to London after several days at Kelham and the S.C.M. Camp at Swanwick,[2] and find this morning a letter from my friend

---

1 – Will Spens (1882–1962), educator and scientist, was Master of Corpus Christi College, Cambridge, 1927–52. Early in his career he gave a course of lectures published as *Belief and Practice* (1915); he wrote on the Eucharist in *Essays Catholic and Critical by Members of the Anglican Communion*, ed. E. Gordon Selwyn (1926), and on birth control in *Theology* (1931). A member of the commission on Christian doctrine appointed by the Archbishops of Canterbury and York, 1922–38, he was knighted in 1939.
2 – Tomlin, *T. S. Eliot*, 92–3, recalled Kelham students commenting 'with a kind of awe on the ardour of devotion which Eliot was seen to display at Mass'.

Robert Sencourt, about his application for a professorship at Bucharest, which appears to be urgent.[1] So at his suggestion I am writing to you privately about him.

I don't know anything about the job in Bucharest, but I should think Sencourt would do admirably for it. He is a New Zealander, and has lived abroad a great deal, largely in Italy and France, and has what would be called a cosmopolitan mind. He gets on well with foreigners – he had three years as Professor of English in Cairo, and is very tolerant of inferior races, and gets on well with them. He is an R.C. convert. He knows everybody or nearly everybody. George Gordon will probably speak for his work as an undergraduate at Oxford (some years ago). He is very much more than competent in English literature (you will learn his official qualifications from other sources), is I believe a first-rate horseman, and of physical courage to the point of recklessness. He is regarded as an odd creature, and a snob: but I know that his kindness and generosity are boundless. I will also say what one could not very well say in a formal testimonial, that I think he is absolutely good enough, and *not too good*, for such a position. It wouldnt be a question of blocks being chopped (rather badly) with a razor; he is just the right sharpness and weight; he wouldnt despise the job and he would do it thoroughly; and he would do his best to like and to understand his pupils. I think the Roumanians would be lucky to get him.

Yours sincerely,
[T. S. Eliot]

1–Sencourt had written to TSE from Oxford on 15 July to say that conditions in Cairo had become 'very insecure', and that he was applying posthaste for a professorship in Bucharest; he asked TSE to write a private letter to Will Spens, who was chairing the appointment committee. Robert Sencourt – originally Robert Esmonde Gordon George (1890–1969): critic, historian, biographer: see Biographical Register L7.

## TO *Wyndham Lewis*[1]

17 July [1936]                    *The Criterion*

Dear Lewis,

I am sorry to hear your news.[2] I will mention you in my prayers. I am here until the 31st July, and again from the 10th August to the 22nd August, after which I expect to be in America until the first week in October. Let me know what happens and when I can see you.[3]

Yours ever,

T. S. E.


## TO *T. R. Henn*                                        cc

20 July 1936                    [Faber & Faber Ltd]

*Private & Confidential*

Dear Mr Henn:

I have been considering your letter of the 14th instant and I should like to be of help to you, but I really don't see that I can.[4] I have met both

---

1 – Wyndham Lewis (1882–1957), artist, novelist, philosopher, critic, was one of the major modernist writers; the leading artist associated with Vorticism, and editor of *BLAST*, the movement's journal, 1914–15. On Lewis's death, TSE wrote to Hugh Kenner, 27 Mar. 1957: 'Wyndham Lewis was in my opinion one of the few men of letters of my generation whom I should call, without qualification, men of genius . . . the most prominent and versatile prose-writer of my time.' TSE, 'Wyndham Lewis', *Observer*, 18 Dec. 1960: 'I not only have a very high opinion of Lewis's achievement as painter and draughtsman, but regard him as one of the most important writers of my generation . . . I had always regarded his genius with admiration, and had always found his conversation stimulating.' See further *The Letters of Wyndham Lewis*, ed. W. K. Rose (1963); Paul O'Keeffe, *Some Sort of Genius: A Life of Wyndham Lewis* (2000).

2 – Lewis wrote on 17 July: 'I entered one hospital, had a rather unpleasant experience & left it. Incompetence was rife. I have a very disagreeable patch to go through; I will let you know.'

3 – Lewis responded on 31 July, from 'Somewhere in Hospital-land': 'I was operated on last Monday, satisfactorily I think. My diverticulum is no more! I feel very fine indeed: but am of course in rather low water for the present. – You will hear from me when I leave the clinic.'

4 – Henn, Secretary of the Faculty Board of English, wrote that the Cambridge University Appointments Committee was considering two candidates for a vacant part-time University Lectureship in English, 'and they wish to invite opinions from outside the University as to the merits, relative or absolute, of these two. They understand that one or both of the candidates are known to you either personally, or through their published work or both. The names of the candidates are: Dr F. R. Leavis (Emmanuel College), and Miss G. Lloyd-Thomas (Girton College).'

Gwyneth Lloyd Thomas (1899–1978) taught at Girton College, Cambridge, 1928–52 – as lecturer, Fellow and Director of Studies – before becoming Headmistress of Channing

Dr Leavis[1] and Miss Lloyd-Thomas once on different occasions. I know absolutely nothing of Miss Lloyd-Thomas's work: I only know that I. A. Richards seemed to think well of her. I know of course a good deal more about Dr Leavis from his books and from his review, but what I know has only indirect bearing on his qualifications as a University lecturer. I cannot say truly that I really have any opinion about their respective suitability, and even if I had I think that as I know so little it would be unfair for me to make any observations.

> With many regrets,
> Yours very truly,
> [T. S. Eliot]

## TO *Michael Roberts* 

TS Keele

20 July 1936                    Faber & Faber Ltd

Dear Roberts:

I have your letter of the 14th which is very satisfactory.[2]

I imagine you can see as we do that a book of this kind can hardly be expected to sell any great numbers on publication, but we consider that a book by you on HULME ought to go on selling for a long time, and I don't think there is much risk of anyone else producing a competitive volume on the subject. What we can offer is £50 advance on a royalty of 10% up to 2,000 copies sold, and 15% thereafter. I hope that this seems to you reasonable. A little later we might discuss questions of the available material. I hope that you will be passing through London again at a moment when I am here.

> Yours ever,
> T. S. Eliot

---

School, London, 1952–64. See H. Gardner and M. G. Lloyd Thomas, *Andrew Marvell* (1940). Other publications include an anthology, *Traveller's Verse* (1946).

1–F. R. Leavis (1895–1978), literary critic; Fellow of Downing College, Cambridge, 1927–62, Reader from 1959; founding editor of *Scrutiny*, 1932–53. His works include *New Bearings in English Poetry* (1932), *The Great Tradition* (1948) and *D. H. Lawrence: Novelist* (1955). See further Ian MacKillop, *F. R. Leavis: A Life in Criticism* (1995).

2–'I had been thinking [apropos his projected book on T. E. Hulme] of 240 pages of 300 words, i.e. 72,000 words. This is quite near to your suggestion of 80,000 words, and if I undertake to do the book I see no reason why I should not aim at exactly the length you want.'

# TO *I. A. Richards*[1]

23 July 1936                    [Faber & Faber Ltd]

Dear Richards:

I was delighted to get your letter of July 2nd.[2] You must know that there is no one whose judgement of my poetry I value more highly than yours, and I am extremely happy to have your commendation of *Burnt Norton*. You are quite right about Tennyson. I had to reread Tennyson in the autumn in order to do a preface to a Nelson cheap edition, and I expanded this into an essay included in *Essays Ancient and Modern*. This book, as well as the *Collected Poems*, was sent to Magdalene College to await your return, as I was thinking that you would be back in September. But if you don't find them when you come back, you shall have other copies.

Your suggestion of my coming to Peking gives me something to think about as a fortnight overland does not seem very long, although I presume

---

1–I. A. Richards (1893–1979): theorist of literature, education and communication studies. At Cambridge University he studied history but switched to moral sciences, graduating from Magdalene College, where in 1922 he was appointed College Lecturer in English and Moral Sciences. A spell-binding lecturer, he was to the fore in the advancement of the English Tripos. His early writings – *The Foundations of Aesthetics* (with C. K. Ogden and James Wood, 1922), *The Meaning of Meaning* (also with Ogden, 1923), *Principles of Literary Criticism* (1924), *Science and Poetry* (1926), *Practical Criticism: A Study of Literary Judgment* (1929) – are foundational texts in modern literary studies. After teaching at National Tsing Hua University in Peking, 1929–30, he repaired for the remainder of his career to Harvard University, where he was made a university professor in 1944. Other works include *Mencius on the Mind* (1932), *Coleridge on Imagination* (1934), *The Philosophy of Rhetoric* (1936), and *Interpretation in Teaching* (1938). He was appointed Companion of Honour in 1963, and awarded the Emerson–Thoreau medal of the American Academy of Arts and Sciences, 1970. See *Selected Letters of I. A. Richards, CH*, ed. John Constable (1990); John Constable, 'I. A. Richards, T. S. Eliot, and the Poetry of Belief', *Essays in Criticism* (July 1990), 222–43; *I. A. Richards and his Critics*, ed. John Constable – vol. 10 of *I. A. Richards: Selected Works 1919–1938* (2001) – John Paul Russo, *I. A. Richards: His Life and Work* (1989).

2–'Up in a Temple in the Western Hills here, I found a copy of Burnt Norton. "I can only say, *there* we have been." . . . I hope you know how good it is. It gathers up so much in the earlier poems, and enriches them without being unduly helped in turn. Certainly your poetry of the past seems now to be contained in the present. I've nothing that feels worth saying about it. Only that I go on reading *Burnt Norton* with ever-increasing wonder and content.

'Jumping down to the status of a literary critic, have you or have you not been reading Tennyson?

> We move above the moving tree
> In light upon the figured leaf [*Burnt Norton* II, 10–11]

strikes my ear as a perfect poetic quotation??' (*Selected Letters*, 96–7. Constable ventures: 'R. may have been thinking of *In Memoriam* which has a similar rhythm.' See further *Poems I*, ed. Ricks and McCue, 916.)

it is expensive.[1] But I am going to spend September in New England with my family, and I must be back here by the beginning of October. In any case the journey from New York to Pekin would be too long and expensive. But I would like to think of it as a possibility the next time you are in China, which I dare say will be within a couple of years.

For myself, I am sorry that you are going to be away longer, but I look forward to seeing you both in January.

Yours ever,

[T. S. E.]

## TO *Marie Rambert*[2]                                                    CC

23 July 1936                          [Faber & Faber Ltd]

Dear Mme Rambert:

Rayner Heppenstall is distressed to learn that some remarks in his recent *Apology for Dancing*, which we published, have suggested that his attitude towards Cecchetti[3] is other than what it is. He has therefore asked me to send you the enclosed statement, both for your private interest and possibly that of your friends and pupils, if you care to circulate it.[4]

With all best wishes,

Yours sincerely,

[T. S. Eliot]

---

1–'Do think seriously of coming out here yourself in the Autumn and staying with us. It only takes a day over the fortnight to arrive via Russia, and the things and scenes there are to see. Do take three months off, or a couple. Oct. & November are perfect weather usually. Peking nowadays is empty . . . So there would be nothing you had to do except lounge in the Forbidden City and the Temple of Heaven. Do be persuaded. It must be true that you need a long holiday!'

2–Marie Rambert (1888–1982) – wife of Ashley Dukes – Polish-born ballet dancer and teacher, founded the Ballet Rambert in 1926. Made a Dame in 1962. See Rambert, *Quicksilver: Autobiography* (1972); Clement Crisp, *Ballet Rambert: 50 Years and on* (1981).

3–Enrico Cecchetti (1850–1928), Italian ballet dancer (his career included a period with the Imperial Ballet, St Petersburg) and teacher; founder of the Cecchetti method of dance training.

4–Rambert replied, 31 July: 'Thank you very much for your letter and for Mr Heppenstall's Apology for Apology. I am afraid that yet another Apology would be needed if the matter were to be put really right. The trouble is, he has involved himself into discussions on purely technical matters and every further explanation he tries to give only proves that he is out of his depth. That is a pity because he had quite a lot of interesting things to say without that.

'Would you be so kind as to send him on this, with my greetings.'

## TO *The Editor,* Dancing Times

23 July 1936                    [Faber & Faber Ltd]

Dear Sir:

Mr Rayner Heppenstall, author of *Apology for Dancing*, which we recently published, is distressed to learn that some of his remarks in that book about Cecchetti have created an impression other than that which he intended to convey. He would therefore be grateful if you were willing to insert his enclosed statement in the form of a letter.

Yours faithfully,

[T. S. Eliot]

## TO *The Guggenheim Foundation*

Undated [July 1936]              [Faber & Faber Ltd]

I have known Miss Aline Lion for some years as an occasional contributor to the *Criterion*.[1] She has struck me as a person of philosophic mind, and of wide learning in philosophic subjects, and of literature both French and English. I have always found her essays, both published and unpublished, to be of a very serious interest, and to exhibit rigorous and conscientious thinking, and I have no doubt that any lectures she gave would contain matter deserving the attention of the most serious audience.

## TO *S. C. Roberts*[2]

24 July 1936                    [Faber & Faber Ltd]

Dear Mr Roberts:

A young man whom I recently examined for a Ph.D. at Cambridge is about to approach you with a suggestion for an edition of the whole or part of a good deal of unpublished matter by and concerning Nicholas

---

1–Aline Lion, DPhil (Oxon), taught at Roedean School; author of *The Pedigree of Fascism: A Popular Essay on the Western Philosophy of Politics* (1927), which TSE discussed in 'The Literature of Fascism', C. 8 (Dec. 1928), 280–90. She wrote (n.d.): 'I am thinking of going next autumn or winter to the U.S. for a short & unimportant tour of lectures. Could you bear to give me a short reference . . . ?'

2–Sydney Castle Roberts (1887–1966), author, publisher, biographer; Secretary of Cambridge University Press, 1922–48; Master of Pembroke College, 1948–58; Vice-Chancellor, Cambridge University, 1949–51; Chairman of the British Film Institute, 1952–6. He was knighted in 1958.

Ferrar and about Little Gidding. I don't know, of course, whether the suggestion is likely to appeal to you and the Syndics, but I promised to put in a word for him. Dr Stewart of Trinity can speak with more authority than I.[1]

Yours sincerely,

[T. S. Eliot]

## TO *Aldous Huxley*                                                      CC

24 July 1936                                    [Faber & Faber Ltd]

My dear Aldous,

I have thought about your suggestion that I should sail to America by way of Marseilles, but I am afraid I cannot manage it.[2] As it is, I can only get to Boston just when I want to and I cannot afford the time to leave here any earlier. Then I have had to take a boat returning which brings me back rather later than I should like. You see even a matter of a week or so makes a great difference to the arrangements I have to make about the *Criterion*. If I were away any longer, I should have to delegate most of the preparation of the December number to somebody else and there isn't anyone obvious at present whom I could ask to do this. So I am afraid my visit will have to be at another time.

Your further observations are very interesting[3] and I am in agreement with them, but I still feel a little unhappy about the psychological mysticism at the end of your pamphlet. It does seem to me that unless one has the space to make this explicit, it may be taken very queerly by some readers.

1–Bernard Blackstone, *The Ferrar Papers* (1938).

2–Huxley had suggested that if TSE were to visit them in the south of France, he might travel on to the USA by way of the American Merchant Line or a cargo ship leaving from Marseille.

3–One or more letters are missing in this brief exchange between TSE and Huxley. Huxley wrote on 8 July: 'I quite agree with you that meditation requires a metaphysical or theological background. Even in the pamphlet, there is a faint hint at such a background; but as I had to get a great deal into thirty-two pages, there really didn't seem to be any possibility of enlarging on the subject . . . There is a very well informed and interesting book by a Catholic priest, Fr Bede Frost, called The Art of Mental Prayer – do you know it? – which summarizes the very numerous techniques of meditation evolved at different times during the last five centuries. There are also a number of distinct techniques among the Indians, Chinese and Tibetans . . . But of course, as you say, one also needs a metaphysic. A man who has a mastery over means without knowing what ends to use them for, or who knows only bad ends, may be a most dangerous character. And conversely a man who knows which are the best ends, but lacks the means to realize them, to put his good intentions into practice, isn't much use to himself or anyone else.'

I do feel that the latter part of your pamphlet shifts to quite a different plane from the first. I feel that it is a much more important plane and that therefore the brevity of that discussion leaves one unsatisfied. I feel that anything like the practice of meditation ought to be clearly founded on some purpose more profound than simply the desire to maintain what we call a state of peace.

Ever yours,
[Tom]


TO *James Joyce*                               TS National Gallery of Ireland

24 July 1936                                   Faber & Faber Ltd

My dear Joyce,

I have a letter from Léon stating that the balance left over for the typing of Part I of *Work in Progress* amounts to F. 243, for which I enclose our cheque. This I think settles the matter. The total sum actually works out at rather more than the £10 which we undertook to contribute. But I have settled the balance myself.[1]

I very much hope that you find it possible to get on with the completion of Part II.

With all best wishes,
Yours ever,
T. S. Eliot


1 – Léon had written, 12 July: 'We have just finished in time for Mrs Léon who is leaving within an hour and a half to take the MS of Parts I & III over completed.

'The balance left over for the typing of Part I amounts to Frcs. 248. [*sic*] – which please kindly send over to Mr Joyce direct.

'Mr Joyce is working now steadfastly on Part II and I hope that I am not oversanguine saying that should the same continue for some time the book could be printed and out within a year.'

FVM, who did the sum at the foot of Léon's letter, totted up the expenses as £10.15s.0d, and commented for TSE's benefit: 'this is more than £10'.

TO *Stephen Spender*

24 July 1936                    [Faber & Faber Ltd]

My dear Stephen:

I hope that this letter, which is really an answer to yours of the 24th, will reach you before you leave your Vienna address.[1] I do hope that we may count upon your play for the Spring List. I am sure that you are right, however, not to hurry it and to be quite sure about it before it is released. I cannot help, nevertheless, grudging the time that you have had to spend on the political book, and I confess that the advance announcement with Gollancz does not make me any happier. Still, I am in a position to sympathize rather than criticize, because I also know quite well that one is from time to time irresistibly urged to do something which isn't one's

1 – 'I think you will remember that I wrote to you about two months ago saying that I had done half of my play, the work on which is now interrupted as I am finishing the book [*Forward from Liberalism*] for Gollancz.

'I think the play will be finished by October, as I am going away directly I have finished this book, which will be on August 1st, for a month, in order to complete the present draft. However, as I pointed out to you, I think that perhaps it would be a mistake to try and bring it out in the Autumn.

'My reasons for thinking this are two. Firstly that if Gollancz gives this communist book a great deal of publicity, it will then compete with the play. Secondly, that I am very anxious only to publish this play after the greatest consideration. It is much the most ambitious work that I have done, and I have been working at this idea on and off for about three years. Before I publish it, I would be very grateful for your criticism, and if I feel that any suggestions you make will enable me to do a better version, I shall certainly want to write it again. (dont say that in the catalogue!)

'My own feeling is that perhaps the "psychological moment" to publish this book would be in January or February, the dead season when it is possible to publish something out of the way without its being completely drowned . . .

'You may though want to announce the book in the Autumn list, so here are particulars. It is called The Death of a Judge [published as *Trial of a Judge: A Tragedy in Five Acts*, 1938], and will be in five scenes, three acts. It is partly in verse partly in prose. The scene is derived from post-war Germany, although I avoid as far as I can making it in any way literal. The incident from which the action springs is the trial just before the Nazi revolution of the Botempa murderers, the five Brownshirts who beat and killed a Polish communist jew. In my play the judge sentences the Nazi murderers to death, and at the same time some Communists who have wounded a policeman in a street fight. After this sentence the revolution takes place and he is compelled to withdraw his sentence from the Nazi prisoners, but not of course, from the communists. The Nazis then try him and sentence him to death. He waits for the sentence with the communist prisoners who he himself condemned. The action of the play is the conflict between three different conceptions of justice, the liberal, the fascist and the communist.

'In the play, the Nazis are simply called the Blacks, and the communists the Reds, as otherwise I do not suppose it could be performed, and even now there may be difficulties. But perhaps for the catalogue all you will want to know is that it will be a full-length play and that the theme is the destruction of an idea of absolute justice.'

proper job, and that the only way to get back to one's job is to get the other thing finished and to forget about it. Anyway, I should be glad to hear, as soon as you can let me know, when the play will be ready, so that it may get into the advance Spring List. It is just as well, however, that I did write a few lines about it for the Autumn List, as by removing these I was able to make room for an announcement of MacNeice's *Agamemnon*.

I don't know anything about Mlle. Sibon.[1] I was in Paris for four days at the beginning of June and saw Sylvia Beach several times, but heard nothing about this friend of hers.

Ever affectionately,
[Tom]

---

1 – 'I think I shall spend my solitary August of writing the play in France, as a Madamoiselle Sibon who is translating some of the stories wants to discuss them with me in Paris. She is a friend of Sylvia Beach. Do you know whether she is nice, young, old, pretty, ugly, etc?'

Marcelle Sibon is perhaps best known as the translator of the novels of Graham Greene.

TO *Mary Trevelyan*[1]                                              CC

24 July 1936                              [Faber & Faber Ltd]

Dear Miss Trevelyan,

Thank you for your kind letter of the 22nd, with its enclosures which
I much enjoyed.[2] I wish that I could have heard the rendering of these

1 – Mary Trevelyan (1897–1983), Warden of Student Movement House, worked devotedly
to support the needs of overseas students in London (her institution was based at 32 Russell
Square, close to the offices of F&F; later at 103 Gower Street); founder and first governor
of International Students House, London. She was appointed OBE in 1968; CBE in 1968.
Lyndall Gordon characterises her as 'a brainy woman . . . with bracing energy . . . a mannish
woman, tall, dark, with a high-handed, even bossy manner. She dominated younger friends,
but was considered a "good pal", generous with help, kind and sensible'. Trevelyan left an
unpublished memoir of her friendship with TSE – 'The Pope of Russell Square' – whom she
long desired to marry. See obituary in *Times*, 12 Jan. 1983; Gordon, *The Imperfect Life of
T. S. Eliot*, 430–65.
    See too TSE's report on Trevelyan's submission, provisionally entitled 'Strangers and
Sojourners', 1 Aug. 1941: 'Mary Trevelyan is an extremely nice woman who runs the
Student Movement House in Gower Street. The Student Movement House is a kind of club
frequented by foreign students of all nationalities and both sexes, who are attending London
University. It is an extremely useful benevolent institution and I think Miss Trevelyan runs it
very well. This book is a kind of autobiography covering only the period during which she
has been warden of the house. It is rather scrappy and includes an account of a journey round
the world. I found her notes on individual cases of foreign students and their difficulties
extraordinarily interesting but I doubt whether the book has enough structure to justify its
publication. I may be wrong on this point and there may be many people who would like
to read about these things, and as Miss Trevelyan is rather a friend of mine I should like to
have another opinion on the book. Perhaps C. W. S. [Stewart] would be willing to look at
it. It is easy reading for anybody.'
    Trevelyan's memoir was accepted for publication, as *From the Ends of the Earth* (1942).
2 – Gordon, *Imperfect Life*, 435–6: '[Mary Trevelyan] had been asked to look after Eliot when
he came to read at the Student Christian Movement conference in Swanwick, Derbyshire.
He had arrived with a cold and a stiff neck, and read *The Waste Land* and "The Hollow
Men" in a harsh voice, with his head on one side. After he left, Mary staged a parody of this
reading – harshness and stiff neck included – and suspecting Eliot of a sense of humour, she
sent him a copy.' Trevelyan explained, 'The enclosed shocking effort, composed by Eric Fenn
& myself in a moment of Conference exhaustion, was read exceedingly cleverly by your
ghost – a young man from Cambridge – who, an ardent student of your poems & admirer of
yourself, produced a most lifelike imitation of the very delightful evening we had with you.
    'If you had been, as some of us anticipated, the aloof poet – we should not send you this
– but because you were so friendly & we so much enjoyed having you here, we send it as a
mark of affection & esteem!'
    The three parodies she enclosed included this kindly spoof of *TWL*:

> Tissington Tatlow, Canon of Canterbury,
> Had a bad cold, nevertheless
> Is known to be the wisest man in Swanwick
> With a wicked memory. Here, he said,
> Is your card, the Archbishop of Canterbury,

poems, because it would no doubt have helped me to criticize and improve my own delivery. And I should like to tell you how much I enjoyed my short visit.[1]

Yours sincerely,
[T. S. Eliot]

## TO *Cheslyn P. M. Jones* CC

25 July 1936           [Faber & Faber Ltd]

Dear Mr Jones:

I have been meaning to reply to your letter ever since you found that you were unable to come to see me, but I have been out of town intermittently.[2] I still think that a private talk would be much more satisfactory than anything I can say in a letter, and less likely to give rise to

---

(Those are pearls that were his eyes – Look!)
Here is Lady Proctor, the Lady of the Week,
The Lady of kind welcomes.
Here is the man with Gumboots, and here is the Bugle,
And here is the famous Poet, and this card,
Which is blank, is the stiffness which he carries
In his neck, which I am forbidden to see. I do not find
The Camp Manager. Fear death by water.
I see crowds of people, walking round in the Mud.
Thankyou. If you see the Musical Director
Tell her I brought my music with me
One must be *so* careful these days.

See too Humphrey Trevelyan, 'Poor Tom: Mary Trevelyan's View of T. S. Eliot', *English* 37: 160 (Spring 1989), 43, which quotes from Trevelyan's memoir of this first encounter with TSE; and Barry Spurr, 'Appendix One: The Unpublished Letters and Diary of Mary Trevelyan', in *Anglo-Catholic in Religion: T. S. Eliot and Christianity* (2010), 250–2.

1 – Trevelyan noted in her memoir that she 'received in reply a kindly and amused letter of which I was extremely proud.'

2 – Cheslyn P. M. Jones, a scholar of Winchester College and a recent convert to Catholicism, wrote on 3 June that he was proposing to read Theology at New College, Oxford, and thereafter to prepare for ordination and perhaps offer himself for service in the Society of the Sacred Mission at Kelham. However, he went on, 'I have at times been rather depressed by the attitude around me to religion in general, let alone the Catholic Faith . . . But recently I seem to have had deeper insight into the situation, and since February I have had a definite call to do something about it. I have thought of writing a short book on the spiritual life in public schools, not a devotional manual nor a theological treatise to combat the agnosticism prevalent amongst us; but a fairly simple statement of Christian belief and practice . . . The book would be designated for all of our age, but I see the special need for it in the "new men" at public schools . . . A book written by one of them while still among them might be rather useful.' At Kelham, Brother George Every had recommended Jones to write to TSE about this ambition; so had others.

misunderstandings. I am extremely interested to know of the book which you want to write. It is certainly true that after people leave their public school they may very quickly forget their attitude towards such matters while still there, and that there would be a good deal of interest in having that point of view put. At the same time, I feel that the perspective gained through the university and afterward is also valuable, and incidentally you do not want to set yourself to any piece of work which will interfere with your necessary undergraduate activities. What I should be inclined to advise, so far as it is possible to give advice to anyone whom I haven't met, is to prepare your material now while the situation is fresh in your mind, but without expecting to publish the book for some time to come. You may or may not, of course, find that you change some of your opinions later. But in any case the work that you do now will help to keep your present point of view fresh for the future.

I shall be away from the latter part of August until the beginning of October, but if you were in London at any time after that, I should be delighted to see you.

Yours sincerely,<br>[T. S. Eliot]

## TO *George Barker*[1]                    TS Texas

27 July 1936                    Faber & Faber Ltd

Dear Barker,

I have your letter of the 16th.[2] I have not yet had time to make up my mind what ought to be done about the *Essays on the Theory of Poetry*, but you know that I expressed my opinion that as your last book was a prose book my desire would be to bring out another volume of poems in the early spring, and it would seem that you will have quite enough

---

In due time Jones took orders as a Catholic priest and became a distinguished liturgical scholar (his Bampton Lectures were published in 1970 as *Christ and Christianity*). He was Principal of Chichester Theological College, 1956–69; Principal of Pusey House, 1970–81.

1 – George Barker (1913–91), poet and author: see Biographical Register.

2 – Barker wrote (10 June) that he had finished his 'theoretical' book. 'It contains four or five essays – five to be precise – and totals 27000 words. <It is now nearer 29 or 30,000.>'... [T]he last two papers, on "Politics & Poetry" and "Reality & Poetry" (although this last title sounds rather shaky) affect me as being definitely better than the first paper on Psychology. It takes me some while to get my hand in to the feeling of critical prose but I think that I have succeeded in the last two papers.' He asked on 17 June 'if you can let me have your opinion of the [essay collection] fairly soon, so that if it is necessary for me to rewrite portions of it I can do so during the next few months'.

material. That being the case the *Essays on the Theory of Poetry* does not raise a very pressing question.

I am sorry about financial difficulties.[1] There will be a payment due on account of the section of your 'Ode' which I am printing in the *Criterion*, and I will see that payment for this is made as soon as possible when we get the proof and are sure of the length.[2] That ought to go a good way toward your quarter's rent, and we will then see what is to be done next.

I am afraid I am not likely to be again in Somerset or Dorset for some time to come, but if I am anywhere near I shall certainly come to see you.

Ever yours,<br>T. S. Eliot

## TO *Donald Brace*

CC

27 July 1936                    [Faber & Faber Ltd]

My dear Brace,

I am rather tardy in writing to thank you for your thoughtfulness and generosity in sending a cheque for my royalties up to date.[3] As I am coming over to New England for the month of September this will be very useful.

I am really coming entirely for a holiday, to be with members of my family, and I don't expect even to be in Boston for more than a few days at a time. It is unlikely that I shall get even as far as New York, but if I have time to do that I shall certainly look you up.

I hope that you will be able to get over again next year.

With grateful thanks,<br>Yours faithfully,<br>[T. S. Eliot]

---

1 – Barker (16 July) asked if he might have an advance on the volume. 'I anticipate having some difficulty in raising the £9 for my quarter's rent the end of this month. But please believe me that if it is not possible to allow me any advance within the next month or so, I shall do my utmost to obtain it by earning . . . The long poem is now going along full load. I will soon be sending you the first six or seven cantos.'

2 – Barker, 'Ode to Man (Part I)', C. 16 (Oct. 1936), 33–7.

3 – Brace advised FVM, 29 June 1936: 'Under the new tax law just passed by Congress, we shall be required on and after July second to withhold from royalty payments a tax at the rate of 10%. The current rate is 4%. In connection with Eliot's royalty, it seems likely that we shall be paying in October in the neighborhood of $700, and accordingly I have decided to make an advance payment now of $750, less 4% for tax. Our check is enclosed accordingly. I expect Eliot won't mind having the money in advance and will be glad to have the saving in the tax.'

TO *D. G. Bridson*[1]                                                    CC

28 July 1936                              [*The Criterion*]

Dear Mr Bridson,

I have only just had time to read *The March of the Forty-Five*,[2] which you sent on May 26th. It seems to me an admirable piece of work, and must have been extremely effective in delivery. I wish that I had heard it, but it is some years since I have had a wireless set of my own, and I can never make up my mind whether I want to spend money on one, or keep it for something else. I don't feel that there is anything in it which could satisfactorily be published apart, but I should like to see more of your poems. It is a long time, apparently, since you have written, except for broadcasting.

I am going away on Friday for ten days, and shall be in London between the 10th and the 22nd August. After that I don't expect to be in town until October, but I hope that you will be coming up either in October or August.

                                        Yours sincerely,
                                        [T. S. Eliot]


TO *Mrs Harry B. Fine*[3]                                              CC

28 July 1936                              [Faber & Faber Ltd]

Dear Mrs Fine,

Mr Louis More, whom I saw this summer, gave me your address and suggested that I should write to you before going to America to ask whether your father would be well enough to see me. I expect to be in New England in the month of September, and am unable to stay longer than that. I shall be either in Boston or in the country or at the sea-side, and I had no intention of going to New York. I do not know whether your father was able to get to his summer home, or whether he has been forced to spend the summer in Princeton. It would of course be easier for me to

---

1 – D. G. Bridson (1910–80), dramatist and poet, was for thirty-five years one of the most creative writer–producers on BBC radio, for which he produced two authoritative series, *The Negro in America* (1964) and *America since the Bomb* (1966). Early writing figured in EP's *Active Anthology* (1933), and later books include *The Filibuster: A Study of the Political Ideas of Wyndham Lewis* (1972) and *Prospero and Ariel: The Rise and Fall of Radio* (1971).
2 – A BBC broadcast.
3 – Mrs Harry B. Fine, daughter of Paul Elmer More, lived on East Nassau Street, Princeton.

get to see him if he is in New England, but if he is in Princeton and would care to see me I could probably manage to come to New York for a night, and run down to Princeton. But it is primarily a question of whether you thought that he would be well enough to see me without getting overtired. I sail for America on the 22nd August, and after that my address will be care of my sister, Mrs A. D. Sheffield,[1] 31 Madison Street, Gray Gardens, Cambridge, Mass.

Yours sincerely,<br>
[T. S. Eliot]

## TO *G. F. Higginson*[2]                                    cc

28 July 1936                          [Faber & Faber Ltd]

Dear Mr Higginson,

I must apologise for my delay in answering your letter of the 10th instant. First, about my regular salary. I am still 'Director of Faber & Faber Ltd. and Editor of *The Criterion* Magazine', and I still receive £500 as inclusive fees and salary for this double employment, in quarterly instalments. The extra £125 that you find was Advance on Royalties (July 6th) paid on publication of *Murder in the Cathedral*.

Queried items:

| | | |
|---|---|---|
| May 16 | £1.2.8d. | I don't know. This ought to be in paying-in book. |
| 27 | £12.1.3d. | ditto          ditto |
| July 13 | £10.10.0d | This was a fee paid to me for reporting on the qualifications of a candidate for a fellowship at C.C.C. Cambridge. |
| July 29 | £3.5.0. | Hutchinson. This item should not have gone through my account at all. It belongs to a separate acct. called 'Barker Acct'. It is part of a collection gathered from various friends for the assistance of a needy poet of that name. |
| Aug. 7 | £2.8.1. | |
| Aug. 12 | £7.0.0. | I don't know. These also ought to be in the paying-in book. |

1–Ada Eliot Sheffield (1869–1943), eldest of the seven Eliot children; author of *The Social Case History*; *Case Study Possibilities*; *Social Insight in Case Situations* (New York, 1937). TSE thought her 'a very exceptional woman': the Mycroft to his Holmes.
2–G. F. Higginson, solicitor, Messrs Bird & Bird.

Perhaps I made notes on the counterfoil which would be unintelligible to anyone but myself? If they are not there at all, we must enquire from the bank. If they are there, I had better come to your office and identify them, as you have not returned the paying-in books.

The same remark applies to two of the items marked on the letter from the bank. The other two for £3.5.0d. each (Mrs Hutchinson and W. de la Mare), fall into the same category as the other item of £3.5.0d. from Mrs Hutchinson mentioned above.

Dec. 3. £25.0.10d. Mercury. This represents royalties on the performances of *Murder in the Cathedral* at the Mercury Theatre. The same explanation applies to all items marked 'Nameless Theatre Ltd'.

Feb 3d. £34.13.0d. This ought to be in paying-in book.

Feb. 19th £110.0.5d. Faber & Faber. This represents half-year's royalties on sale of books.

Feb. 27th £14.0.0d. I will ask Faber & Faber's accountant what this represents.

POSTSCRIPT. I have just found notes of the following items, which I should have entered in paying-in book.

May 16 (1935) £1.2.8d. Royalties from Hogarth Press Ltd.

May 27 £12.1.4d. Of this £8.14.0d. is Royalties from Methuen & Co. Ltd., and £3.7.3d. royalties from Harley Granville-Barker.

August 12 £7.0.0d. repayment of sum loaned to a friend.

Nov 12. 17s.6d. royalties from Gerald Howe Ltd.

Feb. 3, 1936 £34.13.0d. £31.10.0d. payment from University College, Dublin for lectures: of which £5.5.0d. was supposed to represent my expenses. £3.3.0d. is payment for a talk from the Dublin Broadcasting Station.

I observe that you also query Aug. 1st 1935, £103.12.9d. This is royalties from Faber & Faber. I may remark, in case of enquiries, that my royalties from my American publishers do not appear separately, as they are paid by Harcourt Brace & Co. to Faber & Faber, who deduct their commission and incorporate the balance with their half-yearly payments to me in February and July or August.

I think that there only remain two unidentified items, of which one can be identified for me by our accountant.

I will ask the bank about bank interest on deposit account.

Yours sincerely,

[T. S. Eliot]

TO *Dorothy Pound*[1]                                    TS Lilly

28 July 1936                          *The Criterion*

My dear Dorothy,

I am extremely sorry, for my own sake still more than for yours, as I had been looking forward to a quiet talk.[2] I don't wonder that the climate of 1936 has prostrated you, but I hope that you will not be afflicted by all the rheumatic etc. twinges with which the Evil One is allowed to torment the inhabitants of the isles. Please remember that I shall be in London from the 10th August to the 22nd August, and if you should be available within that period, lunch or dinner, tea or breakfast, will be at your disposal. I am rather shaky at the moment, because I ran into my late wife in Wigmore Street an hour ago, and had to take to my heels: only people who have been 'wanted' know the sort of life I lead. If I could afford to live anywhere but London I would. Only I mustnt have any address from which I cannot decamp quickly.

> Hoping to see you before you leave,
> Your affectionate
> TP.

TO *Theodore Spencer*[3]                      TS Harvard Archives

29 July 1936                          *The Criterion*

Dear Ted,

I am somewhat handicapped at the moment. My secretary was recently evacuated from San Sebastian by a British destroyer,[4] but only as far as St Jean de Luz; and she has gone to the Lakes for a peaceful holiday; and De la Mare's secretary, who was doing my work, has had a death in the family. So I am doing my own work, though suffering from neuritis

---

1 – Dorothy Pound, née Shakespear (1886–1973), artist and book illustrator, daughter of Yeats's mistress Olivia Shakespear, married EP in 1914. She was a good friend to TSE and VHE during their years in London.
2 – Letter not traced.
3 – Theodore Spencer (1902–48), writer, poet and critic, taught at Harvard, 1927–49; as Boylston Professor of Rhetoric and Oratory from 1946. Co-editor of *A Garland for John Donne 1631–1931* (Cambridge, Mass., 1931), to which TSE contributed 'Donne in Our Time'; and author of *Shakespeare and the Nature of Man* (1951).
4 – During the Spanish Civil War, the Nationalists in San Sebastián were besieged by anarchists, but the garrison surrendered on 27 July. The Nationalists recovered the city on 13 Sept.

as a result of going to stay at a Student Summer Camp in Derbyshire (one always pays for one's good works). Nevertheless, I am coming for September. I don't expect to have time to visit you among the nobs at Manchester. (I am too timid). The neuritis is in the left arm. But I shall be back again in Cambridge for a few days at the end of the month, and hope to see you in Oxford Street.[1] Address me after the 1st September c/o Mrs Sheffield.

Ever your
T. S. E.[2]

1 – The Spencers had moved in 1935 to a large house at 20 Oxford Street, Cambridge, Mass.
2 – It was probably at about this time that TSE began to assemble several pages of notes relating to the preparation of the *Criterion* during his six-week absence from England beginning in the third week of Aug. Headed 'Criterion for January 1937' – but in fact extending to the next two issues, Jan. and Apr. 1937 – his candid jottings include these comments and rulings:

The following letter is to be sent out to the people listed below:

'As Mr Eliot is absent from England until the middle of October, he would be glad if you would let me have the title of any book appearing early enough in the autumn season, which you would care to review for the January number of the *Criterion*. The book would have to appear early enough for you to let me have the review by ......... This letter requires no answer, but I should be obliged if you would let me know as soon as any book appears which you would be interested to review and could review by the date.'

This circular letter should be sent to:
- A – M. C. D'Arcy S.J.
- A – John Hayward
- A – Bonamy Dobrée
  - Orlo Williams        S
  - Isaiah Berlin
- A – Evelyn Underhill
- A – Revd. V. A. Demant
- A – Revd Chas. Smyth
  - W. H. Auden
  - Stephen Spender
  - A. L. Rowse
  - L. Morton        S
  - J. Middleton Murry
  - Richard Church
  - T. O. Beachcroft
  - Gwilym Price-Jones
  - T. S. Gregory
  - M. de la Bédoyère
  - Michael Roberts
  - Canon Cyril Hudson
  - H. G. Porteus
- A – Bro. George Every S.S.M.

                John Garrett
                L. C. Knights                    S
                G. Scott Moncrieff
                C. M. Bowra
        A –     Louis MacNeice
                Basil Bunting
                Frank Chapman                    S
                J. M. Reeves
                E. W. F. Tomlin
                Charles Madge
        A –     Kenneth Pickthorn
        A –     Philip Mairet

They are allowed more than one book each only when they wish several books to include in one review.

Reviewers marked *A* are to have the book they ask for without question. Others may be referred to Mr Morley.

Books approved for review by the reviewers who apply for them, can be delivered even if the quota is exceeded, as the reviews can be put into the April number.

Reviewers marked *S* are especially favoured for Shorter notices.

People not on this list, who write in for books, should be referred to Mr Morley [. . .]

LETTERS

I presume that everyone who ordinarily writes to me 'personally' will know that I am away. Therefore open all letters, including those marked 'personal'. It is possible that some of the latter may be concerned with matters personal to the authors, if not to me. If you find this, send the letters on to me if there is time, otherwise hold them (in the envelope) against my return.

In replying to general correspondents, say simply that I am out of England until the middle of October. [. . .]

TELEPHONE & OTHER ENQUIRIES

You must use your discretion whether to say that I am 'abroad', or 'in America'; and whether to say that I shall be back 'by the middle of October' or to say that I shall be back 'in the autumn'.

UNSOLICITED CONTRIBUTIONS

Deal drastically with all obviously unsuitable matter. In case of doubt, submit first to FVM and secondarily to GCF, and if opinion favourable ask to retain until my return. After January this rule may naturally be relaxed at your discretion, as most people do not bother about their manuscripts for three or four months.

It is just possible that some very good topical article might appear (or something by a bigwig) which if published at all should be published at once. This is unlikely, but in that event consult FVM and if necessary postpone something else for a quarter.

You will have to use your judgment first. The only valuable articles likely to present themselves will probably be by writers already known to the Criterion. As a rule, poetry and fiction can wait indefinitely: if suitable for the Criterion they are unlikely to find publication elsewhere.

But a really good story or sketch is so rare that when one appears every effort should be made to hold it.

I advise you to study past Criterions carefully to gain familiarity with the names of regular contributors, the kind of subjects dealt with, and the general style of treatment. It will then be comparatively easy to reject (with printed rejection slips) about 80% of the MSS sent in.

N.B. Short story or sketch still urgently required for the June number. [. . .]

REVIEWS: GENERAL REMARKS.

Among those who have carte blanche, it must be first come first served. The two great considerations governing the sending out of books, *after* the first few have been allocated for any one number, are (1) proper diversification of subject matter (2) keeping the size of the number within bounds.

As for point (1) Shakespeare is an example, and is always likely to be the chief booby-trap. We do not want to be landed with more than one long Shakespeare book in a quarter, unless there should happen to be two very important books appearing at the same time which could be reviewed together – even so, one could probably be deferred to the following number. For the rest, we must try to diversify the reviews over the various subject-matter ordinarily dealt with in the Criterion.

As for point (2) I want to try to keep the cost in future for contributions down to £100 if possible. Unfortunately, September must be a heavy number.

It is better to ignore a very important book altogether rather than have a review by an incompetent or uncertain reviewer. On the other hand, a book otherwise negligible *may* be worth while if it is an A reviewer who wants it. The ideal is such a combination that the reader will say 'I wanted an opinion of that book, and that is just the man whose opinion I wanted.'

We are, however, subject [to] the ordinary human vicissitudes, the caprices of reviewers, and the caprices of the publishing season.

UNSOLICITED BOOKS

Occasionally you may get a book in for which nobody asks, but which in your opinion is one that ought to be reviewed. ('Ought' here applies also to books by CRITERION contributors.) Refer to FVM with any suggestions for the reviewer that may occur to you.

Other books are to go in due course to Foyle's, or are perquisites for yourself and the directors. But if any really *expensive* book comes in which is not reviewed, it ought in fairness to be returned to the publishers. That is, the publishers should be invited to send round for it.

There is an enormous collection of unwanted review books. They ought not really to be sent to Foyle's until they have been published for at least six months. When you do want to get rid of them, send the whole lot for an F & F messenger down to Foyle's, asking them to value them and let us have a cheque, payable to the Criterion.

REVIEWS

I divide reviewers into several classes. The first and smallest consists of those who may have carte blanche subject to the general rules of reviewing.

M. C. D'Arcy
C. Dawson
John Hayward
Dobrée
Hamish Miles
Kenneth Pickthorn
H. Read
I. A. Richards

A. W. G. Randall
G. Tandy
A Thorold
Orlo Williams      O.W. is always likely to ask for more books than any one man
                     ought to have.

P. E. More
Roger Hinks
J B Trend

## REVIEWERS: CLASS 2.

These people are of the same grade as Class 1, on the whole, but less experienced and might
go wrong in their choice of books, which will need consideration.

H. Sykes Davies
F. McEachran      (will probably want too many, and not always the right ones).
Joseph Needham      (woolly, shd. be held down to books of definitely scientific subject
                   matter).
I. Berlin

## REVIEWERS: CLASS 3.

These are reviewers who may be given carte blanche within their special provinces, which
you know.

F. W. Bain      (Napoleon & Fr. Rev.)
C. M. Bowra      (Greek scholarship or History but I think is in Vienna).
W. Empson      (same field as I. A. Richards).
John Macmurray      Social Philosophy
Grant Watson      Psychology
W. King      Eccentrics of the 18th Century or period of Marlborough
Keith Feiling  ⎤
Kitson Clarke ⎦      both modern history
Hoffman Nickerson      (history of warfare)
Evelyn Underhill      Mysticism & religion
Fr. Demant      Economics as a reforming sociologist
S. E. Morison      (American History).

## REVIEWERS: CLASS 4.

These are similar to class 3, but inexperienced.

L. C. Knights      Shakespeare
Lymington      Agriculture
Rolf Gardiner      Agriculture

## REVIEWERS: CLASS 5.

This is the largest class, and might be extended indefinitely. It consists of the unreliable, who
are disfigured by one or more of the blemishes mentioned below. 'Inexperience' is the least
of these.

D      May choose dull books.
W      May choose wrong books. 'Wrong' means either unsuitable for the CRITERION, or
        unsuitable for that reviewer, or both.
T      May want too many books.
C      Their reviews may need censoring, from one or another point of view, including
        good taste.

TO *John Hayward*                                                    TS King's

29 July 1936                        *The Criterion*

Dear John,

As I am unlikely to see you before I leave for Wales on the 31st, let us make an appointment for some evening between the 10th and the 22nd August – almost any evening I think except the 12th when I have Miss Manwaring to dinner.[1]

I passed by your window the other night and saw you entertaining some Men – you looked like a good party of old buffers with cigars – I forebore

---

I    Inexperience

| | |
|---|---|
| Chas. Smyth | TC |
| Collingwood | D Ancient History or certain kinds of Philosophy |
| Sencourt | DWTC   (R. E. Gordon George) History |
| Auden | I N.B. Give him Porpoise Press Dunbar to review when published |
| Spender | I |
| Rowse | DWTC |
| Belgion | WTC |
| Morton | WTCI |
| J. G. Fletcher | DWT |
| Murry | W |
| Ingram | DW |
| Marianne Moore | I |
| Quennell | WT |
| Beachcroft | I |

As a general rule no one should be allowed to review a book in the same issue in which he has an article – but while Mr Eliot is away this proves rather hard to avoid with such people as I. A. Richards. But it is a very useful excuse for refusing books to someone like Montgomery Belgion who is rather a menace . . .

SHAKESPEARE REVIEWERS.
I do not propose to circularise the specialists, because that would merely be asking for trouble. They are likely enough to do the asking themselves. When an important book appears it can be offered to one of the following.

| | |
|---|---|
| J. Dover Wilson | (sound: the best man to review Robertson). |
| Robertson | (eccentric, cranky, must be cut down, or cut himself down, ruthlessly. Best man to review Dover Wilson. They may say what they liked about each other). |
| Boas | (Scholarly & dull; for books of the Hotson type). |
| Wilson Knight | (brilliant, but for speculative, rather than scholarly works). |
| L. C. Knights | (seems sound, but inexperienced). |
| G. B. Harrison | (sound, dull, best for books about social life & the underworld of letters in XVI Century). |

1 – Manwaring had written, 21 July: 'I hope that I may see you again before I leave. Perhaps . . . you can give me a luncheon or dinner time – dinner preferred – for August 10th, 11th, or 12th.'

to peer in at you but passed quickly though you were in full view. Why did I pass? Because I have become interested in the game of Darts. Now the licensee of the Bell at Hampton, Mr Widgery, (who addresses me as 'doctor' but refers to me in the third person as 'White Cargo') says that the bullseye of the dart board should be exactly 5 ft. 11 in. from the floor, and that the distance from which the darts are thrown is determined by the hypotenuse <(7 ft. long)> of a right-angled triangle which forms a line from the centre of the bullseye to the floor. Now I remembered that Darts is practised at the public at your corner, so I looked in; and I find that the bullseye is higher and the distance of throwing almost double. I wanted to consult the licensee about that, but the bar was full and he was too busy, so I must go to Gamages to get a copy of the League rules. According to the variation of distance, the stroke in throwing the dart is different. <With the longer distance, the dart is held nearer the point, and *hurled*.> It is all very perplexing. And my right arm is very tired after practising all of Sunday.

I am a bit shaky at the moment after an unpleasant meeting in Wigmore Street. But that will keep.

Yr<br>TP.

TO *Henry Eliot*                                                      TS Houghton

29 July 1936                          *The Criterion*

My dear Henry,

I have not, I think, answered your letter of the 24th June. I heard since from Alida Monro that Elsa had arrived, but as I had my hands full with one thing and another (and had Theodora and also Holmes Smith and Abigail[1] to deal with) and as Sam said in his letter that Elsa would let me know when she arrived, and I have not heard from her, I have done nothing about her. Though I liked her, and though I think her son Mather is one of the most intelligent members of the family of his generation.[2]

I learn from Ada that we are to be at Randolph from the 8th to the 15th September, and that you cannot come when we do, but that you will join

1–TSE's cousin Holmes Smith (1863–1937): husband of Rose Greenleaf Eliot (b. 1862), who had died on 14 Feb. 1936. Abigail Eliot Smith (1900–84) was their daughter, whom TSE took to lunch with the Fabers on Sunday, 24 July.
2–Another cousin, Samuel Ely Eliot (1882–1976), was husband of Elsa von Mandersheid (1880–1978); their son Mather Greenleaf Eliot was born in 1911.

us for a few days. So come as early as you can. I presume that you will be in New York until then and in Cambridge afterwards: I am counting on your being in Cambridge during the last days of the month, as I sail from Montreal on the 2nd October.

I have had a letter from the Old Colony to say that a $1,000 Bond of the Atlantic Refining Company has been repaid, and to ask what I want done about reinvestment. (They say they have sent you a copy of the letter). As I know nothing whatever about American investments, I should be very grateful if you would propose to them some suitable security, as I trust your opinion more than theirs. I shall go in to see them, especially about Income Tax.

Affectionately,
Tom

## TO *Edith Perkins* TS Beinecke

30 July 1936          *The Criterion*

Dear Mrs Perkins,

I am very grateful to you for your letter of the 21st,[1] as the cable last week left me very puzzled and anxious. Several causes seem to have contributed to Emily's illness. She has of course made rather light of health in writing to me, and as I have not an innocent faith in her reports on this subject, it is a great relief to hear from you. I had realised that she was giving herself much too generously to Mrs Hale, but at this distance I could not expostulate effectively, as she would have felt that I did not understand the circumstances. I think also that the appointment to Smith, coming when it did, simply added another burden of anxiety. I think it is most important, if I may say so, that she should be made to realise that she *can*, without extra effort, but merely by being confident and herself and welcoming the work and the pupils, make a great success at Smith: it would be good if she could get some glimmering of how much her personality can impress young girls, and how much good she can do them merely by existing in their presence. She needs to make no effort to have adoring pupils, and when they adore her they are certain to benefit.

Meanwhile, I must thank you for your hospitality, but it turns out that my sister is going away earlier than she expected, and will be back in Cambridge before I arrive: and you will understand that she will expect

1–Letter not traced.

me to stay with her. But I believe that Clement Circle is quite near, and I shall naturally, as naturally as before, be taking every advantage of your hospitality.[1]

> Gratefully,
> Affectionately yours,
> T. S. Eliot

## TO *Philip Mairet*

31 July 1936                    Faber & Faber Ltd

My dear Mairet,

First may I ask your advice? I have been asked by Hilary Pepler (I am not sure whether I know him or not) to become a vice-president of the Distributist League. I don't know whether I ought to do this or not. Personally, I am always disinclined to give my name to projects or societies, however excellent in themselves, in the conduct of which I am not taking an active part. Second I am lamentably ignorant of the present aims and activities of this League. I should be grateful for any opinions you cared to express. How far is the present policy of the League in accord with all or any schemes of monetary reform?[2]

---

1 – Gordon, *The Imperfect Life of T. S. Eliot*, 314–15: 'by 1936, Emily was back in Boston with the Perkinses . . . applying for one post after another (still handicapped by her lack of a college degree). Eventually, Emily found a position at Smith College for the fall of 1936. She was appointed Assistant Professor in the Department of Spoken English . . . But by this time Emily had broken down.

'In the spring she took refuge in a Unitarian retreat called Senexit at Putnam . . . She recalled later "the retreat from this little world of men to the great spaces of the Service". Faith began to heal her when she turned beyond the doorway at the far end of the communal room, and found the chapel . . .

'She was still too ill to write, but the Perkinses kept Eliot informed. In a state of some alarm [Eliot] booked a passage via Montreal in August.'

TSE was to arrive in Cambridge, Massachusetts, on 31 Aug. He lodged with his sister Ada Sheffield and her husband at 31 Madison Street, Gray Gardens; the Perkinses lived nearby at 5 Clement Circle, where Emily was convalescing from her breakdown.

2 – Mairet responded, 4 Aug.: 'So far as I know, the members of the Distributist League have little interest in Credit Reform . . . Various efforts have been made to bridge the differences between their policy and ours, notably by Maurice Reckitt, who, with a few others, has a foot in both camps. Frankly, I think their garb, of a jovial old-Catholic cut, would fit you a little baggily. You might like the more studiously theological members, better than I do . . . [W]hat I think is that the Distr. League without Chesterton is a flock without a shepherd, and I wouldn't like to see you take on the vice-shepherding unless they've got a good new leader. The best would be Belloc. But there again, you'd be odd partners, wouldn't you?'

I am going away tomorrow to Wales until the 10th August, so shall not answer the letter until I come back. If you are still in London on my return, might we not meet for lunch or tea?

Second, I enclose for inspection and return a short review which has been given me on your book on Orage. I have not seen your book but, of course, you will see that the reviewer's opinions are not wholly the same as mine. For one thing he seems to me quite to fail to do justice to Orage's value as a literary critic. But once I have given a book for review, I am always disinclined to suppress the review merely because it does not express opinions with which I agree. What I want to know is how far does the reviewer seem to you to misrepresent your views and your book?[1]

Yours ever,
[T. S. Eliot]

## FROM *Vivien Eliot* TO *Messrs Broad & Sons*   TS Bodleian

5 August 1936                    The Three Arts Club,
                                 19A Marylebone Road,
                                 London N.W.1

Dear Sir,[2]

In reply to yours of 4th inst., I am extremely sorry to hear of your illness, and hope very much that it is not serious, and that you have a good doctor and proper care.

Thank you for the receipt of rent. I am lingering on in London trying to get things cleared up for my friend, but as the maid at the flat had to go away for her holiday before the Bank holiday, I moved out of there and went to a hotel in London, where I still live.

1 – Mairet agreed (4 Aug.) that no review should be suppressed 'except for quite extraordinary causes'. But he did wish 'to know the writer's authority for the first statement he makes, correcting me in a matter of fact. My statement that the school was "elementary" has been passed by Edith Orage and Holbrook Jackson, whom I think authorities enough.' However, for reasons unknown, the review of Mairet's memoir of Orage did not appear: instead, TSE wrote a brief, frank statement on Orage in his 'Commentary', C. 16 (Jan. 1937), 292–3: 'at most, he succeeded in being a mouthpiece for minority thinkers of very different value. He is remarkable, not so much for intellect as for character . . . However he behaved, he had some of the essential selfishness of the saint; whatever he believed, he was seeking one faith; and his greatest deception was to have been offered a magic when he was seeking a religion . . . His distinction as a critic . . . is due not so much to intellectual subtlety or great sensitiveness as to an honesty which could not be deceived except generously and on a large scale.' See also TSE, 'Views and Reviews' – on Orage's *Selected Essays and Critical Writings* – *NEW*, 7 Nov. 1935, 71–2.
2 – This letter is couched in the guise of a 'friend' of VHE – presumably 'Daisy Miller'.

I do wish you could get Selfridge's to fetch their piano away from the flat. No, the Ibach piano was never taken away from the flat, it is still there. The idea had been for them to exchange it for a better one, possibly a Bechstein, when she moved, but when she got the opportunity for a fine instrument through The Royal Academy of Music, from the Wigmore Hall, she understood she could terminate the transaction, which she did by writing, and The Wigmore Hall told her definitely that such was the case.[1] However, she know how terribly nervous and timid she is, and how she [is] apt to lose her wits and go all to pieces, so as her friend, rather than she should have any upset, I suggest that if you cannot get Selfridge to take away their instrument, in quite a friendly and orderly manner, she had perhaps better go on paying their instalments (by cash) as long as you make sure it is for a finite period, *because that Ibach is not a piano she would call her own for anything on earth*. NOT.

No, they cannot fetch it away until Friday morning because the maid will not be there until then.

Yes, I have been very much upset and shaken by what I told you about Mr T. S. Eliot, it would un-nerve Mrs Eliot so much if she knew that I am only thankful she is out of the country.

Yours truly<br>(for Mrs T. S. Eliot)

## TO *Enid Faber*

TS Valerie Eliot

11 August 1936                         *The Criterion*

Dear Enid,

First of all, to be practical, I have arranged for your cup and the two volumes of Lupin[2] to be posted back to you, and I have told Miss O'Donovan to write to Frank to tell him to bring back my striped gown

---

1–In July 1936, VHE had agreed to purchase from the Wigmore Hall and Piano Galleries Ltd – at a cost of £5 per month – 'a good secondhand Bechstein grand pianoforte in satinwood case'. She was at this time studying piano at the Royal Academy of Music.

   See too Seymour-Jones, *Painted Shadow*, 553–4: 'By 1936 the Haigh-Wood estate was funding Vivienne's leases on 68 Clarence Gate Gardens, [a house at] 8 Edge Street, her numerous hotel bills, music lessons and doctors' bills. Although Vivienne kept careful notes on her Irish property, calculating that she was entitled to £569.3.4d in rent between 1927 and 1933, her insouciant attitude towards money was an increasing strain upon the estate.'

2–Novels featuring the gentleman thief and detective Arsène Lupin, by Maurice Leblanc (1864–1941).

and bathing garment which I apologise for leaving. I enclose my directions for making a salad, which I have never released to anyone before; but you will not be able to do much with them until I have got round to the Army and Navy Stores and ordered the materials for you.

I had a peaceful journey, as the crowd that got in at Swansea got out at Cardiff; but was very glad to have the sandwiches, nectarine and chocolate cake, which I finished, instead of having to repair to the restaurant car. I was, however, afflicted in mind, as it was with great unwillingness that I left Ty Glyn Aeron after a very happy week, and I wish that I was among you this evening instead of writing this letter. I have learned to look forward to an annual visit very eagerly, so that I am ashamed to think that I have never succeeded in expressing to you and Geoffrey my appreciation of your perfect hospitality.[1]

I am asking Jones & Evans to send a copy of Marlowe to the leading tragic actor.[2]

Ever yours,
Tom

[Enclosure]
## HOW TO PREPARE A SALAD
A good head of lettuce having been chosen, the salad-maker is to wash his/her hands with some scentless soap, rinsing thoroughly afterwards in running cool water. The lettuce should then be carefully plucked apart with the hands, placed in a collander, and rinsed for several minutes in cool running water. Each leaf should be examined and freed from slugs

---

1–TSE first visited Ty Glyn in 1933. GCF to FVM, 12 Aug. 1933: 'Tell him clothes are of no importance. Flannels (gray) & a white pair if he plays tennis & a bathing suit, if hot; anything he fancies if it's cold. Old clothes preferred. No rules or expectations! But let him be prepared for wet as well as fine, & for struggling with a gun after a rabbit through a briar-bush.'

FVM to GCF, 8 Aug. 1933: 'Tom is very worried about your sun-bathing, and I have insisted that he should take a triangle with him; and if only there are sufficient difficulties here, I shall plead to come along equipped with my false Swedish beard, which is the identical colour of Marlene Dietrich's trousers, that is to say, crimson velvet.'

GCF's diary, 4 Aug. 1936: 'T.S.E.'s observation, on being shown a small waterfall, with Ann posing beside it: "Complete with nymph, I see." Dick [GCF's eldest son] insisted on bowling this on to Ann, who of course couldn't bear it.'

FVM to Donald Brace, 24 Aug. 1936: 'You really don't know what trouble is if you have never been to Wales. The spectacle of Mr Eliot on a precipice is one which will return to me in nightmares, and I have no doubt is already a familiar nightmare to him, for I hope you will meet him soon. You must probe that anguish gently when you meet him . . .'

2–GCF's diary, 9 Aug.: 'Ann's play – Dick as the man who sold his soul to the devil for his lady's love. Interpolated a long speech from Dr Faustus. The audience much impressed, & TSE promised (& sent) Dick an edition of Marlowe.'

etc. The lettuce should then be dried by tossing briskly in a linen napkin, if possible in a current of air. Artificial methods of drying, such as blotting paper or electrical fans, are to be avoided, since the purpose is not to dessicate the lettuce but to remove surface moisture.

Salad dressing is made in a tablespoon, preferably of horn, but a silver spoon, or silver plate if well plated, will do. The best dressing consists of three tablespoonsful, therefore salad should not be made in quantity, but only so much at one time as is suitable for three tablespoonsful of dressing. If the proportion is properly struck, and the salad properly fatigued, there should be left at the bottom of the bowl something between a teaspoonful and a dessertspoonful of dressing after all the salad has been dispensed.

The choice of bowl is a serious matter. The bowl should be just large enough. It should not be too shallow or too deep, and its interior should form one curve, so that the back of the spoon can pass freely from one edge to the other. Experience is one's best guide.

The interior of the bowl should be rubbed with a piece of bread soaked in garlic juice, just before introducing the lettuce. The bread should be a cube the size of a normal sugar lump, and should be deposited at the bottom of the bowl under the salad. It forms what is called in England a *bonne bouche*. Alternatively, one may rub the bowl with a cut garlic piece.

I am assuming that this is to be a lettuce salad. There are other salads permitted, such as chicory, chives, batavia, endive, dandelions, nasturtiums. What is important is not to mix the different salads, and not to introduce foreign substances, such as hardboiled eggs and beetroot. What is fatal to a salad is tomato, as the juice of this fruit completely upsets the balance of the dressing.

We now come to the dressing. There are four ingredients, viz.: SALT, PEPPER, VINEGAR, and OLIVE OIL. I shall not attempt here to deal with the more exotic dressings, such as those which include Roquefort cheese, or lemon juice instead of vinegar. Let us take these ingredients in order.

SALT: Any table salt will do, but the best is rock-salt ground out of a salt-mill. Salt-mills are unobtainable in England, so far as I know.

PEPPER: There is no alternative here. The pepper should be ground out of a pepper-mill, from fresh peppercorns.

VINEGAR: Three kinds should be used: chili vinegar, tarragon vinegar, and malt vinegar or wine vinegar.

OLIVE OIL: I prefer French to Italian, but this is a matter of option. Anyway, you cannot tell the difference.

Now, place in the tablespoon as much salt as will cover a threepenny bit. Grind over it enough pepper completely to cover the salt with a slight margin of a couple of millimetres. Pour on

Chili Vinegar: 9 drops

Tarragon Vinegar: 12 drops

Malt Vinegar: 15 drops

Fill the spoon to the top with olive oil, so that a very little runs over.

Stir briskly for several minutes, and continue stirring while emptying the spoon onto the lettuce.

After three spoonsful have been made and poured on in this way, fatigue or tease the salad with the spoon and fork for several minutes, and again tease or fatigue the salad before each serving.

A little MUSTARD (Dijon preferred) may be added to the dressing, if well stirred up in the spoon, when the salad is to be eaten with beef in any form, but not otherwise, and is especially to be avoided if the salad is to be eaten with any kind of bird.

I should mention that the measuring of vinegar by drops is only intended for the beginner or learner. The practised salad-maker develops an instinctive psycho-physical co-ordination, which rectifies an excess of one vinegar in one spoonful by an excess of another in another. The practised salad-maker, in fact, never makes two salads exactly alike. He will not expect to succeed equally well every time, because it is a matter of inspiration, and a number of imponderable and incalculable elements enter into the preparation of any salad. But it is this uncertainty that makes the preparation of salad so exciting, and that renders the great salad so memorable. Personality plays a large part. I myself should put more vinegar into salad to be eaten with meat, than into salad to be eaten with fowl. On the other hand a definitely high bird can stand a little mustard. There is plenty of room for experiment and variation, and a good deal of latitude to taste. Salad cannot be eaten with any other vegetable except potato (not sweet potato) and should never be served at the same meal with cabbage. Curiously enough, I have never found any authoritative statement of what wine goes best with salad when served as a separate course. I incline to a moderate Burgundy, such as a Chambertin; yet strangely enough I believe that a vin d'Anjou or de Saumur is possible, or one of the rougher Swiss wines. Certainly not claret, or Rhinewine, and certainly not Champagne.

This is all I can think of at the moment.

TO *Reinhold Niebuhr*[1]

12 August 1936                    [Faber & Faber Ltd]

Dear Dr Niebuhr,

Thank you for your letter of August 9th.[2] It is indeed a disappointment to learn that you will not be able to lunch or dine with me while you are in England. I am all the more regretful because it appears unlikely that I shall be in New York at all. I am going to America entirely for a holiday, which means that I expect to be in the hills or at the sea in New England with members of my family, and I shall not be travelling through New York either way. But if I do come to New York I shall certainly hope to see you.

I should mention that I had a letter this morning from my sister Mrs Sheffield, who spoke of meeting your mother at some summer conference, and of finding her highly delightful.[3]

Yours sincerely,

[T. S. Eliot]

1–Reinhold Niebuhr (1892–1971): American theologian, ethicist, philosopher, and polemical commentator on politics and public affairs; Professor of Practical Theology at Union Theological Seminary, New York, 1928–60. From 1915 until 1928 he had worked (like his father) as a minister in the German Evangelical Synod, with socialist and pacifist sympathies; and in the 1930s he helped to develop the Fellowship of Socialist Christians and was active in the Socialist Party. From 1938, however, he rejected (as he publicly declared) 'liberal theological ideals and ideas', and became a leader of the neo-orthodox movement in theology; in 1941 co-founded the Union for Democratic Action, being active in support of American action in the Second World War, and was the group's first president (until 1947). Works include *Moral Man and Immoral Society* (1932), *The Nature and Destiny of Man* (1941–3), *The Self and the Dramas of History* (1955), and *The Structures of Nations and Empires* (1959). Awarded Presidential Medal of Freedom, 1964.

2–Niebuhr wrote from a village near Henley, Oxfordshire: 'You were good enough to suggest when I met you at the dinner with Dr Oldham that I should ring you up on my return from the continent with a view of lunching together. Unfortunately I was deflected from my course, went to Geneva for several lectures to an ecumenical seminar, flew back to London several days late and arrived late in the evening. I left immediately for this little cottage where my family had previously gone for an August holiday. I am terribly sorry that this change in plans robbed me of the opportunity of seeing you again. A luncheon with you and a chance to talk over many common concerns would have been a great privilege. If you are in New York on your American trip would you dine with us some time?'

3–Lydia (Holst) Niebuhr (1869–1961), wife of Gustav Niebuhr, German Evangelical pastor.

12 August 1936                          Faber & Faber Ltd

My dear Miss Barnes,

I am sorry that your letter has been so long unanswered, but I have been away for ten days, and am just trying to catch up with the accumulation.

I went through the two manuscripts carefully, and also consulted Morley about details.[1] He agrees with me that the shorter version is *the* more satisfactory. Not that the Doctor's conversation flags at all, but simply because I think that too much distorts the shape of the book. There is a good deal of the book besides the Doctor, and we don't want him to steal everything. I hope that you will be satisfied when you see the proof, which should be ready in a few weeks. I don't think that I have taken any unfair advantage of the liberty which you have allowed.

I will have the proof sent to 9, rue St Romain unless we meanwhile hear from you [to] the contrary. I shall be leaving for America on 22nd August, and do not expect to be back until about the 10th of October. If any question arises meantime, will you take it up with F. V. Morley, who will be here.[2] I hope to see you either in London or Paris later in the autumn.

And I hope that you have been looking after your cough, and that you had had a satisfactory offer for your flat.

Yours very sincerely,<br>T. S. Eliot

We hope to publish about Oct. 15.


TO *Geoffrey Tandy*                                        CC

12 August 1936                          [*The Criterion*]

Dear Geoffrey,

Your letter of the 2nd was actually forwarded to me in Wales, but I was too lazy there to answer it. Also, I find that using a typewriter still sets my

---

1 – Barnes had left London for Paris, where she was endeavouring to sell her apartment. She wrote on 24 July to ask TSE which of the two manuscripts of *Nightwood* he was 'in favour of. My Doctor of the book is frankly broken hearted because I left out one story about an old lady – I left it out because I thought it a bit on the sentimental line – but I'll send it to you as soon as I can find it among my papers – & if you do not like it either – he will just have to face it.'

2 – Plumb relates (xxiii) that 'according to Barnes's account of Kay Boyle's report, "[Morley] is *positive* he'll go to jail for my book and said he was "proud" to!!' (13 July 1936).'

arm to aching, and as I can't write with a pen anyway I was rather incapacitated.

No objection whatever to the B.B.C. Chronicler of the *Criterion* improving the elocution of the B.B.C.[1] On the contrary I am delighted that you have got hold of this. I have implicit confidence in your not making use of the columns of the *Criterion* to extol the interpretations of poetry and prose by Mr Tandy. The only advice I have to give is to make the B.B.C. pay more than they offer. You may be sure, whatever they offer you, that it is not as much as your work will be worth.

Now about your friend Mr Cox, who is an authority on public house life. I should be delighted to dine with you on the evening of August 19th, and possibly share in the advantages of Mr Cox's knowledge, but I am afraid there is no chance of our wanting to do a book. I showed your letter to Faber and Morley and they share my opinion that this is the sort of book that is very pleasant to do, and that gives a good deal of pleasure to a small number of people: but it would not have enough sale to cover the cost of doing it. The people who want to learn about public house life and public house games will go and acquire their knowledge at first hand, and won't buy a book on the subject.

Anyway, I assume that you will be back at the beginning of the week, and I will keep Wednesday evening open. Please give me a blow on the telephone to announce your return.

With love to the family,

Yours,

[Tom]

## TO *The Editor*, The Times

13 August 1936

Mr T. S. Eliot writes:–[2]

Having been away for a week in the country and inattentive to newspapers, I have only just learned of the death of Dr Charles Harris.

1 – Tandy had been auditioned as a possible reader for the BBC; and the official involved, Ian Cox, had disclosed that he had been gathering information about English public houses and the games played in them. Tandy wondered if there was a book in the subject, and invited TSE to meet Cox (possibly in the evening of 18 Aug.). In addition Tandy had suggested a reading of poems by TSE – 'I think I left the young man in such a highly malleable condition that you may be approached again' – and hoped there would be no conflict of interest in the event that he did such a reading, since he was the radio reviewer for the *Criterion*.
2 – Published as 'Dr Charles Harris', *Times*, 13 Aug. 1936, 12; see further *CProse* 5, 392–3. The *Times* obituary of Harris had appeared on 6 Aug.

Possibly you would care to print the following paragraph by one who was associated with Dr Harris for several years past in the schemes that he had most at heart:–

The death of Charles Harris removes the most powerful force in the publication of theological literature in the Church of England. I say 'publication', because in spite of his considerable learning, his wide interests, and his fertility of ideas, Harris always put his own writing second to his great enthusiasm, which was the work of the Book Committee of the Church Union. Of his work in Convocation, to which he gave equal attention so long as health permitted, I cannot speak with such intimate knowledge.[1] But I have always thought that if he had been a layman, and if he had chosen such a profession, he might have become the most successful publisher in London: he would either have made or lost a fortune. He was, however, indifferent to money and celebrity. His aims were on a grand scale, and sometimes gave pause to the more cautious: some of his most ambitious remain unrealized. But one believed that if anyone could realize them, it was he. Enthusiasm sometimes made him a little tactless, but few men have had a greater power of communicating their enthusiasm. During his last years he lived in continuous discomfort between periods of acute physical suffering, but at all times, even just before or after a serious operation, his cheerfulness, serenity, and zeal were undiminished. He was sometimes misjudged by those who knew him only superficially; but no one could know him at all well without regarding him with great affection and admiration.

1–Elsewhere, TSE wrote this memorandum on Harris's book on Convocation: 'I have glanced at some sections of this book and read two . . . I am bound to say after considering these sections that I think that they need so much recasting – amounting in parts to alterations so extensive that I doubt if Dr Harris were he alive would ever have been brought to agree to them – that I should certainly not be willing myself to take any responsibility for advising the publication of the book. I confess that I write this with great reluctance, but I believe some of Dr Harris' main arguments to be misconceived and his learning misapplied in supporting them. And I am bound to add that that learning at any rate in some of the directions where I am at all qualified to form an opinion is not up to date, and has not been for thirty years or more. I find it difficult to conceive how any student could nowadays take the view that he does of the Decretum [*Decretum Gratiani*: the 12th-century text of canon law compiled by the jurist Gratian], and his account of the proceeding whether as to origin, mode or effect in regard to the Templars seems to me to rest on the kind of misunderstanding which happens to people who approach legal subjects without knowledge of legal practice and with preconceived notions of legal theory . . .
'As it stands the book seems to me rather a tragedy.'

TO *Louis MacNeice*                                                    CC

13 August 1936                        [Faber & Faber Ltd]

Dear MacNeice,

I have been away for ten days and am somewhat in arrears. You yourselves are, I imagine, in Ireland, and as I am leaving for America at the end of next week I shall not see you until the middle of October, when you will be installed in London.

We are anxious to do your *Agamemnon*, although we feel that it is unlikely to command anything like the same sale as your original works. For this reason we propose, instead of the former 10 per cent from the start, to offer a higher royalty after the sale of enough copies to cover our own outlay. We offer then 15 per cent royalty after the sale of 500 copies, which first 500 copies will draw no royalty at all. I hope that you will find this satisfactory. The demand for translations, even by poets in whom the public is interested, is very meagre. I made one attempt of that kind myself with *Anabase*. I don't think that the book paid for itself, but we hope that the *Agamemnon*, after a moderate first sale, will revive later under the stimulus of your own reputation.[1]

                              Yours very sincerely,
                              [T. S. Eliot]


TO *George Barker*                                              TS Texas

13 August 1936                        *The Criterion*

Dear Barker,

I am sending you herewith our cheque for £5 5s. in payment for the section of the *Ode to Man* which will appear in the October number. It is possible, also, that there may be some balance in the subscription account payable at the Michaelmas quarter. <Yes, £9.>

I am extremely sorry to hear of your difficulties, and the exceptional expenses that you have had.[2] I cannot think at the moment of anything

---

1–LM agreed on 24 Aug. to the terms proposed.
2–Barker wrote on 11 Aug.: 'The position . . . is fairly desperate with us now. I learned from the bank this morning that I owe them four pounds. The reason why this state has come about is principally because we have had my wife's younger sister living with us for several months until lately – she was ordered into the country by the West London Hospital where she spent the winter and spring under examination for suspected consumption. I have also had to pay the Ophthalmic Hospital for the eye operation on my brother. This is apart from one or two other things – my dog mauled a sheep and it died and this cost £5.

radical to be done, but you know that I was very much interested and pleased by what you showed me of your long poem, and I wish to give you every encouragement to pursue it to the end, and in any case, even if you get a clerical or other job in London remember that it need not prevent you from writing. I had eight years in the City myself.

I am sailing for America next week, and shall be away until the middle of October. If there was anything you wanted to write me about my office would forward any letter to me, and meanwhile if you were in town and wanted to consult anyone here you had better ask for Mr F. V. Morley. I shall hope to see you and discuss the future soon after my return.

Yours ever,

T. S. Eliot


TO *William Saroyan*                                                        CC

14 August 1936                    [Faber & Faber Ltd]

Dear Saroyan,

I have your letter of July 21st, and hope that your confidence in my choice of stories will be justified.[1] As I said, I have tried to represent your wishes as far as possible.

I have spoken to Mr de la Mare about the dust jacket, and he agrees that Barnett Freedman would be a very suitable person. He tells me however that Freedman is a very busy man, and may not be able to accept. So if we have a dust jacket designed by someone else you will understand the reason. I will have you informed of the publication date when it is settled, and pass on your letter to the proper quarter for dealing with the complimentary copies which you wish sent at your expense. I shall be in America during the month of September, so that I shall not be able to

---

'I feel so disheartened also – I had hoped, a year or eighteen months back, that by this time my finances would have improved so as to leave me free to work hard at writing and reading. I cannot think what to do. I suspect that if the long poem on which I am working now were to collapse, I should try for a clerkship or something in London and see that I abstained from writing.'

1–'I know I shall be satisfied with your choice of stories to include (and exclude) in (and from) the London edition of my book. I am not unaware of the defects of the New York edition . . .

'I forgot to say . . . that I would like to have something of mine published in your magazine, The Criterion . . .

'You speak of an advance of £25; I presume that this sum, by check, will be sent to Random House; that is fine, only it means I won't get a nickel of it, because I am in debt to Random House; but my debt will be fairly reduced.'

handle any of this business myself. I am afraid that I shall not have time to get any further West than New England.

I have also passed on the figures which you enclosed.

I shall be glad to publish at some time something of yours in the *Criterion*, provided that it was previously unpublished elsewhere. If you could send me at some time half a dozen stories and sketches to choose from that would be helpful.

I am afraid that the advance did have to go to Random House. I am sorry to learn that it can't reach your own pocket.

With best regards,
Yours sincerely,
[T. S. Eliot]

## TO *George Barnes* 

TS BBC

14 August 1936                    *The Criterion*

Dear Barnes,

I must apologize for not having answered your first letter of the 30th July, but I was away in Wales for a week, and could do nothing about it.[1] You will presumably not get my reply until you return on September 7th.

I am sailing next week, and could do nothing in any case until the middle of October. I don't see any reason in principle why I should not select Vaughan, Herbert and Crashaw for you, if that is not too late, provided the fee was adequate to recompense the labour of going through the work of these poets and selecting poems which could be fitted into a fifteen minute reading. The difficulty of suiting the poems to the time is the greatest, because another reader might read one or another poem,

---

1–Barnes, 30 July: 'I am sending you a brief account of the scheme for afternoon poetry readings which we have prepared for the autumn and winter. We are inviting several poets and critics to undertake the selections and write the commentaries. I am writing to ask if you would like to make a selection from Dryden or 17th century lyrics for this particular purpose . . .

'If your voice test is satisfactory perhaps you would like to undertake the reading yourself.'

The briefing document explained that the object of the series was to answer the question: 'Why should I read the poems of X? . . . The poetry should be read without comment, but it is probably easier to catch the attention of the listener by introducing it with a short commentary.'

[A few days later] 'My letter to you of 30th July, asking you to contribute to our series of poetry readings in the Autumn and Winter requires a little modification.

'The poets which I can offer you (!) are Dryden and/or Vaughan, Herbert, Crashaw; the selection from the last three would make a single reading.'

or all the poems, more quickly or more slowly than I should read them myself. I know from experience that a considerable variation in the matter of time is possible. The B.B.C. people ought to know by now what my voice is like, and I have been given to understand that they do not like it. In any case I am not going to undergo another voice test.[1]

With best wishes, even if they will reach you retrospectively, for your holiday.

Yours sincerely,
[T. S. Eliot]


TO *Donagh MacDonagh*                    TS Kresge Library

14 August 1936                    *The Criterion*

Dear MacDonagh,

Thank you for your letter of August 5th.[2] I return herewith your volume of poems with apologies for the delay. I ought to have known better than to think that I should have time to give you any detailed criticism of them, but the temptation is always strong when one is at all interested. My general impression is that they do not produce as powerful an effect collectively as many of them do singly. Stretches of the book give an impression of monotony of mood and imagery. What I really think is necessary is to wait until you have accumulated a larger stock to choose from before producing a book. If they were all up to the level of the poem which I published in the *Criterion* I should have only praise.[3]

Besides the two Auden books there will be this autumn a translation of the *Agamemnon* by Louis MacNeice which I think would interest you.

1 – Ian Cox sent this memo (19 Aug.): 'Last night I had some conversation with Mr Eliot. We met on another matter, and I could not with decency introduce directly the subject of his arranging Vaughan, Crashaw and Herbert for the series of poetry readings, but I learnt that he would do it, and was able to say how glad we were to hear this from his letter. Also I gathered that he felt the selection of poems would be a labour; that he appreciated the fact that he had not been asked to read them himself, and he made it clear that he considered the selection of a reader of them very important. (Most actors reading poetry are anathema to him). He expressed a feeling that Mr Geoffrey Tandy, who was with us at the time, would fulfil his requirements as a reader and I rather gathered that he could think of no one else who could do it as well.' (BBC)
2 – MacDonagh was grateful to see his poem in print in C., and he asked for the return of the collection of poems he had originally submitted for consideration.
3 – MacDonagh, 'A Prologue to "Iphigeneia in Aulis"', C. 15 (July 1936), 623–6.

I have no defence to offer for Babette Deutsch. I was not much interested in her book myself.[1]

Your foot-note puzzles me.[2] I shall certainly say nothing to Neil [*sc.* Niall] Montgomery, but why his father should be afraid that I should think he was a Jew, and why he should think that that would make any difference to me anyway, is a complete mystery. Furthermore, I can't remember having had any article on Joyce signed by a Greek pseudonym.

Yours ever,<br>T. S. Eliot

TO *Peter Burra*[3]                                          TS Valerie Eliot

14 August 1936                    *The Criterion*

Dear Mr Burra,

I have read with much interest, though I must admit in considerable darkness through not having read the works referred to, your essay on Forest [*sc.* Forrest] Reid.[4] I don't feel that it is suitable for the *Criterion* as it is considerably too long, and secondly because I don't feel that Forrest Reid is quite a *Criterion* author. I may be mistaken, because I read very little fiction, but your essay does not lead me to any other opinion. I feel, however, that in the *Criterion* there is only space to deal with individual novelists as the subjects of full length essays when the novelist is in some way representative of an important point of view or tendency of contemporary thought and feeling.

---

1 – MacDonagh had written: 'I am looking forward to Auden's "Look, Stranger" and his Poems though the only two Faber books I saw lately I did not much enjoy – Babette Deutsch explaining [*This Modern Poetry* (1935)] and Walter de la Mare sentimentalizing . . . I am also looking forward to your children's (if children's) verses.'

2 – 'P.S. Niall Montgomery whom you may remember meeting sent you an article on Joyce, under a Greek pseudonym. Do not let him know you know however – his father was afraid you would think he was a jew boy. This is all deadly secrecy.' Niall Montgomery (1915–87), distinguished architect, poet and playwright – friend of Samuel Beckett; Irish authority on the work of James Joyce – was a friend of MacDonagh at University College Dublin; his father James Montgomery was the Irish Free State's first film censor. See Christine O'Neill, 'Niall Montgomery: An Early Irish Champion of Joyce', *James Joyce Journal* 1 (2008), 1–16.

3 – Peter Burra (1909–37): critic and essayist; friend of Benjamin Britten and Peter Pears; author of *The Novels of E. M. Forster* (1934), *Van Gogh* (1934), and *Wordsworth* (1936).

4 – Essay and covering letter not traced. Forrest Reid (1875–1947), celebrated Irish novelist, critic and translator. His novel *Young Tom* won the James Tait Black Memorial Prize, 1944.

I shall be glad to see more of your work, and hope also that you will from time to time suggest books that you would like to review.

Yours sincerely,
T. S. Eliot

## TO *Bruce Richmond* CC

17 August 1936 [Faber & Faber Ltd]

My dear Richmond,

I am giving a brief line of introduction to a young man named Basil Bunting.[1] This is to tell you something about him first in the hope that you will let him see you. He has just returned to London after some years abroad and as he has been living for several years past at Tenerife he has acquired the appearance of the most ferocious Spanish bandit, but behind his terrifying exterior there beats a mild Quaker heart. Also he is neither a fascist nor a communist, nor has he any political axe to grind. His special subject is Persian Literature, especially of the classical period. He tells me that he does not regard himself as an authority on contemporary Persia, and has never lived there. He lived in Italy for several years, and thinks that he knows Italian very much better than Spanish, though he knows

1 – Basil Bunting (1900–85), Northumberland-born poet, lived in Paris in the early 1920s, working for Ford Madox Ford at the *Transatlantic Review*. From 1923 he was mentored by EP, whom he followed to Rapallo; and it was through EP that he became acquainted with JJ, Zukofsky and WBY. EP published his work in *Active Anthology* (1933); but his enduring fame came about after WW2 with the publication of *Briggflatts* (1966). TSE wrote of him to J. R. Ackerley, 17 Aug. 1936: 'He is a good poet and an intelligent man'; and provided a reference for the John Simon Guggenheim Memorial Foundation, 30 Dec. 1938 (letter to Henry Allen Moe, below). See Bunting, 'Mr T. S. Eliot', *New English Weekly*, 8 Sept. 1932, 499–500; *The Poems of Basil Bunting*, ed. Don Share (2016); R. Caddel and A. Flowers, *Basil Bunting: A Northern Life* (1997); Richard Burton, *A Strong Song Tows Us: The Life of Basil Bunting* (2013). Bunting had been for tea at 24 Russell Square on 13 Aug.

Richard Price, 'Basil Bunting and the Problem of Patronage', in *The Star You Steer By: Basil Bunting and British Modernism*, ed. James McGonigal and Richard Price (Amsterdam & Atlanta, 2000), p. 101: 'According to John Seed . . . Eliot rejected a Bunting collection both in 1935 . . . and in 1950. Victoria Forde also notes what appears to be a further rejection in 1951.

'As Seed also shows, this was hardly surprising. Bunting had openly criticized Eliot's journal *The Criterion* as "an international disaster", and had described all his poetry after *The Waste Land* as "notoriously harmless, [and] supine", adding that "the ruling powers can encourage its circulation without uneasiness".' See John Seed, 'Poetry and Politics in the 1930s: Basil Bunting's Other History', in *Sharp Study and Long Toil*, ed. Richard Caddel (Durham, 1995), 101. Victoria Forde, *The Poetry of Basil Bunting* (Newcastle upon Tyne, 1991), 52.

both better than I am able to judge. He has done some reviewing for me, and is also a very competent poet. On the whole a very good workman. I think it would be worth while trying him if there is any opportunity.

Yours ever,

[T.S.E.]

## TO *Emily Lina Mirrlees*[1]                                    CC

17 August 1936                    [Faber & Faber Ltd]

Dear Mrs Mirrlees,

I am delighted to hear that you are at last established in the country, and I hope that the house you have found is one which satisfies your most exacting demands, both inside and out.[2] I should be delighted to accept your hospitality, and to see you and Hope again after such a long time, but I am afraid it can't be until after the middle of October. I am sailing for America next week, and expect to start my return voyage at the beginning of October. I do hope that you will ask me again after my return.

With best wishes to Hope and yourself,

Yours very sincerely,

[T. S. Eliot]

## TO *Messrs George Allen & Unwin*                    CC

17 August 1936                    [*The Criterion*]

Dear Sirs,

I have your letter PSU/VL of the 13th instant.[3] While I have kept no record of the proportion of your books that have been selected for review

1 – Emily Lisa Mirrlees, née Moncrieff (1862–1948) – 'Mappie/Mappy' – daughter of a family of lawyers, was born in Edinburgh and married in 1886 a Glasgow tycoon, William Julius Mirrlees (1863–1923). Their daughter was TSE's friend Hope Mirrlees, author of *Paris: a poem* (1919) and *Lud-in-the-Mist* (1926). Through much of WW2, TSE was to retreat from the Blitz by spending long weekends at Shamley Wood, Shamley Green, near Guildford, Surrey, home of Mappy and Hope, of whom he became deeply fond. TSE to Philip Mairet, 21 Feb. 1941: 'My hostess here [at Shamley] . . . is a very intelligent, though not intellectual, Scotch lady – but distinctly high in brains as well as character.'

2 – Mrs Mirrlees wrote on 13 Aug. to say they were getting established at Shamley Wood.

3 – 'On looking through our record of reviews for the past twelve months we are somewhat surprised to find that out of 61 books sent to you in that period only 2 appear to have been reviewed. We fully realise of course that you cannot be expected to review every book which we send to you, but this record does reveal a very much smaller proportion of notices than your generous treatment in the past has taught us to expect!'

in the *Criterion*, I am very well aware that you have indeed sent a great many books which I have not had the pleasure of having reviewed. The reason is sometimes, of course, that I cannot at the right moment get the right man to review a book which fully deserves notice. This difficulty often arises with a quarterly in as much as when there are only a small number of people available who are qualified to review a particular book I often find that they have reviewed that book in some periodical appearing at more frequent intervals, and when I can avoid it I do not like to have a reviewer treat in the *Criterion* any book which he has reviewed elsewhere. Sometimes, also, a book otherwise suitable is ignored simply because the proportion of books published which can be reviewed in a periodical like the *Criterion* is very small, and becomes smaller as the annual output of books in this country increases. Furthermore, there may be a certain element of apparent capriciousness in the choice of books reviewed in the *Criterion* for the reason that I like as far as possible my trusted reviewers to select their own books for review, as I feel that in this way they do their best work. It therefore happens that a very high proportion of the books actually reviewed in the *Criterion* are books which I have ordered from the publishers at the request of particular reviewers and not books which have been sent in.

It would really be more satisfactory to both yourselves and to us if you could give me notice of your books as they appear. I will then ask you to send me such books as I think suitable for the *Criterion*, but I should not ordinarily ask for a book unless I had some particular reviewer in view. My experience has been – I have less reason to complain of yourselves than of some other publishing houses – that very frequently books are sent in for review which are of no particular interest to the *Criterion*, whereas other much more suitable volumes published by the same houses are not received. In other words I should prefer to trust my own judgement and that of our reviewers rather than trust the judgement of the publicity departments.

Alternatively, I could send you a marked copy of your catalogue [but] this might give you more trouble than notifying me as books appear.

---

'It would be very helpful to us if you could say whether you find that we are sending a large proportion of books which you do not consider would be of very great interest to your readers . . . We cannot help feeling that some change may have to be made in the selection and number of books which we send out to you, but we should naturally welcome some expression of your views on the matter.'

I would point out also that it is not desirable to send fiction as we do not ordinarily review novels except in a half-yearly chronicle, which selects only a half dozen or so.

I trust that we may come to some arrangement which will be mutually satisfactory, in as much as those of your books which I do have reviewed in the *Criterion* are books which I very much want.

Yours faithfully.

[T. S. Eliot]

## TO *Edward P. Gough* CC

19 August 1936 [Faber & Faber Ltd]

Dear Father Gough,

I am leaving for America at the end of this week to be absent until the middle of October, and in trying to clear up a good many loose ends, represented both among my papers and in my memory, it occurred to me that you might still have in mind the prospect of a play from me for a future festival.[1] I therefore want to report to you the present situation, so that you may not be deceived or disappointed. Several odd jobs, including the preparation of a volume of essays and my *Collected Poems*, prevented me from beginning work on a play during this past year. I hope to set to work as soon after my return as I can arrange to be able to devote my morning steadily to writing, but the subject is still very vague in my mind, and I do not know what form it will eventually find or how long the work will take. When we discussed the matter over a year ago I was more sanguine about the matter of my plans for the immediate future, and certainly expected to be much further ahead than I am. I think I did say at the time that I did not know whether the play would turn out to be anything suitable for you; that for my next piece of work I did not want to work either to order or to time; but if I did finish a play and if it happened to be suitable I should be very glad to have it applied to such a noble purpose as the Tewkesbury Festival, provided that it could be successful[ly] produced. I still hope, but you will understand that it would be unsafe to depend upon me. I have no particular reason for supposing that you do, but at the same time I feel impelled to let you know how matters stand.

---

1 – EMB alerted TSE, 12 Aug.: 'I met Fr. Gough of Tewkesbury at Malvern, who said you had promised him a new play for a 1937 Festival. He seems to be most definitely expecting it!'

Please remember me kindly to Mrs Gough, and believe me,

Yours very sincerely,

[T. S. Eliot]

## TO *Fred Rea*[1]

CC

19 August 1936                     [Faber & Faber Ltd]

Dear Mr Rea,

I have been considering your kind letter of August 3rd.[2] I still find your invitation quite welcome in principle, and I still feel doubtful about undertaking any engagements so far ahead. If it is not asking you to postpone your selection too long, I should prefer to make my final decision at the beginning of next year.

Meanwhile I should be interested to know what types of student one might expect at such a conference, taking place in Ireland. Would you, for instance, have any Roman Catholics present, or would they all be members of other communions? There is a difficulty about the subject 'Literature and Religion' which you propose, which I might as well mention frankly. I know quite well that the question of the official censorship is one which aroused a good deal of feeling in your country. It would be difficult to talk about the subject which you propose without touching on the question of censorship at least in a very general form, or alternatively appearing to evade it. My own sympathies are certainly with the liberal minded, and I do feel that in Ireland clericalism is something of a menace. I don't want to appear either to avoid the subject, or on the other hand to meddle in the domestic affairs of another country. I shall be interested to learn your views on the matter.[3]

Yours sincerely,

[T. S. Eliot]

---

1–Fred Rea (d. 1984), Irish Baptist missionary, was to join the Irish mission in Southern Rhodesia/Zimbabwe, 1937–84; awarded Hon. Doctor of Laws by the Univ. of Zimbabwe for 'his outstanding contribution to the community'. See further Kathleen Rea, *The best is yet to be: fifty years in Zimbabwe with Fred and Kathleen Rea* (? 1992).

2–Rea, as Secretary of the Student Christian Movement, invited TSE to the first Summer Conference of the SCM in Ireland, 3–9 Aug. 1937 – in particular to take part in a special course of meetings on 'Literature and Religion'. They were hoping to have about 200 students present.

3–Rea responded, 15 Sept.: 'I fear that, with one or two possible exceptions, all will be Protestants. At present there is very little inter-mingling in Ireland. Protestantism is very roughly divided into a Presbyterian North and an Episcopalian South . . .

## TO *Polly Tandy*

TS BL

19 August 1936                    *The Criterion*

Dear Pollytandy 'm:

*Private & Confidential.*

This is to inform you, as I take it to be my beholden duty, that I have been hearing ill reports about the behaviour of my goddaughter. The consequences is as may be: for No one can say as I have not an open & umpartial Mind. But if so, So: there will be trouble when I return and look into Matters. And if not so, So: there will be trouble Also. I may be relied upon to set everyone by the Ears. But one thing I would say and I will say it, for the saying Is: speak the truth & shame the Devill:[1] that if your husband had less affexion for malted liquour he wd. hear Less gossip, & wd. be less inclined to believe all he hears. I wd. Speak Evill of No One:[2] but there are those who have spread ill rumiours afore now. The mind mellowed by malted liquour is softened & inclined to credulity; and there be those that wd. profit by mischief. So I shall close by asking you to pay my proper respects to Mr Widgery, of whom I wd. wish to believe all that one might believe of a fellow Christian. He who subscribes kisses your hand sadly & soberly, & asks you to remember in your prayers

Yr. devoted & obedient
T.possum.

## TO *Kenneth Mackenzie*[3]

TS BL

19 August 1936                    [Faber & Faber Ltd]

My dear Lord Bishop,

I am writing on the assumption that you will be calling a meeting of the Book Committee this autumn. As no doubt you realized at the time

---

'As regards the question of making reference to censorship, I think you need have no fear whatever about making any judgments you choose concerning it. We are still a free country when it comes to expressing our minds about existing laws.

'Strangely enough, the censorship has not been a "live" issue for a long time. Nobody ever seems to bother much about it – except of course in so far as its real aim is to suppress birth control, and there the dilemma is felt by the medical profession.'

1 – *Henry IV, Pt I*: iii. i. 54–5: Hotspur speaks: 'And I can teach thee, coz. To shame the devil / By telling truth; tell truth and shame the devil.'

2 – *Titus* 3: 2–4: 'To speak evil of no man, to be no brawlers, but gentle, shewing all meekness unto all men.'

3 – Kenneth Mackenzie (1876–1966): Bishop of Brechin from 1935.

when I wrote to you about undertaking the Deputy Chairmanship of the Committee, some of us believed that Charles Harris had not very long to live, and in any case would never be able to be fully active again; and I am sure that the Committee will wish to take the first opportunity of electing you as his successor.[1] I therefore wish to let you know that I am leaving for America on Saturday, and do not expect to be back until about the 12th of October, so that if you think fit to call a meeting before that date someone else will have to take the minutes.

As for my own position, I was re-elected Secretary only until the end of the year, and while I am quite willing to continue beyond then if the Committee wishes, I should be equally willing to retire in favour of a young man with more time to give.

> I am, my Lord Bishop,
> Your obedient servant,
> [T. S. Eliot]

## TO *Jeanette McPherrin*[2]    TS Denison Library

20 August 1936    *The Criterion*

Dear Jeanie,

As I am sailing for Montreal on Saturday, I am trying desperately at the last moment to clear my conscience, as far as may be done, by tidying up arrears before entrusting myself to the sea. One thing that has been on my mind, and given me an average of three or four twinges a week for some months past – I don't want to count how many – is your Balzac. Well, I have read a good deal of it. The translation seems to me very good; such faults as it has seem to me due to a usual cause among inexperienced translators: lack of self-confidence. I mean, that there are places where you might have made better English by taking greater liberties with the text. It's erring

---

1 – Mackenzie (author of *The Case for Episcopacy*) was elected to act as chairman of the Book Committee, in succession to Dr Harris, at a meeting held at Pusey House on 22 Oct.
2 – Jeanette McPherrin (1911–92) studied at Scripps College and Claremont College, California, at Harvard University, and at the École Normale Supérieure de Sèvres. She taught French at Reed School, Portland, Oregon, and at Kent School, Denver, Colorado (her home town), and went on to become Director of Admission at Scripps, 1939–43. Following war service in the Women's Reserve of the US Navy, she worked at Wellesley College, Wellesley, Massachusetts. where she was a Lecturer in French from 1948 until retirement in 1975.
   At Scripps College, McPherrin had been befriended by EH, who asked her uncle and aunt, the Perkinses, to extend their hospitality to her in Chipping Campden in Aug.–Sept. 1934: while there, McPherrin was introduced to TSE and became his confidante.

on the right side, of course; and the fault is only overcome by practice. Now, as for the publication, that is less favourable. It is a sort of book which would stand more chance with a New York publisher than with London. There are more people in America who read French literature in translation, than here. If there was a boom in Balzac at present, and he was being read by a lot of folk who can't read him comfortably in French, there might be an opening for a book about him. But in general, I do not know of any French work of literary criticism that has ever paid for itself here in translation. One or two novels, such as Céline's *Voyage au bout de la nuit*, have had a moderate success in translation; but it is very rare. If a translation is well reviewed, that may stimulate a demand for the *French* text, if any at all, rather than for the translation. So, if you still want to try your luck with it, I advise trying in New York.

I don't know whether you have regular news from Emily, but I imagine that lately you have heard little. I have been rather alarmed about her, though less so now; and I shall see her in ten days. The winter with the Perkins's, and trying for one job after another, must have been very trying for her; and she has had a sort of a breakdown. Apparently she is much better, and no one expects her to be unable to start at Smith; but I want her to be able to make a good start, and with confidence: because jobs are hard to get (especially for those who have no college degree) and this is a good one among nice people. The Perkins's have been good in writing to me, during the period now over when Emily could not write herself: but they attribute her breakdown largely to her having worked every day trying to help Mrs Hale, who behaved in her usual irrational fashion. I cannot help feeling that if they assign this reason (whether it is so important or not) one might expect them to reproach themselves a little bit for having allowed it to go so far: because they must have been perfectly aware from day to day what Emily was doing and how Mrs H. was behaving towards her. However, I hope to find out more soon; and if you will let me know that you get this letter, and would like me to write, I will give you the result of my observations. My address will be care of my sister: Mrs A. D. Sheffield, 31 Madison Street, Gray Gardens, Cambridge, Mass.; which is quite near I believe to 5 Clement Circle where Emily has been convalescing with the Perkins's. I shall arrive there on the 31st August.

I would like to hear, too, about your own affairs and where you go from here. Will you be in Denver again next winter?[1]

1 – McPherrin was living at 640 Vine Street, Denver, Colorado.

Ever yours
Tom

Yes, I have just re-read your last letter, and I see that you are to be in Denver. But why did I never hear from Miss Melanie Grant? You never need to ask for my consent when you want to give letters of introduction.

Will you accept my tardy apologies and contrition?

## TO *Ottoline Morrell*                                    TS Texas

20 August 1936                          *The Criterion*

My dear Ottoline,

I was very much touched and pleased by your sending me the Thermogene – it is invaluable stuff.[1] My arm and shoulder are much better; if I have to type for any length of time I pay for it later in the day; but I shall leave my machine behind, and expect to be quite ready for the winter by the time I get back. I look forward to my return – and the winter is to me a warm and anaesthetic season[2] – and I shall invite myself to tea immediately upon my arrival.

Affectionately yours,
Tom

## TO *Gerald Graham*[3]                                    TS Graham

21 August 1936                          Faber & Faber Ltd

My dear Graham,

I am sorry not to have been able to give you any final decision about your book before I sail for America on Saturday. I felt very favourably

---

1 – TSE had been to tea alone with OM on 14 Aug. Thermogene, a treatment for lumbago and neuralgia, was made of cotton wool impregnated with capsicum oleoresin, methyl salicylate and orange dye. Also available as a rub.

2 – Cf. 'Winter kept us warm' (*TWL*).

3 – Gerald S. Graham (1903–88), a graduate of Trinity College, Cambridge, was instructor in History at Harvard, 1930–6. After a period at Queen's University, Kingston, Ontario, he was a Guggenheim Fellow, 1940–1; and during WW2 he served in the Canadian Army. He was to be Rhodes Professor of Imperial History at King's College, London, 1949–70; Life-Fellow and Vice-President of the Royal Commonwealth Society, and general editor of the Oxford *West African History* series. A world authority on naval power and the British Empire, his publications include *Sea Power and British North America, 1783–1820: A Study in British Colonial Policy* (1941) and *The Politics of Naval Supremacy* (1967).

inclined toward the book when I read it myself, and I think that so far the other directors do also, but the principle question involved is one of policy, whether we should undertake this type of book or leave it to the other firms which have already done much more of this kind. The matter is at present in the hands of the Chairman and another director. You say that you are yourself sailing on the 6th, so I suggest that you should write or telephone to Mr F. V. Morley at this address a week or so before you leave, and he will tell you what the situation is. I naturally hope that the position will be favourable.

I don't know when I shall see you again, but you will continue to be in my thoughts and I shall be glad to hear from you from time [to time] as to how your affairs are going. And I hope that you will be over again in England next summer, if possible permanently. Please give my kind regards to your wife, and believe me,

Yours ever
T. S. Eliot

## TO *James Joyce*                                                    CC

21 August 1936                          [Faber & Faber Ltd]

My dear Joyce,

When I last saw you in Paris you promised to let me have a page of type to indicate what you would like better for *Work in Progress* than the specimen pages which you had from us. I have kept forgetting to write to remind you of this and I am about to leave for America, and shall not be back until the middle of October. So if you have anything to send will you please send it to Richard de la Mare at this address.

I hope that your domestic anxieties are diminished and that you have been able to get a good holiday away from Paris, and will find work possible.

With kindest regards to Mrs Joyce,
Yours ever,
[T. S. Eliot]

---

Graham wrote to EVE, 28 July 1984: 'T. S. E. was a most compassionate man. That is why he "picked me up" in Eliot House in 1932. We were brought close to each other because (unbeknownst to me at the time) we shared a common misery.'

21 August 1936                         [Faber & Faber Ltd]

My dear Burns,

I have looked carefully at the poems you sent me by M. A. T. Lyon.[2] I do not think they are quite up to the standard we aim at in originality, but the author has more ability than most. There is a little influence of Hopkins, but not too much, and he [*sic*] has a genuine, though so far rather slight sense of rhythm, which in places recalls Tennyson. If the author is very young I can call the verses very promising indeed. If very young, I should advise waiting for somewhat greater maturity before attempting publication. If not so young as that, I should say that the poems are worth publishing by somebody, but we haven't space to take them on ourselves.

I would have tried to see you and discuss the poems with you, which would have been more satisfactory, but I am leaving for America on Saturday, and therefore of course very rushed.

I shall hope to see you soon after I get back in the middle of October.

Yours ever,
T. S. E.

1–Tom Burns (1906–95), publisher and journalist, was educated at Stonyhurst (where he was taught by Fr Martin D'Arcy) and worked with the publishers Sheed & Ward, 1926–35. From 1935 he worked for Longmans Green – where he arranged to finance Graham Greene's mission to enquire into the persecution of the Catholic Church in Mexico – and he became a director of the Tablet Publishing Co., 1935–85. During WW2 he was press attaché to Sir Samuel Hoare, British Ambassador to Spain: see Jimmy Burns, *Papa Spy: A True Story of Love, Wartime Espionage in Madrid, and the Treachery of the Cambridge Spies* (2011). He was chairman of Burns & Oates, the premier Catholic publishing house, 1948–67; editor of *The Tablet*, 1967–82.

2–Ann Bowes-Lyon (1907–99), cousin of the Duchess of York (wife of the future King George VI); poet; intimate of Burns. Burns to TSE, 17 Aug.: 'I'm afraid you must get snowed under with verse to read – but I haven't been a burden [in] this respect & so I am venturing to send you this little collection. It is offered to F&F for publication: the writer is a shy & diffident person who really wants to know the value of her work. Thus I am sending it to you both as a publisher & a critic. I needn't bother you with my own reflections on its quality – I can only say that I'd have special reason for gratitude if you read these pages carefully – & then saw me or wrote to me.' See Lyon, *Poems* (F&F, 1937).

## TO *Bonamy Dobrée*

TS Brotherton Library

21 August 1936                          *The Criterion*

Dear Bonamy, my skiff is on the shore[1] And my ship is on the sea But before we part, once more Here's a triple health to thee. Thanks for your note of farewell.[2] I shd. like to have seen you all this great while, but assumed that you were moving or worse. I hope it will all straighten out. Yes, I got the Boots, but shall not take them, as I shall be back early in October. Yes, please correct Byron for me, unless it will hold till Oct. 12th; and I hope all the quotations are exact. And I will remember you to the people.

Let me come and see you in the winter – I didnt realise that you were BUILDING. Love to Valentine and Georgina, and believe me,

Ever yr. devoted friend and wellwisher.

Tom

## TO *George Every*

TS Sarah Hamilton

21 August 1936                          *The Criterion*

My dear George,[3]

I must apologise for having had to leave this to the very last: just before the point of deciding where the sponge is to go, or whether to leave out the extra shirt. It is now 11 and I must be up tomorrow at 6.15: so dont take anything I say too seriously. And I forgot to bring back a big envelope, so I can't send back the Gilpin, but that's allright anyway. And perhaps I have mislaid something. But of what I have – it is

---

1 – 'My Skiff is on De Shore' is a traditional black minstrel song.

2 – BD had written on 20 Aug.: 'Oh dear oh dear, my dear Tom, I suppose you'll be flitting off to America soon, and we haven't seen you. Damn oh damn! Life has been hectic . . . By the way, shall I correct the proofs of your Byron? . . . Give my love to your family – such of them as I know, especially your brother, not forgetting, of course, his wife. I am not quite so flattered by her attentions to me since you called her "susceptible". Was that quite kind of you? You know how at my age a man needs to have his vanity supported . . .

'You must come & see us in Leeds when our house is built – 12 miles out – woods, rivers & Wensleydale cheese.

'*Ave viator* [*Hail traveller*] – & did you get the boots?'

3 – This letter was published in *Something of Every-Man: A Celebration for George Every's 80th Birthday* (Oscott College, Birmingham, 1989). Included under TSE's letter was the dedication: 'We felt you had been neglected long enough, George. Hence this modest volume of some of your shorter pieces – sufficient to tantalise till the Collected Poems appear.'

*Reveillé*: 21 March 1936; O SAPIENTIA: 20 May 1936; and 'Is this a complete and final despair?': 13th June 1936:

*Reveillé* still derivative, I think, echoes of *The Rock* and *Murder*. I say this rather diffidently, because one never knows where oneself is involved. But as in earlier poems there was a good deal of unresolved Hopkins, so I *think* there is something here that is not your own.

*O Sapientia*. I think this is the best thing you have done so far. You have had to get rid of Hopkins and me, and perhaps other people. But I think this comes very near to being a good poem: I am not sure that it is not. I can't tell for certain until you send it back to me with something you have done six months later to compare it with.

*Is this a complete*. This page seems to me a fragment of a longer poem. I want to see the context.

Heaven help me if I have mislaid other things. But my feeling after these three is: there is a chance that you are a poet – and that is saying a good deal. I mean that *if* you are a poet, you are too good a poet to be dealt with from a publisher's point of view. It is not a question of a volume to be ready in 1937, etc. It's a question of your being good enough to be discouraged: I mean, of your being encouraged to go on writing and not care about publication, or about anything that may happen to what you write while you are alive. I dont believe that a good poet can be killed by not being published, or by being published and badly reviewed. I think that if you are a good poet, you will KNOW when you have finally done something that hasnt been done before, and it wont matter a fig to you whether you are published in the *Criterion*, or in a book. IF you are a good poet you are good enough to be neglected. You either aren't a poet or else you are so much better than the others that you will, when you have done what you are trying to do, know that you have done it, and nothing else will matter. 'O Sapientia' is quite good enough for the *Criterion*, compared with what I do publish. But to be as good as that isnt good enough: that's why I don't want to publish it.

If this seems to mean anything, my address is c/o Mrs Sheffield, 31 Madison Street, Gray Gardens, Cambridge, Massachusetts, U.S.A., until the end of September.

Affectionately,
T. S. E.

TO *John Hayward*                                    TS King's

21 August 1936                      *The Criterion*[1]

My dear John,

I must thank you for your kind entertainment – generous table – superb cognac – delightful conversation – fireworks musik – and general amiability and tolerance the other evening.[2] Should you care to indite a post card – if you visit Eastbourne or Worthing – it would console the poet in Pontus – address: c/o Mrs Sheffield, 31 Madison Street, Gray Gardens, Cambridge, Massachusetts, United States of America.[3] Go to bed early during my absence. I look forward eagerly to my return to the Kensington Kulture Klub and perhaps even a Game of Peggitty[4] with Mr Jennings[5] –

*Et quand Octobre souffle, émondeur des vieux arbres*[6] . . . I look forward to many evenings

. . . *illuminés par l'ardeur électrique* . . .[7]

*Ton dévoué*, what!

T. S. E.

1 – Actually written from the Sheffields' address – 31 Madison Street, Gray Gardens, Cambridge, Mass.

2 – Smart, *Tarantula's Web*, ventures (123–4) that JDH's dinner guests included 'close friends such as Bunny [*sic*] and Peter Quennell and his wife'.

3 – TSE enclosed a label with this address written out in capitals.

4 – A board game marketed since 1925 by the Parker Brothers.

5 – Richard Jennings (1881–1952): great bibliophile and collector (the term 'Jennings condition' has become a byword among book collectors); literary editor and editorialist of the *Daily Mirror* (where he worked for nearly forty years); brilliant conversationalist.

6 – Charles Baudelaire, *Les fleurs du mal*: '*La servante au grand cœur dont vous étiez jalouse.*'

7 – JDH took the opportunity, in one of his 'London Letters' (*New York Sun*, 12 Sept. 1936), to quote this passage of French by TSE, and to point out that TSE was a 'winter author'.

TO *Blánaid Salkeld*[1]                                    CC

1 September 1936                    [Faber & Faber Ltd]

Dear Miss Salkeld,

I have thought frequently about your plays, and have reread them from time to time.[2] I am afraid, however, that the decision is that plays are a very unprofitable investment for a publisher unless they have already been produced with some success, or are about to be produced. I do not know quite what to advise about your plays and poems. I should like them to be published, but our own poetry quota is more than full for some time to come. If Dent are not interested I should suggest one of the younger firms such as Boriswood. I am keeping the poems you sent me for the *Criterion* in case I am able to use any, and I should always be glad to see more from time to time.

As I am leaving England for some weeks I am obliged to leave this letter for my secretary to sign for me. With best wishes,

Yours very sincerely,
[Brigid O'Donovan]
For T. S. Eliot

1–Blánaid Salkeld (1880–1959), née Florence ffrench Mullen: Irish poet, dramatist, actor (Gate Theatre, Dublin), and reviewer (*Dublin Magazine*). Verse collections include *Hello, Eternity* (1933) – praised by Samuel Beckett – *The Fox's Covert* (1935), and *A Dubliner* (1942). Her son Cecil ffrench Salkeld became a noted artist; her granddaughter Beatrice married Brendan Behan.

2–Salkeld wrote from Dublin, 26 May: 'The enclosed were rejected by the Abbey: they want a plot, naturally enough. Later, sent back almost by return, by the Mercury – unread, I gather.

'My next shall have a plot, or not be . . . Every item I have sent forth this year has been flung back at me; so I can tell you, your silence has been indeed golden.'

1 September 1936                    [The Criterion]

Dear Mr Markoff,

Your letter of August 7th has just reached me, together with two copies of *A Monkey and its Tail*.² As this story is too long to be suitable for the *Criterion* I have forwarded it to A. M. Heath as you requested.

I am sorry that you feel a continuous book about Palestine is out of the question, but I hope that you will give the subject further consideration. It is really more a matter of appearance than of fact, simply for the reason that many more people will read a book which has some semblance of continuity than one which is on the face of it simply a collection of scattered sketches. But even if you think such a book out of the question we might still consider it possible to publish a collection of short stories after seeing some of your material. I shall be very glad in any case if you will let me see the rest of your manuscript as from time to time you have it ready. With a view to considering a collection of stories and sketches I am retaining one of the copies of *A Monkey and its Tail*.

Yours very sincerely,

[T. S. Eliot]

P.S. As I am leaving England for some weeks I am obliged to leave this letter for my secretary to sign for me.

---

1 – Markoff had been introduced to Faber & Faber by the poet Wilfrid Gibson, who wrote of his stories, 'When I came to read them . . . they struck me as remarkable work. The author, a young "White" refugee, who has been educated in England, seems to have that half-oriental mystical temperament of the Russian which seems strange to us; and he certainly manages to convey a convincing atmosphere.'

2 – Markoff wrote from the Orthodox Palestine Society, Jerusalem, on 11 Aug. (not 7 Aug.), to submit a story entitled 'A Monkey and Its Tail' written in collaboration with Miss Khoury – 'The characters are fictitious. They are typically "Palestinian", have been chosen with great care, and are of a type most unlikely to be found in ordinary books on Palestine.'

With regard to TSE's suggestion (17 Dec. 1935) that he write a book on Palestine, Markoff remarked: 'It is very difficult to write frankly about the country one lives in permanently and also one does not feel inclined to cover the ground already covered by people far more competent to do so than one is. And then the very unusualness of my material suggests a book of short stories rather than a continuous narrative.

'For some years I have been interested in the study of religious mentality and as Palestine is admirably suited for this sort of study I have collected a fair amount of interesting material. The original idea was to write a number of stories each illustrating a point.'

6 September 1936                    The Three Arts Club,
                                   19a Marylebone Road, N.W.1

Sir,

   Should you be considering a further edition of T. S. Eliot's poem
*Marina*, which I understand is now out of print, I venture to offer for your
attention an illustration for the cover, or first page, which I have made,
and which I think might be more generally popular than the previous
illustration.[1]

   I am not enclosing it, but will send it on hearing from you that you are
interested.

   Incidentally, a copy of this Poem was accepted (graciously) by T. R. H.
the Duke and Duchess of Kent.

   Thanking you in anticipation for your interest in this matter.

                            I am,
                            Yours faithfully
                            V. H. Eliot.

4 September 1936                    Faber & Faber Ltd

Dear Mrs Eliot,

   Your letter of the 2nd September to the Literary Manager has been
handed to me for reply. I have made enquiries, and find that it is most
unlikely that any further edition of *Marina* will be published, as it has now
been included in the *Collected Poems 1925–35* [*sic*], published last spring.
Once a poem has been included in a collected edition it is not our custom
to publish any further separate editions of it. In other circumstances we
should of course have been very glad to consider your kind suggestion, for
which we thank you very much.

                            Yours sincerely,
                            Brigid O'Donovan


1 – *Marina*, published in Sept. 1930, was illustrated by E. McKnight Kauffer.

FROM *Vivien Eliot* TO *The Literary Manager,*
   *Faber & Faber*          TS copy by Valerie Eliot: Bodleian

6 September 1936                  The Three Arts Club,
                                 19a Marylebone Road, N.W.1

Dear Sir,

I have received a courteous letter in reply to mine of the 2nd inst. to your firm, with regard to T. S. Eliot's Marina.

I am now thinking of having it privately produced with my own illustrations, in a similar way to Miss ~~Julia~~ Lucia Joyce's 'Hymn To The Virgin' by Geoffrey Chaucer.[1]

                      Yours truly,
                      V. H. Eliot[2]


TO *Dorothy Olcott Elsmith*[3]              MS Houghton

23 September 1936                  31 Madison Street,
                                 Gray Gardens, Cambridge

Dear Mrs Elsmith,

First let me apologise for writing to you on the typewriter. It seems a frigid and businesslike vehicle, especially for a letter intended to convey

---

1–VHE to Harriet Weaver, 12 June 1936: 'I remember her [Lucia] very well and liked her very much, when she came to lunch at 68, Clarence Gate Gardens to meet my husband's neices [*sic*], and some other people … I am afraid I am no longer a member of Lady Ottoline's little Court. But I could send a notice of the poem to the Court of Saint James's, where I am sure they would be interested. I sent a copy of Tom's (my husband's) poem, MARINA, to the Duke and Duchess of York, and they have all been extremely nice to me ever since.'

On 28 Nov. 1934 VHE had posted a copy of *Marina* to Prince George, Duke of Kent, and Princess Marina as a wedding present, signing it (as recorded in her diary) 'from VHE and TSE with sincere wishes for their happiness'. She received this unsigned note of courtesy from St James's Palace, 7 Dec. 1934: 'The Comptroller is desired by Their Royal Highnesses the Duke and Duchess of Kent to acknowledge the poem sent them by Mrs T. S. Eliot, and to thank her for her good wishes, which Their Royal Highnesses much appreciate.'

2–F&F responded, 8 Sept. 1936: 'In reply to your letter of the 6th, I must explain that although we do not intend to publish another separate edition of *Marina*, we still hold the copyright, and it is therefore not possible for anyone else to publish the poem in any form without our permission. As we are still publishing it in *Collected Poems 1909–1935* I am afraid that we cannot give such permission. Geoffrey Chaucer's *Hymn to the Virgin*, which has recently been issued in an edition illustrated by Miss Lucia Joyce, is not, of course, copyright. I am so sorry that we cannot for the moment be more helpful.'

3–Dorothy Olcott Elsmith (b. 1891). Gordon, *T. S. Eliot*, 255; *Imperfect Life*, 249–50, remarked of TSE's visit to Elsmith's oceanfront home at Woods Hole, Massachusetts, on

the warmest thanks and gratitude; but I suffer from a sort of writers' [*sic*] cramp, and actually can express myself both more grammatically and more spontaneously on the machine. And then I would like to say that I cannot think of any other place, than your home in Woods Holl [*sic*], which I would have preferred to visit in the circumstances: and I think that you will understand how great a compliment to you and Dr Elsmith and your family I consider that to be! But besides that, and my appreciation of your tact and hospitality, and your kindness in accepting the burden of an unknown guest so willingly, I feel that my life has been enriched by making new friends, and that I shall be deeply distressed if you do not give me the opportunity of seeing you on your next visit to England, where I shall expect you next summer.

Gratefully yours,

T. S. Eliot

---

the southern elbow of Cape Cod, in 1933: 'In the midst of family, in a bookish city where Eliot was a celebrity, he and Emily Hale were less free than in California. Dorothy Elsmith, a friend who lived in Woods Hole, provided a retreat, as she recalled: "Emily and Mr Eliot made several visits to the anonymity of my home here [called Olcotage, or Ros Marinus], where they walked the beach, in quiet retreat from Cambridge publicity."'

TSE wrote in Elsmith's copy of *Collected Poems*:

Inscribed for Mrs. Elsmith

By a grateful guest

T. S. Eliot

Woods Hole Mass. 21 XI 36

Elsmith wrote a brief unpublished memoir of TSE, 'Glimpses of the great': 'I recall one thoughtful gesture of the "grateful guest". At the time, one of the boys was a student at Milton Academy. The first morning he [TSE] appeared at breakfast wearing a Milton tie, a graduate himself. Quiet, courteous, unobtrusive, he had a way, flattering to the person addressed, of stooping a little and focusing his attention of the moment on YOU. He seemed to enjoy the informal family routine of continuous buffet breakfasts, set up from 8 to 10, and tray suppers in front of the open fire when he and Emily came in from beach walks. The youngest child remembers his bringing her up her breakfast tray one morning when a cold kept her in bed.'

In Sept. 1937, during a family visit to London, one of the children wrote in her diary: 'Mr Eliot came to tea today, as sweet, gentle and humorous as ever. Seems so UNfamous.'

TO *John Hayward*                                    TS King's

13 October 1936                    *The Criterion*

Dear John,

I would like you to understand that I would of left earlier as I had
intended and would of been convenient to me having just arrived[1] but I
said to myself that would not be fair to John because Bill[2] would certainly
stay to All Hours in that case and if Bill is left to himself he will certainly
stay until the whisky is gone and Bill wd. think nothing of walking all the
way to Marchmont Street[3] rather than miss any of the whisky Now dont
think Im being malicious because I value Bill and am concerned about
Him was he or was he not tight when he arrived I may be mistaken and
hoping I am but my heart sunk it did when I saw the kind of stealthy
subreptitious way he dived at the whisky without so much as having been
introduced and then also if Bill had not been present I wd. not of drunk
so much whisky which is not good for me especially after being with
my family so long and dishabituated to anything but Grade A milk and
Chocolate ice cream but I could not stand the sight of Bill darting at that
whisky and seeing that he was not appreciating the difference between
12s.6d. and 13s.9d. but to him it was just so much firewater you might
say So I staid later and drunk more whisky than I intended but John I Will
replace that whisky if I live to draw a cheque because that is not fair that
you should sit and see your 13s.9d. whisky comsumed as if it weere so
much methylated spirit But pleasantries apart etc. I emjoyed my Evening
very much and would of more so if it had been more confidential but look
forward to an old buffers evening tonight so will close yours etc.

I must write to Otto I suppose but done you say anything about me until
I do. I had a good welcome at the club today Morgan said now sir I have
got a new chef who cooks the roast beef the way you like it and Smith the
Strangers Room Steward came in and said we have a consignment of Old
Cheshire from Mr Hutchinson (not the K. C. but Mr H. the celebrated
Cheese breeder of Malpas, Cheshire) which I think you will appreciate:
and an old buffer whose name I never knew but whom I met once at
lunch at Mrs Brocklebank's and with whom I frequently discuss *the Times*
X-word puzzle (we got together today over SPOKESHAVE) said where

---

1 – TSE returned from the USA on 10 Oct., being met at Plymouth by FVM who wrote to
Neil M. Gunn, 13 Oct.: 'I am only just back from a quick raid to Plymouth in the Ford to
meet TSE on his return from America. He's in lively spirits.'
2 – TSE and William Empson spent the evening of 12 Oct. with JDH.
3 – Empson rented a flat on Marchmont Street, Bloomsbury: a fair walk from Kensington.

have you been all this time? I have a nephew, said he, who writes plays. He had one performed last year at the Westminster Theatre, said he; I went to see it but I didn't like it, I am too old-fashioned, it was called the *Dog Beneath the Skin*; my nephew Christopher collaborates with a fellow named Auden.

Now then looking forward to 7.45 tonight *heure precise* & no Mistake, I am, (and I have *not* been dining tonight with Sidney Dark and the Archbishop of Canterbury)

Your faithful

TP

Damb it I would of answered your letter but how could I I couldnt remember the Christian name of the Duke of Monmouth which I would of had to use in replying must look him up in the DNB.


TO *Djuna Barnes*                                                          TS Hornbake

15 October 1936                    Faber & Faber Ltd

My dear Miss Barnes,

I have just returned from New England, and Morley has shown me your letter of October 8th, and your note of October 14th.[1] I am extremely sorry to learn too late of your abhorrence for the colour purple. If you had mentioned it to me in time we would of course have chosen another colour in deference to your wishes. The only thing to be said in consolation is that in all probability only a small number of your readers will share that loathing, and there would probably be quite as many to object to any other colour in the binder's spectrum. I don't know whether your objection to tallness and slenderness is as strong, but on that point I am inclined to defend the appearance of the book.

As for the absence of two sets of proofs, and consequently for the appearance of some misprints in the book, I am sorry about that too. I knew nothing of this difficulty, of course, until my return, but I gather that it was at least partly due to the difficulties of communication with you at a distance, and on this point my only consolation is that I have never succeeded in getting a first edition of one of my own books printed without some errors in it, and I sometimes find that when those are corrected new errors appear. But we will try to perfect your book when the second edition is called for.

1–Barnes wrote (14 Oct.) that she would be arriving in London on Fri. 16 Oct. The letter of 8 Oct. has not been traced.

I am sending a copy of the book to Mrs Coleman, and I find that yours were sent off to Paris on the 13th. I should like to see you soon, and I am sure that Morley would also. I should like to have a few words with you on the question of complimentary copies to be sent out, and I wonder if you would ring up and make an appointment to come to see us for a preliminary business meeting. Monday morning would be a good time if that suited you.

With all best wishes,
Yours ever sincerely
T. S. Eliot

## TO *Kenneth Mackenzie*

CC

16 October 1936                    [Faber & Faber Ltd]

My dear Lord Bishop,

Your letter of August 27th and your circular letter of September 1st were forwarded to me in America,[1] and I am sorry that I had so little free time that I was unable to answer them. I believe you understand, however, that the date fixed, Thursday 22nd, is quite convenient for me for the meeting at Pusey House.

Following my previous mention of the subject I should like to place before the meeting my formal resignation from the Secretaryship. As you will be unable to undertake the office of Chairman I feel that the two offices ought to be considered together. It may prove in the future a more possible arrangement to have a Chairman who will not need to take upon his own shoulders so much of the responsibility as Harris did, and to have a secretary who can undertake more of the work than I have done. My duties in the past have not been very onerous, but pressure of other work makes it impossible for me to undertake more. I think, furthermore, that if the office of secretary became more important I should probably cease to be a suitable encumbent.

I am, my Lord Bishop,
Yours very sincerely,
[T. S. Eliot]

1–The Bishop of Brechin notified TSE that he would be calling a meeting at a date during the last fortnight of October. 'I am sure however that I cannot take Dr Harris's place. I was very ready to act as his deputy while he was with us; and I think I was able to be of some service to him. But it seems clear to me that time and space alone supply considerations to make it impossible for me to succeed him.'

## TO *A. H. MacIntyre*[1]                                                    CC

16 October 1936                              [Faber & Faber Ltd]

Dear Mr MacIntyre,

                            *Agency Account*

I have just had a letter from my brother dated October 7th, in which
he tells me that you have no written authority from me to authorize you
to accept his recommendations for re-investments in my agency account.
I think that this must be a mistake, as I wrote, not to you personally, but
to the department in general, the day after our interview on the subject,
and I had an acknowledgement in return, though as I cannot lay my hand
on it at the moment I cannot tell you who signed it. In any case I shall be
glad if you will carry out his recommendations.

                             *Income Tax*

I enclose for your consideration the duplicate form which Mr Hughes at
the Post Office gave me to show the Immigration Officer at the frontier as
evidence that my tax for the first nine months of 1936 had been paid. For
the benefit of any other of your alien clients who may find themselves in
the same fix, I may mention that there was no Immigration Officer at the
frontier, so I had no occasion to make use of this paper. Your people will
probably find it useful in making out my 1936 returns. I was surprised
that the tax was so high, but had no time to enter into a dispute with
Mr Hughes, in which he could certainly get the better of me, so I hope
that you will be so kind as to have these figures checked in due course, in
order to ascertain whether I did or did not pay too much. I certainly paid
a cheque for $192.48.

                                   With best wishes,
                                   Yours sincerely,
                                   [T. S. Eliot]


## TO *Hallie Flanagan*                                         Typed copy

19 October 1936                              Faber & Faber Ltd

Dear Mrs Flanagan,

    Thank you very much for your letter of the 24th and for sending me
the gramophone record, which gave me much surprise and pleasure.[2] I am

1–A. H. MacIntyre, Old Colony Trust Company, Boston.
2–Flanagan wrote on 24 Aug. from the Works Progress Administration, Washington, DC:
'Dear T. S. Elliott [*sic*]: I am very sorry that your name was misspelled on the record we are

very glad to have it, as a memento of a production which I more and more regret, after talking to American friends, that I was unable to see.

I was in New England for the month of September, but did not have time even for a visit to New York. I hope that my next visit will take me as far as Washington, where I hope that you will still be directing the Federal Theatre Project. I cannot compliment you enough on the work that you have done in this capacity, and it is not the least of my reasons for hoping that the November elections will return Mr Roosevelt to the presidency.

With most cordial wishes to Dr Davis[1] and yourself,

Yours very sincerely,

T. S. Eliot

P.S. If it were possible I should like to get a few copies of the record both for friends here and in America.

P.P.S. For the convenience of your secretary the letter head and the signature will give him or her the correct spelling of my name.

## TO *Hope Mirrlees*                                              CC

19 October 1936                    [Faber & Faber Ltd]

Dear Hope,

I must apologize for not having answered your letter at once on getting back, but I was of course plunged into a chaos of things to do, both inside and outside the office, and am much in arrears with my correspondence.[2] I should have loved to come down with you to your mother's on the 23rd, but alas I am afraid no weekend will be possible for some time. Apart from two engagements which I made before I went away I have loaded myself with three speaking engagements to be worked off during November. I hope, therefore, that your mother will take me seriously if I say that I should be delighted to come for any weekend after the end of November. Meanwhile I hope that we may meet in town. I shall write again soon in the hope that you will dine, with perhaps a theatre if there is anything to see. I should have liked to suggest the production of Louis MacNeice's *Agamemnon*, but that is to have only two performances at the Westminster Theatre, November 1st and 8th, and I am not free on

---

sending, under separate cover, but I hope that it will not interfere with your enjoyment of it. I still wish that you could have seen the beautiful production of the play.'

1 – Flanagan's husband, Philip Davis, taught at Vassar College.

2 – Mirrlees wrote on 14 Oct. to invite TSE to spend a weekend at her mother's new house in Surrey, perhaps from 23 Oct. 'The car is coming to fetch me so I could come & pick you up.'

either occasion.[1] I do hope to see you soon. Please tell your mother how sorry I am not to be free to come on the 23rd, and I do hope she will ask me later.

> With many regrets,
> Yours ever,
> [Tom]

## TO *Georges Cattaui*                                            CC

20 October 1936                        [Faber & Faber Ltd]

My dear Cattaui,

Thank you very much for your kind letter of the 13th. I am very interested to know of the new dispositions concerning the translation of *Murder in the Cathedral*, and while I know nothing of the talent of M. d'Erlanger[2] I have no doubt of the superiority of any translation in which you and Jean have co-operated. If the date of your next visit to London is at your own choice I agree that we could accomplish more if I had the translation in my hands some days before your arrival. In that case also I should be able to arrange in advance so that we might have the necessary time for discussion.

As for your questions: 1) I agree that the conversation between Thomas and the first three tempters should be entirely in the plural. I should suggest that the fourth tempter should *tutoyer* Thomas, but that Thomas should *vousvoyer* in return. This is what I should have done certainly if that shade of distinction had not unhappily disappeared from the English language. There is an air of insolence, and of being master of the situation about the fourth tempter which would make him adopt the more intimate discourse, while Thomas on the other hand would prefer to disclaim such intimacy. 2) The difference between the two editions is due to the fact that the beginning of the second act was judged unsuitable for production to a general audience. I am not even sure that the significance of the four introits ending with the introit for St Thomas's day being pronounced in anticipation of the murder did not escape the larger part even of the Canterbury audience. Anyway, that beginning lends itself

---

1–Because of the early production of Louis MacNeice's translation of the *Agamemnon* of Aeschylus, publication was brought forward to 29 Oct. VHE went to the Doone production, in which Robert Speaight played Agamemnon. 'The worst sins are those against one's family,' wrote MacNeice, 'which are punished by the . . . Furies that belong to that family.'
2–Emile B. (Beaumont) d'Erlanger (1866–1939), of the banking family.

rather to pageantry than to dramatics. I think I should prefer on the whole that the second version, in which the chorus is substituted, should be used. 3) As for the punctuation, I should be inclined to defer to the French opinion, but I cannot form any opinion on my own until I see the text.

I believe that there is a certain desire to have the English company give one or two performances in Paris, but I expect to have more news of this in a week or so.

With all best wishes,
Yours very sincerely,
[T. S. Eliot]

TO *Martin Shaw*[1]                                                    CC

20 October 1936                    [Faber & Faber Ltd]

My dear Shaw,

It is a great pleasure to hear from you after such a long time, and I hope that we may meet during this winter, although your letter head suggests that you may have abandoned both Hampstead and West Wickham.[2] As to your kind suggestion and that of Revd Porter Goff,[3] you may remember my doubts about such a project when you discussed the matter some time ago. These were of two kinds. My first objection was that what appears to be wanted is something more in the nature of a pageant than a play. I don't really want to do anything more in the way of pageantry, and in any case it would be a job primarily for Martin to lay out, merely indicating to me what was to be written in, as with *The Rock*. Secondly, as I think I said at the time, what would seem to me worth writing on the subject of war and peace would be one so Aristophanic and libellous both to domestic

1 – Martin Shaw (1875–1958), composer of stage works, choral pieces and recital ballads. Director of Music, Diocese of Chelmsford, 1935–44. Other works include *Anglican Folk Mass* (1918); *Songs of Praise* (co-ed., 1925); *The Oxford Book of Carols* (co-ed., 1928). He wrote the music for TSE's pageant *The Rock* (1934).
2 – Shaw wrote from Kelvedon, Essex, 15 Oct.: 'Am I being a nuisance? I'm not quite sure whether you think the idea of a Peace or League of N. play futile.'
3 – Shaw forwarded a letter from the Revd E. N. Porter Goff, Secretary of the Christian Organisations Committee, League of Nations Union, London, 7 Oct. 1936: 'Dear Dr Martin Shaw, I have been thinking over what you said about the possibility of getting T. S. Eliot to write a play about the League similar to the The Rock. I do not myself feel equal to preparing even a draft scenario, but I am sending you, under separate cover, a book which would, I think, suggest suitable subjects for dramatic treatment.' The book was *The League*, by K. Gibberd.

and foreign politicians that it would be impossible of public presentation. In short, I am not an optimist about the League of Nations, and all my published comments on that institution, acknowledging the probability that very few people have read them, have been rather derogatory.[1] All considerations lead me to the conviction that I am not the man for this sort of job. I should like to look at the book you have so kindly sent, and return it to you in a few days time.

With best wishes to Mrs Shaw,
Yours sincerely
[T. S. Eliot]

## TO *Hans Hennecke*[2]                                                    CC

22 October 1936                      [Faber & Faber Ltd]

Dear Sir,

I thank you for your letter of the 22nd August, which arrived after I had left for America.[3] I hasten to reply now that I have returned. I have been trying to think of a French, if not a German, equivalent for 'pattern' (I think that the word Henry James uses is 'figure', but with practically the same meaning) and have been asking French friends, but so far without any satisfactory result. I have heard, however, from the editor of the *Europäische Revue* to the effect that he wishes to substitute another essay (I agree with him that it is more suitable) so that I imagine the question is less urgent.

On my return I found here a copy of the *Europäische Revue* as well as a proof of your article which you kindly sent me.[4] I wish to express my thanks and appreciation for your most gracious article. The subject of

---

1 – See TSE's lecture 'The Christian in the Modern World', 31 Jan. 1935: 'As for those who wish for peace, their ship has been split on the rock of the League of Nations. This ill-omened organisation, formed from a muddle of ill-founded Christian and humanitarian principles, has finally revealed its true character. It was a league of those idealists who wish peace at any price ... The eventual collapse of the League of Nations should have been apparent to any Christian from the beginning: for the foundations of the League were not really Christian. It has shown one thing: it has shown that no pacifism that is not Christian pacifism is genuine' (*CProse* 5, 187).
2 – Hans Hennecke (1897–1977), noted German literary critic and translator.
3 – Hennecke was working on a German translation of TSE's preface to G. Wilson Knight's *The Wheel of Fire*, and asked TSE to help him grasp the exact meaning of his term 'pattern' and to suggest the German equivalent – or a French equivalent.
4 – Hennecke, 'T. S. Eliot. Der Dichter als Kritiker', *Europäische Revue* 12 (1936), 721–35 – an essay on the 'critical aspect' of TSE's work.

such an essay can hardly be the best judge of its quality, but with respect to such parts of the essay as I can be impartial about, it strikes me as an admirable and penetrating study.

Yours sincerely,
[T. S. Eliot]

## TO *Ezra Pound*                                             TS Beinecke

22 October 1936                    *The Criterion*

Resp. Ezmuz,

The time has not arrived for a reply to your esteemed of thesiebzehnteenth August. I hope your wife is arriving safely bearing a copy of *Nightwood* what a book.[1]

Three cantoes read. Only one query (B) 'see weed' etc. To one raised on the shore of the manymermaidcrowded sea,[2] this collocation suggest ALGAE such as a child I dried and classified on the shores of Massachusetts. Just callin it to your attention thats all in case you didnt notice it livin so far inland and you may not comb any on the Ligurural beach.[3] Otherwise, nothing for the like of me to query: I didnt know such things happened so recently as 1732.

Musical Stuff. What can I do about it? Pleased to see you in the columbariums of the Listener, and may it continue;[4] but short of firin my regular musician from the *Criterion* I havent any room for more music stuff however intelligent and I dare say so I dare indeed, and whre else? Palmberston seems more in my line, I know his face well, but what are

---

1 – EP did not share TSE's enthusiasm for *Nightwood*, and sent this limerick on 12 Jan. 1937:

> There onct wuzza lady named DJuna
> Who wrote rather like a baboon. Her
> blubbery prose
> had no fingers or toes
> and we wish Whale had found this out sooner.

He added: 'This ezzagerates as far to the one side as you blokes to the other.'

(EP to FVM ['Whale'], 23 Sept.: 'The Juna is custard/ like Bridge of Lous Rey bloke. More of a gal than he is a boy, but STILL. Why do Americans novelists waal, I dunno, may try again, but damn bored with start.')

2 – TSE's 'Homeric' epithet presumably takes off from Yeats's 'Sailing to Byzantium' – 'the mackerel-crowded seas' – or else from Joyce.

3 – Rapallo lies on the Tigullio Gulf of the Ligurian Coast, southeast of Genoa.

4 – 'Mostly Quartets', *Listener* 16: 405 (14 Oct. 1936), 743–4. See further Mick Gidley, 'Music crit. Etc.: Ezra Pound and the Listener', *TLS*, 15 Apr. 2016, 14–15.

you doin a bout that? he may turn into a 6000 word article or a cantoe before you are done with that review.[1]

Now you says can anythink be done with rejected bits?[2] In first place are you pleased with our work (M.[3] did a lot of work after I left) or not? Then as to what can be done with rejected bits, now, aint that up to you FIRST. You blow up a cushion and Ill SIT on it.

I know Revd Vincent McNabb O.P. nice old lad but too old to bother with now.[4] There is also a Southearne McNab, a Scot. Your wife says there is a McNab to do with the Blackshirt but you wont expect me to have anything to do with HIM. Dont know anything about Gunther: small American journalist I believe.[5]

We have one Street on our list who sells pretty well, his work accordingly is unknown to me but I see the figures,[6] and so I am doubtful about including another but will raise the point. But if you want something 'lightly amusing' a bloke on the boat who said he was a géologue and we had a couple of drinks every night because of the Sorbonne HE said that 'Clochemerle' by one Gabriel Chevalier was a most amusin book have you read it.[7] I read the latest Bernanos and that WAS amusin.[8]

And now as to politics dont you crab Frankie's chances,[9] say what you like about him after Nov. 4th but leave him alone until hes elected because if he aint you dont realise as I do havin been in Boston what the alternative is. There could be nothing worse than Landon you can take it from me I

---

1–See EP, Cantos XLII–XLIV', C. 16 (Apr. 1937), 405–23. Canto 42 opens with a sharp reference to Prime Minister Lord Palmerston (1784–1865) and his dealings with the Americas.

2–EP (17 Aug.): 'can anything be done for collection of various REJECTED bits & butz of mss. not considered Polite enuff?'

3–FVM.

4–The Revd Vincent McNabb (1868–1943), Irish scholar and Dominican priest, based in London; ecumenist; expert on the *Summa Theologica* of St Thomas Aquinas.

5–EP (17 Aug.): 'Dont know if attack on Gunther wd. be well kum. Have swatted him for Macnab but dunno if Macnab will be allowed to print the swat. any dope on Macnab? ... R.S.V.P. re Gunther as I have borrowed copy here. but won't have it in Venice.' John Gunther (1901–1970): American journalist and writer; author of *Inside Europe* (1936).

6–EP (17 Aug.): 'have I six times drawn attention to G. S. Street?? whose books pubd. 1900–1910 *ought* to sell now if revived. = This is disinterested. Tubby never did nowt fer me – but his bukz wuz readable *lightly* amusin. = & bettern the Hukzly generation.'

A. G. Street (1892–1966): farmer, writer, broadcaster; author of *Farmer's Glory* (1932).

7–*Clochemerle* (1934): bestselling satirical novel by Gabriel Chevallier (1895–1969).

8–Georges Bernanos (1888–1948): French Catholic author; an early adherent of *Action Française*, which he abandoned after 1932 when he became an opponent of Fascism and National Socialism; author of the popular *Journal d'un curé de campagne* (1936).

9–'Frankie': Franklin D. Roosevelt.

know because everybody in Boston wants Landon for president. So dont you let your Little Flower pal interfere with Frankie bein elected.[1]

Kno anything about Kenneth Fearing? some of the lads over there have some ability, but I havent found one of em yet will take any TROUBLE to write, exc. possibly Bob Fitzgerald.[2]

And so<br/>TP.

## TO *James Joyce* CC

23 October 1936                [Faber & Faber Ltd]

My dear Joyce,

Your letter of the 5th September arrived while I was in America, but as you wrote from Copenhagen, and as you said that your hands were full at the moment with the publication of *Ulysses* I trust that the delay has not been an annoyance.[3] We have got hold of a copy of *Mesures* containing the translation of your letter to Sullivan.[4] I have discussed the type with De la Mare, and we agree that to print the book in type of that size would make it intolerably big, certainly well over a thousand pages, so far as we can estimate from the part of the book of which we have the typescript. It is not a type which would do very well in a reduced size, as it is so thin that in a smaller size it would be extremely difficult to read. However, De la Mare is having specimen pages set in another type which we think will be much more what you want than that previously submitted, and I will send these on as soon as they are ready. One point is that the type must be

---

1 – In the event, in the Presidential Election on 3 Nov. 1936, the incumbent Democrat F. D. Roosevelt worsted the moderate Republican Alf Landon (1887–1987), Governor of Kansas.
2 – Robert Fitzgerald (1910–85), poet, critic, translator of Greek and Latin classics including Euripides, Sophocles and Homer, studied at Harvard, 1929–33, and worked in the 1930s for the *New York Herald Tribune* and *Time*. Boylston Professor of Rhetoric and Oratory, Harvard, 1965–81; Consultant in Poetry to the Library of Congress, 1984–5. TSE wrote to Henry Allen Moe, John Simon Guggenheim Memorial Foundation, 22 Dec. 1939: 'Fitzgerald I saw something of during 1932–33 while he was an undergraduate at Harvard . . . [A]t that time I was more interested in the work of Fitzgerald than in that of any other young poet in America . . .'
3 – JJ wrote from Copenhagen: 'a copy of *Mesures* with my letter to Sullivan in French was sent to you one day after you left Paris, for you to read the text and for the board to look at the type. Seemingly neither of you had the pleasure I wanted you to have. There is nothing to be done about it, I fear, at least for the moment as all my spare time is taken up with another of the tribe until *Ulysses* comes out in England's glum and puzzled land on the 25 instant.'
4 – JJ, 'From a Banned Writer to a Banned Singer'.

smaller in order to make a volume of reasonable compass, and a smaller type to be legible should be rather heavier and have slightly more space between the lines – more leaded that is to say.

Thank you for your message from Mr Moller.[1] I hope that the Danish translation is a good one and that your business in Copenhagen has been satisfactory. I have my own copy of L's book, and am going to talk to Miss Weaver about it. I have only been back for a short time and have had a couple of days in bed getting used to the English climate again, so that I am a good deal in arrears.

With best wishes for your family,
Sincerely,
[T. S. Eliot]

## TO *George Every*                                                    CC

23 October 1936                    [Faber & Faber Ltd]

My dear George,

I got back on the 12th, but am still very much in arrears, especially as I have just had two days in bed.[2] I have, however, read the Clarendon, which strikes me decidedly as a brilliant piece of work, and it will certainly be published, I think in the April number, as the December is already pretty full. The only weak spot in it seemed to me the last paragraph.[3] I could not decide why it seemed to me weak until I read the Barth review which seemed to me to have the same weakness. I may be quite wrong, but the trouble seems to me that you have wanted in your final paragraphs of each to say things that you had not already said in the course of the article. They read rather like the last words of a man telephoning a trunk call after he has been warned that the time is up. My own feeling is that a final paragraph in general ought not to attempt to introduce any new point or do more than sum up what has already been said. In the Barth review, too, it seemed to me that you were bothered by having a great deal more to say than you could say in the space. I shall use that review in the

1 – 'Fri. Moller here, who is a great admirer of your work asks me, or words to that effect, to explain that his article is only a summary one on account of the paper it appears in.'
2 – Every had written on 11 Oct.: 'Here is (a) a review of Barth's *Credo*, promised in correspondence with Miss O'Donovan.

'(b) Clarendon (and the Popular Front?). I should like a verdict on Clarendon, who might try his fortune elsewhere, though I shouldn't like to reduce him. But I don't of course ask for an early berth for him. He is too big. He must go where and when there is room.'
3 – 'Clarendon and the Popular Front', C. 16 (Apr. 1937), 432–51.

December number, and I hope you will not take any criticisms like this too seriously. If you considered them and rejected them they would still have served their purpose all the same.[1]

I also got your letter which you sent to me at my sister's, and that is so important as to need a separate reply. It is going to give me more trouble than anything you have sent me before, which you are to take as an encouraging symptom.

Yours ever sincerely,
[T. S. E.]

## TO *Francis Underhill*[2]                                    CC

26 October 1936                    [Faber & Faber Ltd]

Dear Father Underhill,

For several reasons, and incidentally because you should know already that I am a very poor speaker, and should therefore have no reason to be disappointed in what I do, I shall be glad to accept your invitation to address the Friends of Rochester Cathedral on June 4th.[3] I hope that I may receive a reminder a couple of months in advance. While you leave the choice of subject entirely I feel that I ought if possible to deal with some subject in which the Friends of the Cathedral might be expected to take a common interest, and I should be very glad if you had any suggestions.[4]

Yours very sincerely,
[T. S. Eliot]

---

1–Every on Karl Barth, *Credo*: C. 16 (Jan. 1937), 366–9.

2–Revd Francis Underhill, DD (1878–1943) Anglican priest and author; Warden of Liddon House and priest in charge of Grosvenor Chapel, Mayfair, London, 1925–32; later Dean of Rochester, 1932–7. From 1937, Bishop of Bath and Wells. Works include *The Catholic Faith in Practice* (1918) and *Prayer in Modern Life* (1928). George Every told Barry Spurr that 'Eliot preferred to have, as confessor, a priest distinct from his vicar as St Stephen's' (Spurr, Ch. 30: 'Religion', in *T. S. Eliot in Context*, ed. Jason Harding (2011), 310). TSE would notify the Revd D. V. Reed, 30 Mar. 1961, that he 'continued to be a penitent of Father Underhill during his period as Dean of the Cathedral' – i.e. Rochester. He went to Underhill at Liddon House, 24 South Audley Street, for his weekly confession, on Fridays.

3–Underhill invited TSE (19 Oct.) to give a lecture – 'on any subject' – for the Festival of the Friends of Rochester Cathedral in June 1937. 'The Friends . . . are a very young society but they are rather dear to my heart and I cannot help feeling that if someone of your reputation would consent to show your "Friendship" in this way it would be greatly appreciated.'

4–TSE's talk was published as 'Religious Drama: Mediæval and Modern', *University of Edinburgh Journal* 9: 1 (Aut. 1937), 9–17.

26 October 1936                    *The Criterion*

Dear Jeanie,

I am very much in arrear, but I did not want to write again until I had been to Northampton, the Sunday before I left; and the remaining days were crammed with relatives and duty calls. I suppose I could have written on the boat, but apart from the depression of Get-Together Night, Gala Night, and Auld Lang Syne Night, I can't express myself properly on bits of note paper and without a typewriter.

When I first saw Emily I thought her very much changed, chiefly in the lack of any animation, in a kind of numbness to the external world, a narrowing of her field of awareness, and a tendency (though one has noticed this before) to think about her own shortcomings all the time. In a person who ordinarily gives out so much to others, this is very painful. She wanted help, but she had that readiness to accept everything one said as true, which shows low vitality (it is always distressing, and sometimes alarming, to have people accept everything one says). While we were visiting her friends at Woods Hole, I thought she picked up a bit; and when I went down to Northampton to see her I thought she was a good deal better. She had not begun to show any lively interest in the work she was to do, but I hope and believe that that will come. I do not believe that there is anything settled in her depression, and I think that it will pass in the course of the work, and getting to know the better girls, and making friends locally: though of course to go through any such phase must make a mark on anybody. If she should seem to you perhaps in correspondence remote or vague, remember that it is a general phenomenon and has nothing to do with you any more than with anyone else.

I have rather mixed feelings about her spending next summer in Campden with the Perkins's. I wish that she could be with more vital and younger people, no matter where, instead of under what seems to me a rather suffocating influence upon her. And I doubt even whether Dr Perkins's rather woolly counsels are very invigorating for her.

I am always happy to hear from you, remember.

Yours ever,
Tom

TO *John Hayward* TS King's

26 October 1936 *The Criterion*

My dear John,

The text of *Meurtre dans la Cathédrale*, traduit de l'anglais par Emile B. d'Erlanger, has arrived, and its first impression is to make me feel like that morose bird, the scritch-owl, in the words of Thomas Chatterton (the something boy who perisht in his pride),[1] to wit (to who):[2]

> That bird wych in the dark time of the yeerë
> Sitteth in dudgeon (1) on the aspen bouwe
> And cryeth *arsehole arsehole* lhoude and cleerë . . .[3]

(1) The worde does not occur in this sense until 1573.[4]

However, will you have the time to be one of the specialists at the autopsy?

Yrs. in haste<br>T. S. E.

TO *Phyllis M. Potter*[5] TS Marion E. Wade Center, Wheaton College

27 October 1936 Faber & Faber Ltd

Dear Miss Potter,

I have been considering your letter of October 5th and naturally I should be glad to do anything I could to aid the performance of a play by Mr Charles Williams, as I am sure that the play itself will be of very great interest.[6] Would you let me know a little more fully what you would

---

1 – William Wordsworth, 'Resolution and Independence', 43–4; 'I thought of Chesterton, the marvellous Boy, / The sleepless Soul that perished in its pride.'

2 – *Love's Labour's Lost* V: ii: 'Tu-who . . . / To-whit to-who'.

3 – Parody of Thomas Chatterton: see *Poems I*, ed. Ricks and McCue, 998–9.

4 – *OED*: 'A feeling of anger, resentment, or offence; ill humour.' *OED* cites: '1573 G. HARVEY *Let.-bk.* (1884) 28 Who seem'd to take it in marvelus great duggin.'
   See further *Poems I*, 288–9.

5 – Phyllis M. Potter (b. 1886), daughter of a wealthy shipowner; Anglo-Catholic; Hon. Director of the Chelmsford Diocesan Religious Drama Guild.

6 – Potter invited TSE to give a talk about a nativity play by Charles Williams called *Seed of Adam* at the Annual Meeting of the Chelmsford Diocesan Religious Drama Guild in the afternoon of Sat. 9 Jan. 1937 at Brentwood, Essex. (The premiere was on 14 Nov. 1936.) 'We are very anxious that Mr William's [*sic*] play should have a good audience & reception, but his name is little known in these parts; moreover the play is so original that it is unlike anything Essex expects. We know that if we could have your support on that day, you would not only bring an audience, but you would be able to make it accept the play even if it didn't understand it!' TSE was to be introduced by the Bishop of Chelmsford, and he

like me to do? Would you wish me to speak from the stage just before the performance, or during the interval, or at the end? How long would you want me to talk? I assume that I should be able to see the text of the play before hand.[1]

Yours sincerely,
T. S. Eliot

## TO *J. H. Oldham*[2]

CC

27 October 1936                    [Faber & Faber Ltd]

My dear Oldham,

Thank you for your letter of the 22nd.[3] As for what you say in the first paragraph I will keep in mind the suggestion. Indeed, what I intended

---

met Williams for the first time at lunch. 'All went very well,' wrote Williams in an undated letter to his intimate friend Anne Bradby, 'though I don't remember what T.S.E. said very clearly, only that we were all extremely pleasant, arguable, & intimate. My wife discussing the Agamemnon chorus with him was a marvellous sight . . . A fantastic day' (quoted in Lindop, *Charles Williams*, 265).

TSE to Anne Ridler, 25 May 1945: 'I did like *Seed of Adam* very much and as I saw it at Chelmsford I can testify that it was interesting on the stage as well as to read.'

1–Potter advised TSE's secretary on 19 Dec.: 'When we first asked Mr Eliot to speak on this occasion we thought Mr Williams's play would need his protection! Since then we have performed it twice at Hornchurch & its severest critics were converted . . . Will you therefore ask [Mr Eliot] to say exactly what he would like to say on the play itself. If he feels he can get in any thrusts at the sentimental religious play that are usually performed I should be grateful. I do not know if he would be prepared to say that bad plays badly acted do harm to the cause of religion. I am sure the time has come when someone with authority should speak forcibly on the subject & condemn the false sentiment & piety that oozes from the usual Religious drama.'

In the event, TSE talked for about twenty mins., following the performance of *The Seed of Adam*. 'Of course what people do today must be very different from the work of the fourteenth and fifteenth centuries. It cannot be so simple, but then our religious faith is not such a simple thing. It has to have a certain surface simplicity, in order to be good drama at all; but when it is sincere it will have under the surface all the complexity of feeling that we experience ourselves . . . And so I think we must see the Nativity story with a consciousness of everything that has happened in the 1900 odd years since. We have to put ourselves there, and we have to see those events here' (quoted in JDH's 'London Letter', New York *Sun*, 23 Jan. 1937). 'Religious drama is not there to give you the effect of the mass-manufactured plaster saint, or the comfortable deadness of the second-rate religious Christmas card. Religious drama ought to supply something in the religious life of the community that cannot be supplied in any other way and when it is fine drama and poetry, it can have a missionary power that is incalculable.'

2–Joseph ('Joe') Oldham (1874–1969): indefatigable missionary, adviser and organiser: see Biographical Register.

3–'I sent a copy of your notes [for TSE's essay in *Revelation*] to Baillie and find that they have interested him as much as they have me. He says that it is obviously going to interest

my rather chaotic note to convey was as much an analysis of the present situation as anything else.

I am rather baffled by the second paragraph. I certainly intended to confine myself as far as possible to a thesis generally acceptable by Christians of all communions, and I cannot help wondering whether Baillie's question is not rather suggested by a reading of some of my previous writings than by the outline he has just seen.

I had rather deliberately confined my illustrations to British and American writers because I was thinking of an English-speaking audience, which I thought would be unfamiliar with any of the continental writers who might be mentioned. I was afraid that readers might be put off by what would seem to them a remoteness similar to that suggested in your previous paragraph. I think that I could easily introduce a few continental writers.

Yours sincerely,<br>
[T. S. Eliot]

TO *Ottoline Morrell*                                                           TS Texas

27 October 1936                    *The Criterion*

My dear Ottoline,

Thank you for your letter of the 23rd.[1] I saw George Barker on Saturday and he spoke with warm appreciation of having seen you the day before. He also struck me as being more mature and showing a good deal of perceptiveness in discussing other people's poetry. Also I have read some

---

him much more than any of the other papers have done. He notes that the paper is rather a *defence* of the Christian view against modernity than an analysis of the modern situation and problem. Would it be possible for you to develop your paper a little further in the latter direction?

'Baillie also raises the question how far many lay readers will find the high Catholic ground which you take to be *convincing*. He suggests that many readers find what you write on religious topics fascinating but rather remote from what they are able to accept.

'A point which occurred to me and has done also to Baillie is that the illustrations which you give are all British. Would it be possible for you to include one or two people from the Continent? e.g. Rosenberg and someone from France? I do not think that this is necessary. If you prefer to take British writers for purposes of illustration an explanatory sentence would be sufficient to put things right.'

1 – 'I had a long visit from George Barker this evening & I liked him very much. He spoke most gratefully of all you have done for him – & altogether. I thought he was very nice . . . & very much of an artist . . . [H]e is very poor. I felt very inclined to send him a cheque for £5 . . . If you think this would be a help – just now – let me know & I shall send it . . . I do hope he will get a job: he seems willing to take anything. I feel so dreadfully sorry for his poverty.'

Cantos of a new long poem which he has been at work on, and they struck me as well in advance of anything he has done before, so I still feel that he continues to merit help, not merely as a nice lad in difficulty, but as a valuable poet.

He told me that he will be staying up in town for another week as he has an appointment at the B.B.C. next Monday. I did not gather that there was any particular vacancy in view, and I am not too sanguine of his obtaining anything which will provide him with a livelihood. I mean to see him after his interview and find out what happened before he returns to Dorset. At the moment he is staying with his people, and I do not suppose that he is in desperate need during this week. My suggestion is that the assistance you mention might be more needed and also would help to raise his spirits if it came after this interview instead of before. If you agree I will let you know about the situation in a week's time.

Yours ever affectionately,<br>Tom

## TO *G. B. Harrison*[1]

28 October 1936                    [Faber & Faber Ltd]

My dear Harrison,

Your card announcing a meeting of the Council of the Shakespeare Association on Friday brings me to the point of the matter which has been in my head for some time. Since I became a member of the Council my business work has increased and my outside engagements have multiplied with the result that time on time during the last two years I have had to absent myself from the meetings of the Council because of other engagements. I feel that some of my more recent activities are of a kind in which I can be more useful than on the Council of the Shakespeare Association, which is already so well served by members of much more competence than myself. And I do not like to be a member of any board or committee in which I am not doing any work or taking an active part. I should like therefore to take this opportunity to offer with much regret my resignation to the Council. If the Council should be anxious for me to

1–G. B. Harrison (1894–1991), literary scholar, wrote on Shakespeare and his contemporaries, and became renowned as general editor of several series of popular editions of Shakespeare. Having been taught at Queens' College, Cambridge, by E. M. W. Tillyard, Mansfield Forbes, and IAR, he taught at King's College, London, and was Hon. Secretary of the Shakespeare Association.

continue I would perhaps reconsider the decision, but I feel very strongly that inactive members are worse than useless; and on the rare occasions on which I should be able to go I should feel too far out of touch with the work of the Council to have any contribution to make.

Yours very sincerely,<br>
[T. S. Eliot]

TO *Kenneth Fearing*[1]                                                    CC

30 October 1936                    [Faber & Faber Ltd]

My dear Sir,

Your volume of poems has been offered to us for publication, and as I have read them with much interest and enjoyment I want to write to you personally to explain why we do not feel that we can afford to publish them. It is extremely difficult at the present time to sell poetry, especially first books by authors. We make a persistent effort to publish one or more books of new verse every year, although these publications are invariably a financial loss to us. The sale even for English poets, who have the advantage of being better known here beforehand, both in periodicals and through personal contacts, is disgracefully small for a civilized country. The sale of books by American poets is very much smaller. In fact, such a small sale can be expected that the publication cannot be said to do the poet any good. It is for the latter reason, as much as for the former, that we practically never publish books by American poets unless they are authors of some years' standing. There is a third reason which is also operative. It is only by publishing a very small amount of new poetry that we are able to do anything toward establishing any one of the poets, and our influence in this way tends to vary inversely to the number of books of verse that we put forth.

---

1–Kenneth Fearing (1902–61), poet and novelist; contributor to the *New Yorker*; founding editor of *Partisan Review*; author of *Angel Arms* (1924) and *Poems* (1935). He published seven volumes of poetry and eight novels – the best-known being *The Big Clock* (filmed in 1948).

Your poems interested me more than nearly everything that I have seen from New York in recent times, and I should be glad if at any time you would let me see some poems with a view to publication in the *Criterion*.[1]

With best wishes,
Yours sincerely,
[T. S. Eliot]

TO *Tom Faber*                                                TS Valerie Eliot

30 October 1936                          *The Criterion*

Dear Tom,

I was very sorry to hear that you had been so ill at the beginning of your first term – though I should have been still sorrier for you if you had waited to be ill until the Christmas holidays: but I understand that you are now getting better & better at Boar's Hill (there may have been boars there once, but I never met any). I wish that I was coming to Oxford during this term, as I should like to come out and see you; but as it Falls Out, I have to go to Cambridge instead. Twice, which is tiresome. I had a very pleasant holiday in America, mostly in the mountains and at the sea-side, and felt very well when I got back, and Mr and Mrs Morley and Oliver and Susanna motored me back through Devon and Dorset, which was very pleasant. But I had not been home for a week before I caught a cold, and I have not got rid of it yet. I suppose that at Christmas you will motor straight to Wales, so I shall not see you then; but if you should be coming up to Hampstead before then I hope you will let me know.

I enclose the last poem I have Written.[2] I have not yet done any illustrations to it because I think the Poem might be improved a good deal in places, but I send it to you meanwhile and of course should be grateful for any criticism of it. I shall let off something in your honour and that of Guy Fawkes. I suppose you will not feel up to Writing letters for a good while yet, but when you do, please remember your

Uncle Tom

1–FVM to Barthold Fles (Fearing's agent in London), 2 Nov. 1936: 'We have kept Kenneth Fearing's POEMS for a long time, because we are particularly interested in him. Mr Eliot and I have both followed his work for some time, and Mr Eliot, in a personal way, has corresponded with him. But in spite of this real interest we cannot make an offer for the present collection . . . If, in spite of this, you can some time let us see Kenneth Fearing's novel, we should be very interested; and we should also, and always, be interested to know his plans for further work in poetry or prose.' For unknown reasons, Fearing's work did not appear in C.

2–'The Rum Tum Tugger'. TSE noted at the foot of the poem: '(sent on appro.)'.

## TO *Robert Speaight* CC

30 October 1936 [Faber & Faber Ltd]

My dear Bobby,

I have your card of the 26th with enclosure from H.M.V.[1] I am extremely sorry that there has been a misunderstanding, but we appear to have been dealing with different departments. I remember your mentioning the matter to me at Ottoline's some time ago, although I don't remember what we said about terms. However, when the request came from the gramophone company recently I had completely forgotten about our talk, and I left the matter to C. W. Stewart, who ordinarily deals with these matters, as this firm has an interest in my gramophone recordings, etc., as well as in my books. The gramophone company in their letter made no mention of you, so in leaving the terms for Stewart to discuss I only asked them to stipulate that the recording should be of your voice, or at any rate of some voice that met with my approval. I may say that in this correspondence a royalty of 5% was never mentioned. They started by offering 6¼%. Stewart then made enquiries as to what was the proper royalty and gathered that 10% was just. This rate he asked for, and in a letter of the 24th October a Mr C. B. Dawson Payne, reference A1 – EMN, informed us that the gramophone company was willing to pay 10%.

It seems to me, therefore, that the company, having committed themselves, should stick to it. I naturally want to do everything I can to convenience you personally, but you will understand that as the company has accepted our terms, I can't see any reason why I should ask my firm now to reduce them.

Yours ever,<br>[Tom]


## TO *Bruce Richmond* CC

30 October 1936 [Faber & Faber Ltd]

My dear Richmond,

I have asked Miss Harriet Weaver[2] to send you a copy of a book published in Paris, Chaucer's *Hymn to the Holy Virgin*, with rather

---

1–Not traced.
2–Harriet Shaw Weaver (1876–1961), English editor and publisher: see Biographical Register, *L* 4, 5.

remarkable illuminated initials, by Lucia Joyce, the daughter of my friend James Joyce.[1] It would, I know for private reasons which I am not at liberty to mention, be a great satisfaction to the Joyce family if this book were to have a notice in the *Supplement*.

Yours ever,<br>[T. S. E.]

## TO *Charles A. Siepmann*[2]　　　　　　　　　　　　　　　CC

[October/November 1936]　　　　　[Faber & Faber Ltd]

<u>PERSONAL.</u>

My dear Siepmann,

I should be very grateful if you would be willing to interview George Barker, who would like to get some sort of job in broadcasting. The point is that Barker would prefer to get a job in connection with talks in some regional station – his first choice would be Bristol – rather than in London, and I should imagine that you have very few applicants whose preference is for the provinces rather than for town.

You know, I think, something about his poetry, as I once discussed with you the possibility of having a reading of some of it. I am still a believer in his abilities as a poet, because the most recent work that he has shown me is a great advance on anything he has shown me before. Also, he seems to me to have matured, and I think you would find him a very likeable chap, with tastes and abilities which might be made use of.

Also it would be pleasant if you could lunch with me again. I shall leave it to you to suggest a general period within which it would be possible, because I imagine that you are out of London a great deal of the time.

---

1 – *Hymn to the Holy Virgin* in an English version by Geoffrey Chaucer, with capital letters designed and illuminated in gold, silver and numerous other colours by Lucia Joyce, was published by the Obelisk Press, Paris, marking the sexcentenary of the birth of Chaucer.

2 – Charles A. Siepmann (1899–1985), radio producer and educator, was awarded the Military Cross in WW1 (aged nineteen). After a time as a housemaster in a borstal, he joined the BBC in 1927, becoming Director of Talks, 1932–5; Regional Relations, 1935–6; Programme Planning, 1936–9 – whereupon he quit the BBC after a violent argument with the Director General, Lord Reith. He was University Lecturer, Harvard, 1939–42; worked for the Office of War Information, 1942–5; and was Professor of Education, New York University, 1946–67. Works include *Radio's Second Chance* (1946), *Radio, Television and Society* (1950), and *TV and Our School Crisis* (1959). See Richard J. Meyer, 'Charles A. Siepmann and Educational Broadcasting', *Educational Technology Research and Development* 12: 4 (Winter 1964), 413–30.

Yours sincerely,
[T. S. Eliot]

P.S. If you could see Barker at some time he would come up from Dorset at your convenience.


## TO *N. M. Iovetz-Tereshchenko*[1]                                    CC

4 November 1936                    [Faber & Faber Ltd]

Dear Dr Tereshchenko,

I have just been talking to Philip Mairet about you, and although he is as doubtful as I am of his being able to be of practical use he would be very glad to have a talk with you. I suggest therefore you should write to him care of the *New English Weekly*, 7 & 8 Rolls Passage, E.C.4, and arrange a time to see him.

Yours sincerely,
[T. S. Eliot]


## TO *Derek Verschoyle*                                    CC

5 November 1936                    [Faber & Faber Ltd]

Dear Verschoyle,

Thank you for your note of the 3rd.[2] I don't think, however, that I had better try to review Yeats's anthology. It would involve a good many remarks about poets included and excluded, and I have pretty consistently preferred to avoid expressing myself in public about the merits of individual living poets. Being a publisher of poetry as well as an editor puts me in a difficult position.[3]

Yours sincerely,
[T. S. Eliot]


1–N. M. Iovetz-Tereshchenko (1895–1954), B.Litt. (Oxon), PhD (London): Russian exile; Orthodox Catholic Christian; university lecturer in psychology: see Biographical Register.
2–Verschoyle invited TSE to review Yeats's anthology *The Oxford Book of Modern Verse 1895–1935* for the *Spectator*. 'It is a characteristically eccentric volume.'
3–Yeats on TSE: 'Eliot has produced his great effect upon his generation because he has described men and women that get out of bed or into it from mere habit; in describing this life that has lost heart his own art seems grey, cold, dry. He is an Alexander Pope, working without apparent imagination, producing his effects by a rejection of all rhythms and metaphors used by the more popular romantics rather than by the discovery of his own, this rejection giving his work an unexaggerated plainness that has the effect of novelty. He

5 November 1936                    *The Criterion*

Dear Stephen,

Thank you for your two letters and for the copy of the *Left Review*.[1] I liked your notice of Auden,[2] but I wish that Day Lewis wrote better English. I have just read a very painful note by him on Robert Frost in Cape's House organ.[3] There is no reason why I shouldn't let you have a poem except that I have literally nothing. When I can get rid of various petty engagements I hope to get to work on another play, but that is hardly likely to provide any fragments.

I agree with you about Leavis. Not that I have yet read your review, which has gone to the printer, but I agree with your remarks in your letter.[4] Leavis is so good that it is a great pity he is not a great deal better. He has never seemed to me to get any direct emotions from poetry or literature at all.

I only spoke for about 10 minutes the other evening, and you missed nothing by not coming.[5] What are your plans for the immediate future?

---

has the rhythmical flatness of the *Essay on Man* . . . later, in *The Waste Land*, amid much that is moving in symbol and imagery there is much monotony of accent' (*The Oxford Book of Modern Verse: 1892–1935*, ed. W. B. Yeats [1936], xxi).

1–Spender wrote, 1 Nov.: 'I am going to write a literary – & Day Lewis a political article for it [*Left Review*] each month, in order to give it a certain consistent line of writing . . . If you are in sympathy with the general line of the magazine would you care to send a poem to it?'

(TSE seems not to have responded to the other letter, dated 23 Oct., in which SS forwarded a poem by Frank Prince. 'I think the poem is remarkable . . . But you will judge for yourself.' SS remarked too: 'Lady Ottoline phoned desperately warning everyone of a surprise visit by Yeats. He was really very boring today – usually he is interesting in patches. There was such a noise that anyhow we couldn't hear him. So you didn't miss much, I think.')

2–'Fable and Reportage' (on WHA and Christopher Isherwood, *The Ascent of F6*), *Left Review* II (Nov. 1936), 779–82; repr. in *W. H. Auden: The Critical Heritage*, ed. Haffenden (1983), 191–7.

3–C. Day Lewis, 'Robert Frost', *Now and Then* no. 55 (Winter 1936), 19–20.

4–Spender submitted on 3 Nov. his review of F. R. Leavis's *Revaluation: Tradition and Development in English Poetry*. 'I am quite anxious to like Leavis whom I believe to be sincere as a man, but his book left me convinced that he is a parasite of other critics & a moral fake. If he weren't so dull, he would be a purely fashionable phenomenon. He has no opinions about poetry, only opinions about opinions, which he calls Taste. And all his criticism is really only about other critics, except when he is simply a train following lines laid down for him through 18th Century villas.' Spender on Leavis, *Revaluation*: *C.* 16 (Jan. 1937), 350–3.

5–'I lost my way yesterday & never got to your lecture. I was very sorry.'

I should like you to come and lunch with me before long, and tell me how the play is progressing.

Ever affectionately,

Tom

And I wonder if you have any Hölderin you would care to print in the *Criterion?*[1]


## TO *G. D. Rosenthal* CC

10 November 1936          [Faber & Faber Ltd]

Dear Father Rosenthal,

I thank you for your letter of the 6th instant.[2] I had already heard from the Bishop of Brechin, and had written to him saying that in the circumstances I should be glad and should feel honoured to continue acting as Secretary to the General Committee.

Thank you for your information about the Annual Meeting, about which I hope to hear more later.[3]

Yours ever sincerely,

[T. S. Eliot]


## TO *Theodore Spencer* TS Harvard Archives

9 no I mean 10 November 1936      *The Criterion*

My dear Ted,

As I am about to ask you a favour, I cannot do less than enclose this Complimentary Ticket to a Rugger Match or two which may or may not already have taken place: but which will give you the best of excuses for a visit to the Quaker City which I am sure languishes without your presence.[4] I am sure that Mr Charles Wharton Stork and his literary pals

---

1 – SS responded on 18 Nov.: 'I think I can finish one or two translations of Hoelderlin, which I shall send to you fairly soon.'

2 – The Revd G. D. Rosenthal, Secretary of the Church Literature Association, informed TSE that at the meeting of the Book Committee, it was the unanimous wish that he should continue to hold office as Secretary: 'In view of the fact that all the detailed work will be done as heretofore by the C.L.A. staff it was felt that you would be willing to do this.'

3 – The Annual Meeting was fixed for Thurs. 28 Jan.; but they had not yet secured a hall.

4 – Spencer hailed from Pennsylvania, and retained something of the local accent.

need your encouragement. Besides, I understand that there is a boy on the Haverford team who recently CLIPPED THE TIGER'S CLAWS.[1]

What I am asking of you is to stir up Alport [*sc.* Allport][2] and ask him whether he has read my Jovetz Tereshcheschenko's [*sic*] Book, and what he thinks about it and whether anything can be done about Jovetz. Because Jovetz has recently been round to me setting up on his hind legs with his paws out.[3]

I am in the usual maelstrom of the pandemonium of November, if you take my meaning. What I mean is, that I have to address the English club of your university (I forget the name at the moment) on Friday, and do a B.B.C. talk on drama in a series for the 6th form of schools next Friday, and address the Shirley Society of St Catharine's College the following Sunday, and so on. I have bought a new hat like Mr Anthony Eden's, but neater. John H. is as usual in the vortex of society and having Musical Evenings, and last week he asked me in to meet the Duchesse de La Rochefoucauld.[4] It would not surprise me to meet Madame de Guermantes there, or even the Baron de Charlus. We have published one good book: *Nightwood* by Djuna Barnes – *retenez bien le nom*. My play is now in the West End (with a lot more rugs and jugs and candle lights), and I hope to make a little more money; but the problem is always to make money faster than people think you are making it – it can't be done. I have been reading a translation into French of it, by an Egyptian Jew and a Portuguese Jew (confidential) which affects me so deeply that I can only say, in the words of old JHON FOORDE [*sic*] who puts it so pithily in his play *The Broken Wind* –

> It is the silent farts that wet the pantseat!
> Let me die smiling . . .[5]

1–Haverford College, Pennsylvania, played the Princeton Tigers in Intercollegiate League soccer. See too *Poems I*, ed. Ricks and McCue, 496.

2–Gordon Allport (1897–1967), psychologist, taught at Harvard, 1930–67. Author of *Personality Traits: Their Classification and Measurement* (1921), from 1924 he taught a course entitled 'Personality: Its Psychological and Social Aspects'.

3–Spencer replied, 14 Nov.: 'I am sorry to have been slow in doing anything about your Russian "Friendship-Love in Adolescence" man, but the psychologist here has been difficult to get hold of. He says that there isn't any chance of the Russian's getting a job sight unseen: the best thing for him to do is to get, if possible, something like a Rockefeller scholarship, come over here with that as a background, & get himself known on that basis. Merely to come here without some such official parenthesis around him wouldn't do any good.'

4–Edmée de la Rochefoucauld, née Frisch (1895–1991), woman of letters, married in 1917 Count Jean de la Rochefoucauld (1887–1970), who became the thirteenth Duke de la Rochefoucauld following the disappearance of his father in 1926.

5–In 'John Ford', *TLS*, 5 May 1932, 317–18 (repr. *SE*), TSE quoted from Ford's *The Broken Heart*, V. iii: 'They are the silent griefs which cut the heart-strings; / Let me die smiling.'

Remember me to Nancy, John and Mattie. I thought that Frisky was a bit sniffy to me when we were there to tea: was it because I had happened at lunch to speak disrespectfully of General Franco? I hope you won any number of Election Bets,[1] though I have heard no report of Mr Lowell pushing you up Blue Hill in a wheelbarrow.

Yr faithful

TP

## TO *John Hayward*

TS King's

10 November 1936                    *The Criterion*

My dear John,

I should like your advice about the enc. I should love dearly to earn 1c a word and UP . . . though it is not quite clear quite what UP means . . . and the notion of appearing in traveller's size excites me . . . and I have a firm practice of concision, towards my own contributors, so that's all right . . . but I'm afraid that I'm a little weak on little quirks . . . Now it is exactly with little quirks that I am hopeful of your help . . . and if you will collaborate on the little quirks, I think we might split on 1/2c and UP each . . . What do you think? Besides, I know that you are a superior reportager to myself . . . and a good sport who will gladly go to bat with me . . . the deadline, I forgot to say, was yesterday . . . . . . . . . . What say, huh? . . .

I really sat down to the machine to tell you that I had a touching letter from Willie Yeats, saying that some folk had already interpreted his Preface as meaning that he preferred the poetry of MacN and Auden to mine, and denying this allegation . . .[2] So don't go and say in reviewing the book that he said so . . .

Yrs etc.

TP

1 – Democratic President Franklin D. Roosevelt won a landslide victory over his opponent, Republican Governor Alf Landon of Kansas, in the US Presidential Election on 3 Nov. 1936.
2 – Yeats protested, 9 Nov.: 'Dear Eliot / This morning I got, in a letter from a friend, an extract from *The Observer* saying that in my forthcoming anthology I preferred MacNeice & Auden to you. I have done nothing of the kind. / Yrs / W B Yeats.'

10 November 1936:                     *The Criterion*
such a long time after
Guy Fawkes' Day[1]

My dear Alison,

   The last Cat I wrote about, was such a Boastful Brutal Beastly Bloody
Bad Pirate, that you may think that I am a kittenthrope, or Hater of Cats:
but such is not the Case. On the contrary. So I hasten to tell you about
another Kind of Cat, to my knowledge, that is wholly admirable. It is

### THE OLD GUMBIE CAT

I have a Gumbie Cat in mind, her name is Jennyanydots;
Her coat is of the tabby kind, with tiger stripes and leopard spots.
All day she sits upon the stair or on the steps or in the mat;
She sits and sits and sits and sits and that's what makes a Gumbie Cat!

   But when the day's hustle and bustle is done,
   Then the Gumbie Cat's work is but hardly begun.
   And when all the fambly's in bed and asleep,
   She tucks up her skirts and downstairs will creep.
   There she must every night attend to the mice –
   Their behaviour's not good and their manners not nice;
   And when she has got them lined up on the matting,
   She teaches them music, crocheting and tatting.

I have a Gumbie Cat in mind, her name is Jennyanydots;
Her equal would be hard to find, she likes the warm and sunny spots.
All day she sits beside the hearth or on the bed or in my hat:
She sits and sits and sits and sits and that's what makes a Gumbie Cat!

   But when the day's hustle and bustle is done,
   Then the Gumbie Cat's work is but hardly begun.
   As she finds that the mice will not ever keep quiet,
   She is sure it is due to irregular diet.
   And believing that nothing is done without trying,
   She sets straight to work with her baking and frying.
   She makes them a mouse-cake with bread and dried peas,
   And a beautiful fry of lean bacon and cheese.

1 – Envelope addressed to 'Miss Alison Tandy, Hope Hope Hope Hurrah Cottage'.

I have a Gumbie Cat in mind, her name is Jennyanydots;
The window-cord she likes to wind, and tie it up in sailor knots.
She sits upon the window-sill, or anything that's smooth and flat:
She sits and sits and sits and sits and that's what makes a Gumbie Cat!

But when the day's hustle and bustle is done,
Then the Gumbie Cat's work is but hardly begun.
She thinks that the cockroaches just need employment
To preserve them from idle and wanton destroyment.
So she's formed, from that lot of disorderly louts,
A troop of well-disciplined helpful boy-scouts;
With a purpose in life and a great deal to do;
And she's even created a Beetles' Tattoo.

So for Old Gumbie Cats let us now give three cheers –
On whom well-ordered households depend, it appears.

So now! nobody can say that I am UNAPPRECIATIVE of Cats.
                                    Your faithful
                                    Possum


TO *Georges Cattaui*                                    CC

11 November 1936                    [Faber & Faber Ltd]

My dear Cattaui,

Thank you for your letter of the 1st November.[1] I have been very slow, you may think, in replying to it, but I wanted to examine the manuscript of the translation as carefully as possible before committing myself to an opinion. I might as well say at once that I do not think this translation can be considered as more than the first draft which might be useful material upon which a practical translation might be based. I do not pretend to be a French scholar, and I therefore speak with some hesitation, but it seems to me that the translation errs throughout in being much too literal, and therefore fails frequently to arrive at the most appropriate French equivalent. To take only one small detail, I believe I am right in suspecting that 'roue de Catharine' is not a French equivalent for that piece of fire-works so well known in England, and that it would not accordingly convey the English significance of the revolving piece of fire-works

1 – Cattaui had submitted the draft translation of *MiC* made by himself and Emile d'Erlanger.

375

which so frequently fails to revolve. I should have thought that either the general term *feu d'artifice* or else something parallel, such as *la lanterne magique*, would be more satisfactory. Again, on page 45 the translation for 'abroad' is given as *à l'etranger*. Of course in English 'abroad' has a double meaning, but of the two meanings *à l'etranger* is here the less important. The essential meaning is 'all about the place'.

I can't feel that I should like the translation in this stage to be presented to French readers and hearers who are unacquainted with the English text. Of course I can see that the whole thing is exceedingly difficult to translate, and that great parts of it can only be rendered by bold and inspired paraphrase. I don't envy anyone the task.

The best translator in Paris whom I know, and who knows my work, is St-Léger Léger. He worked with me on my translation of his *Anabase*, to the vast improvement of my version, and has also translated a few things of mine into French. The only question would be whether his work at the Quai d'Orsay would allow him time to take an interest in this job. I feel that it is a kind of translation, perhaps, in which several people would have to co-operate, as it requires an intimate and, so to speak, creative knowledge of both languages. I am sorry that this is all I can say at the moment.

Yours ever sincerely,
[T. S. Eliot]

TO *Ashley Dukes*                                                             CC

11 November 1936                    [Faber & Faber Ltd]

My dear Dukes,

Thank you for your letter of the 9th and for sending the cheque to the bank.[1] I should like to ask one question about the royalties from the Federal Theatre Project. It would seem to me on the face of it that so far as I am concerned this is income arising in this country and that therefore I have no need to return it in my annual returns of income to the American Government. I naturally wish to avoid this if possible, because, as you no doubt know, the American tax has risen and will I dare say rise further. So can you give me any information that may help to establish my case? Have you, or has the Nameless Theatre, Limited, accounted to the American Government for tax on the proceeds of the New York production? I assume that as this is a Government venture anyway that

1–Dukes had sent a cheque for £167. 0s. 3d. for sundry royalties on productions of *MiC*.

tax will have been deducted at source before any payment was made to you.[1]

I agree wholeheartedly to your suggestion of a readjustment of my royalties on the Duchess production,[2] and I am particularly glad that it should enable Martin Browne to have something nearer to an adequate remuneration for the work that he has done.[3]

I also have your other letter about the production to be given in Budapest and possibly Italy.[4] I have no doubt that you have arranged for the best possible translations to be made, and in any case the more remote the language the less one cares. But I am especially anxious that nothing should be done in French unless the translation is approved by myself. I raise this point because I have recently had a translation submitted to me by Emile d'Erlanger and Georges Cattaui which seems to me so bad that I have had to tell them that I did not wish any part of it to be printed or, as they had intended, recited by a lady from the Odéon. At least, if it is done, I want a translation which is made by a Frenchman into French, which this is not. It seems to me desirable that before any French version

1–Dukes said on 13 Nov. that the royalties from the Federal Theatre production were paid to his representative (Editor-in-Chief of *Theatre Arts Monthly*) without deduction of tax. 'I think it very likely that payments made to authors by the American Government under this project were tax free as they are so much smaller than the usual scale of fees.' He advised TSE to ignore them in his US tax return – 'unless some demand is made. The amount, of course, is subject to tax in this country.'

2–*MiC* opened at the little Duchess Theatre, Aldwych, London, on 30 Oct. 1936 (two days before the anniversary of its opening at the Mercury Theatre): the *Times* hailed it as 'the one great play by a contemporary dramatist now to be seen in England'. However, the production presently ran up against the Abdication Crisis of of King Edward VIII on 11 Dec. 1936, announced on 10 Dec., which as Ashley Dukes pointed out ('Poet into successful dramatist', *New York Times*, 20 Feb. 1938) 'gave awkward point' to such lines as

> King is forgotten when another shall come.

and

> If the Archbishop cannot trust the Throne
> He has good cause to trust none but God alone.

3–Dukes asked for EMB to receive 'a percentage, however small, on the Duchess receipts, and I am sure you will recognize the present success of the play is very largely due to his direction. He received only a fee of £10 from the Duchess management and is getting a salary of £10 – I consider both of these inadequate and want to do something to make them good.' Thus TSE would earn from the Duchess Theatre 4% of several hundred pounds weekly. (For the month of Dec. 1936, for example, box-office receipts at the Duchess were £1,940. 17. 2d., of which TSE received 5% (£97. 0. 10) minus 20% (£19. 8. 2), yielding him £77. 12. 8d.)

4–Dukes had reported on 7 Nov. that Hans Bartsch, who had acquired the Hungarian rights of *MiC*, had arranged for a production by the National Theatre of Budapest, in a translation by Dr Alexander Szik, Hungarian poet and Professor of Literature at the University of Budapest. Bartsch had offered in addition to purchase the Italian rights, and to pay the translator himself.

is allowed there ought to be some performance in Paris by the English company, which will at least give the audience some information on how the thing ought to sound, even if they can't all follow it. I have had a brief talk recently with Madame de Margerie[1] and the Duchesse de la Rochefoucauld, who seem to think that they are in a position to do something about the matter, and if they are serious you ought to hear from one of them about it.

Yours ever,<br>
[T. S. Eliot]

P.S. I see that your publicity man managed to get a more favourable notice into the *Telegraph*.[2]

## TO *H.M. Undersecretary of State, Aliens' Department, Home Office*   TS UCLA

11 November 1936          *The Criterion*

Sir,

I am glad to offer myself as a sponsor for Mr Edward [*sic*] Roditi in his application to be allowed to reside in this country. I have known Mr Roditi for some years as a poet and man of letters, and neither in my personal acquaintance nor in his literary work – he has been a contributor to the *Criterion* – have I regarded him as a foreigner in any way. He writes English as his native tongue, and his poetry has distinction and beauty. I believe his abilities, experience and education to be such that I should consider it for the good of English letters that he should be allowed to reside here. And so far as I know him personally, my opinion of him supports my opinion of his literary work.[3]

I have the honour to be, Sir,<br>
Your obedient servant,<br>
T. S. Eliot

---

1 – Henriette ('Jenny') de Margerie – née Fabre-Luce (she was the daughter of one of France's foremost bankers) – '*die fromme Jenny*' ('the pious Jenny'), as TSE called her in 'Abschied zur Bina' (*Noctes Binanianae*, 1939) – was wife of the cultured and witty diplomat Ronald de Margerie (1899–1990), nephew of Edmond de Rostand, the creator of *Cyrano de Bergerac*, and a close friend of the theologian Teilhard de Chardin; first secretary at the French Embassy, London, where he established good relations with many politicians including Winston Churchill (and later adviser on foreign policy to Charles de Gaulle, and ultimately French Ambassador to Bonn from 1962). The couple were to become close friends of JDH.
2 – Sydney W. Carroll, 'A fine poetic play', *The Daily Telegraph*, 5 Nov. 1936.
3 – Roditi thanked TSE (n.d.) for his 'extremely kind and appreciative letter, which impressed my solicitor considerably and will, I hope, likewise influence the Home Office in my favour'.

# TO *J. S. Barnes*[1]

TS Buona Barnes

11 November 1936            *The Criterion*

My dear Jim,

It was very pleasant to hear from you after all this time, and I have read your manuscript about Abyssinia with much interest. I am afraid it is not suitable for the *Criterion* and therefore I am returning it to you quickly so that you may make use of it elsewhere. For one thing it is much too long, and I don't quite see how it could be cut. One reason is that it is only incidentally about Abyssinia, and I think really that you ought to reshape it yourself into several different articles. One might be about the decadence of Britain, and another about the rise of the Italian nation; I don't much relish the conjunction, and I feel that either point could be made more plausible to readers if it were not associated with the other. There are other questions of detail which might be put. Your case for the Norman aristocracy of England seems to me to rest on a very slight foundation. I should imagine that the Norman blood of England was now pretty well distributed, and that it was several centuries at least since any perceptibly large part of it was confined to the veins of the aristocracy. Then again the mixing with the new rich to which you call attention during the 19th century seems to me to have begun very much earlier, so that you might

---

1 – James Strachey Barnes (1890–1955): son of Sir Hugh Barnes. Brought up in Florence by his grandparents, Sir John and Lady Strachey, he went on to Eton and King's College, Cambridge. During WW1 he served in the Guards and Royal Flying Corps.

TSE to Sir Robert Vansittart of the Foreign Office, 12 Jan. 1939 (when Barnes was applying to be Assistant Director of the British Institute in Florence): 'Barnes is the younger brother of an old friend of mine, Mrs St John Hutchinson, and I have known him, in this way, off and on for a good many years. He wrote two books on Fascism . . . and was one of its earliest champions in this country. He was brought up in Italy (before going to Eton: he was subsequently in the Blues, then a Major in the Air Force, and at King's after the War), has an Italian wife, and is the most convinced pro-Italian and pro-Fascist that I know. He is a Roman Catholic convert, and has or had some honorary appointment at the Vatican; but manages to combine this with a warm admiration for Mussolini, from which it follows that he has disapproved of British policy whenever that policy did not favour Italian policy. He was for a time a correspondent of Reuter, and in that capacity was with the Italians in Abyssinia. He has since lectured in America on international politics, and I believe took the opportunity of defending Italy. In private life he is rather a bore, and talks more than he listens, somewhat failing to appreciate that the person to whom he is talking may have other interests and other engagements.

'I would not encumber you with these details – which for aught I know may be all in his favour – but that my conscience is uneasy if I give a recommendation in which I do not say all that I know which may be relevant.'

See too David Bradshaw and James Smith, 'Ezra Pound, James Strachey Barnes ("the Italian Lord Haw-Haw") and Italian Fascism', *Review of English Studies* 64 (2013), 672–93.

almost say that the England of any period has consisted largely of the descendants of the new rich of a couple of generations before. There was certainly plenty of plebeian infusion during the 15th and 16th centuries.

I mentioned this sort of point not because I think you are wrong but because I think you have failed to make a case which would persuade readers. I don't deny that there is much in your article which is persuasive and worth saying, but I do think that it attempts to cover far too much ground.[1]

With best wishes to your wife, and hoping to see you whenever you visit England,

Yours ever,<br>T. S. E.

TO *F. A. Iremonger*[2]                                         TS BBC

12 November 1936                    *The Criterion*

My dear Iremonger,

CHURCH COMMUNITY AND STATE[3]

I enclose some notes, to which of course I have not been able to give all the time that I would. You will see that the group of problems that has been handed to me is extremely bristly, and likely to become more so. I can't help feeling that the lot has fallen on me to go down the drain

---

1 – Barnes (New Delhi, 29 Nov.) agreed that his thesis would be better split into several articles: 'But damn it all. How is one to do anything well with the ghastly life which a bread winner must needs live doing donkey work from dawn to dusk.'

2 – The Revd Frederic Athelwold Iremonger, DD (1878–1952): Director of Religion at the BBC, 1933–9; subsequently Dean of Lichfield Cathedral.

3 – Iremonger had first contacted TSE on 20 Aug. 1936 in connection with the Conferences on 'Christian Life and Work' and 'Faith and Order' to be held in England in 1937. The BBC Programme Division was planning a course of six talks to be broadcast in support of the conferences, all delivered by laymen, to be called 'Church, Community, and State', and Iremonger invited TSE to be a speaker: the others were Sir Walter Moberly, Professor Arnold Toynbee, Professor T. E. Jessop, Mr H. G. Wood, and Lord Lothian. TSE's slot was 26 Jan. So eager was Iremonger to secure TSE's cooperation that he wrote this letter to J. H. Oldham, 1 Sept. 1936: 'Here is a copy of a letter I had from Eliot's secretary a day or two ago. I think it is absolutely essential that we should get him, so do you think you could write him a personal note, pleading with him to give the talk for which I ask his help? It is the one, you may remember, on the Church; and I don't think anybody could do it better than Eliot. I am asking his secretary to let me have his address in America, so that a plea from you might reach him before he starts back. This certainly will mean a corresponding delay, but I believe that this would be worth while if only we can get Eliot's help.' (cc at BBC Caversham)

after the man-eating tiger.[1] But otherwise not worth bothering with these questions at all.

Sincerely yours,<br>
T. S. Eliot

## TO *Robert Speaight* CC

12 November 1936            [Faber & Faber Ltd]

Dear Bobby,

I am behind hand in answering your letter of the 1st.[2] Although the gramophone company did accede to our terms I have asked Faber and Faber to stand down in the matter and accept the 5 per cent in view of my previous correspondence with you. So I hope the matter is now settled, and I hope the company will let me have a copy of the record when it is ready. I am very glad indeed that your rendering of the sermon should be preserved in this way.

Yours ever,<br>
[Tom]

## TO *P. S. Richards* CC

18 November 1936            [Faber & Faber Ltd]

My dear Richards,

Thank you for your note of the 15th returning proof of your article.[3] I ought to have written to you before to tell you that I did make a rapid excursion from Boston to see More in Princeton, and spent the day with him. He was not exactly bed-ridden, but was able to get up and spend the day lying on a couch in his library. He also seems to take his meals sitting up. He was shockingly emaciated, which gave him a much stronger

1 – See *The Return of Sherlock Holmes*: a tale referenced by TSE in 'Gus: The Theatre Cat': 'He once played a Tiger – could do it again / Which an Indian Colonel pursued down the drain.'

2 – Speaight thanked TSE for his letter of 30 Oct., which he had forwarded to HMV. 'The only amendment I have to make to it is that you did agree *in writing* to the 5% Royalty. That, however, was in correspondence with me, and I don't know how far it binds you. I did write to you at the Gramophone Co's request, but on the other hand I am quite sure I have lost your letter! I quite see Faber's point in the matter, but it seems a pity for all concerned that the Records should be held up just when they would be likely to have a good sale.'

3 – 'The Religious Philosophy of Paul Elmer More'.

resemblance to his brother than I had ever noticed before, and his skin was of a very striking whiteness, as if there was no blood anywhere near the surface. Though he seemed very weak his mind was as active as ever, and we had a very satisfactory talk. I was with him for about an hour before lunch. He has a rest between lunch and tea time, but at tea time two of the younger members of the Faculty came in to see him and stayed talking for about an hour and a half. There are three of four of these men, who are very devoted to him and visit him constantly, and this provides him with all the conversation that he has. He spoke hopefully of the future, but I could not hope doubting whether he would ever be well enough to do more than linger on in Princeton for the rest of his life.

Would you care to review his new volume of *Shelburne Essays* for me for the March number? If you have not got a copy I will send it.[1]

With best wishes to yourself and Mrs Richards,

Yours ever,

[T. S. Eliot]

## TO *Donald C. Gallup*[2]                                        CC

18 November 1936                    [Faber & Faber Ltd]

Dear Mr Gallup,

Thank you for your letter of November 8th mentioning the forthcoming exhibition, of which I do not think I had heard.[3] I shall be glad to have further news of it when the time comes.

Thank you for enclosing a copy of my correspondence with Arnold Bennett. I am glad to find that there is nothing in it which seems to need to be suppressed, either in the interests of Mr Bennett or of myself.[4]

---

1–P. S. Richards on Paul Elmer More, *On Being Human: New Shelburne Essays*, vol. III: C. 16 (Apr. 1937), 514–16.

2–Donald Gallup (1913–2000): curator, bibliographer and editor: see Biographical Register.

3–Gallup had met TSE, with Sheff and Ada Sheffield, and Henry and Theresa Eliot, on a visit to Wellesley College – 'one of my happiest experiences', he said. Now he was putting on an 'Eliot exhibition' at Yale, and hoped to be able to print a catalogue on the Bibliographical Press in the Library. See Donald C. Gallup, *A Catalogue of English and American First Editions of Writings by T. S. Eliot Exhibited in the Yale University Library 22 February to 20 March, 1937* (1937).

4–'You may remember that at Wellesley I mentioned a letter you wrote, but did not send, to the (London) Evening Standard. I am afraid that my incoherent babble did not give you a very good idea of its content, and so I enclose a copy of it, and of the pertinent letters to Bennett.'

The piece of work which I remember having pirated was one of the two sections of *Sweeney Agonistes*.[1] It was certainly Mr Samuel Roth, however, who published this piece. I remember being the more annoyed because he chose to dedicate that issue of his magazine to myself. Possibly he pirated *Eeldrop and Appleplex* also, but I was not aware of that.[2]

I cannot recall how *Literature and Export Trade* got into the Class List.[3] It must have been either a small leg-pull of my own, or a confusion on the part of somebody else. There is no such work in existence. I was certainly concerned at one time with export trade, and at the time mentioned, 1924–25, I was writing monthly articles on foreign currency movements for the Lloyds Bank Monthly Magazine. I am afraid I have no copies of the magazine with my contributions, which were, like other contributions to that paper, unsigned. It is therefore only by internal evidence that my contributions can be distinguished from those of my predecessor and my successor.

> With best wishes,
> Yours sincerely,
> [T. S. Eliot]


TO *Henry Miller*                                                    CC

18 November 1936                    [Faber & Faber Ltd]

Dear Mr Miller,

Thank you for your letter of the 9th instant.[4] I should be very glad to look at some of the material which you suggest sending. I don't like single contributions to be more than 5,000 words, if possible.

> Yours sincerely,
> [T. S. Eliot]


1–Gallup asked what work by TSE had been pirated in 1927 – was it 'Eeldrop and Appleplex'?

2–Samuel Roth pirated 'Eeldrop and Appleplex' in his *Two Worlds Monthly* 1: 2 (Sept. 1926), 189–92; 'Fragment of a Prologue' in *Two Worlds Monthly* 2: 2 (Jan. 1927), 143–6.

3 – 'In the Fifteenth Report of the Secretary of the (Harvard) Class of 1910, a partial list of your books and periodical contributions is given. Among the former occurs "Literature and Export Trade (1925)". So far as I have been able to ascertain, this work has no existence outside this list. Can you, Sir, tell me anything about it?'

4–Miller proposed to submit one or two letters from the correspondence called *Hamlet* that he was writing with Michael Fraenkel (author of *Bastard Death*.) 'The book is being written

20 November 1936                    [Faber & Faber Ltd]

My dear Joyce,

I am sending you herewith for your choice specimens of two pages of *Work in Progress* printed in the only three types which we have been able to find at all suitable. During the last year we have made a number of experiments, and have had, I think, about 25 specimen pages set up, and of all that are obtainable these seem to be the only three at all possible. We should be glad to leave the final choice between these three to you, if you have any definite preference for one over the others. I should be glad, therefore, if you would let me have back the specimen which you prefer.

I hope that your work will be able to progress satisfactorily through the winter without such anxieties as have hampered you during the past year.[1]

                                        Yours ever,
                                        [T. S. Eliot]


TO *Polly Tandy*                                                   TS BL

20 November 1936                    *The Criterion*

My dear Polligal,

Thank you kindly for your sort of invitation thrown out as to Monday or Wednesday next, and wd. much like to accept same, but Here's it. On Wed. I have to take a Old Lady out to dinner, and on Mon. I shall be too exHausted after reading a Paper at Cambridge on Sunday night. Well whats on the air the following week? or shall I throw a lil party at Eliot's[2] in Ch.X Road instead? Shd. like to see you somehow, esp. after most fatiguing 10 days & have been on the Air my self this p.m. I have arranged with Young George (Barnwell) to make 2 15-min. selections from Herbert Vaughan & Traherne which Y. George is to ask your old man to recite in

---

in the form of letters one to the other. Some of them have a complete quality in themselves.' Miller asked too if TSE had a preferred length for submissions to C.

1 – Paul Léon replied on JJ's behalf, 7 Dec. 1936: 'Mr Joyce who is very busy on w.i.p. ['Work in Progress' – *Finnegans Wake*] at present asked me to thank you for your letter and to return you enclosed the three types of printing marking the one he prefers with the red pencil . . .

'The work itself is progressing and I think I was not greatly mistaken when I wrote to you that it could be out within a year from July last.'

2 – Eliot's Club, Charing Cross Road, London.

February. But what I am spelling for is for Possum to become a regular Feature in the Childrens' Hour, and any suggestions he cd. make to that end in the proper Quarters wd. be appreciated. I am toilin away trying to finish the Marching Song of the Pollicle Dogs, but the Scots dialect or language comes difficult to Me. It starts

> My name it is little Tom Pollicle
> And wha maun meddle wi me?

But there I stuck so far.

I am sorry about your back but when you get to my age you'll be so used to rheumaticky pains you wouldnt know how to live with[out] em. Hoping all flourishes, considering everything, and so will close

Yours faithfull

Tp.

I almost forgot to say, Regards to the Licensee.

## TO *Bonamy Dobrée*                                                    TS Brotherton

21 November 1936[1]

> THE CRITERION
> A QUARTERLY REVIEW
> EDITED BY T. S. Eliot
> [Inserted by hand] without any help
> from his 'friends'
> 24 Russell Square, London W.C.1

Dear BONAMY,

You Are a nice kind of Friend, to take no notice of any body all this time: here I've been back since Oct. 12th and plunged into Arrears and then caught cold and have been having Injections which they say has proved useless in the Post Office, and my doctor has made me promise to address the League of Mercy at Lady Cynthia Crinkley's in Hyde Park Sq. and I have had to talk in Cambridge twice, last week and aiagain [*sic*] tomorrow, which they don't even pay one's fare for, so why does one do it I should like to know, and I addressed the 6th Forms on the Wireless yesterday,[2] and no end of practical problems to solve before I can get to work on trying to write a play. So you might have enquired after me I do Think. And next Sunday evening I have to read poetry to some Students

---

1 – See BD's discussion of this letter, quoted in full, in 'T. S. Eliot: A Personal Reminiscence', in *T. S. Eliot: The Man and His Work*, ed. Allen Tate (1967), 81–2.
2 – 'The Need for Poetic Drama', *Listener* 16: 411 (25 Nov. 1936), 994–5. 'A Schools Broadcast to Sixth Forms . . .'; repr. in *Good Speech* (London) 7: 35 (Apr./June 1937), 1–6.

to please Canon Tissington Tatlow D.D., why does one do it. With all this how can I be expected to attend to Christmas Cards? Well what about it. Leeds, I mean, and Boston Spa. And the History – and what's this queer 6 volume work of yours announced by the Cresset Press?[1] – and that volume I worked so hard for, when is it to appear?[2] John Hayward and I want our 15 guineas we do, what with the doctor and the dentist I think I am going to lose another Tooth. And where is your Soul? at present. Would Georgina[3] whom God preserve be interested in my two latest poems or not? I mean *Growltiger's Last Stand* (picaresque) and *The Old Gumbie Cat* (domestic) or not?[4] And may I hear from you, or not? Now, would you be coming up to London before Xmas if we had a *Criterion* Yuletide Revel? and when? Not worth while unless you could spend two nights, so that we could have a QUiet Evening as well, with some decent vintage instead of the vile sherry and hock which is all that the *Criterion* minions deserve. And seriously, now that you are a Perfesser, may I put you up for the O. & C. Club, which you ought to join, and can join at the moment because the entrance fee is temporarily abrogated. Seriously, I am quite in the dumps about the European Situation, so I need your cheering company. With love to Valentine and Respects to the General will close[5]

T. S. E.


TO *Louis MacNeice*                                                          CC

25 November 1936                    [Faber & Faber Ltd]

Dear MacNeice,

Harcourt, Brace and Company, who are my own publishers in New York, and of whom I think very highly, will, I think, be persuaded to take sheets of the *Agamemnon*. I do not think that we could do better

---

1 – BD had undertaken to be General Editor of a series of Introductions to English Literature.
2 – 'Byron (1788–1824) by T. S. Eliot', in *From Anne to Victoria*, ed. Dobrée (1937), 601–19.
3 – Georgina Dobrée, aet. 6.
4 – TSE posted 'Growltiger' also to young Susan Wolcott, who responded on 23 Nov. 1936: 'Dear Cousin Tom / Thank you for the poem about Growltiger specially about Griddlebones. I would have liked to have been Growltiger myself. I must say the other cats were rather cowards! I havent heard it yet on the radio. / With love from Susan Wolcott.'
5 – BD responded, 24 Nov.: 'I know. I'm a *brutta bestia* and among all the horrid things that creep or crawl amid the fog at Leeds . . . Your serious question as to the O & C Club. Yes, I think I would like to join now, if there is no entrance fee. Thank you very much . . .

'I too am in the dumps about the European situation, and indeed the Berritish one . . .

'I regret the bitterness of your insertion concerning the editing of the Criterion. What can I do? Would you like my Inaugural Lecture?'

for you in the way of a New York publisher than this. They would like, also, to have the control of American dramatic rights, and I am inclined to advise you to agree to this. I think that you ought to have someone in New York to look after dramatic rights in America, and these are honest people. They think that there is a possibility of getting the Federal Theatre Project, who did *Murder in the Cathedral* for six weeks last spring, to put the *Agamemnon* on in New York, and I think it would be a very good thing if this were done, and would not prejudice any future production by any other company. So I wish you would think this over and let me know soon whether you are ready to make an arrangement with Harcourt, Brace on terms satisfactory to yourself.[1]

I'd like to see you soon, and will write again to suggest a day to get you to lunch with me.

Yours sincerely,<br>
[T. S. Eliot]

1–Harcourt, Brace had initially expressed misgivings about the idea of publishing *Agamemnon* in the USA. C. A. Pearce to FVM, 23 Oct. 1936: 'Several of us have read Louis MacNeice's translation of THE AGAMEMNON OF AESCHYLUS, and we were all considerably disappointed by it. Not wishing to rely entirely upon the judgments of people who have necessarily had to read it quickly, I have asked a young friend of mine to examine it carefully. His report convinces us that our estimate of the translation is sound.' The anonymous friend's report ran to four paragraphs, concluding: 'It is decidedly not the style of any spoken English anywhere. So far as the stage requires clarity in a known idiom, or even in a dramatic convention, MacNeice's language is apparently deliberately cut off from the stage. Though you regret this you can understand it easily: a composition so largely made up of choruses and long speeches, confined in its action really to one or two scenes, may as well be treated outright as a poem. MacNeice might well have considered that the choice lay between poetic power and dramatic clarity and decided that in the AGAMEMNON, of all Greek plays, the one should not be sacrificed to the other. Very good. The trouble is that in nine cases out of ten his writing comes short of fine poetry.'

Notwithstanding all such reservations, Pearce wrote again to FVM on 9 Nov.: 'Now that we've had time to swallow our disappointment, we're inclined to do as you suggest, if we can purchase a small quantity of sheets at the proper price. Can you cable us your best price for 250 sheets? . . . After all, Louis MacNeice is more than a respectable name; his translation is sound, if occasionally stilted or academic; and we feel we ought to do the book as you have done ALCESTIS. Naturally, also, we're interested in the Group Theatre's announcement of a new play by MacNeice, and we'll want to see that as soon as we can.'

On 26 Nov., LM replied to TSE's letter that he was happy with the suggestions.

## TO *Montgomery Butchart*[1]                                                    CC

25 November 1936                                    [Faber & Faber Ltd]

Dear Butchart,

In reply to your letter of the 20th I would *a priori* certainly consider publishing a selection of E. E. Cummings' poems, as they have not heretofore appeared in this country,[2] but I happen to know that Roger Roughton[3] has in view in the near future the publication of such a selection under the aegis of his little periodical *Contemporary Prose and Poetry*. I understand from Roughton that he has been in touch with Cummings, and that he considers the publication a certainty.[4] However, if this project falls through, I should be glad to reconsider the matter later.

Yours sincerely,<br>[T. S. Eliot]

## TO *Henry Miller*                                                              CC

26 November 1936                                    [*The Criterion*]

Dear Mr Miller,

I am sorry that the mailing department sent you the *Criterion* for last October instead of for October 1935, and you will receive two copies of the latter in due course. Please accept my apologies.[5]

It would be very interesting to have a review by you on Saroyan's book, but I am afraid my arrangements preclude this. You see I don't have fiction reviewed in the *Criterion* unless it is something very exceptional or unless the review of [*sc.* is] practically an article about the work of an author as a whole. Ordinarily fiction is dealt with by a regular man I have who

---

1–Montgomery Butchart (1902–69), author, editor, economic historian; associate editor of *The Townsman* (ed. Ronald Duncan); editor of *Money: Selected Passages Presenting the Concepts of Money in the English Tradition, 1640–1935* (1935).
2–'Would you consider publishing in the same series as that in which Pound's Selected Poems appeared a volume of selections from the poems of E E Cummings? . . . I should very much like to see him made available at 3/6 in this country . . . As to whether Cummings would be willing I cannot say until you or someone else expresses interest and permits me to approach Cummings with a definite offer.'
  See too TSE to Charles Norman, 13 Sept. 1957: 'I have a very high opinion of Mr Cummings as a poet, in spite of my dislike of his typography.'
3–Roger Roughton, poet and critic: see letter of 31 Dec. 1936, below.
4–Roughton had come into touch with Cummings during his time in Hollywood.
5–Miller had been sent two copies of the Oct. 1936 issue of *C.*, when in fact he had requested two copies of the number in which Montgomery Belgion had reviewed his *Tropic of Cancer*.

does a Fiction Chronicle twice a year, mentioning what seems to him the most important books. I don't really feel justified in taking the Saroyan book away from him for a separate review, but I am always open to fresh suggestions.[1]

I am looking forward with interest to the Hamlet pieces.[2] No, I have not had a chance to look at *Black Spring* yet, but I want to get it back in due course, and certainly mean to read it.[3]

Yours very sincerely,<br>[T. S. Eliot]

## TO *Stephen Spender* TS Northwestern

27 November 1936        *The Criterion*

Dear Stephen,

It was stupid of me to ask you to lunch next week, because you make it clear in your letter that you will be out of town, so I shall expect you to lunch with me on Thursday 10th at the Oxford and Cambridge Club at 1.15.

Thank you very much for your long letter.[4] I think from what you say that we should reckon on the play for the autumn, and not too late in the

---

1 – Miller to Durrell, 6 Dec. 1936: 'He almost permitted me to review Saroyan's book – almost. Was extremely apologetic' (*Lawrence Durrell to Henry Miller: A Private Correspondence*, 6 Dec. 1936, ed. George Wickes [New York, 1964], 30).

2 – Ferguson, *Henry Miller*, 247: 'The *Hamlet* correspondence was an idea conceived one afternoon in September 1935 while Miller, Fraenkel and Alfred Perlès [Czech poet and diarist resident in Paris] sat drinking at the Café Zeyer . . . Fraenkel had for some time been wanting to write a book that would be exactly one thousand pages long, and as the three of them sat philosophizing . . . the idea of writing a joint book emerged. The theme would be an improvisation on Fraenkel's idea of "spiritual death" and "soul death" . . .

'The ensuing correspondence, which Alfred Perlès quickly dropped out of, lasted from November 1935 until October 1938. Fraenkel published a first, abridged volume of the letters on Carrefour in 1939 . . . Miller's contributions are among the best, most relaxed and amusingly provocative pieces he ever wrote. The form of the epistolary duel suited him well, dispelling the claustrophobia that the militant egoism of his solo writing sometimes produces in the reader.'

See *The Michael Fraenkel – Henry Miller Correspondence called Hamlet*, 2 vols (1962).

3 – Miller wrote on 22 Nov., of *Black Spring*: 'I know it's not a book for Faber & Faber, but I am eager to have your personal opinion of its merits.'

4 – Spender wrote on 18 Nov.: 'I have now written over half of my play and am getting on very well with it. I am quite sure that it will be ready within fairly reasonable time, but really I dont feel anxious to publish it till, say, next Autumn . . . I have thought of doing this play ever since I lived in Germany and had started it before my first book was published: so it is immensely important to me . . .

autumn. It seems to me better not to make a contract at this stage. The trouble with making contracts in advance, except when the nature of the book is very clearly understood, is that publishers have to be rather on the cautious side, and often after seeing the manuscript one would be able to offer rather more generous terms. I am not talking about quality, but it is impossible to know anything about the width of appeal and probable size of market until one has seen a book. I should certainly be prepared to recommend the Committee strongly to give you an advance in the usual way, that is to say on publication. Or, if it should be necessary for you, on completion of the contract and receipt of the manuscript. We can discuss this point when we meet.

Affectionately yours,<br>Tom

## TO *Elizabeth Bowen* CC

27 November 1936                    [Faber & Faber Ltd]

Dear Mrs Cameron,

After what I said at our last meeting you will no doubt have come to the conclusion from my silence that I am an extremely unbusinesslike person. I think, however, that I have really done my best to keep things moving, only in respect of a book like this I haven't got things altogether in my own hands. Fiction is a subject with which I ordinarily have nothing to do in a business way, unless it is detective fiction, and I read so little myself, and have so little notion of what other people will like that I am quite rightly considered incompetent. I was only called into this affair because of being fortunate enough to know you, but in fact I am merely an intermediary, and it takes some time to collect the views of men who are quite as busy as I am. Here, however, are the suggestions that I have now gathered:

General opinion that Bates is unnecessary.

If Walter de la Mare [is] to be included could something very much shorter be found. A story called *Physic* is suggested.

---

'If you care to make a contract now I would be very glad, and I would also be glad for an advance. But you may feel you would rather wait until the spring . . .

'Gollancz is going to publish my other book in January in his Left Book Club. I think that is sure to cause a mild stir, not because it is as good as it ought to be, but because it expresses a political predicament which a great many people are in.'

If Isherwood is to be included it is felt that something very much shorter should be found.

General to omit L. P. Hartley, Richard Middleton, Sean O'Faolain (could we have Frank O'Connor instead?), and William Plomer.

Query whether Eddy Sackville West is strong enough to need to be represented by anything of that length.

Agreed that Somerset Maugham ought to be in it, but I am told that he could be represented by something much shorter story [*sic*], of which he has published some in the *Cosmopolitan*.

General feeling that the list as it stands tend to be too much a Cape book, and not quite enough a Modern Book. Of course I don't mean that we want you to find more stories from Faber authors, because we are quite well aware of our weakness in this department.

A number of authors have been suggested besides Beachcroft and Virginia Woolf, whom I mentioned myself. (I told them that you had found a story of Beachcroft's which you thought suitable). Eliminating the Americans on the grounds you convinced me of, the new suggestions are Herbert Read, Richard Hughes, James Hanley, H. A. Manhood, Dylan Thomas, Osbert Sitwell, George Barker, possibly Day Lewis, possibly Henry Williamson. The only one of these whom I can speak about with any conviction myself is Dylan Thomas, whom I think would be very desirable as a representative of the youngest school of writers. Of course these are only suggestions. It is not supposed that you will think fit to include them all.

They say the book can run to about 150,000 words.

I don't know what you will make of all this, but I should be very glad, when you have considered these suggestions, if we could meet soon and talk them over.

Yours very sincerely,
[T. S. Eliot]

TO *Joseph Needham*[1]                                    CC

30 November 1936                    [*The Criterion*]

My dear Needham,

I must apologize for the length of time that I have kept your article.[2] I say your article because the translation you enclose with it, although an odd and interesting bit of work, doesn't seem to me quite to come off, and I have made up my mind to return it to you with thanks. But your article has taken a lot of reading and even now I find myself very puzzled by it. I am not really competent to decide how far it could be called orthodox Communism, though I should like to test my doubts against the opinion of someone better qualified than I. But one thing that makes me wonder about its orthodoxy as Communist is that it strikes me as so extremely heterodox as Christianity as to have almost nothing to do with that religion. You know that I have no objection to printing things that I don't agree with – if I did the *Criterion* would have to be much smaller and probably much duller – but I do like to understand what I print, and I really don't understand your article at all. I should probably have kept it some time longer to puzzle over, but as you say you want to try it elsewhere I am returning it with apologies and best wishes.

                              Yours sincerely,
                              [T. S. Eliot]

1–Joseph Needham (1900–95), biochemist, historian of science and civilisation in China, and Christian socialist, was educated at Gonville and Caius College, Cambridge (a Fellow for life, he served as Master for ten years from 1966). Works include *The Sceptical Biologist* (1929) and *Chemical Embryology* (3 vols, 1931); but his major project – conceived during WW2 when he set up the Sino-British scientific cooperation office and served as scientific counsellor at the British Embassy in Chongqing – was a total history of Chinese science, technology and medicine. A polymath and a pro-Chinese witness (he was for some years declared *persona non grata* by the USA), he was ultimately regaled with honours. He was made a Companion of Honour, 1992; and in 1994 he received the Einstein Medal from UNESCO.

2–Needham had submitted on 22 Sept. two distinct pieces (i) an essay entitled 'Othello & the mangold-wurzels' (about literature in the USSR), by a Polish friend named A. Stawar, which Needham had translated; (ii) an address by Needham himself – taking the form of an opening discussion of the paper contributed by the late Prof. J. S. Haldane – that he had delivered at the recent world congress of faiths organised by Sir Francis Younghusband. Needham wrote again on 15 Nov.: 'I wonder if you could decide fairly soon whether or not you want to print that essay of mine on old Prof. Haldane's "testament" in the Criterion? If not, may I please have it back. "Science and Society", a new quarterly published at Harvard, are bothering me for a paper, and I'll send it to them if you don't want it. I would still prefer it to be in the Criterion.'

30 November 1936　　　　　　　[Faber & Faber Ltd]

Dear Mr Brinton,

I have your letter of the 25th instant enclosing two copies of a manifesto.[1] Ordinarily I am rather sceptical of the value of manifestos as a form of action seldom effectual in itself and still more rarely because of the frequency with which it is attempted. I am, however, in general sympathy with this one, and would only query two points. The first, the comparison between the Boer War and the Great War, seems to me capable of leading to quite different reflections than those it is intended to arouse. The Boer War is associated with a period of imperialistic expansion, and though of course it considerably antedated my own interest in politics, it seems to me that a number of intelligent and patriotic Englishmen regard it with strong disapproval. As for the Great War, allowing for the fact that the ultimate causes took root in every country, and were allied to an economic system throughout Europe of very doubtful validity, it can still be defined as from the British point of view a war of defence, and while I agree in deploring the Treaty of Versailles and the subsequent mishandling of the Germans it is possible to recognize also that the racial problem in South Africa is far from being settled. The second point is that the assertion that 'only through democracy can the Christian spirit be fully expressed' seems to me too absolute. Is it in accordance with the traditions of the Church to associate Christianity so definitely with any one form of government? While I myself prefer a democratic to an absolutist system of government it seems to me that the relation of systems

---

1–Brinton sent a copy of a Manifesto drawn up at a meeting of members of the Church of England and the Free Churches, and presided over by the Archbishop of York. The Manifesto was drafted, following the meeting, by the Archbishop of York, the Bishop of Carlisle, and Brinton himself. 'I hope very much that you will agree to sign this Manifesto, which we propose to issue to the press early next week . . .'

The Manifesto: 'As we consider the world in which we live . . . we see that conflict has robbed us of the fruits of victory. Economic conflict is extending to political conflict . . .

'A very large proportion of the political and economic dangers which threaten us are directly attributable to the unChristian manner in which we treated our enemies of the Great War. One of the most profoundly important lessons of modern history is to be learned from a comparison of the effects of our treatment of South Africa after the Boer War and of Germany at Versailles . . .

'We believe that the immediate and practical step to take is to stimulate and provide for the study of economic and political questions in the light of basic Christian principles . . .

'We therefore invite all those who are in general agreement with this statement and who are willing to take part in a movement for translating Christian ethics into action on democratic lines to communicate with us.'

of government to the life of Christianity can only be determined for the particular problems of particular times and places.

I should like to know a little more about the designs for implementing the Manifesto before agreeing to sign it in any form. Is this simply for publication in *The Times* and other newspapers, or is it to be made use of in other ways? And what form is the movement for translating Christian ethics into action on democratic lines to take? It would be interesting also to know from what types of person the signatories are to be drawn.

Yours very truly,<br>[T. S. Eliot]

## TO *Polly Tandy*

4 December [1936] *The Criterion*

Mrs Tandy ma'am here's a Poem I was just inspired to write; yes it came just like that, but as you will see it's only suitable for adults Cert A. and when you read it you will see why. Anyway it will show you I do now & then write a poem for Adults. It is called

THE COUNTRY WALK.

In the form of an Epistle to a Lady.[1]

Of all the beasts that God allows
In England's green & pleasant land,
I cordially dislike the Cows –
Their ways I do not understand.
It puzzles me why they should stare
At me, who am so innocent;
Their stupid gaze is hard to bear –
It's positively truculent.
I'm very inconspicuous
And scarlet ties I never wear;
I'm not a London Transport Bus,
And yet at me they always stare.
You may reply, to fear a Cow

1 – TSE sent a copy of these verses to their proper dedicatee – 'A Country Walk: An Epistle to Miss E – H – with the humble compliments of her obliged servant, the Author'. Hale added at the foot: 'we often took long walks in the country about Gloucestershire' (Princeton).

is Cowardice the rustic scorns:
But still your reason must allow
That I am weak, and she has horns.
But most I am afraid when walking
With country dames in brogues and tweeds,
Who will persist in hearty talking
And pointing out the different breeds.
To country people Cows are mild,
And flee from any stick they throw;
But I'm a timid town-bred Child
As all the cattle seem to know.
But when in lanes alone I stroll,
O then in vain their horns are tossed,
In vain their bloodshot eyes they roll,
Of me they shall not make their boast.
Beyond the hedge or five-barred gate
My sober wishes never stray;
Their deadly prongs may lie in wait,
But I can always run away.
Or I can take sanctuary
In friendly oak or apple tree.[1]

      Yrs etc.

      TP.

Regards to the licensee.

1 – A signed TS copy of this poem was to be sent on 6 Dec. to JDH, with this preface: 'An Epistle, to John Hayward Esqre., suggested by certain experiences of the Author, in the Countryside of the West of England, and set down after parting from Canon Tissington Tatlow, at the corner of Lime Street and Fenchurch Street.' See JDH, 'London Letter', *New York Sun*, 19 Dec. 1936: 'Mr Eliot is composing nonsense verses and has written me a verse-epistle about cows.' John Smart, *Tarantula's Web: John Hayward, T. S. Eliot and Their Circle* (2013), 103, prints JDH's response beginning 'Your letter makes it clear, dear Tom, / That when you wander out of town . . .'

See too FVM, 'A Few Recollections of Eliot', in *T. S. Eliot: The Man and His Work*, ed. Tate, 115: 'Donald at the age of nine in 1935 had begun to edit *The Family News*, a monthly periodical hand-published once a year. Tom submitted poems, but not until 1938 was a poem of Tom's accepted by Donald. That was a poem on Cows. Poems on cats had been rejected.'

4 December 1936                    [*The Criterion*]

Dear Hoskyns,

I have received a new book by Martin Buber, *Die Frage an den Einzelnen*.[2] I don't know anything about Buber myself except that Joe Oldham has sometimes spoken of him, and I know takes his work seriously. I wonder, therefore, if it is up your street, and if it is something that it would please you to review for the *Criterion* I should be delighted.[3]

At the same time I wonder if you have ever heard of the two following American theologians, Donald Wayne Riddle and Ernest Cadman Colwell. They both seem to be professors at the University of Chicago, and I have been sent books by them suggested for publication in this country. I am always rather suspicious of American theology in this country, but if you happened to know that either of them was a strong man I would take him more seriously.[4]

What I really want to talk to you about when we come down next week is the subject of Divinity books for public schools.[5] It is unfortunate that

1–Edwyn Clement Hoskyns, 13th Baronet (1884–1937): theologian; Fellow of Corpus Christi College, Cambridge, where he was successively Dean of Chapel, Librarian and President. His works in biblical theology include *The Fourth Gospel* (1940) and *Crucifixion-Resurrection* (1981). He published an English translation of Karl Barth's *Epistle to the Romans* (1933). See Gordon S. Wakefield, 'Hoskyns and Raven: The Theological Issue', *Theology*, Nov. 1975, 568–76; Wakefield, 'Edwyn Clement Hoskyns', in E. C. Hoskyns and F. N. Davey, *Crucifixion-Resurrection* (1981); and R. E. Parsons, *Sir Edwyn Hoskyns as Biblical Theologian* (1985).

2–Martin Buber (1878–1965), Austrian Jewish religious philosopher; prolific author of studies including *I and Thou* (1923; first translated into English in 1937); *Die Frage an den Einzelnen* ('The Question to the Single One') (1936).

3–Hoskyns replied on 5 Dec. that while he knew of Buber as an eminent Jewish scholar, 'he is too far off my beat for to me to dare to review him'.

(Asked to add his signature to a letter addressed to the Swedish Academy recommending Buber for the Nobel Prize, TSE wrote on 27 June 1962 to Maurice Friedman (NY): 'I only know the English translation of *I and Thou*. But I once had a conversation with Dr Buber, to whom I had been introduced by Dr Oldham, and I got the strong impression that I was in the company of a great man. There are only a very few men of those who I have met in my lifetime, whose presence has given me that feeling.')

4–Hoskyns wrote on 5 Dec. that he knew nothing of either Riddle or Colwell.

5–GCF asked Hoskyns on 30 Oct.: 'There is another matter about which Eliot and I should very much like to consult you, and that is the possibility of our producing a series of divinity books for the better class secondary and public schools. We should like to know whether you think this a good idea – it arises out of a resolution adopted at the Felsted Conference of public school masters, and we should also like to have your views upon the general editorship of such a series. So far as we are concerned the idea is still in a very vague stage, but it would help us very much to define our own ideas if we could have a talk with you.'

I have to come back again on Saturday morning because I imagine the evening will be pretty well taken up with the Anglo-Saxon Chronicle.[1] I wonder, therefore, if you and if possible Spens as well could spare an hour or so before dinner if we took an earlier train in the afternoon on Friday?

Yours sincerely,
[T. S. Eliot]

TO *Isaiah Berlin*[2]                                                        CC

4 December 1936                    [*The Criterion*]

Dear Berlin,

I wonder if you would tackle for me for the April number of the *Criterion An Examination of Logical Positivism*, by Julius Rudolph Weinberg, published in the International Library of Psychology, Philosophy and Scientific Method, by Kegan Paul. There are a lot of pamphlets which might go with it, or which at least I should invite you to look at to see whether you thought them worth reviewing, which are published by the Congrès International de Philosophie Scientifique in the same field. If you don't want to do these you will have to find a very good excuse indeed, as

1–GCF to Hoskyns, 15 Oct. 1936: 'Eliot is now back and we have had a bit of a talk about it. It seems to us all that while we should very much like to publish a translation of the [Parker] Chronicle edited by the best available university man, we could not very well regard this as an ordinary commercial publication to be financed entirely by ourselves. The principal point seems to be whether Corpus Christi College would be willing either (1) to finance the undertaking itself or to arrange for publication "on commission" or (2) to foot part of the outlay, and to stand with the publishers in a partnership relation.' A. H. Smith was suggested as the best editor.

2–Isaiah Berlin (1909–97), author, philosopher, historian of ideas, was born in Riga, Latvia, but brought to England with his family in 1920. Educated at St Paul's School, London, and at Corpus Christi College, Oxford, where he gained a first in Greats and a second first in Philosophy, Politics and Economics, he won a prize fellowship at All Souls. He taught philosophy at New College until 1950. In 1957 he was appointed Chichele Professor of Social and Political Theory at Oxford; and in the same year he was elected to the British Academy, which he served in the capacity of both Vice-President, 1959–61, and President, 1974–8). He was made CBE in 1946 and knighted in 1957. In 1971 he was appointed to the Order of Merit. Founding President of Wolfson College, Oxford, 1966–75. Works include *Karl Marx* (1939) and *The Hedgehog and the Fox* (1953).

otherwise I shall become discouraged. I am sure that you are the best man to deal with this stuff.[1]

Yours ever,
[T. S. Eliot]

## TO *Ezra Pound*

4 December 1936                    *The Criterion*

Well Ez now let's be Practical.[2] Here we have a number of cantoes[3] which look pretty good and considerably more thrillin than the middle lot for a generation of vipers[4] that dont know so much about Van Buren as you Do; also a admirable retrospective article about Wyndham mostly though of a ramblin kind as befits the garrulity of age, and which I should like to Print.[5] Well what do you Want printed in the next number? To begin with, you did not NOT make it clear at all or if you made it clear to FVM he did not make it clear to me, at the time you Remember that your first three cantoes arrived I was to the Westward, partakin of clam chowder and rum with the boys in Jonesport Maine,[6] anyway when I came Back there was the three cantoes and I thought they were simply an instalment of the next instalment of cantoes which I presume is to be published by Faber & Faber in the autumn the fall of the year anyway thats my readin of it.[7] Well it never occurred to me that Ez would let me have a canto for the Criterion unless he said so through a megaphone many times, not just slippin em in like that. Well I shd. of Course be Proud but Now obviously three THREE cantoes is too high a perportion to print all at once in the

1–Berlin on Julius Weinberg, *An Examination of Logical Positivism: C.* 17 (Oct. 1937), 174–82.
2–EP, 6 Dec.: 'I am endeavouring to be "practical" as you exhort.'
3–EP had delivered in Nov. 1936 what he denominated *The Fifth Decad of Cantos* (XLII–LI) –'Gnu Canters,' as he called them in a letter to FVM.
4–Matthew 12: 34: 'O generation of vipers, how can ye, being evil, speak good things? for out of the abundance of the heart the mouth speaketh.' TSE's ancestor, The Revd Andrew Eliot, had preached to his Boston audience on Easter Day 1765 on the text 'a generation of vipers' – meaning (as Lyndall Gordon notes in *The Imperfect Life of T. S. Eliot*, 240) his audience.
5–EP, 'D'Artagnan Twenty Years After', C. 16 (July 1937), 606–17.
6–TSE to Leon Little, 11 Aug. 1956: 'I wish I could see North Haven again, but how? I should also like to put in to Jonesport (another generation of Dyers and Carvers no doubt – I shall never forget Pete leading the Grand March at the Jonesport Summer Ball with Mrs Willie Carver, you never saw anything more respectable) . . . but I dont suppose the only sort of vessel I should care to travel on now could edge through the Roque Island Thoroughfare.'
7–EP had submitted what he called the 'Siena Cantos', nos 42–4.

Criterion or anywhere else what I mean is that is three out of ten which makes the book to put it concisely that is 3/10th of the book at a bang thats givin the public too much for their money in advance why the rest of the paper by itself is worth 7/6 and say 12/6 in all so in the interests of the book-instalment I say print not more than ONE cantoe and I'd like to have one about Usury. But that wd. mean postponing the Article to the Summer. Thats all right by me but I thought I would like to consult your wishes first.[1] And in these circumstances I cant see where Pam[2] comes in for some time to come. Just you get clear about this and dont get any crooked ideas in yr tortuous Italian mind: I'm already all ready QUA editr. of the Criterion to print a batch of three cantoes all together, BUT QUA dir. of this firm it seems to me serialising too much of the book in advance. I sometimes wish you cd. adopt the same direct blunt kind of downright simple straight-forward style as mine, and write letters like this wch. can be understood and comprehended at a glance. So will close yours[3]

TP.

I aint forgiven yr. wife yet.


TO *Ezra Pound*                                            TS Beinecke

8 December 1936                    *The Criterion*

Wel Ezzum I should say your list was fairly Complete. Of course the name of Forbenius [*sic*] dont arouse any enthusisasm [*sic*] in my centres, but you know that. I dont know about Djuna quite: for I infer that what you are takin account is a OEUVRE and not single Book. I wrote to that chink

---

1–EP responded, 6 Dec.: 'The Wyndham can wait till Summer/ if that is definite.'
2–Henry John Temple, 3rd Viscount Palmerston (1784–1865), Prime Minister, 1859–65.
3–EP showed annoyance in his reply (6 Dec.) to this letter – he addressed TSE not by any fond nickname but as 'Dear Eliot' – protesting that FVM had specifically requested in his letter of 10 Sept. some Cantos for the Dec. issue of C.; and indeed FVM 'had verbally said they (Cantos) wd. go in UNLESS you raised hell . . .' If the three Cantos in question, which 'form a unit' and 'can not be printed one afart [*sic*] from the other two', were not now to be published in the *Criterion* (EP threatened), he might have to withhold the next volume of ten Cantos from F&F. Keeping up his resentfulness, he went on: 'Harriet [Monroe] shat on Propertius and [Scofield] Thayer on Mauberley/ and the Waste Land <as a unit> profited by those insults . . . I don't think I have ever treated a yaller dawg in this manner <i.e. you to me> but my memory may be at fault.' And in 'Second Epistle' (also 6 Dec.): 'The USURY canto was sacrificed to "Prosperity" where they hit it in small print . . . 42/44 can not be printed one afart from the other two . . . What does it matter the pubk/ getting too much. The job for decent men is to keep up the arts FIRST.'
EP, 'Cantos XLII–XLIV', C. 16 (Apr. 1937), 405–23.

to say would he like to shorten his valuable but excessively long article (taint ALL about you) or would he rather I did it for em.[1] No answer. And I aint got round to doin the tiresome job myself yet. Miller at moments yes, certainly, but too much of just spillin it and a kind of a East Side Jew touch: there are spots which wont keep forever.[2] I dont see anybody gettin JJ or WL to ORGANISE with anybody. What you want to do? The only really Strong for [*sc.* form] of PROTEST against Nobel is one wich is not likely to be put in our way. i.e. refusin to accept it when it is passed to us. I am quite Willin to make a Pact with you and even Forbenius to that effect.

TP.

TO *Ezra Pound*                                                    TS Beinecke

9 December 1936                         *The Criterion*

Resp. Podestà,

Well there certainly was a slipup in the organisation just this once, and I for one tender my humble and unreserved apologies. It would seem that the Morley failed to explain to me the terms on which the 3 cantos were received.[3] I would only point out (1) that his letter to which you refer merely said that he would do what he forgot to do – tell me that the 3 cantos were submitted as a unit for the December Criterion, without definitely promising inclusion, and (2) my own letter of the 22nd October is still capable of being interpreted simply as minor comment on what I thought was simply an advance instalment of the Book.

Now, what's undone cant be done,[4] and the December number is in Press. But, I have consulted my colleagues and they disagree with me as to the damage of printing 3/10 of the book in the Criterion, so I would like to print this batch of 3 in the March Criterion antedating publication

1–EP, 3 Dec.: 'By way DID you ever pub/ that chink's article ?? on EZ.'

2–EP to TSE, 3 Dec. 1936: '[Henry] Miller at moments a WRITER does basic seriousness count?' EP had extolled Miller on 28 Mar. 1936: 'Miller having done presumably the only book a man cd/ read fer pleasure/ and if not out-Ulyssesing Joyce at least being infinitely MORE part of permanent literature than such ½ masted slime as the weak mind Wolff female etc.'

3–EP to FVM, 6 Dec.: 'I don't see anything for me to do but withdraw offer of the TEN CANTOS as a volume. If that letter [FVM's letter of 10 Sept. to EP] isn't an invitation of the THREE cantos then under discussion / for the December Criterion; what is it?'

4–Cf. Lady Macbeth: 'What's done cannot be undone.' EP grumbled to TSE, 6 Dec.: 'Morley's letter of 10th. Sept. invited the Cantos for the "Decemberium"/ as the 'Octoberium" was full . . . If the Cantos are n't in the DeC/ Morley has mislead [*sic*] me.'

of the book in the same Season. That means the Wyndham Lewis article in JUNE.

Cantoes 42/44 can be sent to be set up at once and payment can be made as soon as proof arrives, if desirable.

The 3 cantos WOULD have been in Dec. Criterion, had I known they were OFFERED.[1]

subito
TP.

## TO *E. M. W. Tillyard*[2]                                    TS King's

9 December 1936                          *The Criterion*

Dear Tillyard,

I have been very slow in answering your kind letter, but I have had four or five other letters, mostly from rather rambling undergraduates, and I really have not had time yet to tackle them.[3] I am glad you wrote,

---

1–EP replied on 11 Dec., stiffly appeased: 'Waaal: That's all right by me. You set 'em up, videlicet/ Set up Cantos 42/44, and send payment as soon as the workings of the firm permit.'
2–E. M. W. Tillyard (1889–1962): Fellow in English of Jesus College, Cambridge, 1926–59; Master, 1945–59. Works include *The Personal Heresy: A Controversy* (with C. S. Lewis, 1939); *The Elizabethan World Picture: A Study of the Idea of Order in the Age of Shakespeare* (1943), *Shakespeare's History Plays* (1944), and *The Muse Unchained: An Intimate Account of the Revolution in English Studies at Cambridge* (1958).
3–Tillyard wrote from Jesus College, 14 Nov.: 'I really must write to thank you for last night's talk. I've seen enough people since to know that it was very greatly appreciated . . .

'There were a number of things I wanted to speak to you about but some of them wouldn't have been profitable, and, as to the rest, I thought the young men oughtn't to be deprived of their talk with you. I thought the discussion just before the close was taking an interesting turn, even if one which didn't admit of profitable pursuit. The issue had been put as if it were between the materialists and the religious. But isn't it today between the spiritually minded agnostic and those who cannot admit religion without a church? Or rather don't those people among the lovers of poetry who do not embody their religious instincts either in a church or in a mystically conceived state possess, most of them, at least some negative faith, some refusal explicitly to shut out the supernatural? . . .

'What does seem to me to be eminently discussible was your assumption about the language of poetry and its relation to speech. I'm not questioning the rightness of reacting from the idiom of 1906–10. And with my contemporary emotions I found myself, when faced with the language question in Greece in 1911, strongly on the popular side (not having of course enough knowledge to have any opinion either way); and I don't regret those emotions. But isn't there the danger of turning into a law something that is an expedient, however necessary at a certain time? Some growth in the language of poetry congruent with that in the language of speech there must obviously be; but is it certain that it is better for the language of poetry to be always at, say, two removes from the other rather than four removes? . . . [T]o put an English case, was Marlowe's early blank verse – surely rather

---

however, because I was not very well satisfied with my talk. The whole subject really needs a great deal more thinking out, and the only excuse for having ventilated it at that stage is that one sometimes likes to talk about things about which one is still thinking instead of only about things upon which one's thinking is finished. In the first place, I certainly didn't want to confound what you call the spiritually minded agnostic with the positive materialist. Nor was it at all my intention to disparage the religion of those who feel no need for a church. Obviously if one regards institutional religion as a good thing one can't regard non-institutional religion as valueless. One simply believes that those who maintain such a position are holding on to something which should be temporary, and have not yet fully grasped the implications of holding any sort of religious faith at all. Obviously religion without a church is possible, just as living in a caravan is possible, but it is also possible to maintain that a nomadic society fails to produce the highest civilization. Any analogy of this sort, however, is apt to be misleading if pressed very far.

As for the question of the relation of poetry to speech, what I said perhaps amounted to no more than the old and familiar assault upon poetic diction. But as for the difference between, as you say, poetry at two removes from speech and poetry at four removes from it, it seems to make a difference what kind of removes they are. A really great poet like Milton can get away with a considerable separation from speech because his idiom is his own, and though his language can frequently not be called natural, yet one must admit that it is natural to Milton. As for Marlowe it only seems to me that I need to make the point that the blank verse in

---

remote in tone from any conceivable conversation – sufficiently related to contemporary speech for it to be sound in that particular? or did it succeed in spite of an unsoundness in that particular? That's the sort of puzzle I should have liked to ask you to solve, if I had had the chance.

'Another thing I'm not happy about is the badness of Miltonic blank verse in the eighteenth century. It certainly ought to be bad, but was it really? Would Thomson have been better if less Miltonic, and isn't there something to be said for a way of writing which, through men like Akenside, ultimately led to the *Prelude*? And aren't the Miltonisings of the *Prelude*, filtered as they are through the eighteenth century, sounder somehow than the more magnificent and directly borrowed Miltonisings of the first *Hyperion*?

'But I mustn't weary you any more with strings of questions . . .

'I entirely sympathised with your reluctance to pronounce on Leavis for the help of the Appointments Committee. [See TSE's letter to T. R. Henn, 26 July 1936.] It wasn't really a fair request; and the only excuse for its making was . . . we were utterly stuck. Did you see we had appointed him? And I only hope we've done the right thing. Empson didn't get much backing. It seems a pity we've lost ability like his, but I fear there's nothing to be done about it. Some people will feel strongly about his college trouble, even though his college has forgiven him.'

which he gets nearer to speech is greater because more fully developed, than his early attempts, fine as they are.

I confess that I have never been quite happy [with] any blank verse after Milton, though I should have to put not only Wordsworth but Tennyson very high. Of course it is impossible to deny the affiliation through Thomson, etc.[1] I should be inclined to say yes, in theory Thomson's verse should have been better if less Miltonic, except that one cannot in the least imagine what it wouldn't be like. I agree that the Miltonic Wordsworth is finer than the Miltonic Keats. But is this primarily due to Milton's being filtered through the eighteenth century, and is it not mostly due to the originality of his own genius.

I am still fumbling about these matters and it would be much more satisfactory if we could talk about them.

Yours sincerely,
T. S. Eliot

## TO *P. M. Mansell Jones*[2]                                           CC

9 December 1936                    [Faber & Faber Ltd]

Dear Mr Mansell Jones,

Thank you for your letter of the 14th November.[3] I had several other letters as a consequence of my talk in Cambridge, and have so far been

---

1–TSE to Patric Dickinson, 15 Sept. 1961: 'I should at sometime very much like to write a note about James Thomson, since his verse and, of course, above all The City of Dreadful Night was so important to me when I was sixteen or seventeen. I still think very highly of this poem which seems, incidentally, to have made a deep impression on Rudyard Kipling.'
2–P. Mansell Jones (1889–1968) was teaching at the University College of South Wales and Monmouthshire, Cardiff; he was to be Professor of French at the University College of North Wales at Bangor, 1937–51; Professor of Modern French Literature, University of Manchester, 1951–9. His works include *Tradition and Barbarism* (1930), *French Introspectives* (1937), and *The Background of Modern French Poetry* (1951).
3–Mansell Jones had attended TSE's talk in Cambridge on the French influences on his work, but had failed to ask a question. 'I have always been intrigued by what appears to be the omission of Mallarmé from the list of those French poets which influenced the new way of writing English poetry to which you referred. Is there an obvious reason for this omission (if I am right in regarding it as such) which I do not perceive? I can think of one. Mallarmé's way of writing is not, I take it, an approximation to prose, in your sense; & it might be clumsy to suggest that his *verse* had much to offer those who were looking out for new models & stimuli of the kind that was wanted in English poetry thirty years ago. But what about his speculations, cogitations, divagations etc., on the technique & problems of writing poetry, surely the most important corpus *of its kind* in recent literature? Had it no influence on the new formations?'

unable to answer any of them. As for Mallarmé, he seems to me in actual fact to have had less influence on English poetry than any of the other poets whom I named. I should not, however, be prepared to assert that his poetry is not a kind of approximation to prose in a eulogistic sense. I admit to being very fond of it myself, although I cannot trace ever having been much influenced by him. Do you know the very fine essays on Baudelaire and Flaubert by Proust?[1] I haven't seen them for a long time, but as I remember he had some very brilliant observations on the originality of their syntax. But of course if Mallarmé didn't fit into my theory I should have to alter the theory, because generalizations of this sort have to be based on one's own taste in poetry, or they are meaningless.

With best wishes,
Yours sincerely,
[T. S. Eliot]

TO *John Hayward*                                                   TS King's

9 December 1936                    *The Criterion*

My dear John,

I know that at the moment you are giving the whole of your attention to the Crisis;[2] so I hasten to send you a

DIARY OF TODAY'S EVENTS.

10.30 a.m. – Mr Eliot, after attending to various business in Grenville Place and at the Vestry, left Kensington by Underground for a destination unknown. To the reporters assembled at Gloucester Road Station, he said: 'You may say that my journey has no connexion with the crisis'.

11.15 a.m. – Mr Eliot had a private interview with Mr F. V. Morley. To the reporters assembled in Russell Square, he sent out by Miss Swan (Receiver-General for Russell Square) the following bulletin: 'You may say that our interview was entirely informal and friendly, and was concerned exclusively with the situation in Rapallo'.

---

1 – Marcel Proust, 'À propos du "Style" de Flaubert', *Nouvelle revue française*, 1 Mar. 1920, 72–90; 'À propos de Baudelaire', *NRF*, June 1921; repr. in *Contre Saint-Beuve*.
2 – GCF in his diary, 10 Dec.: 'The King's abdication announced – I am able to tell myself "I told you so!" For at the funeral in Jan. [the funeral of King George V, 28 Jan. 1936] I said "I don't believe he'll last", and when this Simpson business blew up I said that abdication was the only way out. The suspense of the last week has been very bad for our West End trade.' On 11 Dec.: 'Edward's broadcast was received in complete silence, & I think most of the audience felt embarrassed by it. TSE thought it wld. have been in better taste if he had said nothing.'

12 a.m. – Mrs Alan Cameron arrived at Russell Square in a closed car, accompanied by a gentleman who described himself as a taxi-driver. She spent forty minutes with Mr Eliot, and on leaving said to the reporters: 'You may say that the interview was entirely informal and friendly, and had no connexion with the crisis'.

1.15 p.m. – The Board of Directors of Faber & Faber lunched in camera and behind closed doors. No secretaries were present. To the reporters in Russell Square the Chairman issued the following statement: 'You may say that the meeting was entirely informal and friendly. Differences of opinion were expressed concerning the smoked salmon sandwiches, but a satisfactory solution is in sight'.

2.30 p.m. – A crisis developed during the Directors Meeting of Faber & Faber. At the moment when the item CRYSTAL PALACE came up for discussion, a bomb was exploded, and the Chairman was heard to exclaim: 'I protest'. Immediately jets of water began to play upon the conflagration from several unidentified sources. The Chairman was heard to exclaim: 'I am wet'. To the reporters in Russell Square Mr Morley issued the following statement: 'The moisture was due to atmospheric precipitation, and the incident is now closed'.

3.30 p.m. – Mr Eliot left hurriedly in a closed car, in the company of an individual who described himself to the reporters as a taxi-driver.

3.45 p.m. – Mr Eliot arrived at 36, Hyde Park Square, to attend a meeting in camera and behind partly closed doors, of the Paddington Branch of the League of Mercy. He made a short address, which received an enthusiastic reception, and overwhelming applause as he said: 'The people of Paddington are the salt of the earth, and I speak with special reference to Lady Barker, the Revd S. Nowell-Rostron, Lt. Col. R. P. Collings-Well, Mrs Bate-Crossley, and the Dowager Lady Dimsdale'. He left hurriedly in a closed car, and was observed to show signs of agitation. Mrs Colquhoun addressed the reporters assembled in Hyde Park Square from the first floor window.

4.30 p.m. – Mr Eliot arrived at the Directors' Meeting in Russell Square, where, according to Reuter, he received a mixed reception.

5.30 p.m. – Mr Eliot and Mr Morley left Russell Square hurriedly in a closed car, the driver of which has not been identified. A bystander heard Mr Morley say: 'Victoria Brighton Side, Jack, and stop at the Shakespeare'.

And that's enough for one day.

If anything else happens I'll let you know.

Yrs etc.

*TP*

## TO *W. H. Auden*                                          CC

10 December 1936                    [Faber & Faber Ltd]

Dear Wystan,

I have read the Byron[1] this morning with some difficulty, because the sheets are very slippery and were imperfectly clipped together, and several times slid out of order. I must say that I started with as much prejudice against it as if you had told me that you had done something like the *Rape of the Lock*, only rather better. But actually it seems to me extremely successful, and is very different from a pastiche. I congratulate you. Will you let me know when you are next available, because Morley would like to join us at lunch.

Yours ever,

[Tom]

## TO *Elizabeth Bowen*                                       CC

10 December 1936                    [Faber & Faber Ltd]

Dear Mrs Cameron,

It seemed to be the opinion of the Committee that the most suitable method would be for you to approach Osbert Sitwell yourself, and explain to him exactly what you want. That is to say, of course, if you are quite sure that there is a story amongst those in *Dumb Animals* which is up to your standard.[2] If you are not sure it would be better to get hold of a copy of the book before approaching Osbert. Nobody here has one, but the London Library has one, and is reserving it for me. If you have a subscription yourself, however, I will ask them to keep it for you.[3]

I will try to get copies of the other periodicals containing short pieces by Dylan Thomas and George Barker,

Yours very sincerely,

[T. S. Eliot]

---

1 – Auden wrote on a PC, 28 Nov. 1936: 'Byron ['Letter to Lord Byron'], a typescript of which should reach you from Curtis Brown soon[,] is for Iceland [*Letters from Iceland* (1937)].'

2 – *Dumb-Animal and Other Stories* (1930) had been withdrawn from circulation when Osbert Sitwell lost a libel case in connection with a story called 'Happy Endings'.

3 – Bowen replied on 17 Dec. that she was not a member of the London Library and would be pleased to take up TSE's offer to take out *Dumb-Animal* (1930) on her behalf.

10 December 1936                          Durrants' Hotel,
                                          Manchester Square, W.1

Dear Geoffrey,

I am obliged to write to you to complain of the fact of which I am quite sure you are unaware that on the very rare occasions when I go to 24 Russell Square, where I find an extremely ~~agreeable~~ & courteous atmosphere – I am OSTENTATIOUSLY FOLLOWED by persons who have no claim on me, & *whose acquaintance I deny*.

I write, merely to make you acquainted with a state of affairs which I am sure you will agree with me is in detestably bad taste, ~~hoping that I may~~ rely on your wisdom in not extending hospitality to such persons who follow in my train to your offices & who are the enemies & the parasites of my husband and myself & no friends to your household.

I write on this day of disaster & defeat for England. The last weeks, which have included the serious illness of my mother preceded by a stroke, have been the severest strain which my existence has ever had to support.[1]

                          Yrs sincerely,
                          V. H. Eliot

1 – VHE was writing on the day of the abdication of King Edward VIII, whom she revered; her mother Rose had been incapacitated by a stroke on 9 Nov. this year: see Carole Seymour-Jones, *Painted Shadow: The Life of Vivienne Eliot* (2001), 551.

GCF replied, 11 Dec. 1936: 'I don't know who the persons, of whom you complain, may be. But I need hardly assure you that, if I *did*, I should share your objections to behaviour of the kind you describe . . . Yours sincerely / Geoffrey Faber.'

TO *Bonamy Dobrée*                                          TS Brotherton Library

14 December [1936]                    *The Criterion*

Damb it Bumbaby it isnt your money I want or Cassells or whooze; what I want is to get that damb essay on BURNS no I mean BYRON printed before I change my mind One doesnt mind one's past every body has to put up with That but when it comes masquerading as the Present and theres another Present then people begin to chalk ones door. So for any sake get the book OUT and pay me after it has paid expenses which it never will but pay John Hayward first. Even as it is people will say Auden put me up to writing about Byron thats it Events move so fast faster than you or me accumulate Grey Hairs. Now then what I wanted was for you & Valentine to dine with me on Saturday night because at the moment I am Rotten with money what with the *Muder* [*sic*] playing to half filled houses but the Rot will be arrested about the 1st of January so I wanted you to play with me before the Rot stops.[1] And so let it be unless it is a question of Georgina going to bed and you both having to be on the premises, so if it is a question of dining at Whitehall, I will dine with you but would like to contribute some decent sherry while it lasts: otherwise would prefer you to dine with me, youse to dine with me. Please reply.

                                        Yours coherently
                                        TP.


TO *Elizabeth Bowen*                                              TS Texas

14 December 1936                      *The Criterion*

Dear Mrs Cameron,

   I am rather agitated but it was agreed that the engagement for Friday night was provisional. Well it appears that my god-son is coming back from school that day and going to the country shortly and that is the only night on which he (and his brother and sister) can go to the theatre and they want very much to go to the theatre before they go to Wales, and I had said in a general way that when they came back from school before going to Wales we would go to the theatre. You see how it is. I am not sure what we are to see but I am not sure it is not 'The Boy who lost

---

1–BD wrote on 2 Dec.: 'Good about the weekend. It is nice of you to say. I'm afraid husband & wife are one flesh, & Georgina must be looked after: so will you dine with us – Claret or Burgundy? – on the 19th?'

his Temper'.[1] Anyway, will you ask me again at any time. I shall be here *continuously*.

Apologetically,

T. S. Eliot

I have re-read the two stories. I think on the whole I like the longer one better – though I think it is much more difficult for readers new to your work to grasp the point of the title – the people may like it as much but there will be a great deal more that it will miss, in the longer than in the shorter story – but I shall be glad if you can reduce other people sufficiently to include the 'Disinherited'.

I am writing to Barker to ask him what short things he has had published.


## TO *Djuna Barnes*                                                TS Hornbake

15 December 1936                     Faber & Faber Ltd

Dear Miss Barnes,

Thank you for your kind letter of the 11th.[2] I was rather nervous about writing such a preface before obtaining the author's approval, and also

---

1 – *The Boy Who Lost His Temper*: musical produced at the Duke of York's Theatre, London, for two weeks from 26 Dec.

2 – TSE's introduction to the first US edition was to be published by Harcourt Brace in Mar. 1937. Barnes wrote on 11 Dec. 1936: 'Thank you for your beautiful preface to Nightwood. No critical appreciation has ever given me so much pleasure; it makes my life a little less terrifying.

'It seems the basest ingratitude to cavil at any word in so splendid an appraisal, yet will you permit me? You say in your last paragraph: "I am not concerned, in such remarks, with what was in the *author*'s mind." Perhaps I do not understand you. It gives me the impression that you believe Nightwood to be the accidental and happy outcome of some other, or lesser intention, some philosophy or emotion not contained in the book itself. I assure you this is not so. However, if this is what you believe, and want to point out, then, of course, it must stand. Yet I cannot but wish it had been otherwise. With "author's mind" underlined, the impression is of a work that is good in spite of the author.

'I do hope you will not be offended with me for making so much of what is really so little when the body of the preface is so much more generous than I could have hoped for.'

According to Faltejskova, however, Barnes commented in a letter to Coleman (30 Dec. 1936) that Eliot's linguistic demeanour in his preface was 'a little overhumble in tone' (112). Barnes quoted to Coleman, on 1 Dec. 1936, FVM's remark: 'A preface to a work of permanence so soon begins to fade, and it would not be fair to have him [TSE] smiled at if the reasons for the book's importance to our generation should look a little odd to future generations.'

See too TSE's 'Note to Second Edition' (1949): 'The foregoing preface, as the reader will have just observed, was written twelve years ago. It appeared only in the American edition

rather apprehensive of the impression it might make upon her. As for the sentence you query, my intention was simply to disclaim any pretence of being a kind of official interpreter to the reader, and merely to try to indicate that the book was there, and I was forming my views on the book and not on anything you had told me. It was really due to a fit of modesty on my own part, but since it appears to convey quite a different meaning to you it may quite well be misunderstood by readers, and I will try to get it deleted. Otherwise I am delighted that you like the preface. I did notice the two 'came's myself when I came to quote, but it did not bother me in the book itself.[1] I will write to Brace and ask him to put that right. Your second point doesn't really seem to me important. If the patron of the café reads the book he ought to be gratified at having attributed to him something which a café ought to have.[2]

I will find out about the *Observer*. My impression was that the design had been to get L. P. Hartley to review it there.

Yours very sincerely,
T. S. Eliot

of *Nightwood*, which was published by Harcourt, Brace & Co. shortly after the publication of the book by Faber & Faber in London. In reprinting the book, Faber & Faber have thought fit to include this preface, which thus appears for the first time in an English edition.

'As my admiration for the book has not diminished, and my only motive for revision would be to remove or conceal evidences of my own immaturity at the time of writing – a temptation which may present itself to any critic reviewing his own words at twelve years distance – I have thought best to leave unaltered a preface which may still, I hope, serve its original purpose of indicating an approach which seems to me helpful for the new reader.'

1 – 'Your quotation (from page 216) catches me in error again. "you came along and kicked my stone over, and out I came, all moss and eyes – " The two "came"s too close together. Would you be kind enough to ask Mr Morley to make correction for Mr Brace thus: "Until you kicked my stone over and out I came – " etc.'

2 – 'Also I have made another mistake on page 63, lines 22 and 23 – "With a roar the steel blind came down over the window of the café de la Mairie du Vie". It sounds nice, but on looking at that window I can see no steel blind. Or do you think this unimportant?'

15 December 1936                    [*The Criterion*]

Dear Sir,

Your review of MacNeice's translation of the *Agamemnon* seems to me excellent so far as it goes. My objection is that there is a good deal too much quotation in proportion to the criticism, but at the same time I think it would be more effective if you would cut down the quotation to the strict purpose of illustrating the points you make and no more. It occurs to me that you would lengthen the review by commenting on the acting qualities of the play. I do not, of course, for this purpose, want much discussion of the merits of Mr Doone's troupe, but the performance could be considered in relation to the acting virtues or faults of MacNeice's text. The suitability of his translation of the chorus for declamation, etc.[2]

Finally, I think it would be better for review form if the quotation from Browning, which is certainly to the point, were embodied in the text or perhaps even referred to by indirect discourse. I return your first draft and hope that you will be encouraged to let me have a revised review which I can publish in the March number.[3]

Yours faithfully,
[T. S. Eliot]

---

1–Guy Manton (b. 1912), a graduate of St John's College, Cambridge, was Assistant Lecturer at Queen Mary College, London, before joining the Department of Greek at Sydney University, where he was senior lecturer in Classics. He then became Professor of Classics at the University of Otago, 1949–65; and from 1965 he was inaugural Dean of Arts at Monash University.

2–LM wrote in his introduction: 'I have written this translation primarily for the stage. I have consciously sacrificed certain things in the original – notably the liturgical flavour of the diction and the metrical complexity of the choruses. It is my hope that the play emerges as a play and not as a museum piece.' Cited by W. B. Stanford, 'The Translation of the "Agamemnon" of Aeschylus', in *Time Was Away* (1974), 64.

3–Manton submitted his revised review on 30 Dec.: see C. 16 (Apr. 1937), 528–32.

TO *John Masefield*[1]                                          CC

15 December 1936                    [Faber & Faber Ltd]

Dear Mr Masefield,

I thank you for your letter of this month addressed to Faber and Faber, Ltd, and shall be glad to send you the volumes of verse published in 1936.[2] I should be obliged, however, if you could enlighten me on one point. The last correspondence I appear to have had with you on the subject of the King's Medal was early in 1935, and at that time in your letter of February 27th you informed me that you and your Committee were considering the books of verse published in 1933. I don't appear to have had any enquiries from you about books published in 1934 or 1935. As in those two years we published several volumes of poetry which would satisfy the requirements for submission to the Committee, I should be glad to have those volumes sent as well if the awards for 1934 and 1935 are still under consideration.

Yours sincerely,

[T. S. Eliot]

1–John Masefield (1878–1967) won popular acclaim with *Salt-Water Ballads* (1902) and other books including *The Everlasting Mercy* (1911). Appointed Poet Laureate in 1930, he also served as President of the Society of Authors in 1937. TSE to John Willett (*TLS*), 19 May 1961: 'If I could find the time at present I should be indeed happy to write something about Masefield because I think he is a poet of more historical importance than is usually put to his credit by writers of my generation and younger. But I should have to give some time to re-reading what I have read and reading for the first time a great deal that I have not read of Masefield's work, and I see no possibility whatever of fitting it in at any time this year. I am very sorry because this is a service which I should have been very happy to do him.' Masefield reciprocated TSE's liking, and wrote on 9 Jan. 1940 that he felt 'very deeply moved and delighted' by *The Family Reunion*. 'Nothing finer has been done in my time,' he told TSE.

2–Masefield requested the submission of volumes published in 1936 for the Royal Medals for poetry – to be awarded to the first or second book of a writer, or to the work of a writer under thirty-five. The judges were Laurence Binyon, Walter de la Mare, Gilbert Murray, IAR.

16 December 1936                    [Faber & Faber Ltd]

Dear Mr Betjeman,

Thank you for your letter of the 10th.[2] I am sorry that we are too late, though I can hardly blame myself, because I took the matter in hand as soon as Auden made the suggestion to me. Still I regret very much that we should not have your book instead of John Murray. Perhaps, however, you are now ready to contemplate starting something else, and with that purpose in view I hope to get you to lunch with me, and will write and suggest a day or two as soon as I have a little more time. I think it would be better for me, and I dare say for you if I suggested a date soon after Christmas. If lunch is inconvenient for you perhaps you would let me know meanwhile what time of day or what kind of meal or refreshment fits in with your engagements.

I am interested that you should think that perhaps you remember me at Highgate, if you really do. I didn't enjoy myself very much there either. I liked some of the boys, but I remember particularly disliking the Head of School and Captain, whose name I remember but will suppress. It always happened that the most popular and successful boys were the ones I didn't like. I don't remember Mr Kelly as at all malevolent, but I remember Mrs Kelly, whose only interest was Anglo-Israel and the great Pyramid, was very trying.[3]

Yours sincerely,

[T. S. Eliot]

1 – John Betjeman (1906–84), poet, journalist, authority on architecture: see Biographical Register.

2 – Betjeman wrote from Garrards Farm, Uffington, Berkshire: 'Dear Mr Eliot, / It is good of you to take an interest in my poems via Wystan Auden. As I explained to him Mt Zion with additions, is about to be reprinted by John Murray. I shd have been tremendously honoured to have had them even considered by Fabers & by you. I should so like to meet you. I just remember that young Mr Eliot at Highgate Junior School. You were very nice to me . . . I loathed the school. They all used to shout "Betjeman's a German spy – a German spy – a German spy" & dance in circles. I came to the conclusion that I was. There was a horrible sadistic Matron with Ginger hair & Mr Kelly should have been shot. He used to shake us till we wee'd – nasty old man. It was a very bad school & I was pleased to leave & go to Lynams in North Oxford where all the laburnums & bicycles are.

'Perhaps we could meet one day when you are free. / Yours sincerely / John Betjeman / P.S I enclose a little Christmas Greetings Telegram as a present for you. J.B.'

3 – Betjeman replied, 17 Dec.: 'I should love to have luncheon with you & discuss the future. After Christmas will certainly be best. I come up on Mon, Tue & Wed of every week . . .

'Indeed I do remember you at Highgate, though I had not identified you as yourself until Wystan Auden reminded me. You were known as the American Master & I remember that

17 December 1936                    [Faber & Faber Ltd]

Dear Mr Masefield,

Thank you for your letter.[1] I did not understand that the awards for
1934 and 1935 had already been given, and I am sorry to have bothered
you with an unnecessary question. I am, therefore, sending copies of *Look,
Stranger* by W. H. Auden[2] and a translation of the *Agamemnon* by Louis
MacNeice, which were published in 1936. Both of these authors satisfy
the conditions. There was also a play by W. H. Auden and Christopher
Isherwood, but this was partly in prose and I should imagine that Auden's
volume of verse was sufficient for your requirements.

I have no objection to raise to the recitation of *Ash Wednesday* that you
propose.[3] I am not sure whether I can get to Oxford at the end of July as I
have to be there for a conference of a fortnight earlier in the month, but
I should be able to let you know when the time comes.

Yours sincerely,

[T. S. Eliot]

---

a boy told me you were a poet, but I didn't believe it. You had hornrimmed spectacles, were
tall & with a pale face. You sometimes smiled. Your hair was dark. I have not seen you since
then, nor to my knowledge a photograph of you.'

In the event, they were to meet for lunch on Tues., 5 Jan. 1937.

1 – Masefield wrote (n.d.) in answer to TSE's last: 'Several books published by your firm
were considered by the judges, both in 1934 and 1935. I happened to have copies of these.

'I shall be most grateful for any of the 1936 vintage which you may care to let me have.'

2 – FVM to WHA, 28 Sept. 1936: 'De la Mare has handed me your card about the title
LOOK STRANGER, with the note that it's too late to make any change. We were in great
difficulty about the title, because you had just gone to Iceland and we couldn't consult you
about it; and LOOK STRANGER was the best that the synod composed of Eliot, Faber
and me, could produce. Actually, though I didn't suggest it, I don't think it's bad as a title –
though I admit you know best about that. But as we are too late to change, there isn't much
that I can say, except that I hope it won't do any harm.' *Look, Stranger!* was published on
22 Oct. 1936.

3 – 'At the end of July, 1937, I hope to help Nevill Coghill in the production of one or two
poetical plays in Oxford. We were hoping to add to the programme, if you will permit this,
a recitation of your "Ash Wednesday" by choice speakers. Would you be so very kind as to
permit this, if we could satisfy you as to the excellence of the speakers? The performance
would be in the Great Hall of Rhodes House, and the audience would be lovers of poetry,
gathered there for the occasion. It would be a great delight to myself, as well as to all these,
if you would consent to be present, and to speak a few words, even if you cannot allow the
recital.'

# TO *John Grierson*[1]                                                      CC

21 December 1936                    [Faber & Faber Ltd]

Dear Mr Grierson,

It has been suggested that we ought to have on our list a book descriptive of the making of documentary and amateur films on the lines of the lectures being given at the Group Theatre. These lectures appear to have aroused a good deal of intelligent interest, and it has been remarked that there is very little literature on the subject which students could read. Possibly such a book might be a collective enterprise with contributions by experts such as those who have been lecturing at the Group Theatre. While the lectures are still going on and the matter fresh in the minds of the lecturers might be a good moment to set something of the sort going.

It would be highly desirable, we think, that in such a book you yourself should appear as editor, with perhaps the co-operation of Basil Wright, but I should think most of the heavy work could be done by someone else.

Possibly something of the sort may have been contemplated, but in any case we wish to suggest ourselves as the firm of publishers most actively interested in the literature of the film. If you would care to talk this over, either before or after Christmas, I should be delighted if you come and see me.[2]

Yours sincerely,
[T. S. Eliot]

1–John Grierson (1898–1972), pioneering documentary film maker; chief of GPO Film Unit.

2–See too TSE's Report on Raymond Spottiswoode, *A Grammar of Film*, 12 June 1934: 'I found this interesting. The author's style is rather heavy, and he has the profound seriousness which tends to afflict writers on film and wireless; but there is sufficient descriptive matter to hold the attention of those like myself who are infrequent patrons of the bioscope. The first chapter is particularly suety; and I suggest that the glossary of terms which follows might better precede, as that would appeal to the human weakness of acquiring new technical terms with which to impress our friends. I am glad to know now what tracking and panning mean. In the glossary, and sometimes elsewhere, there are occasional glimpses of the obvious, as on p. 14: "Dissolves are called quick and slow according to the time occupied by this process." The author's feelings are usually on the right side. He does not appear to have seen "Man of Aran", but has warm praise of Flaherty, also of Disney.

'GCF must read this. Is there a public? I should think that it might pay for itself; but not, I trust, an autumn book. Supposing that Alistair Cooke's booklet turned out to be worth publishing – and I am not convinced that it will – I don't think that there would be any overlapping; Cooke's point of view is that of a critic who is primarily concerned with the theatre.' (*A Grammar of the Film* was to be published by F&F in 1937.)

See further David Trotter, 'T. S. Eliot and Cinema', *Modernism/modernity* 13: 2 (Apr. 2006), 237–65.

22 December 1936                     *The Criterion*

My dear Barker,

I have been meaning to write to you for the last fortnight, but at this time of year everything goes wrong.[1] I presume that the BBC possibilities are indefinite, as I have not heard from you about your interview with the Western Regional. So I want to ask you frankly just what your situation is for the present and the immediate future. I have no desire to pry into your, or anybody's affairs; but on the other hand if I could know definitely what the position is, and is going to be, it would put me in a stronger position myself for seeing what could be done.

I hope you are able to work. As for the title of your book: I don't like anything that suggests that it is a collection of poems. I want to emphasise the *Cantos*, and if there could be enough of them just to make a book I should be for leaving the Ode out of this and publishing the Cantos by themselves. In any case, I want a title which will at least make clear that the bulk of the book is one long poem.

With best wishes to your wife and yourself for Christmas and the New Year (let me hear from you as soon as possible)

Yours ever,

T. S. E.

---

1 – Barker had written on 30 Nov.: 'I am enclosing the texts of the Introductory Verses to Book I and of Cantos IX & X; & this completes the first part of Metamorphoses. I feel that I have taken the poem to a point where for the time being it will have to rest. Book II of the poems I do not hope to write until my interior has subsided after this work. Also I find that the initial X Cantos succeed in stating most of the fundamentals of the whole poem, & in doing so achieve on a minor scale a possible design for the whole poem . . .

'I am concerned about the title of the book. The first title which I suggested, *Poems 1935–1936*, I have now definitely abandoned as irrelevant. The poems move & devolve on much the same matters & these are poverty & war: this is why I propose the title Poems on Poverty and War. You disapproved, I remember, of this title when I mentioned it recently. I can think of only two alternative titles, namely *Political Poems* or *Propaganda Poems*. I wonder will you let me have your opinion of this sort of title? . . . I forgot to mention that a man is coming over from the Western Regional to see me about a job. I shall meet him here tomorrow & will of course let you know what happens.'

TO *Ezra Pound*                                    TS Beinecke

22 December 1936                    *The Criterion*

Well Ez, imprimis
  Nowel Nowel
  And remember what is stated in the Digha Nikaya:[1] that the Practical
Cat (Dirghakarna) has no Theories.[2]
  First of All, please tell me who is the old BITCH on the Monument.
This is important.[3]
  Cantos shall go to Press, but first of all here am I medjin an markin to
callate for advance payment towards the New Year.
  Now as to Palmerston, since you will keep sendin tauntin p.c. to the
Whale, referrin to my profile,[4] well, if you Will do Palmerston, send it in on
appro, but you understand it cant be now till September, because, Cantos
April, Wyndham July, one two three.[5] But I dont see absolutely acceptin
Palmerston without seein, it being neither your beat nor mine, but if it is
up to your level, well then. But I aint commissionin Parlmerstone, no not
for the Cdriterium. Now you couldnt ask to be spoke more fair than that.
  Remember, Dirghakarna NOT Dadhikarna thats another kind of Cat
altogether.[6]

                        Nowel Nowel
                        TP


1 – The Digha Nikaya ('Collection of Long Discourses'): a Buddhist scripture forming a
constituent part of the five *nikayas* in the Sutta Pitaka. The *suttas* in the Digha Nikaya
include the famous account of the last days and death of the Buddha (the Maha-parinibbana
Sutta).
2 – The fable of the long-eared male cat named Dirghakarna and the blind and talonless
vulture Jaradgava can be found in the *Hitopadesa of Narayana*, ed. M. R. Kale (1967).
3 – The draft of Canto 42 that EP submitted for publication included the phrase 'that old
bitch on the monument'. EP replied equivocally, 27 Dec.: '"I have forgotten" but if there is
the least doubt resident in yr occiput that that "old BITCH" refers to a statue of Moses "as
Mrs Siddons" back of the Stefanskirche [St Stephen's Cathedral] in Vienna you better print
it "that etcetera".'
4 – EP to FVM, 26 Nov.: 'Waaal ole Proposcis . . . As I can't get anything out of you re/ Lard
Pumice stone I am sending a note on our extreme conempory, and I want an ANSWER.'
  EP to FVM, 27 Nov.: 'BLAST his retroussé proposcis/ he DONT answer. He wunt say
yaaas or no re/ Palmerston/ does he want me to fergit what I thought and have to reread the
two vols . . . ?'
5 – EP had expressed a wish to review *Lord Palmerston* (2 vols, 1936). '[H. C. F.] Bell (the
biographer) is meritorious (tho' not omniscient) at any rate a book worth noticing at length.'
6 – Dadhikarna is a snake demon and a cat.


                                                    417

TO *Edwyn Hoskyns*                                                                    CC

24 December 1936                          [*The Criterion*]

Dear Hoskyns,

Thank you for your letter of the 18th.[1] I am afraid there was some
misunderstanding, and I must apologise for having given you unnecessary
trouble, as after your last letter I had not intended the Martin Buber book
to be sent to you. I have the benefit, however, of your suggestion for
an article on the contribution of non-expatriate German Jews. Now that
you have made the suggestion may I ask further whether you think that
Porteous of Edinburgh, whom you proposed for the Buber book, would
be the right man to treat the subject really critically? I am assuming, of
course, that you would not care to undertake such an article yourself, but
if you did I would rather have it from you than from anybody. Perhaps,
however, the suggestion can wait until I see you on the 30th January.[2]

Yours sincerely,

[T. S. Eliot]

1 – 'I have looked through Martin Buber "Die Frage an den Einzelnen". It is, I am afraid, off
my beat. I am doubtful whether an isolated booklet of Buber's ought to be reviewed. On the
other hand, an article on the contribution of German Jews who have not left Germany to
the understanding of religion would be a very valuable contribution. M. Buber is one of the
very important figures, others are Beck & Ellbogen. The difficulty is to find anyone who will
not merely say that they are altogether right, and the guardians of truth.

'I should like to talk to you about this, I have a suggestion to make, but I must make some
enquiries first.'

2 – Hoskyns answered on 28 Dec.: 'I should rather like a talk with you about a possible
article on non-expatriate Jews. I doubt whether Porteous is the right man. S. A. Cook, our
Regius Professor of Hebrew, could do it, if he would. There is a man named "Parkes" who
is working on the material and has recently come to live near Cambridge, but I have not
met him yet . . . The third possibility is Gerhard Kittel himself. The Divinity Faculty here
has just invited him to deliver 3 lectures on the vast "Theologisches Wörterbuch zum Neuen
Testament" [5 vols, 1933–79] of which he is the editor . . .

'I am looking forward to your visit on the 30th. I wonder what you have in mind about
"Religious Teaching in Schools". The trouble is two fold:– (a) ignorant schoolmasters
(b) untheologically-minded schoolmasters.'

See too James Bentley, 'The most irresistible temptation', *The Listener*, 16 Nov. 1978,
635–7. Gordon S. Wakefield, 'Hoskyns and Raven: The Theological Issue', *Theology*, Nov.
1975, 574: 'It must be said that neither Hoskyns nor Raven reacted with initial wisdom
to the emergence of the Nazis from the confusions of Weimar. Hoskyns was sympathetic
at first to a movement which appeared to promise moral reformation over against liberal
permissiveness and socialist millenarianism. This was due to his friendship with Kittel,
whose book on the Jews he encouraged Faber and Faber (he had influence with T. S. Eliot)
to consider publishing in an English translation. This caused some embarrassment in his
relations with Martin Buber. But his advocacy anticipated its publication in Germany. When
it appeared in 1934 Hoskyns was so shocked by its contents that he saw the evils of the Nazi
régime, renounced interest in the book and drew away from his friend.'

30 December 1936                          *The Criterion*

My dear Henry,

Your pyjamas arrived duly several days before Christmas, and were opened on Christmas morning. It is curious that I had decided that I needed new pyjamas, and had decided to wait for the January sales before replacing them; so that these arrived just when needed. The buttonless form is a great improvement, and I wonder that it has not become universal: indeed it is curious to consider why it has taken so long for it to come into being at all. I was afraid that they would be too warm, because I am accustomed to cotton all the year round; but this light wool is very comfortable and not at all scratchy. I am only doubtful whether the Model Hand Laundry Ltd of Hanwell will take any notice of the washing directions. I don't suppose that the Laundress exists any more in London, except perhaps in the houses of the very wealthy: and this mass-washing is hard on clothes. (It is useless to buy garments of artificial silk, as they bore holes in them in no time). But even if the pyjamas do shrink, there is a good deal of room for that, and I shall have had pleasant nights while they last. Do you wear them in the summer too?

I hope you received my present in due time, though I don't know what it was.

Now to thank you for your two letters of Dec. 5th. You have done a good deal for Eliot House (assuming that the gifts are worth having). I have been trying to think whether I have anything to contribute. I don't keep newspaper cuttings, or copies of periodicals in which there is anything of mine that I do not care about preserving. A broadcast talk

---

On 1 June 1933, Gerhard Kittel (1888–1948) – a New Testament professor and Christian theologian at the University of Tübingen – gave a speech he called *Die Judenfrage* ('The Jewish Question'), which was presently published as a seventy-eight-page booklet. Kittel's text was candidly anti-Semitic, recommending among other measures that Jews should be designated 'guest people' (i.e. non-citizens), that mixed marriage between Jews and Christians in Germany should not be permitted, and that professions including law, medicine and teaching should be closed to them.

GCF's appalled reaction to the booklet can be gathered from the following extract from a letter he sent to Erich Alport (the letter was primarily concerned with SS's novel *The Temple*), 31 July 1933: 'I am also reading a curious MS. about the Nazis, written by a German Jew, who is *mirabile dictu* not unfriendly to the movement. But how I loathe this ideal of the authoritarian state! I become more and more of a Liberal. Will England go down, too, into this wild beast pit of dogmatic dictatorship?' TSE's thoughts on Kittel's text are not known – nor even whether he ever read it – but he normally agreed with GCF's opinions (his enthusiasm for Djuna Barnes's *Nightwood* was to be a rare exception) – and *Die Judenfrage* was not published by F&F.

of mine came out in *The Listener* a few weeks ago, and I may be able to get a back number of that.[1] As for manuscripts, I do all my prose stuff straight onto the typewriter, so there is never anything of that; and as for verse, I usually make a few rough notes and then draft and redraft on the machine. Sometimes I start with a pencil and then when I have got going work straight on with the typewriter. I gave two mixed manuscripts of this kind, *Anabasis* and *The Rock*, to the Bodleian. I have about fourteen or sixteen pencilled sheets of part of *Murder* which I might send you: I only kept them in case of emergency as somebody told me that they might eventually fetch a considerable sum. But I ought to present something to Eliot House. Since 1929 I have contributed very little to the *Times Literary Supplement*, if at all. I can write to Ants Oras to ask him for a copy of the English edition.[2]

I am pretty sure I never wrote about *Childhood and the Poets*. It sounds as if it might have something to do with Walter de la Mare. And I dont think I reviewed Beaumont and Fletcher, because if I had done so I should have some new edition of their plays as a reminder.

I have one copy of my Trinity lectures. I will write to Bottkol as you suggest about permission to quote from them. I used some of the material when I lectured in Baltimore (but that hasnt been published either). I dont want these lectures ever to be published. They are pretentious and immature. One of them, on Cowley, I am supposed to be revising to publish in a presentation volume of essays to Grierson. I dont remember the ms. which Spencer had: I gave him my lecture notes for the course I delivered to a Harvard class on contemporary literature.

I am glad that the 'collection' should be in memory of mother; and also that you have been made a member of the common room. I thought it was the pleasant company of all the houses. Bottkol is a very nice fellow. I am glad that the stuff should be there rather than anywhere else. In any case, there is no way of preventing one's indifferent periodical contributions from being eventually reprinted, if people want to do it.

About the Old Colony. Dividends and interest are all collected by them, and remitted periodically to my bank here. The chief advantage of having them control everything, or at least of having everything pass through their

---

1–'The Need for Poetic Drama', *The Listener*, 25 Nov. 1936, 994–5. 'But underneath the action, which should be perfectly intelligible, there should be a musical pattern which intensifies our excitement by reinforcing it with feeling from a deeper and less articulate level.'
2–Ants Oras, 'The Critical Ideas of T. S. Eliot' (*Acta et Commentationes Universitatis Tartuensis Dorpatensis*), B. Humaniora 28 (Tartu, 1932).

hands, is that they can make out my Tax Returns, and pay the tax for me. Income Tax has become such a complicated matter that one can hardly understand domestic taxes, let alone foreign ones. I have my solicitors now make out my British returns. It is very irritating that the Old Colony, Macintyre and his people, should make such blunders. My original letter telling them to take instructions from you, you remember, which I wrote immediately I had talked to you, was not acted upon because I didnt address it to Macintyre personally, and his assistant or colleague sat on it. It seems an inefficient organisation. Could things be arranged so that you handled the investments yourself, while the Colony still held the paper, received the interest and dividends and remitted in the same way, and also composed my Tax Return? I should think (so far as one can grasp a situation from such a distance) that this was probably a good time for a certain amount of stock purchase against inflation, and your suggestion about Pere Marquette sounds a good one.

In my British returns I merely include in one sum the total of remittances from America during the fiscal year.

This is all I have time for at present. I have two rather tough little writing jobs to work off before I can try to write a play.

With much love to both of you and wishes for 1937. I wish you would write soon more about yourself, and the Peabody Museum, and your own work. I hope you are not doing too much work for the Museum – they wont appreciate you so highly if you do everything they want you to do.[1]

Affectionately your brother,

Tom

## TO *Ezra Pound*                                              TS Beinecke

30 December 1936                    *The Criterion*

Ezz Yes Goddambit but what I wanted was a Plain Answer: was or is the Old Bitch Queen Victoria (the natural inference) or Edith Cavell or who??? Your answer too subtile[2] and coy. Goddambt it havent you any heart towards a publisher? If its Queen Victoria its troubble: now are you aimin at sending me to Wormbwood Scrubbs or not??? I mean, if you

---

1 – Henry jotted against this last sentence: 'Not responsible for these sentiments!'
2 – *VMP* (Clark Lecture IV), 124, apropos John Donne's 'The Funeral' ('That subtile wreath of hair, which crowns my arm'): 'The adjective "subtile" is exact, though its exactness be not to us immediately apparent in the literal sense of the word which has so suffered from the abuse of the kindred word "subtle".'

want to get me in for a stretch, aint you the man to admit your intentions? After all a publisher like Faber & Faber is the author's best friend

for a Cow's best friend is her udder –
And the milk streamed in the pail
For the sake of dear old Yale . . .

Cards on the tabble, Ez, cards on the tabble. I play straight poker with those that plays straight with me. And what have you to gain, except as a empty political demonbstration, by having me have my hair cut for 6 months in the 2nd division, what have you to gain? It isnt as if I was a pal of Baldwin or anybody else. Well what.[1]

TP.

## TO *John Dover Wilson*

TS National Library of Scotland

31 December 1936      Faber & Faber Ltd

My dear Dover Wilson,

You are, I hope, aware that we have an interest in a small publishing firm in Edinburgh called the Porpoise Press, which has produced not only modern Scottish verse and prose but one or two editions of classical texts, notably Mackenzie's edition of Dunbar.[2] It has been on my mind for a long time that there ought to be a new scholarly edition of Gavin Douglas's *Aenead*.[3] The only edition that I know of within recent years is an

---

1–EP responded on 2 Jan. 1937: 'Wot HI sez EZ EF yew dont like it; LEAVE IT OUT.

'If you think some buggar will think it is Victoriar R// leave it OUT. and don't try to entice me into defining what ought to be LEFT in a beautiful penumbra/ of course IF you as a reader are asking for INDIVIDUAL light, I sez THINK fer yerself cause yer unnderstanink is quite bright enuff.

'I told you to putt/ "and leave that *et cetera*"

which can not be identified as the Juke of Yokk on Mr Landor's epigram.

'LEAVE IT out/ I don't want you jugged, much as I wd like to accellerate yr/ metabolism. I dont FINK that is the way.'

2–*The Poems of William Dunbar*, ed. W. Mackay Mackenzie (Edinburgh: Porpoise Press; London: F&F, 1932). (Faber & Faber had taken over the Porpoise Press on 1 Apr. 1930.)

See TSE to Maurice Lindsay, 17 May 1962: 'I have always been sympathetic to Lallans' verse, though I have felt that it ought to get its support from publishers north of Hadrian's Wall. But I agree with you that it is less and less capable of expressing anything that a Scot today has to say. When one looks back as far as Dunbar one sighs with regret.'

3–On 13 Mar. 1958 the Right Hon. W. S. Morrison (Speaker's House, Westminster) sent TSE an inscribed copy of his Dow Lecture. TSE responded, 19 Mar.: 'I have much enjoyed reading your lecture and all the more because you praise two poets for whom I have a great admiration, Dunbar and Gavin Douglas (it has always been a gratification to me that the Standard Edition of Dunbar should be published by Faber and Faber).'

expensive illustrated limited edition, and I think there ought to be a more practical text at a more reasonable price. I am writing to you therefore to ask if you can suggest the name of any Scots scholar, of the necessary rank, who might be interested in undertaking such a task.

With best wishes for the New Year,
Yours sincerely,
T. S. Eliot

## TO *Roger Roughton*[1]

31 December 1936                    [Faber & Faber Ltd]

Dear Roughton,

I have not thanked you for your letter of December 15th, and for sending me the copies of C. P. & P., including the contributions by Dylan Thomas.[2]

It is true that we are interested in Scarfe's translations from Lautréamont with Dali's illustrations, and I have been waiting for the text.[3] If Scarfe is still in London do tell him that I shall be very glad if he could look in here at some time, and have a word with me. I ought to have attended to this before, but the Christmas rush was prohibitive.

Yours sincerely,
[T. S. Eliot]

---

1 – Roger Roughton (1916–41): English poet and critic; editor of *Contemporary Poetry and Prose*, 1936–7; friend of David Gascoyne, Dylan Thomas and John Davenport; and sometime member of the Communist Party. FVM to C. K. Broadhurst, 8 May 1933, on Roughton's 'interesting' poems: 'On this evidence I should say he had a good deal in him; which means he is on the road which calls inevitably for patience and endurance; for as you know as well as I, or better, it is a painful and well-nigh impossible task to publish poems.'
2 – Roughton sent *Contemporary Poetry and Prose* nos. 1 and 3/4 with 'The Burning Baby' and 'The School for Witches' by Dylan Thomas. 'I hear that you are interested in Scarfe's translations of Lautréamont and are considering publishing a book of MALDOROR with Dali's illustrations; is that a fact? . . . Scarfe himself is coming over from Paris for a few days on the 24th, if you want to see him.'
See too Spencer Curtis Brown to FVM, 5 Feb. 1937: 'Here are the Dylan Thomas short stories about which Richard Church spoke to you. I shall look forward to hearing from you as soon as you have come to a decision on them.' The enclosure was: 'The Burning Baby and other stories'. Handwritten on Curtis Brown's note is the word 'No' – meaning 'Reject'.
3 – Francis Scarfe (1911–86), English poet and novelist; Comte de Lautrémont (pen-name of Isidore Lucien Ducasse, 1846–70), French poet; Salvador Dali (1904–89), Spanish surrealist artist.

TO *William Saroyan*                                          CC

31 December 1936                    [Faber & Faber Ltd]

Dear Mr Saroyan,

I was glad to get your letter of December 11th, and am also glad to report that *Three Times Three* has arrived today, so I will read it soon and pass it on to Morley, and then we will let you know what we think about it. You were not deceiving me when you said that it was short. And just as the original *Inhale and Exhale* was much too long, so I fear that this may prove much too short to publish by itself. However, I look forward at least to the enjoyment of its reading.[1]

I am told that the two other important points in your letter have already been dealt with, so I conclude by sending you my best wishes for 1937.

Yours sincerely,
[T. S. Eliot]


TO *Michael Roberts*                          TS Janet Adam Smith

31 December 1936                    Faber & Faber Ltd

My dear Roberts,

I think it is probable that we shall want to do your essays, but I cannot speak for the firm until another director has had time to read and report on them.[2] I hope that this may be next week. But if we do the book we

---

1–Saroyan wrote, 11 Dec.: 'I had to come to Hollywood in order to get some of the glittering gold with which to pay dull, lustreless, decaying debts. While here, 8 weeks now, I brought out a book, Three Times Three, which in the local and non-Marxian terminology is strictly colossal; and a copy is on its way to you, from me. I hope Mr Faber wants to bring it out; but I daresay he won't . . . Your book [the F&F edn of *Inhale & Exhale*] is excellent; I mean your editing of it was excellent, only I was broken hearted about certain omissions, wept for days, and refused to visit friends . . . (I am very grateful to you for saving the book: the American version is much too long. Yours is fine. I like it very much. Barnett Freedman's jacket is swell; only a trifle misleading; maybe not too; can't tell. Probably very appropriate.) . . . This new one Three Times Three is swell . . . I hope you like it and decide to print it in a hurry. It's short; that's one advantage.'
    Saroyan inscribed a copy of *Three Times Three* (Conference Press, 1936): 'New Year greetings to T. S. Eliot from William Saroyan. Hollywood. Dec. 11, 1936. (The Man with the heart in the highlands.*) would like to have this book published by Mr Faber. W. S.
    '* a very amusing & new kind of story' (TSE Library).
    The volume, made up of nine stories – whence the title *Three Times Three* – was just 160 pages in length; the first production of a new imprint, it was put out in just one month.
2–Roberts wrote on 12 Dec.: 'Here are nine of my ten essays: I still want to make them simpler, more coherent, and more cogent, but your reader will certainly be able to judge from the present draft whether they are worth publishing.

---

424    TSE at forty-eight

shall want if possible to bring it out in this season, so that there is no time to waste. I hope, therefore, that you are getting on with the missing essay, and also that you will be thinking of a suitable title. I think that the word 'essays' ought to be avoided. It's a bad word from the sales manager's point of view, and I think it does injustice to a book which is so coherent and pointed as this.

With best wishes to you both for the New Year,

Yours ever,

T. S. Eliot

## TO *Henry Miller*

cc

31 December 1936                [Faber & Faber Ltd]

Dear Mr Miller,

I have read your correspondence with Fraenkel, that is to say the part which you have sent me, with much interest and enjoyment, as has one of the other directors.[1] We don't see, however, that there would be a sufficient public for a correspondence of this sort. It's more a matter for private enjoyment, or for a limited edition which might circulate amongst the admirers whom you have already gained, but I don't think it is a thing which would be useful from the point of view of extending your public more widely. You may remember also the remarks I passed in criticising your essay on Lawrence: I think that they apply to some extent to this

'The missing essay, No. 9, will deal with psychology and psychological theories of religion and art (e.g. William James), with the value of substitution and sublimation, and with the special problems introduced by consciousnesss of our own motives. Some problems, I think, disappear if we include the human soul, as a moral agent, among our data (e.g. the problem of evil). Others become more acute. Or shall we say the problems are translated?

'I intend to write this last essay in January, and it would not take long to re-polish the others, but I think it better to give them a rest before I start. Therefore I am sending them to you now.'

1 – Miller despatched (4 Dec.): 'ten letters from the Hamlet book in order to aid you in making a selection. Of course I have the utmost doubt that you will want to publish any of it, and why I have nearly broken my back retyping them for you is more than I understand myself. But it's done now and if nothing more comes of it than to apprise you of the book's existence that will be worth while. I am now about to go to bed and stay there for a few days. Have an ulcerated tooth, neuralgia and sinus trouble, all at once! Feel lousy and believe in nothing, for the moment.' *The Michael Fraenkel – Henry Miller Correspondence called Hamlet*, 2 vols (1962).

Miller to Lawrence Durrell, 3 Jan. 1937: 'I am sending you tomorrow the ten letters from the *Hamlet* which I sent Eliot and which of course he has just turned down, with a mildly sarcastic letter about it being more suitable for my "admirers" and not calculated to "widen my public"' (*A Private Correspondence*, 46).

composition also. It isn't what I like to think of as more than a bye-product [sic] of your mental activity, and I hope certainly that it will not distract you from your more creative work.

With best wishes for the New Year,
Yours sincerely,
[T. S. Eliot]

# 1937

TO *George Every*                                                        CC

4 January 1937 (you wrote 1936)     [*The Criterion*]

Dear George,

(Please drop Mr) This letter cannot, alas, concern itself with your poetry or with mine – just as I find myself obliged to postpone from month to month the attempt to begin to write any: it is a reply to yours of the 3d, not, as I hoped before Christmas, something very different.[1] That will come in time.

Your enclosure, as enclosures ought to be returned quickly, precipitates this response. It is true that Mairet has asked me to express myself in the *NEW*. What is uncertain is when I can do it. At the moment, I am all tied up in knots over the 'Church, Community and State' pamphlet – have you seen a copy? if not I will get one for you – and my obligation to broadcast on 'The Church's Message to the World' (not a title of *my* choosing!) on

---

1–Every wrote, 3 Jan.: 'I want to send you this letter from Tomlin, which I think you ought to see at once, if possible before you write for the N.E.W. Of course I too have been concerned about the [Abdication] crisis . . . but Tomlin's reaction is not mine, and I do not suppose it is yours. Nevertheless it may be a reaction which has to be dealt with, in some way. I have never discussed Royalism enough with you to know how far your Royalism and mine are the same or different, though I imagine that they are not so very different. Later, when I have seen Tomlin's article, I might attempt a longer letter, but the whole issue of what is to emerge from the shock to the nation of the last month, which is bound to lead to new, and, I hope, fruitful, constitutional controversies, seems to me so important, that I think you should see Tomlin's letter before you see anything that I have to say.' The letter from Tomlin has not been traced.

Every to TSE, 12 Jan. 1937: 'I have now read Tomlin's NEW article, but I don't think I can intervene. There is nothing to start from, and great risk of unnecessary offence. Tomlin skates solemnly round the rink without going anywhere near the middle. He is no fool, but it does seem to me that in this case his personal hesitations have clouded his insight. The silence of the press must surely be taken as a whole, before as well as in the crisis. So taken, it seems to me to bear all against any theory of a put-up job. I never imagined that the Church had won, but I do believe that an obscured but real sense that there are offences which a private citizen can commit at his own risk, but in the throne would wound the commonweal, did contribute to the outcome. If the identification of the throne with a "sentiment of domesticity" is dangerous, the cult of "the matey monarch" would have been still more so.'

February 16th.[1] If the pamphlet gives any indication, the other talks will be nothing but words; and having undertaken to do this – simply because one usually does what Oldham asks one to do – I want to do the best I can. And in a way, it is the greater that comprehends the less.

I do want to use Clarendon in the April number, which I am now beginning to make up (under difficulties, because Miss O'Donovan has left us for the BBC, and I don't get a new secretary for another week); so send me your alterations as soon as you can.[2]

Would you write something for the *NEW* yourself? I am sure (and if I wasn't sure I would still be sure that Mairet would accept an article from you gratefully on my recommendation) that it would be more than welcome.

I think Tomlin ought to think out what he thinks ought to have happened. My own difficulty is, that while I see what has happened as a disaster, it seems to me that anything else that could have happened would have been, given the contemporary mentality, a disaster too. The politician takes, and has to take, history in the moment; but if one is not a politician, one tends to see everything as the result of a cumulation of errors of preceding generations, and see only the spectacle of teeth being set on edge.

There has been no victory for the Church. *Ne nous félicitons pas.*

Of course Tomlin was too much impressed by the spectacle of the crowd at Buckingham Palace, coupled with the falsification by the press the day after. The crowd was no more important than the press.

This is only an interim letter. You will be on my mind until I have done something better by you; and in my affections always.

Yours

[T. S. E.]

There will also be a deliberated report on Father Kelly's Lectures.[3]

1–'Church Community and State: no. VI: 'The Church's Message to the World', *The Listener* 17: 423 (17 Feb. 1937), 293–4, 326; repr. as App. to *The Idea of a Christian Society*. '[H]ere is the perpetual message of the Church: to affirm, to teach and to apply, true theology . . . The Church has perpetually to answer this question: to what purpose were we born? What is the end of Man?' (326)

2–'Clarendon and the Popular Front', C. 16 (Apr. 1937), 431–51.

3–Dr Herbert Kelly (1860–1950), Director of SSM, 1893–1910. See Kelly, *No Pious Person: Autobiographical Reflections*, ed. George Every (1960).

4 January 1937                    *The Criterion*

My dear Dodo,

I left London on the 31st (Thursday) to go to the Morleys' in Surrey as usual to see the New Year in – not that I have any special sentiment about the New Year, but it has become a custom, and the New Year is much pleasanter in the country, because you walk out into the orchard just before midnight and listen to the chimes: from the surrounding villages – in this instance Crowhurst, Lingfield, Tandridge, Edenbridge, Westerham – one seldom hears East Grinstead – and then go in to drink a glass of champagne to each others' health before going to bed. Only this year was not so satisfactory; it should be a clear still frosty night – but it was warmish and cloudy and windy, so that one only heard a few of the bells one ought to hear. However, this is just to explain that I left on Thursday afternoon, and as Morley's birthday was being celebrated on Saturday I staid over until this morning (Monday) and so I don't know just when your Christmas present arrived, anyway I found it this morning. Well, my dear Dodo, I cannot think of any present that could give me more pleasure than your print of Old St Louis. I had a print of a Mississippi steamboat, of a similar kind (the boat was called the Mayflower) but I did not recover it. I was very fond of that print, but this will take its place in my affections; and tomorrow it shall go to be framed; and I think it will hang in my office, so that it shall be more generally admired than it could be at Grenville Place. It is quite the nicest Christmas present I have had, but please don't tell anyone that. Incidentally, I have a sentiment about St Louis which the St Louis of today (or even of my childhood) hardly justifies. It is in fact one of the most unpleasant large towns in the world, and certainly has the worst climate – the air is more charged with soot than any other, and it encourages adenoids, tonsils, and pulmonary complaints; and the last time I visited St Louis, in January 1933 (just about four years ago) it was more repulsive than ever. Nevertheless (if you don't believe it consult the files of the *St Louis Post-Despatch* for a leading article on me) I have a sentimental feeling which is excited to exaltation by *Show Boat* and *Old Man River* and all that sort of thing: and what I do miss on New Year's Eve is the sound of the steamboat whistles (there aren't any steamboats now, apparently). In short, this print is the nicest present I could have had.

By the way, Agatha Christie's latest Poirot book, *Cards on the Table*, is *very* good: much the best thing of hers that I have read. I think the next best is *Lord Edgware Dies*.[1]

And we went to Oxted on Saturday night to see Harold Lloyd and Adolph Menjou in *The Milky Way*, which I enjoyed extremely.

I can sympathise with your agitation over the Crisis. I only wish it WAS over. Of course all the newspapers said it was NOT a Constitutional crisis; and then they said that it was Over. But it isn't over. I have been asked to write something about it, but I cannot yet simplify my opinion sufficiently. It has done great harm. Nothing is the better for it. Morally, it is a victory for the Great Upper Middle Class, but certainly not for the Church and what it is supposed to stand for. It is a victory for those who object to Divorce Twice, but not for those who object to Divorce Once: that is the difference, in that respect, between Respectability and Catholicism. It is a victory against the Throne. In the circumstances, I can't see what else could have happened; but my objections have to go several steps back of the circumstances. King Edward's state of mind shouldn't have been allowed to happen; still less Mrs S.'s. It's a warning that one can't cut history into slices, and say Right and Wrong at each slice. No, everything's wrong; and I can't explain it in a letter. I hope I shall have got it arranged into words by next summer, when, in spite of what you say, I shall expect to see you in London.

Affectionately,<br>Tom

## TO *Ottoline Morrell*

TS Texas

4 January 1937                    *The Criterion*

My dear Ottoline,

Oh dear this is not very promising. On Friday I have to visit the Community Centre in North Kensington, because I have to do a five-minute Good Cause about it for the BBC on the 24th;[2] on Saturday I have

1–EVE to Robert Speaight, 20 Mar. 1973: 'Incidentally, he always wanted to meet Agatha Christie, but never did, although he did stand behind her at a reception trying to pluck up courage to introduce himself. When I mentioned this to her not long ago she was very disappointed because she returned his admiration' (EVE carbon).

2–The Community Centre at Dalgarno Gardens, North Kensington, London, was intended to serve the needs of the Housing Estate consisting of flats built by the Sutton, Peabody and Kensington Housing Trusts. TSE spoke on behalf of the North Kensington Community Centre in 'The Week's "Good Cause" Appeal'. See Eliot, *CProse* 5, 407–9. TSE's radio

to go to Chelmsford to speak for a mystery play there to be produced and written by Charles Williams,[1] and on Monday I have to dress for dinner at the National Liberal Club at 7.30; and on Sunday I haven't time to go so far, and it wouldn't be very satisfactory anyway. Is the following Friday (Friday week) possible?

I had an interview with George Barker. He says that he is entirely dependent upon occasional gifts from a few friends. He is to give a reading of Early English Poetry at the BBC on the 7th, and he has had an interview with someone from the Western Regional, who has asked him to prepare a programme and submit it – if that is successful there might be a prospect of a regular job there in Bristol in some months time. He seems to need money at once, and even if he ultimately gets a job, will do so for some months to come. So I should like, first, to use your cheque which is still in my pocket. Shall I just pass it on to him or would you prefer it to go through the Barker Account in my bank? This would do for a quarter, but I should like to get two other people to contribute the same, or enough people to make up £26, for two more quarters, and I would do a fourth myself if it is necessary. So I should be grateful if you would think meanwhile of possible (under pressure) benefactors.[2]

I wish I could see you sooner, and I wish I did not fritter away so much time in good causes.

Affectionately,<br>Tom

I was wrong: the Community Centre is on Thursday; Friday is the British Christian Council.

appeal attracted contributions from 160 people, yielding £100. H. B. Vaisey, KC, chairman, wrote on 2 Feb. 1937: 'I can only say that the help which you have given us is, in my view, invaluable.'

TSE to Sir Victor Mallet, 19 May 1949: 'As I learnt some years ago when I appealed on the B.B.C. for funds for a Community Centre in North Kensington, these five-minute broadcasts are the very devil. It is very much like having to send a very long telegram to some remote place to which the rate is 10s. a word: one has to cut and cut and then practise and practise, because in these appeals one thing that is fatal is to give the listeners the appearance of being in a hurry; one has to pick out essentials and avoid saying too much.'

1 – 'One might have supposed, from reading it, that Mr Charles Williams's Epiphany play, *The Three Kings*, could never get a performance; but when it was done last January by the Chelmsford Diocesan Religious Drama Society, it proved extremely effective; and particularly impressive was the enthusiasm and conviction with which the amateur company acted it. One felt that they were happy in having a religious play to do that was really exciting and out of the ordinary' ('Religious Drama: Mediæval and Modern', *University of Edinburgh Journal* 9 [Autumn 1937], 16).

2 – OM replied, 5 Jan.: 'Put Cheque to Barker Account. If he thinks *I* am very opulent he might think that I could be tapped at any time. You could intimate that it is an anonymous fund given by Lovers of Literature.'

## TO *Messrs Bird & Bird*

4 January 1937                    [Faber & Faber Ltd]

Dear Sirs,

I thank you for your letter enclosing my Income Tax Demand Note, which I will settle.[1] I shall ask that the receipt be sent to you. When this is done I hope to settle my account with you up to the last statement.

I enclose a letter received from the Office of the Special Commissioners, dated the 31st ultimo. I obviously cannot make any statement to them about my wife's income, of which I am of course ignorant; and a reply to this letter would be best made by you. I should imagine that the District Bank Limited of 75, Cornhill, would be able to provide details of Mrs Eliot's income.[2]

> Yours faithfully
> [T. S. Eliot]


## TO *Fred Rea*

4 January 1937                    [Faber & Faber Ltd]

Dear Mr Rea,

I owe you a humble and double apology. I ought to have written to you long before, and I ought at least to have spared you the trouble of reminding me that you were awaiting a reply from me. Your invitation has been on my mind; but all this time I have been struggling between the temptation to say that I would come, and the growing realisation that I had been accepting far too many engagements. When engagements are offered far ahead, I accept some because I seem to have no reason to refuse, and others because I want to; and as the time approaches, I contract other engagements of the kind that are difficult to decline because they appear either as a duty or else are urged by people to whom I am under obligation. I had counted upon being free to start upon a piece of work of my own by the beginning of last December: now I shall be fortunate if I can start by the latter part of February. And in June my time is peppered with speeches. So I feel that I must decline all engagements hereafter that

---

1–The instalment of income tax due on 1 Jan. 1937 was £139.14.4d.

2–Ernest E. Bird was to write to TSE on 13 Jan. 1937: 'I venture to acknowledge personally your kind cheque for £48.17.11 in discharge of your indebtedness to my firm . . . In doing so may I be permitted to say once again and from the bottom of my heart that I hope that never again will you be called upon to pay so heavy a lawyer's bill.'

I can possibly decline. You see, I only have practically three hours a day, at the best of times, for my private work apart from my regular business; and it is becoming more and more difficult to preserve this much time, even for a few consecutive months.

I write at some length because I feel that I have let you down. I should have very much enjoyed a visit to Dublin; but it would mean a fortnight (allowing for preparation and for recuperation); and I am getting on in years and must begin to conserve my energy if I can.

With humble regrets and apologies, and best wishes to you and to your interests in the new year, I am,

Yours very sincerely,

[T. S. Eliot]

I have let myself get involved in the Conference of Church Community, and State, and that will take a fortnight in July at Oxford, apart from the work I have to do for it meanwhile.

## TO *Ronald Bottrall*[1] TS Texas

5 January 1937                Faber & Faber Ltd

My dear Bottrall,

I am sorry that I have had to remain so long in silence about your poems.[2] It is not so long as it seems even to myself, because I could not ask a decision of my committee until I had the final and complete manuscript to show them.

I was myself in favour of publishing the book, though it contains no poem of the length, or, to my mind, of the distinction of 'Festivals of Fire', but I cannot get a majority of the committee to accept my view. I do not, of course, have a free hand with poetry, any more than anyone else with other kinds of books. And since my interests are in types of literature from which there is little or no money to be made, I am naturally more restricted. Anyway, the other members are not ready to extend the poetry list as much as I should like, and do not want to do this book.

---

1–Ronald Bottrall (1906–89), poet, critic, teacher, administrator: see Biographical Register.
2–Bottrall submitted on 23 Oct. 1936 what he called 'the final version of my book, *Crooked Eclipses* . . . I promised you in the spring to let you have the finished copy in November, and it therefore seems reasonable to send on the MS now, although I have not had definite word from you. I hope that it will be convenient for you to publish in May, when I shall be back in England.' On 3 Jan. 1937: 'I am waiting to hear from you about *Crooked Eclipses*. It would do me an immense amount of good if you could get the book out in May.'

I am all the more sorry because I should like to see the book published while you are in England this summer. I have made general enquiries and find that Church, of Dent's, is in the same position for 1937 as myself. The possibilities that occur to me are Chatto (Ian Parsons) and Cape (Hamish Miles). But you may have your own views, so I will hold the poems for your instructions. I should be glad to be of any personal use possible.

Yours ever,<br>T. S. Eliot

## TO *Donald Gallup*

TS Beinecke

6 January 1937               Faber & Faber Ltd

Dear Mr Gallup,

Thank you for your kind letter of December 21st and for your amazingly full list of first editions. I am astonished at the relative completeness of your collection, and I can say without flattery that you know a great deal more about my bibliography than I know myself. The only omissions of which I am aware, are certain numbers of *The Little Review*, which was published in New York and edited by Margaret Anderson and Jane Heap. This was a small monthly, which flourished at the end of the War and for a few years later: you may remember that *Ulysses*, or parts of it, first appeared in this review and that one number was suppressed. There are several numbers with contributions from me, including a few poems later included in the next volume, EELDROP AND APPLEPLEX, and some remarks about Henry James. I have not got a complete file. I can only find two numbers with contributions of my own, which I am sending on to my brother for the Eliot House Library. I would also mention that *Nightwood* by Djuna Barnes is shortly to be published by Harcourt Brace and will have a short preface by myself in the first edition.[1]

I don't really feel that it is for me to introduce your Catalogue.[2] I feel rather diffident about it and would probably take refuge in humour, which is always dangerous.

With best wishes and many thanks,<br>Yours sincerely,<br>T. S. Eliot

1 – Barnes told Mary Butts, 8 Feb. 1937, that *Nightwood* was 'coming out shortly with a preface by Eliot which should make me happy for the rest of my life'.
2 – Donald C. Gallup, *A Catalogue of English and American First Editions of Writings by T. S. Eliot Exhibited in the Yale University Library 22 February to 20 March, 1937* (1937).

P.S. I don't suppose there is anything to suppress in the letters in your possession.

## TO *Michael Roberts*                                                      cc

6 January 1937                    [Faber & Faber Ltd]

Dear Roberts,

We definitely want to do your book: I think at 7s.6d. (Same price as *Critique of Poetry*, and a lot more for the money). 10% up to 2000 copies, and 15% thereafter.[1] It's a good book indeed. I am writing immediately to say that, if you are agreeable, and if you can think of a title and let me have it by Monday morning, we could just get the real title into the Catalogue. And we shall want the final text just as soon as we can get it, so as to publish in the spring. Do you want me to send the essays back???

We think decidedly that your introduction is unnecessary. It is too tentative and apologetic; and the book is so good, as soon as it begins, that one feels that the introduction has done more harm than good. A SHORT preface, going straight to the point concisely, would be all to the good.

One of my colleagues, Morley (who would very much like to meet you) and who is a mathematician himself, has written the following note which may be of interest to you:

Passages such as bottom p. 199 are delicate matters. As to what he says there, I say a loud hear hear. But even so the phrase 'emotions about numbers' isn't happy. He is, of course, talking about numbers only in one small sense: but he might (there or elsewhere) protect himself on that point. Plato's numbers, or ......'s, for that matter, are to them emotion – direct force – and many of the big mathematicians (e.g. Gauss) give one the feeling that in this realm they have perfect pitch. If M. R. would put 'emotions about numbers' in quotes to show his despite, as he might for phrases like 'emotions about poetry' or 'emotions about music', he'd safeguard himself and be clearer.

It's the 'emotions about' which is the perversion.

He only offers this for 'what it is worth'.

Best wishes for the New Year to both of you.

Sincerely<br>
[T. S. Eliot]

1 – *The Modern Mind* (published on 27 May 1937).

Epiphany 1937[1]                          *The Criterion*

My dear Alison,
   I am asked by my friend, the Man in White Spats –
      Who, to my way of thinking, has nothing to do
   But attend to the horrible sharps and the flats
      Of his Budgerigars and his prize Cockatoo,
   But who still has one feature we may call redeeming,
      (I've observed him quite closely and know it is true),
   And which briefly and shortly is this: to all seeming
      He has a most touching devotion to YOU –
   I am asked by my friend, as I started to say
      And I may say he said it quite off his own bat –
   I am asked by the Man in White Spats to convey
      This informative poem on a Curious Cat.

### THE RUM TUM TUGGER

The Rum Tum Tugger is a Curious Cat,
If you offer him pheasant then he'd rather have grouse;
If you put him in a house then he'd rather have a flat,
If you put him in a flat then he'd much prefer a house.
If you set him on a mouse then he'd rather have a rat,
If you set him on a rat then he only wants a mouse.
Yes the Rum Tum Tugger is a Curious Cat –
     And there isn't any call for me to shout it!
       For he will do
       As he do do
     And there's no doing anything about it!

The Rum Tum Tugger is a terrible Bore:
When you let him in, he wants to be out;
He's always on the wrong side of every door,
And as soon as he's at home, then he wants to get about.
He likes to lie in the bottom drawer,
But he makes such a fuss if he can't get out.
Yes the Rum Tum Tugger is a Curious Cat –

---

1 – Postmarked 6 January.

And it isn't any use for you to scout it:
>     For he will do
>     As he do do
And there's no doing anything about it!

The Rum Tum Tugger is a Curious Beast,
His exasperating ways are a matter of habit.
If you offer him fish then he always wants a Feast,
When there isn't any fish then he won't eat rabbit.
If you offer him cream then he only sneers,
He only enjoys what he finds for himself;
So you'll find him in it right up to the ears
If you put it away on the larder shelf.
The Rum Tum Tugger is observant and knowing,
The Rum Tum Tugger doesn't care for a cuddle,
But he'll leap on your lap in the middle of your sewing,
For there's nothing he enjoys like a terrible muddle.
Yes the Rum Tum Tugger is a Curious Cat –
>     And there isn't any need for me to spout it:
>         For he will do
>         As he do do
>     And there's no doing anything about it!

Now that's what my friend, the Man in White Spats,
Has asked me to convey, in the matter of Cats.
>             Your fexnite
>             Possum


## TO *Ezra Pound*                               TS Beinecke

Epiphany [6 January] 1937          *The Criterion*

Wal Ole Ez thats it if you say so it is so But you are such a comicker I
didnt kno but what you was pullin my leg and sendin me to Wormbwood
Scrubs. So ETCETERA AND HURRAH FOR ETCETERA I didnt mean
all that to be in Capitals and I know you are worried about my thyroid
and thymus but I Have had injections against influenza.

Acting on information received Messrs Faber and Faber have made
enquiries, not to say *démarches*, of the side of Larry Pollinger and Dave
Hyam respecting the recent history of the United States of America said

to have been written by one Woodward and published by Johnny Farrer.[1] And as we used to say at Harvard: OH RHINEHART!!!

Now I have thats telephathy that Is been tryin for weeks to get the continuation of that Ballet about Mrs Simpson[2] but though I have made contact with a parson from Pittsburgh who says his secretary was at school with her in Baltimore, and though I have been permitted to see Upton Sinclair's memoir of her (Upton's very proud of his family, djykno, has he had the Noebl prize yet or not) I have been unable to contact any authentic carol singers. but I know somebody whose sister in law works in Bermondsey, so it isnt hopeless yet.

Jim Barnes a pal of yours, huh? I spose so.

Wuff

This is goin to work out about 13 pounds (or guineas). I guess I got to trim down some of the other boys.

Jug! and again Jug (jug)![3] I'll lay you a pony to a tanner[4] I land in jail before you do. aint so bienpensant as you is Ez.

TP

Heres a financial mossel for you about the British Film Industry. If you are interested I have a fuller account in the FILM WORLD includin a portrit of Lord Luke of Pavenham.[5] Hes a director of Lloyds Bank, which must have run down since my time, and hadnt so far to go either.

Well Now I most forgot. About that list. Yuss, but you must be fair. That list is a little fuller than I could make it: you includeid one or two blokes unknown to me, I wont sponsor any ~~frogs~~ wops no not the late priandello [sic], and I agree Cocteau allright but you mentioned another frog that I dont kno, and Id like to include Djuna and praps Marianne.

---

1–EP recommended TSE to publish *A New American History*, by W. E. Woodward. He stressed on 2 Jan. 1937: 'I am serious about Bill Woodward's book/ shall blurb it in N.E.W.'
2–EP had written on 2 Jan.: 'Mark the herald angels sing / Mrs Simpson's pinched our king' – adding 'please COLLECT the rest of this aufentik carol.'
3–Cf. *TWL* II, 'A Game of Chess', 102–3: 'And still she cried, and still the world pursues, / "Jug Jug" to dirty ears.'
4–A 'pony' is cockney slang for £25; a tanner is sixpence.
5–George Lawson Johnston (1873–1943), vice-chairman of Bovril Ltd (a business established by his father); director of the *Daily Express* and Lloyds Bank: created 1st Baron Luke in 1929.

## TO *F. A. Iremonger*                                    TS BBC

7 January 1937                    *The Criterion*

My dear Iremonger,

I enclose a copy of the second draft of my talk, which, mindful of your admonition, I have reduced to what I am sure are modest limits. I hope that you will find in it enough challenge, and I should be discomfited if it struck you as defeatist. But I must say, that I have seldom attempted anything more difficult or less able to give satisfaction to the author. The things one has to leave out! . . . for various reasons.

I shall be showing this to two or three friends, and may have occasion, if time permits, to make alterations.[1]

Sincerely yours,
T. S. Eliot


## TO *Henry Eliot*                                    CC

7 January 1937                    [*The Criterion*]

My dear Henry,

I should be grateful if you would do something for me. It may be as much or as little as you choose but please don't let it take any time in excess of its importance.

There is a man whom I have known for some years named Jim Barnes, otherwise Major James Strachey Barnes. I don't know him intimately. It is rather that he is the brother of a Mrs Hutchinson who is an old friend of mine. Jim has been in Reuter's Agency in India and is shortly coming home on leave with his wife by way of America. He has just written to me from New Delhi to ask me for introductions to people in Los Angeles, Chicago, Washington, Baltimore and New York. I cannot think of anybody to give him introductions to except some of the heavier, wealthier and duller relatives and I don't remember any of their addresses. He says nothing about Boston but I should think he would like to go there too if he had introductions. What I should like to do would be to get him to write to you and ask you to supply any introductions you thought fit.

Jim is rather a queer bird. He is a cousin of the Stracheys and I think his father is a head of the Anglo-Persian Oil Company or something of

---

1–The third and final version of the talk on 'Church, Community and State' was to be submitted to the BBC by TSE's secretary on 19 Jan.

the sort. He is very correct, having been to Eton, Cambridge, in the Blues and ended the War in the Air Force. He is a violent Italophile, a pal of Mussolini, and wrote a couple of books about Fascism in its early stages. He is also some kind of honorary valet to the Pope, being a R.C. convert. His wife is Italian and I have only met her once. She seemed to me quite attractive and talks English easily. It is obvious from Jim's politics that he would not go with the Sheffields but I should think he would be quite suitable for the Wolcotts, the Du Boises, Tuckermans and people of that sort. I think you might find them pleasant for an evening if they turned up in Boston. I don't know anybody in Los Angeles. I should think that the Porters in Chicago might be suitable. I don't know anybody in Washington either. I imagine that he would like there to meet official people around the White House, and I don't know who could help him. Baltimore seems equally difficult. I imagine that Chicago, New York, if not Boston, are the places to concentrate on. But it is not worthwhile bothering about very many I don't suppose, as his visit will probably be brief. In any case you won't have to do anything unless you hear from [him] because I don't know where he will be stopping.

Yours ever affectionately,
[Tom]

TO *George Barker*                                    TS Texas

8 January 1937                    *The Criterion*

Dear Barker,

I was sorry to be unable to listen to your selection last night (I should have been still more interested if you had been reading yourself). I am going to buy a set for myself, but my current is being changed over, so I have postponed the purchase. And I couldn't get the use of anybody else's: my landlord's was out of order. I hope that you will be doing some more.

I have got hold of a sum amounting to £13 which could be payable at once. I am not sure on what day you were returning to Dorset, so please let me know where to have the bank send it. I hope that the same amount will be available in three months' time, but that must be seen to.

Yours ever,
T. S. Eliot

10 January 1937                    [Faber & Faber Ltd]

My dear Vaisey,

Here is my second draft, which is considerably shorter than the first. I have counted it word by word, and it seems to amount to 704 words unfinished. You said 600. But I have read it aloud to myself, and did it in just under 5 minutes. And as I always like to have a rehearsal before doing anything for the BBC, it might be tried out and reduced in rehearsal. (By the way will you tell them that I want a rehearsal?)

It is impossible to say what one wants to say in a 600 word telegram. But I should be glad if you would criticise this, and if you think of anything I ought to have stressed, rather than something I have said, I will gladly rewrite it.

I can't do the really sentimental appeal. You need a Barrie for that. I have kept to my own line, which is usually qualified as 'cold and precise', because if one tries to do what one's temperament forbids, one does worse.

I have left the end uncertain. I have no set of my own (I have got to get one, much as I loathe it) and I have not listened to an 'appeal' for a long time. My impression is that people say: 'send your contributions to me (then pronounce their own name carefully) at Broadcasting House, W.C.1.' I don't know how this is worded. But if it would help for me to say 'and I will thank you for them personally', I am willing to sign any number of letters if the BBC or the Centre would type them for me to sign: and of course would be ready to write my own letters in response to any whopping or particularly touching contributions. But my experience in trying to get good money for good causes leads me to believe that if I appeal for £5000 the expectations are £49 and some pence.

Sincerely,

[T. S. Eliot]

---

1–Harry Bevir Vaisey (1877–1965), barrister-at-law; later a senior judge in the Chancery Division of the High Court of Justice in England and Wales. Chairman of the Community Centre, Dalgarno Way, Dalgarno Gardens, North Kensington.

TO *Paul Elmer More*                                    TS Princeton

11 January 1937                    *The Criterion*

My dear More,

I have just been reading your first 'Marginalia' in the November *American Review* (I haven't seen the December yet) and I enjoyed them so much that I must write and thank you. Your quotation from Newman brings out just the point which has always made Newman seem rather alien to me. *We begin by degrees to perceive that there are but two beings in the whole universe, our own soul, and God.*[1] Now I would not dream of setting up my poor religious intuitions to match Newman's, but this is not only a perception that I have never had, but a perception that shocks me a little. I know a little what is the feeling of being alone – I will not say *with* God, but alone in the presence and under the observation of God – with the feeling of being stripped, as of frippery, of the qualifications that ordinarily most identify one: one's heredity, one's abilities, and one's *name*. But to feel at any moment that 'there are but two beings etc.' seems to me almost a denial of the Mystical Body of Christ, a monstrous solipsism bordering on the abyss of the German mystics. But was Newman ever quite orthodox? And is not there the shadow of the error of Cartesianism over this? I should like to know.

What touches me most closely is a suggestion, here and there, of a spiritual biography which, if I may say so without presumption, is oddly, even grotesquely, more like my own, so far as I can see, than that of any human being I have known.[2] And when you say

'I have often wondered what line my experience might have taken had I been brought up in a form of worship from which the office of the imagination and of the aesthetic emotions had not been so ruthlessly evicted . . .'

1 – Paul Elmer More, 'Marginalia Part I', *The American Review* 8: 1 (Nov. 1936), 19–21.
2 – In sections ix–xi of his essay, More reflects upon the religion he inherited in his youth: 'I lived in full security of the old inherited faith of Calvin . . . But it had one terrible weakness. The very rigidity of its logic . . . was a menace . . . Calvin . . . took over for the basis of his systematic theology that definition of God as the absolute unconditioned Cause of all things' – and in due course More found himself questioning 'the very notion of a God so constructed', and he cast it off 'with bitter actual tears of regret': 'I did not know that my revolt was in the main against a particular formulation of theism rather than against the spirit of Christianity. And I have often wondered what line my experience might have taken had I been brought up in a form of belief and a practice of worship from which the office of the imagination and of the aesthetic emotions had not been so ruthlessly evicted.' His life might otherwise have moved happily towards 'that form of wondering faith which we distinguish by the name of sacramentalism'.

I have made the same speculation. But I am inclined to think that I know how to value these things better, just for having (being me) to struggle so long, and for so many years so blindly and errantly, towards them. <– May one say, under the guidance of the Holy Spirit?>

Affectionately and admiringly,

T. S. Eliot

## TO *M. C. D'Arcy*                                                                cc

11 January 1937                    [Faber & Faber Ltd]

My dear D'Arcy,

Thank you for your kindness in replying – I am grateful for your criticisms, which I shall avail myself of – that phrase of St Paul's has long seemed to me one of the 'silver nails' as Henry James would say,[1] but I admit it would not have come to me in this context: and I am mightily relieved that you find no more – allowing for your not having time to search my vitals – to criticise.

Yes, I really must come to see you, but perhaps it will not be until the spring. For my being so jammed up this winter Joe Oldham is to blame. I have to turn to on my preface to your 'Revelation' next. Have you read all the other papers, I wonder. Barth seems to me such a queer mixture of admirable insight and something just so alien that I can't make head or tail of it; and as for Bulgakoff's 'Sophia', it seems to me an unnecessary and rather undesirable character. But that may be my stupidity.[2]

Yours ever gratefully,

[T. S. Eliot]

---

1 – Henry James remarked, in his essay on Gautier: 'His world was all material, and its outlying darkness hardly more suggestive morally than a velvet canopy studded with silver nails' (*French Poets and Novelists*, 33).

2 – *Revelation*, ed. John Baillie (Professor of Divinity, University of Edinburgh) and Hugh Martin (F&F, 1937) – a symposium on the foundations of Christian theology – comprised contributions from TSE, Karl Barth, Professor of Dogmatic Theology, University of Basle; William Temple, Archbishop of York; Sergius Bulgakoff, Professor of Theology at the Orthodox Institute, Paris, and formerly Professor of Economics at Moscow University; M. C. D'Arcy, Master of Campion Hall, Oxford; Walter M. Horton, Professor of Theology, Oberlin Graduate School of Theology; and Gustaf Aulén, Bishop in Strängnäs, Sweden.

The blurb (Spring Books 1936, 52) remarks: 'Everyone who is interested in contemporary theology will recognize the importance of this volume on reading the names of the contributors. Six different Christian communions are represented . . . The book has a special timeliness in view of the International Conference on Church, Community and State, to be held at Oxford in July, and is published under the auspices of the Faith and Order Movement.

TO *Maurice Reckitt*[1]                              TS University of Sussex

13 January 1937                              Faber & Faber Ltd

My dear Reckitt,

I have received yesterday a letter from Bolshakoff enclosing the report of the permanent secretary of the International Academy of Christian Sociologists. I should very much like to know whether you have read this report and if so what you think of it. For me, it rather confirms the suspicion that I have entertained for a long time that the Christian Sociologists were going to turn out to be Fascist Sociologists, and my first impulse was immediately to write to Bolshakoff and insist upon resigning. But I think it is better to let one's feelings cool and I should like very much to have your opinion and counsel.

I have always felt that the so-called Academy was going to be futile, but one can't resign from a thing merely on the suspicion that it will be futile; one has to wait for time enough to prove that. On the other hand, if it is to be noxious as well one can resign at once.

Yours ever,
T. S. Eliot


TO *Theodore Spencer*                              TS Harvard Archives

14 January 1937                              *The Criterion*

Dear Ted,

I hate to worrit you, but you remember that when you so kindly undertook to bring the work and the appeal of Dr Jovetz-Tereshchenko to the attention of Professor Alport [*sc.* Allport], you wrote to me to say that Alport would be communicating direct with the Former. Jovetz has turned up again, and is coming to see me today; but I understand from him that he has never had a word from Alport. Would you be willing to jog, as they say, the Latter's memory? It may prove that he has come to

'This book will need no recommendation to people at all conversant with contemporary Christian thought – they will know at once that it is a book that they must read. But, in connection with the urgent social and political problems of the present time, it should have a general appeal also to the "lay mind". In his introduction, Mr T. S. Eliot endeavours to make clear the reasons for the relevancy of this discussion to questions occupying the minds, and affecting the lives, even of those who take least interest in pure theology. This is not merely a book for the scholar, but a book for the times.'
1 – Maurice Reckitt (1888–1980): Anglo-Catholic and Christian socialist writer; editor of *Christendom: A Quarterly Journal of Christian Sociology*: see Biographical Register.

the conclusion that the stuff is of no use or that there is nothing to be done for the man; but you did say, that the Latter would write direct to the Former when etc. Again I say, and I repeat it, that I am sorry to bother you.[1] I suppose you are up to the ears etc. So am I. If you have an all-wave set, I am broadcasting on Feb. 16th, National Wave Length, 9.20 Greenwich time p.m.[2]

Affectionately in haste,<br>
TP

TO *Willard Thorp*                                              TS Princeton

14 January 1937                    *The Criterion*

Dear Willard,

I enclose a short paper on More, in response to your letter of the 23d December.[3] I am sorry that I could not write it more quickly, and that it

---

1 – On receipt of TSE's enquiry, Spencer went round to Allport's house. But, as he reported back (26 Jan.), he found it 'empty & to rent and he in California on his sabbatical . . . But as I told you before there's practically no chance – according to Allport – of their taking a man sight unseen. He's really got to establish himself here on some sort of fellowship.'

2 – 'The Church's Message to the World'.

3 – Thorp and A. E. Hinds (his colleague in the English Department) requested TSE to write something – 'about 1500 words' – for the *Princeton Alumni Weekly* in honour of the long association with Princeton University of Paul Elmer More (who was rapidly failing in health), in his capacity as lecturer in Greek philosophy and the History of Christianity. They hoped for TSE, with all his sympathy and distinction, to write of More's life and work in a way that might even be read by More himself, if he should happily live longer. They concluded: 'it would give us the deepest satisfaction to feel that the importance of his life and writing had been presented to a Princeton audience by the man whom we know he would most delight to have honor him.'

'Paul Elmer More', *Princeton Alumni Weekly* 37: 17 (5 Feb. 1937): *CProse* 5, 418–23, includes these reflections: 'It was not until my senior year [at Harvard], as a pupil of [Irving] Babbitt's, that More's work was forced on my attention: for one of the obligations of any pupil of Babbitt was to learn a proper respect for "my friend More" . . .

'It was not until one or two of the volumes of *The Greek Tradition* [5 vols, 1917–27] had appeared that More began to have any importance for me . . . The English Church was familiar with the backslider, but it knew nothing of the convert – certainly not of the convert who had come such a long journey. I might almost say that I never met any Christians until after I had made up my mind to become one. It was of the greatest importance, then, to have at hand the work of a man who had come by somewhat the same route, to almost the same conclusions, at almost the same time: with a maturity, a weight of scholarship, a discipline of thinking, which I did not, and never shall, possess . . .

'I still consider *The Greek Tradition* More's greatest work. There are theological points which will always be matters of contention, but I do not know of any book which gives such a masterly treatment of the process through which Greek thought influenced Christianity . . . I dislike to use the worn and soiled phrase "spiritual pilgrimage," but More's works

is not better. I am dissatisfied with it; but in the circumstances it has to be both hurried and a compromise. If I knew that it was obituary, I should be more personal; if I knew that it would not be an obituary, I should be more critical. Please edit it, for the sake of good taste and appropriateness, according to the circumstances of publication. You may want to leave out bits, alter tenses, etc.

This is a eulogy and a 'demonstration'. I think that in some ways More's theology is rather narrow and defective; that he tends to emphasise those things in Anglicanism which were absent from the doctrine of his childhood,[1] and to ignore things which the two have in common. I think he remains a little sectarian, and not wholly orthodox. But this is not the place, nor am I quite the person, to sift his work in this way. Then he is 'anglophile', in that he sees the excellence of English institutions where a person resident here is more likely to see their shortcomings and corruptions. And I suspect that in some of his views on contemporary political affairs he was a somewhat conventional conservative: but I am not sure. It is difficult anyway to be sure except when two people have a common knowledge of one field of political action. When I last saw him he just touched on the Spanish affair, if I remember correctly; but I did not feel then like getting into a contentious argument with him.

If this won't do, don't use it: please use your discretion.

Sincerely yours,

T. S. E.

are, in the deepest sense, his autobiography. One is always aware of the sincerity, and in the later works the Christian humility (a very rare virtue too) of the concentrated mind seeking God . . .

'It must remain a matter of regret that in later years More and Babbitt were obliged to diverge. To those who have found it necessary to take the way of the Catholic Church, the regret will be particularly acute. Yet, in such a generous friendship, I am sure that each regarded the other as the greater man . . . [This divergence] points to the decision that we must all of us, if we follow our thought to the bitter end, find ourselves compelled to make. That is, unless we have already made the easier choice of some shoddy philosophy which they would both of them denounce. The diversity of created beings is very great, and one is hardly likely to do justice to all: but these seem to me the two *wisest* men that I have known.'

1 – More was brought up a Presbyterian.

14 January 1937                    [Faber & Faber Ltd]

My dear Vaisey,

It is a relief to a busy man, and also gratifying, that you should have found my words on the whole satisfactory. There is just one alteration at which I want to cavil. I can quite understand that 'good English stock' might suggest a narrow racialism, and might offend those few who are not of English stock: and this of course I do not wish to do. But I don't like 'fine independence' either.[1] What I am in horror of, in making an appeal of this kind, is any suggestion of being patronising to the less fortunate; and I feel something of this – though others may not – in the word 'independence'. (I welcome the suggestion of altering *my* phrase, and I see that the later reference to Anglo-Saxon self-government is enough). Would it do just to say (as there is question of having too many words anyway): 'They are people of good London breed'?[2]

In haste,

[T. S. Eliot]

1 – Vaisey had sought to amend a phrase in this opening paragraph of TSE's draft appeal:

'In a remote corner of North Kensington, near the line of the Great Western Railway, over against Kensal Green, there are living, in several blocks of Housing Trust flats, some two thousand adults and three thousand children. It is an area you can walk round in ten minutes. They are people of good English stock and London breed. Before they were moved to these flats, they were living in Paddington in overcrowded decaying houses – many of them in damp sunless basements. Very few realise what a struggle the London poor will make to live decently in such surroundings. Now, these five thousand have a better opportunity.'

Vaisey deleted 'good English stock' and substituted 'fine independence'.

2 – Vaisey responded in a letter of even date: 'I ought to have been more explicit. I did not, of course, intend to put any words of mine into your mouth, but I did not think that "good English stock" will do. The people are a very mixed lot racially, and include *many* Irish, and I believe some Jews; and one of the surprising things has been the "community" spirit in a collection of people of very diverse breed. One does not wish to emphasise this, of course, as it is important not to encourage "race consciousness" in any form, but the use of the word "English" is not right (I am sure) especially as the Warden herself is very proud of being a Scotswoman and impatient of the use of any expression of nationality not wholly in accordance with the facts!!!

'I entirely agree on reflection with the objection to any reference to "independence" (which has, I think, a flavour of "patronage") and your proposal to say simply "a good London breed" is quite to my liking. The later allusion to "Anglo-Saxon" seems to me entirely free from any of the objections we have been considering – the thought crossed my mind that you might substitute "native", but you know best.'

TO *Louis MacNeice*                                          CC

15 January 1937                        [*The Criterion*]

Dear MacNeice,

I am sending you the Hopkins notebooks, which have finally arrived. If I had known that they would be so long delayed I would have asked you to do for the March number one of the other books you suggested, because you will need more time for this than is possible. I shall be glad therefore if you will do it for the June number.[1]

If you think seriously of an essay on the futility of books about contemporary poetry I should be delighted. You must come and lunch again before long.

Yours ever,
[T. S. Eliot]


TO *E. W. F. Tomlin*                            TS Lady Marshall

15 January 1937                        *The Criterion*

Dear Tomlin,

Thank you for your note.[2] It is true that I have talked with Mairet about a note on the crisis for the *N.E.W.*, but I simply haven't had the time even to get my ideas in order. I have been very busy ever since, partly with a talk in the Church, Community and State series, of which you may have seen the first, a pretty mediocre production too, by Sir Walter Moberley in the current *Listener*.[3] I should be glad if you could hear or read these talks in the successive five weeks, and I should very much like to have your opinion later about the whole affair. It might even provide an article by you for the *N.E.W.* The fact of my participation rather precluded any discussion in the *Criterion*.

Yours sincerely,
T. S. Eliot

---

1 – MacNeice, untitled review of *The Notebooks and Papers of Gerard Manley Hopkins*, ed. Humphry House: *C.* 16 (July 1937), 698–700.

2 – Tomlin wrote on 12 Jan.: 'Mr Mairet told me that you might perhaps be writing something on the [Abdication] crisis for "The New English Weekly". I do hope that this is so, as I have been looking forward to hearing some of your views on this subject.'

3 – Sir Walter Moberly, 'Church, Community and State: Challenge of the New Faiths', *The Listener* 17: 418 (13 Jan. 1937), 49–50, 84.

TSE, 'The Church's Message to the World', *The Listener* 17: 423 (17 Feb. 1937), 293–4, 326. TSE, 'Mr Reckitt, Mr Tomlin, and the Crisis', *NEW* 10: 20 (25 Feb. 1937), 391–3.

15 January 1937                    [Faber & Faber Ltd]

Dear Miss Macaulay,

Thank you for your letter of 8 January describing your and Mr Richardson's projected book on modern vulgar errors.[2] It promises to be a most amusing volume, and I am honoured at being invited to be one of the contributors. But unless some error flashes into my mind which I find an irresistible temptation to talk about, reason tells me that I have already far too many engagements. It is not even a question at present of getting on with what I want to do: it is a question of interruptions being interrupted by other interruptions; so I must decline, with sincere regrets and best wishes.[3]

Yours sincerely,

[T. S. Eliot]

1 – TSE wrote to Macauley c/o George Routledge & Sons.

2 – Rose Macaulay and Maurice L. Richardson were proposing to compile an entertaining collection of 'Modern Vulgar Errors or pseudodoxia' – 'the mind of the modern public teems with fallacies of a more sociological nature, any one of which could be made the subject of an amusing short light essay' – and invited TSE to contribute a brief essay (up to 3,000 words, at a rate of three guineas per 1,000 words) on a fallacy of his own choosing. They were approaching some thirty prominent writers, ranging from Clive Bell and Isaiah Berlin to Leonard Woolf and Virginia Woolf. The volume, they envisaged, would make up 'quite a revealing commentary on our peculiarly distressing times'.

Macaulay wrote again on 15 Jan., repeating the invitation to TSE to contribute to the planned volume of vulgar errors, and in addition inviting him to a drinks party on 21 Jan.

3 – Nonetheless, TSE was to continue to be mischievously stimulated by Macaulay's prospectus of 'modern vulgar errors'. On 2 Aug. 1938 he was to write – borrowing his title from Sir Thomas Browne's *Pseudodoxia Epidemica* (1646–72) – for JDH's benefit:

I have added one more to my growing collection of

PSEUDODOXIA CONTEMPORANEA

i.e.

*All Policeman have big feet.*

(Janes turns out to have smaller feet than I have).

The previous items in the collection are

*A fart, strained through bath water, loses both odour and inflammability.*

*A cigarette, smoked before breakfast, is sovereign against costiveness.*

(With which may be compared the superstition recorded by Ben Jonson:

*To rub the fingers between the toes, and sniff them, is sovereign against costiveness.*

The number of pseudodoxia turning on the matter of costiveness must be legion. Other specimens welcomed.

On 3 Aug. 1938:      PSEUDODOXIA CONTEMPORANEA.

*That cigar ash, stirred into black coffee, is most urgently aphrodisiac.*

P.S. It is further argued, that the better the cigar (irrespective, it seems of the kind or quality of the coffee) the more powerful its aphrodisiac action.

I cannot find any respectable authority for this further pseudodoxy.

The number of aphrodisiac pseudodoxia must be legion.

TO *Maurice Reckitt*                                    TS University of Sussex

16 January 1937                        *The Criterion*

My dear Reckitt,

Many thanks for your letter of yesterday. I enclose a draft of the letter I propose to send – I do not find my exasperation diminished by waiting! But I shall be glad of any improvements you care to make – or to know of any other line of action that your mature judgement suggests.

I have had in mind most of the doubts about the Academy which you express. I have striven to prevent my attitude from being influenced either by my personal feelings towards Bolshakoff or my prejudice against certain of his Anglican friends.

I incline to the opinion that a blunt withdrawal at this point might be capable of being construed as a pretext for something one had wanted to do anyway. What I want is to put it up to him either to express principles which are impossible to accept, or to be so evasive that one is forced to withdraw. You will observe that I want to get him to commit himself in writing! Quite apart from this 'crisis', I have always found interviews with him merely a fatiguing waste of time.[1]

Yours sincerely,

T. S. Eliot

1 – Evidently TSE did write to Bolshakoff on this subject, though his letter has not been traced. Bolshakoff replied, 22 Jan.: 'Thank you for your letter. The survey of the world situation in the report expresses my point of view only, and I tried to be as impartial as possible . . . The sociological ideals of the Academy are expressed in its Declaration referring to the Encyclicals "Rerum Novarum" and "Quadragesimo Anno" . . . In my description of the Spanish situation and of Austria and Portugal and also about the merits or failings of the communism or of the fascism I followed to the general line of the opinions expressed about this subject by Roman Episcopacy and also of the Orthodox one. I accept that Nazism is inherently antichristian, but you cannot say that Austrian fascism of Dr Dollfuss is inherently antichristian or even the regime of Mussolini must be condemned and fought by Roman Church . . .

'There is not any absolutely Christian regime and never will be. The difference is that the Communism plainly destroys the Church and will have the management with her, but the different Fascist regimes are ready to cooperate with the Church as far as they can; as Mussolini, Franco, Metaxas, Carmona etc. The antichristian principles of the Fascism were denounced by the Pope, several Roman Catholic, Orthodox and Anglican prelates . . . You cannot say that the parliamentary, democratic, republican, feudal or any other regime are the incarnation of the Christian state . . . I try to impress all members that there is not any purely Christian regime and they are all antichristian more or less and the Church is not of this world but it is enough if any regime is ready to collaborate with the Church respecting her essential principles.

'I am not a Fascist, or Republican, or Socialist, but look for Christian Church allowed to exist and to carry on her mission' (University of Sussex).

Whether we should frame a joint letter, or write separately but collusively, is a question which I leave for you to think over.

## TO *Hugh Gordon Porteus*                    TS Beinecke

18 January 1937                    *The Criterion*

Dear Porteus,

Your article in the *N.E.W.* for 24 December suggests something that you might do for me, if you cared to take it on.[1] The summary notes on foreign periodicals at the end of the *Criterion* are something that I like to keep up, and the material is becoming more and more skimpy. America still provides enough reviews to talk about; Russia is very irregular in sending its magazines and there are not many of them; Germany is mostly not very interesting; France is verbose and Italy is deadly. It struck me that we might do something with English periodicals. I don't mean anything systematic, and I certainly don't intend to exchange with the *Quarterly Review*, but a good many of the odd and end things come into the office, and there is really plenty of material for some rather happy-go-lucky sharp-shooting once in six months or so. We get the *Colosseum* and the *Adelphi*, *Life and Letters*, Roughton and all that sort of thing, and if there were any other curiosities that you wanted, such as the *Left Review*, that could be arranged. Anyway, think it over and let me know whether it appeals to you.

And I wish you would come and lunch with me one day before long. What about Friday the 22nd?

Yours ever,
T. S. Eliot

## TO *Rupert Doone*                    CC

18 January 1937                    [Faber & Faber Ltd]

My dear Doone,

I must apologise for my delay in answering your letter of 5 January.[2] I have got Robert Medley's card, and I very much hope to find time to

1–Porteus, 'Views and Reviews: Periodical Drift', *NEW* 10: 11 (24 Dec. 1936), 211–12.
2–'Robert Medley has sent you a card to an Exhibition of Pictures where he is exhibiting . . . I do hope you will be able to get to see them. He is wishing to do illustrations and other kinds of book design. Is it possible you might tell him who to apply to at Fabers.'

go to see the exhibition in which are his pictures.[1] If he would like to do illustrations and book designs he ought to write to Richard de la Mare at this address and make an appointment to see him. There is not, in these days, very much to be done in the way of illustrated books, but there is of course always a demand for book-jackets.

I do hope that you will be able to make some arrangement with Ashley Dukes for producing *The Ascent of F6*.

Yours sincerely,
[T. S. Eliot]

## TO *J. S. Barnes*

ts Buona Barnes

18 January 1937                    *The Criterion*

My dear Jim,

I must apologize for my delay in answering your nice letter from New Delhi of 29 November.[2] I have been extremely busy, and the office has been somewhat disorganized by changes and influenza. I hope that this letter will reach you in time. The point is that I don't know anybody in Los Angeles or Washington, and I cannot think of anyone amongst my small acquaintance in Baltimore who would interest you. I have several relatives in Chicago and New York whom I should like you to meet, but I don't remember their addresses, so what I have done is to write to my brother, who is a very agreeable and hospitable person, to tell him about you and say that I am asking you to get in touch with him as soon as you get this letter, and let him know where you will be and when. I have told him of the sort of people I think you might like to meet in New York and other places. My brother, unfortunately, has now left New York and is living in Cambridge, Massachusetts, where most of my immediate relatives are. The great majority of my relatives and most of my friends in America live in the vicinity of Boston, and I will urge you if you can to take at least a few days in that rather pleasant town, as I think it would be worth your while. My brother's normal address is –

---

Robert Medley (1905–94), artist, theatre designer; teacher; from 1932, artistic director of the Group Theatre, designing sets and costumes for productions by his partner, Rupert Doone, of plays by TSE, WHA, SS and LM. See further Medley, *Drawn from the Life: A Memoir* (1983).

1–Medley exhibited six pictures, including 'Tenement Buildings' and 'The Jokers at Agnews', in a joint exhibition with Francis Bacon, Roy de Maistre and John Piper.

2–Not traced.

H. W. Eliot Esq., 84 Prescott Street, Cambridge, Mass.; and his telephone number is Eliot 0720. The trunk call system, or as it is called in America, long distance, is very good, and people habitually telephone all over the country; furthermore, people in the States are fairly informal about introductions of people from Europe. If you went to Boston and rang up Theodore Spencer, 20 Oxford Street, Cambridge, and told him that you were a friend of mine and that I had asked him to see you, you would be welcome. He is a delightful person; a younger professor at Harvard. There are also at Boston two very charming and intelligent people of whom you may have heard: Mr and Mrs Daniel Sargent.[1] You would find them in the telephone book.

I hope this letter will reach you, and I look forward to seeing you in London.

Yours ever,
Tom Eliot

TO *John Hayward*                                                    TS King's

Monday [18 January 1937]             Faber & Faber Ltd

Forgot to say that the Vaughan Broadcast is on Thursday at 9.45.[2] If you shd. be free that day before dinner I might bring Tandy in for sherry, and you could have a look at him. He will be dining with me before the broadcast. I enjoyed last evening very much and as usual, but I think I drank too much of your whisky, because when I came back I played a game of patience, and I don't do that at that hour when I am completely rational. So I must see about that Marsala and Madeira in my own interest. Possibly my taste for Marsala is due to my admiration for Edward Lear, but I do like it, and like Mr Lear, I never get Tipsy at all.[3] My lunch party broke up at 3.40 which isn't bad. Present, Virginia Woolf,

---

1–Daniel Sargent (1890–1987), historian, biographer, and poet, taught at Harvard, 1914–34, and was thereafter a full-time writer. Author of eleven books including *Thomas More* (1933).

2–TSE's introductory remarks to a selection of the poems of Vaughan and Traherne, made by TSE himself, was broadcast on Thurs. 21 Jan., from 9.45 to 10 p.m. The fee was three guineas.

3–Edward Lear, 'How Pleasant to Know Mr Lear':

He sits in a beautiful parlour,
With hundreds of books on the wall;
He drinks a great deal of Marsala,
But never gets tipsy at all.

Mortimer, Miss Mary Baker (what is the point of Miss Baker? she asked me to come some day to a party at Claridge's) and the Hon. Virginia Brett, who I thought was slightly embarrassed by being crossquestioned by V. W. about the tastes of the Younger Generation.[1] Led V. W. across the street, and returned to interview Charles Madge, who has rejected the *Daily Mirror*. How upsetting for poor Jennings. A broken up kind of a day.

Yrs etc.

*TP*

P.S. I can't see any more point to Miss Baker than I can see to Miss Curtis Brown.

## TO *Elizabeth Bowen*                                                      CC

18 January 1937                          [Faber & Faber Ltd]

Dear Mrs Cameron,

I must thank you for your letter of January 11, and am glad to hear that the work is progressing so satisfactorily.[2] We think now that as it is impossible to get the book out in the early spring it had better come out in the late summer, so that although we have thought best to leave the announcement in the Spring Catalogue you need not feel so pressed for time.[3] As for the order, I think that the best and simplest way is, as

---

1–See *Diary of VW*, vol. 5, 50n: 'Clive's guests in fact were, besides Raymond Mortimer and T. S. Eliot, his rich American flame Mary Baker [See *VW Diary*, 18 July 1932] and the Hon Virginia Brett [1916–70], eldest daughter of the 3rd Viscount Esher.'

2–'I have at last completed, and am giving to my secretary to re-type, the revised list of Short Stories, also my Preface for the collection . . . I have got to go into a nursing home tomorrow evening for a dental operation (wisdom teeth and various complications) so am writing now instead of sending a covering letter with the manuscript . . . *As to order*: I take it that the stories are to be arranged in the order of the writers' ages?'

3–The blurb (Spring Catalogue 1937, 6–7) was probably written by TSE: 'In projecting a volume which should perform, for the modern short story, a service similar to that of Michael Roberts's *Faber Book of Modern Verse*, we agreed that Miss Elizabeth Bowen, distinguished both as a short-story writer and as a novelist, was the obvious choice as editor. The task was in a way more difficult, in that the short story is not always very short; but Miss Bowen has succeeded in choosing a representative selection from the best work of her contemporaries. The book will serve the reader in three ways: first in the pleasure of reading stories of such quality, second as an introduction to the work of writers whom he may not know, and third as evidence of the temper and tendencies of our time as shown in fiction. And we think that the collection shows more *variety* than a selection on any other principles could do.

'Miss Bowen, in an introduction which will be much discussed by critics, considers the development of the modern short story, the specific contribution of our time, and the reasons for making the selection contained in this book.'

---

you say, to arrange the stories according to the writers' ages, or putative ages. After all, the ages are at least as important, and sometimes more important, than the actual dates at which the stories were written. I think that we might, when the time comes, write to any authors whose ages are not yet public property, if you will remind me.

Walter de la Mare's story 'Physic' is in the recent collection *The Wind Blows Over*, and I am having a copy of the book sent to you.[1]

As for Eddie Sackville West's story, the final selection of stories must of course rest with you.[2] None of us knows this story anyway, but the important point is whether its length would require the sacrifice of something else which we should all want to keep.

I sympathize with your troubles, which I share. The worst of it is that the dentist always takes so much time. I hope to see you again when you have recovered.

Very sincerely yours,<br>
[T. S. Eliot]

## TO *J. B. Trend*[3]                                                    CC

18 January 1937                    [Faber & Faber Ltd]

Dear Trend,

I have an appeal from Marichalar to which I haven't yet replied.[4] I wonder if you have heard from him yourself? He is still in St Jean de Luz,

---

1–'I remember but cannot trace among the collections of Walter de la Mare stories I own his story *Physic*.'

2–'I have decided I *should* like to keep in – if you are agreeable – Eddie Sackville West's story: Helmuth lies in the Sun. I like its character – though I could wish it were shorter.'

3–J. B. Trend (1887–1958): journalist, musicologist, critic – he wrote music chronicles for the *Criterion* – Professor of Spanish at Cambridge and a Fellow of Christ's College, 1933–52. See Margaret Joan Anstee, *JB: An Unlikely Spanish Don: The Life & Times of Professor John Brande Trend* (2013).

4–Antonio Marichalar, Marquis of Montesa (1893–1973): author, critic, biographer, journalist; contributor to the newspaper *El Sol* and the periodical *Revista de Occidente* (on subjects including Claudel, JJ, Valéry, and VW). Works include *Mentira desnuda:* 'The Naked Lie' (essays on European and American culture, 1933); *Riesgo y ventura del duque de Osuna* (1932): *The Perils and Fortune of the Duke of Osuna*, trans. H. de Onís.

Marichalar quit Madrid for France in Sept. 1936 – '*après six semaines sous le terreur*', as he told TSE (3 Sept.). Reports said he had signed 'a supposed adhesion to the Alliance of Antifascist Writers and their violent manifesto', which he disputed: 'I had refused to sign it. I belong to no political party, and only gave my name when José Ortega y Gasset consented in making a declaration of not being implicated in the Movement, but in no way an Antifascist declaration.'

and apparently in pretty low water, though with a man like him one does not know whether that is absolute or relative. He wants to get work for some periodical or newspaper, or lectures in a university, and affirms his Anglophilism. I suppose he could only lecture in Spanish. So far as I know he has very little English indeed, and I found his French, like that of so many Spaniards, very difficult to follow. Can you make any suggestions for him? At the moment I can't. Do you think he could write a book about the revolution? I don't know that we should want it ourselves, because we have already two on the way, but he might have some special line to urge.

If you should be in London I would like to talk to you about Marichalar, and it is a long time since we have met.[1]

Yours ever,
[T. S. Eliot]


TO *Henri Fluchère*[2]                                                    CC

18 January 1937                    [Faber & Faber Ltd]

My dear Sir,

In replying to your most interesting letter of 4 January I will pay you the same compliment, and reply *de puissance à puissance*[3] *in English.*[4]

In principle I am extremely pleased that you should be interested in the task of translating *Murder in the Cathedral* into French with a view of getting it taken up by Copeau.[5] I am sure that no French producer would be likely to understand it better or mount it more properly than he, and as for yourself, I have seen your work in *Scrutiny*, and I know the reputation you enjoy in Cambridge.

In a matter like this I would not act without consulting Mr Ashley Dukes, who is my manager and agent, and who holds the dramatic rights

---

1 – Trend replied on 19 Jan. that he had heard nothing directly from Marichalar. He could offer only one lecture, but the return fare from St Jean de Luz would make that unaffordable. 'Have you heard anything about Marichalar's book on *Savanarola*? Wouldn't that be more worthwhile (and not less saleable) than yet another book on the Spanish revolution? . . . The Catholic intellectuals are more unfortunate than anyone else; for Franco's supporters seem to distrust anyone who can read or write.'

2 – Henri Fluchère (1898–1987), translator and critic: see Biographical Register.

3 – 'from power to power'.

4 – Fluchère, who wrote of his enthusiasm for TSE's works, wished to translate *MiC*, paying attention to all aspects of language and rhythm, and hoping to benefit from TSE's advice.

5 – The avant-garde director Jacques Copeau (1879–1949) built and directed the Théâtre de Vieux Colombier. See Maurice Kurtz, *Jacques Copeau: The Biography of a Theatre* (1999).

in all countries. I will take the matter up with Mr Dukes and write to you again.[1]

> With best wishes and sympathy, I am
> Yours very sincerely,
> [T. S. Eliot]

## FROM *Anne Bradby*[2] TO *John Dover Wilson*

TS National Library of Scotland

18 January 1937                    Faber & Faber Ltd

Dear Professor Dover Wilson,

Mr Eliot asks me to write to you to thank you for your letter to him of 4 January, and to ask whether you would be so kind as to write to him

---

1 – GCF to Dukes, 20 Jan. 1937: 'We have taken note of your desire to be consulted before any foreign editions of *Murder in the Cathedral* are arranged and we will certainly do so.'

2 – Anne Barbara Bradby (1912–2001); poet, playwright, editor, worked at F&F from 1934; as TSE's secretary, 1936–40. In 1938 she married Vivian Ridler (1913–2009), manager of the Bunhill Press, London, and later Printer to Oxford University, 1958–78. Her writings include poetry (*A Dream Observed*, 1941; *Collected Poems*, 1994), verse plays (*The Shadow Factory: A Nativity Play*, 1946), librettos and translations of opera (Monteverdi, Cavalli, Mozart); and her posthumous *Memoirs* (2004).

GCF to FVM, 31 Jan. 1936: 'Dick (d l M) has got a new, additional, secretary – one Ann Bradby, niece of Humphrey Milford, a Downe product. Very nice, & very intelligent; said to be a firstclass reader. Probably more suited to the editorial side than to Dick's constantly frustrated purposes!'

Ian Smith, 'I was the Possum's minder', *Oxford Times*, 15 Apr. 1988: 'As Eliot's secretary, she was responsible, among other things, for seeing the quarterly Criterion through the press, and monitoring the unsolicited contributions.

'"When after weeks of vetting the mostly-rubbishy poetry sent in, without finding anything worth his notice, I felt I must pick out something for him to look at and put a couple of manuscripts on his desk with his letters.

'"These were held out to me later, with a blank look, and the monosyllable 'Why?' To which I think I found no better answer than that I didn't understand them, so thought they might be good."

'Mrs Ridler recalls how slight inaccuracies often crept into editions of Eliot's poems. For the proofs, she feels, "were probably too reverentially treated by the correctors". But the only natural fear of being made to look a fool was sometimes challenged by Eliot with his instinct for teasing, against which he expected people, even his underlings, to defend themselves vigorously . . .

'"In dictation he was measured but fluent: as with his normal speech, the sentences were perfectly formed – there might be a pause, but no humming and haaa-ing. Sometimes, his extempore criticism in a letter was so interesting that I found it hard to remember that my business was to take it down, not to listen or comment" . . .

'Mrs Ridler paints a picture of a man whose standards of truthfulness were so high, that those around him tried harder "for the rest of one's life, to be careful of the truth"; who was

again about the lectures which you are expecting him to give at Edinburgh this year.[1] He was under the impression that he had undertaken to give one lecture only, and he would be grateful if you would write to him to let him know what the position is.

Yours truly,
Anne Bradby

## TO *John H. Barber*                                            cc

20 January 1937                        [Faber & Faber Ltd]

Dear Mr Barber,

In reply to your letter of 18 January I enclose my cheque for 15s to pay for a year's subscription to *World Film News*.[2]

While a great deal of the contents are outside of my interests, as I am a very infrequent film-goer, I was very glad to have two articles; one on the financial position of the film industry in Britain, and the other on the use of propagandist films, which seemed to me quite valuable. In the latter case it seems to me that the magazine could continue to do a great deal of good, if it can be completely impartial and call attention to instances of

generous with money, to all kinds of people, and who was so tender-hearted that he could not bear to re-read old letters, "because of the emotion they evoked".'

Ridler to TSE, 7 July 1940, on leaving F&F: 'I do not think it would be possible to find a more considerate, just and kind employer than you are, and at least I can thank you for that, though I owe you more than I could ever tabulate in a letter. To work for you is a joy, and anyone who can do it is lucky; but the best part of it for me was this; that after admiring you as a writer ever since I began to grow up, I should find you so good as a person, and so much to be respected and revered in your dealings with other people. If it made me unpleasantly aware of my own backsliding and impatience, that I suppose was lucky for me too. Then for anyone who thinks at all about words, to take down your letters is not a drudgery but a delightful thing to do, which one never gets tired of . . . Thank you again for your goodness, & God bless you' (EVE).

Ridler to the *TLS*, 13 Apr. 1984 includes the comment: 'While Eliot himself found Vivienne's pursuit of him humiliating and agonizing, he never felt indifference to her pain.'

See obituary of Anne Ridler in the *Times*, 16 Oct. 2001, 19.

1–Dover Wilson had enquired, 4 Jan. 1937: 'I suppose it is too early yet to give me an idea when you are likely to be able to come to us for your promised course of lectures next year. I am keeping the early part of the Lent Term free for you.'

2–*World Film News and Television Progress* was edited from London by Marion A. Grierson.

propaganda for any cause which is disguised as news or entertainment. I feel that the news reel is something that will need careful watching.[1]

Yours very truly,<br>
[T. S. Eliot]

## TO *Dora D. Babbitt*[2] CC

22 January 1937               [Faber & Faber Ltd]

Dear Mrs Babbitt,

I enclose what I have finally been able to do, in the midst of an unfortunate number of other engagements, because I do not like to trust it to the Editors unless it has your approval first.[3] If you like it well enough, please pass it on to them; if not, please tell me so. I also enclose the original notice of 1933 from the *Criterion*. If you liked it better, you could make alterations in it and send that instead: but most of it seemed inappropriate for the present occasion.

Curiously enough, I have been called upon, at the same time, and urgently, to write a note about More for the Princeton gazette.[4]

With my humble apologies,<br>
Yours very sincerely,<br>
[T. S. Eliot]

## TO *Louis MacNeice* The MacNeice Estate

22 January 1937               *The Criterion*

Dear MacNeice,

I have your letter of the 21st.[5] I will call Richard de la Mare's attention to the misprints that you mention. He is away today, but I shall see him on Monday.

---

1 – Barber replied on 25 Jan.: 'The Editor, Miss Grierson, was particularly interested in your comments on disguised propaganda in news films. Recent articles, as you probably know, have dealt with this problem, while the discussion "Is the 'March of Time' Fascist?" originated from this journal.'

2 – Dora D. Babbitt (1877–1944): widow of Irving Babbitt (1865–1933).

3 – Mrs Babbitt had written on 12 Dec. 1936 to urge TSE to contribute to the planned collection *Irving Babbitt: Man and Teacher*, ed. Frederick Manchester and Odell Shepherd.

4 – 'Paul Elmer More', *Princeton Alumni Weekly* 37: 17 (5 Feb. 1937), 373–4.

5 – 'The Iceland book is nearly ready. Dr Auden who has the map says that there are three places where Þ (= th) has been printed as P; also one other misprint. If to correct these in

I am afraid that I shall be unable to use the Eclogue, although I like it, in the March number.[1] Owing to a misunderstanding I found myself committed to publishing three Cantos by Ezra Pound in that number, and there won't be room for anything else.[2] I was also under the impression that *Iceland* was coming out too soon for publication in the *Criterion* to be possible. Apparently the date has not yet been fixed.[3] I am sorry not to publish the Eclogue in the *Criterion*, because I like it.

---

the map itself is too expensive, we might have a note of Errata somewhere?' (See MacNeice, *Letters*, 292.)

1 – 'Are you using the Icelandic Eclogue for the next Criterion?'

2 – 'Cantos XLII–XLIV', C. 16 (Apr. 1937), 405–23.

3 – *Letters from Iceland*, initially scheduled for publication on 8 July 1937, actually came out on 6 August. Faber Spring Books catalogue 1937, 33, on *Iceland* (as the book was provisionally titled): 'We understand that the book will take the form of a series of letters, some in verse, some in prose, written from Iceland in the summer of 1936. The recipients of the letters include Lord Byron, a tourist, an employee of Shell-Mex, a member of the Oxford City Council, a Cambridge lady don, an Icelandic journalist, and a well-known young painter. In addition, Mr MacNeice contributes an eclogue between two tourists and the ghost of Grettir, Mr Auden some amateur photographs, and Mr William Coldstream some pen-and-ink sketches.

'There may be a good many other books about Iceland and about other expeditions, but this is the only book by Mr Auden and Mr MacNeice.'

An unsigned TS memo headed 'ICELAND' is possibly by TSE:

a. I think Chapter IV For Tourists would go better at the end of the book with the Appendix. This book isn't going to be read as a guide book, and information about boats, clothes etc. seems out of place among the letters.

b. Chapter IX Last Will and Testament is much too long, and I should suggest cutting the purely private jokes, say from p. 7 (see pencil mark) to p. 9, and thereafter a few verses easily marked if you agree. As this is the last chapter in the book the rest could be set up while it is being altered; and in any case it ought to be read for libel.

I think Chapter XII Hetty to Nancy goes on too long for the joke to last, and some of the things the schoolgirls say are impossible – but probably that will have to be left.

Minor points

Chapter II I think it should be said that this is by Auden? And that 'Dear Christopher' is to Christopher Isherwood.

Chapter VI I have put the names of the authors at the beginning of the long extracts (p. 20 on) so that you do not have to search to the end to see who they are by.

Chapter IX p. 7 Could there be a translation of the Icelandic rhyme?

They don't say anywhere just how much Icelandic they could speak.

WHA and LM responded with an undated note written in LM's hand:

*Letters from Iceland*.

(1) We are anxious that the book should be entitled 'Letters from Iceland' rather than 'Iceland' which seems to give a false impression.

(2) We purposely inserted Chapter IV for Tourists among the letters to break the run of letters. We want the book to look as varied as possible as one glances through it. The objection to Chapter IV, by the way, would also apply to Chapter VI.

(3) We are afraid that we entirely disagree with the suggestion that Chapter IX, the Will, is too long. We should have liked it to be longer. The point about the Will is that it should

It is not so easy to arrange lecture engagements in America at short notice.[1] The usual way of course is through a lecture agency. You would probably have to stay a month or six weeks to make it interesting to any agency, and I don't recommend that form of labour anyway, because you are completely in the hands of your agency while you are there, and they take, I think, ordinarily about 60% of the receipts. But if you could tell me pretty closely the dates between which you could be in America, I could write to a few people at colleges and find out whether an engagement is possible. The usual fee for a literary lecture by a poet is 100 dollars, and a couple of such engagements would almost cover the cost of a tourist passage both ways. For heaven's sake don't think of going out as a steward, unless you want to find out for yourself what the exploitation of labour by the steamship companies is like. I will talk about this to Morley, who may have some suggestions.

Harcourt Brace & Co. have taken the sheets of 250 copies of *Agamemnon*.[2]

As for *The Rising Venus*, I certainly think that we ought to publish it, but if it is going to be done, as I hope it will, I am a little nervous of premature publication.[3] *The Ascent of F6* has been largely rewritten since

---

appear very circumstantial and should have long lists of private names intermixed with the public. The bequests are not all supposed to be funny or satirical. We put in our friends because it is *our* Will. People who have read it without knowing the people concerned found it quite readable. In any case, this is the sort of book where readers are prepared to do a lot of skipping (?) [*sic*]

(4) This also applies to Chapter XII, Hetty to Nancy, which is not meant merely as a joke but is to serve as an accurate description of an Icelandic trip on ponies. If we cut the jokes, such as they are, the whole thing will become a little heavy but if we cut the factual detail it will become useless as information.

(5) If any passages in the Will are decided to be libellous would this be corrected if we substituted for the proper names in those passages initials, asterisks or something of the sort?'

Ch. XVI of *Letters from Iceland*, 'Letter to Lord Byron: Part V', includes (p. 233):

> Cheer up! There're several singing birds that sing.
>     There's six feet six of Spender for a start;
> Eliot has really stretched his eagle's wing,
>     And Yeats has helped himself to Parnell's heart . . .

1 – 'I am thinking of going to America for two or three weeks at Easter. Could you suggest any way by which at that time I could make a little money to balance some of my expenses? Journalism, lectures, anything like that? And is there a possibility of going out as a steward or something like that?'

2 – 'Talking of America, is there any more news from Harcourt & Brace who, you said, thought of doing the Agamemnon?'

3 – 'And what about "The Rising Venus"? I am thinking at the moment of expanding it, which I shall have to do soon if the Group Theatre do it this spring, as they still hope to.'

we published it, so that the acting version will differ considerably from what we published.[1] This means that when it comes to a new edition it will probably have to be set up again; so that what I should like to have of your play would be the final version, when you have agreed upon it with Rupert Doone. I am referring not to cuts but to alterations. The reading version can afford to be longer than the published version, but it should not be a different version.

Yours ever sincerely,
T. S. Eliot

TO *John Dover Wilson*                    TS National Library of Scotland

22 January 1937                    *The Criterion*

My dear Dover Wilson,

Thank you for your letter of the 20th.[2] At the moment I can't see that it matters to me very much during what part of October I come to Edinburgh, but I think I should prefer you to fix some date towards the end of the month. I should certainly wish to stay two or three days, as it will be my first visit to Edinburgh. Even if I could give you a series of lectures, it would be difficult for me at that time to stay as long as a fortnight, as I always have plenty of work to do here. I should really prefer to give only one lecture, and I have not thought of a subject yet even for one, but I will turn the matter over, and if I can extend it to two I will do so. I very much look forward to my visit.

1–GCF to Ashley Dukes, 20 Jan. 1937: 'As for "The Ascent of F6", I find that Auden has deposited with De la Mare (who is away this week) a good many corrections and alterations against a second edition, and I imagine that these must include the revision of the monks scene.' Donald Gallup, *W. H. Auden: A Bibliography 1924–1969* (2nd edn, 1972), 20–1: 'Auden did not see the play until about a week after the opening [at the Mercury Theatre in Feb. 1937] . . . Faber and Faber had already set up the original draft they received and were loath to incorporate the late revisions; they therefore published the original version. The revisions carried out by Doone and Isherwood were published in the second edition [in Mar. 1937].'

2–'I hoped that you would feel inclined to give us at least two or three lectures but if you would prefer to make it one we must be content with that. In any case, I trust you will be able to stay in Edinburgh for two or three days so as to see something of the people here . . . The ideal thing from our point of view would be for you to make a fortnight of it and give say three lectures in one week and three in the next, but I am afraid that is hoping for too much . . . Between the middle and end of October would suit us very well.'

I hope to hear from you before long about Gavin Douglas.

Yours sincerely,<br>
T. S. Eliot

## TO *Polly Tandy*

TS BL

1937. Feast of the Conversion      *The Criterion*
of St Paul:[1] that's it is, ma'am,
though you may not have known it,
bein occupied with domestic affairs:
and I should add, 1937,
with regards to the Licensee.

Sis Tandy,

I certainly am obligated by your kind letter of the 22nd instant, and more than remunerated for any small services which I may have rendered, though I says it myself. And here its been rainin Eavens Ard and I says to meself, ole Sis Tandy's rheumatics must be painin something cruel, so while she out at the Bell (kind thoughts to the Licensee) havin a drop of Old Kate to cheer her vitals, I just drop her a line so she wont feel so bad in the Mornin. Well Im not goin to advise about that PlenteeSpot, except to begin with I think there's something just a bit wrong with its Name, and that may be the Seat of the Trouble, but I think a very slight adjustment by what is called manipulative surgery would put that right. But pendin a surgical examination which I will give (waiving my fee) at the 1st possible moment, I believe he will get no or not much worse in respect of the symtims mentioned, only I recommend a light diet and especially avoid Pheasant and Port Wine, which might result in fluxions or something to the head, and anything might happen. A little Benger's Food in the morning, and a drink of Horlicks at bedtime, to avoid night starvation, with a occasional dose of castor oil say on any night except Saturday night. Once we locate the Seat of the trouble, as I said, there are bright things to be hoped from that Cat (and polished up his Name a bit, which I suspect is the Seat of the Trouble, but not sure without a examination. He might learn to push a Perambulator. On the other Hand it may be gall-stones: that means that I must teach you how to massage him properly, and for that you will need a rubber sheet. I will bring all the other implements with me. Meanwhile, one good turn deserves a smart

---

1–Postmarked 25 January.

smack in return so: I send you enclosed the first release of a long awaited statement of explanation, so will close, but with kind wishes. yours and cetera

TP

## TO *William Force Stead*[1]

TS Beinecke

25 January 1937             *The Criterion*

My dear Stead,

I am returning to you Robert's manuscript.[2] I have read it and Morley has read it. If I were writing to the author I should of course be obliged to give nice reasons, but as I am writing to a mutual friend, need I say more than that we don't see any possible market for the book, at any rate not as a Faber book? It might be more interesting to a firm like Eyre & Spottiswoode.

As for your own book, that is quite a different affair.[3] I am not sure that that is a Faber book either; I am inclined to think that it is a University Press book. At present it is in Morley's hands, as I thought it would do him good to read it. It really strikes me as a remarkable piece of work, both of thorough scholarship and of interesting criticism. It seems to me, so far as I can judge from one hurried reading – but I did begin at the beginning and read straight through – that you have made an unexpectedly good case for the influence of Southwell on metaphysical poetry. You will hear again from me about it in a week or so.

Yours ever affectionately,<br>T. S. E.

1–William Force Stead (1884–1967), poet and critic; Chaplain of Worcester College, Oxford: see Biographical Register L6.

2–Stead submitted on 13 Jan. Robert Sencourt's work 'The Consecration of Genius' – 'a good title, and many of the chapters I have read with a high sense of pleasure and enlightenment'.

3–Stead had just taken his B.Litt viva, and his examiners, Oliver Elton and Canon Hutchinson, of All Souls (who wrote on George Herbert for the *Cambridge History of English Literature*), were 'especially pleased' with the chapter on George Herbert. Stead asked TSE to look over the work (which ran to 100,000 words but could 'easily be cut down to 75,000') – 'and let me have it back fairly soon, say in a couple of weeks'. He posted it on 21 Dec.; he had aimed, he said, 'to dig down to the roots of English religious poetry – and the examiners agree with me that I have proved [Robert] Southwell to be the chief source of the 17th Cent. religious poets' – including 'the subtle metaphysics of the Incarnation as presented by my Jesuit at the end of the century'.

## TO *John Hayward*                                         TS King's

Feast of the Conversion of St Paul    *The Criterion*
[25 January 1937]

Dear Sir,

On behalf of the North Kensington Community Centre, I thank
you most cordially for your kind response to our appeal to the tune of
twenty shillings.[1] May I, in thanking you on behalf of our little ones, be
allowed to respond by sending you a small parcel of wine, very sovereign
against influenza, which is awarded to the first person to solve the puzzle
successfully.

With blessings etc.,
Yours faithfully,
T. S. Eliot

As from Dalgarno Gardens,
London W.10.


## TO *Cecilia Ady*[2]                                          cc

25 January 1937                   [Faber & Faber Ltd]

Dear Miss Ady,

I have now shown your letter and outline to the other directors, and
have had an opportunity of discussing the project with them. We are not
quite certain that the book which you envisage would be quite that for
which we originally saw a public, before I took the matter up with Dr
Harris; and as it is a long time since I took the matter up with him and
he spoke to you about it, and since then his death and the reorganisation
of the Committee have taken place, there has been plenty of opportunity
for confusion and misunderstanding. I do not say positively that there has
been any misunderstanding, but the possibility makes me anxious to be
as clear as possible.

The book that we had in mind was to deal primarily with the organisation
and operation of the Church today. It would in fact contain in a more
organised and generally palatable form the sort of information which has
been included in the *Churchman's Handbook*, as well as a good deal else.

1–JDH had written, 24 Jan.: 'I hope there are 4999 other people who, having listened to
your admirable appeal, will send you, as I now do, a cheque for one pound. I'm sure each
child is worth a great deal more.'
2–Cecilia Ady (1881–1958), author and academic, taught at Oxford University.

The account of the history of the Church is certainly necessary, not so much for its own interest as for an understanding of how the Church has come to be what it is. We had in mind an analysis of the anatomy and functioning of the Church such as one might find, let us say, in a book about the Civil Service. The public we had in mind was to include not only the educated layman and the enquiring foreigner, but the intelligent Briton who knew nothing whatever about the Church, and whose interest might even require some stimulation.

In order to give the kind of preparation that we wanted it might be advisable to start with the Church as it is today; then go back to its history, and end with a more detailed account of its present organisation and condition.

I find all this very difficult to make clear. If at some time you were in London and I could have a talk with you I think we might arrive at an understanding more easily. It is fundamentally a question of whether what you want to do approximates to what my committee want done or not.

Yours very sincerely,

[T. S. Eliot]

P.S. Meanwhile, do you wish me to return the outline or not?

## TO *Angus Macdonald*[1]                                          CC

26 January 1937                          [Faber & Faber Ltd]

My dear Sir,

I must express our apologies for a departmental error, owing to which our acknowledgment of the 15 January to your letter of the 13th was not followed up.[2] Your suggestion of a new edition of *The Kingis Quhair* [*sic*]

---

1–Angus Macdonald, Lecturer in English Language, University of Edinburgh; assistant editor of the University Journal. See too Macdonald, 'The Kingis Quair' (letter), *TLS*, 20 Mar. 1937, 222; and 'Notes on "The Kingis Quair"', *Modern Language Review* 34: 2 (Oct. 1939), 569–72.

2–Macdonald ventured the possibility of F&F producing a new edition of *The Kingis Quair*, by James I of Scotland. 'On the two occasions on which I have worked on this text with a University class, I have been so severely handicapped by the lack of a good edition that I have ceased to prescribe it. The two English editions, those by Skeat (1886; revised 1911; both for the Scottish Text Society) and by Lawson, are out of print, and unobtainable; an American edition, published by Neilson and Webster in *The Chief British Poets of the Fourteenth and Fifteenth Centuries* (12/6), is by no means an accurate version, and its glossary is confined simply to a few foot-notes.

'The poem, which consists of 197 stanzas of seven lines each, is of considerable importance for the history of Scottish poetry in the Middle Ages, and especially for the

is one which interests us; or which, to put it more exactly, is of interest to the Porpoise Press. I will make enquiries about the possible demand for such an edition in Universities and elsewhere. If we can come to the conclusion that there would be sufficient interest to justify the expenditure. I think that we should be quite likely to proceed with the matter.

With many thanks for the suggestion,
Yours faithfully,
[T. S. Eliot]

## TO *R. W. Chambers*[1]                                              CC

26 January 1937                    [Faber & Faber Ltd]

My dear Chambers,

I expect you to be something of an authority on Scots poetry as well as on everything else, so I am writing to ask you whether you would have any opinion about a) the desirability, b) the possible market for new scholarly editions, first of Gavin Douglas's *Aenead* and second of the *Kingis Quhair*. I am very much interested myself in following up our edition of Dunbar's poems with similar texts of other of the greater Scots poets. This, I may explain, is on behalf of the Porpoise Press of Edinburgh, a firm with which we are associated.[2]

Yours sincerely,
[T. S. Eliot]

———

Scottish Chaucerians, Henryson, Dunbar, etc. In the Scottish Text Society the text occupies 45 pages of print, and with Introduction and notes the resulting book would be at most about the size of your edition of Dunbar.

'If you should be willing to undertake the publication of this text, I shall be glad to edit it, as I have been working on it for several years, and have a great deal of new material. The edition would perhaps be mainly for use in University classes, and therefore I cannot promise a very large sale; but there would be a steady and lengthy sale.'

1–Professor R. W. Chambers, Department of English, University College London.

2–Chambers responded, 27 Feb.: 'My first impression is that for a scholarly edition of the *Kingis Quhair* [1424] and Gavin Douglas's *Aenead* [1513] there would be a slow but steady sale, more especially for the former. A scholarly edition of the *Kingis Quhair* cheap enough to be purchased by students would have a chance . . . This, however, is only my first impression.'

Chambers wrote again on 2 Mar.: '(1) *The Kingis Quhair*. The standard edition of this was done by Skeat for the Scottish Text Society back in the eighties of last century, and a revised version was issued in 1911. I do not know whether the Scottish Text Society keeps all its texts in print: it would be worth while to find out from the Secretary, Dr R. F. Patterson (Graham's Dyke, Bearsden, Dumbartonshire), what the position of the *Kingis Quhair* is. It was a very scholarly work at the time it was done, but since that time there have been a lot

26 January 1937                    *The Criterion*

Dear Hawkins,

Thank you for your letter of the 17th.[1] I only thought that if it were convenient I would like to see you and have a talk about the next Fiction Chronicle before it was written. I am afraid I have left matters too late. Primarily, I had a notion that you might on the next occasion cast your net a little wider, but that will really keep until the third Chronicle. By the way, do you know anything about Calder Marshall, and would his new book be worth a mention? I only know that Elizabeth Bowen, whose opinion I respect, thinks well of him.[2]

However, let me know when it is convenient for you to come and have lunch again.

I am certainly in favour of letting you have any quotations you want for your Donne introduction, but you will have officially to apply to Faber & Faber and not to me for them.[3]

---

of debates, mostly very futile, about the *Kingis Quhair*, and a modern student would feel that he ought to know something about them.

'There was another edition by Alexander Lawson, 1910, A. & C. Black. I do not know whether this is still in print. It is exceedingly bulky, giving (I think unnecessarily) two texts of the *Kingis Quhair* and a supplementary poem, *The Quare of Jelusy*. Lawson seems to me to be wanting in discrimination, chiefly in that he seems to give undue weight to the doubts which have been raised as to whether King James of Scotland is really the author.

'I should have thought that there should be room for an edition, scholarly, but kept within such limits as would enable students to buy and use the book . . . If, as may conceivably be the case, both Lawson's and Skeat's editions are out of print, there would of course be the very strongest reason for a new edition.

'(2) Gavin Douglas's "*Aenead*". The standard edition of the works of Gavin Douglas is that by Small published in 1874, 4 vols, Edinburgh, Paterson; London, Sotheran. The case against a new edition of the "*Aenead*" is its bulk. It fills 859 pages in Small's edition . . . It seems therefore that there is no case for printing the whole of the "*Aenead*". It would be better to make it either the complete works of Gavin Douglas, or a little book of selections from the "*Aenead*". I do not know whether Small's edition is out of print . . . It would be well to make enquiries from Patterson of the Scottish Text Society about that.

'There has been recently an important monograph on the "*Aenead*" (*Douglas's Æneid*, by Laidlaw Maclean Watt), which is an added reason for some new edition.'

1 – 'Thank you for your message that you would like to see me. Is it about something particular and urgent, or just in a sociable way?'

2 – Hawkins replied, 28 Jan.: '[Arthur] Calder Marshall is goodish, I think, but hardly momentous. I have reviewed him in The Criterion (April 1936). I should like to do his next book. He's a good competent craftsman, but no dazzling light shines therefrom.' Arthur Calder-Marshall (1908–92), novelist.

3 – Hawkins had been invited by Nelson's to prepare an edition of the work of John Donne, and requested permission to use some quotations from TSE's writings on the poet.

Herbert Read and Surrealism are matters to be discussed over lunch, I feel, rather than in correspondence!<sup>1</sup>

> With best wishes to your family,
> Yours ever,
> T. S. E.

## TO *John Hayward*  TS King's

27 January 1937  *The Criterion*

Dear John,

You know my aversion to Modernism in all forms, and especially in Poetry; and you know that Movements like Surrealism are things that I cannot make Head or Tail of. But occasionally something comes my way, that makes me catch my breath, rub my eyes, pinch myself, sit up, cut myself shaving, and behave like Housman thinking of one [of] his poems<sup>2</sup> – I mean that we old fogies have something to learn after all from the younger generation, and perhaps it's good for us to have a rude jolt now and again before we get too fossilised. Such a poem came my way yesterday, and I send it to you at once in the hope that you will be able to tell me whether I am awake or dreaming?<sup>3</sup> Is this, or am I mistaken, the dawn of a new era, to which we must learn to adapt ourselves. I feel that what we old ones lack is Understanding, and I mean especially *sympathetic* Understanding. What I enclose is of the modern Allusive kind. I fear that I have not caught all its Allusions – though the subtle reference in line 23 to the 'Othello music' could escape no sensitive reader; it has that reference to 'old, forgotten far off things' that is so fascinating – with that vein of mocking irony running through it so characteristic of the Moderns – there must be many more allusions that you will be able to identify. Am I Right

---

1 – Hawkins asked (17 Jan.): 'What did you think of Read's piece in Surrealism? . . . I never had much of an opinion of Read, but I didn't think he'd commit himself to obvious drivel of that sort. It's almost pathetic, that prim and petulant little mind, wishing he could have a FEELING. And then not daring to let himself go, but pushing himself in the back all the same, in the hope that he might get launched unawares. He's so miserable and dreary and solemn. Oh, Scotsmen, when they're solemn and dreary, and do so earnestly want to have a feeling! I think he must hate himself, he always wants to exchange his identity. Read the austere classicist, Read the wild revolutionary, but always Read the something –' TSE had a low opinion of surrealism.

2 – A. E. Housman, 'The Name and Nature of Poetry': 'if a line of poetry strays into my memory, my skin bristles so that the razor ceases to act'.

3 – The enclosure was some light allusive verses entitled 'Proclamation', attributed to Roger Roughton: see *Poems* I, ed. Ricks and McCue, 292–3, 1200–2.

or am I Wrong? Please return it with any marginal notes you think fit to make. Perhaps you will laugh me to scorn, in your keen incisive Voltairean way, but it still seems to me that I have felt the authentic breath of genius. It was certainly a breath. But was it authentic? That is the question.

Yours exaltedly,<br>
TP

## TO *John Hayward* TS King's

28 January 1937            *The Criterion*

John:

Morley has been away all this week with a cold and his wife I rang up tonight is not at all sure that he will be fit to come out on Monday. So let us share a Car on that evening thats quite fair and I will come with you though I may have to stay on after you want to leave It would not be fair for you to have to have a Car for the whole evening all to yourself as well as the price £1 which is not to say high unless the food is a good deal better than the Savile's ordinary. Martin Browne will bring a gramophone so we can take the record. Think of me this weekend in Cambridge, that cold place, with Master Spens and Sir Hoskyns and Faber, that is if we get there, I have a feeling in my bones that there will again be some kind of accident en route as before and we shall spend Saturday evening either in hospital or at the Everyman Cinema.[1] yrs etc.

TP

## TO *Ezra Pound* TS Beinecke

January 28. St Cyril            *The Criterion*
of Alexandria, 1937

Well Ole Ez, I got your p.c. postmark Rapaloo 25.1.37 and headed by Yourself 'Sunday' though 'Septuagesima' would of been more precise.

1 – GCF's diary, Sat. 30 Jan.: 'To Cambridge with Tom Eliot & Enid. Stayed with Hoskyns's – Lady H in bed with 'flu . . . Meeting at Corpus to talk about A. S. [Anglo-Saxon] Chronicle. Dined with the Spens's.' (The Estates Bursar, Corpus Christi, told GCF on 17 July that the College approved the proposals: the College would guarantee a sale of 600 copies in two years and would also make a payment to the editor.)

'News of Cornford's death in Spain, on Govt side . . . [John Cornford (b. 1915), poet and communist, had been killed on 28 Dec. 1936 while fighting against fascism in Spain.]

'Whole ultra-Toryism of Corpus very repellent to me.'

Never Mind. I know I am slower than most in the uptake, and in the ordinary way I would never of guessed what you was aimin at, but as luck would have it I had been carryin about a cheque – the one elcosed, in fact, just to prove it: and I thinks, well, even if he didnt mean it, it will apply just the same so I might as well. I dont know whether your sense of decorumb, which is ever outstrippin the mark like a giant refreshed, would consider that I had ought of paid this cheque over to Larry:[1] but cant formbality be waved once in a while between friends, and a sterling cheque must look sweet now and again in the land of the Leerer, so here goes, and if conscience says Not, then you can yourself take your little Pollinger and eat yo' supper over on the Golden Shol or wherever yo' laiks. I havent yet yeard from you in response to my broadcast appeal on Sunday (Septuagesima); but you bein a radio fan must keep your ear open for Ole Possum's Popular Lectures on Cats in the Childrens Hour.[2]

yr<br>TP

## TO *Myfanwy Evans*[3]                                                    CC

28 January 1937                    [*The Criterion*]

Dear Madam,

I have been very much fascinated by the Japanese fairy tale which was brought to my notice by Mr Geoffrey Tandy, who gave the reading of it at the B.B.C. I have never come across anything of the kind which concentrates such a strong and definite effect in so few words. It has given me a very strange feeling, which I have found still more oddly to be shared by several other people: the feeling of having either heard the story in some other form at some remote time, or else of having dreamt it. It is possible that I may have read some version of it in Sanskrit folk lore, but I am sure of nothing.

---

1 – EP, in his next letter (30 Jan.) deplored the very idea. 'This, surrr, iz to acknowledge yr/ 12 pound look and to say whotterHell has it got to do with Larry [his agent Pollinger]/ He dont never place no serial rites for ole EZ and why shd/ he git a slice when EZ serials.'

2 – EP replied (30 Jan.): 'Ef I hadda knowd yu wuzza CATekizin or Broadening CATs I sure wd. have gone down stairs an interrupted the lads of the village an' the feetbull returns on, as you say, Septuergizzimah . . . and wot kind of Cat's haz yu been casting to children ANYhow?'

3 – Myfanwy Evans (1911–94), art critic and librettist, married the painter John Piper in 1937; wrote librettos for Benjamin Britten: *The Turn of the Screw, Owen Wingrave, Death in Venice*. See Frances Spalding, *John Piper, Myfanwy Piper: Lives in Art* (2009).

Mr Tandy tells me that you yourself don't recollect the origin of the tale. There can hardly, I imagine, be any copyright in it, except that as in its present form it is in your words we may consider you the proprietor. What I should like to do would be to print it as you have written it out, with due acknowledgements to yourself, and invite any readers who may have come across it before to write to the editor. If this is agreeable to you we should, of course, pay you for it as an ordinary contribution.[1]

Yours very truly,
[T. S. Eliot]

## TO *Hugh Martin*[2]                                                       CC

28 January 1937                    [Faber & Faber Ltd]

Dear Mr Martin,

I am replying to your letter of the 25th addressed to Mr Faber. It might have been answered by Mr Morley, as it was in reply to one by him, but he is at present away ill. In any case it is fitting that I should reply to give you some news of my own contribution to the volume. My work on this was interrupted, as I knew it would be, by having to prepare a broadcast talk in the series on Church Community and State, and you can imagine that a talk on such a subject limited to 20 minutes gives one a great deal more trouble in one way than an essay of this kind in which I have all the scope I need. I felt, however, that my participation in this volume and in the work of the conference made it impossible to decline to give the talk.[3]

I am again at work on my essay, and am giving myself a limit of the next fortnight to complete it. I think it should come to about 8000 words. If I couldn't say what I have to say at that length it would have to be a whole volume by itself, so I am sure it will not be longer.

We will have the essays by Bulgakoff, Horton and the Archbishop of York set in galley proof at once. I quite agree with your remarks about proof reading. I should suggest, however, that the word *Chapter* should be avoided as misleading in a book of this character. It seems to me that it might do if the essays were headed merely I, II, III etc. with the name of

---

1 – 'A Japanese Tale: Written down by Myfanwy Evans', C. 16 (Apr. 1937), 468.
2 – Hugh Martin (1890–1964): Christian student leader; ecumenist; Managing Director and Editor of the Student Christian Movement Press (specialising in theological works).
3 – See further Michael Coyle, '"This rather elusory broadcast technique": T. S. Eliot and the Genre of the Radio Talk', *ANQ: A Quarterly Journal of Short Articles, Notes and Reviews* 11: 4 (Fall 1998), 32–42.

the author beneath the numeral. Just how my own paper ought to come in with this arrangement we can tell better when I have finished it and sent it to you. I have been writing it as Oldham wished me to do, in the form of a kind of prolegomenon to the discussion proper of Revelation.

Yours sincerely,
[T. S. Eliot]

## TO *John Hayward*

TS King's

[29 January 1937]    The Vestry, St Stephen's Church,
Gloucester Road, S.W.7.

Ere. I didn't know you was such a accomplished Illustrater. Maybe you are the appointed Illustrater for my Popular Lectures on Cats. Wd. you care to submit a few speccimim illustrations? In combitition with Mr F. V. Morley, who thinks he can do it. But that Deomon Harpisisichordist is simply Orrible. Go On.

## TO *Ezra Pound*

TS Beinecke

29 January 1937    *The Criterion*

Eg. Sig I forgot to say that there will probably be a slight balance in your favour when the cantoes are properly paged, say a £ or so. Eg. Sig. prego tell me if you know anything about one Luigi Berti who writes to me from Firenze and who has to do with Letteratura. Is he a intelligent Bertie as well as a polite one or no???

TP

TO *Frank Morley*                                              TS Faber Archive

29 January 1937                          *The Criterion*

Now sir you are taking up my very valuable time to tell you this. Yesterday I received a cable from Fresno *ainsi conçu*:

FABER 24 RUSSELL SQUARE LONDON

ELIOT SENDING TODAY EDITED ALL MATERIAL FOR THIRD BOOK

AWAIT ARRIVAL — SAROYAN

which I cant understand what waiting I am to do which I shouldnt do anyway. But does he mean hold up the G & M Flux? But now Stop. There is also a letter which I need not communicate to you All, you know Little Billee's[1] letters, but *dont je donne le relévé suivant*:

'Although I feel that it (3 times 3) is a whole book . . . I will not mind its not being brought out in England as a book, if you believe that that would be unwise – in which case I believe we could take those pieces you like and put them with the pieces left out of Inhale & Exhale and make a book. Among the pieces left out of I & E are a number which I shall not care to have published in England. My agent writes: "F & F still do not feel that they have a completely satisfying title for the forthcoming book of pieces omitted from I & E and would therefore appreciate any further suggestions you can send." I feel that I need a little time during which to think about a title for the book, and also that it will be helpful if I know first if some of the pieces in 3 times 3 are to be included. I shall go to work on the book as soon as I hear from you.'[2]

The G & M Flux stuff is in the hands of the printers and presumably they are starting to set up. This looks to me as if we ought to hold it up? What do you think? I couldnt get Dick today, tarryhootin round

---

1 – 'Little Billee' is a humorous ballad hailing from Bristol, of which William Makepeace Thackeray wrote a version – TSE is funnily adverting to William Saroyan's given name.

2 – Saroyan wrote from California, 16 Jan.: 'Three Times Three [a short volume of short stories published in Los Angeles by a new imprint, The Conference Press, in Dec. 1936] is getting a very interesting press in this country. Without any advertising the book has sold over 700 copies and promises to go through the first edition in the next month or two. We do not know yet if there is to be a second printing. I am curious to know what you think of the book and how you feel about its chances of proving all right in England. I feel that it is likely to irritate some readers and critics, and then again I am not so sure; also, I am not so sure it wouldn't be all right to irritate some readers and critics . . . I shall edit each story to be included in the book, as I feel the stories can be improved by certain small changes. Of course I should be happy to hear that you like Three Times Three and wish to bring it out separately, but in case I am mistaken about it, I should like to know. This book is also to be edited and improved.'

somewheres he was. Lets have a word from you on Monday. So will close yrs etc.

TP

## TO *Stuart Gilbert*

TS Mrs M. Gilbert

1 February 1937                    *The Criterion*

My dear Gilbert,

I have your letter of the 29th.[1] It is certainly flattering to have a musician want to make an opera; I wonder whether it could be done. I have never been faced with this problem before, and it seems largely a question of how singable the words are without destroying the text completely. In any case, I do not think I can take any steps without consulting Ashley Dukes, who controls the dramatic rights of the play. After I have talked to him about it I will write either to you or direct to your friend. I suppose, as you say he is half American, that the libretto would be in English.

I am not sure how soon I can visit Paris again, but what I want to do if I can is to come over in May during Coronation week. I trust you will be there then.

With best wishes to Mrs Gilbert and yourself,

Yours ever sincerely,<br>T. S. Eliot

P.S. I don't suppose you have any definite information as to how far J. J. has got on with the middle part of *Work in Progress?*[2]

1 – Gilbert wrote on behalf of 'a youngish friend', the Swiss-American composer Edward Staempfli (b. 1908), who wished to be given permission to write an opera of *MiC*. Gilbert had heard a good deal of his work, including pieces for piano and a symphony. 'He composes in the modern idiom – somewhat on the lines of Hindemith – but isn't as far as I can judge, derivative. He is too timid to write to you directly and, taking compassion, I consented to act as go-between.'

2 – Gilbert replied, 14 Feb.: 'About Work in Progress – I have information, straight from the poet's mouth. He expects to finish it in May. This is the first time I have heard him commit himself to anything more definite than a year, or a decade; and I really think the chances are in favour of its coming off.'

TO *William Force Stead*                                        CC

1 February 1937                         [*The Criterion*]

Dear Stead,

I have your letter of the 26th, and quite agree with what you say about Robert.[1] One of the troubles in handling these rather impervious people – that is to say, impervious not because they are thick-skinned but because they are protected by a certain fantasy about themselves – is that one is always afraid that if one punches hard enough to get through at all one will be punching hard enough to do serious damage; and if one doesn't one is merely likely to offend without doing any good. But I will try to concoct a letter such as you can show to him or quote to him. To tell the truth, I don't really care for Robert's prose style: his purple passages sometimes make me shudder.

                              Yours ever affectionately,
                              [T. S. E.]


TO *Henry S. Swabey*[2]                                        TS BL

1 February 1937                         *The Criterion*

Dear Mr Swabey,

I have now got your article back from Philip Mairet, who has been so kind as to read it and make a few suggestions: too late, however, for the number which is going to press.

I should like therefore to publish it in the June number. I now return it with a few suggestions. It would be a very great help if you would retype it in double spacing. I had rather that you would omit any references or quotations from myself, except possibly the one at the beginning, which you may think essential for your point. You will find on p. 2, second paragraph from the bottom, the first sentence, a passage which both Mairet and I have queried as it stands; the first sentence does not seem essential anyway.

---

1–Robert Sencourt.
2–Henry Swabey (1916–96) was at this time studying at Durham University and preparing to take orders in the Anglican Church: see further Moody, *Ezra Pound . . . The Epic Years*, 205–7.

On p. 4 you say 'I hear from Rapallo', why adopt this rather coy indirection? Why not say 'I am informed by Ezra Pound'?

On p. 11 it seems to me that the illustration of Montagu Norman[1] going to the Duke of Buccleuch's memorial service is not altogether happy, and does not strengthen your hand. The irony seems to me at this point a little heavy.

But the greatest weakness of the article is, I think, that pointed out by Mairet on p. 7, as indicated by the word *debatable*. It does seem to me that you may be considered to be giving Lancelot Andrewes more credit for repeating views on finance which were current up to his time than he really deserves. In short, you have not been able to show that he is a really strong enough peg to hang such a weighty and important argument on. Would it not be possible for you to recast the article, merely using Lancelot Andrewes as a highly expedient springboard to take your leap from? The quotations from his writings are to the point, but here again I doubt whether the quotation from Lord Clarendon is strong enough to bear the weight you put upon it. It seems hardly likely that Andrewes's preferment to Canterbury would have made all that difference to the course of economic and monetary history in this country, when so many other powerful and concurrent reasons were driving it to the course which it has taken. And it is very improbable that Clarendon himself was thinking of all that.

Mairet adds in his letter to me the following interesting remark: 'Of course the weakness of this approach is that what beat the Church *about usury* was not so much the ideological change that came in with the Renascence as the enormous difficulty of the *practical* problems that multiplied about that time, and became too complex to keep up with. Still, that is no argument against Swabey's view for the moral superiority of the scholastic effort at regulation.'[2]

1–Sir Montagu Norman (1871–1950), banker and Governor of the Bank of England 1920–44, was (according to Mark Carney) 'spectacularly incompetent' and 'helped to tip the world into a depression'. See I. M. Drummond, *The Floating Pound and the Sterling Area, 1931–1939* (1981); P. Williamson, *National Crisis and National Government: British Politics, The Economy and Empire, 1926–1932* (1992); Liaquat Ahamed, *Lords of Finance: 1928, the Great Depression and the Bankers who Broke the World* (2010).

2–TSE quotes from Mairet's letter to himself, 27 Jan. Mairet added: 'There are also roughnesses of writing here and there that impede the reader: but there is a "kick" in the style that should not be smoothed out of it. The argument is pretty clear and good as far as it goes, and tells us a good deal we didn't know about an early chapter of financial history.'

I don't want to discourage you, but on the contrary. The article is full of good meat, and on the whole I like the way it is put; and I do want it back in a revised form so that I may publish it in June.[1]

Yours very sincerely,
T. S. Eliot

TO *Maurice Reckitt*                                               TS University of Sussex

1 February 1937                          *The Criterion*

My dear Reckitt,

Thank you for your letter of the 28th.[2] I have still not quite made up my mind how far to force the issue at once. I think at least that we ought to insist on some declaration of policy, so as to uncover the real sympathies of the majority of Bolshakoff's people. But I am rather anxious to get this matter cleared up quickly, because I have a feeling that the use of such names as yours and mine has probably enabled Bolshakoff to get a certain amount of highly reputable American support. The people over there will have no means of judging personalities, nor do they know anything about the scruples and hesitations with which we have been afflicted since the start.

I feel that Christopher Dawson will probably take quite a different view from ours.

I do think it is a pity, as you say, that this Academy should be quite out of touch with the kind of Roman Catholic thought that we find sympathetic. I should very much like to be in contact with the Oxford Dominicans, and with people like Father Drinkwater. I have heard rumours that such people are not very well thought of in official quarters, and I don't believe that Bolshakoff would like to risk offending official R.C. opinion.

Anyway, I will send you a copy of my next letter to Bolshakoff.

Yours ever,
T. S. Eliot

1–Swabey, 'The English Church and Money', C. 17 (July 1937), 619–37. In the Oct. issue there were letters from EP and Swabey about the latter's confusion in the final paragraph of the article with regard to issuing and lending money.
2–Not traced.

TO *S. L. Bethell*[1]                                                    CC

2 February 1937                    [*The Criterion*]

Dear Mr Bethell,

I must apologize for keeping your essay on George Eliot for such a length of time, but it is always the more interesting manuscripts about which there is the greatest delay.[2] I confess that I realized some time ago that it would be too long, but in view of your previous work I was anxious to read it, nevertheless. It seems to me an admirable piece of work, and your method of estimating the author and her development by the style of particular passages seems to me a very useful and refreshing change from the usual method of criticizing fiction, which ignores the actual writing. I wish that I could publish this, but it is exactly twice too long. You have suggested that it might be serialised in two numbers, but I have found this method of publication in a quarterly extremely unsatisfactory, inasmuch as the lapse of time means that readers of the second part will have forgotten what preceded, and it is only the exceptional reader who will not only preserve the previous issue but will trouble to re-read the first instalment as a preparation for the second part. On the other hand, there seems nothing in the article that could be called superfluous, and I do not see how it could be cut, but if you cared to make that arduous and ungrateful attempt to reduce it to not more than 6,000 words, I should be prepared to consider it very favourably for publication. If not, I hope that you will be able later to send me other things of the suitable length.

Yours sincerely,<br>[T. S. Eliot]

---

1 – S. L. Bethell had just been appointed to a lectureship in English at University College, Cardiff. George Every to TSE, 11 Dec. 1938, of Bethell: 'I like what I've heard of him . . . He is a friend of Knights and Leavis, but I heard of him through D. G. James (of *Scepticism and Poetry*) who deliberately and seriously put us on to one another. He has the advantage of having done Cambridge theology before a temporary intellectual meander permanently turned him from ordination to literary education. But he and Fr. Matthews are hunting together and cutting some intellectual ice in Cardiff now.'
2 – Bethell submitted his essay – 'an attempt to produce (I think for the first time) a real criticism of Geo. Eliot's novels, and an estimate of her significance in relation to her period and from the standpoint of the present day' – on 9 Nov. 1936. He conceded that it 'was rather long . . . I could try to boil it down, which would be easier now I have worked my ideas out at some length. But the treatment would be bound to suffer very considerably.'

TO *A. Desmond Hawkins*                    TS A. Desmond Hawkins

3 February 1937                    *The Criterion*

My dear Hawkins,

Thank you for your letter of the 28th. We can talk about the chronicles when we meet, but meanwhile you have no cause to worry about them. I think this chronicle is much better than the first, partly no doubt because you have a more interesting lot of novels. In fact I think it is very good. I thought your comments on Cyril Connolly and Henry Miller extremely well balanced and just.[1] As for who reads such contributions besides myself, it is really no use for any contributor to the *Criterion* to ask about readers. I don't know any more than you do, but I do think that after a lapse of time such a chronicle as this can show evidence of having made an impression on a surprising number and variety of people. I have some evidence of such interest in the Broadcast Chronicle, and I think that the effect of a good chronicle is cumulative. That is why they are worth keeping up.

I think you are probably right about Elizabeth Bowen, but I think you would agree that she has a very definite place, and a pretty high one, amongst novelists of her kind.[2]

Next week is getting pretty full, but I think lunch on Thursday would be possible if that day suited you and you could tell me at once. Or if lunch doesn't suit, come and have tea here.

Yours ever,

T. S. Eliot

1–'Fiction Chronicle', C. 16 (Apr. 1937), 495–507. '*Black Spring* is not so much a novel as an explosion of a volatile personality . . . The recollection of his early life and of his father's friends is beautifully done, with a rare and moving tenderness . . . Apart from these reminiscences the book is a feat of personality. Its strength, when Mr Miller is not imitating other authors, lies in the freshness of the idiom. This Paris–American idiom, loose and fragmentary as it may be, is the one impersonal contribution to imaginative prose style in our time . . . Mr Miller is not yet a novelist of great stature: he is – wilfully, I think, and with deliberation – a "character", a personality that can be capitalized in literary terms. He goes on a pubcrawl, with words for liquor; and that is all. But put any page of Mr Miller's own authentic writing beside any novel written in England during the last five years, and it will be obvious that he has freshness, vigour, *panache*, and an *intimacy* with his environment that our native gentility has lost' (p. 503).

2–Hawkins had written on 4 Feb.: 'I want occasionally to criticise an author in extenso on the basis of his total extant work, when that seems good enough to warrant it . . . The names that I have had in mind for some time are O'Faolain and Elizabeth Bowen . . . I don't know whether you think them big enough fish to be treated in this way, and I can say nothing as I have not sufficient knowledge of their work.'

4 February 1937                    [*The Criterion*]

My dear Gill,

You disappointed some of us very keenly by not being able to appear at the dinner the other night. I only hope that whatever prevented you is not of serious consequence.

I am now writing on the assumption that you read German. If you don't, you need not bother about what follows, but I have a book in German which was simply sent to me personally by the author, but which I should like to have reviewed. It is a work on aesthetics, called simply *Schönheit ein Versuch*, but unlike most German works on aesthetics it is very short, being only 152 pages, and is happily in Latin type. The reason why I should like you to review it if you can is that Theodor Haecker, the author, is not merely a philosopher, but a Roman Catholic and something of a theologian, and the book must be reviewed by someone who will understand his point of view. I have not read it, but I have a great respect for Haecker as one of the few intelligible and civilised writers in Germany today. I have read a couple of his earlier books. I daresay his name is known to you.[2]

> Yours very sincerely,
> [T. S. Eliot]

---

1-Eric Gill (1882–1940), artist, type designer, sculptor, draughtsman, wood-engraver, essayist, social critic; convert to Catholicism, 1913; member of the third order of St Dominic, the lay order of the Dominicans, 1919–24; neo-Thomist; socialist; practitioner of the ideal craft community; devotee of a 'holy tradition of workmanship'. Writings include *Work and Leisure* (1935); *The Necessity of Belief* (F&F, 1936); and *Autobiography* (1940).
2-Gill replied on 8 Feb. that unfortunately he could not read German ('much as I should like to know what the author says'); he recommended Ananda Coomaraswamy of the Museum of Fine Arts, Boston.

4 February 1937                    [Faber & Faber Ltd]

Dear Prince,

I am sorry to be a month in answering your letter of 1 January.[2] I wanted to show your poem 'For William Maynard' to one or two people to see if their impressions corresponded to my own. I don't think that the poem is quite finished yet. I have a feeling that you will find some polishing required before you put it into a book, but I think it is a good poem, and I want to publish it in the *Criterion* if possible in June.[3]

Now about your collected poems. I have as you know a number of your poems here scattered about and filed. But you would help me if you would let me have all the poems that you want to put into a volume, with a table of contents and in the order in which you would like to see them appear. That will be something more positive to put before my committee than my own collection of various poems and versions.

I never want to mislead people into being too hopeful, but I think at least that I shall, when I have the whole collection before me, be able to recommend it to my committee.[4]

                                   Yours sincerely,
                                   [T. S. Eliot]

---

1 – F. T. Prince (1912–2003), poet, critic, editor, was born in South Africa and educated at Wits University, Balliol College, Oxford, and Princeton University. During WW2 he served in Army Intelligence. From 1946 he taught at the University of Southampton, where he was to be Professor of English, 1957–74. Works include *Poems* (F&F, 1938), *Soldiers Bathing* (1954), *Collected Poems, 1935–1992* (1993). See further 'F. T. Prince: A Tribute', *PN Review* 29: 1 (Sept.–Oct. 2002), 26–38; *Reading F. T. Prince*, ed. Will May (Liverpool, 2017).

2 – 'I am sending you a corrected copy of A Muse for W. M, which you may choose to print instead of Burke ['Words for Edmund Burke']. The shorter pieces go towards the prospective book.' He was anxious to know whether F&F would be commissioning a book from him.

3 – 'A Muse for William Maynard', C. 16 (July 1937), 603–5.

4 – Prince responded on 10 Feb. with 'copies of all the poems [10 in number] I would want to print . . . The whole amounts to about 450 lines of verse. I shall probably have two or three small poems in the next few months which I might like to substitute.'

See *Poems* (F&F, 1938), blurb: 'This is the first volume of a poet whose work is well known to readers of *The Criterion* as being distinguished for metrical accomplishment as well as original sensibility. It is the only volume of verse by a new poet that we have added to our list this year.'

## TO *Ashley Dukes*

8 February 1937                    [Faber & Faber Ltd]

Dear Dukes,

I have written to Fluchère as you suggested, proposing that he should let us see a specimen translation. Now another worry has turned up. I first had a letter from a man in Paris named Stuart Gilbert, a very charming retired I.C.S.[1] man with a French wife, who is a friend of Joyce's and wrote the best book about *Ulysses*; and now I have a letter from the man himself. It is a young Swiss (half American), who wants to turn *Murder in the Cathedral* into an opera. I have never heard of the man, whose name is Edward Staempfli, and I don't know what the devil to say to him.[2] What would you do about this? I am already in difficulties because of two Italians who are both translating *Ash Wednesday* and seem to be at each other's throats over it, and I don't want to get into a row with musicians as well. I don't take the slightest interest in turning *Murder in the Cathedral* into an opera, but if it was to be done one would naturally want the best possible man to do it.

                    Yours ever,
                    [T. S. Eliot]


## TO *Charles Madge*[3]

8 February 1937                    [Faber & Faber Ltd]

My dear Madge,

I return herewith your preface and the draft of the pamphlet.[4] First about the preface; I have again shown it to someone else, and we agree

---

1–Indian Civil Service.

2–Edward Staempfli (1908–2002), Swiss composer and conductor, asked on 3 Feb. for permission in principle 'to transform your play . . . into an opera. It would naturally be an oratorio just as well as an opera.' The idea had been suggested to him by the novelist and poet Pierre-Jean Jouve (1887–1976), who had seen a performance of *MiC*, since Staempfli had written an oratorio 'on one of his poems'.

3–Charles Madge (1912–96), poet and sociologist, was a scholar at Magdalene College, Cambridge (which he left without a degree). In 1935–6 he was a reporter on the *Daily Mirror*: this was thanks to the help of TSE (who also published his first volume of verse, *The Disappearing Castle*, 1937). In 1937 he set up, with the anthropologist Tom Harrisson, the Mass Observation project: their output included *May the Twelfth* (1937) and *Britain by Mass Observation* (1939); and he was Professor of Sociology at Birmingham University, 1950–70.

4–Madge wrote on 6 Jan: 'I am afraid I shall have to come along to your office to draw up a table of contents, but I should be very glad of the opportunity to talk to you about another

that it would be better for you to publish it separately as a pamphlet rather than with the poems. I think that the poems stand perfectly well on their own feet, and would only be interfered with by an essay tacked on to them. But I have said all this before.

At the same time I wonder whether you will want to publish this preface as a pamphlet at the present time, in view of your bringing out the other pamphlet, which is certainly a more adequate treatment of its own subject. But perhaps the second will be quasi anonymous, so as to make little difference.

It is not quite easy to criticize the pamphlet without knowing exactly what audience you have in view for it. I imagine that you aim first at the small number of more intelligent collaborators. Later, if you want to bring in all sorts of people who might be helpful to your purpose without really understanding clearly what you are doing, a shorter and more popular pamphlet might be desirable. But even with this one I feel that for the purpose of an appeal the order is not quite right. As it is, people will plod on for page after page without knowing quite what you are getting at. You have got to give them some inducement to read what appears at first to be an essay in the abstract. Would it not be better to start with a short explanation of the work you want to set on foot, so as to get them curious and excited; then have your long and philosophic section showing your background of ideas, and end finally with what will be a detailed exposition of the first part? This, at any rate, would be the form in which such a pamphlet would most readily capture my attention, and secure my interest.

There are one or two minor points; as you have not numbered the pages I have been obliged to turn down corners. The first reference is to your statement that Copernicus and Galileo put an end to a view of things in which the whole universe depended on man. I don't think this is true, and at least it would be more exact to say – for what these large generalisations are worth – that they assisted in the change from one kind of anthropocentrism to another.

At the end I think you restrict the number of your sympathisers unnecessarily by the final sentence. It suggests that nobody can be in on

question. I think I may have mentioned when you came to see us that I had been planning some research on collective images by means of a large number of observers on the analogy of weather bureaux. This plan has expanded suddenly on account of a letter describing it in the "New Statesman" which seems to have drawn on a latent volume of sympathy from Wigan to the Athenaeum. I have had more than thirty offers of help already. The sudden expansion brings up problems on which I should be most glad of your advice.'

this except those who are convinced that 'science' can explain everything. But surely you don't want to give the impression of appealing only to positivists? You want to enlist also those who are simply inclined to believe that this kind of science can throw a good deal of light on this kind of subject.[1]

Yours ever,
[T. S. Eliot]

## TO *T. F. Burns*                                                    cc

9 February 1937                              [Faber & Faber Ltd]

My dear Tom Burns,

At last I have read twice within a few days your friend's book of verse.[2] I have taken the liberty of making a number of marginal notes in pencil,

1 – These paragraphs adumbrate the beginnings of the social research organisation called 'Mass Observation', which would seek to apply systematic methods, the principles of observation, to the *vox populi* of the United Kingdom, and to penetrate below the level of published public opinion – thus affording a more empirically based alternative to the recently launched Gallup Poll system of question and answer. Teams of observers (including William Empson, filmmaker Humphrey Jennings, photographer Humphrey Spender, and artist Julian Trevelyan) were set to mingle with and to record all aspects of the behaviour, including authentic utterances, of the largest possible cross-section of the people at large. 'We wanted to observe what [people] did, not what they *said* they did . . .,' said Harrisson in a paper on 'The Mass-Observation Archive at Sussex University' read at an Islib Meeting, 19 May 1971. 'At the peak of our activity, which was really from 1937 to near the end of the war, we had up to forty wholetime paid observers, and over one thousand other people, throughout England, who made up our voluntary panel.'

One of their initial undertakings was to document the day of the coronation of George VI on 12 May 1937, following the abdication of Edward VIII. Thanks to TSE, the volume *May the Twelfth: Mass-Observation Day-Survey* (1937) was brought out by F&F.

See Madge and Harrisson, *Mass-Observation* (1937); 'Mass-Observation as Poetics and Science', special issue of *new formations* 44 (Autumn 2001); Nick Hubble, *Mass-Observation and Everyday Life* (2006); James Hinton, *The Mass Observers: A History, 1937–1949* (2013); and David Hall, *Worktown: The Astonishing Story of the Birth of Mass-Observation* (2015).

2 – Burns submitted on 22 Dec. a sheaf of poems by his friend Ann Bowes Lyon. 'You said "Send them at Christmas" and so I do. I know what that means – having these extra jobs at [a] time when one wants to rest a little – I am all the more grateful to you.

'You'll remember that you read these poems & discerned some merit & promise of more. There are 50 or so here. The author wants to cut them down to 30. They are uneven & uncertain in places – & maybe you'll think the whole mode has now passed. But we can't make "contemporary" an essential quality of poetry, can we? These are deeply felt, painfully worked things and I'd give a lot to see them as the beginnings of real achievement. I explained to you, I think, that helpful criticism was going to make all the difference to the author's life. Rough notes would serve – though a meeting & a general talk (which I could easily arrange) would serve as well or better.'

because I think this kind of criticism is often of more use to an author than any amount of separate commentary. My impression of the poems bears up the favourable opinion which I formed when I read them some time ago. The author has I think a very good ear; that is to say, a definite gift for a rhythm which without varying widely from any accepted rhythm – and so much the better – yet has a very personal tune to it. There are a few poems which are more conventional and no better in metric than A. E. Housman's. I have marked two of these, and think they ought to come out.

I think the author has a definite gift within definite limits. If she is a really intelligent poet she will realise that this is high praise. The book is good enough to be published. I will even say that it is good enough not to be published. I mean that I should expect the author's future work in verse would consist in doing very much the same thing over and over, sometimes better and sometimes worse, but she does it so well that it would be worthwhile for her to see that every poem is as perfect as it can possibly be. I mean that she ought to go on writing, although at the end of a lifetime's work her whole volume might not be very much bigger than it is now. But by that time she would have refined it as far as possible, and have developed her own critical faculty, which is so very important, to a degree at which she could distinguish very slight differences of quality which would enable her to select and reject with precision. Her themes are well worth dealing with again and again; in the end a great deal should be destroyed. I think that in a book such as hers would be it is almost more important to leave out what is not quite so good than it is to keep in the high spots.

Burns again, 22 Feb. (1937), following a conversation with TSE about Bowes Lyon's work: 'The point is that [René] Hague wants to print it now and in the normal way would come to Faber's with an agency arrangement . . . De la Mare knows all the details. But it is a little different in this case – where you have already read the book. None of us wants to scoot in by a back door! We see the point about keeping to a certain policy in poetry but we also hope that the suggested arrangement doesn't make so much a breach of your rule as an exception to it in exceptional circumstances. We are agreed that the stuff is good enough to be published and so I hope that Hague's printing of an edition will not compromise your policy any more than his printing of the other books that he has put out through Faber's. Without this arrangement we might go about hunting interminably and you know what a damnable business that would be. I'm very anxious to get things settled up quickly now, so I'd be grateful if you would let me know of Wednesday's decision as soon as possible.'

(Presumably the arrangement included a subsidy towards the publication of the poems.)

Ann Lyon's *Poems* appeared in the July to December catalogue, with this blurb (p. 54): 'Miss Lyon's poems are distinguished by a delicate personal rhythm which makes old forms new and a delicate cultivation of a particular range of feeling. This is a book for those who require of verse not momentary amazement, but quiet satisfaction.'

Of course this is not the Faber sort of poetry; as you know perfectly well, for perfectly practical reasons it is necessary to specialize in poetry if a firm is going to make an impression with its poetry list, and if it does not want to lose money to no purpose. I think this book might well be published, but unless I am over-estimating the abilities of the author and her devotion to poetry, I should say that it should be a still better book in ten years' time.

And with that I can only repeat my apologies to you, and still more to the author, for being something over five weeks in arrears.

Yours ever,

[T. S. Eliot]

## TO *Djuna Barnes*

TS Hornbake

9 February 1937                    *The Criterion*

Dear Miss Barnes,

I have your letter of the 7th.[1] I used to know Roger Cornaz slightly in Lausanne many years ago, and I remember that he was then busy translating something of Lytton Strachey's, but I have never read any of his translations, and cannot say from personal knowledge how good he is. He is certainly quite bilingual – I think his mother was Scotch – and ought to do a good job.[2]

I don't know whether I ought to take the initiative myself in approaching Gide or anybody, because I am not in a position to know who would be most suitable as an introducer. If Roger Cornaz thinks that Gide would be the best man, and if he does not know him himself, I am quite willing to write. I do know Gide, but he is an incalculable character, and I have no idea how I stand with him at present, though I am on very good terms with some of his friends. I am wondering for the moment whether it would be better if I wrote first to Jean Paulhan[3] to engage his interest.

---

1 – Barnes had been approached by Roger Cornaz with a view to translating *Nightwood* into French, along with TSE's preface and perhaps an additional foreword by 'some important Frenchman of letters' such as André Gide. Would TSE be prepared to write to Gide himself, or else give Barnes a letter of introduction to him?

2 – Frédéric Roger Cornaz (1883–1970): translator into French of works by Lytton Strachey, Rabindranath Tagore and D. H. Lawrence (*Lady Chatterley's Lover*).

3 – Jean Paulhan (1884–1968), editor of *Nouvelle Revue Française* (in succession to Jacques Rivière), 1925–40, 1946–68. He was active in the French Resistance during WW2. Works include *Entretiens sur des fait-divers* (1930); *Les Fleurs de Tarbes, ou, La Terreur dans les lettres* (1936); *On Poetry and Politics*, ed. Jennifer Bajorek et al. (2010). See Michael

487

I don't suppose Paulhan has much to do with the book publishing of the N.R.F., but he ought to have some influence with Gallimard. On the other hand, if you should see Gide, or anyone else for that matter, do suggest yourself as a friend of mine.

This sounds a very roundabout kind of letter, but the real point is merely this: I don't know who would be the best person for an introduction, but if you and Roger Cornaz and anybody else you consult agree that Gide is the person, let me know definitely and soon and I will write to him.

Yours sincerely,
T. S. Eliot

## TO *William Empson*                                            CC

9 February 1937                        [*The Criterion*]

Dear Empson,
I like your 'Villanelle', and want to publish it as soon as I can find room.[1]

Yours sincerely,
[T. S. Eliot]

## TO *Frank Morley*                                            TS Berg

St Cyril of Alexandria, B.C.D.        *The Criterion*
[9 February] 1937

Now Sir you listen to Reason. You don't need to worry about MSS. because Enid and Miss Bradby have been havin a pleasant time this afternoon readin em and passin caustic remarks; and I found a nice book on the Ice Age which was sent to us because we published *Moons Mush & Magic*,[2] which will keep Geoffrey quiet; and I offered Miss Wright a choice of two German books one on St Ignatius Loyola (fiction) and one on Sigismondo Malatesta (fiction) and she chose Malatesta which shows

Syrotinski, *Defying Gravity: Jean Paulhan's Interventions in Twentieth-Century French Intellectual History* (1998); Martyn Cornick, *Intellectuals in History: The 'Nouvelle Revue Française' under Jean Paulhan, 1925–1940* (1995); Anna-Louis Milne, *The Extreme In-Between: Jean Paulhan's Place in the Twentieth Century* (2006); William Marx, 'Two Modernisms: T. S. Eliot and *La Nouvelle Revue Française*', in *The International Reception of T. S. Eliot*, ed. Elisabeth Däumer and Shyamal Bagchee (2007), 25–33.
1–C. 16 (July 1937), 618.
2–H. S. Bellamy, *Moons, Myths and Man* (F&F, 1936).

that she has read Ezra's Cantos; and I have sent Ez a cheque for £12 to keep him quiet for a bit until he thinks of the nastiest way of complaining that it aint £40 – which reminds me that that is just about what my appeal has brought in so far including a 6d. postal order from the Misses Linnell in Tunbridge Wells, and I have just made my little speech to the Annual Meeting of the Church Literature Association, and anyway we are to start again on our voyage to Cambridge on Saturday; and I have saved you two nice books, one on the Cooperative Movement in Denmark and the other that Woodward's history of the U.S.A.,[1] so you remember that the Mississippi is still risin and stay in bed. Try to acquire a sense of values and remember that the most important item on the agenda is Monday night, but that even that is less important than the general future. You shd. be occupied with yr. illustrations, for which I will provide a very large Portfolio for the Committee. Just to keep you busy here's another which you may not have seen: get to work and illustrate that. Earp and Tandy and I had a pleasant meeting at Gordon's Wine Bar last night, and I fed the hungry today by givin lunch to Heppenstall. There is a detective story about the Murder of the M.F.H. and a book on what's wrong with the Church by a lady who says that her only distinction is that she is the only female race horse trainer and she thinks if we publish the book in April she will win a race about then and that will help the book. So will close, yrs etc.

TP

## TO *George Rylands*[2]                                    TS King's

10 February 1937                   *The Criterion*

Dear Rylands,

I have your letter of the 8th.[3] I am much interested to know that you are going to produce *The Revenger's Tragedy*, and hope that I may be able

---

1 – W. E. Woodward, *A New American History* (1936).
2 – George 'Dadie' Rylands (1902–99), literary scholar and theatre director, was from 1927 a Fellow of King's College, Cambridge. Early publications included *Russet and Taffeta* (verse, 1925), *Poems* (1931), *Words and Poetry* (1928) – all published by LW and VW at the Hogarth Press (for which he worked for six months in 1924). As director of the Marlowe Society, he became famous above all for his productions of plays by Shakespeare; he taught generations of talented students including Peter Hall, Derek Jacobi and Ian McKellen; and he became chairman of the Arts Theatre in 1946. He was appointed CH in 1987.
3 – 'The Marlowe Society which is the most serious of the dramatic societies here is to produce *The Revenger's Tragedy*, this term. Since the war they have given both the Websters, also

to see it. By the way, I have seen a letter which someone has written to the *Times Literary Supplement* suggesting that a couple of lines in the last act spoken by Spurio should really be attributed to Supervacuo.[1] It struck me as plausible, and I will look up the text and let you know where the alteration comes.

I should be glad to help by writing a prefatory note if possible, but everything I do is against time, and therefore I should like to know when you would need it. Also, as I have not any of your old programmes by me, I should like to know what sort of line this kind of note should take. Perhaps you would even send me an old programme as a guide. I certainly should not have time to do anything in the way of a Montague Summers[2] turn for you, loading it with obscure information.

Yours ever,

T. S. Eliot

## TO *Gregor Ziemer* CC

10 February 1937       [*The Criterion*]

Dear Sir,

I have your letter of 1 February, which asks a number of questions.[3] Please forgive me for saying to begin with that it seems to me you are

---

*Volpone, Arden of Faversham* & the *Fair Maid of the West* apart from the Shakespearean productions. It is a gamble – or rather it will lose us a little money – I think it is worth it. The Society are very anxious that I should persuade you to write a short programme notes – 350–500 words or so. We want to have the programme on view & on sale beforehand to excite interest. You could help us enormously. Whenever I write to you, it is to ask you to do some rather tiresome kindness, I fear, & you may say in this case that you have already written on Tourneur & said your say.

'I wish, however, that you would glance at the play again & give us an impression. It *would* be valuable & would be very much appreciated.'

1 – Major C. S. Napier, 'The Revenger's Tragedy', *TLS*, 13 Mar. 1937, 188.

2 – Montague Summers (1880–1948), scholar of Restoration theatre, occultist and demonologist, graduated in theology from Trinity College, Oxford, and attended Lichfield Theological College, whereafter he was ordained and practised as a deacon. However, in 1909 he migrated to the Roman Catholic Church and thereafter posed and garbed himself as a religious (researchers have found no record of an ordination). A man of considerable scholarly industry, he published editions of works by writers including Aphra Behn, Congreve, Wycherley, Otway and Dryden; and he was instrumental in setting up the Phoenix Theatre, 1919–25, which was followed by the Renaissance Theatre, 1925–8.

3 – Ziemer, Headmaster of the American School in Berlin, wrote on behalf of Professor Schirmer and a class of 25 students who had been worrying TSE's poems inc. *The Waste Land, Journey of the Magi* and *Ash-Wednesday*: 'A few definite questions that are hanging in the air. I'm afraid that only you can answer them . . .

simply creating obstacles for yourself by your over anxiety. You speak of an 'almost heartbreaking effort to understand, be guided by, and assimilate' my poetry. I do not like the idea of people making heartbreaking efforts over poetry, and I think that the desire to understand often stands in the way of understanding, so that quite simple people who merely have a natural ear to catch the rhythms and read them aloud often get more out of poetry than those who are too anxious to dissect it for precise meanings.

Similarly, your question whether you have been brazen is irrelevant, and indicates a self-consciousness which is not desirable.

I do not understand what you mean by being guided by my or anybody's poetry; still less a desire to be guided by something which you say you do not understand.

Please forgive these blunt remarks, for they seem a necessary preface to stating that the majority of the questions you ask seem to me unanswerable. I could certainly invent answers, but they would be as irrelevant as the questions, and would be adding a meaning rather than explaining an existing one. Question 5 can be answered clearly: I do not remember any leopards in the Bible, but I have no Concordance; my leopards represent simply the world, the flesh and the devil. I have been told that there is a similar use of white leopards in certain Sudanese folk lore, but I did not know this at the time.

'(1) Waste Land – Is the note of Shanti at the end a solution? Is doubt still supreme, or is something definitely promised?
'(2) In the Maggi – the idea of death and living. Does the death the Maggi talk about mean the death of an outworn system, or their own spiritual awakening?
'(3) Ash Wednesday – I do not hope to turn again . . . An hour was spent in discussing – Did you turn with regret in your heart? Were you still vague about the future, letting the past go with regret?
'(4) Part II of Ash Wednesday – we found in it, or seemed to find, the whole Catholic Tradition extant. Is that correct?
'(5) Are the Leopards in Ash Wednesday from the Bible?
'(6) We felt that Ash Wednesday, more perhaps than Murder in the Cathedral, had the assurance of salvation. Is that the way it was intended?
'(7) Is the idea of life and death in Ash Wednesday similar to that of Simeon and Maggi?
'(8) Are the notes to Waste Land to be taken seriously?
'(9) The Triumphal March had us beaten. Matthiessen informs us that you were not thinking of any particular dictator. The part dealing with the dictator is clear as long as we think of a modern one, but why the classic allusions? I am beginning to feel that your poetry speaks to me with the greatest economy of words – that you want to approach me, the reader, without handicap of words. But could you not relieve a great emotional vacuum by informing us what the outstanding emotional reaction this poem is to evoke really is?
'Have I been brazen? I am sure of it. But these questions are the result of a most sincere desire, an almost heartbreaking effort to understand, be guided by, and assimilate your poetry.'

6. I cannot see that there is any more assurance of salvation in *Ash Wednesday* than in *Murder in the Cathedral*. I should like to point out here that I should draw a clear distinction between the assurance of the possibility of salvation and the assurance of salvation. The latter, I believe, is only given to Calvinists.

[7.] Probably so, as they were all written during the same period.

8. The notes to the *Waste Land* should be taken at their face value.

9. *Triumphal March* was not concerned with contemporary politics. I am afraid that I cannot give you any more explanation than the very exhaustive one of Mr Matthiesson, who I think already explains a little too much.

With best wishes to yourself and the rest of your class,

> I am,
> Yours sincerely
> [T. S. Eliot]

TO *Henri Fluchère*                                                                 CC

10 February 1937                          [Faber & Faber Ltd]

Dear Mr Fluchere,

Thank you for your kind letter of the 8th.[1] I look forward to receiving some of your translation, and will hold in mind to let you have it back as quickly as possible, though you will understand that I shall want to get one or two other opinions besides my own, and shall have to show it to Mr Ashley Dukes.

I should certainly be very happy if Copeau[2] were interested in producing the French version, because I am sure he could do it better than anyone else in Paris that I know. If the translation interested him he would of course have to be put in touch with Mr Ashley Dukes for getting consent and arranging the rights.

What you say about the difficulties of translation interests me very much, and I quite agree with you that it is above all a question of rhythm.

---

1 – Fluchère was surprised by TSE's request to see a sample of his translation of *MiC*, but he had decided to meet the challenge: he would submit certain 'fragments' and would ask TSE for certain clarifications. The task was not easy, because even apparently banal expressions ('*en apparence banales*') like 'patched-up affair' were hard to render into French. Still, he said, it was all a question of rhythm ('*tout est une question de rythme*'): he believed that above all else.

Fluchère was to complete his translation by July 1939. *Meurtre dans la Cathédrale* was produced by Jean Vilar at the Théâtre du Vieux-Colombier in June 1945.

2 – Jacques Copeau (1879–1949) built and directed the Théâtre du Vieux-Colombier, Paris.

I very much wish that you could have heard a performance by the English company, as I think it would have been, with some reservations, a help to you. There was some question of its going over to Paris for a few performances, but that seems to have fallen through.

The Herald's speech is of course intended to be rather flat and prosy in style. 'Patched up affair' is I agree a difficult phrase to translate. What you want is some equivalent cliché; and indeed you want a certain number of clichés for that speech.

> With many thanks, and best wishes,
> Yours very sincerely,
> [T. S. Eliot]

## TO *Edward Staempfli*[1]                                    CC

10 February 1937                    [Faber & Faber Ltd]

Dear Sir,

I have your letter of the 3rd instant, as well as a previous letter from Mr Stuart Gilbert. I was obliged to take a few days over answering, because I had to consult Mr Ashley Dukes, who holds all the performing rights of *Murder in the Cathedral*. He thinks, and on mature consideration I agree with him, that it is premature to turn the play into an opera, especially as we are anxious that it should become more widely known in its present form first.[2] So I am obliged, with many regrets, to decline. I hope that I may have some opportunity of hearing some of your compositions.

> Yours very truly,
> [T. S. Eliot]

## TO *William Force Stead*                                    CC

12 February 1937                    [*The Criterion*]

My dear Stead,

The manuscript of Robert's book has unfortunately already been returned to you, so I cannot give you any detailed comments upon it, or quote chapter and verse for the reasons of our rejection of it. I do not think that it is our book in any case: one acquires a kind of instinct about what one can sell if anybody can, and what some other firm could sell

1–Edward Staempfli (1908–2002), Swiss composer.
2–Dukes had written to TSE, 9 Feb.: 'Better decline the operatic proposal right away – it would never do you any good, whether as success or failure.'

better. But there are two things which I think he ought certainly to do to the book to make it more acceptable to anybody. One is to prune the purple efflorescences of his style, and try to discipline himself to a more direct, simple and austere prose. This weakness combines with a tendency to ramble about and bring in almost everything in such a way as to make the reader wonder what the book is all about. I think that he ought to write a different kind of introductory chapter, making quite clear what he has set out to do, and after that I think that the book would be improved by being cut down considerably. He seems to have written it with a view to getting in everything that could possibly be made to go in, rather than on the principle of omitting everything that could be left out. I think he has a very interesting case to make, and a subject of his own which he ought to be able to make a very good book with.

Yours ever affectionately,

[T. S. E.]

## TO *John Hayward*

TS King's

Friday [12 February 1937]          [No address given]

Dear John,

It seems that I am to go to Mrs Mirrlees on Sunday morning [illegible] presumably on Monday evening. But she does do [illegible] she sends a car to fetch one, and one has breakfast in one's room, and everything civilised except Hope's dachshund.

Otto asked after you this afternoon.

My old newspaper woman at the Gloucester Road Station (at that corner where there is always a congestion of prams, terriers and policemen) hailed me this morning with 'OY! I see your photo in the Radio Times this morning'. As if it wasnt enough to have had to walk all the way home from Earls Court last night, because we stayed too long tippling with George Barnes last night and I had to deliver Tandy by taxi to Hammersmith to catch the last Twickenham Bus.

If you think of a place where I could conveniently get a Valentine tomorrow between 12–1 (because I shall be at home tapping away at Revelation till then) to send to Jean, I should be grateful for a ring.

Anyway, here's the photo Old Ma saw.[1]

1 – The cutting shows a photograph of a bearded man (not T.S.E.) from the *Radio Times* with this caption: 'T.S. Eliot gives the last talk in the "Church, Community, and State" series tonight, at 9.20. He will discuss "The Church's Message to the World".'

Yrs etc.

TP


## TO *P. Ross Nichols*[1]

17 February 1937                    [Faber & Faber Ltd]

Dear Mr Nichols,

Thank you for your note.[2] I do appreciate the trouble that you are taking on behalf of Franz Pfeifer, and hope that it may lead to a successful issue. I should be surprised if he had done anything very indiscreet myself, beyond wearing English clothes and being rather naively pleased at being taken for an Englishman, but you know that Mrs Culpin is naturally an impetuous and outspoken person, and there may have been indiscretions on her part.[3]

Yours sincerely,

[T. S. Eliot]


1 – Philip Peter Ross Nichols (1902–75): teacher, poet, artist, historian; wrote extensively on Druidism and Celtic mythology; in 1964 he founded the Order of Bards, Ovates and Druids.

2 – Nichols, who lived in London, wrote ('Friday'): 'I am writing to ask if you think anything can be done about obtaining the release of our friend Mrs Culpin's adopted son.

'I have heard twice from her in Paris. The first card indicated that she was going to Köln. I wrote and suggested that she might be interned, and that if instead she sent me full particulars of the lad's name, etc., I might bring some influence to bear. However, she still says she is going to Köln; and I have no particulars.

'Now – as an individual with friends in various parties – I happen to know – well – a very prominent German lady whose name works wonders in the Fatherland – her first cousin in one of Hitler's right-hand men, it seems – Col. Pfeffer; she told me (without my seeking the information) that she obtained within a few hours the release of a Communist friend of hers . . . I am presuming that the boy has not engaged in political activities, but is one of those border-line cases of "politically unreliable" people, owing probably to his English associations.

'On the other hand, any intercession from England might have a prejudicial effect – unless Mrs Pf. might be induced to represent him as a friend of *hers*.

'I would like to confabulate with you upon this for a few moments before possibly putting both feet into it. Perhaps you have already been taking steps yourself?

'Shall attempt to discover your office on Saturday morning sometime between 10 and 1.30, when I hope you may spare a few moments.'

Nichols to TSE, 'Tuesday (morning)': 'I enclose a letter I have just received from Mrs Culpin. You will see that she doesn't say the situation is improved . . .

'I think that if I may have Francis's exact name and address I will now see what Mrs Pfeffer can do, meanwhile dropping another card to Mrs Culpin that influence is being used.'

3 – Nichols wrote again ('Sunday'): 'I thought you would like to know that Frau Pfeffer has very kindly promised to write specially to her cousin the Führer's henchman on Franz's behalf, so soon as I can provide her with the fullest passport & other record particulars . . .

TO *Djuna Barnes*                                               TS Hornbake

17 February 1937                        *The Criterion*

My dear Miss Barnes,

On second consideration it seems to me that the proper person to ask André Gide for an introduction would be Roger Cornaz himself.[1] After all, Gide has had a copy of the English edition, and if he knows enough English has probably read it by now, and what Gide will be having to sponsor is Cornaz' translation. If Cornaz does not know Gide, or does not feel enough confidence, I am quite willing to back him up, but I think that if I write to Gide at all I shall want to say simply that Cornaz is applying to him, and that I hope he will be able to see his way to doing a preface. I could also send Gide a copy of my preface if he has not seen it.

Paulhan is the editor of the *Nouvelle Revue Française*, and presumably is pretty close to Gide, and I think is also a member of the Communist Party.

Yours ever,
T. S. Eliot


TO *J. H. Oldham*                                                    CC

17 February 1937                        [Faber & Faber Ltd]

My dear Oldham,

I am enclosing my essay for your criticism, with apologies for the delay. Unless you think it is wholly unsuitable, I will ask you to send it on after reading it to John Baillie for his consideration. Baillie should then return it to me for the printers.[2]

———

'This means that, if all goes well, Franz should certainly receive his visa; it will cut right across any local red tape or pettinesses. Unless of course he really *has* done something foolish.'

1–Barnes had written on 12 Feb.: 'I wish you would tell me what you think best in the matter – I know *nothing* about French writers of today, or which would be the best to approach for I neither read or speak the tongue. Mr Cornaz said (he has now gone to Zurich, but I've written him about your suggestion, Jean Paulhan) that the very best person would be Gide, I took his word for it. He said if Gide would not do an introduction the next best would be Paul Morand, Vallery Larbeau [*sic*] (you see I can't even spell them!) If you would rather not write Gide, & think it would be any use for me to do so, I will do so immediately. I don't know what is best – I might as well be in China for all the use I am in France. I do not know who Jean Paulhan is.'

2–TSE, 'Introduction', in *Revelation*, ed. Baillie and Hugh Martin (1937), 1–39.

I need not say that I am dissatisfied with what I have done. I have really had to work very much against time, partly but not altogether because the broadcast talk took so much more preparation than I had anticipated. You will no doubt find this paper rather scrappy, and the authors chosen for examination will seem to you to indicate a rather capricious choice, but in any case a thorough examination of secularism in Europe and America could hardly be possible except by writing a rather large book, and if this essay is rather on the short side, I feel that I could not have made it profitably longer without making it too long. It seemed to me more pertinent to discuss a few individualists, and to say very little about political philosophies, which have been discussed to the point of satiety.

It may be however that this is not in the least what you or Baillie want. In that case I am afraid the only thing to do will be to leave it out altogether, because time presses, and it would be impossible for me to start afresh without delaying publication of the book for at least a season.

May I have a card from your secretary to acknowledge receipt of this typescript?[1]

Yours sincerely,
[T. S. Eliot]

1–Oldham replied on 19 Feb. that he found TSE's paper 'more interesting than any of the other contributions. I felt in reading the earlier pages that the treatment of the various authors was perhaps a little scrappy, as you say in your letter, but I do not see what else is possible within the limits of space, and you pull things together splendidly at the end, and I find the conclusion illuminating and helpful.' He was sending the paper on to Baillie for his editorial judgement.

TSE in his essay took issue with Bertrand Russell in *The Conquest of Happiness* – 'which may be called a defence of mediocrity. It comes to the conclusion that so far as happiness depends upon oneself, and not upon circumstances, "the recipe for happiness is a very simple one" . . . Christian morality is not an end but a means. Mr Russell simplifies his contrast by making it one simply between inward and outward. "Professional morality" is for him a kind of egotism . . . For once we have asked the question: what is the end of man? we have put ourselves beyond the possibility of being satisfied with the answer: "there isn't any end, and the only thing to do is to be a nice person and get on with your neighbours."'

Pondering the question of why 'intellectuals in the modern world' turn to Christianity, he notes too: 'The conversion to Christianity is apt to be due, I think, to a latent dissatisfaction with all secular philosophy, becoming, perhaps, with apparent suddenness, explicit and coherent.' (He added in a footnote: 'I am deliberately disregarding the operation of grace in order to keep it to the secular plane.')

Turning to the case of Irving Babbitt, in his posthumous *The Dhammapada: Translated from the Pali with an Essay on Buddha and the Occident*, TSE notes: 'The problem is why Babbitt, with such a mind and equipment, as, it would seem, could only be supported by Christianity, should have turned to Primitive Buddhism (Hinayana) instead . . . One of the reasons why Buddhism appeals to him is apparently his hostility to Platonic ideas, and his dislike of the Platonic influence upon Christian theology.'

He quotes Babbitt to this effect: 'Religion also looks upon life as a process of adjustment. This process as envisaged by the Christian is summed up once for all in Dante's phrase:

TO *Stephen Spender*                                                    CC

17 February 1937                          [*The Criterion*]

My dear Stephen,

I am glad to hear from you, because I had been under the impression
that you had been in Spain all this time, but I am all the more sorry, as you
say that you are leaving on Thursday for Valencia, that I did not know
you were in London, for I should have liked very much to see you.[1]

---

"In his will is our peace." A reading of works like the Dhammapada suggests that the
psychological equivalent of this form of adjustment was not unknown to Buddha.'

TSE's comment on Babbitt's position: 'One might remark . . . that it is not proved that
there can be any "psychological equivalent" . . . I suggest that the Buddhism of Irving Babbitt
is not simply a purified Buddhism . . . but that it is an artificial Buddhism – not only purified
but *canned* . . . It therefore has something in common with the psychological mysticism that
is a phenomenon of decadence rather than of growth. This is the mysticism which seeks
contact with the sources of supernatural power, divorced from religion and theology.'

TSE goes on: 'The mixture of violent prejudice with sympathetic interest in Christianity
displayed in the writings of Babbitt has a curious analogue in the writings of Mr Aldous
Huxley' – specifically as evidenced in his Peace pamphlet *What Are You Going to Do About
It?*: 'From a Christian point of view – from any religious point of view – it cannot be an
ultimate good cause, inasmuch as peace itself (the peace of this world) is not an end but a
means. There is apt to be impurity of motives in our *natural* devotion even to such a good
cause as peace; and in the effort to purify our motives towards peace, the effort to isolate
for contemplation the essential idea of peace, we must, I think, be led to the final theological
problem of the end of man.'

The essay concludes: 'What a discursive reading of the literature of secularism, over a
number of years, leads me to believe, however, is that the religious sentiment – which can
only be completely satisfied by the complete message of revelation – is simply suffering
from a condition of repression painful for those in whom it is repressed, who yearn for
the fulfilment of belief, although too ashamed of that yearning to allow it to come to
consciousness.'

1–Spender wrote on 15 Feb.: 'This letter is to tell you that the International Association
of Writers for the Defence of Culture is holding an exhibition & meeting in about 14 days
time for Spanish Medical aid. We want to get well-known writers to give signed copies of
their books &, if possible their MS, which will be auctioned by some such person as Hugh
Walpole.

'Please will you send some signed copies and – if it's not too much to ask – MS? The
address is to Mrs Amabel Williams-Ellis, I hope that name does not produce a shudder . . .

'Next, my own news. I am going to Valencia on Thursday to do English broadcasting for
the Workers Union (U.G.T.).

'Meanwhile, I have written ¾ of my play which I shall finish in Valencia. I shall leave
a copy of what I have already done with my wife and then post the rest to her, page by
page . . .

'My reasons for going are partly that I am asked & cannot refuse if I am needed, partly
that the anxiety of knowing that my best friends, including Wystan & Tony, are there, is
unbearable. It is simpler to go myself.'

(Amabel Williams-Ellis, née Strachey (1894–1984), cousin of Lytton Strachey and
associate of the Bloomsbury Circle, was a novelist and critic; wife of Clough Williams-Ellis,
with whom she collaborated in the construction of the resort of Portmeirion in north Wales.)

I think I had a letter officially from the International Association of Writers for the Defence of Culture to the same effect as yours.[1] When I got the letter it struck me that one was being asked implicitly not simply to defend culture but to defend a particular politicised view of culture which I did not share. While I see no alternative organisation of culture that I like any better, I don't want to be drawn into the fringe of any political movement of either extreme.

It is good to know that you are so far forward with the play, and I shall look forward eagerly to reading it. I hope that your expectation of being able to finish it in Valencia means that you will be in a position of no physical danger – at any rate not on a firing line. I should love to hear from you from there, and also would like to have news of Wystan.

Yours affectionately,<br>[Tom]

TO *Willard Thorp* TS COPY

17 February 1937 *The Criterion*

Dear Willard:

Thank you for your letter of the 7th.[2] I am more than repaid for my effort; especially as I had a note from More himself (dictated to Mrs Fine)[3] which expressed, I thought, genuine pleasure. Thank you also for your thoughtfulness in sending two dollars for the cable – I can't now remember whether it cost as much as that or not.

---

1 – The writer and journalist Charlotte Haldane invited TSE (8 Feb.) to contribute a copy of 'one or more' of his books (first-edition and/or signed) or 'one or more manuscripts' to a Book Exhibition and Auction to be held on 20 Mar. at the Friends House, Euston Road, on behalf of the International Association of Writers for the Defence of Culture. She added: 'As the Artists' Exhibition raised £500, we have a high standard to live up to as writers.'

2 – 'You have done a most generous and useful thing in sending us the paper on Dr More for the *Alumni Weekly*. I know that one is glad to do things of this sort, but the writing of such a "eulogy and a demonstration", as you call it, may well have been more difficult and exacting than most of the writing which you do.

'Mr More was well enough to have it read to him and to see the proofs . . . Naturally we are all grateful that it came in time to give him pleasure.

'I understand that it is quite literally his will which keeps him alive. Fortunately the science of giving opiates has advanced so far that the doctor can keep him from pain and yet permit his mind to be relatively clear some of the time. Either he does not know that his illness will be fatal or he carries such a brave front before his family and friends that he all but convinces them that he does not know.'

3 – Mrs Harry B. Fine, Paul Elmer More's daughter.

I cannot help thinking that More knows how near to death he is. It would be surprising if a man of so much wisdom was quite unaware of the coming of such an important event. I felt it in his *Marginalia*. He seems to me to be one of the very few great men whom I have known.

Yours sincerely,
T. S. E.

## TO *Marjorie E. Roberts*                                        CC

17 February 1937                        [Faber & Faber Ltd]

Dear Mrs Roberts,

Thank you for your letter of the 11th instant. I cannot see that the order makes very much difference, except that those who speak early and get it over with are rather to be envied. I will come to Lady Hodder Williams's on the 3rd, though I am not clear whether you mean that the six speakers are to have a meeting by themselves, or whether they are merely to make what opportunity they can for discussion while circulating amongst other guests.[1]

Yours sincerely,
[T. S. Eliot]

## TO *Henry Eliot*                                        TS Houghton

17 February 1937                        *The Criterion*

My dear Henry,

I was horrified to get your letter of the 4th today with £50 back.[2] I suppose I must take it, but I had rather you had sent £25. I am quite

1 – The fund-raising entertainment on behalf of the British Red Cross Society – a discussion called 'Authors' Night' – hosted by Lord and Lady Londonderry at Londonderry House on 10 Mar. (preceded by a sherry party on 3 Mar.), was to include addresses of 10–15 minutes each by speakers inc. C. Day Lewis, Canon H. R. L. 'Dick' Sheppard, and Humbert Wolfe. Lord Esher was to take the chair, and Lord Balniel (chair of the Ex-Committee) to propose thanks. (The Society supplied books and magazines to over 2,000 hospitals and other institutions.)

Mrs Roberts reported on 11 Feb. that a special meeting of the Book Trade Advisory Committee had decided upon an order for the six speakers, and that TSE was to be last of all.

GCF's diary, Weds, 10 Mar.: 'Dined alone with Mother, E[nid] being out at her Red X debate with the unfortunate T.S.E. in tow.'

2 – HWE wrote: 'I was staggered by the size of your contribution to the St Louis taxes, and since this amount, with what the others have contributed, would bring the total to nearly

convinced that I ought to be responsible – at any rate, while the going is good and I am getting something every month from my play – about £100 for the run in January – for considerably more than either you or Ada. And I get a good deal of pleasure out of being able to shoulder my share.

You should by now have received various Eliot items in three envelopes in three separate mails: what mss. there are of *Murder in the Cathedral*, and other scraps; also (a fourth parcel) two copies of *The Little Review*. I am also asking Harcourt Brace to send a copy of *Nightwood* with my preface.

I am sorry to hear of Theresa's illness, and hope you will let me know when you get this, how she is progressing.[1] Please give her my love. This makes me all the more unhappy at receiving back from you £50. Please remember that I do not have these anxieties and expenses.

I have just had the usual annual letter from the Old Colony about the Mary C. Stearns Trust. I wrote back to say that I felt sure that Margaret and Marion were still the most needy; but said that I understood that the larger part had been paid to Margaret in the past, and suggested an enquiry into their relative financial positions. There is no obvious reason why Margaret should receive more than Marion. If Margaret makes injudicious investments on her own judgement, then she should suffer from that rather than Marion. Or is it possible that the Old Colony themselves have squandered more of Margaret's money than Marion's?

It's odd that I have not received a copy of *The Southern Review*.[2] Mario wrote to me about his article before he wrote it.

I feel that instead of returning £50 to me, you should have returned dols. 50 to Ada, and dols. 50 to yourself, that's dols. 100 or £20; and then returned me £30. At the most. I shall have to get back at you in some indirect crookt way.

I can well understand that the hospitality of kind relatives interferes with your work.[3] Don't I know it: I have kind (I *mean* kind, not ironically)

---

the whole of the taxes without any contribution from me at all, I feel that I should return half of this sum. That will make my contribution equal to yours. Ada paid $250, Marian and Margaret, without urging, $100 apiece, and Shardy [*sic*] and Theodora $100 apiece.'

1 – 'Theresa is in hospital just now for ten days, for experimentation with diets. It is very pleasant, she has a room with a view over all the countryside, and has only to rest and eat what is put her, which is little enough. She will be back next week.'

2 – 'The Mario Praz article in the Southern Review looks good . . .' Praz, 'T. S. Eliot and Dante', *Southern Review* 2: 3 (Winter 1937), 525–48; repr. in Praz, *The Flaming Heart* (1958).

3 – 'I am being smothered with invitations to meals from relatives. Say it not to any of them, please, but the net result is that what with getting out to see T once in a while, and dining out, I am getting too little time for work. It is agreeable, of course, and I am appreciative.'

friends who are always wanting to do me (as a lonely single man etc.) a kindness by asking me to the country to visit them for weekends, when I should be much more comfortable (especially in winter) snuggling in my club by myself: and I have to accept some of their invitations in order to give them the pleasure of feeling that they are doing something for me. Otherwise, one is ungrateful and unsociable!

But I should like to know how you *are* getting on with your own work; and to know that you are doing just enough for the Peabody Museum for them to appreciate having you, but not so much that they will take you for granted without being grateful to you.

And for goodness' sake take care of your own colds and don't pass them on to Theresa. We are catarrhal: I always use up a handkerchief before breakfast.

I have had a new gold tooth put into my mouth this morning (it has meant the loss of four mornings that tooth) so that I can hold a pipe again, but it is still very uncomfortable. My dentist says that my teeth are just bad, but the longer I can hold on to my stumps before having a plate, the better.

Affectionately,<br>Tom

## TO *Olaf Stapledon*[1]  CC

17 February 1937  [Faber & Faber Ltd]

Dear Mr Stapledon,

I have your letter of 15 February, and remember our meeting, which seems many years ago.[2] Since then I have followed your work with much interest.

---

1–Olaf Stapledon (1886–1950), science-fiction writer and philosopher, took a degree in history at Balliol College, Oxford, and then worked for a while in his father's shipping company in Liverpool. But in 1913 he abandoned business in favour of making his living by teaching for the Workers' Educational Association (WEA). After WW1 (he served as a conscientious objector in the Friends' Ambulance Unit), he earned his doctorate at Liverpool University and subsequently essayed poetry and philosophy: *A Modern Theory of Ethics* was published in 1929. However, fame and fortune came in 1931–44, when he produced a series of celebrated works of science fiction (including *Last Men in London*; *Last and First Men*; *Sirius*) and books of philosophy and cultural criticism. See Richard Crossley, *Olaf Stapledon: Speaking for the Future* (1994).

2–Stapledon (who had met TSE in 1928) asked him to support a petition organised by Caradog Jones, a statistician, 'in the belief that many people in this country, even if they disagree about other aspects of the international problem, can at least pull together to

I have rather a prejudice against signing petitions unless it is about something which is a pretty clear issue on which I have strong convictions. I do not feel, after all the commissions and conventions which we have had since 1918, that the project in view is likely to get us anywhere.[1] It does not seem to me that such an examination would get really to the heart of the matter, even from a purely technical point of view. I do not see how any readjustments of colonies etc. can help very much so long as the countries concerned adhere to the present monetary and commercial system. So long as various countries wish to pursue the economic warfare amongst themselves I suspect that readjustments of the means for carrying on this warfare will [not] accomplish any more than all the abortive schemes for limitation of other armaments. This is by no means to say that I disapprove of such a petition, but only that I do not feel sufficiently convinced of its fundamental value to be able to support it.

Yours sincerely,

[T. S. Eliot]

## TO *Ashley Sampson*

CC

18 February 1937                    [Faber & Faber Ltd]

Dear Mr Sampson,

I have your letter of 15 February, which I am sorry to inform you is in vain, because Berdyaev has never been on our list.[2] My impression is that

---

advocate expert commissions of inquiry into the economic and political facts underlying current disputes.

'The petition is meant to be signed by (a) representative officials of societies, and (b) distinguished individuals in the professions.'

He invited TSE to put his name to a petition to be addressed to leading writers. 'We have secured H. G. Wells, Somerset Maugham, Hugh Walpole . . . We are anxious to have one or two outstanding names with a more distinctively literary reputation. I have therefore asked Spender, but his reply may be too late. I am asking Auden, & Virginia Woolf.'

1–Petition not found.

2–Sampson reported that the first three volumes in the 'Christian Challenge Series' had proved so successful that Centenary Press was thinking of extending them beyond the first twelve titles they had in hand: he wanted to commission a book from Nicolas Berdyaev on a subject such as 'Authority and Freedom', but he did not wish to alienate Berdyaev from his usual publishers – whom he understood to be F&F. Could TSE advise him on this question?

Nicolas Berdyaev (1874–1948): Russian philosopher (sometime a Marxist) and religious thinker; author of *The Russian Revolution*; *Christianity and Class War*; *The End of Our Time*; *Freedom and the Spirit*; *The Fate of Man in the Modern World*; and other works.

Tomlin, *T. S. Eliot*, 94–5, recalled that at Kelham in the late summer of 1937, Eliot had remarked to him that one theologian 'with whom, after an initial enthusiasm, he had

he has been published by several firms, notably Sheed and Ward, and I believe one volume by the Centenary Press. I am pretty sure that nobody has a monopoly of his books, and in any case, as this is a special series of yours, it seems to me that you are entirely at liberty to write direct to him. I feel all the more certain of this because the Rural Dean of Dunmow told me that Berdyaev was extremely unbusinesslike about his books, and that he wanted him to put his affairs in the hands of a literary agent.

I cannot help wondering whether there are not other foreign writers who would be more interesting than Berdyaev in your series, although I do not know whether they would sell as well. It would be interesting if you could get a volume from Karl Barth or Emil Brunner, or even Max Buber; and Theodor Haecker is a very interesting writer too.

> With all good wishes,
> Yours sincerely,
> [T. S. Eliot]

## TO *Katharine Oliver*[1]                                    CC

18 February 1937                    [Faber & Faber Ltd]

Dear Mrs Oliver,

It is very kind of you to write to me about my play, and what you say of it has given me very great pleasure.[2] But I should have been delighted

---

become somewhat disillusioned was Berdyaev. I could well understand why; a "Christian theosophist" or "believing free-thinker" was not quite Eliot's cup of tea.'

1–Katharine Oliver: widow of F. S. Oliver (1864–1934), businessman, author and polemicist, who was educated at Edinburgh and Cambridge before joining forces in 1892 with Ernest Debenham in the firm of Debenham and Freebody (drapers, wholesalers, manufacturers), which they caused to flourish (buying up Marshall & Snelgrove and Harvey Nichols). Oliver, who became a wealthy man, retired as managing director in 1920. A radical Tory, he engaged himself in many public causes. Works include *Alexander Hamilton* (1906), *Ordeal by Battle* (1915), and *The Endless Adventure* (3 vols, 1930–5). He died on 3 June 1934. See 'Mr F. S. Oliver: The Business Man as Historian', *Times*, 5 June 1934, 19.

2–Mrs Oliver wrote from 15 Portman Square, London, 15 Feb.: 'I must write you a few lines to say how much I admired & enjoyed your play – which I saw last week.

'The above address may puzzle you but you will remember coming to stay with us as Kenry House while we were there – and I still live at Edgerston [Jedburgh] most of the time . . .

'Fred would have liked reading your play – I know.

'It is so delightful & so unusual to see a play written & produced like yours – a perfect whole – or so it seemed to me . . .

'The Norman Barons might have walked out of the windows of Tewkesbury Abbey – & their defence is a satire which Fred would have delighted in – I thought too how he would have approved of the last speech of the priest at the end.'

in any case to hear from you, because I have often thought of you and wondered whether you were still at Edgerston. I wish indeed that your husband could have seen the play, and it would have been a great gratification to me had he liked it as much as you suggest. It is perhaps not impertinent to tell you how very much I enjoyed the last volume of *The Endless Adventure*, even in its unfinished state. He was one of the men whom I most admired as a writer amongst what I may call my elder contemporaries. It seems to me that the standards of style in political writing have deteriorated.

With many thanks,
Yours sincerely,
[T. S. Eliot]

## TO *Ezra Pound* TS Beinecke

1937                 *The Criterion*
19 February: feria, this time,
and that reminds me I don't know
anything about S. Savina, or other
local Ligurian deities but that day
you wrote on was properly speaking
CHARLES KING & MARTYR[1]

Now Ez I got a bit of good news. You was right in your suspicions about these 3 cantoes.[2] Paging from your types. was worked out to 13 pp but I have had it done again from galley and it works out nearer 20 pp. so when I confirm that from the final page proof there shd. be a modest balance in your favour to settle promptly. Your corrections to the cantoes for book form seem pretty clear[3] but one point is not clear You put in a little pink slip with on it FIFTH DECAD OF CANTOES Now is that when you want to call the book because it seems to me that it had beeter be uniform with the fourth decad for convenience of collectors with tidy minds, but if you want to wrangle that point with us you better speak

---

1–EP had teasingly sent a letter headed 'S. SAVINIA', i.e. Saint Savina of Milan (d. 311), whose Feast Day is 30 January – for which 'Charles King & Maryr' had clear priority for TSE.
2–TSE had sent EP a cheque for £12 in payment for the Cantos serialised in the *Criterion*. 'How the hell you got three canters onto 12 pages Gorrr knoze,' exclaimed EP.
3–EP sent his comments on the volume on 8 Feb.

quick.[1] Incidentally we appreciate yr. delicacy though you dont carry so far as the Criterion never mind.

It is satisfactory that you have showed understanding and acumen in relation to doubledorans, and we are engaged now in fashioning arrangements about CULTURE.

Know anything about Freeman Tilden?

Havent seen your motherinlaw for a coons age. Hope she aint puny.[2] Theres a good deal of mumps about, in case you dont hear from me again for some time, and when elephants gets mumps the zoo hears about it. (indirectly)[3].

Now you say you don't know BERTI so do you know BALDI? Anyway, Bertie and Baldie are engaged in some all-in wrestling over the Ash Wednesday and I dont like havin to be in the ring with them.[4]

Yrs

TP

1 – EP replied ('D. II di Quaresima' [Lent]): 'I SEZ the "FIFTH DECAD" wot don't mean decay or decaydence/ and when I SEZ DECAD thaZattt/ And I have precedent more or less cause our ole friend Dant Alligator [Dante Alighieri] he divvys 100 inter 3 parts and gets 34 so damn uniformity ANYhow. DECAD sez Ez/ the Fifth Decad/ there is ten of 'em, thazza decad. REEMembur yr/ Livy [. . .] only dont call 'em can TOES. Call 'em CANTOS.' *The Fifth Decad of the Cantos XLII–LI* (1937).
2 – Puny: 'Chiefly U.S. regional (esp. south and south Midland): In poor health; ailing; sickly.' (*OED* 2c).
3 – Word in parenthesis added by hand. EP replied (n.d.): 'No, sfar as I hear me movverin row aint feelin puny. ThankU kindly for the HenQuiry.'
4 – Sergio Baldi (Istituto Magistrale, Aquila degli Abruzzi) to TSE, 2 Feb. 1937: 'The Frontespizio – our Florentine Catholic Review – is going to publish a translation of mine of your Ash Wednesday, which I have tried to translate into Italian verse as well as I was able to. Now, Signor Luigi Berti pretends he has had the right of translating all your works and he is going to give us trouble about it. Then I was obliged to quote the American edition of 1936, the copyright of which, I see, is no longer yours. That would be enough for the Italian law, but notwithstanding, I should be very grateful to you if you would be so kind as to authorize me to translate from these editions, or from any other edition you like better. Being perfectly stranger to you I should not have written you till I had published something worth of your attention, and I hoped to do it very soon. As a matter of fact since five years I was reading and studying as much of your poetry and criticism as I was able to be informed of here in Italy, and some conclusions which I have drawn from these years of studying are going to be published in a long essay (La poesia di T. S. Eliot) which I shall send you as soon as it will appear in print. If you need any reference I may tell you that I got my degree in Letters from the University of Florence, and that my translations (from Ezra Pound and Stephan [*sic*] George) were awarded the second prize in the Littoriali della Cultura . . .

'Hoping to get your grant to translate and publish your poems in the way you like best.'

EP responded (n.d.) : 'Only Tilden I knowz uv is BILL, and he's turned purrfesshunul. And Baldie spells BACON to me, and Bertie is the last and lost of the Russies.'

TO *Emily Lina Mirrlees*                    MS Hornbake Library

21 February 1937                    Faber & Faber Ltd

Dear Mrs Mirrlees,

Your treatment proved effective, so that I have been able to carry out the programme of a very busy week without relapse. I am sure that I was a very dull guest for the most part, but I can offer you some of the satisfaction I am sure you take in beneficence, by saying that your household is an ideal one to be ill in. But I hope earnestly that I shall be free from all ailments the next time you ask me.

I only hope that the situation in Tonbridge is at least not still one of anxiety and suspense for you.[1]

Yours very sincerely<br>T. S. Eliot

P.S. I enclose a dog which I think might interest your brother.[2] What we need is a breed of cats that stay in at night.


TO *Polly Tandy*                    TS BL

Feast of St Joseph of Arimathea C.    *The Criterion*
Also of Geo. Washington H.T.
otherwise 22th Febry [1937].

Now, Sis Tandy, I dont know was you expecting me for this coming weekend and when it come to that I dont know that I was wanted, being as I had proposed the date myself. But here's what's happened: we have had to Fix a meeting of the Parochial Church Council for Sunday morning at 12.15: why? because we must have an Annual Meeting to discuss the Allocation of the Free Will Offerings for the past year, which has mostly been spent already, and it has to be then because it suits old Sir Henry who is the Treasurer of the Fund, and can't get out much because of his

---

1–Hope Mirrlees's sister Margot Coker lived at Tonbridge: the circumstances behind this remark by TSE are not known.

2–TSE sent a cutting from *The Listener*, Feb. 1937, p. 317, with a photograph captioned 'THE DOG THAT NEVER BARKS': 'Dogs of all shapes and sizes turned up in their thousands last week at the Cruft's Coronation Show at the Royal Agricultural Hall, Islington. Cocker-spaniels – 813 of them – made the biggest entry, with the Labradors close on their heels. There were dogs of unusual breeds, exotic colours and all shapes and sizes, including the strange breed from the Congo, shown above, which never barks and which, in order to survive the English winter, grows a special coat.'

Mappy Mirrlees's brother was Maj.-Gen. W. H. B. Mirrlees.

phlebitis etc. and only in the middle of the day at that. So I wonder would it be ekally welcome was I to invite myself for the following weekend or not. Because I don't know about Ole Pop's fixtures for lexuring at the Museum or doing one of his funny turns at Langham Place. I suppose that rumjumbling kind of a child is pretty much of a nuisance nowadays racin about on 2 feet up and down and no peace anywheres, but I hope no vestige or symptom of ailments is at present casting any shadow over your life so will close yrs. respfly

TP

## TO *Christopher Isherwood*[1]                                   cc

23 February 1937                    [Faber & Faber Ltd]

Dear Mr Isherwood,

We have been told by Curtis Brown that you have been making some further alterations in the text of 'F6' during rehearsal. A new edition is in the press, in which we have incorporated some considerable alterations given us by Auden before he left, and the proofs should be in any moment. I hope therefore that [if] you can let us have a copy of your own alterations at once I think we might be able to bring the new edition up to date to the production.[2]

Yours sincerely,<br>[T. S. Eliot]

1 – Novelist, playwright, translator, and writer on religion, Christopher Isherwood (1904– 86) published his first novel, *All the Conspirators*, in 1928; it was followed by successful fictions including *Mr Norris Changes Trains* (1935) and *Goodbye to Berlin* (1939). He collaborated with Auden on three plays, *The Dog Beneath the Skin* (1935), *The Ascent of F6* (1936), and *On the Frontier* (1939); and on *Journey to a War* (1939). His autobiographical novel *Lions and Shadows* (1938) contains a vivid portrait of the young Auden under the guise of 'Hugh Weston'.

2 – No reply has been traced. The second edn of *The Ascent of F6* (Mar. 1937) incorporated revisions made by Rupert Doone and Isherwood for the Group Theatre production, Feb. 1936.

GCF's diary, Fri, 26 Feb.: 'E & I dined with T.S.E. & went to first night of *Ascent of F6*. Met Mrs Auden.'

23 February 1937                    [*The Criterion*]

CONFIDENTIAL

Dear Rothschild,

You may remember that two years ago you very kindly subscribed to a fund for helping a young poet named George Barker. I kept this going a second year, by appealing to different people, and had hoped that at the end of that time there need be no more worry about him. I don't believe in subsidising authors indefinitely, or at all if they can find any decent way of making a living. But Barker is an exceptional case, both in his poetic abilities and in his inability to get the kind of job that is open to university men. He has been trying to get a regular job, and people have been trying for him, and there is some prospect that later in this year he will get some work in the Western Regional and possibly in extension lecturing in the West. But meanwhile he is as badly off as ever, and I want to get a little more money to let him have a pound a week for the rest of the year.

I have got one subscription of £13, and I will do the same myself: I need a total of £26 for the rest of the year.

I am fortunately able to feel more conviction about this, because he has just done a new long poem which seems to me a long way ahead of anything he has done. We are publishing this in the spring.[2] But he is still an author whom we publish at a loss, and my firm have done as much for him as I can ask them to do.

I am limited in the number of people whom I can ask to help, because I don't like to ask people merely because they are kindhearted and can afford it, but only if they care enough about there being contemporary poetry to be really interested. If you feel able to help I should be very grateful: if not, there should be no reason for embarrassment on either side.[3]

Yours sincerely,
[T. S. Eliot]

---

1 – Victor Rothschild (1910–90), Fellow of Trinity College Cambridge, 1935–9, succeeded his uncle as 3rd Baron Rothschild in 1937.
2 – *Calamiterror* (1937).
3 – Rothschild responded, 27 Feb.: 'I should certainly like to do something for George Barker: I am enclosing a cheque which I hope will assist you.' He contributed £10.

TO *F. S. Flint*[1]                                                    CC</>

23 February 1937                    [*The Criterion*]

My dear Frank,

I have been wondering what had become of you, and hope that you have come back from Nice in the best of health and will remain so.[2] Yes, if you can cut out the Keynes and shorten the paper to not more than 6,000 words I should be very glad to print it in the *Criterion*.[3] I don't expect you to cut out the mathematics, but any reductions and simplifications that you can manage would be gratefully appreciated by

                                        Yours ever,
                                        [T. S. Eliot]

1–Frank Stuart ('F. S.') Flint (1885–1960), poet and translator, and civil servant, grew up in terrible poverty – 'gutter-born and gutter-bred', he would say – and left school at thirteen. But he set out to educate himself in European languages and literature, as well as in history and philosophy. In 1908 he started writing articles and reviews for the *New Age*, then for the *Egoist* and for *Poetry* (ed. Harriet Monroe). Gaining in authority (especially on French literature – his influential piece on 'Contemporary French Poetry' appeared in Harold Monro's *Poetry Review* in 1912) – he became associated with T. E. Hulme, EP, RA and Hilda Doolittle; and he contributed poems to the *English Review* (ed. Ford Madox Hueffer) and to EP's anthology *Des Imagistes* (1914). Between 1909 and 1920 he published three volumes of poetry, though his work as essayist, reviewer and translator was the more appreciated: he became a translator and reviewer for the *Criterion* from the 1920s – and a member of the inner circle – even while continuing to work in the statistics division of the Ministry of Labour (where he was Chief of the Overseas Section) until retiring in 1951. See also *The Fourth Imagist: Selected Poems of F. S. Flint*, ed. Michael Copp (2007).

2–Flint wrote on 19 Feb.: 'I have been away in Nice for a month, and have only just recovered sufficient "equanimity" to reply to you . . . on my return.

'I read Frank [Morley]'s notes with great interest, and liked 'em. But I did want to have a kick at Keynes.

'Do I understand that you will publish the essay, with the mathematics, but without the Keynes part? If so, I could make it much more easy to understand with these simple diagrams.'

3–F. S. Flint, 'The Plain Man and the Economists', C. 17 (Oct. 1937), 1–18.

'[W]hat the hell, you want to run Flint for I dunno,' commented EP (19 Oct. 1937); 'looks like dhirty woik to me . . . There is too much REAL writing on the subject to take time out for dead heads. Is he trying to get a raise out of shitten Eden and the bank buggars or what??

'The MOTIVE back of the writing differentiates the man from the stinking frog's terd.'

TO *George Every*

TO *George Every*                                                      CC

23 February 1937                    [Faber & Faber Ltd]

My dear George,

It occurred to me afterwards that possibly you would not want the copies of *Murder in the Cathedral* immediately, and that if your production does not come off you would have had to pay me at half price for 9 copies that you did not want. So if they should be unused you can always return them to me and get your money back. I thought you might have a few students who would be glad to have a copy of a 5s. book for half a crown.

There is one point in your letter which I overlooked; that about the opening to Part II.[1] You will observe that the second edition of the play, which is what I sent you, starts with the Chorus as used in the London production. If you prefer to use the Introits, and they might be more suitable for your purpose, I will type out a copy for you which you could have repeated. It only amounts to about a couple of pages.

I am by no means oblivious of the fact that I owe you a letter for a long time past. I expect it will soon be possible, but last week I had my broadcast, and had to finish up my long article for John Baillie's symposium, and also had to write my own Commentary, and a contribution, for which Mairet has been begging, to the Reckitt–Tomlin dispute. I hope that you will find the last of these more or less to your liking. I have taken issue to some extent with Tomlin, but more importantly with the editor of *Blackfriars*, whose statement I have had to take more seriously.[2]

Yours ever,

[T. S. E.]

1 – Every asked, 28 Jan.: 'I had thought of asking you if we could have a look at the opening chorus of part II as used in London, or even at the London stage-directions, but Br. Edwin and others are rather keen in doing the printed opening of part II, with the Introits, and I think it would suit here.'

2 – Reckitt's article 'Envoi to the Crisis', *NEW*, 28 Jan. 1937, 307–9, was followed by E. W. F. Tomlin's 'Mr. Reckitt and the Crisis', *NEW*, 11 Feb, 351–3. Reckitt replied in *NEW*, 18 Feb, 378–9. These items form the basis of TSE's article – 'Mr Reckitt, Mr Tomlin, and the Crisis', *NEW* 10: 20 (25 Feb. 1937), 391–3; *CProse* 5, 449–56 – on their opposed views of the constitutional 'crisis' – King Edward VIII's abdication on 10 Dec. 1936 on account of his determination to marry Mrs Wallis Simpson (1896–1986), an American socialite twice married and in the midst of her second divorce. Edward VIII and Mrs Simpson were to marry on 3 May 1937. Tomlin and the editor of *Blackfriars* wrote in support of the king, Reckitt in opposition.

TSE remarked in his essay that Tomlin's 'indignation led him to attach too much importance to the feelings of the crowd . . . That the behaviour of any crowd means *something* I do not deny; but it requires interpretation . . . The Editor [the Dominican priest Victor White] of *Blackfriars* (whose January leader, "Catholics and the Crown", is the ablest exposition of

TO *Mary Butts*[1]                           TS BL/Mrs Camilla Bagg

23 February 1937                    *The Criterion*

Dear Miss Butts,[2]

I am returning your story 'Mappa Mundi' to you, with diffidence and
regret, as after several readings it does not seem to me quite successful

---

the point of view held by Mr Tomlin that I have seen) appears to believe that there was
concerted action [by the Press and Government against the monarchy]. He speaks of the
London Press on December 3rd as acting "with a uniformity in diversity that Dr Goebbels
might well envy" and contrasts with it "the obviously spontaneous and unconcerted reaction
of the Catholic press." *Blackfriars* is hardly fair . . . Is the accusation that the secular Press
(including the *Church Times*) received its instructions from the Government [of Stanley
Baldwin], directly or circuitously? . . .

'I would say furthermore, though I dislike saying it, that I do not believe that Mr Tomlin
has any better knowledge than I have, of what King Edward would have tried to do for
improving the condition of the people or righting the wrongs of the distressful areas. It seems
to me that Mr Tomlin does not everywhere keep distinct the notion of power of the Kingship
(which I think we should like to see enhanced) and the "patriot King" as an object of personal
devotion . . . But loyalty to the King is something that we can observe towards any occupant
of the Throne: the possibility of personal devotion is not altogether in our command.'

On the Abdication Crisis: 'No blame can attach to King Edward for forcing the issue, but
force it he apparently did . . . [S]urely the effect of abdication in 1937 or 1938 would have
been a more severe blow to the Kingship than abdication in 1936. In taking the step he did,
or "forcing the issue", King Edward is to be commended . . .

'I suggest that the idea of the Kingship is more fundamental, from a *Royalist* point of view,
than the idea of a "Patriot King" – a phrase which was given currency by an eighteenth-
century writer [the Tory politician Henry St John Bolingbroke, in 1738] whose notions
about the Kingship were not complicated by religious orthodoxy. I suggest that Mr Tomlin's
conception, like that of some of our Roman friends who hold similar views, might point
towards the identification of a Patriot King with a kind of Fascist King – with a conception
of the Monarchy in which the hereditary claimant to our allegiance should double the role
of *duce* or *Fuehrer*.'

For Tomlin's later reflections, see *T. S. Eliot: A Friendship*, 79–82, 86. 'Although Eliot
expressed some liking for Edward VIII as a man, he felt he lacked character. He also referred
to some presumed sexual oddity, which had made the unfortunate Prince lean more heavily
on the one woman, out of a number, who seemed able to cope with it. That Eliot tended to
be curious in such matters, others have noted, and they have sometimes inferred some oddity
in his own make-up. I rather felt it testified to the contrary.'

1–Mary Butts (1890–1937), writer, was married to the poet and publisher John Rodker
(1894–1955) from 1918 to 1926, and to the artist Gabriel Aitken/Atkin (1897–1937) from
1930 to 1934. She lived in France, 1925–30. Her works include *Speed the Plough and Other
Stories* (1923), *Ashe of Rings* (1925), *Imaginary Letters*, illustrated by Jean Cocteau (1928),
*The Macedonian* (1933), *Several Occasions* (1932). Butts remarked on 25 Dec. 1927: 'T. S.
Eliot, with his ear on some stops of english speech which have not been used before, the
only writer of my quality, dislikes me & my work, I think' (*The Journals of Mary Butts*, ed.
Nathalie Blondel [2002], 275). See further Nathalie Blondel, *Mary Butts: Scenes from the
Life* (1998); *A Sacred Quest: The Life and Writings of Mary Butts*, ed. C. Wagstaff (1995).
2–TSE had been tipped off by Charles Williams on 20 Jan. 1937: 'You know Mary Butts?
I had a letter from her the other day which seemed to me rather distressed because her review
work was falling off. You probably know this also, but I mention it privately.'

enough to justify publication by itself in the *Criterion*.[1] I should like however to take this opportunity of mentioning directly a proposal which I made to your agent Mr Leonard Moore some time ago, and to which I have once or twice reverted. We were very much interested indeed by a group of three short stories which you sent in some years ago, and I trust that Mr Moore has reminded you that we should take a very lively interest in any collection of your short stories sufficient to form a volume.[2] I should be interested to know if there is any likelihood in the near future of your having such a collection, assuming of course that you have not promised it to any other publisher.[3]

With best wishes,
Yours sincerely,
T. S. Eliot

1 – Butts, 'Mappa Mundi', in *With and Without Buttons and Other Stories* (Manchester, 1991), 188–201; *Complete Stories*, ed. Bruce R. McPherson (Kingston, New York, 2014).

2 – See TSE's F&F reader's report on Butts's stories, 9 July 1934: 'The three or four here are offered as samples of a projected volume of short stories. The first is a story of a house which was haunted by gloves (odd ones, and without buttons) turning up unexpectedly, and by an old petticoat with holes in it which tried to strangle a man. It doesnt end, it just stops. The second and longest is a rather skilful story, and rather horrible, about an American girl who fell in with some black magicians in Paris. (You see, Mary Butts is Cornish to begin with, and I believe she studied with Alistair Crowley in Sicily. *Without responsibility or prejudice.*) Anyway, this story is about as definite a libel on Gertrude Stein as you could get. She may have had others, such as Nathalie Barney or the Duchesse de Clermont-Tonnerre etc. in mind, but everything points straight to Gertrude as the patron of a gang of sexual maniacs and murderers. Then there is a story which [*sc.* with] a footnote evidently not intended for publication which the footnote says is a straight account of how they all got hysterics after Isadora (Duncan?) died. They certainly did. And then there is a story about a nice man from Boston who looked like a fishing schooner and his wife like a liner and he was in love with a woman who was dead (Isadora again?) and burst into tears in the garden but pulled himself together before his wife reappeared and this one was printed in the *London Mercury*. Mary Butts has some talent but if these stories are fair samples she does draw heavily on real people and events, and the one suggesting Gertrude is too strong. I think Gertrude would have a better chance with a jury than Crowley did. I think somebody else had better look at these however.'

3 – Butts died within a few days, on 5 Mar. 1937.

TO *Walter de la Mare*[1]                                    TS de la Mare Estate

23 February 1937                    *The Criterion*

My dear de la Mare,

I am more punctual in replying to your letter of 11 February than I usually am in dealing with manuscripts, but even so I owe you an apology for a delay which was due to a particular pressure of work throughout the last week.[2]

I have read *Shah Jehan* with much interest. I agree with you that it is something out of the way, and the verse is certainly very competent. It is obviously a piece of work to be taken seriously, but I cannot see my way to recommending my firm to publish it. The publication of books of verse by new poets is, as you will realize, something that we have to undertake in what I may call extreme moderation, and verse plays have to be regarded with still more caution than plain verse. If a verse play is to be produced, that makes all the difference in the world, and I always advise poets who want to write verse plays to write for the theatre first and consider publication only if they can get the plays staged successfully. But I am really rather doubtful of the possible stage success of this play. There is, it seems to me, too much talk and too little straightforward action. The elaborate apparatus of introduction and stage direction is also a deterrent.

With many regrets and all best wishes,

Yours ever,

T. S. Eliot

1–Walter de la Mare (1873–1956), poet, novelist and short-story writer, worked for the Statistics Department of the Anglo-American Oil Company, 1890–1908, before being freed to become a freelance writer by a £200 royal bounty negotiated by Henry Newbolt. He wrote many popular works: poetry including *The Listeners* (1912) and *Peacock Pie* (1913); novels including *Memoirs of a Midget* (1921); anthologies including *Come Hither* (1923). He was appointed CH, 1948; OM, 1953. See TSE's poem 'To Walter de la Mare'; Theresa Whistler, *Imagination of the Heart: The Life of Walter de la Mare* (1993).

2–'I am enclosing with this a play entitled "Shah Jehan" which will best speak for itself. It is the work of a friend of many years' standing, Morna Nicholas, with whom I have corresponded for many years, but whom I met for the first time only recently. She wishes to submit it to F.&F. for publication, and is particularly anxious that you will read it.

'"Shah Jehan", I am sure you will agree, is well out of the beaten track, in theme, conception and technique. The only difficulty is that Mrs Nicholas is very anxious to have a decision as soon as possible. I realise how desperately busy you must be, and especially just now. Could you possibly let her have your decision fairly soon?'

Morna (Nicholas) Stuart (b. 1905), playwright and novelist, a graduate of St Anne's College, Oxford, was a teacher and BBC scriptwriter, 1937–62. Works include *Till She Stoop* (1935) and *Traitor's Gate* (a play about Thomas More, 1939).

## TO *John Baillie*[1] CC

23 February 1937          [Faber & Faber Ltd]

Dear Professor Baillie,

Thank you for your letter of the 22nd.[2] It is a relief to hear that in a general way you approve of my paper. I shall be grateful for any suggestions you care to mark on it, and hope that I may be able to improve it slightly in proof.

Perhaps in your introduction you will say a word as to the purpose and place of my essay in the collection, as otherwise I feel slightly embarrassed at appearing in such learned company.

Yours very sincerely,<br>[T. S. Eliot]

## TO *Frederick May Eliot*[3] CC

24 February 1937          [Faber & Faber Ltd]

My dear Frederick,

Thank you very much for your letter of the 7th February.[4] You veil your supposed offence in such neat and periphrastic compliments that it

---

1 – The Very Revd John Baillie (1886–1960): Scottish theologian; minister of the Church of England; taught at Edinburgh University, 1934–59.

2 – 'I will frankly confess that I read it with greater interest than any of the other contributions. This, however, is partly because the systematic stuff of so many of the other essays is so familiar to me . . .

'My judgment would be that your essay should be printed first as number "I", *without* being headed "Introduction". I am expected to contribute a kind of introductory preface. I do not *want* to do this, but Oldham and Martin think it necessary.'

3 – The Revd Frederick May Eliot (1889–1958), educated at Harvard Divinity School (graduating *summa cum laude* in 1911), was Minister of Unity Church, St Paul, Minnesota, 1917–37; President of the American Unitarian Association, 1937–58. He married in 1915 Elizabeth Berkeley Lee. Works include *Fundamentals of Unitarian Faith* (1927) and *Toward Belief in God* (1929). See too *Frederick May Eliot: An Anthology*, ed. Alfred P. Stiernotte (1959); and John Kielty, 'Frederick May Eliot', *The Inquirer*, 26 Mar. 1960, 489: 'It is rare that in one man are found the qualities of a good executive officer ably directing the day-to-day business of a religious body; the qualities of a mystic with a deep philosophic mind; and those pastoral qualities that reveal a deep concern for men, women and children as persons of infinite worth. Rare indeed that one man should possess all-round qualities to such a high degree.'

4 – Such was Frederick's enthusiasm for *MiC* that he had ventured to speak about it in public, twice – 'I hope you will reserve judgment until I can tell you about it!' He was to visit England in Aug., for an Oxford conference of 'liberal religionists', and hoped to be able to see TSE.

is quite impossible for me to divine what it was. But in any case I assure you of my forgiveness. I had a very pleasant lunch with Martha[1] and Miss Dunham just before they returned to America, and was able to introduce them to a detective story which they enjoyed. It is good news to hear that you will be in England next August. I am myself going to attend a religious conference in Oxford in July (it seems to be a family habit), but the place will no doubt be swept and garnished[2] and ready for your incursion in August.

It is rather a coincidence that you should have written to me, because I had been meaning to write to you ever since the news reached me that the smoke had finally risen from the chimney on Beacon Hill, and the announcement made that you were to wear the triple crown. I congratulate the American Unitarian Association on having made the inevitable choice, and am glad to think that the family retain their proud position of being the Borgias of Unitarianism. I am also glad to think that it means that I am more likely to see you on my next visit to Boston. Meanwhile I look forward to seeing you in August, and hope that Elizabeth and the children will be coming with you.

Ever yours affectionately,
[Tom]


TO *Hugh Gordon Porteus*                                    TS Beinecke

23 February 1937                      *The Criterion*

Dear Porteus,

Thank you for your letter of the 22nd.[3] I am as a matter of fact engaged this evening, and I really don't know that the prospect of failing to hear

---

1 – Martha May Eliot (1898–1979), paediatrician and expert on children's health. A graduate of Radcliffe College and Johns Hopkins School of Medicine, she was a founder of the World Health Organization and UNICEF, and fourth head of the Children's Bureau. She taught at the Harvard School of Public Health, headed the Massachusetts Committee on Children and Youth, and conducted pioneering research on rickets.

2 – Luke 11: 25: 'And when he cometh, he findeth it swept and garnished.' Matthew 12: 44: 'Then he saith, I will return into my house from whence I came out; and when he is come, he findeth it empty, swept, and garnished.'

3 – 'The enclosed invitation [not traced] was forwarded to me by Messrs Faber a few days ago with a request from a friend of mine, Mr Gleb Struve, that I should pass it on to you. It arrived in my absence on a long week-end. I'm sorry the notice is so short. Possibly you are already engaged tomorrow evening: and you might have other reasons for not accepting . . .

'Struve is a pleasant intelligent non-political Russian: he wrote a good book on Russian Literature which you may know. He . . . is a little diffident about this business. Vladimir

a Russian poet read English translations of his works depresses me very much.

I have sent you a number of odds and ends of periodicals to look over. So far as I can see from our list the only ones we appear to exchange with are the *Adelphi, Dublin Review*, and the *Green Quarterly*. But I think that we ought to make sure of exchanges with any that you would like to see regularly. So I will wait until I get your full list, and please we should be glad to have the addresses as well as the names where possible.

I shall be glad to see you again soon, say the second week in March. I am free at present except on Monday evening, the 8th, and Wednesday the 10th.

I had already thought of you for *Polite Essays*, and am sending you a copy for review. I think it makes quite a lively and good book, and am really more pleased at producing it than *Make it New*.[1]

Yours ever,

T. S. E.

---

Sirin is a very young Parisian–Russian poet, some of whose works have been translated into French and German. The next number of the Nouvelle Rev. Française will print his paper on "Le vrai et le vraisemblable'. . . I regard Struve as a trustworthy person, or I should not waste your time with this. If you felt adventurous tomorrow, – (You would be welcome. It is a gamble!)'

1 – 'If *Polite Essays* are [sic] available for review in the Criterion, I should enjoy writing them up (and/or down).

EP's *Polite Essays*, published in Feb. 1937, carried this blurb (almost certainly by TSE): 'This may be described as a companion volume to *Make It New*, with the important difference that it is priced at 7s. 6d. instead of 12s. 6d. in order to make it accessible to a much larger public. Also, the former volume consisted primarily of erudite studies in the classical literature of several languages: its successor is more concerned with contemporary problems. It contains the essays on Housman, Binyon and Monro, which appeared in *The Criterion*; studies of the problems of contemporary poetry and modern education, and other matters of literary actuality. But just as Mr Pound cannot deal with questions of literary history without considering their present application, so his considerations of the present are based upon his knowledge and judgments of the past. In this volume, for instance, he has preserved his essential observations upon the poetry of Dante. The two books together are sufficient to justify the reputation enjoyed by Mr Pound among the discerning – of having been the most fructifying influence upon literary criticism of his time.'

The volume included too the essay 'Mr Eliot's Solid Merit', 98–105, in which EP said (p. 98) he was reminded 'of the days when the *Quarterly* with its usual whatever-it-is employed a certain [Arthur] Waugh to denounce Eliot's best poems [Oct. 1916] as the work of a "drunken helot", possibly hunting for something approaching a pun but at any rate showing that kind of flair and literary sensibility (*à rebours*) which have characterized the Albemarle Street congeries from its inception and will probably last as long as cabbage emits an odour when boiling.

'If Mr Eliot weren't head and shoulders above the rank of the organized pifflers, and if he didn't amply deserve his position as recognized head of English literary criticism I would not be wasting time, typing-ribbon and postage, to discuss his limitations at all.'

(See too EP, 'Drunken Helots and Mr Eliot', *The Egoist*, June 1917, 72–3.)

# TO *Charles Williams*

25 February 1937                    [Faber & Faber Ltd]

My dear Williams,

My colleague Frank Morley, whom I think you have never met, is very keen about *Descent into Hell*, and I should like to arrange a meeting.[1] We

1 – Williams had arranged in Jan. for his agent Higham to send the TS of *Descent into Hell* to TSE. CW explained in a letter, 20 Jan.: 'Collins, after having (he says) glowing reports from certain readers had twilight reports on the possibilities of sales. So they turned it down, as I always suspected they might. I send it therefore, partly to you because you asked about it, and as much to Faber & Faber as you think tolerable. There is one small point in it which a little displeases me, but I am quite certain that I shall not be able to do anything better with it for years yet and I have no intention of revising it any more. I want to do other things, and the chance of making the incredibly necessary money out of this won't be at all heightened by revising it indefinitely.

'You will forgive as a publisher what you invited as a man – the intrusion of yet another manuscript on your invaded time.'

TSE's reader's report on *Descent into Hell*, 25 Jan. 1937: 'To criticise this book properly one should first read Williams's three other supernatural thrillers ("War in Heaven", "The Place of the Lion" and "The Greater Trumps") first. All published by Gollancz. But I should like somebody to read this book without having read the others, and without having read this report.

'Williams has a real gift for this kind of fiction. He can get a thrill out of the Problem of Evil as nobody else can. But the success of this kind of story depends upon a proper balance between the plot and the myth and theology. Most readers are not so interested in the Devil as Williams is; and to be interested they have to have that remarkable personality presented in a more simplified way. In this book one feels that Williams is writing too much to please himself. The action is too crowded, and our attention is taken from one character's situation to another. The plot is a good enough one: the production of a new poetic drama (a great one, so the author must be either Williams or myself, I can't make out which, perhaps both; anyway he is a very wise and fine character named Stanhope and he is what would be the local squire except that the place has become a London suburb) by a local amateur society. Williams knows all about that, and does it very well. But the hanged labourer doesn't help very much and one gets tired of his suicide at the very beginning. I think that with a good deal of work Williams might make this into a first-rate novel. But I don't think he wants to work at it any more at present.'

TSE's blurb for *Descent into Hell* (Faber Catalogue July–Dec. 1937, 7): 'Those who have read Mr Williams's earlier novels – *War in Heaven*, *Many Dimensions*, and the others – will not want to be told anything about *Descent into Hell* except that it is one of his best. Those who do not know the author's work will find that when they have read this novel, they will wait impatiently for a new one. To them we explain that Mr Williams is the best living writer of the thriller with a supernatural element. His novels can be read for pure excitement; beyond that, readers will find as much as they are capable of finding. There is also comedy of manners, and acute analysis of human relationships, and, finally, exploration of abysses of beauty and horror beyond the borders of the material world. This novel, as the title may suggest, is not recommended reading for hypersensitive people alone at night in an empty house.'

TSE would recall, after Williams's death: 'With all his radiant benevolence, there were depths to his nature beyond my plumbing. In *Descent into Hell*, for instance, to my mind

want to talk about that book, as well as about things in general. He tells me that he has no free time for lunch until after the 18th of March. Are you free for lunch on the 19th? If not, let me know what other days you have that week and I will try to get him to put off some other engagement. Monday the 15th might be possible. Wednesday we are never free, as we meet in committee. I don't want to make it the following week if I can help it, because I try to make no engagements during Holy Week.

Yours ever,

[T. S. Eliot]

## TO *John Dover Wilson*      TS National Library of Scotland

26 February 1937      *The Criterion*

My dear Dover Wilson,

Thank you for your letter of the 23rd.[1] So far as I can see Thursday 21 October would be as good a date as any, and if I come then I should be delighted to stay over the weekend. I wanted to put it rather late in the month to be on the safe side in case I have to go to America in September, but I do not think I shall have to go, and I shall not go unless I have to.

Thank you for your perseverance in the matter of the *Aenead*.[2] In making investigations I should be glad also if you could give me your own opinion, and also that of any Scots with whom you discuss the matter, as to the extent and intensity of interest in such an edition that we might expect in Scotland. I do feel that Scots ought to support any attempt to present in scholarly modern editions their own classics. We should not expect really to make money with such a book, judging from our previous experience with Dunbar, but I think we ought, if there is any intelligent interest in literature, to be able to count upon not losing money. I will remind you again that I am speaking primarily on behalf of the Porpoise Press of Edinburgh, and only secondarily on behalf of Faber and Faber of London.

At the same time I should like to place a further burden upon you, and ask your opinion – and again if possible that of anyone you care to

the most impressive of his novels (all of which fascinate me) there is an understanding of evil and of moral collapse which makes me shudder.'

1 – Dover Wilson, 23 Feb.: 'I should guess that Thursday Oct 21 would be a good date (from our side) for your first lecture. That would give you the chance of staying over the weekend.'

2 – 'I have been trying to sound one or two people (without committing you) on the matter of Gavin Douglas's *Aenead* and academic correspondents are so casual! I have not got a name for you yet, but I am going to try one or two others.'

consult – about the possible interest in a new edition of the *Kingis Quhair*. I have had an enquiry about that too, from someone who says that the two English editions are out of print, and that an American edition is inaccurate.

Yours ever sincerely,
T. S. Eliot

## TO *E. W. F. Tomlin*

1 March 1937                                *The Criterion*

Dear Tomlin,

Thank you for your letter of the 27th.[1] I had feared that I might find you in total disagreement with the position which I took up, and I am gratified that you are not. It seemed to me that to a superficial examination I might be appearing as what I am not particularly anxious to be – an apologist for the Baldwin Government.

You must not think that you had any responsibility for driving me to write. I think that Mairet will be quite willing to shoulder the whole of that burden.

Please understand that I am as apprehensive as you are about the mendacity of the Press: not that I attach great importance to *that* incident in itself, but that I think it one piece of evidence amongst many, of something which you justly suggest is more dangerous than 'corruption'. I had rather also consider my general dissatisfaction with the attitude of the Church in a larger frame of reference than that of the *NEW* discussion.

1 – 'I should like to thank you for your article in the "New English Weekly", from which I have derived considerable benefit . . .

'I confess I find your arguments more cogent than some of those advanced to me by Brother George Every, though there are a number of vital points upon which you are naturally in agreement with him. From a personal point of view, your comment upon my reactions to the Palace crowd, and your statement that my position is "idealist" and "undemocratic", interested me most – so much that I must reserve any observations on these topics to some future discussion. I am a little surprised and even embarrassed to find myself grouped with the "Blackfriars" circle, though I certainly found myself very much in sympathy with Father D'Arcy's attitude . . .

'Perhaps I take a somewhat too serious attitude to the whole affair, but I was struck by the difference between the attitude taken up by a paper like "The Daily Telegraph" during the crisis and its gloating at the "progressiveness" of the Church during the debate on divorce. I, too, took a long while to make up my mind (if it is made up) and I certainly wasn't influenced by the *views* of the Palace crowd, merely on the misrepresentation of these views, good or bad . . . But for the moment I must again say how grateful I am for what you have written. Perhaps when you feel able to take a holiday, you will pay us a visit here.'

520    TSE at forty-eight

What are you doing at Merstham?[1] Do you come up daily to the Sloane School? If so, what days of the week are possible for you for lunch, or if lunch is impossible, could you ever stay up and dine?

I told you that I should like to have a contribution for the June number, but now it looks as if I would much rather have it for October. Owing to certain complications and misunderstandings I am printing three whole cantos of Ezra Pound's in the April number, and that has meant shoving forward into June several things which I had hoped to print sooner. In that event, is there anything you would like to review for June? I have, by the way, a small book on the Crown by Erskine of Marr, but it looks popular and rubbishy, and merely part of the expected Coronation litter.

Yours ever sincerely,<br>T. S. Eliot

TO *George Every*           TS Sarah Hamilton

St David [1 March] 1937        *The Criterion*

Dear George,

Having just had two days in bed with a cold, I have read your poems again several times, and have read the new ones. I have a feeling that you know pretty well what you are doing, and do not need to be told much about them. I had read the poems before I had read the letters accompanying them,[2] and I find that our judgements of their relative merits are very much the same.[3] 'Radices' is certainly the best of the new ones, and the only one that is fit to go with the best of the previous, though 'King Charles's Walk' is very agreeable and quite satisfactory. I feel that 'Vivat' tries to cover too wide an idea – though I am not quite sure about this: the end seems too weighty for the beginning, or the transition is not too clear to me. 'Plot for a Novel' seems to me to be an extended epigram, which, if it can't be packed into one stanza, can't be done at all. 'Masks' I am not quite sure about, but I think that from the beginning of Part II to the end is very good indeed; Part I doesn't seem to me quite digested. I put 'Radices' and 'O Sapientia' the highest. 'Bio-Chemistry' doesn't seem to me ever to get quite to the point – I mean the kind of point that *poetry*

---

1 – Tomlin was living at Wychwood House, Merstham, a village in Surrey.
2 – Not found.
3 – Every wrote in a postscript, 25 Feb.: 'On second thoughts I think if you are going to mull over O Sapientia, Biochemistry and Masks soon you had better have those with you as well. Radices is the best . . . I do not want to be shot for the politics of Vivat!'

has to get to, the point at which thinking stops and something is just apprehended or contemplated.

The two poems I like best seem to me certainly to be a great deal more assured than anything you have done before – they are positively *there* and finished. There is incidentally a purgation or assimilation (the two processes go on together of course) of influences which I am very glad to see; you are much more clearly emergent as yourself alone.

I enclose the *NEW* pages with Reckitt's article, Tomlin's reply, and Reckitt's letter, which brings the discussion up to my entrance; and I will send you a copy of mine as soon as I get some more – both of my copies are out on loan. I have heard that Tomlin and Cullis are distressed by my contribution.

I will try to get Turnell's book and look at it (for French) before sending to you.[1]

Affectionately,
T. S.

## TO *Gerald Graham*

2 March 1937                                    *The Criterion*

Dear Graham,

I was very glad to get your letter of the 14th.[2] It seems a very long time since I was in touch with you, and I had often thought of you at Queen's College. I am very glad that at last your position at Queen's is fairly secure, even if badly paid. I hope however that you will advance to something more distinguished after your book has been published and earned the reputation which it deserves.

I should think that either Harvard or Cambridge ought to be glad to publish your book.[3] Both of them produce quite enough rubbish, especially

---

1–Every, 24 Feb.: 'Turnell (of *Colosseum*) threatened me with an Essay in Order called *Poetry and Unbelief*. It very possibly hasn't appeared, but if it has, I think I might find it a profitable subject to discuss in the Criterion, unless you have something else in mind for me. Or someone else in mind for the book. But if he expatiates on French literature it had better go elsewhere.'

2–'Queen's [Kingston, Ontario] have decided (about a week ago) to keep a fourth man in the History Department. I am as the Vice-Principal put it a Luxury appointment, and in a sense they have made a job for me, – a procedure which would be highly gratifying to me were it not for the fact that a Luxury appointment means a salary and status which in no way provides for luxury of living. But it is a great joy to be settled.'

3–'I finally heard from [S. C.] Roberts of the Cambridge Press. Apparently they are well stocked with learned Mss. at the moment, and in any case, refuse to consider the book until

---

Harvard, and they ought to be glad to get such a good book as yours. I don't know what are the international rules of these University presses, but I don't see why a book should not be published by the Harvard Press in America and the Oxford or Cambridge Press here. The catch about publishing books with American University presses is that the Oxford Press is the agent for the best of them, and the Oxford Press does nothing to advertise them or make them known in this country. I don't see how it could, as it represents so many, but it is a pity.

I hope to see you both when you are next in England. Please give my kindest regards to your wife, and join with them my best wishes for your son.[1]

Yours ever,<br>T. S. Eliot

## TO *Mary Butts*  TS Texas

2 March 1937  [Faber & Faber Ltd]

Dear Miss Butts,

Thank you for your letter of the 26th.[2] I have looked up the previous submissions of any of your manuscripts, and find that we have not had anything of yours since 20 July 1934. These were the stories – three of them I think – to which I referred in my previous letter. You speak as if there must be considerably more than that. We should certainly be glad to see the lot of them, and I hope that there are enough for a normal sized book.

Yours sincerely,<br>[T. S. Eliot]

---

it is completed. Under the circumstances, I shall probably submit it to Harvard this coming winter.'

1 – 'Emily joined me on December 31st, and seems very much better. She says there is no reason why she should ever be ill again. I am beginning to have a new respect for Psycho-analysis . . . The infant John flourishes and gives me great joy.'

2 – 'I have just heard from Moore, my agent, a letter [*sic*] in which he said that he, recently – say eighteen months ago at most, or less, sent you my stories & you refused them.

'Certainly he said nothing to me about it.

'If that is so, do you wish to see them again? Largely reprinted from the old *Life & Letters*, one more recent, from *The Cornhill*, & another from *The Mercury*.'

## TO *Charles Madge*                                    CC

4 March 1937                          [Faber & Faber Ltd]

Dear Madge,

My committee do not like *Poets and Descriptions* [*sic*].[1] I see the point
of the title myself, and it is all right for anybody who has read the book,
but unfortunately titles have to be chosen for the benefit of people who
have not yet read the books. They want to call the book *Poems* simply.
Is there any objection to this? I don't think you have ever published any
book with this title have you? If you don't object, we shall go ahead with
it.[2]

Yours sincerely,
[T. S. Eliot]

P.S. We have had another idea of a possible book which I should like
to talk to you about, but I imagine it is no use trying to interest you in
anything when your hands are so full with the observation work.


## TO *Ada Sheffield*                                    CC

9 March 1937                          [No address given]

Dear Ada,

This is to tell you that I am giving an introduction to you to a young
man named Charles Siepmann, who in spite of his name is English, and is
an official of the British Broadcasting Corporation. He has been asked to
America for three months by the Rockefeller Foundation, to investigate
the situation of regional broadcasting. He is a serious person, whose
political sympathies are rather of the left, and I think he would like to
meet the sort of people in the various places to whom you could introduce
him; that is if you are satisfied with him when you see him. He is not the
sort of person who would be particularly interested in the Wolcotts or the
Lambs.[3]

---

1 – Madge wrote on 1 Mar.: 'Instead of DELUSIONS, would POEMS AND DESCRIPTIONS
be a better title for my book of poems?
    'I prefer it myself to HOURS OF THE PLANETS.'
2 – *The Disappearing Castle* (1937), as the volume was ultimately called, carried this spare
blurb by TSE: 'This is the first volume of Charles Madge's verse to appear. His work is well
known to readers of the younger literary periodicals, and is represented both in Mr Yeats's
and in Mr Michael Roberts's collections. His own selection of his poems up to date will be
received with eager curiosity.'
3 – Roger and Barbara Wolcott. Aimée and Rosamund Lamb.

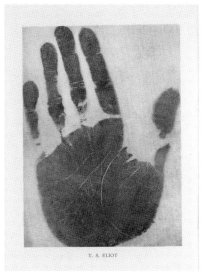

TSE reading from his poetry at
Shakespeare & Company,
Paris, 1936.

Eliot's handprint, taken by
Charlotte Wolff, published in her
*Studies in Hand-Reading*, 1936.

TSE on the porch at Randolph,
New Hampshire, 1936.
Photograph by Henry Eliot.

TSE and Emily Hale
at Woods Hole, Massachusetts,
September 1936.

Paul Elmer More, 1937.

Elizabeth Bowen, 25 July 1939.

TSE with the son of Count
Michael de la Bédoyère.
Photograph accompanying a
review by G. M. Turnell in the
*Catholic Herald*, 10 July 1936.

Emily Hale with her dog Boerre,
1939.

Djuna Barnes, November 1939.

Brother George Every at the
Society of the Sacred Mission,
Kelham, 1937–8.

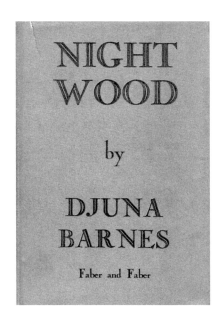

Djuna Barnes, *Nightwood*,
London: Faber & Faber, 1936.

Frontispiece illustration by David
Jones for *In Parenthesis*, London:
Faber & Faber, 1937.

Alan Pringle handing over the proofs of the first part
of *Finnegans Wake* to TSE, April/May 1937.

Henry Miller, Paris, *c.* 1933.

Anaïs Nin, Paris, 3 April 1934.

Frank Morley, Geoffrey Faber and W. J. Crawley at the Faber offices,
September 1936.

Geoffrey Faber, reading a
newspaper, 1930s.

Enid Faber, seated, 1937–8.

TSE with Tom Faber
and the new telescope
at Tyglyn Aeron, Ciliau Aeron,
August 1938.

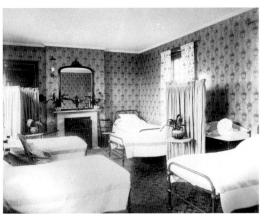

Northumberland
House in Finsbury
Park, North London,
exterior and interior.

Vivien Eliot, a studio portrait she
sent to Theresa and Henry Eliot in
December 1935.

TSE with the Camões Prize jury, in Lisbon, including
Massimo Bontempelli (*second left*), José Silva Dias (*third*),
Jacques de Lacretelle (*fifth*), José Caeiro da Mata (*sixth*),
Robert de Traz (*seventh*) and António Ferro (*right*), 29 April 1938.

TSE addresses the assembly on Speech Day,
Truro School, 3 June 1938.

Wyndham Lewis with his rejected portrait of TSE,
at the Royal Academy, London, 21 April 1938.

Please tell Sheff[1] that I am very grateful to him for all his trouble and correspondence on behalf of Tereshchenko.[2] The Tereshchenko problem remains acute. He came in to see me a few days ago in such a state of mind that I was completely exhausted by him. Being a thoroughly unpractical Russian, he had formed a notion of getting enough money somehow to go to America in the spring for six weeks and look about for jobs. But I warned him that this would involve him in considerable travelling expenses, and that furthermore I doubted whether, going in that way – and as I did not add, in his present state of mind – he would have sufficient prestige. He is going to find out for himself about the necessary conditions for applying to the Rockefeller Foundation, and to something called the American University Union of Europe, but I should be glad for any information from Sheff that I can pass on to him. He mentioned, by the way, in case Sheff can make any use of the information, that he had sent a copy of his book to one Professor William Clark Trow, at the University of Michigan, and received a polite acknowledgement. He also says that he knows a specialist in his own subject, Professor William Stern, at Duke University, North Carolina, and he has a friend at Harvard named H. F. Schwarz,[3] a lecturer in a rather minor position.

[no valediction]

[Tom]

## TO *Henry Eliot*                                             cc

9 March 1937                          [*The Criterion*]

My dear Henry,

I have two rather impersonal matters to mention. First of all, I shall be sending off to you for your collection at Eliot House a batch of old copies of the *Egoist*, which turned up the other day during a house-cleaning of Morley's room – which used to be my room. It is not quite complete, but it contains most of the issues during the period while I was assistant editor, and I think that you will find some things, of no importance in

---

1 – Alfred Dwight ('Sheff') Sheffield (1871–1961), husband of TSE's eldest sister Ada (1869–1943), taught English at University School, Cleveland, Ohio, and was an English instructor, later Professor, of Group Work at Wellesley College.

2 – In Feb. 1937, 'Sheff' had written on behalf of Tereshchenko to the Director of the Institute of Human Relations at Yale University, to the Yale Department of Psychology, and to R. M. Elliott, Chair, Department of Psychology, University of Minnesota (who did express interest).

3 – Author of *The Imperial Privy Council in the Seventeenth Century* (1943).

themselves, which you have never seen. Any contributions signed Apterix [*sic*] are by myself.[1] Please let me know if you don't receive the parcel within say a week of this letter, because I have a duplicate set in reserve, and if you receive the first lot I will give the duplicates to a friend here.

The second point is that I am giving a letter of introduction to you to a man named Charles Siepmann, who is leaving for America in a week or two. In spite of his name he is in all appearance a perfectly English person, and was educated at Rugby and Oxford. I think his father or grandfather was German. Siepmann is an extremely serious, not to say solemn, young man, of about 36, who has been in the British Broadcasting Corporation longer than anyone I have ever heard of except Sir John Reith himself. He is coming to America at the expense of the Rockefeller Foundation, who want him to investigate regional broadcasting in the U.S.A. and make a report on it comparing the American system with that here. The B.B.C. are lending him for about three months. But he is also anxious to meet people worth talking to, and find out as much about America as he can. He is not anxious to meet wealthy or fashionable people, although of course if he is to understand America he ought to see something of them too. He is a very different kettle of fish from the last man I recommended to you, and his political sympathies are rather liberal and left. He is a very nice fellow, although somewhat humourless. I shall give him an introduction to Ada and Sheff also. I shall suggest to him that he should write to you when he reaches New York, and let you know where else he is going besides Boston. He will certainly go to Chicago, and I advised him to go to Saint Paul as well as to California, and New Orleans, Richmond and Charleston as well. I should think he might like to meet Horace Kallen,[2] and perhaps the Lawrence Smiths. People like Bobby Strauss he will probably meet in the way of business.

Affectionately,
[Tom]

---

1 – 'Verse Pleasant and Unpleasant' – review of *Georgian Poetry, 1916–1917*, ed. E. Marsh, and *Wheels, A Second Cycle* – *Egoist* 5: 3 (Mar. 1918), 43–4; 'Professional, or . . .', *Egoist* 5: 4 (Apr. 1918), 61; 'Observations' [signed. T. S. Apteryx], *Egoist* 5: 5 (May 1918), 69–70.
2 – Horace Kallen, philosopher: see letter of 6 Dec. 1938, below.

9 March 1937                    Faber & Faber Ltd

Dear Mr Corrie,

I am enclosing herewith a list of the poems which I have selected for the volume.[2] I should like to say at once that I feel that it is presumptuous to attempt to make a selection from the work of another poet who is still alive, although it is true that I have performed the same office before, and I think not unsuccessfully, for two other poets, Ezra Pound and Marianne Moore. But I am in any case submitting this list for your consideration and approval, as we shall not let the printers start on the book until we have your confirmation. I therefore return herewith all of the poems which have been omitted.

Of course any selection like this from a considerable number of poems is likely to appear to another person slightly capricious, and indeed it is possible that one might oneself make a somewhat different choice in six months' time. I can only say that I have given a good deal of time to it, and gone over all the poems carefully. According to the terms of my commission the reduction, you will remember, is for the purpose of making a book small enough to sell at the best price, so that my choice is by no means an absolute one, but merely guided by the exigencies of the situation.

I should like particularly to call your attention to one bold act on my part, which you may not approve. I read the poem 'Urvasi' a number of

1–Joe Corrie (1894–1968), Scottish miner (he went down the pit at fourteen), poet and playwright who wrote in the Scottish vernacular. Works include the plays *In Time O' Strife* (1926), *Martha* (1935), and *And So To War* (1936); and *The Image O' God* (poems, 1937).
2–FVM had written to Corrie, 23 Dec. 1936: 'I am now able to write about the Poems and to say that we should be glad to publish them in the spring, under the Porpoise Press imprint, if you will allow us to suggest cutting out a few of them so as to make the length suitable for publication at 3/6. I should like to make use of Mr Eliot's advice as to the proposed cuts; and will do so just as soon as possible after Christmas and write again.' Corrie replied, 28 Dec.: 'If Mr Eliot agrees to do this I leave him with a free hand.'
*The Image o' God and other poems* (a pamphlet of the same title had appeared in 1927) was published by the Porpoise Press (1937), with this blurb – most probably by TSE – 'The forceful genius of Joe Corrie, ex-miner from Fife, is well known to all who follow the most vigorous expression of modern Scotland, the drama. This volume of his poems has been published in response to frequent urgings, for in the revival of Scottish poetry Corrie has taken an assured place as a genuine poet. His verse is tender and bitter, with a proper Scots twist to the tail of it. Not since Burns has the voice of Scotland spoken with such authentic lyric note.'

times at intervals, and always came to the same conclusion – that it is more effective if the second page is omitted. I do not mean that I think the second page inferior; only sometimes one has to sacrifice in a poem lines and whole pages equally good in themselves for the sake of making the poem a whole. I find the first page complete in itself, and quite fascinating. I hope you will do more in this kind of rhythm. But if you are convinced that the poem needs the rest of it – and you ought to be the best judge – please countermand my order. In any case, however, will you please indicate yourself one or two more poems which you would be willing to omit if the volume proves to run a page or two longer than the 64 pages estimated for?

I hope that you will be able to let me have your final verdict quickly, as of course we can do nothing further until we hear from you. In closing I should like to say that I hope there will be many readers to enjoy your poems as much as I have enjoyed them myself. If you feel that the *order* should be different in the abridged book, please send a revised Table of Contents.

Yours sincerely,
T. S. Eliot

Enclosures: List of Contents; rejected poems.

## TO *Elizabeth Bowen* CC

9 March 1937 [Faber & Faber Ltd]

Dear Mrs Cameron,

I understand that we are getting on gradually with the inevitably slow negotiations about the prices of the stories in your list, so that it is now time for me to bring up a question which I should have mentioned the other evening had there been occasion for any private and professional conversation. At the beginning of your introduction (of which I think we have no other criticism to make) you say that the short story in England is 'the child of this century'. It struck us that this statement needs qualification. As it stands it immediately makes the reader rack his brains to think of all the important short stories – and there are a good many – which were written in the 19th century. Is it not necessary to say 'the short story in its contemporary form', and then, somewhere near the beginning, indicate the difference at the back of your mind between the modern short story and its predecessors or archetypes? Anyway, I shall be very interested to know what your reply will be.[1]

Yours sincerely,
[T. S. Eliot]

## TO *Richard Sheppard*[2]                                        CC

9 March 1937                          [Faber & Faber Ltd]

Dear Canon Sheppard,

Thank you for your kind note of the 3rd.[3] I should be very glad indeed to lunch and have a talk with you, but I have had to make another appointment for Tuesday 16th. Perhaps when we meet again on Wednesday evening we could discuss possible dates.

With best wishes,
Yours sincerely,
[T. S. Eliot]

## TO *Daniel Starch*[4]                                          CC

11 March 1937                         [Faber & Faber Ltd]

My dear Mr Starch,

I have your letter of February 24th, and regret that I am unable to give you much help in your project, because it is not a kind of undertaking which I can really approve.[5] This sort of attempt to make a selection of the world's greatest books was started, or at least given standing, by

---

1–Bowen replied on 11 Mar.: 'I note the point you make, or suggest, about the early paragraphs of my preface for the Short Story collection, and I will certainly go through my carbon copy of the preface and revise these on the lines you suggest.'

2–Richard 'Dick' Sheppard (1880–1937), vicar of St Martin-in-the-Fields, London, 1914–26; Dean of Canterbury, 1929–31; foremost pacifist: author of *We say "No": the plain man's guide to pacifism* (1935); and organiser of the Peace Pledge Union, 1936.

3 – 'I lacked courage yesterday to tell you how much I should like to see you if you had time to see me. I know you have to lunch with authors most days but can you lunch with one whose literary style is terrible at 1.15 on March 16th here? Ivor Nicholson is coming but no one else.'

4–Daniel Starch (1883–1979): American psychologist and pioneer of market research.

5–Starch was approaching a hundred 'distinguished persons' to help him 'construct a list of the world's greatest books . . . Your own selection will, of course, be kept confidential and will be used only in combination with others. I hope to use the results in a book on Educational Psychology which I am writing.'

the late Charles W. Eliot of Harvard, whose ideas on this subject seem to me as misguided as most of his educational theories. I do not believe that there is any one selection of great books which can be recommended for everybody, and I think it is misleading the half-educated public if one allows them to believe that they will be educated, or as it is said, 'cultured', if they have got through a certain prescribed course of reading.

I cannot help mentioning, however, that there are certain authors who seem to me definitely to deserve no place on your list; namely, Henry Adams, Mary Baker Eddy, Albert Einstein, Richard Dana, and O. W. Holmes.[1] I think that Henry James is very inadequately represented by *Portrait of a Lady*, and I consider that if Milton and Shakespeare are to be included they ought to be included entire. I object to Thomas Mann on the ground that he is a contemporary, and contemporary values in literature are never certain. There are several other contemporaries who have as good or better right to be represented as Mann. I also regret that you have not included any of the works of Saint John of the Cross.

Yours faithfully,
[T. S. Eliot]

## TO *Angus Macdonald* CC

12 March 1937 [Faber & Faber Ltd]

My dear Sir,

I am following up my letter to you of 26 February. As you have expressed interest in a new edition of THE KINGIS QUHAIR, you could be of help to us in finding out the present position of previous editions. From one or two enquiries that I have made the project seems well worth following up. What is desirable to know is whether the edition of the Scottish Text Society (1911) is kept in print, and also whether the edition of Alexander Lawson (A. & C. Black 1910) is still in print. Such enquiries would come more fittingly from someone like yourself than they would from me. I believe that for information about the Scottish Text Society texts one should apply to the Secretary, Dr R. F. Patterson (Graham's Dyke, Bearsden, Dumbartonshire). While I understand that these editions are both out of date, and that the latter is extremely bulky, the project of

1 – Starch's large provisional list included Henry Adams, *Education of Henry Adams*; Mary Baker Eddy, *Science and Health*; Albert Einstein, *Papers on Relativity*; Richard Dana, *Two Years Before the Mast*; and O. W. Holmes, *The Autocrat of the Breakfast Table*.

a new edition would be much more attractive if we were sure that there was nothing kept in print.

It may interest you to know that I have lately been pursuing a similar enquiry with a view to a possible new edition of Gavin Douglas's AENEAD. I found that there was a text by Small published in 1874: 4 volumes, published by Paterson of Edinburgh. I think that Dr Patterson of the Scottish Text Society should also know whether this edition is in print, and whether anybody has a new edition in preparation. If therefore you will be so kind as to write to Dr Patterson, I should be more than grateful if you would ask him about the situation of Douglas's AENEAD as well.[1]

Yours very truly,
[T. S. Eliot]

## TO *Edward Marsh*[2]

12 March 1937                    [Faber & Faber Ltd]

Dear Mr Marsh,

I have your letter of the 10th instant.[3] The project for helping the Old Vic and Sadler's Wells is a very desirable one, and I feel that as a member

1 – Macdonald replied by return, 13 Mar.: 'I am writing tonight to Dr Patterson, to make the enquiries you suggested. I happen to know, from information from a friend of mine, now retired, but formerly a partner in the firm of A. & C. Black, that the edition of Kingis Quair by Lawson has years ago been sold out. The copy which I have was picked up some years ago second-hand. You must understand also that volumes of the Scottish Text Society's publications are available only to members, and that copies may otherwise be got only when the libraries of members are sold. I myself paid 10/- for a copy of the first edition of the S.T.S. edition some years since . . . I can assure you, also, that the Scottish Text Society has done nothing towards getting an edition of the Aeneid done. As a matter of fact, the Scottish Text Society has been more or less moribund for years!'
2 – Edward Marsh (1872–1953), civil servant; man of letters; translator; and patron of the arts; friend and advocate of poets including Rupert Brooke and Siegfried Sassoon. Knighted in 1937.
   TSE was to write to the Hon. Harold Nicolson, 13 Oct. 1952: 'My dear Harold . . . I have no objection whatever to being implicated in the celebration of Eddie Marsh's eightieth birthday, but I should think that Eddie Marsh himself might be happier without me. I am under the impression that he has always regarded me as the great corrupter of English poetry, and that he almost bursts into tears when my name is mentioned. I only know that he always seems to look the other way when I am in sight. That, of course, may be due to myopia or mental concentration, but his expression on such occasions, which is like that of a man who has just bitten into an unripe persimmon, has suggested that he was not unaware of a noxious atmosphere in the street, so I think that out of modesty, I ought to decline.'
3 – It was proposed to open a fund – the Vic–Wells Completion Fund – to put the work of the Old Vic and Sadler's Wells on its feet by providing a capital sum of £15,000 for extensions at

of the Executive Committee of the Sadler's Wells Society I ought to give it my support. I feel that I ought to ask you first, however, exactly what will be expected of the committee which you are forming, and how often it is likely to meet. I am anxious to do what I can, but it would not be fair to the committee to undertake anything for which I have not the time.

Yours sincerely,<br>[T. S. Eliot]

## TO *Bernard Blackstone*[1]                                              CC

12 March 1937                          [Faber & Faber Ltd]

Dear Blackstone,

I have your letter of the 9th. As for your manuscript, I am only sorry that the misunderstanding in Cambridge caused delay in getting the manuscript back to you.[2]

I am not altogether surprised that you are considering the possibility of taking Holy Orders, as I had imagined that you might have a vocation.[3] I am afraid however that Sir Edwyn Hoskyns or Dr Stewart is mistaken in thinking that I have ever been active in the question of funds for ordinands. It is of course a matter in which everyone should be interested, but about which I have no more knowledge than the next man. I should be very glad to be of help to you in the matter, but it would have to be for you to indicate to me how that help could be given. Have you had in view any particular training college? I wonder whether you have considered the possibility of Mirfield or Kelham? I could write to people at either of these places and make enquiries. I think there is something to be said for both of them – I have not yet visited Mirfield, but I know Kelham pretty intimately – for men who are already University graduates, partly for the

---

Sadler's Wells which would enable the two theatres to save a heavy expenditure on cartage of scenery, and to pay off building debts. Marsh invited TSE to serve on the committee.

1–Bernard Blackstone (b. 1911), a research student at Trinity College, Cambridge, was to go on to teach at University College, Swansea; in South America, Cuba and Turkey; and as Byron Professor of English at Athens University. Works include *The Ferrar Papers* (1938), *English Blake* (1949), *Virginia Woolf: A Commentary* (1949), *Byron: A Survey* (1975), and *The Consecrated Urn: An Interpretation of Keats in Terms of Growth and Form* (1959).

2–Blackstone had asked TSE on 10 Jan. to return his work on Herbert, which he was submitting for a Fellowship at St John's.

3–Blackstone was thinking of taking Holy Orders. His trouble was that he had no money to forward the plan; he could get assistance from the diocesan board, but not enough. He had been advised that TSE would know something about how he might secure financial aid.

reason that in these two places you would come in contact with students many of whom had not had such advantages, and I think that is a good discipline for one's spirit. There are some very intelligent people indeed at Kelham. But I am afraid I do not know enough in general to be able to be of use until you can get more information from other quarters.

With best wishes,
Yours sincerely,
[T. S. Eliot]

## TO *Angus Davidson*[1]

12 March 1937                    [Faber & Faber Ltd]

Dear Mr Davidson,

Thank you for your letter of March 10.[2] I am very much shocked and extremely sorry to hear of the death of Mrs Aitken. I had not even known that she was in poor health. It is a good many years since I last saw her, but I feel that if she had lived she might have made some remarkable contributions to literature.

I imagine, as you say, that the stories which she promised me were never sent off. I shall be very glad if you will let me see whatever stories you find, and after reading them I shall be very glad to discuss with you the problems of publication.

I do indeed remember meeting you some years ago. I think that at that time you were assisting the Woolfs with the Hogarth Press.

Yours very sincerely,
[T. S. Eliot]

---

1–Angus Davidson (b. 1898), a graduate of Magdalene College, Cambridge, had worked for the Hogarth Press, 1924–7.

2–'I am writing in reply to your letter of March 9th to Miss Mary Butts (Mrs Aitken), to tell you that she was taken suddenly ill last Thursday & died on Friday after an operation. She had not been well for some weeks . . .

'She told me about the proposed volume of stories, & I understood that she had already sent them to you, but I suppose this cannot have been so. (I don't think she can have sent them to Christy & Moore, or you would have had them by now). I am her literary executor, & shall be going through her papers shortly: I may find that she had already made a selection. But in any case, if I may, I will send you what stories I can find . . .

'I don't suppose you will remember me, but we met once or twice some years ago – at the Woolfs', I think.'

TO *John Hayward*                                                    TS King's

13 March [1937]                          *The Criterion*

Dear John,

I did forget.[1] I am sorry. I have Carew Hunt's paper here to return to you.[2] I was uncertain about it myself, but Faber and Morley are convinced that it would not make our book. Probably Allen & Unwin. I apologise for the delay. I knew that there was something on my mind the other evening, but I persuaded myself that it was merely to return the periodicals. I will drop the typescript at your door one evening.

I don't like *Life*. What a nasty paper. I thought of doing some drawings to illustrate how the Perfect Husband should undress, but it would be unwise to send them through the Post.

I must try to remember that it is not good for me to tipple Brandy, much as I appreciate both your Brandy and your generosity with it. Brandy and Beethoven together are too much, anyway. The mild after-dinner wine is my beverage. I think I will add some of Williams & Humbert's Walnut Brown[3] as a variety.

Yrs etc.
TP


TO *Eric Cheetham*[4]                                                cc

14 March 1937                          [9 Grenville Place, S.W.7]

Dear Father Cheetham,

I saw the flat in Emperor's Gate on Friday, and I should like to come.[5] The exposure is rather northerly, that's my only criticism. And I hope the Gas Company can be induced to put in new gas heaters in the rooms (I should like the bedroom to have a gas ring too).[6] I don't see where you are going to put Miss Cowan, though![7]

1–Letter not traced.
2–R. N. Carew Hunt (1890–1959), author; writer on Marxism. His 'paper' not traced.
3–Walnut Brown is a sweet Oloroso sherry marketed by the house of Williams and Humbert.
4–The Revd Eric Cheetham (1892–1957): Vicar of St Stephen's Church, Gloucester Road, London, 1929–56 – 'a fine ecclesiastical showman', as E. W. F. Tomlin dubbed him. TSE's landlord and friend at presbytery-houses in S. Kensington, 1934–9. See further *L7*, 34–8.
5–TSE was to write *East Coker* at 11 Emperor's Gate (EVE to Helen Gardner, 24 July 1973).
6–Cheetham replied, 15 Mar.: 'I am glad you like the two rooms. I will, of course, see the Gas Company put in good gas heaters and a gas ring in the bedroom.'
7–Miss Cowan was presumably the housekeeper.

I have only hesitated because there seemed to be an opportunity for me to go to Bina Gardens.[1] But for me, at the moment, there would be serious disadvantages in that, and I only wavered because I know that it would be comforting to my crippled friend to have a friend in the house, in case of emergency. I may eventually want to set up for myself, but I don't know. In any case, I think you ought to have three months' notice.

I want to pay my share of the cost of moving – that is, moving everything in these two rooms.

Now for Miss Forwood's letter,[2] which you sent up without comment. Knowing nothing of this scheme except what she says in the letter, I can't pronounce any opinion – I would like to know more about it and what, if anything, there is to be said against it.

I gather from Captain Rawlinson that as the dilapidation fund on this house has been paid out of Church Expenses, he thinks that Church Expenses ought to be reimbursed. I am not sure that that is very important, because the Church will benefit in another fund. But what I do feel is that some provision ought to be made, in the future, out of current income (and the church income will benefit by the sale of the property) for dilapidations to the church itself. Major McGowan had read of some insurance scheme in the *Church Times* which seems at least to deserve investigation. I feel that if any serious structural weakness appears, the next generation will have great difficulty in getting together the money to correct it.

What reminded me of this (which has been in my mind for some time) was the enclosed estimate of Claxton's. It sounds to me moderate enough, but Prewett thought that you were considering getting another estimate. I do not know what you think of Claxton. I understood from Prewett that if we do not accept this estimate we shall have to pay for the time already spent by Claxton in investigating; and that if we do accept it, the cost of those preliminaries is included; but this needs confirmation.[3]

Sincerely yours,<br>
[T. S. Eliot]

1 – JDH lived at 22 Bina Gardens, London S.W.7, from 23 Mar. 1933 until Nov. 1938.
2 – Muriel Forwood: Hon. Sec. of the Pivot Club (President, Elsie Fogerty) – the Social Club of the Central School of Speech and Drama. Robert Sencourt explains that next door to Eliot's lodgings in Courtfield Road 'lived a prominent Anglo-Catholic, Miss Muriel Forwood' (*T. S. Eliot*, 121). 'Miss Forwood . . . would drive him about in her car. Once she was taking him to a poetry reading. "I hate reading my poetry aloud like this," he told her. "It's like undressing in public." "You needn't worry," she reassured him. "You never take off too much"' (Ibid., 130).
3 – Cheetham, 15 Mar.: 'Claxton is expensive . . . Prewett lives in his house; he is a friend of his, and consequently always gives him all the Church work. I do feel this ought to be stopped.'

TO *John Hayward*                                         TS King's

14 March 1937                              *The Criterion*

Dear John,

I have devoted considerable thought to the matter. I am glad that you broached it with Mrs W., so as to know her disposition for the sake of the future. But as it turns out, it would be the most inconvenient moment for a change. The situation is, that the Vicar wants to move out from here soon after Ladyday, as he has found a flat in Emperor's Gate which suits him, and they won't hold it for him; and as he has to be near the church, he doesn't want to miss an opportunity. I have seen the flat, which is on two stories; and I can have two rooms at the top, rather better than this. The exposure is rather northerly, which is against it. But one important point is this: if I decided to come to Bina Gardens now, I should have to pack up and spend three months in a hotel, just when I look forward to having that length of time more or less free in the mornings for my own work, at last. So I think it is better for me to go there for a time and try it; and certainly it will be advantageous for the vicar to have a p.g. through the change when there are exceptional expenses, instead of having the rooms vacant for some time perhaps. But if later Mrs Morris should leave voluntarily, then I would like the chance, and I could also at a later time go straight from one to the other without having to have any considerable interval in temporary quarters.

That's how I see it at the moment, anyway. I don't know whether I am influenced by liking to feel safe, or not. Six months hence I may feel much more like setting up for myself.

Affectionately,<br>
TP.

TO *Cleanth Brooks*[1]                                   TS Beinecke

15 March 1937                              *The Criterion*

Dear Mr Brooks,

I have read with interest the commentary on *The Waste Land* enclosed with your letter of February 25th, and appreciate your caring to have my

---

1–Cleanth Brooks Jr (1906–94), American critic, graduate of Vanderbilt University, Nashville, Tennessee; close associate of Robert Penn Warren, John Crowe Ransom and Donald Davidson; identified with the Southern Agrarians and the Fugitives; a loyal founding father of the so-called 'formalist' approach to literature known as New Criticism. Brooks

own criticisms of it.[1] But with a criticism of this kind I am afraid that the author can be of very little help. It seems to me on the whole excellent, and much better than H. R. Williamson's,[2] which went to rather fantastic lengths. I think that this kind of analysis is perfectly justified so long as it does not profess to be a reconstruction of the author's method of writing. Reading your essay made me feel, for instance, that I had been a great deal more ingenious than I had been aware of, because the conscious problems with which one is concerned in the actual writing are more those of a quasi musical nature, in the arrangement of metric and pattern, than those of a conscious exposition of ideas. There is one criticism which interests me, in which you follow Mr Mathiessen [*sic*] in suggesting that a certain passage was probably a reminiscence of a letter of Rupert Brooke's.[3] It is

---

taught English at Louisiana State University, Baton Rouge, 1932–47; and from 1947 at Yale University, where he became Gray Professor of Rhetoric. Co-founder and co-editor with Robert Penn Warren of the *Southern Review*, 1935–42, he was co-author, with Warren, of *An Approach to Literature* (1936), *Understanding Poetry* (1938) and other collaborations; author of *Modern Poetry and the Tradition* (1939), *The Well Wrought Urn: Studies in the Structure of Poetry* (1947) – which includes a notable critique of *TWL* – and *The Shaping Joy: Studies in the Writer's Craft* (1971).

1–'I am enclosing a rather full commentary on The Waste Land, first, because I would like for you to see it, and second, because I hope that I may prevail upon you to make some sort of comment upon it. I feel that this is a matter of some delicacy, for I can think of many reasons quite apart from the goodness or badness of this particular commentary which would prompt you to reserve any comment whatsoever. I hope, of course, that the interpretation that I have given is fairly accurate and not too clumsy, and I am encouraged somewhat in this hope by favorable comments of my friends, Mr Warren and Mr Tate, who have read this essay.'

See 'The Waste Land: An Analysis', *Southern Review* 3 (Summer 1937), 106–36; repr. in *Modern Poetry and the Tradition* (Chapel Hill: University of North Carolina Press, 1939), 136–72; and in *T. S. Eliot: Critical Assessments*, vol. II, ed. Graham Clarke (London, 1990).

2–H. R. Williamson, *The Poetry of T. S. Eliot* (1932).

3–Matthiessen, *The Achievement of T. S. Eliot*, 92–3: 'My friend John Finley, Jr., pointed out to me a certain similarity between the following sentences from Rupert Brooke's description of the first shocked impression made upon one of his friends by the announcement, "We're at war with Germany", and the "heap of broken images" that set the tone of the opening of "The Waste Land":

"My friend ate and drank, and then climbed a hill of gorse, and sat alone, looking at the sea. His mind was full of confused images, and the sense of strain. In answer to the word "Germany", a train of vague thoughts dragged across his brain. The pompous middle-class vulgarity of the building of Berlin; the wide and restful beauty of Munich; the taste of beer; innumerable quiet, glittering cafés; the *Ring*; the swish of evening air in the face, as one skies down past the pines; a certain angle of the eyes in the face; long nights of drinking and singing and laughter . . . certain friends; some tunes; the quiet length of evening over the Starnbergersee."

'In [such a case], however, it is wholly a question of the possible suggestion of some of the material which Eliot's imagination seized upon, and transmuted into quite a new context; not of any effect on the actual movement of his lines.'

quite possible that I read this letter, and I cannot say that it was not at the back of my mind, but actually this particular passage approximates more closely to a recollection of a personal experience of my own than anything else, and indeed is as nearly as I could remember a verbatim report.[1]

With all best wishes,
Yours sincerely,
T. S. Eliot

TO *George Every*                                                         CC

16 March 1937                                    [Faber & Faber Ltd]

My dear George,

Although I do not seem to have room for any more reviews in the June number of the *Criterion*, I should like to ask you now whether you would review for me, for publication in September if not June, Kenneth Ingram's new book *Christianity – Right or Left?* I have always felt rather doubtful of Ingram,[2] and this is I think a rather dangerous book, perhaps more because of what it does not say than of what it does say. I think that you will find it concerns subjects to which you have already given a good deal of thought. In one place he quotes you as a representative of the point of view which he opposes to his own, but in such a way, I think, as to make you the more suitable and not the less suitable reviewer.[3]

Affectionately yours,
[T. S.]

1–Brooks to EVE, 4 Dec. 1988: 'My essay on *The Waste Land* was published in the Summer 1937 issue of *The Southern Review* but I did not print TSE's comments on it on that occasion. My reasons for not doing so were several and I shall not go into them here. Years later, in 1950, when Robert Penn Warren and I brought out a revised second edition of our text-book, *Understanding Poetry*, we added a long essay on "How Poems Come About: Intention and Meaning." We felt that what TSE had said in his letter to me bore rather precisely on that problem and (along with other such citations) did quote two sentences from his letter to me. They make up the passage beginning "I think that this kind of analysis" and ending ". . . of a conscious exposition of ideas." The passage we quoted made a special point and did not involve any expression of agreement with what I had had to say about the meaning of the poem.' See Brooks, 'The Waste Land: A Prophetic Document', *Yale Review* 78: 2 (Winter 1989), 318–32 – which includes a reproduction of this letter from TSE on 320–1.

2–Kenneth Ingram (1882–1965), author, founded and edited *Green Quarterly* (Society of SS Peter & Paul, London) in 1924. His works include *Why I Believe* (1928) and *Has the Church Failed?* (1929).

3–Untitled review of Kenneth Ingram, *Christianity – Right or Left*: C. 16 (July 1937), 711–13. 'Mr Ingram, like so many others, pins his faith to the Popular Front. The atrocities of Fascism are duly catalogued. (But excesses in Russia are due to the Slav temperament.)

16 March 1937                    *The Criterion*

My dear Praz,

I have just received a copy of the *Southern Review* containing your article about my obligations to Dante.[1] In so far as the subject of such an article is capable of judging, it seems to me a highly successful piece of work, and I feel more confident because it throws some light on the matter even to myself. I was not really aware, for instance, of the extent to which I was indebted to Pound on certain points.

> With many thanks,
> Yours ever sincerely,
> T. S. Eliot

TO *Jeanette McPherrin*                    TS Denison Library

17 March 1937                    *The Criterion*

Dear Jeanie,

I was very glad to get your letter, although it made me the more annoyed with myself for not having managed it first.[2] I was going to send you a card at Christmas, and then I thought I would write to you instead: and then I didn't, and it has been on my mind ever since. I am glad that something is eventually to happen about Miss Grant, and I shall wait daily in expectation of hearing from her, and I shall be prepared for Mrs Grant too. It will really be a great pleasure to meet

---

Fascism perpetuates class, is nationalist, "aims at the permanent sublimation of the individual in the racial unit" (whatever that may mean). Worst of all, it is reactionary. The Fascist man goes back to sword and ploughshare, his woman to hearth and cradle, but Communism is an adventure, a new civilization, knowing neither class nor nation . . .

'Christian orthodoxy is a standard which we confess with the dead and with the unborn, which will be true and right whatever the world thinks, however seriously the Church militant may distort or misapply it. It need not therefore issue in an alliance with the secular Right. It is bound to issue in a total rejection of the monist attitude to the world common to Fascism and Communism, which makes the "general line" of present day politics determinant of all interest, all activity, all value. Mr Ingram resents the suggestion that Christian belief limits political loyalty, but for that limit the martyrs died.'

1 – 'T. S. Eliot and Dante', *Southern Review* 2: 3 (Winter 1937), 525–48. Published as 'T. S. Eliot e Dante', *Da Letteratura* 15 (Luglio 1937), 12–28 – offprint sent 'with M. Praz's compliments Rome July 1937': TSE Library. Repr. in *The Flaming Heart: Essays on Crashaw, Machiavelli, and Other Studies in the Relations between Italian and English Literature from Chaucer to T. S. Eliot* (1958, 1973), 348–56.
2 – Not traced.

them; and I hope that they will have more news of you than you choose to give me of yourself.

I also wish that Emily might be coming to England in almost any other circumstances. I have even taken it seriously enough, and have felt unselfishly enough, to wish that she might rather be spending the summer in America, if among the right people! However, I shall do what I can – though one's battling has to be so *very* indirect! The fact that she has been reappointed at Smith is very helpful: but I wish that Smith was a few hundred miles, at least, away from where it is. I agree that on the whole her letters seem more wholesome, though she is still, I think, much too concerned with 'self-improvement'. But I was cheered by her last letter, because she was exercised about trying to get public opinion in Northampton working for the improvement of a hideous café or coffee stall in the main street, patronised by the girls. That kind of activity is all to the good, in her case.

The Archbishop is still being murdered by Robert Speaight every night. I understand that they have somehow secured Queen Mary for Friday night! Not yet in French or German, but I understand that a production in Budapesth is under weigh.

I dont suppose you are arriving for the coronation (I shall try to get over to Paris for that week if I can), but I wish you might be coming in the summer. I expect to give your love to Inverness in about three weeks.[1]

> Yours ever,
> Tom

TO *Henry Eliot*                                                                  TS Houghton

St Patrick's Day [17 March] 1937     *The Criterion*

My dear Henry,

I think the best thing for me to do is to enquire about seats at a good agency and cable Frank.[2] He could probably have good seats for fifteen guineas apiece, but I don't know how much he is willing to pay. I see that

---

1–TSE sent McPherrin a postcard depicting 'Glencoe from Rest and Be Thankful, near Arrochar' [*sic*], dated 6 Apr. 1937: 'This is to let you know that there is still a good deal of snow about Inverness, which I left yesterday morning. Crocuses are out, however. T. S. E.' (Denison)

2–Frank M. Eliot (Washington, DC) and his wife Lucy wished to secure seats for the Coronation. Frank to TSE, 16 Apr.: 'I received your wire saying that you had gotten three seats for the procession and telling us of the need to get hotel reservations at once.'

the little girl is about 14, which is old enough if she is sturdy; but it will be pretty exhausting, because even if you have good seats you have to get there early in the morning in order to get there at all. I intend to go to Paris, or at least to the country (but it is better to get abroad) for that week.

I have dug out for you three numbers of *Commerce*, but there is one (with the translation, not a good one, of 'Difficulties of a Statesman') which I think I must have torn up to use for the printers of the book.[1] As there proved to be several copies of what I had, I sent two of each: dispose of the duplicate as you like. I also found a copy of the *Nouvelle Revue Française* which contained my obituary note on Jacques Rivière,[2] and a French anthology of American verse with a translation of 'Portrait of a Lady',[3] and sent these too. I hope you will be able to let me know that you have received the *Egoists*, as these are rather more interesting. The *Nightwood* should have reached you direct from Brace some time since, as a copy I ordered has been received in England. I have no copy of the *Navire d'Argent*.[4] There is another book (just out) which I will send you called *From Anne to Victoria* with an essay of mine on Byron;[5] and another symposium to be published this spring called *Revelation* will contain an essay by me: I will send you that when it appears.

I shall be interested to hear about the production at the Fogg.[6] The play is again in London for the last two weeks of Lent; Dukes tells me that they have arranged for Queen Mary to see it, and that sort of visit is supposed to help, by the theatrical world.

Affectionately,
Tom

1 – '*Difficultés d'un homme d'état*', trans. Georges Limbour, *Commerce* 29 (Winter 1931/32), 79–87.

2 – 'Rencontre', *Nouvelle Revue Française* 12: 139 (1 Apr. 1925), 657–8.

3 – *Anthologie de la nouvelle poésie Américaine*, par Eugène Jolas (Paris, 1928), 64–9.

4 – *Le Navire d'Argent* 1 (1 June 1925) included '*La chanson d'amour de J. Alfred Prufrock*', trans. Sylvia Beach and Adrienne Monnier, 23–9.

5 – 'Byron', in *From Anne to Victoria: Essays by various hands*, ed. BD (1937), 601–19.

6 – HWE replied on 29 Mar.: 'We were busy while "Murder" was being given in Fogg. I have sent you all notices, programme, etc. of this. We took Ada and Shef and Gallup, who came from New Haven and was much delighted, as I took him to Eliot House for lunch and let him look at the collection (which now numbers some 600 items, an item being either a large book or a small clipping, as may be). The performance was very successful, well attended for five evenings.'

TO *André Gide*[1]                                           cc

S. Patrice [17 March] 1937          [Faber & Faber Ltd]

Cher monsieur et maître,

J'ai la témérité de vous envoyer, ci-inclus, les feuilles d'un préface que j'ai écrite pour l'édition américaine de *Nightwood* qui vient de paraître.

Je suppose que Miss Barnes (malgré sa timidité naturelle) aura déjà fait des démarches chez vous au sujet d'un préface de vous pour la traduction française que M. Roger-Cornaz est en train de faire. Est-ce trop, exprimer mon espoir que vous consentirez à accorder votre appui inappréciable à un projet que j'ai beaucoup à cœur? *Nightwood* me semble un ouvrage magnifique; je suis bien fier d'avoir pu faciliter la publication de ce chef d'œuvre en Angleterre et en Amérique.

Je vous prie, cher monsieur Gide, de recevoir l'expression de mon admiration soutenue.

[T. S. Eliot][2]


TO *William Temple*                                         cc

18 March 1937                       [Faber & Faber Ltd]

My dear Lord Archbishop,

I am venturing to write to Your Grace concerning the problem of publishing the lecture notes of Father Kelly of Kelham on early Church history. I was given to understand by Brother George Every that Your Grace had expressed the hope that these notes might be published, otherwise I might not have ventured to write.

---

1 – André Gide (1869–1951), novelist, essayist, diarist, travel writer and translator, critic and anti-colonialist; co-founder of the *Nouvelle Revue Française*, 1908; author of numerous works in various genres including the novels *L'immoraliste* (1902), *La porte étroite* (1909), *Les Caves du Vatican* (1914), *Corydon* (1924), and *Les faux-monnayeurs* (1925); and journals and autobiographies including *Si le grain ne meurt* (1924). Nobel Prize laureate, 1947.

2 – *Translation*: Dear Sir and Master, / I am taking the liberty of sending you herewith the pages of a preface I have written for the American edition of *Nightwood* which has just been published.

I imagine that Miss Barnes (despite her natural shyness) will have already approached you about a preface for the French translation, which is currently being undertaken by M. Roger-Cornaz. I hope it will not seem excessive, if I too express my hope that you will agree to lend your invaluable support to a project I hold dear? I consider *Nightwood* a magnificent work, and I am very proud of having been able to facilitate the publication of this masterpiece in England and America.

Please allow me, dear Monsieur Gide, to express my lasting admiration. / [T. S. Eliot]

We have formed a high opinion of these lecture notes, and agree that they ought to be published. At the same time it would seem that the market for such a book in this country would be very small. Kelham is already supplied with mimeographed copies, and it may be that for the students there the notes are more effective in that form than they would be if published as a book, which would be necessarily too expensive for them to buy individually. It is hardly likely that the demand from theological colleges would be very great. At the same time we should be very glad to publish the book, if we had a reasonable hope of recovering our outlay. The only possible direction in which to look for assistance appears to be New York, and we are exploring the possibility of inducing one of the best New York publishing houses to buy enough sheets of the book when printed to assure us against any considerable loss. It is with regard to our approach to the possible American publishers that I am now applying to Your Grace. A brief letter from Your Grace expressing a favourable opinion of the lecture notes and a desire that they might be published would, we feel, make a deeper impression on our American correspondents than any recommendation from any other source, and I should be extremely grateful if it were possible for us to be given this advantage.[1]

I remain, my Lord Archbishop,
Yours Grace's obedient servant,
[T. S. Eliot]

1 – Temple responded, 23 Mar.: 'I have read a good many of the sections of Father Kelly's Notes and regard them as stimulating in a peculiarly high degree. He is a student of singularly fresh mind and is able to revive the human problem with which those theologians of an earlier date were dealing as very few students of the subject have ever done. This makes his treatment vital and vivid, and I have always wished that the Notes should be available for a wider circle.'

Thereupon TSE drew up a 'Memorandum' entitled 'Lecture Notes on Church History by Rev. Herbert Kelly S.S.M.' including the full statement by the Archbishop of Canterbury, and headed by this manifesto by TSE: 'Father Kelly was the founder of the Society of the Sacred Mission, and although now, by reason of his advanced age, no longer its director, still takes some part in the teaching. As the founder he devised and instituted a system of education for theological students which is, I think, remarkably fine. I mention this point because the merit of these lecture notes is due not only to his knowledge of Church history and abilities of presentation, but to his acknowledged outstanding abilities as educationalist.

'I think that these notes ought to be published in almost exactly their present form, with very little polishing. To any intelligent reader the tersenesss and simplicity of the mode of presentation is an added virtue. I should recommend them not only to students of the subject but for all intelligent readers who wish to acquaint themselves with Church history through one condensed and comprehensive book. Father Kelly has a lively and sometimes humorous style which is also to his advantage. I should aim at the general public as well as the libraries of theological seminaries. T. S. Eliot.'

18 March 1937                          [Faber & Faber Ltd]

My dear George,

I ought to let you know the results of my enquiries so far about Gavin Douglas. I wrote to Dover Wilson, who consulted, I think, some of his colleagues at Edinburgh, and who believed that a new edition of Douglas's AENEAD was desirable and needed. I elicited the same opinion from R. W. Chambers, who added a good deal of information about existing editions: one of the problems about the AENEAD seems to be that it is a pretty big book, but I have not yet had time to see if the London Library has a copy of the edition, which is now out of date, published by the Scottish Text Society. If it is not there I shall have to have it looked up in the British Museum.

Meanwhile I had a letter from a certain Angus Macdonald, whom I do not know, but who appears to be in the English Department at Edinburgh, suggesting that there ought to be a new critical edition of the KINGIS QUHAIR. This also looked interesting to me, and I have had some encouragement from Dover Wilson and Chambers about that project too. I am not sure that it would not an easier thing to tackle first than the Gavin Douglas. Dover Wilson was going to make enquiries with a view to proposing possible editors for the Douglas texts. I have asked Macdonald to make enquiries on his own account to find out what texts of both of these works, if any, are kept in print, and also whether any other new edition is in preparation. I am informed, by the way, that Macdonald himself would not be ~~a very satisfactory editor~~ the right man to edit – not that he has proposed himself.[2]

---

1–George Blake (1893–1961), novelist, journalist, publisher – author of *The Shipbuilders* (1935) – co-founded the Porpoise Press in hopes of refashioning a national publishing industry in Scotland. The Press was taken over by F&F in 1930. GCF wrote to H. M. Cohen, 14 Oct. 1930: 'We recently acquired the stock and good will of a small private business in Edinburgh called The Porpoise Press. The Porpoise Press exists for the purpose of publishing pamphlets, books and poems of Scottish national interest. It has hitherto been run in a very haphazard way by a single individual, and has just about paid its way. There are, however, considerable possibilities in it; and we are now working it up, with the assistance of two Scotchmen, named Blake and Thomson.' (See further Alistair McCleery, *The Porpoise Press* 1922–39 [1988].) On 10 Oct. 1930 FVM told Henry S. Canby (editor of the *Saturday Review of Literature)* that 'my very good friend' was 'the recently appointed Fiction Editor to Faber and Faber . . . The fact that we have been able to snaffle him for Faber and Faber, shows the happy reputation which we have been establishing . . . There is a very interesting Scottish nationalistic movement; and it is really producing some brilliant writers.'

2–Deletion and revised sentence closure in TSE's hand. The 'informant' was Dover Wilson.

Of course this is only the beginning, and I have no idea, if we were to undertake either of these jobs, what the expense would be. I hope I may have some more information before we come up to Scotland, and we can discuss these matters then.

I told Frank that it would suit me just as well to come up on Wednesday night, the 31st, if that is going to give us the time [to] take in a bit of Galloway as well. I don't know, however, how you are fixed. I should be quite ready to cut out Edinburgh on this occasion, because I have to come up there in July and again at the end of October.

Yours ever,<br>[Tom]

## TO *Cecil Day Lewis*[1]                                           cc

19 March 1937                    [Faber & Faber Ltd]

Dear Mr Day Lewis,

I was reminded by meeting you the other night of a project which we have had in mind for some time past, and which I should like to discuss with you. So far as I know there has been no good history of literature from a Marxist point of view, at any rate not by an English author, and I have been wondering whether you would be interested in undertaking such a book yourself. I have not discussed the matter with any other writer, and it seems to me that you would be as appropriate an author as could be found, if you cared to undertake it.

I don't know how frequently you come to London – I hope not often for such questionable and thankless purposes as that of the occasion of our meeting – but when you are next in London I should be delighted if you

---

1 – Cecil Day Lewis (1904–72), Anglo-Irish poet and novelist (author of an admired series of mystery novels under the pseudonym Nicholas Blake); Oxford Professor of Poetry, 1951–6; Norton Professor at Harvard, 1962–3; Poet Laureate, 1968–72. Educated at Wadham College, Oxford, he edited with his friend W. H. Auden the anthology *Oxford Poetry 1927*; and for a period in the mid-1930s he was a member of the Communist Party. After WW2 he worked as a director and senior editor of the publishers Chatto & Windus. His publications include *Transitional Poem* (1929), *From Feathers to Iron* (1932), *The Complete Poems of C. Day-Lewis* (1992); and critical works include *A Hope for Poetry* (1934); *The Poetic Image* (1947); and *The Buried Day* (autobiography, 1960). See Sean Day-Lewis, *C. Day Lewis: An English Literary Life* (1980); Peter Stanford, *C. Day-Lewis: A Life* (1998).

On 2 May 1933, GCF had written to Day Lewis: 'By the way, if you are not permanently associated with a particular publisher, I hope you will remember that we cast covetous glances in your direction. You and Auden ought surely to have the same imprint?'

would have lunch or dinner with me, even if you feel no interest in what I have just suggested.

Yours sincerely,<br>[T. S. Eliot]

## TO *Geoffrey Grigson*

TS Texas

19 March 1937                                      *The Criterion*

Dear Grigson,

I have your letter of the 17th.[1] I shall be delighted to propose the matter of a *New Verse* anthology again. Would you intend it to be bigger than the first collection, or merely more drastically selective?

I will think over your suggestion of a contribution to an Auden number.[2] It is a little embarrassing for everybody, making these public testimonials on behalf of one's friends, and perhaps especially if one happens to be the publisher as well. I should like a little clearer idea of what other people are doing.

Yours sincerely,<br>T. S. Eliot

## TO *Djuna Barnes*

TS Hornbake

23 March 1937                                      *The Criterion*

Dear Miss Barnes,

I have your note of the 22nd, and I also have a letter from Andre Gide, of which I send you a copy.[3] It is I think a very characteristic letter, coy

---

1 – Grigson wondered whether the autumn would be a good time to bring out a 'New Verse' anthology. 'Anthologies have died away a bit, and the flower bed will be fairly empty.'

2 – 'Also would you give your verbal blessing to an Auden number of "New Verse" . . . ? I mean, would you write for it a paragraph approving of anything you do approve of in Auden?'

3 – Barnes wrote from Paris, 22 Mar.: 'I have heard nothing from Mr Gide as yet – have you?'

Gide to TSE, 21 Mar. 1937: '*Je lis avec un vif intérêt votre trop courte étude sur NIGHTWOOD. Elle me donne un vif desir de connaître le livre – que je n'ai pas encore reçu. (Peut-être m'attend-la à Paris). Mais accablé de travail, je crains bien de ne pouvoir écrire cette preface dont vous me parlez; j'attends d'avoir lu le livre pour répondre définitivement: tout engagement nouveau me fait peur et j'en viens a refuser systematiquement même ce qui me serait la plus agréable.*

'*Veuillez croire à l'assurance de mes sentiments tres attentifs.*'

and evasive. I don't think that it is worthwhile waiting in the hope of getting Gide. Very likely after the book has been acclaimed Gide will turn up and let the world know that he was the first person to recognise its merit. Have you or Roger Cornaz any ideas about the next best man?

Thank you for the *New Yorker* review, which I should have attributed to Clifton Fadiman even if you had not written his name on it.[1] He is quite an intelligent Jew I think, and this review ought to help. I am also informed that the intense intelligentsia of Harvard are engaged on the delicate task of deciding what they ought to think.

I am very happy to have the copy of the New York edition, with your inscription. It is the first copy that I had seen. I can't say that I like its appearance so well as ours, although you will certainly prefer the cover. I have had copies sent to various people in America.

Sincerely,<br>T. S. Eliot

## TO *Cecil Day Lewis* CC

24 March 1937                    [Faber & Faber Ltd]

Dear Mr Day Lewis,

Thank you for your letter of Monday.[2] I rather feared that you would be booked up for some time to come, but I hope that you will keep that

---

('I read with great interest your short study of NIGHTWOOD. It gives me a keen desire to know the book – which I have not yet received. (Maybe it's waiting for me in Paris). But being overwhelmed with work, I fear I can't write this preface for which you ask; I wait to read the book to answer definitively: any new engagement scares me and I tend to reject absolutely even that which would be most pleasant to me.

'Please believe in the assurance of my very attentive feelings.')

1–Clifton Fadiman, 'Djuna Barnes', *New Yorker*, 13 Mar. 1937, 103: 'One hopes devoutly that Djuna Barnes' *Nightwood* may not be visited with a *succès de snobisme* or served up as caviar to the general . . .

'I have wit enough to realize that this extraordinary novel, like *Ulysses*, requires for complete understanding half a dozen readings. I have read it only twice and am persuaded, at least, that it is an original, not an eccentric, book. Its obscurities are not willful but imposed by the weird materials of the story . . . *Nightwood* seems to Edwin Muir, whose standards are inflexible, "an undeniable work of genius". I am not competent either to dispute or confirm his judgment, but my hunch is that *Nightwood*, if not a work of genius, has genius in it.'

2–Day Lewis wrote that while he thought it 'nice' of TSE to suggest he write a Marxist history of literature, he was contracted to another publisher, Jonathan Cape, for another eighteen months; and he felt he did not 'know nearly enough about literature (or marxism) at present'; all the same, he would be willing to reconsider the idea 'in the more or less remote future'.

idea in mind, because except for the remote possibility of our asking someone else to do it, we should be delighted to pursue the matter further with you when you saw your way free. I admit that it is a pretty big job for anyone who takes it conscientiously.

I am sorry to say that April 1st is no use for me.[1] I have got to be in Scotland at that time until the 7th of April. After that I shall be in London except, I hope, for Coronation week, when I shall try to go abroad.

It is hardly worth bothering about the humiliation, is it?[2] I certainly knew in advance what I was in for, from a previous experience, but the circumstances were such that it was impossible for me to refuse. One will probably have to do this sort of thing again, but one never treats the audience seriously more than once.

Yours sincerely,<br>
[T. S. Eliot]

## TO *George Barker*

TS Texas

24 March 1937            *The Criterion*

Dear Barker,

Thanks for yours of the 21st.[3] I was very glad that you did raise that quibble about the blurb, because it drew my attention to the fact that what I had written for the catalogue had been copied on to the jacket, for which it was not quite suitable. I was therefore able to modify the paragraph still further.[4]

---

1 – Day Lewis suggested lunch with TSE on 1 Apr.

2 – 'That meeting was the most humiliating thing I've ever gone through: it should be a lesson to all of us.'

3 – 'I have received from de la Mare the jacket and cover designs for Calamiterror: I think that it should be an extremely elegant book. I hope that my quibble about the blurb was nothing worse than a quibble.'

4 – Barker to RdlM, 20 Mar. 1937: 'I see that you remarked about the blurb to Eliot – thanks so much. As for the book, I imagine it should be one of the best you have yet designed.' *Calamiterror* was published on 4 Mar. 1937.

Faber Spring Books 1937, 55, on *New Poems* (the provisional title): 'This volume, the title of which is still unsettled, consists chiefly of a number of cantos of a new long poem. These cantos, with their greater simplification of style and concentration of energy, will substantially add to Mr Barker's growing reputation.'

The blurb for *Calamiterror*, in F&F Books July–Dec. 1937: 'A new volume, consisting of a number of cantos of a new long poem. These cantos, with their greater simplification of style and concentration of energy, will substantially add to Mr Barker's growing reputation.'

*Calamiterror* eventually carried this blurb: '*Calamiterror* is a long poem, or the first ten cantos of a longer poem. Readers of his first volume of *Poems*, and readers of *The*

I am afraid that *Quia Amore Langueo* will not be out in time for the June number, but I will try to think of something else.[1] I am afraid however that such is the pressure of books that the review list for June is pretty well filled. You shall have the book you want, or something else if that is not ready, in time for September.

There will be the small sum of £13 available on the 25th, and the bank will pay it over to you.[2] I am sorry that it is not more, but I am certain of the same amount for the June quarter, and also I hope for September.

Yours ever,

T. S. Eliot

---

*Faber Book of Modern Verse* and *The Oxford Book of Modern Verse* have awaited with impatience Mr Barker's second volume of verse. We are convinced that *Calamiterror* will show that the author has an astonishing power in a new and more difficult form, and that his work has gained in both simplicity and concentration.'

1–Barker asked to review *Quia Amore Langueo* (F&F, 1937). Fraser, *The Chameleon Poet*, 97: 'For some time [Barker] had been attempting to interest the author of "Ash Wednesday" in a scheme which had been dear to him since the months in Kimmeridge [1935]: the preparation of a proper edition of "Quia Amore Langueo" ['Because I languish for love']. In 1925 Arthur Quiller-Couch had included the section headed "The Appeal of Christ to Mankind" in his *Oxford Book of English Verse, 1250–1900*, but this was only half of what had come down from the late fourteenth century. Eight variant manuscripts of a complementary lyric, "The Appeal of the Blessed Virgin Mary to Man", also existed which, ever since George and Kit had got to know it in the Harleian manuscripts, had seemed to them incomparably more lovely. Persuaded by Barker, Eliot commissioned H. S. Bennett, the medievalist and Fellow of Emmanuel College, Cambridge, to bring the two halves of the poem together in a slim volume illustrated with woodcuts by Eric Gill. The restitution had the effect of re-investing the poem with the lingering sexual ambiguity to be found in "The Song of Solomon".'

*Quia Amore Langueo*, ed. H. S. Bennett, Emmanuel College, Cambridge, University Lecturer in English, with four full-page engravings by Eric Gill. Printed by Hague & Gill for Faber & Faber, 1937: 400 copies only.

2–'I wonder also,' asked Barker, 'if you will let me know whether I stand to receive any money from the quarterly source? I have begun a catchpenny novel with the notion of making money, but the things [*sic*] got stuck so I am writing some poems.'

## TO *D. L. Sandford*[1]                                          CC

24 March 1937                          [Faber & Faber Ltd]

Dear Miss Sandford,

I have your letter of the 22nd.[2] I was staying in Rochester with the Dean[3] over the weekend, and discussed the matter with him. I told him that I was not the right person for a talk on Mediaeval Religious Drama, because for that purpose they ought to have someone of greater scholastic authority, like E. K. Chambers, or alternatively someone who had actual experience in producing it, like Martin Browne. What I said I thought I could do would be to give a talk on Mediaeval and Modern Religious Drama, stressing the differences of conditions, and therefore the differences of treatment which we ought to expect. I think the production of contemporary religious drama is rather hampered by people measuring it by entirely irrelevant standards, because the conditions under which it can be written today are utterly different from those of the 14th and 15th centuries. I thought that some title like 'Religious Drama: Mediaeval and Modern' might do. I should be glad to know, however, if you have any further suggestions.[4]

Yours sincerely,<br>[T. S. Eliot]

## TO *N. M. Iovetz-Tereshchenko*                               CC

24 March 1937                          [Faber & Faber Ltd]

Dear Dr Iovetz-Tereschenko,

I called on Mr Willard Connely[5] the day before yesterday and had a talk with him. He seemed extremely amiable and well disposed, but could not help directly in the way of research scholarships. He suggested however that he would be very glad to arrange a meeting for you with

---

1–D. L. Sandford: Hon. Festival Manager, Friends of Rochester Cathedral.
2–Sandford requested a title for TSE's talk. 'What do you think of something on Mediaeval Drama? . . . The lecture is for the general public and not only for the Friends of Cathedral.'
3–Francis Underhill.
4–Sandford replied (30 Mar.) that she thought the proposed talk 'excellent'. TSE, 'Religious Drama: Mediaeval and Modern', *University of Edinburgh Journal* 9 (1937–1938), Aut. 1937, 8–17; repr. as *Religious Drama: Mediaeval and Modern* (New York: House of Books, 1954).
5–Willard Connely, Director of the American University Union: see letter of 14 June 1937, below.

Professor McDougall, who he said was arriving in London within a day or two, and could probably give useful advice. He undertook to write to you direct, and put you in touch with McDougall. He also suggested that if nothing happens meanwhile I should myself go and see President Nicholas Murray Butler of Columbia,[1] whom I know slightly, when he arrives in London in July. This I shall be glad to do, but I believe that McDougall is the more likely to be helpful.

Yours sincerely,

[T. S. Eliot]

TO *Margaret Trouncer*[2]                                                     CC

24 March 1937                         [Faber & Faber Ltd]

Dear Mrs Trouncer,

Thank you for your letter of 22 March. I was very glad to hear from you again, and I am much interested by your suggestion, although I have to admit a good deal of ignorance.[3] I will lay it before my committee, who I am sure are all equally ignorant, and see how it affects them.

I have not had the opportunity to look at the *Pompadour* since I saw the original typescript, but I am confident that it will be even more interesting than *La Vallière*.[4]

---

1–Nicholas Murray Butler (1862–1947), American philosopher, diplomat, educator; President of Columbia University, 1901–45. President of the Carnegie Endowment for International Peace, 1925–45; winner of the Nobel Peace Prize, 1931.

2–Margaret Trouncer (1903–82), author.

3–Trouncer aired an idea for her next book: 'Madame Elizabeth de France, sister of Louis XVI . . . Elizabeth was beautiful, proud, wrote virile letters full of "bonhomie" & was, to begin with, a violent young woman. Unfortunately, from the point of view of the English reading public, she never fell in love, for her soul was espoused to God. So, the story, so to speak, has no plot. But she is a darling, & I love her.'

4–Trouncer, *The Pompadour* (F&F, 1937); the blurb, Spring Books 1937, was probably by TSE: 'In her previous book the author told the extraordinary life of Louise de La Vallière, the first mistress of Louis XIV. Turning now from the seventeenth to the eighteenth century, she paints a portrait of the Pompadour, the most eminent of Louis XV's mistresses, on a larger canvas and against a more crowded background. We see Louis XV, his Queen, and his early mistresses, before we meet the Pompadour herself and follow her career from the convent school to the place behind the throne. The Pompadour exercised her power for public as well as private ends: she was influential in politics, was a patroness of art and letters, while maintaining her position against her many enemies. In writing her biography, Mrs Trouncer has given a fascinating picture of Paris from its salons to its low life: we see Voltaire and the *philosophes*, and encounter the art, the fashion, and the superstition of the time. The death of the heroine, in full court dress with rouge and patches, is the visible symbol of the end of a dissolute age.'

With best wishes to yourself and your family,

Yours sincerely,

[T. S. Eliot]


TO *James Laughlin*                                        TS Houghton

30 March 1937                         *The Criterion*

Dear Mr Laughlin,

I have your letter of March 8th, and we are looking forward with
interest to the Williams book that you promised to send.[1]

I am glad that you have been interested in *Nightwood*, which I am more
pleased with than anything for a long time.[2] I am sorry that Harcourt
could not let you have my poems for your collection.[3] If I write any of the
right size in time for your next I will be glad to let you have something,
but I do not think this is very likely, as I am trying to work on a play
instead.

Yours ever,

T. S. Eliot


1–Laughlin drew TSE's attention to the novel *White Mule*, by William Carlos Williams.
'Williams' poetry of course you know. His prose has I think equal quality. WHITE MULE is
by way of being his life work. He has been at it for a great many years, and it is a thing of,
as they say, "enduring worth". The book is in itself, in its story, a definition of what makes
Americans american and not something else.' (TSE to Richard A. Macksey, 15 Feb. 1959,
of Williams: 'Poetry springs from the most unexpected soil . . . He continues to split rocks
and find poems' – quoted by Louis L. Martz, 'The Unicorn in Paterson: William Carlos
Williams', in *William Carlos Williams: A Collection of Critical Essays*, ed. J. Hillis Miller
(1966), 76–7.)
2–Laughlin had talked with Theodore Spencer. 'We discussed NIGHT WOOD which has
the community pretty much in a twitter. It is a wonderful book, though I'm not sure I'm
"up" to it all yet.'
3–'I wonder if you liked my NEW DIRECTIONS IN PROSE & POETRY? I wanted to use
the poems you had given me for the magazine, but Harcourt wanted more money for them
than I could then pay.'

30 March 1937                    [Faber & Faber Ltd]

Dear Mr Miller,

Thank you for your letter of the 24th.[1] I am sending you a copy of
the *Criterion* with a notice of *Black Spring* in the Fiction Chronicle. The
*Criterion* has only just come out.[2]

As for your book, we should be delighted to consider for publication
anything of yours that is publishable in this country.[3] It is entirely a
practical question, and I cannot say without seeing the material. I am not
optimistic, but we are always ready to see what is possible.

We know Lawrence Durrell already, of course,[4] as we are doing one
book of his, and we certainly want to have the chance of his next one.
What you say about it makes me very eager to read it.

With best wishes,

Yours sincerely,

[T. S. Eliot]

P.S. I hope that you will be able to send Durrell's book along quite soon.

---

1 – Miller asked whether TSE had managed to run a review of *The Black Book* in *C*.
2 – A. Desmond Hawkins, 'Fiction Chronicle', *C*. 16 (Apr. 1937), 502–3. '[Mr Miller's]
words spout in gushers and he seems to let them lie where they fall. *Black Spring* starts
interminably, goes on interminably, and only ends for the sake of stopping somewhere – or
perhaps because Mr Miller has no more paper handy. For my part, I enjoyed it enormously.
Mr Miller is, I suppose, the last American *enfant terrible* left in Paris.'
3 – 'I shall have a very long book finished in a very short time – a collection of stories, essays
and portraits – not all of which are censorable. Is it any use submitting it to you through
Kahane, or are you *off me*? I have the impression that it's almost hopeless with the English
and American publishers. So advise me frankly – no harm done.

'On the other hand it is encouraging to learn that in America it is the censor himself who
is waging a fight for me. He is submitting my books to the critics on his own responsibility
– says there is still hope!'
4 – 'I must also tell you that I have in my hands a book (or manuscript rather) of Lawrence
Durrell's [*The Black Book*] from Corfu, Greece, which he has asked me to send to your
firm. I am holding it up in order to have carbon copies made. It seems to me a work of
genius – with glaring faults but with a content really extraordinary. And I know in advance
it is doomed. But what a day if an Englishman ever made a fight to launch a book like
that!' Miller had first mentioned Durrell on 4 Dec. 1936: 'This morning I had a letter from
Lawrence Durrell . . . who informs me that Faber & Faber are reading two of his books
now. Again I stick my oar in – forgive me. I never read any of Durrell's poetry or novels, but
I do know that no man has ever written me such letters as he writes. If he is not a talented
young author then I am very much mistaken. Anyway, I take the liberty of calling your
attention to his name. I have just persuaded Philip Mairet to publish a letter he wrote me
about Hamlet – the best thing on Hamlet I have seen to date! He knows what he is talking
about, apparently. I don't.'

TO *John Purves*[1]                                            CC

30 March 1937                        [Faber & Faber Ltd]

Dear Mr Purves,

I must explain that when I went seriously to work to revise my lecture on Cowley, I found that after ten years I was too dissatisfied with it to be able to make use of more than a part. To have prepared a new essay on the subject would have taken me more time than I had at my disposal. I hope therefore that you will accept, with my apologies, the enclosed short trifle of eleven pages, which is all that time has allowed me to prepare. If you find it too short, or otherwise unsuitable, I shall quite understand any disinclination on your part to print it.[2]

Yours very truly,
[T. S. Eliot]

## TO *The Old Colony Trust Company*                          CC

31 March 1937                        [Faber & Faber Ltd]

Dear Sirs,

You will recall that when I left America at the end of September you prepared a statement of my American income tax for the first nine months of 1936, and that I paid in Boston the tax on this amount, in satisfaction of the requirements concerning the departure from the country of non-resident aliens. In order to enable you to make my returns for the last three months of the year, I give you hereunder the items of income other than those which have passed through your hands.

I received 125 dollars in payment for a reading which I gave while in the States, and an odd sum of 25 dollars, paid direct to me for anthology rights.

---

Miller to Durrell, 6 Dec. 1936: 'I just wrote Eliot about you, hope it will do you some good. He seems to treat me very gingerly and cavalierly. He means to be warm-hearted, I suppose, but has grown such a crust that it is almost impossible. I just sent him about a hundred pages of the *Hamlet* book (ten letters), saying I know he won't take it, but read it.' (*Lawrence Durrell and Henry Miller: A Private Correspondence*, ed. George Wickes [NY, 1964], 30.)

1 – John Purves (1877–1961), Lecturer in Italian, University of Edinburgh; from 1938, Reader.

2 – 'A Note on Two Odes by Cowley by T. S. Eliot', *Seventeenth Century Studies presented to Sir Herbert Grierson* (Oxford, 1938), 235–42.

In October I received the payment for the performance of my play in New York under the Federal Theatre project. The sum amounts to 483 dollars, 35 cents, from which 10% should be deducted as that represents my agent's commission.

I have subsequently received in royalties from Harcourt Brace & Co. the sum of 86 dollars, 67 cents, and 122 dollars, 36 cents, from both of which sums 10% should be deducted, as that was taken by my agents.

I trust that this information will enable you to complete my income tax returns for the year 1936.

Yours faithfully,<br>
[T. S. Eliot]

## TO *John Hayward*

MS King's

Tuesday [31 March 1937]  Oxford & Cambridge Club

My dear John

On the eve of my departure for the Northern Kingdom, I employ a short respite to pen these hasty lines by way of valedictory. From the frequentation of my society, and my abundant conversation (it afflicts me to think how often I must have wearied you with my dilatations on this and other topicks) (O noctes Binanianae!!)[1] you will be fully acquainted with my abhorrence of the uncouth manners, the barbarous repasts, and the heady liquours of our northern neighbours. You will also know, that at my advanc'd age, and with the physical infirmities under which I suffer, the tour of the Hebrides is one not to be undertaken without misgiving and anxiety. Try to pourtray to yourself my distrefs and affliction of spirit, in relinquishing the urbanity of Kensington for the hardship of Scotia (as ill an exile as Ovid's, while it lasts) and pray for the safe restoration to civility of one who commends himself as

Your oblig<sup>d</sup> obt. serv<sup>t</sup><br>
Th. Eliot<br>
of Somerset.

1–'O nights at Bina [Gardens]': an allusion to Horace: 'O noctes coenæquae deum!' ('O nights and suppers of the gods!'). The volume of light verses called *Noctes Binanianae* (privately printed, 1939) – co-written by TSE, GCF, JDH, FVM – was titled after *Noctes Ambrosianae* (Ricks/McCue). Other precedents include Alexander Pope's *Notae Bentleianae* (1734). JDH lived at 22 Bina Gardens, London.

6 April 1937                          *The Criterion*

Dear Enid,

Thank you for your letter, which I found this morning on my return from Scotland.[1] I am rather exhausted, not so much by the potations of the heady liquors which (with a somewhat simple humour) they call the Wine of the Country, as by the baps, bannocks, potato scones, and mutton pies that one has to consume; by an evening with George Blake's Uncle George at the Inn on Loch Fyne; by spending two nights with Frank in a Caravan in Neil Gunn's back garden; by having no opportunity to wash during several days; by the intelligentzia of Glasgow; and by the universal goofiness of the Highlands in general and Neil Gunn in particular. My heart is in the highlands,[2] but I am very glad that my digestive system is back in London. I am sorry that your letter strikes such a mournful note, and I am sorry to hear about the trees. I have a letter from Ann who seems to be somewhere else. I hope that everyone is now in good health. I am moving to Emperor's Gate on Monday. I have brought back a bottle of ginger wine for Geoffrey, to refresh him after his holiday labours on *Jowett*. I am trying to write a play: but Crawley[3] is trying to persuade me to go and talk at a teaparty organised by a Bournemouth bookseller whom he knows, next week. I am very unhappy because of my indigestion on account of baps and bannocks etc. I visited the Grave of Robert Burns and his birthplace. I hope you will be back soon. Your depressed

TP.

And Daisy Gunn is sad company too. We had a picnic.[4]

1 – Not traced.
2 – Robert Burns's 'My Heart's in The Highlands' (1789): sung to the tune of *Fáilte na Miosg*.
3 – W. J. Crawley, formerly senior country representative of Methuen & Co., was appointed in Sept. 1933 to be Faber's sales manager and chief London representative, in succession to A. J. B. Patterson.
4 – FVM to the Gunns, 6 Apr. 1937: 'Hurrah. George's driving was magnificent as usual, and got us through fog and in one place – believe it or not – through a good ten feet of snow – smack through the middle of it – which if you think I am exaggerating, will be proved by photographs, if they develop. I forget just where the snow was, but there was really a lot of it. After that we had to pass through a cloud . . .

'As to our great and lasting gratitude to both of you, I will record that more fittingly later. Just now I am not in a condition to write . . . partly because Uncle Tom was so jealous of what he called Daisy's preferential treatment towards me, that he certainly scarified me all night long. I told him that he, being the successful dramatist and all was spoiled by being lionised in London; and that it was the highlands that rightly brought out the essential verities. The lowlands too, for when we got to Helensburgh last night we were just in time to be taken up to say good night to Sally Blake. We had to go up because Sally was asking

7 April 1937                          [*The Criterion*]

Dear Mairet,

I have just returned from Scotland to find your two notes. I am afraid the mistake about the Cotman book was due to my not having explained to my secretary what it was intended for.¹ The book is not for review in the *Criterion*, but for you to use in the *N.E.W.* Of course if you will deal with it yourself I shall be all the more pleased.

I have read the letter by Rilke.² It may be due to dullness on my part, or to an unjustifiable lack of sympathy, but I simply cannot get on with

---

for us, and in these terms. First she asked for the man (meaning me) and when I had had my dismissal, she asked for the boy. So the boy (Uncle Tom) was once more put in his proper place . . . Hurrah once more, and all great gratitude for your nobilities towards us. I hope the legs of the caravan are not permanently splayed – we are enormously the better for it . . .'

FVM to his brother Christopher, 6 Apr.: 'I myself am just this morning back from a strenuous foray in Scotland. Eliot and I went up by train last Wednesday night; emerged from the train at Dumfries, where we discovered George Blake, looking very burly, in the station hotel; and we spent that day very happily routing around Galloway with George. As you once remarked, George has a good nose for routing, and it was a very agreeable and beautiful stretch of lowlands hitherto unknown to us. We blazed a good trail and thought of you at various moments. The weather on that Thursday was good though cold, and we were glad that Ellie had a good fire when we eventually reached Helensburgh. It was our first inspection of George's seat, The Glenan; which is an old mansion in the heart of Helensburgh pleasantly protected and very comfortable. On the Friday we called on the Glasgow booksellers and flushed a very odd covey at lunch; the most remarkable person being James Bridie who in private life is Dr Mavor. After lunch – that's to say what in London we should regard as after tea – we collected Ellie and set forth in George's little Singer (which is really no larger than a sewing-machine so that portions of me were at all times exposed to the airts [*sic*]) and successfully reached and spent the night at Cairndow; where a most remarkable thing happened – we found staying in that same inn, the real George Blake: George's formidable Uncle George who rapidly had all of us in thrall and before whom our George quailed as in childhood. It was a good evening, with Uncle George holding the platform with an account of the building of the highland railway back in the '80s. On Saturday we travelled under an unfortunately cold and gloomy sky, sometimes through the sky, by way of Inverary (which, though Campbell's headquarters, is the most remarkable and beautiful town in Scotland) up the glen and past the new and very pleasing rough stone memorial of Neil Munro, towards Appin. Appin was new to us, and is very good; after Appin it was the familiar road by Mr Carmichael past Loch Ness (no monster visible on so cold a day) to Neil Gunn's quarters. We spent two nights with Gunn, Uncle Tom and I sleeping in a caravan in his back garden; or perhaps I should say spending what remnant there was of each night in the caravan. Yesterday we left Inverness in good time and plugged along through snow and fog to reach Helensburgh in time to catch a connection for the Night Scot, which has just landed us back.'

1 – Sydney D. Kitson, *The Life of John Sell Cotman* (F&F, 1937).

2 – Mairet to TSE, 1 Apr.: 'I thought you might like to have a look at this letter of Rilke. It is translated by R. F. C. Hull, and I understand never published here. It is much too long for

this sort of thing. It may be very good indeed, but I don't like to publish anything about which I feel no sort of conviction.

I have a card from Symons[1] indicating the next four meetings of Chandos. It would be a help if you would let me know as far in advance as possible which meetings would be most profitable for me to attend.

Yours ever sincerely,

[T. S. Eliot]

P.S. We have written to the publishers of Dalbiez, but we think it would be an advantage if you, or particularly Ludovici, could write to them as well in our favour. The point is that they seem to have been negotiating with another firm here – I don't know who – and a little support might just make the difference in bringing the book our way.[2]

TO *Daisy Gunn*[3]                     MS National Library of Scotland

9 April 1937                     Faber & Faber Ltd

Dear Daisy

We got back on Tuesday morning, tired but contented, after what was for me certainly the most delightful visit to the Highlands that I have yet had. I am so glad that there was the caravan for us to sleep in – I should not have enjoyed my visit half so much if we had had to go to the Hotel. Thank you very much for all your hospitality, which with the picnic, gave memories not to be forgotten. Whether we meet next in the Hebrides or in

---

the N.E.W. and probably for the "Criterion" too, for which I feel unable to judge of its suitability.'

1 – W. T. (Travers) Symons, journalist, was editor of *Purpose*; an editor of the *New English Weekly*, and a director of C. W. Daniel, London publishers.

2 – Mairet to TSE, 19 Mar.: 'I have had a talk with Ludovici today, and he spoke of the [Roland] Dalbiez book on Freud, which he is reviewing for the N.E.W. He has just finished the first volume, and is prostrate with admiration, as I was.

'I wonder if you have yet been able to obtain a decision from Faber's as to whether they would care to publish a translation. There is, of course, something of a slump in the literature of the Viennese psychologists generally, but Freud himself is in a class apart, and this book is of unique and permanent value.'

*La méthode psychanalytique et le doctrine freudienne*, by the philosopher Roland Dalbiez (1893–1976), with a preface by Henri Claude (2 vols, Desclée de Brouwer, 1936), was translated as *Psychoanalytical Methods and the Doctrine of Freud* (Longmans, 1941).

3 – Jessie (Daisy) Gunn (1887/8–1963): wife of the Scottish novelist Neil Gunn, whose works were published by the Porpoise Press (see TSE to George Blake, 9 Aug. 1932) and subsequently by F&F. The Gunns lived in a bungalow they had built at Inverness.

your wooden house – barring your visit to London, which I hope you will not cancel – here are my thanks and blessing to both of you.

Yours very sincerely

T. S. Eliot

## TO *William Greenleaf Eliot*[1]

CC

9 April 1937                               [*The Criterion*]

My dear Will,

It was very kind of you to write to me about the death of Paul More.[2] I did indeed feel it as a very deep loss, which is somewhat mitigated, first by the fact that it had been expected for some months in advance, and second by my good fortune in being able to run down to Princeton and spend a day with him during my visit to New England in September. I found him completely lucid, and his same delightful and affectionate self, although obviously with very little physical strength.

I had not remembered that you had seen so much of him at the University.

I am delighted to have the photograph of my father, as I had never seen a copy of this photograph, and I have no other portrait of him at that age.[3] If you happen to know in what year it was taken, I should be very glad to have the date. I should imagine it was in the later 'sixties.

I hope that you received safely the walking-stick of Grandfather's, which I left for you with Ada three years ago. I should like to think that it would always be in the possession of one of his namesakes.

I shall look forward to seeing the biography of your father.[4]

With love to Minna and yourself,

Affectionately yours,

[Tom]

1 – William Greenleaf Eliot, 3rd (1897–1990).

2 – Will Eliot wrote from Portland, Oregon, on 25 Mar.: 'The death of Paul More moves me to write to you, for you will feel the loss deeply. It brings *me* sorrow, though there had never been such intimacy between us as you & he had enjoyed. I have read his books through the years & often wished I might acknowledge my indebtedness & tell him of my gratitude. But I suspect, perhaps erroneously, that he had forgotten me! When we were in college together he was a year ahead, & his kindness and encouragement meant much to me. I remember with happiness a long walk one afternoon in the open country west of St Louis. I do not remember what we talked about, but I am sure we settled all the affairs of the universe.'

3 – 'You have probably seen this photograph of your father, but may not yourself have one; in which case I hope you will be pleased to keep it.'

4 – Earl Wilbur had written a biography of Will Eliot's father: *Thomas Lamb Eliot: 1841–1936* (1937). Later in the year he sent a copy to TSE, which was acknowledged.

TO *Allen Tate*[1]                                               TS Princeton

12 April 1937                           *The Criterion*

My dear Tate,

I was very much pleased by your sending me your poems, which I have read with great pleasure.[2] They seem to me to make a volume which stands up extremely well, and I am very glad that Scribner's will be doing them. But as for us, I am afraid that at present it is quite out of the question for me to get my committee to accept them here. It is hard enough to sell English poetry here, and they naturally feel that what we can do in the way of verse ought to be first in support of what is produced in England. I wish I could be more optimistic, but at the same time I don't want to discourage you from trying elsewhere. The best person to approach is certainly Richard Church of J. M. Dent & Sons. There are only three or four firms, anyway, worth approaching with poetry. If you want me to do anything about it, I shall be delighted to be what use I can.

I wish that we might meet again some time, but my visits to America have to be too brief for me to get very far beyond the borders of New England.

Yours ever,
T. S. Eliot

1 – Allen Tate (1899–1979), poet, critic and editor, grew up in Kentucky and attended Vanderbilt University (where he was taught by John Crowe Ransom and became associated with the group of writers known as the Fugitives). He taught at various universities before becoming Poet-in-Residence at Princeton, 1939–42; Poetry Consultant to the Library of Congress, 1944–5; and editor of *The Sewanee Review*, 1944–6; and he was Professor of Humanities at the University of Minnesota (where colleagues included Saul Bellow and John Berryman), 1951–68. Eliot wrote of him in 1959: 'Allen Tate is a good poet and a good literary critic who is distinguished for the sagacity of his social judgment and the consistency with which he has maintained the least popular of political attitudes – that of the sage' (*The Sewanee Review*, 67; 4 [Oct.–Dec. 1959], 576). Tate's works include *Ode to the Confederate Dead* (1930), *Poems: 1928–1931* (1932), *The Mediterranean and Other Poems* (1936), and *The Fathers* (novel, 1938).

2 – Tate sent (6 Mar.) the MS of a volume coming out in the autumn, made up of the three volumes he had published since 1928. 'I should be very much pleased should Faber & Faber decide to bring the book out in England where my verse has not been printed in book form.'

TO *F. T. Prince*                                                          CC

13 April 1937                          [Faber & Faber Ltd]

Dear Mr Prince,

It is a long time that I have had your poems without having let you
have word about them. I think, however, I told you that I hoped to use
the 'Tears for William Maynard' in the June number of the *Criterion.*[1]
I should like to propose your poems to my committee with a view to
publication, but I think that your selection is really rather small. Ten
pages or so more would be helpful. Have you been writing anything lately
that you would care to let me see? and in any case, what about the final
version of *Tchaka*?[2]

                              Yours sincerely,
                              [T. S. Eliot]


TO *Alison Tandy*[3]                                                       TS BL

Friday, the 16th Day of April: 1937 *The Criterion*

Dear Alison,
          Poor Poony now is meek and mild,
          And very like a Christian Child.
          She must be peaceable and good:
          She could not Bite me if she would.
          I know it's very hard in youth
          To be without a sweetened Tooth,
          And so I send this floral wreath
          In memory of Poony's teeth.
          But Oh! when you would like to gnash
          On Food more firm than Succotash,
          And Oh! when you would like to grind
          The tough refract'ry bacon rind,
          And Oh! when you would like to champ

---

1–Prince, 'A Muse for William Maynard', C. 16 (July 1937), 603–5.
2–Prince replied on 15 Apr. that he would remedy the length of his proposed book within
a short while. 'As for *Tchaka* I have not yet taken it up again as a whole because I have
assumed that it wouldn't fit into the present selection in any form.' He was now working at
Chatham House, but hoped not to keep TSE waiting more than a couple of weeks. Prince
resubmitted the collection, with almost double the number of poems, on 2 June.
3–Alison Tandy (b. 1930).

Some food more firm than porridge damp –
The sorrow from your face efface
And think upon Poor Possum's case.
For he is much worse off than you
In losing teeth: but two by two
And year by year, they are extracted.
His agony is more protracted.
And though you now must feed on mushes,
You very soon will have new tushes
(To crack a nut or chicken bone)
Which you can call your very own.
But Poor Old Possum has to wait
For something called a Dental Plate
That's not in any way so good
For human nature's daily food
And not so powerful to bite
And not so beautiful and white.
I hope this Letter will convey
A mite of all I'd like to say
And will express in Microcosm
The sympathy of faithful

POSSUM[1]


то *John Hayward*                                          тs King's

Friday [16 April 1937]          *The Criterion*

Good news for the voracious readers of the *Sun*, but I don't know how
soon. Our Wystan lets me know that he is taking the King's Medal from
Mr Masefield this June. Me avin bin a bit be'ind the scenes as you might
say, wiv I.A.R. on the subjcct, there's a couple of laughtts in that. I have
written to Wystan to ask whether and how soon the news may be released,
and will let you know. And I have suggested to him (1) that he should take
over the Coronation Duties from Masefield, and (2) meanwhile try a half
column Ode for *The Times* (I mean Geoffrey Dawson's *Times* newspaper)[2]
on the subject of Potato Jones.

Tp.

1–A carbon copy of this verse epistle was sent to EH (Scripps).
2–Geoffrey Dawson (1874–1944): editor of *The Times*, 1912–19 and 1922–41.

If you see those Maxesses[1] again, there might be a couple of laughs in Mrs M.'s account of the Mad Tea Party at Lady Darnley's. I forgot to mention that before.

tp.

TO *John Hayward*                                                    TS King's

Friday [16 April 1937]                    *The Criterion*

Dear John,

A subsequent invitation has just reminded me of Bradfield. I will write to Geoffrey, but I doubt whether in his condition of mumps and mopes he will feel like making an engagement. But if he doesn't, I'd like us to go anyway, and will stand the cost of a car with great pleasure. It may be high time to see about tickets. I cant go on the 26th, and prefer not on the 24th, but either the 19th or the 22nd would be allright.

I have just had another cold under difficulties. I suspect due to sleeping in a newly papered room that had not been dried out. In bed two days with the plumbers camping in the bathroom both days – no hot water – part of the time no gas – didnt wash – could only rear in the evening: one day Elizabeth collapsed from overwork and I depended upon odd unknown parochial females who poked cups of bovril and tea at me from time to time and said 'Are you sure that's all you want?' All settled now and just going out. The place has drawbacks – 79 steps. Must get a rope ladder.

Yrs
TP

I dont know the telephone yet, but the address is Flat 3, 11, Emperor's Gate (Hemprer's) S.W.7.[2]

---

1 – Major John Herbert Maxse (1901–78), educated at Eton and the Royal Military College, Sandhurst, and his wife Dorinda, née Thorne (1901–88), were close friends of JDH.
2 – FVM to Ada Sheffield, 16 Apr. 1937: 'We very much hope for Uncle Tom this week-end. He has been having a cold, and moving; and if extra attention is required to recuperate him, we will certainly do our best. I have read the first act of his new play and am very pleased with it.'

16 April 1937                    [Faber & Faber Ltd]

My dear George,

Thank you for your letter of the 14th, and your short sharp slap at Ingram, which will do nicely.[1] I have also read your essay on modern poetry, which I like, and I am afraid I have no comments to make, except two trifling ones.

In the Epigraph, did MacNeice really write 'osculation'? It looks as if it ought to be 'oscillation', but I cannot lay my hands on the book at the moment.[2]

The other point is also a small one. Aren't you rather exaggerating the unity of the Middle Ages? Half the time at least it seems to me that they were tearing down what the previous period had erected. At Rochester I know the Norman nave only remains because their money gave out after they had reconstructed the transept, and the junction is rather an ugly one. I may be prejudiced in favour of the Norman style, but I do suspect that the later Middle Ages destroyed a considerable amount of good Norman work in order to replace it with styles which I don't like so much. The Norman nave of Southwell is to my mind much the finest part of the building, and does not fit at all with the spirit of the Chapter House. I wonder if you know the little church of Hardham in Sussex, where the lovely frescoes of the 12th century were plastered over by the 13th century, as the style was too crude to suit their more cultivated taste.[3]

I should like to settle a date to come to Kelham, because I see that if I do not do so well in advance, the time will get taken up. Would either the weekend of the 22nd or the 29th May be convenient for you and the Prior? Or if my plans fell through for going abroad during Coronation week, I should be glad to take sanctuary with you then.[4]

                              Yours ever affectionately,
                              [T. S.]

1 – Letter not traced: it covered what Every called his 'S.C.M. poetry paper'. Untitled rev. of Kenneth Ingram, *Christianity – Right or Left*: C. 16 (July 1937), 711–13.

2 – MacNeice, 'Eclogue for Christmas': 'With an osculation of yellow light, with a glory like chrysanthemums' (*Poems* [1935], 16).

3 – St Botolph's Church, Hardham, W. Sussex, a late Saxon or early Norman building (completed *c.* 1125) has extensive wall paintings, dating from the twelfth century (including the earliest known representation of St George in England), uncovered in 1868.

4 – Every, 21 Apr.: 'There will be *no wireless*, not even (I think) on coronation day. So this would be an effective sanctuary, and perhaps not such an escape as a continental trip.' The coronation of George VI on 12 May 1937 was the first coronation to be broadcast live on radio.

20 April 1937                    *The Criterion*

Dear Geoffrey,

I meant to write a week ago, on hearing of the Mumps: but I was immediately stricken myself. I think through moving into a flat which had recently been papered and not dried out. Anyway, I went to bed on Monday night after spending an evening with my Old Buffers dining club listening to our Baptist member, Mr Le Quesne K.C.[1] explain the principle of Adult Baptism, and waked up on Tuesday with my head full of cold. On the same morning arrived the receipted bill from my doctor, for the anti-cold inoculations he had given me. I mention this point, not in a spirit of grievance, but so that others may learn from my experience. I struggled through that day, but the next day kept my bed. It was not the best occasion, because, although the moving was done, the plumbers camped in the bathroom for two days, jingling their silly tools and conversing gruffly with each other: for two days I did not wash, and could only rear either early in the morning or after 6 p.m. Then Elizabeth the housekeeper collapsed temporarily from over work and running up and down stairs, so that one day I was entirely dependent upon odd unknown parochial women poking cups of bovril at me and saying 'Are you sure that's all you want?' When I got up and looked at myself after three days I discovered that my beard is really quite grizzly, or like Hamlet's ghost, 'a sable silver'd'; and it was quite painful to shave. I staggered out on Friday, and lunched with Pickthorn at the House of Commons, which is like lunching at a railway station, except that the food is not so good. He was hoping to speak on the marriage bill, but apparently he didnt. Anyway I discussed the Hancock proposal with him, and he liked it very much, only he said there was already a first-rate book covering the subject, called *Jesus and Civil Government*.[2] It didnt sound to me as if it could be exactly the same thing, but I have got it out of the London Library and shall have to read it. But Pickthorn seemed pleased with the notion of doing a book for us, and I think it is well worth while finding a subject and hammering at him – he is shy and diffident. He is the most intelligent Tory that I know. On Saturday I crept down to Pike's Farm (where I didnt get any baths

---

1 – Charles Thomas Le Quesne (1885–1954): Jersey-born Liberal Party politican and barrister: King's Counsel, 1925. President of the Baptist Union of Great Britain and Ireland, 1946–7.
2 – Arthur Temple Cadoux, *Jesus and Civil Government: a contribution to the problem of Christianity and coercion* (1923).

either, because they let the boiler go out; but I got one this morning and feel better, except that my chest feels very tight. I was too annoyed with my doctor to send for him, so I treated myself with Pulmo and Cascara Evacuant (Parke Davis) and now with the Prophyll Portable Atomiser and Regesan Bronchial Mixture which is cheap at one and three a bottle and some say does good; but this tight chest catches me coming in as I have 79 steps to climb to get to my roost and I MUST get a rope fire escape). That would have done me a lot of good if the weather had been better, but I did get a bellyfull of Beethoven, starting before breakfast. Michael Roberts and Janet Adam Smith turned up for the day on Sunday.

Well I looked at your X-word puzzle and it is indeed a teaser; I think too difficult for me – I got two words. Why do the Welsh chemists keep whiskey? does that mean that they do Not keep whisky? There is a bottle of the latter, imported from Glasgow, in your cupboard. (There wasnt much washing in Scotland either, and sleeping in the back garden in Inverness in a caravan with the corners precariously propped and Frank at the other end is a very strange experience indeed, but appropriate to that goofy country; but I am glad I went to Scotland because (1) a nip of delicious Islay malt whisky in a shop in Helensburgh (2) I got a photograph of George which I will send you, standing in front of a wrought iron fountain in Stranraer looking wonderfully monumental (3) I saw Inverary (4) Gunn showed me a book called *Carmina Gadelica* from which I got a hint for my play).[1] I am encouraged by hearing that you have been doing Alcaics, or as I might write 'alcaics'; it would seem to indicate that the mumps are not badly ravaging, though they must be VERY unpleasant at best, and that you have your mind still.[2] And as for the other parts, congratulations: but don't be so elated as to behave like Old Ike Carver of Mosquito Cove, who strained himself . . . but I

---

1 – *Carmina Gadelica: Hymns and Incantations, with illustrative notes on words, rites, and customs, dying and obsolete: orally collected in the Highlands and Islands of Scotland and translated into English* by Alexander Carmichael (Edinburgh, 1900), III, 201). A. W. R. Miller to TSE (Sept./Oct. 1934): 'have you ever come across Carmichael's "Ortha nan Gaidheal"? – a collection, with excellent translations (mercifully), of Gaelic incantations and hymns of the Celtic Church; and with enthralling notes on Celtic mythology and rites . . . It completely redeems Gaelic literature from the ghastly hash that Fiona Macleod made of it. It contains a few poems (one above all) that I should rank as high as anything.' TSE to Miller, 3 Oct. 1934: 'I don't know the Carmichael book of which you speak. The title is formidable. I will see if they have it in the London Library.' The collection was to be an acknowledged influence on *FR*.
2 – GCF's diary, Thurs, 8 Apr.: 'Definitely mumps – & must have had it for past week, so to bed & stay there, writing mock alcaics for T. S. E. (subsequently published in *Criterion* over anagram of name Offa E. Freyberg).' See 'Poetae Cuiusdam Ignoti: Carmen Singulare', *C.* 16 (July 1937), 655–65.

mustn't get gossiping, although there's really no secret about it, at the time I remember everybody was laughing about it all the way from Moose-a-Bec[1] to Boot Cove.[2] Well, I can't write alcaics, because I was never taught: did plenty of Latin and Greek proses in my time, but no verses, not even hexameters. I wish I had, because I believe that one would appreciate Horace more sensitively for having done so (by the way, I'm not SURE that I'm not going to have mumps too, my throat seems a little sore, and the O'Donovan came to see me last week). And I was only made to read selected Horace – just the things that young people used to be supposed to be able to quote in order to get on in smoking rooms etc. – and left to oneself at that age one takes more readily as I did to Catullus and Propertius (it's years now since I read it, but when you feel stronger look at the Marriage of Peleus and Thetis again and see if it doesn't knock you out).[3] Well I wish things would stop happening so that I could get on with my play. It is a gloomy play, I rather think it is going to be much the grimmest thing I have ever written: when I tell you it is about a birthday party you will see the possibilities: everything goes wrong except the cake. That sounds as if I had been influenced by Chehov, Tchechoff, Checkhov, and perhaps I have. Oh, I have just remembered something important enough to need a new paragraph.

John Hayward wants to know if you would care to come to the Bradfield College Play (Oedipous Turannos in Greek) on either June 19th (Saturday) or June 22nd (Tuesday) afternoon. The applications have to be in by May 1st, but he can get three tickets or four I dare say if he applies in time. If you do come, we Hope that you will drive us (it's somewhere near Reading isnt it) but that is not obligatory, because otherwise I shall stand for a car and chauffeur for the day and there would be room for everybody in a hire Daimler. Anyway, we hope that you will come, but you must decide before May 1st.[4]

. . . . .

Well, I want to get back to this play, but there are so many interruptions. The Coronation, for one. I want to be out of town, because my cousin Frank's wife, sister-in-law and daughter Caroline,[5] none of whom I have

1 – Moose-a-bec: a reach of water by Jonesport, Maine.
2 – Boot Cove: a bay close to Boot Head, Maine.
3 – Catullus's epyllion, or little epic, *The Marriage of Peleus and Thetis*.
4 – GCF's diary, Sat. 19 June: 'To Bradfield with TSE & JH. Enjoyable day, tho' I don't think Oedipus T. ideally suited. Liked our hosts (Mr & Mrs Norman Saunders) – he goes as Master of the XX to Rugby next term.'
5 – TSE's first cousin Frank Monroe Eliot (1886–1964) was brought up in St Louis, Missouri; he married Lucy Byrd Morton (b. 1887), and their daughter was Mary Caroline Eliot (b. 1923).

ever seen, are going to be here; in fact, Right here, in Queen's Gate: and obviously, I can't be here too. I have seen about their seats, and that's enough for ties of blood. Besides, when Frank was eleven or twelve he used to wrestle with me and always tripped me up. I haven't seen him since, but I don't want to meet his family. And no sooner is that over than I have to write out a lecture to deliver to the Friends of Canterbury; and damn it, now that the Dean (I dont mean Canterbury, I meant to write Rochester, but you cant alter with single spacing) has gone to Bath & Wells I suppose I shall have to become a Friend of Bath & Wells too and go through this all over again another year. So I'm getting worried about this play. And Presently I must go and give lunch to John Betjeman and ask him whether he would like to write a book on English Architecture. So I think I must stop. That seems a good idea for you to go to Bruges (pronounce Bru-jez) for a week to convalesce.

Yours (and all the family's)<br>TP

## TO *Ezra Pound*

TS Beinecke

21 April 1937                    *The Criterion*

Dear Ez,

The enclosed letter indicates a responsibility such as you ought not to elude. As you seem to have done so much already to modify the author's life, perhaps you would be willing to do a bit more. Actually I think he might be worth it. He is a lad whom I fell in with coming back from Montreal last summer, age about 20 or 21, comes from a paper manufacturing town in Northern Ontario, which must be a pretty awful place, to judge from some of the sketches he has written about it.[1] Some of his stuff seemed to me distinctly promising, and I have warned him off trying to imitate the later Joyce. I think you might help him to do something good. At any rate, if anyone can it is yourself. He is introverted, but not in a tiresome way, very modest, anxious not to take up one's time and very easy to shoo away when one has had enough of him. You need not worry about his getting out of hand. Will you see him a few times if he comes out to Rapallo? If you like you can have some specimens of his stuff in advance, but I think there is more in the boy than yet comes out in anything he writes. All prose, and wants to do a kind of novel about the paper town.

1–J. A. Reid.

I told him I would write to you and intercede. He is not the kind that tries to borrow money.[1]

Yours,

TP


## TO *E. R. Curtius*[2] CC

21 April 1937            [Faber & Faber Ltd]

My dear Curtius,

I was very happy indeed to get your letter of the 16th, and wish to assure you that I quite understand long periods of silence on your part, and hope that you will accept my own silences in the same way.[3] I only wish that we could occasionally meet, but I do not know when it will be possible for me to visit you in Bonn.

1–EP responded, 23 Apr.: 'To the Big cheef Protopherias Wattahatamie Possum WHOOGUMM! All right, ship the kid along. I can't take things with quite the solemnity of yr/ coverin' epistl. Can he play tennis? . . . You tellink me of REEsponserbiLLY /tea izza gnu one.'

2–Ernst Robert Curtius (1886–1956), scholar of philology and Romance literature. Scion of a family of scholars, he studied philology and philosophy at Strasbourg, Berlin and Heidelberg, and taught in turn at Marburg, Heidelberg and Bonn. Author of *Die Französische Kultur* (1931; *The Civilization of France*, trans. Olive Wyon, 1932); his most substantial work was *Europäische Literatur und Lateinisches Mittelalter* (1948; trans. by Willard R. Trask as *European Literature and the Latin Middle Ages*, 1953), a study of Medieval Latin literature and its fructifying influence upon the literatures of modern Europe. TSE to Max Rychner (24 Oct. 1955): 'I have . . . my own personal debt of gratitude to acknowledge to Curtius, for translating, and introducing, *The Waste Land*. Curtius was also, I think, the first critic in Germany to recognise the importance of James Joyce.' TSE praised too 'that masterly work, *Europaeische Litteratur und Lateinisches Mittelalter*, on which he had been at work during the years when freedom of speech and freedom of travel were suspended. It bears testimony to his integrity and indomitable spirit . . . Curtius deserves, in his life and in his work, the gratitude and admiration of his fellow writers of every European nation' (TSE's letter is printed in 'Brief über Ernst Robert Curtius', in *Freundesgabe für Ernest Robert Curtius zum 14. April 1956* [1956], 25–7.) See too Peter Godman, 'T. S. Eliot and E. R. Curtius: A European dialogue', *Liber: A European Review of Books*, 1: 1 (Oct. 1989), 5, 7; J. H. Copley, '"The Politics of Friendship": T. S. Eliot in Germany Through E. R. Curtius's Looking Glass', in *The International Reception of T. S. Eliot*, ed. Elisabeth Däumer and Shyamal Bagchee (2007), 243–67.

3–Curtius wrote that he was sorry for his long silence: 'Few people now living mean as much to me as you, and I follow your progress from a distance and hold conversations with you in my mind. But in the periodicity of life there are times to keep silent and times to speak. There are times of which one can say: *Bene vixit qui bene latuit* [to live well is to keep well concealed].' He went on: 'In the meantime I'm sending you a letter from someone unknown to me. I replied to him at once asking him to let me know what arrangements he had made with you [. . .] I've received no reply. I suspect that a certain amount of reserve would be sensible — at least on my side.'

As for the writer of the letter which I return herewith, he is as unknown to me as he is to you. He wrote to me a considerable time ago, making a suggestion which apparently was for a complete edition of my prose and verse in German. He did not make it clear what part, if any, he wished to take in this project, which struck me as over-ambitious; and I must confess to having suggested to him that he should consult you. His present letter does not seem to throw much more light on the subject.

I am interested to read what you say about Hennecke's article in the *Europaische Revue*.[1] I was puzzled at the time, but I am still more mystified now.

> With best wishes to Frau Curtius,
> Always cordially your friend,
> [T. S. Eliot]

## TO *Ian Cox*[2]                                                      CC

21 April 1937                                    [Faber & Faber Ltd]

My dear Cox,

I must apologize for the delay in writing to you about *Desire Provoketh*, which I hope you will interpret in a favourable sense.[3] That is to say, I was very much interested and struck by it indeed, as a very unusual piece of work, and my delay in writing has been due to awareness of the difficulty of putting to you or to anybody exactly how I feel about it. I can perhaps express it better in conversation when we meet, but to put it crudely, what the material seems to lack is anatomy; certainly something which will not be supplied simply by the chapters which are missing. You have put in a great deal of the inapprehensible and unnameable emotion and feeling which one wants to get in to any work of poetry or imaginative prose, but you have left out the structure of ordinary action which is the necessary vehicle for conveying these things. I mean that what is missing is the part which ought to take one's conscious attention, at least at a first reading,

---

1–H. Hennecke, 'T. S. Eliot. Der Dichter als Kritiker', *Europäische Revue* 12 (1936), 721–35.

Curtius wrote: 'You will have read the essay on you by Hennecke in the Europ. Revue, where we learn that until now no German critic has dealt with your work. The editor of this journal, a pupil of mine, wrote to me subsequently to say that my name had not been mentioned "so as not to harm me". *Voilà les moeurs de notre époque littéraire* [so much for the manners of our literary epoch].'

2–Ian Cox, a scientist by training, was BBC Talks Producer from 1936.

3–At Tandy's suggestion, Cox had submitted his 'rather skeletal script' on 1 Mar.

and what you have put in is the part which ought to affect the reader at first while he is attending to something else. I mean that one ought to be able to look at what you have set down out of the margins of one's eye, the part in which the rods and cones are less worn, just as one can count more of the Pleiades on a clear night when one is not looking directly at them.[1]

This is a periphrastical way of putting it,[2] but I don't think I can make it any clearer by labouring after analogies. The point is, what is to be done to supply a body to carry all this stuff? You see, if it were published just as it is, it would fall into a category of literature where it does not belong, and which is very much below its level of intensity; that of the quiet meditative observation of nature plus reflection, say. This may seem to you quite beside the point, but ridiculous as the confusion would be, it would be made, and it is a pity that it should be made. What you have to supply, I think, is something for which you would not need to tear your vitals, but simply a practical method for getting it over.

I will try to develop these points in conversation.

Yours sincerely,

[T. S. Eliot]

TO *Caresse Crosby*                                                        CC

22 April 1937                    [Faber & Faber Ltd]

Dear Mrs Crosby,

I must apologize for my delay in thanking you for sending the George Grosz drawings, but I had hoped to give you sooner a decision from my committee.[3] We do compliment you on having produced a very beautiful

---

1 – TSE is alluding to the technique called 'averted vision'. The retina contains two types of photoreceptors, rods and cones. The rods, being far more numerous, are more sensitive than the cones, yet they are not sensitive to colour. Cones are sensitive to colour, but not in conditions of low light. The rods retain sensitivity in darkness, but since they are located slightly off the centre of the retina, night vision works best when exercised sidewise.

2 – Cf. *EC* II: 'That was a way of putting it – not very satisfactory: / A periphrastic study in a worn-out poetical fashion'.

3 – Crosby had written from New York, 10 Mar., about *Interregnum* (Black Sun Press, 1936), her edition in twenty-eight numbered copies of George Grosz's satirical drawings: sixty-four black-and-white lithographs and one full-colour lithograph. Sold at $50 a volume, she reported, the edition was 'going very slowly, although there is a continued interest':

'However, I should be glad to negotiate with you for reproduction of the 64 lithographs in the trade edition, or else perhaps send you some of the sheets in the volume as it is, if you cared to use it with your imprint in London. The book has been very much admired here,

book. It is not, as I think you know, the kind of production which we felt we could dispose of in this country, where the market for this sort of expensive fine edition has almost completely disappeared. What we were, and are still, interested in is the possibility of an ordinary trade edition, such as I understand Simon and Schuster were thinking of producing in New York. If there is any prospect of such an edition, I should be very glad if you would let me know. Meanwhile, if you are interested in approaching any other firm with a view to their taking sheets of the expensive edition, I will hold the copy for your instructions.

The business of the Joyce poems is not in my hands,[1] and it depends on coming to some agreement with Jonathan Cape, who controls Joyce's first volume of verse.

With best wishes,
Yours very sincerely,
[T. S. Eliot]

## TO *Geoffrey Grigson*                                                    CC

22 April 1937                        [Faber & Faber Ltd]

Dear Grigson,

I look forward to seeing your re-selections of the *New Verse* anthology as soon as you have it ready. I think that we ought to do it.[2]

About contributing to your Auden number.[3] I have thought this over pretty carefully, and I feel that considering that I am in a difficult position

---

and was chosen as one of the 50 finest books of the year by the Society of Graphic Arts; but I do not find that there is the same interest in book collecting that I found with my clientele in Paris, and I should be glad to dispose of some of this edition abroad. I could sell the sheets, which include the hand set introduction by John Dos Passos . . . for $15.00 a volume . . . I will at any rate send you a copy of the book and you may judge for yourself if you care to do anything with it.'

1 – Crosby wrote in her letter, 'The Joyce poems have also received mention in the 50 books of the year, and are going very well. I do not think that I will have any difficulty with them. They sell for $5.00, and $20.00 for the Japan copies signed. If you would care to get the rights through Joyce's agent, I should be very glad to make some arrangement with you to copy my edition in phototype, or have some sheets run off from the original text on ordinary paper.'

2 – Grigson wrote on 6 Apr.: 'My idea about the *New Verse* anthology is to weed out the selection I sent you last year, and add a few more poems. The size I think of as roughly that of Louis MacNeice's poems or Auden's *Look, Stranger*. I will send you the material.'

3 – 'About the Auden number . . . if you were to write even a paragraph of commendation or approval, it would be good: English poets or writers always seem hesitant about other English poets or writers . . . I think probably that anything said by you acknowledging

for saying everything that I should like to say about contemporaries, it is really unnecessary for me to be included. It seems to me that I have committed myself generally and perfectly clearly to approval of Auden and his works in the capacity of editor and publisher. But for me to say anything worth saying about his poetry would involve either mentioning or conspicuously refraining from mentioning other poets of his generation, and I feel that any such expression, or alternatively implication, on my part, would be unfair both to other poets whom we publish and to some of the poets whom we do not. I cannot say publicly that I think Auden very much the best poet of his generation, because that would be of more damage to other poets than it would be of use to him. After all, Auden has now arrived, and I am very glad of it, but I feel that if I raised my voice at all it ought to be on behalf of young poets who are still not accepted.

Yours ever sincerely<br>[T. S. Eliot]

## TO *W. B. Yeats* CC

22 April 1937 [Faber & Faber Ltd]

My dear Yeats,

I should have written to you yesterday if I had had time, and there was no opportunity for discussing business matters with you at dinner. I am writing to ask about the Swami's Patanjali translation. We now have the text and the illustrations. That is all right as far as it goes, but I am not sure whether there is any W.B.Y. in the translation, and in any case we are not keen to do the book without a preface by you. From a publisher's point of view it is only your co-operation and introductions that make it possible to market the Swami's work, and if you are not going to figure conspicuously in this Patanjali, we shall have to think more than twice about doing it. But I should like to do it, and therefore I very much hope to hear that you are having at least a hand in the translation, and that you will also provide an introduction.[1]

Ever yours sincerely,<br>[T. S. Eliot]

---

Auden would be valuable publicly. It would help readers to a confidence; and that kind of confidence is needed by most people, whether it becomes academic or not.'

1 – Yeats replied from Dublin ('May') agreeing to this undertaking, though he made clear there would be a delay before he could get to it – he had other obligations to attend to.

See Bhagwan Shree Patanjali, *Aphorisms of Yoga*, trans. Shri Purohit Swami, with an introduction by W. B. Yeats (F&F, 1938).

22 April 1937                                    [Faber & Faber Ltd]

Dear MacNeice,

I am told that the revised version of *Out of the Picture* has reached us and is now in the hands of the printer.[1] Also that we could probably produce the book early in June. That being so, it seems to me that it would be a good thing if the publication of the text could approximate to the date of the dramatic production; that is to say, if the play could be put on before the summer holidays for a run, both the book and the play would benefit. Will you let me know what the prospects are, and suggest this as an inducement to Doone? Last time I spoke to Ashley Dukes he had still heard nothing from Doone, but expressed warm interest in the play.

Yours ever,<br>[T. S. Eliot]

## TO *Virginia Woolf*                                        TS Berg

22 April 1937                                    *The Criterion*

My dear Virginia,

I was very much pleased, and not a little annoyed, to get your card today,[2] because I had intended to write to you yesterday, and would have done so had I not had to go to an evening party given by the *New English Weekly*. I shall be very glad to dine with you on Monday 3rd at 8 o'clock, which I perceive is Bank Holiday in Scotland.

I have been seeing your portraits, mostly pretty well garbled, in every American periodical that comes my way. They are decorating both advertisements and reviews of *The Years*.[3] It is so long since I have heard

---

1–The blurb for *Out of the Picture*, F&F New Books July–Dec. 1937, was almost certainly written by TSE: 'This is the verse play on which Mr MacNeice has been at work for a considerable time. Mr MacNeice is already an established younger poet; with the *Agamemnon* he proved that Greek Tragedy can be accurately translated into vigorously dramatic verse in contemporary metre and idiom. We predict that his first original play – which is to be produced in the autumn – will take its place in the repertory of the new poetic theatre.' The play was put on by the Group Theatre at the Westminster Theatre on 2 Dec. 1937, for just two performances.

2–Not traced.

3–On Sunday, 11 Apr. a full-page advertisement for *The Years*, featuring the Man Ray portrait of VW, appeared in *New York Herald Tribune Books* (a rave review by Isabel Paterson appeared on the front page); two days later (12 Apr.), *Time* magazine ran a feature on VW. See further Brenda R. Silver, *Virginia Woolf Icon* (2000), 91.

from you that I wondered whether you had not risen completely above literary and academic society, and were not [?now] moving in a world consisting of K.C.s, belted surgeons, chartered accountants, generals, admirals of the blue, retired pro-consuls (e.g. Ronald Storrs[1]), and higher ecclesiastics. But I am glad that you have not forgotten me.

Affy

T. S. E.

## TO *Cecilia Ady*

CC

23 April 1937                    [Faber & Faber Ltd]

Dear Miss Ady,

You will think that I have been a very long time considering your synopsis of 20 March, which I might have made up my mind about within a few days.[2] As a matter of fact I did, but I had to pass it on to two other directors in succession for them to consider. They both like your outline as much as I do. We are inclined to think that it would probably be a mistake to deal at any length with conjectures or aspirations about the Church of England in the future, and that the conception of something parallel to a book explaining the Civil Service remains good. You express some doubts yourself on this point, and I think that we have come to a sufficient accord to invite you to undertake the book. We have in mind a book which would be priced, at least in its first edition, at 12s. 6d., and we propose a royalty of 10% up to 1500 copies; thereafter 12% to 3000; and thereafter 15%. We should want to be able to control American and foreign editions.

I hope that this proposal will commend itself to you, and assure you that I look forward greatly to the book.[3]

With best wishes,

Yours sincerely,

[T. S. Eliot]

P.S. Unless you wish me to return it, I will retain your synopsis.

---

1 – Sir Ronald Storrs (1881–1955) had served as Military Governor of Jerusalem, Governor of Cyprus, and Governor of Northern Rhodesia.
2 – Ady said of her scheme: 'I found it best to work by subjects & to treat each subject historically, as so much of the present organization of the Church has its roots in the past.'
3 – Ady, *The English Church and How It Works* (F&F, 1940).

575

TO *Christopher Dawson*[1]                                              CC

23 April 1937                              [Faber & Faber Ltd]

My dear Dawson,

You will remember that before you left England we had a discussion about *Christianity and Sex*, and about the possibility of finding a subject on which you might be able to write a similar book for us while you were abroad and separated from reference libraries. I have thought of the matter repeatedly during the winter, and I am sorry that it is only just recently that an idea has suggested itself to me. I hope very much that it does not come too late to be of any use.

The suggestion arose out of your contribution to the symposium on 'Peace and War' in the *Colosseum*, which was reprinted in the *Tablet*.[2] Apart from questions of agreement, yours seemed to me the strongest piece of reasoning of all the contributions, and I have been wondering whether you might not be willing to develop this subject into a small book, which might be comprehensive enough to be entitled 'Christianity and Civil Government'. In a way it might comprehend the subject matter of your pamphlet on *Christianity and Sex* as well as that of 'Christianity and War', at any rate to the extent of taking up the problem of Christian

---

1–Christopher Dawson (1889–1970), cultural historian: see Biographical Register.
2–'Mr Christopher Dawson writes' – 'Symposium on War and Peace' – *The Colosseum* 4: 13 (Mar. 1936), 26–35. 'The denial of the possibility of a just war under modern conditions would seem to reduce modern warfare to a sub-moral level in which the justice or injustice of the particular issue goes by the board . . .

'The real case against modern war is that it is unnecessary and avoidable: that war between nations is as anomalous as private war had become by the end of the Middle Ages . . .

'If there is a great European war in the near future it will not be a capitalist war for markets, but a war of creeds for the possession of men's minds. And each side will be firmly convinced of the justice of its cause. The Fascist Powers will believe that they are defending Christendom and European culture against Communist atheism, while the democratic and socialist states will believe that they are defending justice and peace against militarist and capitalist tyranny . . .

'What is the duty of Catholics under these circumstances? No doubt to work for peace: but how? Certainly not by co-operating with the professional pacifists, for they are just the people who are most ready to beat the drum for a crusade against Peace with Fascism, and who write letters in favour of recruiting for the Spanish civil war in *The Times*. What we want are not pacifists but peace-makers . . . The vital problem we have to solve is . . . how to effect a reconciliation here and now between the rivalries and animosities of the existing national states – above all, how to heal the wound made by the last war (or rather by the last peace) between the four great Powers of Western Europe . . . But any peace propaganda which shuts the eyes to realities is worthless and may even increase the danger which it sets out to combat.'

Reprinted as 'The Catholic Attitude to War', *Tablet*, 13 Mar. 1937, 5.

marriage and the secular state, which is one very much in people's minds at present and likely to remain so. Anyway, I should be glad to hear what you think of this suggestion.

[T. S. Eliot]

TO *Virginia Woolf*                                                    TS Berg

27 April 1937                          *The Criterion*

Thank you, Virginia, I WILL come to Tea on Tuesday the 4th May at 4.30 and I hope that Leonard will perhaps be in before I leave: anyway, it seems the only possibility between now and the end of May. But I don't see why you should be broadcasting without pay, unless you are appealing for a Good Cause (which is hard work at that): I should say that there was quite enough unpaid work to be had without adding broadcasting to it. To go to the Opera in a box is the only endurable way of going to the Opera: I have not been under such conditions for many a long year. Perhaps I shall go to Vienna and see if they have any cheap Opera there. I wish I might see you oftener, because as things are I seem to be degenerating into an Old Buffer. All my sports are getting to be Old Buffers' sports – e.g. I went to Wisbech last weekend, by way of the high table of Magdalene, to drink Port, and I have taken to the vice of Dining Clubs. It would not surprise me if I ended as a member of the Wine Committee of something or other; and this June I am to deliver the Prize Day Speech at Kingswood (Methodist) School. A respected citizen. And I have gone to live in Emperor's Gate. O dear. Am I a humbug? I envy you having finished an opus so recently as not to be expected to be working on a new one. I am trying to write a play, but it is very difficult, irritating when interrupted and tedious when not interrupted. O dear.

Your faithful<br>Tom

28 April 1937[1]                          *The Criterion*

Dear Geoffrey,

We're off for Bradfield: John says he can get four tickets for Tuesday June 22nd with the greatest ease (what a life, I have got to go to Bath on the 24th to give the Prize Day Address at the Kingswood (Methodist) School) and that will be great fun.[2] The only question is whether your new car will take John's wheel chair, folded up, on the luggage grid or somehow – that is essential. A picnic lunch is indicated: and as John is providing the tickets and you the transport I think I can do no less than save Enid a little trouble and see what Fortnum's can do in the way of a basket lunch. Is lobster and Bollinger '23 your idea? I wonder. By the way, I should like to take you down some day to the Rose & Crown at Wisbech where they have nearly every vintage Port beginning with Dow '51. Even what I drank, a Cockburn 1900, almost persuaded me to become a portdrinker. Now then Geoffrey, I must admit that you have got me stalemated, counted out, or whatever you like. There's no way in which I can hit back: I might as well be tied to a lamppost. Well, those Alcaics are first rate: commentary, introduction and notes brilliant. I can only collapse in quiet admiration.[3]

A hard day yesterday: lunched the Archdeacon of Auckland till 4 o'clock (Divinity Books); directly I reached Russell Square ready for a peaceful tea by myself Djuna Barnes arrived in a state of hysterics and smelling salts because Liveright want to collar her royalties: had to get Frank up to soothe her, but managed to send her away tranquillised. Then H. Gordon Porteus to dinner, and that's the way the money goes. And this morning I must pay for my new spectacles and have a fitting for a new suit and I have had such a charming letter from a wine merchant that I am tempted to drop in and sample his fine Macharnudo Supremo as he invites me.

---

1 – The envelope, postmarked 28 Apr. 1937, is addressed to: 'Dm. Galfridus Faber'.
2 – JDH to OM, 16 June 1937: 'On Saturday Tom & I are going to the Bradfield Greek Play – Tom as a guest of honour who will have to pretend that he understands Greek, for I'm sure he's no classical scholar! The following week that mysterious lady-friend of his arrives from America – Emily Hale: do you remember her? A grim, prim, schoolma'amish female who takes a dreadful proprietary interest in poor Tom!' (Texas)
3 – See GCF, 'Poetae Cuiusdam Ignoti: Carmen Singulare', C. 16 (July 1937), 655–65. GCF to FVM, Friday [Apr. 1937?]: 'All my spare strength has gone into those Alcaics for TSE – now finished & being annotated.'

But first I must have another lick at my unhappy family and their birthday party. Somehow I think of a new misfortune for them every time I sit down.[1]

Otherwise, everything is quiet.

Yr. oblgd. & obt. servt.

TP

## TO *Alexis St-Léger Léger*[2]

CC

29 April 1937                    [Faber & Faber Ltd]

*Personal*

My dear Monsieur St-Léger,

It is such a long time since I have had occasion to write to you that you may almost have forgotten my existence; but we now wish to revive the question of the English edition of *Anabase*, which you will remember was published with my translation. For a long time the sales were only moderate, and we recently decided to reduce the price from 10s. 6d. to 6s. This has had a favourable effect, and we are confident of selling the rest of the stock. We believe also that the revival of interest due to the reduction to a reasonable price is likely to continue, and we feel that we could before long undertake a second edition. You will remember, however, that in our contract with you we were limited to the publication of 2,000, and I am therefore writing to ask if you would agree to the publication of a second edition.

One reason which makes a second edition highly desirable is that we have firm assurance of being able to make an advantageous arrangement with one of the best New York publishing houses. At present we have not enough stock to satisfy their demands, and we should be very sorry if an opportunity advantageous to us and to yourself should be missed.

I do not believe that such continued publication would have any disadvantages from the point of view of the sale of the Paris edition. If however you were averse to the re-publication of the French text in this country and in America, we should still be interested in publishing my translation by itself, with your consent. I should regret this, because I think that the interest and value of such a translation is greatly diminished if it is

1 – The reference is to *FR*.
2 – Alexis St-Léger Léger (1887–1975) – St-John Perse – poet and diplomat; Nobel Laureate, 1960: see Biographical Register.

not read in conjunction with the original work, and from a practical point of view I believe there to be a considerable public, still more in America than here, which would have difficulty in appreciating the original poem without the aid of a translation.

My committee suggest that if you license us to publish another edition of both French text and English translation, the whole royalty should go to you without further payment to myself, but that if the translation only were published, a moiety of the royalty should be paid to me. I have no opinions of my own on this point, except to say that the matter of royalty is not of great moment to me, and I should be extremely sorry if my translation were not accompanied by the original poem.

I may say that at the present moment something more than half of the original advance of £50 has been earned, but that with a second edition we should hope soon to be in a position to be paying further royalties.

I hope that you will think this over and come to a favourable decision. Had I any prospect of visiting Paris in the near future I should like to have a talk with you, but I do not imagine that your work is any less, or that you are any more accessible, than when we last met.

Please receive, my dear monsieur St-Léger, the assurance of my warm admiration,

[T. S. Eliot]

TO *James Laughlin*                                          TS Houghton

30 April 1937                          *The Criterion*

Dear Laughlin,

I have your letter of 14 April. We have been expecting the *White Mule*, and I am looking forward to it with much interest.[1]

As for Dudley Fitts's poems, I do not know that I can say anything about them until I have seen them.[2] It is a considerable time since I have seen any of his work. In principle I am against praising people's work in public, unless it seems to me absolutely first rate, because once one

---

1–Laughlin reported that an advance copy of William Carlos Williams's *White Mule* would reach TSE as soon as possible. But see too EP to FVM, 9 Apr. 1936 – with reference to an unidentified text – 'I suspect Possum of having EATEN the Williams, as he cant stand the gynecological medico . . .' (EVE)

2–Laughlin would be sending a copy of *Poems* (1937) by Dudley Fitts. 'Fitts once said that you had praised his work. I wonder, if you really think, as I hope you do, that he is a good poet, if you would care to send me a statement that I could use in "pushing" the book.'

descends below that level, there seems no point at which it is possible to stop, under the impulse of amiability. So I shall not do it to please you or Fitts, but only if I am really knocked all of a heap by the poems.

Yours ever sincerely,

T. S. Eliot

## to *A. Desmond Hawkins* ‎ ‎ ‎ ‎ ‎ ‎ ‎ ‎ ‎ ‎ ‎ ‎ ‎ ‎ ‎ ‎ ‎ TS Desmond Hawkins

30 April 1937 ‎ ‎ ‎ ‎ ‎ ‎ ‎ ‎ ‎ ‎ ‎ ‎ ‎ ‎ ‎ ‎ ‎ ‎ *The Criterion*

My dear Hawkins,

Thank you for your Lawrence review, which is not too long considering the size and nature of the book, and which treats it in the best way possible for the immediate purpose.[1]

Djuna Barnes is an American, though I understand that her mother was English.[2] I should think she was older than that, because she was writing in the *Little Review* in its early days, 1917 and 18. She has produced a previous book called *Ryder*, which was published in New York, but which was not nearly so good as *Nightwood*. It is more in the way of preliminary exercises, preparatory to the later book. I don't think there is anything else of hers so far that you need to read, and what the future will produce nobody knows.

About the Chronicles:[3] I think you had better stick to your present method, as it produced a very satisfactory result last time. The only difficulty is to find enough novels every six months on a high enough level to provide you with the material. Has this year brought you anything so far that is worth talking about in October?

As for your suggestion of a Christmas book, I shall have to meditate on this and discuss it with the committee, and will write to you again.[4]

---

1–Hawkins, untitled review of D. H. Lawrence, *Phoenix*: C. 16 (July 1937), 748–52.

2–Hawkins asked (n.d): 'Will you tell me something about Djuna Barnes? Is she American, and if so why Djuna? Just because it's a nice name, or is she only one generation out of Europe? . . . I take her to be thirty-fiveish, and suppose she must have written something else before Nightwood. Is anything extant? Nightwood "pulled" me from page to page, but I look back on it with a certain degree of doubt . . . She's certainly amazingly accomplished.'

3 – 'When we lunched together we never seem to have got down to the advertised subject: at least I'm still not clear how I am to cast my net wider.'

4–'I have an idea for a book which may interest you. I saw recently a Christmas symposium published by Knopf in America, which contained verse, one or two short novels, essays, short stories etc. The whole thing sold at a usual omnibus price and I was told that it was quite a usual type of publication in America. I expect you know about that. Well, this was a random collection, having the sole virtue of quantity; but a schoolmaster friend who

It is certainly interesting, but it is the sort of book which is chiefly a sales problem, and we shall have to have the Sales Manager's opinion.

Thank you for your invitation.[1] I might be able to come down to you in August, and I should like to do so very much, but it is impossible to tell far ahead, as the summer always brings an incursion of American relatives and friends, to whose movements I have to shape my own to some extent. I expect to get away for a fortnight's holiday at the end of next week, and hope you will lunch with me when I return. Meanwhile I see you are acquiring experience in the ways of country people, and of the East Anglians in particular.[2]

Yours ever,<br>T. S. E.

## TO *Richard Church* CC

3 May 1937                         [Faber & Faber Ltd]

My dear Richard,

I am doing what we all do to each other constantly, and sending you some poems.[3] I think Allen Tate's poems are very interesting poems, and some of them very good, and I hope they will have in America the success they fully deserve. I told him that we could not do them, and that I should be glad to send them on to another publisher, and he naturally chose you.

---

was staying with me suggested that I should collect a similar volume in England, made up entirely of what is known as "modern" literature . . .

'I should propose the inclusion of Sweeney Agonistes, Dance of Death, some of Joyce's Work in Progress, Barker's Documents of a Death *or* The Bacchant, Spender's essay on Yeats, some short stories from Elizabeth Bowen's new collection, Pound's How to Read, essays by Lewis, yourself, Roberts etc., and poems by ten or a dozen I don't need to name. This would be a homogeneous, purposive collection . . . It could be aimed at the Christmas market. What do you think of this?'

1 – 'Would you care to spend a weekend here in June or August?'

2 – 'You'll be interested to know that an Anglo-Catholic battle rages in this village. The Vestry Meeting split the inhabitants into factions over the eleven o'clock Sung Eucharist versus Mattins controversy. Meanwhile Kensit-ites invade from Saffron Walden and shout "Papists!" After urban paganism it's quite bewildering to find religious opinions passionately held and fought over. I'm neutral, though I like Matins and can't see the point of a Communion at which no-one is allowed to commune. Still, I was born into nonconformity and no doubt some taint of it lingers; even although I fled, as soon as I could speak, into the C. of E.'

3 – Tate asked TSE (21 Apr.) to pass his poems on to Church – 'with any comment you care to make . . . I've read some of Church's verse, and I met him in 1928, but of that meeting all I can remember if his asking me, as somebody in the 18th century might have asked Captain Cook about the anthropophagi, "Have you ever seen any Poor Whites?"'

Needless to say that I think you would not make any money, but that you would be publishing a good man. Incidentally I think Tate is really of considerable importance as a critic and prose writer, and it might be worth your while to take his poems for the sake of his other work, or some book that you could make him write.

Yours ever,<br>
[T. S. Eliot]

## TO *John C. MacKenzie* CC

3 May 1937 [Faber & Faber Ltd]

My dear Sir,

I have lingered for some time over your letter of the 27th, waiting for light as to what I should do.[1] It seems highly ungracious to decline an invitation which does me such honour, especially when I learn that the occasion has been put forward to make it possible for me to come. But public speaking is always very irksome to me: it comes no easier, and I do not perform it any more gracefully, with practice; and the amount of time and energy spent is usually out of all proportion to any satisfaction I give. I have had to do a good deal in the last few years; during the last year particularly it has very much obstructed the kind of work which I feel best fitted to do. I find myself growing old, with very little to show for it in the way of writing in verse; and if I am to accomplish anything with the years that remain I must decline every public engagement that I can possibly avoid. I am committed to lecturing once, or twice, in Edinburgh in October; at the present time I am very little interested in critical writing, and have almost nothing to say. Sometimes invitations have to be declined with subterfuge or dissimulation: I am now sticking to truth, and laying before you candidly considerations which circumstances have been pressing more and more upon my attention, during the past months.

With many regrets, and with the highest respect to the Society,

I am,<br>
Yours very sincerely,<br>
[T. S. Eliot]

1 – John C. MacKenzie, Secretary of the Dialectic Society, Edinburgh, wrote to advise TSE that the members of the Society had decided to postpone their 'Ter-Jubilee' celebrations until Dec. 1937 or even Feb. 1938 – 'in the hope that you might be able to attend as guest of honour'.

TO *Kenneth Pickthorn*

My dear Pickthorn,

I have now read *Jesus and Civil Government*,[1] and agree with you that it is an exceedingly able work. I am grateful to you for having brought it to my attention, and I wish that the book might be more widely known than it appears to be.

There are places where it seems to me that the author is clear and logical rather than profound, but these are where he gets to the edge of the problem of Good and Evil, and this criticism does not detract from the value of his work. The point is that as I expected the book does not cover ground that I had in mind in talking to you. It might certainly overlap at points, but that does not matter. This is a book which is written primarily for Christians wishing to settle their problems of conscience in the world. The book we had in mind was not aimed at the small number of people sufficiently Christian to be interested in books of this sort. You would get a better notion of what I meant by thinking of the point of view taken in the third and posthumous volume of Fred Oliver's *Endless Adventure*.[2] That is not, I think, a very good book, except for those who, as I did, knew Oliver personally, and his previous work. I did not have in mind either a book which would concern itself solely with the question of peace and war, but largely with the general moral problem of government and of foreign policy. It seems to me, for example, that a great many of the people who voice their opinions about Spain with the greatest confidence, whether so-called artists of the Left, or Liberal Deans, or Totalitarian Papists, have not thought out the distinction between attitudes proper for individuals and attitudes proper for nations, and that none of them seem to take enough account of what are the interests and the necessities of Britain in any particular circumstances. I of course do not mean that I want a defence of the present government or of any particular government, but perhaps an exposition of the nature of government in contrast to the emotions of individuals and the programmes of ideologues.

My notion is still rather vague, as I think it should be, because for such a book the precision should be left to the potential author to make. But I am quite certain that it wants a layman, and one who will be writing from

1–Arthur Temple Cadoux, *Jesus and Civil Government: A Contribution to The Problem of Christianity and Coercion* (1923).
2–*The Endless Adventure* comprises a trilogy surveying English politics through the lifetime of Sir Robert Walpole (1676–1745). Vol. 3 appeared in 1935.

the point of view of the State rather than of the Church. I am quite sure that if you were disposed to undertake the book for us, you would be the best person to do it, shaping it according to your own mind.

I do want a book from Smyth, and I think his recent sermon 'On Saint George's Day' printed in the last *Church Times* would make a very good starting point.[1] I wonder if you have read this, and if you agree with me. But this would be a very different type of book from what I hope you will do, and would not have quite the same public, though the two might reinforce each other.

Yours ever,
[T. S. Eliot]

## TO *Hugh Gordon Porteus*

TS Beinecke

4 May 1937                              *The Criterion*

Dear Porteus,

This business about teeth and gastric trouble sounds rather worrying. It seems as if you both needed punctilious diet and other things. If it's a question of financial problems making the proper treatment more difficult, I wish you'd let me know confidentially. *Murder in the Cathedral* ought to contribute a bit.

Yrs in haste,
T. S. E.

Pound review O.K. I think.[2] He will write a furious letter, which I shall have to suppress in his own interest. But it may sink in. I shall not cut

---

1–Charles Smyth, 'The Anglo-Catholic Pulpit: Loyalties: A Sermon preached at St Mary's, Graham Street, for the Church Union, on St George's Day, April 21', *Church Times*, 30 Apr. 1937, 539–40. 'The task of the Church is to preserve to the individual his right, under any given circumstances, to obey the dictates of his conscience: *ergo*, his right to fight in what he honestly believes to be a just war, his right to refuse to fight in what he honestly believes to be an unjust war. Therefore the Church is bound to oppose those whose deliberate object is antecedently to shackle his moral freedom by making him sign a Pleace Pledge or a War Pledge or any other sort of pledge designed to control his action on a moral issue in contingencies which it is quite impossible to foresee ... It is not the function of the Church to stabilize Western civilization, or to hold the structure of society together without unwelcome alterations ... The function of the Church is to be a perfect instrument in the hand of God for the accomplishment of His purpose and the achievement of His Kingdom upon earth.'

2–Porteus on EP, *Polite Essays*: C. 16 (July 1937), 744–8. 'It is characteristic of Pound that he can always drop, even if he can seldom take, a useful hint. Like the bulk of his work, this volume is suggestive rather than conclusive or convincing ... As a critic, Pound's most peculiar quality probably comes from his ability to perceive and define, with an extraordinary precision, his own worst vices – in the work of other people.'

unless general space requires it. I am going away on Monday for a fortnight's holiday.

## TO *F. S. Flint*                                                     CC

4 May 1937                              [*The Criterion*]

Dear Frank,

I have read all that I can understand of this essay, and I must say that the part of it that is in English impressed me very much. As for the part that is in mathematics, I gave the paper to Frank Morley to puzzle over, and he has produced a report which seems to me interesting enough to send you herewith.[1] I cannot say myself what his suggestion about doubling the income tax has to do with it, but no doubt you will. Could you produce this in such a form that ordinary readers of the *Criterion* like myself could understand say 3/5 of it?[2]

And by the way, how are you?

Yours ever,
[T. S. Eliot]

## TO *John Hayward*                                               TS King's

4 May [1937]                            *The Criterion*

Dear John,

I wish I was sure that it was a thief.[3] I have a dim impression that it may have been included in a lot of other junk that I cast out for a few shillings, nearly two decades ago, without thinking about inscriptions being in them. What is distressing is that this may go on circulating forever with

---

1 – Not found.

2 – F. S. Flint, 'The Plain Man and the Economists', C. 17 (Oct. 1937), 1–18.

3 – JDH had sent a catalogue clipping from the Frank Hollings Bookshop (London) offering for sale a copy of *Jonah* by Aldous Huxley, one of about only fifty copies privately printed. It was inscribed 'To T. S. Eliot, with best wishes from Aldous Huxley, Xmas, 1917'. The advertisement states: 'As a link between two of the greatest and most influential figures in the modern world of letters, it is not too much to claim that no choicer copy of this very rare book is likely to exist.' Donald Gallup to EVE, 7 Nov. 1989: 'I have always assumed that it must have been one of the books from Tom's library that Vivien is rumored to have sold, and am much interested that Tom himself may have been responsible.'

the damaging word UNCUT. Do not mention this to a soul. It cannot be drowned in Armagnac.

Yrs. etc.

*TP*

I had a wild impulse to go and buy it in, but £25 is really too much for trash & honour.

But preserve this letter, and in this harsh world draw thy breath in pain etc. What I mean is, absent thee from felicity.[1]

P.S. But praps this letter may be worth £25 too to your executors. You never know. The eventual possessor of both the book and this letter will have one of the real rarities of literature.

At a pinch, offer this letter to Mr Gallupp [*sic*] for £25.[2]


TO *Ashley Dukes*                                                    CC

4 May 1937                              [Faber & Faber Ltd]

Now then Ashley don't you be so sly. How dare you give Maynard Keynes the impression that I am earning and being paid £7000 a year from *Murder in the Cathedral*? It may be good for business but it's bad for me, and it shakes my confidence in Maynard's statistics in *The Times*. A man who would believe that, especially hearing it from you, would believe anything. Do you want to get your auditors to prepare an exact statement of what I have received and send it to him? I would contribute within reason to their fee. Besides, this is a double edged tool: do you realise that people are saying that you have already cleared £30,000 out of it???[3]

Yrs. distractedly

[T. S. Eliot]

1 – *Hamlet* V. ii. 344–6: If thou didst ever hold me in thy heart / Absent thee from felicity a while, / And in this harsh world draw thy breath in pain.'

2 – Gallup to EVE, 7 Nov. 1989: 'I was overjoyed to see Tom's letter to John of 4 May 1937 with its reference to me. Although *A Catalogue of English and American First Editions of Writings by T. S. Eliot Exhibited in the Yale University Library 22 February to 20 March, 1937* – to give it its full title – had indeed been published in February that year, Tom was, I am sure, thinking of me primarily as an extremely avid collector of his writings.'

3 – Dukes replied, 5 May 1937: 'Maynard Keynes is the most modest of exaggerators, for he has apparently multiplied your figures only four or five times, while the Observer on learning that I needed £30,000 for the new Mercury charged me outright with having made that sum from your play. We shall both be pursued by tax gatherers, but I hope you are not taking any notice and getting on with that new play.'

TO *W. B. Yeats*                                                    CC

7 May 1937                          [Faber & Faber Ltd]

My dear Yeats,

I will write to Shri Purohit Swami as you suggest.[1] I understand from
Mrs Shakespear that his address is simply c/o Thomas cook, Bombay,
and I will write to him there. We propose the same terms as for the ten
Upanishads, and as soon as I have his concurrence we can have the
typescript set up, and proof sent to you so that you may write your
introduction.[2]

> Yours ever sincerely,
> [T. S. Eliot]


TO *Shri Purohit Swami*[3]                                          CC

7 May 1937                          [Faber & Faber Ltd]

My dear Swami,

I have been in communication with Yeats about *Patanjali*, and he
suggested that I should write to you. We shall be glad to do this book
on the same terms as the ten Upanishads, provided that Yeats writes an
introduction. As you know, an introduction by him is of great value in

1–WBY had written, 'May' (1937): 'I would be greatly obliged if you would write to
Purohit Swami and make your suggestion about my introduction or preface to his work.'
2–The blurb for *Aphorisms of Yoga, by Bhagwan Shree Patanjali: Done into English from
the original Sanskrit, with a commentary where necessary*, by Shree Purohit Swami, and an
Introduction by W. B. Yeats – in Faber Books Spring 1938, 66 – was probably penned by
TSE: 'Those who are interested in the philosophy of India already owe a great debt to Shree
Purohit Swami and Mr Yeats for their edition of *Ten Upanishads*. They have discerned an
unusual combination of talents: an Indian scholar who learned his Sanskrit in the traditional
Indian way – not through grammars written by Englishmen or Germans – and for whom
therefore it is a living language of thought; and the greatest living poet, himself a student of
Indian mysticism.

'Patanjali was one of the earliest and greatest of Indian philosophers and systematic
mystics; and after the Upanishads and the Bhagavad-Gita his commentary is the most
important text for any reader who would penetrate Indian thought. This translation will be
of value to all students of Sanskrit philosophy; and to those who cannot read the original it
will be indispensable.'
3–Shri Purohit Swami (1882–1941): Hindu teacher; scion of a wealthy Maharashtran
Brahmin family; educated at Calcutta University, Deccan College and Bombay University;
author of *Autobiography of an Indian Monk* (1932); translator into English of the *Bhagavad
Gita* and *The Ten Principal Upanishads* (F&F, 1938). See John Harwood, 'Appendix: Yeats,
Shri Purohit Swami and Mrs Foden', *Yeats Annual* no. 6, ed. Warwick Gould (1988), 102–7;
Harwood, *Olivia Shakespear and W. B. Yeats* (1989).

starting a book on the market. As soon as I hear from you that you concur with this proposal, we can send the material to press, and Yeats will write his introduction when he receives proof from us.

With all best wishes for your happiness and progress,

I am, yours sincerely,

[T. S. Eliot]

## TO *John Betjeman* CC

7 May 1937 [Faber & Faber Ltd]

Dear Betjeman,

I confess that the name of Ashbee means nothing to me, but I will accept him as important on your recommendation.[1] I should like very much to meet him one day if you could arrange it. That will have to be some time after the 24th of May, as I am just leaving for a fortnight's holiday. Meanwhile, I will leave your letter behind for my committee to consider when it meets again on Wednesday week. Our office, like most publishing offices, will be shut for a week, so that nothing can be done quickly.

With many thanks,

Yours ever

[T. S. Eliot]

1 – Betjeman wrote ('Ascension Day 1937'): 'I hasten to write to you because I have been staying with that great veteran pioneer of modern architecture, student of aesthetics & sociology, King's scholar & aesthete C. R. ASHBEE – ARCHITECT METAL WORKER LECTURER WHO DAZZLED AMERICA FOUNDER OF THE GUILD OF HANDICRAFT (150 men chosen from the East End before the war) PUBLISHER & PRINTER (ESSEX HOUSE PRESS) whom everyone suspects is dead. He was put up for the Art Worker's Guild by his friend William Morris, worked with Roger Fry in the latter's Arts & Crafts Days, is now a fervent admirer of Gropius & Regency architecture . . . He is now writing his reminiscences & has completed some of them. I honestly think it would be worth your while to see them. He is famous in U.S.A. & among the cognoscenti in English architecture & typography.

'Will you meet him at lunch with me one day? He has a drooping moustache & an imperial & a Cambridge voice – a charming & great man. I am sure you will like his work & might want to publish it. Perhaps he had better send you the MS & *then* have lunch, if you think Faber's can do anything with it. It certainly *ought* to be published. Will you let me know.

'Love to the left wing poets.'

TO *Martin Shaw*                                        TS Houghton

7 May 1937                      *The Criterion*

Dear Martin,

I have your letter of May 4th, with its very interesting suggestion.[1]
I must say first of all that this again is a field which is quite unknown to
me, and in which if I did any work at all I should only want to work with
some intelligent producer like John Grierson. I am very diffident about
what I could do, and, I confess, not very anxious to undertake a job at
the present time. In fact, I could not even think of it until the beginning
of next year, as I have a play on which I am working, which will certainly
take me until then to get into working order, to say nothing of the various
engagements which interfere. I do not know whom to suggest meanwhile,
but I will keep the matter in mind both for myself and in general.

With all best wishes to you both,
Yours ever sincerely.
T. S. Eliot

There's a lad named Rayner Heppenstall who might be interested. Poet
with religious proclivities.

1 – 'I happened to be under the same roof as the Bp of Croydon (now Bp Designate of
Lichfield) when this appeared in *The Times*.

'He thinks it is of the utmost importance that something fine should be created before the
usual slops are spread about.

'I had a talk with him & he welcomed with enthusiasm a suggestion of mine that I should
ask you if you wd consider the writing of a film of the nature of The Rock as regards
dimensions i.e. with crowds choruses & other music. I believe his Council have the use of a
studio & all appliances.

'He wd. very much like to be in a position to put something forward to his Council in a
fortnight or three weeks time & if he could say that in principle you were sympathetic he
would be overjoyed I know & details could be gone into later.

'The prospect of working again with you gives me a joyous marrow thrill.'

The article in question was a letter to the Editor of *The Times* (28 Apr. 1937) by Edward
Croydon, chairman of the Cinema Christian Council – 'Religious Films: An Undeveloped
Field: Richness of Biographical Material': 'There is a growing demand all over the country
for films which can be used for education or definitely religious purposes . . . The Cinema
Christian Council, with which is closely associated the Religious Film Society, is in friendly
touch with the film industry in this matter of the making of religious films . . . I am confident
that I am speaking for the Archbishop of Canterbury [president of the Council] and the
leaders of all the Churches when I express the earnest hope that the present opportunity to
take a wise and fruitful line in the development of religious films will not be missed.'

7 May 1937                    *The Criterion*

Dear Maynard,

Louis MacNeice came in to see me a few days ago, and reported that Rupert Doone had given you the text of his play *Out of the Picture* to read with a view possibly to producing it first in Cambridge during August. The point of my writing about it is that we are just about to send the book to press, and if you do accept the play for this purpose we should like to know, both in order to adjust the publication date and to make some announcements of a forthcoming production. So I should be grateful for any information you care to release, one way or the other, as soon as you have come to a decision. I have not seen the final version of the play, but the text that I have seen seemed to me well worth putting on, with some modifications. As for the business of a wireless apparatus chorus, I objected to that on the ground that people would say that he had taken it over from *The Ascent of F6*, but MacNeice was rather grieved by this, because it appears that he thought of the idea before Auden did. I think certainly he was working on this play before Auden and Isherwood began theirs.[2]

Incidentally, I have complained to Ashley Dukes for grossly exaggerating the amount of my income from *Murder in the Cathedral*. His reply is that he didn't. I suppose your reply will be that you didn't either, but that it is due to the imagination of Virginia, who told me that you told her.[3]

Yours ever sincerely,
T. S. Eliot

1–John Maynard Keynes (1883–1946), economist and theorist of money; patron of the arts: see Biographical Register.

2–Keynes responded, 10 May: 'Rylands and I have now read MacNeice's play and have, I am sorry to say, decided not to do it. I wish we could have decided otherwise. It is in many ways a very gifted work, but too much, as Lydia puts it, "an unhappy reaction against life". This attitude and these feelings of course exist, but should they be exhibited for our delectation? I am growing into the opinion that they should be hushed up.

'I agreed with you in thinking that the wireless apparatus chorus would seem dreadfully stale after "F.6". But it is bad luck for MacNeice if he has been anticipated.'

3–Keynes, 10 May: 'God knows what your income may have become by the time it reached you through Virginia! But I hope the truth is not too remote from fiction. For that would mean that Ashley and the other per-feshionals are keeping too much.'

TO *Bryan Guinness*

8 May 1937                              [24 Russell Square]

*Confidential*

Dear Guinness,

I have just sent you, as one of the previous contributors for the benefit of George Barker, a copy of his new volume of poems. I hope that you will think, as I do, that it shows a considerable increase of power and even some gain in directness and lucidity.

I have kept going a small fund for him for two years, by appealing to various people, and had hoped that by this time there would be no reason to worry about him. I don't believe in subsidising authors indefinitely, or at all, if they can find any decent way of making a living. But Barker is a peculiarly difficult case, both in the kind of ability he has and the kind of inability. He had very little education, I fancy, except his own reading, which is unusual and erratic and there seems very little that he can do except to write poetry. He has been trying to get a job, and there is still some hope of regular work in Western Regional broadcasting, and possibly some extension lectures in the West. He might have more prospect in London, but that would increase his expenses first of all.

This year, I have managed to get enough to let him have a pound a week; and I need a total of £16 to continue to the end of the year. I don't ask people to contribute to anything unless I contribute myself; and I am limited in the number of people whom I can ask – I don't like to ask people merely because they are generous or because they can afford it, but only if they care about poetry in general and can appreciate the merits of this particular case. And as I say, I don't want this to go on any longer than necessary, though on the other hand I feel more conviction because of the development in his work.

If you felt able to help I should be grateful; if not, I understand that you must have many claims, and there need be no embarrassment on either side.

Yours sincerely,

[T. S. Eliot]

I shall, by the way, be going abroad on Monday for a fortnight, and shall be back on the 24th.

## TO *Henry Miller*                                        CC

10 May 1937                          [*The Criterion*]

Dear Mr Miller,

I don't know anything about Anais Nin yet, but after reading your
essay I must find out more about her. This is merely to say that I was
very much impressed by the essay you sent me, and want to use it. At the
moment I am just rushing off for a fortnight's holiday, and am not able to
give you further particulars, but I will write to you again on my return.
I congratulate you on a fine piece of critical writing.[1]

Yours sincerely,
[T. S. Eliot]


## TO *Mervyn Wall*[2]                                     CC

27 May 1937                          [Faber & Faber Ltd]

Dear Mr Wall,

I have read your play with a good deal of interest, and think that it
ought to have a definite success upon the stage.[3] I should rather expect it
to do better as a repertory piece than for a long run, as I am afraid there is
not a very extensive public for a play of such a sombre nature. I submitted
it to my committee, and to my regret they do not feel that it would be
wise for them to attempt publication. It would probably have a better
success with some firm with more experience in the publication of plays,
and I should suggest either Jonathan Cape, who I believe publish Denis
Johnston, or the firm of Frederick Muller, Ltd.[4]

---

1 – Miller, 'Un Etre Etoilique' (on Nin and her diaries), *C.* 17 (Oct. 1937), 33–52.
2 – Mervyn Wall (1908–97), Irish playwright, novelist, short-story writer, journalist;
worked for the Irish Civil Service, 1934–48; later for Radio Éireann, 1948–57; and he was
Secretary of the Irish Arts Council/Chomhairle Ealaíon, 1957–75. Publications include *The
Unfortunate Fursey* (1946); *Leaves for the Burning* (Best European Novel of the Year, 1952).
3 – At the suggestion of Brian Coffey, on 28 Apr. Wall wrote from Dalkey, Co. Dublin, to
submit to TSE his play *Alarm among the Clerks*, which had been performed that month
at the opening of the new Abbey Experimental Theatre, Dublin; and Seán O'Casey had
read it with enthusiasm. Denis Johnston (a director of Productions for the BBC in Belfast)
prompted him to send it to the St Martin's Theatre in London, and had also asked for a copy
for broadcasting.
4 – *Alarm among the Clerks* was to be published in 1940.

Thanking you for the enjoyment I have had, and with many regrets,

I am,

Yours sincerely,

[T. S. Eliot]

## TO *Montgomery Butchart*

27 May 1937                     [Faber & Faber Ltd]

Dear Mr Butchart,

I should very much like to see Robert Sutherland's novel when it is ready, but the enclosed bits do not seem to me good enough to pick out under a spotlight.[1] The first one is very lively, and the Doric seems to me to go very well, but like a good many fantasies of this thought, it lies too deeply under the shadow of the night town section of *Ulysses*.

The second I don't like half as much: it seems to me an essentially commonplace account of a commonplace incident. I am probably doing him injustice, but in that case it is possible that a good many other readers would do so as well, and I had rather see his work in the mass before judging it.

Yours sincerely,

[T. S. Eliot]

1–Butchart (Gilbert White literary agency) wrote on 14 May: 'Christopher Grieve has commended Robert Sutherland, an Edinburgh man who writes in the dialect, to send me a novel. It proves to be uneven but the high places in it, are, I think very high indeed, and as a few of them may be read out of their context I have asked him to let me show them to you as interesting in themselves and as (barely?) possible material for Criterion. I am enclosing therefore one chapter, AN IDYLL ON SOUTRA, in prose, and a MASQUE OF EDINBURGH, as well as two shorter poems, in verse. The Masque appeared in *The Scot's Observer* of 8 July 1933.

'An agent is of course always prejudiced. Nevertheless if Sutherland, who chooses the pseudonym of Robert Garioch, can rewrite his novel, as he is now attempting to do, I shall do all I can to find him a publisher who will recognise adequately what is I feel a genius of at least a middle order.'

Robert Garioch (1909–81), poet, worked as a schoolteacher, 1945–64; later as a magazine editor. See *Selected Poems* (1966); *Complete Poetical Works*, ed. Robin Fulton (1983).

Corpus Christi [27 May] 1937      *The Criterion*

My dear Ottoline,

I am recently back from my fortnight's holiday in Austria, and hear from John that you are still at Tunbridge Wells.[1] <I rang up to enquire just before I left.> I am sorry not to find you back in London, but I hope that you have been making progress. I was more fortunate in weather, as I found it extremely warm and sunny – one day too much so, a real sirocco and sandstorm – and returned to England just as the good weather began here. I feel very much better – the Austrians attractive – I had not been in that country since 1911 – and the contrast between Austria and Germany (we spent a day in Berchtesgaden, and an afternoon in Munich) interesting.[2] There is an agreeable democracy in Austria – due to the *hoehere Herrshaften*[3] sinking (rather than other people rising) (they seem to be serving in shops and taking in lodgers) and a feeling of decayed empire that gives it a dignity over the more bustling nations. I do not expect to go away for any length of time this summer – I have to spend a week at a conference in Oxford in July – and I hope that you will let me come to see you as soon as you are back. Meanwhile, I will pray for your restoration to health.

Affectionately<br>
Tom

1 – TSE had called on JDH on 27 May.

2 – Tomlin, *T. S. Eliot*, 85: 'On 25 May [1937] I dined with Eliot at the Oxford and Cambridge Club. On meeting him again, I at once noticed that he was looking unusually well and bronzed. He told me that he had been in Austria and he mentioned how "handsome" he had found the people. Altogether he struck me as being in better spirits than usual; and I learnt later, though not from him and I cannot vouch for its veracity, that he had had himself psychoanalysed. I doubt whether this implied anything lurid; it may have been just a consultation.'

Cf. TSE to Eva Le Gallienne, 28 Oct. 1953: 'I am myself rather sceptical of psychogical explanations and analyses – at least, of any psychological analyses I have seen of my own work, but then the psychologists always seem to discover that I am really a rather unpleasant or despicable person!'

3 – *hoehere Herrshaften*: upper classes.

TO *The Secretary, Universities Bureau*
*of the British Empire*                                    CC

28 May 1937                          [Faber & Faber Ltd]

Dear Sir,

I have received your unsigned letter of the 27th May, asking my opinion of the suitability of Mr F. J. R. Bottrall for the post of Professor of English Literature in the University of Athens. I had already heard from Mr Bottrall, and had gladly given my consent to his using my name as a referee.[1]

I have known Mr Bottrall since he was an undergraduate at Cambridge, and regard him not only as one of the abler poets of his generation, but as a critic of unusual intelligence and sensibility. I have no hesitation in recommending Mr Bottrall warmly for such a post. He has already had some years of experience in teaching English Literature to foreign students both at Helsingfors and at Singapore, and I consider him to be ably equipped. I cannot think of any of the younger men of my acquaintance whom I should recommend with more confidence.

I may mention also that although I have only met Mrs Bottrall once, she also strikes me as a suitable person.[2]

I recommend Mr Bottrall not only on general grounds, but taking into account the special responsibility of an English teacher of English literature in a foreign capital.

Yours faithfully,
[T. S. Eliot]

1–Bottrall had written, 11 May: 'I am afraid that the Liverpool job is not going to come off; but I have some hopes of the Byron Chair of English Literature and Institutions which the British Council has founded at Athens . . .

'I hope you will not mind my sending your name as a referee. If you can make your remarks *ad hoc* (it is a Byron chair!) I shall be very obliged.'

2–Margaret Saumarez Smith (1909–96), English scholar and teacher (born in Sydney, Australia, where her father was Archbishop), became Tutor and Fellow, Hughes Hall, Cambridge (where she also served as Vice-President), 1959–70; Fellow of Lucy Cavendish College, Cambridge, 1961–76. In 1934 she was married in Singapore to Ronald Bottrall (they had met as Harkness Commonwealth Fellows while in the USA), who was then Raffles Professor of English. Her publications include *The Divine Image: A Study of Blake's Christianity* (1950), *George Herbert* (1954), and *Traherne's Way of Blessedness* (1962).

## TO *Richard Church*

31 May 1937                    [*The Criterion*]

My dear Richard,

In reply to your letter of the 11th,[1] I do agree with you on the whole about Allen Tate. His work does seem just to fall short, and since as you say one has to leave a margin for the possible work of a genius, one can hardly afford to support work which not only just misses genius, but also misses the qualities which are necessary to support it on both sides of the Atlantic. I am very glad that you have got a new volume from Edwin Muir. His best stuff seems to me very good. His work in the bulk has generally suffered from unevenness, and from his apparently being unable to distinguish in his own work the good from the indifferent.

Yours ever,

[T. S. Eliot]

## TO *W. B. Brander*[2]

31 May 1937                    [Faber & Faber Ltd]

Dear Sir,

I have your letter of the 28th May, stating that Mr G. Wilson Knight has mentioned my name in connection with the post of Professor of English Literature at the University of Athens, for which he has applied.

You will remember that I recently wrote to you in support of the candidature of Mr F. J. R. Bottrall. I shall, however, be glad to speak in favour of Mr Wilson Knight, if I can do so without prejudice to my support of Mr Bottrall. I am still of opinion that Mr Bottrall is as suitable a candidate as any known to me.

---

1 – 'I have the same difficulty as you about Allen Tate's poems. Our allotment for publishing verse can necessarily only be a small one, and I have to space this out accordingly, trying to keep in hand a sum to cover the work of genius that might, but which never, comes along. For this year I have already filled my list, intending to conclude with a new set of poems by Edwin Muir which take him a considerable stride forward in poetic experience.

'Finally, I do not feel more than a mild interest in Tate's work. As a man and a critic I found him stimulating; but his verse seems to me always to have a sense of nervous over-effort in it, a fault which tends to intellectualism and to a "dying fall" in his rhythmic structure. Were he easier in his work, there would be more emphasis of personality in his phrase. Were his work unsigned, I should not be able to recognise it.'

2 – W. B. Brander, Secretary, Universities Bureau of the British Empire.

I have known Mr Wilson Knight[1] in connexion with his essays on Shakespeare's plays, which have attained a considerable reputation. My opinion of these essays is sufficiently indicated by my having committed myself in writing the introduction to the first of the volumes, which was published by the Oxford University Press (*The Wheel of Fire*). Although I think Mr Wilson Knight sometimes presses a point too far, I have a very high opinion of his Shakespeare scholarship. I do not know anything of Mr Wilson Knight's success as a teacher, but I imagine that authorities in Canada will speak for his abilities in this profession. I know that while in Ontario he was very active in forwarding amateur productions of Shakespeare's plays by the students, and I have no doubt that his enthusiasm and knowledge made them very successful.[2]

> I am,
> Yours faithfully,
> [T. S. Eliot]

## TO *Henry Miller*                                                    CC

31 May 1937                              [*The Criterion*]

Dear Mr Miller,

Thank you for your letter of the 21st.[3] If it is impossible to use the name of Anais Nin, then I think it is important to use whatever name she

---

1—G. Wilson Knight (1897–1985) served in WW1 and took a degree in English at St Edmund Hall, Oxford, in 1923. In the 1920s he held a variety of teaching posts before being appointed Professor of English at Toronto University, where he worked until 1940; thereafter he taught at Leeds, ultimately as Professor, until 1962. Works include *The Wheel of Fire* (1930) – for which TSE wrote the introduction, having recommended the work to OUP – *The Imperial Theme* (1931), and *Principles of Shakespearian Production* (1936). On 29 Oct. 1956, TSE was to write to Helen Gardner, of Wilson Knight: 'I found his first book about Shakespeare's imagery very stimulating indeed – in fact, I wrote a preface to it, but by the time the third volume came out, I began to feel that it was enough to submit a few of Shakespeare's plays to such analysis, but I did not want to read any more.' Wilson Knight situated himself in relation to TSE in 'My Romantic Tendencies', *Studies in Romanticism* 9: 1 (Winter 1967), 556–7.

2—The appointment was awarded to H. V. Routh (1878–1951).

3—On Anaïs Nin's diary: 'if you are going to publish it I am sorry to say that we must avoid using her name. Miss Nin has asked me to write you upon the advice of her agent here in Paris. It will be absolutely necessary for her to guard her anonymity. The diary will be published under a pseudonym and the names of all the persons referred to in it altered.

'Perhaps I should also make it clear that the diary has not yet been accepted by a publisher. Some twelve or fifteen volumes, selected, have been shown to a dozen publishers in England and America and have received the most enthusiastic reception, but owing to the length of

adopts for the purpose of publication. Furthermore, I think it would add very much to the effect of your criticism if we knew that Miss Nin's diary was actually going to be published, so that the work itself and your essay could co-operate. But that will not mean delaying publication of your essay on that account. I could not use it much before the end of the year in any case, and I hope that some definite arrangement will be made about the Diaries before then.

I have never read *The House of Incest*, but I got the impression, from your article and from what I have heard about her, that this diary form is the one in which she expresses herself best, and I should imagine that anything in the way of pure fiction would be a by-product.[1]

---

the work and the nakedness of it no publisher has had the courage to accept it. It is now in the hands of Little Brown & Co. in America . . .

'I might add that Anais Nin is the author of a short critical work on D. H. Lawrence, published by Edward Titus (D. H. Lawrence, An Unprofessional Study) which Rebecca West praised very highly. Also the author of "The House of Incest", published by Carrefour, Bruges. My Scenario, which Kahane is bringing out in a few weeks, is based on this little book, a sort of phantasy of neurosis. Perhaps you forgot too that it was Anais Nin who wrote the preface (without which Kahane would not have published the book) to Tropic of Cancer. And the fact that the Black Spring was dedicated to her. In addition she has written two novels as yet unpublished. It is quite possible that one will be taken by Kahane next year, called "The Father". She is now compiling a book about myself, from her diary. A book about my writings principally . . .

'I mention all this because from your letter, which I appreciated, I had the feeling that perhaps you were under the illusion that the diary had already been published. I had no intention of deceiving you. This little essay forms a chapter of the forthcoming book, "Max and the White Phagocytes", which Kahane will bring out in the spring of 1938 . . .

'I am sending in the same mail a manuscript called "Money and How it Gets that Way", also from this book. Suggest it as a brochure to be printed separately by Faber & Faber. A little joke on Ezra Pound and his ilk.'

1 – See TSE's 'Interim Report on the DIARY of ANAIS NIN' for F&F, 5 June 1937: 'I find this book (into parts of which I have dipped, both French and English) very different from the GUIDE TO KULCHER. The difference is this: that while Pound is concerned with things which interest me, and which have solidity and shape and objective value, Nin is concerned with the vague emotions of herself and other people all of whom seem to me to be crashing bores. This is a book which should prove fascinating to anyone who is interested, say, in the psychology of woodlice. I assume that woodlice, living as they do mostly under stones and logs, are tremendously interested in each other and themselves, unused to sunlight, and indifferent to plastic values. Anais and her friends, her father, Hans, Alaune, David, Miguel and the rest of the riffraff, seem to live a life designed for them by Jewish psychologists: they are phantasmata of limbo, or spawnings of the diabolic imagination before the Creation, if that is conceivable.

'But mind you, this is only my personal re-action, as you would say. (Up into the upas-tree / Who should climb but little me?) And I have a powerful but restricted emotional range. This is off my key-board, outside of my auditory range, like bats, bagpipes, and welsh miners. This stuff has appealed to giants like Rebecca West and Henry Miller (Miller indeed has been inspired by it to writing a remarkable piece which will probably appear

I look forward to seeing your book, although I am glad that it is not coming out until next Spring, so that I shall have time to publish the essay first.

I am looking forward now to reading Lawrence Durrell's book.[1]

> With best wishes,
> Yours sincerely,
> [T. S. Eliot]

## TO *Janet Adam Smith*[2]                                      CC

1 June 1937                                    [*The Criterion*]

Dear Mrs Roberts,

Thank you very much for your letter of the 27th.[3] I have had very little news of how *Murder in the Cathedral* has been received outside of London and information, especially when satisfactory, is always welcome. I have always thought myself that the clowning of the golfing Tempter was overdone, so that I am somewhat relieved to find that you did not object to it. I remain, however, of the opinion that golf is hardly the sport to associate with that type.

> With many thanks,
> Yours sincerely,
> [T. S. Eliot]

---

in the CRITERION); and if wisely selected and edited and pushed by Cyril Connolly and Peter Quennell and such, it might appeal to a large public of lavatory-snipes. To me, it seems ludicrous to compare this dripping to Proust: one waits in vain to find out how anything Looked or Sounded or Smelt

'P.S. I have a very MUCH higher opinion of L. Durrell.'

1 – *The Black Book*: see below for TSE's letter to Durrell, 28 June 1937.

2 – Janet Adam Smith (1905–99), who read English at Somerville College, Oxford, married the poet and editor Michael Roberts in 1935. She was assistant editor of the *Listener*, 1930–5; assistant literary editor, 1949–52, and literary editor, 1952–60, of the *New Statesman*. Her works include *Mountain Holidays* (1946) and *John Buchan: A Biography* (1965), as well as anthologies including *The Faber Book of Children's Verse* (1953). See further Jason Harding, 'The Criterion: Cultural Politics and Periodical Networks in Inter-War Britain (2002), ch. 8: 'Michael Roberts and Janet Adam Smith'.

3 – 'I have managed at last to see *Murder in the Cathedral*; I was staying with my people near Edinburgh, and we went in and saw it there. The King's Theatre is a big one, but nearly every seat was taken, and, being General Assembly Week, the place was black with ministers. I don't think there can have been such an outing since they crowded to hear John Home's *Douglas* in 1756 ... It was an extremely attentive audience, and a very serious one too. I laughed out loud at the golfing Tempter [i.e. Third Tempter], and there were disapproving looks. I enjoyed it very much, and so did my mother; though we both felt that the Canterbury Women's voices became too wailing and whiney towards the end.'

3 June 1937                    [Faber & Faber Ltd]

Dear Canon Bell,

It is possible that you may be at sea or in this country before this letter reaches you, but as I do not know how to find out, I must go ahead.

I assume that you are acquainted with Father Kelly, the founder of Kelham. I have been interested for some months past in the possibility of getting his lecture notes on early Church history published. The Archbishop of York is also very anxious that this should be done. There does not seem to be enough demand for such a book to justify our publishing it without American support, and I wonder if you could make any suggestions? The notes are extremely good, and although naturally in a very condensed form, I think they would be none the worse for publication, and Father Kelly is now too old and infirm to go through the considerable labour of expanding them. There are several volumes, but what we have in mind is to publish as one volume all the notes on Church history up to the 5th century.

If you are interested, and think that anything could be done, I can have a copy sent to you. If you get this letter, please at least let me know where you are, and I will either write more fully or await your arrival and explain vocally. I very much hope that we shall see you in England this summer. I wish that you might be coming to the Conference in Oxford.[2]

Yours very sincerely,
[T. S. Eliot]

TO *Paul Léon*                    TS National Gallery of Ireland

3 June 1937                    *The Criterion*

Dear Monsieur Léon,

I must apologize for the delay in answering your letter of the 24th, due to my absence abroad.[3] I have noted that the rest of the galleys of Part

1–Bernard Iddings Bell (1886–1958), American Episcopal priest, author and cultural commentator; warden of Bard College, 1919–33.
2–Iddings Bell wrote back on 23 June from the British Empire Hotel, De Vere Gardens, Kensington, where he and his wife were staying until 22 July ('Fr. Cheetham is good enough to let me say my mass in your pleasant St Stephen's Church'): 'I know the Kelly outlines. He gave me a typescript of them some three years ago. I'll be glad to talk to you about them.'
3–'Mr Joyce is for the moment getting through a first reading of the galleys after which he will read it again with someone to make the necessary corrections of which, so he tells me,

III are to be sent to Mr Joyce as quickly as they are ready.[1] As for Part II, Lord Carlow[2] is coming to see me on Monday, but I understand that he is only bringing with him the certain parts of Part II which he is to print privately. I do not think that I had heard anything about this private edition before, and I am rather puzzled, but he is to explain to me about that on Monday. Meanwhile I hope you will understand that we dare not ourselves take the responsibility for assembling the parts of Part II published in *Transition*. May I ask you therefore, as soon as Part II or any considerable section of it is ready, to let us have the necessary pages of *Transition*? If we get them from you, we shall be able to assume that Mr Joyce has passed them for our printers.

With best wishes to Madame Léon and yourself,

Yours sincerely,

T. S. Eliot

<hr />

there are not many. But could you have the rest of the galleys sent to him so that Part III is completed?

'The text of Part II is partly (or should I say greatly) to be found in *Transition* – and Lord Carlow will send you a few corrections introduced in a fragment published therein in 1934, so that you may have everything ready for composition as soon as is necessary.'

1 – FVM had written to Edmond Segrave (*The Bookseller*), 11 May 1937: 'Would you like to see, would you like to use, a photograph of a startling kind? It records a very great moment in the history of literature – the handing over of proofs of the first part of James Joyce's WORK IN PROGRESS by Mr A. J. Pringle (on the left) of the house of Faber & Faber, to Mr T. S. Eliot (on the right) for transmission to the author. How's that for excitement?'

2 – George Lionel Seymour Dawson-Damer, Viscount Carlow: see letter of 10 June 1937, below.

3 June 1937                    *The Criterion*

Dear John,
    First of all, I wish to invite you to a

> **.A.**   LECTURE.   T. S. ELIOT on "Religious Drama : Mediaeval and Modern "  **.A.**
>      in the King's School Hall (by permission of the Headmaster.)
>                    *Reserved seats 2/6 and 1/6.*

which will prove much more amusing if you tear off the strip marked
A A.[1]
    Second, I am tired because I have been to tea at the Zoo with the
Huxleys, and there was a Raft of people, with Robert Nichols[2] and Miss

---

1 – A strip of paper is stuck to the letter at this point: it cannot be removed.
2 – Robert Nichols (1893–1944), poet and playwright, educated at Trinity College, Oxford,
served in WW1 as a second lieutenant in the Royal Field Artillery (shell shock cut short his
service): his war poetry, *Invocation* (1915) and *Ardours and Endurances* (1917), brought
him renown. He was Professor of English at Tokyo Imperial University, 1921–4, and then
worked for a time as adviser to Douglas Fairbanks in Hollywood. Other works include
*Aurelia* (verse, 1920) and *Guilty Souls* (play, 1922). See William and Anne Charlton, *Putting
Poetry First: A Life of Robert Nichols, 1893–1944* (2003).

Ruth Pitter[1] and a half-grown Lion named Jim who padded around the walls and glared and I thought at one moment that he wanted one of my trouser legs but he was called off, and a Himalayan Bear Cub named Teeny or Weeny who snuffled very loud. I hope that I was not very depressing the other evening but the fact is that I had a touch o' sun from roaming about at Kelham for two days with no hat on because the monks were not wearing hats, but I got a queer headache the kind that clutches your throat and it took me in the evening and that is why I was so quiet and I hope Jack was not upset about the carnation. And I had to dine last night with Tom Burns to meet our poet Miss Bowes-Lyon and our prosateur Mr Davy (Dai) Jones.[2] Whose book I will send as well as Barker & Madge which I have ordered. And the headache took me again.

I am in a jam over Bradfield, because I have decided I want to meet Emily on the 22nd, and I had hoped in that case to say can they have me on the 19th, although that would be a very moderate pleasure in lieu of going with you and Geoffrey. But that is Geoffrey's fault. Just as I had it nicely arranged that I was to be picked up at Bath on the 25th after distributing the Prizes to the Methodist Boys, and transported by Faber or Morley to Wales for the weekend there in honour of Donald Brace, Faber now says that he wants to make it the weekend of the 19th instead, only he is not quite sure whether he is free that weekend for a day or two, and will I keep it open. Well this matter of giving Donald Brace a weekend in Wales has been mooted for many moons, and of course business is business and Donald Brace is business though *I* think Ida Brace is bad business but you should ask Morley about that, and I mustn't put a spoke in my confreres' wheel being only a 5th wheel myself so that is imperative. By the time I can say that I am free on the 19th it will be too late to get admitted to Bradfield; and I can't say the 26th, because how can I be sure of getting from Bath to Bradfield on that day? Everything works out wrong, and I shall not be able to consult you until Monday and

---

1–Emma Thomas 'Ruth' Pitter (1897–1992), poet; winner of the Queen's Gold Medal for Poetry, 1955; elected Companion of Literature (Royal Society of Literature), 1974; CBE, 1979.

2–David Jones (1895–1974), poet and painter; author of *In Parenthesis*.

Thomas Dilworth, *David Jones: Engraver, Soldier, Painter, Poet* (2017), 191: 'Jones and Eliot were seeing more of each other. In the summer of 1936, at dinner with Eliot and others, Jones had liked him "a great lot". In the second week of July 1937 at Faber, they talked alone for the first time. Eliot said with apologies that *In Parenthesis* reminded him of Kipling. Jones said, "Yes, I can believe it." In the poem, soldiers sing "Casey Jones" (68), which Eliot told him was his favourite song, one he sang to himself while shaving. Jones found him "quiet & unpretentious to talk with".'

I hope that you will have balmy weather at Cambridge and success to Mr Rhodes.

Yours for the present

*TP*

I am going to bed and will perhaps post this first or perhaps in the morning. The only gleam of sunlight is that I have bought 3 pairs of socks. But *Murder* will have to pay my dress account.


## TO *Polly Tandy*                                                   TS BL

6 June 1937                    *The Criterion*

Dear Ma Tandy, Ma'am,

Now then ma'am I know that the Old Possum is going motheaten in the fur and shaky in the toofs and uncertain the claws[1] and sometimes he can't even hold on to a branch with his Tail: but I take it hard, I think it crool of you to reb it into him that he is going wambling in the memory. Well well if you says it was the 12th then it is the 12th and Im not going to make any argle-bargle about that, so I says anythink for the sake of Peace the 12th it is and the 12th let it Be. Can I come on the Friday or the Sat. that is to say the 11th or the 12th assuming that the Friday is the 11th or the 12th whichever it is. That is the question and I dont rightly know the answer, but I will communicate early in the week. I mean, I will ask my secretary what day which day is and what I am doing. I am prepared to bring with me a

> Tyrolese Hat
> Wettermantel[2]
> sandals with toes
> backless sunsuit
> sock suspenders
> orange stick & cuticle scissors
> bottle Macharnudo sherry

but I expect the household to provide

> Solar Topee
> Bee Veil
> shooting stick

---

1 – Cf. a chorus in *MiC*: 'Ill the wind, ill the time, uncertain the profit, certain the danger.'
2 – *Wettermantel* (Ger.): raincoat.

automatic

    scarlet & decorations

as heretofore.

    Yours respfly and hastly to catch the pst.

TP

---

TO *John Hayward*                                              TS King's

6 June 1937                          *The Criterion*

Dear John,

Thank you for yrs. of the 4th.[1] I have written to Geoffrey & Enid, and I hope that you will all have none the less pleasant time, though it is agreeable to think that one may be missed. But I want to be missed directly, and not simply because everybody thinks that somebody else will miss me etc. wch. would be foolish. I hope Geoffrey will be able to settle about the 19th however, because if it isnt Wales I should like to pay my respects to Mr Sanders [*sic*].[2]

I am glad to hear that you have been tippling with Lord Vernon.[3] I hope all is well at Clarence Terrace.[4] I had a line of invitation to the Connolly party – should have been glad to oblidge, but feared it would be as you say it was. I made my Speach at Rochester,[5] which will be reported I think in the *Kent Messenger*. Have had a quiet weekend, reading and reporting on MSS. Old Mr Isherwood has at last been to see *The Ascent of F6* and doesn't like it.[6] I did not ask him why. I was more more [*sic*] interested in finding out when he was leaving London for his Place in Cheshire, which I advised him to do at once. The Vicar is up North for the funeral of his mother – God rest her soul – and meanwhile I have eaten some excellent asparagus which somebody sent to him and Elizabeth cooked for me, as she says he said when he was away never keep anything for him. I am glad that you have had a benign weekend at Cambridge, and hope you will ring me up in the Afternoon. No more headaches: I was so exhilarated this afternoon by the halcyon weather and my new Austin Reed semi-

---

1 – Not traced.

2 – Norman Saunders, of Bradfield School.

3 – Francis Lawrence William Venables-Vernon, 9th Baron Vernon (1889–1963).

4 – No. 2, Clarence Terrace, Regent's Park; home to the novelist Elizabeth Bowen from 1935.

5 – 'Religious Drama: Mediæval and Modern', *University of Edinburgh Journal* 9 (1937–1938), Autumn 1937, 8–17. See *Prose* V, 519–30.

6 – Henry Isherwood (d. 1940), uncle of Christopher Isherwood (his deceased father's elder brother), had inherited Marple Hall and family estates in Cheshire in 1924.

tropical suit that I walked all the way from Pall Mall to Emperor's Gate, taking in a Communist Procession (the same that I saw last week in the Charing Cross Road) on the way.

Yr. faithful<br>TP

## TO *Edith Perkins*

7 June 1937                    *The Criterion*

Dear Mrs Perkins,

Thank you very much for your letter. I trust that by now you have had more hopeful news from America. I have no idea how well Emily will be when she arrives; I only know that there seems no doubt of her being able to sail.[1] I propose to meet her at Waterloo (unless she wants to be met at Southampton, but ordinarily, and especially on the arrival of a large and crowded ship, there is nothing that one can do for anyone there) and as it will be tea-time at the very earliest, she had better have my rooms for the night – Elizabeth and the vicar will be glad to see her I am sure. I can take her heavy luggage over to Paddington to be ready for the next day.

I am vexed to have had no free weekends so far, and the prospects for the immediate future are not bright; but I want to let you know what my fixtures are, because I should like to arrange a visit as early as possible, and whatever is possible, before other engagements come crowding in. I have to be away again the coming weekend and probably the next in Wales, but am not sure of the latter. On the 25th, most unfortunately, I have to be in Bath to make the prize-day speech at the Methodist School there;[2] I don't know when I can get away, or whether anything can be done with the remains of that weekend. On the 2nd July I have to be in

---

1 – The Revd John Carroll Perkins and his wife Edith had reached Liverpool by ship on 24 Apr. He had written to TSE on 2 Apr.: 'We shall hope to see you as soon as it is convenient for you. And I am sending you our united cordial invitation to spend the first week end in May with us.

'Emily has been with us for her Easter vacation. She is not as strong as we could wish, but I am sure the year at [Smith College in] Northampton has been good for her; and her spirit is good and fine. Emily and I saw the performance of your widely acceptable "Becket". The actors were definitely amateur in the Harvard presentation . . .

'Hoping that we may see you on May 1st I send our united affectionate greetings.'

2 – The text of TSE's Prize Day Address at Kingswood School, Bath, on 25 June has not survived; but it was reported in the *Kingswood Magazine* 25: 3 (July 1937), 86–9: *CProse* 5, 510–13.

Edinburgh for the weekend.[1] Emily expressed some wish to be present at the ceremony; but although I have applied for three tickets, I don't advise this, as it seems a tiring journey and considerable expense, and I don't expect to have any free time – that day is wholly taken up with formal parties at the University, and I expect my host, John Baillie, will have filled up the rest of my time.[2] Then from the 12th to the 18th I have to be in Oxford for a Conference. I shall try to keep the week before quite free, and of course it would be easy to combine Oxford and Campden. The following week is also free except that I have to pay a final visit to Rochester on the 23d. And after that I have no engagements yet! though I imagine I will be wanted for a week in Wales about then – Faber likes to fit me in before the 12th August, as I do not shoot.

So that we have a possibility of the weekend of the 19th, but that is very doubtful, and I don't want you to keep it; and the weekend of the 26th, if it is possible to get from Bath to Campden on a Saturday, and then the time after the 4th July.

I hope you are enjoying this good weather at last. And may it persist for another three months!

Affectionately yours,<br>Tom

## TO *George Blake*

CC

7 June 1937            [Faber & Faber Ltd]

Dear George,

I have been rather dilatory about the enclosed,[3] but it arrived while I was away in Salzburg, and since then I have been pretty busy. I have not discussed this with anyone here, and I should like to know your views on the subject before I take it up with the committee.

Personally I am all for exploring *The Kingis Quair*, which ought not to be a very expensive job to produce. Of course I had nothing to do with the arrangements about the Dunbar, and do not know whether the Porpoise

---

1 – For the award of the hon. degree of D.Litt.
2 – EH did accompany TSE to Edinburgh for his hon. degree. Gordon, *The Imperfect Life of T. S. Eliot*, 398–9: 'At the last minute she discovered that a long dress was obligatory, sped out, and returned in a dress splashed with a dramatic print. Eliot teased her about her brightness at so sober a gathering. Emily herself liked to tell of being snubbed. She was admiring a private garden when Lady Drummond, looking pointedly at the floral colours of her guest's dress, said: "I see that Miss *Hale* has brought her garden with her."'
3 – Not traced.

Press paid Mackenzie for the job, or how much. But I should not think that the *Kingis Quair* would be such an expensive piece of editing.

As for the *Aenead*, that might let the Press in for a white elephant, and I should not advise its committing itself, at least until one knows how the *Kingis Quair* is likely to do. There might be some sale to American universities, and possibly some New York firm would come in on it and undertake a definite number of sheets in advance. I do think, however, subject to the opinion of the members of the Porpoise Press, that it might be worthwhile having some pourparler with the Scottish Texts Society and investigating the problem of expense in co-operating with them. At any rate it might be a good thing to establish some sort of claim on Gavin Douglas before any other general publisher does.

Best wishes to Elly and the boys, and in particular Sally.

Yours ever,

[Tom]

TO *Joyce Ridley*                                                          CC

9 June 1937                    [Faber & Faber Ltd]

Dear Miss Ridley,

My committee have now considered fully the question of the publication of your and Mr Scarfe's translation of the works of Lautreamont.[1] I regret

---

1 – Joyce Ridley (Newcastle upon Tyne) submitted the translation on 4 May 1937.

TSE in his reader's report (n.d.): 'This is to be a translation of the complete works of Lautreamont, made by two young people [Ridley and Francis Scarfe] whom Herbert Read has recommended and sent our way. The translations here are of the CHANTS DE MALDOROR only, but these constitute the bulk and much the most important part of Lautreamont's work.

'Personally I have always considered Lautreamont to be pretty nearly rubbish, and not in the same class with Rimbaud. I shall be surprised if any member of the committee reading either text or translation does not come to the same opinion. The point is, however, that Lautreamont is one of the classics in the Surrealist racket, and that we should not need to like the stuff ourselves to feel perfectly respectable in publishing it. The question is, however, is it worth while? Only if we think the Surrealist game is going to continue to pay well enough. In that case, to publish this volume would be a further stage of ingratiating ourselves with the Surrealist boys.

'If you think the book is worth publishing, which I don't, especially in view of our already having more books than we want, I think that someone ought to go through a part of the text carefully to judge the translation. It is not necessary for anyone to read it all, but I suggest that it would be a nice way of letting John Hayward earn a guinea, by asking him to look through it sufficiently to give us his opinion. He is very conscientious in these matters, and would probably consult some of his friends at the Embassy on [incomplete].

An unknown hand wrote on TSE's report: 'GCF says NO' and 'Committee *dubious*.'

to say that they do not feel on mature consideration that this is a book with which we are the most suitable people to deal. They do not feel that we could market it profitably, and they are of the opinion that it would be better in the hands of a smaller firm which could give it more attention. I should suggest trying Boriswood or the Parton Press. The Corvinus Press might also be interested, but they only do very fine editions in small numbers, and therefore would not reach the public at which you are aiming.

With many regrets,
I am,
Yours sincerely,
[T. S. Eliot]

TO *John Hayward*                                                    TS King's

9 June 1937                          *The Criterion*

My dear John,

Thank you very much for your informative letter. It was all the more welcome, as I was still frothing and fuming over John Masefield's letter in *The Times* newspaper yesterday.[1] The English Verse Speaking Association is a monstrous cancer in this Land, stretching now its foul tentacles towards the public house. In old times it was said that an Englishman's public house was his castle – but what is it now? and what is it to be?

---

1 – 'Art in the Inn: Halls for Readings and Drama: An Oxford Experiment' (letter), *Times*, 8 June 1937, 17: 'Sir – You have lately remarked on the improved publichouses and inns up and down the country, which are a feature of our changing England . . . There are now many improved houses with large rooms or halls which challenge a search for the uses to which they can be put.

'It is proposed to make the experiment of using some of these halls for verse-speaking, drama, and readings of prose, and thus encouraging a wider appreciation of our language and literature in its higher forms. By way of opening the experiment, the Oxford University Dramatic Society has kindly promised to give an evening performance (subject to permission) of *Twelfth Night* at the Downham Tavern, on the L.C.C. housing estate, S.E., on June 24 . . . We do not fear to aim high. It is easy to underrate the power of popular appreciation. And we are fortunate in having won sympathetic interest not only from a sufficient number of owners of publichouses, but also from the English Association and the British Drama League . . .

'We trust that all who are interested in the experiment will watch its progress and that those who are able to help will do so . . .

'We are, Sir, your obedient servants,

'John Masefield [plus fourteen other signatories including Francis Underhill and Sybil Thorndike] / 35, Belgrave Square, S.W., June 7.'

the scene of choral recitations of Jerry Hopkins's The Leaden Echo.[1] The last of the Oxford Giants, Father Kelly of Kelham who still travels with a hip bath, would not approve of this. He must not know. I am aware of a changing world. This evening, on my after-dinner perambulation to take the air, I encountered a strange concert party in Hereford Square. They had a very old taxi, into which they had mounted a piano in place of the back seat. The side of the taxi was hung with those metal tubes which give a sound bearing the same resemblance to bells that the fiddle with a horn and one string (I have never understood how the sound of the string comes through the horn) bears to a Stradivarius. There were two men dressed I regret to say as Pierrots; and three women (one on the piano, one singing, and one *faisant la quête*)[2] dressed as Tzigauner. It was ominous. After they had collected all the money they could get from the Hereford Arms, apparently, they cranked the taxi and moved on. It all seems ominous. It reminds me of Butler Barker – but that story (which is Mary Hutchinson's story) will wait.

I am very sorry that you are so *umgebaut von Amerikanischen Publikum*.[3] In some way or other it must be your fault.[4] I am sorry to hear that Rosamund Lehmann's husband has been blown up.[5] It is ominous. I am sorry to hear of anybody being blown up. I have nothing to set against it but Lister's twins. Faber is still gloomy with jaundice, and Morley's guffaws and twinkles ring hollow, because he too is hounded by American visitors. A small black cat darts in and out of my window. I have written to Mr Saunders.[6] My life may be put in the form of a catechism:

Q. Have you a lunch engagement tomorrow?
A. Yes. Miss Bradby is to ring up to tell me where and with whom.
Q. Who is Miss Bradby?

1 – Gerard Manley Hopkins, 'The Leaden Echo and the Golden Echo'.
2 – *Faisant la quête* (Fr.): lit. 'doing the quest' – taking round the hat.
3 – *umgebaut von Amerikanischen Publikum*: 'rebuilt by an American audience'.
4 – JDH had written, in a letter dated 10 June (it is not known whether he or TSE got the date wrong): 'My days and nights are given over to your former countrymen . . . And then on Monday a Guggenheim birthday revel! Oh lor! And now my dear Lehmann's husband has been knocked out by a bomb in Spain.'
5 – Wogan Philipps (1902–93), politician and artist, Rosamond Lehmann's husband since 1928, had joined Medical Aid for Spain and worked (for eighteen months from 1936) as an ambulance driver for the Republicans. After being wounded by shell-fire he returned home, whereupon he joined the Communist Party of Great Britain. He succeeded his father as 2nd Baron Milford in 1962 and sat in the House of Lords as representative of the Communist Party.
6 – Norman Saunders, Bradfield College.

A. A young lady receiving a small weekly salary to act as a professional Fury.

Q. Have you anything to do after that?

A. Yes, but I shall not get it done; because someone is coming to see me at 3.30 and at 4.45, but I forget who or why.

Q. Have you anything to do in the evening.

A. Yes.

Q. What?

A. I have to dine with Miss Mirrlees. I should not be surprised to find Desmond MacCarthy there too.

Q. Have you any lunch engagement on Friday?

A. Yes. Dr Oldham is lunching with me to discuss Dr Wissert t'hooft's essay,[1] and the question of my making a reply of 20 minutes to pp. 41–45 thereof.

Q. Have you anything to do in the afternoon?

A. Yes. But I shall not get it done, because two people are coming to see me.

Q. Have you anything to do in the evening?

A. Yes.

Q. What?

A. Davy (Dai) Jones is dining with me. I don't know why, but he is a very nice man.

Q. Have you anything to do at the weekend.

A. Yes. To be brief, I have to go to Morley's to help him entertain Donald Brace, New York publisher. I don't know how.

Q. If you did not have to go to Morley's, what would you do?

A. I should have to spend the weekend with Tandy.

Q. If you did not have to spend the weekend with Tandy, what would you do?

A. I should have to listen to two sermons, and count up three collections and balance the returns for the week: including threepenny bits of both the old and the new style.

Q. Do you ever relax?

A. No.

---

1–Willem A. Visser 't Hooft (1900–85), Dutch theologian; from 1932, general secretary of the World Student Christian Federation; editor of *The Student World*, 1929–39; General Secretary of the World Council of Churches, 1948–66. His works include *Students Find the Truth to Serve: The Story of the World Student Christian Federation 1931–1935* (1935).

So no more for the present. I did have something to write to you about, but I have forgotten it.

Yrs.

TP

P.S. I am still fretting about Masefield and the public House. Is there anything to be done or not? Must we just be Cynical and leave the public Houses to Masefield?[1] Gropius has gone to America, that's one good thing.

JUST REMEMBERED what I had to write about. Henri Fluchère has sent in specimen translations of *Der Dommord*. Can you spare the time to go through them and make comments? Immensely grateful. It looks much better than Cattaui–Erlanger[2] anyway.

TP

P.P.S. Everything seems ominous.

I have dealt with Arthur. He smashed up a milk cart in Ebury St.[3]


TO *Polly Tandy*                                                    TS BL

9 June [1937]                    *The Criterion*

Dear Ma,

Here's a kettle of fish. An important American publisher has just arrived in London (he happens to be my publisher there) and Morley has got him to come down to his Farm for the weekend, and he particularly wants me to come too – there are complicated reasons not strictly my own private affair why I should, yunnerstan, and I should have preferred to come to

---

1 – See too TSE's 'Commentary', C. 17 (Oct. 1937), 85: 'I have always thought of the public-house as one of the few places to which one could escape from "verse-speaking, drama and readings of prose" . . . I am appalled at the thought of turning into the saloon bar at five-thirty for quiet refreshment, and finding that it has been converted into a *Poet's Pub* . . . If the public-house is to fall into the hands of the English Association and the British Drama League, where, one must ask bluntly, is a man to go for a drink?'

Geoffrey Whitworth, Director of the British Drama League, invited TSE (17 June) 'to be present at the performance' by the Oxford University Drama Society at the Downham Tavern on 24 June, 'at which the Poet Laureate will be present and speak'. TSE declined the invitation.

Tomlin, *T. S. Eliot*, 88: 'He was always against the Poet's Pub idea. To him, the poetry of taverns resided in their authentic atmosphere, not one rendered bogus by the intrusion of "art".'

2 – The draft translation of *MiC* by Georges Cattaui and Emile d'Erlanger.

3 – This refers to the developing plot of *The Family Reunion*.

Hampton.[1] And there's furthermore a complication about the 19th. I had made an engagement to go to Bradfield College on the 22nd to see the OEdipous play they are doing there, with a party. Now I find I cant go on the 22nd and said so, and I find they are taking a lot of trouble to get me a seat on the 19th instead – I mean, that if they do, it's too late to stop them and I should feel that I ought to go in recognition and those folks particularly wanted me to go etc. So I MAY not be able to get down on the 19th until late in the evening, but I hope that you will not be Furious and will accept me even on those terms, because I am really pathetic if you only see it in that light, and also from pillar to post I am as they say. Though not quite so also as yr. husband between the Devil and the B.B.C. So now I have made a clean Brest of it and there it is and I am truly sorry oh dear, well will close hoping for your favour and am very sorry indeed. yours faithful

TP.

There is neither (P.S.) pleasure nor personal profit in all this, it's just conscience.


## TO *A. Desmond Hawkins*                    TS A. Desmond Hawkins

10 June 1937                    *The Criterion*

My dear Hawkins,

Your suggestion for a modern omnibus, which got submerged during my absence on holiday, has now been discussed by the committee, who express keen interest. They think it inadvisable to plan such a book for the coming autumn, which would mean working under pressure anyway, inasmuch as our Elizabeth Bowen volume, the *Faber Book of Modern Stories*, is to come out then, and they don't want to launch both at the same time. They would like to go further with you into plans for a volume in 1938, and indeed not necessarily in the autumn, so the next step is to ask you to let us have a more detailed outline of contents, so that estimates of expense can be gone into. You would presumably do a preface discussing your choice, but this of course could be left to the last. As you yourself suggest, to make such a book profitable the bulk of the

1–FVM to Donald Brace, 9 Apr. 1937: 'Eliot says that Pike's Farm is more endurable now that we have electricity and electric fires wherever you want them; and he promises to spend whatever week-end you would like at the Farm – as a competitor in inertia, if you will come there. I will have the fish polished up and ready for you.'

The Tandys lived at Hope Cottage, 82 High Street, Hampton-on-Thames, Middlesex.

contents would have to be taken from Faber authors. I do not think that it ought to be exclusively taken from Faber authors, however, and it does not seem that you think so either. Anyway, the Sales Manager thinks well of the project, so I hope we can put it through.[1]

Yours ever,
T. S. Eliot

## TO *Montgomery Belgion*[2] CC

10 June 1937           [*The Criterion*]

Dear Belgion,

As you are in the vortex of the newspaper world, perhaps you can help me with a problem which arises in a play which I am trying to write.

I want to know whether the country edition of the *Evening News* or the *Evening Standard*, assuming there to be a country edition, could be supposed to reach a remote country house in the North of England by 10 o'clock in the evening.[3] I should imagine, from what experience I have had of country places, that this would be impossible. In my experience of places equally remote, the morning London papers arrived about tea-time, and the evening papers the next day. If this is invariably so, then a new question arises. I want to know how late in the evening a motor accident could occur in London and be mentioned in next morning's paper.

I have your note, for which I thank you. I look forward to seeing you at tea on Tuesday at Barbellion[4] and at lunch on Thursday at L'Ecu de France.[5]

Yours ever,
[T. S. Eliot]

1 – Hawkins responded, 11 June 1937, that he was glad to know his suggestion was 'working out so far'; he submitted a provisional list of contents.
2 – Montgomery ('Monty') Belgion (1892–1973), author and journalist: see Biographical Register.
3 – This question relates to the plot of TSE's play-in-progress *The Family Reunion*.
4 – Barbellion: a restaurant at 79 New Bond Street, London.
5 – A l'Ecu de France, Jermyn Street, London.

TO *Viscount Carlow*[1]                                              CC

10 June 1937                          [Faber & Faber Ltd]

My dear Lord Carlow,

Since talking to you, and since receiving your letter of the 7th instant,[2] I have looked up our agreement with James Joyce for the publication of *Work in Progress*, and find that it gives us exclusive rights for the British Empire. I have discussed with the Board of Directors your publication of a section of Part II in a limited edition of 125 copies, to be priced at about 2 guineas. We understand that you will be bringing out this book during the course of the current year, so that there is no danger of its appearing simultaneously with the complete text. In the circumstances my Board consider that we should ask from you a fee of £25 for the licence to publish this limited edition. I hope that you will find these terms satisfactory.[3]

Yours sincerely,
[T. S. Eliot]

1–George Lionel Seymour Dawson-Damer, Viscount Carlow (1907–44), founded in 1936 the Corvinus Press, publishing fine limited editions of works by writers including T. E. Lawrence (a close friend), Walter de la Mare, Wyndham Lewis and Stefan Zweig.

2–Lord Carlow had talked with TSE on 7 June about his plan to publish a section of JJ's 'Work in Progress', and wrote further on the same day: 'I have already explained to you the circumstance in which James Joyce offered to let me print this section; so I do not think it necessary to refer to it again here. I propose to print approximately 125 copies, all of which will be numbered, and the edition will be strictly limited. The cost of each volume is uncertain until the book is finished and in the hands of the binders, but I imagine it would be about two guineas.

'I hope to have it ready for issue in about two to three months' time, as I am now only waiting for Joyce's final comments on my last corrections before I begin printing.

'I hope that my limited edition is not in any way interfering with your plans for the publication of the whole work.'

3–In reply, Lord Carlow said he felt 'confounded' by TSE's letter. 'This press is purely a hobby of mine, done because I am interested in fine printing, limited editions, and trying out experiments that the other printers are commercially unable to do, and this, as you may fully realise, is not lucrative in any degree whatsoever.' Indeed, he went on, the Corvinus Press ran at a heavy annual loss, and no private press had ever paid a dividend. If he had anticipated that a licence fee of £25 was to be paid, he would have reconsidered printing the JJ piece; and heretofore he had never been charged a fee. 'I no more wish to pay the £25 than come to cross-purposes with your firm, as our combined interest is, I believe, to perpetuate modern literature.' They settled for £10.

See *Storiella As She Is Syung* (London: Corvinus Press, 1937), with a decorated initial letter designed by Lucia Joyce adorning the first page of the text: 175 copies (25 signed).

14 June 1937                          [Faber & Faber Ltd]

Dear Mr Connely,

Thank you for your letter of June 11th, and for returning *The Dhammapada*.² I have also to thank you for your kindness toward Dr Tereshchenko and the trouble you have taken on his behalf. I was not myself sanguine that anything could be done for him in the States. It is one of the most difficult problems with which I have had anything to do.

I think it would be a capital idea to get your man from Hopkins in touch with Auden.³ As you know, the fee for the Turnbull Lectures is not really enough to tempt anyone to visit America for that purpose alone, but it happens that Auden is to be lecturing in America during the coming winter in any case, so I think it would fit in admirably. In the circumstances, although of course it is contrary to office rules, I will give you his address, as follows:

The Downs School, Colwall, near Malvern.

Yours sincerely,
[T. S. Eliot]

1 – Willard Connely (1888–1967), critic, biographer and lecturer, was at this time Director of the American University Union, 1 Gordon Square, London.
2 – Connely had borrowed TSE's copy of *The Dhammapada*, trans. Irving Babbitt (1936). 'I found your marginal notes frequently quite as thought-provoking as what Babbitt himself said. It is curious how much Babbitt's characteristic prejudices recur . . . For all his condemnation of literature of escape, I have always thought that Babbitt was fond of the Orient somewhat because he wanted to get away from thinking about the Occident. I am not sure he makes too good a case for the spineless East, which would have a sadder time in this world were it not for the strength, inner if you like, which is in the character of the fallible West.'
   Connely reported that he had been able to introduce Tereshchenko to Professor McDougall, and would put him in touch with any other psychologists who came to London. 'It is of course most unfortunate that a man of his abilities should have nothing to do, and yet, the way to get something to do might be to take any sort of work which offered, even manual labour, and then watch for chances to get something better. But I gathered that Mr Tereshchenko would not be very venturous along such lines.'
3 – 'I have a man here from Hopkins looking for candidates for the Turnbull Lectures next year. I think he would be interested in having a talk with Auden, and I should like to bring them together.'

TO *E. Martin Browne*                                                    CC

17 June 1937                          [Faber & Faber Ltd]

My dear Martin,

It appears that we are rapidly approaching the time when *Murder in the Cathedral* will have to be reprinted, and I want to make that the occasion for a third edition. That is to say, I propose to incorporate as a kind of appendix the opening of Act II which appears in the first edition but not in the second. It seemed to me that this might be useful for amateurs performing the play in religious surroundings where the introits might be effective.

Also, I want to incorporate the alterations in the part of the Fourth Knight which we made when we went through the part together recently. You will remember that there are one or two places which you were going to try out and see whether the original rendering was more effective, or whether the lines should be taken away from that character. And, of course, before making any of these changes I want to know that you are satisfied with the way they work out on the stage, so I should be glad of confirmation, and of any other suggestions in connexion with the new edition.[1]

Yours ever,
[T. S. E.]


TO *John Hayward*                                                        TS King's

21 [June 1937]                        *The Criterion*

Dear John

Just a line to say hit as struck me I shuld like to give you a birthday Pressent when is your birth Day It come to me you need a new Chair[2] now I suppose theres new Kinds of Chairs steam Lined stop and Go etc more solid and pneumatic but Would not suppose necessary to cuncult

1–EMB replied (? 18 June): 'The Fourth Knight now has
        "How much longer will you keep us waiting?"
        "God bless him!"
in first scene, & nothing but the meeting-speech in the second. These work very well.
    'Should you not make some note, however tentative, about the correspondence of Tempter/Knight characters if you make these alterations?
    'I've now incorporated "Is it the owl that calls" and the centre section of "Clear the air" in the show, with excellent results.'
2–JDH had to use a wheelchair: he was severely disabled.

Herbt Read and with centrel heating etc please excuse my impertnence but have enjoyed much Hospitality and nothing for It but part of the liquour most of what I drink upp and so will close[1]

                              yours Respcfully
                              T. S. Eliot

hoep to here or see you soon

I had lunch with Mr Faber and Mr Morly and Sir Hug Walpole I had pruins with cream thay was lovely thay had Cherry trat[2]


## TO *Vernon Watkins*[3]                                    TS Berg

23 June 1937                    *The Criterion*

Dear Mr Watkins,

I must apologize for having been unable to see you when you called, but I am not ordinarily here in the morning. I must also apologize for the delay in reporting to you about your masque.[4]

---

1 – JDH replied, 22 June: 'My birthday was years ago but that only makes it more delightful to be asked what one would like for a present. I'm afraid the chair business is more complicated (and more extravagant) than you possibly realize. I've often brooded on the matter. The trouble is that my chair has to do too many things. It has to be able to go at racing speed on the flat (and in the flat); it has to be narrow enough to go through the eye of a needle; it has to go up and downstairs and must thus (design for elevating apart) be as light as possible; and finally it must fold up into the smallest possible space. You see, it is really a kind of surrealist's dream. The old pram I have – 1930 model – fulfills these requirements in its clumsy fashion and is not uncomfortable to ride in. But I have sometimes wondered if it might not be possible to construct such a chair from duralumin instead of wood – duralumin being the infinitely light, infinitely strong material used in aircraft – and improve the general design and make the folding business neater. I should like to discuss the matter with you – at any rate in theory, for no one has ever had the pleasant idea of suggesting an improvement. And one might go so far as to make enquiries in the Welbech district where these mysteries are understood. Meanwhile, you must guess how delighted I am with such a warm hearted gesture.'
2 – GCF's diary, Mon., 21 June: 'Lunched at Oxf. & Camb. With FVM, TSE, & Hugh Walpole, who was in good form. He is a diabetic; has had to give himself 2 injections of insulin a day for last 10 years. Has given up alcohol, because if you don't, at Hollywood, where he has been most of last 2 years, you either die or collapse. Hollywood filled him with despair – he began to feel he wld never escape from it. Is helping [Charles] Laughton to do a picture – writing it – but never again; it's like working with neurotic madmen.'
3 – Vernon Watkins (1906–67), Welsh poet and lifelong friend (from 1935) of Dylan Thomas, was educated at Magdalene College, Cambridge (which he left without a degree). He worked for thirty-eight years at Lloyds Bank in Swansea: he was a cryptographer at Bletchley Park during the war, and resumed his banking straight after. Writings include *The Ballad of the Mari Llwyd* (1941) and *The Lady with the Unicorn* (1948).
4 – Watkins submitted his masque, 'The Influences', in June 1936: for some reason, it seems not to have come to TSE's attention until 1937. (On 8 Dec. 1936 Watkins even issued this

The masque seems to me to show quite considerable facility and accomplishment. I think it fails, for two reasons: one is that it hesitates between something intended to be performed and something intended for reading. If you examine the short plays of Mr Yeats, by whom you seem to have been considerably influenced, you will find that however lyrical they are, there is always some effective dramatic trick of suspense and surprise. I think, on the other hand, that, for reading, this masque becomes simply a sequence of poems rather thinly connected; and in the versification itself I think there is a tendency to monotony in a measure, and indeed a kind of vocabulary, which Mr Yeats has made very familiar, and in the use of which he cannot be equalled. In short, I think that this is an interesting experiment which should be useful to you, but which is not in itself satisfactory for publication.

I shall look forward to seeing more of your work.[1]

Yours sincerely,
T. S. Eliot

TO *Ashley Dukes*                                                                 CC

23 June 1937                        [Faber & Faber Ltd]

Dear Ashley,

You will remember that we had some discussion about a Frenchman named Henri Fluchère, who wanted to translate *Murder in the Cathedral* for stage purposes, and who seemed a possible candidate. He has now translated some of the first pages, which I enclose for your consideration, together with his letter, which is relevant.

---

reproach: 'I hope you will not think me unduly persistent but I am working in an office where letters have to be answered by return, and it seems odd to me that replies should take weeks, even months.') See Watkins, *The Influences: A Masque* (1977).

1–Watkins responded on 3 July: 'Your criticism is not merely just, it is extraordinarily penetrative. I think if it were less so you would have called me an imitator; but although I have borrowed the dresses from Mr Yeats and even had my dancers trained in his measures, I cannot find in any one of his plays the particular allegory which is the subject of the masque. And because this allegory seems to me as profound as anything in the whole of art (– it is, indeed, touched upon in your later single poems for which I have a very great admiration) I feel I cannot discard the masque in the way you mention – as "an interesting experiment which should be useful to you, but which is not in itself satisfactory for publication." Instead, I intend to attempt a new version with your criticism to guide me. Perhaps I shall use prose to break the monotony. At any rate, I shall try to convey my idea, which I feel has not yet been conveyed, in either a dramatic or a reading form, with my eye and ear on one or the other.'

You will notice that John Hayward and I have queried a few passages. I should not want to accept any translation without getting also the opinion of some qualified Frenchman with a knowledge of English. But what I enclose strikes me as a quite competent, if not highly inspired, rendering. I should expect to find that the rest of his translation would have to be combed through pretty thoroughly for errors and imprecisions. I am a little disconcerted by his confession that he translated *The Duchess of Malfi* in a month. One cannot help wondering whether anyone who can do such a job, even under pressure, in that time, has been able to maintain the highest standards.

Still, I should be glad if you would let me have this back, at your leisure, with your comments and opinion. You will notice that he himself seems over anxious to get the thing done quickly. I don't know anything about Madame Renaud-Thévenet of Brussels or her intention of rendering the choruses: it sounds rather depressing.[1]

Yours ever,
[T. S. Eliot][2]

## TO *A. Desmond Hawkins*                TS A. Desmond Hawkins

24 June 1937                *The Criterion*

My dear Hawkins,

In the circumstances I don't see what else you can do. I will certainly try to get *Such Is Life*[3] for you, and will send you a copy of *In Parenthesis*.[4]

---

1 – Fluchère reported on 5 June that Mme Renaud-Thévenet, of the Conservatoire Royal de Musique de Bruxelles, wanted to work on the chorus as soon as possible.
2 – Dukes responded on 7 July: 'You and Hayward seem to have noticed most of the mistakes in detail – and there are plenty of them – but I really do think the rhythm is so beautifully preserved that it compensates for the small weaknesses.

'Therefore on the whole I would advise asking him to go ahead. It is a little surprising that anyone able to write such an excellent English letter should have failed to understand '*some not able to* . . .' This line was always appreciated at the Mercury.'
3 – *Such is Life* (London, 1937), by Tom Collins, was first published in Australia in 1903.
4 – *In Parenthesis*, by David Jones, was published on 10 June 1937.

TSE wrote in his undated reader's report (Sept. 1936) on *In Parenthesis*: 'The Committee is not to think that it can escape the necessity for re-reading this book by relying on my opinion. That is to say that although I found this book quite fascinating, it is definitely not a one-man opinion book, whether mine or anyone else's. I should certainly recommend it if I thought that it had any chance of paying for itself, but a book dealing with Flanders between December 1915 and July 1916 in a kind of prose which is frequently on the edge of verse is hardly likely to be popular at the present time. What makes the book interesting is not so much its documentation, which seems pretty good, subject to G.C.F.'s correction. The interest is rather in the refraction through a rather odd personality. There are things about the book which give it somewhat the same kick that you get from something by Kipling, and I almost think that Kipling himself might have liked it. I don't mean that it is full of ordinary jingo or empire sentiment, but that the author has a kind of sense of history and a sort of sense of glory in the relation of races which is somewhat Kiplingesque. F.V.M. ought to be pleased by the constant recurrence to the Arthurian Cycle, and the author really succeeds in presenting a genuine poetic aspect of Welshness. But I haven't the slightest notion whether what I see in the book is really there, or if it is there, whether it will reach more than a few people. But the references to Welsh literature are extremely effective. I recommend the book for serious consideration.'

RdlM to Jones, 1 Oct. 1936: 'I am afraid I have kept you waiting longer for our decision about *In Parenthesis* than I hoped . . . Of course we have no doubts about it at all – it is a splendid piece of work, and we should be proud to publish it.'

Jones to TSE, 19 Nov. 1936: 'Thank you so much for my typescript returned.

'I did so much enjoy yr coming to dinner that night at Tom Burns & I do hope we may meet again when I am in London.

'I am glad to have the mss back for making final corrections – one feels one would like to work on a thing, not for four or five, but for 20 or 30 years, before its publication!

'I was more pleased than I can say that you found something to like in it – there is much that I'm doubtful about.

'I hope we meet again.'

TSE's blurb (first published in Faber Spring Books 1937, 28) reads: 'David Jones is already well known as a painter and draughtsman: he will be known equally as a writer. This is the record of a period between December 1915 and July 1916; it is not a "war book" so much as a distillation of the essence of war books, and in particular it is the *chanson de gestes* of the Cockney and the Welsh and the Welsh Cockney in the Great War, men and ghosts, and behind them the shadows of all their ancestors who fought and toiled and died in the Britain of the Celt and of the Saxon. Having said this, we may describe the book as an *early epic*: one of the strangest, most sombre and most exciting books that we have published.'

TSE would later relate, in a BBC talks feature on David Jones, compiled and introd. by Goronwy Rees and broadcast on 29 Oct. 1954: '[P]eople like to classify . . . *In Parenthesis* could be regarded as a "war book", a book about the first world war; even though the author had said "I did not intend this as a 'War Book' – it happens to be concerned with war." The distinction is important. But if *In Parenthesis* was a "War Book", then, people could say, it was probably intended to be prose, even though you could not take the typography as a reliable guide.'

See too 'A Note of Introduction' (1961): '*In Parenthesis* was first published in London in 1937. I am proud to share the responsibility for that first publication. On reading the book in typescript I was deeply moved. I then regarded it, and I still regard it, as a work of genius . . .

'When *In Parenthesis* is widely enough known – as it will be in time – it will no doubt undergo the same sort of detective analysis and exegesis as the later work of James Joyce and the *Cantos* of Ezra Pound. It is true that *In Parenthesis* and David Jones's later and equally remarkable work *The Anathemata*, are provided by the author with notes; but author's notes (as is illustrated by *The Waste Land*) are no prophylactic against interpretation and dissection; they merely provide the serious researcher with more material to interpret and dissect. The work of David Jones has some affinity with that of James Joyce (both men seem to me to have the Celtic ear for the music of words) and with the later work of Ezra Pound, and with my own. I stress the affinity, as any possible influence seems to me slight and of no importance. David Jones is a representative of the same literary generation as Joyce and

I think that the latter can be treated in several ways, and I think it deserves to be treated twice, so you could confine yourself to what you really want to say about it, on the assumption that it will have a separate review. I may possibly write a review notice of it myself, as I cannot review our own books elsewhere than in the *Criterion*.[1]

I will pass your request for a copy of *Revelation* over to our review department, over which I have no control.

Yours ever,
T. S. E.

## TO *Henry Miller*                                            CC

28 June 1937                          [*The Criterion*]

Dear Mr Miller,

Thank you for your note.[2] I am glad that neither you nor Miss Nin sees any objection to the disclosure of her name in your article as the author of the Diary.

I am afraid that the publication of such a voluminous work is indeed remote. I do not think, however, that the commercial publisher is lacking

---

Pound and myself, if four men born between 1882 and 1895 can be regarded as of the same literary generation. David Jones is the youngest, and the tardiest to publish. The lives of all of us were altered by that War, but David Jones is the only one to have fought in it.'

1–Hawkins, 'Fiction Chronicle', C. 17 (Oct. 1937), 107–18. '*In Parenthesis* is not fiction, but I propose discussing it because it takes an important place in contemporary imaginative prose . . . *In Parenthesis* is as near to being folk-epic as any self-conscious work can be.

'But it is self-conscious. We have to some extent surrendered the innocence in which epic flowers naturally, and *In Parenthesis* has at times the appearance of being contrived, factitious, pedantic in the care of construction . . .

'This synthetic element weakens the force of the book, but nevertheless Mr Jones has produced many passages of remarkably fine prose. I wish some novelists would emulate his personal restraint, his inventiveness, his sense of the dignity of his subject, and his freedom from irrelevant commonplaces.'

2–Miller wrote, 24 June 1938: 'I'm glad to say that you may keep the name of Anaïs Nin in that essay after all. Miss Nin feels, and I believe she is right, that the possibilities of any one ever publishing the diary in its entirety and unexpurgated, as she wishes, is so remote that even if it did happen no one would remember the article about her.

'If I ever earn any money I shall bring it out for her myself, bit by bit. I have dissuaded her from accepting any offers to publish a collapsed, castrated revision of the work. It is a big work and demands someone equally big to bring it forth. Such people do exist always, but one must search for them. The commercial publisher has no soul and little guts . . .

'P.S. Can you tell me of any art review in England to which I could send a short, poetic essay on a painter here in Paris – Hans Reichel? Studio & the Burlington are out of the question.'

merely in soul or guts, but also frequently in the spare capital necessary to finance a venture, which on such a scale would mean a very considerable loss.

I do not know what art review at the moment is the most likely for your essay. They are constantly being founded, and do not always last long. I should suggest your writing to Herbert Read for his advice, because although he is the editor of the *Burlington*, his soul is elsewhere, and he would be as well informed as anyone, and probably better qualified to advise.

Yours sincerely<br>[T. S. Eliot]

## TO *Lawrence Durrell*[1]                                          TS Morris Library

28 June 1937                                          Faber & Faber Ltd

Dear Mr Durrell,

I am writing informally to tell you that I am very much impressed indeed by *The Black Book*, which I have now read through.[2] It seems to me to have both promise and performance. I say both, because the term 'promise' used by itself is apt to be a disparagement of the accomplishment, and because one often has occasion to say about a book which is a good job in itself that the author is not likely to go any further. So I say that this is a book which ought to be published, but also that I think you ought to proceed from it to something still better.

---

1 – Lawrence Durrell (1912–90), novelist, poet, dramatist, travel writer: see Biographical Register.
2 – TSE wrote in his reader's report on Durrell's *The Black Book*, 5 June 1937: 'This man has some ability. One can see why Henry Miller thinks so highly of him, and all the wrong reasons, as well as possibly some right, why Henry Miller does so think. It is a pity that such a genial talent should go to waste, and something must be done about it. Another ten years growing up, and working away with the language and literary form, would help. The sort of book this aims to be is that which takes ten years to write, and I doubt whether it took him more than two. There is some imagination, and some good reportage. The Surrey Side atmosphere is good, or at least persuasive (I don't know that side as well as one ought to) but the author does seem to know his Catford, Lea Green, Brixton etc. The story of Gracie is good; its weakness is that Gracie IS a type rather than an individual and you cannot do much about that. I like the piece about her father coming down to Bournemouth to look at her in the coffin. And there is a nice page about Thibet; but there is a lot else that could be dispensed with. The book as it is is unprintable, and it could not be printed merely by excisions: the author would have to rewrite it himself. I think that the book would be none the worse for being rewritten in a printable form. There are some good bits in the account of the commercial school and teaching the African lady to read Chaucer. In its present form, the book is a mess. Somebody else must look at it.'

The Corfu passages, which to the superficial reader might seem irrelevant, strike me as being quite essential to the form, and it is in fact the existence of a certain formal pattern, in a kind of book which might very easily be nothing more than a succession of scenes of greater or less intensity, that makes me sanguine for the future.

I do not intend, in this letter, to praise or to criticize in detail. The immediate point is obviously this: that, as you are quite well aware, the book as it stands could not possibly be published in this country. Opinions will probably differ as to the amount of alteration that would be necessary. The only thing that counts is your own feeling about it, and whether you wish to alter this book at all for the sake of having it published in England and getting a larger currency for it. Sometimes one feels about a thing of one's own that it has done its job just as it stands, and that alteration from such motives is a matter of indifference. One may even have lost interest when a thing is done, and want to devote all one's energy to the next thing. So I am not going to try to press you to alter this book: I will only say that I very much wish that it might be put into a practicable form, and that I am anxious to know how you feel about it.

I think almost any real writer might want to write one book in which he said exactly what he pleased without deference to practical possibilities. But I do not think any real writer is likely to find himself under that necessity indefinitely, for in that case what begins as freedom ends as a kind of bondage. So I shall be glad, first, if anything can be done to make this book publishable in England; if not, I shall be glad to see it published abroad; and in any case I look forward with keen anticipation to the next book you write after this.[1]

Yours sincerely,

T. S. Eliot

1 – Durrell replied from Corfu, July 1937: 'Thank you very much for your kind letter. I value your good opinion of the Black Book; and rejoice in the hopes expressed for my future. I am not at all sure that I have one, to tell the truth. By this I don't mean that I can't write better books in future, but simply that my problems are not technical but personal. It remains only to see whether I develop as a person; the mere writing is nothing compared to the grind of the personality against its own sicknesses . . .

'About the actual book. If the English edition didn't stand in the way of a simultaneous unexpurgated Paris edition I would be only too glad for Fabers to take it. I can't imagine any better home for it . . . It isnt every day that an author can feel his publishers backing him with such general goodwill and spontaneous friendliness.' (Published in full in 'Letters to T. S. Eliot', *Twentieth Century Literature* Lawrence Durrell Issue, Part 1 [Fall 1987], 348–9.)

Durrell to Miller [July 1937]: 'Bombardment from the directors of Fabers. Enthusiastic letters from Morley and Pringle and a typical "kind letter" from Eliot. In short they want an altered English edition. I have replied that provided it does not stand in the way of the

TO *H. David Jackson*                                    CC

30 June 1937                        [Faber & Faber Ltd]

Dear Mr Jackson,

I have your letter of the 27th.[1] It is always difficult for an author to explain his own work when it is verse, because any explanation given has the disadvantage of excluding other possible interpretations, all of which are better held in solution than definitely accepted or rejected. The part of the Chorus is certainly not meant to be that of Destiny, except so far as you may be inclined to affirm that such a character as Cassandra represents Destiny. One may perhaps accept the convention that the Chorus as onlookers are collectively somewhat more intuitive than any of them individually would be. There is however an intention of intensifying or relaxing the versification according to the character of the speaker, and you are right in supposing that the Herald, or as he should be called, the Messenger, has a slightly comic role.

With many thanks for your approval,

I am,
Yours faithfully,
[T. S. Eliot]


TO *John Hayward*                                    TS King's

30 June 1937                        *The Criterion*

Dear John,

For the last week or more I have not had time to Breathe, and unless you are as practised in holding your Breath as we both are in holding

---

Paris unexpurgated, I don't mind. It will be advertisement, I suppose. Will you, however, immediately ask Kahane whether he would like to do the book in its full-dress uniform regardless of Faber? . . . Will he take it? If not I'd better castrate for Faber and wait until I have money enough to do the full version myself. It's rather a fix' (*A Private Correspondence*, 102).

1 – H. David Jackson – 'a rather impecunious teacher-student of music' (as he called himself) – ventured to ask whether 'the part of the Chorus [in *MiC*] is meant to be that of Destiny (particularly in the first scenes) and as such they speak continually in poetry (which I personally consider superb). The degree of poetic utterance given to the other characters is in direct proportion to their world[l]iness. Is this the case[?] The Archbishop stands first – half saint, half politician (or at this stage in his life 90% churchman 15% statesman). The three priests present a fine gradation in contrast, the herald and the knights coming of course at the bottom of the scale.

'Is this conclusion correctly drawn?'

our Bladders, you cannot conceive the joy with which I look forward to the novelty of a few inhalations & exhalations on Monday next. But that motion will have to stop by the end of the week, when I sink again – but the analogy is not good, because I believe that scaphandres[1] have breathing apparatus – ah yes, the comparison is to the oriental pearl diver (richer than all his tribe, I believe?)[2] and not to the scaphandre. It is well to be able to hold one's breath, when in the company of such folk as the Bishop of Winnepesaukee[3] and Sir Josiah Stamp.[4] But the meaning is, now on to Edinburgh! on to the exchange of civilities with the Picts! and then, between Monday and Friday, could we have a private evening together? I have strange things to tell about the Methodists in Bath. Perhaps stranger shall I have, about the Presbyterians of Auld Reekie.[5] Meanwhile imagine the clashing of claymores, and the jokes about Galloway Elliots, the porridge, and baps an' scones etc.

Yrs. and no more,
TP

## TO *George Blake*                                                    CC

8 July 1937                          [Faber & Faber Ltd]

My dear George,

The situation is this: I find that the edition of 2,000 copies of *Dunbar* cost £300.[6] Mackay Mackenzie received 60 guineas fee, and so far the net

---

1 – *Scaphandre*: from the Greek *skaphe* (barque) and *andros* (man), the term derives from a treatise by the Abbot of Chapelle on the Theoretical and Practical Construction of the Diving Bell or the Human Boat (1775): a form of snorkel. The diver descends with a breathing apparatus connected by a tube to the surface.

2 – *Othello* V. ii. 342–8: 'one whose hand / Like the base Indian, threw a pearl away / Richer than all his tribe.'

3 – Lake Winnipesaukee is in New Hampshire, USA.

4 – Sir Josiah Stamp (1880–1941), industrialist, economist, civil servant, statistician, writer; a director of the Bank of England. In June 1938 he was to be raised to the peerage as Baron Stamp of Shortlands

5 – 'Auld Reekie' ('Old Smoky') is a nickname for Edinburgh.

6 – Blake noted, 13 June, 'It would seem necessary, whether desirable or not, to postpone the Aenead . . . As for collaborating with the S.T.S. [over Douglas's *Aenead*], the difficulty, though not formidable, is that Blackwood's production is of a standard we could hardly approve.

'Taking the Quhair as the job in hand, however, the fact is that we did pay Mackenzie quite a substantial fee for the Dunbar – so [*sic*] much as £75, I think. To be sure, he had to handle a considerable corpus of poetry and accomplish something definitive; and while the relative lengths and difficulties of the jobs are not clear in my mind at the moment, my

loss has been £43. There is no reason to grumble at this: I do not think anybody could have expected to show a profit on such a book in less than ten years' time, and I think it will be all right in the end. Also, what seems to me important, this sort of book makes a great difference to the back list of the Porpoise Press. So everybody is ready to go forward with *The Kingis Quair*, if we can arrange suitable terms. I have been telling them that there ought to be more demand for this than for *Dunbar* in schools and colleges as well as with the general public, and I hope I am right. I am also assuming that the job of editorship would be much less laborious. I should think that it would not be more than a third as big a book as *Dunbar*, if that, and we think that 20 guineas ought to be the reasonable fee for Mackay Mackenzie.

If you are in accord, would you care to take the matter up with Mackenzie himself? It might be as well to find out in corresponding with him how elaborate a job of bookmaking he thinks it would be. I do not see how we could go beyond 20 guineas, partly because I think that the book ought to be priced lower than *Dunbar*, in order to give it as wide a circulation as possible.

I assume that you know Mackenzie: in any case I shall have to be away for about ten days from the end of this week. I shall be at the Isis Hotel, Iffley Road, Oxford, all of next week, and I expect to be in here again on Thursday 22nd, and do not suppose that you will have anything to communicate before that.

Much interested but not at all surprised to hear of Neil's misadventures. I am afraid that boat is going to prove a rather expensive home for them.

Yours ever,
[Tom]


TO *Virginia Woolf*                                                    TS Berg

8 July 1937                          *The Criterion*

My dear Virginia,

In my case-book for June I find noted the adventure of the Rochester Skeleton, the mystery of the Methodist School, and the case of the abominable vice-chancellor and his toy ducks: but I have not seen Virginia Woolf. I hardly hoped to meet you at Dorothy Bussy's kettledrum

---

impression is that the Quhair is a much less onerous job than the Dunbar, so that a sort of *pro rata* offer to Mackenzie would probably be acceptable.'

yesterday. At the end of this week I go to Oxford to investigate the Heretical Theologians,[1] and I shall not be settled in London again until

1–Kenneth Paul Kramer, *Redeeming Time: T. S. Eliot's 'Four Quartets'* (2007), 227–8: 'By 1936, Eliot had become a member of the Archbishop's committee, charged with preparing for a conference on the church to be held at Oxford on the impending wartime topic of "community, church and state", where Eliot delivered "The Ecumenical Nature of the Church and Its Responsibility toward the World." ...

'Gathered at the Oxford Conference were delegates for forty countries and hundreds of denominations ranging from Orthodox Catholics to the Disciplines (U.S.A.) and the Salvation Army. The Oxford Conference was divided into two sections. Eliot's section dealt with the economic order. On the evening of July 16, Eliot addressed a plenary session in the Town Hall, titled "The Church as an Ecumenical Society". He opened by saying,

'"The question of War and Peace, of absolute or relative Pacifism, is the most conspicuous. Not one communion, I venture to say – and my own is not one of the least divided – has an unanimous opinion about the relation of the temporal and the spiritual power. I only mention this, to remind you of the obvious fact that before the various communions can agree completely, each must agree with itself. Each must decide for itself what is obligatory for its members, and what may be left to private judgment."'

See TSE, TS 'The Church as an Ecumenical Society', delivered on 16 July 1937 (Houghton), in *CProse* 5, 497–503.

'The Church and the World: Problem of common social action' (from our special correspondent, Oxford), *Church Times*, 16 July 1937: 'Mr T. S. Eliot was the first speaker at today's plenary session of the conference on Church, Community and State, when the general subject under treatment was "The Ecumenical Nature of the Church and its Responsibility towards the World". The Bishop of Dornakal, South India (Dr Azariah) presided.

'Mr Eliot said he did not believe there was a single Christian community which had, within the realm of social action, solved the questions, "To what are we all as common believers committed?" and "In what matters are differences of private judgment permissible?" Before the various communions could agree, obviously each must agree with itself. Meanwhile, what cooperation in social action was possible between the various branches of the Christian Church? He described the great difficulty of arriving at such action on the part of a Christianity as disrupted as it is today, when forms of worship and theology had alike been fractured by the forces of nation and race and language. A sensible Christian philosophy would neither exalt race, nation, and class to an unnatural primacy, nor attempt to eradicate these differences, which should be left to represent differences of function, rather than a struggle. For lack of this, in a world which for many generations had done its theological and other thinking in compartments of nation and class the communions, in not knowing each other, had ceased to know themselves.

'Mr Eliot proceeded:– "I think that the present interest of different Christian communions in finding out more about each other is one of the most hopeful signs we have" ... but the problem of more union ... "is not one of legislating ourselves together, but that of the slow process of growing together." Without this reintegration, agreement and common action in social matters could only be partial and occasional. But common action, in matters of social justice, need not wait upon reunion. At the same time they must keep in mind that the problem was truly a theological problem. Christian sociology was a department of theology. He therefore pleaded for "more theology".' ...

'Wanted: More Theology'
'On Friday, a particularly long session was held to deal with the general subject. "The Œcumenical Nature of the Church and its Responsibility Towards the World." The four

the 24th. Just before Bank Holiday I must be off again to look into the affair of the Netherhampton Squire[1] and his imperfect drainage; and by that time I suspect that you will be away to Rodmell or elsewhere. Is there any time between the 24th and the 31st (except the 26th) when it would be possible to see you at some time of day? For otherwise, I shall hardly hope to see you again until October.

Aff.

T. S. E.

## TO *Polly Tandy*

TS BL

8 July 1937                                    *The Criterion*

Dear Pollyma'am,

What was the meaning of the great Revival of Spiritual Gifts and Power, which broke out in 1904–5, in Los Angeles and in Wales simultaneously?[2]

---

speakers were Mr T. S. Eliot, the Rev. S. McCrea Cavert, a co-opted delegate from New York, the French Protestant pastor, M. Pierre Maury, and the Rev. Chukichi Yasuda of Kyoto in Japan. Mr Yasuda gave a brief description of the political, social and industrial conditions in Japan, and then analysed the difficulties facing the Christian Church in view of the emergence of a re-invigorated nationalistic Shintoism.

'Mr Eliot made several interesting points. Thus he asserted that the question of common action among various communions is preceded by the question of common action within one communion; and no communion today, not even the Roman, has solved the problem, to what all its members as common believers are committed. Again, he distinguished co-operation between separated Churches under the pressure of external persecution from the search for common grounds of action when all are enjoying liberty: the former may only last so long as the enemy remains strong. He also stressed (without depreciating questions of faith and order) those local, racial, linguistic and psychological differences which divide Christians and which were apparent even before the disruption of Christianity. Finally, if the Church was to present a united front against the foe, he pleaded for more theology. "Where we hear fundamental principles clearly enunciated, we often fail to hear the explicit pronouncement on the particular act; and where we hear the explicit pronouncement on the particular act, we are not always sure of the theological foundations."'

1 – Bruce Richmond, whom TSE was to visit at his home. (See Sheila M. Wilkinson, 'Netherhampton House, Near Salisbury', *Virginia Woolf Bulletin*, issue 9, Jan. 2002, 39–41.)

2 – The Azusa Street Revival, in Los Angeles, California, was launched at a meeting in Apr. 1906 led by William J. Seymour, an African-American preacher: there occurred ecstatic experiences, speaking and singing in tongues, and supposed miracles – it was if the terms of Acts 2: 4 had come to pass: 'And they were all filled with the Holy Ghost and began to speak with other tongues, as the Spirit gave them utterance.' Within a month, a crowd of between 300 and 1,500 people would congregate at the mission. 'Pentecost has come,' it was proclaimed. The revival of Pentecostalism is said to have been initiated by Seymour's revival.

The Religious Revival in Wales was started in 1904. Sparked by Evan Roberts (1878–1951), a former collier and minister in training, the awakening gathered thousands of converts; aided by animated newspaper reports, it spread through Britain and abroad:

I am not going to keep you waiting for the answer. Here it is: The meaning was this. The Lord was appearing in Ambassadorial – that is – Apolostolic Presence, unto His Baptized Peoples, and standing outside of the official door (to which place the Episcopacy of this C. A. Church had excommunicated him in His Apostolic or Ministerial presence in 1905) [. . .].[1] Well, even apart from that, the World is full of troubulation. Here it is. You know I thought that praps I could go from Salisbury to Yeovil and thence to wherever you will be in Dorset. Well now. I have to go to the Fabers at that time. I trust I am speaking in Confidence. For one thing, the Fabers always want me to come before August the 12th for a spell, because I am not one given to blood sports, expert neither with stirrup nor with gun nor with hook nor with gin. For another thing, it is complicated by the fact that this year the Morleys are not going to visit the Fabers. Hit seems, that first they were to take a fambly holiday in Donegal instead, and they couldnt afford both excursions (Hit seems like evy time theyse a excursion I'm always broke); and now they find they cant afford to go to Donegal but they cant afford to go do Donegal I mean Wales either. BUT for the last two years the Fabers have had me to visit them in Wales simultaneiously with the Morleys. So I hope I dont need to dot every I: I mean that as the Morleys are not going I must go – not that it is not very pleasant, very pleasant indeed ma'am. But the only time seems to be directly from Salisbury possibly cutting out the old homestead (not that there is any trace of one, any trace whatever, ma'am) and so I shall get back to London by the middle of the month and will find plenty to do there, plenty, for a few days, and by that time I suppose you will have left your Dorset site. So nothing to do. As for the immediate future. I have to go to Oxford for a week for a conference and then to stay with American friends in Gloucestershire and then back and to Rochester for a night returning to London for a week on the 24th: and I must be in London for a week then because there will be a fortnight's work not attended to in arrears and another fortnight's work in advance. So sorrow it is, sorrow. So where are we? Right into the autumn or fall of the year, when I hope to see you, but meanwhile hope to see your husband and send you a bottle of Macharnudo for your stomach's sake, and the old piece of soap I left please keep until my return so will close for the moment yours respfly

TP

---

Scandinavia, parts of Europe and N. America. The Holy Spirit was ascendant, and the influence of what began as a local revival spread even to the apparently coincidental Pentecostal Movement in California.

1 – The end of the sentence is illegible: cut, pasted and obscured.

12 July 1937                              [Faber & Faber Ltd]

Dear Mr Fluchère,

Mr Ashley Dukes and myself have both read the 12 pages of translation of *Murder in the Cathedral* which you sent, and though we have, as you will see, queried a number of expressions, we are much pleased with the movement of the translation as a whole.[1] We shall be glad if you will complete the translation, but before authorising its publication or its production on the stage or in any other public place, we should reserve the right to make detailed criticisms such as you will find enclosed. I am extremely busy at the moment, and therefore will not make any suggestions for improvement, but we will give the matter our close attention when we have the complete translation. You may rest assured that meanwhile, up to reasonable limits, we shall not entertain suggestions from anyone else wishing to translate the play.

I would remind you again, for regularity's sake, that for the publication of the text a French publisher should address himself to Faber & Faber, and for the rights of performance of any kind, application should be made to Mr Ashley Dukes.

I am asking my secretary to sign this letter for me, as I have to leave without waiting for it to be typed.

With best wishes and congratulations,

> Yours very sincerely,
> for T. S. Eliot
> Anne Bradby

1–Fluchère had sent his sample passages on 5 June. 'I have done my best to keep a certain rhythm, in accordance with the atmosphere of mixed grandeur and prosy flatness here and there, and also with what I could detect of the original rhythm.' He asked: 'Should my translation be published in a magazine (or parts of it) would you object to giving me half the rights? – and should it be published in a volume, would you think it fair to divide between ourselves in the same way?'

## TO *Virginia Woolf*                                  MS Berg

23 July 1937                        *The Criterion*

My dear Virginia,

Of course you can't see me at present.[1] I knew nothing about it until I got your letter. I am very sorry. I am writing to Vanessa.

Well, I shall hope that I may see you at Rodmell in September or October.

Affectionately

Tom

## TO *Vanessa Bell*[2]                                  MS King's

23 July 1937                        *The Criterion*

Dear Vanessa

I got back to London yesterday after ten days' absence, and found a note from Virginia about Julian. I am very very sorry. Please accept my sympathy.

Also, I found the mss. which you had left. I have read a part, and am much impressed. When I have read the rest, and had someone else read it, I will write again. I think it should be accompanied by some sort of memoir.[3]

Yours ever

T. S. E.

---

1 – VW wrote, 23 July: 'As you may have seen, Julian [Bell] has been killed in Spain. I am with Vanessa as much as possible, and if she is able, we may go down to Charleston on Sunday. So we must put you off – but I'll write later and hope to see you.' (*Letters* 6, 147). Elder son of Clive and Vanessa Bell, Julian Bell (b. 1908) grew up at the centre of the Bloomsbury circle. Educated at King's College, Cambridge, he published a volume of poems, *Winter Movement*, in 1930; and his work was represented (with poems by Empson, WHA and SS) in Michael Roberts's watershed anthology *New Signatures* (1932). After teaching at the University of Wuhan, 1935–7, he participated in the Spanish Civil War, serving as an ambulance driver with Spanish Medical Aid: he was killed on 18 July.

2 – Vanessa Bell, née Stephen (1879–1961) – sister of VW; wife of Clive Bell – was an artist, illustrator and designer; member of the Bloomsbury Group.

3 – Bell replied from Charleston, 17 Aug.:

Dear Tom

Thank you for writing to me. I would have written before but have not been able to do much – but I liked hearing from you.

Virginia told me that Faber's cannot publish the essays. I understand. But I hope it may be arranged that someone will do so, because though there may be much that

TO *John Hayward*                                          TS King's

26 July [1937]                        *The Criterion*

Dear John,

There were three matters which, in my state of anaemia after Oxford,
I forgot to mention. The first is the Problem of the Pocket Pram.[1] I don't
expect to have time to make any investigations now before the middle of
August at the earliest, but perhaps meanwhile you might have time to find
out who are the people (in the Welbeck district?) to be consulted.

The second is the Problem of the Resident Patient.[2] After teetering for
some time my inclination is to stay where I am, if I can find a practical Fire
Escape. The reasons will cross your mind, but I might review them again
when I see you. And perhaps I have become like Bernard-Lazare: '*je ne
suis chez moi que dans un hotel*'.[3] (Blessington *is* Sutton, of course; and
Biddle, Hayward and Moffatt are on the loose).

And the third I have forgotten for the moment.

Yrs
TP


TO *Alexis St-Léger Léger*                                    CC

27 juillet 1937                        [Faber & Faber Ltd]

Cher ami,

Je viens de rentrer d'un congrès à Oxford, et j'ai accueilli avec joie votre
charmante lettre du 15 courant.[4] Vous êtes bien aimable d'accorder un
assentiment si compréhensif, et je crois que vous ne serez pas déçu, à la

---

could be better expressed & perhaps Julian himself would have changed I think they
say something he wanted to say. But I know you did what you could.
    I hope to see you later.
        Yours ever
        Vanessa Bell   (EVE)

1 – The lightweight wheelchair that TSE was hoping to purchase for JDH.
2 – Conan Doyle, 'The Adventure of the Resident Patient' (1893), in *The Memoirs of
Sherlock Holmes*.
3 – Bernard Lazare (1865–1903): French Jewish literary critic and political journalist;
outspoken in his defence of Captain Alfred Dreyfus.
4 – Alexis St-Léger Léger, Ministère des Affaires Etrangères, Paris, blamed his long silence
on the huge workload he had been labouring under for many months. Happily he gave his
consent to TSE's proposal. He had imposed a ban on any plans to reprint his work in France,
and so TSE's bilingual edition would ensure the sole survival of his text in the French.

longue, par les ventes en Angleterre et en Amérique d'une édition meilleur marché.

Je devrais vous signaler que l'édition première, malgré le prix élevé, s'est pleinement justifiée au point de vue de l'influence littéraire. L'œuvre de plusieurs des plus doués de nos jeunes poètes s'est déjà imprégnée, d'une façon assez frappante, de l'influence d'*Anabase*; je me réjouis que ma traduction (ou il existe encore des erreurs qu'il faut rectifier plus tard) a servi à renvoyer ces auteurs au texte français. J'espère, pour une édition à prix modeste et d'un format plus commode, un succès plus répandu.

Je suis content que nous sommes d'accord, d'autant plus que vous me dites que vous allez interdire la publication ultérieure en France. Nous nous félicitons de pouvoir accomplir une tâche bienfaisante en prolongeant la célébrité du poème en pays de langue anglaise, jusqu'a ce que l'interdiction soit levée.

Le bruit a couru à Londres que vous étiez ici au moment des sacres, en qualité officielle, mais je croyais bien que vous étiez trop affairé d'avoir les loisirs pour les amitiés personnelles. Je ne manquerai point de vous avertir de ma prochaine visite à Paris, toutefois sans trop d'espoir de vous trouver un moment libre. En attendant le rendez-vous éventuel, croyez-moi, cher poète et ami, votre admirateur dévoué

[T. S. Eliot][1]

---

1 – *Translation*: Dear friend, / I have just returned from a conference at Oxford, and I am overjoyed to find your charming letter of the 15th inst. You are most kind to approve all the details, and I do believe you will not be disappointed, in the long term, with the sales procured by a cheaper edition in England and America.

I should also draw your attention to the fact that the first edition, despite its high price, has been more than justified in terms of literary influence. The work of several of the most gifted of our young poets has already been infused, in a striking way, with the influence of *Anabase*; I am delighted that my translation (in which errors persist, to be corrected later) has sent these authors back to the French text. It is my hope that a second, cheaper edition, in a handier format, will enjoy wider success.

I am gratified that we are in agreement, especially as you inform me that you intend to forbid its publication in France for the time being. We are happy to be able to pursue a worthy cause by prolonging the fame of the poem in English-speaking countries, at least until the ban is lifted.

Rumour has it in London that you were here, in an official capacity, for the Coronation, but I can well believe you were much too busy to have time to catch up with friends. I shall not fail to alert you when I expect to be in Paris next, though you may well have no time. In anticipation of that future meeting, believe me, dear poet and friend, your devoted admirer / [T. S. Eliot]

TO *Marion Dorn*[1]                                            CC

27 July 1937                          [*The Criterion*]

My dear Marion,

I am so sorry that I was not able to speak to you on the telephone, but I understand that your second call came through just after I had left. It is sweet of you to remember that I wanted to meet James Thurber. I do hope this is possible, but unfortunately I have got to be away on visits to the country from next Saturday until the 12th. Will he be here after that, and will you? It would be delightful to have an invitation from you even if Thurber has left.[2]

                              Ever yours sincerely,
                              [T. S. E.]


TO *William Empson*                                           CC

27 July 1937                          [*The Criterion*]

My dear Empson,

I have been thinking about your book on Buddhas, which was held over for me, as I was away last week and the week before.[3] I wish that we

---

1 – Marion Dorn (1896–1964), textile designer – she contributed work to the Savoy Hotel and Claridges in London, and to the *Queen Mary* – lived in London with the artist and illustrator E. McKnight Kauffer, 1920–40: they were to marry in New York in 1950.
2 – TSE was to write a 'puff' for the jacket of Thurber's collection of short fantasy stories for children *The Wonderful O* (1957): 'It is a form of humour which is also a way of saying something serious. There is criticism of life at the bottom of it . . . His writings and also his illustrations are capable of surviving the immediate environment and time out of which they spring. To some extent, they will be a document of the age they belong to.' TSE subsequently commented on his own words: 'This is from some statement of mine about Jim Thurber's work. I don't remember it, but I stand by it. He is my favourite humourist. And I liked him personally. It does not have any particular application to his children's stories, however.'
3 – Empson wrote from 71 Marchmont Street, London W.C.1 (n.d.): 'I wonder whether Faber's would consider a small book about Buddhas, which Chatto's wouldn't do. There *ought* to be a little book of photographs of Japanese and Chinese stuff with short introduction for halfcrown – the best Far Eastern sculpture ought to be as easily accessible in photographs as Greek. I have a lot of good photographs and have been to the main places – could write an introduction. Of course I know extremely little, but the experts won't do the job of popularizing. However this simple plan (the one Chatto's refused, also Cambridge University Press) is muddled by my wanting to chatter about the left side of statue heads as apart from the right, and the machinery of facial expression, and why they have archaic smiles when they do, and so on. Even so the letterpress would be short, say 25000 words, and the main thing would be the photographs. I enclose an article which I have been unable to get published anywhere in England, also an old Listener article, to show the kind of

could do it, but I simply feel that the cost of producing a book like this would make any profit unlikely, and to produce it at anything like half a crown would be out of the question, unless there was a prospect of a very large sale indeed. I am very sorry that Chatto's won't consider it, because it seems to me really a job for your regular publishers, which we, alas, are not.

I am interested in your paper on asymmetry, and should like to have that for use in a future number of the *Criterion*, unless you wish to keep it for other purposes.

I am going away on visits at the end of the week, and shall not be back until the 12th or 13th of August. I very much hope to see you again before you leave for China, and will try to get hold of you for dinner one evening toward the end of August or early in September. I hope that you are not leaving too soon to make that possible.[1]

Yours ever,<br>[T. S. Eliot]

## TO *George Barker*

TS Texas

27 July 1937                    *The Criterion*

My dear Barker,

I have now read the sections of *Jerusalem*.[2] I find it very difficult to make up my mind what to say about it, and I should like to keep the typescript for a time so that I may get another director to read it.

The first point is a very simple one. Here are three sections of a book, which according to your note is to consist of five sections. Unless the two

---

thing. It would be an ignorant book as serious knowledge goes in these things, but serious knowledge is pretty rare. I am not quite clear that I wouldn't have to give Chatto's a refusal of this, though they refused the first plan. But if you think the plan hopeful it will seem worth trying to write the book in China. Supposing I get there with this war on. I hope anyway that you can come to my farewell party on July 27.'

A note on WE's letter (hand unknown) reports for TSE: 'This was brought up at the Book Committee, but they returned it without, I think, deciding anything, for you to look at.'

1–Empson replied at the end of July: 'I daresay it's rather a good thing if I don't churn out an ignorant book on Buddhas. The article I should like to have in the Criterion, as it can't be published anywhere with the photographs; but to go without photographs it wants re-writing a bit. I am planning to leave for Peking next Tuesday, the tenth, and will send the article on later.'

See further Empson, *The Face of the Buddha*, ed. Rupert Arrowsmith (2016).

2–'[R]eviving his earlier passion for the Crusades, Barker produced a historical saga written in a prose style resembling mock Walter Scott' (Robert Fraser, *The Chameleon Poet: A Life of George Barker* [2002], 99).

others are a great deal longer than any of these, the book is going to be a very short one indeed.

It probably seemed to you that in this story you have been doing something of quite a different kind from any of your previous prose work. I should say, on the contrary, that what seems to me best in what you have submitted is essentially of the same kind, but much better done. That is to say, from the standpoint of your usual style this is very much more lucid, and the pictures are clearer and more satisfying. But what this sort of writing will do, I think, is to give more pleasure to the sort of people who are already interested in your work, rather than to put you in touch with a wholly different public. So far as I can yet see, the narrative and dramatic elements are the weakest. The beginning reads to me somewhat like a caricature of the medieval romances of Scott, but after one has read on, a succession of scenes become fixed on the mind in a rather peculiar and impressive way. The spirit of the book seems to me not 12th century at all, nor is it that of a modern novelist writing about the 12th century. It is much more *quattro cento*, or to put it in terms of English literature, the imagination and the method are much more akin to Spenser than to any other author I can think of. There is the same queer sharply defined dream imagery, in which one scene seems to melt imperceptibly into another. I think that in this way you might make something very fine indeed, but only by discarding the attempt to do anything in the way of a conventional historical novel.

I find blemishes of two kinds: one is that I think your prefatory defence of anachronism is more suitable to the kind of book you could write than to the kind of book which, part of the time at least, you appear to be trying to write; and also I think one has to remember that anachronism and other vagaries can be all right when the author is committing them deliberately, but are never all right when they give the appearance of ignorance. My second criticism is that there is still rather too much of the digestive and intestinal sort of imagery, of which some of the critics of your poetry have complained. It is more out of place here than in the poems, and sometimes gives me the effect simply of grotesque absurdity. Similarly, I do not like the incident of the man breaking his own finger. It is the more unpleasant for seeming rather absurd.

This must be taken as interim criticism only, because I do not yet see where you are going, or whether the final effect will be more than that of a succession of lovely dissolving views; and I want somebody else to read this part before I return it.

I have picked out the essay on Poetry and Reality, which I think I can get into the September number. At any rate I am having it set up now.[1]

Yours ever,
T. S. Eliot

TO *Matthew Nathan*[2]                                                                    CC

27 July 1937                                        [Faber & Faber Ltd]

My dear Sir,

My friend Dorothy Bussy informs me that you are engaged on a history of the Coker parishes. I am expecting to come to East Coker for the night of August 3rd, as I shall have been staying with the Richmonds at Salisbury, and it would be a great pleasure to me to call on you on that day, if you happened to be at home and found it convenient. Otherwise pray do not bother to answer this letter.

Yours very truly,
[T. S. Eliot]

TO *Antonio de Mendonça*                                                          CC

27 July 1937                                        [Faber & Faber Ltd]

Dear Senhor de Mendonca,

I have received a copy of the French edition of President Salazar's addresses, *Une Révolution dans La Paix*, and have been reading it with interest. It seems to me that this book would be more easily translated than that of Senhor Ferro, and I shall recommend it to my firm. At the same time, I cannot ask them to enter upon very definite negotiations

1–Barker, 'Poetry and Reality', C. 17 (Oct. 1937), 54–66.
2–Sir Matthew Nathan (1862–1939), soldier, engineer and colonial administrator. Educated at the Royal Military Academy, Woolwich, and completing his training as an engineer at the School of Military Engineering, Chatham, he was commissioned in the Royal Engineers and served in Sierra Leone, Egypt, India and Burma. He was Acting Governor of Sierra Leone, 1899–1900; Governor of the Gold Coast, 1900–3; Governor of Hong Kong, 1903–7; and Governor of Natal, 1907–9. He was appointed Under-Secretary of State for Ireland in Aug. 1914, but the single blemish on his career was that he failed to anticipate the Easter Rising of 1916: he resigned two days later. Later he took office as Governor of Queensland, 1920–5; serving as Chancellor of the University of Queensland, 1922–6. In retirement he settled at the Manor House, West Coker, where he served until 1934 as High Sheriff of Somerset. Absorbing himself in local history, he was author of the posthumous *The Annals of West Coker* (1957).

about it at the present time. The book by Senhor Ferro should obviously appear first, and as you know, we have received neither the translation nor the agreement, and remain completely in the dark as to when the book can go to press, and be published. I hope therefore that it will be possible to press matters forward as rapidly as possible with Senhor Ferro's book. There is not, as I see it, the same necessity of haste with this book by President Salazar, which, with all due respect to Senhor Ferro, is obviously something which will have a more permanent interest. It might be worthwhile to keep in mind that there may be – either already or in future – other addresses by President Salazar which would bring the book as nearly as possible up to date at the time of publication.

Yours sincerely,<br>[T. S. Eliot]

## TO *Enid Faber*

TS Valerie Eliot

28 July [1937]                    *The Criterion*

Dear Enid,

The Dye is Cast, and the 3-speed bicycle with two saddles one higher one lower has started on its long journey across England and Wales. If it is still the wrong size it must come back with me.[1]

Now I expect to arrive at Carmarthen at 4.45 on Wednesday afternoon next. I suppose that there will be a train from there to Lampeter, and shall hope to be met at the latter place. I hope that the chemists will be open, as I shall have to buy a toothbrush, as I shall have lost my luggage in the course of the journey: Yeovil to Westbury, Westbury to Bristol (Temple Meads), Bristol (Temple Meads) to Bristol (Stapledon Road), Bristol (Stapledon Road) to Cardiff (with an hour for lunch), and Cardiff to Carmarthen. I shall see a great deal of the railway system, but I do not see how I can expect to keep my bags.

But the next step is to buy the white flannels which will be in one of the bags to be lost between Salisbury and Lampeter.

Yrs etc.<br>Tp

---

1–Presumably the bicycle was for Richard (b. 6 Dec. 1924) or Tom (b. 25 Apr. 1927).

## TO *Virginia Woolf*

30 July 1937                    *The Criterion*

My dear Virginia,

I wish you would advise me whether I should write to Vanessa at once about Julian's essays, or wait a little. I found them very interesting myself, and recommended them, but other opinions are contrary, and the decision is that it won't make a book for us. I do hope that someone will publish the essays, and of course with a memoir.[1] But should I write to her at once, or wait till I get back? I don't know how she is or where she is at the present moment. I am just going off to Wiltshire and Wales, but your reply to this would be forwarded to me, and I could write from there.

I still hope to see you in September.[2]

Affectionately,
Tom

## TO *Sidney Dark*[3]

30 July 1937                    [*The Criterion*]

My dear Dark,

I waited for the *Church Times* to pronounce upon the Oxford Conference as a whole – which you only did today.[4] And you find me in the midst of preparations for a round of country visits for a fortnight

1 – Julian Bell, *Essays, Poems and Letters*, ed. Quentin Bell (1938).
2 – VW replied, 7 Aug.: 'I showed Vanessa your letter, as I knew she was anxious to hear. She thanks you very much, and would I am sure like it if you would write to her some time yourself about Julian's essays . . . Yes, do come down . . . [W]ould you come the first week end or the third or late in August? I know Vanessa would very much like to see you, and so should we' (*Letters* 6, 154–5).
3 – Sidney Dark (1872–1947), editor of the Anglo-Catholic *Church Times*, 1924–41.
4 – See Keith Clements, *Faith on the Frontier: A Life of J. H. Oldham* (1999), 307–8, 328: 'The world conference on "Church, Community and State" . . . is easily described as one of the great ecumenical landmarks of the 20th century. It brought together over 400 delegates from 120 churches in forty countries to study, debate and formulate lines of thought and action for the churches in relation to contemporary society. It met at a time of deepening political crisis in Europe and the Far East. In Nazi Germany Hitler had just put Martin Niemöller in prison, and had banned any delegates from the German Evangelical Church from attending Oxford – which paradoxically made their witness even more powerfully present . . . Oxford 1937 represented an attempt to bring the churches together to face these brute realities and to identify the directions of response . . . It was an ecumenical study conference on a world scale . . .

leaving early tomorrow morning. So the enclosed letter was perhaps not written under the best conditions.

If you think this too short, brutish and nasty,[1] ignore it. But my motive was similar to that of André Gide, who, when asked, you remember, why he wrote Si le grain ne meurt, replied: '*J'avais honte de les voir tous mentir*'.[2]

Yours sincerely,

[T. S. Eliot]

## TO *The Editor,* The Church Times

30 July 1937[3]                    24 Russell Square, London W.C.1

Sir,

May I be permitted, as a delegate to the recent Conference on Church, Community and State, to offer a brief postscript to your leading article of last week?[4] I do not wish to make any extended criticism until the

---

'Reinhold Niebuhr [came] to Oxford. So did the 425 official delegates – 300 of them appointees of the churches, and 125 invited by the Universal Council – and nearly all the other main speakers hoped for, from Emil Brunner to T. S. Eliot.'

1 – '[T]he life of man [is] solitary, poor, nasty, brutish and short' (Thomas Hobbes, *Leviathan*, ch. xiii).

2 – Source not located. TSE may have learned the phrase from Charles du Bos or Dorothy Bussy – or it may be that it was something Gide said to him in person in Paris in 1936.

3 – Published 6 Aug. 1937, 130. See further *CProse* 5, 514–16.

4 – TSE delivered his address to the Conference, entitled 'The Church as an Ecumenical Society' – it is published in full for the first time in *CProse* 5, 497–503 – as the first of three plenary speakers under the session title 'The Ecumenical Nature of the Church and its Responsibility toward the World', in the Town Hall, on 16 July. The address was reported in the *Times* of 17 July under the heading 'The Church and the World: Problem of Common Social Action' (18). A further article in the *Church Times* (23 July, 83) – 'Church, Community and State: A Busy Week at the Oxford Conference' – included a brief summary of TSE's talk.

See too the *Church Times* editorial on Fri. 6 Aug.: 'The Life and Work Conference has come to an end. We report elsewhere the proceedings of the Catholic School of Sociology. During the next fortnight the Faith and Order Conference will be sitting in Edinburgh. We have no possible desire to minimize the value and significance of these meetings. They are evidence both of the longing for Christian unity and of the yearning to see Christian principles applied to the solution of contemporary problems. At the same time, as Mr T. S. Eliot urges in a letter which we print this week, there is a grave danger that the significance of these meetings may be over-estimated. The true understanding of their value is only to be obtained when their constituents are remembered.

'Mr Eliot points out that the Life and Work Conference was dominated by American Protestantism. The Coloured Methodist Episcopal Church and the United Brethren in Christ had exactly the same representation as the Church of Wales and the Episcopal Church of Scotland. Of the four hundred delegates, the Church of England only had eighteen, and of

printed reports of the sections are available and until the reports of the Conference on Faith and Order are available.[1] But at the moment the following two points seem to be pertinent.

1. Was the Conference 'representative'? That depends on what one thinks ought to be represented. Of the full delegates, the number of whom was, I believe, supposed to be four hundred, the Church of England had eighteen, of whom I was one. The Church of Wales and the Episcopal Church of Scotland had one delegate each; and the Unitarian Church in England was represented by one delegate. From America, the Methodist Episcopal Church (coloured), the Five Year Meeting of Friends, the Methodist Episcopal Church (African), the Reformed Church in America, and the United Brethren in Christ, were all as fully represented, numerically, as the Church of Wales and the Episcopal Church of Scotland. Of the eighteen full delegates of the Church of England, at most five could be qualified as Catholic. How many delegates of the Episcopal Church in America were Catholic I do not know, as all the names were unknown to me.

2. Did the Conference arrive at any 'unity'? It is impossible for such a Conference to arrive at any unity. There were far too many delegates – far too many Americans, some of whom did not strike me as having any theological qualifications whatever. The report of the section with which I was associated was prepared by a small number of delegates chosen because of their intelligence and vigour, irrespective of proportional representation or theological views, and the section as a whole was expected to accept it. I do not know of any other method by which it would have been possible to prepare a report at all.

I was only present throughout the first week of the fortnight. What made that week valuable to me is this, that it made me much more clearly aware of the profundity of the differences between Christians. The official languages were English, French, and German. But these linguistic divisions were trifling compared to the differences of language even between those who spoke the same language. I for one learned a greater respect, though no greater liking, for the Orthodox and the Lutheran theologies. I wish I could say the same about American Protestantism. I conclude that the

---

these "at most five could be qualified as Catholic". It seems to us obvious that to describe a body of this sort as "œcumenical" is such a misuse of terms as to lead to misunderstanding and illusion. It is a good thing, as Mr Eliot says, that we should have a closer understanding and a keener appreciation of the members of other Christian communities. But it is an evil thing when fundamental differences are obscured.'

1 – The report on the Oxford Conference, entitled *The Churches Survey Their Task*, was to be published by Allen & Unwin in Oct. 1937.

Conference will have done much good if it makes these fundamental differences clearer; and conversely only harm if it serves to obscure them.

T. S. Eliot

## TO *Elena Richmond*

MS William Rathbone

5 August 1937

Tyglyn Aeron, Ciliau Aeron, Lampeter, Cardiganshire[1]

Dear Lady Richmond,

The fine weather of Salisbury lasted through Yeovil – I walked from East to West Coker in great heat and saw Sir Matthew Nathan, who struck me as a remarkable man, even in discussing matters of moment no greater than local feuds during the Wars of the Roses.[2] And I was rather surprised by arriving here with all my luggage, though of course the route turned out to be quite different from that shown by *Bradshaw*.[3]

The fine weather only completed what was a particularly delightful visit – the most memorable that I have enjoyed for a long time. And incidentally, if I may say so without impertinence, I very much enjoyed the company of the other guests.

Yours very sincerely
T. S. Eliot

## TO *Geoffrey Faber*

TS Faber Archive

16 August 1937

*The Criterion*

Dear Geoffrey,

Both letter & enclosure very welcome.[4] If this is a fair specimen of Aubrey's epistolary style, it strikes me as having some points in common with my own, at any rate an equally difficult exercise for you to translate in the manner of Cicero to Atticus (an idea! when things get to the worst, we must make you write a letter to Ezra in Ciceronian Latin (no Priscian).[5]

1–TSE stayed with the Fabers at Ty Glyn Aeron, 4–13 Aug. FVM to GCF, 16 Aug. 1937: 'I had lunch today with Uncle Tom who gave me a most pleasant account of his stay at Tyglyn.'
2–TSE owned the 8th edition of *Somerset*, by G. W. Wade and J. H. Wade (1929). See also David Foot, 'When dad had T. S. Eliot caught behind the font', *The Guardian*, 22 July 2008.
3–*Bradshaw's Descriptive Railway Hand-Book of Great Britain and Ireland*.
4–Not traced.
5–Priscian: Priscianus Caesariensis (*fl.* 500 AD): author of the textbook *Institutiones Grammaticae* ('Institutes of Grammar').

That will stun him. It is pretty near to the necessary moment now, as Ez is thinking of writing his autobiography). Frank fairly cheerful. Apparently eager to visit you in December – anxious to explain that things had altered since they were first invited, because then Christina thought it not right always to take Donald and never Oliver, and she felt that Oliver at Ty Glyn would be a sort of Samson at Gaza; but since then she has taken Oliver to the Tandys, who have been inhabiting a ramshackle cottage in Dorset where nothing mattered, so she is ready to go away without him. Conversation then turned to Mass Observation. The United University[1] not a safe place, partly because the Reform[2] is turned loose there too, and I ran bang into Erich Alport[3] (that's what the Reform has come to).

It really was a delightful and happy visit, though I felt myself that a slightly less proportion of the Jerrihoppers[4] (nice as they are) to my time with the family alone would have been acceptable. All the more because I never see you in London – a little more of that would help the winter, even if we have to get lost in a fog to manage it.

Ever,<br>TP

As for the Australian poet,[5] I have seldom had more thanks for less work.


## TO *Virginia Woolf* TS Berg

16 August [1937] Faber & Faber Ltd

My dear Virginia,

When I got your letter I at once sent orders to have Julian's papers despatched to you.[6] It was deuced uncivil of me not to have written at

---

1 – The United University Club, founded in 1821.
2 – The Reform Club, founded 1836.
3 – Dr Erich Alport (b. 1903), educated in Germany and at Oxford, was author of *Nation und Reich in der politischen Willenbildung des britischen Weltreiches* (1933). He features as Dr Ernest Stockmann in SS's autobiographical fiction *The Temple* (1988). In the early 1930s GCF sought his advice about German books suitable for translation into English.
4 – Gerard ('Gerry') Hopkins (1892–1961), publisher and translator, and his wife Mabel. A nephew of Gerard Manley Hopkins – whose poetry, letters and diaries he would put into print – he was educated at Balliol College, Oxford, and won the Military Cross in WW1. In 1920 he joined Oxford University Press, serving as publicity manager and later editorial adviser. Fluent in French, he became well known for feats of translation: his output included vols 7–27 of Jules Romain's *Men of Good Will*; biographies by André Maurois; Proust's *Jean Santeuil*; memoirs, broadcasts, plays. He was made Chevalier de la Légion d'Honneur, 1951.
5 – Not identified.
6 – VW had asked on 7 Aug., '[Vanessa] wants us to the read the essays [by Julian Bell], only

the same time, but in Wales there was no typewriter available, and my natural disability with the pen was exaggerated by a gorse spine festering in my thumb – the result of scrambling on a cliff and holding on tight to anything. Now, will you still have me in September? The very best date (and one which I think you offered) would be the weekend of the 25th September. A weekend earlier would be difficult: but alternatively I might consider myself justified, for such a cause, in taking a night or two off during that week if the weekend didnt suit.

They want me to give a lecture on Shakespeare in Edinburgh in October, so I have been reading him over the weekend. It is very good reading; but I dont really see that there is anything to be said about it.[1]

Affectionately
Tom

TO *Enid Faber*                                    TS Valerie Eliot

16 August 1937                    The Vestry, St Stephen's Church

Dear Enid,

The only solace of my weekend in town after the delights of Wales was that I didnt have to see anybody (except the verger, with whom I discussed our quarrel with the Kensington & Knightsbridge Electricity Co.). If I had had to see people I couldnt have endured London. Slept (during the afternoons) at the United University, where the waiters have the same irritating habit of taking away one's own *Times* with the x-word unfinished while one is asleep that our waiters have. Read 'Found Floating' by Wills Croft:[2] not good. 'These Names Make Clues' by Lorac[3] is better, though some ancient wheezes in it. Read six plays of Shakespeare. Very good, and recommended for the library list, but I dont think there is anything to say about them, and I have to give a lecture in Edinburgh on Shakespeare at the end of Oct. I hope the last lecture I shall give, or public speech, for 1 year.

Thumb recovered, with thanks; but still wondering whether to see the doctor about the toe. Returning to London brings a positive feeling

one of which, the Roger Fry letter, we have seen. Would you therefore tell whoever has them to forward them to me here as soon as convenient?' (*Letters* 6, 154).

1 – VW commented on this letter: 'A letter from Tom; uneasily egotistic also. Or do I impute this?' (*Diary* V [17 Aug. 1937], 108).

2 – Freeman Wills Crofts, *Found Floating* (1937).

3 – E. C. R. Lorac, *These Names Make Clues* (1937). Robert Macdonald series.

of autumn – summer will persist until the end of holidays in Wales, I am sure. My shoulder is peeling and the floor is littered with it – a pleasant reminder of my visit. Frank has rung up and wants to lunch, which probably means sorrow and too much beer. My cousin Fred is coming to tea, and my niece Dodo will turn up presently.[1] My black cat (Tumblecat) has turned up again: he really belongs next door. I have a feeling that everyone in Kensington is dead. That is the effect of Wales, no doubt. There is nothing to do but order a winter suit and overcoat, and look forward to next summer. The right word at this point is 'Heigh-oh' I believe. Dont forget about Fred Astaire. I wish I was back in Wales with you, but perhaps I shall be somewhat less melancholic when I see you next: Sep. 20th I believe in Regents Park.

> Droopingly
> TP

## TO *Maurice Haigh-Wood* CC

16 August 1937            [Faber & Faber Ltd]

Dear Maurice,

Hayes's explanations, as repeated in your letter of the 12th, seem quite satisfactory, and I have signed the duplicate agreements and returned them to Hayes.

I shall hope to see you when you return.[2] Your club is quartered with us for September, so I might see you there; or drop me a line and I will come to the City. I hope that you will have a restful holiday; I imagine that you have had a good deal of worry of late. On one point I am not clear: that of the disposition of the cash. I take it that one third goes to you, one third to V., and one third to the estate for re-investment. I hope you will persuade V. to let you or her bank re-invest her share for her, and not to treat it as petty cash.

> Yours ever,
> [Tom]

---

1 – Theodora Eliot Smith was visiting London: TSE gave her a munificent gift of money on her departure, and some books – for which she thanked him in a letter (19 Sept.) written from the *Ascania* (Cunard White Star Line) on her voyage back to New York.
2 – MH-W was going for a holiday at Hotel Victoria, Menaggio, Italy.

16 August 1937                         [Faber & Faber Ltd]

My dear Henry,

I have picked out from among my books the following to send you for your Eliot House Library. I should like to get rid of my most valuable books while I am alive, except those which are likely to be of use to me; and if they go to Eliot House, there is some assurance of their being valued. The books which will reach you in several parcels are:

1. *L'Anglais qui a connu la France*. This is a somewhat rare pamphlet by a great French writer, Charles Maurras; the copy of the first edition which he inscribed to me.

2. *Lettre à Jacques Maritain* by Jean Cocteau, inscribed by him to me; and the *Réponse à Jean Cocteau* by Jacques Maritain, inscribed to me. Both must be rare, and the two copies certainly unique.

3. *Lettres à Mélisande* by Julien Benda, inscribed to me.

4. *Morceaux Choisis* by André Gide, together with a letter from Gide inviting me to become a regular contributor to the *Nouvelle Revue Française* (1921) with a reference to Lytton Strachey.

5. *Picasso* by Jean Cocteau, inscribed to me. A somewhat rare pamphlet.

6. *Souffrances et bonheur du chrétien* by François Mauriac, inscribed to me.

7. *Byron* by Charles du Bos, inscribed to me.

8. *Das Schrifttum als Geistiger Raum der Nation* by Hugo von Hofmannsthal, a rare pamphlet inscribed to me.

9. *From Ritual to Romance* by Jessie Weston. My original copy, which I used in preparing *The Waste Land*. I think it is out of print.

I should think that the total value of these books at the present time might be about £250. So if Eliot House isn't appreciative, keep them for yourself. If Eliot House wants them, they ought to be willing to have the paper ones properly bound in morocco.

There are two books which I am afraid V[ivien] has managed to retain; Chapman's *Handbook of Birds of North-eastern North America* (my original copy) and the first edition of Pater's *Renaissance*, with my notes to the Epilogue. No good crying over spilt milk.

If these are favourably received, I may have others to send later.

That was an Elliot tartan, but it's nothing to do with us, though the Scots all believe in a mythical Norman conqueror who settled in Northamptonshire, and whose brood spread into Devon and Galloway. East Coker is good enough for me; I was there a fortnight ago, and took

some photographs which are being developed, and which I will send you.[1]
Called on the Squire of West Coker, an impressive old Jew named Sir
Matthew Nathan, formerly governor of the Sudan – a member of a dining
club to which I belong.

Affectionately,
[Tom]

## TO *John Hayward*                                                TS King's

17 August 1937                     *The Criterion*

My dear Jhon: yourlettert hrills me. Herehav eI been whi ling away
amongst count rysquires, the squire of Netherhampton, the squire of West
Coker and the squire of Glyn Aeron, un til I stink of the stableand the
gunroom, and you have been, as we used to say in St Looey, among the
high rollers. Not tha ttherewere nota few treats: a memorable Phillips
Oppenheimer 1923 (Auslese) a jerriboam of Pigham, Bollinger & Hearn
1933 (young but lively) and other toothsome toothfuls. I look forward
to drinkin gyour lealth in a Whiteway 1937. Have had the company of
the charming and knidly Jerrihoppers also. Whether it is possible to meet
before Saturday I do notk now, but a blow on the telephone would be
cheering to your faithful

TP

But as for beards! how they did wag.[2]

   P.S. My hand is still full of throns thorns working their way out, grasped
on the precipes precipices of Cardinganshire.

## TO *Charles Clayton Morrison*[3]                                    CC

19 August 1937                   [Faber & Faber Ltd]

Dear Dr Morrison,
   I imagine that you have just left Edinburgh, and hope that this will
catch you in London, otherwise it will have to pursue you to Chicago.
I have read *I Yahweh*[4] with a good deal of interest, but I am very much

---

1 – This was TSE's second visit to East Coker: he had been there first in June 1936.
2 – Shakespeare, *Henry IV, Part II*, V. iii: ''Tis merry in hall when beards wag all.'
3 – Charles Clayton Morrison (1874–1966): American Disciples of Christ minister; Christian
socialist; ecumenist; proprietor-editor of the *Christian Century* magazine.
4 – Robert Munson Grey, *I Yahweh: A Novel in the form of an Autobiography* (1937).

of the opinion that there are several other publishers, such as Hodder & Stoughton, who are better equipped to launch a book of this type than ourselves. Our theological list is being built up very slowly, and our present procedure is to attempt to expand it from connexions with the type of stuff that we already have, and I do not think that we are prepared yet to make a leap to something as different as this. I am holding the advance copy until you let me have your instructions what to do with it.

With many thanks, and best wishes,

Yours sincerely,

[T. S. Eliot]

## TO *The Editor,* The Church Times

20 August 1937, 184[1]                    24 Russell Square, London W.C.1

'The Oxford Conference'

Sir,

Having been away in a rather remote part of the country, I have only just seen your issue of August 6, and apologise for the following comment being a week overdue.

In your first leading article you say, 'Mr Eliot points out that the Life and Work Conference was dominated by American Protestantism.' This is not quite what I was trying to convey. I said that there were too many Americans (indeed I think that were too many delegates altogether), but this is not the same thing. So far as I was aware, the few Americans who could be called 'dominant' owed their position, like the representatives of other countries, to their individual abilities; the Conference was very much in debt to Professor Reinhold Niebuhr, among others. But the policy of statesmen has to be shaped according to the temper of the majority of the people whom they have to rule. What I fear for such assemblies in the future is the insensible influence of the mass; and there appeared to be a larger mass of American liberal Protestantism than of anything else. I doubt whether a Conference can be 'oecumenical' and at the same time 'democratic'.

T. S. Eliot

---

1–Letter written on 16 Aug. See further *CProse* 5, 517–18.

TO *Henry Miller*                                           CC

20 August 1937                    [*The Criterion*]

Dear Mr Miller,

Your letter of the 17th, together with the corrected proof, has arrived.[1]
The corrections are not heavy enough to bother seriously about, or to
need a second galley proof.

The *Criterion* pays for prose articles in the body of the issue a flat rate
of £2 per thousand words. When I say 'flat rate' I mean that nobody has
ever got better or worse terms than these. So as your essay is of some
length there will be at least a cheque worth the bother of cashing. We can
let you have extra copies at trade rates, that is to say, 5s per copy, but we
could also probably scrape up a few extra copies of the proofs to send
you, if you want them.

We have no objection to your reprinting the essay in any way you like,
three months after publication in the *Criterion*. After that date all rights
revert to the author. In case of need I should have no objection to re-
publication in America quite soon after the appearance of the *Criterion*,
which is scheduled for the end of September.

I have discussed your suggestion with the committee, and we should
very much like to see the collection which you have ready, *Max and the
White Phagocytes*. We should certainly like to do this if possible, so would
you send it along to me? the sooner the better.

I hope that I shall see Durrell when he gets to London[2] – if he does –
especially as I have never met him.

---

1 – 'Herewith a corrected proof copy . . . I wish to apologise for making these last minute
changes, but as they are all for the good perhaps you will more readily forgive me . . .

'I suppose the Criterion pays for contributions – have no idea what. Am curious because,
if possible, I should like to order perhaps 10 or 12 copies of the October issue to send to
certain individuals who may be interested in knowing about Anaïs Nin's work . . .

'I also should like to know immediately if I may have permission to reprint this article
after its publication? . . .

'Another thing, perhaps quite pertinent – the first book I am offering Knopf's, which is
finished now, a collection of stories, essays, etc. called "Max and the White Phagocytes"
is practically free of obscenity . . . I am wondering if you would seriously consider it for
England – for Faber & Faber . . . I like this book very much myself because it covers a very
wide range – it is a voluminous affair. Kahane (Obelisk) has not yet decided whether he
intends to publish it . . .

'Now I should very gladly give *you* (Faber + Faber) first chance, if there is a contract to
be made with an English firm. Because you have, I feel, always shown a genuine interest in
my work. Knopf know that it is very problematical whether they can print me in America.'
2 – 'My friend Durrell is going to England in a few days . . . I believe he intends calling on
you.'

651

*Scenario* has also arrived, but I have not had time to read it yet.[1]

> With best wishes,
> Yours sincerely,
> [T. S. Eliot]

## FROM *Anne Bradby* TO *Edward Ainger*[2]

CC

20 August 1937                    [Faber & Faber Ltd]

Dear Sir,

Mr Eliot has asked me to write in reply to your letter, and to say that it is impossible for him to answer your letter in detail, but that he can reply on one or two points.[3] He did not intend there to be any separation of the medieval and modern Knights, and did intend a certain relationship between Knights and Tempters to appear. He cannot agree, however, that the temptations of Becket are such as might equally well present themselves to the Prime Minister.

> Yours truly,
> [Anne Bradby]
> Secretary to Mr Eliot

## TO *Stephen Spender*

TS Northwestern

2 September 1937                    *The Criterion*

Dear Stephen,

I am very sorry to hear of your appendicitis.[4] I trust that it is a simple case, and hope you will let me know as soon as you are out and about again.

I have been laid up with a cold for a day, and have been reading *The Death of a Judge*. I am eager to see the missing act. You suggest

---

1 – 'I mailed you a copy of "Scenario" today. It is for you – not for review.'

2 – Edward Ainger (1893–1947), army officer.

3 – Ainger asked on 5 Aug.: 'In so far as the Tempters, the Knights and the modern Knights are different, but yet their parts are played by the same actors, is it your meaning that the three are in a sense indissolubly linked[?]

'As I see it the temptations which came to Becket might equally come to say Mr Chamberlain and their real roots would lie in certain defects in the British character which are the same today, in essence (though their form has changed) as they were in medieval times.'

4 – Letter from SS not traced.

showing it to Speaight, but I wonder whether what is wanted first is not the opinion of a producer rather than of an actor. I should like Martin Browne to see it, but of course I won't show it to anybody until I receive your permission. Various comments come to my mind, but I have got to sort out those which I am competent to make from those which are the theatrical people's business. What I'm not sure about at the first reading is whether there is enough action in it for a play of that length. But I will write to you again during your convalescence.

Affectionately,<br>Tom

## TO *Lawrence Durrell*

TS Morris Library

9 September 1937                    *The Criterion*

Dear Mr Durrell,

Thank you for your letter making quite clear the context in which you would wish to use my remarks in advertising *The Black Book*.[1] I hope that your project will be realised, and when the time comes I suggest your bringing the matter up with me again, as I might, for that purpose, be able to improve on the sentence you quoted from my letter.

I have been rather dilatory in dealing with the sections from Anais Nin's *Diary*. I am just going to read them again, and will send them back to her as I must write to her about them in any case.

It was a great pleasure to meet you, and I hope you will be in London again before long and will be able to have a meal with me.[2]

Yours sincerely,<br>T. S. Eliot

1 – Durrell wrote (n.d.): 'I believe I mislead [*sic*] you when I asked you to let me use the phrase from your letter as a blurb to the Black Book: I did not mean for Kahane's edition, should that materialise, but only for my own edition, should such a one be necessary. If I canvass the book a bit now, it is not for a possible Obelisk printing which will have to find its backers after publication – in the ordinary way – via review copies etc. It is only if I start it, alone and anonymous that help such as you offer me would be the first necessity. I just wrote this little note to assure you, in case I wasn't explicit when we met, that I was not doing Kahane's work for him – simply gathering nuts against a hard winter of my own.'
2 – Durrell responded from Paris, n.d.: 'Very many thanks for the letter . . . I hope to be able to return to England in a little while and look forward to meeting you again. Your sympathy and generosity did me good. I met KAHANE day before yesterday and addressed him as if I were Dante himself, which rather surprised him . . . He is a man of no taste, I feel, and no faith in what he does. His books have to be backed by other opinion before he works up enough courage to print them. Also he informed me that he is a genius himself; which is a little trying. Everyone is a genius here. The clashing of ego's can be heard a mile off!'

to *Michael Roberts*                                   ts Janet Adam Smith

9 September 1937                      *The Criterion*

My dear Roberts,

I have just heard from a friend who has heard from Lady Adam Smith and write to congratulate you and hope that both Janet and your son are in good health.[1]

I ought to have written to you, in any case, first to say that I like the short poems you sent me in July and want to publish them together, but I am inclined to agree that the fourth poem might be omitted.[2]

---

Durrell to Miller, [Sept.–Oct. 1937]: 'I have met Eliot who is a very charming person, believe it or not.' (*Lawrence Durrell and Henry Miller: A Private Correspondence*, 118)

Durrell recalled in 1965 ('The Other T. S. Eliot', 61–2.): 'Henry Miller, who said that he always visualized Eliot as a "lean-faced Calvinist", was most astonished and intrigued when I returned to Paris with an account of my first two meetings with him. So much so, in fact, that he started reading him with attention and prevailed upon me to engineer a meeting with him in London, a meeting which duly took place in a little flat in Notting Hill Gate, loaned to me by Anaïs Nin's husband, Hugh Guiler, the painter. I think Eliot himself was a little intimidated by the thought of meeting the renegade hero of Tropic of Cancer in the flesh, while Miller was still half convinced that Eliot would be dressed like a Swiss pastor. At any rate, the relief on both sides was very apparent, and I remember a great deal of laughter. They got on famously; and it was now that Eliot made one of those gestures which displayed not only his kindness but the unswerving, uncompromising truthfulness which from then on was to characterize for me everything he did and thought. He offered Miller a blurb for his book, and myself a prefatory note for The Black Book. This could have compromised his reputation somewhat, for by the standards of the day both of us were "unsavory writers" (choice phrase), while Eliot's own great reputation was tremendously respectable. But no; he liked the books, and without thought to himself offered us his help. He always had this unfaltering honesty in his dealings. From this delightful evening one small scrap of conversation comes back.

'Eliot: Of course there is more than one kind of pornography; often it has nothing to do with four-letter words.

'Miller: Who are you thinking of?

'Eliot [with immense seraphic gravity]: Actually, Charles Morgan.'

1–Birth of son Andrew. (A year later, on 12 Sept. 1938, Roberts would write: 'Andrew, whose working name is Hokey, is very gay and lively.') Andrew D. Roberts was to become Professor of the History of Africa at the School of Oriental and African Studies, University of London.

2–Roberts, 25 July: 'I enclose four short poems, but the fourth is out of key with the others.' See 'Three Poems: If It Were the Cry; It is a Bold Man; Taller the Cornflower Grew', C. 17 (Jan. 1938), 235–63. The fourth poem, not printed in C., was 'It is your own finger.'

654   TSE at forty-eight

I have not acknowledged your letter of the 11th July either as I have been away a good deal off and on during the summer.[1] I am glad to hear that you have been getting on with Hulme. Whatever the Committee may think, I think that you ought to take your time about it and not feel hurried by keeping to any date. In any case the end of the year would do capitally. I quite realise that the job cannot be adequately done without a great deal of reading and re-reading, and if you are so conscientious as to attack Husserl, I applaud but I am sorry for you. One of his books was translated into English some years ago but I thought not particularly competently though I have not read the original. I went through his *Logische Untersuchungen* twenty-three years ago, and it was about as difficult reading as anything I have ever done; but if you want the two volumes of that work, I shall be glad to let you have my copy.[2]

With regard to reprinting either the Notes on Language or printing any of the unpublished poems, I have forgotten, if I ever knew, who owns the rights to Hulme's unpublished work.[3] No doubt you are up on that point. I think it is a good idea and the only question is what, if anything, we should have to pay for the right.

Yours ever,
T. S. Eliot

1 – Roberts, 11 July: 'I am working steadily at Hulme, but I find that it involves a lot of supplementary reading and re-reading, Pascal, Sorel, Husserl, and so on, and I find that I can't get on with my own part of the book until that is finished and forgotten. I really don't think I can get the manuscript finished till the end of the year. I hope Fabers won't mind.'

2 – Edmund Husserl, *Logische Untersuchungen* ('Logical Investigations'), two vols, 1901–2.

Janet Adam Smith later added a note at the foot of this letter: 'Mr Eliot's copy of Husserl, with some ms annotations, was presented by me to the London Library of which he was then President, in 1955 or thereabouts'.

Roberts to TSE, 29 Sept. 1937: 'Husserl is very relevant: I've found some of Hulme's notes on him and on Scheler.'

3 – 'Among Hulme's notes there are a number of drafts of poems – some of them re-written four or five times. I enclose copies of what seem to be the latest drafts of some of them. *The Man in the Crow's Nest* ought to be printed, I think, and perhaps *Susan Ann* and *A City Sunset*, but I'm doubtful about the others.

'I propose to print an expanded version of the *Notes on Language and on Style* as an appendix on my book, if you don't mind.'

## TO *Anaïs Nin*[1]                                              CC

9 September 1937                        [*The Criterion*]

Dear Miss Nin,

I must apologise for the delay in answering your letter and reporting on the two pieces which you sent me.[2] As you expected, I fear that the passage about the stillborn child would hardly do for isolated publication in the *Criterion* although it is very impressive, and will be perfectly fitting in its text.[3] As for the beginning of 'Father', I confess that I find this unsatisfactory for publication itself. I feel that its significance will only fully appear in the light of the rest of the book, and that it would not be appreciated by itself. I should be very glad if you would keep the *Criterion* in mind, and send me any further selections which seem to you suitable for separate publication.

With best wishes,
Yours sincerely,
[T. S. Eliot]

## TO *Henry Miller*                                            CC

10 September 1937                       [*The Criterion*]

Dear Mr Miller,

I have your letter of September the 8th and wish you success with your edition of Anais Nin's Diary.[4] I shall be glad to subscribe for the first volume to begin with.

---

1 – Anaïs Nin (1903–77), Cuban-American diarist, essayist, novelist and writer of erotica. Works include *D. H. Lawrence: An Unprofessional Study* (1932); *House of Incest* (fiction, 1936); *The Diary of Anaïs Nin*, I: *1932–1934* (1966), II: *1934–1939* (1967); *Henry and June: From A Journal of Love* (1986); *A Literate Passion: Letters of Anaïs Nin and Henry Miller* (1987). See too Noël Riley Fitch, *Anaïs: The Erotic Life of Anaïs Nin* (1993); Deirdre Bair, *Anaïs Nin: A Biography* (1995).

2 – Nin wrote (n.d.): 'Henry Miller asked me to write you because he wanted you to see this First Part of a novel on my Father. He thought this might present less of a problem than the birth piece which Lawrence Durrell mailed you. As you have read volumes of my Diary I would like you to see the created work which was done en marge of it. I received a letter from Faber and Faber explaining the difficulties which I understand very well. If you ever have any time I would like to know what you personally felt as you read. I have so little communication, because of the problem which blocks all the routes, that humanly, I am happy to know that I have in a way, communicated with a poet.'

3 – Nin had delivered a stillborn child in Aug. 1934: see *Incest: from A Journal of Love: The Unexpurgated Diary of Anäis Nin: 1932–1934* (1992).

4 – Miller wrote on notepaper headed '*The Booster*: Founded by the American Club of France' – he and Lawrence Durrell were Associate Editors – 'Anaïs Nin has now given me

I gather you would like the *Criterion* printers to strike off two hundred and fifty off-prints of your paper and I will look into the matter and let you know what the price will be.[1]

I hope you will encourage Miss Nin to let me see some more fragments for possible publication in the *Criterion*.[2] I sent her back two which, for different reasons, seemed unsuitable and I am afraid she may be discouraged. Perhaps it would be as well if she took your advice on what kinds of passage to send in.

I look forward to seeing the *Booster*.[3] I met Durrell last week and liked him very much.

Yours sincerely,
[T. S. Eliot]

authority to act as publisher for her diary. I am going to bring it out slowly, volume by volume, in an integral edition. The first volume, in a child's French, will be brought out through subscription – 200 numbered, signed copies at a hundred francs a copy, with 50 unnumbered copies for the press . . .

'The date of publication for the first volume of the diary is March 1st, 1938.'

1 – 'We should like to enclose with the subscription blank a reprint of the Criterion essay. I hope it is not too late to inquire about this, to know how much it would cost us to have reprinted in the same format as your Criterion pages [. . .] 250 copies of this essay.'

(TSE's Acting Secretary advised on 10 Sept. that 250 off-prints would cost £2.10s.)

2 – 'While I am at it I should like to add that I have suggested to Anaïs Nin that she prepare to submit fragments of the later volumes of the diary to editors of important reviews such as the Criterion and one or two in America. There are two full portrait-studies I should like to have you see soon, if you think you would be interested – one on Antonin Artaud.'

3 – 'A copy of the first number of the new Booster will be sent to you in a day or two. I wish you well and am full of warm appreciation for your continued interest in my welfare. And my best wishes also to Frank Morley whom Durrell tells me "is a man after my own heart." More power to him!'

Ferguson, *Henry Miller*, 253: 'An American businessman named Elmer Prather had started a country club and golf course for the amusement of Americans and Englishmen in Paris and employed [Alfred] Perlès as the club's subscriptions manager and editor of the club magazine *The Booster*. Perlès proved a charming but untalented manager.' The first issue (of three in all) appeared in Sept. 1937. See *The Booster: September 1937 to Easter 1939* (1968).

My dear Alison,

### HOW TO PICK A POSSUM:

When the flowering nettle's in blossom,
    And spring is about in the air,
How delightful to meet Uncle Possum
    With fragments of hay in his hair.

When the bullocks have horns (and they toss 'em)
    And summer's about on the lea,
How delightful to meet Uncle Possum
    As he swings from a neighbouring tree.

At home, he is drest in a mitre
    And a cope, or a cape and a cowl.
Although he's not known as a fighter
    He has a most terrible growl.

On some days he's duller or brighter,
    He objects to both pencil and ink;
Yet he bangs on an ancient typewriter,
    Without ever stopping to think.

He is apt to frequent railway stations,
    Where he studies the maps on the wall;
He is skilful at solitaire-patience,
    And never reads poetry at all.

From April to middle-December
    He is apt to occur in the parks,
For which reason it's well to remember
    His important distinguishing marks: –

VIZ. a nose which in summer is pinky,
    And in winter a beautiful blue;

He has hair, which is straight and not kinky,
   Which I wouldn't say but that it's true.

He has ears, which are almost symmetrical,
   And of use when the wind is behind;
And a mouth, which is small and upsetrical
   And not very easy to find.

At the sound of a sudden sub-poena
   He will quickly retire to his lair,
Very much like the spotted hyaena
   Imitating the cinnamon bear.

In the winter, when fields are forsaken,
   He develops a casual laugh,
Which prevents him from being mistaken
   For the hyperborean giraffe.

In the summer, when flowers are blooming,
   His voice is uncertain and gruff,
Which distinguishes it from the booming
   Of the bittern, the raven or chough.

He has teeth, which are false and quite beautiful,
   And a wigg, with an elegant queue,
And he asks me to send his most dutiful
   Respects to your fambly and you.

                    (Signed)
                    THE MAN IN WHITE SPATS.[1]

---

1 – This poem – ultimately the opening gambit of the collection *Noctes Binanianae* (1939) – was sent too, at about the same time, to GCF – with dedication, and with this additional stanza:

   P.S. His habits are strictly arboreal
   Affording protection from cows;
   And in spring he affects such sartorial
      Display as the fashion allows.

## TO A. W. G. Randall[1]

15 September 1937                    [*The Criterion*]

My dear Randall,

I have your letter of September the 8th and have ordered Franz Werfel's book to be sent to you for a review of any length that you choose.[2] I am also taking the liberty of sending you two books, *Gottesdienst* and *Shakespeare in Germany* to do notices of or not as you think best.

I should be very glad if you could let me have some notices of German periodicals for the December number, that is to say before the end of October, if you have accumulated enough material to be ready to write.

I am somewhat ashamed of my evasiveness towards the Dano-British Association. I heard from them in the Spring but have done nothing about fixing a date, and I hope that they will not think me very uncivil. I was waiting to see what I should have to offer and when. I have got to go up to Edinburgh at the end of October to deliver two lectures on Shakespeare which I am now at work on. Does the Dano-British Association want lectures which have never been delivered before or would it accept a repetition of these lectures which will not have been published? Possibly they will think public lectures in Edinburgh too public to be suitable for repetition; but I find that it would be very inconvenient for me to come over before the end of the year.

It is, in fact, very inconvenient for me to have to go to Edinburgh because I have a piece of work of my own which has been in preparation for some time, and which I am anxious to finish before it goes bad.[3] If the Association would have me sometime in the late winter or early spring, I think that would give me time to improve these lectures considerably before the second reading; but if they very much prefer to have something

---

1–Alec (later Sir Alec) Randall (1892–1977), diplomat and writer. In the early 1920s he was Second Secretary to the Holy See. He ended his career as Ambassador to Denmark (Grand Cross, Order of Dannebrog), 1947–52. He wrote on German literature for *C.* and the *TLS*. Later works include *Vatican Assignment* (1956) and *The Pope, the Jews and the Nazis* (1963).

2–Werfel's *Twilight of a World* (just published in English) was not reviewed.

3–FVM to Janet Leeper, 22 Nov. 1937: 'A matter which is of great significance to him and to us is that Mr Eliot should finish the new play, called FAMILY REUNION, by the end of the year. The first draft of the first act is completed and is wonderfully good; but if he is to get the job done, he must really roll himself up like a hedgehog and not go out during the winter. To my considerable irritation he got behind with this much more important work by accepting an invitation to give two lectures on Shakespeare in Edinburgh. I am all the more urgent, so far as my urge goes, which isn't very far, that for the next months he must be ascetic and deny himself a great many pleasures.'

fresh, I had rather know now, but would, in that case, have to set the date rather later.

Yours ever,<br>
[T. S. Eliot]

TO *Stephen Spender*                                    TS Northwestern

15 September 1937                    *The Criterion*

Dear Stephen,

Thank you for your letter of the 13th.[1] It is reassuring to have a letter in your own hand and in ink, and I hope that I may see you as soon as you come back from Salcombe.

I am sorry that I did not say more about the play when I wrote to you but I had only given it one reading and was writing in rather a hurry. I found it extremely interesting and impressive to read, and felt very much in the dark as to how much alteration it would need for acting purposes. The question of whether to publish one version which may differ considerably from the acting version is a problem that we shall have to discuss. Producers don't like it and if it is to be done the two things ought, perhaps, to be made to appear to be quite different even to the extent of giving them different names; but it is more important to find out first how much alteration for acting purposes the producer thinks is likely to be necessary. I have only just heard from Martin Browne who has had a slight breakdown from overwork and is resting at his home in Dorset,

---

1 – 'I am out of the Nursing Home now & am up & feeling better . . . On Friday we are going to Salcombe in Devon for 14 days convalescence.

'You don't say whether you like the play and what I feel about publication in book form rather depends on whether you do or don't. So I will consult your wishes by saying that I myself am in favour of publishing it as soon as possible, either in the late Autumn or early Spring. I am very keen to finish it now & get it done with, partly because I have three other books in mind, a novel, a book of stories and poems since my last book, including perhaps a new version of *Vienna*. Also, I feel that the alterations I may have to make in the acting version won't necessarily improve the literary quality of what I have written, so I don't see why the literary version shouldn't be published as something rather different. E.g. Auden & Isherwood object to the parrot which they say is a literary conception. Well, I am quite willing to take it out for the stage, but I would like it to remain in the published poem. I hope this view of the "poetic drama" doesn't shock you.

'*Business*. Can I have an advance now from Faber, for the play & two other books. If I could have £100 down I should be very grateful because this operation and all has come very expensive. You will let me know if this is too much to ask.'

and I shall send the play to him directly. Meanwhile I know that the Mercury Theatre is clamouring for new plays.

Business – I will bring the matter up with Faber and the Committee this afternoon and will write to you in a few days. If you should not hear from me before you leave for Salcombe, please drop me a line with your address.

Yours affectionately,
Tom

## TO *John Hayward*

TS King's

Thursday [16 September 1937]      *The Criterion*

My dear John,

I thank you for your cordial invitation, which I shall be unable to accept.[1] It would have been a pleasure to meet Mr Thurber at last, and I hope you will salute him for me.[2] To say nothing of Mr Marx and his four brothers.[3] But it is a still greater pleasure to look forward to seeing you on Sunday evening.

Yours etc.
TP

1 – GCF's sonnet to TSE, opening 'Arboreal though the natural habitat', was sent to JDH by TSE on 15 Sept. 1937, with the parenthetical subtitle '(Addressed to the Rev. Uncle Possum by his unworthy coadjutor, Father Faber, who, also, will be unable to be present.)'
2 – Thurber was to write to JDH, 20 Feb. 1950: 'Time runs on too fast, and so many of the great joys are in the past, a lot of them in the London of John Hayward twelve years ago.'
3 – The Marx Brothers: Groucho, Chico, Harpo, Zeppo, accompanied possibly by another brother, Gummo, a performer in his youth but by this time a theatrical agent.

## TO *Eugene Jolas*[1]

CC marker

CC

21 September 1937             [Faber & Faber Ltd]

Dear Mr Jolas,

I am afraid I cannot be of much use to you with your questionnaire.[2] Questions number 1 and 2 are really matters I prefer to keep to myself. The answer to number 3 is definitely no. I am not, as a matter of fact, particularly interested in my 'night-mind'. This is not a general assertion about night-minds, nor does it carry any suggestion about other people's interest in their night-minds. It is only that I find my own quite uninteresting.[3]

Yours very truly,
[T. S. Eliot]

## TO *Virginia Woolf*

TS Berg

23 September [1937]          *The Criterion*

Dear Virginia,

I hope you are still expecting me for this weekend? If not, would you send me a wire (to 11, Emperor's Gate, S.W.7.)? If you are expecting me, I will look for a train to bring me down just before lunch on Saturday, and

---

1–Eugene Jolas (1894–1952), poet and editor, was born in the USA (his father was French, his mother German) but educated until the age of fifteen in France. Back in the USA, he found employment as a newspaperman, and in the 1920s returned to France, working for a while for the Paris edition of the *Chicago Tribune*. An ally of JJ, he promoted the interests of the work that became *Finnegans Wake*. In 1927 Jolas co-founded (with his wife and Elliot Paul) the avante-garde magazine *transition*. Other works include *Secession in Astropolis* (1929) and posthumous memoirs, *Man from Babel*, ed. Andreas Kramer and Rainer Rumold (1998).

2–The questions were posed in a letter from Jolas, 15 Sept. 1937, for *transition*:
  1. What has been your most recent characteristic dream? (Or day-dream, waking–sleeping hallucination, eidetic impression, phantasma)?
  2. What ancestral myths or symbols have you observed in your 'collective unconscious'?
  3. As a creative artist have you ever felt the need for a new language to express the experience of your night-mind?

3–TSE's letter was published in the symposium 'Inquiry into the Spirit and Language of Night', in the tenth-anniversary edition of *transition*, no 27 (Spring 1938), 236. In the copy of the magazine supplied to him, TSE would later write against his entry: 'for Valerie. This seems to me the right answer to a silly question. T.S.E.'

Other contributors to the symposium included Sherwood Anderson, Kenneth Burke, Malcolm Cowley, Ernest Hemingway, Robinson Jeffers and Archibald Macleish.

663

send a wire; alternatively, if it is more convenient to have me come in the afternoon, send me a wire to tell me what train to take.[1]

Affectionately,

T. S. E.

TO *George Barker*                                                       TS Texas

26 September 1937                    *The Criterion*

My dear Barker,

It seemed to me I might as well write to give you the content of the letter which, as I told you, I had drafted and was going to rewrite to you.

The Chairman and I had discussed the unfinished draft of JERUSALEM, and agreed that if you eventually made out of it a book of a possible length and of the right kind, it ought to be something that we should publish. When I say the right kind, I mean that you should make it a Barker book, abandon any attempt to make a popular seller of it, and write it seriously as literature. It seems to me that if you really feel that it is something you want to go on with, and will consider what I am saying in the light of my previous letter, you will discover for yourself a new and personal form in which to recast it. You certainly are not at ease when endeavouring to write down to the supposed larger public, and I think that the freedom from this intention would tell you how to write the book. The fact that the best passages occur later on suggests that you were expanding as you forgot the original intention.

I think, however, that this effort to write something saleable to an ordinary public, however mistaken, has been a very good exercise, and has brought about some simplification and clarification of your prose style. So it might not be a bad thing to keep in mind a public, even in rewriting without thought of a large sale. I say *a* public, but do not mean the large public, whose tastes, as the Chairman and I both think, you are not equipped either to understand or to gratify. But it seems to me desirable for you, in your verse as well as your prose, to remember that a work of any length needs some pattern of tension and relaxation; that

1–VW noted on Sun. 26 Sept.: 'Tom in some ways – with his sensitive, shrinking, timid but idiosyncratic nature – is very like myself. This morning, as Priestley's play [*Time and the Conways*] is praised, he is uneasy, as I shd be, & insinuates, as I should, distrust of critics, yet reads them, as I do, furtively. Tom is liverish looking, tired; but revives under the effect of Judith [Stephen]'s fresh & downright & able but not sophisticated, or I daresay, highly aesthetic, youth' (*Diary* V, 112).

if you produce pure poetry all the time, the best trained reader will be stunned and fatigued, and you will lose the resources of emphasis. To write a poem of any length one ought to have at command verse as well as poetry – verse which shall be good verse without being poetry of the first intensity.

At the moment, the foregoing appears to be superseded by the results of our conversation. You may change your mind about some of the material in JERUSALEM later on, but if you do take it up again, it must be only because it is something that you want to write, that is, something which we should expect, written in that spirit, would deserve our support as publishers; but would not be a book upon which an advance of royalties would be justified.

I will not repeat the remarks that I was going to make about looking for a livelihood to some other occupation than literature, because you seem to have come to this conclusion yourself. The thing for us to do now is to try to find the paths which would lead to a steady and tolerable job of any kind, but preferably remote from literature.

I will repeat the part of the last paragraph that I read to you: I believe in your genius, so far as one is ever justified in believing in genius except in retrospect, and I believe that it is genius if anything and not talent. If I am right, that is the best reason for not blunting your gifts on hack-work. Although it may be natural for you to write a good deal, I believe that yours is a concentrated kind of gift – you should scrap a good deal and publish little. I cannot believe that you are one of those – nearly always second-rate – persons who can expect to make a living out of writing. You ought to be in a position in which you could be indifferent to frequent publication and its immediate financial rewards, and cultivate an attitude which would enable you to observe without envy the prosperous parade of more facile and accommodating talents. You should be prepared to be acclaimed late, if at all.

As I said, I don't think that the subsidy can be continued any longer, as the number of people from whom I am able to ask financial support for any purpose is very limited. So I hope that some dependable occupation will turn up in the near future.

> With best wishes,
> Yours ever,
> T. S. E.

27 September 1937                    *The Criterion*

Dear George,

*The English Renaissance* has now been read by my colleague Morley, and has had the effect of making him very anxious to meet you; so I hope you will let me arrange it when you are next up in London. Let me know if there is any possibility of your coming up before Christmas time, or at that time.

In any case, I think I must try to get down to Kelham some time in November or early in Advent – I shall certainly be unable to do so until the middle of November – and have a talk with you about it. I find it difficult to express in writing exactly what I feel, and the results of my conference with Morley about it. So what I say now must be taken as a preface to a conversation.[1]

We both feel, first of all, that the book is not commercially practicable. Second, we are doubtful about the attempt to convey what you are trying to convey in this form, which seems, so to speak, too delicate a pattern to be apprehended by the public mind. I mean that I am very much aware myself that there is a pattern, and a unifying principle to the book, but I feel that this would not be apparent except to people like myself who know you and what you are after, or to a very few people who will have the perceptiveness to divine the nature of your personality behind it. It is the meaning of the thing as a whole, rather than the good bits which readers may very well pick up here and there, that gives the book its value, and if they don't get this unity, as I don't think they will, they may get not merely nothing, but a wrong impression. It would certainly be a positively wrong impression if the book were taken, as I am sure it would be taken, merely as a collection of leisurely and dispersed essays. In this way everything that they got from it would be slightly askew; for, in short, what is the unifying principle is your personality.

You know that I like the book myself, but I think that now and then there is such a thing as a very good book which there is no point in publishing, and I think that before this appears you will have done something of a very different kind.

---

1 – Every submitted his book on 6 Aug.: 'Of course I am not satisfied with it . . . But I have come to the conclusion that this book can only have a chance with Faber, i.e. if you reject it or prefer it without the poetry it will have to be made in another book of a more orthodox kind.'

So much for my preface, and I look forward to a talk with you.

Affectionately,

T. S.


## TO *George Every*                                                    CC

27 September 1937                    [*The Criterion*]

Dear George,

I am sending you back Nicholson's poems as you request, and apologize for the delay.[1] I do think there is very likely something there, if he is young enough, and I am pleased by an interest in a variety of things outside himself, and a livelier experimentation with varieties of metre than is usual. It is still very unformed, of course. I agree with you that Roberts might be as useful to him as anybody

Yours ever,

[T. S.]


## TO *Henry Miller*                                                    CC

27 September 1937                    [Faber & Faber Ltd]

Dear Miller,

Morley, Pringle[2] and myself have all had a go at *Max and the White Phagocytes*. I think you may be hearing from the others as well as from me. Some of the things, of course, I had seen before, so these do not need

---

1 – Every submitted on 6 Aug. 'some poems by a T.B. case [Norman Nicholson], aged 23, t.b. since 17, which I want you to see . . . If they are important, and I think they are, I should like the poor lad to have some more appreciation before he dies. I got them from a sensitive girl friend of his [C. B. ('Bessie') Satterthwaite, of Millom] who has just passed out of L. C. Knights' school of English at Manchester and is going to teach near her home and his at Whitehaven in Cumberland. He evidently reads, but also sees. And he makes words.'

Nicholson (1914–87) had contracted pulmonary tuberculosis at the age of sixteen and spent two years in a sanatorium: see his memoir *Wednesday Early Closing* (1975).

Every to TSE, 23 Sept.: 'I have been having some interesting letters and some more poems from Norman Nicholson . . . I cannot quite decide whether to say more to Nicholson himself than I have done – critically as well as by way of encouragement, or to hand it over to [Michael] Roberts as in many ways, I think, a more suitable adviser perhaps than (for different reasons) either you or me. I wonder whether therefore you could let me have Nicholson's poems which I sent you back with or without comment . . . I am sure your comment would be very valuable but I don't see that I can say anything to Nicholson about what he is writing now without them.'

2 – Alan Pringle (1911–77), editor at Faber & Faber.

any new floral decorations. The simple point is this: there is a lot of good stuff in the collection, as you know, and it will have to be published sooner or later. But I think it would be a very bad policy to use this book to start publication in England with. The publication of a collection like this implies the existence of a considerable public which is already familiar with several big works of an author, and is ready for the dessert of miscellanea. It is a bad idea to produce the pudding and cheese before the soup and fish. As a collection which would not yet have a chance of a wide circulation, and therefore as a comparative failure, it would take the edge off the appetite of booksellers and reviewers for an important continuous book. I think strongly that this ought to be held up for a couple of years at least. What we should like would be some book of the bigness of *Tropic of Cancer* or *Black Spring*, which at the same time was a possibility for publication in the English-speaking countries. With something like that to begin with we could make something much more like a success with this collection. Let me know if you don't get my point, or don't agree with it, and I will say it all over again in different words. At any rate, I think you will get the same tune set to different instruments from the others. We are certainly hoping for something from you on a large scale.[1]

> Yours ever sincerely,
> T. S. Eliot

## TO *Louis MacNeice*                                                CC

28 September 1937                    [*The Criterion*]

Dear MacNeice,

Thank you for your letter of the 25th.[2] I am keeping 'On those Islands', which seems to me the most suitable, and sending it to the printers for the next number.[3] I return the other poem and the dialogue herewith.

I am sorry to say I found the committee rather inflexible on the subject of a further advance on *Iceland*.[4] The only thing I can suggest at the moment is that you should put up any suggestion for a further book which occurs to you as desirable. I have also been wondering whether, as

---

1 – *Max and the White Phagocytes* was to be published by Obelisk Press (1938).
2 – 'Here are two poems & the dialogue which I mentioned, in case you like any of them for the December Criterion?'
3 – 'On Those Islands', C. 17 (Jan. 1938), 214–17.
4 – 'As to my money difficulties previously mentioned, *would* it be possible to wangle any advance on the Iceland royalties?'

a tolerable means of making a little money from time to time, you might not get something out of the BBC. I have just suggested your name for one purpose, but there may be others still better.[1]

> Yours ever sincerely,
> [T. S. Eliot]

## TO *A. L. Rowse*[2]                                                    TS Exeter/CC

28 September 1937                [Envelope postmarked
                                 South Kensington, S.W.7][3]

*Private and Confidential.*
My good friend Postman, do not falter,
But hasten to Sir ARTHUR SALTER,
And then enquire for LESLIE ROWSE,
Who's hidden somewhere in the house –
For having fled from dons and wardens
He must be sought in CORNWALL GARDENS,
Among the stucco, stones and bricks
You'll ask for him at SIXTY-SIX.
And now to make my rhyming even,
Observe the district,

> S.W.7.

You hardly need a lens bi-focal
To see that this address is LOCAL.

---

1–See Barbara Coulton, *Louis MacNeice at the BBC* (1980).
2–A. L. Rowse (1903–97), historian; Fellow of All Souls, Oxford: see Biographical Register.
3–Rowse wrote, 25 Sept.: 'I'm going to be in town all this week, at Sir Arthur Salter's flat, 66 Cornwall Gardens, S.W.7. actually digging, as usual, in the Public Record Office. Perhaps we may meet?'

See further *The Diaries of A. L. Rowse*, ed. Richard Ollard (2003), 358, where ALR reports a conversation with EVE, 24 Nov. 1965:

'There was another story – of the admirer of Eliot's, who followed him out of church in Kensington hoping to hear the great man say something remarkable. What he heard when Eliot got to his car was: "That bloody bird's done it again."

'I told her in return the story of T.S.E.'s little practical joke in the 1930s, when I was staying in Sir Arthur Salter's flat, to ring up the Vicar of St Mary's Kensington. I half-knew that something was afoot for the address to the postman was in verse: to the effect

> Postman, do not falter
> Till you come to the house
> Of Sir Arthur Salter
> Where you'll find A. L. Rowse etc.

'When I rang up, the Vicar didn't know what it was about, nor who I was, any more than I knew who he was. T. S. E.'s little joke came off.'

TO *John Dover Wilson*                                        CC

28 September 1937                    [Faber & Faber Ltd]

My dear Dover Wilson,

Thank you for your letter of the 26th.[1] I take it that I should arrive on the morning of Tuesday 26th October, and go straight to the Maitlands.[2] If your previous suggestion still stands, you will arrange for me to transfer myself to your house in due course, and I believe I am to attend Grierson's Inaugural on Friday, and return to London that night. This is what I remember the suggested arrangement to be, but I leave myself in your hands. I trust that you will also let me know what forms of clothing to bring, as I imagine that Edinburgh is inclined to be rather more formal than London.

I am working now on the second lecture. It is difficult to arrange a really good title for anything until it is finished, but the subject matter suggests a title of one of two kinds. The first is 'Shakespeare: the popular and the unpopular plays'; and the second is 'The development of Shakespeare's dramatic verse'.[3] Perhaps it is not immediately apparent how the same pair of lectures could bear two such different titles, but I think the two things do manage to fit in fairly well. Neither title sounds very attractive to me, and perhaps improvements can be found on both.

Yours ever,
[T. S. Eliot]


1 – 'I am arranging for you to give [your] lectures on Oct 26 & 27 at 5 o'clock & have told the English Association that you will read them some of your poetry at some hour on Oct. 28th.'

2 – The Maitlands lived at 6 Heriot Row, Edinburgh. JDW advised TSE, 2 Mar. 1937: 'He is a K.C. [King's Counsel] with literary interests, and she is a first-rate musician . . . They have heaps of money and their house is one of the old houses in Edinburgh which they have filled with beautiful pictures. They are charming people.'

3 – 'Shakespeare as Poet and Dramatist' (two parts: 20 pp. & 20 pp.): published as 'The Development of Shakespeare's Verse: Two Lectures' in *CProse* 5, 531–61. Steven Matthews, *T. S. Eliot and Early Modern Literature* (2013), 180: 'Eliot's title for his series echoes and differs from that of his Harvard tutor George P. Baker's *The Development of Shakespeare as a Dramatist*. Baker too emphasised the need for Shakespeare to be viewed alongside his contemporaries, and promoted the idea that what made drama "poetic" was that it should be shaped around a "unifying idea" . . . Eliot included Baker's book in his Extension list.'

EVE to Franz Wurm, 16 Feb. 1966: 'You were quite right in thinking that "The Development of Shakespeare's Verse", which my husband gave in Germany in 1949, has not been published in English, and I am interested to learn that you do not think very highly of the German translation [*Der Vers: Vier Essays* (1952)] . . . This lecture was based on earlier unpublished lectures which my husband gave in Edinburgh in 1937, and he did not wish it to be published in English, but I may include it in due course in his collected works.'

## TO *John Hayward*

30 September 1937                    *The Criterion*

Dear John,

I shd. welcome a suggestion as to who might review G. M. Young's essays (*Plains & Champagnes* it is called or something like that) for the *Criterion*.[1] He seems to be a man of a certain stoutness, though he didnt seem interested in writing a book for F&F when I wrote to him. But if I gave him to any of the young sparks they would be very scornful, because he dont think much of what I once overheard a man in the club call the Eliot school of poetry (I dont know who he was, but he is one of the regulars and I have seen him frisking about in court dress and once when Osbert was lunching with me which as you may imagine was some years ago Osbert said is that C. B. Cochran but I am sure it is not because this bird has a moustache, and hair, a sable silver'd)[2] or anything nowadays, which I dont either for the most part but that is between ourselves. So can you suggest a reliable man of balanced mind.

                                       yrs etc.
                                       TP


## TO *Louis MacNeice*

30 September 1937                [Faber & Faber Ltd]

My dear MacNeice,

It now appears that we are within measurable distance of having to reprint your poems. Some time ago you spoke of bringing the book up to date by including a number of new poems, including one from *Iceland*, for the New York edition. Whether you are doing this or not, it seems to me that such additions, enough to form a second edition of the book, would be a good thing and stimulate sales here. If you think well of this, the sooner we have the material the better.

---

TSE's lecture remarks – 'With Marlowe, dramatic poetry is for the most part speeches: with Shakespeare it becomes for the first time conversation. He learned, gradually, to write poetry in which we can hear ordinary human beings talking: at the same time ordinary conversation and great poetry' – correspond to what TSE wished for his own dramatic verse.
1 – Richard Jennings on G. M. Young, *Daylight and Champagne*: C. 17 (Jan. 1938), 319–22.
2 – Horatio describes the dead King Hamlet's beard as a 'sable silvered' (*Hamlet* I. ii. 239).

Have you ever thought of trying your hand at a detective story?

Yours ever,

[T. S. Eliot]

## TO *Geoffrey Faber*

TS Faber Archive

[Undated ? 1 Ocober? 1937]    *The Criterion*

There is some question whether the enclosed Poem, the manuscript of which has just been discovered in the British Museum, is correctly attributed to the late Mr GAY; and it is therefore sent to the chief living authority on that Author, for the benefit of his opinion. One reason why the attribution has been doubted, is that the identity of the Gentleman to whom the Poem is addressed, is completely obscure. Had there been such a Person among the Poet's acquaintance, we might expect to have heard of him before.

### AN EPISTLE

To the *Learned* and *Ingenious* <u>*Dr Morley*</u>.
The *Elephant* of forty-nine[1]
Cannot be caught with *hook* and *line*,
Especially when it leads into
The Precincts of the *Hamburg Zoo.*
The *Whale*, of nearly thirty-eight,
Has less grey matter in his pate.
The *Elephant*, of beasts alive,
Is quite the most *Conservative*:
While other creatures change and roam,
He lingers in his jungle home
In vegetarian flatulence,
*Slow* in attack, *strong* in defence.
The *Whale*, of more *mercurial* mind,
Is driven about by Tide and Wind;
A mammal with no nobler wish
Than live like *fish* among the *fish*,
A Monster who escap'd the *Flood*

1 – See FVM's poem 'For Doctor Thomas Eliot' (*Noctes Binanianae*), written on TSE's forty-ninth birthday this year.

With watery diluted blood,
And, sacrificing *hoof* to *fin*,
Perpetuates pre-diluvial Sin.
Yet ah! might even *Whales* repent?
And leave their fluid Element?
Prepare the higher life to meet
And stand at last upon their feet?
With *fatted calves* we'd welcome them
Into the New Jerusalem.

Anon.

## TO *John Hayward*

TS King's

1 October 1937                    *The Criterion*

Dear John,

Here is a very curious item on which you must prove your scholarship. The manuscript of the enclosed poem was recently found inserted in a copy of the first edition of *A Tale of a Tub* in the British Museum. It was immediately submitted to Mr G. C. Faber, the recognised authority on the works of Mr GAY. Mr Faber has pronounced against its ascription to that poet – I think myself, with some over-confidence in his own knowledge, for he writes: 'Had GAY had any friend or correspondent of that name, I should certainly know of his existence'. However, I am now authorised to submit it to the recognised authority on the works of the late DEAN of ST PATRICK'S, in the hope that you will be able to assign it to that author. If you deny the authorship, a curious situation arises: can it be that there was another Poet, a luminary obviously equal in magnitude to these two giants, whose other works and even whose name have completely disappeared? The suggestion is absurd. I await your pronouncement with vast curiosity.

Yours etc.
T. S. E.

TO *John Hayward*                                                    TS King's

2 October [1937]                          *The Criterion*

Dear John,
    The enclosure will explain itself. Does it?
    Or does it not?[1]

                                          In haste,
                                          TP


TO *Geoffrey Faber*                                          TS Faber Archive

2 October [? 1937]                        *The Criterion*

Dear Geoffrey,
    I am writing in haste to prevent you from spending any more time over
the problem which, as it now appears, I presented prematurely. I hope that
you have not begun to write your full report, questioning, if not wholly
disproving, the ascription to Mr GAY. Because meanwhile a new copy of
the Poem has turned up in the British Museum, this time entitled simply
'A Fable'. It was found by a research student from Nigeria, between the
leaves of vol. III of *The Complete Works of Harold J. Laski*. It is identical
in dedication and in every other respect, including paper and ink, except
that after the lines
            The *Elephant*, of beasts alive,
            Is quite the most *Conservative*,
we have a couplet which does not occur in the first version, viz.:
            (Of *beasts conservative*, the most
            Have perish'd, like *The Morning Post*):

1 – JDH responded on 17 Nov.: 'My dear Tom: I was overcome with amusement – and by the
brilliance of "Vers pour La Foulque" [*Noctes Binaninae*]. For sheer virtuosity, and indeed
for everything else, it surpasses all the poems in the canon! I showed them to Louis Roché,
a secretary of Embassy who was here last night, and asked him to make any necessary
corrections. I find that the few he suggested have been incorporated in the improved and
emended version which came this morning. But there are still two small revisions needed to
make the verses perfect. "Tu vois bien, que c'est bien grotesque" is apparently not French
as she is spoke. Roché suggests: "Ne vois tu pas combien c'est grotesque". Also, "grincer"
being an intransitive verb, the first line of the third stanza must read: "Le facteur meme
grince *des* dents". "Peu de vivant", by the way, which you've now altered, was incorrect.
I hope to hear in due course if there are any more poems, apart from this one, to be added to
the list I sent to F.V.M. You see I'm not in a funny mood this morning – so I'll just subscribe
myself / Aillevard, duc et pair.'
    The letter was adorned with a drawing of spider, whale, elephant and coot.

Which appears to give us an approximate date for the Poem. Doesn't it? or does it not?

In haste (as I said above) and apologetically,[1]

TP

## TO *Virginia Woolf*

TS Faber Archive

[?4 October 1937]                    [Faber & Faber Ltd]

AMONG the various Middle Classes[2]
(Who live on treacle and molasses)
A custom has (for want of better)
Been called the Bread & Butter Letter.
But Mrs Woolf would not rejoice
In anything that's so bourgeoise,
So what can poor Old Possum do,
Who's upper-middle through and through?
For centuries and centuries
And under President or King,
He's always told the proper lies
And always done the proper thing.
Still growing longer in the tooth,
He sometimes yearns to speak the truth,
And would express his gratitude
For conversation, bed and food,
And quiet walks on downs and knolls,
And Sunday morning game of bowls.[3]
Whoever gives him their approval -
He only hopes that Mrs Woolf'll.[4]

1 – GCF's diary, Sat. 2 Oct.: 'Wrote a poem for FVM & TSE after tea.'

2 – TSE had visited the Woolfs at Rodmell, 2–3 Oct.

3 – On the Sunday, VW wrote to Angelica Bell: 'Tom was miraculous at bowls, dignified, supple, regretted you, and showed up well, Judith [Stephen] thought, beside William Plomer' (*Letters* 6, ed. Nicolson, 178).

4 – These lines were written on the verso of a letter – 'Dear Mr Elliott' – from Ursula Cooke (Secretary of St Stephen's Bridge Tournament), dated Oct. 1937, inviting TSE to take a Bridge Table, or to send a donation. Against 'bridge table' (which he underlined), TSE wrote: 'I am using this in my next play.' See this speech by Violet, in *FR*: 'I should have been helping Lady Bumpus, at the Vicar's American Tea.'

6 October 1937                          [No address given]

Dear Mr Winston,

I am sorry to have delayed so long in replying to your enquiries about children's verse in schools,[1] but I must point out in extenuation that the subject was not raised by me, and also that it is a subject on which I cannot speak with any more authority than anyone else.

The anthology you sent certainly has some interest. I should say that up to about fourteen – no age of course can be definitely fixed – the most that can be said is that there is no harm in children writing verse if they want to. I mean that before that age I cannot see any particular reason for encouraging them to write verse, or for using it as a school exercise. I cannot feel that all of the pupils represented in this book have benefited particularly by the exercise, because the poems do not appear to have been corrected by their teachers.

After about that age, I think that there is a good deal to be said for a certain amount of verse writing in connexion with their work in prose composition. It ought I think to be set in traditional forms, because this is what they need, whether they are poets or not. Even quite complicated forms, such as the sonnet or the sestina, might be tried, and an intelligent and enthusiastic teacher could make the attempt to solve the technical problems very exciting. I should certainly discourage young people from writing in that formless and rhythmless speech which is called vers libre. Nobody ought to attempt free rhythms until he has served an apprenticeship in strict ones.

Yours faithfully,<br>
T. S. Eliot

## TO *Louis MacNeice*                                        cc

7 October 1937                          [Faber & Faber Ltd]

Dear MacNeice,

I have discussed your letter of October 4 with the committee.[2] We agree, on second thoughts, with your opinion that it would be better to make

---

1 – Letter not found.

2 – 'I am glad to hear that the Poems may soon need reprinting but I am not at all sure that it is a good idea to include my new poems in the book. I now have nearly twenty, including three long ones, which would almost make a new book by themselves. From talking to

another book of the new poems, rather than enlarge the first book into a second edition, and we are strongly of opinion that the same procedure should be followed in America also.[1] You speak as if you had not yet got quite enough material, so I hope that you will be writing some poetry this winter, and be able to let us have a new book in the spring.[2]

The suggestion of a book on the teaching of the classics sounds an extremely good one, but our opinion is that it ought not to be too 'impressionistic', but to be a really serious book, which might have a real influence on the future. And *a priori* I am not enthusiastic about having part of the book in verse. I think it would restrict the public, and the *Iceland* design is not one that can bear repeating too often. But I hope you will produce some kind of outline of such a book soon, and let me submit it to the committee.[3]

Yours ever,
[T. S. Eliot]

## TO *Theodore Spencer*[4] TS Harvard Archives

8 October 1937 *The Criterion*

*PRIVATE AND PERSONAL*

Dear Ted,

This is a kind of business letter. Several times in the last few years I have thought of someone here who would be just right for the Norton

---

people I am pretty sure that while many of the people who bought the original volume of "Poems" would buy an entirely new book, very few of them would buy a new edition of the original book even if it were announced as containing some new poems.

'I do not feel like trying a detective story at the moment, but someone has made a suggestion to me which I think rather good. Namely, that I should write a shortish book about my experience of the teaching of the Classics (at two English schools & three universities). Not however in the form of a treatise but impressionistically – e.g. presentation of the classroom or lecture room, specimens of Greek & Latin literature *as they appear* in translationese, some good translations for contrast, the point of the whole thing being to show the very different & distorted ideas people in schools (& universities) get of the "Classics". One might have also a few words against pseudo-Hellenism etc. Some of the book could be in verse' (MacNeice, *Selected Letters*, 303–4).

1 – The second impression of *Poems* (Dec. 1937) included no new additions.
2 – *The Earth Compels* (1938).
3 – Not published.
4 – Spencer had taken notes – 'Evening with T. S. Eliot' – on 21 Sept. 1936; they included:

> Job getting out 1936 vol. of poems: had to have new poem [*BN*] at end so as not to have vol. trailing off into little fragments.
> Discussion of *Murder in the C.*

Professorship, but as the Committee don't ask me to make suggestions I naturally don't want to approach them. I wonder if you have any direct or indirect influence in these matters? I should suppose, without flattery, that your influence was in the ascendant. I have often thought, of course, of Herbert Read in this capacity, and I am wondering whether there would be any possibility of his being appointed for 1938–39. I am sure he would do a good job, and I think that the job would do him good too. He has had to do a good deal of work during the last few years which has been more or less hack work, or at any rate under excessive pressure, and I think that with an opportunity like that he would blossom out and do some really first rate work again; and it does seem a pity to me that Harvard should not get the best men for this job while they are still young enough. I don't know who has held it since Binyon was there,[1] but if there had been anyone really eminent in the world of letters I think I should have known about it.

Is there any chance of seeing you during 1938? You know we are expecting you over here some time after Christmas.

Yours ever,
Tom

## TO *Clive Bell* Envelope & PC[2]: Berg

12 October 1937  [Postmarked 'London']

> Good Postman, leave this at the door
> Of FIFTY GORDON SQUARE to-day:
> I want it to arrive before
> The bailey beareth CLIVE Bell away.[3]
> W. C. 1

---

Agreed with me that murderers speeches sh'd go so fast that audience shouldn't know what was happening to them till it was over.

He said he thought its greatest weakness as a play was that the audience didn't know when it was going to stop. Many people puzzled by this – unless, of course, they'd read it before.

1 – Laurence Binyon, CH (1869–1943), Keeper of Prints and Drawings in the British Museum, 1932–3; noted translator of Dante. In 1933 he had succeeded TSE as Charles Eliot Norton Professor of Poetry at Harvard.

2 – Photograph of the Lincoln Building, New York City.

3 – 'The bailey beareth the bell away; / The lily, the rose, the rose I lay' ('The Bridal Morn', anon., 15th–16th C.).

[Message]

the destined walls

. . .

Turkestan bore . . .[1]

T. S. E.

## TO *W. H. Auden*                                                      CC

12 October 1937                    [Faber & Faber Ltd]

Dear Wystan,

Grateful thanks for your prompt reply.[2] I quite agree that publication ought to be at or about the time of production, and I hope you will see that we are informed when that is likely to be. When the date is definitely settled *and* the script in its final form, I think it ought to go to press at once.

If you are going to edit an anthology for Oxford, I hope you will take warning by W.B.Y.'s horrid example; and if it is a book of light verse, I think you ought to remember to do your friends a good turn when possible. But I imagine that my Practical Poems about Cats are more suitable for the *Oxford Book of Children's Verse*, which you will no doubt edit next year.[3]

---

1–From Milton, *Paradise Lost*.

2–WHA replied on 10 Oct. to TSE's letter of 7 Oct.: 'Yes, the new play is finished, but I'm sure you will agree that it is better to withhold publication till after production. Negotiations are going on about that – Maynard Keynes is interested – but when or how it will be, I don't know.'

3–WHA, 10 Oct.: 'The Oxford University Press have asked me to edit The Oxford Book Of Light Verse for them. If you think of anything that no one knows of, but which simply must be in, please let me know. We range from The wife of Bath's Prologue to Frankie and Johnny.' Compare Lindop, *Charles Williams*, 275–6: 'In July [1937], he [Williams] was in touch with W. H. Auden, who proposed to edit an Oxford Book of Light Verse. The two poets met in Oxford on 28 July . . . The book was approved, and they met again to sign the contract on 20 September (Auden received £100; *Light Verse* appeared in 1938). Williams noted:

'Auden looked in today (accompanied by Isherwood, who, I understand, is the Force Behind). He goes to China in January – he and Isherwood . . . to do a similar book to the Iceland volume. I gather that Faber are putting up some money but hardly enough.'

FVM to Spencer Curtis Brown, 29 Dec. 1937 'about an idea which Faber and Eliot and Auden discussed at lunch together as far back, I believe, as the 9th December. The idea was that we should publish, more or less uniform with the FABER BOOK OF MODERN VERSE (which, as you know, is 7/6) an anthology of verse for the young. The purpose would be to give children, and anybody else with an unspoiled mind, a straightforward road

I don't sing very well, but I might accompany you on the guitar.[1]

Let me know, in advance if possible, when there is any chance of meeting.

Yours ever,
[T. S. E.]

P.S. Stephen's play is extremely interesting, and I have put him in touch with Martin Browne, who likes it.

## TO *Barbara Wootton*[2]                                    cc

12 October 1937                          [Faber & Faber Ltd]

Dear Madam,

I have your communication of the 6th instant, 2178.02, inquiring about the qualifications of Mr E. W. F. Tomlin, who had asked permission to mention my name in connexion with his application for tutorial class work.

Whilst I have no first-hand knowledge of Mr Tomlin's abilities as a lecturer and tutor, I have no hesitation in recommending him warmly. I have known him for about seven years, and have been in touch with him throughout his career at Oxford and subsequently. He is one of the most brilliant and promising of the young men with whom I have come in contact during that period, and I am very much interested in his future. He has frequently contributed to the quarterly review, the *Criterion* which I edit. I also regard him as a young man of high character, who would be extremely conscientious in any work that he did, and I feel sure that he would be a valuable acquisition to the University Extension staff.

I should be glad to answer any further detailed questions if requested.

Yours very truly,
[T. S. Eliot]

---

towards modern poetry; creating potential customers for the best modern work. Of course the anthology which Auden took part in for George Bell is along this road, and is very good; but I think I am right in saying that Auden felt that there was plenty of room for the present suggestion too.'

GCF's diary: 'Thurs, 9 Dec. Lunched with Eliot & Auden at Tom's club. First time I've really met Auden – I liked him, & thought him obviously a man of real talent, & not mere surface stuff. We took him back to the office, so that he cld. work in the waiting-room.'

1 – WHA, 10 Oct.: 'I've developed an unhealthy passion myself for writing ballads, which has ruined greater poets than I before now. Do you sing? If so, we might try and earn an honest penny at street corners.'

2 – Barbara Wootton, Baroness Wotton of Abinger, CH (1897–1988), University of London: sociologist and criminologist; President of the British Sociological Association, 1959–64. She was one of the first four life peers appointed under the Life Peerages Act 1958.

13 October 1937                    Faber & Faber Ltd

Dear Valentine,

I was particularly sorry to learn your news from Bonamy, because I remember your father so well[2] – I mean, more clearly & definitely than one usually remembers the relatives of one's friends, meeting them in that way; and I have a strong impression of the respect and regard in which he was evidently held by the villagers of Mendham. You have my warm sympathy.

I hope that you and Georgina will be in town during the Christmas holidays, and that I may see you.

Yours ever,
T. S. Eliot

He was so very nice to me, too!


TO *Harley Granville-Barker*[3]                    cc

13 October 1937                    [Faber & Faber Ltd]

My dear Barker,

I have just got round to answering your letter of July 28th.[4] I wanted to wait until I had finished my two Shakespeare lectures for Edinburgh, and make up my mind whether they would be of any use to you. I have got to deliver them at the end of this month. I don't want to publish them for a year or more, because I think that they will be very much the better for revision from time to time, and thinking still more about the subject. I shall probably, however, send you a copy of them in due course, partly because I have used some sentences of yours in your Romanes lecture as

---

1 – Valentine Dobrée (1894–1974) – née Gladys May Mabel Brooke-Pechell, daughter of Sir Augustus Brooke-Pechell, 7th Baronet – was a well-regarded artist, novelist and short-story writer. In addition to *Your Cuckoo Sings by Kind* (1927), she published one further novel, *The Emperor's Tigers* (1929); a collection of stories, *To Blush Unseen* (1935); and a volume of verse, *This Green Tide* (1965). She married BD in 1913. See further *Valentine Dobrée 1894–1974* (University Gallery Leeds, 2000).
2 – Valentine Dobrée's father had died on 6 Oct.
3 – Harley Granville-Barker (1877– 1946), English actor, director, playwright and critic.
4 – Granville-Barker repeated his invitation to TSE to participate in his planned course at the British Institute of Paris.

starting points for some of my hares, and I shall be very glad of your comments.[1]

But as for their possibility for Paris, that is rather involved with a promise I made some time ago, before you approached me at all, to lecture at some time in Copenhagen. I ought to have gone this autumn, but put it off; now I find that they don't want me after March 15th, and I don't believe I shall be ready to undertake anything before that, so that my visit will probably be a year hence. That would be, if all goes well, just about the time when these two lectures would be ready to take their final form, and I may use them there. In that case they probably would not do for Paris also, which would mean postponing Paris for another year, in order to have time to produce something else that might be worthy. But I will write to you again some time in the New Year, and let you know how my other work is going.

Yours ever,<br>[T. S. Eliot]

## TO *Alexis St-Léger Léger*                                        CC

13 October 1937                              [Faber & Faber Ltd]

*Personnelle*

Cher poète et ami,

Dans le contrat que nous venons de réaffirmer avec vous au sujet d'*Anabase*, se trouve une clause réglant les conditions des royautés dans le cas d'achat de feuilles par une maison américaine. Or, on n'a pas prévu la possibilité d'une édition imprimée en Amérique: ce qui est justement ce que nos amis de la maison Harcourt, Brace & Co. – une des meilleures maisons new-yorkaises – veulent faire; et ce qui indique, de leur part, un

---

1 – Granville-Barker's Romanes Lecture (Taylor Institution, Oxford University, 4 June 1937) was published as *On Poetry in Drama* (1937). TSE remarked of Granville-Barker's lecture, in his Edinburgh lecture 'The Development of Shakespeare's Verse':

'It is related to my subject, it is an admirable essay, and it presents the advantage of offering several statements for me to disagree with.

'In this lecture Sir Harley says: "Some poets may have proved poor dramatists enough" – that is a statement with which I can agree – "but what great dramatist has not been a poet? But, if poets are born, dramatists are made. For playwriting is a craft as well as an art, and a craft must be learnt."'

'I should like to believe that dramatists can be made, without having been born, but I am sure that poets are not merely born but made too, partly by circumstance and partly by hard work.'

intérêt plus sérieux. Il parait qu'ils croient à la possibilité d'une vente plus haute à la longue que l'on n'aurait crue.

Je peux vous donner les détails exactes si cela vous intéresse – c'est un calcul un peu technique – mais peut-être suffit-il de vous dire que la différence remonte à une penny l'exemplaire: au lieu à un penny vous recevrez deux pence pour chaque exemplaire vendu. Un rendement global de 10 pour cent, sera divisé en trois parties: vous recevrez la troisième, moi la troisième, et Faber & Faber la troisième.

Je ne veux pas vous imposer – affairé comme vous êtes – l'ennui de me répondre. Si vous y voyez des obstacles (qui me sont invisibles) je vous prie de me notifier immédiatement, par lettre ou par télégramme; sinon, nous prendrons le silence pour l'assentiment.[1]

Croyez-moi, cher ami, toujours votre admirateur dévoué,[2]

[T. S. Eliot]

---

1–FVM to Donald Brace, 19 Nov. 1937: 'Cap [C. A. Pearce] is . . . quite right to prod me, and would be justified in prodding more violently, about ANABASIS. I never knew such a pair of men as Eliot and St-Léger Léger for magnificent politesse without any crystallization of decision. The present delay occurred because I found that after the last long delay which did result in permission from St-Léger Léger to extend the contract, that Eliot hadn't suggested any terms, and I had a feeling we ought to get Léger's consent to a share of royalty before rather than after publication. I know that a lot of beautiful chess play has been taking place between the two of them, and I will see if we can't boil something out of it by next mail.'

2–*Translation*: Dear poet and friend, / In the contract we have just confirmed with you concerning *Anabase*, there is a clause concerning royalties in case an American publisher should buy up the pages. We did not, however, foresee the possibility of an entirely separate American edition: which is precisely what our colleagues at Harcourt, Brace & Co. – one of the best New York publishing houses – are proposing; it is proof of a more serious interest on their part. Evidently, they believe that higher sales over the longer term is more of a possibility than originally believed.

I can supply you with all the details if you are interested – the calculation is rather technical – but perhaps it is sufficient to say that the difference amounts to a penny per copy: instead of one penny you will receive twopence for each copy sold. The total royalty will be 10%, divided into three parts: you will receive a third, I shall receive a third, and Faber and Faber a third.

Busy as I know you to be, I do not want to burden you with having to reply. If you see any difficulties (I see none) please let me know immediately, by letter or telegram; otherwise, we shall take your silence to mean assent.

Believe me, dear friend, ever your devoted admirer, [T. S. Eliot]

TO *Henry Miller*                                          CC

13 October 1937                    [*The Criterion*]

Dear Mr Miller,

I have read your letter pretty carefully (by the way, you did not date it), and it is a very good letter indeed.[1] But I say that it does not really apply to what I was telling you in my letter. Perhaps the difficulty is partly that I am a publisher as well as a critic, and the two roles are not the same, and I was writing in the former and not the latter capacity. If *Max and the White Phagocytes* was a book and not a collection of various things of different kinds of interest, produced on various occasions, what you are saying would apply perfectly; but you don't really controvert, it seems to me, the simple contention that I made: which is that to launch your work successfully in London we need something which is a whole book. We don't want to publish it simply for the people who know your work already; we want to get a lot more people interested in it, and you cannot do that with a collection like this. Whether you can or cannot produce one connected piece of creative and imaginative writing which could be published in England is a matter for your own aims and your own conscience. I continue to hope that you will; but in the meantime, as *Max and the White Phagocytes* will, I think, only get hold of your present readers, and perhaps a few more, there is not much advantage in producing it in London rather than in Paris. If the book that I want could precede it, that is a very different matter, but I suppose for the moment we must leave it at that.

---

1 – 'Of course I get the point: I am afraid I understand only too well. I am torn always between my understanding of life and of people and my determination to push on regardless of consequences. Your voice is like the voice of the world answering me, and yet I will not believe it, it is not the final word. You must realize, too, with the high intelligence you have, that you have anchored yourself in a contradiction which it is not easy to resolve. In asking something from me on a large scale, as you put it, you are asking ipso facto for something which the English-speaking countries dare not publish . . .

'I ask myself sometimes why I keep pegging away at you. You have never given me very much hope, and yet somehow you always manage to leave the door open . . . I know you have an entirely different attitude towards life than I have and I respect it . . . I think you have been very fair to me, all things considered . . .

'Look, I am not an absolutely crack-brained individual. I know how difficult it is to put my books before the public – most any public . . .

'What is at the bottom of the whole question, let me be so bold as to say, is fear. Nobody wants to assume the responsibility of saying "I believe in this man!" Some will go so far as to say – "this book is a great book," or "this book merits attention", and such like phrases. I am grateful for even this much support – *moral* support, as it is called. But the true moral support lies in deeds.'

I shall be writing to you again soon about your Lawrence paper, which, it is hardly necessary to say, has interested me enormously.

Yours ever sincerely,

[T. S. Eliot]


## TO *Ian Cox*

13 October 1937                    [*The Criterion*]

### PRIVATE AND PERSONAL

Dear Cox,

I have read your poem several times, and am very much interested in it, and as with your other work, I find it extremely difficult to put into words just what I feel about it.[1]

My feelings are, however, very similar to those on reading your prose book. It is exciting and queerly disturbing, just as your prose is. It seems to me that you have the right material for poetry, but have not yet succeeded in making a poem out of it. To say that much is already to say a good deal, because people whose experience fabricates the right material inside them are by no means common. With most of the poetry that I see, not only is the workmanship bad, but the material itself is bogus. Your material and experience is quite real to me. Where I find the poem fails is both in rhythm and in the control of imagery. There is still a lack of musical pattern in the poem, and one does not feel inevitability in the line arrangement. This is one reason why my attention tends to wander from time to time. A poem, like anything else, must be constructed in such a way as to keep the reader's attention: I don't mean to keep it taut the whole time, because that itself is fatiguing and leads to inattention, but, in a poem of any length, by a right alternation of tension and relaxation. And when I say that a poem must keep the attention, I do not necessarily mean that it should be very simple and easy to understand. A poem can be very obscure and yet be extremely exciting to read.

I also feel that the imagery of the dead leaves is something which is very real to you, which is not conscious invention, but a real experience. Yet I find that you seem rather obsessed by it than making use of it, and it reappears from time to time without enough difference in identity to make its reassurance necessary to the reader. The total effect, therefore,

---

1–Cox submitted his poem (title unknown) for C. on 25 Sept.: 'Quite honestly what I should value much more would be any comments you might care to make on it.'

is rather of notes for a poem than of a poem – although they are the very best quality of notes.

I do hope therefore that you will go on and put in a good deal more work on this. I shall be keenly interested to see it again, or anything else that you do.

> With best wishes,
> Yours very sincerely,
> [T. S. Eliot]

## TO *Antonio de Mendonça*

15 October 1937 [Faber & Faber Ltd]

Dear Senhor de Mendonça,

I have discussed with my committee the flattering suggestion of Senhor Ferro that I should myself contribute a short preface to *Salazar*. The opinion was unanimous, that such a preface would not be desirable from any point of view. If I confined myself to remarks on style and translation, I should only be doing what could be as well done anonymously; if I said more, I should be going outside my province. Furthermore, a preface by myself, who am not only intimately connected with this firm, but by no means the obvious person to introduce such a book, might very well give the impression that we felt that the book could not sell on its own merits, and needed any bolstering that we could give. Such is by no means the case, and the majority of people who will buy the book will either know nothing about me, or if they do, will wonder why I rather than a statesman or political theorist should be the introducer.

I have made quite clear to my committee why it is impossible to use the preface by the late Sir Austen Chamberlain. We still think that an introduction by a political celebrity would be desirable, though not essential. The name that most obviously presents itself is that of Mr Winston Churchill, as probably the one Conservative politician out of office whose name carries most weight, and would appeal to the largest public. I make the suggestion that perhaps you might best get in touch with him through the intermediary of your ambassador, and shall be interested to know what you think.

I trust that you received the amended contract, and that Senhor Ferro will be able to let us have both contracts back within a short time. I also hope that I shall be kept informed about the progress of the translation of the Salazar speeches.

Yours very sincerely,<br>
[T. S. Eliot]

## TO *Howard Morris*[1]

TS Morgan

16 October 1937                    *The Criterion*

Dear Howard (sometime known as 'The General'),

This is just to let you know that I am getting around to answering your kind letter of December 31st, 1935,[2] and that maybe some day I will. But what does one do, the world being what it is? If it isnt one thing it's another, and next week I have to go to Edinburgh on business; and I don't often get to New York (in fact I havent been there since 1933, except that in September 1936 I was in the Grand Central Station for two hours, waiting for a train back to Boston, having come from Princeton N.J., from 10 to 12 p.m., and what can you do in New York with just that amount of time to spare except eat oysters and wash them down with Irish whiskey which I did?). At any rate I want to acknowledge your photographs of Howard age 12 and Lewis age 9 (that's a good name, Lewis, there was a poet of that name once, Lewis Morris, but I never read his works,[3] and I think somebody of that name discovered Oregon,[4] which is probably a cousin of yours) and I calculate that they are now 14 and 11 or so. Well well. Have you put on any weight in the last few years? I hope so. I am just as lean as ever, because what has gone on the waist has come off the chest. Anyway heres your health.

So will close ever yours<br>
T. S. E.

1–Howard Morris (b. 1887), from Milwaukee, Wisc., who had been a friend at Milton Academy, MA, and at Harvard, was a successful dealer in investment bonds.
2–Not traced.
3–Sir Lewis Morris (1833–1907): Welsh academic and politician; poet of the Anglo-Welsh school.
4–TSE was probably thinking of Lewis Morris (1671–1746), chief justice of New York and Governor of New Jersey; first lord of the manor of Morrisania in New York (now the Bronx).

TO *William Greenleaf Eliot*                    TS William G. Eliot III

16 October 1937                    *The Criterion*

Dear Cousin Will,

Thank you very much for your letter.¹ It is a satisfaction to me to know that the stick was received, and that it will go down in the right line. The photograph of my father and myself I am very glad to have. It was taken by Henry. The inscription strikes me, as father was at that time only three years older than I am now.

I have been meaning to write and thank Earl for the biography of your father, which I read with great interest.² There was a great deal in it which was new to me, and I was struck by the close resemblance of his life to *his* father's. What astonishingly full and varied achievement, besides which one's own seems trifling. But for that generation life was simpler in many ways.

I was interested by what you say of Paul More, and I hope that it will find its way into some fuller account of him, if Schafer takes advantage of it. More became a very close friend of mine, in his last five years; it is a satisfaction to me to have gone down to Princeton to spend a day with him in his last illness, in September of last year.

Please give my regards to your mother – if she will remember me; and with affectionate wishes to Cousin Minna³ and yourself, I am,

                    Tom S.


TO *Ezra Pound*                    TS Beinecke

16 October 1937                    *The Criterion*

Well podesta you will certainly be surprised to hear from me, but here I am as usual lookin around for some fat of the land to live off of if there was any fat in this land but Sir Jos. Stamp has eat it up. Well, I havent any a priori objection to Leopardi, as they say, except that he is a gloomy cuss and I like cheerful light reading and if anybody presents a essay of the right length 5,000 words (not pages) with your O.K. on it, it will be most respectfully considered.⁴ You should receive prooves of Paideuma

---

1 – Not traced.
2 – Earl Morse Wilbur, *Thomas Lamb Eliot 1841–1936* (Portland, Oregon, 1937).
3 – Minna Charlotte Sessinghaus Eliot (1868–1944).
4 – EP announced on 26 Sept. – in this year of the centenary of the death of the great Italian poet, philosopher and essayist Giacomo Leopardi (1798–1837) – that his friend M. T. Dazzi

before long,[1] and *Kulcher* is coming on as fast as Morley and I and the fulll editorial staff can rewrite it.[2] I can use stuff already printed if it is

---

(who was librarian of the Biblioteca Querini Stampalia, Venice) had written 'a huge and careful essay 166 pages' about Leopardi's ideas on the novel – 'which is too long for you, but the matter might be recast and shortened'. EP explained further that Dazzi was 'a worthy bloke . . . The Leopardi material I think IS Criterion material . . . I forget whether you used translation of stuff already printed. The Leop is in typescript. forget where it is to appear . . .

'The POINT of the Leop apart from Centenary fuss is [that] Leop thought a good deal about writing several novels and didn't but did more or less anticipate what others did later, and that a good deal of his thought still has bearing on the subject NOW. I mean Daz. [is] not doing a simple retrospect but hunting for life in the old Leop yet.'

1 – EP, 'For a New Paideuma', C. 17 (Jan. 1938), 205–13. 'The term Paideuma has been resurrected in our time because of a need. The term Zeitgeist or Time Spirit might be taken to include passive attitudes and aptitudes of an era. The term Paideuma as used in a dozen german volumes has been given the sense of an active element in the era, the complex of ideas which is in a given time germinal, reaching into the next epoch, but conditioning actively all the thought and action of its own time.'

2 – EP had initially proposed a different title for his new book of prose, as he wrote to FVM on 24 Feb. 1937: 'I suggest "The New Learning" as a be'r titl than Guide ter Kulchur. The public mightn't take the Guide idear seereeyus.

'However, if yr/ pubic [*sic*] is rough you kin call it the Guide ter Kulchur, so long as you dont call it the Gide.'

TSE's report on *Guide to Kulchur* – 'The Book of Ezra,' as TSE styled it – 5 June 1937: 'We asked for this and we have got it. It is only a damned kulchered person who will be able to find his way about in this book, but for the perceptive there are a good many plums, and for the judicious who know how to trim the boat with their own intelligence there is a good deal of wisdom. It is quite impossible to reduce this to order: because it is part of Ezra's method to stimulate the reader by assuming that he knows all about the subject already, and instead of finishing off one topic at once to revert to it again and again. You have the effort of finding out what are Ezra's principal themes (e.g. Kung, whom the person seeking guidance will not immediately recognise as Confucius; and a certain Vivaldi, who seems to have been an early Italian composer of some merit, drawn upon by Bach J. S.) and then noting their frequencies and contexts. I suppose somebody ought to check his references to Aristotle (there is surely something wrong about the hearing of a man who spells Xenophon Zenophon) but I admit that there is some rightness in his perception of Aristotle although he puts it as unacceptably as possible. Anyway, he stands up for medieval Latin. I think the only thing to be done is to divide the book into sections with titles. It will help readers to be told to PAUSE at points indicated.'

(EP to FVM, 9 Apr. 1936: 'Possum has been perfectly poisonous about Kung.')

FVM to EP, 31 Aug. 1937: 'While you have been looking forward to the future, Elephant and I has been patiently antiquarian studying Kulchur and dusting up his eyebrows . . . The work we has done on it is just one of those unremembered things which kulchur is. I aint even mentioning to you the variety of ways in which we have improved your notions . . . The text remains to his honourable proboscis as to me, a very considerable and provokative pleasure. So soon now as the thing can be printed I will send proofs.'

Blurb – possibly by TSE, but more probably by FVM – 'We take the liberty of boasting that it was our idea that Mr Pound should write this book – knowing perfectly well that it is impossible to say what kind of book Mr Pound is going to write until he has written it. Mr Pound has fulfilled our demand in his own way, and we are quite satisfied with his way of doing the job.

important enough (which it never is) or if it has appeared in only some inconspicuous magazine like the Cornhill or the *Revista de Bahia*. But I doant give a damn about centenaries, my own is too near at Hand. And incidentally how are you. And why do I not hear from Wyndham. Yrs etc.

TP

review copies were dealt with at the time (abt. 1st oct.)

Please give my regards to your Pa.

## TO *Lilian Morley*[1]

TS Berg

18 October 1937                              *The Criterion*

Dear Mrs Morley,

I have just heard today from Frank of the death of Dr Morley.[2] Although he seemed to me very frail when I saw him, I was very much surprised and shocked to have this news. I cannot help feeling very glad, and very honoured, at having had the privilege of dining with you on your last evening in London. I enjoyed the evening very much, but it now becomes memorable. Dr Morley had always seemed to me a man of very unusual charm, reminding one in a fascinating way of Frank and his other sons, and with a very definite individuality of his own. I hope you will pardon this note of sympathy from one who feels very much a friend of the family, although not often seen; and my expression of hope of seeing you again next year.

Yours very sincerely,<br>T. S. Eliot

---

'This is, as the title implies, Pound's guide to kulchur: a digest of all the wisdom he has acquired about art and life during the course of fifty years. In another fifty years, we shall ask him to write a sequel: meanwhile, this can stand. It is emphatically a book of *wisdom* – a concentration of the "new paideuma" – there is of course information as well – about Confucius, Aristotle and many other subjects. But Pound is not a pedagogue in the style of any of the popular encyclopaedists of the present time: he is writing for young people intelligent enough to realise how badly they have been taught, and who actually want to learn to think for themselves.'

1–Lilian Morley, née Lilian Janet Bird – FVM's mother – of Hayward's Heath, Sussex; married Frank Morley in 1899.

2–Dr Frank Morley (1860–1937) was born at Woodbridge, Suffolk, and became a scholar of King's College, Cambridge, where he was placed in the first class in both parts of the Mathematical Tripos. A fine chess player, he was in the Cambridge University chess team, 1880–4. After a period as mathematics master at Bath College, he went on to teach at Haverford College, Pennsylvania, where he was ultimately Professor of Mathematics. He was for a while President of the American Mathematical Society. His three sons were all Rhodes scholars – Christopher, the novelist; Felix, editor of the *Washington Post*; and FVM.

Please excuse typewriter: a kind of cramp makes it hard for me to express myself with a pen.

## TO *J. S. Barnes*                                                                 CC

18 October 1937                    [*The Criterion*]

Dear Jim,

I am always glad to hear from you, and venture to hope that you may be going to America by way of England, so that I may see you.[1] I should be interested to know your itinerary, if you know it yourself, and I will write again to my brother and tell him that you are finally coming.

I have read your article, as always, with much interest.[2] Whether I agree with your point of view or not is a side issue. If I only printed in the *Criterion* what I absolutely agreed with, I should have to write a large part of it myself, and even that would not be completely satisfactory, because one changes one's own mind from time to time. But it seems to me, again, that you have tried to do too much in the space, and therefore have not done anything quite convincingly. We will agree that the views you maintain are antipathetic to the ordinary Englishman of today, and even though I do not agree with you myself, I will agree with you that the ordinary Englishman is wrong. When he is wrong and stupid there is not much to be done about it, but the small number who are wrong and intelligent need to be dealt with by something more than assumptions. I quite agree with you about the decline of population and the probable decay of the empire, and I do not think we can hope for serious improvement without radical economic changes. This question, however, you do not take up. I cannot accept your view of the necessity for imperialism, because if it is right it seems to imply a future of perpetual armed conflict of more and more horrible kinds, and more widely destructive consequences. But in any case I don't see that your division of the two aspects of the British Empire into Catholic and Protestant is very convincing, especially when you identify the Protestant with the Carthaginian. I agree however about the ruin of Empire by capitalistic aims. My ultimate quarrel with you is simply, as I said, that I think you try to cover too much ground in 15

1 – Barnes wrote on 10 Oct., 'Actually I am off to Libya at the end of the month and to America at the end of the year.'
2 – Article not traced. In his covering letter (10 Oct.), Barnes conceded: 'I should not be surprised if even the Criterion hesitated to accept the enclosed. Yet I think it is a perfectly balanced appraisement of the situation and that it should be known in the public interest.'

pages. There is material enough in this essay for any number of separate papers. One thing which I would like to see, and which you ought to be able to do, is an analysis of the difference between the ideal imperialism and the imperialism of exploitation, which would insist on the importance of the land as a mode of life, and not as something to be exploited and abandoned.

Do let me hear from you again before long.

Yours ever,<br>
[T. S. Eliot]

## TO *Alison Tandy*                                                    TS BL

21 October 1937                          *The Criterion*

Dear Alison,

Some time ago I mentioned in a letter that I was meaning to write a Poem about TWO Cats, named Mungojerrie and Rumpelteazer – and here it is. You may not like it, because those two Cats have turned out to be even Worse than I expected. Anyway, I am looking forward to seeing you and also your Fambly on the anniversary of the Gunpowder Plot, and so will close, your affectionate

Possum[1]

## TO *Marion Dorn*                                                     CC

21 October 1937                          [*The Criterion*]

My dear Marion,

I am so very sorry I cannot accept your invitation, as I have to go to Edinburgh on Monday, and shall be there the whole week.[2] I hope that you will be so kind as to ask me again before the year is out.

What do you mean by saying 'don't I want the table'? Of course I want a table, as I said, a small table tall enough for me to play the typewriter

---

1–Alison replied, in an undated letter: 'Dear Possum, thank you for the poem. I liked it very much. Here is a picture of Mungojerrie and a picture of Rumpelteazer. I think they are funny don't you. LOVE FROM ALISON xxxxxx.'

2–Dorn (141 Swan Court, London) wrote on 20 Oct.: 'Ted and I would be very pleased if you could dine with us next Monday the 25th at 8 o'clock in Chelsea. John [Hayward] is coming.

'Didn't you want the table, after all?'

standing up, light if possible but steady. Where can I get it? I shall be wanting it, in fact, any time after I get back from Edinburgh. Did you at any time suggest a way in which I could get such a table? If so, I am afraid I have forgotten. If you can help, I shall be very grateful.

With love to Ted and yourself,

Yours ever,

[T. S. E.]

## TO *Leonard Woolf*[1]                                                            CC

21 October 1937                            [*The Criterion*]

Dear Leonard,

I don't mind in the least.[2] It is much less villainous than the photograph of me which Faber & Faber have used at the Book Exhibition in the past. Would you mind our using it too, if I can persuade the authorities to make the substitution? Alternatively, might we use it as a portrait of Prinz Hubertus von and zu Loewenstein?[3]

I take it that you have now returned from Rodmell. May I come to tea after I get back from Edinburgh, where I shall be next week? That is, unless you are both too busy with the Sunday Times Book Exhibition, which I myself regard as a waste of time for everybody.

Yours ever,

[Tom]

---

1–Leonard Woolf (1880–1969): writer and publisher; husband of VW. A friend of Lytton Strachey and J. M. Keynes at Cambridge, he played a central part in the Bloomsbury Group. He wrote a number of novels, including *The Village and the Jungle* (1913), and political studies including *Imperialism and Civilization* (1928). As founder-editor, with VW, of the Hogarth Press, he published TSE's *Poems* (1919) and *The Waste Land* (1922). In 1923 he became literary editor of *The Nation & Athenaeum* (after TSE had turned it down), and he remained a firm friend. See *An Autobiography* (2 vols, 1980); *Letters of Leonard Woolf*, ed. Frederic Spotts (1990); Victoria Glendinning, *Leonard Woolf: A Life* (2006).

2–LW sent (20 Oct.) a photograph he had taken of TSE at Monks' House. 'We are having a good many photographs of our authors on the stall at the Sunday Times Book Exhibition. Would you dislike our using this one with HOMAGE TO DRYDEN [*sic*]?'

3–Prince Hubertus zu Loewenstein-Werthelm-Freudenberg (1906–84): historian; exiled from Germany, he was an active anti-Nazi.

LW replied on 22 Oct.: 'I don't mind Faber using the photograph at all, in fact I should be flattered, and it would certainly do very well as Prinz Hubertus.'

TO *George Blake*                                                    CC

22 October 1937                        [Faber & Faber Ltd]

Dear George,

A man named Robert McLellan of Milngavie has sent in two plays
with a view to the Porpoise Press: one is called *Toom Byres* and the other
*King Jamie the Saxt*. As you will infer, they are both in Scots. He says that
they have both been produced by the Curtain Theatre in Glasgow, and
well received – indeed he encloses cuttings. He also reminds us that he
submitted *Toom Byres* by itself last year, and was told that single plays
in book form were not likely to be marketable, and that is why he is now
sending two.[1]

I have just read *Toom Byres*, and it strikes me as a very skilful piece of
stage work indeed. I don't see how it could fail to be a good stage play
when well acted: in fact I envy him his skill in dramatic technique. It is
extremely readable at that, though not in the least highbrow, and full of
good old-fashioned sentiment and humour. The language sounds good
to me, for what a Southron's opinion is worth, and at any rate there is
almost nothing I really need a dictionary for, and the writing is very much
alive.

There is the problem for you: what are we to do about it? Can you
give us any information about McLellan; about his success on the stage,
and the possible sale of the book in Scotland? He seems to me quite good
enough for the Porpoise Press to have to take seriously, and possibly do
something about if it is likely to cover expenses. This may be transient
enthusiasm on my part, and I await the confirmation of your soberer
judgment.

                                        Yours ever,
                                        [Tom]

---

1–Robert McLellan (1907–85), Scottish dramatist and poet; author of plays in Scots
including *Toom Byres* ('Empty Cowsheds') and *Jamie the Saxt*, first produced at the Lyric
Theatre, Glasgow: the work made a star of the actor Duncan Macrae. OBE, 1978. See
*Playing Scotland's Story: Collected Dramatic Works*, ed. Colin Donati (2013).

TO *Dorothy Norman*[1]

25 October 1937                    [*The Criterion*]

Dear Miss Norman,

I have your letter of October 4, and have written to a young man who is a regular contributor of the *Criterion*, and who I think would do the job very well. His name is A. Desmond Hawkins, and his address is School Lane, Radwinter, Essex. So if you are interested in pursuing the matter, will you write to him direct?

As for questionnaires, it seems that there are always a good many people quite willing to answer any questions in print, but I confess myself to having little love for this form of self expression.[2] I really don't think that I should care to answer on dotted lines the kind of question that you suggest. Put in so few words one's views can easily give a false impression, and I think it would take a whole article on each question to express myself satisfactorily. That is merely my personal attitude about questionnaires, which seems to be that of only a small minority. I do feel that I express my views on public affairs from time to time in writing, and if people want to know what they are, they can always find out.

I have not at present anything available for publication anywhere, but I shall keep the *American Quarterly* in mind, and look forward to receiving a copy of the first number.

> With best wishes,
> Yours sincerely,
> [T. S. Eliot]

1 – Dorothy Norman (1905–97): photographer, writer, editor; patron of the arts; liberal activist.
2 – 'I am afraid that you are correct in your decision that it would be necessary for the authors to remain anonymous . . . It might be of great value to find out the political affiliations and sympathies of the outstanding men of letters of today, and to coordinate these answers so that a general picture would be available . . . If it would not be too inconvenient for you, I would appreciate knowing whether you feel that this kind of question could be answered by yourself, for example, and whether you feel it would be of value to the young person evolving to see a group of answers to these questions by outstanding creative men of today . . . ?'

25 October 1937                    [Faber & Faber Ltd]

Dear Canon Tatlow,

I am very much interested in your letter of the 18th instant in connexion with the Friends of Reunion.[2] It is true that this is a subject to which I have not devoted any very particular attention, though I was obliged to allude to it in my formal speech at the Oxford Conference. The outlines of my opinions may perhaps be visible behind the pleasant haze of words in which ideas have to be somewhat screened on such occasions.

My doubts about writing an open letter for you as a four-page leaflet are not only caused by lack of time, but by my belief that I am not quite the right sort of person to speak for such publicity purposes with the simple straightforward conviction necessary in such a message. I believe, of course, that eventual reunion is something which every Christian must desire and pray for, as he must desire and pray for permanent peace throughout the world. I think it is more likely to come about than permanent peace, but I think it will be a slow process, and that it will be aided by gradual social and economic development, of which people are still hardly conscious. I am also afraid of a good many mistakes being made on the way, and

---

1 – The Revd Canon Tissington Tatlow, MA, DD (1876–1957) studied engineering, arts, and subsequently theology at Trinity College, Dublin. He had been general secretary of the Student Christian Movement, 1903–29, and Hon. Chaplain. He was Hon. Director of the Institute of Christian Education at Home and Overseas (which he launched in 1936); Chairman of International Student Service; Hon. Canon of Canterbury Cathedral; and Rector from 1926 to 1937 of All Hallows, Lombard Street – which served as a spiritual centre for students in London. See Tatlow, *The Story of the Student Christian Movement* (1933).

2 – 'As you know, the World Conference on Faith and Order held an extremely important gathering at Edinburgh this summer, which indicates that the leaders of the religious bodies throughout the world, including the eight autonomous Orthodox Churches as well as the Anglican communion and the different elements in it, are moving forward very steadily in the direction of closer rapprochement. An absolutely central position in all this movement is held by the Anglican Church because of its knowledge and contact with the non-episcopal churches . . .

'One great concern of many in England who are interested in this whole question of reunion is how much more rapidly the leaders are moving than the rank and file . . .

'A few years ago an organisation was started in this country, Friends of Reunion, with the churches acting alongside the official World Conference on Faith and Order, in order to try and stir general interest. I was at its Executive Committee recently. They were there discussing the question of how best to extend interest in reunion, and as a result I was asked if I would approach you to see if you would be willing to write an open letter which Friends of Reunion might print as a four-page leaflet, in the hope that it would perhaps reach fresh people.'

Oxford and Edinburgh have made me for the moment more interested in these possibilities than in anything else. I really think you could get someone more suitable than myself at the moment.

With best wishes,<br>
Yours very sincerely,<br>
[T. S. Eliot]

## TO *Ashley Dukes*

25 October 1937                    [Faber & Faber Ltd]

Dear Ashley,

I have got this copy of Fluchère's translation back from John Hayward, and as I am off to Edinburgh and shan't have a chance of looking at it for a week anyway, I am taking the liberty of sending it on to you. The heavy pencil writing is Fluchère's, the light writing is John Hayward's. He wants me to rub out any suggestions that we don't use. I see no reason why you should not put your own suggestions on wherever you like.

The nuisance of having one's work translated into French is that one has to go through the translation, and it takes such a devil of a lot of time.

Anyway I am not pressing you. Let me have it back when you have made all the comments you want to make; and the main thing is whether in principle it seems to you a good enough translation. I should be inclined to say yes.[1]

Yours ever,<br>
[T. S. Eliot]

1 – Dukes replied on 3 Nov. that he thought Fluchère's translation 'generally good enough'.

TO *Geoffrey Faber*                                    TS Valerie Eliot

29 October 1937                    *The Criterion*

*Private & Confidential*

The Chairman,
Faber & Faber Ltd.,
24 Russell Square, W.C.1.

Dear Sir,

### O.H.M.S.

Having just arrived from Edinburgh by the Night Mail, your Agent has the honour to submit the following report.[1]

Acting on instructions received, your Agent saw Professor Sir Donald Tovey.[2] It was not difficult to see Sir Donald Tovey, as your Agent met him wherever he went, and bade good-bye to him affectionately last night at 10.30. Sir Donald Tovey is a good scout, but he talks too much. It is a matter of somewhat more difficulty to see Sir Donald Tovey in private, but your Agent was able to arrange an interview at 9.45 on Thursday morning, by the intervention of his hostess, Mrs Maitland, who happened to have been Sir D. T.'s first pupil and herself an accomplished musician, and who had, as things fell out, already had Sir D. T. and Lady T. to lunch on Tuesday so that your Agent might meet them.

---

1–GCF to TSE, 26 Oct. 1937: 'If you can manage it while you are in Edinburgh, would you try to sound out Donald Tovey as to his willingness to lend a hand with the one-volume Musical Dictionary, which Oscar Thompson is editing for Dodd Mead, and which we are almost certainly going to publish here.

'I stressed the importance (a) of having English (British) music adequately handled (b) of having the name of a first-rate English music critic or musician on the title page as Associate Editor. The point has been well taken, as the enclosed letter from Thompson to Dodd shows. I have discussed names with Lewis and Dodd Mead; and we think that Tovey is the best man to try for. We would run, between us, to £200 editorial fee.

'Actually, not very much work would be needed. Thompson is evidently a first-class editor: the book is his idea; and he is all out to make it as good as he possibly can. The English Associate Editor's main task would be to read the English stuff, and make such comments as he thought necessary . . .

'I enclose also the American Publishers' draft announcement. Note that the book, though planned originally for 1938, can't possibly be published before 1939.

'I write in great haste: so forgive a laconic epistle. Och aye!'

2–Sir Donald Tovey (1875–1940): musicologist, writer on music, composer, conductor, pianist; Reid Professor of Music, University of Edinburgh; noted for his *Essays in Musical Analysis* as well as editions of works by Bach and Beethoven.

Your Agent regrets to report that although Sir D. T. professed himself in entire sympathy with the project, and said that a successor to Grove[1] was badly needed, he could not see his way to undertaking the work required. Your Agent pointed out how little work there was for Sir D. T. to do, and said that the Dictionary in question was not scheduled to appear for two years. Sir D. T. said that it didn't matter how little work there was: the point is that he is tied up with contracts with the O.U.P. which are already three years overdue, that he has enough in that way to keep him busy (apart from his other work, and he does keep himself busy, to say nothing of dining out and appearing everywhere) for the next ten years; and that if his name appeared on any other book in the meantime his name would, in effect, be Mud in Oxford; though those were not the precise words used by Sir D. T., but the words used were equally vigorous.

Finding Sir D. T. obdurate, your Agent pressed him to express an opinion about a possible editor. Sir D. T. opined strongly that Dent of Cambridge[2] was the next best man to himself, and that his only weakness would be that Dent would exaggerate the importance of contemporary music, and somewhat undervalue music between Purcell and the present time. Your Agent, judging from the memorandum submitted to him that this was what was wanted, held his peace. Sir D. T. seemed to think that for this purpose a good music-journalist would do as well as a real musician, though he expressed himself strongly and contemptuously about music-journalists in general and about one in particular whose name I will not give in case this report goes astray or is opened (steam) by any unauthorised person. Said he had never heard of Oscar Thompson,[3] but that that meant nothing and he didnt know much about American music-journalists anyway. At the end of half an hour Sir D. T. excused himself as he had to prepare to go to the Rectorial Inauguration, as also did your Agent. In closing, he wished us luck.

Your Agent also did a little work elsewhere on behalf of the Porpoise Press, because the Scotch don't know what's good for them, but Dover Wilson and I do. To allow myself to drop into the 1st person, I find that of the two, Edimbourg is nearer to being my spiritual home than is Glasgow.

1–A Dictionary of Music and Musicians, ed. George Grove, was first published in four volumes (1879, 1880, 1883, 1889) The second edition, in five volumes, with the proper title Grove's Dictionary of Music and Musicians, was published between 1901 and 1910. The third edition, also in five vols, came out in 1927, and the fourth was to appear in 1940.
2–E. J. Dent (1876–1957), musicologist and composer, Fellow of King's College, Cambridge, was Cambridge Professor of Music, 1926–41.
3–Oscar Thompson (1887–1945), American critic and writer on music; editor of International Cyclopedia of Music and Musicians (1938).

The Scots are extremely hospitable, and I am tired; but had only a sip or two of whisky and a couple of glasses of Scotch Ale; for the rest, wine nothing out of the ordinary, except Kemp Smith's (a good soul Kemp Smith)[1] which was nearer to vinegar than anything I have ever drunk except vinegar. (That N.B. is why this letter is so *Confidential*). Also there is another thing about the Scots which is not usually credited to them, and that is that they are full of blarney, and much more plausible than the Irish at that. Auld Reekie is still reeking. Also I went under the impression that I was to get £20 for two lectures, and I got £20 each. That is another queer thing. I found myself at dinner next to Winifred Peck,[2] whom I thought very nice indeed, but why did she marry Peck?[3] I can't make that out. Because I had to go to a lunch given in honour of Peck and he made a speech. Also have been hobbing & nobbing with Law Lords, who are mysterious; the most mysterious is that one of them is named Lord Salvarsan, and he is a Norwegian at that.[4] Do you know the difference between a Scot and an Orcadian? All the difference in the world, apparently. Lord Normand agreed with me about Lord Nuffield.[5]

1 – Norman Kemp Smith (1872–1958), philosopher; held professorships at various times at Princeton and Edinburgh.
2 – Winifred Peck, née Knox (1882–1962): novelist and biographer; her siblings included E. V. Knox, editor of *Punch*, and the theologian Ronald Knox.
3 – James Wallace Peck (1875–1964), civil servant and local government officer; from 1936, Permanent Secretary to the Scottish Education Department. Knighted in 1938.
4 – Edward Salvesen, Lord Salvesen (1857–1942): Scottish lawyer, politician and judge. His father was Christian Salvesen (1827–1911), Norwegian-born founder of the shipping company. Salvarsan was a drug used to treat syphilis.
5 – Wilfrid Normand – Baron Normand, PC, KC (1884–1962) – Scottish Unionist Party politician (MP, 1931–5) and judge: from 1935 Lord President of the Court of Session; appointed Law Lord in 1947 – wrote to TSE, 10 Nov. 1937: 'I am grateful to you for sending to me your incisive criticism of Oxford's new adventures in education. It was time that someone should speak to whom people who set some store by education and who venerate Oxford will listen. I confidently expect that you will release a flood of censure which has been pent up till now.

'One may hope that Nuffield College will be sterilized by ridicule before it does much actual harm. But it may succeed in imposing itself on the world as the Oxford College, and the pronouncements of the cranks who are to be invited to make it their meeting place may come to be regarded as the voice of Oxford. It is not possible to set limits to the evils which may flow from the headlong acceptance of these benefactions.

'It was to me a very great pleasure to meet you here and to attend one of your lectures. I was prevented from coming more often. I think that you must feel sure that Edinburgh will always delight to welcome you when you choose to return.'

William Morris (1877–1963), successful motor manufacturer and entrepreneur; founder of Morris Motors Ltd, Oxford; designer of the bullnosed Morris and manufacturer of the Morris Minor, 1928; the MG Midget, 1929. Raised to the peerage as Baron Nuffield, 1934.

Ended last evening with J. C. Smith, retired Inspector of Schools,[1] and Sir Robert Greg[2] arguing across me about Tennyson's having called Catullus the tenderest of Roman poets.[3] All agreed that Virgil is the tenderest etc. So will close.

TP

P.S. One does feel a Swell leaving by sleeping car & walking up and down the station platform in a dinner jacket.

## TO *Michael Roberts* CC

1 November 1937            [Faber & Faber Ltd]

Dear Roberts,

Your review arrived during my absence in Edinburgh, and I shall see it in proof.[4] I am glad to hear that Hulme is progressing nicely, and I should be grateful if you could give me a tentative date for the delivery of the manuscript, so that I can satisfy the committee.[5] Remember however that I don't want you to be pressed for time, and we can always postpone the book if that is really necessary. But we should like to bring it out as early as possible next spring.

I had a very pleasant lunch with Sir George and Lady Adam Smith during my week in Edinburgh, and we spoke of you.[6]

Yours ever,<br>[T. S. Eliot]

1 – James Cruickshank Smith was better known as editor of Shakespeare and other texts for Oxford University Press; friend of Robert Frost.

2 – Sir Robert Hyde Greg (1876–1953), diplomat; British Commissioner for the Egyptian Debt; collector of Egyptian antiquities and works of art.

3 – 'Tenderest of Roman poets nineteen-hundred years ago' (Tennyson, 'Frater Ave Atque Vale').

4 – Roberts (29 Sept.) called the book in question, *The Birth of Language* (by R. A. Wilson, Professor of English Language and Literature, University of Saskatchewan) 'interesting but entirely speculative'. On 28 Oct., 'I spent some time on the book on language, and found it, in the end, disappointing. I don't think my review says anything important and I shall be happy if, finding yourself overburdened with reviews for the next Criterion, you throw it in the wastepaper basket.' The review was not printed.

5 – Roberts, 29 Sept.: 'I have written six chapters of Hulme, and I have made notes for the remaining four, but the book will need a lot of re-writing; it is very stodgy at present.' 28 Oct.: 'Hulme is coming along nicely: at one stage there was a complete first draft of the book. He's gone into the melting pot again, and I hope to get a better cast this time. He will certainly be ready for your Spring List.'

6 – Sir George Adam Smith, FBA (1856–1941): Scottish theologian; Principal, University of Aberdeen, 1909–35. His wife was Lilian, née Buchanan (1866–1949). Their sixth child (of seven) was Janet Adam Smith (1905–99), wife of Michael Roberts.

2 November 1937

Dear Mr Eliot (may I drop the Dr?)

We are getting together our little Spring list of pretty pretties, and the boys have deputed me to write the announcement of the Play, which it is rumoured you may have ready some time for publication.[1]

I don't know how you feel about it, but you know it is customary for publishers to consult their favourite authors before committing either of themselves to such important things as catalogue announcements; and I wouldn't like you to feel that we are casual in such consultations.

I need, therefore, to know whether you wish the title to be mentioned, or whether you would prefer the firm to be mysterious.[2]

> I have the honour to be,
> Yours faithfully,
> F. V. Morley.

---

1 – *The Family Reunion*. EMB records (*The Making of T. S. Eliot's Plays*, 90) that on 14 Nov. 1937, 'Eliot came to supper and read new play.' Ashley Dukes to TSE, 18 Dec. 1937: 'Your play is immensely exciting so far, and both Martin and I want to see it on stage as soon as possible . . . We are of course prepared to make a proper contract for the production as soon as the play is finished.'

2 – See FVM's blurb in Faber & Faber Spring Books 1938, 79:

> ### The Family Reunion: A Verse Play
>
> It was not long ago that the wise men of the theatre took the death of poetic drama for an obvious, irretrievable fact. Plays might, certainly, be written in verse; they might even, as a tour de force, be produced upon the stage. But they could be no more than curious revivals of a mode no longer suited to the modern realistic temper.
>
> And now the corpse, over which so many literary tears have been shed, has sat up and confounded all the pundits and pessimists. There is no question about it. The one and only test which the theatre accepts – the box-office test – proves it. *Murder in the Cathedral* plays to capacity wherever it goes, and "the book of the words" is a best-seller.
>
> It is not Mr Eliot alone who has worked this miracle. In Mr Auden, Mr Isherwood, Mr MacNeice, Mr Spender and others a new school of dramatists, relying upon a modern poetic medium, is beginning to make successful contact even with West End audiences. But it is Mr Eliot who, with his poetic dramatisation of Thomas Becket's martyrdom, scored a bullseye in every sizable town in the kingdom. And it is on Mr Eliot's next move that the attention of critics and playgoers is focussed.
>
> *The Family Reunion* – a verse play with a contemporary setting – is that move.

TO *Leonard Woolf*                                    cc

4 November 1937                    [Faber & Faber Ltd]

Dear Leonard,

We discussed at our Book Committee yesterday a suggestion, which was favourably received, for doing a small selection for the Faber Library of the four younger poets who, at least in the public estimation, belong together: Day Lewis, Auden, Spender and MacNeice. The best of Day Lewis's work, of course, is included in what he published with the Hogarth Press, so I am naturally writing to you before mentioning the matter to any of the authors concerned, to know what would be your attitude in principle to a selection of any 25 or 30 pages in the Faber Library format. If you are generally opposed to releasing so much Day Lewis for anthology purposes, we must abandon the scheme, or reorganize it differently; but if you have no objection in principle, we can proceed to discuss terms.[1]

Yours ever,
[Tom]


TO *Lawrence Durrell*                          TS Morris Library

5 November 1937                    *The Criterion*

Dear Durrell,

I have read the *Poet's Horn-Book* with interest, and with some apprehension. Let me say at once that for reasons which have nothing to do with its merit I don't think that the *Criterion* is quite the place for it. It is certainly too long, but that is not the point. I don't like to publish articles in the *Criterion* in which my own work is one of the subjects discussed, and on the other hand, if you cut me out of this article it would not only mutilate the article, but would have in a way as bad an effect as if you left me in. That is to say, it might give the impression that I liked to publish articles which criticized several of my contemporaries but left me alone. So if you publish it, I think it had better appear elsewhere.

Now first considering the article without relation to yourself. It seems to me that you make out an admirable case, if the presuppositions are admitted. But these presuppositions are very great, and it would indeed

---

1–LW replied, 5 Nov.: 'I do not think that I can possibly agree to releasing twenty-five or thirty pages of Day Lewis in the way suggested. We sell him in a Collected Poems edition and it is not a very large volume.'

take a good deal of study to find out exactly what they are, as I am not sure that they are all quite conscious. But one can use as some test of the validity of the premises one's instinctive feeling about the conclusions. It seems to me that there must be something wrong about the presumptions behind a course of reasoning which leads you to dismiss Ezra Pound in a phrase, and to deal with Wyndham Lewis, one of the most living of living writers, in the same category as – and indeed as somewhat less significant than – Aldous Huxley, who is one of the deadest. Surely the fact that Wyndham Lewis writes good English, and the fact that Aldous Huxley does not, are relevant.

Secondly, as for this kind of critical activity as an occupation for yourself, which is the cause of my apprehension. There seems to me to lie a danger for you as a creative writer in the critical work which is particularly concerned with making conscious the activity of your creative mind. If you were concerned with building theories which had nothing to do with, or conflicted with, your creative activity, I should consider this sort of writing a healthy outlet, and also desirable for bringing in a little money. You will doubtless remark that this point of mine is a bit of disingenuous apologetics, to which I will only say that the opinion crossed my mind before it crossed yours. But I have lately had to give a couple of lectures on Shakespeare, without having realized in advance what it was going to let me in for, and I am so alarmed at finding that my interpretation of Shakespeare was really concerned with what I myself am interested in doing in the theatre, that I think I had better leave Shakespeare alone for some time to come. If I am writing a play I think I am better concerned with becoming conscious of how to do it than with becoming conscious of what I am trying to do.

All this could be elaborated at considerable length, but I know that you are quite capable of doing that for yourself, whether you agree with my point or not. I have certain opinions which you will no doubt discount: I think for instance that you and Miller make far too much fuss about D. H. Lawrence; but that really has nothing to do with it. What I want from you for the *Criterion* is something of a creative kind first, and I am going through a copy of the *Black Book*, which I have here, in the hope of suggesting some passage which you will let me use.

Yours ever sincerely,

T. S. Eliot

P.S. I am sending the typescript of the *Poet's Horn-Book* to Curtis Brown, as you instruct me.

# TO *Wilma Gregory*[1]                                        TS Kathy Lee

9 November 1937                    Faber & Faber Ltd

Dear Madam,[2]

I have read your long and interesting letter about your young friend Laurie Lee, and sympathize with your interest and anxieties about him.[3] It is with regret that I must say that his poems do not seem to me, so far,

---

1 – Valerie Grove, 'Fiercely unconventional and rampantly seductive: Lorna Wishart, the muse who made Laurie Lee', *New Statesman*, 30 May 2014: 'While in Spain, he had been taken in by Wilma Gregory, the middle-aged wife of Professor Theodore Gregory of the LSE. A former suffragist, a friend of Rebecca West and a formidable busybody. Wilma virtually adopted him, astonished by his gifts for music, poetry and drawing. It was Wilma (never publicly acknowledged by Laurie) who engineered the rescue of Laurie and herself by a British warship, when they were stranded on the Andalusian coast as the Spanish civil war broke out. Back in England, Wilma rented a comfortless cottage in the Berkshire woodland so that Laurie could study art at Reading. After his first year, when his tutors declared him to be "the English Picasso", Wilma enrolled him in the École des Beaux Arts in Montpellier. But first she enabled him to go to Cornwall, where he encountered the woman she described as "the most beautiful, aggressive and dangerous of his mistresses".'

2 – This letter was first published in Valerie Grove, *The Life and Loves of Laurie Lee* (2014).

3 – Mrs Gregory wrote on 25 Oct. 1937: 'Dear Sirs / I am venturing to send you with this letter some of the poems of my young friend Laurie Lee, who is much too lazy and too devoid of ambition to bother to send them to a publisher himself . . .

'Consequently, with a total lack of principle and of ordinary decent scruples, I have stolen as many of his poems as I can lay hands on (Laurie Lee being away from Montpellier for a few days) . . . And there are probably other poems, very likely better ones, which I have not been able to find among the loose leaves and scraps of paper, thrust into notebooks and left lying about his room, which I have unlawfully ransacked . . .

'I hold strongly that a poet has no right to keep his work to himself, nor even for a privileged circle of friends.

'I think his work is remarkable.'

She went on to outline the early life of Lee (b. June 1914), in a labourer's cottage in the tiny village of Slad, Gloucestershire, where he went to the local school and took art classes and violin lessons. Then he worked for a while in an accountant's office, which he detested. But at the age of seventeen or eighteen, he began to have epileptic seizures. 'I think myself that they may have been caused by semi-starvation, and by a very great emotional strain and a series of emotional shocks,' said Gregory. Later still, he worked for a while as a 'navvy' in London. However, for his twenty-first birthday, a member of the family gifted him some money – enough for him to travel to Spain, where he spent several months tramping, sleeping rough and earning a pittance by playing his fiddle. By Jan. 1936, when Gregory met him, he was working in a hotel in Andalucia, washing dishes and cleaning fish, and in the evenings playing for the guests. In Aug. 1936 he was among those evacuated from Spain by a British destroyer.

Back in the UK, he passed several months as an (irregular) half-time student at the art school in Reading, where his tutors were impressed by his artistic talent. There was a hope that he would go to the Ecole des Beaux Arts in Montpellier, but this he declined to do. He preferred his humble, vagrant existence – his material needs were nearly non-existent – though his well-being was hampered by his 'malady' (he did not even always have enough money to buy the drugs he needed to manage the epilepsy).

remarkable enough to justify our undertaking their publication. This is, however, only the opinion of one man, who often feels that excessive reading of manuscript verse may have dulled his sensibility, and I therefore advise you to make a fresh attempt elsewhere. I suggest your showing the poems to Mr Richard Church of Messrs J. M. Dent & Sons, Aldine House, Bedford Street, W.C.2. I shall not meanwhile mention to Mr Church the fact that I have seen these poems.[1]

Yours very truly,
T. S. Eliot

## TO *Christopher Dawson*

CC

12 November 1937                    [Faber & Faber Ltd]

My dear Dawson,

Thank you for your letter, the tenor of which does not surprise me.[2] I quite agree that there are too many books, and that most books are

---

He was well liked 'by people of all types, classes, and nations' who encountered him; but in Gregory's passionate opinion he needed above all else to fulfil 'his most important gift' for poetry. She earnestly implored F&F to read the poems enclosed – 'not just one or two, but the whole lot'.

'I have a hope that the excitement of publication (if you, or failing you, some other publisher, decides to publish his poems) will reconcile him to remaining outside Spain. All this last year it has been very difficult to dissuade him from returning there as a volunteer, and now there is a renewed and very ardent desire to go there, and I am afraid he may manage to get across the frontier somehow.'

1 – Laurie Lee himself wrote to TSE in Nov. 1937, from the Hotel Regina, Perpignan, France:

'Dear Sir, / Some weeks ago you may remember Mrs W. Gregory sent a very odd assortment of my poems to you for consideration. I knew nothing about it, but that doesn't matter. Judging by the letter she received, however, your reactions were most unfavourable. Having a great respect and an even greater admiration for your powers of poetical criticism such a condemnation should by rights have done me considerable damage. Yet I possess a resillient [*sic*] vanity & it leads me to believe you could only have looked at a very few verses and those by unfortunate chance the worst and most inarticulate. Whilst thanking you very sincerely for having taken even that trouble I hope one day to be able to confound your opinion.'

2 – Dawson wrote, 9 Nov. (in response to a letter from TSE of 4 Nov. 1937, available on www.tseliot.com): 'As to Xty & Sex, I wish it had been possible to keep it in print, as I think it is quite useful: indeed, I wish it could be sold as a 6d pamphlet. The alternative of expanding it seems to me less satisfactory. Of course if I was free to devote plenty of time to it, a book on the subject would be well worth while, but unfortunately I have not the time. But if one simply padded it out to make an excuse for a 3/o book, I think it would be fatal. There is too much of that kind of thing. In fact I think that the habit of dilating 6 pennyworth of material to a fill a shillingsworth of paper & letterpress is destroying religious literature in this country.'

too long. The tendency for books to say what they have to say at much greater length than necessary no doubt has something to do with the deterioration of the reading public into mere ruminants, who can only nourish themselves by a great deal of grass, and reject more concentrated food. The more condensed the book, the more mental effort is required on the part of the reader. But we as publishers have to take things as we find them, and when there is something to be said that everyone ought to listen to, there is all the more reason for considering in what form the public will take it. I therefore beg you, in the interests of society, to reconsider your verdict. To republish your pamphlet at sixpence instead of a shilling is ideal, but an unattainable ideal, because we should merely lose money on it. I do beg you to put your mind on the problem, and see whether a longer book can be provided, either by expansion, development, or accretion.

I hope you will be up, and able to see me, next week or the week after. I have much more time free the second week, but if next week, Friday is available, or Tuesday afternoon or evening.

Yours ever,
[T. S. Eliot]

## TO *Hope Mirrlees*                                          cc

15 November 1937                    [Faber & Faber Ltd]

Dear Hope,

Thank you for your letter. I am afraid I had to give up *The Elephant never forgets*.[1] I tried to read it yesterday afternoon, but I saw it was going to be more of an agony of nightmare than I could bear, and I got the suspicion in my head that it was something more of a set piece, a too deliberate torture, than the previous books. It may be very good, but it is too disturbing.

---

1–HM wrote on 14 Nov., of Ethel Lina White's *The Elephant Never Forgets* (1937): 'Many thanks for letting me know about Ethel Lina. As a matter of fact mother got it for me when I was at Shamley. Personally, I liked it the least of all her books. I do wonder what you thought of it.

'At the moment I am reading Agatha's latest. I always think one can't say whether or not a detective book is *good* until it is finished. But it is certainly very *enjoyable*.'

I should love to come to dinner again soon, but this week is very full, and I have got to go away for the weekend. Is there any evening of the week of Monday 29th that would suit you?

Yours ever,<br>
[Tom]

## TO *George Blake* CC

15 November 1937 [Faber & Faber Ltd]

Dear George,

Thank you for your letter of the 14th.[1] That is somewhat as I expected. The plays are not really suitable to amateur productions, for the reasons you suggest. I don't know how a play in Scots would go in London, and it might be very difficult to cast it with good actors who could speak the lines properly, but I believe that *Toom Byres* is better than any contemporary play in London at present.[2] It seems pitiable that nothing can be done with this stuff. I should very much like you to read it for yourself before it is returned to him. May I send the plays on to you, at the same time writing to McLellan to explain why their publication is not practicable, but saying that I wanted you to know something about them? You could then return them to him with a word of approval or in silence if you prefer.

Yours ever,<br>
[Tom]

1–Blake had met McLellan and wished to report his impressions. 'He is a fine, quietly decisive, red-haired lad with good ideas and, I should think, a future. As to the plays, I gather they were well-received by good audiences when produced in Glasgow. The producing company, however, lost money on both, and that is against their revival by other groups. I also understand from the dramatic enthusiasts that their demand for elaborate costume – especially JAMIE THE SAXT – almost completely rules them out from the consideration of community players, and that they have had, in fact, nothing but the original production by the Masque Theatre.

'So it comes to be a question of their reading merits, and my fear would be that the two factors, play *plus* Scots, do not make a hopeful publishing proposition. I could only suggest that you intimate your interest to the young man and hold out a hope of publishing him when his market can be more clearly discerned.'

2–Robert MacLennan, *Toom Byres: A comedy of the Scottish border in three acts* (first performed in 1936).

TO *Alison Tandy*                                            TS BL

15 November 1937                    *The Criterion*

Dear Alison,

   I have written a number of Poems about Cats, and I thought it was time
to write a Poem about a Very Old Cat; because he has only forty or fifty
years more to live, and I wanted him to have the glory of a Poem about
him now while he could appreciate it. Why is he called Old Deuteronomy?
Well, you see, that is Greek, and it means 'second name' – at least, it
means as near that as makes no difference, though perhaps not quite that;
and you see when he was young he had quite an ordinary name, but when
he became quite old – I mean about forty-eight or nine[1] – the people
thought that he deserved a Distinction, or a grander name, so that is the
name they gave him, so will close.[2]

                              Your fexnite
                              Possum


TO *Henri Fluchère*                                          CC

16 November 1937                    [Faber & Faber Ltd]

Dear M. Fluchère,

   I must apologize for the long delay in returning the typescript of your
translation of *Murder in the Cathedral*, but I have been extremely busy,
and it is only within the last few days that I have been able to go through
it and consider the criticisms made by one or two of my friends.[3] You
will find that I have noted on the left-hand blank pages the criticisms of
which I feel absolutely sure, and the answers to your own queries. The
suggestions in pencil among the text itself are more tentative, but I have
retained all those with which I am inclined to agree. There are one or two
places in the chorus parts where I think you should make a new start.
I am particularly uncomfortable about the translation of the *Dies Irae*
chorus in Part 2, which I think should attempt at the beginning and end to

---

1 – TSE's own age.
2 – TSE enclosed 'Old Deuteronomy', together with what he called 'a minor OPUSS': 'The
Practical Cat'.
3 – Fluchère had sent his translation on 4 Aug.: 'My ambition has been: to be faithful to the
text, in so far as the rendering with an equivalent is possible – then, to preserve a rhythm all
through, at the cost of slight deviations of meaning.' He wrote again on 7 Nov. to ask after
his MS at TSE's 'earliest convenience': Jean Paulhan hoped to place it with *Nouvelle Revue
Française* or *Mesures*. In addition, Fluchère wanted to send the corrected text to Jacques
Copeau.

preserve the rhythm of the Latin sequence, in order to fit into the familiar tune. That is what I endeavoured to do in English.

It has been interesting to see where occasionally my phrases and syntax have an ambiguity which I had not suspected. You in one or two places, and my English friends also, have taken me to mean something quite different from what I intended. This will show you that my sentence constructions are sometimes as unusual to an English ear as to a French ear. On the whole I like your translation very much indeed, and with the alterations recommended and suggested, Mr Ashley Dukes and I think that it will do very well.

With best wishes,<br>
I am,<br>
Yours very sincerely,<br>
[T. S. Eliot]

TO *John Hayward*                                                    TS King's

22 November [1937]                    *The Criterion*
                                      au Portail Imperial: ce 19 novembre[1]

Dear John,

This matter of the en-tête[2] is very difficult. Your suggestion is admirable in itself but I wonder . . . I mean . . . perhaps there is enough Vapulation of the Coot in the text, and I should like the Title to suggest collaboration between the Coot and others . . . Besides, the possum should not be too forward . . . perhaps some such title as originally proposed by me
NOCTES BINANIANAE

Wherein are contained such Voluntary & Satyrical Compliments and Verses as were lately Exchang'd between some of the *Choicest Wits* and *Most Profound Deipnosophists* of the AGE

(Ornament or Emblem of a Coot,
or other Absurd Bird), or Figure
in which is tapaster'd an Elephant,
upon whose back capers a Whale, upon
whose head a Coot with wings extended,
holding in his mouth a *stockfish*, and
above all a *Vesperal Spider* suspended,
which spinneth his Web about all.

1 – Typed on *Criterion* headed notepaper, with TS addition of place and date.
2 – *en-tête* (Fr.): title/heading.

Imprinted for Rchd. de la Mare, His Maiestie's Printer, dwelling in Paules Churchyard, at the South west doore of *Saint Paules* Church, and are there to be had.

But I am mixing the periods. Anyway, what about the capital point?

TP.

<FROGNAL'S HELICON?

A PARADISE OF . . . .

On my way back this afternoon from St Stephen's Hospital in the *Fulham Road*, where I had been to visit Mr W. L. Janes, who there lies sick,[1] I happened to pass yr. doore.>

## TO *Ezra Pound*                                                    TS Beinecke

22 novembre 1937                    *The Criterion*

O Ez, fiorello mio,[2] La Guardia qui ne se rend pas,[3] it is nice to get that lil point cleared up wich has been worrying us; because I think, the more lil points, political, personal, economical, or what not that the Podesta gets cleared up, well, the more time he will have to kill lyin around and writing poetry.[4] Yet it aint so hellesklar and durchsichtig as all not that,

---

1 – Janes had turned eighty-three on 11 July this year.

2 – *fiorello mio* (Ital.): 'my flower'.

3 – '*La Guardia qui ne se rend pas*' (Fr.): 'The Guard who does not give up.'

4 – For reasons known only to himself, EP in a letter of 17 Nov. chose to hark back to an innocuous occasion dating from nearly three years earlier, in Jan. 1935, when TSE had kindly taken Olga Rudge (1895–1996) out to lunch in London. TSE had reported to EP, 17 Jan. 1935: 'Brother, the trouble with Miss Rudge is not only that she dont eat much but that she dont drink ANYTHING. Now one can understand that in Alida Monro, but I hope Miss Rudge hasnt got some secret sorrow; dont she drink with anybody or just wont she drink with me? Nevertheless, I hope she was not too bored.' Rudge was an American-born violinist and musicologist; brought up in London and Paris. In 1936 she began to champion the work of Vivaldi, having unearthed in Turin twenty-five volumes of his music (309 concertos for violin and orchestra): she formed a Vivaldi Society in Venice and published a comprehensive catalogue (1939). See obituaries of Rudge in *Times*, 21 Mar. 1996; *Guardian*, 20 Mar. 1996; and Anne Conover, *Olga Rudge and Ezra Pound: 'What Thou Lovest Well . . .'* (2001).

EP worried at the memory in his letter to TSE, 17 Nov. 1937: 'As bearin on the elucidation of somfink long wot has puzzle me/ a phrase in one of yr/ Ezsteemed letters of yester season or that before it/

'Sez you "Don't the gal ever DRINK anyfink?" waal thet I cdn't make out, she bein tactful on most occasions.

'So tother day I sez to the gal (she was bein modest and I sez waaaal sfar as I know no one aint never said nothing against you Ezscrpt th Possum an all he sez wuz "Dont th gal never DRINK anything").

'an she sez "But I had just had a large SPESHUL beer". Wot sez I sez I? (the term special worrit me)

no not yet.[1] What I mean is this, When that young lady met me at that highly respectable bourgeois bouge[2] in Soho for what I had laid out to be a rather expensive lunch, she was not only sober as a Judge, but a great deal sobrer than most english judges seem to be if you estimate them by their decisions, if you take my meaning, for instance that recent notorious case of that poor bloke and that other one more recent what I mustnt mention. Sober as a Stone, she was, unless she was exercisin more than superhuman control, which I dont believe women can do unless they are very practised drunkards, which I dont believe this young lady is, not if I am any judge of character. Well then what about it? You may say, without thinkin, Imagination; but anyone that can imagine that they were at Fenchurch St Station drinkin special beer with a friend is either loony or a genius, and I dont believe that her genius lies in the direction of that peculiar kind of Imagination, not that kind. Well then, she probly was at Fenchurch St drinking special beer with a friend; it would certainly not occur to me (and I am considered or used to be once, an Imaginative kind of card) either to think of drinkin beer with a friend or with a enemy or neither at Fenchurch St station or to do it; there is so many other possibilities would occur to me first, either in action or in imagination. Very well then. Either she had only a sip or so of this special beer; or else it wasnt so very special; and if she is interested in special beer I could show her willingly some special beer that would put her in a very different state from cool and cultured animation long before she got the distance between Fenchurch St station and that bouge in SohO. Well now to get to action, Action I say and I mean it. What does she want? Does she want a real English meal? If so there is a hotel in Wisbech I can think of, or there is fish and chips in the Waterloo Road, and there is Liverpool St station for Boiled turbot, Im only anxious to please; so you do what you can to

---

'Yes she sez; I was seein some frien's off at Fenchurch St Station an he had some special beer that etc/etc/

"so when I got to the table [with TSE] she sez I didn't want any more. Fenchurch St she says, vurry English, (Dickens) sez she is payrenthesis.

'and then she sez it wuz embarrassin "I answerd wiffout LOOKIN' at the MeNU, an sed 'Oh I like ENGLISH food.'"

'She bein impressed wiff the honour of the occasion and then looked down at the MeNU an see Ezcargot, and nothing but curlycues an SNAILS, and all supposed (by her) to have been such EElite consideration fer her Parisian antecedence, and she have so putt her fut in it that she never caught up.

'Wot sez I you git axd to a luncheon and go fill up on beer and bloaters/ no sez she THEY had lunch, I hadda sanwich.'

1 – *hellesklar* . . . *durchsichtig* (Ger.): 'clear . . . straightforward'.

2 – *bouge* (Fr.): 'hole'.

put things right, damb it I am only anxious to please. And what about that too, it is not imaginable that anyone especially a young lady should have any fear of Old Possum, what is the timidest of all lil beasts, and I dont know what to think of it all, so will close[1]

TP

WHAT O! EPITAFF.
O wot avails the noble race,
   O wot the form divine,
The statesman's gift, the artist's grace???
   Ole Possum, all were thine.[2]

1 – EP responded to this letter on 25 Nov.: 'Waaal Possum yew old Wombat

'The LADY don't want nuffin but to clear "er name ov the orful shayme ov TEETOTALISM. She warnt pleadin' inebriety or that orful carefullness due to being onthe inebrititious VERGE/

'I jess raises the pint or olbow to plague her a bit fer LOOKIN so SEErEEyus; and I sez "dont yew ever drink nuffink" and she then after all the interval Ezplanes/

'And all them graces and hesitations of yourn avails fer to purrjewes an effek of charm (fatal woid) registered by the said interlocutress of yr/ correspondent/

'And as it is the age of memoirs/ vide Wyndham re/ Joyce and Mr T.S.E. in Paree/ etc. I jes registers the scene of two so correct Americans muchooly inhaling with utmost constraint in the Bostonian fear that either has not been efficiently deferetial, one in offering a snail and the other in absently unfeeling the import of the offer and gruffly palpitatin "beer and taters".'

2 – Walter Savage Landor, 'Rose Aylmer': 'Oh what avails the sceptred race, / Ah what the form divine! / What every virtue, every grace! / Rose Aylmer, all were thine!' (Ricks/McCue).

EP, 25 Nov.: 'Wall as to the Hepptaft/ You sure IZ accomplished; as I never did, and never do an never shall denye.'

[?22 November 1937]                    [Faber & Faber Ltd]

[Re Enid Starkie, *Rimbaud*][1]

Well, allright, but one can't be expected to comb through a ms which has already been accepted, looking for things that the author ought to have told us. It would have been natural (exc. that she is Irish) for her to have explained at beginning that the little book was only notes to the big one. The public won't know that.

*If* she will explain, without hysteria, what she has written 3pp *without* doing: just *why* the little book isn't going to affect our sales, I think we might proceed as before, & do the best we can.

[T. S. Eliot]


TO *Theodore Spencer*                    TS Harvard Archives

23 November 1937                    *The Criterion*

Dear Ted,

Thank you very much for your letter in connexion with the Norton professorship. I am very much of the opinion that if Herbert Read should be asked to come, he should be invited to lecture on poetry or literature rather than on fine arts. He has had to do a great deal of writing about art in the last few years, I think rather more than he would have done of his

---

1–Enid Starkie's *Arthur Rimbaud* was brought before the Faber Book Committee on 28 Aug. 1937. There is no trace in the Faber Archive of a book report, but the record has it that TSE offered 'remarks'. The decision was to accept the book.

GCF had a strong predeliction for the book, writing to Richard de la Mare, 23 Aug. 1937: 'Enclosed explains itself. This is TSE's meat, & if he is available will you give it to him with E. S.'s typescript, which I am asking her to send direct to you.

'I feel strongly that we should do this book, in spite of Gascoigne. Enid Starkie is a first-rater, & her Baudelaire was well spoken of – tho' I never read it myself.

'If TSE is not available, use your own judgment of what's best to do.'

Starkie herself wrote to TSE, 24 Aug. 1937: 'I hear that it is you who are to read my T.S. of Rimbaud. I am sorry that you, particularly should be reading it in this rough state. I began writing the book on the 1st of Aug. and I finished it this morning at 3 A.M. Of course I had planned the book first and have been thinking about it for 4 years, but the actual writing has taken me three weeks. I have next term off and I intend to spend the next four months rewriting and polishing it. You are having it now with all its roughness and all its repetitions. Now that it is finished I see many changes that I wish to make.

'It is only the urgency of wishing to be certain of publication as soon as possible that drives me to allow any one to see it in this state. I have a rival, David Gascoigne [*sic*], writing a book on Rimbaud, and it is to get finished before him, that I applied for sabbatical leave.

own choice, because there is more of a market for art criticism than for literary criticism. Furthermore, he is pretty well soaked in the art business,

---

'If I were not so exhausted, and were not leaving for Ireland this afternoon, I would rewrite certain pages which I think atrocious, but they will now have to remain.'

But see too GCF to Enid Starkie (Rome), 16 Nov. 1937: 'Eliot has just seen an announcement of your *Rimbaud in Abyssinia* and is greatly disturbed by it. He says that, in his opinion, it cannot but seriously affect the sales of the book which we undertook to publish; and that, had he known of it, when you offered us your bigger book, he would have advised us against the publication of the latter.

'I have this morning, read through all our correspondence. There is not a word in it about *Rimbaud in Abyssinia*, before your letter of October the 3rd. Without doubt this was an entirely unintentional mistake on your part; the reference in your letter makes it clear that you thought we knew all about it. But in fact we knew nothing at all about it when we made our offer; and it is, on any view, a very material fact.

'You will realise that this puts you – and us – into a most awkward position. And I do not see how we can decide what to do, until we have had an opportunity of talking the whole thing over with you, when you come back to London – which is, I believe, to be early next month?'

GCF to Starkie, 23 Nov. 1937: 'Thank you for your long and candid letter.

'Let me assure you in the first place that I did not for a moment intend to accuse you of intentionally keeping us in the dark about the little book. Indeed, I hoped I had made that clear in my last letter . . .

'We accept the situation as it stands, and will publish the book on the terms previously agreed. But may I add that I have *not* in any way at all been attempting to exploit the situation, with the object of obtaining the book on better terms. We find it difficult to think that the Oxford book will have no adverse effect upon the sales of the big book. If it doesn't do so – and, of course, there is not likely to be any means of ascertaining whether it has done so or not – it will run contrary to all our experience. Unfortunately, not a few people begin and end their meals with the hors d'oeuvres! . . .

'I am very sorry that this fly should have got into the ointment, but I hope that when the book comes out it will justify both your attitude and our acquiesence in it.'

The blurb for *Arthur Rimbaud* – published in an edition of 1,000 copies – is almost certainly by TSE:

'This is the first comprehensive book in English – and the fullest biography in any language – about a man who is interesting for two reasons. He was one of the most original and important poets of the nineteenth century, who has influenced the poetry in every European language; and he had one of the strangest and most romantic careers in the whole of history.

'Miss Starkie – whose previous book on Baudelaire is necessary to any student of that poet – has aimed primarily at a biography. But Rimbaud's life is essential to Rimbaud's poems: and anyone who reads this book will feel that he never before understood Rimbaud's poetry. On the other hand, Miss Starkie gives the fullest possible account of Rimbaud's amazing career during the years after he had abandoned the practice of verse, and of his extraordinary life in the Levant and in Abyssinia as trader and explorer – a career at once picaresque, at times grotesque, and deeply tragic. In writing this book she has been fortunate in gaining access to much hitherto unused material.

'Miss Starkie's book makes absorbing reading, even for those who want only romantic biography; and it will also be the standard life of the poet.'

Enid Starkie to GCF, 7 July 1945: 'I think it is my best book.'

See further Joanna Richardson, 'The One and Only Enid', *Sunday Times*, 19 Aug. 1973; and Richardson, *Enid Starkie: A Biography* (1973).

being editor of the *Burlington Magazine*. I think it would be good for him, and I think he would welcome the opportunity of taking the time to produce something fresh in the way of literary criticism, and I think he would certainly give you something very interesting.

There is another thing you could do for me, if it came handy, and were not too much trouble. There is a young Italian who is spending a year, perhaps two, at Harvard, and is specialising in political economy. His name is Camillo Caetani.[1] He is a very distant relative of mine, but of course has a good many closer relatives in Boston, because his mother was a Chapin from Springfield. He is also related through his father to Ronald Lindsay, our Ambassador in Washington. He ought therefore to have plenty of introductions, but his family do not appear to know anyone on the faculty, and the economists, unless they are different from economists elsewhere, must be a pretty dull lot. It would be good of you if you could get hold of him sometime, and possibly have him meet one or two selected undergraduates. He is a very nice youth, and is a sort of heir presumptive of the Duke of Sermoneta. He is living at Dunster House.

Ever yours,
Tom


TO *Ian Cox*                                                    TS BBC

30 November 1937                    *The Criterion*

Dear Cox,

Thank you for your letter of the 27th, reference PP/IC.[2] Very well: I agree with you that it would be best to confine yourselves to cats for the

---

1–Camillo Caetani: son of the American-born Marguerite Caetani, née Chapin (1880–1963) – half-sister to Mrs Katherine Biddle, and a cousin of TSE – who was married in 1911 to the composer Roffredo Caetani, 17th Duke of Sermoneta and Prince di Bassiano.

2–'Geoffrey and I have been looking over the material available for the reading on Christmas Day, and we find that there is enough for two programmes. We would like to suggest, therefore, that the programme we discussed last week should be confined to cats, and I will be sending you our suggestions for the poems to be included as soon as they are typed out next week.

'Meanwhile, could I trouble you to peruse the enclosed programme note which I was thinking of sending to "The Radio Times". If you could possibly let me know what you think about this as soon as possible it would be a help, because they make up that paper a very long time in advance.

'I feel reluctant to trouble you further in this matter now, but since we have all the material here I should like to ask if you could permit us to make up a second programme on the lines of the first, to be broadcast at a later date.' (CC BBC)

The Programme note read:

Christmas programme, but I think it would be best to wait until you find out how that programme is received before fixing any further reading. I must say, in parenthesis, that why Geoffrey should want to take the time to come up to town on Christmas Day to read poems about cats, passes my comprehension! However, if he is going to do so, and if I cannot prevent him from wasting his time, I suggest that the heading had better be PRACTICAL CATS, as that term is much more comprehensive than JELLICLE.

I wait for Geoffrey's selection, which of course has to have my approval. I must also demand a fee from the BBC for the reading, and I am likely to ask more for unpublished poems than I should for poems previously published. So it is a question whether the BBC will agree. This is a matter of principle: I don't want the money myself, and I should like it to be added to Geoffrey's fee for reading, if that can be done without his having previous knowledge of it. Another point upon which I insist is that the copyright remains in my hands, and that the BBC shall not have the right

---

JELLICLE CATS
For some time past Mr Eliot has been amusing and instructing the offspring of some of his friends in verse on the subject of cats.

These poems are not of the kind that have been usually associated with Mr Eliot's name – they have not yet been published. With his permission, we have arranged some of them into a programme, and they will be read by Geoffrey Tandy.

The idea for such a programme had first been raised nearly a year earlier, on 9 Dec. 1936, in a letter from Ian Cox (BBC Manchester) to TSE: 'I was very happy when the question of your broadcasting, pseudonymously, some of your Nonsense Rhymes arose in the course of our conversation on Victoria station the other day, and have taken the liberty of making the suggestion to the Children's Hour Organiser in London. I now hear that he is very interested but, naturally, cannot make a definite decision without first seeing them.

'If you would like to do this, I wonder if I could trouble you to let me have copies of such as you would like to broadcast . . . Perhaps you would like to suggest a pseudonym at the same time as you send these.'

(Cox recorded in a memo, Fri. 19 Nov. 1937, a note of his conversation with TSE on the subject of 'his unpublished Children's verses': 'I met Mr Eliot and Mr Geoffrey Tandy and we discussed more materially a question we have reviewed several times before – the possibility of a broadcast reading of Mr Eliot's unpublished Children's verses about cats and dogs.

'Eliot said that he couldn't possibly do anything before next May, but if Tandy liked to do the reading he would have no objection to our making a programme up and broadcasting it on Christmas Day. He only stipulated that he would reserve copyright and wished to go over the script for possible emendations.

'Eliot said he would be glad to come to a rehearsal if one could be arranged at a suitable time.

'Accordingly Tandy and I are going ahead preparing a reading for December 25th, 2.30–2.45 p.m. – Tandy collecting the various original poems.')

to print the poems in *The Listener* or anywhere else, or to prevent me from doing anything with them that I like.[1]

With best wishes,
Yours sincerely,
T. S. Eliot

## FROM *Charles Williams*[2] TS Valerie Eliot

30 November 1937

> I am not one of those who squabble for a penny,
> I am as little conceited as any, and always on guard
> against discontent; praise of others is my second nature.
> But I must say I do think it hard
> at my own play[3] on my own day
> to have an elderlyish woman meet me afterwards
> and look silently at me for a great while –
> and I? I looked back – for minutes – with an inquiring smile.
> Presently she said: 'Do you know Mr Eliot?'
> I said: 'Yes'.
> More minutes went by; we still gazed –
> I gravely now, partly out of respect to Mr Eliot,
> partly in my own patience, partly to play up to her.
> Presently she said: 'Do you know *Murder in the Cathedral*?'
> I said: 'Yes'.
> Time slipped into a crack and slept and came back.

---

So successful was the broadcast that the BBC repeated it in 1938. It was followed by *Cats Mostly Practical*, 25 June 1938, and by *Pollicles and Jellicles: Tales of Cats and Dogs in Verse*, 7 Oct. 1939, which the *Radio Times* trailed: 'Before Christmas Day 1937, when the first selection was broadcast, nobody would have associated a set of cheery, yet at the same time profound, verses on the subjects of cats and dogs with the name of T. S. Eliot. Nevertheless the author of The Waste Land has written such verses, originally for the amusement of his friends' children.'

1–Cox, 2 Dec.: 'As to the fee and the request you make, I am unable to answer myself, but will pass the information on to the relative quarter. I have made clear to our Copyright Section that all rights of these poems must remain unquestionably and at all times with yourself.'

2–Williams wrote on 30 Nov.: 'I enclose a copy of the verses of which I spoke to you. The joyous fact is that it records an actual incident.'

3–Williams's verse play *A Rite of the Passion* – which Grevel Lindop terms 'hardly a play at all, more a kind of ritual' (*Charles Williams*, 272) – was performed on 22 and 23 March 1937 at the Congregational Church, Duke Street, London.

She said: 'I think that's a very fine play'.
(No emphasis, no hostility, nothing, a mere fact
discovered in a voice.) I said: 'Yes'.
She looked at me again for some time and then went away.
That was all. As I say
against bitterness I am always on guard, but I *do* think
                              it hard.


TO *Charles Williams*                                    CC

[December 1937]

### AN EXHORTATION[1]
To Chas. Williams Esqre.


Beware, my boy, the aged maid,
    Beware the tongue which is so ven-
omous, but be thou not dismayed
    by the austere *paroissienne*![2]

Her taste in poetry is obs-
    olete, she gives her benison
only to sentimental daubs
    of imitation Tennyson.

Your verses look like crazy rhomb-
    oid shapes to her; for she enjoys
no verse more new than that of Thom-
    as Eliot, or the nobler Noyes.


1–Anne Ridler to EVE, 24 Nov. 1966: 'I have started to sort out a box of typescripts consigned to me by someone who typed all Charles Williams's unpublished writings for him, and I find in it this delightful poem by T.S.E. I vaguely remember being shown it, probably by Charles, and I recall that some lady had written that she wished he wrote like Humbert Wolfe! Perhaps you have already got the poem – and I do not know where T.S.E.'s own typescript may be, for this that I have is copied into a looseleaf book, where I have left it, making this further copy for you. I propose to deposit these scripts in the Bodleian, but I shall have to put a time ban on their being shown to students, so I don't suppose you object to the copy going in with the rest?' See further *Poems*, ed. Ricks/McCue.
2–*paroissienne* (Fr.): parishioner.

She, educated in the pur-
    lieus of some dim suburban Surrey,
Admires the nonconformist vir-
    tues of prophetic John Macmurray.

Of subtle thought like Tom Aqui-
    nas's she is quite ignorant;
Perhaps she is a press propri-
    etor's relict or maiden aunt.

Between her mind and yours is fixt
    A canyon or abyss or gulf.
Her values are completely mixed,
    And she admires Humbert Wolfe.[1]

She's probably a Kensitite,
    Or else of Bishop Barnes's band:
So cease thou not from mental fight,
    Nor let thy sword sleep in thy hand!

1–Humbert Wolfe (1885–1940) – originally Umberto Wolff (the family became British citizens in 1891, and he changed his name in 1918) – poet, satirist, critic, civil servant. The son of Jewish parents (his father was German, his mother Italian), he was born in Bradford (where his father was in a wool business), and went to the Grammar School there. A graduate of Wadham College, Oxford, he worked at the Board of Trade and the Ministry of Labour. He found fame with *Requiem* (1927), and in 1930 was mooted as a successor to Robert Bridges as Poet Laureate. He edited over forty books of verse and prose, and wrote many reviews. See Philip Bagguley, *Harlequin in Whitehall: A Life of Humbert Wolfe, Poet and Civil Servant, 1885–1940* (1997).

TO *Susanna Morley*                    TS Susanna Smithson[1]

1 December 1937                    The Zoological Society,
                                   24 Russell Square, W.C.1

DEAR SUSANNA,
   This is a story about

## SOSERA THE CAT.

Sosera looked in at the window:

Sosera jumped down onto the floor:

Sosera saw the Loom:

And thought he ought to look into it!

So he looked into it:

And after he had looked into it:

He found that he could not get out:

1 – From Susanna Morley, *Family News 1938*.

So what did the Family DO about it? Well,

Mother got excited:

Daddy played the piano:

And Oliver did a few sums:

But SUKEY knew what to do about it. She . . .

Fed Sosera-the-Cat on Cheese
out of a Spoon!

And I hope this is only a STORY –

About SOSERA-THE-CAT.

UNCLE TOM[1]

1 – Susanna Morley replied, 2 Dec. 1937:
    'Dear Uncle Tom
    'The way you spelled Sosera is wrong I will show you how it goes.
    'Sorcerer!
    'Thank you very much for your lovely story. I liked all the pictures but
    especially Daddy playing the piano because of the pick-axe behind him.
    'With love from Susanna'
Cf. FVM, 'A Few Recollections of Eliot', 115: 'Donald had his own cat, which he had named
Saucerer.'

## TO *Polly Tandy*

TS BL

1 December 1937                    *The Criterion*

Dear Pollicle Ma'am,

Now then here's a Go. I do not refer to the date of my next visit during Christmastide, because I have just arranged that with your Husband on the telephone, I am to come out on St Stephens afternoon for the night and get back in time for 10.30 oly Hinnocents next morning so thats all right. But about Christmas presents. There's one idea which is not a good one but I must put it to you. Would Anthea[1] like to have a Labrador puppy either sex? because the Morleys have some very nice wellbread [*sic*] ones. I am not trying to pass anything off on you, and I may just pass the remark as evidence of seriousness that I would pay the market price for that puppy, so it's no question of Peter and Paul at all; and its not my responsibility to help them get rid of their puppies; but I saw the puppies and it occurred to me. Well if not a live dog (which I would not suggest but that your household seems a little short of livestock at the moment) I should welcome other suggestions, including for her elder sister and brother. So thats all thats on my mind at the moment, and with best wishes I remain your faithful

Tp

## TO *Virginia Woolf*

TS Berg

1 December [1937]                    *The Criterion*

My dear Virginia,

Alas! on Thursday the 9th I am going to see *Mourning Becomes Electra*.[2] My bosses (Ashley Dukes and Martin Browne) tell me that I ought to see it, because they think it has enough in common with *The Family Reunion* to make it desirable to postpone my play from the spring to the autumn. And I am alarmed, on looking at my calendar, to see how many evenings are taken, in one way or another. I am always trying not

---

1–Anthea Tandy (b. 1935), third child of Geoffrey and Polly Tandy: TSE's godchild.

2–VW had written, 29 Nov.: 'The woods decay, the woods decay & fall … And why doesn't the old Possum (see poem) come to dine?

'What about Thursday 9th at 8? And who would, or whom shouldn't he, would you, or he should it be, like to meet?

'Anyhow come, before all the vapours have wept their burthen to the ground.'

(For VW's quotation, see the opening lines of Tennyson's 'Tithonus'.)

to, but December is a bad month anyway, what with Christmas cards and presents, and the dentist too (I expect to do myself rather well in false teeth presently). Is either the 7th or the 20th possible? Failing that, can we arrange a day for me to come to tea? I should be sorry for any longer period to elapse without seeing you, and I suppose you will be off to Rodmell towards the end of the month to eat a Fortnum & Mason Yorkshire Pye there. But as to whom else you invite, is that not, to me, a matter of comparatively trifling importance? Let that arrangement be for your entertainment, which is superfluous for mine.

Affectionately,<br>Tom

## TO *Jacob Bronowski*[1]                              CC

3 December 1937                    [Faber & Faber Ltd]

Dear Bronowski,

I have read your book with much interest and sympathy, and have shown it to my committee,[2] but I am afraid that this is a type of book for which, especially as an author's first book, there is very little sale, and furthermore, we are so overloaded with books for next year that we cannot take on anything more, unless it shows every prospect of great success. I am not quite sure to whom you should take it. Cape would be very good; and a University Press is possible.

As for criticism: the only immediate and obvious suggestion that occurs to me is that while the use of the short sentence is erring on the right side, I do find that you use it to such an extent that your style tends to become

---

1 – Jacob Bronowski (1908–74) – Polish-born scientist, humanist, writer and broadcaster, whose family came to the UK in 1920 – read mathematics at Jesus College, Cambridge. After gaining his doctorate in 1933, he taught at the University College of Hull, 1934–42; and after WW2 he became scientific deputy to the British Joint Chiefs of Staff mission to Japan (where he wrote a report on the effects of the atomic bombs on Hiroshima and Nagasaki). From 1950 he was Director of the Coal Research Establishment of the National Coal Board, working on the development of smokeless fuel; and in 1964 he became Senior Fellow at the Salk Institute for Biological Studies in San Diego, California. Works include a critical study of William Blake (1944). In later years he won acclaim for his thirteen-part TV series *The Ascent of Man* (1973).

2 – Bronowski submitted on 1 Nov. a book of literary criticism (*c.* 65,000 words) on which he had been working for three years, dealing with 'the literary theories of a number of poets, and with their own poems in the light of their theories. The poets whom I have chosen are Sidney, Dryden (and Jonson), Wordsworth, Coleridge, Shelley, Swinburne, Housman, and Yeats.'

monotonous and wearying; unnecessarily so, as the matter is not tedious
in the least.

Yours sincerely,
[T. S. Eliot]

## TO *James Laughlin*                                        TS Houghton

3 December 1937                    *The Criterion*

Dear Laughlin,

Thanks for your letter of November 4. I have received from the Rydal
Press (Santa Fe) a set of galley proofs of some poems, with no indication of
who the author may be. I imagine that these must be Kay Boyle's poems,
although you said in your letter that you did not expect to send them for
a month; but I should be glad of your confirmation.

I look forward to Stuart Gilbert's translation.[1] I read Dujardin's book
some years ago, and I am doubtful of our being able to do anything with
it. It is rather short, to begin with, and rather slight, and I am doubtful
whether it is important in the long run, except because Joyce mentioned
it as the original 'Dialogue Interieure'. However, if you send it, it will be
examined without prejudice.

As for *Anabase*,[2] I am afraid that has been arranged with Harcourt
Brace, who are, as you know, my regular publishers in America, and who
will probably be bringing it out early next year.

Yours ever sincerely,
T. S. Eliot

## TO *William Force Stead*                                   TS Beinecke

3 December 1937                    *The Criterion*

Dear Stead,

I have read your essay on Two Poets and Two Cats with enjoyment. I am
afraid however that in its present form it is either too light or too heavy for

---

1 – Laughlin was to publish Stuart Gilbert's translation of Édouard Dujardin's *Les Lauriers
sont coupés* [1888], under the title *We'll to the Woods No More* (1938). 'I am sure you know
this admirable book, which has great merit in itself apart from its historical importance.'
(JJ had acknowledged the work as an influence on his use of the interior monologue in
*Ulysses*.)
2 – 'Might I ask again about your plans for an American edition of Perse's ANABASE?'

the *Criterion*. As a general essay comparing the life of Christopher Smart with that of Thomas Gray,[1] it is informative but more suitable for such a review as *English*. What I like, and what is quite new, is the comparison of Smart's admirable cat poem with that of Gray. You say that the poem of Smart is still unpublished and unknown: it would be very jolly for the *Criterion* to have an essay on this poem, including large chunks of the text (for I take it that the whole poem is much too long to publish in this way), and comparing it with Gray's 'Selima'. But with all deference, it seems to me that you praise Gray's poem much too highly. It has always seemed to me a piece of very prim and frigid wit, and the fact that it was not his own cat, but Horace Walpole's, is no excuse. It would be a bad poem, I think, if it were about a china cat, but about a real cat it is unforgivable. Smart has real feeling for cats, and Gray has none. Anyway, you may or may not feel inclined to make a different paper of it.

Affectionately yours,<br>T. S. E.

TO *Enid Faber*                                           TS Valerie Eliot

4 December 1937                    *The Criterion*

Dear Enid,

This is a bad time of year for everybody, and I know you have your share of trouble; but I do want two suggestions. Can you propose anything that *Tom* wants for Christmas, or that he ought to want? And

Can you suggest what I should give *Miss Swan* this year? Last year I gave a handbag from John Pound's.[2]

Now as for Geoffrey. If you want to give him a bottle of Hock, then Williams, Standring & Co. of 59 Duke Street, Grosvenor Square, have a

Wachenheimer Boehling Riesling 1921
Estate Bottling – Excellenz v. Boecklin-Wolff
@ 210s. a dozen, which would work out about
right for one bottle. It ought to be very
choice; and at that price would be rather an
after dinner wine, being somewhat strong.

1 – Christopher Smart (1722–71), Thomas Gray (1716–71), English poets.
2 – John Pound & Son, with several retail outlets in London, made and sold handbags; the firm was ultimately taken over by John Lewis.

On the other hand, if you want to give something that would LAST longer, why not a Grande Chartreuse – the Yellow at about a guinea, the green a little dearer, say twenty-five shillings; which you could get equally well from Chalié, Richards or indeed from Fortnum's.

If neither of these suggestions meets with your approval, I shall be happy to investigate further.

Affy.<br>TP

## TO *Louis MacNeice* CC

6 December 1937                    [Faber & Faber Ltd]

Dear MacNeice,

I have been meaning to write to tell you that the proposed book of selections from four poets is off. I was not too keen on the idea myself, and I am rather relieved. Accordingly there is no complication about your next book of poems, which I hope you can let me have by the beginning of January.

I did not go to *Out of the Picture* last night, but I am looking forward to seeing it next Sunday.[1]

Now what about *Station Bell*? I have read it, and it seems to me very amusing farce, but it is emphatically a play to be produced first and published afterward. Have the Group Theatre made up their minds about it or not?[2]

Yours ever,<br>[T. S. Eliot]

1 – Produced by Rupert Doone with the Group Theatre at the Westminster Theatre, London, for two Sunday performances (5th and 12th Dec.), with décor by Robert Medley and Geoffrey Monk, and music by Benjamin Britten.

Blurb by TSE in Faber Books catalogue July–Dec. 1937, 52: 'This is the verse play on which Mr MacNeice has been at work for a considerable time. Mr MacNeice is already an established younger poet; with the *Agamemnon* he proved that Greek Tragedy can be accurately translated into vigorously dramatic verse in contemporary metre and idiom. We predict that his first original play – which is to be produced in the autumn – will take its place in the repertory of the new poetic theatre.'

2 – *Station Bell*, a farcical fantasy that MacNeice had been putting together in 1934–5.

TO *Philip Mairet*                                                    cc

8 December 1937                         [Faber & Faber Ltd]

Dear Mairet,

I am sending back the copy of *La Fin de la Peur*, which I have now read, and which has impressed me considerably.[1] I cannot be sure that my Board will be interested in a small book of this type, but I should like very much to see your translation as soon as it is ready, and find out how it impresses one or two of my colleagues. I should certainly like to see a translation published.

Yours ever,
[T. S. Eliot]

TO *Guy Boas*[2]                                                     cc

9 December 1937                         [Faber & Faber Ltd]

Dear Mr Boas,

Thank you for your charming letter of December 6.[3] I very much dislike making myself disagreeable: partly on principle; partly from an easy-going nature, and partly because opposition to other people's designs always entails an expenditure of energy which one wishes to conserve for other purposes. But I am afraid that I remain unmoved in my preference not to release my poems for the English Association anthology.

I would rather prefer, with all due respect, not to go any further into this matter.

With best wishes,
Yours very sincerely,
[T. S. Eliot]

1–Denis Saurat, *La Fin de la Peur* (1937): published as *The End of Fear*, with a preface by Mairet (F&F, 1938).
2–Guy Boas (1896–1966), Headmaster of Sloane School, Chelsea, London, 1929–61; author of *Shakespeare and the Young Actor* (1955); *A Teacher's Story* (1963).
3–TSE had been asked by the Executive Committee of the English Association to release some poems for the third series of their anthology *Poems of To-Day*. F. S. Boas wrote a personal appeal in Nov. 1937; and on 6 Dec. his son, Guy Boas – 'the instigator, on the Publications Committee of the English Association, of Poems of Today 3rd series' – asked TSE to think again about his decision not to release poems for use in a volume which would aim 'to give to the public, and chiefly to the public of young people in schools, a collection of poetry as good as we can make it, to illustrate the work of the last fifteen years'.

TO *Polly Tandy*                                                TS BL

9 December 1937                         *The Criterion*

Dear Polly Tandy m'm,

I have thought over the matter of this Misterperkins, and have come
to the conclusion that there is nothing to be done about it.[1] When a Cat
adopts you, and I am not superstitious at all I don't mean only Black cats,
there is nothing to be done about it except to put up with it and wait until
the wind changes, and perhaps he will go away of his own accord and
never be heard of again; but as I say there is nothing you can do about it.
You must for the present provide liver and rabbit, and a comfortable seat
by the fire; and perhaps he will disappear. I am sorry to give such cold
consolation, but one might as well face facts.

I am going to investigate punching bags on Monday;[2] and when you
say attaché case (shouldn't it be attach*ée* case in this case) I suppose you
mean one fitted with writing paper and cubby holes, or it will not come
amiss. And I suppose a Dog with cotton wool inside him.

Yrs etc.

Tp


TO *Frank Morley*                                               CC

13 December 1937                      [Faber & Faber]

*Memorandum to Mr Morley*

Herewith the corrected copy of ANABASIS for the use of HarBrace.[3] If
you will glance through it, you will notice that the alterations are more
extensive than at first contemplated, and what HarBrace will have will

---

1–See final line of 'Mungojerrie and Rumpelteazer': 'It was Mungojerrie – AND
Rumpelteazer!' – and there's nothing at all to be done about that.'
2–TSE had been enquiring about Christmas presents suitable for Alison and Richard Tandy.
Richard Tandy was to write to him in Jan. 1938: 'Dear Possum / Last Thursday Alison and
I went to Gamages and we bought a punch-ball and a dynamo lighting set and a bag for the
crossbar of my bicycle. So I want to thank you for it all. From Richard.
  'P.S. We changed the big punch-ball for all these things.
  'P.P.S. Come and have a whack at the new punch-ball.'
3–EVE to Richard Owen Abel, 3 July 1967: '[TSE] felt that St John Perse had done
something highly original [in *Anabase*], and in a language in which such originality is not
easily attained. Towards the end of his life my husband remarked that Léger was the only
French poet amongst his contemporaries – with the solitary exception of Supervielle – whose
work continued to interest him. He also acknowledged that he had felt an influence which
was visible in some of his poems written after the *Anabase*.'

really be a second edition superior to that which we have been publishing. This information in case HarBrace wish to make any publicity use of it.[1]

I should like to add that most of the work on this has been done as a labour of love by John Hayward, who has not only taken a great deal of trouble himself, but has also consulted French friends. I think that he has done so much work, and that the result is so valuable, that I should very much appreciate it if HarBrace could see their way to offering Hayward some fee for his work in the matter.

Beyond a few errors which I had already spotted for myself, my own labour has been confined to spending yesterday afternoon with Hayward, going through the suggestions which he has accumulated.[2]

T. S. E.   13.12.37

## TO *Michael Roberts* CC

13 December 1937                    [*The Criterion*]

Dear Roberts,

Thank you for your letter of the 11th.[3] I was under the impression that the text of *Hulme* which you sent was intended as the final version, and was therefore rather puzzled by your remarks about embodying further matter in the first chapter. I now gather that you merely sent this for me to read. I should have been quite willing to take as read anything that

---

1–FVM cabled Harcourt, Brace in Apr. 1937: 'Anabasis published originally under limited licence stop attempting to get extension stop would spring suit instead fall stop.'

C. A. Pearce to FVM, 30 Apr.: 'Your cable about Eliot's translation of St-J. Perse's ANABASIS arrived yesterday and, as a result, we are no longer counting upon this book for fall. If you are successful in securing permission for the publication of the American edition, we will be glad to put it in the spring list. Presumably, the proposal outlined by Mr Brace in his letter of March 9th is acceptable to Eliot, and, therefore, if you do secure proper release, we will expect you to draw up the publishing agreement and send it along.'

2–FVM to Brace, 14 Dec.: 'At long last I am able to send the corrected copy of ANABASIS, which Eliot gave me yesterday, along with a memorandum which I enclose with this. It is true what Eliot says about Hayward's trouble over the text, which is now as near perfection as humanly possible. It now amounts, as Eliot says, to a second edition superior to that which we have been publishing.

'I don't quite know what to say about the fee Eliot suggests for John Hayward. Would it, do you think, stand a couple of guineas?'

The corrected copy of the first edn of *Anabasis* (1930) is in the T. S. Eliot Library.

3–'I am still working on Hulme, but if you have no serious objection to the book as it stands, I could let you have a copy fit to go to the printers by Dec 31st. I have straightened out the last three chapters since I sent you a draft, and I have introduced a few more anecdotes into Chapter I.'

you sent as the final text. I have read as much as I have had time to read up to the present moment, and like the book very much. I think we can take it that the book is what you call 'reasonably satisfactory', so I am returning this draft, and we shall be glad to have the copy for press on December 31.[1]

Ever yours,
[T. S. Eliot]

TO *Paul Léon*                                        TS National Gallery of Ireland

14 December 1937                        *The Criterion*

Dear Mr Léon,

I thank you for your letter of 11 December with enclosures.[2] Another section of Part 2, printed evidently by Lord Carlow, arrived several days ago, but without any covering letter, so I had been waiting in expectation of an explanatory letter from someone, as I did not know to whom to acknowledge it. This portion is the one which formed the subject of conversations between Lord Carlow and myself some time ago, in consequence of which we gave him a licence to publish this section.

I take it that I am to understand that the section above-mentioned is the beginning of Part 2, and that the parts enclosed with your letter of 11 December constitute <the next section of> Part 2.

1–*T. E. Hulme* (1938) carried this blurb: 'The case of T. E. Hulme, author of *Speculation* [*sic*], is a singular one. This philosopher and poet who was killed in action in 1917, having published nothing but a few articles, has proved to be perhaps the most influential mind of his generation. A critical introduction to his work has been badly needed; and now, twenty years after Hulme's death, Mr Michael Roberts – obviously the person best equipped in mind and learning, and in perspective as a representative of a younger generation than Hulme's – has fulfilled that need.

'Mr Roberts has made an exhaustive study of Hulme's sources, and a critical examination of the tendencies of his thought in æsthetics, in politics, and even in theology. He has added a few unpublished documents of great interest, including several poems. The book is important for every one who would understand the philosophy, the æsthetics and the art of the present time and probably of the future; but the general reader also will find great interest in the study of a fascinating, puzzling and adventurous mind.'

2–Léon wrote: 'I have been withholding the second section of Work in Progress as I was expecting to hear from you about the safe arrival of section 1. As it has not come yet, I do not want to wait any longer and am enclosing section 2: section 3 will follow in due course.

'Here is the rule to read this section:

'First comes the first portion printed by Lord Carlow (20 pages). Then comes the typescript consisting itself of four portions. But I have paginated them uniformly in red ink, as they have to be printed one after the other. Finally comes the last portion of the printed text (7 pages).'

I should be interested to know how much more matter there will be before the book is complete. You speak of a Section 3 to come. Am I to understand that Section 3 will complete Part 2, or will there be further sections?

Furthermore, I take it that the printed pages which you enclose with your letter of 11 December will make another book, as a limited edition to be published by the Corvinus Press, in other words, Lord Carlow; but I am not aware that we had had any intimation that Lord Carlow wished to publish this section as well, and I should like to be informed about the actual situation. You will understand that for any parts of *Work in Progress* which the Corvinus Press wish to publish in a limited edition, they have to obtain a licence from ourselves.

With all best wishes to yourself and Madame Léon,

Yours very sincerely,
T. S. Eliot

TO *John Hayward*                                                TS King's

16 December 1937                    *The Criterion*

Dear John,

You were so wise and helpful last year, that I think I ought not to buy a present for Miss Swan without consulting you first. (Last year, at your suggestion, a bag from John Pounds; I think I paid thirty shillings). I have some suggestions from Enid, viz.:

umbrella
travelling clock
silk scarf           ('this should be square and very gay to be
                       in the fashion – i.e. the Tyrolean one,
                       which though slightly over in Bond Street
                       would, I fancy, just be Miss Swan's mark
                       now'. sic). [*sic*]
evening bag, of some kind of sparkly stuff
handkerchiefs with initials
thermos in a case, for hiking

If you approve any of these, or have (as I shall expect) some quite unique and superior inspiration, I shall be grateful for a blow on the telephone.

yrs. distractedly
TP

## TO *Virginia Woolf*                                         TS Berg

16 December [1937]                    Faber & Faber Ltd

Dear Virginia,

Unless you have come by the book in some other way, as I dare say you have, I should like to make you a Christmas present of *Men Women and Things* by the Duke of Portland.[1] It surpasses his previous books in fatuity, and is altogether delightful reading.[2]

aff.

TP

I could bring it on Monday.


## TO *Wilma Gregory*                                          CC

16 December 1937                      [Faber & Faber Ltd]

Dear Madam,

Thank you for your letter of December 8th.[3] I am writing in reply to ask you not to take too seriously my single opinion, and to ask you to persuade Mr Laurie Lee not to exaggerate the value of my opinion either. No one is infallible in these matters, and I often feel particularly that my own taste has become blunted by excessive reading of the indifferent verse which is sent to me in large quantities. I should be distressed if either you or your friend took my opinion more seriously than I take it myself, and I wish to urge you to see that the poems are submitted to other critics.

---

1 – Published by F&F on 29 Nov.

2 – VW replied with a note of even date: 'Of course I should cherish a copy – just my line; to the very t.'

3 – Mrs Gregory had replied to TSE's letter of 9 Nov.: 'I am sorry that you did not think Laurie Lee's poems worth publishing – the more sorry, because your eminence as poet and critic obliges me to think that I must have been mistaken in thinking so highly of them.

'It was so very kind of you to read them with so much care, that I ought to have written long ago to thank you for doing so. But I have been almost exclusively occupied in trying to persuade the boy not to go to Spain . . .

'I had to confess that I had sent you his poems, and I tried to persuade him to let me send them to Mr Church. He refused *nettement*; his respect for the opinion of Mr T. S. Eliot made him accept your verdict as final.'

Beside Mr Church, I would suggest that Mr Herbert Read would give a valuable opinion, and with a taste less dulled by the constant reading of verse than either my own or Mr Church's.[1]

Yours very truly,<br>[T. S. Eliot]

## TO *John Macmurray*[2]　　　　　　　　　　　　　　　　　CC

16 December 1937　　　　　　　　[Faber & Faber Ltd]

Dear Macmurray,

I have taken the liberty of giving a card of introduction to you to a young poet of my acquaintance named George Barker. I will add at once that he would have been trying to see you in any case, as it was Walter de la Mare who advised him to see you, and I am merely supporting him by this letter.

George Barker is in my opinion one of the most interesting of the younger poets, and we have published several of his volumes. He has found it difficult to get any suitable regular employment, as he has no University degree, and no kind of diploma. But I think that in some fields of English literature he might do very well. What he wants to see you about is the possibilities of any sort of Extension lecturing. According to Walter de la Mare, you might be in a position to give him some advice. At any rate, I should be personally very grateful to you if you would see him.

---

1–Gregory responded to this letter on 1 Jan. 1938: 'It was immensely kind of you to bother to write again ... Unfortunately on December 4th he stole across the frontier to join the International Brigade. As an epileptic is obviously unfit for war service, steps were immediately taken to inform the authorities of his malady and do everything possible to have him sent back ...

'If he returns safely, I will certainly try to persuade him to send his poems to Mr Church and Mr Read.

'May I say that this is the first time I have ever so much as heard of a critic's being kind enough to write a second time about rejected poems, and that the memory of your having done so will increase the already very great pleasure with which I read your poems and essays.'

2–John Macmurray (1891–1976), Scottish philosopher, educated at Glasgow and Oxford, served in WW1 as a lieutenant in the Cameron Highlanders (MC); Grote Professor of the Philosophy of Mind and Logic at University College, London, 1928–44; Professor of Moral Philosophy at Edinburgh University, 1944–58. Works include *Freedom in the Modern World* (1932); *The Self as Agent* (1957). See J. E. Costello, *John Macmurray: A Biography* (2002); *John Macmurray: Critical Perspectives*, ed. D. Fergusson and N. Dower (2002).

Incidentally, he is a very nice person, and when he comes to see me never takes an unreasonable length of time.[1]

> With all best wishes,
> Yours sincerely,
> [T. S. Eliot]

## TO *Cosmo Gordon Lang*[2]                                    CC

17 December 1937                    [Faber & Faber Ltd]

My dear Lord Archbishop,

I have the honour to acknowledge the receipt of Your Grace's communication of 14 December.[3] While I should feel it a duty to attend any particular meeting at Your Grace's request, I am anxious to avoid for some time to come committing myself to activity on committees and councils which may extend over some period of time. If I felt that my presence in such meetings were really valuable I might feel obliged to accept, but experience has led me to believe that I am not amongst the most useful or best qualified persons for such activities. I am also moved by the consideration that I already have as much to do as I should undertake, but I do not urge that point, as it might no doubt be equally true of all those whom Your Grace would consider fit to undertake this responsibility.

1–Barker to TSE, 28 Dec. 1937: 'I wrote to Professor Macmurray before Christmas, and have not yet had a reply.'

2–Cosmo Gordon Lang (1864–1945), Scottish Anglican prelate: Archbishop of York, 1908–28; Archbishop of Canterbury, 1928–42.

3–'As a result of the Conference held at Oxford during the course of last Summer on the subject of Church, Community and State, informal conversations have taken place among representatives of the Churches concerned in that Conference with regard to the possibility of forming a Council of the Churches in Great Britain on the Relation of the Christian Faith to the National Life.

'I have agreed to take the initiative in calling a meeting of representatives of Churches to consider this question [and] should be glad to know whether you would be willing and able to attend the meeting which is to be held here [Lambeth] on Friday, January 14th, at 2.30 p.m.'

I should prefer to state my position in the following way: that in view of other activities I would ask Your Grace's permission not to be joined in this undertaking, which does me an undeserved honour.

I have the honour to remain,
my Lord Archbishop,
Your Grace's devoted
and obedient servant,
[T. S. Eliot]

## TO *Ezra Pound*                                    Beinecke

19 December 1937                    [Faber & Faber Ltd]

Well Ez that is very nice of You and I am by no means unfavourably disposed and should be glad to do it if at all Gratis, because money is scarce and I am always happy to carry light into foreign parts for the love I bear to human beings.[1] But now question is have I got time and have I got anything to say that nobody knows already? that is to be doubted. you know how modest and un presumin Possum is; and it strikes him, he'd better get on and see if he can't or can or can not write a play first; he says that, knowing that he aint written a play yet, and thinks, aint it better to devote one's energy for a bit to trying to contribute in that direction rather than go blatherin about what a play ought OUGHT to be: a argument or line or reasonin which ought OUGHT to appeal to Ez, as well as bein in line with the Possum family's mottoe which is: say nothin & saw wood. And here were [*sic*] are in December and Possum has got a kind of a play 3/4 written and to be finished by Easter or so; so would your lil friend like to wait a bit until Possum has finished his play and THEN Possum can tell him exactly what a play ought to be, or he can just look at this for himself and draw his own conclusions; for so far the Possum's opionions about the writin of a play is simply this:

1 – Cf. John 3: 16: 'For God so loved the world . . .'

EP relayed on 14 Dec. a request from a 'Bloke' – the editor of a European periodical – who 'SEZ: will th POSSUM rite piece sayin just and PLAIN wot he fink a styge (noota stooge) playe orter beee.

'He pays somfink, not much acc/ Threadneedle standards, bUTT you cd/ sell the piece later in the orry/ginal wiff the kudos of itz havin been requested an published nearer the centres of European culture.

'dew yew git me/ It needn't be LONG az I kno youre lazy.

'But also its needn't be in that keerful Criterese which so successfully protkks you in the stinking and foggy climik agin the bare/ boreians.

'de yew git meh?'

1) You got to keep the audience's attention all the time.

2) if you lose it you got to get it back QUICK.

3) Everythin about plot & charactyar and all else what Aristotle and others says is secondary to the foregoin.

4) But IF you can keep the bloody audience's attention engaged, then you can perform any monkey tricks you like when they arent lookin, and its what you do behind the audience's back so to speak that makes yr. play IMMORTAL for a while.

If the audience gets its strip tease it will swallow the poetry.

Dja get me?

I spose it is a good think they are awakin, but I wish yr. lil brown bros. in Nippon wd. go to sleep again, they look pleasanter that way. How come Ez so fond of lil brown men.[1] Know anything about the Resorgimento in Mindanao? Its a comin on, its a comin on.

> So wot I sez
> To ole Ez
> Is wot the 'ell,
> NOEL NOEL.

TP

my best Compliments of the Season to your Pa & Ma, also to yr. Wife, Bless her heart.

When is yr. young friend comin over for her annual Do of hot-pot and jam roly-poly. The season is ON, tell her.

## TO *The Editor,* The Times

22 December 1937, 8

Mr Wyndham Lewis's Works

Sir, –

Many years have passed since the strange mind of Wyndham Lewis began to invigorate English painting and letters.

Mr Lewis is now holding his first exhibition since 1921,[2] and it seems to us an appropriate time to suggest that Lewis's deep and original art should be publicly recognized. Social change has made it inevitable that

---

1 – EP responded, 22 Dec.: 'I like my li'l brown bruvvers cause I has know'd some GOOD ones, an [. . .] there is a CIVILIZATION in one of their li'l fingers wot we aint got in th whole of our corpus.'

2 – The Wyndham Lewis exhibition at the Leicester Galleries, London, included 'The Surrender of Barcelona' (1936–7).

in these days the place and duties of the private patron should be handed over, in a large degree, to the public galleries; and those rarer artists whose vision and energy are too great to be confined in small or decorative pieces must depend on the wise discernment of the galleries more and more.

We believe Wyndham Lewis to be such an artist, and we are convinced that every serious painter and serious writer in England is much in debt to his integrity, and to the originality and strength of his vision: and we hope that the opportunity of acquiring a representative work by him for the national collection will not be overlooked.[1]

Yours, &c.

Henry Moore, Eric Gill, Paul Nash, Mark Gertler, Edmund Dulac, Edward Wadsworth, P. H. Jowett, Randolph Schwabe, John Piper, Serge Chermayeff, Raymond McGrath, Arthur Bliss, Michael E. Sadler, T. S. Eliot, W. H. Auden, Herbert Read, Rhondda, Rebecca West, Naomi Mitchison, Stephen Spender, Geoffrey Grigson.


## TO *John Hayward*  TS King's

22 December 1937  *The Criterion*

Dear John,

I am a worried man. Perhaps you, as a man with profound understanding of etiquette and diplomacy, a master of high pollicie, a very matchavel,[2] will look at the enclosed and outline the proper letter to write to a sister who wants me to return the card she sent me a year ago, so that she can show it to my brother instead of giving him a new one? I may say that the word 'Toby' conveys nothing at all to me.[3]

Also, what does Clara Webster mean by saying 'it is more than I expected after your being such a good friend to my sister'? This also is disturbing.

But I am glad to be able to enclose a tribute to the nurses at St Stephen's Hospital, Fulham Road.

1 – Lewis (29A Kensington Gardens Studios, Notting Hill Gate, W.11) responded to TSE, 24 Dec.: 'Very many thanks for two things – first for so kindly writing something for Julian Symons little paper [*Twentieth Century Verse*]; and second for so kindly consenting to add your name to the *Times* letter of last Wednesday about my paintings. Immediately after Christmas I shall suggest a dinner-date.'

(Prompted by this letter in the *Times*, the Tate Gallery purchased 'Red Scene'.)

2 – *The Merry Wives of Windsor* (Quarto I, 1602): '[A]m I polliticke? am I Matchauil?'

3 – TSE is referring throughout this paragraph to a letter he enclosed (not found) with this missive to JDH.

The Xmas card game is in full swing. So far I am holding my own, except for a flood this morning from Americans whom I had forgotten. I am just even with Ottoline, except that the diary has arrived before the flowers have been despatched; the Camerons have beaten me by one post, and now they will never believe that I had them on my list at the beginning. On the other hand, I am well ahead of the Hutchinsons, the Wolmers, and Elsie Fogerty, though behind the Dean of Chichester and Mr Norman Carter; and I am well off the mark with the Kauffers. Which reminds me, what am I to do about that desk thing? Am I to take it as a gift, and just wait for it? or can I treat it as a kind office, and ask them how much I owe? As I said at the beginning, I am a worried man.

yrs distractedly,<br>TP

I gave Virginia the Duke of Portland,[1] and she came straight back at me with a handsome silk handkerchief. My brother has sent me a gadget suit case to put one's evening clothes into for weekends (I think he imagines I spend all my weekends at Hatfield and such like places) and the niece I don't care about has sent me a very large photograph of herself (I havent opened it but that is obviously what it is). The vicar has given me what is obviously a devout book, and I can think of nothing for him but a bottle of Berry's Talisker 1924. Please take no notice of me, I am nearly at breaking point. So will see you on Sat. evening so will close.

TP

Anyway all the children have been provided for.

The sister in question is the one who never buys a 5¢ stamp because they have Theodore Roosevelt on them.

## TO *Alison Tandy*

TS Alison Tandy

23 December 1937 *The Criterion*

> DEAR ALISON, I fear I can-
> not join you on the First of Jan-
> uary for your Birthday Part-
> y and it nearly breaks my Heart.
> Unhappily I have a pre-
> vious engagement: were I free,

---

1 – *Men, Women and Things: Memories of the Duke of Portland, KG, GCVO* (F&F, 1937).

there is no doubt but I would scam-
per gleefully to you at Ham-
pton, singing Yankee Doodle Dand-
y to the family of Tand-
y on the afternoon of Sat-
urday the First. Alas, I must
go where I was invited fust,
because that is considered yet
a rigid rule of etiquette.
So on that day I have to hurry
to Mr Morley's house in Surrey –
the reason being, strange but true,
he was born on the same day as you.[1]
But still I find it very vex-
ing not to be in Middlesex
at Hampton in the street called High
among the Tandy family.
At least, I'm glad that I shall be
with you on Sunday next for tea
and in the Tandy family buzzim,
and sign myself, with love, your
                              Possum[2]


## TO *Ezra Pound*

TS Beinecke

23 December 1937                    *The Criterion*

Well Ez you are surely untiring in good gorks works and may you be
suitably rewarded here or hereafter and the least I can to is to wish you
very heartily the compts. of the season and all the double cream of 1938.
And I have nowt but good wishes for the Townsman[3] though there is

1–FVM was in fact born on 4 Jan. TSE's error may be tactful.
2–Alison Tandy wrote on 2 Jan. 1938 (the day after her birthday): 'Dear Possum, Thank
you very much for the Telegram. I have had a very Happy Birthday and I got lot of Presents.
And I am so sorry you could not come to the Party it was lovely. With love from Alison.' At
the foot of the page she drew a picture of 'Old Deuteronomy' – looking less like a cat than
a perky rat.
3–EP (20 Dec.) forwarded a letter from the editor of the *Townsman* soliciting a contribution
from TSE. 'I whope you will send 'em at least a few firvolous lines/ or unearth a passage of
"BOLO the KING", or a citation from scripture.

'OV course my idear of the Townsman IZ that it shd/ delouse the HIGH POSSUM, and
deestinguish between the ORTHer of AGON and the bloke wot prints crap in the Criterion.'

things more excitin to me than nipponese verse but then you have to suit all tastes but what can pore ole possum do[1] to help except to allow himself to be baked with sweet pertaters which he is always ready to do, knowin what savoury gravoury he exudes under sufficient heat and with the judicious garnishments etc. As for present however, there is naught available except

> children's poems, not to be released yet
>
> certain private lampoons etc. too esoteric for general public
>
> a few translations from the Telugu (the lascars is awakin up and producin)
>
> part of a play, which a play is difft. from a epic in that you cant release chunks in advance, on the contrary you have to keep it in a safe

and I refuse to write PROSE damb it you know I cant write PROSE and I dont like to either. So what is there for the Present except benevolence?

Have been in correspondence with the Butch/[2] and am composing of a letter to Him to fit the eys of Reid Pere[3]

& so will close etc.

TP

---

TSE was to reflect on *Townsman*, in his *Criterion* 'Commentary': 'Ideas with which I am familiar and at ease (though I can claim no part in originating them) turn up with some slight difference in their features. Even Christianity, even the Church, is not ignored – not at all: I find my immediate fear to be rather lest it be compromised. Communism is contemned; monetary reform, decentralisation, the revival of agriculture and the agricultural life are demanded, mob rule is denounced – yet I feel like a Tory who becomes aware that he is also (having been born when he was, and not several generations earlier) something of a Liberal ...

'The air may clear a bit after "Townsman" has fully assimilated the influence of Mr Pound, whose powerful personality inspires its pages, and some of whose sillier sallies have decorated them. I believe that this influence is all to the good, so long as it takes the proper course of an influence and does not become a possession (there is an essay on the Earl of Rochester by the editor which is excellent, and which might be a ringer for one of Pound's): I only fear the apparition of Mr Pound's imaginary hero, the Strong Man.' TSE recommended *Townsman* 'to all readers who have the imperturbability to be irritated by it in the right way'.

1 – 'And what can poor old Possum do' (letter to VW).

2 – Montgomery Butchart.

3 – EP remarked (11 Dec.) that the youth John Reid, whom TSE had encouraged to go and visit EP, 'seems a thoughtful bloke, not so depressin' not NEAR so depressin as you made out', and he asked TSE to write an explanatory letter to Reid's parents, 'tellin 'em a NUVVLE takes long to write' and that 'the heads of the profession look calmly on the tadpole: and that old EZ is a post grad university INCARNATE, and that they shdn't deprive the lad of such as chanct ... IF his fambly can afford 10 bucks a week, shdn't he have two years to turn round in.' On 20 Dec.: 'waaal I am trying to edderkate the y:man ... anyhow, I aint kussin yuh fer interjuicink him (not YET, at any rate).'

TO *Mary Hutchinson*                                        TS Texas

Childermass [28 December] 1937    *The Criterion*

Dear Mary,

It was sweet of you to remember me with the gift of the Giotto reproductions – which are extremely good – to tell the truth, I like Giotto frescoes (I only know Padua, I have never been to Assisi) as I do Magdalenian rock-paintings, better in such good reproductions than *in situ*. And I hope you had a pleasant Christmas, and that we shall meet again when the theatre next presents anything worth seeing, and I hope that Barbara is flourishing under the French treatment, and that Jack is well, and that 1938 will be a happy year for you.

Ever affectionately,<br>Tom


TO *Ezra Pound*                                            TS Beinecke

Childermass [28 December] 1937    *The Criterion*

Well Ez, now your letter of the 22 dec it would have arrived in time but for the Office bein closed over Christmas but I got it today and none the less welcome, none the less. And as for the Dramtix, you can quote me if you like till the cows come home & you are blue in the face, and by all means keep the Praxes down, keep 'em down.[1] ONLY, I aint goin to allow that the Igorots, and they do talk a lot about Bali and the Trobriand Islanders too, has got so much CIVILISATION as, what? what is CIVILISATION? a moot point, brother, a moot point, and you may say the sootier the brethren the less mooty, but you remember what I am a N. Englander born south of M. & Dixon's line, and I DEW draw a kind of a colour bar, and a lot of other bars too. well I hope thaat after the Nyu Year you will instruct me in brown culcher etc. & meanwhile I better let yr. friend Dunk Dunkum have the dope on the cultural revival of Pago Pago tell the gal when she's sick of spaghetti theres a warm toad in the ole waitin for her

---

1 – After sending (22 Dec.) his 'besss XXXmas or Ezmus wishes', EP asked: 'And as to wit yo sez erbaht DRAMERDY . . . praps I might quote yo' letter?? which wd/ keep the Prazites under salootary discipline/ so to speak vs. PraXis which is different.'

and a pint of mild & bitter at the Old Swan in Commercial Road and the company of a couple of churchwardens me and a bloke named Alfred.

Best wishes for the New Year from<br>TP

Old Possum & his Performin Practical Cats

## TO *Rayner Heppenstall* TS Texas

29 December 1937 *The Criterion*

Dear Heppenstall,

I am sorry that Hanley's books are both very bad, but I am afraid I must ask you to do a short note on them, because I had to order one especially.[1] A very short note will do, and you need not pretend to think well of them; only I think that in the circumstances some notice ought to appear.[2]

When I send you poetry to review you may take it that I have given up the expectation of your ever writing any more yourself.[3] In other words, I would rather for your own sake you reviewed some other kind of books, and I am always open to suggestions.

I don't know whether I have had a lapse of memory, but at the moment the word *Pelagia* fails to attach itself to anything in my mind.[4] I am sorry, so will you refresh my memory, which is rather jaded by the confusions of December?[5]

My only impression of Waldo Frank's work is that what I have seen struck me as rather dull, but I daresay I am doing him an injustice.[6]

With best wishes,<br>Yours ever,<br>T. S. Eliot

1 – Heppenstall reported (n.d.): '"Grey Children" and "Broken Water" are both very bad books, and though I could find plenty to say about them I don't think it would interest *Criterion* readers.'

2 – Heppenstall on James Hanley, *Broken Water* and *Grey Children*: C. 17 (Apr. 1938), 586.

3 – '[C]an I have something else to review? . . . I would still like to have a whole quarter's batch of verse – just once – but you may have arranged that.'

4 – 'Do you like Pelagia at all? I am at present doing a series of monochrome illustrations to it . . . I should be glad if you like the text well enough to print [it] in the Criterion meanwhile.'

5 – Heppenstall replied (n.d.): 'Pelagia is a play partly in verse which I gave you in a text as for broadcasting three weeks ago with some poems. I have now done eight illustrations to it which I would like you to see.'

6 – 'Waldo Frank [1889–1967] is very sad. He thought that literary London would come to sit at his feet, and it hasn't . . . His English friends are trying to persuade him that he fails to catch on here because of the quantity of sex in his books which upsets English prudery. As a matter of fact I did hear an English reader venture the opinion that he was a dirty old sod.'

29 December 1937                    [*The Criterion*]

Dear Gascoyne,

I have your letter of 10 December with a copy of the *Nouvelle Revue Française*, and would have written to you before, but for the Christmas rush.[2] I have taken the opportunity of reading the article, and agree with you about its merit. But I do not like reprinting an article which has already appeared in that paper, the point being that I think our circle of readers is likely to include most of the people in this country who would read the *N.R.F.* I am much interested to learn that you have got on to the work of Jouve, who has always seemed to me one of the best French poets of his generation. If you find yourself moved to translate any of his poetry I would consider publishing some of that, especially if we could get permission to publish the French text as well.

I should very much like to see your new poems, and hope that you will soon let me have the opportunity.

                              Yours very sincerely,
                              [T. S. Eliot]

---

1 – David Gascoyne (1916–2001), poet, playwright, translator and novelist, by this date had published *Opening Day* (1933) and *A Short Survey of Surrealism* (1935); and *Hölderlin's Madness* would appear from Dent in 1938. See too Robert Fraser, *Night Thoughts: The Surreal Life of the Poet David Gascoyne* (2012).

2 – Gascoyne wrote from Paris with a copy of the Nov. issue of *Nouvelle Revue Française* containing an essay by Pierre Jean Jouve entitled 'Grandeur Actuelle de Mozart' which he wished to translate for the *Criterion*. Jouve, he felt, was 'a poet of very rare quality and of an importance difficult to exaggerate . . . As far as I know, he is one of the first men to perform a truly satisfying integration of the findings of psych-analytical research with the traditional cosmogony of the poet, and to relate the life of the instincts with the profounder life of the spirit . . . [H]e does implicitly rather the same kind of thing as Jung has explicitly attempted in his "Modern Man in Search of a Soul".'

Pierre Jean Jouve (1887–1976): esteemed writer, novelist, poet; works include *Vagadu* (1931), *Noces* (1931), *Sueur de sang* (1935).

Gascoyne added: 'Since I came to live in Paris last August, I have been writing a number of new poems, which I should like to send you presently, if you could be bothered to read them . . . I hope that you will find the new poems better worth your consideration, at any rate considerably more mature, than any previous work of mine that you have seen.'

30 December 1937                    *The Criterion*

Dear Bridson,

Thank you for your letter of the 29th, with a list of rehearsals.[1] I will come to the one on the 6th, unless you particularly want me to come sooner. But the mornings are very precious to me for work, and I hate to give them up if I can avoid it, especially because the loss of even one morning means a further delay in getting the machinery started again.

What I am afraid of is over-dramatisation on the part of the speakers. It is always a trouble in verse speaking in a play, (and would be still worse in something which is not intended for the stage), that as every speaker wants to make all that he can dramatically out of his own part, instead of accepting his position as that of an instrument in an orchestra. You need to be a producer who can thoroughly cow all the performers, and keep them in their proper place!

Yours ever sincerely,
T. S. Eliot

1–On 8 Nov. Bridson had sent 'a rough script of "The Waste Land" adapted for broadcasting': 'You will see that I have split it up into various characters, all of whom are mentioned by name in the announcement. You will probably feel that the ascription of certain remarks or paragraphs to certain of the characters is wrong and I should be glad if we could get together sometime to make the adjustments which I know are necessary. On the other hand, I have taken the liberty of mixing the characters up slightly (in view of the fact that most of them telescope anyway) and have used the Phoenician Sailor now and again for passages which you may think should be given to the commentator or even Tiresias. Similarly the Fisher King and the Hanged Man crop up in places which may or may not appear a trifle arbitrary. On the other hand, I have had to bear in mind the fact that in most instances the voices will appear solely *as* voices and not as characters and by allowing myself a little latitude here and there I have been able to obtain antiphonal effects for purposes of emphasis which I think justify the juggling about . . .

'I might say that the job of arranging the script (for better or worse) has proved most fascinating and I am very anxious indeed to get the thing into production as soon as possible.'

On 29 Dec. Bridson sent a list of rehearsal dates – including 6 Jan., 4.40–7.30 p.m. – and wrote further: 'I understand that Cox has been in touch with you about the preliminary patter and that a plan of action has been decided upon. He also tells me that there is a possibility of your saying at the end exactly what you thought of the whole business, and this promises to be good fun.

'I have secured an Indian (I believe) for the last four lines, and have booked a cast which – if not the best I could have thought of – in view of the money allowed me appears to be more or less adequate.'

TO *Wyndham Lewis*                                                    CC

30 December 1937                    [*The Criterion*]

Dear Lewis,

Thursday of next week, the 6th, will suit me very well, and I will meet you at the Kensington Palace for dinner, unless you have other views.[1]

Don't conclude anything yet about the proposal you made.[2] The fact is that in the scramble of December it had escaped my mind, and I have never brought it up. We have another meeting on Wednesday next, and I will sound the committee about it then. Please excuse my oversight.

John Reid is a young man from Northern Ontario, who wants to write a good novel.[3] I put him on to Ezra, and I believe they have been getting on quite nicely together in Rapallo.

Yours ever,
[T. S. E.]


TO *Polly Tandy*                                                    TS BL

30 December 1937                    *The Criterion*

Pollicle Ma'am,

Ole Possum presents his compliments & apologies for having left his bedroom Slippers behind; but hopes that Pa Tandy will make them the Pretex for a glass of the inwariable one evening next week, to be arranged by telephone, giving ole Possum 24 hours to thaw out after returning from Lingfield on Monday morning, because that clay soil of Surrey is something terrible damp this January weather, not like our West Country soil.

Have you seen that remarkable Piece in the Standard about Mr Woodiwiss the bull-dog breeder? Well it seems Mr Woodiwiss went to some dog show some years ago and he noticed a 'smell of cats'; so he went upstairs and there was a cat show in progress, and his attention was caught by a short-haired tabby named Champion Xenophon. 'Within a few minutes he was mine'. And that's how Mr Woodiwiss began to breed cats. You do get yr. 1d. worth out of the Evening Standard, and no

1–WL had written on 29 Dec.: 'Thurs, Friday or Sat of next week at present will suit me.'
2–'Am I to conclude that the proposal that I made re book of photographs (20 or 30) of pictures, & critical dope, & introduction by self, is unacceptable to Fabers? Should know now, as I need a thing of the sort out.'
3–'Who in Hells name is "John Read", who writes me letters & talks always about *you*?'

mistake, every time.[1] So will close, and thanking you for your hospitality, which was much appreciated & enjoyed,

Tp

## TO *Michael Roberts* TS Janet Adam Smith

30 December 1937  *The Criterion*

Dear Roberts,

Thank you for your letter of the 29th.[2] Your typescript has not yet arrived, but I have no doubt it will in a day or two, and will be acknowledged. Meanwhile I will pass your letter on to Richard de la Mare, for your comments on the setting and the jacket. Have you, by the way, ever seen the bust itself? It belongs to Ashley Dukes, and I saw it a little while ago for the first time. It seemed to me one of Epstein's best portrait busts, and there are some very interesting angles which throw more light on the character than the photograph in *Speculations*.

I look forward to seeing you when you are back in London, although your reference to the evening of the 11th is a mystery to me.[3]

1–On another day, TSE sent Polly Tandy a cutting from the *Evening Standard* identifying class winners at the Southern Counties Cat Show. Category winners in the show included (shorthaired) 'Major E. Sydney Woodiwiss's Abyssinian male Ras Seyum as reserve'; (short-haired kitten) 'Major E. Sydney Woodiwiss's Abyssinian male Ras Aylu as reserve and best foreign kitten'; (long-haired) 'White male, Mrs Cattermole's Lotus Leander; female, Mrs Cattermole's Lotus Lizana.' Alongside the cutting TSE pasted these verses in typescript:

> Now my idea of Bliss
> Were this –
> Upon the whole –
> Eternal Chats
> About Cats
> With Major Sidney Woodiwiss
> And Mrs. Cattermole.

2–'I am now sending you the typescript of Hulme, ready for the printer. It looks rather messy . . . I have been over it carefully, checking such things as the style in which references & quotations are given; and I think that it ought to need very little correction in proof.

'When you are considering a jacket for the book, there might be something to be said for using the photograph of the Epstein head, which was used as a frontispiece to *Speculations*.'

3–The Roberts family had been spending the Christmas holiday in Savoie, France. 'On the 12th, I shall be in London, but I gather that we are likely to meet on the evening of the 11th.' On 11 Jan. 1938 the BBC broadcast *The Waste Land* for the first time – produced by D. G. Bridson: with comments on the broadcast by Michael Roberts and Freddie Grisewood (later famous for the programme *Any Questions*). The Programme Contracts Executive (Robert Gillott) contacted TSE on 4 Jan.: 'We understand from Mr Cox that you may wish to be present in the studio during the broadcast of the "Waste Land" programme on Tuesday,

With best wishes to you and your family for the new year,

Yours ever,<br>T. S. E.

## TO *E. Martin Browne*                    TS Houghton

31 December 1937                    *The Criterion*

Dear Martin,

Here is my new version of the Knights' parting words. I don't like it very well, because it adds three lines; but I don't quite see how to omit anything so as to keep the speech the same length:

> *Knights.*
> Let this be the end of your quibbling words:
> We go for our arms, we go for our men;
> We return with the argument of our swords.
> Priest! monk! and servant! . . .
> . . . we come again.

As for the public meeting. 'My neighbour in the country' seems to me quite right. I cannot get anything so concise for Morville. I thought that if I could suggest that he was an ambitious young politician, it might both sound contemporary and make a good contrast to Traci:

'I shall next call upon Hugh de Morville – a name to remember. He is one of our younger statesmen, whom rumour has marked for high office (in the next ministerial shuffle?): there is no one better qualified to expound the constitutional aspect.'

This is too long, I know.

I can't think of any improvement for Brito, except that I think 'coming as he does of a family distinguished for its *loyalty* to the Church' would be better than *fidelity*.

I offer everything tentatively, and you or Ashley may be able to improve.

Yours ever<br>T. S. E.

I shall see you on Monday evening.

<With the first speech, the Knights might first clap their hands to their sides automatically, and then, finding that they have left their swords behind, speak as follows.>

---

January 11th, from 10.15 to 11.0 p.m., and that you may possibly be broadcasting for about five to eight minutes at the end of the programme.' TSE did not contribute to the broadcast.

# 1938

## TO *Ian Cox*

4 January 1938                              [Faber & Faber Ltd]

Dear Cox,

Thank you for your letter of the 3rd, and for sending me the script.[1]
I have not yet had time to read carefully the text, but I don't suppose it
differs materially from that which Bridson originally submitted. As for
the dialogue, this is certainly an improvement on what was originally
contemplated, though it rather reminds me of a conversation between Mr
Drage and Mr Everyman[2] and seems about as elementary. What worries
me chiefly at the moment is this. According to the script it would seem that
the list of characters is to be read out, but it does not appear that anything
is being said to indicate that several characters are introduced who have
no part in the original poem, or in general to indicate that the poem in its
original intention is any different from the broadcast version. It seems to
me most desirable that there should be some explanatory note somewhere
to explain that the original was a poem, and that this is a dramatized
interpretation, which inevitably takes a number of liberties with the poem,
and which is somewhat different from the poem. Otherwise the innocent

---

1 – Cox had written in an internal BBC memo to 'D.T.', 20 Dec. 1937, on the topic of 'T. S.
Eliot and F. & D.'s experimental hour "The Waste Land"' – 10.15–11.00 p.m. 11.1.38:
   'We have been asked to provide 15 minutes talk in contribution to this programme. In
consultation with Mr Bridson I have arranged for:
       An introductory dialogue between Michael Roberts and F. H. Grisewood to make
       clear the intention of the programme.
       T. S. Eliot (the author of the poem) to speak after the programme to give his views
       on it.
   'Eliot says he will speak only if he has anything to say after hearing the programme: he
does not therefore wish to appear in the "Radio Times". From my personal knowledge of
him I would say that there's very little doubt that he will find something to say, but this
means he will have to speak without a script. I understand from our telephone conversation
that you approve of this.
   'D. F. D. has approved by telephone.'
2 – The furniture retailer Drage's Ltd used the concept of 'Mr Everyman' in its marketing
campaigns from the early 1920s.

listener may imagine that all this is exactly what I intended when I wrote the poem. This seems to me a matter of some importance.[1]

I am intending to come on Thursday afternoon at 4.30 to hear a rehearsal.

Yours in haste,

[T. S. Eliot]

---

1 – 'The Waste Land' – a 'dramatised' adaptation – was broadcast on 11 Jan. 1938, with the text divvied up (at some moments bizarrely) between a series of speakers including Tiresias (played by Robert Farquharson), a Commentator, Phoenician Sailor, Belladonna the Lady of Situations, Belladonna the Cockney, Fisher King, Three Thames Daughters, Angel, God, Hanged Man (the voice of the Thunder), Lithuanian Girl and Archduke.

The script opened:

'This is the National Programme. We present "The Waste Land", a poem by T. S. Eliot, conceived for broadcasting by D. G. Bridson. The poem is in five parts . . .

    TIRESIAS:          April is the cruellest month, breeding
                          Lilacs out of the dead land [. . .]'

For unknown reason, the 'Commentator' recites the opening lines of this passage:

                          In the mountains, there you feel free.
                          I read, much of the night, and go south in the winter.

BEHIND THE LAST TWO LINES, HELPED OFF BY A FADE ON THE GIRL'S LAUGH, THE CONVERSATION HAS GRADUALLY FADED AWAY TO SILENCE, WITH SUFFICIENT OVERLAP TO ROUND OFF THE SEQUENCE. SLIGHT PAUSE, AND UTTER QUIET FOR:

    THE HANGED MAN:    What are the roots that clutch, what branches grow
                          Out of this stony rubbish? Son of man,
                          You cannot say, or guess [. . .]

Belladonna speaks the lines opening:

                          My nerves are bad to-night. Yes, bad. Stay with me.

Later, the Commentator 'hums to himself': 'O O O O that Shakespeherian Rag'; and a 'Cockney' sings the lines beginning 'The river sweats / Oil and tar [. . .]'.

The production concludes:

    THE MAN:               Datta.
    THE ANGEL:           Dayadhvam.
    THE GOD:             Damyata.
    THE HANGED MAN:    Shantih   shantih   shantih.

Val Gielgud wrote to Bridson at the North Regional Offices, Manchester, 19 Jan. 1938: 'Many thanks for your letter about "THE WASTE LAND". I imagine that by now you have had Eliot's letter which I forwarded to you.

'The general view here was the thing was well worth doing. Personally, I don't agree: I am inclined to the opinion that to those who were unfamiliar with the poem the result was pretty well meaningless, while to those who were the radio presentation was disagreeable rather than agreeable. But the Powers that Be here do not agree with me, so no doubt I am wrong! Anyway, I'm glad that you should have had an opportunity of doing something that I believe was rather dear to your heart.'

TO *Louis MacNeice*                                    CC

6 January 1938                    [Faber & Faber Ltd]

Dear MacNeice,

I have read *The Earth Compels* last night, and am very much pleased with it. It seems to me quite up to standard, quite up to what we expect of you, and I am very glad that we are publishing it.

I have only two queries in connexion with 'Eclogue between the Motherless': you mark a number of divisions with parallel ink lines; does this mean that you want separate lines, or what other form of indication that two people are speaking? And a smaller point: is the split infinitive 'to nonchalantly' necessary? It doesn't seem to me so, but perhaps you feel that it is. I don't like using them myself unless an important difference of meaning is conveyed.[1]

Otherwise the poems can go straight to the printer.

Yours ever,
[T. S. Eliot]


TO *Paul Léon*                    TS National Gallery of Ireland

6 January 1938                    Faber & Faber Ltd

Dear Mr Léon,

I have your letter of 1 January, together with the letter from Mr Huebsch of the Viking Press. I will return the latter letter in a few days, as it is at present in the hands of my colleague Mr Morley, who deals with our New York interests, and who is writing to Mr Huebsch.[2]

I must say that your letter of the 1st came to me as a complete surprise, as I was no more aware than was apparently Mr Huebsch of how near

---

1 – MacNeice responded on 8 Jan.: 'I am so glad you like The Earth Compels.

'About the two points you raise:–

'(i) "to melancholy open" in Eclogue between the Motherless can be changed to "nonchalantly to open".

'(ii) I put in the vertical lines thinking that similar lines could be supplied by the printer. Otherwise the change of speaker had better be represented as in my Eclogues in the first book of poems. Only I do not in this case wish to have any initials or numbers.'

*The Earth Compels* was advertised in F&F Spring Books 1938, 78: 'Mr MacNeice's position as a poet was incontestably established in 1935 by his first volume of *Poems* (6s.). He is one of the few poets today none of whose poems could have been written by anyone else. His second volume has been awaited for some time: now that it has arrived, it needs no advertisement.'

2 – Anne Ridler added by hand, at the foot of the page: 'It is after all enclosed herewith.'

the book was to completion. You will remember that in my letter of 14 December last I asked how much more matter there would be before the book was complete. In your letter of 18 December, after discussing the sections which you had recently sent, you say merely: 'All this will constitute by far the greatest body of the text, which is to be followed by an Epilogue to complete the whole work.' I understood from this that there was some more of the text to come, as well as the Epilogue. But we have had no indication from you or from Mr Joyce himself as to when the remaining matter was to be delivered to us. Furthermore, although the bulk of the proof had been sent over, some of it a considerable time back, we have had no corrected proof returned to us, and no indication from Mr Joyce that he was working on the proof and intended to let us have it all back at once. We were for every reason in complete ignorance that Mr Joyce was working at high pressure, or aiming to finish the book by any fixed date.

I am sorry to say that it is quite certain that it is physically impossible for either ourselves or the Viking Press to produce the book in the spring. Mr Joyce's efforts, however, will by no means have been wasted, for if we have the complete material in hand in a final form by 2 February, it will I assure you be none too soon for our needs if we are to bring the book out in the autumn. Even were this book something in the ordinary routine, and making all speed, we should find it quite impossible to bring it out before the summer, and I am sure you will agree that with a book of the importance and of the character of Mr Joyce's, the greatest care is necessary if we are to produce it in a way which will be satisfactory both to Mr Joyce and to ourselves. Furthermore, the programme of publicity has to be very carefully studied.

I hope therefore that you will make it clear to Mr Joyce that we must have the remaining matter and the corrected proofs at the earliest possible moment, in order to launch the book in the autumn.

There are one or two points which I should like to emphasise at this moment, which concern the printing of the book. In the first place, the production department ask that in returning the galleys Mr Joyce should make his divisions very clear, and should state how he wants the page proofs arranged: where he wants sub-headings, and where he would like to have half-titles and titles. By half-titles I mean a blank page with the title of the following section of the book upon it. It is vital for the production of the book in the autumn that we should have on the corrected galleys every indication needed for paging as Mr Joyce would have it done. Otherwise there may be indefinite delay through reprinting the page sheets.

The second point is this. In one of the sections you have recently sent there are side notes. There were no side notes to any of the previous sections of the book, and we had not been warned that such notes might be required in later sections. We had therefore not allowed for this possibility in arranging the format of the page. Does Mr Joyce wish these side notes to be printed in our edition, and if so, will it be satisfactory to him if these notes are indented into the page? We should also like to know whether there will be more side notes in the parts of the book yet to come.

We are expediting the preparation of the proofs of the fresh material in our hands, and will send them as soon as possible. Meanwhile we need to know the answers to the questions I have asked. Also, it would be a help if we could know the title of the book. We quite understand that Mr Joyce does not wish at this point that the title should be generally known, but if we could be given it in confidence it would help to hasten the printing.

With best wishes to yourself and Mrs Léon for the new year,

> I am
> Yours very sincerely,
> T. S. Eliot

## TO *W. H. Auden*                                                    CC

6 January 1938                    [Faber & Faber Ltd]

Dear Wystan,

I have spoken to Stewart about the advance on the Far East book, and he will settle that with Curtis Brown at once. About the advance for *On the Frontier* I cannot report so satisfactorily. I found my committee adamant on the point. As the play cannot be published until the autumn – and I agree with you that it would be a great mistake to publish a play a season in advance of the production – they do not see why we should stand out of all this money for eight months or so. I am sorry, but there seems to be nothing to be done.

I am drafting a letter for you, to whomever it may concern, and sending it on to Wales to Faber, as I think that such a letter should be signed by the Chairman. Besides, it is just possible that they might be suspicious if I signed it.

Let me know when I can see you before you go, and when you are having your party.

> Yours ever,
> [Tom]

TO *Geoffrey Faber*                                        cc

6 January 1938                          [*The Criterion*]

Dear Geoffrey,

Auden came in the other day, and asked if we would supply him and Isherwood with a letter such as the one which I enclose.[1] His point was that they wished to go to Japan as well as China, and that they thought they were more likely to get the necessary visas from the Japanese Consulate in Hong Kong than in London. It seemed to him possible that the Japanese in London might either know something about them, or make enquiries, which might result in the visa being denied. I discussed the matter with the committee yesterday, and we were in accord, and all thought that such a letter ought to be signed by the Chairman. So if you agree, will you sign it and let me have it back, so that I can pass it on to Auden?

They are leaving on the 19th, to sail from Marseilles. We are paying over the instalment of the advance on the book, as arranged, to Curtis Brown. They also asked, by the way, whether they could have the advance on the play, which they have just delivered; but as the play cannot be produced until the autumn when they return to London, and as I feel quite certain that it would be a mistake in the long run to bring it out a season before the production, the committee could see no reason why we should pay over this £75 before the stipulated date, which is that of publication.

Yours ever,<br>[Tom]

TO *Polly Tandy*                                          ts BL

7 January 1938                          *The Criterion*

Well, Pollicle ma'am, I am certainly astonished and gratified and deeply touched by the Oriental Superba or remarkable gift which you and the Old Man have given me – and why? – there seems no reason at all but pure gratuitousness and megaloprepeia etc. And it does reproach me when I looked at those scarlet superbas and compared them with the

---

1 – TSE's draft letter, dated 6 Jan. 1938, read:
'To *whomever it may concern*.
'This is to certify that Mr W. H. Auden and Mr Christopher Isherwood are leaving England for a journey of indefinite extent, for the purpose of travel in preparation for a non-political book on the Far East, which this firm has commissioned them to write. / Chairman.'

tattered clogs which you kindly returned, the latter stained with Calox[1] and Philips's Dental Magnesia froth, torn by toes inside and worn by floors outside, I said well this is a delicate and tactful way of reminding me that I am a slattern, and I will bear it in mind I will indeed. But I shall specially rejoice when I look at my Feet clad in those Scarlet Slippers, to think of what Kind Friends & Generous I have, and that (when you get to my age) is a Comfort and warming to the organ. So three Cheers and a Tear of gratitude, and I hope I will be a Better man for it, I hope so.

> So will close,
> with scarlet toes,
> Tp

## TO *A. Desmond Hawkins*                 TS A. Desmond Hawkins

9 January 1938                 *The Criterion*

Dear Hawkins,

I wrote a letter to Ezra and then scrapped it, because with such a proud and touchy man as he, it is just as likely that a well-meant intervention may only incense him more. I now think it best to wait; and if you do get a roaring letter from him about Stonier, let me know at once, and I will then try to soothe him down. It is obviously much better that you should print a letter from me than one from Ezra – better for Ez I mean.[2]

By the way, I think I ought to have your friend Barlow[3] reviewing for the *Criterion*. Would he? and what sort of books?

I enjoyed seeing you. Let us lunch again early in February.

> Yours
> T. S. E.

---

1 – Calox Tooth Powder, marketed by McKesson and Robbins, Bridgeport, Connecticut.
2 – TSE, 'On a Recent Piece of Criticism' – a response to 'The Mystery of Ezra Pound' by G. W. Stonier – *Purpose: A Quarterly Magazine* 10 (Apr.–June 1938), 90–4; *CProse* 5, 602–8.
3 – Kenneth Barlow.

Dear Bonamy,

Yes, your paper on blank verse (Shakespearean) seems to me O.K.[1] But I speak with diffidence on matters of prosody; because I was quite hopeless at it at school; because I never was set to write even Latin verse; and because what I was taught was never of the slightest use to me in English composition; and because I have always had the greatest difficulty in remembering the difference between a spondee and an amphibrach. All I am certain of is that (1) Nobody knows anything about either the pronunciation of Greek or the reading of Greek verse (2) Latin verse is fundamentally different from Greek but overlaid by it; otherwise it is more like modern European verse and is probably at its best (most itself) in mediaeval hymns (3) English verse is really directed by something that is not present in the Latin languages, and P. S. German verse may be ignored for our present purposes.

I am inclined to think that the iambic pentameter business accounts for the inferiority of post-Miltonic blank verse, and for the puzzling difference between Shakespearean blank verse and later imitations. Why is it that the versification of *The Cenci*[2] etc. ought to be as good as minor Jacobean tragedy and actually is as the worst margerine [*sc.* margarine] to bad butter?

The stress on stressing is I am sure right. The number of syllables doesnt matter.

Procrustes.

However, my own criticism (and its faults) will be apparent rather from my next play, when you see the text. It is in lines mostly of four stresses (irregularly placed) varied by lines of three and sometimes (for choral purposes) of two. Every now and then there is a line that could be scanned as regular iambic pentameter. (It is interesting that when actors have to declaim real verse (Shakespeare) they try to turn it into prose, whereas when they have to declaim what is obviously bad verse (*cf.* Shaw: *The*

---

1–Dobrée (n.d.) sent a lecture he had recently written, 'Note on Shakespeare's Verse', which the 'Warwick editors' insisted upon – 'so I did 'em something different from the vainly repetitive, prosodic nonsense. Perhaps it may amuse you to read it. Luckily I hadn't seen your lectures before I wrote it. I should like it back before very long . . . It is meant for schoolboys.'
2–Percy B. Shelley, *The Cenci: A Tragedy, in five acts* (1819).

*Admirable Bashville*)[1] they do make it sound like verse). I have kept in mind two assumptions:

1. If you can't make the most commonplace remark and still make it sound manifestly VERSE and not prose,

2. If you cant utter the most exalted sentiments, express the most rarified or intense emotions, without the audience thinking at once: 'this is poetry!'

then it isnt dramatic verse.

The audience ought not to be aware continuously that your characters are talking verse. It ought to be too interested to stop to notice that you are talking verse instead of prose.

When I read the first scene of *Hamlet*, or the Recognition Scene in *Pericles*, I am too interested to worry about Poetry, Verse, and Prose.

*The Way of the World* isnt prose while it's going on: it's prose after it's over. *Hamlet* isn't poetry while it's going on: it's poetry after it's over.

Are these ideas right or wrong?

Yours<br>Tom

I am coming up directly after EASTER.[2] Until then, I shall be stewing over what is provisionally called *The Family Reunion*.

## TO *Geoffrey Curtis*                                    TS Houghton

10 January 1938                          *The Criterion*

My dear Curtis,

It was good of you to write in acknowledgement of my card. I rejoice to hear of your profession;[3] you are often in my thoughts, and will be especially remembered on the 13th.

I have always had in mind that I should like to come to visit Mirfield, but I think it will have to be after Easter, because I have a piece of work which I want to finish before then, and don't want to leave London at

---

1 – George Bernard Shaw, *The Admirable Bashville* (1901): a short play based on his novel *Cashel Byron's Profession*.

2 – Dobrée wanted TSE to visit him at home: Southbank, Collingham, Leeds.

3 – Curtis (7 Jan. 1938): 'You will rejoice with me, I know, and remember me in your prayers at the time of complete consecration, that I may really belong to God, and thus the more faithfully to those whom I love. God bless you + ever yours devotedly in Christ / Geoffrey Curtis CR / member elect CR.'

weekends, as I find it is such an interruption. When I come I shall be combining it with a visit to Bonamy Dobrée in Leeds.

Ever yours in Christo,<br>
T. S. Eliot

## TO *Laurence Munns*

CC

10 January 1938                    [Faber & Faber Ltd]

Dear Sir,

I have your letter of 4 January, and must say that I am rather surprised that you have been asked to write a thesis in the Medieval History School on the subject of *Murder in the Cathedral*.[1] It does not seem to me to offer very much scope, unless you depart from the play to consider the constitutional issues involved between the King and the Archbishop. I really feel that your advisers have been themselves ill-advised, and sympathise with your bewilderment. I think you had better take the play as a springboard, and find your subject in the historical documents, which after all is all that I did myself.

With best wishes,<br>
Yours sincerely,<br>
[T. S. Eliot]

## TO *Montgomery Butchart*

CC

11 January 1938                    [*The Criterion*]

Dear Butchart,

I have been very favourably impressed by John Reid ever since I met him crossing from Montreal. Nothing that he has shown me could be called *achieved*, but what do you expect of a boy of twenty? He has a good deal clearer idea of what he wants to do, than I had at his age; and his letters show an unusual power of self-criticism and of humility and abnegation of self before the work to be done. What he needs at present is opportunity for growth and development, and not in the conventional

---

1–Laurence Munns (Birmingham) wrote, 'I am a student of Mediaeval History, & am required to write a thesis for my final examination in June. The subject I have been given is your well-known poetic drama "Murder in the Cathedral".

'I am no dramatic or literary critic, but a historian . . . I therefore take the liberty of appealing to you to suggest some points which may have appealed to you as the author, & yet are lost by the average member of the public.'

way of academic progress. If his family can keep him, on a modest scale, in Europe, for another two years, I can't promise them that they will have made a great author, because one never can predict that; but on the one hand there is just the possibility that he may produce something quite first rate; and on the other, he should be all the better equipped for anything else.

As for his present novel, this may be the nucleus of an important work, but he needs a couple of years development to put it through the melting pot.

Yours,
[T. S. Eliot]

## TO *L. K. Hindmarsh*[1]                                                      CC

11 January 1938                  [*The Criterion*]

Dear Sir,

I must apologise for my delay in answering your letter of the 3rd instant, but I thought it best to wait and see Mr George Barker, and find out from him what subjects he proposed to offer, before answering your enquiry.[2]

Mr Barker has no academic qualifications, but he has a distinguished reputation as a poet, and I can speak for the excellence of his prose writing, both imaginative and critical. His writings have appeared in the *Criterion*, and have been published by Faber & Faber, so that I have shown my interest in them in the most practical way. I have no knowledge of his ability as a lecturer, but (having had considerable experience of extension lecturing myself in the past) I can say that he would bring to the work a literary sensibility, and enthusiasm and an originality which his students ought to receive with gratitude as exceptional amongst lecturers. I recommend him warmly for a trial course.

---

1–L. K. Hindmarsh, Secretary, Delegacy for Extra-Mural Studies, University of Oxford.
2–'I have received a letter from Mr George Barker (if I have read the signature correctly) in which he states that he has been recommended by you and by Mr de la Mare to seek an opportunity of giving extension lectures for the Delegacy. Mr Barker does not give very much detailed information about his qualifications but he refers in particular to the fact that you are well acquainted with his work.

'I am afraid there is not at the moment any very definite prospect of the Delegacy being able to offer Mr Barker any courses, but there is always the possibility of the unexpected opportunity arising. I should therefore be very glad to have your confidential opinion of him both from the point of view of his competence as an authority on his subjects and his suitability as a Lecturer.'

I have advised him to include among his suggested subjects a course on fourteenth and fifteenth century poetry, as I know that he has an unusual sympathy with the poetry of that period.

Yours very truly,
T. S. Eliot
Director of Faber & Faber Ltd.
Editor of *The Criterion*

## TO *Val Gielgud*

TS BBC

13 January 1938 *The Criterion*

Dear Mr Gielgud,

Thank you for your letter of the 11th.[1] I appreciate your generosity in exculpating Bridson from responsibility about the cutting of *The Waste Land*. I did have a talk with him about it, and I have never for a moment supposed that he would voluntarily have altered the text in any way. By the time I saw Bridson and knew that a cut had been made, the performers had already been engaged and were rehearsing, and I told Bridson that in view of that fact I felt that it would be inconsiderate of me to call a halt to the production, and thus presumably deprive the performers of the fees which they would otherwise have earned. I told him however that I did take very strong exception to the principle of such cutting, while holding him in no way responsible, and I want to make it quite clear that in any future production of any of my work, no cuts are to be made to which I have not agreed in advance. I feel that if there is any question of doubtful passages the B.B.C. should make up its mind before coming to an arrangement with the author, and of course with the producer and speakers.

I should like to give Bridson high marks for having done as well as he did with what seemed to me a quite impossible task, but I should like to say that I cannot agree with the suggestion in your last sentence. With all praise and good wishes, it seems to me much better that *The Waste Land*

---

1 – 'It is, I think, only fair to Geoffrey Bridson to let you know that while he was given a free hand with the broadcasting presentation of "The Waste Land", he only submitted to the cutting of the script under the influence of *force majeure*.

'I should like personally to express to you my regret that any cutting seemed to me to be necessary . . . This, however, is probably inevitable when dealing with material acknowledged to be, from a broadcasting point of view, experimental, and I hope that ultimately you may be disposed to agree that it is preferable for "The Waste Land" to be heard by a listening audience even in an imperfect form than that it should not be broadcast at all.'

should never be broadcast at all than that it should be broadcast in this form![1]

Yours sincerely,
T. S. Eliot

## TO *D. G. Bridson* CC

13 January 1938           [Faber & Faber Ltd]

My dear Bridson,

I must congratulate you at least on having improved the performance of your actors certainly out of all recognition to their behaviour during the rehearsal that I heard. Assuming for the moment that it is suitable to produce *The Waste Land* in this way, I have three criticisms of detail which it might interest you to know. The first is that there were moments when the incidental business and off noises were so much to the foreground that it was a strain to hear the words, and I don't believe that anyone who had never read the poem could have followed the words in these places. This was particularly evident in the last paragraph of Section I.

Secondly, while I did not otherwise object to the bit about the barges being sung, I thought that it led to an unfortunate reversal; I mean, it is a pity that the refrain should have been spoken (which makes it sound foolish) instead of being sung to the excellent bit of music which Wagner

1–D. G. Bridson, *Prospero and Ariel: The Rise and Fall of Radio: A Personal Recollection* (1971), 64–5, 67: 'The only production that I had time to mount in London was a radio dramatisation of *The Waste Land*, for which I had Eliot's blessing. So far as I was concerned, this made quite remarkable radio, but I have to confess that Eliot did not share my own enthusiasm for the result. It will be remembered that the substance of the poem, on Eliot's own showing, is "what Tiresias sees". As dramatised, the substance of the poem becomes "what Tiresias says". Apart from his linking narration, therefore, the poem resolved itself into a medley of remembered sounds and voices – the Lithuanian woman, Madame Sosostris, the girl in the pub, and the rest of them. As it transpired, the girl in the pub faced me with my only serious problem; for unlike poor Lil, the BBC flatly refused to swallow any abortion pills. I suddenly found myself under strict orders to omit all mention of them – vital as they were to the argument of the poem! Eliot was so incensed by this ridiculous censorship, that he only allowed the mangled text to go on the air at all out of a friendly feeling for me as producer. But what principally dismayed him about the production was Robert Farquharson's performance in the key role of Tiresias.

'Farquharson took to his role of the old man-woman with natural relish; his interpretation gave to it new shades of implication which Eliot little supposed were there. Never was sexual ambivalence heard more convincingly on the air . . . Even so, an audience of millions accepted *The Waste Land* on the air with surprising enthusiasm. For one thing, resolution into its different parts made it a great deal easier to follow. The mail which reached me after the broadcast was something of a surprise even to Eliot himself.'

provided for the purpose. But what shocked me most of all was that the words of the Thames Daughters which follow were also sung, to the accompaniment of an irrelevant and trivial strumming, instead of being spoken as they should be.

The experiment may have been worth making, as an experiment, and I feel sure that you did the best with it that anyone could do with such material. But that confidence in your own accomplishment only confirms my belief that this sort of poetry is quite wrong for dramatising in that sort of way.

But finally I should like to congratulate you on the conversation between Roberts and Grisewood which followed the poem. It really seemed to me a very courageous thing to do, and I am quite certain that it was much better from every point of view than having me speak myself.[1]

Yours ever,<br>[T. S. Eliot]

## TO *Stephen Spender*

13 January 1938                    *The Criterion*

Dear Stephen,

Your letter of the 11th arrived opportunely for discussion by the committee yesterday afternoon.[2] I am afraid that our opinion is

---

1 – Bridson replied, 18 Jan.: 'I was very glad to hear that you found the actors more satisfying than at the rehearsal, as I rather fancied you would. Your criticism of the music could very likely have been cleared up to our mutual satisfaction if we had been able to include it at the session you attended. (Incidentally, "irrelevant and trivial strumming" which you mention gets full marks from the Musical Adviser to the City of Birmingham, who picked it out for special mention!) . . .

'As regards exegesis, I still think that the real raison d'être of the programme consisted in its presentation of your raw material as opposed to your comment upon it. For all your note to the contrary, the substance of the poem is not so much of what Tiresias *sees* as what he thinks or says about what he sees. This simple fact will, I think, clear up for you the essential differences in tone between the poem as read and the production as heard . . .

'Finally, I really do wish to thank you again for the extremely aimiable [*sic*] way in which you received not merely one cut but two cuts in the text, for which, as you know, I was in no way responsible. I believe Gielgud has written you on this point, but I should like to say once more that I absolutely deplore any such interference with other people's work.'

2 – SS wrote on behalf of the Group Theatre. 'We are organising a series of Lectures, given on Sunday nights, by distinguished men of letters. For example, next Sunday, John Betjeman is giving a Lecture on "Antiquarian Prejudice". Christopher Isherwood has already given one (which was such a success that people were turned away), and also Masefield and others; John Grierson and myself are each giving one soon, and there is to be a Debate on painting between William Coldstream and John Piper.

unanimous about any proposal for the production of pamphlets. We have found in the past that the amount of overhead charges, so far as both the production and the selling departments are concerned, are so high with pamphlets in relation to the possible sale as to make them an impossible luxury. Of a pamphlet one wants to be sure of selling at least 10,000 copies in order to make the expense of time and thought justifiable, and it is a very rare pamphlet indeed which will sell to that amount; in fact, our experience with the *Criterion Miscellany* was that the items which sold conspicuously better than anything else were not really bought as pamphlets at all, as they were first editions of bits of unpublished work by Joyce and D. H. Lawrence.

There might be a limited advertisement value for the Group Theatre in publishing the pamphlets at their own expense, and certainly the probable sale would not encourage any publisher to undertake it in view of the fact that a pamphlet takes almost as much trouble to lay out, and certainly as much trouble to sell, as a full-sized book. I think however that if your committee seriously wants to get these lectures published in this way, the only way to do it is to go direct to a printer and get the work done according to your specifications and the amount you are able to spend, and then give a good deal of time yourselves to pushing the sales and distribution. Or you could approach some firm like W. H. Smith, but I don't believe that a huge commercial organisation like that would want to bother with what from their point of view would be of such trifling value.

If your committee wish to pursue the matter, I shall be glad to be of any use I can personally, but I could not see my way to recommending the scheme to Faber & Faber, and they would not have looked at it any more favourably if I had done so.

There is one point in which I am interested in a different way, and that is your publishing a lecture covering the ground of your book on *Aspects of Modern Poetry*. I think it is a very commendable scheme for you to lecture on this subject as much as you can: it might do no harm to publish the lecture in a periodical, but I should strongly urge you not to publish it separately, as I think it would seriously interfere with the sales

---

'It has occurred to us that it might be a good idea to start a series of pamphlets, called the Group Theatre Lectures, to be published by Faber. I think that the Writers would be in agreement. Betjeman, for instance, was delighted at the proposal. I myself would like to write a Lecture covering the ground of my book on Aspects of Modern Poetry. Perhaps I might even express the hope that you yourself will again contribute a Lecture to the series. We could let you have the manuscript of the first Lecture by Betjeman within the next few days, if you would care to see it, and after that we could probably arrange to send a manuscript every two months.'

of the book. Indeed if we are to publish the book, I think we have [a] very serious interest in your not publishing a pamphlet on the same subject!

It occurs to me that if you abandon the pamphlet project, I might suggest the *Criterion* as a medium in which to present some at least of the lectures, especially if they do not come too rapidly and are not too long for our limits.

I note what you say about the manuscript of the play, which I hope to be able to have a good look at before it goes to press; and I will make a note that you want to have galley proofs.[1]

With best wishes,<br>
Yours ever affectionately<br>
Tom

## TO *Theodora Eliot Smith*

TS Houghton

14 January 1938 *The Criterion*

Dear Dodo,

Here I am at last getting round to writing you a post-Christmas letter. The more formal ones go first. I got your letter in time,[2] and also the two photographs: neither of which – may I say – I liked *very* much! The one of you is rather stiff and frozen, and looks as if you did *not* enjoy the operation (as many photographs do), though at the same time it has a pleasing mediaeval aspect, like a late Gothic head on a corbel (NOT a gargoyle). The one of Priscilla is at least a good deal better than the large cabinet one which I received from Chardy, and that is all I can say about it: but of course I have never seen the child herself. This does not sound very thankful, but I AM pleased to have them, and with you for sending them.

Well, I am thinking of buying a portable radio too, as my present to myself. I have done very well without one for some years, but now and then there are things which I ought to have heard. But I don't want one that will take up much room, or that will get remote foreign stations (which is a fraud anyway, as they are mostly explosions); I have listened

---

1 – 'I shall be sending you my own manuscript of the play, in its completely rewritten form, at the end of this week . . . If you can let me have galley proofs (not page proofs), I would be very glad, as there may still be alterations which I want to make when I see it set up.'

On 16 Jan. SS submitted to RdlM the text of *Trial of a Judge* (1938); he returned galley proofs on 14 Feb. The production was scheduled for 18 Mar.

2 – Letter not found.

to Schenectady. And sometimes some of my own works are done: though the production of *The Waste Land* a few days ago gave me some mirth, but not much pleasure.

You will, I believe, have the *Murder* in Baltimore, unless it collapses under criticism before it gets there, by way of Philadelphia. Anyway, they are starting out from Liverpool tomorrow to open in Boston on the 31st; and any reports you get of their reception in Boston may give you some notion of whether they will survive to Baltimore. I hope if they do they will send you tickets for the first night. I can say (having spent a good deal of time last week with rehearsals) that the Chorus is quite the best they have ever had, and some of the new actors (two new knights) are very good.

Well, about the school. One can hardly give advice knowing so little: but it sounds to me wise for you to resign, even with nothing definite in view, if you are convinced that a collapse will come. If you hung on to the end, people might then, when you were applying elsewhere, wonder whether you were not one of the reasons for the collapse! But when you have anything to communicate, I shall be eager to know what you are doing about next year, and what the prospects are. And if you don't get a job in time, you probably won't feel inclined to come over next summer. But I at least may be able to go over for a month in the autumn.

With much love and 1938 wishes, from

Tom

## TO *Elsie Fogerty*[1]                                     CC

14 January 1938                    [Faber & Faber Ltd]

Dear Miss Fogerty,

Thank you for your note of 12 January.[2] I return herewith the list of 100 names for seats. I feel that I am unqualified to make any suggestions about actors or workers in or for the theatre, but one or two suggestions occur to me in the list of dramatists. Of course there are several dramatists in the list whose names are unknown to me, and several more, such as

---

1–Elsie Fogerty, CBE, LRAM (1865–1945) – teacher of elocution and drama training; founder in 1906 of the Central School of Speech and Drama (Laurence Olivier and Peggy Ashcroft were favourite pupils) – had trained the chorus for the Canterbury première in 1935 of *MiC*. See further *Fogie: The life of Elsie Fogerty, C.B.E.*, compiled and ed. Marion Cole (1967), 164–8.
2–Not traced.

St John Hankin,[1] who seem to me pretty small beer. I would like to suggest that Christopher Marlowe, who is omitted, is more important in national drama than Stephen Phillips,[2] or even Henry Arthur Jones;[3] and the same might be said, although less emphatically, about Otway.[4] Indeed there are three or four other Elizabethan or Jacobean dramatists who seem to me more important than Alfred Sutro.[5]

With best wishes,
Yours very sincerely,
[T. S. Eliot]

TO *Paul Léon*                                   TS National Gallery of Ireland

18 January 1938                                  *The Criterion*

Dear Mr Léon,

I am enclosing two more specimen pages for Mr Joyce. I am now able to inform you that the last galleys of the remaining matter which we have in hand will be ready by the end of the first week in February,

Lord Carlow came in to see me, and gave me the dummy for the page arrangement of the book, which I have handed to Mr de la Mare. Lord Carlow also intimated that Mr Joyce would like to have the book published on 4 July. I am afraid this date also is much too soon to be possible for either us or the Viking Press, and has the additional disadvantage that it is a public holiday in America, and therefore no books can be published there on that day. We think that a date at the beginning of September should be possible, and that it would be the right moment.[6]

---

1–St John Hankin (1869–1909), Edwardian playwright and essayist; associated with the Stage Society and the Royal Court Theatre; author of *The Return of the Prodigal* (1905).
2–Stephen Phillips (1864–1915), poet and dramatist; cousin of Laurence Binyon; author of plays including *Paolo and Francesca* (1900) and *Herod: A Tragedy*, prod. by Beerbohm Tree in 1900.
3–Henry Arthur Jones (1851–1929), dramatist. *The Silver King* (1882), *Saints and Sinners* (1884), *The Middleman* (1889), *Judah* (1890), enjoyed great success in their day.
4–Thomas Otway (1652–85), Restoration dramatist; best known for *Venice Preserv'd* (1682).
5–Alfred Sutro (1863–1933), author, dramatist, translator; friend and translator of the Belgian author Maurice Maeterlinck (1862–1949), winner of the Nobel Prize for Literature, 1911; author of many popular plays including *The Walls of Jericho* (1904).
6–Paul Léon responded from Paris on 23 Jan. that JJ had asked him to 'transmit' to TSE this message: 'After the receipt of your letter of the 18th he called to his son (at present on

With best wishes,

Yours very sincerely,

T. S. Eliot

---

a visit to New York) to telephone Mr Huebsch on the subject. His son replied by cable to say Mr Huebsch considered publication on the 4th of July undesirable but would await the arrival in New York early in February of Mr Morley of your firm in order to confer with him before deciding. Mr Joyce wishes me to remind you, in view of this proposed conference, that Mr Huebsch is the person who always believed that a publication of Ulysses in the United States was impracticable and that Mr Morley is the person who believed, even after Mr Huebsch had been proved in every way to be wrong, that a publication of Ulysses in England was also impracticable. Mr Joyce is perfectly well aware of the fact that the 4th of July is the American National holiday (five members of his family owe their Christian names to this fact including his dog) and it is precisely for this reason, among others, that he wished his book to be published in England on that day and in the U.S.A. on its eve (his father's birthday).

'If no intelligent effort will be made to comply with his wish he sees no use in continuing to work night and day as he has done and plans to leave from Switzerland after his own birthday (2 February) for a holiday of several months, reserving the work on his work for the autumn.'

TSE was so exasperated by Léon's missive that he passed it to GCF, with this note penned at the top: 'Will you be dealing with this? You can control your temper better than I can.'

GCF duly wrote direct to JJ, 26 Jan., with exaggerated patience and firm courtesy:

> Eliot has given me his recent correspondence with M. Léon concerning the publication of WORK IN PROGRESS, and has asked me to continue it, since he feels that M. Léon's last letter (of January 23rd) needs to be answered by the head of the firm.
>
> I haven't taken any personal part in the correspondence and pourparlers over WORK IN PROGRESS hitherto, because – rightly or wrongly – I imagined that you would rather be dealing with a friend of long standing like Eliot. But impar congressus Achilli ['no match for Achilles': words spoken by Troilus in Virgil, *Aeneid* 1: 475] though I am – it is clear that M. Léon's letter of the 23rd brings matters to a point at which I must take over responsibility.
>
> In matters of importance, and especially in matters which are threatened by any kind of misunderstanding, my own instinct prompts me to get into direct communication with the other party. The publication of WORK IN PROGRESS is a matter of unique importance. So I make no apology for writing to you direct; especially as M. Léon was writing under your instructions. I am sending M. Léon a copy of this letter.
>
> Although I have only had the pleasure of meeting you once, some years ago, at Eliot's flat, I know that I can ask you to dismiss from your mind the irritation, which is expressed in the message conveyed to us by M. Léon, and to consider the simple facts of the situation. They are as follows:
>
> So far as we are concerned, we could publish on the date, which you so earnestly desire, July 4, provided that (1) we received the rest of the MS within the next two or three weeks (2) both you and we could be sure that the correction of the proofs would not take you too long a time. On the first point, we have no definite information. And on the second point, is it not probable you will find the correction of the proofs a rather slow process?

19 January 1938                    *The Criterion*

Dear Hawkins,

Yes, I got quite to the end of your letter, and in fact I read it twice.[1] I can see your point about a short article (I think it should be very short) instead of a letter to the Editor. It might be effective in making Ezra keep quiet, and if there is no response except a letter he may still think that a letter from himself is called for. I also think that it has editorial advantages.

---

It would certainly be very difficult for the Viking Press to publish on July 3 (which M. Léon now tells us is the date you want in the U.S.A.), since they cannot begin until they have our corrected proofs to work from. Moreover, American publishers need a considerably longer time in which to prepare the ground for the publication even of ordinary books than English publishers need, because of the enormously greater size of the territory which their travellers have to cover. They cannot bring their publication dates forward so easily as we can. In the case of a book so unusually important as WORK IN PROGRESS their need of sufficient time is all the greater.

M. Léon tells us that Mr Huebsch is waiting for Morley's arrival in New York in order to discuss the date of publication with him. Morley sails tomorrow morning; but unless Huebsch knows when he can expect final proofs from us, how can he possibly commit himself to a date? And we cannot say, even approximately, when such proofs will be available for him, unless we know when we shall have the rest of the MS and how long a time your proof-corrections will take.

If we published in July and the Americans in the autumn copyright would not be affected; but the Viking Press could not be expected to agree to so long a gap, since it would be impossible to prevent the leakage of English copies into the American market.

So you will see that the difficulties in the way of promising publication for July 4 aren't of our making, and we can't remove them. The only person who could conceivably remove them is yourself; but I don't see how you can be sufficiently sure over the amount of time that will be needed for proof-corrections.

These being the facts of the situation, will you not ease the relations between yourself and your publishers by giving them fair recognition, instead of instructing M. Léon to write in the extraordinary terms of his letter of the 23rd? As it is, I propose to treat M. Léon's letter as if it had not been written, and to end simply with an appeal to you to reconcile yourself to publication in September, if publication in early July proves to be impracticable; and not to carry out the idea of breaking off your work now, just when its completion is in sight.

1–Hawkins wrote on 16 Jan. (from Radwinter, nr. Saffron Walden, Essex) a three-page letter ending 'What a length this letter is. Are you still with me?' He asked 'about your reply. I know you said it was to be in the form of a letter, but I should be very happy if I could disguise it as a short article. Would you object to that? What I had in mind was a commencement on the lines of "In the Jan. number of Purpose Mr Stonier – etc. etc. and I should like to – etc."'

I will meditate on that over the weekend, and in any case would be glad to know when you want copy for the next number.[1]

Also the symposium in *Purpose*.[2] I think I should have time to do something for you toward the end of the year, and you will at least be justified in including my name amongst the contributors.

I particularly don't want you to think that I had any line in mind for the Fiction Chronicle other than what you have taken.[3] I don't know anybody else who I think would have done it better, and I am very glad to have had what you have done, and I imagine that you have quite enough material to do a good one for the next number. But I have been very doubtful whether after the start we should find enough fiction of importance regularly to give you the food to digest. I was also looking at it – I will not say from your point of view, but from my point of view of what was to your interest, and it seemed to me that a man who was interested in writing a novel himself had nothing to gain from writing about other people's, especially when they are not masterpieces, and that your mind would be better occupied for a little while on reviewing the American intellectual scene. Whether I am right or not, this is what I want to try next!

I hope that I shall be hearing from Barlow.[4]

I should be glad to meet the Swinglers, and to meet your wife and yourself in town, but I am afraid Thursday and Friday nights are impossible.[5] If I should find myself free on Friday evening I would ring up on the chance of possibly finding you at home so that I might come in after dinner.

---

1–TSE, 'On a Recent Piece of Criticism' (concerning *The Mystery of Ezra Pound* by G. W. Stonier), *Purpose: A Quarterly Magazine* 9: 2 (Apr.–June 1938), 90–4. *CProse* V.

2–'The other matter is the Symposium series. I wanted to take Western culture as the subject and define the kind of perspective within which thinking can usefully go on . . . Bluntly, what have we got, what can we salvage from the past, what can we expect, and what do we want?'

3–'I'm glad about doing the American periodicals. It's the sort of thing that will interest me, but I have a twinge of regret at the disappearance of my Chronicle as such. Were you dissatisfied with it? I have a feeling I didn't strike the line you wanted.'

4–'I'll pass your message on to [Kenneth] Barlow and he had better ask you for the books he thinks he could best review. His ground is science in general, and particularly the attempt to deduce a philosophy from scientific method. I should say his root is a kind of modified vitalism.'

5–'We are coming up to Town on Wednesday and staying until Saturday with the Randall Swinglers. Would you care to come one evening to dinner . . .? I think you would like them. I expect you will have heard of Randall. He took over Auden's job with the Group Theatre, is a friend of Auden and George B., writes verse, edits Left Review, is consequently Left, and in spite of all that is one of the pleasantest men I know.' Swingler (1909–67) joined the Communist Party in 1934, and was founder-editor of *Left Review*. See Andy Croft, *Comrade Heart* (2003).

As for Growltiger (one word) I have no spare copy at the moment, but I will let you have one as soon as I can get round to retyping it.[1] Many thanks.

Yours ever,

T. S. E.

TO *John Middleton Murry*[2]                                    TS Northwestern

19 January 1938                              *The Criterion*

Dear John,

I have just read your pamphlet 'God or the Nation?' which only came my way recently from a young man who came to see me, and I like it very much.[3] I am not speaking specifically of your attitude about Peace – in this respect I am as near to Maritain as to anybody (v. his preface to Mendizabal's *Aux origines d'une tragédie*)[4] – but in general. It is very

---

1 – 'Lastly a request: have you a spare typescript of Growl Tiger? As I have two children AND a siamese cat, I feel I'm the ideal audience for which you wrote.'

2 – John Middleton Murry (1889–1957), English writer and editor: see Biographical Register.

3 – Peace Pledge Union: 'bewildered mankind will find release and salvation only when it knows that by the death of Caesar it is to be absolved from allegiance to Caesars; and that it has but one way now; to render unto God the things that are God's . . . I am deadly serious and completely sincere when I say that the problem of establishing a supra-national authority is none other than the problem of discovering, or rediscovering God.' (11–12)

'And the manner of the re-birth of Christianity appears plain to me. Christianity will be re-born in that form of the Christian Church that has the courage really to break with Nationalism. That means necessarily a re-birth of the Christian Church into the catholicism it has now finally betrayed' (16). 'The one political problem of the European world today is the establishment of the necessity and authority of God: of the Christian God' (17). 'Thus I have come to believe that a re-birth of the Christian religion . . . is necessary to the life of humanity and the continuity of civilisation' (23).

4 – Alfred Mendizabal, *Aux origines d'une tragédie: la politique espagnole de 1923 à 1936*; preface by Jacques Maritain (Paris, 1937): *The Martyrdom of Spain: Origins of a Civil War*, trans. Charles Hope Lumley (London, 1938). 'We do not condemn the use of force in itself. We have endeavoured to point out elsewhere that in the hierarchy of means, this particular means is far from being the most glorious, and by reason of the axiom, "The order of means corresponds to that of ends," temporal history places Christians under the obligation of preferring a host of other means to force [cf. Maritain, *Humanisme Intégrale* (1936), 261–9]; but the use of force is not bad in itself, is not intrinsically bad. Nor do we think that recourse to this means should be excluded on principle where there is question of the defence of religion (although this is assuredly the least admirable way of defending it). If, in certain extreme cases, people have recourse to force in order to defend their religious liberties, it would be because, on account of their superior virtue, these liberties interest the common good of the temporal city and of civilisation . . . If they believe it to be just, let them invoke the justice of the war they are waging, but do not let them invoke its sanctity! If they believe they have to kill, let them kill, in the name of the social order or of the nation; that is

---

nearly Christian in spirit (please take this remark as made in an intention of measurement and definition, not of a kind of approval which might sound impertinently patronising): only not so, I think, because the centre of values is rather this-worldly. But everything that you say about parish life, about the difference between town and country, the mistaken policy of some town-bred clergy in country parishes, is very true according to my own observation, and puts better several things that had occurred to my mind before.[1]

Ever yours,
Tom

## TO *Idris Davies*[2]                                                CC

20 January 1938                     [Faber & Faber Ltd]

Dear Sir,

I must apologise for having held your poems for such a long time, but I am very slow in making up my mind about poetry, and like to read poems several times, at considerable intervals.[3] I am afraid this is not the

---

horrible enough as it is; but do not let them kill in the name of Christ the King, who is not a leader of war, but a King of grace and charity, who died for all men and whose Kingdom is not of this world.' (31–3)

1–JMM to TSE, 20 Jan. 1938: 'I daresay I'm a good deal of the heretic still' (cited in F. A. Lea, *The Life of John Middleton Murry* [1959], 249). See too TSE to Philip Mairet, 19 Jan. 1938: 'Middleton Murry's pamphlet, "God or the Nation?" is worth a notice. It's a Peace Pledge Union pamphlet, but it has some good points apart from the pacifism business. A reliable informant tells me Murry is taking Orders, which rather alarms me; for unless Murry has taken to sticking to the same skin and the same spots, I think him less inconvenient outside the Church than in.'

2–Idris Davies (1905–53). *The Collected Poems*, ed. Islwyn Jenkins was to be published by Gemerian Press of Llandysul, Cardiganshire. TSE to the Revd Islwyn Jenkins, 7 Nov. 1957: 'I am very glad that there should exist such a biographical and critical account of Idris Davies and his work as you have produced, and like to think that the copies will be available for future students in the National Library and in University College, Cardiff. I do regard Davies's poetry as a valuable document on a particular moment of civilization in a particular place and I hope that his work will not be wholly forgotten. At the same time, I must say that I am very doubtful of the possibilities of publication of such a book. I am very happy to have been instrumental in publishing so much of Davies's work and indeed I gave a good deal of time to selecting the poems of a writer who, as you say most justly, was rather too fluent; but I cannot see any publisher risking publication.'

3–Davies submitted the first fourteen sections of his long poem 'Gwalia Deserta' on 20 July 1937. 'And this is definitely my last attempt to deal with "modern" South Wales in English verse. Recently, I have been very interested in the legends of pre-Christian Wales, and I believe that I shall find plenty of material there, in the near future, for something like good poetry, poetry that will be "purer", and in less danger of being contaminated (or cursed?)

type of poetry which fits into our list, which, as every publisher's must be with verse, has to be very definitely limited. It is simple, straightforward, and is definitely impressive by its sincerity, and by the author's obviously knowing what he is talking about. I should like very much to see your poems published, and to see this sequence of poems published as one volume. It would seem most suitable to suggest local publication in Wales, if I did not know that the tendency for everything to centre in London had destroyed the life of local publishing activity. I really don't know what publisher to suggest, and I can only say that if you are writing to one, I shall be glad if you care to say that I have expressed interest, and am quite prepared to write direct about the poems to any publisher who cares to communicate with me.[1]

With many regrets,<br>
Yours sincerely,<br>
[T. S. Eliot]

## TO F. T. *Prince*                                                  CC

20 January 1938                          [Faber & Faber Ltd]

Dear Prince,

I am glad to tell you that yesterday the committee agreed to publish your volume of poems.[2]

It is now impracticable to produce the book in the spring, so we propose to bring it out in September. We are offering the terms which we have now made our rule with first books of verse: that is, no royalty is paid on the first 500 copies sold – that is to say, until we have covered our expenses – and in view of this we offer a 15% royalty thereafter, instead of the 10% which we should give if we were paying a royalty from the beginning.

---

by politics. For, though my verse may sound Socialistic here and there, I detest Communism as much as I detest Fascism, To be frank, I desire a Wales knowing neither Christianity, nor Communism, nor Fascism. I shall try to recreate the peculiar beauty of the Wales of the pagan princes.'

1 – On 11 Aug. 1937 he sent the concluding sixteen sections of the poem. 'I know that you will be merciful with my verses.' *Gwalia Deserta* was to be published by J. M. Dent (1938).

2 – Final blurb for Prince's *Poems* (1938): 'The title *Poems* usually means that the book is the first volume of poems by that author. Poems by F. T. Prince have appeared in *The Criterion* and other periodicals: this is his first volume.'

See too Anthony Rudolf, 'F. T. Prince: A Tribute', *PN Review* 29: 1 (Sept.–Oct. 2002), 26–38: 'On 17 May 1976, Prince wrote to me, his quondam latest publisher, from the University of the West Indies: "the blurb to *Poems* (1938) was indeed a supreme example of Eliot's art as a blurb writer"' (147).

A contract will be sent to you in due course, but I should like to have your general agreement first.

Meanwhile, I should like you to consider whether you wish to call the book *Poems*, or give it some particular title. For my part, I think that *Poems* is quite satisfactory for a first book. I shall also, when I have meditated the matter a little, offer a suggestion or two about some alteration in the order of the poems.

Yours ever,
[T. S. Eliot]

## to *E. McKnight Kauffer*[1]                                    ts Morgan

21 January 1938                          *The Criterion*

Dear Ted,

I don't know exactly what your relations are with the advertising world at present, and if this request is merely a nuisance please say so. I am trying to find a job of some kind for George Barker, who is an interesting young poet, several of whose volumes we have published. He suffers both from malnutrition and a tendency to write too much, and a steady job, even at a very small salary, would help in both ways. He says that he would be very much interested in advertising. He draws and sketches, but I have not seen any of his work of this kind; and he is also much interested in typography.

I sent him to Tom Beachcroft, who was very nice to him, and gave him an introduction to some people in Walter Thompson's, but there was nothing doing there. If you cared to let him come to see you at some time and give him advice, I should be very grateful; but if you feel that you have nothing to say, I don't want to waste your time.[2]

Yours ever,
T. S. E.

P.S. Did Marion ever get a letter from me about the drawing desk?[3]

T

---

1 – Edward McKnight Kauffer (1890–1954), American artist and illustrator; friend of TSE.
2 – McKnight Kauffer responded, 29 Jan.: 'I have seen Mr J. L. Beddington of Shell Mex & B.P. Ltd. . . . I have spoken to him about George Barker and he would be very pleased and interested to see Barker. It may be possible that he can offer him something, but this I am not sure of. Mr Beddington assures me, however, that there are openings for people of Barker's calibre.'
3 – Marion Dorn replied, 22 Jan.: 'The table is ordered and should be delivered on Monday . . . The price was £4. 15. 0. . . . Ted & I missed the "Waste Land" by the B.B.C. but John tells me that you will probably be pleased we did.'

## TO *E. McKnight Kauffer*                                    TS Morgan

24 January 1938                          *The Criterion*

Dear Ted,

Thank you very much for your letter of the 23rd.[1] I am answering at once to say that while I am sure Barker would rather have a part-time job than none, I think that he had in mind a whole-time job, and I am quite sure that a whole-time job would be better for him, as I think that the less time he has for writing poetry the better it will be for the poetry he does write.

I am looking forward with much excitement to the table, which may have arrived in my absence, and will write to Marion as soon as it comes. I am extremely grateful to her for the trouble she has been at.

I am free on the evening of February 2nd, Candlemas Day,[2] and if there is to be a birthday dinner for John I should be delighted to be allowed to come, though rather jaded I fear after having to appear at a do at the Mansion House on behalf of Southwark Cathedral.

Ever yours,
Tom


## TO *Philip Mairet*                                              CC

24 January 1938                          [Faber & Faber Ltd]

Dear Mairet,

Thank you very much for your letter. I hope that the recipients of the N.E.W. will be properly appreciative of the benefits they are receiving.

I quite agree with you that there is danger in a precipitate rush of unprepared entrants into the Church.[3] I find it very difficult to think of

---

The Coller Table Easel with Imperial Triple Drawing Board with fittings was marketed by Clifford Milburn of Fleet Street, London. It enabled TSE to type while standing.

1 – 'I will ask one or two people I know about Mr Barker. I take it he would only wish a part time job. Peter Quennell has such a job with Shell-Mex and I believe it was quite agreeable.'

2 – 'John's [JDH] birthday is on February 2nd. We are hoping to have a birthday dinner for him – could you come?'

3 – Mairet wrote, 21 Jan.: 'The rumour about [JMM] is a bit of a shock to me, too, although I have been for some time expecting a trek of lost intellectuals towards the true fold. Perhaps the Church had better get beforehand and make a rule that those who have lived by the publishing of more or less heretical views should spend the same length of time as good laymen before seeking ordination! I suppose Murry would have been a first-class mind but for some psychic mess-up that dates a long way back, and is unlikely to get much better. Indeed I lately wondered if it hasn't got much worse: I don't know if he wrote the "Last

Middleton Murry as a vicar, except as one of the kind who eventually get into trouble with their bishop. Whatever he went into, I am sure he would carry any number of heresies in with him, as he did into Marxism, and these will breed and make trouble later.

I will keep Thursday 3 February. Prada's[1] would suit me as well as anywhere, but if you prefer another place, let me know. Say 7.30.

Yours ever,

[T. S. Eliot]

## TO *George Barker*                                      TS Texas

24 January 1938                      *The Criterion*

Dear Barker,

Here is the letter I had been writing to you, which of course will have to be read in the light of our conversation of Friday afternoon, in spite of which conversation however I think the main points worth making.[2]

---

Romantic": I can hardly debit him with anything so dreadfully written, yet I cannot see how anyone could have written a hardly-disguised autobiographical novel about an amour with K. M. [Katherine Mansfield, Murry's late wife], printing letters of hers, without Murry prosecuting, unless it were Murry himself. If it was, it's rather pathological: I hope it was not, but several people I know feel sure he did it.

'My own belief, for what it's worth, is that as an increasing number of intellectuals become converted to Christian philosophy, they'd do better not to hurry to get into the organized religious bodies, still less to take orders to teach in them.'

1 – Casa Prada, Marylebone Road, London.

2 – Barker wrote to TSE on the same day: 'Friday after our conversation on the matter of my verse I realised that I have never yet written you giving my own notions of how I suppose a development of my powers of writing poetry might evolve . . . I owe you a letter about my work in reply to your letter about Jerusalem.

'First I am conscious of having searched assiduously and so far unsuccessfully for a technical form adapted to taking the subjects I have to write about . . . and I now feel that I must make experiments to evolve a stanza that will carry what I want to say and facilitate my saying it well . . . It seems to me that my growth has gone roughly along this sort of line: I wrote my first poems from an adolescent obsession with two facts: how nice to be alive, and how nice to be dead. And then in the first book of *Calamiterror* I wrote about how horrible but exhilarating my own life had been . . . And now, in the poems I have recently been writing, I write how these matters, the complexion and colour of one's life, can have very little meaning, if in fact one ever succeeds in dying, because it is better to die . . . [W]hat I await is the completion and consummation of my death and not of my life.' The first book of *Calamiterror*, he went on, 'ends with the hope that sooner or later ones life can be lived decently if things can be put into some sort of order . . . Left alone with oneself there is nothing but the core of rot that in the end spreads all over . . . What I am now trying to do is to write poems discrediting the expensive, the gay, and the exhilarating, and substantiating the enemy of substance . . . But now I propose to devote myself to work on the play I mentioned to you.'

I have delayed writing to you for some time, not because I did not know pretty well what I thought about these poems, but because of the difficulty of expressing it.[1]

I do not think that these poems make a volume which it is advisable to print as it stands. To you, no doubt, these poems appear new, and a development on your previous work: but they will not so appear to the reader. I do not say that they are not, take them all round, just as good as your first volume: the point is, that after two volumes they are not the right stuff for a third. There comes a point, and it comes very quickly, where the reader of poetry – and I mean the most intelligent and sensitive reader – demands not merely more of the same, but something new. The ordinary novel reader is quite happy to have 'another Edgar Wallace' or 'another Ethel Mannin' as the case may be; and would be annoyed if he got anything very different from the last. He is not going to re-read the author's previous novels, and he wants the same thing made to look just different enough. But in publishing poetry you are publishing primarily for the hundred or so best readers – if you get a larger public, that is all to the good, but it can't be aimed at. And the best poetry readers don't want more of the same: until you do something quite new they prefer to re-read what you have done already.

Whether you stop writing poetry for a time, or merely stop printing it, is a point upon which no one can advise you; but I do feel that for the present you should stop publishing: except, of course, for 'trying things out' in periodicals. Poetry is either a matter of a brief outburst, or it is a matter of a lifetime's work: in either case it is a nuisance to be a poet. When it is a life work, you are sure to find from time to time that your inspiration is exhausted, and that you either repeat yourself, or stop writing. These are painful, but necessary periods. I do not say that this has happened to everybody who has been accounted a great poet. A few men, like Shakespeare, have gone on growing so fast that they simply could not repeat themselves; you could almost say that Shakespeare was a new man every time he started a new play. But more often a poet has

---

1 – TSE's reader's report on 'New Poems' by George Barker, 31 Dec. 1937: 'I take it that we ought to go on publishing Barker, but I must say that these poems do not seem to me to show the advance in maturity that Barker ought to be making, and the question is whether it is worth while merely publishing more of the same, or whether we should make him wait until he has succeeded in doing something riper.

'I would even say that these poems irritate me. Do they or do they not show a kind of intellectual laziness, and an attempt to take heaven by storm with a good deal of fake imagination mixed in with the genuine? Some of his tricks seem to me to be becoming positive affectations. One gets tired of the pseudo Blake and the false infantile.'

gone on writing without knowing that he has not developed sufficiently to justify it. Swinburne wrote many good poems in later life – poems that nobody else could have written. But at the same time it is not *necessary* to read them, in a world crammed with reading-matter. In the long run, it is only *necessary* poems that count, and only the necessary poems that will be read.

I think, as I say, that it is a right part of the labour of going on writing poetry, to have these periods of sterility and bafflement of which I speak. They should recur throughout one's active life. There have been several periods of considerable extent in my own life, when I have felt *almost* convinced that I should never be able to write again; or when I have produced something with great labour and found it still-born. In fact, these periods seem to make up the greater part of my life. My published work might be much larger than it is, if I had not kept in mind that *nothing is worth doing twice*. It is quite possible that my later work is not so good as my earlier – I must prepare myself not to be too depressed if I ever see that to be so; but at any rate I can make sure that it shall be *different*. Whether we develop or not is a mysterious business, not directly under our control. But one must try to be clear about this: in what way do I feel things differently from last year? and let one's work be faithful to the change. One's emotional life is in constant change; one wakes up astonished to find that one does not feel the same about something as one did yesterday; feelings disappear from which we part with regret; but there is always the fascination of the new, or perpetually adapting oneself as an artist to the change in oneself as a man, and as one grows older restating the problems of life from the older point of view.

Now in these periods of sterility one has to have recourse partly to patience and waiting: that is the passive side. But one can also do much by filling up one's mind – partly from books, from interesting oneself in new subjects in the outside world, and partly from one's experience and study of human beings. Also, one can do much by widening one's taste in poetry, and saturating oneself in authors who are not immediately congenial; and by technical experiments in verse of various kinds. All these activities will help to preserve you from the common danger – which I see in your own verse – of diffuseness; and help you to gain concentration.

Ever yours,<br>T. S. Eliot

P.S. There is a common error nowadays of making a distinction between poetry for 'the few' and poetry for 'the many'. This is introducing an irrelevance based on political premises. Poetry should be written, not for the 'few' in the sense of a small group of highly refined, or socially superior, triflers who are trained to enjoy the obscure and the eccentric and the perverse: but for the 'few' in the sense that there are never more than a very small number of people who are competent to judge poetry at all. One must aim to satisfy the *best* readers of poetry – whoever they may be, because one only knows a *very* few oneself; the rest are scattered and often obscure; and not more than a very small percentage of newspaper critics – sometimes none – is included among them. And the larger public, or 'the people', is only the shadow of this unknown or only partly known elite. To aim directly at 'the people' is to aim to write the ephemeral, because that is what the people wants.[1]

<I have written to Ackerley and Verschoyle, and to my friend who may know about advertising.[2]>

## TO *Djuna Barnes*

TS Hornbake

28 January 1938                    *The Criterion*

Now then Djuna don't be a Goose. I knew you would write like that and I would have tried to anticipate you but I had to go out to dinner that night with an old widow lady from Portland Maine, and the next night to the pantomime and I got ptomaine poisoning I think just before the pantomime but I am feeling better now.[3] For one thing I want to arrange for you to come with me to see my friend John Hayward, who is a cripple and most intelligent and admires *Nightwood* which he had the privilege of reading in typescript in order that he might support Morley and me as his opinion is much respected: and he would very much like to meet you. He has been in bed with a cold, and I will write and suggest a possible occasion next week.

And stop worrying about the Baroness. I think that the chief use of the Baroness is to start you off, and if the result shows very little of the Baroness and mostly yourself well that's what we shall like best. So don't

---

1 – In response to this letter, Barker wrote again on 26 Jan.: 'How right you were about my having lately experienced a passive period was proved I feel by the fiddling and fumbling manner in which I have been failing to deal with my play for the last six months.'

On 27 Jan., he announced that he had completed the first draft of his play.

2 – E. McKnight Kauffer.

3 – GCF's diary, Tues. 22 Jan.: 'Dined with Hopkins, & to Pantomime, with them & TSE.'

have any scruples about historical accuracy etc. but just make USE of her. She will approve, I am sure.

Yrs etc.

TP

TO *Lawrence Durrell*                               TS Morris Library

31 January 1938                    *The Criterion*

My dear Durrell,

Some time ago we discussed the possibility of my finding a bit out of the *Black Book* which I could publish in the *Criterion*. I think I could use a piece in June, and even if Kahane's edition[1] has already appeared I shall have no objection, if he has none.

I have gone through the copy of the book here with this in view, and naturally cannot find anything of any length. Inevitably also, no selection would give any impression of what the book as a whole is like. It would be simply a specimen of one of the styles. The passages which I have noted are – pp. 131–138 inclusive; pp. 181–185 inclusive; and 202–206 inclusive. Have you a copy with the same paging as the bound copy you left here, and if you have any preference between these three would you send me a set of pages including the one you prefer? Of course if your copy is paged differently this indication is no use, but you might also have a spare proof copy from Kahane which you could let me borrow.[2]

Yours sincerely,

signed for T. S. Eliot (Anne Bradby)

1 – The Obelisk Press, Paris.
2 – Durrell responded (n.d.): 'the book has already gone to press, but owing to some hang-up in French printing it looks as if February is premature as a publication date. There is certainly no trouble about this Criterion section; did I make it clear that where an obscenity destroyed the sequence of any of your choices it could be cut? I hope so. Tomorrow I will go through a paged copy and see the pieces you have marked. It *is* rather hopelessly mixed in styles and stories. It must have been a fiendish job to choose anything at all. My gratitude as ever.'

Jack Kahane wrote to TSE as late as 11 Oct. 1938, in response to a letter from TSE to Henry Miller dated 19 Sept., 1938 (not found): 'I have a poor explanation to make of the non-departure of THE BLACK BOOK fragments. This was due entirely to the abominable treatment the book received from the printer . . . simply one of those rotten things which happen when one deals with foreigners.' Review copies had been sent out by *c.* 11 Aug. 1938, but evidently none had arrived at the offices of the *Criterion*. 'I hope that it will be possible for a review to appear in the Criterion as this is the best thing that can happen to any book published by me.'

## TO *Virginia Woolf*

TS Berg

3 February [1938]¹            *The Criterion*

Possum now wishes to explain his silence
And to apologise (as only right is);
He had an attack of poisoning of some violence,
Followed presently by some days in bed with laryngitis.
Yesterday he had to get up and dress –
His voice very thick and his head feeling tetrahedral,
To go and meet the Lord Mayor & Lady Mayoress
At a meeting which had something to do with repairs to Southwark
    Cathedral.
His legs are not yet ready for much strain & stress
And his words continue to come thick and soupy all:
These are afflictions tending to depress
Even the most ebullient marsupial.²
But he would like to come to tea
One day next week (not a Wednesday)
If that can be arranged
And to finish off this letter
Hopes that you are no worse and that Leonard is much better ³

1–First published under the heading 'T. S. Eliot: A Verse Letter' in the *New York Times*, 31
Jan. 1974, C 33; and in facsimile in *Other People's Mail* (1973), ed. Lola Szladits.
2–The common, or Virginian, opossum is *Didelphis Marsupialis*.
3–Cf. Alfred Austin, 'On the Illness of the Prince of Wales, Afterwards Edward VII': 'Across
the wires the electric message came / "He is no better, he is much the same".'

VW replied, 'Wednesday' (9 Feb.): 'The Wolves hope that The O'Possum, who is hereby
created King of all Possums, & an Irish Monarch, will come to tea, 4.30, on Tuesday 15th:
one Wolf has now recovered, it is hoped, from kidney disease, the other from influenza:
recurring; & both would relish a little cheerful talk about ptomaine poisoning & laryngitis,
– the Wolf who is holding the pen cant spell tonight or form her letters, but thats nothing
to the discredit of her heart, which is true & tender as the poet says the North is: & oh god
what a good poem Venus & Adonis is compared with Mr. — I forget his name but must now
read his MS' (*Letters*, 213).

VW alludes to Tennyson, 'The Princess', 6: 'And dark and true and tender is the North.'

TO *Marion Dorn*                                                    CC

4 February 1938                    [*The Criterion*]

My dear Marion,

I was very sorry indeed to have to miss your dinner party, which I should very much have enjoyed.[1] I did get out that afternoon, to fill an engagement of long standing, but was allowed to do that by my doctor only on the condition that I should not go out in the evening for the rest of this week. I should have been glad to see the Moores. I think I have met both of them in past years, and probably before they knew each other.

Let me know when the Etruscan statue is nearly ready, and I will see what I can do in the way of a poem. I do hope I shall see you both again soon.

Yours ever,
[Tom]


TO *Pamela Murray*                                                 CC

4 February 1938                    [*The Criterion*]

Dear Miss Murray,

I should like to help you with your difficulty, which I can well understand, but it is difficult for an author to think of any new approach to his own work for another person to take.[2] I can at least answer two of

---

1–Dorn had written on 28 Jan.: 'Wednesday's, being John's birthday, we are expecting you to come to dinner at 8 o'clock . . . There are 2 other people coming of whom John is fond – Lord Moore & his wife. She will play my clavichord very beautifully for us, which I feel you will enjoy . . . John has told me that you don't always like meeting people, but we hope you won't mind about the Moores because we are all fond of them. I wanted Elizabeth Bowen – but John wanted me to ask her without Allen [Alan Cameron, Bowen's husband] & somehow, I felt that I just couldn't, because I don't know her well enough . . .

'The Etruscan statue that I am having made for John's birthday at the British Museum will not be ready in time because I have been ill & was unable to order it in time. You had said that Sunday night at dinner that you would write a poem to go with it, as John did for Ted's at Xmas. And I am sad because my illness has made all of that impossible. But, perhaps, you will be relieved!'

2–The seventeen-year-old Pamela Murray wrote from St Leonards School, St Andrews, Fife, on 26 Jan.: 'I'm writing a paper on you – it sounds awfully rude just written blatantly like that – but you know what I mean. To be more explicit, we have a Literary Society here at school which meets once or twice a term & then someone reads a paper on some poet or novelist: just like any ordinary Literary Society. Anyway, I have to write a paper and at the moment I'm rather stuck . . .

'Can you give me any ideas?

your questions. I do experiment consciously, in the sense that everything I undertake is like setting myself a new problem to solve. If one wants to say something that one has not said before, one must find a new way of saying it. It does not seem to me worthwhile ever to do the same thing twice. And as for the way of working, that depends upon the kind of poem. If it is only a little poem, well, it probably shapes itself quite quickly (though it may have been at the back of my head for a long time) and gets written in an hour or two at any time. If it is a long poem, or a play, then it is a matter of sitting down every morning after breakfast and working regularly for two or three hours a day at it, over a period of perhaps many months.

It is perhaps useful to remember that there are three generations of poets alive, each with its own characteristics. The oldest is Mr Yeats; the middle generation may be represented by Mr Ezra Pound and myself; and the third by Mr Auden and Mr Spender. Of course there are younger poets still, but there has not yet been time for a distinct 'fourth' generation to be established. One may take 'generation' as meaning a space of about twenty years in age between each. But it is a mistake to treat all the poets of any one generation as if they were very much alike – if they are any good they are very different from each other. And of course they vary according to the forms in which they prefer to express themselves. What interests me is the dramatic, and I think that the chief interest in the best of my early poems is the sketching, however slightly, of character; you will observe a middle period ('Ash Wednesday') in which there is no dramatic interest; and now I am chiefly interested in the theatre. But I am also interested ('Burnt Norton') in possible approximations to musical form and musical effect.

Yours sincerely,
[T. S. Eliot]

---

'This seems to be extremely vague but there is so much I do want to know that I dont know how to set about asking. I have heard it said that while other modern poets tend to go back to earlier forms whether consciously or not, you "experiment" realising that you are doing it? When you write poetry do you write it suddenly by an impulse or can you, as it were, sit down & write? What do you think of W. H. Auden, as a poet?

'These questions are silly, & not worth answering, but if you aren't bored by getting letters like this of mine, & too busy, – I should be *very* pleased by an answer.'

TO *Hugh Gordon Porteus*                          TS Beinecke

4 February 1938                    *The Criterion*

Dear Porteus,

Many thanks for your English Periodicals, which is as interesting as ever. I have made three alterations which I ought to tell you about. First I have slightly altered your remark about regretting that some of the contributors to the *Twentieth Century Verse* Lewis number had not been invited to contribute to the Auden number of *New Verse*, because I was myself invited by Grigson, and declined, thinking it inappropriate for me.

Second, I have put back into lower case the phrase 'While I am naturally sympathetic' from my contribution to the Spain questionnaire. The point is that the capitals are not mine, but introduced by the ingenious editor of the collection. As a matter of fact I never intended to contribute at all. I thought I was merely writing a polite note to Nancy, declining to take part. The phrase only means that I was naturally sympathetic with Nancy or with any lady, as a polite way of writing, but I did not mean to express sympathy with anything political, so that the phrase as it stands in the collection has a really comic meaninglessness![1]

1 – *Authors Take Sides on the Spanish War* (Left Review, 1937):

'The Question' . . .
    This is the question we are asking you:
    Are you for, or against, the legal Government and the People of Republican Spain?
    Are you for, or against, Franco and Fascism?
    For it is impossible any longer to take no side.
    Writers and Poets, we wish to print your answers. We wish the world to know what you, writers and poets, who are amongst the most sensitive instruments of a nation, feel.

TSE's answer was placed in the category of 'Neutral?':

'WHILE I AM NATURALLY SYMPATHETIC, I still feel convinced that it is best that at least a few men of letters should remain isolated, and take no part in these collective activities.' – reprinted in *Spanish Front: Writers on the Civil War*, ed. Valentine Cunningham (1986), 56.
    EP commented to TSE in a letter of 11 Dec. 1937:
'Upon reading Mr Eliot's remarks in the Left Review pamphlet
The thoughtful lady commented:
I know now why you call him the Possum.'
    See further Nancy Cunard to GCF, 16 Oct. 1938: 'I am going to propose something to you soon; that is, I am going to send you a representative part of two or three pages of the translation from the Spanish original into English of a new long poem [*España*] by Nicolas Guillen which has just come out in Valencia; it is very fine indeed . . . I have written, all too briefly perforce, on Guillen along with two other poets of colour in this month's "Left Review". When I send you the aforementioned pages I shall ask you to tell me if you think

Third, I must apologise for your having received by mistake three American periodicals. These really belong to Desmond Hawkins, who has now taken over that department on Bridson's retirement. So I think I ought to cut out those short paragraphs, to avoid confusion. I am sorry about this. Otherwise everything is straightforward. I have had in mind that I have been wanting to see you again. I have just been in bed for a few days, and will write again as soon as I have got things straightened out.

Yours ever,
T. S. Eliot

---

an edition in English published by yourselves can be considered. Guillen is now in Spain and has given me permission to translate him and look for a publisher. He is extremely well known in all Latin America, unknown in England, getting to be known in the States, and of course, in Spain.'

Cunard to GCF, 21 Dec. 1938: 'Here is the translation of Nicolas Guillen's poem ['España'] – He is a Cuban, most famous in all Latin America and considered the best of the Hispano-American poets of today . . .

'Please note that the Title as it now is in English ['Spain'] will be changed. I could not find one at the time of translating, so this is just temporary . . .

'Could the poem be shown to T. S. Eliot – he is with you I believe? I know him.'

GCF to Nancy Cunard, 4 Jan. 1939: 'Eliot and I have considered Spain – both together and in consultation with our colleagues – with every wish to convince ourselves that we could publish it successfully. By which I don't mean commercial success, because the cost of publication would be so small as to be almost negligible. Our trouble is of a different kind – as you know, we have had to cultivate the art of making modern poetry saleable; and we have only succeeded by keeping out everything which didn't fit in as an essential part of our programme. (Once or twice, we have not done this, and have always regretted it!) Spain is a vigorous poem, and your translation is a very good one. But – though it is parallel in some ways to Auden's Spain – it is really too much of a sideturning off our own carefully planned route. We should have to do it in a style and at a price which wouldn't suit it; even so we feel very doubtful about putting it over; and if we did it cheaply, we shouldn't be able to make any impression with it.

'It seems to us that the Hogarth Press would be the better publishers for it – or possibly Boriswood.'

See too TSE's 'Commentary', C., Jan. 1937: 'Now an ideally unprejudiced person, with an intimate knowledge of Spain, its history, its racial characteristics, and its contemporary personalities, might be in a position to come to the conclusion that he should, in the longest view that could be seen, support one side rather than the other. But so long as we are not compelled in our own interest to take sides, I do not see why we should do so on insufficient knowledge: and even any eventual partisanship should be held with reservations, humility and misgiving. That balance of mind which a few highly-civilized individuals, such as Arjuna, the hero of the Bhagavad Gita, can maintain in action, is difficult for most of us even as observers, and, as I say, is not encouraged by the greater part of the Press.'

## TO *George Barnes*                                                    TS Beinecke

4 February 1938                        *The Criterion*

My dear Barnes,

Thank you very much for your kind letter of the 30th.[1] It is very encouraging to receive such approval from the right kind of critic. The verses were certainly intended for children, in so far as they were intended to amuse anyone but myself, and unless they do really amuse children there is no point in their existing. I don't want, like one or two popular authors whom I can think of, to write children's poems which will appeal primarily to sentimental adults. That kind of verse seems to me definitely unpleasant.

I should like very much to dine with you again a little later.[2] I have just had several days in bed, partly as a result of the fatigue of dining out five nights in succession, and am going to try to be careful to keep down my evening engagements for the rest of the winter, and if possible never dine out two nights in succession. So I hope you will give me a reasonable amount of notice when you ask me again.

> With many thanks,
> Yours ever,
> T. S. Eliot

## TO *John Middleton Murry*                                        TS Northwestern

4 February 1938                        *The Criterion*

Dear John,

I should have written this note before, but have been in bed.

You may have wondered what Maritain had to do with it, if you have now read his preface.[3] To tell the truth, my mind was thinking of two

---

1 – 'Practical Cats has given so much pleasure that I must write and tell you about its reception in this house. My child (6½) was playing in the room on Christmas Day, and stopped unbidden to listen entranced to the end. He has been looking forward ever since to the repeat, and yesterday extended his "favourite poems" from Growltiger and Deuteronomy, to those two and Gumby, Practical Cats, the Naming of Cats. He is fast learning them all by heart, a process helped by the purloining of a copy of the script.'

2 – 'Would you come to dine with us one night or is that impossible while the Play is being written? It would be very nice to see you again and to singe your white beard.

'Perhaps you will give a curt command to Ersatz O'Donovan to type me a p.c.'

3 – JMM wrote, 20 Jan.: 'I was glad to have your letter [of 19 Jan.], and to know that you liked my pamphlet. I should very much like to see that preface of Maritain's, which, you say,

things at once – what Maritain does give, is a view about *Spain* which I find congenial, and the bearing of what he says on 'pacifism' is here only indirect. The view about *Peace* which I find most acceptable is that of Demant, whose pamphlet you know. So it would have been more to the point if I had written 'Demant' instead of 'Maritain'.

Also, when I wrote, I was overlooking the fact that you were addressing a primarily pacifist, and probably only in small proportion somewhat Christian audience.

And is it not implicit in the meaning of the term 'the Catholic Faith' that there should be *the* meaning (not merely meanings) whether any one of us apprehends it or not. I doubt if anyone can hope to grasp *the* meaning, but we must assume its subsistence, surely. But I am inclined to believe that in one's private and individual thinking there is bound to be a considerable residuum of heterodoxy – if not heresy; and that to call any individual 'orthodox' is to misuse terms – unless the looseness of the application is kept in mind. Of course such a view can be dangerous if misapplied.

Yours ever
Tom


## TO *Maurice Haigh-Wood* CC

4 February 1938 [Faber & Faber Ltd]

Dear Maurice,

I should have answered your letter of the 26th ultimo earlier, but I have been in bed with laryngitis (due to fatigue I think) and only crawled out prematurely on Wednesday to fill an engagement at the Mansion House, so that my recuperation has been rather delayed.[1]

---

approximates to your own view about Peace; I wonder whether you would be good enough to lend it to me.

'On the question whether "the centre of values is this-worldly", I cannot speak with assurance: nor am I quite certain whether you are referring to the *visible* centre of values or to the *invisible* one. But I presume the latter: because the visible centre is bound to be this-worldly in an address to a mixed audience of Pacifists, of whom probably not more than a quarter were Christians professed.

'Whether my invisible centre of values is sufficiently other-worldly to satisfy – I don't know; but I daresay I'm a good deal of the heretic still. I find a full, and sufficient, and illimitable meaning in most of the formulas of the Catholic faith; but whether it is *the* meaning, or whether *the* meaning exists, who shall say?'

1 – Haigh-Wood (John R. Sutro & Partners, London) wrote on 26 Jan.: 'For the investment of the balance on the Trustees' account, which is roughly £645, or for part of it, I would

I am quite ready to accept your opinion about investing most of the balance of £645 in gold shares (I say most, because it seems desirable to keep a very little cash on hand). I recently objected to such an investment on behalf of another trust in which I am involved; but that was because the trust, though small, is rather complicated, and I felt that where it is nobody's business in particular to keep a constant eye on investments, mines were unsuitable. But here I feel that you are in a position to know the right moment for changes; and for that reason gold shares are possible – and I see their advantage at the present time – and not what you say about hedging against industrial setbacks. It will mean, of course, your getting Vivienne's approval? I don't see how we can make such an investment without her consent.

If you happen to have any day free for lunch next week, or alternatively would prefer to look in for a quiet glass of Tio Pepe at the end of the day, do ring me up here any afternoon.

Yours ever,
[Tom]

TO *Henry Eliot*                                                        TS Houghton

4 February 1938                        *The Criterion*

Dear Henry,

I don't know what has become of Mrs Charlotte Woolf.[1] She was living in Paris, I believe, being a Jewish refugee from Germany. The Huxleys

---

suggest a holding of Union Corporation shares and a holding of Consolidated Gold Fields of S. Africa, in about equal proportions.

'These as you know are two of the leading mining finance houses, and I do believe that the gold mining industry is one of the safest things to put money in under present conditions.

'Present prices of these two shares are 8 3/8 and 3 7/8 respectively, which is considerably below the high levels of a year ago before the "gold scare". The gold scare which never had any reasonable basis is now dead and buried, and never likely to revive. On the contrary further devaluation of currencies in terms of gold is not altogether impossible. The principal argument in favour of gold shares, however, is the negative one that they provide the best hedge against an industrial recession or slump.

'Both the Union Corporation and Consolidated Gold Fields are very strong financially. The Union Corporation has a capital of £962,500 and Reserves of £1,320,000. Dividends for the three years 1934/5/6 were 64%, 64% and 68%. The yield at the present price works out at a little over 5% ...

'I should be very glad to have your opinion on this suggestion.'

1–HWE wrote on 18 Jan.: 'I am sending you herewith several imprints of the palm of my left hand, which I had made at the printers' who printed my letterheads, and this is what, in the interest of science and truth, I would ask you to do with them:

might have known but they are in America. I might be able to reach her through Chatto & Windus. But meanwhile something better has occurred to me. There is a man whose book we published, named Jaquin I think, who is said to be better. I have never had anything to do with him (which is an advantage) but a friend of mine, a biologist, has been in correspondence with Jaquin in the past, and has sent him impressions to read and has been impressed by the results.[1] I will get this man to send your impressions to Jaquin, together with some that he has taken of my hand. Anonymously, of course. J. has never seen my hand; so it will be interesting to see whether he can detect family relationships.

Then afterwards I can try to reach Mrs Wolff (I spelt it wrong above). But the chances are that I might never hear anything further, and the first idea seems to me more interesting anyway. I was not much impressed by Mrs Wolff's diagnosis: even if she knew nothing of me, still she has some very strong prejudices I should say.

I am waiting eagerly to hear how the *Murder* has been received in Boston; and whether you have seen Dukes and the Brownes and any of the crew.[2]

Affectionately,
Tom

----

'Will you hand or forward them (perhaps preferably the latter) to Dr Charlotte Wolff, the author of the interesting book, Studies in Hand-Reading, published last year by Knopf over here; and ask her to read my palm and send you a character analysis, and then send the analysis to me, with the hand prints.

'I am frankly sceptical about chiromancy, and my object in this is to test Dr Wolff's abilities. I can believe that there is something in handwriting, which reveals personality, and I can even put a little faith in phrenology, though I think both are highly unreliable. But I cannot see why the human hand, which is, one might say, a human tool, should reflect anything more than, perhaps, the general physical type of a person and his occupation and status in society. My belief is that a *bone fide* reading of my hand would tell just about as much as is common to us both, and no more. I suspect that in the case of Dr Wolff's reading of your hand she displays too much foreknowledge gleaned from the public prints. I have not her book at hand for comparison, but I imagine that all the hands of our family are much alike and that their features can all be laid to hereditary factors.

'I don't know but that it might be best to let Frank Morley, if he will lend himself to this plot, transact the matter . . . I hope that you are not so busy as to find this a nuisance.'

Wolff, *Studies in Hand-Reading* (London: Chatto & Windus, 1936).

1 – Geoffrey Tandy had been in communication in early 1938 with Noel Jaquin (1893–1974) – 'Consulting Psychologist and Diagnostician' – who was based in London. Jaquin was convinced that chirology and hand-reading could serve as a diagnostic tool in the analysis of psychological and pathological conditions. Tandy to TSE, 9 Feb.: 'I shall send both prints to Jaquin and tell him that I want detailed diagnoses much as I might expect from a respectable taxonomist in the botanical line.' See too Jaquin, *The Hand of Man* (F&F, 1933); *The Signature of Time: The Revealing Symbol – the Human Hand* (F&F, 1940).

2 – *MiC* was playing in Boston for two weeks from 31 Jan.; then in Philadelphia for two weeks.

5 February 1938                    [24 Russell Street, London W.C.1]

Reverend Sir,

In your always admirable 'Extracts and Comments' which I invariably read with profit, I am vexed <a little nettled> to find, in the current number, a brief reference to my having commented 'charitably' on Lord Nuffield's benefactions to Oxford.[1] While I hope that my comments always show Christian charity (I fear that sometimes they do not) I take <a mild> exception – not to the brevity of the reference – but to the use of the word 'charitably' in such a brief reference. Are you sure that all your readers will take it <simply> that I have shown Christian charity toward this appalling blunder? and that they will not interpret your remark as meaning what in journalistic language may be called 'qualified approval'? I wished to express unqualified disapproval. – The point might not matter if any considerable part of the press had taken a similar view to mine. But so far as I know, mine was a solitary voice of warning against the subjection of <the> Oxford of 'Dominus illuminatio mea'[2] to the purposes of materialism. And, so far as I know, <mine was> the only voice raised in criticism of the preposterous appeal for Funds signed by Lord Halifax and the Master of Balliol.

I need hardly say, that this letter is not intended for publication.[3]

> I am, Reverend Sir,
> Your obedient servant,
> [T. S. Eliot]

1 – *Blackfriars* 19: 215 (Feb. 1938), 'Extracts and Comments', 142: 'CRITERION (Jan.): . . . T. S. Eliot comments charitably on Lord Nuffield's "benefactions" to Oxford University.'

TSE had in fact expressed misgivings – in his 'Commentary', *C.* 17 (Jan. 1938), 254–9 – about Nuffield's benefactions (which, as it was said by the Vice-Chancellor, were intended to meet the needs of 'humanistic studies' as much as the sciences), including the endowment of a new Nuffield College: 'The increase of University machinery and activity, as distinct from that of the Colleges, may lead to the necessity of greater centralization of authority, and greater continuity of direction. The universities will thus tend to assimilate themselves to the provincial universities, and ultimately to the megalopolitan American universities . . . The finger points towards centralization, towards the further Americanization of Oxford, and perhaps further still: to the ultimate incorporation of Oxford, with Cambridge and the Scottish universities, into one vast system manipulated from Whitehall.'

2 – Psalm 27: 'The Lord is my light': the motto of the University of Oxford.

3 – Hilary J. Carpenter, editor of *Blackfriars*, replied on 9 Feb. 1938: 'Thank you for your letter which (let me say at once) I regret you did not offer for publication.

'I am quite sure that the writer of EXTRACTS & COMMENTS did not misunderstand your intentions, nor I do think that the majority of our readers would misunderstand his comment. However I have passed on your letter to him and he will probably write to you himself.'

See further *CProse* 5, 599–600.

TO *Djuna Barnes*                                    TS Hornbake

8 February [1938]                    *The Criterion*

Now then Djuna Barnes, you are coming with me to see John Hayward
on the evening of Thursday the 17th instant – Thursday week that is – and
so please meet me at the Queens Restaurant in Sloane Square that evening
at 7.30, and if you have another engagement put it OFF. And I shan't have
had more than three double Booths, I don't expect, before I meet you.

   So don't worry about either the Baroness OR yourself, worry about the
Book.[1]

                                        Yrs faithful
                                        TP.


TO *C. M. Grieve*[2]                              TS Edinburgh University

8 February 1938                       Faber & Faber Ltd

Dear Mr Grieve,

   I am very glad to hear from you after this long time, and shall be very glad
indeed if you will let me see your long poem.[3] It sounds very interesting,

1 – Barnes (who was staying at 60 Old Church Street, Chelsea) replied, 9 Feb.: 'Delighted to
meet you Thursday the 17, at the Queens (thats one restaurant I *do* know, so if I am late this
time it will be unpardonable) at 7.30, the double Booths or no Booths, I am bound to be in
a state of the jitters – I've had them for some years now – & am very tired of it.

   'When I said I was worried about myself I meant the book – because I can't get on with it.
I can't make out whether it's the book that is making me ill, or if I am making the book ill – I
am really afraid to see people in such a state; like Proust's aunt I think seriously of taking to
my bed for the rest of my life. / Always / Djuna.'
2 – Christopher Murray Grieve (1892–1978): pseud. Hugh MacDiarmid – poet, journalist,
critic, cultural activist, self-styled 'Anglophobe', Scottish Nationalist and Communist;
founder member of the Scottish National Party, 1928; founder of the Scottish Centre of PEN.
His works include *A Drunk Man Looks at the Thistle* (1926), *To Circumjack Cencrastus*
(1930), '*First Hymn to Lenin*' *and Other Poems* (1931), *Hugh MacDiarmid: Complete
Poems, 1920–1976* (2 vols, 1978). See further Alan Bold, *MacDiarmid, Christopher Murray
Grieve: A Critical Biography* (1988); *The Letters of Hugh MacDiarmid*, ed. A. Bold (1984);
and *Dear Grieve: Letters to Hugh MacDiarmid (C. M. Grieve)*, ed. John Manson (2011).

   Joseph Chiari, *T. S. Eliot: A Memoir* (1982), noted: 'Strange as it will appear to some,
[Eliot], the self-proclaimed royalist and conservative, liked and respected the rebellious, ever
explosive anti-monarchist Hugh MacDiarmid, whose poetry he admired and whose efforts
to raise the Scots language to the level of a mature medium for all aspects of literature he
applauded.'
3 – Grieve wrote on 4 Feb. that he had completed an 'important long poem' – between 4,000
and 5,000 lines – entitled "Mature Art" – which he wanted to submit to the *Criterion*.

   'I define it as a "hapax legomenon [ἅπαξ λεγόμενον: 'something said only once'] of a

though I must say the title 'Mature Art' is somewhat forbidding! I look forward also to reading your essay.

> With best wishes,
> Yours sincerely,
> T. S. Eliot

## TO *Frederic Prokosch*[1]                                    CC

9 February 1938                    [*The Criterion*]

Dear Mr Prokosch,

I like extremely your long ode, and only regret that it is now too late to include it in the next *Criterion*.[2] I could only do so by postponing several things which have already been kept waiting for a long time, and that would not be fair.

I have very few criticisms to make. You will find one or two marked. I don't feel quite sure that the terminal 'the' at the end of the first line of the last stanza of the first page is quite justified. These hanging particles

---

poem – an exercise in schlabone, bordatini, and prolonged scordatuna", and it is, I am very safe in saying, a very advanced example of "learnèd poetry", much of it written in a multi-linguistic diction embracing not only many European but also Asiatic languages, and prolific in allusions and "synthetic poetry", demanding for their complete comprehension an extremely detailed knowledge of numerous fields of world literature. At the same time the logic of the whole is quite clear.'

He hoped also to offer 'an essay on what may be called the British Question in the light of dialectical materialism. Socialist thought has sedulously avoided the British Question – paying lip-service to Scottish, Welsh etc. autonomy, but in practice doing nothing to further these causes, and in fact steadily supporting British Imperialism. While the essay is written from the Dialectical Materialist standpoint and I am a member of the Communist Party, it is, of course, severely critical of Communist Party policy, and is full of very important, and little understood, implications in view of recent developments in Ireland, the growth of the Welsh movement, and the changing situation in Scotland. The article is a political counterpart to the article on "English Ascendancy in British Literature" I contributed to the "Criterion" a few years ago.'

1–Frederic Prokosch (1908–89), American novelist and poet – son of Edouard Prokosch, Sterling Professor of Linguistics at Yale – graduated from Haverford College, Pennsylvania, and taught English at Yale for two years. His novel, *The Asiatics*, published to acclaim when he was just twenty-three, was translated into seventeen languages: André Gide hailed it as an 'authentic masterpiece', and Thomas Mann as 'this astonishing, picaresque romance'. Later novels included *The Seven Who Fled* (1937) and *The Skies of Europe* (1941). Accomplished as a printer of small private editions (including a pamphlet of verse by TSE called *Words for Music* in 1934), he also translated poems by Hölderlin and Louise Labé. He was squash-rackets champion of France, 1933–9; of Sweden, 1944. See Robert Greenfield, *Dreamer's Journey: The Life and Writings of Frederic Prokosch* (2010).

2–See 'Ode', in *The Carnival* (1938), 41–9.

justify themselves better in some forms of verse than in others, and of course it is a trick which Marianne Moore in her own way has handled to perfection. But the end of a line is a light pause in itself, and I cannot see that such a break between 'the' and 'pageants' has any particular significance here. I much like the second part, chiefly because it seems to me that you have managed just the right selection of images to convey a compressed account of thirty years or so of life. I am a bit bothered by 'the infinite magic of human memory' in connexion with Asia. You may be quite justified, and Asia is more your business than mine, but indifference to time seems more characteristic of the past of Asia than memory. Perhaps you can explain this.

In the sixth section I felt that the verb 'explore', which I have marked at the top of a page, struck me as a little artificial in that context; a little too artful. I have marked lower down a line which seems to me not to read well aloud, because of its sibilance. I hope you will keep 'puzzles', and I think you could get round the difficulty by some substitution for 'mists'.[1]

I shall look forward with keen interest to your book, and hope that you will come to see me when you are in London in March.

Yours sincerely,<br>[T. S. Eliot]

## TO *Geoffrey Tandy*

TS BL

10 February 1938                    Faber & Faber Ltd

Dear Geoffrey,

Many thanks for your letter of the 8th. Well, I fear that if Gus is too antiquated for a young man like you, it will be completely unintelligible to a youngster like Cox. But you have my permission to try him on anybody you please.[2]

---

1 – Most of TSE's criticisms were adopted for the published volume.
2 – 'GUS: THE THEATRE CAT is for a limited audience I think. I haven't been very successful in finding reasons for this opinion. I think there is some weight in the objection that the figure of the broken-down actor, making a poor living and living on his past triumphs, is more than a little dim and unfamiliar to most people under the age of thirty. Perhaps there's something to be said for the poor old has-beens, as it might be you or me and why shouldn't they have their bit of fun. I've just been listening to Mr Agate telling the young folks how they don't know what acting is because they didn't see Irving: that he was the greatest actor Mr Agate has ever seen or hopes to see. (Beg pardon! ever will see). Would you like to try Gus on somebody younger (I. Cox say); or may I have your permission to do so.'

About *Burnt Norton*. I do not feel quite sure about this idea of yours, although I recognise its profundity in principle.[1] I had rather wait until I can manage to do something that I have had in mind for some time past: write a few pieces of Chamber Music, somewhat on the same lines, but deliberately with the intention of distribution between a definite number of voices, probably four. It may turn out that the stuff does not look any different from *Burnt Norton*, I mean that one kind will be as suitable or as unsuitable for several voices as the other, but there may turn out to be a difference, and as that seems just possible I had rather wait, and not confuse myself by bothering at present with an adaptation. However, I will go on thinking about the matter.

Yours,

TP

What about Monday for the transfer of 'Bring 'Em Back Alive'? At either wineroom, as usual.

---

Tandy wrote again on 9 Feb.: 'Talk about a patent never-stop sassidge machine! Some peoples' typewriters would make it look like a case of arrested development; as the greyhound fancier said as he looked at the Peke. I shd think Monday p.m. wd do very well for a drink of sherry wine and it might be as well to see how I. Cox is fixed at that time. I shd think Gordon's is as good a place as any so I shall be there about 5.30 or so unless warned to the contrairy [*sic*]. I will see about IC and if he can't make it we'll have to think up the next move.'

1 – 'An idea came to me the other evening which you may think is a silly bloody idea. I was reading *Burnt Norton* and I remembered that you once spoke of it as a quartet for strings. It seems possible that four voices, corresponding more or less to the four instruments of the classical string quartet, could make a very effective presentation of the poem. I am not, especially in view of recent experiences, proposing anything even faintly "dramatic" and I think it would have to be done by Talks and not by the Drama dept. If doing *Burnt Norton* this way doesn't appeal to you (and I can see a number of reasons why it won't) will you consider the possibility of writing something for such a combination . . . Have you ever wanted to hear different words being spoken simultaneously in a contrapuntal relation? I can see that a *tutti*, even of four voices, might not be able to do more than use different pitches for the same words and remain intelligible; but it would be highly interesting (to say least) if they could.' (EVE)

TO *Stephen Spender*                                    TS Northwestern

10 February 1938                    *The Criterion*

Dear Stephen,

I have just received your letter of the 8th, but cannot get hold of de la Mare at the moment to discuss the question of publication dates.[1] I will of course urge the desirability of earlier publication, and I am sure that de la Mare will agree, if it is possible for the printers. I will let you know about this as soon as I can talk to him.

I am handing on your letter to the publicity expert for the use of your advance paragraph, and will ask him to write to you about mailing lists.

Yours affectionately,

Tom

1 – Since *Trial of a Judge* was to be staged from 18 Mar., SS was anxious for early publication. *Trial of a Judge: a tragedy in five acts* (advertised both in F&F Spring Books 1938 and on the dust jacket of the volume with the subtitle 'A Tragic Statement in Five Acts') was published in Mar. 1938: 'This is the poetic drama on which Mr Spender has been at work for the last three years. The material is political, but the readers and the audience will, according to their abilities, find deeper levels of meaning. The theme is a struggle of conscience, a tragedy of human weakness which is of timeless significance; and the liberal-minded judge, striving to maintain his conception of justice between contending political factions, becomes at the end a figure of tragic greatness. Mr Spender's dramatic method, as well as his versification, is something distinctly his own; and with this play he should take a distinguished place among the poetic dramatists of our time. This is a play which will be seen – it is to be produced by the *Group Theatre* – but which must also be read again and again.'

TSE, 'The Future of Poetic Drama', *Drama: A Monthly Record of the Theatre in Town and Country at Home & Abroad* 17 (Oct. 1938), 3–5: 'One of the most promising attempts in poetic drama, amongst those of my younger contemporaries, is the *Trial of a Judge* by my friend Stephen Spender. But when I consider the number of interests that occupy Mr Spender, I wonder whether he will ever find the time to perfect the art he has begun.'

'The Last Twenty-Five Years of English Poetry', a lecture composed in 1939 for an Italian tour (but not in fact given: the tour was cancelled): 'The most promising play so far, is in my opinion the *Trial of a Judge* by Stephen Spender, a play which has faced all the difficulties of being all in verse. I will quote a few lines merely to indicate the kind of versification:

I speak from the centre of a stage
Not of a tragedy, but a farce
Where I am the spiritual unsmiling clown
Defeated by the brutal swearing giant
Whose law is power, his order
Nature's intolerant chaos.

'The play has serious technical defects, and I do not think that the author has a perfect control of his medium, but the possibilities of development are evident.'

GCF's diary, Fri. 25 Mar. 1938: 'E[nid] & I went to Stephen Spender's play at the charming little Unity Theatre. "Trial of a Judge." Very passionate, & intense; in parts very fine & moving. But it's a defence of liberalism, whether Stephen meant it so or not. A very shrewd article on it in the New Statesman by Desmond MacCarthy.'

*Trial of a Judge* sold 3,086 copies by 1944 (3,660 were printed).

10 February 1938                    [Faber & Faber Ltd]

Dear Lord Lytton,

I must confess to reading with some surprise your letter of the 8th instant.[2] It is true that I had a conversation with Miss Fogerty about the schemes for the financial establishment of the National Theatre, but I was left with an impression at the end that Miss Fogerty intended to approach me only in a general way for the purpose of enlisting my sympathy with programmes not yet settled, and that I should hear from her at a later date when vague designs had taken a definite form. It may be that my memory is quite at fault, but I have no recollection of such a term being used as 'public relations committee', nor indeed do I recall having been invited by Miss Fogerty to join any committee. Whatever the explanation of this surprise may be, you will realise that it is a surprise, and that I must consider it entirely afresh, as if no earlier approach had been made.

As you may not know, I had never hitherto felt any enthusiasm about the foundation of a National Theatre. If I should come to give it whatever assistance lies within my power, it would be in the spirit of one who accepts the inevitable and is anxious that it should be made as useful as possible. As I say, my impression is that I parted from Miss Fogerty only with general expressions of good-will, which I could hardly have withheld from a lady to whom I am so deeply indebted. I should be glad however to be given as much information as possible about the function and personnel of the Public Relations Committee, so that I may consider whether I can exercise any useful activity in that connexion.

> I am,
> Yours very sincerely,
> [T. S. Eliot]

1 – Victor Bulwer-Lytton, 2nd Earl of Lytton (1876–1947), politician and colonial administrator.
2 – 'Miss Fogerty tells me that you have been good enough to join the Public Relations Committee [for the proposed National Theatre], which is being formed in connection with the National Theatre Appeal. I am very grateful to you for your help in this matter.'

TO *The Universities Bureau of the British Empire*    cc

11 February 1938                    [Faber & Faber Ltd]

Dear Sirs,

I understand from my friend Mr Robert Sencourt, that he is applying for the professorship of English at Raffles College, Singapore.[1] I am eager to add my recommendation, as I am sure that no more suitable incumbent could be found: Mr Sencourt is qualified for such a position to an unusual degree, both by his academic and literary attainments, by his experience of teaching, and in particular by his experience in teaching Orientals. He has furthermore all the social and personal qualifications – such as patience, tactfulness, and a cosmopolitan experience which gives him a sympathy with foreign minds. I believe that I was one of those who recommended his predecessor, Mr Ronald Bottrall; and I would vouch for Mr Sencourt equally.

> Yours faithfully,
> [T. S. Eliot]

If something more, or different from this letter is required, I shall be happy to write again.


TO *Ian Cox*                        TS BBC

11 February 1938                *The Criterion*

Dear Cox,

As for more cats, I quite agree in principle, if we can arrange a programme which will satisfy everyone concerned.[2] There are several that I don't think good enough, and Geoffrey did not seem particularly enthusiastic about the last two I sent him, so I don't know whether there

---

1–Sencourt wrote to TSE, on Candlemas (2 Feb.) 1938, from Prinknash Priory, Gloucester: 'In Singapore there is a Professorship of English now vacant and so well paid that I feel that though it is not what I would have chosen I ought to apply for it. I wonder if you would repeat something of the same kind of thing as you said for me in 1936.'

2–Cox wrote on 10 Feb.: 'Everyone is anxious for more cats, or to hear something about dogs too, and I am wondering if you could possibly allow some of the unpublished poems which we did not use last time to be made up into a further programme . . .

'If you could I should be most grateful if you would let me know your wishes about the reading of them. You know, I think, that we should be most happy if you did that yourself but if the position remains the same as when we last discussed this, we should of course be glad for Geoffrey to do it. His reading of "Practical Cats" was very greatly appreciated.'

is enough for a new programme.[1] I have suggested to him that we should meet for a glass of sherry on Monday afternoon, and if you are free to join us, I suggest that you should ring him up and find out whether he is coming, and where we are to meet.

Yours ever sincerely,
T. S. Eliot

## TO *John Middleton Murry*                                    TS Northwestern

11 February 1938                            *The Criterion*

Dear John,

I can't lay my hand on a copy of Demant's pamphlet at the moment; I think it may have got thrown away unintentionally with other papers.[2]

---

1 – Tandy wrote on 6 Feb.:

> 'Report on *MACAVITY: THE MYSTERY CAT*:
> The *General Impression* is entirely favourable. It has been read to Mr Richard Tandy and Miss Alison Tandy who received it very well and said that they liked it very much.
> Mr Richard Tandy observed that "it's like Growltiger, but not so rough and tumble". Of the corpus known to him he places *Old Deuteronomy* 1st and *The Old Gumbie Cat* second. He says he would like to hear about other *Kinds* of Cat. He does not find any troublesome obscurity in *Macavity*.
> Miss Alison Tandy, examined separately, expressed herself well pleased with *Macavity*; but exhibited the same preferences and order of merit as her brother.
> On Moral Grounds I regret to see that, unlike Growltiger, the criminal seems to escape the due reward of his deeds.
> Stanza III, l. 2. ? "for".
> V, l. 4 A box, a safe or a bag can be rifled; but can jewels?
> VI, ll. 1, 2, 5. Do you like Foreign Office, Admiralty and Secret Service as plural nouns?
> I think it "sounds" well.' (EVE)

2 – JMM had responded to TSE's letter of 4 Feb.: 'I'm sorry you've been ill. I found Maritain very interesting, and congenial; and thought that he indicated an attitude to Peace which was respectworthy & not very far removed from mine.

'But I am very anxious, for some reason, to get hold of yours; and I'm ashamed to say I don't know (or don't think I know) Demant's pamphlet. Will you tell me what is its name, & where I can get it?

'Yes, I accept your contention that there is *the* meaning, and that its subsistence is implicit in the idea of the Catholic faith; it is the claim that any individual man should apprehend it, that I cannot admit. The Church – in the fullest sense of the word, may (indeed must) apprehend it: indeed must in some sense be *the* meaning. But that takes us into deep waters where I should sink.

'The simple point I wanted to make, and on which you seem to agree (unless I am reading too much into what you say in your letter) is that the subsistence of *the* meaning, in the catholic sense, is perfectly compatible with the interpretation by the individual of *the* credal

But I will ask him to send you it. Yet I had been under the impression that it was the substance of a talk he gave at the Adelphi Centre.

Yes, I accept your remark about interpretation of the creeds so far as I understand it, and with the reservation that again, more than one interpretation could be put upon *your* words (and perhaps on *any* words). But I am very wary of anything that looks like Modernism, or any 'interpretation' which makes a set of words mean something inconsistent with what they seem to mean. In short, I can't really tell how far we are in agreement, merely by our swapping a few phrases: we should need to understand the whole complex background behind the statements of each.

I am very glad that you have got in touch with Oldham.[1] He seems to me as great a man as I know – and that is an opinion which has stood the test of five years or more and only become strengthened. There is very little I would not do, I think, if he asked me. We could not meet under better auspices.

Yours ever,
Tom

TO *Rayner Heppenstall*                                                TS Texas

14 February 1938                        *The Criterion*

Dear Heppenstall,

I have your further undated letter, with enclosures.[2] I am glad to see that you have got a new typewriter ribbon. About *Pelagia*. I feel that if it is not to be broadcast, then it ought to be redrafted in a purely literary form. As it stands it would give the impression of being merely a dud broadcast play, and I don't think that closet broadcast plays are any more desirable than closet drama of the ordinary kind. But there is some good stuff in it, as you know.

---

formularies in the deepest fashion he knows. All that is required of him is the recognition that the profession of the catholic Christian faith is *the* expression of his deepest fashion of knowing.'

1 – 'I learn, through Dr Oldham, that there is some chance of our working together. That would be very satisfying for me.'

2 – 'Pelagia is not good broadcasting as I was told by Howard Rose and Val Gielgud at any rate. I intended it to be seen as reading matter and want it to be printed as such if any good . . . If no good as reading matter in a lump then I shall extract the nice bits to go in a book of poems.' He enclosed 'a few more poems'.

I have indeed read and noted with pleasure several contributions of Bernard Kelly in *Blackfriars* and perhaps elsewhere.[1] I should very much like to meet him and get him to write for the *Criterion*. From what you say he sounds the right stuff.

I will write to you again when I have read what you enclose.

Yours ever,
T. S. Eliot

I return *Pelagia* herewith, but retain the poems.

TO *John Hayward*                                                    TS King's

15 February [1938]                              *The Criterion*

Dear John,

Christina will be happy to come to 5 o'clock tea on Friday. I said I would meet her at Gloucester Road Station, but if I should be delayed she volunteered to come on by herself, so perhaps she is not quite so frightened as Frank thinks. At any rate, we shall have got Djuna over with, and anything else will seem child's play after that.

I am not going to press you to be Literary Executor if you are disinclined for any reason, and you don't need to give any reason. But before dropping the matter, I do want to say this. I always count on making a new will every five years: I don't expect a will to stand good until I die full of years at 95, like my Uncle Tom. So that is the only period ever in question. A will is in case I am knocked (as the saying is) arse over tea-kettle by a Buss, or some other unexpected calamity cuts me down like a flower ('as a child cuts down a flower')[2]. In my circumstances, a will can only be a temporary one. I have no obvious person or persons to leave all my worldly goods to, in the long run; my beneficiaries, from period to period,

---

1 – 'Have you ever seen a man called Bernard Kelly? . . . [He] is I think very good and quite the nicest Catholic mind in this country . . .

'What I really mean is could I say to him that you would be pleased to see him and that he could arrange to call on you at Faber's with a view to writing something for The Criterion? He's terribly modest and shy and ought to be allowed to expand a little . . .

'None of your bright-boy, thumb-to-my-nose, young, sixth-form Turnell fascists and Bernard Walls. None of your careful Jesuits crying Holy War, celibates crying for blood, fashionable priests in drawing rooms, virgins in black petticoats, quoting St Thomas's texts on copulation. None of your Douglas Jerrolds. None of your mighty quaffers of chemical beer in the home counties. None of your coughing Watkins and Dawsons either.

'No, something really handsome, like Maritain and Eric G. and some of the Dominicans.'

2 – Ernest Dowson, 'Impenitent Ultima'.

may be changed; furthermore, any considerable increase or diminution of my fortunes would mean altering the will too. The immediate occasion for a new will, for instance, is the fact that my actual will makes no provision for dramatic royalties, which ought to be dealt with separately from my publishing royalties. And the putting in or knocking out of a Literary Executor is a very simple matter, as my instructions would stand for whoever it was. But at present, I don't know anyone else besides yourself whom I should altogether trust in that capacity.

The functions would be chiefly negative. I have had to write at one time or another a lot of junk in periodicals the greater portion of which ought never to be reprinted. If any of this came to light, you would have to decide; but I wouldn't expect you to collect it yourself: you could take it in general that what I have not published in books by the time of my death I don't consider worth publishing. F. & F. might be tempted, and your job would be to say no. And I don't want any biography written, or any letters printed that I wrote prior to 1933, or any letters at all of any intimacy to anybody. In fact, I have a mania for posthumous privacy. So again, your job would be to discourage any attempt to make books of me or about me, and to suppress everything suppressable. And I would leave instructions with the will, to this effect.

Possibly a careful selection might be made of the best commentaries: I don't know.

I shall not refer to the matter again, if you don't.

Yours<br>TP

Items: A queer letter from Cambridge – the Kitten Menace – another Cat Broadcast – a Portrait in the Academy? – probably not – Geo. Barker off to Norwich.

## TO *E. Martin Browne*                    TS Houghton

15 February 1938                    [*The Criterion*]

Dear Martin,[1]

I am sending under separate cover a copy of the complete text of *The Family Reunion* to you, and also to Ashley. I should be grateful if when you receive it you would send me a short wire, merely saying 'manuscript received', as if the manuscript went astray without my knowing of it, much valuable time would be lost.

1 – This letter was given in full in Browne, *The Making of T. S. Eliot's Plays*, 101–2.

I can imagine how little time you have at present, and I am very sorry to add to your burdens, but if the play is to be produced and published in the autumn, it is really important that I should have your and Ashley's criticisms at the earliest possible moment, especially if they involve any drastic changes.

I should like from you if possible both fundamental and minor suggestions for alteration. It is a pity that we cannot discuss points in conversation, as the play must really go to press early in June in order to be ready for publication. I want any criticisms therefore of the plot as a whole, of the characters, and of any inaccuracies or weaknesses that suggest themselves.

I am not certain of all of my entrances and exits. I have an uncomfortable feeling that some of the entrances may appear fortuitous and unmotivated, and especially the entrance of Mary in the last scene.

Incidentally, you are much more at home, naturally, in foxhunting society than I am, and you may find minor points which could be improved from this point of view.

You will notice that I have rewritten Act I Scene 2, and I think have improved it by giving it more relation to plot and character, and I hope relieving some of the slowness which seemed to me to afflict that Act.

If I think of any other points of detail, I will send them on later, but I must get this letter off to catch the *Queen Mary*.

I hope that you are keeping well in spite of the strain, and that you have not suffered from excessive hospitality in Boston.

> In haste,
> Yours ever,
> [Tom]

## TO *Enid Faber*                                            TS Valerie Eliot

16 February [1938]                    Faber & Faber Ltd

Dear Enid,

You have given me a bad two hours' work. How can a peer (who inherited his father's title, in fact the peerage dates back to George IV) be the younger brother of his two younger brothers who survive him?[1] Well that has got me fair beat. I cant solve that any more than I can solve today's cross-word puzzle. Something might be done if he wasn't a peer, but all

---

1 – TSE was trying to place his hero 'Harry' – Lord Monchensey – in *FR*.

things considered it's hopeless. There's nothing for him but to abdicate his position as the youngest of the family. As I see it, he will have to be the eldest. And I am willing to appear on the balcony and make an apologetic speech to the infuriated crowd milling about in the street in front of the offices of *Burke's Peerage*. The next thing I expect you will do is to point out that somebody has made two dramatic entrances without having had the opportunity to leave the room. Will MAN'S HIDDEN POWERS be a boon to the distracted amateur dramatist? I doubt it. Meanwhile please continue your search for cavities, and I remain,

Yr, demented<br>Tp.

TO *Frank Morley*                                        TS Faber Archive

17 February 1938                    *The Criterion*

Dear Frank,

Thanks for your cheering letter.[1] One point that neither you nor Brace nor John seems to have picked up is that a man who had two younger brothers couldn't have been the youngest of his family. I owe that to Enid, and it's what I call Useful Criticism.

Doxology at end of Part I has gone out anyway.

Don't agree with you yet about PUSHED, because I *wanted* the comic associations. Besides, how else, without a good deal of machinery, or how else with equal ease, can you get something on the borderline where it might have been murder, might have been an accident, or might have been imaginary? For all we know, he may have been standing several feet away thinking about this or that but with the lower level of day-dream mind fancying himself pushing her over. When you want to kill somebody the imagination of doing it, in a particular way, can be very vivid; and everyone knows that a realistic dream can come back to the mind later and you can wonder indefinitely whether it was dream or actuality. And there is a suggestion of triviality about 'pushed' which pleases me.

As for birthday cake, I knew when I wrote it that it was tentative and might have to go out. So you may very well be right there and I shall shed no tears if it goes out: but I still might want to keep it in the printed text.

I have now sent copies (Part I, scene II quite re-written and improved I think so as to give more speed) to Dukes and Browne, so if you run across

1–Not traced.

them you can ask them how they like it. They had a good press in Boston, and I should say too many tea-parties, but financial success still doubtful.

I am also encouraged by hearing that Brace likes it.

You are lucky to be out of the way while we are all having to sign away all our goods and chattels to get an overdraft from the bank: your children may bless you for going to America at this moment. I have thought for some time that we were over-trading, and I suppose we shall go on doing so. But it's going to be awkward, some time, if a war breaks out when we are right up to the limit with our overdraft.

Give my love to Donald & Ida, and my warm respects to your mother, my more boisterous compliments to yr. brothers, and appropriate remarks to anyone else. (Before you leave the States, I am sure Emily would appreciate a card from you: you will not be seeing her, as she is professing at Smith College: her address is 22 Paradise Road, Northampton, Mass.)

Christina seems well, and seems satisfied about all the children. She has a nice flat: but I hope she eats enough. She says she is getting a good deal of sleep, but is coming to tea with John tomorrow. By the way, John has finally agreed to be Literary Executor, which will relieve you – though he says he doesnt expect to outlive me, but I tell him this is only in case I am run over by a bus, or done in by political opponents, or anything else in the next few years. My instructions will be simple: he is to obstruct everything, and prevent you and Geoffrey from trying to print posthumous books of papers that ought to be suppressed. I have done a new Cat, modelled on the late Prof. Moriarty, but he doesn't seem very popular: too sophisticated perhaps.[1] Geoffrey seems satisfied with Paris (like the Hotel de Beaujolais) and had a large and appreciative audience who laughed at his jokes.

So no more for the present from yr.

TP

Here Ive left out the most important news, which is that Wyndham Lewis is painting a portrait of me for the Academy.[2] Any offers from the U.S.A.? Cheaper than Gerald Kelly R.A. and should be worth more after a time.

---

1 – 'Macavity: The Mystery Cat'.
2 – FVM had written to HWE on 14 Jan. 1938: 'I have had a serious and important idea. Oughtn't Harvard University, or Eliot House, or whatever foundation has the title and funds to answer it, to commission an oil painting of Uncle Tom while the bloom of youth is still on his cheeks, while his hair still waves in the battle, and while his two remaining teeth can still gnash.

'I am not suggesting that the golden bowl is breaking, but the sound of the grasshopper is always in the man – and seriously this is the moment to have a portrait made.'

TO *Henry Eliot*                                                    TS Houghton

17 February 1938                              *The Criterion*

Dear Henry,

Very many thanks for your long letter, the fullest account of the play, as
well as of the attendant festivities, that I have had.[1] I very much appreciate
all that you have done for Dukes and the company. They seem to have
had plenty of entertainment in Boston: perhaps some of the entertainers
need no thanks from me, as they may merely have been getting in on the
excitement and publicity. I shall be very sorry if the run is not a financial
success – not only on my own account! – though, the earlier Browne
comes back, the better we can get on with the plans for my new play,
which we have intended to produce here in the autumn. (And the necessity
of waiting on the programme of work in preparation of this play, prevents
me from making any plans for the summer or autumn: so I don't know
when I shall be over next). I couldn't have come now in any case, as Frank
Morley is in America till the latter part of March; also I only finished my
first draft a couple of weeks ago: and in any case I had rather come when
there is less publicity and no formal parties.

I thought myself that the company on the whole was working better,
at the last rehearsals, than it had for a long time; and that the chorus was
the best we had had. And to judge from the cuttings, Speaight has pulled
himself together again: during the latter part of the English run he had
deteriorated. His voice is magnificent, but I think Browne delivers verse
better.

Anyway, they must have enjoyed their visit to Boston.[2]

---

'His friend Wyndham Lewis would be certain to do a brilliant job; I know Tom has a high
opinion of his portraits. There are also the romantic, the stolid, and conventional portrait
artists of every degree.

'You may perhaps feel that it is a suggestion which you would prefer somebody else to
put forward. If so, couldn't you please pass this note to Theodore Spencer for him to start
the excitement? Tom's position is so large and secure that no possible mistake could be made
by having paintings – and so far as paintings are concerned, there is more glory, don't you
think, to have them young – genius ought to be nipped in the bud.'

Frederick Tomlin, *T. S. Eliot*, 92: '[Wyndham Lewis] spoke often of Eliot . . . As Lewis
was very fond of champagne, he had offered Eliot some during a sitting in the spring of 1937
[*sc.* 1938]. Eliot had apparently declined it on the plea that it was Lent. He murmured that
he would have some whisky instead. This had greatly tickled Lewis.'

1 – Not traced.

2 – Ashley Dukes (New York) to HWE, 21 Feb. 1938: 'We began very slowly here, in great
contrast to our splendid welcome in the second week of Boston; and even now we are only
beginning to bring in the right kind of audience, but there is evidence they are coming . . .

There is to be a broadcast of some more Cats, London Regional on April 7th at 9.30 p.m. Greenwich time, for anybody who has a radio set that will take it.

I don't know what I shall do with three more sets of pyjamas! I have never had so many in my life: but I suppose I can use three in winter and three in summer.

When I said £200 I meant that, and not dollars; and if you and the authorities on the spot should think best to pay the taxes, there it is.

I have had a curious request from a little curate here. He is a Yorkshireman, and it appears that his grandmother was the last of the family of Saltonstall there. He is interested in establishing the relationship with the American Saltonstalls, and finding out more about them. He would like to know if anything is known of the ancestry before 1500, and something of the descent of the family in America. He has a notion of writing a thesis on the Saltonstalls for an M.Litt. degree at Durham – which shows that you can get degrees on just as trivial research in this country as you can in America. I thought that possibly some time when you were in the Widener you might ask whether there was any book of Saltonstall genealogy; or if you knew any Saltonstall who was interested in genealogy you might put him in touch with my little man. I believe the Tuckermans are related to the Saltonstalls, and Cousin Jenny used to be an indefatigable genealogist. But I don't want you to put yourself to much trouble. Anyway, I enclose his letter.

I must stop now.

> With love to Theresa,
> Affectionately,
> Tom

---

'I want to take this opportunity of thanking you both for your kindness to us in Cambridge. I have already had a message from *Time* and we are discreetly giving them some information about Tom's new play' (Houghton).

*Time* duly reported (28 Feb. 1938): 'At present Eliot is working on a modern play laid in an English country house, but with a substratum of Greek drama.'

The London *Times* ('"Murder in the Cathedral": English Company in New York', 18 Feb. 1938, 12) reported on the New York production of *MiC*: 'The critics were bound to compare this performance with that given by the Federal Theatre two years ago. They found the English presentation less vividly theatrical but more fervently religious than its forerunner, and by that much at least the gainer. There was unlimited admiration for Mr Robert Speaight's portrayal of Becket. It was not too much to say of him, as Mr Brooks Atkinson did in the *New York Times* [17 Feb. 1938] that he played "with the exaltation of an actor whose reverence for a Christian martyr has become a way of life." There was scarcely less praise for all the other players. But some felt that the chorus chants, varied as they were at times by distributing lines to individual voices, "drugged the ear more than stimulated it" because of the droning of the women's voices.'

17 February 1938                         *The Criterion*

Well Ez I ought to have written to you before about your lil kinderbuch which I take it you have translated from a Italian translation from the Swedish (or have you got so proficient that you do Scandinavian straight off).[1] Well its a nice little book and I agree it is well written and the life is well pourtrayed but there is just one objection: you couldnt SELL it. I am sorry but there it is I believe. Anyway that is not my opinion only but everybody's so what next.

You ought to have a look at *The Black Book* by Laurence Durrell when Jack Kahane produces it in the spring. I think he is better than Henry Miller, unless Miller gets him down: but I think this is more serious as a whole than *Tropic of Cancer*. I dont believe Miller could do Brooklyn as well as Durrell does the Surrey Side; and besides Miller is all gummed up in D. H. Lawrence anyway.

That young Prokosch does some nice verses sometimes, although a bit too literary and devitalised as a rule. Something the same applies to Frank Prince: but these boys do take a little trouble over composing their verses, which is rare nowadays.

And Wyndham is starting a portrait of me to send to the Academy. Well well.

A aint heard nothing of yr. mother-in-law for a long time, but hope she aint puny.

Well Ez anyway I have done a play which is a lot better than *Murder in the Cathedral* anyway. And I expect to get some nice teeth before long.

So whats the next item. Mencius in June I expect.

yrs
TP

---

1 – EP wrote, 16 Jan.: 'To the Rt/ Rev the POSSUM and Omnobospherous WHALE . . .
'I have just dambit finished the clean copy of thet li'l CheeYild's buk I wrote of.

'They tell me it is a FIND . . .

'Out of my line, but I found it interesting to translate. Child of twelve/ stylistic influence if any, Miss Matrineau's "Norway" [Harriet Martineau, *Feats on the Fjord: A Tale of Norway* (1865)] . . .

'EF a cheeyild wrut it, it must be comprehensible to other ingFangs??? . . . I think you will admit sound sense and the peasant point of view.

'Enny haow, wotter baht it?'

According to EP in a subsequent letter (23 Feb.), the story was written in German and not Swedish. 'Oh yes, en passant/ the Tirol has never been Sweedish,' he wrote sarcastically.

I hope youre happy with young Reid. Have seen young Duncan, but none*
of his work yet, except Townsman, which wont last, he's not practical,
but he seems to know something about Cornish fishermen.

[*] Here, this isn't true. Some scenes of a play – begins quite nicely, but
second scene not so good. Told him I can't judge it as theatre until I see
the whole.[1]

## TO *Laurence Pollinger*[2]                                        CC

18 February 1938                    [Faber & Faber Ltd]

Dear Pollinger,

Your two letters of the 15th received, and I will try to get the Saroyan
dealt with quickly. About Pound I am rather in the dark. I have not seen
any list of contents for a *Less Polite Essays* volume myself, and I am
having it looked up. And I do wish that Ezra would make his suggestions
much more explicit, especially for a musical ignoramus like myself. How
can we get any further from Ezra's cryptic note? I take it he wants us to
publish the score of a concerto, with some illustrations and Miss Rudge's
article about the composer. Do you know anything about Vivaldi?[3] I had
not been in on any previous suggestion of Ezra's about going in for music
publication, although he has babbled at times about microphotography.
But I thought that was for use on something like a home cinema outfit.
However, I suppose I had better try to decipher his recent correspondence
with Morley, and then write to him myself.

                                Yours sincerely,
                                [T. S. Eliot]

P.S. Yours of the 17th with enclosure from Ezra received. I haven't been
in on this music business before, but I have just read a letter to him from
Frank of 17 December, asking for more information, and I am brooding
over a reply from Ezra of the 19th. I think the best thing I can do is
to bring it up in the committee on Monday, and find out what further

1–This handwritten postscript is linked by a line to the word 'none' in the previous
paragraph.
2–GCF's diary, Thurs. 3 Mar.: 'Lunched with Larry Pollinger [of Pearn, Pollinger &
Higham] at Café Royal. He is, I must say, a soothing & most admirable person!
3–EP to TSE, 23 Jan.: 'If Possum is capable of looking at some sample reproductions/ of
music, and getting ready fer THEM with some other matter (did you see the Vivaldi letters in
Listener or do you WANT to see them?) I will send EM.' 8 Feb.: 'Are you capable of dealink
wiff this probbubbUlum or do we aWAIT the Whhale?'

information the committee think we need. Then I will let you know, and write to Ezra also.[1]

## TO *Donald Brace*                                                CC

18 February 1938                    [Faber & Faber Ltd]

Dear Brace,

I cannot tell you how much pleasure your letter of 11 February gave me.[2] I value your good opinion highly, and also, just as it is almost more important to me that the actors should be keen on the play than that the audience should be so, it matters a great deal to me that my publishers should like a book. I had heard from Frank that you were pleased with *The Family Reunion*, but it is very much more convincing to hear from you direct.

We might as well have the agreement with Faber & Faber as before.[3] It is impossible yet, however, to say what the sale price of the book can be, because when Martin Browne, the prospective producer of the play, gets

1 – EP to FVM, 7 Dec., launched without preamble into his characteristic idiolect: 'Also fer the good of the FIRM ! these here microfoto and photostat processes ARE before forever and hell's day GOING to work.

'esp/ in MuZIK and chinkese studies . . .

'Now the question IS If a interestin brochure were provided, what sort of allowance wd. you blokes make for proper illistrations. Where wd. you thik them sound bizniz? . . .

'Suppose I offer you 64 pages of pretty reprods . . . And wd. you be interested in 'em AT ALL if they were aimed at reading machines only, and not at the nude and average EYE?'

FVM to EP, 17 Dec.: 'Your letter of the 7th stirred receptive responses all the way down Whale's backbone, for he has for years past been cogitating about photography and the musical score . . .

'But what I mean to say is that if you will tell me what you are talking about in your letter of the 7th, we may be able to get forrader. The curiosity is titivated; what are the facts?'

Laurence Pollinger passed to TSE a letter he had received from EP dated 14 Feb.: 'Dear LarriPOL / QUESTION IZ, can the Rev Eliot act without WHALE?

'Whale's wanting to horn in on Music publication, might miss A BOAT.

'I mean the FIRST piece of music published with new process (plus preface by me) will get attention and sale beyond that of the second and third pieces published by anybody unless it were Strawinsky or somfink of that sort.

'Happens that I have a GOOD piece ready. I can send up illustrations of process NOW . . . Better wake the possum NOW tenderly and see if any use my sending up the swag.'

2 – 'I want to tell you how much I enjoyed reading the draft of your new play . . . It is extraordinarily fine, I think; it is rich in memorable passages and implications. It will be fascinating to see it on the stage and, at least for me, even more exciting to publish it.'

3 – Brace wrote: 'I find that the agreement for *Murder in the Cathedral* was with Faber and Faber. Before drawing up an agreement, however, I had better ask you what your wishes are.'

to work on it, he may want to cut as well as to alter. As it stands I think the play is a good bit longer than *Murder in the Cathedral*.

I am sorry that I did not have time before Frank left to prepare a copy of the third revise of the play for him to take, because it contains substantial alterations of Act I, Scene 2, which I think improve it considerably.

With many thanks, and best wishes,<br>
Yours sincerely,<br>
[T. S. Eliot]

TO *Ian Cox*                                                          TS BBC

18 February 1938                    *The Criterion*

Dear Cox,

I have your letter of the 17th, and will as I promised think a little more about 'The Poet and the Public'.[1] But I must warn you that much as I dislike to give pain, I don't at present feel that this is my job.

As for next Friday, I still hope that it will be possible, but since I saw you I have agreed to sit to Wyndham Lewis for an oil portrait, and as it suits him to work in the evenings, this may take all my free evenings for a fortnight or so to come.[2] I will let you know on Monday.

It seems to me that your new programme might have the original title of *POLLICLE DOGS AND JELLICLE CATS*, as you have put both of them in. How does that strike you?

Yours ever sincerely,<br>
T. S. Eliot

1 – 'Quite honestly I am miserable at the thought of this series "The Poet and the Public" without you taking part in it, and I do hope that your "thinking about it" will result in your deciding to contribute . . . I enjoyed our short meeting on Monday exceedingly and do hope that Friday, 25th February at about 9.00 p.m. continues to be a possible time for our next meeting.'

2 – See Wyndham Lewis, *Blasting and Bombardiering* (1937; revised edn, 1967), 286–7: 'Appearing at one's front door, or arriving at a dinner-rendezvous (I am thinking of the late thirties, not his more vernal years of course) his face would be haggard, he would seem at his last gasp. (Did he know?) To ask *him* to lie down for a short while at once was what I always felt I ought to do. However, when he had taken his place at a table, given his face a dry wash with his hands, and having had a little refreshment, Mr Eliot would rapidly shed all resemblance to the harassed and exhausted refugee, in flight from some Scourge of God. Apparently a modest reserve of power, prudently set aside, would be drawn on. He would be as lively as ever he could be or any one need be – for of course it is not necessary to fly about on the tips of one's toes with one's scarf and coat-tails flying.'

TO *Lawrence Durrell*                                    TS Morris Library

18 February 1938                        *The Criterion*

Dear Durrell,

Blurb writing is the most difficult and also the most unsatisfactory form of art that I know, and I could always go on writing the same blurb over and over for weeks without getting any nearer to anything that would content me.[1] However, one cannot labour indefinitely over these things, and I hope the enclosed will do. If not, send it back, & I'll try again.[2]

Yours sincerely,

T. S. Eliot

[Enclosure]

Lawrence Durrell's *The Black Book* is the first piece of work by a new English writer to give me any hope for the future of prose fiction. If he has been influenced by any writers of my generation, the influences have been digested, and he has produced something different. One test of the book's quality, for me, is the way in which reminiscences of it keep turning up in my mind: evocations of South London or of the Adriatic, or of individual characters. What is still more unusual is the sense of pattern and of organisation of moods which emerges gradually during the reading, and remains in the mind afterwards. *The Black Book* is not a scrap-book, but a carefully executed whole. There is nothing of the second-hand literary about the material; but what is most unusual is the structure which the author has made of it.[3]

1 – Durrell wrote (n.d.) that Jack Kahane was 'delighted with the news that you are printing parts of the Book and is grateful for the blurb which he asked me to get as soon as possible'.
2 – Durrell responded (n.d.): 'Very many thanks for the blurb; I think it is excellent and am grateful to you for it. Sorry it took such effort: but it is a dreadful thing to have to write. There is only one thing harder – to write a blurb for oneself! I have been slaving away at the dust-jacket blurb for the book, trying to say just how wonderful I think I am and to appear modest withal.'
3 – *The Black Book: An Agon* (Paris: Obelisk Press, 1938) – the first volume of the Villa Seurat Series, ed. Henry Miller – quotes TSE's statement on the front flap. When the book was republished by the Olympia Press (Traveller's Companion series) in 1959 – as *The Black Book tout court* – Durrell sent a copy to TSE with this inscription: 'My dear TSE Lio T / I didn't come and bother you knowing how busy you must be. But I thought you might like to have a copy of the newly reissued Black Book as a testimony of my affectionate admiration and gratitude for all your patience and kindness to / Yours sincerely / Larry Durrell' (TSE Library).

18 February 1938                    *The Criterion*

Dear Frank,
    Two business points.

### 1) *EDMUND WILSON*

I have read a fair amount of Bunny Wilson's *Triple Thinkers*, and am glad to see that his mind is working as well as ever. The same intelligent, conscientious, rather solemn Puritan.[1] There is some very good stuff amongst this, but I simply cannot see it as a Wilson item for us to start off with. *Axel's Castle* was well worth publishing, and I wish we had had that, but that had a continuous idea running throughout it, although the continuous idea was not a very good one, and what was good was the criticism of individual authors. But this book is merely a collection of essays with nothing to hold them together; furthermore, there is too much cold mutton for the English market: you cannot warm up essays on Paul More and John J. Chapman for the English public unless your name carries a great deal more weight here than Wilson's. I am holding the galleys, subject to your instructions, and meanwhile am suggesting, with the approval of the committee, that you might have a talk with Brace about Wilson's future, and see whether anything could be suggested to him in the way of a whole book on some subject which might have a better market here than the *Triple Thinkers*.

### 2) *JOHN GRIERSON*

I had Grierson to lunch again the other day, as Geoffrey and I had both trusted the other to remember our previous conversation, and neither of us could remember anything.[2] To refresh your memory I send you herewith a copy of the synopsis which you have already seen. What Grierson wants to write will come to about 100,000 words. He wants to have appendices amounting to another 20,000 words, written one by Tallents, and the others by two or three other people. You know Grierson, and will not be surprised to learn that he believes that Tallents and the other people

---

1–Peter Quennell recorded in *The Wanton Chase: An Autobiography from 1939* (1980) that when he once suggested, in an exchange of letters with TSE, 'that the author of *The Waste Land* was still a Puritan at heart, [TSE] had asserted that he was proud of his Puritan ancestry, and that a long line of studious clergymen and judges had firmly fixed his mental pattern'.

2–Grierson to GCF, 17 Mar. 1938: 'We are anxious to get out a small book telling teachers how best to use our various documentary films in the teaching of Civics . . . This is a job we want to have done very quickly, in time for distribution of the book to teachers at the Empire Exhibition in Glasgow.'

will do the work for him for nothing. What he wants himself is £250 in advance. Apparently Geoffrey and I told him before that the English market would not bear more than £150, and he is quite ready to let us see what we can get out of the American market to make up the balance. In short, £250 means world rights. It will be a fairly bulky book of course. Grierson says he is going off to Canada shortly, and he wants to go and see people in Washington – he says he knows whom he will see – and also to go out to Hollywood and talk to two or three of the biggest producers there, so he naturally wants a little cash. I don't myself want us to put up more than £150, so will you see whether you can sell the American rights to anybody? That, in short, is the idea.

Yours,<br>TP.

C.W.S.[1] has just rung up to say a Miss Evans, representing Houghton Mifflin, says they approached Grierson to do a film book, & he referred her to us. So will you tackle Houghton Mifflin about it?[2]

## TO *Henry Miller*                                                      CC

18 February 1938                         [*The Criterion*]

Dear Mr Miller,

   The length of time that I have kept your paper on Lawrence must have cost you intense exasperation,[3] but it also means that the essay itself has given me no end of trouble. I have wrestled with it I don't know how many times. It so obviously means a great deal to you, that I feel that it ought to mean much more to me. But apart from some lucid moments at which I am able to applaud, I find myself merely grasping at something in the dark, and seemingly only pulling off handfuls of cotton-wool. What I really want is more of yourself and less of Lawrence, an author whom I have always found difficult and irritating. I would very much like to see an essay by you on Nijinsky or on Amiel, as you suggest.[4]

1 – C. W. Stewart, a director of Faber & Faber.
2 – FVM noted at the foot that the book had been rejected by both Harcourt Brace and Macmillan; and that he had 'left synopsis with HM Co. [Houghton Mifflin Company]'.
3 – Miller had written on 8 Nov. 1937: 'I don't mean to press you for a reply about the Lawrence ms. which you acknowledged some weeks ago [13 Oct. 1937], but write merely to say that should you reject it, I wish you would mail it to me recommandé [registered] as I find that the copy is either lost or misplaced – or mislaid. That always give me a certain angoisse.'
4 – Henri Frédéric Amiel (1821–81), Swiss philosopher, poet, critic; author of *Journal Intime*.

Well, I am very sorry. And for quite other reasons I cannot make much of Anaïs Nin's fragment about Woman.[1] I have taken other opinions on it, but without correction. I hope that I shall see more in Anaïs Nin later, but I think it will have to be something different from this. It seemed to me almost as if she was writing it under your influence, and of course not doing it so well. I thought that the bit about her father was better, and I suspect that she might be better at exact reporting of experience than at these generalisations.

Always with the best of all wishes,
Yours sincerely,
[T. S. Eliot]

TO *Bonamy Dobrée*                                    TS Brotherton

18 February 1938                    *The Criterion*

Dear Bonamy,

I have read your essay on English Poetic Drama at once, and as you request, return it at once.[2] It seems to me very good, especially for a foreign audience. The prefatory matter about the decline of English poetic drama in the last 300 years would I think be unnecessary for any intelligent English audience, but I think is desirable for foreigners.

What of course you have not been able to prove, and I don't think there is any material available which would prove it, is that verse drama today has yet found a suitable medium for dialogue. The bits you quote from *Murder in the Cathedral* are more lyrical. I think that I have now found

1 – Nin had replied to TSE (n.d): 'Let me thank you for the copy of The Criterion. I was not discouraged by your letter and return of the manuscripts perhaps because Lawrence Durrell reported his talk with you and conveyed to me a feeling of your interest, more than I could feel it in a letter. Ever since I have been looking through the diaries with the hope of finding a block of it that would be right for The Criterion. So far I have found nothing. All I read is too mixed with the personal, not sufficiently objective. As soon as I find something you may be sure I will send it to you. Meanwhile I am enclosing an essay I wrote on woman's creation.'
The passage enclosed – which was to be published, in slightly revised form, in *The Diary of Anaïs Nin*, vol. 2: 1934–1939 (1967), 233ff – opened: 'Woman never communicated directly with god but through the priest or through the artist; she never communicated with her own meaning except by way of man's interpretation. She never created.'
2 – Dobrée (15 Feb.) sent TSE a lecture that he was to deliver at three universities in France the following week. 'Would you honour me by glancing over it, & telling me if you want anything special said about yourself – if I have misrepresented you in any way, & if you cannot tolerate my truncating your chorus? I have, as usual, stolen freely from you without acknowledgment.'

a better medium for dialogue than I had in *Murder*, and I admit that you could not make out a very good case for the dialogue in that, I only mention it as what an astute member of the audience might recognise as the weakness in the case you make out for contemporary work.

I think the point about the transparency of dramatic poetry is most important. One reason why I am dissatisfied with *Murder* is that there are too many bumps of poetry sticking up like outcrop, and the poetry is not sufficiently integrated into the drama. This was partly a weakness of the situation; the plot material is so scanty that I had rather to overweight the play with lyrical outbursts, and now I also think that I have got nearer to this integration.

I shall have to read my Shakespeare lectures again before I answer your previous letter. My first impression is that I did not mean quite what you seem to say that I meant; but perhaps it is simpler than that.

Yours ever,
Tom


TO *Henri Fluchère* TS Fluchère

18 February 1938 *The Criterion*

Dear Mr Fluchère,

I was glad to receive your letter of 14 February, to reassure me that *Meurtre dans la Cathèdrale* is going forward. I quite see the difficulty of the *Dies Irae*, but I look forward to seeing your revision.[1]

If Paulhan decides that he would like to publish it in the *N.R.F.*, I hope that means that he will be able to publish it all in one number, and not in parts. Even if serial publication is decided on, however, he ought to write to Faber & Faber first for permission, and not to me. The division of the payment is quite acceptable to me, as I know that that is the custom, but my moiety would have to be paid to Faber & Faber and not direct to myself. Will you therefore ask Paulhan, if he decides that he wants it, to write to this firm?

1 – Fluchère had finished his translation of *MiC* – 'The most difficult part, so far, remains that of the Dies Irae rhythm" – and wished to show it to Jean Paulhan. Since the play was now a set text for the *agrégation*, students would be interested in it. 'As regards royalties for publication, the custom is that they should be divided between the author and the translator – but it concerns only, as you justly said, the first serial rights in the French language.'

I confess that my primary interest is that your translation should be performed, as publication alone of a play does not seem to me so important.

There is, by the way, an article about the play in the current number of *Études Anglaises* by one Jean Farenc, whom I do not know, which struck me as quite good.[1] I think that Dr Leavis's book is on the whole excellent and useful. I think the Matthiessen book as good as one can expect any such book to be; on the whole it seemed to me an excellent piece of work.[2]

Anglo-Catholics are not a separate body, but are regular members of the Anglican Communion.[3] The term is somewhat vague, and it is becoming more and more difficult to draw any definite line between those who can be called Anglo-Catholics and those who cannot. It is sometimes applied, and indeed sometimes abused, as a term only regarding those who employ a greater amount of Catholic ritual, but the ritual of the Church in general tends to become more Catholic, and therefore this distinction is not a very clear one. The term may also be applied to those who lay more emphasis on orthodoxy in doctrine, which is the true tradition of the Oxford Movement, which at the beginning paid very little attention to reform of ritual and completion of liturgy. But I think the term is a dying one, and I personally shall not be sorry to see it disappear. Even in its present use, however, it cannot be taken to apply only to the small number in the Church of England who accept the whole of post Tridentine doctrine in the Roman Church. But the Church of England is one of the most difficult institutions of the country to explain to anyone outside, and one really has to live in England in order to understand how the English mind works in theological matters!

With best wishes,
Yours very sincerely,
T. S. Eliot

1 – Jean Farenc, '*Murder in the Cathedral* à la scène', '*Études Anglaises* 2 (1938), 27–35.
2 – Fluchère was lecturing on TSE's work. 'I have found Dr Leavis very helpful – indeed, I owe him much. I know he disagrees with you, now and then, but still his *New Bearings* [*New Bearings in English Poetry*, 1932] are [*sic*] most illuminating, and I believe contain the best criticism on recent English poetry that I know of . . .

'*In fine*, is the Matthiessen book any good?'
3 – 'A point which remains obscure, is the position of "Anglo-Catholics". Are they included in the body of the Anglican Church, differing from them only on the question of ritual? Why "anglo"? Is not "catholic" a word for "universal"? I know one says "roman catholic". But still, the difference is not clear to me.'

TO *Ronald Duncan*[1]                                   TS Valerie Eliot

21 February 1938                    London W.C.1

Dear Mr Duncan,

I see no objection to your printing the extract from my letter to Ezra, so long as you make it quite clear that it *is* taken from a letter to Ezra.[2] If printed without that explanation the style might appear affected and pert. And I would be glad if you would add a point 5. 'If you write a play in verse, then the verse ought to be a medium to look THROUGH, and not a pretty decoration to look AT.'

Yours sincerely,
[T. S. Eliot]


TO *Ezra Pound*                                        TS Beinecke

21 February 1938                    *The Criterion*

Dear EZ

I am trying to decipher your correspondence with Whale about MUSIC PUBLICATION. Well and good, but he went off to America without talking to me (or apparently anybody else) about this, and now I says, I should like to get this settled one way or another, as it might be a big thing. Well I cant figger out much from your cryptograms, which, like most of yr. explanations, assume that the Reader knows all about it already. And I have read Olga Rudge's contribution to UMBROLLO, which is a good deal more lucid, but still fails to tell me some necessary facts.

1. WHAT is the process? what sort of machinery necessary? how can I find out all about it? has anything been done in this country? WHAT does the result look like? I take it you dont mean to publish these little film things (either *pellicole rotolate* or *pellicole rigide*) which you look at through a projector, but a full-size music score which you can put on a music stand and play from?

---

1 – Ronald Duncan (1914–82), poet, playwright, journalist; editor of *Townsman*, 1938–45; librettist of Benjamin Britten's opera *The Rape of Lucretia* (1945); author of plays including *This Way to the Tomb* (1945); *Our Lady's Tumbler* (1951); *Don Juan* (1953). He was instrumental in setting up the English Stage Company at the Royal Court Theatre, 1956.
2 – Duncan wrote (14 Feb.) that EP had suggested he print in *Townsman* no. 3 an extract from TSE's letter to EP of 16 Dec. [*sc.* 19 Dec. 1937] giving the Possum's requisites for a play. See above.

2. IF you mean books of music, full size, how big would they be, and have you a specific list of composers in mind? I take it what you are eager about is the making of OLD composers available to the public at a low price. I suppose that VIVALDI is your first item. What others?

3. Could I get more information from Dott. Leonard Sayce of Newcastle?[1]

Start from the beginning and make it plain. You could probably make yourself more intelligible in Italian than in English; or better still, get Olga Rudge or Dorothy to put it into English for me, as yr. ejaculations must be more intelligible on the SPOT than when put into writing. The Possum is not quite asleep but has finished a play and is laying off it for a spell, and is only anxious to do good to his fellow creatures.

Yr

TP

P.S. DID YOU OR DID YOU NOT SEND WHALE A OUTLINE OF MORE IMPROPER ESSAYS???[2]

---

1–Dr Leonard Sayce (1905–86): pioneer in the development of microphotography. *Ezra Pound and Globe Magazine: The Complete Correspondence*, ed. Michael T. Davis and Cameron McWhirter (2015), 224: 'Dr Sayce of Kings College, Newcastle, calculates he can register 500 pages of music on a grid of grainless film the size of a post card. This means an absolute revolution in all study of unpublished music.' EP to FVM, 19 Dec. 1938: 'Doc Sayce system is fer projection only/ buttt marrvelous.'

2–EP replied, 23 Feb., with regard to a volume of outspoken essays that he thought to call 'Less Polite Essays' (having published *Polite Essays* in 1937): 'I done sent Larry [Pollinger] or Whale or some boko a list of LESS Polecat // But fer yr/ CONsiderashun I repeet . . .

'Less Perlite essays
    1. D'Artagnan (from Criterium) 20 years after.
    2. Gaudier / the chapter of personal impressions from my Gaudier Brzeska.
    3. Immediate Need of Confucius (from Aryan Path)
    4. Jefferson and/or Mussolini
    5. The Ethics of Mencius
    6. Rene Crevel
    7. Pavannes, 46 pages of light licherchoor from Pavs and Divs.
Some brief PEPS/ re/ the little brown brothers, and possibly a few words on music.
    'vide next Townsman.
'I think this is all that can be got into one vol/ . . .
'Of course there are my EyeTalYan writings but I reckon they are still in advance of the SIÈCLE as seen from Grenwich willitch and Russul Sqzeer.'

TO *Enid Faber*                                          TS Valerie Eliot

21 February 1938                          Faber & Faber Ltd

Dear Enid,

I hasten to cheer you up: yes, there is a gleam of hope for Harry, as for Orestes, OEdipus, and all the other men who got into hereditary Greek jams. That shall be shewn in the sequel, if there ever is a sequel. No pistol-shots in this play. Harry may come back to Wishwood in forty years' time. No death but Amy's, and she had a weak heart. Monchensey. From a verse quoted by Browning:

> 'Ivy and Violet, what do ye here
> With blossom and shoot in the warm spring weather
> Hiding the arms of Moncenci and Vere?'[1]

Monchensy and Piper have this advantage, that no such names are found in *Burke's Peerage*. But there are five Dr Warburtons in the Medical Directory, all in the country (though none has a Cambridge M.D.) and I am rather worried by that. Your suggestion that the Eumenides should do a strip tease act is novel, and I believe has box-office possibilities. But there is one difficulty. If they don't wear any clothes, how do we distinguish between their evening dress and their travelling costume? That is important. When I have cleared up these Cats (labouring over two more, but I fear the vein is exhausted) I shall be able to turn my mind to the great Sherlock Holmes play.

                                          Yr. pathetic
                                          TP.


TO *Bruce Richmond*                                          CC

22 February 1938                          [*The Criterion*]

Dear Richmond,

Well, I suppose I ought to do it, under the double pressure of a cathedral and yourself.[2] I cannot plead inexperience in this sort of thing, as I had to

---

1 – Robert Browning's epigraph to his play *Colombe's Birthday* (1844) is taken from a poem by his friend Sir John Hanmer, MP (1809–81) entitled 'Written After Reading Horace Walpole's Account of Castle Henningham' (*Fra Cipollo, and Other Poems*, 1839). The poem is about the history of a great house, specifically the vicissitudes of the illustrious de Veres, Earls of Oxford.

2 – Bruce Richmond wrote on 18 Feb.: 'The "Friends of Salisbury Cathedral", of which I have just been put onto the Executive Committee, are having a two days' celebration on May 25 & 26 – mainly enlarged musical services, choral singing in the cloisters & so forth –

give an address last year for Rochester, of which I am one of the Friends, and a few weeks ago for Southwark. But that doesn't make it any easier to think of what to say on a third occasion, and I shall be very grateful if you will make suggestions, and even if you cannot, I should like to know how long they will want me to speak.[1]

It is a consolation to know that this visit will be without prejudice to my regular visit in the summer.

Yours ever,
[T. S. Eliot]


TO *Herbert Read*                                    TS Victoria

22 February 1938                    *The Criterion*

Dear Herbert,

I should have answered your letter yesterday, but was in rather a rush.[2] I will certainly bring up the question of *Poetry and Anarchism* at the committee tomorrow, and shall urge them to take it on. I have no doubt that they will feel as I do, and wish that the book might be longer. But if you are convinced that 25,000 words is the right length for what you say, don't let yourself be influenced.[3]

Many thanks for reporting the enthusiasm of Mr and Mrs Gropius.[4] I only hope that a large number of people will feel the same way. I am looking forward to a visit to Seer Green as soon as the season and other

---

and I am writing at the request of the Dean (but with my own very warm hope also) to ask if you would come and address the Friends in the Chapter House on the afternoon of May 25 – a wonderful setting and a good cause – the subject to be such as the setting and the cause may suggest to you. It would be grand if you would. In that case I hope you would spend the night with us here – "but be it noted, and it is hereby expressly declared, that such visit is without prejudice to and is entirely independent of your regular summer visit, the time and details of which are to be as hereinafter determined" – .'

1 – See 'Report on a lecture on George Herbert', *The Salisbury and Winchester Journal*, 27 May 1938, 12: *CProse* 5, 617–22. TSE celebrated Herbert as '*the* poet of Anglicanism'.

2 – HR wrote on 17 Feb.: 'I have been putting together a final statement of my heresies which will make a tract of about 25,000 words. I propose to call it POETRY AND ANARCHISM and would like to see it published in a format like AFTER STRANGE GODS . . . Would Fabers like to consider it? I am so desperately hard up that I would like an advance of £25, but I don't insist.

'Meanwhile I am not neglecting COLLECTED ESSAYS and have got some way with them.'

3 – Read, *Poetry and Anarchism* (F&F, 1938).

4 – 'I had an extraordinary dithyrambic epistle from Mrs Gropius the other day; she and Gropius had just seen Murder in the Cathedral in Boston and they were "as happy as only

conditions are favourable, and meanwhile send my love to Ludo and blessing to your son.

Ever yours,
Tom

## TO *Philip Mairet* CC

23 February 1938                    [Faber & Faber Ltd]

Dear Mairet,

I asked my secretary to ring you up this afternoon, because we have had today an estimate for the production of Saurat's book which makes it possible for us to make an offer without waiting to hear from America. If you are prepared to allow your translation to be used without translator's fee, we can offer a royalty of 10% after sale of the first 250 copies. Such terms are admittedly meagre, but I think that you and Saurat both realise that the demand for such a book will probably be small, that the book cannot be priced higher than 5s., and that we desire to publish it, not in the expectation of making money by it, but because of our enthusiasm for the book itself. I shall be glad to hear whether you and Saurat agree to this proposal.

Incidentally, we all think that it would be better for the English edition simply to translate Saurat's title and call the book *The End of Fear*, instead of adopting your longer title.[1]

Yours ever,
[T. S. Eliot]

---

the encounter of perfection can make us".' (Walter Gropius [1883–1969]: pioneering German architect; founder of the Bauhaus School; briefly resident in London; married since 1923 to Ise Frank.)

1 – TSE almost certainly wrote the blurb for Denis Saurat, *The End of Fear*, with Introduction by Philip Mairet, and Commentary by Neil Montgomery (F&F, 1938): 'Professor Denis Saurat, of the University of London, is well known as an authority on the literatures of two languages. His studies of Milton and Blake are necessary to all students of those poets. But this is a book which will surprise even Professor Saurat's admirers. Its point of departure is the death of his father, and its effect upon his peasant mother, and through his mother upon himself. He finds a relationship between the beliefs about death held by French peasants, and dreams that he has dreamt; furthermore, between their primitive superstitions and the beliefs that he has come to hold as a philosopher; and he sees his own philosophy foreshadowed and directed by the beliefs of his ancestors. This is first a vivid portrait of M. Saurat's mother, in her French village, given by means of her sayings; and second, the exposition of M. Saurat's own account of the *fear of death*, and its explanation. It is a very queer book, and will have a very queer effect upon the reader.'

## TO *Mary Hutchinson*                        TS Texas

Wednesday [23 February 1938]        Faber & Faber Ltd

Dear Mary,

About Olga's development, one point that only struck me afterwards as of complex significance was that of the old Nurse when she reappears in the last Act.[1] She says that Olga has taken her to live in a flat where she has her own bedroom and bedstead, and 'all at the expense of the government'. Apart from the significance of the Nurse's being the only person at the end to feel really happy, this seems to me to indicate, not only Olga's kindness in taking the Nurse to live with her, but also her delicacy in giving the Nurse to understand that it was the Government that paid for it – whereas presumably the Government only paid for the Nurse by paying Olga a (probably not very large) salary as Headmistress of the High School.

T.

## TO *Enid Faber*                        TS Valerie Eliot

24 February 1938        Faber & Faber Ltd

Dear Enid,

It would be Uncouth of me not to thank you for your Extream Civility in writing again – a delightful surprise.[2] People will say all sorts of nice things, but are often shy of saying straight out that they LIKE what one has written. Yes, I hope it is quite clear that nobody dies except Amy (who, as you must have gathered, had a weak heart). The tragedy, as with my Master, Tchehov, is as much for the people who have to go on living, as for those who die. And may I urge you (I did mention it to Geoffrey) to go to see St Denis' superb production of *Three Sisters* at the Queen's while it is still on.[3] It's the best production of a great play that I have seen for a long time.

---

1 – This exchange follows TSE's attendance with MH at a performance of Chekhov's *Three Sisters*.
2 – Letter not traced.
3 – TSE and Michel Saint-Denis (Managing Director, London Theatre Studio) exchanged letters in Mar. 1938. TSE's letter – it was presumably a fan letter about *The Three Sisters* – has not been traced, but Saint-Denis responded on 16 Mar.: 'I am not very well at present; it's why I am late to tell you the great pleasure I have had in receiving your letter. Your appreciation means much to me and I feel encouraged to go the way I want to go, which is to form a permanent company of actors, supported by my studio.'

I think Tom is very wise. I hope that he will contrive to preserve his wisdom as he grows up. Some folk have failed to do that. But I am not pessimistic in his case.

Affy<br>
TP.

But there is Hope for Harry – the hope of learning to want something different, rather than of getting anything he wanted.

## TO *Laurence Pollinger* CC

24 February 1938                 [Faber & Faber Ltd]

Dear Pollinger,

I have written to Ezra to ask for more complete and business-like details about the microphotography affair, and suggested that in order to make it intelligible he should either write in Italian or get somebody else to write for him. I expect I shall have an explosion from him by Monday, but meanwhile we can turn to other business.

It is about Saroyan that we are worried; see your letter of the 15th enclosing galleys. I have looked at the new stuff, some parts of which I had seen before, and it is all right, but of course it is merely more of the same. As you know, I have been fearful for some time that Saroyan's fluency might kill his market. He seems convinced that the public here must have an insatiable appetite for his work, such that two volumes a year from him can only just keep people alive. He really has been exceeding his market, and I should like to miss a beat this season, in the hope of catching up. We don't want to let this go, and in any case I am sure there is not enough market for Saroyan to distribute amongst two or more publishers, but if there is any prospect of a novel from him in the autumn, I think that

---

Later, at the behest of Alliance Française, TSE wrote this untitled tribute, 21 Dec. 1953: 'I cannot speak of Michel St Denis as one man of the theatre of another, or, what is more important from the profitable experience of being associated with him in any production. It is only as a member of the theatre-loving public that I can pay my homage: having seen some of his London productions (his production of Tchehov's *The Three Sisters* was an unforgettable experience – my only experience, I think, of weeping visibly in a theatre) and knowing indirectly but by reliable report, of the work he did for the *Old Vic* and for the training of its young actors. His mere presence in London was an encouragement: it gave one the feeling that at any moment something important and memorable might happen on the London stage. When he left us, he was mourned not only by all those who had experienced the charm of his personality in social intercourse, but by a great many people unknown to him, who were aware of his very great influence and contribution to the vitality of the English Theatre.'

ought to be the next item. It remains to be seen whether Saroyan can write a good novel, but if he can, I am sure that the market will be the better prepared for it by a rest this season than by having a fifth volume of short stories forced upon it.

It would be a pity if anyone so clever as Saroyan should go dead after such a short run, and we don't want him to have a meteoric Damon Runyon career. Can you keep him quiet, and persuade him that the best thing to do is to let us keep *Love Here is my Hat* in cold storage and prepare to do a really good novel?

Yours ever,
[T. S. Eliot]

## TO *J. H. Oldham* CC

24 February 1938        [*The Criterion*]

My dear Oldham,

Thank you for your letter of the 23rd, enclosing the new draft,[1] which I shall read over the weekend, and hope to write to you about next week. I have reserved March 17th for the conference, which I suppose is to be at Lambeth, and am very much looking forward to the weekend conference of April 1st or 2nd.[2]

---

1–Not found. Keith Clements, *Faith on the Frontier*, 367–8: 'Oldham had circulated a prepatory paper setting out his understanding of the "crisis" facing British society and the need for an "order" to counteract the slide into moral uncertainty and state absolutism . . . Members reacted variously . . . Eliot wanted both a long historical perspective and a more precise definition of the problem . . .

'The discussion developed into a long debate on whether a Christian regeneration of society could involve anything other than some form of "Christian totalitarianism".'

2–The discussion group – in today's parlance the 'think-tank' – known as 'The Moot' was first suggested by J. H. Oldham in Dec. 1936. See Clements, *Faith on the Frontier*, 363: 'it is clear that even as he was preparing for [the Oxford Conference of July 1937] Oldham was looking beyond the conference to a variety of ways in which some of its main themes and concerns could be pursued in depth by "the best minds". It was to be small in size and exclusive in nature, yet in retrospect the Moot is justly viewed as one of Oldham's most creative ventures, largely due to the unusual calibre and extraordinarily contrasting personality of those whom he drew together in it . . . [F]rom the start his goal was not thinking for thinking's sake, but action . . .

'So Oldham envisaged "a multitude of centres of spontaneous activity" whereby Christians in neighbourhoods or professions combated evils in social and political life. The Moot was, in part, a particularization of this idea. Those whom he would invite would indeed be original, intellectually sharp thinkers, but among them would be people in highly influential roles in public life. As well as "cells" among the population at large, the idea of an *order* of people in key positions began to take shape in his mind; and the Moot could be the genesis of such an order . . .

I return herewith Loewe's paper, which you sent me on the 10th.[1] It has a very good idea, although I confess I was somewhat disappointed by the sketchiness of this paper itself. The notion of the necessity for studying the culture patterns at the background of Western Liberal democracy seems to me very pregnant, and I think might take us a long way, but Loewe's actual comments on University education in Germany and in England don't seem to me to go far enough back. He may be justified in touching on German University education simply from about the Napoleonic era – of that I cannot judge – but his view of the Oxford and Cambridge system does not seem to me to reach far enough back into its origins. When he says that originally the English Universities were not 'intellectual gymnasia but rearing grounds for a social type' I wonder what period he has in mind. Surely that is not true of the 17th century in the same sense that it is of the 18th, and surely the situation is very different again before the Reformation. It seems to me that he rather overlooks the importance, even in the deteriorated contemporary situation, of the original ecclesiastical foundation and character.

Yours ever,

[T. S. Eliot]

P.S. I could manage a couple of days in the middle of the week if it suited everybody else better, but for myself the weekend is distinctly preferable.

---

'Twelve people, including Joe and Mary Oldham, met for the first meeting of the Moot from 1 to 4 April at High Leigh in Hertfordshire. It was ... a highly eclectic group' – including TSE, JMM (Christian pacifist and communist); John Baillie, Professor of Divinity at New College, Edinburgh; H. A. Hodges, Professor of Philosophy at Reading; Sir Walter Moberley, sometime Professor of Philosophy at Birmingham, then Principal of University College, London, and Vice-Chancellor of Manchester University, and since 1935 Chair of the University Grants Committee; and Adolf Löwe.

1 – Not identified. Adolf Löwe (1893–1995), a German Jew, had taught at the University of Kiel, 1925–31; at the Institute of World Economics, where he was Associate Professor of Economics, 1930–1; and as Professor of Political Economy at the University of Frankfurt am Main, 1931–3. Having been dismissed from his teaching position under Nazi laws against 'non-Aryans', he emigrated with his family to England, where he was a Rockefeller Foundation fellow, 1933–8, and Lecturer in Economics and Sociology at the University of Manchester, 1933–40. After being naturalised as a British citizen in 1939, he then emigrated to the USA. His works include *Economics and Sociology: A Plea for Co-operation in the Social Sciences* (1935).

TO *Montgomery Butchart*                                    CC

25 February 1938                    [*The Criterion*]

Dear Butchart,

Thank you for sending Ronald Duncan's review. I am rather disappointed, or rather, irritated. He seems to have something to say, but to have a quite unnecessary and irritating irritability, and it is really intolerable that a man who is supposed to have been educated at Cambridge[1] should write with such deliberate carelessness, leaving out verbs and other desirable parts of speech. I think I can use his review, but somebody will have to rewrite it for him, in order to make it usable.[2]

I will keep a note of the books you mention, and will certainly pass on something of that kind to you for review for June.

1 – Duncan had studied with FRL at Downing College, Cambridge, from 1933.
2 – Duncan on H. G. Rawlinson, *India*: C. 17 (July 1938), 775–7.
    Ronald Duncan, *All Men Are Islands: An Autobiography* (1964), 168–9, 185: 'I received a note from T. S. Eliot suggesting that I go to see him with a view to contributing something to the Criterion. I was delighted at the prospect of meeting him, but was not very enthusiastic about writing for his magazine, which, with my youthful arrogance, I then dismissed as academic and stuffy. Like Eliot's prose-style, I thought it was too cautious, a collection of parentheses. Obviously Pound had written to Eliot and made the suggestion that we should meet.

'We had tea in his tiny room at Faber's. He already had the habit, I suppose because his room was so small, of littering the floor with books, which he would occasionally consult while they were still in that position. I think it was this method of reading that gave him his stoop.

'He suggested that I review a book for the Criterion. I said I would like to review some new poetry.

'"No," he said; "that wouldn't do you any good. Don't read any modern verse; it will only distract you from your own. I'd like you to review this book on India."

'He handed me a dull-looking tome and generously suggested that I should send him some of my play when I got down to writing it . . .

'I persisted with the review, trying to hammer out a telegraphic style. My aim was to pack as much meaning into as few words as possible, dispensing with any word that could be taken for granted. The first draft of the article ran to fifteen hundred words, but by pruning out the dead and unnecessary words I reduced it eventually to three hundred without any sacrifice of meaning . . .

'Eventually I posted the review to Eliot. He sent me thirty shillings, the first money I ever earned as a writer. I was thrilled with the cheque. I would have had to spend nearly a whole week down the pit to earn that much.'

    Montgomery Butchart told TSE at the time (9 Feb. 1938): 'You were very encouraging to Ronald Duncan when he came to see you, and for that I am personally grateful.'

I return your memorandum on Sixpenny Books, which the Chairman has read with care, and has reported to me about. We both query some of your assumptions, and the Chairman in particular is averse to taking up an enterprise of this kind. He cannot see that at present there are the conditions necessary to bring about the production of new books at this price.

Yours ever sincerely,
[T. S. Eliot]

## TO *Hugh Gordon Porteus*                                        MS Beinecke

29 February? [1938]                          24 Russell Square?
6:30?

Waited till after 7: never get that ½ hr. back. Might have used it in meditation – OR if you have acquired a bucolic principle of adhering to winter time, why didn't you tell me?[1]

Yrs etc –
ANNOYED.

1 –Porteus replied ('Friday') to TSE's *faux-féroce* note:
  'What can I say or do? I am very sorry indeed
    (a) to have missed you.
    (b) to have caused you to waste precious time.
    (c) to have ANNOYED.
  'It was *because* I know that I have no time-sense that I made a note of the time at the time. For some reason, diabolical very likely, my hand put down very plainly the figure 7 (i.e. 7.30 p.m.). I am very sensible of the enormity; and though I see no way of compensating you for your lost hour, I hope that there may be a way.
  'If, malgré tout, you will permit me to offer *you* dinner again, let us meet when you will, and it shall be a condition that I am at my post to the minute.
  'Your humble disciple, still at sixes & sevens, prostrates his unworthy self at your feet.'

TO *Virginia Woolf*                                    TS copy Valerie Eliot

[? late February 1938]                    The Vestry,
                                          St Stephen's Church,
                                          Gloucester Road, S.W.7.

Be sure that Possums can't refuse[1]
A Tea with Mrs Woolf on Tues.
And eagerly, if still alive,
I'll come to Tea with you at five.
I'd like to come at half past four,
But have a business lunch before,
And feel responsability [*sic*]
To do some work before my Tea.
But please don't let the kettle wait,
But keep for me a cup and plate,
And keep the water on the bile,
A chair, and (as I hope) a Smile.


TO *Alison Tandy*                                      TS Alison Tandy

Ash Wednesday [2 March] 1938        *The Criterion*

Dear Alison,

I have been meaning to write to thank you for two fine drawings, but I
have been ill for some days and am only now on the Mend. I liked those
drawings very much, both the Pegasus and the Cat, which latter seems to
me one of the best drawings that you have drawn, and a remarkably fine
Cat: it is a better Cat than I could draw, I know that. I only hope that you
will do something similar in COLOURS, because I have two paintings of
yours on my Walls, one of the Dog Lost and one of the Dog Found.

---

1 – These undated verses seem to be a response to an undated note from VW:

52 T.S. / Sunday.
Dear Tom,
    I have been away, or I would have written.
    I'm afraid this week is nothing but horror.
    Would you come to tea, finding me alone, on Tuesday week, which is the 8th –
at 4.30 sharp? So that we may have time for a gossip. A long way off I'm afraid.
    Yours ever / V.

See too *Poems II*, ed. Ricks/McCue, 186–7. Original not traced; text here from a typed
copy headed 'From T. S. Eliot' (EVE).

I am trying to do a Poem about a Railway Train Cat, and if I can do it I will send it to you in due course.

I don't know whether I shall see you before Easter or not, but if not then soon after, and meanwhile send you my Love from your affectionate

Possum

TO *Ezra Pound* TS Beinecke

4 marzo 1938 *The Criterion*

Ezzumpo:

Ho yuss, an when it come to latrines which I cleans, well, some of em is modern sanitation and some of em is more like Indiana earth privies or Serial Dumps and where does cirrespondence with Ez come in?[1] Well after a page or two of Sears Roebuck and a dustin of Sanitas[2] round the figger nails what I says is title is Not Kulch it is Kulcher[3] and instead of startin series numbers put your correspondence in Order. Well Crevel I thought that was Crape on the doorknob and memories of P. J. Jouce and L. P. Fargue and the like, but if you say he is aLIVe why dont you do something about it?[4] I mean serially seriously three months after Mencius if you

---

1 – EP replied, 1 Apr.: 'If you dont READ what is sent you/ or if you dont git letters/ and spend AWL yr/ time as you so elegantly phrase it "cleaning latrines" (and goddam it printing UNcleaned one in the Critererium/

'I shall have to start a series number and REFER to previous

'As to titles/ the title is KULCH OR [. . .]

're/ CREVEL/ he wuzza good guy and he is dead/ and damned mortician like yourself/ OUGHT to appreciate my decency in wanting to write a decent and decorous tomb stone/ The boy deserved it; being about the only Frawg litterater since Cocteau who WROTE any books.'

2 – The firm of Sanitas, which produces and markets medicinal products, was founded in 1922.

3 – *Guide to Kulchur*: see note to TSE to EP, 16 Oct. 1937, above.

Evidently TSE expressed reservations about the work in a letter (now lost) to Philip Mairet in Oct. 1938. Mairet replied, 1 Nov.: 'I am not surprised at the misgivings you expressed in your letter. Actually I am just discovering where I do not fit with E.P. at all: and it makes the business of reviewing his "Kulchur" somewhat onerous. I cannot, as I did with his ABC of Reading, merely praise and defer to the exquisite eclecticism of his taste. A general conspectus of culture is a bigger matter and reveals the teacher in his human wholeness of lack of it.

'Hence the delay in producing this review: I'll try to get it off in the next day or two; for I believe you want it for the New Year number: but you will appreciate the difficulty.'

Mairet on EP, *Guide to Kulchur*: C. 18 (Jan. 1939), 326–9.

4 – EP, 1 Mar.: 'a proper note of Rene Crevel OUGHT to have appeared two years ago/ you git all behind hand if you dont never move more'n enuff fer ter burn up th waGon.'

like unless in the form of a short obituarary note; and MEANWHILE
if you got the book then a short note on Maister Lewis Golding wd. be
acceptable doggonit nobody has stopped you[1] and if you think that 3
latin poets is NOT worth reviewing why do you aggravate me about it[2]
and as for BRELOTTO[3] I did show Wyndham yr. inspired note on Hitler
and he larfed in his coarse way and said nothing and if you want him to
be interested why not write to W. L. 29A Notting Hill Gate W.11???? But
I am not sure that advt. in *Townsman* is not worth money to keep it out
no it aint, but I am irriratated with that Duncomb[4] for his litrary style and
damb it if you have so much curiosity as to read letters you YOU read the
enclosed I cant my pore old eyes dazzles[5] but YOU answer it so will close

TP

TO *Henry Miller*                                                          CC

7 March 1938                    [*The Criterion*]

Dear Miller,

I trust I still know as well as you do what I like and what I don't like,
but I should be in my own opinion a rather poor editor, at any rate of a
periodical like this, if I went entirely by immediate likes.[6] I don't know in
the least whether I am at the opposite pole from you or not, and I don't

1 – EP, 1 Mar.: 'life of Golding, the Ovid bloke just recd/ worth couple of pages in yr shorter
reviewes/ WHEN do you want it? . . . The Golding very carefully done/ MERITS notice/ and
ought to be done by someone who knows a bit about the matter. i; e; EZ.' 1 Apr.: 'A SHORT
. . . shd/ ALSO be given to the life of Golding/ I have no need to negotiate a review cawpy.'
2 – EP remarked, 1 Apr.: 'I also boned a rev/ cop of a dirry book on "Three Latin Poets"
out of the pubr/ this I do NOT care to review/ the author having discovered that copulation
was practiced in Rome under the Emperors. And that being his chief message to the reader.'
3 – EP, 1 Apr.: 'I again cawl yr/ attention to BROLETTO which is reviewing real stuff.'
4 – Ronald Duncan.
5 – Webster, *The Duchess of Malfi*, IV. ii: 'Cover her face. Mine eyes dazzle. She died young.'
6 – Miller wrote on 26 Feb., in response to TSE's letter of 18 Feb.: 'The only exasperation
you caused me was through your temporizing, your indecision. I don't understand that. I
can decide *immediately* whether I like a thing or not. And tomorrow, if I change my mind,
I say so. It seems to me that you are unduly worried about the "value" of everything.
That I feel is wrong. And especially in dealing with a type like myself, you ought not to be
squeamish. I know that you are at quite the opposite pole from me. It is only by a miracle
that you should have found something to praise in "Tropic of Cancer" – and what that
book represents is the least part of me, the rebellious part, which I have outlived quicker
than Lawrence. You seem to be so concerned about my not putting myself into the Lawrence
book. Wait – wait till the book appears. The criticism will be of just the reverse order. I don't
give a fuck about any man whom I may happen to admire or be influenced by, except in the
measure that he does something to me, for me. I have no innate reverence for persons . . .

think the phrase means anything unless the terms of reference are carefully defined in advance. Anyway, I am not worried about that. I daresay your Lawrence article is as simple to you and to those who know the language as you say it is. There is very likely plenty of literature in tongues like Pushtu and Tamil which is perfectly simple to those who can read them, but I cannot. And again, I just don't know what you mean by suggesting that I am trying to fit you in to my own scheme of things, or just accepting or not accepting people.

I will take your word about Anaïs Nin, and I do see your point about the difference of aim between you and herself. Meanwhile, as we are not meeting immediately, I will write to Butchart and ask him to unload some of your stuff here.

Yours ever,
[T. S. Eliot]

## TO *George Every*                                     TS Sarah Hamilton

7 March 1938                          *The Criterion*

Dear George,

Thank you for your letter of the 3rd. I continue to rejoice at the thought of the handbells tinkling away on the banks of the Trent.

---

'And if you find a simple, honest, straightforward man like Lawrence "difficult and irritating", then what can you expect of me should I decide to tell you about Nijinsky & Amiel?

'No, I must repeat what I suppose I have already told you – though it will probably get us nowhere – that I deplore your attitude of trying to "fit me in" to your scheme of things. Why don't you just *accept* me, for what I am? Isn't my integrity or my difference worth more to you than the frame of the "Criterion"?

'Really, you amuse me when you say you "wrestled" with a mss. of mine. There is nothing to wrestle with. Either you get it or you don't get it. I don't mind at all if you reject on the grounds of not liking. That's legitimate. I object to the "wrestling". And to a certain obtuseness, if you will forgive me being so crude. For example – Anaïs Nin. She is not at all under my influence. If anything, *I* am the one who has been influenced. But there is really no meeting point. My vision and my technique is absolutely other than hers. I hold things in and explode. She writes like water flowing. I want to be much more than a writer. She will be happy if she becomes a writer. She is very human – I am inhuman. She is intelligence and clarity itself – I want only a modicum of intelligence, and fuck your clarity! Do you follow me?'

Butchart to TSE, 8 Mar. 1938: 'Many of the short pieces for Miller's *Plasma and Magma* are in the hands of editors. I shall catch a number as they return and send a representative selection to you in the course of the month.'

I also have been concerned about Middleton Murry.[1] I have had a little correspondence with him, by the way, arising out of his pamphlet, which I praised; and he has, as you know, been in touch with Oldham. I believe we may meet at a weekend party which Oldham is arranging for a discussion in April. While of course Murry's previous record is such as to lead one to fear his rapidly bursting into almost any heresy, I feel that he ought at the moment to be given the benefit of the doubt and treated on the assumption that he will become a sound Christian. The best thing, of course, will be for him to be in contact with as many as possible of those Christian and Catholic minds that he will feel obliged to respect, so that he may get the impression that Christianity is first of all something to be accepted, that there is such a thing as authority, and that it is not merely a starting off place for new improvisations. And I hope that we can get him in time to visit Kelham.

I note with appreciation your good missionary work in the direction of the Archbishop of York.[2]

> Yours ever,
> T. S.

## TO *The Editor,* The New English Weekly                    CC

8 March 1938[3]                    [Faber & Faber Ltd]

Dear Sir,

Having in mind the attention which you have recently given to the relations of Agriculture and Industry, I was struck by a note in *The*

---

1 – Every wrote, 3 Mar.: 'I am rather concerned at the news of Middleton Murry's conversion. This may be no news to you, but in case you don't know I think you should know that he is going to Westcott House Cambridge in the summer as an ordinand. Davison says he knew this was in his mind as long ago as November, and Fr Demant told me last August that he had got on well with him at the Centre. So it isn't quite so precipitate as it looks, though it is a little terrifying. What I really want you to know is that in a copy of Peace News . . . for February 12th, there is an important qualification of the P.P.U. pamphlet "God or the Nation", which is definitely reassuring. Christianity is not the same as pacifism. Murry believes that soldiers can be Christians. He doesn't blame the Church for giving non-pacifists holy communion but for lack of faith and love and expectation of the second coming . . .
'What is going to happen to Murry's disciples?'
See further Every's review of JMM, *Heaven – and Earth*: C. 18 (Jan. 1939), 352
2 – 'Fr Hebert sent the Hawkins articles to the Archbp of York, and we have just had a most kind and helpful letter back. He seems particularly interested in Roberts. I think it might be [a] good idea if he had a copy of the Hulme book.'
3 – Published as 'Who controls population-distribution?', *NEW* 12: 23 (17 Mar. 1938), 459.

*Evening News* of March 7.[1] Mr Robert Holland-Martin, chairman of the South Railway, had been addressing members of the British Railway Stockholders' Union at a lunch. He observed that his railway's electrification policy had proved a 'gold mine'; and added that the company was 'fortunate in having and, possibly, in *making* (italics mine) a very large development of suburban London south of the Thames'. It would seem therefore that the railways not only have a considerable interest in the further suburbanisation of greater Greater London, but make an overt policy of it. Other authorities, I believe, have expressed alarm at the concentration of such a large proportion of the population in south-eastern England.

Mr Holland-Martin is also a country squire in Gloucestershire, but I do not know how much interest he takes in agriculture.

Yours faithfully,
[T. S. Eliot]

TO *Enid Faber*                                              TS Valerie Eliot

8 March [1938]                        *The Criterion*

Dear Enid,

I wish to write to thank you for a very pleasant evening. I enjoyed your hospitality (in particular, and on the gastronomic plane, the savoury) and I found Mrs Feiling very agreeable company.[2]

The Two points about F. Reunion are these.

F. V. MORLEY in a letter written on the ship: objects to 'pushed' – thinks the verb has too comic associations. But the association with the trivial and sordid is what I want; and I cant see that any other verb would

---

1 – 'Southern Railway's "Gold Mine": What electrification has done', *Evening News*, 7 Mar. 1938: 'Mr Robert Holland-Martin, chairman of the Southern Railway, told members of the British Railway Stockholders' Union at a luncheon in London today that the Southern's electrification policy had proved a "gold mine".

'The company, he said, was fortunate in having and, possibly, in making a very large development of suburban London south of the Thames.

'Future profits of the company would depend to a large extent on the population trend, but he did not share the prophecies that the population of the country would suffer a heavy decline in the immediate future.'

2 – GCF's diary, Mon. 7 Mar. 1938: 'Dinner at No. 1 with the Feilings, Knox's, Adele B.-Ward, & T.S.E. (who was a noble guest). A successful evening; & TSE made the right impression on Keith Feiling, who liked him enormously, & on Mrs F who is as good company as ever.' (Feiling was Professor of History, and a Fellow of All Souls College. ALR, *All Souls in My Time*, 145: 'Feiling had real feeling for history, but he was not a good writer.')

do. Besides, I want it left quite uncertain whether he really *did* kill her or not; and *pushing over* is exactly the easiest thing to imagine that you had done. If you poisoned or shot or strangled somebody there could be no mistake about it. So I dont see this point myself.

TANDY queries the age of Amy. As her eldest son is 30 I meant her to be 60 – she married at 30 and her husband I imagine as having been 27 at the time: it seems appropriate that she should have been rather older than he, and that she married him rather than vice versa. But Tandy thinks that Amy gives the impression throughout of being a much older woman than that. This criticism shakes me more.

I should like your reflexions on these points when you have time to meditate upon them.

Yours

TP.

The Railway Cat (L.M.S.) is rather stuck.[1]


## TO *Frank Morley*                                   TS Faber Archive

8 March 1938                          *The Criterion*

F. V. Morley Esq.
c/o Messrs Harcourt, Brace & Co. Inc.,
383 Madison Avenue, New York City


Dear Frank,

I was under the impression that you had got a lien on Hart Crane's poems, and when I got a letter yesterday from Greenwood of Boriswood's, saying that they were going to publish them, and having the cheek to ask me to write an introduction, I got Miss Evans to dig for any correspondence you might have had. I find a carbon of a letter from you to Pell of 9 July, from which I learn that Philip Horton wrote to you that he had told Pell that we might be interested in publishing the poems, and apparently Pell sent you a copy of the American edition. That seems to be all, and we don't appear to have any legal claim, but it is odd that Pell should not have let us know that he had come to terms with Boriswood. I merely pass on this information to you in case you think fit to make any enquiries. Perhaps it

---

1 – The TS of 'Skimbleshanks: The Railway Car' was to be sent to Enid Faber on 15 Mar. 1938. See EVE, 'Apropos of *Practical Cats*', *Cats: The Book of the Musical* (New York, 1983), 8: '"Skimbleshanks" is based on Kipling's "The Long Trail".'

is just as well that Boriswood should publish the poems if they want to, but it is somewhat annoying.

Yours ever,
TP.

FROM *Ashley Dukes*                                                       TS Houghton

8 March 1938                          Hotel Great Northern,
                                      118 East 57th Street,
                                      New York City

Dear Tom,

Martin will have told you something of our sad history, and I will let you have the whole tale in London about March 22, for I am sailing with about half the company on Thursday by the *Antonia* for that port, Martin and others remaining for a few days.

We are both eagerly interested in the new play, which I have read several times. First the title. I wanted to suggest something like pursuit or horizontal doom – rather than the perpendicularity generally associated with doom, and asked why you could not have a hunting metaphor implicit in the name. Martin then thought of *Meet at Wishwood Manor*, which was a development of an old suggestion about the name of the house. I think on reflection *Meet at Wishwood* would seem to me expressive enough. Does it not also contain the same basic idea as *A Family Reunion*, or would not *The Meet at Wishwood* say the same thing in a satiric way as *The Family Reunion*? And still bring in the Furies as a pack?[1]

Martin and I both feel that the controversy bound to centre in the poetic use of the word 'push', and the image conjured up by 'push', especially in the case of the well, will be disturbing to the play. This is almost certainly the word dearest to you, and we have no hope that you will give it up, but think you ought to. And Martin does not quite see the chorus yet but will write to you himself on that matter.

Meantime it is all deep and exciting and must go on to the stage soon.

Yours
Ashley Dukes

1–See too HWE to Donald Gallup, 9 Feb. 1938: '"The Family Reunion" will probably not be the title of the new play, if Dukes has his way (though I like the title myself[)]. It has to do with the Eumenides, or Erinyes, or Furies, who I believe appear in evening dress of the present day, and concerns the actions, interactions and reactions of an English family upon one particular member of the younger generation.'

[TSE numbered the two main paragraphs of this letter, and wrote by hand at the foot:]

For consideration –
  *I* don't hold with (1) [the suggested title] at all.
  As for (2) I think that the push into *the well* might go out, but I hold to the pushing in Part I sc. 1.


# TO *R. G. Collingwood*[1]                                                    CC

11 March 1938                          [Faber & Faber Ltd]

Dear Mr Collingwood,

  Thank you very much for your very flattering letter of the 8th.[2] You may be sure that I shall look forward with the keenest interest to reading *The Principles of Art* when I receive a copy, and I feel very much honoured.

---

1–R. G. Collingwood (1889–1943), philosopher and historian; Fellow of Pembroke College, Oxford; later Waynflete Professor of Metaphysical Philosophy, Magdalen College. Works include *Outlines of a Philosophy of Art* (1925) and *The Idea of History* (1945). See Fred Inglis, *History Man: The Life of R. G. Collingwood* (2009).

2–Collingwood asked his publishers to send TSE a copy of his forthcoming *The Principles of Art* (1938). 'It is primarily a treatise on aesthetics, but intended as bearing in a strictly practical way on the present state & situation of the arts; and it necessarily contains a summary of my general philosophical position, which readers mainly interested in art will probably find boring. My primary reason for asking you to accept a copy is that in a sense the book is dedicated to you; the concluding pages are all about *The Waste Land*, regarded not so much as the greatest poem of this century (which though true so far as it goes would be rather an empty compliment) but rather as a demonstration of what poetry has got to be if my aesthetic theory is to be true! I hope you will be able to forgive me for treating you as a *corpus vile*, and will understand that it is the highest compliment a poor devil of a philosopher has it in his power to pay you.'

(*The Principles of Art* closes with this praise of *TWL*, p. 336: 'no community altogether knows its own heart; and by failing in this knowledge a community deceives itself on the one subject concerning which ignorance means death. For the evils which come from that ignorance the poet as prophet suggests no remedy because he has already given one. The remedy is the poem itself. Art is the community's medicine for the worst disease of the mind, the corruption of consciousness.')

See too TSE to Thomas Stauffer, 17 Aug. 1944: 'Aesthetics was never my strong suit. In fact, it is one department of philosophy which I always shied away from, even in the days when I thought I was going to be a philosopher, and that is a long time ago. I think that instinct told me that the less I thought about general aesthetic theory the better for me. (Incidentally, do you know Collingwood's book *In Praise of Art*? <*Principles of Art* – I am not sure of the title, but I have the book somewhere> To a plain literary practitioner like myself, who, as F. H. Bradley said of himself, has no capacity for the abstruse, Collingwood seems very good.)'

I will write to you again when I have read it; but aesthetics has never been my field, and my comments may [be] of little value.

Yours very sincerely,
[T. S. Eliot]

TO *James Joyce*                    TS National Gallery of Ireland

11 March 1938                      Faber & Faber Ltd

Dear Joyce,

I enclose herewith a specimen page to show the best that can be done with this section.[1] The only possible alteration to suggest is that the notes on the right-hand side should be set out in italics instead of capitals. Will you let me know which you prefer?

The point is that if we had known at the beginning that one section of the book would present these features, we could have adopted a format which would have made its lay-out easier to arrange; but as the greater part of the book had been set up before we were presented with this difficulty, we have had to do what is possible in the circumstances.

I am not quite clear how much more fresh matter there is to come, apart from the galley proofs which are all in your hands. Will you let me know, or have someone else let me know, as soon as possible, how much more is to come before the book will be complete?

I do hope that you have been making further progress in Zurich, and that you will soon be able to return to Paris.

With best wishes,
Yours ever sincerely,
T. S. Eliot

1 – JJ had written to TSE from the Carlton-Elite-Hotel, Bahnhofstrasse 41, Zürich, 27 Feb. 1938 – his letter was taken down from dictation, so the errors are those of the amanuensis – 'My eyes, which had improved, are not so well since yesterday, so I am dictating this. Please tell Mr Faber I shall take up the matter of the date of publication after my return to France.

'In the meantime I have been shown the galleys of part II section 2 in which left hand annotations have been indented into the body of the text. This incorporates them with the text and very successfully nullifies my intention, which was that: the text should be accompanied on the right side and on the left side by comments of a completely different character, which change sides after the indefinite Syncope of the parenthesis, while indifferent to her twin brothers, the girls garroulous independence runs on unbroken in her footnotes.

'I have gone to a great deal of trouble and a great deal of expence, to prepare a perfectly plain typescript, but apparantly there was one place, where the printer could put his foot in it and the honnest fellow has found it out. I told Lord Carlow to say, that if this section was printed exactly like his printing of it, it would be all right, if not, it would be all wrong.'

P.S. I am sending a carbon of this letter, with another copy of the specimen galley, to your Paris address.

## FROM *E. Martin Browne* MS Houghton

11 March 1938 Hotel Great Northern,<br>118 West 57 Street, New York City

My dear Tom,

Our efforts to prolong 'Murder's' chances in New York have finally ceased after a week of frantic ups and downs, so I am free to write about the much-more-important new play. I am very tired and it may not have had the best of my brain, so if you find some of my ideas about it trivial or stupid, don't be surprised or mind them, but just discard them. I think though, that Ashley and I are in agreement about the main questions, and that these are what you most want to hear of now.

We both feel the play to be weak in plot.[1] Reading it again, one is once more enthralled as at the first reading by the skill and wit of the versification of natural country-house speech, and by the strong & authentic atmosphere of the house, family and retainers. This is splendid, and so long as development is not called for, is good for the stage. But later one begins to feel the need of stronger on-stage plot, and at the end one is definitely disappointed for lack of it. Two or three ideas have come up which I put for consideration:–

(1) *Mary*. The scene with her leaves her indeterminate: and she fades out after it. This is a pity as she comes at so crucial a point: & also she can be of great use: she is or has been a *way of escape*. Henzie suggests that, as she is a distant cousin, to marry her might have been Harry's right way of nullifying the curse: there might have been a real love between them: then Harry feeling the oppression of Wishwood and unwilling to face and overcome it; ran off with his alien woman and so was led from crime to crime – from desertion to murder. This would make material for real use of Mary, and would bring out the now-obscure genesis of the push (that *most* dangerous word!).

It is also possible to draw a parallel between the child – the next heir to Wishwood – that Harry did not give to Mary, and Harry himself whom his father tried to destroy in the womb. So can be established that struggle, so tragically typical of English country families, between the conscious need

1 – The draft of *The Family Reunion*.

of an heir and the subconscious curse of barrenness in the soul which fears the power of the unborn generations. All this can be on-stage (tho' not contemporary) plot. (like Ibsen).

(2) Gerald & Charles, Ashley suggests, should be Arthur and John. It is true that the accidents are impossibly weak, happening to people one never sees: they also don't develop the plot at all, and because we don't see those people, your effect in Mary doesn't register. You want, don't you, to show Amy unmoved by the physical disasters but killed by Harry's physical one? This needs defining far more clearly: & if Arthur & John appeared it would be easy. I don't think their part in the Chorus need be invalidated either.

(3) In this connection I suggest that the Winchell scene could be far more strongly planned, still preserving the wit of your dialogue. Winchell could come *to arrest* Arthur, unwillingly of course; and the matter could be arranged with him and hushed up – a contrast between the physical arrest which the power of the Manor can avert and the spiritual arrest by the Furies, which is unavoidable because Wishwood is itself one with them.[1]

(4) *Ivy & Violet* are also nebulous,[2] & it would, I believe, be of great value to get a *quarrel* between them, in which both characters would define themselves more clearly, about Harry and the future – we should see them jealous of Agatha as being closer to Harry, and afflicted by the sense of barrenness and isolation, yet feeling their roots strong in the family and house – this study of two of the thousands of such women could be very poignant. By reconstructing pp. 60–69[3] (the newspaper stuff will probably come out anyway now?) you could make a good join also between scenes 1 & 2 – this is now a bad stage-join, with no motivated entrances or exits.

(5) Amy's death is brilliantly done: and I like the ritual enormously. I suggest two things. (a) Amy's acceptance of Harry's going seems far too meek. If she is the strongest person in the play, she would either *fight* to keep him, or would expressly recognise his going as the working of the Fates (see below). There's a necessary scene here, & one of the strongest in the play, perhaps the *climax*.

---

1 – Pencil note by TSE: '(3) Is this really needed?'
2 – Pencil note: 'but they're vague, woolly types'.
3 – Note by HWE in Houghton MS Am 1691 (11) – HWE's typed copy of the exchange of letters – 'Page references here are to the MS loaned by Miss Hale. Pp. 60–69 begin with (Harry) "They don't understand what it is to be awake," and end with (Scene II, Harry): "I only feel the repetition of it / Over and over. When I am outside".'

(b) The *cake* should be carried on, unlit, on p. 93 (Charles' speech): the candles lit during the Chorus p. 97. So we get time to appreciate its significance.

(6) *The curse.* (a) What started it? *Surely* we need some indication of its origin or at least of its *deep* past.

(b) Is it a curse (doesn't some human pronounce a curse?) or a *fate*?

(c) If it is connected with house or family & not just with the two pushers, wouldn't all the family know it in some form? It needs this *grandeur*: and at the end we need to sense its expiation more definitely.

These are the big questions I see needing answers. I have noted smaller ones on a separate sheet.

You'll realise, I hope & think, that we all three feel this draft to have magnificent possibilities. I hope this analysis will seem constructively useful and to be in tune with your aims. It is directed towards making the play the overwhelmingly strong work it *implicitly* is now, without destroying the quiet, witty, loving observation of character which makes it so valuable.

We are planning to stay here a couple of weeks anyway, but most likely shall be back in mid-April. I should *very* much like to know, however, when you've seen Ashley, whether it would be of material assistance to you to have me on the spot by that time, as I should try to make my plans accordingly. Could you send me a deferred cable saying 'should appreciate your presence' if you want me: I do want to help over this, more than anything else I might be doing, so don't hesitate to call on me, if Ashley wants to make an early production. I haven't told you how enormously we enjoyed your Boston friends & especially your brother Henry & his lovely wife.

Henzie sends her love: and finds comfort in your lines in this time of stress.

Yours ever,
Martin.

Notes on Minor Points.

16/17 Harry is very abstract in these speeches.[1]

28 the scene needs an end – this might be made out of the *car*, which needs to be made significant – the chariot that bears him away.

34 Harry's second speech is very hard to follow, as spoken.[2]

43/4 This for the end of Part I is going to be a bit flat on the stage: the Chorus' point of view is negative and the Rune is mysterious, and they

---

1 – TSE's note: 'I don't agree. This is apparently a criticism of the poetry.'
2 – TSE notes: 'Not a criticism – depends on effort made.'

follow a scene of several pages with no happening. Here is where revision of plot may be a great help. *Don't* cut the Rune!

48ff. This excellent dialogue needs sharpening up – the dramatic point of each speech needs defining and they need to have more pressure & less reflection, so that one gets the excitement of conflict – the *reaction* on each other of two men each in a difficulty.

67. Is Amy's speech a little too resigned?[1]

69. Could more concrete facts & pictures enliven this very important past history?

70. Could Agatha *discover* on the stage 'you have not known what crime you expiate'? If this were *new* it would be thrilling: & it should be explicitly connected with his father, etc. for the audience to grasp it.

71. the description of father has a few phrases like 'common realities' which need sharpening.

74/80. This scene seems to stand still here – to deal with *states*, rather than *developments*, of mind: & some of the very fine abstract phrases need linking to the story. They tend to seem almost absurd if there are too many, spoken by two characters only, in close continuity.[2]

83. Amy (bottom of page) – does she speak too elaborately for so single [?simple][3] an emotion?[4]

90. the house is suddenly called 'damned' – we ask why? Here would come in the advantages of some history of the curse.

Do reflections of "Murder" matter:–

'seven years'.

'end or beginning' (75)

'wait and witness' (88) ?[5]


## TO *George Barker*                                                    CC

14 March 1938                          [*The Criterion*]

My dear Barker,

I have now read your manuscript through twice, and I am afraid that you will find this copy useless for any other purpose, because I have covered it with detailed comments and queries. I thought that this was the

1–TSE notes: 'I don't think so.'
2–TSE notes: 'Cf. G.C.F. comment on definite articles.'
3–Transcription 'single' confirmed by HWE.
4–TSE notes: 'No.'
5–TSE notes: 'Of course not.'

only way in which I could make my points clear and specific, so I hope you won't mind. It seems to me that you need several months' work on this, both for construction and for purifying the language, but I suggest that meanwhile you might show another copy to Stephen Spender, because you have had a fair amount of my opinions, and I think that they could be usefully balanced with some other poet's opinion. Hereafter follow my more general comments on the play.

For a 'Missionary Play' this would of course be unsuitable. It is humanitarian in spirit, but there is nothing particularly Christian about it. And St George does not seem to appear in a very favourable light.

This would also be unactable in public as it stands, unless you changed Roosevelt and Ford into historical figures. The Censor would never pass a play which put on the stage known living men, especially in the bad company of Satan.

This is not a play, and you rightly call it a masque. It has enough plot for a masque – if the plot were easier to grasp. If I cannot make it out clearly on two readings, it is very unlikely that an audience would make head or tail of it.

Even for a masque, not enough HAPPENS. I mean that there are moments – indeed it is most of the time – when the characters are simply talking, and talking incomprehensibly.

A masque can afford to be more heavily loaded with decorative language than a play, but this is much too overloaded even for a masque. The style is much too metaphorical, and there is a great deal of interference between metaphors. They follow each other so closely as to get suffocated. Many of them appear to have nothing inevitable about them. A metaphor or simile is supposed to throw light on an idea, or to intensify or make more apprehensible an emotion. A metaphor should be explanatory or elucidatory; yours too often make the meaning more obscure than before.

One is not always convinced that you yourself know what you mean. You would do well to analyse every sentence you write, see whether it has a defensible grammatical form, make sure that you know what it means and that its meaning is relevant to the situation.

Some of the lines have no perceptible metrical form.

You can sometimes write poetry, but you need to learn to write VERSE. No long poem can afford to be all poetry. Your technique up to date is only suitable for short lyric flights.

See if you could explain the plot of this briefly enough for the back of a postcard.

And this needs several months' hard work. Don't depend on inspiration. Don't despise *simple*, *clear* and *distinct* ideas.

Also, you should have a dictionary, and look up EVERY WORD THAT YOU DO NOT ORDINARILY USE IN CONVERSATION.[1]

Yours ever,

T. S. E.

## TO *Allen Tate*

TS Princeton

14 March 1938                    *The Criterion*

Dear Tate,

Thank you very much for your interesting letter of 3rd March.[2] I have completely forgotten now what I said in my lecture notes on *The Turn*

---

1–Barker next wrote from a new address – Boxholm, Balls Cross, Petworth, Sussex (a cottage given to the Barkers for a year by Emily Coleman) – on 26 Apr.: 'I may say that I rewrote my masque before I left London and forwarded Stephen Spender a text of the new version. I saw him for an hour or so just before Easter and gathered that he liked it quite a lot: he was particularly anxious that I should publish it. The text has since, I understand, passed into Rupert Doone's hands . . . I am most anxious to have you read the new version, which embodies many of the suggestions you appended to the first text.'

On 27 May: 'I have abandoned the writing of the Johannesburg Masque firstly because I dislike it very much and again because Rupert Doone assures me that it is "not suitable for stage production". . . . I now regard it at best as a private experiment and at worst a false birth.'

2–'When I was in Cambridge a couple of weeks ago Ted Spencer showed me a lecture note of yours on James' "The Turn of the Screw". I had told him that I had made a dramatic version of the story, and I was astonished to see that your note perhaps indicates that you are [the] only other person besides myself who understands the work. I mean your distinction between Bad and Evil. No other critic has described the substance of the story in that way . . . James himself in his Preface offers a clue to the difference between Bad and Evil, in his remark about "weak specifications", which would, if made, lower the tale to the plane of mere Bad. One kind of specification would have been to make the spectres objective, rather than (apart from the actual plot) symbolic; that is, James could have let the Governess in "real life" work the evil upon the children without the spectres, which are merely necessary as symbols in a work of fiction. For the Governess, as you see, is not an immoral person; she doesn't "do" anything; she *is* Evil. And of course it is she who corrupts the children merely by *being* evil: the spectres are only the medium of this corruption, its exhibit as psychological self-deception.

'One day I tested all the dialogue in the story: if you subtract from the conversation between Governess and children the Governess' remarks, what the children say is invariably innocent. The Governess' gloss violently puts it into a context of which they know nothing. Technically this is one of the perfect instances of what James called the "central intelligence" in fiction, that which controls and heightens every detail of the work.

'This clue to the consistent ambiguity of the dialogue led me to write (with a collaborator whose chief work was to make me work) a dramatic version. Do you want to see it? It is a

---

*of the Screw*, but your own account seems to me fundamentally right. I should be most interested indeed to read your dramatic version of the play, and hope you will let me see it. *A priori*, I don't know quite what could be done with it in a publishing way, and also we should have to go into the question of whether it might not be an infringement of copyright. That sounds rather absurd, but I remember some years ago somebody had the idea of writing all the unwritten Sherlock Holmes stories, the names of which are so exciting, and that proved to be an infringement of copyright. On the other hand, I very much hope that your dramatisation is a really actable version. It would, I should imagine, demand supreme acting, but if well done might be very thrilling.

> With best wishes,
> Yours ever,
> T. S. Eliot

## TO *António Eça de Queiroz*[1]                                   CC

16 March 1938                         [Faber & Faber Ltd]

My dear Sir,

In reply to your letter of the 4th instant, which reached me on Friday last, I sent you as quickly as possible (for the matter demanded some reflexion) a telegram indicating my acceptance of the kind invitation of your Government to take part in the jury concerned with the award of the Camoens Prize.[2]

---

pretty crude article compared to the original. The point I have made had to be worked very hard. But without this clue to the ambiguity, the stage version would have been even cruder than I have made it – possibly as crude as the ordinary thriller, like Dracula.'

1 – António Eça de Queiroz, Sub-Director, Secretariado da Propaganda Nacional, Portugal.

2 – 'The Secretariado de Propaganda Nacional will distribute this year for the first time the Camoens Prize which is to be awarded for the best literary or scientific work on Portugal published abroad by a foreign author during the last two years.

'Since the respective regulations state that the language of each book produced for the competition should be represented and also because some of the competitors are English, we have the honour . . . to invite you to kindly participate of the jury which will classify the works.

'The jury will be constituted by the most eminent names in the European intellect and the meeting will be held in Lisbon towards the end of April next.

'All travelling expenses will be paid by the Portuguese Government which will have the honour to consider you as a guest during your stay in Portugal which will be of 6 to 10 days.'

TSE, 'Class of 1910: Fiftieth Anniversary Report': 'In 1938 I was the guest of the Portuguese Government for three weeks as a membro do jury for the Camoens Prize.'

Permit me to express more fully my appreciation of the honour, and of the hospitality of the Portuguese Government.

I understand that the session of the jury will be during the latter part of April. Engagements here make it necessary for me to be back in London early in May.

I do not know how much responsibility the members of the jury are expected to take, so it is only fair to remark that I should not feel qualified to pass an opinion on books in any languages except English and French, and to a less degree German.

I shall hope to receive more detailed instructions later, and I presume that I should reserve a passage as soon as the exact date of the meeting is fixed.

I remain,
Yours Very Sincerely,
[T. S. Eliot]

## TO *E. Martin Browne*

TS Houghton

19 March 1938                    *The Criterion*

Dear Martin,[1]

Your good letter arrived yesterday, and I cabled at once, as there was no point in waiting for Ashley. The fact is that after Easter I am going to Lisbon (I do not yet know the exact date) to sit on a jury to decide the award of the 'Camoens Prize' – at the expense of the Portuguese government! This sounds rather silly; but I had thought of taking a short holiday after Easter, as I found it beneficial last year. Then when I got this invitation I had the opportunity of enquiring about it in a very high quarter, and was urged to accept – to contribute my mite to the Ancient Alliance! I shall have to be back early in May in any case, as I have to speak in Salisbury. I thought you ought to know at once that I should not call upon you to change your plans: it was good of you to offer to return sooner.

Your examination of the play was no more painful than I had anticipated – I had been looking forward to the moment with dread. I shall try to do some work on it before I see you; but first I have to sort out, of course, the criticisms I can accept from those I can't! And where I think you may have misunderstood me, that is significant too, as indicating that I have

1 – This letter was printed in full in EMB, *The Making of T. S. Eliot's Plays*, 106–8.

not made the meaning transparent. First, I am ready to admit my own apprehension that the play has not enough plot, or that what plot it has is too much in the background. That must be remedied somehow. Second, I confess that some of your criticism seems to me tantamount to asking me to write a new play: but if I do that I shall start with quite another situation and another set of characters! This includes, first, the suggestion that I should substitute Arthur and John for Gerald and Charles. But, apart from my affection for Charles (as the character most like myself) and apart from the fact that we are meant to realise that John and Arthur, though we never see them, are weaker images of Gerald and Charles respectively <I mean Gerald – John; Charles – Arthur> I still feel that there is a good deal of point in their not being there. This needs a lot of thinking about; all I am quite sure of at the moment is that if I re-write the play in this way it will not be finished until next year. That does not matter in theory, but political events make one feel that one is working against time, and may lose the race anyway.

Next, as to Mary. I do feel that there is a weakness in having her turn up only for two big scenes, and disappear in between. Of course, if I accepted Henzie's suggestion, I should have to make her much older, because as it is she was hardly more than a child when she last saw Harry, and he could hardly have been interested in her then. This could be done, but altering her age would mean altering her character. And there is meant also to be some point in the parallel between her starting life now as a teacher, and Agatha's debut in that profession.

Now, as to Harry's marrying Mary as the right way of ending the 'curse', here I feel on surer ground. The point of Mary, in relation to Harry, was meant to be this. The effect of his married life upon him was one of such horror as to leave him for the time at least in a state that may be called one of being psychologically partially desexed: or rather, it has given him a horror of women as of unclean creatures. The scene with Mary is meant to bring out, as I am aware it fails to, the conflict inside him between this repulsion for Mary as a woman, and the attraction which the *normal* part of him that is still left, feels towards her personally *for the first time*. This is the first time since his marriage ('there was no ecstacy') that he has been attracted towards any woman. This attraction glimmers for a moment in his mind, half-consciously as a possible 'way of escape'; and the Furies (for the Furies are *divine* instruments, not simple hell-hounds) come in the nick of time to warn him away from this evasion – though at that moment he misunderstands their function. Now, this attraction towards Mary has stirred him up, but, owing to his mental state, is incapable of developing:

therefore he finds a refuge in an ambiguous relation – the attraction, half of a son and half of a lover, to Agatha, who reciprocates in somewhat the same way. And this gives the cue for the second appearance of the Furies, more patently in their role of divine messengers, to let him know clearly that the only way out is the way of purgation and holiness.[1] They become exactly 'hounds of heaven'.[2] And Agatha understands this clearly, though Harry only understands it yet in flashes. So Harry's career needs to be completed by an *Orestes* or an *OEdipus at Colonus*.

Mary understands nothing, and is in a fair way to having to follow exactly the footsteps of Agatha, in order eventually to reach the point that Agatha has reached.

Amy also understands nothing: she is merely a person of tremendous personality *on one plane*. What happens to Arthur and John are not meant to be 'disasters', but minor accidents typical of each: she *is* affected by these. But I admit that her behaviour on Harry's departure needs clearing up. But Harry's departure is not a disaster for *him*, but a triumph. The tragedy is the tragedy of Amy, of a person living on Will alone.

There is one point which is meant to be left in doubt: did Harry kill his wife or not? This is the justification of the word 'push'. In what other *simple* way can one person imagine that he has killed another, except by pushing? Suppose that the desire for her death was strong in his mind, out of touch with reality in her company. He is standing on the deck, perhaps a few feet away, and she is leaning over the rail. She has sometimes talked of suicide. The whole scene of pushing her over – or giving her just a little tip – passes through his mind. She is trying to play one of her comedies with him – to arouse *any* emotion in him is better than to feel that he is not noticing her – and she overdoes it, and just at the moment, plump, in she goes. Harry thinks he has pushed her; and certainly, he has not called for help, or behaved in any normal way, to say nothing of jumping in after her.

Harry therefore is really expiating the crime of having wanted to kill his wife, like his father before him. Only, his father did not succeed; he only dragged out a miserable existence first at Wishwood and then abroad. So the crime, and the necessity for expiation, repeat themselves. But Harry is still not quite conscious. At the beginning of the play he is aware of the past only as *pollution*, and he does not dissociate the pollution of his

1 – EMB ringed, in pencil, the terms 'purgation' and 'holiness', and wrote in the margin of the letter: 'not stated?'
2 – See Francis Thompson, *The Hound of Heaven* (1893).

wife's life from that of her death. He still wants to *forget*, and that is the way forbidden. (It is not I who have forbidden it, I see it as Law). Only after the second visit of the Furies does he begin to understand what the Way of Liberation is; and he follows the Furies as immediately and as unintelligibly as the Disciples dropping their nets.

As for the pushing, I had already felt some doubt of the advisability of the second pushing ('into a well') and I am ready to drop that. But I thought I had made things clear enough to the audience by having Harry say, in his dialogue with Agatha, that perhaps he only dreamt he pushed her.

I do attach a good deal of importance to Charles, and what I get out of him (a different attitude from that of any of the other choral figures) I could not get out of a younger man. What just saves Charles is his capacity for being surprised by the bulldog in the Burlington Arcade.

Of course there is meant to be a marked difference between Amy's attitude towards her eldest son and towards the two younger sons whom she 'created', whom she has already recognised to be second-rate, and who, ironically, take after the less interesting members of her husband's family. She is as near to real affection for Harry as she is capable of being. Not that I mean her to be a terrifying stone image, but her capacity for love has been atrophied by a loveless marriage, a humiliating marriage as it turned out to be, and that humiliation working on a character whose great sin was pride. I mean her to be pathetic as well as powerful and jealous.

Well, I think this must do for the present. I can imagine what 'scare' headlines the New York papers have been printing. Of course anything may happen, but no one seems to expect war in the immediate future.

With many thanks, and love to Henzie,

Yours ever affectionately,

Tom[1]

1–EMB's scribbled notes at the foot of this letter include: 'Long patch after Harry's first exit wh. doesn't advance the spiritual development at all . . . Mary & Harry re childhood & Wishwood: should this theme be more definite?

'End of Part I is very low theatrically, & for a long time.'

# TO *A. L. Rowse*

TS Exeter/CC

21 March 1938 [No address given]

My dear Rowse,

You know that at all times I am ready to be of use to you for such small services as are in my power, and I shall be very glad to give *Essex and Elizabeth* to Ashley Dukes to read.[1] He returns from America in a few days' time, and I shall be seeing him this week. I doubt if it is a play of a type which Dukes is likely to want to handle; it ought to be done on a rather generous scale, on a large stage, with no expense spared on scenery, costumes or supers,[2] but I am sure that his criticism and advice would be valuable, and he could also be of help in directing it to the right quarter.

For myself, I have read it through with continuous interest, and was at times moved. It is not for me to make theatrical criticisms, but I questioned the effectiveness of soliloquies once or twice in a play which is so very realistic, and I also could not quite envisage the arrangement on the stage in one or two scenes which are rather crowded. One of the great difficulties, I find, in dramatic writing, is that of remembering all the characters at every moment. You cannot simply leave people doing nothing, and I think turning them into corners to whisper is usually a painful device. Anyway, time and time again I have found that I have left characters on the stage with nothing to do! My only other criticism is not a criticism but a warning that I think a producer would be very like to deprive you of the last scene, which is really an Epilogue, although I can

1–Rowse wrote on 14 Mar. '(Personal)': 'I wonder if you wd do me a great service and add one more to the immeasurable kindnesses I have had at your hands? You know about the play "*Essex and Elizabeth*" . . . ? Could you bear to read it for me, and if you think well enough of it to hand it on to Ashley Dukes with a word of commendation – for I don't know him?

'I think I told you about my writing it – over two years ago now; that Shaw very kindly read it for me, said that the characterisation was very well realised, but that it was too long and needed cutting down. He also made several useful criticisms and suggestions. I simply hadn't time to do anything about it . . .

'But the other day Stephen Spender read the play and seemed so enthusiastic about it that it encouraged me to get down to revising it, which I did last vac. Since then one or two people here whose judgments I much respect have also read it:– e.g. Nevill Coghill, who has a streak of genius as a producer, an amateur, great friend of Wystan Auden. And he also was so enthusiastic, that I venture to send it on to you; otherwise I shouldn't dare to bother you . . .

'I should tell you that I am sending the play to Edith Evans, whom it is my great ambition to see as Elizabeth.'
2–*Super*: 'A person employed on a casual basis to perform a non-speaking or other minor part in the theatre . . . an extra' (*OED*).

see that it might in itself be made very effective. Anyway, I can tell you that I enjoyed the play very much indeed, and congratulate you upon it.

I wonder why you are going to meetings in Cork.[1] Apparently you did not have time to look me up while you were in London, but I hope that we shall meet again soon. – I think we agree at least upon the necessity of supporting France: you because it is a democratic country, and I through thick and thin, whatever kind of government it had, even one to my own liking.

Yours ever affectionately,
T. S. E.


## TO *Montgomery Belgion*                                                    CC

21 March 1938                          [Faber & Faber Ltd]

Dear Belgion,

I have been reading Céline's *Bagatelles*,[2] not quite consecutively, because I don't see how anyone could do that, but with a great deal of pleasure in the language. But I confess myself completely baffled to understand what you think could be made of it for English publication. The brilliance of the book in style and in its inexhaustible flow of slang and coined words is incontestable, but what will be left of that, even in the most accomplished translation? And at the present time it seems to me that there would be a less favourable reception in this country for Jew-baiting than ever previously. I am so perplexed by your suggesting this book that I can't help feeling I have made some mistake, and failed to get the point of it, so I hope you will reply and state your case for it as persuasively as possible.

Pending your reply, I should like to keep the book to refer to when I hear from you.

Yours ever,
[T. S. Eliot]

---

1 – 'I am going to be up in town tomorrow & Wed at Salter's flat . . . Then I go to Cork for a week's meetings. Back here after Mar 27 then abroad – if there isn't a war by then.

'I saw yr charming reference to me as "our ferocious friend" – but really I am rendered desperate by what has been happened in Europe since 1931. I should like to publish my poems, full of hatred & fury, this year before the deluge descends on us. If it doesn't, I'll have a large work of historical scholarship, "Tudor Cornwall", next year.'

2 – Louis-Ferdinand Céline, *Bagatelles pour un massacre* (1937). Belgion was reviewing the book for the *TLS*, and had lent his copy to TSE.

Louis-Ferdinand Céline (1894–1961): French novelist and doctor, whose high reputation was marred by virulent anti-Semitism and collaborationism; works include *Voyage au bout de la nuit* (1932); trans. by J. H. P. Marks as *Journey to the End of the Night* (1934).

## TO *T. F. Burns*                                                     CC

21 March 1938                          [Faber & Faber Ltd]

My dear Burns,

I had really made up my mind about the question of the suitability of my introducing Bobbie's book[1] before I saw the galleys, indeed, if my decision had depended upon the quality of the book, I should have felt more disposed to write the introduction than not, because it seems to me on the whole an excellent piece of work which does Bobbie much credit, especially as the writing of it was so much interrupted by his other work. But I do feel that there is no real justification for my introducing it. I am not an authority on the history of the period, and Bobbie certainly has made it his business to learn a great deal more about St Thomas than I know or ever did know. The book is very satisfactory to me, in that it will serve as evidence of my having followed the historical records very closely myself, but there is nothing I could say in a preface except to commend it, and I think it would be so obvious that my providing a preface was merely a matter of friendship, that my standing as an introducer would decline. I do hope you see what I mean.

With best wishes,
Yours ever,
[T. S. Eliot]

## FROM *Henry Eliot* TO *The Editors*, Time

21 March 1938                          Cambridge, Mass.

Eliots

Sirs:[2]

Your critical comment on T. S. Eliot and *Murder in the Cathedral* contains a number of absurdities, which I will point out *seriatim. Imprimis*, you

---

1 – Robert Speaight, *Thomas Becket* (1938).
2 – Published in *Time*, 21 Mar. 1938, 2–6. HWE's letter responds to a review of the production, by Gilbert Miller and Ashley Dukes, of *MiC*: 'New & Old Plays in Manhattan', *Time*, 28 Feb. 1938: 'Poetic drama by modern writers has been chiefly the plaything of the Little Theatres or the largess [*sic*] of high-minded or highfalutin producers. With a contemporary background poetic drama seems nerveless, artificial, grandiose. But with a historical background it can still, in the right hands, achieve a noble movement.

'This was proved nearly two years ago in Manhattan, when the Federal Theatre successfully produced *Murder in the Cathedral*. The proof still seemed valid last week when the English production of the play opened in Manhattan after 600 performances abroad.

call him dandiacal in appearance; this is a decided exaggeration. To offset the picture which you have of him in slicks, I enclose one in slacks; it is a much more characteristic portrait . . . *Item*, you say his U. S. relations (meaning relatives) regard him as the black sheep of the family; all I can say is, that this is the first that I have heard of it. Possibly some of them may have 'confessed that "his poetry still fuddles a lot of us"', but on the other hand some of them regard themselves as in an uniquely favorable position to understand his poetry, some of which is unintelligible unless you know the man. *Item*, your review of the play shows a more nearly complete misunderstanding of it than any that I have read, and I have read nearly all of them. You speak of the play's lack of psychological drama; on the contrary, it *is* a psychological drama; that is the essence of it; the reason that the murder scene itself is so symbolically presented (in accordance with T. S. Eliot's own wishes) by the English players is to throw the emphasis on the spiritual struggle. You state that Becket is *not* inwardly lacerated, whereas the whole play is about his inward laceration; it is because the play is so introspective that it is hard to follow. As for your 'Eliot gets in a brutal and final punch', I must say, that even if

---

'Playwright Eliot's subject is the slaying of Thomas à Becket, Archbishop of Canterbury, in 1170. In Anglo-Catholic Eliot's hands, Becket (Robert Speaight) stands forth as a tremendous spiritual figure who, before the play begins, has made his choice between Heaven and Earth. Tempters only arouse his scorn. Assassins only increase his submission. Out of such an attitude comes the play's blazing religious exaltation, its lack of psychological drama. The great heroes of tragedy are inwardly lacerated; Becket is not. Hence the first half of the play is mainly declamatory. But in the second half Poet Eliot's richly cumulative rhetoric takes fire, makes antiphonal voices of his despairing chorus of women, his truculent band of murderers, his central, uplifted archbishop. Then, at a stroke, the murder. Then, with a counterstroke, the murderers, using mealy-mouthed journalese, try to justify their crime. In this sudden contrast of shoddy human self-seeking with rapt spiritual self-abnegation, Eliot gets in a brutal and final punch.

'The Author. Thomas Stearns Eliot is, with Novelist James Joyce and Gertrude Stein, the most famed of living highbrows. Like them, he is an expatriate. A poet and critic long before he was a playwright alike, in his long poem *The Waste Land* (1922) and in his brilliant literary essays, he founded a movement. Becoming ever more conservative and religious-minded, Eliot, finally, in 1927, stated his position as "classicist in literature, royalist in politics, and Anglo-Catholic in religion". All his later works are colored by this credo.

'Born in St Louis in 1888 and a member of the famed Harvard class of 1910 (Columnist Walter Lippmann, Economist Stuart Chase, Radical John Reed, etc.), Eliot left the U.S. in 1914, settled in England, eventually became a British subject. Dandiacal in appearance, he has acquired an ostentatiously English accent. He once taught baseball in an English school, today writes long letters to the London *Times* about cheese, edits the London *Criterion*. His U.S. relations regard him as the black sheep of the family, confess that "his poetry still fuddles a lot of us". At present Eliot is working on a modern play laid in an English country house, but with a substratum of Greek drama.'

(as I presume) your dramatic editor is down with the flu, that is no excuse for your turning the job over to the sporting editor.

Henry W. Eliot Jr.

Embarrassed at having horrified an Eliot, TIME gladly prints Brother T. S. Eliot's 'much more characteristic' portrait (see cut, p. 4). – ED.

## TO *Stephen Spender*

TS Northwestern

22 March [1938]                     *The Criterion*

Dear Stephen,

I want to repeat that I was very much impressed and moved.[1] I think that you ought to be very well contented with your first play, and I hope that there will be more. It was also much better produced than I expected, and my only criticism of the acting was that the Judge tottered more frequently than seemed to me necessary. But I might change my mind when I saw it again, or I might find other criticisms.

My chief criticism of the play itself, on the stage, is that I thought there was *too much* poetry. It seems to me that for the stage one needs a good deal of straightforward simple *verse*. So much poetry is deadening to one's sensibility, and also doesn't leave any reserve for hammering with particular passages and phrases. Some phrases (such as the one about Beethoven's silences) and some passages (such as that between Petra's fiancée and his dying brother – and the repetition of the theme here is very good) seemed to me to lose some of their proper effect by not being surrounded by a rather flatter verse.

But you are aiming at the right thing and not evading any of the difficulties of verse plays, and have tackled a noble theme, and I feel encouraged.

Affectionately,
T. S. E.

I am not certain about some of the scansion, though.

1–On Mon., 21 Mar. TSE had accompanied VW and LW to the Group Theatre production of Spender's play *Trial of a Judge*, staged for a short run at the Unity Theatre Club in Camden Town, London. VW noted: 'A moving play: genuine; simple; sincere . . . Too much poetic eloquence. But I was given the release of poetry' (*Diary* V, 131).

TO *Ezra Pound*                                                    TS Beinecke

24 March 1938                        *The Criterion*

Dear Ezzum,

Resistance to entering upon music publication proved too high, and I have passed the stuff back to Larripol to deal with. Music publisher probably the most like approach. Nobody keen to experiments [*sic*] just now. As for GUIDE TO KULCHUR

We think – and *I* think strongly, in fact I hold strong views on the subject –

that the title should be simply

      GUIDE TO KULCHUR

and *not*

GUIDE TO CULTURE OR KULCHUR or anything like that. Suggests lack of Conviction – timid advance to supposed British publickum. Come out Strong with GUIDE TO KULCHUR simple.

Very rushed until after this week, o/a Wyndham painting a portrite. *I* think it's going to be a good picture.

           TP


TO *Montgomery Belgion*                                             CC

24 March 1938                        [Faber & Faber Ltd]

My dear Belgion,

I don't at all contest the unusual brilliance of Celine's book, but I am still extremely doubtful about translating a work the fascination of which is so largely linguistic.[1] It seems to me that it could only be adequately

1–Belgion had replied on 22 Mar. to TSE's letter of 21 Mar.: 'You rather surprise me. I thought that all I had found to say about the Céline [*Bagatelles pour un massacre*] I told you in our last two sessions at the Écu de France and that you had been inclined to agree with it. Moreover, that is now so long ago that I am not sure I can remember what I said.

'It was more or less, I fancy, that both Céline's two novels and his anti-Russian pamphlet had been translated, but that it is only in *Bagatelles* that he has disclosed his true vein – the vein of invective. Whatever reasons, therefore, there may have been for translating the earlier books are stronger reasons for translating this one. In addition, the novels are thoroughly French, but the subject of *Bagatelles* is not. If it has any appeal anywhere, that appeal is universal. Finally, I said, I fancy, that no Jew can be either hurt or offended by the book, because the invective is hyperbolical. The sources of Céline's "data" are, it seems, a book and two 1d. pamphlets, none perhaps thoroughly trustworthy; but he has not hesitated to exaggerate their information where it suited him. *Bagatelles* is thus simply a huge joke; and with the parts I have indicated to you lopped off or dropped out it becomes one which can be appreciated as well in London as in Marseilles, in New York and in Paris.

translated in somewhat the manner of Sir Thomas Urquhart's *Rabelais*, using both all the existing resources of the language in vocabulary, and drawing also on your own invention for new words. And it seems to me that to do this properly would take more of your time, energy and skill than the probable returns could justify. It would be a pity also to have to bowdlerize the book.

This is only my individual opinion, and I should like the book to be read by someone else in order to check my view. It is a question of how soon you need the book back, or how soon you would be able to spare it again. I should not be happy that anything which I recognise as so impressive, or anything that you yourself believe to have translation possibilities should be rejected on my own unsupported opinion.

As to the proposed book of essays, I am myself strongly of the opinion that we ought to do it, but I think that it should be easier to manipulate the matter when Morley is back, which should be in less than three weeks, and I think it is prudent to hold the matter over until then.

As we are taking a train on Saturday at 2.25, I believe for Worthing, could we not meet for a late meal beforehand?[1] You usually have more ideas than I about where to eat, but if you have no better suggestion, we could meet at say 1.15 at the chromium snack bar just outside the station, which communicates with the ordinary bar at the end of the Brighton side.

Yours ever,
[T. S. Eliot]

## TO *The Trust Officer, Old Colony Trust Company*     cc

24 March 1938            [Faber & Faber Ltd]

Dear Sir,

### *FEDERAL INCOME TAX*

With reference to my letter of 23 February, I am now able to inform you that my dramatic royalties from productions of my work in the U.S.A.

---

'There, I think, is more or less what I said. I may add that Céline is the French equivalent of Kafka as regards originality; and I don't believe Gollancz needed to know the innermost meaning of Kafka before he took on a translation of *The Trial*.'

1 – Belgion had notified TSE, on 5 Mar.: 'Richards tells me that he has secured "the cream of the rooms" at Storrington for the 26th. He will very kindly meet us at Worthing. I am saying to him we shall get there by the train due at 3.47. This leaves Victoria at 2.25. Perhaps Miss Bradby will make a note of the times.'

during 1937 amounted to 720 dollars, 24 cents, which should be included in the return which you are kindly making for me for that year.

Yours faithfully,<br>[T. S. Eliot]

TO *A. L. Rowse*                                                    TS Exeter/CC

28 March 1938                     *The Criterion*

My dear Rowse,

Thank you for your undated letter.[1] This is just to say that I think the proper procedure is to explore first the possibilities of getting your play produced, before considering publication. This has two advantages: for one thing, if a play is going to be produced, it will probably have to undergo a good many alterations at the suggestion of the producer, and it is irritating to people who are both readers and play-goers to find a text which differs materially from the acted version. Secondly, if a play is produced first with even moderate success, it means very much better prospects for the sale of the book. I think that the book ought to be published in any case; it is merely a question of trying a theatre first, and when it is published, I should certainly approve of the introduction you suggest, and make it as long as you like. And before committing yourself

---

1 – 'You have already helped me a great deal by your kind and encouraging words. For you know beneath the over-confident exterior of yr ferocious friend, there is more hesitation and caution, – and over literary matters such as this play, more want of confidence than appears. (I am sure you in yr wisdom about human beings have known that; and perhaps that is why it is confidence you have given me all along.) But I really shouldn't have taken out this play and revived it at all, if it hadn't been for the enthusiastic approval of Stephen Spender and Nevill Coghill.

'And you really think I may publish it now? About producing it, I know nothing, and shall be grateful for Ashley Dukes' advice . . .

'But you evidently think the play is *readable*. At the cost of bothering you again, I should be grateful if you'd tell me if you think it worth publishing; and whether it oughtn't to have a longish preface defining what I think about the personality of Elizabeth, about whom so much nonsense appears.

'I don't suppose Geoffrey [Faber] wd want to publish it – he was rather discouraging once when I tentatively mentioned it before writing "Grenville". (Hence what happened about publishing "Grenville", – which I shd certainly have published with him otherwise, and which you almost won back from Cape by sheer niceness about it that day we lunched together!)

'I'll remember those points you mention in criticism, and try to revise & cut down a bit more. I quite agree about the last scene: it *is* an epilogue & was intended as such, incorporating the actual words of Elizabeth's last speech, the "Golden Speech" it was called.'

anywhere else this time, I should like to have the opportunity of discussing it with Geoffrey. But I must first see what Dukes says tomorrow night.

I have no prejudice against Blum whatever, and I have every sympathy with him in his present difficulties.[1] And at the present time, it seems of minor importance what sort of government France has: it is a matter of great anxiety that it should have some kind of stable government.

Ever yours,<br>T. S. E.

## to *T. F. Burns*

CC

28 March 1938                    [Faber & Faber Ltd]

Dear Burns,

I am very willing to write a little note to use amongst others for blurbing, but that again has proved a difficulty, as it would not do anybody any good if I committed myself to indiscreet historical assertions, which the historians might make game of. The following note seems rather egotistic, but I submit it for your consideration.

> I hope that everyone who has read or seen *Murder in the Cathedral* will read Mr Speaight's biography. He not only makes the subject extremely interesting but has been, I think, ~~scrupulously~~ quite fair to King Henry and Becket's opponents. And his book, as an historical and biographical study, is distinguished by the fact that he has written, not merely the Life of a great ecclesiastic who influenced the course of English history, but the Life of a Saint.[2]

Yours ever,<br>[T. S. Eliot]

1 – 'I am glad you think as you do about France, – though really I shdn't have thought there was much to put you off in [Léon] Blum. He is about the only figure in French politics who is incorrupt; he is a charming, civilized man. I once had a long talk with him in his flat on the Ile St Louis, very much the surroundings of a reading man, full of books, and every evidence of taste and culture. The chief thing against him is that he is old now and exhausted.' Léon Blum (1872–1950), politician, French prime minister at the time of this letter.

2 – Speaight, *The Property Basket: Recollections of a Divided Life* (1970), 184–5: 'a proposal from Tom Burns – who had left Sheed & Ward for Longmans – offered not exactly to release me from the "crypt of St Eliot's", but to remove me to a different corner of it. Would I care to write a short, popular life of St Thomas of Canterbury? Evelyn Waugh's life of Edmund Campion had been deservedly acclaimed by everyone except James Agate; this should be a book of similar scope and size . . . I could see what Eliot [in *Murder in the Cathedral*] had taken from [the historical sources], and his guess at the character of Becket – a man cast

29 March 1938                    *The Criterion*

Dear Dr Perkins,

I feel that I have been negligent in not writing to thank you for your kind letter of February 18th[1] – and furthermore, to thank Mrs Perkins for her kind hospitality to the members of my troupe. I know that they enjoyed their visit to Boston very much. I have not yet seen any of them, but am seeing Ashley Dukes tonight, and expect to hear from him, for the first time, a full account of their adventures and vicissitudes. While I am very sorry for him especially, and also for the company, the comparative failure of the tour is not a cause of personal grief to myself, as I had not set my hopes high, and as the success of the play in the past had exceeded my hopes, and as I am now more interested in the play which I hope may be produced in the autumn.

I was much gratified by the *Transcript* article by Bishop Sherrill.[2]

I hope that the disorderly state of Europe (I should say, in some respects, excess of order) will not have affected your plans for next summer, and I trust that Stamford House will be available for you. It does not appear likely that this summer will be particularly disturbed. So I hope that you have by this time seen your History of King's Chapel through the press, and that you will be able to return having accomplished the task for which you returned last autumn.

With many thanks, and affectionate good wishes,

Yours very sincerely,

T. S. Eliot

I am so glad to think that Emily is having a holiday in the South, which ought to refresh her very much. So far as I can gather from herself (not perhaps the most reliable source of information on that point) she has got through the winter pretty well.

----

in heroic mould, but tempted to exhibitionism – seemed to me a very shrewd one. I had always felt that [King] Henry had more native genius than the brilliant civil servant who disappointed his hopes, and I was anxious to be fair to him. Eliot, who for good reasons of his own had kept Henry out of the play altogether, obliged the publishers by saying that he thought I had succeeded. If the truth be told, I was more attracted to the character of Henry than to the character of Becket . . . I cannot say that I warmed to Becket by writing about him any more than by acting him.'

See too TSE to R. P. Adalbert Hamman, 27 Oct. 1955: 'There is an excellent brief biography of St Thomas of Canterbury in English by my friend, Mr Robert Speaight.'

1–Not traced.

2–Henry Knox Sherrill, 'Bishop Sherrill Writes Review of "Murder in the Cathedral": Finds Becket a Symbol of Today', *Boston Evening Transcript*, 2 Feb. 1938, 1.

TO *Charles Williams*                    TS Marion E. Wade Collection

29 March 1938                    *The Criterion*

My dear Williams,

Your outline looks very satisfactory to me, and the Chairman was also pleased with it.[1] At the moment somebody else is brooding on it, but I hope we can get that settled tomorrow, and tell you to go ahead, and then we must arrange terms.

Only we think the title possibly a bit high-flown: perhaps it would be better to have something matter of fact, which would make clear to the uninitiated public what the book is about.[2]

I want to suggest, with some timidity, that I should feel very honoured if you cared to review Tillyard's new book on Milton for the *Criterion*. I say 'with some timidity' because I don't often dare to ask people so busy as you are, when the *Criterion* doesn't really pay enough to make it worthwhile. It is only that I feel more curiosity to know your opinion on this matter than that of anybody else. If you review the book, you will find that the author devotes a good deal of time to belabouring myself. It would be equally profitable and instructive to me, whether you felt impelled to take a different view or to reinforce his blows with your own.[3]

Ever yours,

T. S. E.

1–CW wrote on 14 Mar.: 'Herewith the paragraph I showed you and a set of chapter headings. I will not swear to the title, though I think it makes a pleasant suggestion of strangeness or of horror according to the reader's information. I have not bothered to put in all sorts of allusions to poems and things because they will be scattered all over it. But tell me if it ought to be altered in any way.

'Let me add one more murmur of shy thanks for our last week's lunch. You almost emanated light.'

2–The book was initially to be called *History of Magic*; it then turned into *History of Witchcraft*, and was finally published as *Witchcraft* (F&F, 1941).

CW responded, 30 Mar.: 'By now I entirely agree with you about the title. It is the kind of romantic phrase one first thinks of, and ever afterwards regrets. Besides it formally confines the book too much to Black magic as such, and it would be more satisfactory to leave the faintest loophole for occasional squinting at whatever may be meant by White. Let me meditate.'

3–Williams, 30 Mar.: 'Does it matter that I have already written 300 words on it for the *London Mercury*? – they will probably be unsigned, and they certainly said nothing except about Milton. I rather delicately avoided going between the incensèd bounds of such opposites. But under your protection – ! If the *Mercury* note make no difference to the *Criterion* I should be very glad to do it.' CW on E. M. W. Tillyard, *The Miltonic Setting: Past and Present*: C. 17 (July 1938), 738–40.

TO *Ezra Pound*                                                    TS Beinecke

30 March 1938                    *The Criterion*

Ezzumpo,

That's right, it's GUIDE TO KULCHUR.[1] And you don't always make things CLEAR. What do you mean, what did you mean, about CREVEL?[2] I thought praps if I left the matter you would deign to talk more about it. I remember his name years ago, but don't know what he's been up to. What do you want to DO about him?

I know something about the Tate there is a larfable anecdote about that which one of your gossips will no doubt retail to you, but aint you seen that Mr Manson has resigned on grounds of ill health.[3] Yes, and we don't know what we'll get next.

I don't think I enraged Larripol????? I thought we was on very affable terms?????[4]

Wyndham is all in paint at the moment,[5] can't think of anything else. I think its a very handsome portrite indeed. Its a grand chance for the local Museum or Tate or Temio Tempio at Rappaloo to acquire a GOOD pixture.

TP.

1–EP wrote, 26 Mar.: 'YAAAAAS Kuss it/ you nacherly wd/ use yr/ three minutes on the NEGATIVE rather than the constructive point in my correspondence.

'The TITLE of the book is KULCH OR

    EZ Guide to Kulchur

'only title that wd/ get into Amurikah/ but the contract sez Culture or Kulchur?? Or dont it??'

2–EP, 26 Mar.: 'What about CREVEL? what about Golding?'

3–James Bolivar Manson (1879–1945), artist; director of the Tate Gallery, London, 1930–8. An alcoholic, Manson disgraced himself on 4 Mar. 1938 at a lunch organised by Kenneth Clark at the Hotel George V, Paris, to mark the opening of a British exhibition at the Louvre. Resistant to avant-garde art, when he was asked to vouch for the artistic authenticity of certain sculptures selected by Marcel Duchamp for exhibition at Peggy Guggenheim's London Gallery (they were being held by customs officers pending a ruling as to whether the sculptures were in fact art and therefore to be exempt from duty), he dismissed Constantin Brancusi's *Sculpture for the Blind* as 'idiotic' and 'not art'. There followed a big outcry against him in both press and parliament.

4–EP, 26 Mar.: 'Any how no need to enrage Larry [Pollinger] so he destroys all the specimen material sent up/ and one proposal was NOT for publication of MUSIC but for biography and damned interesting material at that.'

5–EP, 26 Mar.: 'And getting free advt/ from Wyndham; ARE you going to PRINT him in Criterion??'

TO *John Hayward*                                                        TS King's

31 March 1938                          *The Criterion*

Dear John,

Just a Line to tell you that the up Shot of my evening with Dukes was this. He began by wanting me to remove Gerald and Charles and substitute Arthur and John: at the end he wanted me to leave Gerald and Charles and leave Arthur and John out altogether. He sticks to the point that it is a weakness to have people mentioned throughout a play but never seen. He also has the idea that it would be much more effective and tragic for Amy if Harry was the only son. In the event of Harry's death, therefore, Gerald would come in to the title; so he would like Gerald to be turned into an elderly sot who is to get into trouble with the local police.

One point seems indisputable. He points out that such a report about Arthur could never appear in a newspaper except after he had been tried and fined – if all this was reported at the moment of his being taken up it would be libellous. Geoffrey (the barrister) believes that this is true. In this case, the news should be conveyed in some other way. But Dukes sees the advantage of working in a passage of quotidian prose, for setting the verse into relief.

Also, he queries the use of the word 'curse', inasmuch as in the exact sense there seems to be no curse on the house (nobody cursed it) but only a 'doom'. This may be right. I can't tell till I get my other copy back from Tandy.

I will communicate on Monday.

                                                                        TP


TO *Eric Maclagan*[1]                                                    CC

1 April 1938                          [Faber & Faber Ltd]

Dear Maclagan,

One of the young men in whom I am interested has I understand decided to put in for a vacancy at the Victoria and Albert, and rang this

---

1–Eric Maclagan (1879–1951): Director of the Victoria and Albert Museum, London, 1924–45. Distinguished as scholar and lecturer, and an expert on early Christian and Italian Renaissance art, his works include *Catalogue of Italian Sculpture* (with Margaret Longhurst, 1932) and *The Bayeux Tapestry* (1943), translations from poets including Rimbaud and Valéry, and editions of the works of William Blake. His offices included Vice-President of the Society of Antiquaries, 1932–6; President of the Museums Association, 1935–6. A devout

TSE at forty-nine

morning while I was not here to ask if I would let him have a testimonial tomorrow.[1] I do not know why he should need it at such short notice, but in the circumstances it seems to me better to drop you a line informally to tell you what I know and do not know about him.

His name is E. W. F. Tomlin, and I have known him for about seven years. When he was still a schoolboy he came to me with a very precocious book he had written, which was a rejoinder and attack upon A. L. Rowse's *Politics and the Younger Generation*, which had just come out. The book was of course too immature to publish, but it showed great promise, and I have kept in touch with him ever since. At Oxford he did Modern Greats, a subject for Schools of which I have my doubts, and I know that Tomlin himself would have preferred to take Greats, but through no fault of his own did not have enough Greek. He has frequently contributed to the *Criterion*, to *Scrutiny*, and to other papers. I regard him as one of the most brilliant of the young men with whom I have come in contact, and I am very much interested in his future. I also believe him to be a young man of high character, and extremely conscientious, I think to the point of being inclined to worry, over his work.

Heretofore I had looked upon him rather as a coming political thinker with a great deal of interest in and respect for the Christian faith. My friend George Every at Kelham has taken a great deal of interest in him. He represents the younger type of constructive Tory. I was therefore surprised to hear that he wished to apply for a position in the Museum, but having only learnt of it this morning, I have had no opportunity to talk to him about it. I do not know what your requirements are of candidates, beyond the intellectual attainments, character and social suitability. But for these things I can speak of him most warmly, and I hope that he will be able to prove his suitability to your satisfaction.

Sincerely yours,
[T. S. Eliot]

Anglo-Catholic, he served too on the Cathedrals Advisory Council and the Central Council for the Care of Churches, and as a member of the Church Assembly. Knighted in 1933, he was appointed KCVO in 1945.

1 – Applications for the post of Assistant Keeper at the Victoria & Albert Museum were to close on 2 Apr. 'I don't imagine that my qualifications are exactly what is wanted,' Tomlin told TSE on 31 Mar.; 'but the advertisement in "The Times" seemed to suggest that I should be eligible.'

6 April 1938                              [*The Criterion*]

Dear Bonamy,

Thank you for your letter and review. As you are off to France, from which I hope you will return with the headgear of Montpellier, I don't suppose you will get this note for some days. I only want to question whether it is not rather unnecessarily violent, and also not especially called for in this place, to refer to Leavis as 'an academic gangster'? It seems rather hard, especially as a mere passing shot. It will be easy enough to alter this in proof. Let me know when you get back.[1]

Yours ever,

[Tom]


TO *A. Desmond Hawkins*                    TS A. Desmond Hawkins

7 April 1938                              *The Criterion*

Dear Hawkins,

Your new address is noted.[2] I hope you will find Saffron Walden satisfactory. I suppose that from some points of view it is more convenient than Radwinter.

It seems to me all to the good that the *Southern Review* should publish your series of articles simultaneously, and I cannot see that anyone could have any objection.[3] As for my own contribution, I should like it to come well into 1939, so I expect you will have had one or two others before me, and I should certainly like to take account of my predecessors, as far as possible.

Perhaps you will try Lewis again when you have got the others settled.

1 – 'Books of the Quarter' – on E. M. W. Tillyard, *Shakespeare's Last Plays* – C. 17 (July 1938), 740–3. Dobrée's closing sentence was duly amended to read: '. . . Dr Tillyard is not to be numbered among the academic gangsters' – without identifying the gangster F. R. Leavis.

2 – Hawkins and his family had moved home from his 'Log Cabin' in the Essex countryside to 'The White House', 18 West Road, Saffron Walden, Essex.

3 – Hawkins wrote, 5 Apr.: '*The Southern Review* is undertaking simultaneous publication of the whole *Symposium* issue [of *Purpose*], & I should like to know if you have any objection to this.' Other contributors were to include EP and Allen Tate, and he proposed also to invite Michael Roberts and Tomlin. 'Wyndham Lewis has been asked but has not replied; which is rather disappointing.'

Unless I have to be abroad at that moment, I certainly expect to go to Reckitt's lunch on the 21st, and am looking forward to it with keen interest.[1]

Yours ever,
T. S. E.

TO *Christina Morley*                                    TS Berg

7 April 1938                    *The Criterion*

Dear Christina,

Many thanks for your letter.[2] I was going to write today in any case, because I had a sort of message yesterday from Morley K.,[3] to the effect that you were going to motor down to Southampton on Monday, and offered me transport. Whether you did or not, I should have been delighted to come, but next week is impossible, I can't get away from London until after Easter. I wonder whether Frank is to be expected at Russell Square next week or not. Tell him that we should be glad to have him look in for Wednesday, but I don't see why he should do any more than that. And Miss Evans has plenty to do, because she is typing out my Complete Cats, which will presently be offered to Faber & Faber. (I didn't get home after the Committee yesterday until 8.35, because I had to go to the B.B.C. and rehearse Tandy for another performance tonight).

Your vicissitudes on returning to the Farm are just about what I expected, except for the fox getting the hens, which I hadn't thought of. (Does a fox only kill as many hens as he can eat, or is he a real killer?) (I mean, I could eat only half a hen myself, so how can a small creature like a fox eat four in a night). On the other hand, it is refreshing to have such very satisfactory news of the children. But I should think that your feelings towards Jill might be hard to keep under control. And I thought she was supposed to be good with animals. When your colleens arrive there will be plenty of uproar, no doubt. I hope they won't expect you to get up to take them to early Mass every Sunday at Lingfield. There's something I've thought of which perhaps you haven't.

I gather that Frank is anxious to get back, judging from his express statement, written in the train near St Paul, that he is sick of fried chicken

1 – 'I hear I may see you at lunch on the 21st at Reckitt's. I'm looking forward to that party.'
2 – Not traced.
3 – Morley Kennerley (1902–85), a director of F&F.

and even of ice cream, and that he finds St John of the Cross agreeable. These admissions, taken together, come as near to conversion as I have ever known him.

No word from the Portuguese. Blast them, this is just what I ought to have expected, after my previous experiences with them. They have sent me a lot of books to read; and I have found out from Gaselee[1] what to eat and drink. It wouldn't surprise me if the whole thing were put off, nor would it surprise me if I received a cable telling me to come at once. So the next six weeks are in suspense. I am certainly keeping the first available and mutually convenient weekend in May for the Farm, and that will help me to deal with 1. the Tandys, 2. the Hopkins's, 3. the Maxse's, 4. the Aikens (I particularly don't want to sit for another portrait), and will carry me over till I have to go to Salisbury.

But I hope, as you suggest, that we can have a weekend in town before that, because I want to thrash out this question of whether I am to re-write the play as completely as Browne and Dukes wish me to, or not.

Ever yours,<br>TP

TO *John Hayward*                                                    TS King's

11 April 1938                          *The Criterion*

Dear John,

Here's a How d'ye Do – or, for a different tune of thought, a Pretty kettle of Fish. I am reserving a passage on the only Boat possible (according to Cook's), that is the 'Highland Princess' from London arriving at Lisbon the 27th of this month. Gaselee told me particularly to avoid the 'Highland' boats of the R.M.S.P. Coy., but that is the only sailing for Lisbon to arrive anywhere near my date. But there is no return sailing, by ANY line, before the 13th May. Am I to spend a fortnight in that country, and will the Government pay for my entertainment all that time? It is most inconvenient. If the Government entertain me all that time, they will surely expect me to write a book about Portugal – and you know how many other things I have to do. Also, I shall have to go straight to work on returning, to devise what to say to the Friends of Salisbury Cathedral (I have just declined an invitation from Miss Edith Olivier[2]

---

1 – Stephen Gaselee; see letter of 28 June 1938, below.
2 – Edith Olivier (1872–1948): writer, and well-known hostess based in Wiltshire.

on the ground that I am invited by the Richmonds). I inquired about Air travel, and was told that there was no direct Air Service to Lisbon (what's the use of my going to all this trouble, if the Air people don't do their duty?) so I should have to fly from Lisbon to Casablanca, and thence go to Tangiers in the hope of picking up a Boat to England. As for the through trains, you not only have to get permission from the Foreign Office and the Franco Representative in London, but you can only buy your ticket to the frontier, and after that you have to buy another ticket from Spain to the Portuguese Frontier etc., <or *vice versa*> so unless the Foreign Office and the Portuguese can guarantee my getting back by train (and besides you have to stay the night in Paris) without being badgered by Franco officials I won't come back that way. So what am I to Do? If I had never met the great-grandson of Leigh Hunt, none of this would have happened. Have you any powerful friend who can console a distracted Possum? Meanwhile Morley has arrived in England; I don't know whether he was active when Lily Pons[1] slid across the floor: anyway he was uninjured in the tempest, and I expect to see him tomorrow. And meanwhile here is a

SPOTLIGHT ON 22, BINA GARDENS:
THROWN BY JOHN FOSTER –

Will the Goblin nuisance be put an End to?

Mr Foster said that the club was the resort of undesirables, habitual disorder and drunkenness occurred there, and the police had frequently been called in to quell disturbances.

'The premises are badly conducted, and the police regard them as one of the worst in the district,' the inspector added.[2]

Things don't look too good for Mrs Walker

Yrs. etc.
TP

---

1 – Lily Pons (1898–1976): successful French-American opera star and actress.
2 – Unidentified newspaper clipping. TSE has typed glosses on either side.

TO *John Middleton Murry*                          TS Northwestern

11 April 1938                          *The Criterion*

Dear John:

Thank you for your letter of the 8th.[1] I look forward, after what you have told me, to reading your piece on Chaucer with the keenest interest. I will certainly use it in the June number if I can, but I know that I have already made this promise concerning several other contributions and I cannot promise definitely at the moment. I shall be working out the body of the *Criterion* in the next few days and will then let you know the prospects.

I wonder if you have made any progress with the written report, if that is what it should be called, which you and I were both commanded to compose after our meeting last week?[2] I hope to try my hand at something before Easter, but it is going to be extremely difficult. I think, however, that the meeting was certainly a success, at least in the very satisfactory personal relations which subsisted between the members – largely, I think, owing to Joe Oldham's genius for managing that sort of affair. I was certainly very happy to see you, and I think that we are likely to meet and communicate more often.

Yours ever,<br>Tom

TO *Philip Mairet*                                    CC

11 April 1938                          [Faber & Faber Ltd]

My dear Mairet,

I return herewith the carbon of your long and interesting letter to Montgomery.[3]

---

1 – 'The piece on *Chaucer & the Village Community* needs to be typewritten . . . I . . . hope to let you have it by Wednesday next. As it stands, it is 18pp of my writing (i.e. 4–8,000 words) . . .

'It was a real happiness to me to meet you again, in that fashion. Whether anything still divides us, I don't know; but I do know that, if there is any such thing, it is inessential.'

The essay on Chaucer did not appear in C: see JMM, *Heaven – and Earth* (1938).

2 – At the first meeting of the Moot, JMM and TSE had agreed to write preparatory papers for the second meeting in Sept.: TSE to respond to JMM's 'Towards a Christian Theory of Society'.

3 – Not traced. Mairet wrote, 9 Apr.: 'I wrote a long letter to Dr Montgomery last week, which I copied for Chandos to see, and it should reach you via Rands very shortly. I mention this in case you might wonder why it comes: the matter I thought of interest to us all.'

Any comments that I can make are very much limited by the fact that I do not know Hargrave[1] or his associates personally, and by the fact that I have not been following their activities on paper. I did subscribe to the Social Credit paper for a year or two, but gave it up because it seemed only to repeat itself.

Any general remarks that I might make would have to be qualified by my opinion, if I had any, of Hargrave's general political abilities. One of the particular difficulties of thought and action at the present time is – as I think you rather suggest yourself – the separation, the confusion, and the substitution one for another, of three things: religion, politics and economics. To attend to a different aspect of this tangle than that which you mentioned to Montgomery, I think that there is, and always will be, something called politics which is not embraced by economics. The consistent conduct of Social Crediters – including the *N.E.W.* – has been, and I am sure very rightly, to call attention again and again to the economic basis of politics. But to have a firm grasp of the economic problem, or to be a sound Social Crediter, is not enough in itself for political action. Any party which seeks to prepare itself for the exercise of power must have two things besides sound economics: the ability to inflame the emotions of the mass of people (I don't mean proletariat, but everybody who is incapable of political thinking, or who prefers not to think about politics – and that is nearly everybody) and the ability to apply central principles to every department of government. It needs a political *ethics*. Have Hargrave and his friends thought out any line of action on such matters as Education, the Balance of Industry and Agriculture, or (it is not so remote as it may seem) Church and State?

I find that I tend more and more to concede that any practical effort for the regeneration of Britain within the visible future must involve the exercise of a more absolute central power. It seems too late for anything else. And this involves all the risks of building up a secular mass-morality which will end in a conflict between the temporal and the spiritual. How this culmination is to be avoided I don't know. But, looking at the immediate future, I can't see how any merely negative action – the mere removal of economic and financial oppression – is going to check, to say nothing of reversing, the industrialisation and metropolitanisation of the *minds* of the great mass of the people.

---

1 – John Hargrave (1894–1982): author, commercial artist, inventor, lexicographer, pacifist; youth leader (Head Man of the Kindred of the Kibbo Kift, a co-educational youth movement in the 1920s); prominent proponent of Social Credit.

The question is, what are Hargrave and his people doing to prepare themselves, not only to *gain* political power, but to qualify themselves for exercising it? Since this power, if gained, would have to be exercised not merely for revolutionising the banking system, but over the whole life of the nation? What I am afraid of is a Social Credit which may go to the extreme of a kind of economic materialism, assuming that if you have the power to scrap and replace certain parts of the machinery, everything else that is desirable will follow of itself. I object to this not because it is 'materialistic' (not because of the connotations of that word) but because I don't think it would work; because I think those in power would find that if chaos was to be avoided, or some order worse than the present, they would have to deal, unprepared, with a number of vital issues not dreamt of in their orthodoxy.

It depends there, upon how broad a mind Hargrave has, upon how much he could be led to see the *practical necessity* for the future of his own designs, whether cooperation could be fruitful. He would have to be made to see that he himself had a great deal to gain from the collaboration of people like the Chandos – who, among them, represent I think several important problems which I dare say he has never thought of.

It is perhaps not irrelevant to explain that Germany today, far from being in a state of renascence, seems to me to be in a long view so much nearer to decadence. It may have vitality in the sense that it may be able to destroy the British Empire, but in so doing will be infecting itself hopelessly with the same disease and creating an empire which won't last as long as ours has. And one very bad symptom in Germany is the new movement for duping the workers into a kind of contentment by sending select parties of them on Mediterranean tours (Kraft durch Freude![1]) If we are merely going to compete with existing totalitarian states for their own ends and by their own means, then we might as well leave it to Chamberlain and not bother about Hargrave. And our difference, to be worth the trouble, has got to be more than that of having a different economic and monetary theory – important as that is.

You see, I am willing to part company with 'secular humanitarianism' and 'liberal democracy' – but I think we must at the same time realise the risks to be run.

And I really don't know whether this letter has any useful bearing on the problems in your mind in writing to Montgomery or not.

Yours ever,

[T. S. Eliot]

1 – 'Strength through joy!'

12 April 1938                    *The Criterion*

Dear Tate:

I have now read your version of *The Turn of the Screw* and can say that I liked it very much.[1] There are two possible objections that occur to me. The first is that the opinion of anyone like myself, who is very familiar with Henry James's story, is useful in one way but not in another. The fact that as an admirer of the story I also like the play you have made of it is one person's testimony of your fidelity to the spirit of James; but on the other hand the play as a play ought to make a very definite impression on the audience whether they are familiar with Henry James's story or not, and I simply cannot tell in the least how intelligible the play will be to anybody who is unfamiliar with the original. Possibly you have already tried out your version on such people, but if not, I think that it is an important point.

The second difficulty is about the use of child actors. I may be unnecessarily squeamish, and I may also be quite out of touch with the minds of at least some children, but I confess that I am rather disturbed at the thought of having real children taking part in an action of such horror as this, and the fact that the horror is, from the ordinary point of view, of a vague and supernatural kind doesn't minimise my aversion. I should like to know your own response to this criticism.

Finally, I should like Herbert Read to have the opportunity of reading your play and hope for your permission to show it to him.[2]

Yours ever,

T. S. Eliot

---

1 – Tate had posted off his dramatic version of *The Turn of the Screw* on 22 Mar. – 'but if you read it don't think about publication; read it for whatever amusement it may give you. I don't think I should like to see it published. Of course I should like to see it produced somewhere.'

2 – Tate responded (20 Apr.) that he was 'glad' TSE liked his version; 'glad' for HR to see it. In answer to TSE's criticisms: 'The question of putting children in that situation on the stage is a very serious one. The relative "distance" of a character in fiction is one thing; but the immediacy of the stage is quite another, and possibly actual children would tend to make the thing, in the literal sense, obscene . . . I had already considered it desirable to increase the children's ages from eight and ten to eleven and thirteen, so that perhaps an ingenue could take Flora's part, and a grown boy Miles'.

'The other problem you raise may throw light on it. I've read the play to three or four mixed groups of persons, and the response has been on two levels. The naive response presupposed the physical reality of the apparitions, and the attention here focussed upon the struggle between the Governess and the spooks; the suffering of the children became to an

TO *Messrs Faber & Faber*                          TS copy Valerie Eliot

18 April 1938                          The Pines, Putney, S.W.15[1]

Dear Sirs,

I enclose herewith stamps for the return of the enclosed poems.[2] The publishers to whom I have previously offered them all tell me that the only firm which publishes poetry is Faber & Faber. Is this true? If so, I shall take your rejection as final.

I must explain that these poems are meant to be illustrated; and that, if you should look upon them with a not unfavourable eye, my friend the Man in White Spats is prepared to submit specimen illustrations. If you should consider the poems worthy of publication, or alternatively if you should wish to publish them, and should approve of the speciment [*sic*] illustrations, then I suggest a royalty of 10% and an advance on royalty of £30 to be paid not to me but to my friend the Man in White Spats.

I enclose some opinions on the enclosed poems.

Faithfully yours,

O. Possum

[Enclosures]

Report on PRACTICAL CATS

I take it that the author is as much of an authority on Cats as he claims to be. If that is so, the Committee has to consider whether what I see in the poems is really there or not; and if it is there, whether anyone else will want to read them. That I think is antecedently improbable. What the poems convey to me is the sense of a particular Cat in a particular place at a particular time; and here I must warn the Committee against approaching these Cats from the standpoint of Thomas Gray, Old Mother Tabbyskins, or the callow polyps of the Faber Book of Animal Verse. Nor is it to use my report as an excuse for avoiding a second opinion.

[Unsigned][3]

---

extent the occasion of the Governess' heroic efforts to save them. The critical response, of course, assumed their innocence and the guilt of the Governess, and this "rationalising" of the conflict seemed to minimize the horror.

'But on neither level, apparently, was any of the dramatic effect lost. I say this in reply to your question about the effect of the play on persons who have not read James. That was the first test we made after the MS was finished; we selected for the purpose only people who had not read the story. The result was far beyond our hopes.'

1 – The address at which A. C. Swinburne lived for thirty years with Theodore Watts-Dunton.
2 – 'Old Possum's Book of Practical Cats'.
3 – See further *Poems* II, 45–7.

Report on PRACTICAL CATS

I have had this manuscript for six weeks and haven't had a minute in which to look at them so I bring them back.

R. de la M.

Report on PRACTICAL CATS

Mrs Crawley was delighted with the first two or three that she read, but after a time she found that she couldn't get on with them. So I started at the other end and very much enjoyed the two or three that I read, but when I had worked back to about the middle I found my attention wandering. Since then I have spoken to Minchell and rung up Sampson Low and been on the telephone to Blackie's, and everybody agrees that the market for Cats is pretty dead. If we could get the author to do a book on Herrings, I believe I could interest the trade in Hull, Grimsby and Lossiemouth.

[W. J. Crawley]

Report on PRACTICAL CATS

These poems are apparently the product of some member of the would-be Chelsea intelligentsia of the Blue Cockatoo variety. Personally, I find them pretentious, and cannot recommend publication. They might sell. I think they should be read through carefully with a view to the possibility of libel, that is, if you think seriously of publishing them. In view of the attitude of Colonel James Moriarty on a previous occasion, and the likelihood of legal proceedings, I think that one of these poems should be omitted. That is, if you decide to publish them. Personally, I think that the author should be seen and encouraged to offer us his next book, on the understanding that we might publish this book subsequently if his next book proved a success. I think a second opinion is needed. Would Mr Morley look at this ms.?

A. P. [Alan Pringle]

Report on PRACTICAL CATS

Here's a book that F. & F. ought to publish, Frank: I think I could get Heinemann's to do it, but it's much more F. & F. stuff. O.P. is the real surrealist poet we have been waiting for; he's going to knock Gascoyne and Barker stiff; and what's more, he needs the money. If F. & F. don't see the point, I despair of modern society. There are enough complexes in this book to keep all of Freud's disciples busy for a generation. Ludo and Thomas send you their love. Yrs.

H. R. [Herbert Read]

TO *William Force Stead*                                    TS Beinecke

20 April 1938                          *The Criterion*

My dear Stead,

How very kind of you to remember me at Easter, and give me such a very valuable and welcome gift. I don't know Johnson's Prayers and Meditations, and I am very glad indeed to have them. I am going away on Saturday, and shall take them as part of my reading matter. Morley, by the way, is familiar with them, and thinks very highly of them. I shall prize your gift.[1]

The manuscript of Christopher Smart's Cat appears to have been returned to you. Unless you have changed your mind about it, would you send it back to my secretary, so that it can go to press for the next number?[2]

With grateful thanks,
Yours ever affectionately,
T. S. Eliot

1–Force Stead inscribed the volume – *Prayers and Meditations* composed by Samuel Johnson, LL.D, third new and revised edn (1928) – 'T. S. Eliot / from W. F. S. / Lent 1938' (TSE Library).

TSE sometime marked two passages. Against the prayer 'On Easter Day' (14–15) – specifically 'And, O Lord, so far as it may be lawful for me, I commend to Thy fatherly goodness the soul of my departed wife; beseeching Thee to grant her whatever is best in her present state, and finally to receive her to eternal happiness' – TSE pencilled in the margin, simply: 'Purgatory'. In addition, he pencilled a line alongside 'Prayer against vain scruples' (58–9): 'O LORD, who wouldest that all men should be saved, and who knowest that without Thy grace we can do nothing acceptable to Thee, have mercy upon me. Enable me to break the chain of my sins, to reject sensuality of thought, and to overcome and suppress vain scruples, and to use such diligence in lawful employment as may enable me to support myself and do good to others. O LORD, forgive me the time lost in idleness, pardon the sins which I have committed, and grant that I may redeem the time misspent, and be reconciled to Thee by true repentance, that I may live and die in peace and be received to everlasting happiness. Take not from me, O LORD, THY HOLY SPIRIT, but let me have support and comfort for JESUS CHRIST's sake. Amen.'

2–Stead, 'Christopher's Cat', C. 17 (July 1938), 679–85. Stead's discovery of *Jubilate Agno* – published as *Rejoice in the Lamb: A Song from Bedlam* (1939) – introduced the cat 'Jeoffry'.

21 April 1938                    *The Criterion*

Dear Lewis,

I learn from the *Telegraph* that your portrait of me has been rejected by
the Academy. ~~I am not in the least surprised. And~~ For my own part, I will
not disguise my feeling of relief. Had the portrait been accepted, I should
have been pleased – that a portrait by you should have been accepted by
the Academy would have been a good augury – at least, I should have
been gratified by the spectacle of the Royal Academy at Canossa, so to
speak. But so far as the sitter is able to judge, it seems to me a very good
portrait, and one by which I am quite willing that posterity should know
me, if it takes an interest in me at all. And though I may not be the best
judge of it as portraiture, I am sure that it is a very fine painting. But
I am glad to think that a portrait of myself should *not* appear in the
exhibition of the Royal Academy, and I certainly have no desire, now, that
my portrait should be painted by any painter whose portrait of me would
be accepted by the Royal Academy.[1]

Yours,
T. S. Eliot

1–On 21 Apr. the Hanging Committee of the Royal Academy rejected WL's portrait of TSE.
    See too FVM to WL, 26 Apr. 1938: 'The grand publicity should help to get a grand price
for the Eliot portrait. I have been very eager to see it, but on my return from a long trip in
America I have been so tangled up that I haven't been able to try yet.

'While I was in Boston I talked with several people there about possibly getting an offer
for the portrait from Harvard, so that it could be hung in Eliot House. Of course I don't
know what your plans are, but if an offer from them would be of any interest, I would be
delighted to promote it to the best of my ability. Such a sale would have the advantage of
being free of any commissions. If you would like me to follow up Harvard, a photograph –
such as Tom said you were in any case going to send to his brother Henry, would, of course,
be very useful.

'On the other hand, I don't want to butt in. Maybe you've sold it already.'

See too TSE, 'Wyndham Lewis', *The Observer*, 18 Dec. 1960 (letter in response to Edith
Sitwell's 'gossipy account of her acquaintance with the late Wyndham Lewis' published in
the issue of 27 Nov.): 'I not only have a very high opinion of Lewis's achievements as painter
and draughtsman, but regard him as one of the most important writers of my generation.

'I presume that I came to know him better in his later years than did Dame Edith, but she
had one privilege which was not vouchsafed to me. Lewis painted my portrait twice, but for
neither portrait did I sit for him daily (barring Sundays) for ten months. I had what seemed
to me only a normal number of sittings, even for the second portrait, which cost him great
pains. He was obliged to peer closely at me every few minutes, as it was the last picture he
was able to paint before complete blindness put an end to his practice of this art.

'I had always regarded his genius with admiration, and had always found his conversation
stimulating; but I came to feel for him in his later years a warmth of sympathy and friendship
which no one would suspect, from Dame Edith's account, that he would ever arouse.'

TO *John Hayward*                                          TS King's

Dear John,

I enclose a pound note with a visiting card; but you can spend as much as you think fit for the flowers, up to the limit of ostentatiousness. Ottoline meant a good deal for me, first as one of the first landmarks of London for me, and later, especially in the last five years, when I think she had become a much nicer person than when I first knew her. Anything more is for conversation.[1]

I will now write (in long hand) to Milly and Julian.

I have received the programme from Lisbon. My goodness, there is not much free time; the only mention is '9 *(lundi) la journée libre* . . . *Le soir, spectacle dans un théâtre de Lisbonne*'. Most of it is

'*A neuf heures, départ pour* .... *Visite à la plage et déjeuner dans un restaurant typique de* .... *Après-midi, visite à* ...... *et diner dans un restaurant typique de* ......

---

See too 'Augustus John Resigns', *Evening News*, 25 Apr. 1938: 'Mr Augustus John has resigned his membership of the Royal Academy following the Academy's rejection of Mr Wyndham Lewis's portrait of Mr T. S. Eliot, the poet.

'Interviewed at Fordingbridge, Hants, today, he said the Academy's action in this matter was the culminating point.

'"There is a lack of understanding and a difference of outlook between the Academy and myself. I have many personal regrets at resigning, and I am very sorry to do anything so drastic and sensational, but I shall be far more at home outside."

'Mr Lewis was an old friend of his, and he had written to him expressing his strong disapproval of the Academy's action, which he described as "an inept act."

'So far Mr John has not received any formal acceptance from the Academy of his resignation . . .

'One of the most famous artists of the day, he was appointed a Royal Academician in 1928, having seven years previously been elected an A.R.A.

'He has been a trustee of the Tate Gallery since 1933 . . .

'Mr Wyndham Lewis said today: "A situation has been created by the resignation of Mr Augustus John which must lead to radical reform of that sinister institution, which has been a millstone round the neck of English art for three or four generations.

'"This resignation . . . should be a mortal blow to the Royal Academy, if it is possible for one to use the expression 'mortal blow' with reference to a corpse."'

See also EVE to Neil Hughes-Onslow, 18 Mar. 1986: 'I agree with you about the painting, and must confess that if I had the opportunity I would steal it. Augustus John used the Royal Academy's rejection of the portrait as an excuse for his resignation. He had not seen the picture at the time, and was later to tell Laura Knight that he did not "give a damn for it". His real reason was supposed to be his dislike of the President, Sir William Llewellyn.'

1–OM had died on 21 Apr. Julian Vinogradoff (OM's daughter) to EVE, 3 Mar. 1985: 'almost the last signature in [OM's Visitors' Book at Gower Street] February 21st 1938 is T. S. Eliot alone. After that I think she was too ill to go on seeing people.'

What indigestion. I am taking cascara pills and chlorodyne. But if I
dont get an interview I shall be grossly indignated, not personally but as
representative of his publishers, FABER & FABER – I mean interview
with Dr Oliviera Salazar. It ends up on the 11th with

*Banquet au Palace d'Estoril* (Estoril seems to be the Blackpool of
Portugal) *avec l'assistance des intellectuels portugais.*

Well, well. I commend you to the Saints,

yrs etc.

TP.

## то *J. H. Oldham* cc

22 April 1938                    [Faber & Faber Ltd]

My dear Oldham,

I was only able to read Murry's report last night, but as George Every
was dining with me I showed it to him. He also thought the first three
pages excellent. I am returning the copy to you, as I have pencilled some
notes on the last two pages. The following is all that the report has had
the time to provoke from me.

I can see, on the first few readings, nothing that I would wish to qualify
on the first three pages, which seem to me an admirable statement. The
notes which I have scribbled on the following two pages indicate rather
queries as to what is the background of certain phrases in Murry's mind,
than a cavilling at the phrases themselves. We must be very careful to avoid
confusion (and in consequence heterodoxy) in the meanings of the term
'the Church' in different contexts. I can see what Murry means, I think,
but I want to be sure that he has the other meanings in his consciousness
too. For there is surely a sense, and that the most fundamental one, in
which the Church cannot be described as a 'grouping'? Certainly the
Communion of Saints is not correctly described as a 'group'.

Murry's second pair of questions I approve in themselves: I only query
their being the 'resolution' of the first pair.

I am very doubtful about the formulation at the bottom of p. 4. It
suggests rather an individual doctrine for Murry himself, than one
universally acceptable.

I am afraid of slipping into an anthropocentric version of Christianity,
of a pragmatist attitude which is so easy for the modern world to adopt
unconsciously – one which will forget that the first duty of the Christian is
Worship, or which will dissimulate the pessimistic view of this world which

Barthianism over-emphasises, but which seems to me an essential element in Catholicism just the same – that one has to be optimist and pessimist at once and in the extreme – happy and suffering: the tag which I keep as a reminder of what I fear we may tend to forget is the sentence of Pascal: *le Christ sera en agonie jusqu'à la fin du monde.*[1] And I feel that our effort will be lopsided if it is confined to *thinking* – even Christian thinking – and does not impose upon the members a further duty of devotions and even ascetic theology. I am always afraid of departmentalisation of the theologian, the ascetic, and the 'Christian sociologist'. This paragraph is not a criticism of Murry, but the statement of an anxiety which is not wholly dispelled by his notes.[2]

Yours ever,
[T. S. Eliot]

## TO *Robert Waller*

TS BL

22 April 1938                                  *The Criterion*

Dear Waller,

I should like to use the supplementary poem, 'Apology', which you sent me. I am having it set up, but I think there are two lines that could be improved. The fifth line is rather clumsy to speak, with the words 'welcomed' and 'unprisoned' coming so near together, and the meaning is not immediately clear. In the 10th line 'trees' sensual' (I presume that 'trees'' is in the possessive case) is an unpleasant combination of sibilants. I am sending the poem to press, but I should like you to consider these objections when it comes to correcting proof.[3]

Yours sincerely,
T. S. Eliot

1 – Blaise Pascal, *Les Pensées*: 'Le Mystère de Jésus': '*Jésus ~~est~~ sera en agonie jusqu'à la fin du monde. It ne fault pas dormier pendant ce temps-là.*'
2 – See Appendix for TSE's response to JMM's paper 'Towards a Christian Theory of Society', read at the second meeting of the Moot, 23–6 Sept. (see Clements, *Faith on the Frontier*, 371).
3 – 'Apology', C. 17 (July 1938), 678.

TO *Ezra Pound*                                            MS Beinecke

25 April 1938                          Blue Star Line

Now, podesta, it is time the Old Possum had a rest, after workin like a nigger all the winter on behalf of you & everybody else – so Whale is takin over for a bit, and if you want a holiday join me in ole Lisboa at the Hotel Aviz, but let me know you are a comin c/o Secretariado da Propaganda Nacional that's where I work, so come and brush up yr Camões.[1] Yrs etc.
                                          TP


TO *Geoffrey Faber*                                        MS Valerie Eliot

4 May 1938                             Aviz Hotel, Avenida Fontes,
                                       Lisboa, Portugal

Dear Geoffrey,

    In case the railway disaster at Viana do Castelho was reported (which I doubt) this will inform you that we only arrived at the crossing ten minutes afterwards, while the victims – some of them – were being scraped off the locomotive. We have had a rapid tour of the North: rapid because one is rushed through a town or a monastery, so as to have time for a lunch of 2½ hours. The diet would suit Frank, as there is much meat & very little vegetable. A lunch of 9 courses, 6 of which are meat, is a pleasantry once, but a torture when repeated regularly. And the only thing I have baulked at was pork chops from a special kind of pig – a '*specialité de la region*' – which is fed on fish to give it a peculiar flavour. The fish is excellent, as soon as you get used to the seasoning, which makes it taste putrid. Another cause of fatigue is being asked every 15 minutes whether you are enjoying yourself. I must give you a detailed account later of the scenes at the Festa do Trabalho, attended by several Spanish generals. The company of the French & Swiss members is a great support.[2] The

---

1 – On 2 May, EP sent FVM this limerick – 'the larst epode', as he called it:
    When Possum went to Portugal
    Twas thought he wd/ debauch a gal
    But the juicy young red
    Who divided his bed
    Found this thoughts purely theological.
2 – In addition to TSE, the jury comprised the French writer Jacques de Lacretelle (1888–1985) and the Swiss writer Robert de Traz (1884–1951). Two other judges, who were not able to be present in Lisbon, were the Italian Massimo Bontempelli (1878–1960) and the German playwright Hanns Johst (1890–1978), a committed Nazi and sometime President of the German Academy of Writers.

hospitality is overwhelming, & I don't know how I can survive another week of it. Today is a day of rest, & we are permitted to eat light food. I arrive in London, D.V., on the 15th or 16th via Southampton.

Yrs –
TP.

TO *John Hayward*                                                    MS King's

4 May 1938                          Aviz Hotel

Dear John

I shall have to report

1. The Festival at Viana do Castelho, attended by several Spanish generals.
2. Diner dans un restaurant typique de Viana.
3. Porguguese cuisine, including a special regional delicacy, pork fed on fish.
4. The beauties of Batalha, Coimbra, & Tomar.
5. Still to come: feast at Estoril with Portuguese intellectuals, and feast of reception to Gonzague de Reynold.[1]

I hope to be back on the 15th. I met Selby by accident, at Alcobaça. I have no news from Europe. Let me have enclosure back when we meet.

TP.

---

1–Gonzague de Reynold (1880–1970), a Swiss writer, was the winner of the 1937 Prémio Camões for his book *Portugal* (Paris: Éditions Spes, 1936).

Reinaldo Silva makes this claim: 'Before even accepting to sit on the jury of this literary prize, Eliot was fascinated with the personality and beliefs of the author of *Portugal*' ('T. S. Eliot and the Prémio Camões: A Brief Honeymoon and Anointment of Portuguese Fascist Politics', *Yeats Eliot Review* 26: 2 [Summer 2009], 18).

Silva writes further of Reynold and his book, p. 19: '[T]he Christian, authoritarian – but not totalitarian – State he envisaged could only be found in Portugal. Since 1935, he regarded Salazar's regime as a beacon and Salazar as the only politican in contemporary Europe capable of bringing about a European regeneration. Reynold's views in Portugal undoubtedly made Eliot realize that he was not the only one in Europe who was actually afraid of atheist politics . . . Throughout the book, Reynold praises Salazar's authoritarian regime. To him, Salazar was a savior who, through his perseverance and austere politics, placed Portugal once again on the path of development and international recognition . . . The other major reason why he chose to write about Portugal was that Salazar's *Estado Novo* (New State) inaugurated in 1926, was a Christian State and that it was radically different from Mussolini's fascist politics, Hitler's Nazi ideology, or even Russia's Bolshevism . . . Reynold maintains that the nation's revolution on 26 May 1926 brought a new direction to Portugal and that Salazar established order, financial prosperity, and morality. To him, Salazar was not a dictator because he did not seize power through violent means . . . Reynold

10 May 1938                          Aviz Hotel

À Signaler:

1. The mechanical bidet in my bathroom. It is fascinating.
2. My radio-diffusion last night, ending with the words: VIVA PORTUGAL.
3. Tea this afternoon with Sna. de Oliveira Reis.
4. Grand reception to night chez les Ferro.
5. Grand dîner tomorrow night to meet the Portuguese intellectuals.[1]
6. Grand dîner Thursday in honour of Gonzague de Reynold.
7. Départ de Lisbonne.

I am beginning to like the nasty soup. You must meet the Lacretelles in London (he knows the Margérys).[2] He is slick and superficial I suspect, but intelligent, & well-bred as foreigners go.

The English here seem very dull. Actually, the Portuguese are much the nicest people in Lisbon.

We have *not* been taken to see a bull-fight. Or Salazar.

TP.

---

notes Salazar's Catholic upbringing and states that even if Salazar admired Mussolini's fascist program, the differences between both – and even Hitler – are astounding.'

1 – See António Ferro, 'O Primeiro Júri do Prémio Camões', *Prémios Literários (1934–1947)* (Lisbon, 1950), 63–9.

Reinaldo Silva writes ('T. S. Eliot and the *Prémio Camões*', 20–1): 'Without a doubt, the banquet speech [by Ferro, Director of the Portuguese Secretariado da Propaganda Nacional] delivered in French the day before (11 May 1938) at the fancy Tavares Restaurant [. . .] to honor the members of the jury is very illustrative of fascist propaganda. Furthermore, the regime later used this event to convince both the Portuguese citizens and foreigners that Salazar's government was respectable and credible since a group of prominent European intellectuals travelled from so far away to attest to it . . . To attest to this interest, Ferro notes that Reynold's book had to compete with three additional works, namely: Stefan Zweig's *Magalhães*; Sieburg's *Novo Portugal*; and Lautenzach's *Portugal*.

'After these introductory remarks, Ferro addresses each member of the jury . . .

'When speaking to Eliot . . . Ferro notes the performance of *Murder in the Cathedral* in a London theatre for two consecutive years and states that Eliot is a "pure poet" who does not "forgive prose-writing." Eliot had become a literary critic so as to criticize the moral degradation in fiction. Eliot, notes Ferro, cannot tolerate "moral degradation, the part of the devil in the world of the spirit." Moreover, Eliot cannot even "acknowledge that a book is well written when it wallows in the mire, when the breath of poetry does not air it out and elevates [*sic*] it" (66; my [Silva's] translation). That is why, notes Ferro, Eliot writes so harshly about D. H. Lawrence's books, which he considers "splendid and extremely badly written." That is why, notes Ferro, Eliot applies a *coup de grace* to the author of *Lady Chatterley's Lover*, a novel where the protagonists regress to a fundamental and repulsive primitivism.'

2 – Jacques de Lacretelle (1888–1985), novelist: elected to the Académie Française in Nov. 1936.

TO *Delia Christian Craig*                                                CC

Dear Madam,

I find your letter of April 8th, on returning from abroad, and feel that it requires an answer.[1] I do not, as a rule, care to take part in collective manifestoes on political subjects by literary folk, most of whom are incompetent to judge the rights and wrongs of the matters. The short communication by me which you read was not intended for publication, and was only an attempt to excuse myself politely, to the lady who wrote to me, from taking part. Had I intended it for publication I should have written differently: I was very much surprised to see it in print. The 'sympathy' offered was sympathy only with the good intentions of the persons involved, and not with anything else.

My own views on the matter of the Spanish conflict are very close to those of my friend M. Jacques Maritain, which he has expounded in the *Nouvelle Revue Française* and at greater length in the preface to a book by Senor Mendizabal.

Yours very truly,<br>[T. S. Eliot]

1–Craig wrote from Melbourne, Australia: 'Some time ago I discovered, in one of our Australian newspapers, a reprint of your sentiments (among other writers) regarding the Civil War in Spain . . . Reading your opinion of the war in Spain I have been both surprised and pained. I will quote your words as printed – "While naturally sympathetic to the Government of Spain, I think it best that at least a few men of letters should remain isolated." This was under the heading of Neutral – but the opinion was nonetheless expressed.

'Now, Mr Eliot, I am going to speak plainly and beg you to excuse me and take it in good part, for it is no light matter. Do you realize what you are saying when you are "naturally sympathetic" to the Spanish "Government"? The Church of St Thomas, the Catholic church, is fighting against that Government today just as it fought in the person of St Thomas the Erastianism of Henry II in Twelfth century England.

'It is no use quibbling the point. Russia, i.e. Bolshevism, is behind the Spanish "Government", & we know what that means. If you refuse to see this, are you more honest, more sincere than the four murderous knights whose casuistry you paint [in *MiC*] with such unforgettable satire? Perhaps you would argue that Fascism is behind General Franco – (and why Franco is automatically wrong & his antagonists automatically right is rather above my comprehension) – even so, it pains me that you should be "*naturally* sympathetic" to a system of Government which you so bitterly decry in another land. If you expect to be taken as a sincere thinker as well as a poetic genius, how can you contradict yourself in so flagrant a manner? How you ever thought of the harm you may do by the prejudice you express? For prejudice pure and simple it must be against the unfortunate Spanish Catholics. After all they have as much & far greater right to govern Spain with the Faith of their ancestors than the upholders of the recent insidious régime. Is it fair to persist in old-fashioned bogies of the Inquisition?'

TO *Stephen Spender*                                                    CC

19 May 1938                        [*The Criterion*]

Dear Stephen,

I have just got back from Lisbon and your letter of the 17th to de la Mare has been handed to me.¹ Goronwy Rees² doesn't seem to have said anything about the translation of Buchner's play to Faber, but he is away ill at the moment so I am not sure. Anyway, we should always be interested in anything to which your name was attached. But I must confess that I was unable to enlighten the Committee about *Dantons Tod*. Could you tell us more about the play? If it is in verse, so much the better; but we would like to know a good deal about it in order to come to a decision.³

                          Yours ever affectionately,
                          [Tom]


TO *Virginia Woolf*                                              TS Sussex

21 May 1938                        *The Criterion*

Dear Virginia,

On arriving back from Portugal – bearing triumphantly a large three volume History of the Colonisation of Brazil, in Portuguese, weighing something over a hundredweight, and flatteringly inscribed to me by the Minister of Education, Exmo. Senhor Pacheco⁴ – I was told that Mrs Woolf was on the telephone, and had been ringing up constantly. Judge then of my chagrin, on discovering that it was the Wrong Mrs Wolfe – or one of the Wrong Mrs Wolves. But it is a pretext for writing to apprize you of my return. The immediate future is dark: I have to go to Salisbury (at Richmond's command, of course) to chat to the locals about George Herbert: and next week I have to to to <stet>⁵ Truro and to Penzance to

1–SS to RdlM, 17 May: 'I do not know whether Goronwy Rees has approached Faber yet with the proposal that he should publish the translation of Buchner's Dantons Tod which Rees & I are doing for the Group Theatre's next production; if Faber is publishing it, it might be worth while to advertise the fact by inserting a slip in the new edition of Trial of A Judge, as an advertisement both for the book & the production.'
2–Goronwy Rees (1909–79), Welsh writer and academic.
3–*Danton's Death: A Play* by Georg Büchner, trans. SS and Goronwy Rees (F&F: 1939).
4–The presentation set of *Historia da Colonizacao Portuguesa do Brasil* (1921–4) was given to the London Library by TSE In Feb. 1943.
5–This marginal 'stet' is in TSE's hand; he has also dotted the corresponding proofreading marks '_ _ _ _' under 'to to to'.

distribute prizes to the boys and the girls respectively of the Methodist persuasion.[1] But I hope that the Right Mrs Woolf is well and that I may see her soon, perhaps for a Cup of Tea. And also I wish to thank you in person for representing me (as well as yourself) at Ottoline's funeral.[2]

Affectionately,

TP

## TO *D. L. Murray*[3]

23 May 1938                                [Faber & Faber Ltd]

Dear Mr Murray,

I must apologise for the delay in answering your letter of May the 12th,[4] but I have only just returned from Lisbon and have had to deal

---

1 – See further E. H. Magson (Headmaster, Truro School) to TSE, 16 June 1938: 'Some of the Senior boys have asked whether it would be possible to have the manuscript of your Speech so that it may be printed in the School Magazine. The Press report was very inadequate, and they would like to study it again at leisure . . .

'We had a great time on Speech Day, and it may interest you to know that your remarks on the need for continuous development in religious thought and belief were made the basis of the next sermon in the School Chapel, by our Second Master.'

'On Christianity and a Useful Life' was printed in *The Truronian*, Dec. 1938, 2–9: see *CProse* 5.

2 – VW responded to this letter on 26 May: 'Whichever Woolf it was, it wasnt this Woolf; but now it is this Woolf – which sounds like a passage from the works of the inspired Miss Stein.

'This is only to say in soberer language, that we go away for Whitsun on Wednesday; would therefore suggest tea on Sunday next at 4.30; failing that, tea on Tuesday next . . .

'I'm longing I needn't say to hear how the visit to the water closet at Netherhampton [Sir Bruce Richmond's residence] went off . . . Yes, I murmured "I'm Mrs Woolf," at Ottolines funeral; then in a bold loud voice BUT I REPRESENT T. S. Eliot – the proudest moment of my life; passing, alas, like spring flowers' (*Letters*, 230–1).

However, VW had also commented in her diary, 26 Apr.: 'I must . . . go to Ott's memorial service, representing also T. S. Eliot at his absurd command' (*Diary* V, 135).

TSE did see VW again on the following Sun., 29 May: 'Tom came, most respectable; swallow tails & grey silk tie, having he explained to slip into his evening service in time to take round the plate – a churchwarden in South Kensington. Very friendly; & elaborate description of his triumphal progress through Portugal as Brit. Rep. on some prize giving commission. And then he spoke at Salisbury on George Herbert, in aid of the Cathedral, staying with the Richmonds. I was amused at the careful analysis he gave Juliette . . . of his own play's failure, & of Priestley's artistic nonentity, scupulously, painfully conscientious in detail; with his wild hazel eyes' (*Diary* V, 146).

3 – D. L. Murray (1888–1962): editor of the *TLS*, 1937–45.

4 – 'I realise that you have probably no leisure for doing book reviews in these days, but I am wondering whether we might not hope some time to have an article of yours under your signature.

with many arrears. It gives me much pleasure to feel that you would like me to contribute occasionally to the *Literary Supplement*, and I should be glad to retain a connection of which I have always been proud. It is true that I have less and less time for critical journalism. Nevertheless, I am glad to feel that the columns of the Supplement will occasionally be open to me for an article. I presume, of course, that you mean unsigned leaders such as I have had pleasure in writing in the past, because a great deal of the pleasure as well as of the discipline which I have derived from writing for the Supplement has been due to its anonymity. I have only one article in mind at present, and that is not due until 1946. I had much rather, when the time comes, that R. W. Chambers wrote it instead of myself, as he can do it very much better. But if any more timely ideas occur to me, I will certainly suggest them to you.

Many thanks,
Yours sincerely,
[T. S. Eliot]

## TO *John Cournos*                                                CC

27 May 1938                    [*The Criterion*]

Dear John,

I have been several weeks in Lisbon, hence the delay in answering your letter of 19 April.[1] I am truly sorry to hear of your further disasters: you seem indeed to be a descendant of the man who had seen affliction.[2] And as the Russian Periodicals are so few and irregular, I should be glad to have some other kind of contribution from you. The American periodicals I cannot honourably tamper with at present, as I have only recently put them into the hands of a man who also needs all of such meagre support

---

'If you had any ideas for articles of about 2,000 to 2,500 words which you might think suitable for our columns I can only say that we should be very proud to have the offer of them.'

1 – 'A series of fatalities during the past six months has almost landed me on the "sidewalk" ... In any event, not in a position to pay the rent where I have been and am (for the moment), I don't yet know where I shall settle for good ... [I]t has occurred [to me] that you may be willing to let me do the American periodicals for you (in addition to the Russian). I am on the spot ...

'Occasionally, too, there may be an opportunity for an American chronicle, covering books, etc. Let me hear about this too.

'I hope I may be forgiven for having been born under an ill star!'

2 – *Lamentations* 3: 1: 'I am the man that hath seen affliction by the rod of his wrath.'

as the *Criterion* can supply. But it has occurred to me that possibly the *American Chronicle*, which was once done by Gilbert Seldes, and which has fallen into desuetude for a long time, might very well be revived by you. What do you say to this? You have read, I presume, some of the other Chronicles which appear in the *Criterion* from France, Italy and Germany, and you know that a good deal of latitude is allowed in treating of the contemporary intellectual situation in each country according to local conditions and their form at the moment. It is not quite so remunerative as doing the periodicals, because it involves much less drudgery in the way of reading, but from the point of view of the *Criterion* is of considerable importance.

If this appeals to you, I will write again and suggest a date for a Chronicle.

> Yours ever,
> [Tom]

## TO *António Ferro*[1]          CC

27 May 1938                [Faber & Faber Ltd]

Cher monsieur et ami,

All the preoccupations which I was so happy to put aside, for the sake of spending three weeks in your country, have encompassed me since my return, and I have been obliged to wait until now, for the hour to devote to trying to frame an adequate expression of recognition and gratitude to Portugal, to the Secretariado, and especially to yourself and Madame Ferro.

In retrospect of three weeks of intellectual and aesthetic interest in most congenial society, permit me to felicitate you first on the perfection of the organisation of everything connected with the award of the Camoes Prize, and with the entertainment of the Members of the Jury. I am sure that the others must have been as much impressed as was I, with the efficiency of the organisation; and that they must furthermore have carried away with them, as did I, permanent memories of the generous, thoughtful and

---

1 – António Ferro (1895–1956), Portuguese writer, journalist, politician – author of *Viagem à Volta das Ditaduras* ('Journey round the Dictatorships', 1927) and *Salazar: o Homem e a Obra* ('Salazar: The Man and his Work', 1927; eventually published in revised translation as *Salazar: Portugal and Her Leader* [F&F, 1939]) – was a firm supporter of the authoritarian regime of António de Oliveira Salazar (1889–1970), Prime Minister of Portugal, 1932–68. Ferro served as Director of the Secretariado de Propaganda Nacional.

cordial hospitality of our hosts – as well as of the great beauty of your country, the charm of its people, and the strength of an enlightened and far-seeing Government. And the impressions of respect and admiration for Dr Salazar, formed by reading, were confirmed by having the privilege of meeting him.[1]

I look forward to seeing you and Madame Ferro, at an early date, in London. Incidentally, I may say that the officials of the Natural History Museum – an institution which has had a long connexion with the University of Coimbra, and is now collaborating on a catalogue of the flora of Angola – would be very pleased to see you.

And may I, in closing, remind you of our interest in receiving very soon your new preface and your proofs!

With most grateful memories,
Yours very sincerely,
[T. S. Eliot]

1 – TSE was later to recall of his brief meeting with Dr Salazar in Lisbon that he 'has never encouraged the adoption of the "Leader Principle," and no leader has ever won his position with less personal ambition, or less appeal to mass emotion. Nor did he rise to power through a "party." He simply happens to be the ablest statesman in Portugal, all the more distinguished by never appearing in a uniform or wearing a decoration. He looks what he is by profession, a university professor: but a very brief meeting with him gave me the impression of a university professor who is also an extremely acute judge of men. His interest and importance for us is that without being in any dubious political sense pro-clerical he is a Christian at the head of a Christian country' (*The Christian News-Letter* 42 (14 Aug. 1940): *CProse* 6, 108–9).

TO *Merrill Moore*[1]                    TS John Hay Library, Brown University

27 May 1938

Dear Dr Moore,

Thank you very much for your letter of 30 April, which gave me much pleasure and amusement.[2] I should be interested to hear whether the patients who submitted themselves to this discipline are being kept under observation with a view to discovering whether they have suffered any permanent ill effects from making use of my verse in this way.

With best wishes to yourself and Mrs Moore,

Yours sincerely,

[T. S. Eliot]

1 – Merrill Moore (1903–57), poet and psychiatrist, was educated at Vanderbilt University where he joined the circle called 'Fugitives' (including Allen Tate, Robert Penn Warren and John Crowe Ransom) and contributed sonnets and other short poems to the *Fugitive*, 1922–5; he also edited *Fugitives: An Anthology of Verse* (1927). He studied medicine and psychiatry at Vanderbilt Medical School, and in 1929 moved to Boston where he specialised in neuropathology and psychiatry – one of his later patients was Robert Lowell, about whom he was to correspond with TSE. Author of innumerable sonnets (he would write sonnets every day of his life), his publications include *The Noise that Time Makes* (1929), *M: A Thousand Autobiographical Sonnets* (1938); and contributions to scientific journals: he was an authority on alcoholism and suicide. FVM told the publisher Donald Brace, 15 Feb. 1935: 'Eliot has a great respect for Merrill Moore, and I have been gaining one by reading the new sonnets, *Six Sides to a Man* [1935]. But we have got a heavy deck load of poetry ahead of us . . . Will he understand that it is no disrespect if we feel we cannot make an offer for this book?'

2 – 'I thought you might be interested and possibly amused at this little fragment. In Harvard College I have a student friend who is much interested in hypnosis. He has gone to work and has written a thesis on the subject entitled, "The Recall Ability in Hypnosis". This has been done with the Department of Psychology . . . He just did a splendid job involving an extraordinarily interesting experiment. The experiment consisted as follows. (1) Patients were taught to learn perfectly (that is memorize) seventeen lines of "Murder in the Cathedral". They were then shown some motion pictures. They were then subjected to light hypnosis. Then they were tested for their ability to recall under hypnosis the poem.

'They were tested for casual, immediate, and longer recall. The results were extremely interesting when compared with a group of non-hypnotized patients.

'The thesis is very interesting and of definite scientific value but most interesting was the fact that your poem was used (on my suggestion) as part of the subject matter of the scientific experiment. I hope you do not mind such abuse of your gift.'

TO *Richard Fuchs*[1]                                                    CC

30 May 1938                        [Faber & Faber Ltd]

My dear Sir,

I must apologize for my delay in answering your letter of 25 April, but my secretary explained to you that I was abroad for some time after it arrived.[2] I am very much pleased that you should have been interested to set to music *A Song for Simeon*, and can understand its special appeal to you. I must explain that I have no particular standing amongst musical circles in England, but if you will let me see a copy of the score I shall be very glad to consult musical friends, and see what could be done about getting a performance in England. It seems to me possible that the Broadcasting Association might be interested.

With many thanks, and best wishes,
Yours very truly,
[T. S. Eliot]

1–Richard Fuchs (1887–1947), German Jewish architect and composer from Karlsruhe, Baden, fought with high patriotic valour in the First World War (he was at the Battle of the Somme and at other engagements, and was awarded the Iron Cross for his four years on the Western Front). After studying at the Karlsruhe University of Applied Sciences, where he earned his doctorate in architecture, he pursued a successful practice as an architect; and his musical compositions – symphonies, chamber music, choral works and songs – enjoyed recognition in Jewish circles. But from 1933 he was increasingly subjected to Nazi persecution; and in Nov. 1938 he was arrested and despatched to Dachau concentration camp. However, his wife produced for the authorities a New Zealand visa and immigrant permit that had been secured for them, and happily Fuchs was released: the family left Germany for New Zealand, via the UK, on 26 Dec. 1938. For the remainder of his life he worked as an architect in New Zealand, though his music was still neglected. His papers are in the Alexander Turnbull Library, Wellington. See further: www.richardfuchs.org.nz/publications/Fuchsbiography.pdf.

2–Fuchs wrote on 25 Apr. 1938 to introduce himself as a composer well known in Jewish circles. He had won first prize in a competition with the choral work 'Jewish Fate' – 'but of course there is no possibility to get it performed in Germany'.

Recently he felt inspired to set TSE's 'A Song for Simeon' for bass and orchestra. 'The words you found for yonder old man in the gospel must in a strange and undivined sense produce an answer and echo in the very soul and heart of a man, who is forced to bear at our days the mediaeval Jewish fate to be homeless in his own country and to have lost perhaps all possibility to work for wife and children henceforth. Imagine how a modern Ahasuerus must feel your poetical words!'

He hoped TSE might help him to get the work performed in England, and would be happy to let TSE see a copy of the score, or at least the piano-score. He hoped to hear back soon.

'As my elder daughter is at school near London I would in any case like to come to England during the next months.'

Fuchs managed to visit England during June 1938.

## TO *Hamilton Marr*

30 May 1938                    [Faber & Faber Ltd]

Dear Mr Marr,

   In reply to your letter of the 27th[1] I have pleasure in authorising Mr Geoffrey Tandy's broadcast of five unpublished poems on 25 June, at a fee of two guineas for the reading of each poem.[2] I am not sure that I like the title which Mr Tandy appears to have given to this future reading, but no doubt I can arrange that privately with him in good time.

                              Yours sincerely,
                              [T. S. Eliot]


## TO *Enid Faber*

TS Valerie Eliot

31 May 1938                    *The Criterion*

Dear Enid,

   Well this is very cheering etc. and portends well. That you should write to me so early about the summer, if there is a summer, and may it come soon. Whether it means

   a) What an Honour to ask Dr Eliot    OR

   b) We must ask Pore Ole Possum, better get it settled –

that's all One to me, so long as I may look Forward to the Hospitality of Tugglungairyon (Portuguese phonetics).


1 – The Tandy broadcast was to be entitled 'Jellicle and Other Cats', at a fee of two guineas for the reading of each poem.

2 – It appears that on 24 June 1938, Marr circulated at the BBC a minute regretting the 'high' fees that TSE was demanding for his poems. However, a later Internal Circulating Memo (author unknown), dated 7 Oct. 1938, entered this more qualified judgement: 'At the time it was written the Programme Copyright Section were experiencing a great deal of difficulty with Faber & Faber over Eliot's work in that very high rates were being asked, and consequently there was the natural fear that easy agreement to them would affect the rates for verse generally. The position now is that the attitude is much more reasonable and there need be no hesitation in considering Eliot's works for inclusion in programmes. He is, however, capricious and might easily ask for an exceptionally high fee in respect of a work that, for the time being, he valued highly. We should, in that event, be very glad to have the co-operation of the Programme department concerned to the extent of considering the deletion of the item in question. A firm attitude about fees has never yet proved to be of any permanent disadvantage to programmes.

   'I am sorry that the easier position regarding Eliot's works was not subsequently made known, but you will observe that Mr Marr's memo of the 24th June did not ask for the complete exclusion of the poems from programmes.'

Well. I suppose the Summer begins towards the end of July, though you don't say: but I am sure that I could fit in a week or so well before the 12th August. Or, if it happened to suit you better to have me later, I could come any time from the 25th August on. But the beginning of August would suit me quite well, so long as I dont have to leave London on the Saturday before Bank Holiday, which I did last year (not your doing) and don't want to do it again.

Is this Clear? I hope, as you says yourself, that this is intelligible. The point being that I am so Tormented by the speeches I have to make to the Methodist children in Cornwall on Friday (I suppose I shall have to eat meat with them) and by getting a letter saying 'don't talk more than twenty minutes' and a telegram saying 'talk up to forty minutes' and what with talking about George Herbert at Salisbury last Thursday and being introduced by the Bp. as 'Mr Herbert': that I can't really talk sense for another week or so.

Yr. grateful but afflicted

TP.

## TO *Susan Hinkley*

TS Houghton

6 June 1938                     *The Criterion*

Dear Aunt Susie,

Your letter arrived while I was away in Lisbon, and since my return I have been very busy with chores – that is to say, works of benevolence in the way of speeches; so that I am badly in arrears with personal correspondence. I congratulate you with all my heart on your first great-grand-daughter, and Eleanor on her namesake. (I had a letter from Susan in which she said that she now had five nephews as well as a niece – surely this is an overstatement – or am I that much behindhand?)[1] I look forward to seeing Barbara and Roger[2] this summer, but wish still more that you and Eleanor could come. My own plans cannot be fixed. I had hoped to get over in the autumn, and it is still possible; but I shall not know until August, perhaps, whether and when I shall be free to leave London; and by that time it may be difficult to secure a passage until late in the year.

1 – The young Susan Wolcott had announced to TSE on 15 May 1938: 'P.P.S. did you know my sister Barbie had a daughter on May 4th.

'P.P.P.S. her name is Eleanor.

'P.P.P.P.S. now I have five nephews and one niece.'

2 – TSE's cousin Barbara Hinkley and her husband Roger Wolcott, from Boston.

That notice about Harry Child's marriage sounds very odd. I may hear the details eventually from the Clements.

Always your affectionate nephew,<br>Tom

Did the Bloods ever live in Ireland? The only Bloods I have ever come across came from Ireland.

## TO *C. M. Grieve*

TS Edinburgh University

8 June 1938       *The Criterion*

Dear Mr Grieve,

You will have to understand that my delay in writing to you about 'Mature Art' was due to my absence abroad. I tackled it on my return, and I must say that it seems to me an extremely interesting, individual, and indeed very remarkable piece of work. There can be no doubt that it is something that ought to be published, but the question is how, and by whom. For in the first place, any publisher who undertook it ought to have the courage and conviction to be prepared to publish the whole poem when it is complete.

I am sorry that I cannot get my colleagues to consider undertaking a work in verse of this size. I cannot afford to lose much money for them on poetry. You will understand that to say frankly that a book of poetry is going to make a considerable loss for its publisher is no criticism of its value: it may even be a compliment. But while I can sometimes urge them to publish a small book of verse which I know will lose money, I cannot ask them to tie up so much capital in anything so monumental as this. I would like to see it published, and I would be willing to give my personal support, for what it is worth, if you approached some other firm. Until hearing from you, as the manuscript is large and the distance great, I will keep it here for further orders.

Yours very sincerely,<br>T. S. Eliot

TO *Ian Cox*                                          CC

16 June 1938                    [Faber & Faber Ltd]

Dear Cox,

I have just had a visit from a rather touching German Jew named Dr Richard Fuchs, who is over here for a short time, and who had written to me about this matter before arriving in England.[1] He has produced an orchestral setting of *A Song for Simeon*, which is intended to be accompanied by a bass voice singing the words in English or German. He would very much like, of course, to have this produced in England, and what I want to know is how I can get it read by the right person at the BBC. He tells me that the whole setting would take about 15 minutes to perform. I have the score here, but as I am now completely incapable of reading music, and should not be a very good judge even if I could, I am wholly in the dark as to the nature and value of this composition. But as he has appealed to me – his only claim being that he has chosen to set to music a poem of mine, which appeals to him for obvious reasons – I feel that I ought to do what I can for him. I shall be very grateful if you can tell me how I ought to proceed to get this score read by the right person at the BBC.

                           Yours ever,
                           [T. S. Eliot]

1 – Having met up with Dr Fuchs, TSE had arranged a second appointment to hear his setting of 'Song of Solomon' as performed on a piano; but Fuchs could not make the meeting.

'Unfortunately I could not remain in London, the whole situation is always so difficult for us with respect to the financial troubles as you know. I hope we will hear soon of the B.B.C. about the possibility of performing the work . . .

'In the meantime our whole situation [in Germany] is once more turning so badly that I must think to come out as soon as possible . . .

'I confess to be ashamed to force you to deal with such troubles and I must apologize – perhaps you may understand how care-worn I must needs be, I have indeed no other idea but how to come away.'

TO *Reginald Tribe*[1]                                         CC

Dear Father Reginald,

You have a very difficult task, and I doubt my capacity to give much help.[2] I do not think that the picture of the Oxford Conference suggested by Demant's report is at all too sombre. A large group of individuals – too large a group – most of whom did not previously know each other, and most of whom, I think, had little knowledge of any theological tradition except their own, were given a week in which to find a formula: a week in which a good deal of time was necessarily wasted by performers on hobby-horses. I do not want to appear to take a wholly gloomy view, because I think that a good deal might be accomplished more slowly by meetings of select groups from selected churches. I annoyed some of my American friends by saying, in a letter to *The Church Times*, that there were too many Americans: I thought at the time that I was perhaps in a better position to put this unpleasant fact than anybody else. But it might be put differently by saying that too many bodies were represented, some of which did not seem to have any living theology at all.

I quite agree that the question of Christian social action, except on occasions for which nothing more is required than a common *negation* of protest against something that is happening, is dependent upon theology. And confusion ensued not merely from the differences of theological background, but also from the differences in the way in which the social

1 – The Revd Reginald Tribe, SSM (1881–1943) – a sometime consulting gynaecologist – was Director of the Society of the Sacred Mission, 1925–43: 'a professional Anglo-Catholic . . . one of the founders and a leading light in the Anglo-Catholic Summer School of Sociology. Sociology had a wider sense then: as Tribe himself wrote "Every Act of Parliament . . . is an act of practical sociology." His book, *The Christian Social Tradition* (SPCK, 1935), deals with political and economic questions, but much more cautiously than the Catholic Crusade' (Mason, 173, 181).

2 – Tribe wrote on 4 June: 'I am chairman of the Research Ctee of that sprawling jellyfish – the Christian Social Council . . . Demant brought to our ctee this very penetrating & stimulating document on Theological problems . . . He has not time to revise, & the ctee with no very clear notion of its purpose asked me to revise it. I gave an unwilling consent . . . but I jib. I think I can see some sort of purpose for the thing, as set out in my preamble to the outline, which I enclose.

'What I want from you is this. You were at Oxford, & I was not. Do you think Demant's is a fair critique of things theological there. I am wondering [whether] he has seen shadows & rifts that were not there, especially in view of the tendenciousness he always shows against "humanitarian liberalism" . . .

'You will see that I have used only a very small amount of Demant's stuff. But I don't want to plant it on the C.S.C. if it is not right.'

problem appears in different countries. The effort to find a common formulation of Christian action for all countries, instead of resulting in the abstraction of principles of universal application, led simply to an obsession with totalitarianism. That is to say, English and American delegates were in danger of taking the line of the average Englishman or American towards a situation existing in other countries, rather than taking the line of Christians towards situations in their own countries. Hence a certain unreality about much of the discussion.

An important question which I do not think was adequately explored, is the question whether a 'Christian sociology' is possible at all; and if so, what are its limits. It seemed to me that only very few of the persons present at Oxford had threshed their own beliefs and social emotions sufficiently to know what was the result of their Christian faith, and what was the result of their heredity and environment. There was a strong prejudice, which I fear was no more than a prejudice, in favour of 'democracy'. And with the exception of the few extreme Lutherans, it seemed to me that the content (during the sessions at least) of most of the minds was this-worldly. I mean, that in the context of the occasion, people seemed to forget that what happens to a man after death is more important than what happens to him in his life.

Now I am not sure that Demant himself has wholly thought out the possible limits of meaning of the term 'Christian sociology'.

I do not know how your C. S. C. is composed, but I take it, from the addition of a note by Garvie, that it is interdenominational. That makes the task very difficult.

I agree very strongly about the Church speaking 'in the indicative'; also that the first need is to re-unite the fractured truths and expel the fractional errors (equally important, and perhaps more difficult, because error is frequently less explicit than truth) – in short that the need is for theology, though I confess I do not like the connotations of the adjective 'synthetic'.

Incidentally, it is unfortunate that a man with so profound a mind as Demant should not be able to write better.

All this may be quite irrelevant and useless, so I offer it with humble apologies.

Yours very sincerely,
[T. S. Eliot]

TO *Michel Saint-Denis*                                                                                     CC

17 June 1938                                    [Faber & Faber Ltd]

Dear Mr Saint-Denis,

Your suggestion of a play about Oliver Cromwell is an interesting one, but who is going to write it?[1] If, of course, I can be of any use with suggestions I shall be delighted to talk the matter over with you, and you have only to ring up my secretary and let her know when you would like to come. But I haven't anybody in mind, and don't quite see what use I can be on this point.

Yours very sincerely,
[T. S. Eliot]

TO *H. D. C. Pepler*[2]                                                                                     CC

17 June 1938                                    [Faber & Faber Ltd]

My dear Pepler,

I have received back from you a revision of Mrs Mairet's book, but I confess that I am left in some perplexity.[3] As I no longer have the previous text, which has been, I believe, returned, I cannot make comparisons, but this seems to me essentially the same book, and certainly no longer.

I am afraid that I cannot have made our suggestions clear. What we had in mind as something that Mrs Mairet ought to do, was a much longer, quite exhaustive book on the whole subject of weaving, though of course from the point of view of an authority primarily interested in hand weaving. I was under the impression that you agreed with me that it was

1 – Michel Saint-Denis (Managing Director, London Theatre Studio) wrote on 13 June 1938: 'I happened to come across a play about Sir Thomas More and Thomas Cromwell. This seemed to me a very interesting subject for our time and it put into my mind that perhaps a play on Oliver Cromwell would arouse a lot of interest. But it ought to be treated in a broad way, according to the real conventions of the stage, instead of the rather naturalistic way in which the play I have been reading about Thomas More is written. That is only an idea, but I would be interested to talk with you about it.'
2 – Hilary Pepler (1878–1951), printer, writer, poet; founder of St Dominic's Press, *fl. c.* 1915–36. An associate of Eric Gill and G. K. Chesterton and Roman Catholic convert, he was co-founder (with Gill and Desmond Chute) of the community of craftsmen at Ditchling, Sussex, in 1920.
3 – Philip Mairet had written to TSE on 28 May: 'I see Faber's have announced another edition of Ethel Mairet's Vegetable Dyes: and I heard she was doing another, but we have been parted for a good many years now, you know. I certainly think she ought to do a book on Weaving.'

desirable that Mrs Mairet should write such a book, and that you would put our suggestion to her.

I do not wish to appear to be depreciating the virtues of the text which you have sent, but the book is very brief, and somewhat incoherent; and even for such a short book it seems to me that the arrangement of the matter is somewhat capricious. If Mrs Mairet is not prepared to consider a longer and more systematic book, we will consider this one on its merits, but I shall personally be keenly disappointed if this is all that we may ever expect from her.

With you let me know, therefore, what is Mrs Mairet's attitude?[1]

Sincerely yours,

[T. S. Eliot]

## TO *Henry S. Swabey*

TS Henry Swabey

17 June 1938 *The Criterion*

Dear Swabey,

I have been thinking about your letter of June 7th.[2] It is difficult, knowing nothing about the personnel at Chichester, or the curriculum, to know how much is wrong with it, or to what extent you are looking for something which it may be rather your business to bring with you. Certainly, I do not suppose that anybody is likely to acquire, by stopping in a theological college, the convictions that he has not brought with him. In any sort of college or university, one expects surely to get merely certain things, information or knowledge, that one cannot do without: and beyond that one is fortunate if one finds a very few persons there who have the root of the matter in them.[3] I should, I confess, feel more

1 – See Ethel Mairet, *Hand-weaving To-day: Traditions and Changes* (F&F, 1944).
2 – Swabey wrote from the Theological College, Chichester: 'I have two charges to bring against Chichester. In the first place, there is a lack of moral drive. "The Church has no revelation for society". "But surely, that's not our business." Get the people to mass and confession, and the evil world can do them no further harm . . . And what is the use of a church that manifests the seven deadly sins severally if it has no message for society; if, that is, it does not drive against social injustice?

'Secondly: Who'd be a celibate? The homosexual type. And are these the right men to instruct the laity? Excellent for knocking all morals out of religion, and leaving an aesthetic-intellectual skeleton . . .

'These are not charges against individuals or the college, but against tendencies that I have induced from many cases. A priestly therefore is not substitute for moral effort! I hope this theological news is not depressing, but you asked me if I was satisfied.'
3 – 'But ye should say, Why persecute we him, seeing the Root of the matter is found in me?' (Job 12: 28).

unqualified sympathy with your revolt against social deadness, if it wasn't coupled so oddly with a protest against celibacy. For one thing, you are not compelled to remain unmarried, in the Church of England; and I ought not to need to remark that the 'homosexual type' hardly makes the best celibate: though I dare say that if one is homosexual (that is, of a feeble or incomplete sexuality) it is very easy to imagine that one has a vocation for celibacy. But to deny that celibacy is the highest ideal (however few people may be fitted to practise it) seems to me to be in a very bad spiritual muddle. I am really wondering whether you are called to be a priest at all! Not that I want to shake anybody's determination: only I can't imagine anybody making such a serious decision without a great deal of self-examination.

Sincerely yours,<br>
T. S. Eliot

## TO *Anne Bradby*

MS Anne Ridler

18 June 1938                    *The Criterion*

Dear Miss Bradby

After deep thought on the subject of wedding presents,[1] it still seems to me that this is the most useful form. People are always given so many things that they don't want (and changing them is such a nuisance, & has its limits of possibility) and are always left without so many things that they *need*, that I think they should have some opportunities to choose for themselves. So perhaps you will put down in the list of presents: 'From Mr T. S. Eliot, three rolls of lino, several pyrex dishes, and a few curtain rods'.

With most heartfelt wishes for your happiness,

Yours very sincerely,<br>
T. S. Eliot

1–Anne Bradby was to marry Vivian Ridler on 2 July 1938.

## TO *Nevill Coghill*                                               cc

22 June 1938                                    [*The Criterion*]

Dear Coghill,

It is only be accident that I find in the *Oxford Magazine* an article which
interests me, and as your name is appended to it, I am writing to you.[1]
I say by accident, because that periodical is so dreary and conventional
that most weeks I hardly open it. I liked very much what you said, and
if you should ever care to deliver yourself at more length on this or a
kindred subject, I should be glad if you would keep the *Criterion* in mind.

Yours sincerely,<br>[T. S. Eliot]


## TO *Geoffrey Whitworth*[2]                                        cc

22 June 1938                                    [*The Criterion*]

Dear Mr Whitworth,

I was glad to get your letter of the 20th,[3] because I had written to you
to enquire about 5 July, I think to your Chelsea address, but the letter
seems to have gone astray. I take it from our conversation that what I
am expected to do is to talk for about half an hour, and I was under the
impression that other persons would continue the discussion. Is this right?
I see that in the programme I am described rather alarmingly as giving
*une conference*, and I should like to know exactly how long you want
me to speak. I suppose that that meeting will be over by six o'clock? The
reason why I ask is that some friends have asked me to spend the night
at Campden, and I shall have to arrange to get a car to take me over. Or
my friends could arrange to have a car sent to fetch me, in which case I

---

1 – Coghill, 'Gym-Lido', *The Oxford Magazine* 56: 24 (16 June 1938), 764–5. '[I]n private,
schoolmasters will for the most part admit (what is indeed no more than a commonly
observed fact) that athletics, taken as a cult, are inimical to intellectual work . . . [T]o suggest
mulcting colleges to the tune of a hundred a year in the interests of gym-instructors and
channel-swimmers, when many Faculties, such as those of English Language and Literature
or the Physical Sciences, are urgently in need of more teachers and new laboratories, reveals
a view of the function of a University with which I earnestly hope few will sympathise.'
2 – Geoffrey Whitworth (1883–1951): lecturer and author; founder of the British Drama
League and editor of its periodical, *Drama: A Monthly Record of the Theatre in Town and
Country at Home & Abroad*, 1918–44; hon. secretary of the Shakespeare Memorial Theatre
Committee.
3 – Whitworth invited TSE to speak on 'The Future of Verse Drama' at the International
Theatre Congress to be held at Stratford-upon-Avon in the afternoon of Tues. 5 July 1938.

should like to know as closely as possible when that afternoon meeting will end, and where it will take place. I suppose in some room connected with the theatre.[1]

Yours sincerely,
[T. S. Eliot]

TO *Frederic Prokosch*                                                    CC

22 June 1938                          [*The Criterion*]

My dear Mr Prokosch,

First of all I wish to congratulate you on your book,[2] which I hope will have the press that it deserves, and in particular on the 'Ode' which you showed me in typescript, and which bears rereading very well indeed. It seems to me a very fine poem.

I must apologize for not replying to your objection to the notice of *The Seven Who Fled* in the April *Criterion*.[3] I have reread our commentator's remarks several times, with your objections in mind. You will realise that while I try to exercise careful choice of regular reviewers, and as far as possible their suitability for particular books, I should not wish to give them anything but a free hand in saying what they like. The only limits are

---

1 – Whitworth responded: 'the session on the Tuesday afternoon will begin with the Verse Play item. I think half-an-hour should be the maximum for your address as there will be other speakers to follow. Indeed, it might be even a little shorter . . .

'There is no doubt that the meeting will be over by six o'clock.'

TSE, 'The Future of Poetic Drama', *Drama* 17 (Oct. 1938), 3–5; *CProse* 5, 653–8. 'I have said elsewhere that we cannot expect actors to speak Shakespeare properly until we can give them good contemporary dramatic verse to speak: until then the verse of Shakespeare must remain largely a dead language . . . failing the appearance of a spontaneous genius who should have equal and supreme gifts as both dramatist and poet, we are more likely to get tolerable verse plays from poets who have laboured to learn the art of the theatre, than from dramatists who have toiled to write verse . . . It is not sufficient to learn the craft of the theatre and then fill your play with good poetry; you have to learn to write a special kind of poetry which is different from what you have written before. To put it in the simplest terms: a poet writes his ordinary poetry implicitly to be spoken by himself: he must write dramatic poetry remembering that it is to be spoken by someone else. This is an important distinction. I find that in my first draft of a play there are passages which seem to me first-rate, and they are likely to be the ones that I have to remove. They may be plums, but if so it is right that plums should be pulled out; they are poetry, but they are my poetry and not that of my character who speaks them.'

Whitworth wrote to thank TSE on 13 July: 'May I . . . say how very much your participation in the Congress was appreciated by all concerned?'

2 – Prokosch, *The Carnival* (1938).

3 – Desmond Hawkins, 'Fiction Chronicle', *C.* 17 (Apr. 1938), 508–11.

those of libel or of extreme breaches of good taste. Now in the case of a book which I have not read, like *The Seven Who Fled*, I am in no position to judge how fairly the book has been treated. I can see in what ways the reviewer may have given you annoyance, and I am very sorry that you have felt annoyed. But I am still unable to see that there is anything in this particular notice to which the Editor would have been justified in taking exception.

With many regrets, and all best wishes,

Yours sincerely,
[T. S. Eliot]


TO *Henry Nelson Lansdale*[1]                                        CC

22 June 1938                    [Faber & Faber Ltd]

Dear Mr Lansdale,

I have your letter of 13 June, asking me whether I am an American or an English writer.[2] That is a very difficult question to decide, and I submit that I am in no better position to answer it than is anyone else in possession of the published facts. I take it that the question of legal status is not raised, but only that of literary status. If one is to appeal to the year books, I can point out that for several years I appeared in both the British and the American *Who's Who*. The editors of the American *Who's Who* eventually dropped me without any notification. Possibly their opinion on this vexed question might be of some value, as no doubt they would not have proceeded to such a step without consideration. It might be argued that this question is one which cannot be decided by itself, but is only a special case in a general category. Is Napoleon, for instance, to be considered as an Italian or a Frenchman? We know that his native language was Italian, and that his Corsican family were probably of Genoese extraction. His case however is not quite parallel to mine, because he changed the spelling of his name, which I have not done.

1–Henry Nelson Lansdale (1915–64), art and music editor of *Newsweek: The Magazine of News Significance*.
2–'Your friend and my acquaintance, Gilbert Seldes, now a Columbia Broadcasting Company official, has suggested I ask you the question I put to him at luncheon the other day: "Is T. S. Eliot an American writer?" I particularly want to know because I'm writing a master's thesis at Columbia University on "Poetic Drama in America since 1900".

'You appear in the British *Who's Who*, but not in the American edition. *Living Authors* neatly avoids the point. *The International Who's Who* flatly labels you a "British writer", and you seem to be almost the only member of your family not listed in *The Dictionary of American Biography*.'

A case perhaps more pertinent is that of Cardinal Newman. Is Cardinal Newman to be considered an Anglican or a Roman writer? One notes of both these men that they are claimed or repudiated according to the disposition of the individual critic.

I am not sure whether *The Rock* has ever been produced in America. I know that someone once considered producing it in West Virginia, but I think that the project fell through. The first production of *Sweeney Agonistes*, however, was that of Miss Hallie Flanagan in her experimental theatre at [Vassar] College, which took place in the early summer of 1933, and a very good production it was, too. The fragment has since been performed by the Group Theatre in London.

With best wishes,
Yours very truly,
[T. S. Eliot]

TO *John Betjeman*                                          TS Victoria

22 June 1938                     *The Criterion*

My dear Betjeman,

I have your telephone message, and it is very sweet of you to suggest fetching me from Bristol.[1] I should enjoy very much spending the week-end with you, and I am sure that you would not only be the best, but a unique guide to Bristol. But there are two difficulties in the way. One is that I don't know at what time I shall be able to get away from my hosts, as there is an official lunch, and I do not know what after that, and I should not know where to tell you to call for me. The other is that I have got to go to Stratford on the Tuesday morning in order to open a discussion which takes place at an international conference of dramatists on the subject of the Future of Verse Drama. I cannot help thinking at the moment that if people will ask me to talk about Verse Drama, it is all the less likely to have any future at all, and I don't like international conventions, but I accepted in order to get out of a rather difficult position in connexion with the National Theatre, which I don't want to be concerned with.

But there it is, and I think that the only thing I can do in the circumstances is to get home from Bristol as quickly as I can, and spend Sunday – that is

---

1 – JB had invited TSE to spend a weekend with him at Gerrards Farm, Uffington, Berkshire.

to say, the fragments of Sunday which are allowed to a churchwarden – in thinking of what I am going to say at Stratford.

Are we dining together on the 30th? And does it mean a white tie? I suppose five or ten minutes' talk is quite enough, but if there are any topics which ought to be mentioned, or any people who need to be flattered, I wish you would prime me as soon as possible.

Yours regretfully,

T. S. Eliot

## TO *Harry Brown*[1]

24 June 1938                                    [*The Criterion*]

Dear Mr Brown,

I have your kind letter of the 13th instant, and am naturally flattered by the honour which the *Harvard Advocate* intends to offer one of its former editors.[2] I will not insist further on my appreciation, and will proceed to reply to your questions.

I have literally nothing unpublished that would be at all suitable for the occasion; the reason is that I have been occupied for the past year with a new play, which is not yet quite ready. No piece of that would be suitable by itself: any fragment would be unintelligible, and would, I dare to say,

---

1 – Harry Brown (1917–86), poet, novelist, screenwriter, was a friend at Harvard of the poet Robert Lowell – though Brown dropped out after his sophomore year and went to work in literary journalism. Writings include *The End of a Decade* (1940), *The Poem of Bunker Hill* (1941), *A Sound of Hunting* (play, 1946, produced on Broadway with Burt Lancaster), and *A Walk in the Sun* (novel, 1944); and he wrote the screenplays for *Sands of Iwo Jima* (1949), *A Place in the Sun* (1951) – for which he won an Oscar – and *Ocean's 11* (1960).

2 – The *Harvard Advocate*, to mark TSE's fiftieth birthday, was bringing out a special T. S. Eliot number: 125: 3 (Dec. 1938). Eight early poems, written and published while he was at Harvard 1906–10, were to be reprinted, with a commentary by Lawrence B. Leighton. Articles were to include F. O. Matthiessen's 'Notes for an Unwritten Chapter' (of *The Achievement of T. S. Eliot*), and Theodore Spencer's 'On "Murder in the Cathedral"'. Contributors to a symposium included Richard Eberhart, Archibald MacLeish, Merrill Moore, Wallace Stevens, Allen Tate, William Carlos Williams and Robert Penn Warren. 600 copies had been ordered by the class of 1910, and over 150 advance orders had been received from America and England.

'I'm in complete charge,' wrote Brown, 'and am trying to get everyone from Yeats to George Barker, on both sides of the Atlantic, to write something for this issue. Response thus far have [*sic*] been splendid; and I assure you that the homage will be sincere and interesting . . . And now comes the hard part. It's going to be an imposition to ask you for something. I don't like to do it – for it's like asking someone to beat the batter for his own birthday cake – but I've got to do it just the same. Would you have something you could give us, a Five-Finger Exercise, or anything at all, to head off the issue?'

not do itself justice apart from the whole. If any idea occurs to me in the immediate future I will try to produce something, but at this time of year such extra efforts are almost impossible.

On the other hand, I should feel no shame in seeing my undergraduate verse for the *Advocate* reappear, so long as each of the poems that you choose is dated. You probably would not want to use them all, but I leave the decision entirely in the hands of yourself and the other editors.

With many thanks, and best wishes,
Yours very sincerely,
[T. S. Eliot]

## TO *Maurice Haigh-Wood* cc

27 June 1938    [Faber & Faber Ltd]

Dear Maurice,

I have been thinking a good deal about your letter of the 20th: excuse my delay for answering.[1] First of all, so far as I understand the financial

---

1 – 'You will remember that the Bank of England stock was sold in March because at that time according to all the authorities undated Government securities were expected to slide down to lower values. The slide has not yet actually begun although it is still regarded as inevitable sooner or later . . .

'The circumstances in which the Irish property was held made it a very risky investment. Situated in a foreign country; no possibility of proper supervision; under the control of one agent in whom none of us have very much confidence; income subject to severe fluctuation in the event of voids, exceptional repairs & so on.

'There is no doubt in my mind that we were very wise to sell when we had the chance.

'Now the income from the capital sum involved worked out in good years at a return of between 7% and 8%. If the proceeds are invested in gilt edged stocks the return is only 3%, which means a material reduction in mother's income.

'Quite apart from the special circumstances of this case (in which mother's income is one of the main considerations) I do not regard fixed interest & gilt-edged securities at the present time as the soundest class of investment.

'Inflationary influences are evident everywhere. Budget expenditures in this country for 1938/9 will be over £1,000,000,000 & chances of any recession from this level in the next four years are slight. Some rise in the cost of living is already taking place, & a further gradual rise seems inevitable.

'In these conditions cash & fixed interest bearing securities giving a low return are wasting assets.

'The objection to making any constructive investment is that V's concurrence is desirable, but is unobtainable. It is a superhuman task to induce her to express any opinion assent or dissent on any matter of this kind, quite hopeless, & beyond my powers to attempt.

'It took me months of trouble & effort to get her consent to the sale of the Irish property, & then she finally expressed her definite assent on condition that Haigh Terrace should remain.

situation, I agree with your prognostic about inflation for the near future: although when so much depends upon waves of political tension and relaxation it of course needs watching all the time. Second, the Anglo-Iranian Oil sounds very reliable to me, and I am willing to accept your judgement about the mining shares, though any mining stock seems to me uncertain, and not to be looked on as a permanent investment. And obviously, neither of these at present is any more uncertain than Irish real estate.

I wish you would remind me of the exact degree of legal responsibility that we should be taking, if you make these purchases and give me the undertaking. (I am rather doubtful whether any undertaking on your part would relieve me of any responsibility, but that is a lawyer's problem). I ought to have a copy of your father's will: but was there not a codicil clause putting this sort of investment in our power? I mean, so far as this would be reinvestment of money realised from sale of speculative property, are we strictly required to reinvest in ordinary trustee stock? As you suggest, with the ordinary safeguards of attention, this reinvestment is in some respects less risky than the original holding.

In any case, I don't see that I should be justified morally in withholding my assent to any reasonable improvement of your mother's income –

---

'If it were possible to sell Haigh Terrace on decent terms it would obviously be to our advantage to do so, but I shudder at the thought of having to get V's concurrence. However, that doesn't arise at present.

'To return to the question of re-investment. You will remember that when I urged a switch from Canadian Pacific Common to International Nickel, I wrote you a letter in which I took sole responsibility for doing so. Incidentally that switch has saved the Trust a considerable sum of money, & has added a little to mother's income.

'At the present time I should very much like to invest a good part of the money lying at the Bank in certain first class shares, particularly General Mining & Finance Corp$^n$ £1 standing at £5. These give a yield of 5% on their 25% dividend. They are the pick of the gold mining investment stocks, & not only give a good yield, but also have really fine prospects of gradual improvement in value. These first class gold shares are not subject to the risks attached to ordinary industrials.

'Another share I have in mind is Anglo-Iranian Oil (the old Anglo-Persian) of which the British Government has a large shareholding, reputed to be over £11,000,000 worth. The £1 shares at about 4½ give a yield of 6%. The company is enormously strong. The use of its product has a "secular" upward trend, which is important as a long-term stabilizing factor.

'I enclose some particulars of both those concerns, which please return. I should like to invest five or six hundred pounds in each of these two concerns. If you agree, I shall be glad to write you a letter releasing you from all responsibility in the matter, similar to that which I sent you over the International Nickel.

'I haven't seen you for a long time. I tried to get to the Leicester Galleries to view your portrait, but didn't succeed.

'My affairs are still very much in the melting pot. We might have a quiet glass of sherry one day soon, next week perhaps?'

having in mind the very peculiar circumstances – but I should like to be clear how far this would be overstepping the restrictions of the Will or the regular fiduciary restrictions. (But for the sake of simplifying procedure in future cases, I am wondering whether it would not be simplest for me to withdraw from the trust). If you could let me know quickly, we can get the particular matter settled this week. I expect to go away for ten days in about a fortnight's time.

Yours ever,<br>[Tom]

[P.S.] I want to post this at once, so as I have no long envelope here, I will send on the reports this afternoon.

## TO *Arthur Winnington-Ingram*[1]                                        cc

[?27 June 1938]                          [Faber & Faber Ltd]

My Lord Bishop,

I am venturing to put in a word which I hope will not be considered impertinent concerning my friend Canon Iddings Bell of Rhode Island. I understand that Canon Iddings Bell's present position in the Diocese of Rhode Island will shortly be terminated owing to the lack of the necessary funds to support his work there. I have known Canon Bell for some years, and have had a good deal of conversation with him, especially on the subject of religious education in secondary schools. I believe that he would be a very valuable man in any position which would make it possible for him to work with and for young people.

I would not wish to say more at this moment, because I don't know whether it is to the point that I should raise the subject at all, and I would not venture to do so but that I have heard from Canon Bell that the matter had been discussed between him and yourself.

I have the honour to remain,<br>Your Lordship's obedient servant,<br>[T. S. Eliot]

---

1 – Arthur Winnington-Ingram (1858–1946), Bishop of London, 1901–39.

28 June 1938                    [Faber & Faber Ltd]

*PRIVATE AND CONFIDENTIAL*

Dear Gaselee,

Here is something I am worrying about. I understand that António Ferro, head of the Secretariado Nacionale de Propaganda, is coming to London for a visit in a few days time. I understood that he expected to be here for several weeks, but this hasn't been lately confirmed. I feel I ought to entertain him to lunch or to dinner, and I should like to get your company if possible.

The point is that Ferro occupies a fairly high position in Portugal, and ought to be flattered. He is, I think, a very superficial person with a sort of contemporary culture, a good deal of cleverness, great ambition and considerable native vulgarity. He is just the sort of Portuguese whose appearance is the worst advertisement for his country, because he looks just like what Nordic peoples are apt to think all Portuguese look. If he is accompanied by his wife, the situation is still more difficult, because it is very hard to think of people to have with them in a social way. They both, incidentally, have more than a lick of the tar brush in them, and are absurdly fat.

If Ferro is coming in any official way, I suppose Vansittart will do something for him, and even if he is coming unofficially isn't it a suitable job for the British Council? I have a strong intuitive feeling that Ferro's ambition is to be Minister in Paris and possibly an eventual Ambassador here. I should think that Salazar was much too shrewd a man to let him get as far as that. But one never knows. If he is going to get any official entertainment, I don't feel obliged to do so much, but if not I feel that these two great black babies present something of a problem for me. So I should like to arrange some lunch or dinner at which I could persuade you to come and suffer with me.[2]

Yours sincerely,

[T. S. Eliot]

---

1 – Stephen Gaselee (1882–1943), librarian, bibliographer; Fellow of Magdalene College, Cambridge; Pepys Librarian, 1909–19; Librarian and Keeper of the Foreign Office from 1920; President of the Bibliographical Society, 1932; Hon. Librarian of the Athenaeum Club; President of the Classical Association, 1939; Fellow of the British Academy, 1939. Works include *The Oxford Book of Medieval Latin Verse* (1928). Knighted in 1935.

2 – Gaselee (Foreign Office), 6 July: 'In continuation of my letter of June 29th, I now hear that Senhor Ferro may arrive here in a couple of days unless he is detained on his way in Paris.

1 July 1938                          *The Criterion*

Dear Roberts,

Thank you for your letter of the 28th which arrived simultaneously with an official invitation from the Literary and Philosophical Society.[1] I am afraid that I cannot possibly fit it in. I do not know just when my play will be finished or how much work I shall have to put in at the last moment, and I must keep the autumn free. Furthermore, as soon as that is off my hands I must set to work thinking seriously about the two Boutwood lectures which I have to deliver at Corpus in February, so I am afraid it is out of the question.[2] I only regret that it deprives me of the pleasure of visiting you in Newcastle.

I am doubtful whether Fabers would be inclined to take on a book about Ortega unless it were something of the most superlative brilliance.[3] However, it is not our policy to decline MSS in advance and if Galbraith is willing to show me some of his stuff or come and see me, I shall be very glad to give him any help I can.

I do not think we have been sending any books to Bill Empson, but if you know of any you think he would particularly like and can provide me with any reasonable excuse for sending them, which I can offer to the department concerned, I will see what can be done.[4] It may be difficult to persuade them that the possible sales in Yunnan would justify the cost.

With best wishes to Janet and your son.

Yours ever,

T. S. E.

---

'It is proposed to ask Sir Robert Vansittart [head of the Foreign Office] to receive him and, when he comes, I shall see him and find out the kind of things he wants from Governmental circles. Our Ambassador at Lisbon has warned us to be careful to avoid anything in the nature of "bear leading".'

1 – 'At a meeting of the lecture sub-committee of the local Lit. and Phil. tonight we decided to ask you to give the Spence Watson lecture this year . . . I hope you will be able to come.'

2 – Will Spens, Master of Corpus Christi College, Cambridge, had invited TSE (4 Mar. 1938) to deliver the Boutwood Lectures: 'two lectures on any subject in political or religious philosophy or in the borderline between these. There is an endowment of £20 for the lectures. You could give them either next Autumn or in the Lent term of 1939.' TSE accepted the invitation and opted, in a now lost reply, for Lent 1939.

3 – A colleague and friend at the Grammar School, W. O. Galbraith (a graduate of Durham University, aged twenty-five), was working on a book on Ortega y Gasset: Roberts hoped TSE would be able to advise him about publishing possibilities.

4 – 'I had a letter from Bill Empson the other day: he is at the Combined University, Mengtzu, Yunnan, China, and is likely to be there for some time. He has asked me to send him some books: if you happen to know that Fabers have sent him something, I'd be glad to hear, to avoid duplicating them. I sent him a copy of *Hulme* some time ago.'

## TO *Mary Trevelyan*

1 July 1938                    [Faber & Faber Ltd]

Dear Miss Trevelyan,

I must apologize for my oversight in not answering your kind letter of the 6th June.[1] It is a compliment which I appreciate to be asked to repeat my performance at The Student Movement House, but I have for some time been declining invitations for the rest of this year. I have a play to finish and after that have two lectures to prepare, to which I feel I should give all my time. I should be very happy to come at the end of the winter, if that were of any use to you.

> With apologies and regrets,
> Yours sincerely,
> [T. S. Eliot]


## TO *Maurice Haigh-Wood*

6 July 1938                    [Faber & Faber Ltd]

Dear Maurice,

Your letter of the 5th arrives opportunely as I return from one of my vexatious excursions.[2]

1–Trevelyan invited TSE to 'help our Club in a special way by coming to read your poems again in the autumn, when we are hoping to arrange an "all star" programme to celebrate the Club's coming of age . . . If . . . you could help us would Saturday, October 29th be possible?'

The date of TSE's first reading at the Club is not known, but Trevelyan recalled it in her memoir: 'He arrived with a lady whom I took to be (but wasn't) his wife . . . [Presumably the lady in question was EH.] After the reading I asked a selected few [of the students] to meet him. This was not an unqualified success. The students were nervous and gauche. The poet looked terrified. Perhaps this was the only occasion on which I was really thankful to see him go.'

2–'The Codicil of father's Will reads as follows:-

"Whereas I appear to have in & by my said Will charged my Trustees to sell & convert into money my leasehold property, stocks, shares & other investments I now declare that there should be no obligation on the part of my Trustees to sell but that at their discretion they are empowered to dispose of any investment of a wasting nature or that does not appear to be sufficiently secure, & to reinvest the proceeds in trustee *or other high class stocks* or mortages."

'I think this is pretty clear. The words underlined mean non-trustee stocks. There might be room for difference of opinion as to what stocks are high class, but I should imagine that the general Stock Exchange view is about the only criterion on that . . .

'It seems to me that Mr James took this view when the matter cropped up many years ago in connection with various re-investments from time to time . . .

The terms of your father's Will which you quote appear to give the Trustees power to exercise their discretion among 'high class stocks'. I do not see that we should be exceeding these terms in investing in either of the stocks that you suggest. I think that the letter of indemnity from you to me that you propose to write, will be useful as far as my responsibility to you as a beneficiary is concerned, and although I do not see how it would exculpate me otherwise, I shall be glad to have it – though I do not see that it is necessary.

My doubt about mining stocks bore only on the impossibility of knowing whether and how long any particular mine would continue to yield; not on the value of gold itself. The only difference, so far as *I* know, between gold and oil, is that gold has been mined in the Rand for a good many years, whereas the attempt to exhaust the supplies of oil has begun more recently. I will gladly give you discretion to invest in either Anglo-Iranian or Shell Transport, as you find best at the moment, for part of the capital to be invested, and in General Mining, if you still think it desirable, or some other mining stock, for the other half.

Yours ever,

[Tom]

TO *Michael Roberts*                                    PC TS Janet Adam Smith

[Postmarked 6 July 1938]                    Faber & Faber Ltd

Had you had the text before you, you could not have fallen into the error of supposing that Macavity had anything to do with Lupin.[1] We know ('813') that *Arsène Lupin ne tue pas.* A study of the text would have shown you immediately that Macavity is the feline analogue of the late Professor Moriarty, the mathematician and amateur of Greuze.[2]

---

'I think Mr James considered it desirable that Vivienne, as one of the beneficiaries, should know of & concur in these investments, & she probably did so in the case of some of the earlier ones. But Mr James didn't appear to consider it important enough to get any written agreement from Vivienne at any time.'

1–Roberts had written, 3 July: 'Having no wireless, we haven't heard "Practical Cats" yet, but I hear reports of McCavity [*sic*], who seems to have a dash of Arsène Lupin in his composition.'

2–TSE's secretary to Mrs Yvonne S. Dickens (Lexington, VA), 24 Sept. 1962: 'Mr Eliot has asked me to acknowledge your letter of 4th September and to say that he based Macavity's character entirely on that of [Sir Arthur Conan Doyle's] Professor Moriarty; he is glad to see that you have recognised the likeness in detail as he hoped his other readers would do.'

In 'The Valley of Fear' we learn that Sherlock Holmes's arch-enemy Professor James Moriarty possesses a painting by Jean-Baptiste Greuze (1725–1805) – proof of his ill-gotten

14 July 1938                              42 Gresham House,
                                          Old Broad Street, London E.C.2.

Dear Tom,[1]

I am very sorry to have to write to you on your holiday but I'm afraid I must.

V. was found wandering in the streets at 5 o'clock this morning & was taken in to Marylebone Police Station. I was telephoned & immediately went there, & I took her back to my flat where she had some breakfast & recovered fairly well. Ahmé[2] & I wanted her to stay & rest, but she insisted on going off. However I persuaded her to let me take her wherever she wanted to go, & we went (with 2 attaché cases & a parcel which she was carrying around) to Burleigh Mansions where she has a flat (No 21).

The Inspector at the Police Station told me that she had talked in a very confused & unintelligible manner & appeared to have various illusions, & if it had not been possible to get hold of me or someone to take charge of her, he would have felt obliged to place her under mental observation.

As soon as I got to the City I rang up Dr Miller,[3] who said that he was at that moment on the point of writing to me.

Some 3 or 4 months ago Dr Miller went to see V. at the Constance Hotel in Lancaster Gate. He was *fairly* satisfied with her condition, & he had a talk with the manageress of the Constance, who has been very kind & considerate with V. Although the manageress told him of certain awkward & unpleasant incidents that had taken place from time to time, he felt that V. was in good & friendly hands there.

I may say that this was my own impression from several calls I had made at the Constance while V. was there.

---

gains, since his wealth so far exceeds his modest academic salary. If only it was ever thus.

1 – This letter was first published, in excerpted form, in Blake Morrison, 'The Two Mrs Eliots', *Too True* (1998), 139–40.

2 – MH-W's American wife Ahmé Haigh-Wood (1905–70).

3 – Dr Reginald Miller (1879–1948) of 110 Harley Street, London, W.1.; Consulting Physician to St Mary's Hospital and to Paddington Green Children's Hospital, London; a general physician with a special interest in children, he was expert in the problems of mental deficiency in children and in rheumatic diseases and heart diseases in childhood (on which he wrote several articles). He was the first editor, with Dr Hugh Thursfield, of the *Archives on Disease in Childhood*. Brought up in Hampstead, it is probable that he was an early friend of the Haigh-Wood family.

Dr Miller took the opportunity at that time of materially reducing the strength of V's doses.[1]

Since that time V. has been away at Eastbourne & also in London, & no one knew her address – she gave it to no one.

Having heard nothing for so long Dr Miller wrote to Allen & Hanbury's to ask them if they knew whether all was going well, & he got a reply from them this morning in which they said that V. called every day for her medicine, that she appeared to be in a deplorable condition & that they had no idea of her address.

Dr Miller was therefore on the point of writing to me because he feels that something must be done without much more delay.

When I told him of what happened this morning he begged me to get hold of you as soon as possible, so that we could both go & discuss the matter with him.

Dr Miller feels that the time has come when V. *must* go either to Malmaison or to some home, & I also am inclined to think that, because there is no telling what will happen next.

V. had apparently been wandering about for two nights, afraid to go anywhere. She is full of the most fantastic suspicions & ideas. She asked me if it was true that you had been beheaded. She says she has been in hiding from various mysterious people, & so on.

It would be deplorable if she were again to be found wandering in the early hours & taken into custody.

How urgent the matter is it is difficult to judge. She seemed much calmer & more normal when I left her at Burleigh Mansions, fairly normal & contented. I shall call there again this evening, but she says she never sleeps there & is rarely there at any time. However I rather think she must be staying there at present.

I have made a provisional appointment with Dr Miller for 3.15 pm tomorrow (this was before I discovered that you were away).

I really don't know whether to suggest your running up to town tomorrow & returning to Gloucestershire in the evening, or not. You will be able to decide that yourself, but I would be grateful if you would send me a telegram in the morning to say what you decide.[2]

---

1 – Three-and-a-half years earlier, on 8 Jan. 1935, Allen & Hanbury's (Chemist, 7 Vere Street, Cavendish Square, London) had written to VHE to advise her that she was using perhaps too large a quantity of the Faivres' Cachets. See *L7*.

2 – The following day, 15 July, MH-W cabled TSE (at Stamford House, Chipping Campden, Glos.): 'Have provisionally fixed appointment Miller 3: 30 Monday.'

Yours ever
Maurice.

---

Dr Miller to MH-W, 21 July 1938: 'As to the difficult matter of what is best to be done in the present circumstances, I do not think that it is much good forcing some mental specialist upon her just now. She is apparently better and able to carry on, and it would be difficult for a new man to certify her as needing special care and restraint even in view of the recent breakdown; nor do we want actual certification if it can be avoided . . .

'The best advice that I can give you, though necessarily unsatisfactory, is as follows:

(1) To instruct the Manager of Allen and Hanbury's, 7 Vere Street, W.1., that during my absence in August symptoms of any serious sort should be communicated to you at once. When I am back at work this would be done automatically to me, as happened recently.

(2) Should such a report reach you during August you must consult Dr [R. D.] Gillespie, or if he is not back, Dr Edward Mapother or Dr Bernard Hart who are said to be doing his work while he is away.

(3) The question of our seeing Dr Gillespie in September without Mrs Eliot might be reconsidered then in the light of Mrs Eliot's condition.

(4) If Mrs Eliot again comes into the hands of the police I think that you must definitely determine to adopt one of two courses:– (a) if you are called to her, as before, before she is charged, you must refuse to care for her unless she will promise to undertake treatment; or (b) let her appear before the Magistrate and refuse to be responsible for her unless she promises the Court to undertake treatment in a home. I know this sounds unpleasant and harsh, but it is highly probable that her proper care and supervision will ultimately only be initiated through some sort of action by the public authorities.

'If you agree, perhaps it would be best if I gave the necessary instructions to Allen and Hanbury, on your behalf, as what little actual responsibility they have is to me rather than to you.' (Copy with EVE)

MH-W wrote on the same day (21 July 1938) to TSE: 'Very many thanks for your letter [not traced] about the appointment with Gillespie. I very much appreciate your undertaking to be responsible for the fee, and in fact I need hardly tell you that at the present time I am in no position financially to assume any burdens other than that of trying to keep body and soul together of myself and family.

'At our interview the other day I told what I know of V's finances. This morning the manager of the District Bank rang me up and asked me to call around to see him. I did so and he said that he was worried about V's account and by the manner in which she had been drawing cheques. At first he was very reluctant to give me any details owing to the very strict banking rule about the divulging of information to a third party. But I pointed out the exceptional nature of the case and he finally told me that:–

'a) Last November at the time when the Irish proceeds were paid in the account was some 700 pounds overdrawn. The Irish proceeds were 1700 pounds odd. Of this amount 800 pounds were invested in gilt-edged. After paying off the overdraft this left her 200 pounds in credit. She is now overdrawn again to the extent of some 500 pounds.

'b) Recently, i.e. within the last two weeks she has been uttering cheques irregularly and very carelessly drawn. Unfortunately she has a Bearer cheque book and various cheques have come into the bank without any Payee entered in and with words and figures in the wrong places etc.

'With regard to (b) the Manager said that he would see that when the present cheque book is exhausted, any new one issued to her would be crossed and to-order. In any case I think this irregularity in drawing cheques is only due to the particularly bad condition in which

19 July 1938                    [Faber & Faber Ltd]

My dear Trend,

A German Jew named Dr Fuchs has recently turned up here with a
score of his setting *A Song for Simeon,* for orchestra and – I think –
baritone voice. He wanted me, of course, to do something about getting it
performed in England, but apart from the occasion of his using my words,
I am as useless a person as he could have chosen to apply to. Incidentally,
I have completely lost my youthful ability to read music, and it might as
well be Hindustani to me. Would you be willing to look at it, if I send it

---

V. has been during the last two or three weeks. She is still at 3 Compayne, and I understand
that she is now considerably better.

'The question of (a) is very serious indeed.

'I had a letter from Dr Miller today in which he says that Gillespie is away until the 15th
of August. I enclose the letter herewith and shall be glad if you will return it to me when
you have read it.

'I promised the manager of the District Bank that I would treat the information which he
gave me with the utmost discretion, but it is obviously my duty to pass it on to you.'

Two days later (23 July 1938), Dr Miller wrote to TSE – in reply to a (now lost) letter
from TSE ('I note what it tells me') – 'From what I hear there is reason to hope that the bad
phase is over; and I have written to Mr Haigh-Wood giving him the best advice that seems
possible at the present moment. He will no doubt communicate with your solicitor and I
expect to be told presently if they are ready to agree to the plan I have put forward to cover
at least the holiday period.

'We have in Allen and Hanbury's someone who is in daily contact with the patient and
my idea is to get them to report to whoever is available (Mr Haigh-Wood or myself) if signs
of deterioration are again observed. It seems almost impossible to do more just now, at all
events without running the danger of doing more harm than good.'

G. F. Higginson, solicitor, to TSE, 28 Sept. 1938: 'Dr Miller has sent me a note of his fee
for our consultation on July 18th amounting to £5.5.0. I think at the time you said that
this was one of the expenses that you would wish to bear personally, and if that is the case
perhaps you will kindly let me have a cheque in settlement.

'I should, however, perhaps add that this is an expense which could quite properly be met
out of the patient's estate and need not therefore fall upon either you or Mr Haigh-Wood.'

In response to a (now lost) letter from TSE, dated 2 Oct., Higginson responded: 'I note
your views with regard to Dr Miller's fee, with which, if I may say so, I am entirely in
agreement. I will therefore place the account with the others that are to be brought to the
notice of the Master on the 17th inst.'

The 'Master' in question here was one of the two Masters in Lunacy – as they were called
after 1845 – who represented the Lord Chancellor's jurisdiction in cases of lunacy. (From
1947 the Office of Master in Lunacy was to be replaced by the Court of Protection.)

on to you, and give me a frank opinion of its value? Then I shall at least feel that I have done all I could for him.[1]

Yours ever,

[T. S. Eliot]

## TO *Richard Fuchs*

19 July 1938                                   [Faber & Faber Ltd]

Dear Dr Fuchs,

I am sorry that your letter of July 8th has remained unanswered, due to my absence from London.[2] I am afraid I am very doubtful of my having the right connexions in America to be of any use to you. Do you by any chance happen to know Professor Gropius,[3] with whom I had a slight acquaintance while he was in London, and who is now Professor of Architecture at Harvard? If he were interested, he might be able to let us know what the possibilities are.

Yours sincerely,

[T. S. Eliot]

---

1 – Trend replied, 5 Aug.: 'Both [Philip] Radcliffe and I have looked at this, and we agreed that it is Strauss and water – a mixture which (as Radcliffe said) is peculiarly unsuitable for your poem! His themes are Strauss and his harmonies generally Wagnerian, and I don't think anyone would undertake to perform a thing of that kind, at this time of day, in England. I'm sorry for the man; but so few of his kind realize that things have moved on, in this country – in music as well as in poetry!'

Fuchs did receive an endorsement from Ralph Vaughan Williams: 'I have heard and seen several compositions, including works for orchestra, for choir and solo songs by Dr Fuchs and in my opinion he is a competent and well trained composer with an excellent technique in all branches of composition of which he had shown me examples' (Turnbull Library).

2 – Fuchs wrote that 'the whole situation' was becoming so bad that he had to think of quitting Germany 'as soon as possible. I remember our talking about my main profession as architect – I would be glad if I could find a way to U.S.A. . . . Could perhaps you help me to find a goodhearted man or family to help me in this situation?'

3 – Walter Gropius (1883–1969), German modernist architect; founder of the Bauhaus School. See Fiona MacCarthy, *Walter Gropius: Visionary Founder of the Bauhaus* (2019).

TO *John Betjeman*                                        TS Victoria

19 July 1938                        *The Criterion*

Respected Betje,

Soft you, a word or two before you go: I have done the Shell some service, and I know't.[1] Now is the chance for your good deed, I mean your interim good deed so long as it does not hold up the Bressey Report.[2] So listen. By none but me may the tale be told, the butcher of Rouen, Big Berold.[3]

> Betjeman must betake himself to Swanwick
> To prattle about Art and Architectonic.

1 – 'Soft you, a word or two before you go. / I have done the state some service, as they know't' (*Othello* V. ii. 354–55). TSE's adaptation of Othello's words is explained by this letter from Betjeman, writing on behalf of his employer Shell-Mex and B.P., on 31 May 1938:

> Dear and Great Poet,
>     This is to confirm yesterday's telephone conversation in which you kindly agreed to open our Exhibition of the original drawings for lorry bills etc., which we are holding in Shell-Mex House [Victoria Embankment, London] on June 30th at 9.30 p.m. You will, I trust, have a nice little literary dinner beforehand with me.
>     I hereby undertake to fulfil my part of the bargain, which will be to let you have:-
>> (1) The syllabus of architecture book
>> (2) Article on Bressey Report
>> (3) Book by the end of the year.
> and it looks to me as though, onerous as your job is, mine is going to be more so . . .

On 1 July Betjeman thanked TSE for his speech – 'which was an unqualified success. The more I read your poetry, the more I got a conscience about having let a sensitive person into such a predicament. But my eye! how well you acquitted yourself. The Directors were pleased, the audience was happy & still & Field Marshal Sir Philip Chetwode said to me "Who was the young man who made the speech?" Nothing I can ever do will repay you for your kindness.'

2 – Betjeman added to his letter of 1 July: 'Anyhow the article on the planning of London will be ready in time PROVIDED YOU CAN GET THEM TO LET YOU HAVE A COPY OF THE *BRESSEY REPORT* for me – either from H. M. Stationary Office or the L.C.C. Publications Dept.' In 1935 the Minister of Transport Leslie Hore-Belisha commissioned Sir Charles Bressey to make a survey of the traffic problems of London: his comprehensive and in parts visionary paper was to be published as 'London Traffic Improvement' in 1938.

3 – The opening lines of Dante Gabriel Rossetti's poem 'The White Ship' (1880), from *Ballads and Sonnets* (1881), about the wreck in the English Channel on 25 Nov. 1120 of the White Ship, a vessel conveying close members of the family of Henry I of England – his only legitimate son and heir William, along with his half-sister Matilda and half-brother Richard – from Normandy to England. The only survivor of the shipwreck was a butcher of Rouen named Berold:

> By none but me can the tale be told,
> The butcher of Rouen, poor Berold.

The good Bro. George Every, S.S.M. of Kelham, a charming and saintly young man whom you ought to know, has arranged a set of informal lectures for the summer course of the S.C.M. at Swanwick – a place very conveniently situated in relation to the railway junction of Swindon. He only wants the best: Michael Roberts is doing one of the talks. He had Porteus for Art, but Porteus has fallen down, I think he funks speaking in public, and you can't get anything at Swanwick to cheer you up. It is supposed to be a talk on Modern Art, but you could quickly divert it to the Bressey Report, 18th century box pews, or anything else you like, embellished from your inexhaustible fund of wit & humour. He wants you, YOU, and has probably written, and this is to back him up. You will deliver your talk either Saturday *next* or the following Monday: preferably Saturday in order to draw the crowd away from the rival attraction on that morning, C. E. M. Joad. I am sure that your public spirit will compel you to accept.[1]

Yrs. in haste,
T. S. E.

TO *George Bell*[2]                          Lambeth Palace Library

21 July 1938                          *The Criterion*

My dear Lord Bishop,

I have to acknowledge your two letters of the 13th instant with apologies, as I was away in the country last week. I shall be very glad to

---

1–George Every to TSE, 29 July: 'Thank you for writing to Betjeman. He could not come, but his letter was most friendly.'

2–Rt Revd George Bell, DD (1883–1958): Dean of Canterbury, 1924–9; Bishop of Chichester, 1929–58; President of the Religious Drama Society of Great Britain from its foundation in 1929; chairman of the Universal Christian Council for Life and Work, 1934–6; President of the World Council of Churches from 1954 – he has been called both a true 'world churchman' and 'the father of modern religious drama'. Though shy, modest and soft-spoken, with a high voice, he was a man of uncompromising conscience, courage and energetic commitment, especially to the work of international ecumenism and the place of the Church in public life. 'Not for me', he said, 'a fugitive and cloistered Church, which refuses to face the problems and crises of the modern world.' In 1944 his denunciation in the House of Lords of the Allied policy of bombing cities and civilian homes in Germany caused much resentment: his stance was believed to have dashed his chances of succeeding William Temple as Archbishop of Canterbury later that year. His works include *Randall Davidson, Archbishop of Canterbury* (2 vols, 1935), *Christianity and World Order* (1940), *The Church and Humanity* (1946). In 1935 Bell invited TSE to write for the Canterbury Festival the play that would turn out to be *MiC*. See further Ronald C. D. Jasper, *George Bell: Bishop of Chichester* (1967); Kenneth Pickering, *Drama in the Cathedral: A Twentieth*

---

talk to Christopher Fry, and see his work, and will write to him and let him know that I am ready to make an appointment.[1]

As for your second suggestion, it is very interesting,[2] but seems to me to be an exploration of somewhat the same kind as those which Joe Oldham has this year initiated. I am pledged to go for a weekend to the meeting of a group assembled by Oldham at the end of September: therefore the question in my mind is how far, with the limited time at my disposal, I can afford to disperse my attention to other groups of similar purpose. I should like, if possible, to leave the matter open until some time in October, if you were willing to do so, and could have me reminded of the meeting a fortnight or so beforehand, as it is possible that my time may be wholly occupied. I should like you to understand, however, that I should be very happy to be one of your group if I find myself free.

I am, my dear Lord Bishop,

Your obedient servant,

T. S. Eliot

---

Century Encounter of Church and Stage (1986, 2001); Andrew Chandler, George Bell, Bishop of Chichester: Church, State, and Resistance in the Age of Dictatorship (2016).

1 – 'I want to introduce you to a young poet called Christopher Fry. He is a young man of about 30. He has just written and produced an admirable poetic drama <for the open air: performed at Coleman's Hatch [Sussex]> about St Cuthman's called "The Boy with the Cart". I saw it and indeed I spoke the closing words, a kind of epilogue. Fry owes much to the rock [The Rock], it had to do with the building of Churches, but he is a poet to keep your eyes on. I think if you could perhaps get him to come and see you one day it would be a real help.'

Christopher Fry (1907–2005) taught at Hazlewood Preparatory School, 1928–31, before founding the Tunbridge Wells Repertory Playhouse, 1931–5. He was Director of the Oxford Playhouse, 1939–40, 1944–6; and from 1947 was a director and staff dramatist at the Arts Theatre, London. Other plays include A Phoenix Too Frequent (1946), The Lady's Not For Burning (1948), and Venus Observed (1950), and adaptations of Anouilh, Ibsen and Rostand. He wrote the screenplays for Ben Hur (1959) and The Bible: In the Beginning (1966); and was awarded the Queen's Gold Medal for Poetry 1962.

2 – 'Rom Landau, the author of various religious books, has had various talks with me in Chichester. He and I are both anxious to get a few people to meet at this house for a weekend to consider what I think you and Oldham might fairly describe as "bridge building", that is, the interpretation of things spiritual in the context of concrete modern life. It is Rom Landau's great passion. So I have agreed to hold a Conference at Chichester from October 29–31. Rom Landau has already secured Ronald Cartland, M.P., F. A. Beame, Vice-Chairman of Lloyds Bank, and Sir Francis Younghusband. We have several other ideas, but it is naturally of first class importance that the Christian view should be stated and supported by people who realise the problems of modern life . . . I am most anxious that you should come.' Bell wrote again on 27 Sept. to express the hope that TSE would come to the conference with Landau on 29–31 Oct.

(Rom Landau [1899–1974]: Polish-born British sculptor, author, and educator; later an expert on Arab and Islamic culture; noted for God is My Adventure [1935]. See too Landau's Love for a Country: Contemplations and Conversations [1939], in which the author reports

TO *Jacques Maritain*[1]    TS Strasbourg

24 Juillet 1938        *The Criterion*

Mon cher ami,

Je ne sais pas si vous serez à Meudon, au moment du passage à Paris de mon jeune ami M. E. W. F. Tomlin. Mais si vous êtes là, je vous dirai que voici un des ceux, parmi mes cadets de la *Criterion*, que je veux vous présenter – un philosophe qui s'intéresse à l'esthétique, à la sociologie, à la philosophie de la politique, – et qui comprend l'importance fondamentale, pour notre époque, d'une théologie exacte. Si vous pouvez le voir, ce n'est pas simplement moi ou lui, mais aussi la jeunesse anglaise, qui vous sera redevable.

Je suis encore votre débiteur pour un beau livre: je lirai, avec l'intérêt le plus vif, tout ce que vous et Madame Maritain [ont écrit] sur la poésie.

Toujours votre admirateur dévoué
T. S. Eliot[2]

Monsieur Jacques Maritain, 10, rue du Parc, MEUDON

---

these deliberated remarks by TSE: 'All that matters to a poet while he's writing poetry is the poetry . . . All that matters to the bee is the making of honey . . . Can a poet whilst writing poetry be preoccupied with anything but the technique of his craft?')

1 – Jacques Maritain (1882–1973), philosopher and littérateur, was at first a disciple of Bergson, but revoked that allegiance (*L'Evolutionnisme de M. Bergson*, 1911; *La Philosophie bergsonienne*, 1914) and became a Roman Catholic and foremost exponent of Neo-Thomism. For a while in the 1920s he was associated with *Action Française*, but the connection ended in 1926. His works include *Art et scolastique* (1920); *Saint Thomas d'Aquin apôtre des temps modernes* (1923); *Trois Réformateurs* (1925); *Primauté du spirituel* (1927); *Humanisme integral* (1936); *Creative Intuition in Art and Poetry* (1953). Tomlin, *T. S. Eliot*, 73: '[A]lthough he much liked Maritain as a person (as who could not?), he felt that the French post-Bergsonian intellectual approach, even if called "Neo-scholastique", differed markedly from that of St Thomas himself: it was the difference between a hovering darting kestrel and a "dumb ox pawing the ground".' See Walter Raubicheck, 'Jacques Maritain, T. S. Eliot, and the Romantics', *Renascence* 46: 1 (Fall 1993), 71–9; Shun'ichi Takayanagi, 'T. S. Eliot, Jacques Maritain, and Neo-Thomism', *The Modern Schoolman* 73: 1 (Nov. 1995), 71–90; Jason Harding, '"The Just Impartiality of a Christian Philosopher": Jacques Maritain and T. S. Eliot', in *The Maritain Factor: Taking Religion into Interwar Modernism*, ed. J. Heynickx and J. De Maeyer (Leuven, 2010), 180–91; and James Matthew Wilson, '"I bought and praised but did not read Aquinas": T. S. Eliot, Jacques Maritain, and the Ontology of the Sign', *Yeats Eliot Review* 27: 1–2 (Spring–Summer 2010), 21.

2 – *Translation*: My dear friend, / I do not know if you will be at Meudon, when my young friend Mr E. W. F. Tomlin will be visiting Paris. But if you are, let me explain that he is one of the people, among my younger colleagues at the *Criterion*, I should like you to meet – a philosopher, interested in aesthetics, sociology, the philosophy of politics, – and he also understands the fundamental importance, for our age, of an exact theology. If you can receive him, it will not be just me or him, but the youth of England, that will be in your debt. I am also in debt to you for a beautiful book: I shall read, with the keenest interest, everything that you and Mme Maritain [write] about poetry. / Ever your devoted admirer [T. S. Eliot]

TO *Robert Melville*[1]                                                              CC

27 July 1938

Dear Mr Melville,

    We have read with enjoyment your lively and interesting essay on
Picasso, but I candidly do not see how we or any other firm at the present
time could sell it.[2] I should be glad, however, to hear more about your
work, and to see other specimens of it from time to time.

                                                    Yours very truly,
                                                    [T. S. Eliot]


TO *Jacques Maritain*                                               TS Strasbourg

2 August 1938                          *The Criterion*

Mon cher ami,

    Vous êtes un des hommes les plus affairés qui soient, néanmoins
ai-je l'effronterie d'écrire pour demander votre conseil. L'excellent
Henri Fluchère, qui a mis tant de soins à traduire mon "Murder in the
Cathedral", n'a pas réussi à trouver un éditeur complaisant. Je sais qu'il
a fait des démarches chez Gallimard, et peut-être chez Grasset (le dernier
a, néanmoins, témoigné d'un certain intérêt dans un volume de proses).
Je ne veux pas qu'il perde sa peine: mais jusqu'à présent personne ne
s'est interessé à Murder in the Cathedral excepté un R. P. Flouquet, qui
serait disposé à le présenter dans les 'Cahiers des Poètes Catholiques' en
Belgique.

    Je ne serais pas du tout exigeant au point de vue financier (quoiqu'il faut
remarquer que c'est la maison Faber, et non moi, qui détient les droits),
mais je voudrais que les droits de traduction durent [soient] remis à la
maison la plus capable de donner si cela la publicité la plus propice. Mais
je vous demande, si cela ne vous gêne pas, de me conseiller: devrions-

---

1–Robert Melville (1905–86), art critic, was based at this time in Birmingham, where he
was associated during the 1930s with the Surrealist movement. In the 1940s he wrote for
the Birmingham *Evening Despatch*, as well as for *The Listener* and *Horizon*. Art critic of
the *New Statesman*, 1954–76, he also wrote a regular column in the *Architectural Review*,
1950–77. His writings helped to establish the reputations of Francis Bacon and Sidney
Nolan.

2–Melville wrote on 20 June 1938 to offer an essay on Picasso entitled 'The Multiplication
of Progress', with illustrations taken mostly from the Hugh Willoughby collection: 'No
volume on Picasso has so far been published in this country.'

    His pioneering study was to appear as *Picasso: Master of the Phantom* (OUP, 1939).

nous céder les droits aux 'Cahiers des Poètes Catholiques', ou tâcher d'intéresser une maison plus connue à Paris?

Vous auriez dû recevoir le dernier numéro du Criterion qui contient un petit article de Murry sur le livre de Mendizabal et sur votre préface. Dans le prochain je reparlerai de vous à l'occasion des vilaines paroles de Senor Suner. J'espère que l'appui de quelques amis anglais vous apportera quelque soulagement. Ici les fanatiques de la gauche sont plus nombreux, et plus pseudo-chrétiens, que les bigots de la droite.

Toujours votre dévoué,<br>T. S. Eliot[1]

## TO *Aldous Huxley* CC

3 August 1938 [Faber & Faber Ltd]

My dear Aldous,

It was pleasant to get a letter from you after such a long silence, during which I have heard very few and meagre rumours. I shall of course be delighted to see your friends, who will be able to give me further news of you, and I hope that they will not turn up while I am away in the country, into the beginning of September.[2]

---

1 – *Translation*: My dear friend, / You are one of the busiest of men, and yet I have the temerity to ask your advice. The excellent Henri Fluchère, who has taken such pains in translating my *Murder in the Cathedral*, has failed to find a willing publisher. I know he has approached Gallimard, and possibly Grasset (who have shown, however, tentative interest in publishing a volume of essays). I do not want his labour to be lost: but up until now no one has shown interest in *Murder in the Cathedral* except a certain R. P. Flouquet, who is ready to present it in the 'Cahiers des Poètes Catholiques' in Belgium.

I am not disposed to be in any way exigent about the financial side (although it is the publishing house of Faber, and not myself, that holds the rights), but I would like the translation rights to be sold to a house capable of promoting the book in the best way. But I should like to ask you, if you don't mind, for your advice: should we sell the rights to the 'Cahiers des Poètes Catholiques', or should we try and interest a better known house in Paris?

You should have received the latest issue of the *Criterion* which contains a little article by Murry on the book by Mendizabal, and on your preface. In the next issue I shall also be writing about you in connection with Senor Suner's ugly words. I trust that the support of a few English friends will afford you some comfort. Here the fanatics on the Left are more numerous, and more pseudo-Christian, than the bigots on the Right. / Ever your devoted, [T. S. Eliot]

JMM on Alfred Mendizabal, *Aux Origines d'une Tragédie*, C. 17 (July 1938), 718–21.

2 – Huxley (Beverly Hills, California) wrote on 12 July to say that he had given a letter of introduction to TSE to his friends Edwin Corle (1906–56), novelist, and his wife, the actress Helen Freeman (1886–1960). 'I think you will find them a very pleasant and intelligent couple.'

I wish we might see you here again, as I think one visit to California will have to do me for a lifetime. Such a journey can only be undertaken at the cost of giving a number of lectures, and unless poverty compels, I have no wish to reappear on a lecture platform.

With love to Maria,
Ever yours affectionately,
[T. S. E.]

## TO *John Betjeman*  TS Victoria

3 August 1938  *The Criterion*

Respected Betj.,

First, you have my forgiveness for being in Westmeath instead of available for Swanwick, as you have written so charmingly to both Every and myself.[1] Second, I am very much pleased by your essay on the Bressey Report, and am having it set up.[2] I warn you that there may be possible danger spots, which will come to light when the text is released into print, from the comparative obscurity of your handwriting, but these we will deal with in proof. I know that the whole subject bristles, so to speak, with difficulties which can hardly be handled without offence to somebody. You may not be aware, for instance, that the head of this firm is Estates Bursar of All Souls College, which possesses considerable housing property within the Archdeaconry of Middlesex. I was pleased by your reference to the Southern Railway: you would not have seen an acid comment of mine in the *New English Weekly* on a speech made at its last general meeting by the Chairman, a respectable Gloucestershire squire, Robert Holland Martin; and I imagine that the only branch of my family which has ever made any money is among the rackrenters of South London to whom you refer. There was a great deal in the essay for me to enjoy, and for my own part I hope it will come out quite intact.

---

1–Betjeman wrote on 21 July to excuse himself from giving the talk which TSE had commanded of him: he was coincidentally visiting Ireland, staying at Pakenham Hall, Castlepollard, County Meath, and it would have inconvenienced several people if he had changed his plans. 'As it is, I feel a frightful cad to have let down you & your friend in a crisis, when you so kindly helped me out with Shell. I have written today to your friend . . .

'What can I do in return for my delinquency? Finish the Bressey Report article in time for Aug. 1st. That I will do. I have brought it over with me & other necessary books . . . I am so happy that my conscience jabs at me for not having gone [to Swanwick] . . . I really was honoured to be asked to talk among such distinguished people – broad church though the whole thing seemed to be . . . I will willingly go next year, if they ask me.'

2–'The Bressey Report', C. 18 (Oct. 1938), 1–12.

Now about your book and the memorandum, which I return herewith. The memorandum is accepted, largely because of our confidence that you will do the book best by doing it according to your own design. There is a difference of opinion, however, about details of size and price. The committee want a book which will sell, at first, at the price of 10s.6d. or 12s.6d. They don't see how any money can be made, especially with so many illustrations, except by starting in this way, with the intention of producing a cheaper edition later on at a price which you would approve. The book will also need to be at least 70,000 words in length. I hope the prospect of doing a book of this kind will not be too disagreeable to you. We are prepared to offer a 15% royalty, and, if you want an advance, £50; but I am ready to appeal for a somewhat larger sum if that seems to you an inadequate advance for so much work.

I am writing to Ireland, as you still give that address on your last card (by the way, your picture of the Church of Ireland at work seems to contain a microphone on the table. Is that what it is meant to be, or not?).[1]

Let us meet as soon as we are both in London at the same time. I shall be away from the end of this week for a fortnight, and again from the 26th August for ten days. If we can meet in the interval I shall be very glad.

Yours ever,
T. S. Eliot

## TO *Frank Morley*

TS Frank Morley

4 August 1938                    *The Criterion*

Dear Frank,

I hope you liked the spoon. I have your letter of the 2nd instant.[2] I am glad to hear about Jeremy Taylor. Everything one reads needs some antidote (this has nothing to do with literary education of course) and well, just as Dom Chapman and our D'Arcy require the complement of say Bp. Gore, Bp. Talbot and even Joe Oldham, so the Tractarians (but I

---

1–On 27 Aug. 1938 Betjeman sent a note with his piece on the Bressey Report. 'I am so sorry I have no typewriter here & do pray that you can read this MS. London Traffic seems gloriously remote from here.

'Overleaf is a picture of the Church of England at work.'

On the back of the card was a drawing by Betjeman himself of a cleric at prayer: the object on the table, which TSE took for a microphone, is more probably a small book-stand.

2–Not traced.

recommend strongly Pusey's Private Prayers – in some respects Pusey was much more one of us than was Newman)[1] seem narrow and limited when you get into the large style of the XVII Century. Its only the real giants that one is required to face without any alternative: S. Paul, S. Augustine, and of course S. John of the Cross. I hope that the spoon will be useful. After a course of XVII Century theology it is well to look at Geo. Herbert again, but not before. And Geo. Herbert brings us back to S. John of the Cross, who I suspect was a greater poet, though not so great a craftsman. And whatever one reads I think it is well to come back to Coleridge's marginalia, but I suspect that Coleridge cannot mean very much for one, or is likely to mean the wrong things, unless one knows a fair amount of what Coleridge knew – i.e. Coleridge was the immense marginalian. I should be glad to think that that spoon might be of use. Which brings us back to E. V. Lucas, as the puny marginalian: but the sight of poor Lucas always increased my terror of death. And about that abyss, which brings us back again to S. John of the Cross (I hope that you can make some use of that spoon) the sorrow is that until you get to the point of S. John of the Cross all abysses look different, so that probably I can be of no use to Wheen or Wheen to me or either of us to Oliver until we are all so conscious as to see that it comes to the same thing. As for the abyss (do you think you can make any use of that spoon?) the ordinary mistake is to think that 'Religion' saves one from it, for the people who are saved from the abyss by religion would be saved by anything say a Sunday excursion to Scarborough for the fact is that religion to use the ordinary word can make one feel that one is walking on the edge all the time and it shows the abyss to be deeper so I dont know what you will do about that spoon unless you get some marrow bones and know how to cook them so may the B.V.M. pray for us sinners now and at the hour of our death, yours etc.,

TP.

TO *David Gascoyne*                                          cc

4 August 1938                          [*The Criterion*]

Dear Gascoyne,

Thank you for your letter of the 18th July, with the copies of the poems of P. J. Jouve, which I was unable to use for the number which is now in

---

1 – E. B. Pusey, *Private Prayers* (1883): see *Poems* I, 738.

the press.[1] I hope, however, to use them soon, and should like to be quite clear about the question of copyright and payment. I wonder if you would be so good as to get for me a note from Jouve authorising the publication of these poems on the terms I propose. Our ordinary payment for verse is at the rate of £1 per page, and as I shall print the text and translation on opposite pages, it seems to me fair to pay Jouve and yourself £1 a page each, for one, two, or all of the poems.

I have sounded my committee about an anthology of modern French poetry, and I do not find them sufficiently enthusiastic so I must return your outline herewith.[2] Incidentally, it occurs to me that if your anthology is to be comprehensive, you cannot very well ignore completely either Verlaine or Valery. There was a good translation of *Le Serpent* made some years ago by Mark Wardle, and published under the auspices of the *Criterion*. And Tristan Corbière is a really important poet, whom you ought not to ignore. So far as I know, nothing of his has ever been translated. You might also find it useful to consult the small anthology, with a running commentary, made some years ago by Ezra Pound. His anthology does not, of course, cover all the ground that you have marked out.

I am having review copies sent you[3] of Auden's *Selected Poems*, MacNeice's *The Earth Compels*, and Spender's *The Trial of a Judge*. *The Family Reunion*[4] and *On The Frontier* have not yet gone to press. I am not quite clear what set of Pound's *Cantos* you want. There has been no group of *Cantos* published recently: the last volume was *XI Cantos*. If that is the one you want, I will have it sent.

Yours very sincerely,

[T. S. Eliot]

1 – Gascoyne had submitted four translations of the most recent poems of Pierre Jean Jouve.
2 – Gascoyne proposed to put together an anthology entitled *Modern Poetry in France*; he had already written part of the introduction, and the anthology was to include translations of about 150 poems by poets including St John Perse, Mallarmé, Rimbaud, Louis Aragon, Lautréamont, Jarry, Fargue, Eluard, Bertrand, Apollinaire, Jacob, Supervielle, Cendrars, Jouve, Breton, Tzara, Peret, Char and Picasso. 'This anthology, together with a detailed analytical introduction and copious explanatory, biographical and bibliographical notes at the end, ought to constitute a really complete study and reference book on all the most modern tendencies in French poetry.'
3 – Jean Le Louët, editor of an 'important new review' called *Les Nouvelles Lettres*, had invited Gascoyne to write a piece on 'the most recently published collections of English poetry; to that end, he requested review copies of *The Family Reunion*, Auden's *Selected Poems*, MacNeice's *The Earth Compels*, SS's *The Trial of a Judge* and *Over the Frontier*, and EP's 'new "Cantos"'.
4 – The F&F agreement to publish *FR* is dated 13 June 1938.

## TO *The Editor,* The Times

4 August 1938, 12                    [Faber & Faber Ltd]

### PROFESSOR H. H. JOACHIM

I trust it will not be amiss for an old pupil to add a postscript to your obituary notice of the late Professor Joachim.[1] To him I owe not only whatever knowledge of the philosophy of Aristotle I may once have possessed but also whatever command of prose style I may still possess. There are other teachers also to whom I owe a debt of gratitude for stimulation of thought and curiosity, and for direction of studies: to Joachim alone am I aware of any debt for instruction in the writing of English. All readers of *The Nature of Truth* will acknowledge the distinction of Joachim's own writing: only those who have been his pupils know his influence upon the writing of others. He taught me, in the course of criticizing weekly essays with a sarcasm the more authoritative because of its gentle impersonality, and because he was concerned with clearing up confusion rather than with scoring off his victim, that one should know exactly what one meant before venturing to put words to paper, and that one should avoid metaphor wherever a plain statement can be found. To his *explication de texte* of the Posterior Analytics I owe an appreciation of the importance of punctuation; to his criticism of my papers I owe an appreciation of the fact that good writing is impossible without clear and distinct ideas. Any virtues my prose writing may exhibit are due to his correction; my vices are too obviously my own for me to need to disclaim his responsibility. I would not offer you this note, did I not believe that I write, not as a singular example, but as a representative of those who have had the good fortune to have been taught by Harold Joachim.

## TO *J. H. Oldham*                                        cc

4 August 1938                        [Faber & Faber Ltd]

My dear Oldham,

I am sorry that we cannot meet for so long to come, but I suppose that most of the subjects we discuss are of the kind that are almost too serious to be urgent. There is one topic, however, which I had proposed to mention to you in conversation, and will give you now, simply in the

1 – 'Professor H. H. Joachim', *The Times*, 2 Aug. 1938, 12. Joachim was a Fellow of Merton College, Oxford, 1897–1919; Wykeham Professor of Logic at New College, Oxford, 1919–35. TSE was his pupil at Merton in 1914–15. See further *CProse* 5, 646–7.

hope that you may have time to devote a few minutes' thought to it, and let me know your opinion when we meet. My Chairman has had the thought that there might be some interest in a book about Niemöller:[1] the adventurousness of his earlier life, and the present impressiveness of his behaviour and condition. I said that I would get your opinion on the subject, as you were likely to know better than anybody whether there is the material for a kind of biography of Niemöller, whether a good book could be made, and whether there is anybody who could write it.[2]

Yours ever sincerely,

[T. S. Eliot]

1–Martin Niemöller (1892–1984), who served during WWI as a resourceful U-Boat commander (being awarded the Iron Cross First Class), became a Lutheran pastor and anti-Nazi theologian. A staunch nationalist from early years, he endorsed the belief that Germany required strong leadership, and he voted for the Nazi Party in Mar. 1933. He hailed the advent of the Third Reich and even endorsed antisemitic sentiment (he credited the diehard notion that the Jews were guilty of deicide). However, when the German Christians adopted racialist policies by banning even 'non-Aryan' converts from holding positions in the ministry or as religious teachers (the so-called 'Aryan Paragraph'), Niemöller found himself in opposition (he believed the sacrament of baptism was not to be overriden by Nazi rule): he thereupon co-founded the Pastors Emergency League in Sept. 1933 to combat the intrusion of racialised criteria into church affairs: this organisation was the forerunner of the Confessing Church, co-founded in May 1934 by Niemöller and other Lutheran and Protestant churchmen, including Karl Barth and Dietrich Bonhoeffer, to oppose the Nazification of German Protestant churches – though Niemöller would admit that he continued to share certain aspects of anti-semitic prejudice through much of the 1930s. Accordingly, from the mid-1930s Niemöller became an outspoken critic of Nazi interference in Church affairs – denouncing from his pulpit the neo-paganism of Nazism – and in consequence he was arrested in July 1937, and after a lengthy spell in solitary confinement was found guilty of crimes against the Law for the Prevention of Treacherous Attacks on State and Party and the Law for the Maintenance of Respect for Party Uniforms. Himmler's SS then incarcerated him in Sachsenhausen concentration camp, and from 1941 in Dachau. Following Liberation, he was elected President of the Hesse-Nassau Lutheran Church, 1947–61, and unequivocally preached the necessity to accept collective guilt for Nazi crimes and persecutions: his views on this question informed the Stuttgart Confession of Guilt (*Stuttgarter Schuldbekenntnis*), issued in the name of the German Evangelical Church. From the 1950s he was a pacifist, and served a period as President of the World Council of Churches. He is still seen as an ambivalent figure because his stated nationalism in the 1930s led him to oppose not the totality of Nazi doctrines but only in so far as Nazi ideology interfered with the governance of Christian affairs. Niemöller's ultimate enduring shame for his early failure to speak out unequivocally against all Nazi ideology, including the abomination of anti-semitism, is enunciated in his line, 'First they came for the Socialists, and I did not speak out . . .' See further *'God is my Führer', being the last twenty-eight Sermons by Martin Niemöller* . . . with a Preface by Thomas Mann (New York, 1941); James Bentley, *Martin Niemöller: 1892–1984* (1984); Victoria Barnett, *For the Soul of the People: Protestant Protest Against Hitler* (1992); and Wolfgang Gerlach, *And the Witnesses were Silent: The Confessing Church and the Jews* (2000).

2–Oldham replied, 7 Aug.: 'I think that a book on Niemöller, if it were well done, might not only have a considerable circulation but be of great value. Unfortunately I have no idea at all

## TO *J. R. Culpin*                                              CC

4 August 1938                            [Faber & Faber Ltd]

Dear Jack,

I am returning Singer's essays herewith. Even if they were of the very
highest quality, I could still do no more than give encouragement for
future work, because a volume of essays by an unknown writer is about
as unsaleable as anything can be. Mr Singer seems to have some good
material, and a gift for affectionate observation of London life. What
he lacks is a first-rate style, and essays of this kind are only possible by
perfection of writing. I was under the impression before I saw the essays
that the author was a foreigner. I find that he is someone who knows the
English language only too well, and in the wrong way. His style shows a
certain lack of ease: it reminds me somewhat of the epistolary style of a
skilled and highly intelligent metal-worker whom I know; a man who can
talk perfectly good and simple English, but who cannot put pen to paper
without using words like *maelstrom* or *pandemonium*, a sort of language
drawn I imagine from the leading articles of the penny press. I should,
however, be glad to look at his novel when it comes along, because it is
just possible in the case of a novel that he may have other gifts which will
justify an effort to improve the writing.

Yours ever,
[T. S. Eliot]

## TO *G. F. Higginson*                                          CC

9 August 1938                            [Stamford House,
                                          Chipping Campden]

Dear Higginson,

Thank you for your letter of the 8th instant and for your conduct of the
affair. I enclose a letter from Mr Haigh-Wood, forwarded from Russell
Square, and my reply to his request for an authorisation to show to Dr
Hart.[1] I shall be obliged if you will scrutinise this reply and send it on to

---

about the material that would be available, nor have I any idea about a possible writer . . . In
the meantime the best person in this country to consult would be the Bishop of Chichester.'
1 – Higginson wrote, 8 Aug.: 'I was relieved to learn that [MH-W] had succeeded in getting
into touch with Dr Bernard Hart, who is, I understand, to see the Nurse today and your wife
probably on Wednesday . . . I am hopeful therefore that before long we shall arrive at what
seems both to Mr Bird and myself the only real solution of this most unhappy business.'

Haigh-Wood immediately if you pass it. If you think it should be couched differently, or with more restrictions, I authorise you (if that is possible and you think fit) to write a letter of authorisation to Haigh-Wood on my behalf.

I take it that Haigh-Wood has not forgotten that I am already paying five pounds a week (a payment on which I have always assumed that my wife pays no income tax). As for increasing this payment, I confirm what you have said to him according to your letter of the 8th. I think however that it was made clear, at the meeting I had with you and Bird, that no increase of payment could be contemplated unless my wife's financial affairs were taken completely out of her hands, and put under the control of some responsible administrator, presumably Haigh-Wood himself. To contribute to the expenses of some voluntary sequestration, as at the Malmaison, which she could terminate at will, would be merely to throw money away.[1] In other words, the supplementing of her income seems inseparable from certification.

Incidentally, it might be worthwhile, I suggest, at the next interview with her Bank Manager, to enquire whether the Bank have been preparing and seeing to the payment of any Income Tax that she makes. But as I imagine nearly all her income has tax deducted at source, this should not be much: indeed, perhaps she might have refund claims to make.

Yours sincerely,

[T. S. Eliot]

---

Bernard Hart, MD, MRCS, LRCP (1879–1966) – 1 Harcourt House, Cavendish House, London W.1 – author of *The Psychology of Insanity* (1912): for many years a standard textbook. Assistant Medical Officer at the Hertfordshire County Asylum, Hill End, St Albans, and at Long Grove Asylum, Epsom; Lecturer in Medical Diseases, University College Hospital, London. Appointed in 1913 the first physician for psychological medicine at University College Hospital, London, he was also on the staff of the National Hospital, Queen Square, and of the Maudsley Hospital. President of the medical section of the British Psychological Council, 1926; President of the section of psychiatry at the Royal Society of Medicine. Medical superintendent of Northumberland House Private Asylum, 344–354 Green Lanes, Finsbury Park, London N.7.

1 – VHE had been a voluntary patient at the Sanatorium de la Malmaison, nr. Paris, in 1926.

TO *Maurice Haigh-Wood*                                           CC

9 August 1938                           [Stamford House,
                                        Chipping Campden]

Dear Maurice,

In reply to your letter of the 5th instant, so far as my authority is concerned and so far as my authorisation is necessary, I give you my authority to apply for certification of your sister, Mrs T. S. Eliot, if Dr Bernard Hart thinks advisable, or to take any steps leading thereto which he thinks advisable, which may require my authorisation as well as yours.[1]

                                        Yours sincerely,
                                        [T. S. E.]


FROM *G. F. Higginson*                                  TS Valerie Eliot

10 August 1938                          Bird & Bird,
                                        5 Gray's Inn Square,
                                        London

Dear Mr Eliot,

Many thanks for your letter of yesterday with its enclosures.

The authority which you have signed, in my opinion, entirely meets the case and I have accordingly forwarded it immediately to Mr Haigh-Wood. I have also spoken to him again through the telephone this morning. He tells me that Dr Bernard Hart has seen your wife and that while he is satisfied beyond all doubt that she is certifiable he does not think that the case is one of sufficient immediate urgency to justify the issue of a certificate without a second opinion. The difficulty will be to arrange for your wife to see another Doctor but Mr Haigh-Wood tells me that he is doing everything possible to that end and hopes for some further developments today or tomorrow. He will then write to you himself and report.

---

1 – This letter contradicts Seymour-Jones's comments, in *Painted Shadow*, 559: "'Tom would not sign the committal order," remembered a resentful Maurice [in an interview with Michael Hastings in 1980]. Eliot was not prepared to take responsibility for Vivienne's final committal. According to Maurice, it was Jack Hutchinson, who had met Vivienne in 1936, who signed the order. Enid Faber confirmed to Michael Hastings, in a letter of 26 August 1983, that she did not sign an involuntary reception order on behalf of Vivienne Eliot – "And I do not think my husband Geoffrey did." Enid remembered that "some member of the family did". Maurice later said: "I don't think I did. If I did I can't remember," but guilt clouded his memory.'

It appears that the fact that you are already paying your wife £5 a week[1] had for the moment slipped his memory, but after taking this allowance into consideration he thinks that the means that are available will after all be sufficient to maintain Mrs Eliot without calling upon you for a further contribution and does not desire to trouble you further with the financial situation for the time being. It is of course an essential part of the certification that a Receiver should be appointed to take over complete control of your wife's financial affairs. I agree with you that Mr Haigh-Wood is probably the most suitable person for this purpose, and when the time comes will get into touch with him and arrange to do what is necessary. We shall then have to go fully into her affairs – which will be scrutinised by the Court by whom the Receiver will be appointed – and I will take the opportunity of going into the question of tax to which you refer.

Yours sincerely,<br>
G. F. Higginson

## TO *A. Desmond Hawkins*

TS A. Desmond Hawkins

11 August 1938                    *The Criterion*

Dear Hawkins,

Your letter of the 5th was forwarded to me in the country.[2] The suggestion is a very ingenious one, which might lead to very interesting consequences; and I should be very glad to see it gone into thoroughly. Perhaps the first question is, up to what size book will the educational presses print, having the instruction of their pupils in mind? Then, how many books (or how much total printed matter) would any one school undertake during the course of a year? and finally, how many copies would they print? (I suppose binding is taught in the same schools, but I am ignorant). Upon the answers to these questions (especially the first) must depend the suggestions to be made by the men of letters who interest themselves. I suggest that the organisation should be as loose as possible, beginning by getting half a dozen people, such as those you name, to

---

1–£5 per week in 1938 is roughly equivalent to £330 in today's value.

2–Letter not traced. This had to do with an 'Authors Guild Editions' project – 'to make available works of lesser known authors which are out of print or virtually inaccessible' (to be printed by the L.C.C. Printing School), and 'to deposit copies in the principal libraries of England, the British Empire and the United States, including the central depots of the public library exchange system' – that ADH was planning.

make suggestions: but a central group (I think yourself and two others) would have to determine at least the order of precedence.

It sounds like the germ of a sort of cooperative movement among men of letters. Something of the sort may eventually be necessary to preserve civilisation – i.e. to preserve and circulate all the books that wont sell from 10,000 copies up in sixpenny editions.

Yours ever,<br>T. S. E.

Yes, I was glad to hear about the *N.E.W.* arrangement.


## FROM *Maurice Haigh-Wood*                    MS Valerie Eliot

14 August 1938                    36 Cranley Gardens, S.W.7

Dear Tom,[1]

Vivienne is now at Northumberland House, Green Lanes, N.4.[2]

---

1 – This letter was published, in excerpted form, in Blake Morrison, *Too True* (1998), 140–1. EVE to Frederick Tomlin, 5 May 1987: 'I can state categorically that Tom never visited Vivien at Northumberland House' (EVE). 'The doctors had told him he mustn't,' said EVE to Blake Morrison (*Too True*, 139–40).

Michael Hastings, 'Introduction', *Tom & Viv* (1985), 39: 'Her doctors were only obliged to show "she is an individual, no longer able to fulfil her duty because of unsoundness of mind, and is therefore a fit and proper person to be detained", under the Government Reception Order, Section 4, 1890 Lunacy Act.'

See *Law Reports: The Statutes, 53 Victoriae, chs. 1–5, May 1, 1890*, vol. xxvii, Part 1: 'An Act to consolidate certain of the Enactments respecting Lunatics', 7ff; Charles Mercier, *Lunacy Law for Medical Men* (1894): 'Private Patients: Placing Under Control', 7ff.

Evidently TSE wrote about Vivien's committal to both his brother and his sister Ada Sheffield. HWE replied on 27 Sept. 1938: 'I was glad to get your letter of the 14th [not traced] yesterday, and also glad to hear from Ada that she had heard from you. We are of course glad to hear that Vivien has been placed in an asylum. As I understand it from Ada, she had bought a house and a car, besides keeping the Clarence Gate apartment and I know not what else. I am glad that it was Maurice that took this step and that you are relieved of the responsibility; also I suppose that you will now be able to get possession of your library, personal papers, and family heirlooms that she has retained. And I am glad that now you will be able to come and go without fear of annoyance or attack. And I am of course glad for her own sake, since the next thing she would have been hit by an automobile while wandering around demented' (Houghton).

2 – Northumberland House was run as a private asylum by the Stocker family from 1912 to 1954, when the site was acquired by the London County Council and demolished in 1955. Situated to the south of the New River on the east side of Green Lanes, on the border of Finsbury Park and Stoke Newington, the building was constructed in 1821 as a late Georgian Palladian country house of three storeys, with a pillared entrance, balustrade and urns on its roof, and with two-storeyed wings; and it was presently sold in 1826 for conversion into a 'private lunatic asylum'. Opened in 1829, the asylum accommodated forty private patients (male and female). The women were housed in ground-floor 'Ladies' Apartments' within

I took Dr Bernard Hart up to see her on Wednesday morning, & arranged for Dr Edward Mapother[1] to go to see her at Dr Cyriax[2] on Friday, where she had an appointment for massage.

I saw Dr Mapother afterwards. Both doctors felt strongly that she should be put into a home. They handed me their certificates. I then had to go before a magistrate to obtain his order. I got hold of one in Hampstead.

I then went up to Northumberland House, saw the doctor there, & arranged for a car to go with 2 nurses to Compayne Gardens that evening.

The car went at about 10 p.m. Vivienne went very quietly with them after a good deal of discussion.

I spoke to the doctor yesterday evening, & was told that Vivienne had been fairly cheerful, had slept well & eaten well, & had sat out in the garden & read a certain amount.

The head doctor is Dr Dillon[3] & his assistant is Dr Edwards.

---

both wings: each patient being afforded a room measuring 10 x 10 feet, with fireplace and window, and accessed by a door from a central gallery. In 1877 it was taken over as a going concern by the experienced and humane Dr Alonzo Stocker (owner of Peckham House Asylum), who made improvements to the patients' accommodation, including a bath, toilets and indoor plumbing.

A descriptive advertisement for Northumberland House appears in William H. Gattie, *Lunacy Practice: A Practical Guide for the Certification and Detention of Persons of Unsound Mind* (London: Shaw & Sons, 2nd edn, 1913): 'A Private Home for the reception and treatment of patients suffering from Nervous and Mental Diseases: This House was established in 1814 [*sic*] for the care and treatment of Ladies and Gentlemen of the upper and middle classes. Its buildings and gardens extend over seven acres of ground highly situated facing Finsbury Park.

'Arrangements are made for the classification of the patients according to their various mental conditions, and separate villas away from the main Institution afford excellent accommodation for suitable cases, and have nothing of the asylum character about them.

'Besides medical treatment, every effort is made to promote recovery by means of occupation and recreation, the patients having daily opportunities for out-door exercise and excursions, whilst various in-door amusements such as Dances, Re-unions, Billiards, Music, etc., are provided.

'Religious services are conducted in the House once a week by the Chaplain.

'Convalescent establishment and Seaside Branch at Worthing.

'Voluntary Boarders are received without certificate.'

1–Dr Edward Mapother (1881–1940), physician; progressive psychiatrist; from 1919, Medical Superintendent of the Maudsley Hospital, which became in 1923 the main institution for the treatment of psychiatric ailments, as well as for teaching and research in psychiatry; creator of the Institute of Psychiatry at King's College London, where he was first Professor of Psychiatry.

2–Dr Anna Cyriax, a physiotherapist, practised with her husband Dr James Cyriax and father-in-law Dr Edgar Cyriax at 41 Welbeck Street. Seymour-Jones, *Painted Shadow*, 507, notes that Anna Cyriax was VHE's 'favourite doctor'.

3–Frederick Dillon was Medical Superintendent of Northumberland House.

The fee is 6 gns a week plus £1 per month for Laundry.[1]

This evening I went to see Janes, who told me about the house at Edge St & the flat at 34 Russell Chambers. I knew of the one at 21 Burleigh Mansions. Janes also took me round to the Belgravia Garage, Caroline Terrace, where I saw her car. I believe she is also paying heavily for storage of furniture somewhere or other.

I gather that a 'receiver' will now have to be appointed, & I suppose it will be his job to liquidate all this business.

I don't know yet what the procedure is. I imagine that the Commissioners of the Board of Control are the proper body.

I find from what Janes told me & also Nurse Moore, that Vivienne was in the habit often of saving up her drugs & then taking an enormous dose all at once, which I suppose accounts for the periodical crises.

As soon as you get back I should very much like to see you.

From all I hear Northumberland House is very good. There are 3 separate houses & patients are graded according to the severity of their case, rather like Malmaison.[2]

It has been a rather harrowing week. I do hope she will settle down & find some peace there.[3]

---

1–In anticipation of the committal of VHE, TSE's solicitor G. F. Higginson had written to him on 8 Aug., following a telephone discussion with MH-W, to report that VHE's finances were 'in a serious condition'. Although MH-W did 'not yet know exactly how far her income has been reduced, he thinks that it may well be inadequate to provide the expenses in the Home, and this will obviously become of some importance in considering the most suitable establishment to which to send her. In brief, he feels that he may have to ask whether you would be prepared to supplement her income to some small extent for the time being until her Mother dies.'

2–See too EVE to Blake Morrison (*Too True*, 141): 'Vivienne was in the nicest part, the Villas, where the patients who needed least watching lived. They only moved her when she began stealing from and worrying other patients. She stirred up a lot of havoc in the place, apparently.'

3–EVE to Peter Ackroyd, 2 Oct. 1984: 'it is clear from a handwritten letter of 14 August 1938 that Maurice Haigh-Wood collected certificates from the two doctors and then went before a magistrate to obtain his order before arranging for a car to go with two nurses to collect Vivien and take her to Northumberland House. As he attended to all the details I think it is a fair assumption that he signed the certificate. My husband made regular payments to Vivien throughout the rest of her life which covered most of her expenses.'

Enid Faber (who wrote down in 1950 her personal memories of VHE) to EVE, 18 Feb. 1984: 'I do not now remember seeing a Doctor [during her visits to VHE at Northumberland House], & would have said that I went to see Vivienne much more often than 2 or 3 times a year . . . I do remember seeing a Nurse once, & so on.'

EVE to Revd Canon Christopher G. Colven (vicar of St Stephen's), 9 Sept. 1993: 'Lady Faber visited her fairly regularly, and said that Vivien had to be supervised after a while because she was stealing from the other patients, and upsetting them in various ways.'

EVE to Harman Grisewood, 23 Sept. 1993: 'Enid used to visit her, and on one occasion Vivien protested that an eye was being kept on her, and would Enid please find out why. She

I shall look forward to seeing you on your return.

Yrs ever<br>Maurice

## FROM *G. F. Higginson*                                             TS Valerie Eliot

17 August 1938                           Bird & Bird,
                                         5 Gray's Inn Square,
                                         London

Dear Mr Eliot,[1]

From a letter received from Mr Haigh-Wood this morning I gather that he has already reported to you that your Wife was seen by a second Doctor on Friday last and has now been certified. She is at present in Northumberland House, Green Lanes, Finsbury Park. I have no doubt whatever that this is by far the best thing for her in the unhappy circumstances of her case and I think it will be a relief to you to know that she is now under proper supervision.

At Mr Haigh-Wood's request I enclose an account of Dr Mapother's fee – the second Doctor to see your Wife – which you have kindly undertaken to pay.

The next question to be considered is the appointment of a Receiver to take over the control of Mrs Eliot's affairs. I spoke to Mr Haigh-Wood through the telephone this afternoon and understand that owing to the difficulties of his own private affairs he does not feel he can take on any further commitments and although he is quite prepared to assist to the best of his ability in the application for the appointment of a Receiver he does not feel able to act in that capacity himself. You I know would not wish to do so, and as I do not think there are any other near relatives who could be expected to undertake the task, I would suggest that the Official Solicitor be appointed. This is the normal procedure under similar circumstances and I think quite appropriate to your Wife's case.

The Manager of the Trustee Department of the District Bank telephoned to me this afternoon and suggested that the Bank might act if the Court

---

was told by the doctors that Vivien had been stealing from the other patients and causing disruption . . . Please do not believe anything you read in any newspaper. You and your friend can rest assured that Tom did not ill-treat his first wife – in fact friends from that period have said they did not know how he put up with the situation for so long. It was all very sad.'

1 – Letter addressed to TSE at Stamford House, Chipping Campden, Gloucestershire.

would agree. It is certainly not usual for Banks to be appointed, and indeed until recently the Court would not entertain such a proposition at all. I believe, however, that they have modified their views now, but there is no case of a Bank having actually been appointed within my own knowledge, nor do I think that the Bank offers any advantage over the Official Solicitor in the present case. I should, however, be glad to have your views on the matter.[1]

Yours sincerely,
G. F. Higginson

## TO *John Hayward*                                                TS King's

17 August 1938                          *The Criterion*

Dear John,

Many thanks for your letter.[2] I am glad to hear that the essential features seem to have been 'embodied', though I regret that those I wished to have incorporated, such as the Tickford roof, conduite intèrieure, outboard motor, and hydroplane undercarriage for taxiing across the Round Pond, would have added too much to the tonnage, displacement and tare. However, I look forward to a walk to test the advantages for myself.

As you see, Gloucestershire has provided no new freaks of nature for the post card industry, and I am reduced to the familiar letter head. Weather variable. I return on Monday and will telephone.

Yours &c.,
TP.

## TO *G. F. Higginson*                                              CC

18 August 1938                          [Faber & Faber Ltd]

Dear Mr Higginson,

Thank you for your letter of the 17th. I had already had an account of the events from Mr Haigh-Wood, and everything appears to have been arranged satisfactorily so far.

---

1 – EVE to Stella Newton, 15 Mar. 1984: 'Those who claim that [TSE] had her put away to get his hands on her money are talking rubbish, because under our law the official solicitor takes charge of the finances of anybody certified. The press seems to have little regard for truth.'

2 – Not traced. TSE had purchased a bespoke wheelchair for JDH.

I take it that it is in order for me to send a cheque direct to Dr Mapother, and will do so unless I hear from you to the contrary. I presume that there will also be an account from Dr Hart.[1]

I am not surprised, from what I know of Mr Haigh-Wood's affairs, that he should be unwilling to take over the conduct of Mrs Eliot's affairs. He has quite enough on his hands looking after his mother's finances. And I imagine that there will be considerable work to be done at the beginning: I gather from his letter that there is not only the car, and a flat at Burleigh Mansions to be disposed of, but a house in Edge Street, Campden Hill,[2] and a flat in Russell Chambers. I do not know how much the Official Solicitor takes upon himself, and whether his office would dispose of these properties immediately for whatever they would fetch, or would make serious efforts in the patient's interest, to obtain the best market price for them. Nevertheless, I am a priori in favour of appointing the Solicitor rather than the Bank, which has primarily its own interests to consult in the matter of the overdraft. I think that the views of Mr Haigh-Wood ought to be obtained before making a decision.[3]

I shall be in London during next week, and come up to town on Monday morning.

Yours sincerely,<br>
[T. S. Eliot]

---

1–Higginson responded, 19 Aug.: 'It will be quite in order for you to send your cheque direct to Dr Mapother. Mr Haigh-Wood will no doubt let me have Dr Hart's account in due course.'

2–By July 1936 VHE had signed a six-year lease on 8 Edge Street, Church Street, Notting Hill, at a rent of £160 a year; she was still paying £215 per annum for 68 Clarence Gate Gardens.

3–Higginson, 19 Aug.: 'I am glad to note that you agree with my view that the Official Solicitor is the most suitable person to be appointed as Receiver and I think Mr Haigh-Wood is of the same opinion . . .

'Although I hope to be able to issue the Summons for the appointment of a Receiver in the near future it is unlikely, owing to the Vacation, that the matter will actually be dealt with by the Court before October. I have therefore asked Mr Haigh-Wood to arrange with the authorities at the Home for their account to stand over for the time being until the Receiver is appointed. This is not unusual as there is always some delay between certification and the appointment of a Receiver during which time there is no one officially in a position to deal with the patient's estate. It would, I think, perhaps be advisable for you temporarily to discontinue the weekly payments of £5 which I take it are made under Banker's order direct to your Wife's account, until we see our way more clearly with regard to the financial position, otherwise they will merely be absorbed in reduction of her overdraft whereas if you allow them to accumulate on your account they will gradually provide a small sum of cash which would be available in the case of any emergency arising before the Receiver is appointed.'

TO *The Manager, Lloyds Bank*                              CC

21 August 1938                    [Faber & Faber Ltd]

Dear Sir,

On the advice of my Solicitors, I am writing to request you to discontinue until further notice the weekly payment of £5 which you have been making from my account to the District Bank, Cornhill, for the benefit of Mrs Eliot.

I may explain that Mrs Eliot has been certified of unsound mind, and it has been suggested that no further payments should be made to her account until a Receiver has been appointed to clear up her affairs.

Yours faithfully,

[T. S. Eliot]


TO *A. Desmond Hawkins*                    TS A. Desmond Hawkins

22 August 1938                    *The Criterion*

Dear Hawkins,

Your letter of the 12th has awaited my return from the country. I have to be away again throughout next week, but I expect to be in London after that, and should like to arrange a meal with you about three weeks hence.

I am quite willing to be a member of a *preliminary* committee in the company of Roberts and yourself, to examine the scheme and decide on the next steps.[1] I don't think I could undertake to be a member of any permanent committee to deal with material and the machinery for printing and circulating it, because I should not have the time, but I shall be very glad to help as much as I can at the beginning. Incidentally, I don't suppose that Roberts will be back from his mountain climbing until some time in September.

---

1 – 'I am very pleased to know that the printing idea interests you . . . Once the thing starts it should be fairly easy to keep it alive. I accept your suggestions about organisation, which are much to my own way of thinking. I don't think we want to start with a rigid idea of membership . . . If I am to be one of a central group of three I should like Michael Roberts and yourself as the other two. Would you be prepared to consider yourself as "appointed" to that as a preliminary committee to examine the scheme[?] . . . [M]ore bluntly, can I quote you as being (with Michael and myself) sponsor of a preliminary enquiry?'

I am very interested to hear of your programme for the *N.E.W.*, and of course shall be glad to help when I can.[1] This is another subject which I should like to discuss in conversation.

I also have received the Maritains' book on poetry.[2] I have not yet had time to read it, but I think it should certainly deserve a note. When you have read it, would you write and tell me what you think of it, and whether you are still interested to write a note on it for the December *Criterion*?

Yours ever,
T. S. E.

## TO *George Bell* CC

23 August 1938               [Faber & Faber Ltd]

My dear Lord Bishop,

I should be grateful if you would give me your opinion of the following suggestion. We have been considering for some time whether it might not be desirable and interesting to have a book on the life and opinions of Pastor Niemöller. The question remained in abeyance for some time, as I had been hoping for an opportunity to see Oldham and discuss it with him. As we were unable to meet I finally wrote to ask his opinion, and I find that he believes that such a book might have some success, and be of considerable value. He professes ignorance, however, both about the availability of material and the suitability of an author. I therefore write to you to ask for your opinion, first on the desirability of such a book; second on the possibility of collecting the necessary material, covering the whole life and career of the man; and third, a possible author.

I should be very grateful for any observations you care to make.[3]

---

1 – 'I'm very hopeful about my job with the New English [Weekly]. I'm expecting to bring in a fair number of new people who will strengthen it. Wyn Griffith, Elizabeth Bowen, James Hanley have already undertaken reviews. I want to make a big splash of Views and Reviews ... No, I can't restrain myself from asking you to come in once in a way – even once a year ... I thought of asking Read, Dobrée and Muir – as well as yourself – to come back at long enough intervals for you to have forgotten what a nuisance it is. My other possibles are Charles Smyth, V. S. Pritchett and Richard Church – and old hands like Porteus, Every, Barlow, Cullis etc.'

2 – 'Maritain has just sent me a new book by his wife and himself. Would you like a short note from me about it for the next Cri?' No review of *Situation du poé*sie (1938) appeared in C.

3 – Bell replied, 24 Aug.: 'It so happens that Pastor Hildebrandt, a very able man, Niemoller's Curate and a Non-Aryan Christian has just written anonymously (for his name must be kept

937

With most cordial good wishes to Mrs Bell and yourself,
I am, my dear Lord Bishop,
Yours very sincerely,
[T. S. Eliot]

## TO *Enid Faber*                                         TS Valerie Eliot

23 August 1938                    *The Criterion*

Dear Enid,

Referring to the message above,[1] I dare say you will be annoyed with
me for changing my mind and not bringing a leelow,[2] but there are several
reasons for the Telescope.[3] (1) It was my own idea (2) it is more of a
gadget (3) it is more edifying and mind-broadening for Tom than a day-
bed (4) in spite of your graphic description I was uncertain about the kind
of leelow, I saw one in Gloucestershire like an elongated wheelbarrow,
with two wheels and two legs, easily moved about. I meant to buy a
Cotswold Dog Bed for Gyp, but forgot to get his measurements. If I had
known as much about telescopes as I do since this morning, I would have
seen about it six months ago. Apparently a telescope is like a gun, you
get yourself measured and have it built to order. Mr Negretti, or perhaps
Mr Zambra,[4] seemed to look down on me for expecting to get a telescope
ready made. There was not a great deal of choice: the standard 'Public
School Telescope' costs twenty guineas, so I thought that might wait until
Tom developed an alarming passion for astronomy; besides, it is too big
for him to lug about himself. So I have secured one which is not quite

---

absolutely confidential) a short book about Pastor Niemoller which has been published in
Switzerland, and is certain to have a large sale there. It is now being translated into English,
and Hildebrandt has asked me to see what I can do about getting a publisher. He wants me
to write a foreword, but his name must be kept out. I enclose you the book as he has given
it to me without myself having read it, for I am no good at German. I am certain, however,
it will be a good piece of work, and it will be interesting. I do not know really there is quite
the material for a full scale study of the life and opinions of Niemoller. But I have no doubt
material could be added to what Hildebrandt has written, either by himself or by some other
person. But I would venture to suggest for your consideration the possibility of publishing
Hildebrandt's book in English for the Christmas season, and if it is any help I would write
a preface or something of that kind.' Pastor Hildebrandt was living in Blackheath, London.
1 – A handwritten note attached to the letter: 'Mr Faber rang up & said they would very
much like a telescope.'
2 – Li-Lo: an inflatable mattress or bed.
3 – See photo of TSE standing in plus-fours, with godson Tom peering through the telescope.
4 – Negretti and Zambra – founded by Henry Negretti (1818–79) and Joseph Zambra
(1822–97) – was a well-known firm of instrument makers.

what I wanted, but which is guaranteed to reach the rings of Saturn etc. and has a cap you put on if you want to look at the Sun. Now if I can obtain a Prayer Book, a Bible, a Guide to the Heavens, and an elementary handbook of navigation and knot-making, I shall be ready to start.[1] Having begun the day by shopping, I fell to buying things for myself: item, a Waterproof Jacket, which should be the admiration of the county, and a pair of heavy walking shoes (in CASE I am led onto a precipice again) guaranteed to hold if you walk on the ceiling.

Now, I want you to let me know what train is most convenient for you for me to take on Friday. I hope that is clear. I mean that I should prefer the Aberystwyth route because the scenery is more cheerful, but I will come either to Aberystwyth or Carmarthen & Lampeter whichever fits in.[2] There are trains to either about 11 to 12 in the morning: but just send me a WIRE to say what train to take and I will take it. I shall, Alas, have to leave on Saturday the 3d, unless I take a sleeping car on the Friday night; because I Must spend that weekend Sunday with some American friends who are sailing the following week. I have to get from Wales to Campden Glos., so if there is a train that stops at Oxford I will make a connexion there. I hope you have recovered from Oliver and so will close, your respectful

TP.

N.B. To bring electric torch for Bats.


TO *Edith Perkins*                                   TS Beinecke

24 August 1938                    *The Criterion*

My dear Lady,

It was, one would say, but a question of sitting down and addressing oneself to the, however, always formidable typewriter – all the more formidable because of the comparative, blessed release from the thumping of the keys, enjoyed in Campden: yet for the first two days after return to the discipline of the so massive and overwhelming Emperor's Gate, the oppression of the matter of gratitude insistent to be expressed battered

---

1 – At some point during this year, TSE gave his godson a copy of the *Book of Common Prayer*, inscribed 'Thomas Erle Faber / from his godfather / Thomas Stearns Eliot / 1938.' (Sold at Bonhams, 20 Sept. 2005.) He also gave a Bible and Prayer Book to Susanna Morley in the summer of this year.
2 – GCF's diary, Fri. 26 Aug.: 'Enid met TSE at Lampeter at 6.40.' TSE stayed with the Fabers from 26 Aug. to 3 Sept.

in vain against the too narrow gates, as it were, of expression; oh, it was obvious from the start, as one might in an indolent and relaxed moment say, that ultimately those gates would have to be forced by this turbid torrent, at the cost, one had already surmised, of disorder and even rout in the ranks of syntax and vocabulary. The result, as you may already have conjectured, was likely to be, and indeed is, a commixture of verbiage, idiom and imagery, which could not by the furthest stretch of generosity be said to 'come off': yet I hope that you will nevertheless accept, with the confidently expected tolerant interpretativeness, such babblings as one can pay only a few friends the honour of assuming their ability to decipher the clue of. It wasn't, one adds hastily, and conscious all at once of the incalculable number of separate and particular moments, each one of which deserved detailed and singular analytical record – it wasn't conceived or executed with the clarity of Swift, or the gravity of Johnson, or the urbanity of Walpole (not poor dear Hugh, but dear Horace) or even the directness of Byron: but could it be, one wondered pensively, that the lingo had changed with the times, or perhaps that these authors had never experienced a situation, in relation to or *vis à vis* a hostess, which taxed their powers of elucidation to the extent to which this taxes his? However that may be, my Dear Mrs Perkins, I cannot feel that, *le cas échéant*,[1] any more signally than the author, they would have triumphed over the difficulties of expression: no, not even our dear, our cherished, our venerated Flaubert.

> I remain, my dear Mrs Perkins,
> Your obliged obedient servant,
> T. Possum

## TO *John Betjeman*                                    TS Victoria

25 August 1938                          *The Criterion*

Respected Betje,

I have had a word with de la Mare about the illustrations, size and make-up for your book,[2] and there seem to be several minor questions to settle, so that I think it would really save much time and trouble if you would find an opportunity, at your convenience, to look in and have

---

1 – *le cas échéant* (Fr.): 'where appropriate'.
2 – F&F was taking over publication of the Shell Guides: starting with *Somerset*, ed. Betjeman and Peter Quennell (1939).

a talk with him. He would prefer this himself, and besides being keenly interested in the book, he would like to make your acquaintance. So when you feel ready to do so, ring up and arrange an appointment to see him.

Yours ever,<br>T. S. E.

## TO *E. Martin Browne* cc

25 August 1938                [*The Criterion*]

My dear Martin,

Thank you for your letter. Gielgud's reply seems promising, and I shall be very glad if we can meet him and have a discussion in September.[1] I expect to be back again myself on the 5th or 6th.

Yours ever,<br>[Tom]

P.S. I have been reading Christopher Fry's stuff, and it seems to me quite promising. Has he anything more to show? But as I am getting this note off to you before leaving for Wales, I should like to discuss his work further with you when we are both in town again.[2]

---

1 – The actor John Gielgud (see letter of 24 Oct 1938, below) had expressed an interest in appearing in *The Family Reunion*. See also letter to John Hayward, 20 Oct. 1938 below.
2 – Christopher Fry was induced to write verse for the Tewkesbury Festival pageant 1939.

EMB had been trying for many months to get TSE involved; and as late as 25 Oct 1938 he wrote to him: 'I enclose the scenario for Tewkesbury. I have still not got the concrete material for the last scenes, but that does not affect the structure of the whole or the verse-framework: and I have verified the times for the Choruses. 10 lines a minute is a liberal allowance – you would be safe with 8 or 9 decasyllabic lines, for instance, in the open air: and for the characters on the roof I have allowed 5 lines a minute.

'I have done some cutting of my original scenario to get this result: and of course it is open to the most thorough overhauling.

'Let me say that I do appreciate your reluctance to overburden yourself. I would not go further with it did I not feel that one or two of the chances it gives – such as the study of spiritual development within the Chorus, and the Babel chorus as a piece of craftsmanship – might lead to the exploration of useful avenues for verse-drama. And I hope that, in its present severely restricted form, the job is not an unweildy [*sic*] one. If you see ways of further reducing it, do let me know.'

## TO *H. J. C. Marshall*[1]                              TS Royal Literary Fund

1 September 1938                              24 Russell Square

Dear Sir,[2]

Mr Dylan Thomas has requested me to write to you, in connexion with his application for a grant from the Royal Literary Fund.[3]

Mr Thomas has informed me of his present reasons for distress and anxiety, and I have heard from other sources, from time to time, of the desperate state of his financial affairs.

Mr Thomas has, from time to time, contributed both prose and verse to the *Criterion*, which I edit; and I am publishing another poem of his in the next issue.[4] I consider him one of a very small number of notable poets of his generation whose names will survive the test of time; he has the additional distinction of being the most brilliant (in my opinion) of younger Welsh writers. I wish to support wholeheartedly his application; and I do not know of any way at the present moment in which a grant

---

1–H. J. C. Marshall (1873–1947): Secretary of the Royal Literary Fund, 1919–45.

2–This letter is evidently typed by TSE himself.

3–Dylan Thomas wrote from Sea View, Laugharne, Carmarthenshire, 23 Aug.: 'Dear Mr Eliot, / I am applying to the Royal Literary Fund for a grant of money, because of my present desparate [*sic*] position and because my wife is soon going to have a baby. We have no support at all apart from my earnings as a writer, which are extremely little, and I hope the Fund will see that my cause is deserving. I'm told that in my application I should give the names of two or three wellknown writers who will say a word for me. Could I please use your name, which would be of very great help? As far as I can gather, all you would have to do – if you did agree to help me in this way – would be to answer the enquiries of the Fund trustees and to say that, in your opinion, I was deserving of their charity. Without some such immediate grant I will have to give up the house that with difficulty we rented and furnished here & take again to lodgings and running from debts and instability and less and less opportunities for doing my own work. But above all I have to consider the wellfare [*sic*] of my wife and her baby, and I do very much hope that you will allow me to use your name. / Yours sincerely, / Dylan Thomas.' (EVE)

Thomas wrote again on 31 Aug.: 'Thank you very much for your letter, and for being so kind as to allow me to use your name as a reference to the Royal Literary Fund. / This morning I heard from the Fund Secretary, who said that my application "must be accompanied by letters from two or three respectable persons authenticating the merits of my case. Although the Fund does not meet until October, the Secretary, Mr Marshall, wishes me to have these letters sent to him at once as he intends approaching the Government on my behalf for an immediate bit of money to keep me going until October. Would you send Mr Marshall a letter to his Welsh address?: H. J. C. Marshall, O.B.E., M.C., Y Gell, Trelyllyn, near Towyn. It would help my cause a great deal and, I am sure, enable me to get something quite soon. / Thank you again. / Yours sincerely, / Dylan Thomas. / [P.S.] If on your holiday you come near Laugharne, which isn't far from Lampeter, I do hope you'll call to see us' (EVE).

4–'Poem' ('How shall my animal'), C. 18 (Oct. 1938), 20–30.

from the Royal Literary Fund could be more suitably bestowed. If it should prove desirable, I should be very glad to do anything further in my power to advance his claim to the beneficence of the Crown.

Yours very truly,
T. S. Eliot
Litt.D., LL.D.,
Editor of *The Criterion*

## TO *George Every*

TS Sarah Hamilton

8 September 1938                    *The Criterion*

Dear George,

Your letter of 28 August was forwarded to me in the country, but I am very lazy when I am out of town, and indisposed to cope, while a visitor in the house of friends with the problem of time, space, and an unfamiliar typewriter. I am very sorry indeed to have missed Nicholson, but I shall write to him a word of encouragement, and hope that there will be another opportunity of meeting before long.[1] I must explain that I was somewhat delayed in returning by a cold, due to several circumstances, probably including imprudent sea-bathing on a cold day.

I am keenly interested in your suggestion of a group to consider the problems of education in conjunction with the ~~original~~ Moot.[2] It was certainly inherent in Oldham's original idea that the Moot itself should only be one of a number of groups dealing with more or less specialised problems, somewhat according to the nature of the composition of each;

1 – The young poet Norman Nicholson (1914–87).
2 – Every wrote on 28 Aug. of 'an idea that has been in my mind since I corresponded with [F. R.] Leavis . . . I touched on it with Geoffrey Curtis. And that has been that a group might be formed of people concerned with education and radically critical of the existing state of affairs, people who think education ought to have something to do with Weltanschaaung, without being necessarily Christians. This could co-operate with the Moot, and include some people who were left out of the Moot as I was simply from lack of space . . . In many ways I should be glad to have Dobrée as I believe I could make contact with him more easily than with most people and he would make it possible to approach others without the appearance of a clerical plot.'

and that it might to some extent develop ~~peripherally~~ fissiparously.[1] I do hope that you and Curtis and others will push on towards its realisation, and I should be very glad to participate as far as possible. I think that it is important that such a group should have a nucleus of persons who realise the radical nature of the task to be undertaken. You do not want it to be littered and hampered at the beginning by distinguished official educators whose aims are rather toward patchwork improvement and compromise. From this point of view I think that at the beginning such an association would be of more value to Dobrée than Dobrée would be to the group. Even with this limitation, however, I think he would be worth having, and might prove very helpful in the long run, and even immediately, in forming contracts [*sc.* contacts] with a less clerical world. He has his nose to the grindstone of the provincial university machine, and is at present a very tired man, but he is not without perception of the futilities of contemporary education. His mental formation is Liberal, but he has the rare advantage of being a man of breeding, so that his instincts with regard, for instance, to society, the community and the land, are likely to be right. He is also a person of strong, and I imagine hereditary, public spirit.

I will write again next week, when I get a bit straightened out.

Yours ever,

T. S.

1–Oldham in *The Church and Its Function in Society* (1937), 198: 'Wherever there has been a revival of Christianity of an enduring kind it has generally found expression in the spontaneous activity of small groups meeting for mutual encouragement, fellowship, and common effort. The conception of "cells" is wholly congruous with the genius of Christianity. May not the formation of such cells of Christian witness and service be the distinctive Christian contribution to the social and political struggles of our time? To be effectively changed a social system must be changed from within and in all its parts' (cited in Clements, *Faith on the Frontier*, 365).

11 September 1938      *The Criterion*

Dear Mrs Perkins,

The dog was safely fetched on Saturday morning, and a very handsome animal he is. Emily stopped long enough to have some conversation with the two agreeable young women who run the Kennels, and I think elicited enough information to start with. The dog is fifteen months old, and has reached his full stature, but not his mature weight and thickness. He seems a very gentle affectionate creature, but has the advantage of appearing very formidable, and as most people appear to think that he is a dark Alsatian, he proved very useful in clearing a way through the crowd at Victoria. I believe that he is just the right kind of dog for her to have. Certainly he was the right kind for this moment, for being highly (though pleasantly) excited by his first acquaintance with trains and taxis, he required a good deal of attention, and I think by doing so made the day of departure less painful than it might have been.

I confess that with the political situation what it is, I felt acute relief at getting Emily off. I had felt anxiety for some weeks; as from no point of view that I can admit, would it be desirable for her to be here in time of war. Please God that may not happen; but the position is still so delicate that I shall, on balance, be glad to think of her on the other side of the water while it lasts. And while she has not gained so much as I should wish, yet she is obviously better in health than a year ago.

I must thank you again, and this time in more serious fashion, for your kindness and hospitality this summer. I must always remain your debtor, and must always feel that my expression of obligation remains inadequate. I look forward to seeing you again in October: meanwhile best wishes for your lecture at Rochester. I am sorry that to my thanks I must add an apology: for leaving behind, in the cupboard, a double-breasted dinner jacket! (jacket only). I left it out till the last moment to put on the top of the case, and then forgot it. I have always said, and shall say, that to leave things behind is very bad manners in a guest. You need not forward it to me unless that suits you best: if more convenient, bring it with you when you come, as I have another which I wear in town.

I enclose a leaflet for Dr Perkins.

I had a short wire from the boat to say that all was well, and was relieved to know that she and the dog (Boerre his name is,[1] and I said that was the kind of name that should stick to a dog) had had no mishap on the way.

Always affectionately yours,<br>Tom

My cold is cured, thank you for letting me have it at Stamford House!

## TO *Messrs Macmillan & Co.* CC

13 September 1938 [Faber & Faber Ltd]

Dear Sirs,

I understand from Mr C. M. Grieve (Hugh MacDiarmid) that he has already communicated with you about his long poem *Mature Art*, which he is offering for publication. I therefore send on herewith the manuscript, which he gave me the opportunity of examining. I should like to say that it seems to me a remarkable work, which well deserves to be published, and I for one shall be very happy if you think favourably of it. I should willingly have recommended it for publication to my own firm, but as you see, it is a book of considerable length, and with our other commitments for volumes of verse we did not feel prepared at this moment to extend our expenses in this particular field.

Yours faithfully,<br>[T. S. Eliot]

1 – TSE had bought for EH a Norwegian Elkhound, a hunting dog recognised by the Kennel Club in 1901. (*Norsk Elghund*: 'Norwegian moose dog'). See photo of EH with dog, in Denison Library: 'For Jeanie, June 1939 Wendy & Boïre [*sic*]'. T. S. Matthews, *Great Tom*, 146: 'More than her faculty mates she liked her dog, a great Norwegian elkhound with a name no one could spell – pronounced Brrrr, like a shiver. She was devoted to this handsome and dignified animal.' TSE puns on the noun 'burr' – as if the name refers to a prickly seed-vessel or flower-head.

# TO *Ralph Hodgson*[1] TS Beinecke

13 September 1938                    *The Criterion*

Dear RALPH HODGSON,

My spies tell me that you are about. When can we meet? I am willing to lunch at Ridgway's on Friday, Saturday, or almost any day next week. I want to have a private conversation with you about CATS, and have waited impatiently for some months.[2]

Yr. faithful<br>T. S. E.

1 – Ralph Hodgson (1871–1962), Yorkshire-born poet – author of *The Last Blackbird* (1907); winner of the 1914 Edmond de Polignac Prize of the Royal Society of Literature – taught English at Sendai University, Japan, 1924–38. He was awarded the Order of the Rising Sun, 1938; Annual Award of the Institute of Arts and Letters, 1946; Queen's Gold Medal, 1954. See further Stanford S. Apseloff, 'T. S. Eliot and Ralph Hodgson Esqre', *Journal of Modern Literature* 10: 2 (June 1983), 342–6; Vinni Marie D'Ambrosio, 'Meeting Eliot and Hodgson in Five-finger Exercises', *Yeats Eliot Review* (2005); John Harding, *Dreaming of Babylon: The Life and Times of Ralph Hodgson* (2008).

2 – Hodgson wrote to his wife Aurelia (who was in the USA): 'Solemnly at the door of Ridgeway's [tea rooms] we met. He placed my old walking stick in my hand. I his own in his. Then we went upstairs. Eliot had a manuscript of a book of nonsense poems he has written about cats which they insist upon my illustrating. It seems absurd, but there it is' (cited in Harding, *Dreaming of Babylon*, 156).

Harding relates further: 'Hodgson, under some pressure, agreed to do the drawings as long as his name did not appear in the book. Eliot agreed, suggesting Hodgson be referred to only as "The Man in White Spats". Aurelia, however, could sense Hodgson's reluctance and wrote back to him, "Your illustration for TSE's book quite surprises me. Do you still want a loophole out of that? Here it is. If it means you must have a cat in the house for observation, I veto it. I really don't see how a cat will fit into this menagerie" (the menagerie being various cages full of birds, plus two dogs the Hodgsons had already accumulated).

'In 1938, Hodgson was 67 years old, his mind still totally absorbed in his "long poem". He was also anxious to rejoin Aurelia in America, and the *Cats* idea was one he felt he couldn't pursue in any practical way. At the same time, that he should dismiss such an idea out of hand was courageous. In 1939, Eliot was the country's pre-eminent poet and the *Cats* idea would have meant a useful fee . . .

'*Old Possum's Book of Practical Cats* went ahead without Ralph Hodgson. On 5th October 1939 an edition of 3005 copies priced at 3/6d appeared with Eliot's own drawings

13 September 1938 [*The Criterion*]

My dear Smyth,

I owe you an apology for a delay which is due to the usual summer confusion of trying to get too much work done in between holiday visits. I passed the galley proof of your review without comment, and it was not until I went through the page proof that I was held up by a few remarks which seemed to me indiscreet, if not positively libellous. The first was the reference to the Vigilance Committee of the Westminster Catholic Federation. This was the longest passage that I queried, but, there were also one or two remarks about Belloc, such as the suggestion of his incapacity to report honestly, which also seemed to me undesirable. Reading through the whole of the second part of your review, that dealing with Belloc, in order to see what could be done at this stage to make it less dangerous, I became more and more convinced that the whole section needed recasting. I hold no brief whatever for Belloc, but on the contrary I feel that your invective somewhat overshoots the mark, and is capable of arousing sympathy for Belloc, just as Belloc's attack excited your sympathy for Coulton. I decided therefore that the only thing to do was to cut out the whole of this half of the review from the present number at the eleventh hour, fill up the space with a couple of reviews which I had in reserve, and suggest that if you consent, it would be a good thing for you to revise your review of the Belloc pamphlet in a less incandescent state of emotion, and let me print it in December.

If you agree, I would suggest that I think it might be more effective to reverse your order, and instead of starting with general remarks about Belloc, proceed from the particular to the general, after first allowing the facts to speak for themselves, as apparently they are perfectly able to do. Your general denunciation of Belloc might easily persuade the reader in advance that you were approaching the pamphlet prepared only to find what was worst in it. In a case like this, the less emotion the reviewer betrays in advance, the more effective his review upon the reader. In any case, the point is not to betray one's own feelings so much as to excite those of the reader; and the most effective denunciation is that which

---

on the front cover and the dustwrapper. Inside was a small dedication to "The Man in White Spats"' (*Dreaming of Babylon*, 156, 158).

On 18 July 1938 TSE inscribed an early TS of *Old Possum's Book of Cats* 'for Miss Emily Hale, / this not quite final text. / from Old Possum. / 18.vii.38.' Now in the Ella Strong Denison Library, Scripps College, Claremont.

makes the reader more excited than he believes the writer to be. In any case, I hope you will not think my criticisms impertinent, as their aim is to assist you to produce the effect at which you aim, and certainly not to diminish it.

Yours ever,
[T. S. Eliot]

TO *Enid Faber*                                                   TS Valerie Eliot

14 September 1938                    *The Criterion*

Dear Enid,

Well this is a nice business, this is, me being 11 days late in writing my bread and butter letter, but let me explain, and if Geoffrey has anything to say about it, just ask him meanwhile what is an OUBIT? (It is *not* a variety of OUAKARI).[1] As I say, let me explain: well, I got to Cheltenham finally, but it would have been better if the lad at Aberystwyth had explained that that train goes on to Stratford on its way to Birmingham, and Stratford was 13 miles nearer where I was going than Cheltenham was, but as I had ordered a car to Cheltenham I had to get out there, however when I got there I took to my Bed for two days with that cold of Alan Watt's which Geoffrey passed on to me,[2] and after that returned to London and then had to see off a friend to America with an elkhound so was very busy and then had to write to my relatives in America by the last post before the crisis; and now Frank has been sneezing his cold all over the board room this afternoon before going to meet Tom, so I suppose I shall be in bed again over the next weekend. Well that cold makes no odds, but what with Janes being ill with gastric and Frank's cold and the elkhound and breaking my umbrella in the escalator and writing to my family before the crisis I have been very busy, and I am going tomorrow to John Pound to see about a studcase for Dick.[3] Anyway, I want to say that I enjoyed my holiday very much, even though the weather did not permit of the expected bathing and sunbathing; but my triumphant afternoon of victories on the grounds of the Peterwell Tennis Club made up for that; the excursion to St David's and Nevern and Newgate Sands was something to remember permanently, the day on the Moors was very pleasant, and

1 – Oubit: a hairy caterpillar – a 'woolly bear'. Ouakari: a short-tailed Amazonian monkey.
2 – GCF's diary, Sun. 24 July: 'Bill & Alan Watt called, & stayed to lunch with T. S. E. & his niece (? Miss Smith).' TSE's niece was Theodora Eliot Smith ('Dodo').
3 – Young Dick Faber had recently won a scholarship to Westminster School.

what I particularly enjoyed was being the only guest and evenings with you and Geoffrey alone.[1] And it is most pleasant to think that we are to meet again for the evening of Monday the 19th and Harold Lloyd, so I hope nothing will go wrong meanwhile,[2] and so I will close, with Love to Miss Davies, and still more to yourselves, and I have not forgotten about my contribution to the Magazine, your faithful

TP.

P.S. Give my love to Miss Davies.


## TO *Michael Roberts*                                    TS Janet Adam Smith

16 September 1938                          *The Criterion*

Dear Roberts,

Morley had told me about his conversation with you, and I was therefore glad to get your letter.[3] First of all I must say that we all feel that

---

1–GCF's diary, Sun. 28 Aug.: 'went for a family walk, with TSE . . .

'Interesting discussion with Tom after dinner & Pickwick about forms of poetry. I said I feared *we* might miss the inevitable English reaction from modernism; & he said that whatever form it took it wld. certainly be something so different from what we anticipated that it was better not to try to anticipate it. We argued much abt "classicism & romanticism" & the elimination of nature from poetry by the modern, & sat up rather too late.

'Fri, 2 Sept. Final expedition with TSE & family to St David's.'

2–GCF's diary,Mon. 19 Sept.: 'Tom Eliot to dinner, with Ann & Dick; & we all went to the cinema. Spawn of the North at the Plaza.' (*Spawn of the North* [1938], a movie about Alaskan fishermen, starred George Raft with Henry Fonda, Dorothy Lamour and John Barrymore.)

3–Roberts wrote on 12 Sept.: 'Perhaps [Frank] Morley has told you that I have been thinking about writing a book of criticism dealing with Tennyson, Housman, Valery, Rilke and yourself. Hopkins might come in, but a great deal has been said about him already. These headings would give me a chance to describe the changes in poetic taste in the last sixty years and to try to understand them. Other poets – Morris, Meredith, Laforgue, for example – would come in incidentally. Pound I omit because he does not fit in with the scheme I have in mind, though I shall have to mention him often enough in talking of the sound of poetry. I don't think it's time to talk about Pound in general until the Cantos are finished: it's like watching a climber on a difficult pitch – one can't judge the line he's taken until one sees how he gets out.

'I see several themes running through a book of this kind: there is the sort of thing I talked about at the end of *The Modern Mind*, there is the question of private religions (Yeats and Rilke both make me uneasy; there is a touch of humbug that always creeps in when the poet pitches his claim as high as they do), there is the change in imagery and in verbal music. After my last two books it would be a relief to get back to some real criticism.

'If I settle down to do this book, it will take me some time. For one thing, I mean to leave myself elbow-room to write a few poems; for another, I want to give the book a chance to grow, so that it add something to what I could say at the moment.'

any book that you really want to write is a book that we ought to publish. It remains, therefore, with you to do this book, if it is the book that you really want to do next.

At the same time, this does not, I confess, on the face of it strike me as the most advantageous next step from any point of view. My first thought was to wonder whether you were sure that the *Critique of Poetry* was far enough behind you for you to start afresh on these lines. I welcome your hint of wanting to take time over it and give yourself intervals for writing your own poetry, but I should have thought from that point of view that it would be better to have a subject for a prose book further away from poetry.

These are just my scruples in expressing the fact that my first impulse was unfavourable. You ought to know best what you want to do, and the main thing is that whatever you do should be in the direct line of your major thinking. If you remain firm on the point, go ahead; only I should like to hear from you again about it in a few weeks' time.[1]

Yours ever,
T. S. E.


TO *Maurice Haigh-Wood*                                    CC

16 September 1938              [Faber & Faber Ltd]

Dear Maurice,

What I am writing is no way to treat a man on his holiday, if anything can be a holiday at a moment like this: but it does concern you.

To take the simpler matter first, I enclose a letter from V. to Janes which he sent me.[2] He felt quite properly, that he could not undertake such a commission without authority. If she does need underwear I suppose that the matron of the home will notify you. In any case, I told Janes that he was quite right not to undertake any commissions. What puzzles me is that the home should send out a letter like this without notifying you.

Janes says he would like to go to see her, but says that he has written to you twice to ask your permission, and has had no reply. I can't see any harm in his going to see her. Whether he can is another matter. I went to see him on Wednesday and found him looking very ill and emaciated,

1–Roberts responded, 10 Oct.: 'I dare say you are right about my projected book: at any rate you voice misgivings of my own. I'll leave the matter for a time and see what happens.'
2–Not traced.

saying he had eaten nothing for two days, but obstinately determined not to call the doctor. The point being that on the last occasion the doctor sent him to a hospital in Fulham, where he was well looked after, but the hospital pursued him afterwards with requests for payment as I thought quite in excess of his means – in the end I paid for him. I went in tonight with some beef tea etc. but he was out for his walk: I shall look in again tomorrow.

The other matter is quite unrelated. I have had some correspondence with, and visits from, Maurice Lamb, the husband of your cousin Pat.[1] According to him, they are absolutely destitute, are on the point of being thrown out from their rooms in Cliveden Place by the bailiffs, and the doctor says that unless Pat is taken away from London he won't guarantee her life for a year. What he wanted was a considerable sum, in order to go to live in the country. I told him at this point that I couldn't consider doing anything more for them unless they consented to my consulting you first, because (a) I could not do anything more without probable sacrifice of relatives with needs and a stronger claim on me (b) my income was diminishing and my possible liabilities increasing (c) I felt that it had become improper unless it was an open Haigh-Wood family matter. Furthermore, I felt that it had got to a point at which I wanted more than the Lambs' own view of things, and needed to have an outside opinion about them and what ought to be done for them. So now he has presented me with a statement of his needs and wishes. It begins with £50 to pay arrears of rent before they can start on anything new, and amounts to about £185 to start a venture of market gardening near Horley. I am not in a position to hand out £185 like that. Also, even if it is a matter of life and death to Pat (whom I have not seen for about twenty-three years), I did not feel sure that young Lamb was the best judge of how any money to help her should be expended, or that if the money was provided they would get anywhere with it. So they agreed to my consulting you, with a view to considering what your mother would have done for them if she were able to appreciate the situation.[2]

1–Pat Lamb was the daughter of Aunt Lillia: that is, aunt of VHE and MH-W.
2–MH-W to TSE, 5 Oct.: 'I have had a talk with Nurse Moore about the man [Lamb] we discussed & she is convinced that he is nothing but a sponge & will never attempt to do any work as long as he manages to get finance in other ways. Also that the wife is not really ill at all, but her nerves [*sic*] & ought to do a job of work, which would be the best thing for her. I merely repeat this. I have no first hand knowledge.'

MH-W to TSE, 29 Sept. 1938: 'My dear Tom, / I have intended to tell you that mother has always very much wanted to see you again. Long ago before her illness she told me this. I didn't mention it to you because I realized that there was always a possibility that if you

I should like a talk with you as soon as you return. I shall be out of town (or rather, at a conference in Hampstead) over the weekend of the 24th, but I shall be back again on the 26th.[1] Meanwhile, if you can say anything in writing, I shall be glad of it, and I hope you will get what benefit you can from being at the seaside.

Affectionately yours,

[Tom]

## TO *C. M. Grieve* CC

[Mid-September 1938]                    [Faber & Faber Ltd]

Dear Mr Grieve,

I must apologise humbly for my unpardonable delay in dealing with your manuscripts, for which I can only give the excuse of the disorganisation of life and work which overtakes me every year during the summer months.[2] I have sent the 'Mature Art' to Macmillan & Co. with my warm recommendation, and I should like to accept your suggestion of publishing the first Appendix (on Cornwall) in the *Criterion*. As I have sent this on with the rest of the poem, could you, at your convenience, provide me with another copy?[3]

I must say that I think this Appendix will be very much more impressive and effective in the *Criterion* than your article on Scottish Politics in

---

were ever to go up to see her you might quite easily happen to hit on a time when Vivienne was also up there.

'Nowadays Mother is often not at all lucid, but she always knows me perfectly well, & although she sometimes appears quite absent at first, after a few minutes quietly, she becomes lucid enough.

'I believe that if you were ever to find a spare half hour to go up there some afternoon or evening, it would give her great happiness. You know she has always had the greatest affection for you & she understood very well indeed the compelling reasons which caused the separation.

'She has not been at all well the past week or two, I wonder whether you could manage just to go in & see her for a few minutes one day soon? I am sure it would be a great comfort to her, even although she might not appear to realize very much at the time.

'Yours affectionately / Maurice.'

1 – The second meeting of the Moot, held at Westfield College, London, 23–6 Sept.

2 – Grieve (18 June) appreciated the difficulties of publishing a large work like 'Mature Art'; he would be pleased if TSE could pass it on to Messrs Macmillan with his recommendation. He now enclosed some appendices to that work, and hoped TSE would consider the first for *C*.

3 – 'Cornish Heroic Song for Valda Trevlyn', *C*. 18 (Jan. 1939), 195–203. A footnote remarks: 'This is the opening section of an extremely long unpublished poem by Mr MacDiarmid.'

953

its present form.[1] For one thing, the article is about twice as long as is convenient to publish. For a second point, I had much rather have a contribution which you could sign with your own name, than a manifesto from the Red Scotland Committee. Third, I feel that for the purpose of the *Criterion* your article covers far too much ground. There is no objection to your slanging the English, but I think it could be made more effective in a different form, and in more minute particulars. In this essay you seem to me to make too many charges to be able to convince the reader of the force of all of them, and a detailed forensic on one point might be more effective than making too many points which you have not the space to justify in detail. For our purpose an essay like this includes the germs of a number of single articles, such as one on MacLean,[2] although I do not suggest that as one particularly suitable for the *Criterion*.[3]

Yours very sincerely,
[T. S. Eliot]

## TO *Merrill Moore*

TS John Hay Library, Brown University

21 September 1938

Dear Dr Moore,

I have your letter of the 13th, and should certainly welcome the appearance of any new poet of promise, even if his name is Lowell, but I do not see what I can do about this lad until I have read some of his poetry.[4] If you are writing to him at any time, you might care to suggest

---

1 – 'Brief Survey of Modern Scottish Politics in the light of Dialectical Material.'
2 – Sorley MacLean (1911–96), Scottish poet, writing in both Gaelic and English.
3 – Grieve responded (17 Sept.), 'I shall think over very carefully what you say about dealing with aspects of the wide-ranging theme of the essay on Scottish Politics, and thus bring a more detailed forensic to bear on specific matters.'
4 – 'As you have not been to Boston for some time you might be interested to know that a young poet is beginning to appear on the horizon of whom you have probably not yet heard. His name is Robert T. S. Lowell. He lives in Boston and is a cousin of Amy Lowell. He is about 21 years old and I feel really has poetic talent.

'I just wanted you to know about him as you may hear from him later. I have advised him to go to Kenyon College in Gambier, Ohio and live and work there with John Crowe Ransom, whom I feel is a wholesome poetic influence. He has been profoundly stimulated and influenced by your work and I am sure would deeply appreciate a line from you some day, if you care to drop him one. His address is R. T. S. Lowell, Kenyon College, Gambier, Ohio.

'Next summer he will probably go abroad (He is a man of independent means, superior social background and considerable tact and personality.) and I do hope that it might be possible for him to have the pleasure of meeting you.

his sending on something, or still better, of letting you pick out some specimens to send to me for him. If he is in England next summer, I should of course be glad to see him.

With best wishes to Mrs Moore and yourself,

Yours sincerely,

T. S. Eliot

## TO *V. A. Demant*                                                      CC

21 September 1938                    [Faber & Faber Ltd]

Dear Demant,

I have your letter of the 19th instant.[1] While it is a commonplace that *Theology* is quite mediocre, and also sometimes inclusive of people who were better left out, I wonder whether the present moment is a good one for launching a competing review. For one thing, I understand that *Theology* is to be edited in future by Vidler.[2] Might it not be better to wait and see what he makes of it? For another thing, I am a little fearful of dispersing energy and possible subscriptions by multiplying Church papers, and I should like to consider the possibility whether such a periodical as you desire might not be achieved by an enlargement of the scope of *Christendom*.

I should be very glad to see Dom Gregory Dix,[3] whom I have for some time wished to meet, but I am also a little hesitant about suggesting a meeting, because I am quite sure in advance that Faber & Faber would

---

'May I impose on your good nature and kindness and your interest in poetry to the extent of asking you to keep him in mind.'

Robert Lowell (1917–77), scion of a Boston Brahmin family, poet; author of *Land of Unlikeness* (1944); *Lord Weary's Castle* (1946); *Life Studies* (1959: National Book Award, 1960). Pulitzer Prize for Poetry, 1947, 1974; National Book Critics' Circle Award, 1977.

TSE to Aimée Lamb, St Andrew's Day 1954: 'I am quite fond of Robert Lowell . . . But (in confidence) I hope that he is not under the care of Dr Merrill Moore' (Boston Athenaeum).

1 – 'I am interested in a project for starting a monthly journal which will be a much needed rival to "Theology", in the sense that its object will be to vindicate the Orthodoxy of the Church of England, and will also be much more interesting, showing the relevance of dogma to current secular issues as well as ecclesiastical.

'Dom Gregory Dix, O.S.B. of Nashdom Abbey, Burnham, Bucks, is taking the initiative in this matter and would very much value a talk with you about the project.'

2 – Revd Alec Vidler, theologian; see letter of 4 Oct. 1938, below.

3 – Dom Gregory Dix (1901–52), Anglican monk, who studied at Merton College, Oxford, and taught modern history at Keble College. He entered the Benedictine community of Nashdom Abbey in 1926, and was to be Prior, 1948–52. A noted liturgical scholar and Anglican Papalist, he published *The Shape of the Liturgy* (1945).

be disinclined to consider taking on the publication of another periodical. The reasons in favour of our doing the *Criterion* would not apply to any other review; and as we have had several proposals made to us from time to time in the past, we have gone into the matter and decided in general that we should not be able to recoup ourselves for the extra labour and overhead expenses.

Might it not be a good thing to thrash out the prospects for a new periodical review with a few people like George Every? In any case, before talking to Dom Gregory Dix I had rather have a talk with you about it. Is there any possibility of your being able to meet me in Town within the next few weeks?

Yours ever sincerely,<br>[T. S. Eliot]

## TO *Geoffrey Grigson* TS Texas

26 September 1938             Faber & Faber Ltd

My dear Grigson,

We have now had time to examine the *New Verse Anthology*,[1] and I hope that you will not mind my making one or two suggestions before it goes to press; suggestions of a kind which had better be made directly and informally to you than through the official medium of Pinker. The chief point is that we were somewhat disappointed not to have something in the nature of a longer and more animated manifesto of *New Verse* policy as a preface. I know that this is very difficult to do, but the desire is only a recognition of the fact that what has made *New Verse* so welcome amongst periodicals has been the red pepper or vitriol of the editor, as much as the major part of the verse contributions. Of course in a preface like this you don't want to go in, I know, for personalities, saucing Edith

---

1 – See *New Verse: An Anthology* (F&F, 1939).

Blurb, F&F New Books Autumn 1938, 52: '*New Verse* was the first of several periodicals of its kind, and it has won, under its editor, Mr Geoffrey Grigson, a reputation such that the first question asked about any young poet is, whether his work has appeared in *New Verse*. Mr Grigson has made a selection from the poetry which he considers the best that has been published in his periodical since it was founded. The anthology differs from all others, in that it is at once a record of the achievement of the most distinguished poetry review in England, and a document of the development of poetry in England during the last five years. It will be a necessary addition to the libraries of all students of contemporary poetry. And to those who have so far failed to acquaint themselves with contemporary accomplishment, it will be an introduction to a new world of experience.'

Sitwell etc., and it may be that you have already thought this over and decided that a purely formal preface was best. If, however, you have not already dismissed the possibility, we feel that a rather longer introduction with more Grigson in it would help the book a good deal.

May I ask, by the way, why there is nothing of Allen Tate in the anthology? He seems to me a more interesting poet than MacLeish, if one is going to have Americans; and if you disagree, that is simply a point on which it would interest me personally to know your opinion. I just wanted to be sure that Tate had not been overlooked.

We think that the translations ought to be listed uniformly under the names of the translators rather than under those of the original authors, or alternatively one might have cross-indexing.

Yours ever sincerely,
T. S. Eliot

## TO *Meg Nason*[1]                                         CC

27 September 1938                    [Faber & Faber Ltd]

Dear Miss Nason,

Your letter of the 25th arrived this morning.[2] By the same post I have a letter from Mrs Perkins from Minehead, saying that they are coming up to London today, so I suppose that they will be at the Aban Court Hotel, South Kensington. But Brown Shipley would be sure to reach them. I gathered that they intended to leave for America in about ten days, if not sooner.

I have just heard of Emily's arrival, but have no particulars about either herself or Boerre. I know that she is in Northampton, and trust that he is also.

---

1 – Margaret (Meg) Geraldine Nason (1900–86): proprietor of the Bindery tea rooms, Broadway, Worcestershire.

2 – Nason asked (25 Sept.) after the whereabouts of John Carroll Perkins and his wife Edith, whom she had seen at Chipping Campden, but whom she thought might have returned to the USA in the face of the worsening situation in Europe.

'Also I wonder if you have heard yet of Emily's arrival, I do hope she has had a good journey, and that Boerre has not minded the crossing too much.

'I am terribly glad Emily has him, as I know he will be a great joy to her. I hope this may reach you in time to wish you a very happy birthday . . .

'If you have not yet found the perfect "Double Gloucester", I hear that you can get it at the "Army and Navy" stores.

'We look forward to another supper picnic next summer.'

I have had a discussion with my chief authority, the head steward of my club, about Double Gloster, and he gave it as his opinion that the mysterious white cheese about which there was so much discussion was probably a very new Double Gloster, which would require perhaps several months' ripening before it attained the right colour and consistency. He gets his Double Glosters from the Army and Navy Stores, but I gather that the Stores are somewhat secretive about the source of their supply.

I did indeed enjoy the picnic supper immensely, and it will remain a very pleasant memory, only to be superseded, I hope, by another picnic next year.

With best wishes for the winter to yourself and Miss Milne,

Yours very sincerely,

[T. S. Eliot]

TO *Edith Perkins*                                        TS Beinecke

27 September 1938                    *The Criterion*

Dear Mrs Perkins,

Welcome back to London: and thank you for your two letters received this morning. I am happy to tell you that I had a cable from Emily from Northampton yesterday morning, on the occasion of my anniversary:[1] so

1 – TSE's fiftieth birthday.
  See HWE to FVM, 15 Sept. 1938: 'Tom's birthday, in case you do not know it, comes on the 26th of September. This year, however, is his fiftieth, and deserves special observance. What could be more fitting than to present him some public office, dignified but not too arduous and in no way interfering with his literary and editorial activities? As you know, the office of a Senator of the United States entails very little mental and only a slight physical effort, such as shouting "Hear, hear" when the President's name is mentioned, or "Aye" in a loud voice when any measure sponsored by him is put to vote.
  'I am sending you therefore some publicity matter to that end. There may be some slight technical questions about citizenship, etc., and the matter of voting without being physically present at legislative sessions, but I doubt not that in the general atmosphere of good-fellowship engendered that could all be straightened out; and besides, the gesture is largely honorific and complimentary . . .*
  'Best regards to all, and Pip, Pip, for TOM Eliot.'
  FVM to HWE, 27 Sept. 1938: 'Your letter was perfectly timed. I had not forgotten that yesterday was Tom's birthday, and in addition to more private ceremonial, we had arranged a small stunt for his pleasure. Yesterday we were having one of the many councils of war which are incumbent on us in these times; Tom does not bother to attend such meetings when they are concerned with tedious detail, but is of course brought in on matters of great urgency or importance. So, yesterday afternoon while the rest of us were in conclave in my room and while Tom was up in his, chattering on the phone to John Hayward, I rang to interrupt him, told the telephone operator to cut off the telephone conversation, and

it would not seem that the hurricane has affected Northampton. I also have letters from her this evening, not, to be sure, much after her arrival, but recounting her passage. It would appear that her cabin companions, though foreigners, were not unpleasant; and that the exercising of Boerre happily occupied most of her attention on the voyage. And her last letter, just after arrival in Northampton, reveals that her landlady was most pleased by her first impression of him.

One still does not know whether Hitler will pipe down, in the face of so much opposition from so many sides, or not; but if you are leaving, alas, as early as the 7th, then if you can get an equally good accommodation earlier I should advise you to take it.

I wrote to Emily by the last mail, pointing out very firmly and perhaps brutally, that in the event of war her business would be to stick to her job at Smith. I said that I thought another war might well be a long war, and that in my opinion it would be won by one side starving out the other – not by anything so quick and spectacular as air raids – and that England needed its food, more than it would need volunteers who would consume food. Indeed, if I did not find that I could be of any use here, I think I should do best to go to America so as to leave my food for others to eat. On the other hand, if I were in the government service, it is quite likely that I should be sent somewhere abroad.

I will look in tomorrow before lunch – perhaps before you get this letter.

Affectionately yours

Tom

If you are leaving this week, instead of next, will you ask Dr Perkins whether he could lunch with me at my club on Thursday?

---

simultaneously sent Kennerley to find him. This extraordinary procedure always means a matter of grande vitesse. In truth, it was, for I had provided a birthday cake with fifty candles which were burning away with such fury that it was vital that he should rush down. Rush down he did, thinking, until he put his head round the door, that nothing less than immediate bankruptcy and destruction were threatening the business. When he did put his head round the door, into the darkened room the blaze of candlelight was as dramatic as the final scene in THE FAMILY REUNION.

'Your election material also came in very handy. His room and Faber's and, I am sorry to say, even mine are plastered with the invitation to vote for Eliot for Congress.

'Such are the stern ways and rigid discipline in which we approach war. That we are approaching war rapidly is now the universal feeling, some of the preparations now supervene to prevent a longer letter.'

* (Henry's 'publicity matter' related to the 1938 campaign by TSE's cousin Thomas Hopkinson Eliot (1907–91), lawyer, politician, academic – a Democrat – for a place in the Seventy-sixth Congress, which he lost; at a rematch in 1940 Thomas Eliot won the seat for the Seventy-seventh Congress, 1941–43.)

TO *George Every*                                          TS Sarah Hamilton

27 September 1938                    *The Criterion*

Dear George,

I have been approached by Victor Demant, who is anxious to start another review for people who have been dissatisfied with *Theology*. I wrote to him in reply, saying that I thought this was a bad moment to put anything under ~~way~~ weigh, as I knew that *Theology* was to be reorganised by Vidler, and I thought it would be best to wait a bit and see what came of that. In any case, it seems to me that it might be better to take hold of *Christendom* and widen its scope, rather than to start still another religious review. Demant is, I think, coming to see me tomorrow. Meanwhile I had a talk with Vidler at the Moot on Sunday, and have now a circular letter from him. I have no doubt you have received the same letter, as your name is mentioned in the list of collaborators. I can see no objection to giving my name, but I should like to hear from you before I reply.

I am due to go up to Mirfield for the weekend of the 7th, but if war broke out I should feel obliged to cancel it, as the first thing I must do in that contingency is to finish my play, on which there appear to be several weeks of work to be done.

I have no time to tell you about the meeting of the Moot just yet. It was very curious, though extremely interesting. I am not quite sure yet what I think of the views of Gilbert Shaw.[1]

Yours affectionately
T. S.


TO *Geoffrey Faber*                                        TS Valerie Eliot

1 October 1938                       *The Criterion*

Dear Geoffrey,

It occurs to me to suggest that nothing should be said about the termination of the *Criterion*, and that no rumour should reach even the secretaries, until we have decided exactly how and when. The alternative seems to be winding up now, and issuing some sort of firm circular, to subscribers and the trade, or publishing another (January) number, which

---

1 – See Keith Clements, *The Moot Papers: Faith, Freedom and Society 1938–1947* (2010). Gilbert Shaw (1886–1967), Anglican priest.

might or might not include some editorial statement. I don't want to put myself forward, but it seems to me difficult to avoid some editorial statement in any case. The main thing is to find good reasons to offer, so that it will not merely be supposed that the firm is obliged to retrench. I suppose that this rumour is bound to circulate in any case, but we, and especially I, must give such good reasons for ceasing publication that it will be no more than a rumour.

I cannot myself see any reason for completing the *Criterion* year. I think it will be found that the subscriptions date from every issue, so that whenever we stop there will be some subscriptions to be adjusted by refunding.

I wanted to say something more than this. It occurs to me that the thought may lurk in your mind that I may feel a good deal of regret. But you ought to know that for several years I have had doubts. These doubts do not merely stand for a conscientious thought that it is a waste of money for the firm. It is impossible to run a one-man show like this for fifteen years without feeling that it is going stale. I have run it without conviction for several years; only I felt that so long as you and Frank felt that it was of some advertising value to the firm – or that my chief use to the firm was running the *Criterion* – I couldn't well give it up.

It is not the kind of paper that could be handed over to another editor, even were there any possible editor visible. If the firm should want a review, then it would be better for a new editor, as well as for myself, that it should be a different paper under a different name.

So far as the *Criterion* was of use to the firm, I conceived that its work was to render itself unnecessary. I don't think that it is likely to attract now many desirable authors, who would not think of coming to us anyway.

Incidentally, I am not at all happy about the position of the firm and its commitments. It seems to me that if we were going to war now, the position would be highly critical: even as things are, it is delicate. And as I think that possibly war has merely been postponed to a still less favourable moment, I should like to see the decks kept a bit clearer.

Yours ever,

T. S. E.

P.S. Of course there are other considerations, reinforcing, but not strictly relevant. E.G. when one is young, one can say things in one's own periodical which one would not be at liberty to say elsewhere; but at my age, it tends to the reverse: one has to be much more cautious, as editor, than one would need to be as a contributor elsewhere. And there are some bitter memories of the early years – before your time! – it was in no mood of enthusiasm, but more nearly of desperation, that I consented to launch the review: certainly the happiest editorial years have been those when the review belonged exclusively to Faber & Faber. For this, as for many things, I am grateful to you. Incidentally, I do not forget that it was on the pretext of the *Criterion* that I was insinuated – with some difficulty – into Faber & Gwyer's.

TO *Jacques Maritain*                                              CC

2 octobre 1938                        [Faber & Faber Ltd]

Mon cher ami,

Je parais bien ingrat, ou du moins coupable d'une grande négligence, en manquant de vous remercier de vos soins et de votre lettre aimable du 6 août.[1] Pendant le mois d'août j'étais en villégiature la plupart du temps; et pendant le mois passé les présages politiques paraissaient-ils si mauvais que j'avais délaissé mes entreprises personnelles, en exceptant un travail dur a l'égard de ma prochaine pièce, que j'avais envie d'achever avant qu'une nouvelle guerre fût arrivée de terminer mes besognes d'une autre façon.

---

1–Thrilled to know that Henri Fluchère had translated *MiC*, Maritain offered to secure publication of the French version in the collection called *Les Iles* (of which he was in charge), published by Desclée-De-Brouwer. Regrettably, the play could not appear in the series before May or June 1939, but the publisher did offer good distribution and financing considerations.

He wrote too: '*J'ai été très touché de l'article de Murry sur le livre de Mendizabal et sur ma préface. Dupuis que j'ai reçu ce numéro du Criterion, j'ai dans mes plans d'écrire à Murry pour le remercier, et je pense bien le faire un jour, bien que je sois submergé de travail (je dois partir le 1er Octobre pour les États-Unis). En attendant rendriez-vous dire à Murry que j'attache le plus grand prix à son témoignage et que je lui en sois très reconnaissant, étant donné notamment l'attitude générale de las press catholique anglaise dans cette affaire. J'imagine qu'en Angleterre vous êtes pris entre deux pharisaïsmes, un pharisaïsme de gauche et un droite. Ici la droite est pharisienne et tout à fait sépulcre blanche; et la gauche serait plutôt sadducéenne, dissipatrice et jacobine.*' ('I was very touched by Murry's article on Mendizabal's book and on my preface. Since I received that issue of the Criterion, I have been intending to write and thank him, and I hope I get round to it one day, even though I am drowned in work (I am due to leave for the US on 1 October). Meanwhile, could you please tell Murry how much his remarks have meant to me, and how very grateful I am, especially considering the general attitude of the English Catholic Press over this matter. I presume that in England you are caught between two pharisaical attitudes, one on the Left and the other on the Right. Here the Right is Pharisee and entirely of the Whited Sepulchre; while the Left is rather Sadducee, Profligate and Jacobin.')

He asked in a postscript whether TSE had received the book entitled *Situation de la Poésie*, written by Maritain himself with his wife Raïssa?

Je serais tout-à-fait content de voir paraître *Murder in the Cathedral* dans la collection *Les Iles*. Toutefois, vous comprendrez que je dois consulter M. Fluchère, qui y a travaillé si consciencieusement, et sans la certitude d'un rendement quelconque. Or, M. Flouquet à offert une certaine somme (1000 francs, je crois, mais je n'ai pas la lettre sous la main) pour être partagé entre auteur et traducteur. Quant à moi, les droits restent chez Faber & Faber, qui ne seraient pas, je crois, plus exigeants que moi. Pourraient Desclée de Brouwer offrir une somme comparable au traducteur?

En attendant de vos nouvelles, j'avertirai Fluchère de vos démarches, et je lui proposerai de vous envoyer le texte français.

Toujours fidèlement à vous,
[T. S. Eliot][1]

## TO *George Bell* CC

4 October 1938 [Faber & Faber Ltd]

My dear Lord Bishop,

I certainly owe you an apology for my delay in writing to you.[2] When you wrote to me on 24 August, you were just leaving for a holiday in Ireland so that I did not reply. I have since read the pamphlet, and have discussed the matter with Oldham. He said he did not know either the pamphlet or Pastor Hildebrandt, but his general opinion was that the book we had in mind for English readers ought to be one written by

1 – *Translation*: My dear friend, / I must seem most ungrateful, or at the very least guilty of gross negligence, for not thanking you for your help and for your good letter of 6 August. During most of August I was out of town; and during the last month the political climate has turned so bad that I abandoned my personal projects, except for some hard work on my next play, which I had hoped to finish before another war arrived to interrupt my tasks in a different way.

I would be delighted for *Murder in the Cathedral* to appear in the collection *Les Iles*. However, you will understand that I must consult Mr Fluchère, who has been working on it so conscientiously, and without any certainty of recompense. Mr Flouquet, for his part, has offered a certain sum (1,000 francs I believe, but I don't have the letter to hand) to be shared between author and translator. As far as I am concerned, the rights are with Faber and Faber, and they will not, I suspect, ask for more than I do. Do you think Descléé de Brouwer could offer a comparable sum to the translator?

I look forward to your reply, and I shall in the meantime inform Fluchère of your offer, and ask him to send you the French text. / Yours faithfully, [T. S. Eliot]

2 – Bell asked on 3 Oct., 'What happened about the proposal for a life or study of Niemöller? I wrote at once and sent you my presentation copy from Pastor Hildebrandt of his anonymous study of Niemöller. But I heard no more.'

an Englishman. This was confirmed by the impression I formed of the pamphlet, which though very earnest and pleasing, is not to my mind quite informative enough, and should in any case be amplified. Oldham thought that the two people who knew most about Niemöller were the Dean of Chichester and Nat Micklem.[1] I felt that probably Duncan Jones had said all that he wanted to say in his recent book *The Struggle for Religious Freedom In Germany*, and it transpired that Micklem had been at Rugby with Geoffrey Faber. Faber has written to consult him. As I do not yet know the outcome, I give you this last piece of information in confidence.

It would have been a pleasure to me to meet Pastor Hildebrandt, but I felt that any suggestion that he should come to see me might raise false hopes, and might be a waste of his time, so I have not communicated with him, and I return the pamphlet to you herewith.

> With renewed apologies,
> I am, my dear Lord Bishop,
> Yours ever sincerely,
> [T. S. Eliot]

## TO *Alec R. Vidler*[2]                                         CC

4 October 1938                    [Faber & Faber Ltd]

Dear Father Vidler,

I have no objection to your including my name in the list of collaborators for *Theology*. As for the questions you ask, a) I cannot see any immediate prospect of having time to review any books, and should only be likely to do so when there was a very special pertinence. b) I should be willing

1–Nathaniel Micklem (1888–1976): theologian; Principal of Mansfield College, Oxford, 1933–53. In the 1930s he visited Germany, conferring with the German Confessing Church, and in 1939 he published *National Socialism and the Roman Catholic Church*. He wrote to TSE, 17 Nov. 1938 that 'a possible writer would be a student from Wycliffe Hall who has had some journalistic experience. His name is D. L. Williams . . . I should perhaps add that he went to Germany this year taking some letters from me and with some introductions from me.'
2–The Revd Alec R. Vidler (1899–1991), Anglican priest, theologian and periodical editor, was from 1938 librarian of St Deiniol's Library at Hawarden, Chester (later Warden), and editor of *Theology*. He was to be a noted participant in the discussion group 'The Moot' convened by J. H. Oldham. Dean of King's College, Cambridge, 1956–66. His writings include *The Modernist Movement in The Roman Church: Its Origins and Outcome* (1934), *A Plain Man's Guide to Christianity: Essays in Liberal Catholicism* (1936), *Windsor Sermons* (1958), and *Scenes from a Clerical Life: An Autobiography* (1977).

to give an opinion from time to time on any manuscripts which I was specially qualified to criticise, but of course could only undertake a really limited amount of such collaboration. c) The list of collaborators seems to me so long, so mixed and so inclusive, that I wonder what would be accomplished by anything in the way of a full meeting. I should think that shorter meetings of selected groups, called together for special purposes, might be more to the point. It would be unwise for me to promise to attend anything so extensive as a three days' meeting, because I occasionally, as you know, have other meetings of this sort, and it is very difficult to spare the time.

Yours sincerely,
[T. S. Eliot]

TO *Henri Fluchère*                                                    TS Fluchère

5 October 1938                          Faber & Faber Ltd

Dear Mr Fluchère,

I owe you the profoundest apologies for my dilatory handling of the problem of publishing your translation of *Murder in the Cathedral*. To put it briefly, I have been in communication with my friend Jacques Maritain, as I wished to exhaust the possibilities of Paris before agreeing to the proposals of Mr Flouquet, who has, I must say, shown extraordinary kindness and patience. Maritain expresses a warm interest in publishing your translation, and is reasonably sure that it could be included in the collection *Les Iles* with Desclée de Brouwer, which he edits, and could probably be published in the spring. I have now, after further dawdling, written to him again to explain that the Belgian firm offered an advance, to be divided between you and myself, and that while I was not disposed to press for particularly advantageous terms for myself, I felt it unfair to you if you did not receive at least the equivalent of what the Belgian publishers could pay. I have therefore asked him to let me know what Desclée de Brouwer would be inclined to do in the way of a translator's fee, and when I hear from him I will write to you again.

Meanwhile, Maritain wished me to let you know that if you were favourably disposed, he would be very glad if you would send him the manuscript of *Meurtre dans la Cathedrale*, to his private address at 10 rue de Parc, Meudon, S & O.[1]

---

1 – Fluchère noted on TSE's letter that he wrote to Maritain on 10 Oct.

I can only explain that I am apt to be extremely unbusinesslike where my private affairs are concerned, but this is no excuse for having treated you with such neglect, after all the pains that you have taken in connexion with this matter.

With deep apologies, and best wishes,

Yours very sincerely,

T. S. Eliot

## TO *Alfred Duff Cooper*[1]                                          TS

5 October 1938                                    *The Criterion*

Dear Duff Cooper,

Although our acquaintance is but slight, this is a moment when I feel that some communication is not only justified, but called for, from everyone who not only admired your courage and integrity (as everyone must) but also feels that the general position you have taken up, as expressed in your speech of Monday, is the right one.[2]

Yours sincerely,

T. S. Eliot

Needless to say, this letter calls for no acknowledgement.[3]

1–Alfred Duff Cooper, 1st Viscount Norwich of Aldwick (1890–1954), First Lord of the Admiralty since 1937, resigned from the Government on 3 Oct. in consequence of the Munich Agreement (30 Sept.) which permitted Hitler to annex the Sudetenland in W. Czechoslovakia in return for the false prospectus of 'Peace in our time', signed by Germany, the UK, France and Italy. Prime Minister Neville Chamberlain called it 'peace with honour' – a claim derided by Winston Churchill. Given that Germany had been allowed to annex Austria (the *Anschluss*) in Mar. 1938, Duff Cooper declared it the gravest error to pursue a policy of appeasement against an expansionist dictator: 'sweet reasonableness' was never the right way to deal with the Führer.

Hitler was to annex the remainder of Czechoslovakia on 13 Mar. 1939.

2–See Tomlin, *T. S. Eliot*, 106–7: 'Eliot reiterated his view that, as between a Communist world and a world dominated by the Nazis . . . the latter would be the more horrible immediately to contemplate . . . What particularly shocked him, from then until the outbreak of war, was the repeated humiliations heaped on Czechoslovakia, especially at the Munich conference in September. For although Britain, France, German and Italy had guaranteed the frontiers of that country (minus the Sudetenland) at that same conference, the Czech Republic was fragmented a few weeks later, and by the following March Germany had completed her design by totally absorbing an independent state. Eliot felt that at Munich there had been a betrayal which seemed to demand an act of almost personal contrition.'

3–Cooper replied from the Admiralty, Whitehall, London, on 6 Oct.: 'The good opinion of people like yourself is of great value to me.

'I hope we may meet again at the Literary Society.'

9 October 1938                     *The Criterion*

Dear Martin,[1]

The reason why I am anxious to get the play right without delay, is that I have to look at it from a publisher's point of view. If (as I hope) the play is to be produced at the beginning of February, then we want to have it on sale at the same moment – not before nor after. The point being that the production will in any case stimulate sale of the book: if the play is a success we lose nothing by having the text on sale from the start; and if it fails, then we shall get some additional sale at the beginning anyway. On the other hand, I especially don't want the literary critics to review it before the performance.

Two things in particular for you to scrutinise: (1) the chronology, which is improved, but as you will see not yet quite cleared up – I mean the ages etc. (2) exits and entrances, also improved but not perfect. And, of course, anything else. What I should like to hear from you on Wednesday is, whether the text is right enough to go to the printers, or whether it needs some drastic re-casting anywhere, which I should try to get done within a week.

Yours ever,<br>T. S. E.

1 – This letter is given in full in Browne, *Making*, 144–5.

TO *Stephen Spender*                                    TS Northwestern

12 October 1938                        *The Criterion*

Dear Stephen,

I got your letter of the 11th this morning, and after going through it carefully, discussed it with Faber in the light of the various contracts and the firm's accounts.[1] I think there is a certain amount of misunderstanding about the whole position, which could much more easily be put right in conversation with Faber and myself than by correspondence. As you are not coming back until Monday, the first day when we are both free for

---

1–SS, 11 Oct.: 'I've been looking through my contracts for POEMS and TRIAL OF A JUDGE and as far as I can see I am contracted to Fabers for 1 novel, 1 volume of short stories, 1 book on Modern Poetry but not for a volume of poems.

'As I told you, I want very much to do a book for the Hogarth Press, so I think I would like to give this one <of poems> to them, especially since they offer me far better terms than Faber do. At the moment, I can't afford to disregard a better offer, because I want to be able to work concentratedly on books and give up doing so much journalism.

'Fabers sent me their six monthly accounts a few days ago. In these accounts, they add up all the money that has been given to me in advances, add to that what I owe them for Goods and Corrections to proofs, and subtract from the whole my total royalties, arriving at the conclusion that I owe them £67.

'When we discussed the book of poems a few days ago, I said that I was willing for a clause to be inserted in my contract that *after the advance had been repaid by my royalties* further royalties could go to repaying any of the advance on TRIAL OF A JUDGE which was still outstanding.

'But the position now is that all my advances, including £25 for a book that I have not yet written on modern poetry, are set as a debit against my current royalties. A situation might easily arise at this rate in which you gave me £25 for advance on a book one month and deducted it the next month from my six-monthly royalties. That does not seem to me at all satisfactory, especially as it has been done without consulting me or even notifying me that you intended to do it.

'In addition to this, I can point out that up till now in all the time I have published with Fabers I have only had a debit of £10 – on the Burning Cactus. Moreover, you yourself have written to me justifying the fact that Fabers take 50% of my American royalties, on the grounds that they were insuring the risks involved in publishing my first book. It seems to me that this insurance policy has certainly covered any subsequent loss on my books, but now they are asking me to repay that loss out of my royalties on POEMS.

'As I see it, I owe Fabers about £18 for Proof Corrections and To Goods; which £18 has been almost exactly covered, as it happens, by my royalties for POEMS, which came to £18/18s this time.

'I don't think Fabers need be so nervous about £10 which I have not made up to the advance on THE BURNING CACTUS, nor £55 which I have still to make on TRIAL OF A JUDGE. The latter has only just been published in America and is still selling a bit, I suppose, over here. Moreover, as I told you I am willing to insert a clause in future contracts to repay past advances after and if the current advances are more than covered by royalties.

'As I want to publish the new book of poems with the Hogarth press, this applies to the novel and the other two books.'

---

lunch is Friday the 21st. Could you lunch with me then at the Oxford and Cambridge at 1.15?

If you should not be free for lunch on Friday, I suggest that you should ring me up and fix some time when you could look in here during the week. I should like to get this matter cleared up as quickly as possible.

Meanwhile, I hope earnestly that you will not commit yourself to publish your volume of poems with any other firm until we have had a chance to talk. This suggestion, I may say, comes as a complete surprise to me, especially after we had discussed the terms, and the contract drawn up was all but signed. On behalf of the firm, I should feel very regretful to see your poems go elsewhere; in your own interest I think it would be a serious mistake not to keep all your poetry together under one imprint, however you disperse your prose books; and personally I admit that I should feel rather hurt at your withdrawing the new poems, especially with such unexpected precipitation.

Yours affectionately,

Tom

TO *Louis MacNeice*                                                                    CC

14 October 1938                       [Faber & Faber Ltd]

Dear MacNeice,

I have two points to mention: first, I don't want to hurry you in the preparation of your long poem, because this is the sort of thing about which an author should not allow himself to be hurried, but I ought to hint that the sooner we can have the manuscript, the better it will be for giving the book an advantageous moment in the spring publications. In any case, I trust that it will not be after the end of December.

Second, I mentioned to my committee the information which I had from you and from Doone that you were to translate the *Hippolytus* for the Group Theatre, and they agreed with me that we ought to interest ourselves in publishing that also. So may I ask whether you will let us have a copy of your translation when it is ready? as I remember, you are going to work to some date in February.

It came to my mind that possibly the *Trojan Women* might have more topical bearing, but it is a long time since I have looked at that play.

Yours ever,

[T. S. Eliot]

P.S. Could you let me have a statement about your new poem which would serve for the catalogue advertisement, or at least provide me with something that I could work up? The spring catalogue is going to press pretty soon. If you can, make your note on the long side, so that it can either be used in full or cut down as the make-up of the catalogue dictates.


TO *Ian Cox*                                                                    TS BBC

14 October 1938                        *The Criterion*

My dear Cox,

I have your letter of even date, delivered by hand, and am pleased and honoured that you should think of me in connexion with a broadcast of *Moby Dick*.[1] I think I see dimly the connexion, although I have never really read that novel; I have only dipped into it here and there, and thought its style rather tumid. It is true that my great-grandfather was an owner of whaling ships in New Bedford, and his business was ruined by the British fleet in 1812.[2] But that is as near as I come to a connexion with Nantucket. My own associations have all been with the North Shore, and so I have not the slightest ability to handle the South Shore dialect. You may remember my mentioning that Kipling made some mistakes in *Captains Courageous* in confusing the speech of Gloucester fishermen with that of Cape Cod fishermen. But it is so long since I have even heard my own North Shore speech, that I should be in danger of confusing even that with the speech to the Eastward of Cape Porpoise.[3] So it is evident that I know just enough about these matters not to dare to meddle with them.

1 – Cox was preparing a broadcast serial of *Moby-Dick*, read by Geoffrey Tandy, and thought it desirable to produce a dramatic version of the material from chapters XXXV to XL 'Often while I've been working on this book, I've found myself thinking of you . . . particularly so in the forecastle scene, when I kept recalling the sound of conversations between Frank Morley and yourself, varied with "Frankie and Johnnie" and "The reconstructed rebel". Would TSE 'care at all to take a part (say First and Third Nantucket Sailor, etc., for we shall have to duplicate a lot) in the scene "Midnight, forecastle" XXXIX?'
2 – William Greenleaf Eliot, Sr. (1781–1853), merchant and ship-owner of New Bedford, Mass. (where TSE's grandfather of the same name was born in 1811), was ruined by the British embargo on trade imposed in the war of 1812–15; he subsequently relocated to Washington, where he worked as an inspector in the Postal Service auditing office.
3 – Cape Porpoise is in Maine, some sixty miles north of Gloucester, Mass.

However, I should like to know more about it, and if I am free I should like to drop in and hear your rehearsal at 5.30 on All Saints Day, and have a pint with you afterward.

> With many thanks,
> Yours very sincerely,
> T. S. E.

## to *George Barnes*                                        ts Valerie Eliot?

17 October 1938                    *The Criterion*

My dear Barnes,

My goodness I am not eager to meet anyone so grand as the new Director General (sounds like the head of the Jesuits) (white tie):[1] unless the future of Britain depends upon it (and I know better) (but I have done more than that for the country, I have eaten Portuguese pork) I had *rather* dine quietly with yourselves and the Boatswain: but in any case DON'T RING UP MISS O'DONOVAN. That is where my patriotism calls a halt. When you want me, ring up MISS BRADBY (Mrs Ridler) at this number. Preferably, dine with yourselves and the Boatswain and have some cheerful nautical chorales.

> Yours appreciatively,
> T. S. E.

## to *Ezra Pound*                                              ts Yale

17 October 1938                    *The Criterion*

Resp. Ez.,

This aint as much of a Sprise to me as it wd. of been had I not met Daphne yesterday morning and learned the news.[2]

---

1–Barnes wrote from 3 Albert Terrace, Regent's Park, London, 17 Oct.: 'Anne and I are entertaining my new Director-General and his wife to dinner on November 3rd at 8 °/c, and we should both be very happy if you would join us.

'If you are not eager to meet them and would prefer to dine quietly here with the Bosun [Geoffrey Tandy] and ourselves one other day, please say so; then I will ring up *Miss O'Donovan* and suggest an evening.

'The Bosun is now reading Moby Dick twice weekly on the wireless. It is a long book so I hope he's happy.'
2–Olivia Shakespear, EP's mother-in-law, had died on 3 Oct. 1938 of complications brought on by gall bladder disease.

I immediately, however late, repaired to Ch.Cr.Rd. Post Office and despatched a telegram of condolence to Signora Pound.

Who I understand from Daphne has recently been in the hands of the surgeon. Had I known that, I wd. of send affectionate messages earlier.

This comes of not always reading The Times Newspaper.

In my telegram I observed the decorums of S. Kensington.

Well anyway I will come to 34, Abingdon Ct. tomorrow night (Tuesday) at 7.30 and see what happens.[1] If there aint any dinner there Maybe Ez will dine with O?P. [*sic*]

And maybe you will buy some new shirts.

And pending etc.

yrs. etc.

TP.

## TO *G. F. Higginson*

CC

17 October 1938                    [Faber & Faber Ltd]

Dear Mr Higginson,

I have your letter of the 12th, and will settle the account for super-tax.[2]

I enclose two cards from my wife,[3] further to a letter which I sent you. One was sent to me by an aunt who had been to see her, the other was enclosed in an envelope addressed by the institution. If you consider that their receipt should be acknowledged, will you kindly do so? otherwise do nothing about them.

I hear indirectly (my source of information is not particularly reliable) that Mrs Eliot again attempted to escape, but could get no farther than the roof of the building.[4] My informant (my old servant, who had the

---

1 – EP had in fact (14 Oct.) invited TSE to dinner that evening.

2 – 'I now enclose notice of assessment to sur-tax for the year 1937/38 shewing the amount due from you to be £39.15.1. This figure has been carefully checked and is quite in order.'

3 – Not traced.

4 – Bird & Bird had written to TSE on 21 Sept. 1938, in response to a (now lost) letter from him of 20 Sept.: 'We knew that Mrs Eliot escaped from the custody of her attendant on Thursday, the 15th inst. And was not discovered until the following evening. During this time she went to the Old Bond Street Branch of the District Bank Ltd to obtain some money and also wrote to the Head Office of the Bank asking for money to be sent to her c/o Messrs Brown Shipley & Co., but on our instructions her requests were refused.

'We assume that you do not require us to write to Northumberland House inviting the Medical Superintendent to take special care of Mrs Eliot as we imagine that, having regard to her conduct, this precaution will now be taken.

'We have issued a summons for the appointment of a Receiver.' (EVE)

information, he said, from Mrs Haigh-Wood's nurse) added that the home did not wish to keep her. In a case which I regard as incurable (though the possibility must be faced that she will eventually be released under some kind of financial supervision) I wonder whether it would not be better for her to be removed to some institution situated in the country at some distance from London: it should not only be pleasanter and healthier, but a further removal out of London might make her more docile and less restless. I do not know whether I should make this suggestion to her brother or not.

Yours sincerely,<br>[T. S. Eliot]

## TO *Medical Superintendent, St Stephen's Hospital*  CC

18 October 1938  [Faber & Faber Ltd]

Dear Sir,

I have been making enquiries with a view to visiting Mr W. L. Janes, who I understand has just entered your hospital as a patient in Ward 2b.[1] My secretary informs me that he is in a ward to which visitors are

---

Higginson to TSE, 3 Oct. 1938: 'The letter which Mrs Eliot has apparently written to the Court suggesting that you should act as one of her trustees is no doubt as a result of a notice on the Summons – which had to be served upon her in accordance with the rules – to the effect that the patient may make any observations he or she desires upon the proposed appointment. It is not unusual for patients to write to the Court accordingly but you may take it that her communication is not likely seriously to interfere with the appointment of the Official Receiver.'

See Lyndall Gordon, *Imperfect Life*, 303–4, for letter from Basil Saunders about VHE's attempt to escape and gain the protection of her close friend Louie Purdon – 'a somewhat earnest spinster [with] plenty of humour'. Seymour-Jones, *Painted Shadow*, 560–1: 'Marjorie Saunders, a Christian scientist, provided a refuge for escaped psychiatric patients at her pebble-dashed semi-detached house in Parkside Way, Harrow; it was to this liberal household that [Purdon] intended to bring Vivienne. Basil Saunders [son of Marjorie] takes up the story.

"One evening my mother went up to a café near Allen & Hanbury's off Oxford Street. There she was to receive Vivien and take her home to stay. Instead she was told that 'Mrs Eliot' would not be coming and that the arrangement was off. I believe Vivien had been apprehended before she got to Louie.

"Thereafter Louie was not able to communicate with Vivien. The 'home' she was in would not pass on telephone messages. Louie's letters were returned."'

1 – TSE had been infomed by letter from Mrs C. Webster (17 Oct.) that Janes had been found very ill on Sunday – 'There is a growth in the stomach' – and had been admitted to hospital. TSE was advised by Mrs Webster, 28 Oct., 'I think he is soon leaving us. He scarcely knew me . . . on the danger list.'

only admitted on Wednesday and Sunday afternoons, but that special permission can sometimes be obtained by people who are unable to visit patients during those afternoons. I am never free on Wednesday afternoons, as I have a regular committee on that day, and I have to be in Oxford on business next Sunday, so that I should be unable to visit Mr Janes for another ten days. I had been seeing him frequently during the last week or two, and had been alarmed about his condition, and therefore would like to visit him, if permission can be given to call on some other day. I shall be grateful if you can see your way to granting this permission.[1]

Yours faithfully,
[T. S. Eliot]

TO *Donagh MacDonagh*

18 October 1938                     *The Criterion*

Dear MacDonagh,

I am very sorry to have to express dissatisfaction with your review of Martin Turnell's book, but I have thought about it carefully, and it still seems to me unsatisfactory. I have not read the book myself; I only looked into it with a curiosity to see what might be his general attitude to myself; I hardly know him, and I hold no brief for his work. Nevertheless, your first paragraph seems to me to adopt a slightly offensive attitude toward English Roman Catholics. If you are going to make such a sharp distinction between the Catholic point of view and the point of view of English Catholics, then I think you ought to take pains to make clear what you mean by the former. Furthermore, I do not feel it is enough to dismiss Turnell for being dull, or his theories for clogging up his sentences, unless you are going to prove your case. All this would, of course, take more space, but unless it is worth doing at adequate length, I question whether the book is worth reviewing at all.

Do you think you can do anything about it?[2]

With best wishes,
Yours very sincerely,
T. S. Eliot

1 – 'When Janes fell ill, Tom visited him in hospital and took him champagne, which Janes hid and shared with other patients in the middle of the night' (Trevelyan, memoir, 134).
2 – MacDonagh responded on 19 Oct.: 'I am sorry I did not make it sufficiently clear that when I drew a distinction between the words Catholic and English Catholic, I was really comparing the intolerant Irish attitude towards all non-Catholic literature and art, with the

19 October 1938                    [Faber & Faber Ltd]

Dear Mr Higginson,

Thank you for your letter of the 18th.[1] It is satisfactory to learn that
the Master has in hand the liquidation of Mrs Eliot's liabilities, and that
he considers that she should be removed to a home in the country. It only
occurs to me to suggest that it might be more satisfactory to consult Dr
Hart, or Dr Mapother, rather than Dr Miller; but no doubt you will have
considered the alternatives.[2]

---

broad-minded acceptance of their honesty in England. I did not adopt a slightly offensive
attitude towards English Roman Catholics – if I was offensive it was towards Irish Roman
Catholics, though on rereading the paragraph I find I did not make that clear.' He submitted
a revised version of his review on 28 Oct.: 'I find myself in disagreement with him on almost
every page of his book so that a complete review would necessarily be longer than his whole
work.'

MacDonagh on Martin Turnell, *Poetry and Crisis*: C. 18 (Jan. 1939), 378–9.

1 – Higginson had responded to TSE's letter of 7 Oct.: 'I do not think that any useful purpose
would be served by acknowledging the two postcards from your Wife . . .

'The application for the appointment of a Receiver came before the Master [in Lunacy]
yesterday, and in the result, as I anticipated, the Official Solicitor was appointed without
difficulty. The necessary directions were given by the Master to enable him to dispose of
the piano, the cars, and the flats on the best possible terms. Certain of your wife's shares
are to be sold to discharge the Bank overdraft, while others are to be lodged in Court. The
certificates for the remainder, together with Mrs Eliot's Will, are to be handed over to the
Official Solicitor. He was also directed to investigate the outstanding claim for income tax,
the contents of the safes at Selfridges, the boxes from Messrs. Broad & Son and the packages
at the Bank, and will in due course report again to the Master . . . The whole of the net
income from the patient's estate is to be allowed for her maintenance. The exact financial
position will not clearly emerge until after the Official Solicitor has been able to complete
his enquiries . . .

'In the meanwhile, I have informed the Master that without binding yourself in any way
you are prepared for the moment to continue the allowance of £5 per week which you
have been making to your wife for some time past. He accepts this position and asks that
arrangements should be made for the payment of the sum in question direct to the Official
Solicitor . . .

'Although your letter did not reach me in time to enable me to inform the Master of your
wife's second attempt to escape from the Home and your view that it was desirable that she
should be moved to a Home some distance from London, he came quite independently to the
same conclusion and stated that he did not consider it at all desirable that she should remain
in a Home practically in the heart of London. With Mr Haigh-Wood's approval therefore I
am proposing to communicate with Dr Miller or one of the other medical advisers who have
been consulted with a view to discovering some more suitable establishment in the country.'

2 – Higginson replied by return (20 Oct.): 'I am entirely in agreement with your suggestion
that in considering some alternative Home for Mrs Eliot we should do well to rely rather
upon the more expert advice of either Dr Hart or Dr Mapother, than upon that of Dr Miller,
who does not after all pretend to be a Specialist in complaints of this nature. I have indeed
communicated this view to Mr Haigh-Wood from whom I am now awaiting to hear further.'

I enclose a receipt from the Legal and General Assurance Society, which you will file with my papers. I also enclose a letter from Lloyds Bank, concerning my payment of premium on my Life Assurance Policy, which explains itself.

Yours sincerely,
[T. S. Eliot]

## TO *John Hayward*                                      TS King's

20 October 1938                        *The Criterion*

Dear John,

I got a ticket permitting me to visit Mr W. L. Janes on Thursday afternoons at 6; dashed down to Fulham, and found him sound asleep. I fear he was disappointed when he woke up. Looked pretty grey. Nurse said cryptically, 'we don't think we can do much for him'.[1]

Had your John Gielgud to dinner last night, with Browne. This time he chose oysters, guinness, and a tournedos. Oysters for three make quite a hole in a pound note.

The Gielgud business is not yet released.[2] Still more CONFIDENTIAL is the news about the *Criterion*. Have started composing the obituary.

1 – JDH responded, 30 Oct.: 'Poor old Janes! I'm glad he's comfortable in the place whither he dreaded to go & I hope he will have no pain but will slip away quietly & easily.'

2 – Gielgud to Browne, 23 Sept. 1938: 'Now that this play [*Dear Octopus*, by Dodie Smith] is safely launched I am very anxious to see the Eliot script if it is ready. Perhaps you could come and see me one day during a performance or have supper with me after the play one night – provided all this trouble [i.e. Munich] blows over . . . I'm sorry to hurry you but the B.B.C. have approached me about doing a Shakespeare play in November, and I have been asked to appear for one or two charities; I'd like to know whether there is any question of doing the Eliot play for matinees instead, as if it seemed possible I'd rather do that in my spare time than anything else' (Browne, *The Making of T. S. Eliot's Plays*, 145).

Gielgud, *An Actor and His Time* (rev. edn,1989), 163–4: 'I got on better with Christopher Fry than I did with T. S. Eliot. In some way I seemed to alarm him. In 1939 [*sc.* 1938] I had intended to direct and act the leading part in *The Family Reunion*, which had intrigued me, though I did not understand it very well. I had lined up a wonderful cast – Dame May Whitty, Sybil Thorndike, Martita Hunt – and had scheduled the play for matinées at the Globe Theatre. I was then asked to go to meet Eliot for the first time at the Reform Club. To my surprise he was a rather sober-looking gentleman in a black coat and striped trousers. We had oysters, I remember, and it was very formal. I was rather nervous and began to draw patterns on the table cloth. "Should the set be like this?" I asked him. "The French windows, should they be there?" and "How do you want the Eumenides to be seen? Or should they be invisible, or perhaps in masks?" The more I talked, the more silent Eliot became. However, I left thinking that I had created quite a good impression. I continued to think so until, a few days later, I met Sybil Thorndike who said "You know, Eliot's not going to let you have his

Shant know whether I can catch the down train to reach Paddington at 7.45. Geoffrey has a day of committees there. Perhaps best thing, if you are alone that evening, ring me up and if I am back I will come round. If I dont hear, I shall understand that you have visitors.

TODAY'S SPOT OF BAD NEWS

The Ledbury have had the worst possible luck during the last few seasons. Mr A. W. Strickland, who promised to solve their problems two or three years ago by becoming Joint-Master with Mr Young, was stricken with sudden ill-health and, <u>indeed</u>,[1] has died this summer.[2]

Yrs. etc.<br>
TP.

I hope so for Sunday, as next week is pretty full till weekend, when I shall be at home.

## TO *John Gielgud*[3]    cc

24 October 1938    [Faber & Faber Ltd]

Dear Mr Gielgud,

I was surprised to see a notice of my play in *The Sunday Times*, based on information apparently supplied by you; and I cannot help feeling that the announcement was a little premature. The more so because a play of this kind requires centralised control, if it is not to be a chaos of individual parts; and I have come more clearly to the conclusion, since I first thought about the matter, that as Martin Browne has had unique experience in

---

play – he says you have no faith." Evidently he feared I was going to turn it into a fashionable Shaftesbury Avenue comedy, though he never wrote to me to explain his decision.

'Many years later I went to Marrakesh for a holiday and found that Eliot was staying in the same hotel with his second wife. He was already ill – it was not long before his death. I spoke to him and said how sorry I was I had not done *Family Reunion*, but he still did not reveal what he had felt about me or why he had turned me down. I said I had played it on the radio with some success and had made a recording of his Journey of the Magi which people liked. He asked me to send it to him, and he wrote me a very nice letter about it. I am sure that, over *The Family Reunion*, he had found me over-assertive – perhaps he was right.'

1 – Underline added by TSE.

2 – This paragraph is an unidentified cutting pasted onto the letter.

3 – John Gielgud (1904–2000): distinguished actor and theatre director. Knighted in 1953; awarded Legion of Honour, 1960; created Companion of Honour, 1977; OM, 1996.

producing my work, I should wish him to have the sole ultimate responsibility and authority with this also.[1]

1–Richard Clowes, 'New Work by T. S. Eliot: Mr Gielgud's Interest', *The Sunday Times*, 23 Oct. 1938: 'John Gielgud tells me that he has read with great interest and admiration a new dramatic work by T. S. Eliot. The play is called *The Family Reunion*; it is in verse, and has a modern setting. A series of matinée performances will be given after Christmas. Mr Gielgud hopes to appear in the play, and to direct it in association with Martin Browne, who produced Mr Eliot's *Murder in the Cathedral*.'

Gielgud's developing interest in becoming involved with *The Family Reunion* is evidenced by a letter he wrote to Browne on 30 Sept. 1938: 'I am enormously interested in the Eliot play. I think it will be better if we don't discuss it in greater detail until the final revision has been done, as I agree with the letter I found in the back (which you may or may not have meant me to read) that the play is far more lucid and easy to understand in the early part. I do certainly think the thing needs a good deal of clearing up, and I am very troubled about the Furies, as I cannot quite see them, as he has conceived them, making anything but a comic effect. But as soon as you have talked again with him, and had the revised script, do let me have it and we can talk in detail about the play. Meanwhile I will read it again more carefully . . . It seems to me that if the financial aspect could be arranged it is the kind of play which would do better for a series of matinées than in an evening bill, but of course Eliot may feel that this is not giving him much chance of making any money out of it. But if it has to be kept for a regular run you might have to wait till next autumn, which does seem rather a pity. From my own point of view it would amuse me very much to do it for matinées while this present play is running, because (a) I should love the interest of the extra work and (b) I am sure it would be fun to point the contrast between the two plays; this one of Dodie's has so many of the same main characteristics – the family theme, and the return of the prodigal etc. – but how differently treated. I think this would intrigue people very much' (quoted in Browne, *Making*, 145–6).

See too *Gielgud's Letters*, ed. Richard Mangan (2004), 51–2: [To Mrs Patrick Campbell, 11 Oct. 1938] 'There are not many interesting plays to see, but I have a play by T. S. Eliot which I am hoping to do for matinées after Christmas, very original and lovely poetry, I think. Quite a modern setting almost in the manner of Aldous Huxley, but with choruses and a sort of Greek tragedy analogy, only much better than [Eugene] O'Neill's. I saw *Mourning Becomes Electra* last year and thought it very pretentious and unreal.'

*Gielgud's Letters*, 344: [To EMB, 6 Aug. 1968]: 'Perhaps you never heard the full story. I agreed with T. S. Eliot to co-direct the play [*The Family Reunion*] with you. We lunched – twice, I think – at the Reform Club – surely you were there on one of the occasions. We had a fine cast lined up – May Whitty (Dowager), Sybil [Thorndike] (Agatha), Martita Hunt, Freddie Lloyd for two of the chorus. All seemed to be going very amicably. Suddenly one day I met Sybil who said gaily "You know Eliot won't let you do his play. He says you have no Faith, and therefore are not right to play it." I was amazed. I don't know how he told Binkie Beaumont but the upshot was that we did *The Importance* instead! Later I met Eliot and he was nice but vague. I sent him a record I had made of "The Journey of the Magi" and he said he had wanted to hear me do *Family Reunion* on the air but he had missed it. He was quite ill already, so I never really found out what tactless thing I may have said or done, and of course I was sorry never to have played Harry. I think he got alarmed at the idea of Shaftesbury Avenue and feared I should put a vulgar commercial smear on his writing and force him to accept it.'

EMB comments in *Making* (146), whether forgetfully or disingenuously: 'This opened up a most attractive prospect. Gielgud agreed to co-direct the play with me. He was to play Harry; and he pencilled into my draft his suggested casting for other parts: May Whitty

I feel rather apologetic for not having let you know sooner, but I have had to be very busy with other matters.

Yours sincerely,

[T. S. Eliot]

## TO *Ian Dawson* CC

25 October 1938 [Faber & Faber Ltd]

Dear Mr Dawson,

Thank you for your letter of the 21st.[1] I am very interested in what you say about the way in which you propose to play the part of Becket. I agree

---

as Amy, Sybil Thorndike as Agatha, Margaret Rutherford, Martita Hunt, Frederick Lloyd as aunts and uncles, Ernest Thesiger as Downing. I do not know why it never came to anything.'

Ashley Dukes to TSE, 14 Feb. 1945: 'When any proposals are made about a copyright *which do not materialize*, any announcement about them is damaging to the copyright. This happened in the case of *The Family Reunion*, which John Gielgud announced he was going to produce; a paragraph to that effect that was put prominently into a Sunday paper. I must remind you that you took strong exception to this, and asked me on your behalf to point out to Gielgud that your essential condition for the proposed production (the direction of Martin Browne) had not yet been agreed. Gielgud then made many apologies for the indiscretion, and gave up the project for the play forthwith. He was well aware that no announcement should have been made before the exchange of contracts. The eventual production was made at the Westminster; the prospects of the play were not improved by everybody's knowledge that Gielgud had announced the play and changed his mind.'

John Gielgud to Peter Quennell, 5 Oct. 1982: '[Eliot] I met one day for lunch at the Reform Club, when he seemed very conventional in his black coat and striped trousers. We discussed "The Family Reunion" which had rather intrigued me, and I had tentatively engaged a distinguished cast to present some matinees of the play at the Globe where I was then acting. But a few days later, Sybil Thorndike, who was to have played the Dowager, met me in the street and said "You know, Eliot won't let you do his play because he says you have no Faith." I was naturally disappointed, but as we substituted a production of "The Importance of Being Earnest" which was to be a huge success, and stood me in good luck for several years, I managed to survive the snub, though first rather surprised that Eliot had never written to me himself.'

Levy and Scherle contribute this nugget (41): '"John Gielgud," he [Eliot] reminisced, "wanted to play Harry Monchensey in *The Family Reunion*, but I was opposed to it on the grounds that he wasn't religious enough to fully understand the motivation of the character."'

1–Ian Dawson (who had been for some years a classics master at Charterhouse School) was to take the part of Becket in a production at Croydon Repertory Theatre for the week beginning 31 Oct. 'You saw me at the Duchess in the part of the Third Priest on the occasion of Queen Mary's visit, and earlier you may remember the York Nativity at the Mercury, in which I played Joachim . . . I should very much like to know what you think of my reading of Becket. Much as I admired Bobby's performance, the beauty of voice, the dignity, the spiritual quality, I found myself all along dissenting from the characterisation and shape

with you that it is a part which can be played in more than one way, and I think it would be a very good thing if you followed out this line, and did not adhere to the interpretation of Bobbie Speaight. I share your admiration for his performance, but there is no reason for supposing that even the first interpretation of a part is anything but an interpretation, or that it is necessarily the nearest to what the author himself intended. Furthermore, I agree with you that a character becomes in a sense public property. It will be interesting to see what you can do in the way of making the temptations appear more genuine. I think, however, that Speaight did attempt to follow my suggestion that the temptations were meant to be increasingly real. The first one, in my intention, was for Becket only the temptation to think with a certain amount of pleasure and regret of a period in the remote past; it was definitely not intended to be a temptation to action. The second and third are much more genuine struggles, although of course very much easier to cope with than the last.

If it is possible, I shall certainly want to see your performance, and I hope you will let me have particulars as the time approaches.

With best wishes,
Yours sincerely,
[T. S. Eliot]

---

of the part as he played it. He came on the stage a martyr-elect, the tempters were quite obviously wasting their time, and the distress and conflict were at most narrative, rather than dramatic: the sermon was quite admirable and right; then in the second half the human side of Becket came out more strongly in conflict with the Knights, and one felt a certain arrogance and pride in the strong *man*, for all the spirituality in the quieter passages and the final dedication. In my view, all this should appear unequivocally in Part I, and the temptations should be resisted in act as well as in fact, the pride, the ambition and the human strength should be amply conveyed to the emotions of the audience until the final conquest of personality by spirit takes place before their eyes. The sermon then becomes the reflective recognition of the implications of an experience they have just been through, and in part 2 Becket is seen to be a changed man: although many of the lines are superficially debating-points scored off the Knights, one should never feel the conflict is on the same plane or that Becket is enjoying the exercise of his undoubted personal strength. So the "thee times traitor, you" becomes an echo of our Lord's "you will betray me thrice", with an admixture of sorrow and pain in the tone. If all this does some violence to your own intentions, "I will be bold to say" that a great work of the imagination, as I recognise this to be, transcends the "conscious" intentions of the artist and becomes public property for anyone that has eyes to see. Whether what I see in it has any value or not depends upon the validity of my mental processes, which theoretically may be quite fanciful and irresponsible: in fact, they are sincerely and impersonally felt, and I hope they do have a basis in objective fact.'

## TO *John Middleton Murry*                    TS Northwestern

27 October 1938                    *The Criterion*

Dear John,

I do not know whether Herbert will be distressed by your review or not, but it seems to me to be courageous, intelligent and right, and I am ready to print it if you are.[1] Indeed, I think it ought to be good for Read to have this point of view so well stated, because it is one which I believe he will hardly have met with from his other critics.

Yours ever,
Tom


## TO *George Barker*                    TS Texas

28 October 1938                    *The Criterion*

Dear Barker,

I am sorry that I was unable to answer your letter of the 24th at once.[2] I am very glad that you have been able to get so much done: I have not yet looked at Book II, because I know that it will take a good deal of time and close attention, which I shall not be able to give for perhaps another week.

I am very sorry to hear that there is a jam. I enclose a small contribution: send something to Barclay's Bank, Dorchester, and I hope that the rest will help to keep things going.

Yours sincerely,
T. S. Eliot

1–JMM on HR, *Collected Essays in Literary Criticism*: C. 18 (Jan. 1939), 333–9.
    The blurb for HR's collection (1938) was probably written by TSE: 'This volume is a selection from the author's essays in literary criticism written during the last fifteen years. It includes such part of *Reason and Romanticism* as he wishes to preserve, the essays formerly published as *The Sense of Glory* and *Form in Modern Poetry* (now out of print), together with a few detachable essays from other publications and one essay hitherto unpublished in book form. All the essays have been revised, and as now arranged they fall naturally into two parts – one dealing with the general theory of poetry and criticism, the other comprising particular studies of individual authors, from Froissart and Malory to Gerard Manley Hopkins and Henry James. The general tendency of Mr Read's criticism becomes much clearer in this new arrangement, and has a special interest in that it represents one of the first and most consistent attempts to reinforce literary criticism with the principles of modern psychology.'
2–Barker (24 July): 'The 2nd Book or rather 2nd half of *Calamiterror* is now in the process of completion . . . I have no very accurate notion of how much longer it will be in hand, but this question does not bother me much, for the sensation of relief at having at last got under weigh with it is so good that I cannot worry about how much or how long.'
    On 24 Oct.: 'at last Ive got the 2nd book of Calamiterror finished'.

## TO *Ralph Hodgson*

TS Beinecke

28 October 1938                    *The Criterion*

Respected Towser,

I need the refreshment of your company again as soon as possible. The days fill up quickly, with this or that futility, and you will soon be leaving for Madison. Will you lunch with me say ten days hence? Say Tuesday week? Let me have a provisional reply. Would you be willing to meet one or two carefully hand picked vintage characters who recognise the importance of Mr R. H., or alternatively lunch alone with your

faithful old
Possum[1]

To
  The Man in White Spats,
    c/o S. S. Koteliansky Esqre.,[2]
    5, Acacia Road,
      S. John's Wood,
      N. W. 8.

STOP PRESS: Ezra is in town. Address him at 34, Abingdon Court, W.8. His mother-in-law has died, and he is winding up.


## TO *Bonamy Dobrée*

TS Brotherton

2 November 1938                    *The Criterion*

Dear Bonamy,

I am highly gratified to receive the *Troilus* with inscription, and of course flattered to be mentioned:[3] but as I expostulated before, it suggests that my assistance went a good deal farther and deeper than merely recalling to your notice one or two of the elementary principles of rhetoric. When shall we meet again? Will you be up in London for part of the holidays or

---

1–Hodgson replied, 2 Nov.: 'I need yours. Tuesday would be the 8th: a good selection.

'As to the Table: yourself alone, a trio or any & so many as you can or care to assemble: no one can pick guests so discreetly. But there's a snag: can you pick a gooseberry pie? I'm not certain about this. You notice I say nothing about Saddle of Mutton. / 'Towser.'

2–See Galya Diment, *A Russian Jew of Bloomsbury: The Life and Times of Samuel Koteliansky* (2011).

3–*Troilus and Cressida*, ed. BD (The Warwick Shakespeare, 1938), vi: 'I would like to express my sincere thanks . . . to Mr T. S. Eliot for commenting upon my Introduction, and enabling me to better it.'

for the pantomime? Otherwise, I believe it will probably be March before I can get as far as the kingdom of Northumbria.

Well, how is Social Credit coming? at the cost of letting Mosley bring it? I count the month of October as the most dismal month in public affairs that I have ever experienced. Is that objective, or have I merely become more sensitive to public affairs as I mature?

With Love to Valentine and Georgina,

Yrs ever

Tom

## TO *Herbert Read* CC

3 November 1938                    [*The Criterion*]

Dear Herbert,

Faber & Faber's readers have decided that Pasternak's short stories are not our meat.[1] We think decidedly that this is the right stuff for the Hogarth Press. You don't say whether it should be returned to Robert Payne (a lad, I believe, of considerable ability) or to yourself. Much better that it should not reach the Hogarth Press from another publisher. Let me know where to send it.[2]

---

1–HR wrote, 13 Oct.: 'Robert Payne (Robert Young to Fabers) has asked me to send on to you his translation of some short stories by Pasternak. Pasternak seems to be the most important of contemporary Russian poets, & pleasantly free from "ideology" (which perhaps explains why he is at present in prison). Payne is ambitious to translate all his works, & has done many of the poems as well as the stories. I think the title story is very fine, & the others interesting enough. But it is perhaps rather a question of taking over the man rather than this particular work . . . It is perhaps more in the line of the Hogarth Press. But you ought to see it first.'

Boris Pasternak (1890–1960), poet, novelist, translator. Early work includes the influential collection *My Sister, Life* (poems, 1917). Later best known for *Doctor Zhivago* (first published in 1957 after being smuggled out of Soviet Russia). Nobel Prize, 1958.

2–HR commented, 6 Nov. 1938: 'I am not surprised to hear your decision about Pasternak. Payne has now sent me the poems, but they do not change the position.'

TSE was to write to Dr Prafulla Das, 4 Dec. 1959: 'I am highly honoured by your suggestion that I should write a prefatory note to the Oriya translation of the poems of Boris Pasternak. From what I am told, and from what impression I can receive from translation into English, Mr Pasternak is a very fine poet indeed. Furthermore I am much in sympathy with him and took part in an expression of protest against his being prevented from accepting the Nobel Prize. But I feel that it would be absurd for me to write an introductory note to poems which I have not read and cannot read in the original language, and that you would do best to approach some distinguished man of letters who knows Boris Pasternak and is appreciative of poetry. I venture to suggest the name of Sir Maurice Bowra, Warden of Wadham College, Oxford.'

By all means let us meet soon. What about Thursday the 10th for lunch? I don't know whether Frank will be on hand by then, but in any case.

Yours ever,

[Tom]

## TO *I. Husain*[1]

CC

4 November 1938                    [Faber & Faber Ltd]

Dear Mr Hussain,

Thank you for your letter dated the 2nd September, which has however only reached me within the last day or two. I do indeed remember very well having met you, and remember very well your anthology of the prose works of John Donne, which I was glad to see had a favourable reception.[2]

I confess that the publication of your new book on Donne had escaped my notice, but the number of books published nowadays is so large that I cannot attempt to keep in touch with publication except when books are drawn specially to my notice. Now that you have mentioned the book, I shall certainly keep it in mind for the *Criterion*.

I am naturally much flattered that you should contemplate writing a monograph on my own work. I shall be very glad to fulfil my promise to look through it when it is ready. You will of course not expect me to consider myself qualified to criticize your criticism, because that is an impossible activity for the subject of a monograph to engage in. But my perusal might result, as in other cases, in correcting minor errors of fact, or supplying relevant information of which you were unaware. The brief summary in your letter promises me much interest. There is only one

1–Dr Itrât Husain, MA, PhD, Professor of English, Islamia College, Calcutta, was at this time Carnegie Research Scholar at Edinburgh University.

2–'I hope you remember having met me in June 1936, after you had kindly seen an anthology of the Prose Works of John Donne prepared under the guidance of Sir Herbert Grierson.

'I have this year published a book on John Donne "The Dogmatic and mystical Theology of John Donne" (S.P.C.K London) . . .

'Perhaps you remember that I had told you that when I finish my research work on the 17th century Poetry, I would write a monograph on your poetry "T. S. Eliot as a Metaphysical Poet", and you had kindly promised to go through it when it was ready. I am busy writing it now . . . Please let me know if you will be able to go through it before its publication. I also require an autographed copy of your photo which will form the front piece [*sic*] of the book.'

point on which I must decline to be helpful: I have a certain aversion to having any photograph of myself appear in any book.

Yours sincerely,

[T. S. Eliot]

## TO *Ralph Hodgson* PC TS Beinecke

4 November 1938          Faber & Faber Ltd

Saddle of mutton arranged, but I cannot promise gooseberry tart.

O. P.

## TO *Edith Sitwell*[1] CC

7 November 1938          [Faber & Faber Ltd]

Dear Edith,

It was a very pleasant surprise to hear from you and I am extremely flattered to learn that you want to put me into an anthology along with Yeats.[2] So far as I am concerned I should be delighted, but the rights are vested in Faber and Faber, who will have to be approached formally with full particulars of the anthology and who will, I warn you, demand a fee for publication. So will you have your agent or publisher write to Faber and Fabers or Mr C. W. Stewart, who deals with such matters.

I should very much like to see you while you are in London. Unfortunately I have an engagement for Thursday night, the 17th. I am dining I find with

---

1 – Edith Sitwell (1887–1964): poet, biographer, novelist; editor of *Wheels* 1916–21. Her collection *The Mother and Other Poems* (1915) was followed by *Clown's Houses* (1918) and *The Wooden Pegasus* (1920). In 1923, her performance at the Aeolian Hall in London of her cycle of poems, *Façade* (1922), with music by William Walton, placed her briefly at the centre of modernistic experimentation. Other writings include *Collected Poems* (1930) and *Taken Care Of* (memoirs, 1965). She was appointed DBE in 1954. See John Pearson, *Façades: Edith, Osbert and Sacheverell Sitwell* (1978); *Selected Letters of Edith Sitwell*, ed. Richard Greene (1997); Greene, *Edith Sitwell: Avant-Garde Poet, English Genius* (2011).

TSE to Mary Trevelyan, 16 Oct. 1949: 'Edith and Osbert [Sitwell] are 70% humbug – but kind – and cruel' ('The Pope of Russell Square').

2 – ES wrote from Paris, 6 Nov. 1938: 'I am compiling an enormous anthology, with a very long preface. It begins somewhere about the time of Chaucer. I am only going to include two living poets, (that, of course, is if they consent, as I hope with all my heart they will,) – yourself and Mr Yeats; though there will be quotations from others in the preface.

'I am writing, therefore, to ask you if you will do me the great honour and give me the joy, of allowing me to include "The Waste Land", 'Whispers of Immortality" and "Sweeney among the Nightingales". No anthology could be complete without them.'

Charles Williams, and I can't put it off because I was in bed with a cold last week and this is one of the postponed engagements which result from taking a few days in bed. And on Saturday I expect to be going up to Kelham. Would you, by any chance, be free to lunch with me on Friday the 18th? I am very sorry about Thursday, because otherwise I would willingly have faced the terrors of your club.[1]

Yours ever,<br>[T. S. E.]

## TO *G. F. Higginson*                                                        CC

8 November 1938                    [24 Russell Square, W.C.1]

Dear Mr Higginson,

Thank you for your letter of the 2nd and 4th instant.[2] Were my position different, I should be inclined to maintain that it would be better for Mrs Eliot to be in a suitably enclosed institution at a distance from London,

---

1 – ES wrote, 'I am coming to England next Saturday, to the Sesame Club, 49 Grosvenor Street. It would be such a delight to me if you would come and dine with me there, on Thursday the 17th . . . It will not be a party, but Mr Maugham is coming, and Osbert, and Madame Wiel, poor Helen's sister. Helen died this year, after the most dreadful agony . . .

'P.S. Dining at a woman's club may terrify you. But have no fear. The chefs are *not* allowed to kill my guests.'

2 – Higginson's letter of 2 Nov. enclosed a letter to himself from Dr Bernard Hart, 31 Oct.:

'With regard to homes in the country, I might mention that Northumberland House has a good country home at Kearsney Court, nr Dover and, from what I saw of Mrs Eliot's case, I should think that she would be suitable for a home of this kind where the patients are naturally more free than in a London home. I do not know exactly what fees would be charged, but they would certainly come within the patient's means, and you could get particulars from Northumberland House.' Other possible country Homes, he went on, were St Andrew's Hospital, Northampton; the Holloway Sanatorium, Virginia Water, Surrey; and Ticehurst House, Sussex – though the fees at Ticehurst 'would be rather beyond the available income'.

Higginson commented on Hart's letter: 'In the circumstances I am inclined to think that Kearsney Court sounds the most suitable but I shall be glad to have your views. I have written to Mr Haigh-Wood on the subject and assuming that you are both in agreement I will inform the Official Solicitor.'

However, on 4 Nov. Higginson received this letter of 3 Nov. from Frederick Dillon, Medical Superintendent of Northumberland House: 'our fees for Kearsney Court, Dover, are the same as for Northumberland House, namely, 6 guineas per week and we could receive the patient there at any time. An objection to this course would be that Mrs Eliot would be liable to escape as she would have a good deal more liberty there and the opportunities would be greater.

'With regard to the suggestion of her transfer, however I discussed it with Mrs Eliot this morning and she tells me that she would definitely prefer to remain here, one reason being that she can receive visits here much more conveniently than at Dover. Before any

as I think that it would be better for her to be where she could not receive frequent visits from her relatives. But unless her brother took the same view, it would obviously be unsuitable for me to urge this opinion. So I do not propose to take any initiative further.

Yours sincerely,
[T. S. Eliot]

## TO *A. Desmond Hawkins*　　　　TS A. Desmond Hawkins

9 November 1938　　　　　*The Criterion*

Dear Hawkins,

I have your letter of the 8th, with a draft circular.[1] I have not had time to give it very close attention, but one or two points occur to me. First, although paragraph 6 makes it fairly clear what sort of book is in the minds of the promoters, it might be as well for public purposes to make clear that what you have in mind at present is reprints of scarce old works which are out of copyright.[2] Otherwise you might find yourself deluged with MSS of unpublishable contemporary poets.

I should like to know how many copies would have to be printed in order to present them to all the libraries you have in mind.[3] How much extra expense both in publishing and postage would this entail? It seems to me that you might be letting yourself in for a good deal of unpaid work, and for minor expenses which the committee would have to defray. Is public generosity on such a scale feasible?

---

arrangements are made to transfer the patient to the country I consider it would be advisable to be sure of the patient's wishes in this respect.'

Higginson commented to TSE: 'In the circumstances you will probably agree that it would be preferable to allow Mrs Eliot to remain there, but I shall be glad to have your views.'

1 – Hawkins circulated a draft manifesto outlining a scheme for 'Authors' Guild Editions' – for which the General Committee was TSE, Michael Roberts, William Johnstone (Principal of the L.C.C. Printing School), and Hawkins himself. Point 1: 'The purpose of this guild is to reprint rare or inaccessible books which are of some interest to students and critics of literature but are unlikely to be published in the ordinary way because there is very little demand for them.'

2 – Point 6 read: 'The works of the following poets are among those already suggested – Thomas Beedome, Thomas Tusser, William Broome, Mildmay Fane, William Warner, Thomas Churchyard, Leonard William, Rowland Watkyns, Samuel Daniel, Joshua Sylvester, Giles Fletcher, William Shenstone, William Cleland, William Hunnis and David Gray.'

3 – Point 4: 'Copies of the books printed will be deposited in the principal libraries of England, the British Empire and the United States, including the central depots of the public library exchange system; so that any reader will be able to *borrow* the books through the ordinary public libraries.'

Hawkins had it in mind to print between 100 and 200 copies of each edition.

I don't remember how many copies of any particular book the school would be willing to print. The chief extra expense of course would not be in the printing but in the binding. I think that such books ought to be bound as cheaply as possible in paper, leaving it to the possessors to have them bound at their own expense if they wish.

I think that suggestions made by various volunteers should, except of course when they are unanimously rejected, be pooled for some time, and the selection and order of books made by the committee for, say, a period of six months ahead. This would somewhat diminish the danger of accepting suggestions of minor importance, and being obliged to defer other suggestions of books of greater value. That is all I can think of at the moment.

Yours ever,<br>T. S. E.

P.S. Before any first list of books is settled upon, there are several people who have curious knowledge and might have useful suggestions: for instance, Ralph Hodgson or John Betjeman.

## TO *Theodore Spencer*                    TS Harvard Archives

9 November 1938                    *The Criterion*

Dear Ted,

Thank you very much for your letter[1] and for the trouble you have taken over MacNeice. I have written to all the folk you mention so carefully with addresses, and have told MacNeice that he is to write and thank you and I hope he will hit it off with Frisky[2] better than the last man I sent (Jim Barnes: I thought that Eton and the Blues would be allright with the Master, but apparently it didnt work at all). I have not yet heard from Good Queen Bess (Miss Prof. Elizabeth Manwaring of Wellesley, to whom I wrote when I wrote to you).

You may be presented within a month or two with a letter of introduction from me for a man named Jim Fowler, or he may call himself James Fowler-Seaverns. He is a very nice lad (Harrow and Magdalene) not a bit literary, runs a business in London and Australia which has some mysterious connexion with Needham, Mass. Amongst other things he is

---

1 – Spencer's letter of 28 Oct. is paraphrased in part in TSE's letter to MacNeice of 8 Dec. 1938, available on tseliot.com.
2 – Roger Bigelow Merriman (1876–1945), known as 'Frisky', Gurney Professor of History and Political Science, was the first Master of Eliot House, Harvard University, 1931–42.

marketing the Iron Lung. He has adoptive parents from Portland Maine but has never been in America before. He married a girl named Roper who is some collateral of St Thos. More, she died this summer, and he is a widower with two small children. You will find him a nice innocent fellow who will appreciate anything convivial.

John has just moved to Swan Court, Chelsea.[1] I have not yet seen him in his new abode. I am sinking myself into the problem of Church and State, on which I have to lecture at Corpus in February, under the protection of Pickthorn, in the absence of Spens, who is going to South Africa to recuperate. Meanwhile Ashley Dukes is concerning himself with trying to arrange a production of *The Family Reunion*, which is in the press (Maclehose of Glasgow).

Yours affectionately<br>T. S. E.

## TO *Polly Tandy* TS BL

11 November 1938          *The Criterion*

Dear Polly,[2]

I was very grieved, ma'am, to have my opes so rudely dashed last night by hearing that you were laid low with the influenza ('Con-fined, as the lady said'). I trust that the malady is not serious and that you and your household are being looked after; but I don't know how well Mrs Reddick figures in the role of Sairey Gamp.

Now that I am on the subject, it has been on my mind for some time to mention, if a suitable opportunity presented itself, the fact that I am more than somewhat worried by your Old Man not getting on with that Natural History book he has been writing for us, by fits and starts, over a period of I don't know how many years. I know he has that costive kind of mind, like my own, which isn't satisfied to say anything at all unless

---

1–On 7 Nov. JDH moved from Bina Gardens to 115 Swan Court, London S.W.3, where he was to live until 25 Aug. 1939.

2–The Tandy family – Geoffrey, Polly, Richard, Alison, Anthea ('Poppet') – had written to TSE on 25 Sept. 1938 (the day before his fiftieth birthday):

'The Tandy Fambly wish to convey their humble greetings and their love to you on this anniversary of your birthday.

'Yassuh! B'rer Possum, suh! We sho'ly hopes as yo' toofies am holding up aft' all deze long years. En ef yo' ain't proud 'er bein' ha'f a hundred years old, den all we got ter say is: dey aint no satisfyin' some fokes. Ef so be as yo' wants a bit er comfort on dis sollum ercazyum you jest gimme a ring on dis yer lectric tellifun' (EVE).

every possible shade and qualification demanded by the strictest criteria of scruple can be got down on paper. Nevertheless, not writing the book is no way out, and the only way to get the book written is to write it, and take his friends' advice as to whether it is satisfactory or not. From my own experience I say that it would be very soothing to his nerves to get it done, even if he isn't satisfied with it, which he never will be anyway. Furthermore, while this broadcasting is all very well, for the meagre sums grudgingly paid by that Corporation do help to keep kettles boiling, on the other hand it doesn't get you anywhere; and this book would do more for his reputation, and so for his pocket in the long run. So now it's for you to say whether you agree with me or not, and if so, to exert any kind of constant gentle pressure that seems to you suitable and tactful. So hoping you won't mind my making so bold, and wishing you a speedy recovery, I remain,

Yours affectionately,
O Possum

## TO *John Maynard Keynes* TS King's

15 November 1938         *The Criterion*

Dear Maynard,

I feel impelled to write and thank you for your hospitality of last night, dinner, theatre and supper.[1] The kitchen of the theatre has unquestionably not deteriorated. I was sorry not to see you afterwards and hope you were not overtired. You certainly gave the boys a great send-off, for which they must be very grateful.

Lydia's part did improve and was at its best in the last act (the best act of the play, I thought), and she did the lines admirably.[2] I still think her dress unbecoming! and I didn't like the lighting on her in the ghostly scenes. I think the part of Valerian might have been played with more

---

1 – The Group Theatre produced *On the Frontier*, by Auden and Isherwood, at the Arts Theatre, Cambridge.
2 – Judith Mackrell notes that Keynes's wife, the ballet dancer Lydia Lopokova, 'took pleasure in [TSE's] company. She thought he had a "kind nature" and was intrigued by his and Maynard's friendship' (*Bloomsbury Ballerina: Lydia Lopokova, Imperial Dancer and Mrs John Maynard Keynes* [2008], 346).

subtlety (Felix Aylmer[1] might have done it well); and I am afraid that Hitler is not the simpleton that the authors made him out to be.[2]

Yours ever,

T. S. Eliot

TO *Geoffrey Grigson*                                     TS Texas

16 November 1938                    Faber & Faber Ltd

My dear Grigson,

I acknowledged your letter of the 7th instant, and I think intimated that I would write again. About the preface, I now see that my criticism of your actual preface was purely negative. I agree with you that a preface to such an anthology should not express all the personal antipathies which have made the editorial matter of *New Verse* itself so delightful to its readers. But I find I still feel that I was right in being dissatisfied with the present preface. It seems to me that in your anxiety not to do in the preface what you have done with so much point in a periodical, you have gone too far and been merely the colourless impersonal introducer. So would you not reconsider it in this way? The volume wants a preface which, while avoiding doing what you so rightly wish to avoid, should be a good deal longer and a good deal more personally Grigson than this almost anonymous note. As I would now put it, what the volume needs is a Grigsonian statement of the art of poetry in 1939.

It is possible that this sort of cross purpose is one that can only be straightened out in conversation. Therefore, may I suggest your lunching with me on Tuesday of next week, the 22nd, and discussing that point?

Your last point can be answered by letter.[3] After a discussion by committee, the answer is yes. If the photographs can be really good, and

---

1 – Felix Aylmer (1889–1979), stage and screen actor; knighted in 1965.

2 – 'The play that was performed at Cambridge was virtually identical to the published text apart from various small alterations demanded by the censor to make the parallels between Westland and Nazi Germany less obvious . . . Such alterations are sad testimony to the dishonesty underlying the official British policy of appeasement in 1938. Not that anyone in the audience was unaware of the parallels being drawn between the Leader and Hitler: the grotesque caricature of the Führer was all too obvious' (Brian Finney, *Christopher Isherwood: A Critical Biography* [1979], 166).

3 – Grigson wrote on 7 Nov.: 'I may have jibbed, over the preface, at something which would help the book adventitiously. Another irrelevant aid, but one which I would prefer, would be to have 2 pp. of illustrations, i.e. 2pp of halftones of the faces of some of the chief contributors . . . This would help the sale very much, I believe. It would be unexpected and

neither too conventional nor affectedly eccentric (i.e. it might or might not be well to present MacNeice with a beard), we think that it is a good idea and would help to point the distinction between this and other anthologies. The detail however will have to be discussed. I call your attention to the end of the preceding paragraph.

Yours sincerely,<br>T. S. Eliot

## TO *Donald Brace*

CC

18 November 1938                    [Faber & Faber Ltd]

Dear Brace,

I enclose a copy of the letter which I have just written to Harry Brown of the *Harvard Advocate*. The editors of the *Advocate* have been designing a special number for my jubilee, including a number of articles about me, to appear in December; and for this I naturally raised no objection to their reprinting eight undergraduate poems of mine, which appeared in that periodical (of which I was an editor) between 1906 and 1910. But a possibility which Cap Pierce brought to Frank's attention seems now to be in danger of sprouting: a literary agent has persuaded them into thinking of reprinting the whole issue as a pamphlet, and trying to get some publisher here to take it on. It is not clear to me whether they would publish the pamphlet in America themselves, or get some publisher to undertake it; but I wanted to let you know at once that I definitely object to having these poems reprinted except in the *Advocate*. If they choose to reprint the articles about me, that is their affair and I cannot object, but I have no desire to have my old undergraduate verse broadcast. Mr Harry Brown appear[s] to be under the impression that the *Advocate* holds all rights. They can hardly maintain this after receiving my veto: if they should, we must come down on them. I shall be glad and grateful if you will take steps if you hear any rumours of such a pamphlet being published.

Yours ever,<br>[T. S. Eliot]

---

interesting, and not very expensive; and I have some odd photographs. I hope you will think well of this.'

22 November 1938                    *The Criterion*

Dear Mr Fluchère,

Thank you for your letter of the 10th. First, as to the theatrical part, I have sent a copy of this section of your letter to Mr Ashley Dukes as my manager and agent, and I believe he will be writing to you, if he has not already done so.[1]

As for the final decision of publishers of your translation, I confess that I have a preference for publishing the play in Paris, as I think it would be more beneficial in the long run.[2] I have myself no objection to waiting until next autumn, apart from the inevitable thought which must be in everyone's mind of the uncertainty of human affairs at that distance of time. But I think that if Desclée de Brouwer are really interested, they ought to be prepared to state their terms at once, and if these terms are less advantageous than those of Mr Flouquet, we should consider allowing the latter to publish the play. I shall write to Desclée de Brouwer, and ask them to indicate their terms both to you and to me, so that the matter may soon be decided.

Yours very sincerely,
T. S. Eliot

1 – The Abbé Busson – vicar of the '*petit séminaire de Flers de l'Orne*' – had been in contact with Fluchère with a request to put on a production of his translation of MiC in the seminary.
2 – Fluchère deferred to TSE's wishes with respect to a decision on where his translation should appear: whether immediately from P.-L. Flouquet in Brussels, or else from Desclée et Brouwer (Paris) as late as the close of 1939. As for payment, Desclée et Brouwer had told Fluchère that they would pay him '*mes honoraires de traducteur*' – without making him any definite offer. 'But I think I could get at least the same sum as from Flouquet, so that wouldn't be an obstacle.'

29 November 1938                    [Faber & Faber Ltd]

My dear Prince,

I have read with much interest *The Interpreter*, by your friend Vincent Swart.[1] I return the manuscript to you for two reasons. The first is that there is nothing to be done under present conditions with a thing of this length by itself. The second is that I don't think his work is yet ripe. He strikes me as a writer of considerable promise, who ought to be encouraged, but he is at present in a stage of unassimilated influences, and there is no need to do the *Portrait of the Artist as a Young Man* again. There [is] something directly original in this, but it will have to wait until he has found the right original way of saying it, and meanwhile he will have to overcome the allusive style, which is now obsolete. All these literary quotations become irritating, and give the style an effect of spuriousness which it does not deserve. There is, of course, something of early Joyce in the syntax as well, but he seems to me very promising, and I should think that it was probably for the good that he should be working under I. A. Richards. I should be very glad to meet him at some time when he is up in London. At present I am trying to keep my evenings as free as possible, as I find that more than two evenings a week out are very tiring. Is it ever possible for you to lunch on a Saturday? If so, Saturday the 17th December is possible, and I hope you will lunch with me.

Yours sincerely,<br>[T. S. Eliot]

1 – Prince wrote on 19 Nov.: 'I send you the enclosed MS. because I know the author – he is a fellow countryman I met three years ago, and has just come to England to work under Richards at Cambridge. I would have sent you this story (which he calls a prose poem) even without reading it, because I don't doubt that he is a person of genius. I think you will agree with me that in this thing (which has many obvious defects) the genius is sometimes quite demonic.'

Edward Vincent Swart (1911–61?): South African poet and activist. See Francis Nenik, 'Burning Bright, Burning Out: the story of poet and anti-apartheid activist Edward Vincent Swart' (trans. Anna Aitken), *transition* 119 (2016), 155–67.

TO *Enid Faber*                                          TS Valerie Eliot

29 November [1938]                    *The Criterion*

Dear Enid,

I shall be very happy to dine with you on Monday the 12th, on the conditions specified in your letter of the 25th. What a whirl of festivity December brings! On the following Saturday the Stewarts' musical tea.

As for Charlotte Bonham-Carter,[1] she may know more than we do, if she is in St Denis' confidence: but all I know is that he has had the play to read, but so far, perhaps owing to preoccupation with *Twelfth Night*, my management have had no sign from him.[2]

                              Affectionately,
                              TP.


TO *Lawrence Durrell*                                    TS Morris Library

1 December 1938                       *The Criterion*

Dear Durrell,

I was sorry to hear that you had found it advisable to return to Paris immediately, especially as apprehension about the general strike seems to have been unfounded. It did look, however, as if it was going to be very much more serious. I hope that you will be back again in London before very long.

I have read your prefatory letter from God with a great deal of interest, and frequent admiration.[3] I do feel, of course, that God uses the very characteristic idioms of Lawrence Durrell, but I suppose that He may be expected to speak to each of us in our own language. What I am not sure about is that this is going to be the best bit out of the book to exhibit in the *Criterion*. It is of course much too long for the purpose, and I might be able to choose an extract which would meet with your approval. But I

---

1–Lady Charlotte Bonham Carter, née Winkleman (1893–1989), patron of the arts; wife of Sir Edgar Bonham Carter, barrister and administrator in Sudan and Iraq.
2–Saint-Denis was to write on 7 Dec.: 'I am sorry to have had to remain silent for so long about your play, but I have been entirely absorbed by the preparation of Twelfth Night. Ashley Dukes rang me up this morning and I will meet Martin Browne to know his views about casting. I have read the play only once and cannot say that I have understood it all. I suppose I would if I were more familiar with the text. I think the production of the play is difficult but the kind of problems that have to be solved are of the greatest interest. Could I meet with you after I have seen Martin Browne?'
3–Durrell had sent the Introduction to *The Book of the Dead*.

had rather see a good deal more of the book before choosing. One thing that I have in mind in such cases is that a preliminary serialisation of a piece from a book is a kind of advance publicity, and that it is important to choose a piece which will make the right impression for prospective readers. I think myself that it would be better to wait until the book is practically finished.

But also, is there going to be any serious reason why Faber & Faber should not be allowed to have a chance to decide for themselves whether the book could be published in England? This is what I hope, and I trust you will give us a chance. I daresay Pringle will have written to you to the same effect.

Yours very sincerely,
T. S. Eliot


TO *Evelyn M. Harvey*                                                   cc

1 December 1938                   [Faber & Faber Ltd]

Dear Madam,

I have your letter of the 28th November, and am very sorry to hear of the unexpected misfortunes which have fallen upon the head of Dr Fuchs.[1] I hope that he and his family will arrive safely in England, and that he will be able to find a comfortable livelihood in New Zealand.

I took up the matter of his *Song for Simeon* with the B.B.C., and showed them the score. I also consulted two friends of general standing in the musical world, but to my regret I was unable to obtain any hope of production. For some reason or other I find that this score was never

---

1 – Mrs Harvey (Dorking, Surrey) had been asked to write to TSE 'by a friend in Germany – Dr Richard Fuchs, who says he called on you in June last. You were kind enough then to take the musical score of his setting of "A Song for Simeon" and forward it to the B.B.C.

'You may not have heard that he has since been arrested, in company with all other Jewish men in Karlsruhe, and imprisoned at Dachau – but has just been released, as we were able to produce a visa for him & his family for England. They will I hope shortly be coming to stay with us here until they can travel to New Zealand, probably in February.

'Though people of means they will, like all others, be almost penniless when they are at last allowed to leave Germany. My husband & I are anxious to help them in any way we can, which is my only excuse for troubling you – & Richard Fuchs thinks perhaps his compositions *might* bring in something – either through the B.B.C. or a publisher. I fear it is a forlorn hope – but possibly you may be able to be more encouraging.'

returned to Dr Fuchs in Germany, and I shall be glad to hear whether I should return it to him in your care.

With many regrets,
Yours sincerely,
[T. S. Eliot]

TO *Lawrence Durrell*                                    TS Morris Library

5 December 1938                    *The Criterion*

My dear Durrell,

Thank you for your letter.[1] My only excuse for answering briefly a letter which should be answered, if at all, at some length is that I fear you may have misunderstood me about the question of the appropriateness of your introductory letter to *The Book of the Dead* for the *Criterion*. I was not suggesting that I did not like it, that it was not good enough to use a chunk of in the *Criterion*, or that I wanted anything more startling or different. It was simply that it is obviously impossible to publish more than one chunk of the book in the *Criterion* unless it is going to be a book which will occupy you for at least a couple of years. I was, therefore, tempted to ask to see the whole book or the greater part of it when it was ready, so as to decide for myself what piece would be most effective for prepublication, and I look forward to the book with much excitement.

1–Durrell wrote: 'Many thanks for your letter; I don't know quite how to answer it. I only sent in the portion from the new book because I felt that Kahane had forced me to let you down over the Black Book excerpt and I wanted to atone by letting you have a piece of the new child, equal if not better in temper and style. I don't see quite what it has to do with Faber ultimately publishing the book. If, however, the extract does not seem startling enough please send it back – as I have no copy of it, and need the whole book with me before proceeding with it . . . You seem a trifle hard to please, but no doubt you have excellent reasons to curb my impatience . . .

'I was looking forward to meeting you again, because I feel that a talk with you now and again is a great help to me, living as I do miles from the english and their horrid ways; and having so few contacts in england which I value . . .

'The new book so far is printable; only superstition prevents me letting it be read until it is done. I can't say what the puppets will do in advance since they have their destiny as I have mine. And I learn in life from their actions in fiction. I hope sincerely that Faber will be able to do the book. The style will not be inferior in any way to that of the Black Book; and the poise should be twice as divine. More than that I can't honestly say because I don't honestly know.

'If this letter sounds a trifle despondent it is because today Miller has just received a cutting from American Time in which we are linked together and flayed for being mere smut-hounds!'

If possible let me have a word in advance to say when you are coming again to London and where I can get hold of you.

Yours ever,

T. S. Eliot

TO *George Every*                                     TS Sarah Hamilton

5 December 1938                        *The Criterion*

Dear George,

Thank you very much for your letter of the 30th.[1] I see your point about Coleridge and I have reread the essay with that in mind. Your point is a very useful corrective and it was absence of mind on my part not to mention myself the chapter on regrets and apprehensions which is indeed very relevant. I possess Dawson's *Making of Europe* and will go through it again. I don't think that I ever read it thoroughly. Possibly I can get hold of Maurice's Life from the London Library. I have asked Charles Smyth to let me see his lectures of last year, and I shall also pounce upon your own manuscript, when it comes, without shame, as I believe that my subject is sufficiently different for me not to be in any danger of lawless pilfering.

I am glad to have your news and hope to see you at the end of the year.[2] The 31st is an impossible date. I have a tradition which I cannot break of spending the last day of the year with certain friends in the country. But any time, except that very weekend, will be convenient. Let me know as soon as you can.

Yours affectionately,

T. S.

1 – 'I will find someone who has a copy of Maurice's life [*The Life of Frederick Denison Maurice: Chiefly Told in His Own Letters* (1884)] that they can lend you. It is very well indexed, and the letters might illuminate the illuminating passage in The Kingdom of Christ [by Maurice, 1838]. There is a lot under Church, State, Monarchy, Democracy, Socialism, which is quite invaluable. Coleridge and the English Tradition you shall have as soon as possible. If you take the Church and State by and large without the digressions, I do not think it is irrelevant but very relevant, in that Coleridge recognized the natural, sociological, non-Christian necessity for a *nation* to have a religion, "true or false". If you have no "establishment" you will invent one or disintegrate politically. The regrets and apprehensions chapter seems to me very relevant indeed.

'What about a look at [Christopher] Dawson's *Making of Europe* [1932] for the old dark ages seen with a very contemporary reference.'

2 – 'I will try and spend the night when the year turns in town. Could we finish this year with a dinner together again? – i.e. on the 31st.'

5 December 1938                    [Faber & Faber Ltd]

My dear Mr Dark,

I have your letter of November 30th, enclosing a copy of a draft letter which you wish me to sign.[1]

I must say, at once, that I am naturally sympathetic with any protest against maltreatment of Jews, whether abroad or in this country. In other words, I take what seems to me the only possible Christian position. It is, therefore, all the more difficult for me to make clear why I do not feel that a letter like this is going to be profitable at the present time.

It seems to me that there are two distinct movements or possibility of movements of an Anti-Semitic character in this country. One is the increasing irritability and consciousness of the Jews amongst the ordinary middle and lower middle class population in England. The second, which must be kept quite distinct, is the exploitation of this discontent by a political group hopeful of gaining power by exciting racial passions. If

---

1–Dark (*Church Times*) wrote in his letter: 'I am profoundly disturbed by the evident growth of anti-Semitism in this country, and I hope that you will agree with me that there should be without delay a clearly expressed repudiation by Christian men and women of any sympathy with a movement that feeds on prejudice and inevitably leads to cruelty.

'I am, therefore, asking representatives of the bishops, priests and laity of the Church of England to sign the accompanying letter to the chairman of the Jewish Board of Deputies. I am only approaching my fellow churchmen, Catholics and Evangelicals, knowing, of course, that the protest will be approved by the vast majority of our fellow Christians.

'I feel that it is not enough that we should express horror of the German persecutions. It is our business to endeavour to stay at the beginning the encouragement of insensate and wicked racialism in our own country.

'If you feel able to sign this letter, I should be grateful . . .'

The letter enclosed was addressed to Neville Laski, Chairman of the Jewish Board of Deputies: 'Sir, / Reference has recently been made by the Home Secretary and by certain speakers in the House of Commons, to a possible anti-Semitic movement in this country as a result of the present world turmoil. We are convinced that this is made improbable by the sense of justice, the sense of humour, and the abundant kindliness of the English people.

'None the less, it seems to us necessary that there should be a public expression of the feeling of the vast majority of Christian English people, that in whatever form and however modified it may be, anti-Semitism remains wicked folly, utterly opposed to the spirit and the letter of the teaching of Our Lord.

'We are addressing this letter to you as members of the Church of England, priests and laymen of differing ecclesiastical views and varying political attachments. We know that we are speaking the mind of our brethren, and indeed, of the greater Christian public.

'We would assure our Jewish fellow countrymen that we have the fullest appreciation of the contribution that they have made and are making in various ways to the national life. We would assure them that we utterly repudiate racial discrimination . . .

'"Let us join hands and help one another, for today we are together".'

the second is in mind, that can be more effectively dealt with by specific reference. It is a matter for judgement whether the Anti-Semitic Fascist political movement in this country has reached a point at which it is desirable that all Christians, whose names carry any public weight, should publicly insist on the impossibility of Christians taking part or countenancing such a movement.

But if what your letter has in view is something more dispersed and as yet unorganised, then I do not feel that it is profitable to protest against it in this way. This letter will not be read by bus conductors or small tobacconists or clerks or any of the unemployed or discontented members of the lower middle class. The proper way to deal with and dispel such public feeling seems to me to be to examine and lay bare the sources of this feeling which are economic and not doctrinaire, and to draw the attention of authority to the necessity for dealing with the causes. The best, and indeed the only, consideration of the problem which I have seen in print is that in last Thursday's issue of the *New English Weekly*, which I very much hope I may persuade you to read.[1]

Yours sincerely,

[T. S. Eliot]

1 – 'Notes of the Week', *NEW* 14: 8 (1 Dec. 1938), 113–15. 'Sir Samuel Hoare's dark hint that an "evil movement" might begin in the United Kingdom if too many refugees were admitted from Central Europe, was weighted by his authority as Home Secretary and rendered more impressive by his evident sympathy with the tragic sufferings of the Jews today . . . But of the deeper and determining cause of this wave of so-called "anti-Semitism" now spreading over the world, there has been vouchsafed no glimmer of enlightenment in Parliament any more than in the local Press . . .

'In England and America, the first reaction to the persecution is naturally humanitarian, and one would suppose from the tone of the Press and the public platform, that some moral or rational superiority could be depended upon in those countries to preclude any such treatment of minorities as Germany now exhibits. Anyone who reflects, however, upon the situation we have described must see that a nation can no more escape a dangerous change of feeling towards Jewry by reliance upon humane sentiments, or on a sense of justice transcending racial difference, than we can abolish war by mere propaganda for universal peace. So long as the course of action we pursue, as a nation, is leading us inevitably into situations where the interests men regard as vital are brought into opposition, we do little to safeguard ourselves by proclaiming our hatred of violence in advance . . . Unless the supreme economic evil of our days, which is not the position of the Jews, but the preying of secondary upon primary industry throughout Britain and the Empire, is published broadcast [*sic*] where it is now whispered in secret; these false emotional issues will take precedence, obscuring both physical and spiritual reality . . .

'The letter from Major C. H. Douglas which we print this week upon another page, expresses an attitude towards the present tribulations of Jewry which he has recently disclosed elsewhere, to the consternation of certain of his followers. But in appending his remarks upon the Jews to a warm appreciation of Dr K. E. Barlow's article in our issue of November 17th, on Economic Justice, we hope Major Douglas intended to set things in

TO *Eleanor Follansbee*                                    CC

5 December 1938                    [Faber & Faber Ltd]

Dear Mrs Follansbee,

Thank you for your interesting letter of the 11th November concerning the rights for a ballet to be based on my poem *The Waste Land*.[1] May I be permitted in passing to call your attention to the fact that the title is not 'Wasteland' but 'The Waste Land'.

---

the right order of their importance. For Dr Barlow is one of that body of our contributors . . . who are now compelling attention to the deepest aspect of our modern economy – its incapability not only to distribute wealth, but even to continue producing it without progressive destruction of its ultimate sources . . . The financial delusion we had exposed was revealed as but one portion of a tissue of falsity which had captured the mind of the West, removing it far from the ground of reason, and into the weaving of that web of delusion, incidentally, there has entered far more negation than affirmation of the traditional wisdom of either Christianity or Jewry. The assault upon the financial system, interwoven with the whole as it is, is now indicated as not less necessary but as much more urgent. This is a tragic day of reckoning for a great civilization, in which the Jews are involved as they were in Egypt, Nineveh, Babylon and Rome. The thinker, however, must take care never to write as though the Fate of Jewry could be our Providence; for that is only a retreat to a popular and superficial view.'

See further C. H. Douglas, 'Economic Justice and Jewry', *NEW*, 1 Dec. 1938, 126; K. E. Barlow, 'Economic Justice' (letter), *NEW*, 8 Dec. 1938, 142–3.

Evidently TSE wrote an approving personal letter – not traced – on the subject of 'last Thursday's issue of the *New English Weekly*', to which Philip Mairet responded on 1 Dec.:

'Thanks for your letter. I felt it was time to show that we had a view of the Jewish question, and that we were not afraid to state it.

'After *such* a defence of them, there ought to be silence in Jewry for the space of half an hour! And the anti-Semites ought to think again.'

Sidney Dark replied to this letter by TSE, 9 Dec.: 'I am grateful for your kind letter, and I entirely understand your point of view. You will doubtless remember that in his remarkable article on anti-Semitism in the Encyclopedia Britannica the late Lucien Wolff declared that all anti-Semitic movements were political and economic rather than religious and racial. While, therefore, I value the criticisms you make, I feel that the protest I have in mind is worth while, particularly as I have been able to secure a sufficient representative support.'

1 – Eleanor Follansbee (Chicago, Illinois) – author of *Heavenly History: An Account of Heavenly Architecture* (1927) – wrote: 'I am writing to ask for an option on the rights for a ballet based on your poem, Wasteland.

'The ancient initiation ritual and related subjects have been the object of long study on my part, and I have always admired your use of the material in your poem. The ballet seemed to me a form in which one could solve the problem of presenting simultaneously the text and the notes. Taking a suggestion from J. L. Weston, I have expanded the story of Rishyacinga into a Fisher-king sequence laid in India. This appears as a vision to Albert consulting Madame Sosostris. I have tried to preserve the original spirit and characters of Wasteland while fitting them into the frame of the dance.

'With your permission, I shall present the ballet to M. Leonide Massine of the Ballet Russe of Monto Carlo and send the synopsis in its final form for your approval.

'I have had the pleasure of conversations with Mr Henry Eliot who is an old friend of my family's.'

I am uncertain what the position is with regard to ballet rights and in any case must refer the matter to my agents, Harcourt Brace and Company of New York, whom I will ask to write direct to you.

I do not think that we can permit any of the words to be used, and, candidly, it seems to me that it would be better for you to give the ballet a different title, merely stating that it is suggested by 'The Waste Land'. The fresh use of Indian Folk Lore and the collocation of Albert with Madame Sosostris suggest that what you have in mind is a pretty free departure from the text and intentions of the poem.

Yours very sincerely,<br>[T. S. Eliot]

## TO *Donald Brace* CC

5 December 1938          [Faber & Faber Ltd]

Dear Brace,

I enclose herewith a letter from a woman whom I don't know and don't want to know. I don't like the idea of her making a ballet about *The Waste Land* which definitely will be, in any case, merely a travesty of the intentions of the poem. Can we prevent her from using the title? She says nothing about wanting to use any of the lines of the poem: I rather wish she did want to use some because that would be easy to prevent. There is nothing in this for either author or publishers. It isn't going to [do] the poem any good so I should be very grateful if you can think of anything to say to her yourself which will stop her.

I shall be writing to you again either this week or next with corrected galleys of *The Family Reunion*. Our provisional arrangements are for publication in the middle of February, but I am waiting from day to day in the hope of hearing something definite about the production.

Yours ever,<br>[T. S. Eliot]

6 December 1938                    [*The Criterion*]

Dear Mr Montgomery,

I have read and thought over your letter of the 4th and the enclosure which I return herewith.[2] I am not surprised that your review of the architecture book was censored, especially in view of the position of the authors. But I think that the same fate might have attended it in some periodical in London. The R.I.B.A. stinks and it has power.

The question of free lance journalism is, I take it, secondary to that of getting work as an architect. If your idea is simply to earn what money you can by odds and ends of writing and reviewing while waiting and pursuing your attempt to get settled in your profession, that is a reasonable one. If, however, you are thinking of taking up literary journalism as a livelihood, I can only say that I don't see anything in it. The best thing I could do for you, however, if you hold to the latter intention, is I think to give you a letter of introduction to Desmond MacCarthy, who is extremely amiable, knows all there is to know about literary journalism and is better equipped than anybody for advising you and getting you introductions. But the life of anybody whose interest is in literature and not merely in book making is hard, unless he has an independent income, and reviewing for a living can be heartbreaking.

I will, of course, keep you in mind for reviews and for translations. But there is, I am afraid, very little translation from the French to be done, and what anybody can get from the *Criterion* for reviewing in the course of the year can only amount to a little pin money.

But come and see me again if you would rather talk than write.

Yours sincerely,

[T. S. Eliot]

1–Niall Montgomery (1915–87): Irish architect, poet, playwright, artist and critic, graduated in architecture from University College Dublin, 1938, and pursued a successful career in private practice in Dublin. For thirty years from 1951 he served on the Council of the Royal Institute of the Architects of Ireland; President, 1976–7. Close friend of writers including Samuel Beckett and Flann O'Brien. See further Christine O'Neill, *Niall Montgomery – Dublinman* (2015).

2–Montgomery's letter opened: 'Since I called on you a week or so ago I have been very unlucky and unsuccessful in my search for work: I hope you will not be disgusted if I venture to ask you if you would, perhaps, have some work for which I might be suited.' See below for the bulk of Montgomery's letter, quoted *in extenso* in TSE's letter to Desmond McCarthy, 13 Dec.

TO *Horace Kallen*[1]       TS Yivo Institute for Jewish Research

6 December 1938       *The Criterion*

Dear Horace,

My young friend Louis MacNeice, whose name you will know as that of one of the most interesting of the younger English poets already established, is lecturer in Greek at Bedford College in London. He is intending to spend his Easter holidays by visiting New York, and would like to get a small number of engagements to speak or read simply in order to help defray his expenses. I have put him in touch with people at Harvard, Wellesley, Columbia and Bowdoin, and I think that the first two of these have already arranged with him, but he means to be longer in New York than anywhere else and is open to one or two more engagements there. Do you think that the New School would be interested in having him speak?

He will be able to leave his college work on 18 March, and has to be back in London on April 25. As he has such a narrow margin, he may not be able to fix absolutely formal dates until the list of sailings for that season is settled.

I have heard nothing of you for a long time, but I hope that you and your family are flourishing.

Yours ever,
T. S. Eliot

---

1–Horace Meyer Kallen (1882–1974): German-born philosopher, taught at Harvard, Princeton and Wisconsin before co-founding in 1918 the New School for Social Research, New York. Educated at Harvard (where William James was his mentor), he was an ardent cultural pluralist. His works include *William James and Henri Bergson: A Study in Contrasting Theories of Life* (1914), *Judaism at Bay: Essays Toward the Adjustment of Judaism to Modernity* (1933), *Art and Freedom* (1942), *The Liberal Spirit* (1948). Fellow of the Jewish Academy of Arts and Sciences, and Fellow of the International Institute of Arts and Letters, he was a leader of the American Jewish Congress, a member of the executive board of the World Jewish Congress, Chair of the YIVO Institute for Jewish Research.

See further *The Legacy of Horace Kallen*, ed. Milton R. Konvitz (1987); Sarah L. Schmidt, *Horace M. Kallen: Prophet of American Zionism* (1995); Ranen Omer, '"It Is I Who Have Been Defending a Religion Called Judaism": The T. S. Eliot and Horace M. Kallen Correspondence', *Texas Studies in Literature and Language* 39: 4 (Winter 1997), 321–56.

8 December 1938                          [Faber & Faber Ltd]

Dear MacNeice,

I enclose two further letters I have received, one from Mark Van Doren at Columbia University, and the other from the President of Bowdoin College.[1] I have acknowledged them, but I leave it to you to write and discuss terms. I should be inclined to accept Columbia, even for 75 dollars, because you will be in New York anyway. The question of whether it is worthwhile to go up to Maine for a small fee depends on how it fits in with the rest of your programme, but as I said, it would be a pleasant excursion.

I have also written to the New School of Social Research, which I had forgotten, but I have not yet had time for a reply.

I also enclose a letter from Bryn Mawr, saying that they have no further funds for lecturers this year; and a letter from Bennington College, Vermont, affirming that they can only pay 25 dollars plus expenses. You might keep the latter in reserve, and write to Professor Wallace Fowlie (who is I believe also a poet) if the invitation should later seem acceptable.

We shall expect your poem, then, at the end of the year.[2] As for the *Hippolytus*, I am somewhat worried for fear there will not be time to publish it before Doone's production.[3] We can only leave the matter open, however, and I will discuss it with Doone when I next see him.

I am sorry I could not get to your party, and I hear from Doone that it was very successful.

Yours ever,
[T. S. Eliot]

1 – Not traced.

2 – TSE slightly misread MacNeice's letter of 5 Dec.: 'I am afraid I cannot promise the long poem before the end of the year. There are 1700 lines written but I have several more sections to write. Also I am going abroad for Christmas and I feel that I might be moved, as they say, to write the final section then.'

3 – MacNeice wrote on 5 Dec.: 'As to the Hippolytus: it is to be ready for the Group Theatre according to schedule by the end of February. I shall translate it roughly on the same principles as the Agamemnon but the choruses will be treated more formally and less literally (this is because Euripides' choruses seem to me less integral to the play). I cannot think of anything to say about it in the blurb unless you say that the Hippolytus is a very actable play & that this is intended to be the most actable version in English' (MacNeice, *Letters*, 313).

MacNeice's version of *Hippolytus* was never completed: an extract is featured in G. Nelson, *Oxford Poetry* 11 (2000), 50–68.

TS Beinecke

9 December 1938                    Faber & Faber Ltd

I have known Mr William Force Stead for over fifteen years and count him as a valued friend. He is, first, a poet of established position and an individual inspiration. What is not so well known, except to a small number of the more fastidious readers, is that he is also a prose writer of great distinction: his book *Mount Carmel* is recognised as a classic of prose style in its kind. And while the bulk of his published writing on English literature is small, those who know his conversation can testify that he is a man of wide reading and a fine critical sense.

Mr Stead is, moreover, a man of the world in the best sense, who has lived in several countries and is saturated in European culture. By both natural social gifts and cultivation, he has a remarkable ability of sympathy with all sorts and conditions of men.

I would say finally that I know from several sources, that Mr Stead was most successful as a teacher of young men at Oxford; that he gained both the affection and the respect of his students; and that he exercised upon them a most beneficial influence. He has the scholarship necessary to teach English literature accurately, and the personal qualities necessary to make the subject interesting to his pupils; and I could not recommend anyone for the purpose with more confidence.

T. S. Eliot


TO *John Hayward*                                        TS King's

9 December [1938]                    *The Criterion*

Dear John,

This is just a line of farewell, as the Camerons are motoring me down to Butting Hill to the Jerrihoppers tomorrow afternoon, so if we do not meet again this is a line of farewell and please see that the *Family Reunion* is published and that my uncollected papers are not collected. Why on earth am I going away again for a weekend, and just at the time of year when I am worried to death with the problems of Christmas cards and what not. All I want is to curl up and rest, and why don't I? And going visiting only means that you meet other people or people that you have not seen for years, such as Ethel Sands[1] and the Sassoons and you get involved. Shall we ever meet again? I doubt it, but if this is the last anybody hears of me don't print it. We might meet at Jenyns[2] on Friday and I shall be here at the weekend, so will close

TP.

TO *Enid Faber*                                                    TS Valerie Eliot
9 December 1938                    *The Criterion*

Dear Enid,
   A line of condolence only: I can't think of any news to convey, except that the Marx Brothers are deteriorating.[3] Your disaster has been the cause of general grief, especially keen as it has occurred at this time of year. You will, I hope, be able to have Christmas at home, though supinely; but I grieve to think that you will not be attending the pantomime. Lady Rhonnda Rhondda Rrohnda[4] on Monday is a mere bagatelle. But why do these misfortunes always occur while one is occupied in good works? I speak from minor but significant experience: it was while attending a Student Christian Movement hallelujah Camp in Derbyshire in 1936 that I contracted neuritis, and it was in jumping out of bed at the Isis Private Hotel, Iffley Road, where I was stopping to attend as a delegate (at the personal request, I may add, of the Abp. of Canterbury) of the International Convention on Church, Community and State, that I strained a toe; and I still suffer and always shall from these as well as other minor ailments, which I am not comparing to yours, but only mentioning to reinforce my question: why do these disasters always happen while one is engaged in good works? I hear from Dick that he is now Junior Prompter in the Latin Play, so he seems to have been getting on very rapidly.[5] I can't think of any other good news: the best will be reports of your progress.

Yr. compassionate
TP

1–Ethel Sands (1873–1962): wealthy American-born artist, patron and collector: at her London home, 15 Vale, Chelsea, she courted many of the artists and writers of the age.
2–Soame Jenyns (1904–76), art historian; expert on Chinese art, ceramics and jades; Assistant Keeper of Oriental Antiquities, British Museum, 1931–67. Author of *A Background to Chinese Painting* (1935) and other monographs.
3–TSE was referring to the Marx Brothers' movie *Room Service*, released in Sept. 1938.
4–Margaret Haig Thomas, Viscountess Rhondda (1883–1958), writer and feminist, was owner and editor from 1926 of *Time and Tide*.
5–Richard Faber was at Westminster School.

## TO *Stephen Spender*

TS Northwestern

12 December 1938          Faber & Faber Ltd

Dear Stephen,

If you have not already decided on a title for the volume of poems, I hope that you will now put your mind to it and let me have one. The book appears so far in the proof of the Catalogue simply as *New Poems*, but we don't think that is at all satisfactory on the book itself. The book will go on selling until it is incorporated in some collected edition, and the title *New Poems* obviously will get out of date rapidly, and would make the choice of title for the next volume after it very difficult. So I hope you can let me have a new title.[1]

Yours ever,
Tom

## TO *Marguerite Caetani*[2]

CC

13 December 1938          [Faber & Faber Ltd]

Dear Marguerite,

Thank you for your letter of December 9.[3] I did receive a draft from your bankers in New York, and assumed that you were still there.

---

1 – Published as *The Still Centre* (1939).
2 – Marguerite Caetani, née Chapin (1880–1963) – born in the USA, she was half-sister to Mrs Katherine Biddle, and cousin of TSE – was married in 1911 to the composer Roffredo Caetani, 17th Duke of Sermoneta and Prince di Bassiano (a godson of Lizst), whose ancestors included two Popes (one of whom had the distinction of being put in Hell by Dante). A patron of the arts, she founded in Paris the review *Commerce* – the title being taken from a line in St-John Perse's *Anabase* ('*ce pur commerce de mon âme*') – which ran from 1924 to 1932 (see Sophie Levie, *La rivista Commerce e il ruolo di Marguerite Caetani nella letteratura europea 1924–1932* [Rome, 1985]); and then, in Rome, *Botteghe oscure*, 1949–60, a biannual review featuring poetry and fiction from many nations – Britain, Germany, Italy, France, Spain, USA – with contributions published in their original languages. Contributors included André Malraux, Albert Camus, Paul Valéry, Ignazio Silone, Robert Graves, E. E. Cummings, Marianne Moore.
3 – TSE had at some point lent Caetani some money, which she had recently repaid. 'Many, many thanks. It was really cousinly of you!' She wrote too that she had enjoyed the US edition of *Anabasis*, and had indeed given away 'many copies to friends and am at present without one'. She was shocked to note, however, that Léger's name had been omitted from the jacket. 'Really! How could you consent to such a thing. Maybe you didn't see the proofs!' She added that she had noticed in America 'the extraordinary influence that *Anabase* has had on American poetry'.

I am very sorry about the point you mention in connexion with the American edition of *Anabase*. I received some copies from the publishers, and am sending one as you request, but I had overlooked the omission of the name of Perse on the cover or jacket. It is of course on the title page, but that is not enough. I had not even seen proofs of the book, but sent Harcourt, Brace & Co. a revised copy of the original edition, so that I had no knowledge of what the appearance of the book would be. I will mention the matter to Harcourt, Brace in the hope that they will alter the jacket wrapper. They are excellent publishers, and this is not evidence of any particular unscrupulousness on their part. The fact is that I am a good deal better known in New York than Léger is, and they naturally want to sell the book; so that an action of this kind is evidence only of the moral turpitude of all publishers, and not of that firm in particular.

With best wishes for Christmas,
Yours affectionately,
[Tom]

P.S. Perhaps you had better remove the jacket before presenting the copy to Léger. But I had assumed that Harcourt, Brace & Co. would have sent him six author's copies. If this was not done, it must have been an oversight.


## TO *Mabel Hopkins*                                      TS Princeton

13 December 1938                    *The Criterion*

Dear Mrs Hopkins (or perhaps Mabel)

If you have already consulted the Ouija-board to find out whether your guests enjoyed their weekend, this letter is superfluous; but in any case I hope that you will, at some time next year, ask it when I am coming again and let me know. I do not think, however, that I could enjoy a weekend in the summer any more than one like this in the winter – and at this time the country is most beautiful, and the weather likely to be better than one expects – whereas summer visits in this country are likely to mean baffled attempts at nudism, and head colds. And the incidence of American relatives, friends, and friends of relatives and friends with introductions makes the summer very uncertain. I hope at least that I may come again at the end of the next American season, and meanwhile look forward to seeing you both at the pantomime. And I hear that there is some possibility of Enid being able to come.

Yours very sincerely,
T. S. Eliot

TO *John Hayward*                                              TS King's

13 December [1938]                    *The Criterion*

Dear John,

No sooner had I got over the visit to the Jerrihoppers with the Kameroons, than I had to go last night to help Geoffrey entertain Lady Rhonnda Ronndha Rhondda and Sarah Gertrude Millin.[1] Tonight to a serious dining club at Lord Wolmer's.[2] But I hope (1) to see you on Friday, and trust you will ring up before the party. On Sunday I have to sup with the Woolves. but (2) to have a quiet Christmastide; the only night not free is Boxing night, when George Every will be dining with me. Am free for the whole of Christmas Day, and all other times.

I fear that there is to be another explosion of poetry. I have received a neatly typed copy of some couplets addressed by the Whale to the Tarantula,[3] but I don't propose to intervene (in either *persona*) at the moment, as I have my Christmas cards to address and post, and the usual agony of shopping for the children. Which reminds me, have you any fresh suggestions for this season, with respect to a gift to Miss SWAN?[4]

Hastily

TP.

---

1 – GCF's diary, Mon., 12 Dec. 1938: 'Relic of dinner-party – viz. T.S.E., Lady Rhondda, and Mrs Millin. All going well, except that at the end Mrs M got off with Tom about modern poetry (esp. [Frank] Prince, whom she knows), & Lady R confesses that nothing interests her except politics. Still, I think the evening was a success.' Sarah Millin (1889–1968), South African author.

2 – Roundell Cecil Palmer (1887–1971), Viscount Wolmer, 1895–41; Conservative politician (MP for Aldershot, 1918–40); Minister for Economic Warfare (running the Special Operations Executive), 1942–5. In 1940, on the death of his father, he became 3rd Earl of Selborne.

3 – TSE enclosed a copy of FVM's poem 'The Mark of the Spider is 666' (*Noctes Binanianae*).

4 – Ethel Swan, a Faber & Gwyer 'pioneer', joined the firm on 12 Oct. 1925, as telephonist and receptionist, retiring only in 1972 after forty-seven years. Peter du Sautoy reported in 1971: 'These duties she still performs with admirable skill and charm . . . She has an amazing memory for voices and it is certain that if James Joyce were to return to earth to telephone a complaint (he called us "Feebler and Fumbler") she would say "Good morning, Mr Joyce" before he could introduce himself, as if he had previously been telephoning only yesterday. Many a visiting author or publisher from overseas has felt more kindly towards Faber & Faber as a result of Miss Swan's friendly recognition' ('Farewell, Russell Square', *The Bookseller* no. 3410 [1 May 1971], 2040).

A profile of 'Swannie' in retirement noted that she had built up an 'extraordinary range of warm and wide personal friendships which later made her a unique character in the publishing trade': 'Miss Swan had a great affection and respect for Walter de la Mare, but her favourite was T. S. Eliot, whom she admired both as poet and playwright and also as a Faber colleague . . . He was a devoted sender of postcards to "Swannie"' ('At the Faber Switchboard', *The Bookseller*, 2 June 1971, 2662).

TO *Virginia Woolf*                                        TS Sussex

13 December 1938                 *The Criterion*

Dear Virginia,

Sunday evening will suit me capitally, except that 7.30 is impossible: if you could say 8 instead, that would be perfection. When in town on Sunday I have to check the week's cash receipts after church in the evening, which means that I never get away before 7.30. Alternatively, start your supper at 7.30 and keep a little cold pie for me; otherwise, I will come after dinner: but come I shall. And unless I hear from you I shall come at 8.[1]

Foreigners shouldn't try to produce Shakespeare in England.

Aff.

TP


TO *Desmond MacCarthy*                                          CC

13 December 1938                 [Faber & Faber Ltd]

Dear Desmond,

There is a very nice young Irishman of my acquaintance named Niall Montgomery, who has been educated as an architect, and has been over here for a little time, trying to get a job in some architect's office. I am afraid I cannot help him very much in that direction, but he is also of course a poet and a man of letters, and would like to get reviewing or any literary work that would help him out. I advised him against attempting to become a professional man of letters, but I find that is not his intention; he wants to go on in the hope of making architecture his livelihood, but

---

1 – VW, *Diary* V, 192–3: 'The last dinner of the year was to Tom Eliot last night. Physically he is a little mutton faced; sallow & shadowed; but intent (as I am) on the art of writing. His play – Family Reunion? – was the staple of the very bitter cold evening . . . It has taken him off & on 2 years to write, is an advance upon Murder; in poetry; a new line, with 3 stresses; "I dont seem popular this evening"; "What for do we talk of cancer again" (no: this is not accurate). When the crisis came, his only thought was annoyance that now his play would not be acted. And he hurried up the revision . . .

'Tom said the young don't take art or politics seriously enough. Disappointed in the Auden–Ish[erwoo]d. He has his grandeur. He said that there are flaws in the new play that are congenital. Inalterable. I suspect in the department of humour. He defined the different kinds of influence: a subtle, splitting mind: a man of simple integrity, & the artists ingenuous egotism. Dines out & goes to musical teas; reads poems at Londonderry house; has a humorous sardonic gift which mitigates his egotism; & is on the side of authority. A nice old friends evening.'

in the meantime is in need of anything he can pick up in the way of journalism.

What I can do for anyone financially on the *Criterion* is very little, and it struck me that if you would be willing to see him and advise him, it would help him, and you would probably make up your own mind as to whether you could recommend him to any editors. At the worst, you would be in a better position to tell him to abandon the idea than I should.

If you are in London and would be so kind as to see him, I will tell him to write to you and ask for an appointment. Meanwhile, I think I cannot do better than enclose the relevant portion of a letter he wrote to me about himself.

'At first, in Dublin, I worked with a friend of mine on a book of interviews with young writers and artists: though this was – mercifully – never published as a book, some of the interviews appeared in the *New York Sun*.

Later, with Denis Devlin, I translated a very large amount of French poetry into modern Irish, poems by Nerval, Baudelaire, Verlaine, Rimbaud, Valéry, Apollinaire, Laforgue, Cocteau, Eluard, Reverdy, Supervielle and even Tzara: this large anthology the Government refused to publish saying: "We do not want high-brow poetry; we are catering for the people." I also translated Yeats' *Hour-Glass* – the verse version, but they would not have it, giving as excuse that even in English its meaning was obscure. Some of our work appeared in the *Irish Press* and *Ireland To-day*.

I have always been very interested in films: my father is the official film censor. I worked with Denis Johnston when he filmed Frank O'Connor's story *Guests of the Nation* and I reviewed Arnheim's *Film* for the Dublin Magazine in 1932 or 3.

My own verse – which is very inferior and written in pidgin English – has been published in *Transition, Contemporary Poetry and Prose, Ireland To-Day, The National Student* and Keridrych Rhys is publishing some in a forthcoming number of *Wales*.

I am very interested in painting and I have read much, listened much and danced much to "jazz" music.

My own profession is very absorbing: I am a qualified architect, our Dublin degree giving exemption from the final examination of the RIBA and I venture to enclose – hoping you might some time glance through them – two versions of a review I did recently for *The Irish Times*. The book was a very bad one and had in addition been written by two extern [*sic*] professors of our University. But I had not expected to be censored so.

If it would be possible to let me have some books to review, or if, perhaps, there were some translation work available, I should be very pleased. I hope you will not think it very forward of me to write you this begging letter and I shall not be in the least hurt if you tell me how unsuitable I am: I can always turn round in my mind and contemplate myself as a qualified if unemployed architect.'

Yours ever sincerely,
[T. S. Eliot]

## TO *Polly Tandy*                                              TS BL

13 December [1938]                    *The Criterion*

Dear Polly,

Now Then, this is urgent. I should like to know at once, and as early as yesterday if possible, whether you have any knowledge of notions of what those Children would like for Christmas Presents. As you have on one or two previous occasions been helpful in this way, I hope you will be able to help me again, and so will close

Yr. respectful
Tp

I shall hope to see you soon after Christmas; and as I shall hope to see the Aged for a glass of sherry shortly before the festival, I hope that something can be arranged.

## TO *Ronald Bottrall*                                          TS Texas

16 December 1938                      *The Criterion*

My dear Bottrall,

Thank you for your letter of the 10th.[1] I was very glad to hear of your appointment at the School of Oriental Studies, and write primarily to congratulate you. I look forward to seeing more of you and your wife when you are settled in London.

1–'You have probably seen from the Times that I have been appointed Secretary of the School of Oriental and African Studies of London University. The School is an Institution to which I shall be proud to belong.'

I have not heard from your friend Professor Rebora.[1] Whether I could attend or not would depend partly on the date.

May I ask at the same time whether the post which you have vacated in Florence is yet filled? I have a young friend, E. W. F. Tomlin, who I think might suit extremely well, whom I should like to recommend if there is any chance of doing so.

With best wishes for Christmas to you both,

Yours ever,
T. S. Eliot

## TO *Enid Faber*                                              TS Valerie Eliot

Sunday the 19th [December 1938]   *The Criterion*

Dear Enid,

Thank you for your note. It was gratifying to see that you had so far recovered mobility as to be able to write and even to address the envelope in ink. I ought to have written before to convey the verbal condolences of the Jerrihoppers and of the Kameroons who were also there.

The final revision is not complete! That is to say, there is a small patch near the end where about 20 new lines are needed. So at present I can't give you anything that you have not seen, as Geoffrey has the only spare copy of the proof, except the one which is to go to Harcourt. But as soon as I can finish . . . delayed of course by Christmas. I hope I may see you at home on Friday, though you may not want to be visible unless you were coming too – which I should hardly expect. Yet they say that young bones heal quickly.

Affectionately,
TP.

1 – 'My friend Piero Rebora, formerly Professor at Manchester and now Professor at the Institute, has, I believe, written to you to invite you to represent England in a lecture series at the Institute of Renaissance Studies here [Florence]. Paul Valéry, Keyserling and others are coming. I hope you will be able to accept. It will be a great thing for England and English poetry if you can. I am sorry that I shall not be here to welcome you.'

TO *Sister Mary Beatrice*[1]                                    CC

20 December 1938                    [Faber & Faber Ltd]

Dear Sister Mary Beatrice,

I have been somewhat backward in replying to your letter of enquiry
of November 17. The reference by Mr Gielgud to a possible play of mine
for the radio has no specific bearing on *The Family Reunion*, but on a
possible play which I was to write. I had some correspondence with Mr
Gielgud a year or two ago, and was entertaining a proposal that if I wrote
a suitable play the B.B.C. might do a preliminary broadcast version. As
it has turned out, I do not feel that *The Family Reunion* is suitable for
treatment in this form before it is published. The play is now in proof,
and will be ready to be published by the middle of February, but I have
not fixed any date for publication, because I should like if possible to have
publication coincide with theatrical production, and no production has
yet been settled.

As for the term Poetic Drama, it is quite true that I, and I think my
younger contemporaries, prefer to say Verse Drama, although I should
like to retain the older and more respectable term of Dramatic Poetry, not
so much in reference to the plays themselves, but to draw the distinction,
which is frequently overlooked, between dramatic poetry and other
poetry. It is not merely that a play is written in poetry; it must be written
in poetry of a particular kind, which we call dramatic.

The early experiment in verse drama referred to in my lectures was of
course *Sweeney Agonistes*.

With best wishes for the success of your dissertation.

Yours very truly,
[T. S. Eliot]


TO *Djuna Barnes*                                    TS Hornbake

22 December 1938                    *The Criterion*

Dear Djuna,

Well this is a surprise.[2] I was just on the point of posting a small
Christmas card (enclosed) and was going to write as soon as the Christmas

1 – Sister Mary Beatrice, OSF, College of St Francis, Joliet, Illinois.
2 – Barnes to Emily Coleman, 1 Nov. 1938: 'I almost wanted to weep on his [TSE's] neck,
I said "I can't write" (I would!) he said "If anyone in this age can write it is you' (cited
in Faltejskova, *Djuna Barnes, T. S. Eliot and the Gender Dynamics of Modernism*, 115).

card business was over. So there you are at a mysterious resort apparently named after the Dionne Quins (I hope they are not with you) a long way from the Friend at Hand and the smell of Plymouth Gin. And if you are writing poetry in spite of trying not to, there ought to be some pressure in the boiler. As soon as I have cleared up a lot of arrears (I will send the approaching *Criterion* which will show you what I am up to) I shall be reporting on those already in my possession. Not sure that I approve of Keyserling[1] though. I am glad to hear about the nasty cough, but be careful not to come back too soon: I think you had better stay in the mountains, or at least in a better climate than this, until April, otherwise you may lose all the benefit. That is, if your credit is good with the five infants. So will close for the present wishing you the Best for another year.

Yr. faithful & affectionate<br>T. S. E.

## TO *Ashley Sampson* CC

22 December 1938                  [Faber & Faber Ltd]

Dear Mr Sampson,

I am afraid that a short work of fiction of under 30,000 words is not in our line, and my committee must decline your manuscript on the ground that it is not a type of book with which we are qualified to deal.[2]

Possibly Messrs Chatto & Windus or Boriswood would be in a better position to handle it.

I read the story with much interest, and must make only the qualification that it seems to me a theme almost impossible for anyone to handle successfully. I noticed, of course, minor difficulties which I think you will have to put right; the first is the solidity of the ghost. Although

---

And on 15 Dec. 1938: 'I love him [TSE] ... not only because he has been angelic to me, but because I know he is unhappy without my capacity to shed it in ink, no outlet in him' (Faltejskova, 114).

1–Count Hermann Keyserling (1880–1946), literary philosopher; founded the 'School of Wisdom' at Darmstadt. Author of *Creative Understanding* (1929).

2–Sampson submitted his *nouvelle* 'The Ghost of Mr Brown' on 12 Dec. 'This fantasy has already appeared in "The English Review" as a long short story; and is, in fact, more in the nature of an experiment in fantasy than a novel in the conventional sense. It drew a letter from David Garnett which told me how much he would like to see it achieve some more permanent form; and ... I finally decided to work it up into a short novel and offer it for publication ... This is, I realise, short for a novel; but, as you will doubtless remember, "The Bridge of San Luis Rey" and other works of fiction have been of about this length.'

ghosts have been known to perform physical actions upon furniture and human beings, nevertheless they are ordinarily supposed to be themselves insubstantial, and I think that when you give your ghost solidity some explanation is needed. Also there is no explanation of how the ghost managed to commit his narrative to paper. Incidentally, I myself find the story extremely unpleasant, but this is a personal matter, and is certainly not one which could have influenced its rejection by my firm.[1]

> With many regrets,
> Yours sincerely,
> [T. S. Eliot]

TO *Henry Eliot*                                                    TS Beinecke

23 December 1938                    *The Criterion*

Dear Henry,

This ought to have been a Christmas letter, but I am always so worried by the burden of sending cards, and buying presents for children etc. that I do not get the peace of mind to write letters until all that is over; and it is never over with me until it is too late to do anything more.

I was sorry that Theodora returned the woolen samples which were passed on to her, because Ada and Marian and she all appear so pleased with the stuff they got that I wanted Theresa to have some if she could use it. I will, however, send the samples back to her after Christmas. I ought to explain. I was taken over a hand-loom mill this summer at a little place called Talybont, in Cardiganshire, and was so pleased with the goods that I took samples.[2] It is hand woven tweed from Cardiganshire sheep. I have had a country suit made for myself, which has been invaluable for the country, and during this present cold spell in town as well, for it is very warm. I fear that you might find it too hot indoors to have a suit of, but you might like an overcoat. Anyway, the arrangement is that if you like any of the samples, I will pay for the material (it is only 6s.6d. a yard here) and you pay the duty when you get it. The others seemed to think that even paying the duty and having the goods made up in Boston, they got better stuff than they could at home for anything like the price.

1–Sampson responded, 30 Dec. 1938: 'It is . . . kind of you to have taken so much trouble over it; and I am sorry (though a little mystified) that your reactions to it are "unpleasant"! Somehow the possibility of anyone finding it that had never occurred to me.'
2–Lerry Mills, Talybont, Cardiganshire.

I am glad you met my friend Maritain, and grateful to you for giving him tea. He is not only a very important man, but a very good man, one of the very few saintly men I know. He has also shown himself a man of great moral courage, by the position he has taken up – where very few French or English Catholics have followed him – over the Spanish war. Mercier I met once or twice in Cambridge, and he was very nice to me – gave me a first edition of an essay by Mallarmé. He was, as far as a Catholic can be, a disciple of Irving Babbitt.

I hope that Mr Harry Brown was not downcast by my putting a veto upon the re-issue of the *Advocate* number in England, which he had ingenuously undertaken. My point was simply that I did not want this undergraduate verse to re-appear except as a part of a number of the *Advocate*, not in a pamphlet form. Of course it is none of my business what they do with the rest of the contents of the number. He replied very respectfully, but seemed to think that I did not even want the poems mentioned or quoted in any review of the *Advocate* in any other periodical – which far exceeded my prohibition.

*The Family Reunion* (which, I repeat, has nothing to do with the Eliot family, nor are there any characters which could possibly be supposed to resemble any Eliots) will not appear until February or March. I have had proof, and it is practically ready for press, but as I wish if possible to synchronise publication with production, and as nothing has yet been settled about the latter, I have been holding it up. I do not want to produce it at the Mercury Theatre if a larger theatre can be found; and one or two star actors would be a help. John Gielgud and Sibyl Thorndike have been interested, but they would be available only for matinée performances. The other two possible items for 1939 are the *Book of Practical Cats*, which waits for illustrations, and a short series of lectures upon which I am working.

Tonight I go to the Pantomime with the Faber family. On Christmas Day I shall dine with my friend John Hayward, alone; as the friend with whom I usually spend Christmas, the retired policeman,[1] is in hospital and not likely to come out – I shall visit him in the afternoon.

The weather has been phenomenal for London: it snowed this week for three days on end. The result is not very impressive from New England standards, but has been enough to disorganise English railways, and provide the newspapers with plenty of copy – a temporary relief from politics and police-court cases.

1 – W. L. Janes.

I hope that you are well, and should like to know what you are working on.

With love and best Christmas (too late) and New Year (almost in time) wishes to both,

Affectionately,
Tom


## TO *John Hayward*                                        TS King's

27 December [1938]                    *The Criterion*

Dear John,

It has just occurred to me that it is probably inadvisable for me to release any information about the *Criterion* for next Sunday, because I can't be sure that the copies will be in and sent out to contributors by then. It would give umbrage to some of them – I think especially of Belgion, who is touchy, and who, if as I hear he is in very pinched circumstances at present, will be disturbed anyway by the prospect of losing a small but dependable income – to read of the end of the *Criterion* in a paper before they had been notified directly. I am sorry about this. But I don't suppose that anybody else will consider the event of enough importance to comment on in the daily or weekly press, so the following week might offer a similar opportunity if you were hard up for material. Please forgive me.

Turtle Oil Soap lovely. I shall in future use no other.

Aff.
TP.

Also, perhaps better not let people know that you had any previous knowledge, as I shall say that the secret was kept inside the office.


## TO *Lawrence Durrell*                                    TS Morris Library

28 December [1938]                    *The Criterion*

Dear Durrell,

I suppose that you are expecting me to supper tomorrow (Thursday) as I am proposing to come. I got a message that Miller has landed: I am ready to arrange to meet him under whatever conditions you judge most propitious, if he is willing, or if he can be reduced to a state of anaesthesia in which he might be willing to meet anybody. It doesnt matter to me whether the noises are significant or not.[1] But I must thank you and your wife for the copy of the *Black Book* with the very pretty and innocent looking St Dionysian cover – this is for myself – another copy must be obtained for my brother – I am very proud to have it.

Sincerely,

T. S. Eliot

## TO *Henry Allen Moe*[2]                       CC

30 December 1938          [Faber & Faber Ltd]

Dear Mr Moe,

I am appalled to find that in a jam of affairs in the last month or so I have quite overlooked your letter of enquiry about three candidates (Nov. 22nd). Now, inasmuch as I can dispose of them – so far as my knowledge goes – quite briefly, may I do so in one letter, disregarding your sheaf of forms.[3]

---

1 – Robert Ferguson, *Henry Miller*, 254: '[Durrell] and Miller crossed the Channel to spend Christmas and the New Year [1938] in London where he introduced Henry to some of his friends. There was a meeting with T. S. Eliot at Durrell's Notting Hill Gate flat at which the Paleface and the Redskin got on quite well together. Eliot was in a grave and composed mood, and surprised to discover that Miller did not use bad language in person. Eliot's admiration for *Tropic of Cancer* had been qualified by what he had seen of Miller's subsequent work, and he suspected that a cult was on the way; in 1937 he returned ten *Hamlet* letters which Miller had sent him for consideration for *The Criterion* with what Miller described as "a mildly sarcastic letter about it being more suitable for my 'admirers'".' (That letter has not been traced.)

2 – Henry Allen Moe (1894–1975), Secretary, John Simon Guggenheim Memorial Foundation, New York, 1925–60; President, 1961–3.

3 – Moe had written: 'Comparative judgments, if you can give them, are always very useful. Of course, anything you may say will be held strictly confidential . . . As always, my question is this: Which of these candidates, if any, is in your judgment, first-rate?' The candidates who had nominated TSE as referee were Basil Bunting, Raymond E. F. Larsson, and Louis Zukofsky.

See too Moe to TSE (addressed to Eliot House, B-11, Cambridge, Mass.), 22 Nov. 1938: 'Dear Mr Eliot: / Five years ago you wrote me about Mr James R. Agee who was then an applicant for a Fellowship of this Foundation. Mr Agee is not an applicant this year but I plan to place his name before the Committee of Selection on my own initiative. Before doing that, however, I want – if they please – to take the opinions of Mr Agee's previous sponsors on the question whether or not Mr Agee has in their view lived up to his earlier promise. Will you give me your judgment, please, if you have had an opportunity to familiarize yourself with Mr Agee's later work – confidentially? / Sincerely yours, / Henry Allen Moe.'

Unfortunately it has not been possible to trace any statement by TSE relating to James Agee (1909–55), novelist, journalist, poet, screenwriter and film critic; author of *Let Us Now Praise Famous Men* (1941) and the Pulitzer Prize-winning novel *A Death in the Family* (1958).

From what I have seen of the work of Mr Zukovsky [*sic*], I should judge him to be a minor follower of Ezra Pound. Mr Larsson is on the other hand rather a minor imitator of myself, on the devotional side: but there I speak with more diffidence. Neither of them seemed to me in the past to give very strong promise as a poet, but it must be kept in mind that I have not looked at the work of either for several years. Bunting, on the other hand, is a very intelligent man and an able poet. I say 'able', because I am still doubtful whether he will ever accomplish anything of great importance as an original author. I think he has just the qualities to qualify him as a translator of poetry. As he says, I have published some of his translation of Firdausi [*sic*] in the *Criterion*, and was well pleased with it; he has done well with Horace too. I back him strongly for the sort of work that he proposes to do – work, also, which is in itself worth doing. You will understand that I am wholly ignorant of Persian and of Bunting's qualifications as a scholar in that language: presumably he can give other references for that. He is not only much the strongest of these three candidates, but positively a man worth helping.

Will this do?

With apologies for the delay – and best wishes for 1939.

Yours sincerely,

[T. S. Eliot]

## TO *Ezra Pound*

TS Yale

30 December [1938]                    *The Criterion*

Dear Ez,

Can anything be done about this abomination? Do you know KNOW anything about Moo? I have just written to back Bunting, but this List turns ones stummick. Id have told Moo what I thought about it but it wouldnt have helped bunting.

Merry 1939 (anno XIX)

& to yourself

TP

30 December 1938                    *The Criterion*

Dear Richard, Alison, Poppett,

Thank you very much INDEED for the lovely Box of Cosmetic Articles which I received from you tonight. Especially as French Fern is what I like, as you must have discovered: so now I have (1) Powder (2) Shaving Soap (3) Oil to Slick my Hair down. Now I shall be able to look very neat when I next see you; and if I don't then it will be my fault. I don't quite know what to do about the Safety Razor; it looks to me as if it was the kind that your Father used: but I keep my Beard in a drawer, and only wear it on full-dress occasions such as Guy Faux Day. Anyway, I thank you very much for everything, and, hoping to see you soon, remain your faithful

Possum[1]


TO *Donald Brace*                    CC

30 December 1938              [Faber & Faber Ltd]

My dear Brace,

I have sent you, under separate cover, the corrected galley proofs of *The Family Reunion*, and hope that I shall not feel impelled to make any further corrections in the page. Unfortunately I have not yet been able to fix the publication date, because I have been anxious if possible to synchronise it with the opening of the production, and so far nothing about the production has been settled. This should be in February or March. If for any reason production should be delayed until another season, I do not intend to hold the book over. If you like I will send you a cable as soon as the production and publication date are fixed.

I should like the following, or something like the following, statement to go on one of the front pages of the American edition, I suppose on the same page with the usual copyright statement.

---

1–Richard Tandy replied (n.d.): 'dear Possum / Thank you for the camera and gun I have not used all the caps and noise. You see I am useing [*sic*] a typewriter but take a long time to do it and make a lot of mistakes. Have you used any of your Hair grease. We had a rather posh party but no ballons [*sic*] to go off POP BANG. I hope you will be able to come to the next. Will you write a poem about a cat that likes everything even smacks. FROM RICHARD.'

It appears that we have lost money through a number of unauthorised American amateur performances of *Murder in the Cathedral*, and this is the form of statement which Ashley Dukes suggested to me as useful at any rate in preventing honest amateurs from piracy.

　　　　　　　　　　　With best wishes for the New Year,
　　　　　　　　　　　Yours ever,
　　　　　　　　　　　[T. S. Eliot]

P.S. I hear from a mutual friend that St-Léger, the author of *Anabase*, never received any author's copies of your edition. As this edition is so much revised, I think that he ought to have a set of copies; if you do not feel that this should fall on Harcourt, Brace & Co, please send him six and debit them to me. Incidentally, my informant also expressed horror at the fact that Léger's name – i.e. St J. Perse – did not appear on the cover or jacket of the book. I had no defence to make, except that I had nothing to do with it, but I was considerably embarrassed. I wonder if it would be possible at least to have his name appear on the jacket in future? If you have no address for him, his private name is Alexis St-Léger Léger, and his address is: Ministère des Affaires Etrangères, Quai d'Orsay, Paris.[1]

1–Brace responded, 13 Jan. 1939: 'We did not send copies of ANABASIS to St-Léger. I am afraid it didn't occur to us, and anyway we didn't have any address for him. We only sent the usual "author's copies" to you in the usual way. I am now having six copies sent to St-Léger, and of course we don't want to charge these to you. It is too bad that his name does not appear on the jacket. I find that in preparing the jacket for our edition, we followed the English edition (Faber & Faber, 1930) exactly. We are making a note to add the name to the jacket whenever it is printed again.'

30 December 1938                    *The Criterion*

Dear Alison,

Oh dear, I am so miserable that I cannot come to your Party tomorrow. But I have got to go to the Morleys, and I can't be in two places at once. But I shall think of you and Toast you on your Birthday. But it is so long since I have been to your birthday party that I think the best thing to do, if you want me to come next year, is this. Write to me as soon as possible and say: Dear Possum, you will say, I invite you to my party on December 31st, 1939. And I will say: Dear Alison, I shall be delighted to come to your Party on December 31st, 1939. And if anyone asks me after that, even the Morleys, I shall say: I have a Previous Engagement. Besides, next year's party will be still more important than this, because you will be a year older.

And as it is, I hope to see you within two weeks, in 1939, and meanwhile wish you a HAPPY NEW YEAR.

> Your affectionate
> Possum

P.S. Will you Perhaps let me have one of your PHOTOGRAPHS?

# APPENDIX

## On John Middleton Murry's
## Christian Theory of Society

For the second meeting of the Moot (held at Westfield College, London, 23–6 Sept. 1938), JMM produced a paper entitled 'Towards a Christian Theory of Society'. Keith Clements notes: 'Middleton Murry's paper . . . was a fascinating argument, drawing upon Rousseau, Coleridge and Thomas Arnold, for the state to be a moral organization and for the "national church" to be inclusive of the whole of society and at one with the state. In the modern industrial age, Christian civilization could continue to exist only as an inclusively national and Christian society, led by the national church with the state as its organ. In response some Moot members – Baillie, Löwe and Eliot in particular – jumped on Murry's assumption of the nation as the boundary of society, especially as far as the church, which was universal in nature, was concerned' (*Faith on the Frontier: A Life of J. H. Oldham* [1999], 370).

TSE's draft TS response to Murry's paper is hitherto unpublished.

I think that I may best begin by mentioning several points in Murry's paper which represent not so much positive disagreement, but apprehension about tendency. My hope is that an examination of these points will reveal fundamental agreement.

1. Murry's preliminary remarks about the necessity of a Christian theory of *modern* society are very much to the point. But I have considerable sympathy with Para. 3 of Fr. Vidler's Comment. The Christian theory has to keep firm hold on what is valid and necessary for *any* society. Some of the features of 'modern' society may be transient, some may be positively lethal: and against the latter it is the business of the Christian theory to protest. The extent to which 'modern' – or even 'contemporary' – conditions have to be accepted as a basis for construction is a question requiring long study, as well perhaps as intuitive perception. The point is that our attitude towards the contemporary situation must be determined in relation to a body of belief held to be permanent truth. I agree of course that there are respects in which we cannot go back: but there will

always be various views possible as to the direction in which we should go forward.

2. I am in doubt as to what Murry means by a 'national' Church, and this doubt gives rise to anxiety. He seems to be preoccupied with the relation of the Church to a national society, and at least, does not consider the nature of the Church as a supra-national body. And in using this term I have in mind not only the Church of Rome, but the ideal nature of even the smallest sect. In omitting any discussion of this character of the Church, Murry seems to me to fail to provide for any control of the process he desiderates, by which the State shall be made Christian. The danger for any 'national' Church, even in the sense in which there are already 'national' Churches, is that it may become contaminated by the State, and that its values local and universal may become distorted. There must be an outside standard. And as the State as such must be a restricted set of values, there must always be a tension between the State and the Church, and an inner tension in the person who is both citizen and churchman. I cannot see that Murry provides any safeguard against the *national* Church becoming a *nationalistic* Church – of which the most thorough-going formulation that I know is that of Wilhelm Hauer (v. 'Germany's New Religion': Allen & Unwin).

It seems to me that a distinction must be made between the 'Christian State' and the 'Christian community'. In an ideal state of affairs, the two might be in effect indistinguishable. England still represents, I think, the nearest approach to a Christian State: for the Concordat situation seems to me to assume that the State is not Christian. The most patent evidence of what I call a Christian State appears on the occasion of a Coronation (those who urged that other bodies than the Anglican Church should take part in the Coronation did not realise that the effect would be not to strengthen but to weaken the consecration). The Christianity of a State is a matter of form: it does not require that the individual constituents should be good Christians, and it only becomes a hollow form when the majority of the constituents become positively anti-Christian. And as I suggest that the Christian State is a matter of form, so I suggest that the Christian community is a matter of behaviour, and that it must be clearly distinguished from a community of Christians. I know of one small country parish, which I imagine to be typical, in which the inhabitants are by no means distinguished for religious fervour or regular church-going, though they are married, baptised and buried. But when a proposal was afoot for amalgamating the parish with a neighbouring parish, the parishioners were bitterly opposed to this loss of identity, and I believe that even the chapel-goers shared this feeling. Such a parish is, however dimly, aware of itself as a Christian community.

In discussing such terms as 'Christian society', 'Christian State' and 'Christian community', I think we should keep in mind the difference of meaning, primarily a slight shift of emphasis, which the adjective has in these different contexts. There is one point of view to be kept in mind, from which everyone is to be regarded as a Christian who is not of non-Christian heredity, and who does not maintain explicitly non-Christian or anti-Christian beliefs. (I might explain, merely to make the point sharper, that I am not a Christian in this sense: with a hundred years of Deism as my immediate background, I am only a Christian by individual, not by collective belief).

I am not at all clear – and this is perhaps the most important item in my doubts – what the term 'Christian' means to Murry. Dawson has already commented on the inclusion of Rousseau; I confess myself also surprised to find Matthew Arnold cited as a Christian thinker. I should have thought of Arnold as having the same relation to a Christian, that a boned fowl has to an animated member of barnyard society. This is a matter for discussion.

I am not on firm ground in discussing Dr Arnold, because I have never studied his life and writings. I suspect that Murry makes out the best possible case for him, and that severe criticism could be made of the 'public school religion' which he encouraged. 'In a national society thus conceived,' says Murry, 'after an education thus conducted, disinterested service of the *res publica* was a dedicated Christian life'. Such a statement could not meet, I fancy, with any opposition in Germany: but is not a dedicated Christian life something more and higher than disinterested service of the *res publica*? I have a friend who is a product of Dr Arnold's institution, who approves of compulsory chapel for schoolboys on the sole ground that it is a good discipline for them to be forced to attend regularly something that they so much dislike.

I deprecate Murry's diminishment of the importance of the clergy, at the same time that I welcome his assertion of the importance of the clerisy. I do not think that you will get a better clerisy by derogating the authority of the clergy. What you do get is what you have: a situation in which the clerisy (and what a clerisy!) is cut off from the clergy, and the clergy from the clerisy, so that they not only do not hold the same views, but do not even speak the same language. Indeed, a closer association of clergy and clerisy seems to me exactly when [*sc.* what] is needed: that is something definite about which something could be done.

I think that Murry's view of the Christianisation of the State needs to be complemented by the assertion of the necessity of some repository of immutable Christian truth; otherwise, instead of the State being christianised, it may well be Christianity which is adapted to the purposes of the State. The recognition of such necessity should make us, I think, not only more appreciative of the importance of the Papacy, but more sympathetic than Murry appears to be to the development of Lutheran theology in German in recent times.

I should also like to query Murry's assertion (bottom of p. 1) that the visible Church and secular society are of quite the same order. The visible Church is, I take it, of divine institution, and that seems to me to constitute an important difference. Such a claim can hardly be made even for 'democracy', whatever meaning we assign to the term.

I agree with Murry that the State has, and will probably have increasingly within the utmost range of our operation and design, the modern importance which he gives it. And his conception of a 'national Christian society' seems to me of great value. My comments have chiefly been concerned with the necessity for safeguarding Christianity itself, in our enthusiasm for society. And I think we need to remember, in the heat of social zeal, that the point of living is to be found in Death, and that we are concerned as Christians with what happens to us after that. I mean that the fear of Hell is not merely a matter of individual temperament, but is essential for collective Christianity.

# BIOGRAPHICAL REGISTER

**W. H. Auden** (1907–73): poet, playwright, librettist, translator, essayist and editor. He was educated at Gresham's School, Holt, Norfolk, and at Christ Church, Oxford, where he co-edited *Oxford Poetry* (1926, 1927), and where his friend Stephen Spender hand-set about 30 copies of his first book, a pamphlet entitled *Poems* (1928). After going down from Oxford with a third-class degree in English in 1928, he visited Belgium and then lived for a year in Berlin. He worked as a tutor in London, 1929–30; then as a schoolmaster at Larchfield Academy, Helensburgh, Dunbartonshire, 1930–2, and at the Downs School, Colwall, Herefordshire, 1932–5. Although Eliot turned down his initial submission of a book of poems in 1927, he would presently accept 'Paid on Both Sides: A Charade' for the *Criterion*; and Eliot went on for the rest of his life to publish all of Auden's books at Faber & Faber: *Poems* (1930); *The Orators* (1932); *Look, Stranger!* (1937); *Spain* (1936); *Another Time* (1940); *New Year Letter* (1941; published in the USA as *The Double Man*); *The Age of Anxiety* (1947); *For the Time Being* (1945); *The Age of Anxiety: A Baroque Eclogue* (1948); *Nones* (1952); *The Shield of Achilles* (1955); *Homage to Clio* (1960); *About the House* (1966). Eliot was happy, too, to publish Auden's play *The Dance of Death* (1933), which was performed by the Group Theatre in 1934 and 1935; and three further plays written with Christopher Isherwood: *The Dog Beneath the Skin* (1935), which would be performed by the Group Theatre in 1936; *The Ascent of F6* (1936); and *On the Frontier* (1937). In 1935–6 Auden went to work for the General Post Office film unit, writing verse commentaries for two celebrated documentary films, *Coal Face* and *Night Mail*. He collaborated with Louis MacNeice on *Letters from Iceland* (1937); and with Isherwood again on *Journey to a War* (1939). His first libretto was *Paul Bunyan* (performed with music by Benjamin Britten, 1941); and in 1947 he began collaborating with Igor Stravinsky on *The Rake's Progress* (performed in Venice, 1951); and he co-wrote two librettos for Hans Werner Henze. Other works include *The Oxford Book of Light Verse* (1938); *The Enchafed Flood: The Romantic Iconography of the Sea* (1951); *The Dyer's Hand* (1963); *Secondary Worlds* (1968). Cyril Connolly, 'Poet and privacy', *Sunday Times*, 18 Aug. 1974 (on T. S. Matthews's *Great Tom*): 'Auden told me that he got on particularly well with Eliot because he knew how to tease him . . . Great men like to be teased as large predators like to be scratched.' See further Humphrey Carpenter, *W. H. Auden: A Biography* (1981); Richard Davenport-Hines, *Auden* (1995); Edward Mendelson, *Early Auden* (1981), *Later Auden* (1999); David Collard, 'More worthy than Lark: a television tribute to T. S. Eliot, by W. H. Auden and others', *TLS,* 9 Mar. 2012, 14.

**George Barker** (1913–91), poet and author. Works include *Poems* (1933); *Calamiterror* (1937); *The True Confession of George Barker* (1950); *Collected Poems,* ed. Robert Fraser (1987). With support from TSE, he became Professor of English Literature, Tohoku University, Sendai, Japan, 1939–40. His liaison with Elizabeth Smart is memorialised in her novel *By Grand Central Station I Sat Down and Wept* (1945). Barker told EVE, 5 Jan. 1965: '[TSE] was kind to me, as he was, I know, to many others. Most of all I think of the constant help he gave to me in matters of circumstance when I was young. If it had not been for him, I would not (to speak too much of myself) have had a chance.' Robert Fraser, *The Chameleon Poet: A Life of George Barker* (2001): 'As the years passed, [Barker] would weave anecdotes portraying his erstwhile mentor as lounge lizard, footpad, Sweeney, nightbird, Mr Hyde. Eliot, he would grow accustomed to relating, had worn green eyeshadow. He had prowled the back streets of London after hours dressed as a policeman. He had kept a secret *pied-à-terre* in the Charing Cross Road, visitors to which were obliged to ask the porter for "the Captain".' (Fraser's source was Barker himself.) See too Barker, 'A Note for T. S. Eliot', *New English Weekly,* 11 (Mar. 1949), 188–92.

**Djuna Barnes** (1892–1982), American novelist, journalist, poet, playwright; author of *Ryder* (1928); *Nightwood* (1936); *Antiphon* (play, 1958). See further 'A Rational Exchange', *New Yorker,* 24 June and 1 July 1996, 107–9; *Nightwood: The Original Version and Related Drafts,* ed. Cheryl J. Plumb (1995); Miriam Fuchs, 'Djuna Barnes and T. S. Eliot: Authority, Resistance, and Acquiescence', *Tulsa Studies in Women's Literature* 12: 2 (Fall 1993), 289–313. See too Andrew Field, *Djuna: The Formidable Miss Barnes* (1983, 1985), 218: 'Willa Muir was struck by the difference that came over Eliot when he was with Barnes. She thought that the way Barnes had of treating him with an easy affectionate camaraderie caused him to respond with an equally easy gaiety that she had never seen in Eliot before.'

Montgomery ('Monty') Belgion (1892–1973), author, was born in Paris of British parents and grew up with a deep feeling for the culture of France. In 1915–16 he was editor-in-charge of the European edition of the *New York Herald*; and for the remainder of WW1 he joined up in the Honourable Artillery Company, 1916–18, and was commissioned in the Dorsetshire Regiment. Between the wars he worked for the Paris review *This Quarter* and for newspapers including the *Daily Mail* and *Daily Mirror*, and for a while he was an editor for Harcourt, Brace & Co., New York. In WW2 he was a captain in the Royal Engineers, and spent two years in prison camps in Germany. In 1929 Faber & Faber brought out (on TSE's recommendation) *Our Present Philosophy of Life*. Later works include *Reading for Profit* (1945) and booklets on H. G. Wells and David Hume. See further Belgion, 'T. S. Eliot edited "The Criterion"', *Monday World: The magazine of the radical right* (Summer 1972), 7–8; Jason Harding, '*The Criterion': Cultural Politics and Periodical Networks in Inter-War Britain* (2002), 143–58.

John Betjeman (1906–84), poet, journalist, authority on architecture (he was for many years on the staff of the *Architectural Review*); radio and TV broadcaster. He was taught by TSE at Highgate School, London, in 1916, and was C. S. Lewis's first pupil at Magdalen College, Oxford – which he left without a degree. Volumes of verse include *Mount Zion* (1931), *Ghastly Good Taste* (1933), *Continual Dew* (1937), *Old Lights for New Chancels* (1940), *A Few Late Chrysanthemums* (1954), *Poems in the Porch* (1954), *Collected Poems* (1958), and the sequence *Summoned by Bells* (1960). Awarded the Queen's Gold Medal for Poetry in 1960. Knighted 1969. Poet Laureate, 1972.

TSE on Betjeman, on 18 Nov. 1944, to the British Council: 'I have known Mr Betjeman for some years: I was first impressed by his ability when he was ten years old or so, and a pupil at a preparatory school in which I was an assistant master. He is exceptionally able, highly knowledgeable in literature and the arts, and has good taste both in these matters and in social affairs. He has also personal charm, an easy flow of conversation, and ability to get on with all sorts of people.'

Ronald Bottrall (1906–89), poet, critic, teacher and administrator, studied at Pembroke College, Cambridge, and taught in Helsinki before spending two years at Princeton University. He was Johore Professor of English at Raffles University, Singapore, 1933–7, and taught for a year at the English Institute, Florence, before serving as British Council representative in

Sweden, Rome, Brazil, Greece and Japan. He was head of the Fellowships and Training Branch of the Food and Agricultural Organisation of the United Nations in Rome. His poetry includes *The Loosening* (1931) and *Festivals of Fire* (1934).

**Donald Brace** (1881–1955): founder in 1919 – with Alfred Harcourt, whom he befriended at Columbia College, New York – of the publishing firm of Harcourt, Brace & Howe. See *The History of Harcourt Brace and Company: 75 Years of Publishing Excellence* (1994). TSE in *The Times*, 1955: 'No American publisher was better known or better liked in the literary world of my generation. His English friends will remember his keen sense of humour, which, expressed in his very slow and deliberate speech, was at times irresistibly droll. And they will remember most gratefully the confidence which he inspired as a publisher, by his combination of Yankee shrewdness, loyalty to his authors' interests, and sweetness of temper.'

**E. (Elliott) Martin Browne** (1900–80), theatre director, read history and theology at Christ Church, Oxford, before working for the British Drama League and the Adult Education Movement. He then went to the USA as Assistant Professor of Speech and Drama at the Carnegie Institute of Technology, Pittsburgh, 1927–30, before being appointed in 1930, by Bishop George Bell, as Director of Religious Drama for the diocese of Chichester. He collaborated with TSE on *The Rock*, produced at Sadler's Wells, May–June 1934, and thereafter directed all of TSE's plays: see his *The Making of T. S. Eliot's Plays* (1969). He was director of a touring company called the Pilgrim Players, 1939–49; Director of the British Drama League, 1948–57; and in 1951 he directed the first revival since 1572 of the medieval cycle of York Mystery Plays. He was Visiting Professor of Religious Drama at Union Theological College, New York, 1956–62; Drama Advisor to Coventry Cathedral, 1962–5; and in 1967–8 he directed plays at the Yvonne Arnaud Theatre, Guildford. Appointed CBE, 1952. His first wife was the actress Henzie Raeburn (1901–73).

**Emily Holmes Coleman** (1899–1974), novelist and poet; author of *The Shutter of Snow* (novel, 1930). See Andrew Field, *Djuna: The Formidable Miss Barnes* (1983, 1985): 'Coleman was a Californian who graduated from Wellesley College in 1920, came to Europe with her husband in 1926, and two years later separated from him. She threw herself into slightly more than a decade of various countries and passionate loves, beginning with a wild affair with an Italian and progressing to several poets, chief among them Dylan Thomas ... When she first went to Europe, [she] worked on the European edition of *The Chicago Tribune*. Then for a while she was the society editor of the Paris *Tribune*. Her poetry appeared in *transition*. When Peggy [Guggenheim] met her in 1928 [Coleman] was installed at St Tropez as the literary secretary to Emma Goldman ... Though jealousy and rage were very much a part of Emily's character, generosity was too, and she was, happily, convinced of her own genius as well as Djuna's – *Make it marvellous!!!* she exhorted Djuna as she was finishing writing the novel ... Difficult Emily Coleman is one of the heroines of this story, because, when Barnes returned from America with her much-rejected manuscript in 1934, Emily turned all of her considerable energy to getting it published in England and – after Edwin Muir had pressed the manuscript on Eliot – literally bearded the poet-editor in his office and made it clear to him that Faber would publish the novel, or else.'

**Martin D'Arcy** (1888–1976), Jesuit priest and theologian, entered the Novitiate in 1906, took a first in Literae Humaniores at Pope's Hall – the Jesuit private hall of Oxford University – and was ordained in 1921. After teaching at Stonyhurst College, in 1925 he undertook doctoral research, at the Gregorian University in Rome and at the Jesuit House at Farm Street, London. In 1927 he returned to Campion Hall (successor to Pope's Hall), where he taught philosophy at the university. He was Rector and Master of Campion Hall, 1933–45; Provincial of the British Province of the Jesuits in London, 1945–50. Charismatic as a lecturer, and as an apologist for Roman Catholicism (his prominent converts included Evelyn Waugh), he also wrote studies including *The Nature of Belief* (1931) and *The Mind and Heart of Love* (1945). See H. J. A. Sire, *Father Martin D'Arcy: Philosopher of Christian Love* (1997); Richard Harp, 'A conjuror at the Xmas party', *TLS*, 11 Dec. 2009, 13–15.

**Christopher Dawson** (1889–1970), cultural historian. An independent and erudite scholar of private means (in 1933 he inherited estates in Yorkshire), he taught for a while, part-time, at the University College of Exeter, 1925–33; and, though not a professional academic, was ultimately appointed at the good age of sixty-eight to a chair in Roman Catholic Studies at Harvard, 1958–62. A convert to Catholicism, he devoted much of his research to the idea of religion as the driver of social culture. Works include *Progress and Religion* (1929), *The Making of Europe* (1932), and *Religion and the Rise of Western Culture* (1950), as well as a series entitled *Essays in Order* which he edited for the Catholic publishers Sheed and Ward: his own contributions included *Enquiries into Religion and Culture* (1934) and *Medieval Religion* (1934). For TSE he wrote Criterion Miscellany pamphlet no. 13: *Christianity and Sex* (1930). See Christina Scott – Dawson's daughter – *An Historian and His World: A Life of Christopher Dawson 1889–1970* (1984); Bradley H. Birzer, *Sanctifying the World: The Augustinian Life and Mind of Christopher Dawson* (2007); Christopher McVey, 'Backgrounds to *The Idea of a Christian Society*: Charles Maurras, Christopher Dawson, and Jacques Maritain', and Benjamin G. Lockerd, 'T. S. Eliot and Christopher Dawson on Religion and Culture': both in *T. S. Eliot and Christian Tradition*, ed. Lockerd (2014). See too Dawson, 'Mr T. S. Eliot and the Meaning of Culture', *The Month* 1 (Mar. 1949), 151–7.

**Vigo Auguste Demant** (1893–1983) trained as an engineer but embraced a wholly different career when he converted to Christianity and became a deacon in 1919, priest in 1920. Following various curacies, he became, while working at St Silas, Kentish Town, London, Director of Research for the Christian Social Council – the Council of Churches in England for Social Questions – 1929–33. As noted in the *ODNB*, he was 'the major theoretician in the Christendom Group of Anglican Catholic thinkers, whose concern was to establish the centrality of what they termed "Christian sociology", an analysis of society fundamentally rooted in a Catholic and incarnational theology'. The group's quarterly, *Christendom*, ran from 1931 to 1950. He was vicar of St John-the-Divine, Richmond, Surrey, 1933–42; Canon Residentiary, St Paul's Cathedral, 1942–9; Canon of Christ Church and Regius Professor of Moral and Pastoral Theology, Oxford, 1949–71. Works include *God, Man and Society* (1933); *Christian Polity* (1936); *The Religious Prospect* (1939).

TSE to the Archbishop of Canterbury, 29 Mar. 1939: 'I regard him as quite one of the most profound and subtle of younger theologians. I have observed also that his earnestness and sincerity always win the closest attention when he speaks before any group (as at the Oxford Conference). His book *Christian Polity* seems to me a very valuable contribution.'

Demant remarked at the Requiem Mass for TSE at St Stephen's Church, Kensington, 17 Feb. 1965: 'The Revd Frank Hillier, to whom Eliot used to go for confession and spiritual direction after the death of Father Philip Bacon [at St Simon's, Kentish Town], writes to me: "Eliot had, along with that full grown stature of mind, a truly child-like heart – the result of his sense of dependence on GOD. And along with it he had the sense of responsibility to GOD for the use of his talents. To his refinedness of character is due the fact that like his poetry he himself was not easily understood – but unbelievers always recognized his faith"' (*St Stephen's Church Magazine*, Apr. 1965, 9).

**Bonamy Dobrée** (1891–1974), scholar and critic, was Professor of English Literature at Leeds University, 1936–55. After service in the army during WW1 (he was twice mentioned in despatches and attained the rank of major), he read English at Christ's College, Cambridge, and taught in London and as a professor of English at the Egyptian University, Cairo, 1925–9. Works include *Restoration Comedy* (1924), *Essays in Biography* (1925), *Restoration Tragedy, 1660–1720* (1929), *Alexander Pope* (1951). See also Harding, *The 'Criterion': Cultural Politics and Periodical Networks in Inter-War Britain* (2002).

**Rupert Doone** (1903–66), dancer, choreographer, and producer, founded the Group Theatre, London, in 1932. See obituary by Tyrone Guthrie and John Moody in *The Times*, 8 Mar. 1966. Browne (*Making*, 38) thought Doone 'one of the most intriguing personalities of the theatre of the 'thirties. He came from a Worcestershire family in humble circumstances . . . Leaving home at sixteen he became, through many struggles and privations, a ballet dancer, and finally rose to the most coveted position in that profession – *premier danseur* in the Diaghileff company. But only for a few weeks: the great impresario died in the same year, 1929.

'Doone left the ballet to enter a new field: he went to the Festival Theatre, Cambridge, where Tyrone Guthrie was working with Anmer Hall [Alderson Burrell Horne (1863–1953), theatre manager and owner, producer, actor, who was to become proprietor of the Westminster Theatre, 1931–46], to learn acting and production. This was typical of his endlessly questing mind; and there, as before in the ballet, he found natural friendship with the most imaginative artists of the day. From a play-reading circle at Cambridge there developed the Group Theatre.

'Within a year the Group had its own rooms on the top floor of a building in Great Newport Street . . . Its purpose was the synthesis of all the elements of theatre – movement, mime, rhythm, speech and design – the "total theatre" . . . Doone associated with himself such artists (then hardly known to fame) as Benjamin Britten, Brian Easdale, John Piper, Henry Moore. The reputation of his seasons rests on the series of original plays he produced between 1934 and 1939, by such writers as W. H.

Auden and Christopher Isherwood, Louis MacNeice, Stephen Spender and, to begin with, T. S. Eliot.'

**Ashley Dukes** (1885–1959), theatre manager, playwright, critic, translator, author. Educated in Manchester and Munich, Dukes started out as theatre critic for *New Age, Vanity Fair,* and other journals; he was co-editor of *Theatre Arts Monthly,* 1926–42; and from 1941 he served on the first panel of the Council for the Encouragement of Music and the Arts (later the Arts Council). In 1933, with a royalty of £10,000 from his play *The Man with a Load of Mischief* (1924), he established – with his wife Marie Rambert, dancer, teacher, and founder of the Ballet Rambert (she studied with Nijinksy and Karsavina, joined Diaghileff's ballet corps, and trained Frederick Ashton and other great figures) – the Mercury Theatre in Notting Hill, which (with support from WBY and TSE) became in 1933 a poet's theatre. *MiC,* the first hit – the production ran for 255 performances – was followed by works by WHA and Isherwood, Ronald Duncan, Anne Ridler, and Norman Nicolson. (The Mercury Theatre features in the movie *The Red Shoes,* 1948.) See Dukes, *The Scene is Changed* (1942); TSE in *The Times,* 7 May 1959: 'It was Mr Dukes who, after seeing a performance of *Murder in the Cathedral* at the Canterbury Festival for which it was written, saw that the play had further possibilities, and brought the whole production to London. Owing to his enterprise a play designed for a special occasion and for a very brief run, came to the notice of the general public.'

**Lawrence Durrell** (1912–90), novelist, poet, dramatist, travel writer; author of *The Alexandria Quartet* (1957–60). Early works included *Panic Spring* (published under the pseudonym 'Charles Norden': F&F, 1937) and *The Black Book: An Agon* (1938).

TSE advised S. W. White, British Council, in connection with Durrell's application for a Research Fellowship of the Council of Europe, 19 Mar. 1957: 'I have known Mr Lawrence Durrell for a good many years during which most of his work has been published under my recommendation by the firm of Faber & Faber. In this connection I have seen, over a number of years, a good deal of Mr Durrell personally and like him very much. I know him first as a poet and can say that his work is outstanding amongst that of the poets of his generation. He is also a distinguished prose writer, having written more than one admirable travel book, and recently a novel, *Justine,* which has won high commendation from the critics. Mr Lawrence Durrell is in fact one of the most distinguished writers of his generation.'

Durrell would recall, in a memorial essay 'The Other T. S. Eliot', *The Atlantic Monthly* 215 (May 1965): 'If this was for me a fruitful and rewarding relationship, it was entirely due to this painstaking and gentle man whose mind had so fine a cutting edge, and who undertook his duties so seriously and with such method that he went far beyond them in his dealing with the young writers of the house. I cannot believe that my experiences with Eliot the publisher were any different from those enjoyed by other poets and writers from the same stable. The real mystery is where the devil he found time to deal with us all in such detail, criticizing, consoling, and encouraging. In my case it can only be accounted for by suggesting that he was some sort of saint; poor man, he had to deal with an argumentative, combative, opinionated young man – a self-inflated ego betraying all the marks of insecurity and vanity. At times it was necessary to cut me down to size, and whenever I succeeded in irritating him too much, he would do it with such breathtaking elegance and style that it left me gasping. But always without heat, without vanity, charitably . . .

'A wicked man indeed, for he was seldom wrong, and what is worse, he was never splenetic or small-minded . . . The public image of him at that time was of a rather humorless literary bonze of the Sainte-Beuve type . . . Needless to say he did not correspond at all to this literary image. When first I met him I found his gravity rather intimidating; but as I saw more of him I found that laughter was very near the surface. It came in sudden little flashes.'

**Henry Ware Eliot, Jr** (1879–1947), TSE's elder brother, went to school at Smith Academy, and then studied for two years at Washington University, St Louis, before progressing to Harvard, 1897–9, where he was an editor of *Student Life*. At Harvard, he displayed a gift for light verse in *Harvard Celebrities* (1901), illustrated with 'Caricatures and Decorative Drawings' by two fellow undergraduates. After graduating, he spent a year at Law School, but subsequently followed a career in printing, publishing and advertising. He attained a partnership in Husband & Thomas Co. (later the Buchen Company), a Chicago advertising agency of which he became Vice-President, from 1917 to 1929, during which time he gave financial assistance to TSE and advised him on investments. He accompanied their mother on her visit to London in the summer of 1921, his first trip away from the USA. In February 1926, he married Theresa Anne Garrett (1884–1981), an alumna of the School of Fine Arts. But it was not until late in life that he found his true calling, as a Research Fellow in Near Eastern Archaeology at the Peabody Museum of American Archaeology and

Ethnology, Harvard, where he published a discussion of the prehistoric chronology of Northern Mesopotamia, together with a description of the pottery from Kudish Saghir (1939): see *Excavations in Mesopotamia and Western Iran: Sites of 4000–500 B.C.: Graphic Analyses* (1950), prefaced by Lauriston Ward: 'It was a labor of love, of such magnitude as to be practically unique in the annals of archaeology . . . a monument to his scholarship and devotion . . . Eliot had all the qualities of the true scholar, which include modesty as well as ability.' In 1932 he published a detective novel, *The Rumble Murders*, under the pseudonym Mason Deal. He was instrumental in building up the T. S. Eliot collection at Eliot House (Houghton Library). Of slighter build than his brother – who noted his 'Fred Astaire figure' – Henry suffered from deafness owing to scarlet fever as a child, and this may have contributed to his diffidence. It was with his dear brother in mind that TSE wrote: 'The notion of some infinitely gentle/ Infinitely suffering thing' ('Preludes' IV).

**Vivien (Vivienne) Eliot**, née Haigh-Wood (1888–1947). Born in Bury, Lancashire, on 28 May 1888, 'Vivy' was brought up in Hampstead from the age of 3. After meeting TSE in company with Scofield Thayer in Oxford early in 1915, she and TSE hastened to be married just a few weeks later, on 26 June 1915. (TSE, who was lodging at 35 Greek Street, London, was recorded in the marriage certificate as 'of no occupation'.) She developed close friendships with MH, OM and others in TSE's circle. Despite chronic personal and medical difficulties, they remained together until 1933, when TSE resolved to separate from her following his academic year in the USA. She was never reconciled to the separation, became increasingly ill, and in 1938 was confined to a psychiatric hospital, where she died (of 'syncope' and 'cardiovascular degeneration') on 22 January 1947. She is the dedicatee of *Ash-Wednesday* (1930). She published sketches in the *Criterion* (under pseudonyms with the initials 'F. M.'). See Michael Karwoski, 'The Bride from Bury', *Lancashire Life*, Mar. 1984, 52–3; Carole Seymour-Jones, *Painted Shadow: The Life of Vivienne Eliot* (2001); Ken Craven, *The Victorian Painter and the Poet's Wife: A Biography of the Haigh-Wood Family* (e-book, 2012); Robert Crawford, *Young Eliot: From St Louis to 'The Waste Land'* (2015).

**George Every**, SSM (1909–2003): historian and poet. Educated at the University College, Exeter (he was tutored by Christopher Dawson), he joined in 1929 the Anglican theological college, House of the Sacred Mission, at Kelham, where he lived until 1973. Works include *Christian*

*Discrimination* (1940) and *The Byzantine Patriarchate* (1947); and articles and reviews in periodicals including *Eastern Churches Review* (of which for a time he was editor). Converting in 1973 to Roman Catholicism, he resided thereafter at St Mary's College, Oscott (seminary of the Archdiocese of Birmingham). His friends included Charles Williams, C. S. Lewis, Norman Nicholson and Kathleen Raine. See Every, 'The Way of Rejections', in *T. S. Eliot: A Symposium*, ed. Richard March and Tambimuttu (1948), 181–8; 'T. S. Eliot 1888–1965', *I.C.F. [Industrial Christian Fellowship] Quarterly*, Apr. 1965, 8–11; 'Recollections of Charles Williams and Eliot', *Mythprint: The Monthly Bulletin of the Mythopoeic Society* (Whittier, Calif.), 2: 4 (Apr. 1975), 2–3; and F. R. Leavis, 'The Logic of Christian Discrimination', in *The Common Pursuit* (1952), 248–54. TSE regarded Every as 'a charming and saintly young man'.

**Geoffrey Faber** (1889–1961), publisher and poet, was educated at Malvern College and Christ Church, Oxford, where he took a double first in classical moderations (1910) and Literae Humaniores (1912). He was called to the bar by the Inner Temple (1921), though he was never to practise law. In 1919 he was elected a prize fellow of All Souls College, Oxford, which he went on to serve in the capacity of Estates Bursar, 1923–51. Before WW1 – in which he served with the London Regiment (Post Office Rifles), seeing action in France and Belgium – he spent eighteen months as assistant to Humphrey Milford, publisher of Oxford University Press. After the war he passed three years working for Strong & Co., brewers (there was a family connection), before going in for publishing on a full-time basis by joining forces with his All Souls colleague Maurice Gwyer and his wife, Lady Alsina Gwyer, who were trying to run a specialised imprint called the Scientific Press that Lady Gwyer had inherited from her father, Sir Henry Burdett: its weekly journal, the *Nursing Mirror*, was their most successful production. Following protractedly difficult negotiations, in 1925 Faber became chair of their restructured general publishing house, which was provisionally styled Faber & Gwyer. After being introduced by Charles Whibley to T. S. Eliot, Faber was so impressed by the personality and aptitude of the 37-year-old American that he chose both to take on the running of the *Criterion* and to appoint Eliot to the board of his company (Eliot's *Poems 1909–1925* was one of the first books to be put out by the new imprint, and one of the first best-sellers), which was relocated from Southampton Row to 24 Russell Square. By 1929 both the Gwyers and the *Nursing Mirror* were disposed of to advantage, and the firm took final shape as Faber & Faber, with Richard de la Mare and two additional Americans, Frank Morley and Morley Kennerley, joining the board. Faber chaired the Publishers' Association, 1939–41 – campaigning successfully for the repeal of a wartime tax on books – and helping to set up the National Book League. He was knighted in 1954, and gave up the chairmanship of Faber & Faber in 1960. His publications as poet include *The Buried Stream* (1941), and his works of non-fiction were *Oxford Apostles* (1933), *Jowett* (1957), and an edition of the works of John Gay (1926). In 1920 he married Enid Richards, with whom he had two sons and a daughter.

**Henri Fluchère** (1898–1987), translator and critic, taught until 1941 at the Lycée Thiers, Marseilles, then as lecturer in English at the University of Aix-Marseille; and during WW2 he played a heroic part in the Resistance. From 1946 he was director of the newly founded Maison Française in Oxford – a role in which he enjoyed great success – and he returned to his home university as professor in 1963. Works include *Shakespeare and the Elizabethans* (1957) and *Laurence Sterne: From Tristram to Yorick* (1965). He wrote a review of *MiC* – 'Lettres Étrangères, *Nouvelle Revue Française* 47 (1936), 556–8 – and produced a fine translation of the play. In addition, he translated works by AH, DHL, Henry Miller and T. F. Powys; and he made versions of *The Tempest* and *Macbeth*, and of Peele's *The Old Wives' Tale*. To Valerie Eliot, 19 Dec. 1978: 'You'll never know what T. S. E. meant to me.'

**Donald Gallup** (1913–2000) was for thirty-three years curator of the Yale Collection of American Literature (Beinecke Library), and edited works on literary figures including TSE (1952, 1963), EP (1969), Gertrude Stein, Thorton Wilder and Eugene O'Neill. See his memoirs: *Pigeons on the Granite: Memories of a Yale Librarian* (1988) and *What Mad Pursuits!: More Memories of a Yale Librarian* (1998). TSE advised the Guggenheim Foundation: 'I have known Dr Donald C. Gallup for a number of years and both from personal friendship and from knowledge of his work am prepared to recommend him most warmly ... [H]is bibliography of my own work deserves the highest praise. It is most desirable that a biography [*sc.* bibliography] should at this stage be made of the work of Ezra Pound. It is a most difficult undertaking, but I do not know anyone so well qualified as Dr Gallup to carry it out with success.'

Stuart Gilbert (1883–1969), literary scholar and translator, was educated at Hertford College, Oxford (first class in Classics), and worked in the Indian Civil Service; and then, following military service, as a judge on the Court of Assizes in Burma. It was only after his retirement in 1925 that he undertook work on Joyce, having admired *Ulysses* while in Burma. After befriending JJ and others in Paris (including Sylvia Beach), he wrote *James Joyce's 'Ulysses': A Study* (F&F, 1930). Beach described him as 'this delightfully humorous, witty, paradoxical, rather cynical, extremely kind Englishman' (*Shakespeare and Company*, 1960). He helped JJ with the French translation of *Ulysses;* and in 1957 edited *Letters of James Joyce* (with advice from TSE). In addition, he translated works by Antoine de Saint-Exupéry, Paul Valéry, André Malraux, Jean Cocteau, Albert Camus, Jean-Paul Sartre and Georges Simenon.

Maurice Haigh-Wood (1896–1980): TSE's brother-in-law. He was eight years younger than his sister Vivien, and after attending Ovingdean prep school and Malvern School, trained at Sandhurst Military Academy before receiving his commission on 11 May 1915 as a second lieutenant in the 2nd Battalion, the Manchester Regiment. He served in the infantry throughout the war, and on regular visits home gave TSE his closest contact with the nightmare of the trenches. After the war, he found it difficult to get himself established, but became a stockbroker, and he remained friends with, and respectful towards, TSE even after his separation from Vivien in 1933. In September 1968 he told Robert Sencourt – as he related to Valerie Eliot (2 Sept. 1968) – 'I had the greatest admiration & love for Tom whom I regarded as my elder brother for fifty years, & I would never think of acting against his wishes.' In 1930 he married a 25-year-old American, Ahmé Hoagland, and they had two children.

Emily Hale (1891–1969) came from a similar Bostonian milieu to the Eliot family. Her father was an architect turned Unitarian preacher who taught at Harvard Divinity School, and her uncle was music critic for the *Boston Herald*. Eliot met Emily at the home of his cousin Eleanor Hinkley in 1912, and in an unpublished memoir wrote that he fell in love with her before leaving for Europe in 1914. However, after his marriage in 1915, he did not see her again for many years. Although she did not go to college, a fact which handicapped her career, Emily was a passionate theatre-goer, amateur actor and director, and was to forge a career as a drama teacher. In 1921 she took a post as administrator and drama tutor at Milwaukee-Downer College, a private women's school, and later taught at Scripps College, Smith College, Concord Academy and Abbott Academy. During the 1930s and 1940s, Eliot once again took up his relationship with her, and they saw a lot of one another both in England, where they visited Burnt Norton together in 1934–5, and during his trips to the USA. She joked to her students at Scripps, 'Emily Hale speaks only to Eliot, and Eliot speaks only to God.' However, following Vivien's death in 1947, Emily was dismayed that Eliot did not wish to marry her, and there was a cooling of their friendship. According to Emily (in a letter to a friend, 7 August 1947), Eliot had given her to understand that his love was 'not in the way usual to men less gifted i.e. with complete love through a married relationship': she thought this an 'abnormal reaction'. However, Tomlin recounted – this is a report of what he said that Theresa Eliot told him – HWE had been categorical: 'Tom has made one mistake, and if he marries Emily he will make another.' Towards the end of his life Eliot ordered her letters to him to be destroyed, while she deposited his letters to her at Princeton University, where they are sealed until 2020. See Lyndall Gordon, *T. S. Eliot: An Imperfect Life* (1998); Robert Crawford, *Young Eliot: From St Louis to 'The Waste Land'* (2015).

**A. Desmond Hawkins** (1908–99), novelist, critic, broadcaster, worked in the 1930s as literary editor of the *New English Weekly*, then of the quarterly *Purpose* (where TSE persuaded the owner-editor to allow Hawkins a free hand), and as fiction reviewer for the *Criterion*. In 1946 he became Features Producer, BBC West Region, and Head of Programmes in 1955. He founded the BBC Natural History Unit in 1959. His writings include *The BBC Naturalist* (1957), *Hardy the Novelist* (1965), and *When I Was* (memoir, 1989). TSE to the British Council, 31 May 1940: 'I am happy to regard him as a personal friend, as well as a valued contributor in the past on the *Criterion* . . . He writes admirably both imaginative and critical prose, has keen sensibility and distinguished intelligence, a good knowledge and exceptional critical appreciation of English literature. I believe also that his combination of intellectual gifts, character and personal charm make him very well qualified to fill with success a post in a foreign country.'

**John Hayward** (1905–1965), editor, critic and anthologist, read modern languages at King's College, Cambridge. Despite the early onset of muscular dystrophy, he became a prolific and eminent critic and editor, bringing out in quick succession editions of the works of Rochester, Saint-Évremond, Jonathan Swift, Robert Herrick and Samuel Johnson. Other publications included *Complete Poems and Selected Prose of John Donne* (1929), *Donne* (1950), *T. S. Eliot: Selected Prose* (1953), and *The Penguin Book of English Verse* (1958). Celebrated as the learned and acerbic editor of *The Book Collector*, he was made a chevalier of the Légion d'honneur in 1952; CBE in 1953. Writers including Graham Greene and Stevie Smith valued his editorial counsel. Hayward advised TSE on essays, poems and plays including *The Cocktail Party* and *The Confidential Clerk*, and most helpfully of all on *Four Quartets*. See further Helen Gardner, *The Composition of 'Four Quartets'* (1978); John Smart, *Tarantula's Web: John Hayward, T. S. Eliot and Their Circle* (2013).

**Arthur Gabriel Hebert** (1886–1963), liturgist, New Testament scholar, ecumenist, of the Society of the Sacred Mission, Kelham Theological College, Nottinghamshire. Educated at Harrow School and New College, Oxford (where he gained a first in Greats in 1908, and a first in Theology in 1909), he was ordained priest in 1912. After a year as tutor at Kelham Theological College (where he taught the Gospels, the Epistle to the Hebrews, and Aquinas), he began his novitiate with the SSM in 1915, making his profession in 1921. He taught at Kelham from 1926 to 1952. Ideologically committed to the liturgical reform movement – which worked to bring the laity within the rites of the Church – he wrote *Liturgy and Society* (F&F, 1935) and edited *The Parish Communion* (1937). See Christopher Irvine, *Worship, Church and Society: An exposition of the work of Arthur Gabriel Hebert to mark the Centenary of the Society of the Sacred Mission (Kelham), of which he was a member* (1993).

See too Alistair Mason, *History of the Society of the Sacred Mission* (Norwich, 1993): '[Fr Hebert's] systematic theology tended towards Thomism . . . In these days, [Hebert], and very largely Kelham . . . were clear-cut anti-liberal, quite ready to confront apparent heresy . . . He was a great friend of T. S. Eliot, who loved coming to Kelham, where he could speak freely without fear of being quoted. His *Idea of a Christian Society* originated in lectures at Kelham, and was discussed with Gabriel.'

**Mary Hutchinson**, née Barnes (1889–1977), a half-cousin of Lytton Strachey, married St John ('Jack') Hutchinson (eminent criminal lawyer, connoisseur and collector) in 1910. A prominent Bloomsbury hostess, she was for several years the acknowledged mistress of the art critic Clive Bell, and became a close friend of TSE and VHE. Eliot published one of her stories ('War') in the *Egoist*, and she later brought out a book of sketches, *Fugitive Pieces* (Hogarth Press, 1927). She wrote a brief unpublished memoir of TSE (Harry Ransom Humanities Research Center). See James Strachey Barnes, 'My Sister Mary', chapter 14, in *Half a Life* (1933), 87–93; David Bradshaw, '"Those Extraordinary Parakeets": Clive Bell and Mary Hutchinson', *The Charleston Magazine*: 16 (Autumn/Winter 1997), 5–12; 17 (Spring/Summer 1998), 5–11; and Nancy Hargrove, 'The Remarkable Relationship of T. S. Eliot and Mary Hutchinson', *Yeats Eliot Review* 28: 3–4 (Fall/Winter 2011), 3–15.

**Aldous Huxley** (1894–1963), novelist, poet and essayist, whose novels *Crome Yellow* (1921) and *Antic Hay* (1923) were successful satires of post-war English culture. While teaching at Eton, Aldous told his brother Julian in Dec. 1916 that he 'ought to read' Eliot's 'things', which are 'all the more remarkable when one knows the man, ordinarily just an Europeanized American, overwhelmingly cultured, talking about French literature in the most uninspired fashion imaginable'. He went on to become, not only a popular novelist, but, as author of *Brave New World* and *The Doors of Perception*, an influential intellectual. According to Mary Trevelyan's memoir, TSE remarked of Huxley (in 1950): 'No, he isn't a great writer – his characters are not real, not alive. Sometimes characters are created by an author, though they may come basically from someone known to him – like Mrs Gamp – a real person, but never alive. A second-rate author's characters are usually smaller than himself, whereas a greater writer sometimes creates characters which become greater than himself. Aldous is not interested in people except in so far as they can be used by him.' See further Nicholas Murray, *Aldous Huxley: An English Intellectual* (2002); Huxley, *Selected Letters*, ed. James Sexton (2007).

**N. M. Iovetz-Tereshchenko** (1895–1954), BLitt (Oxon), PhD (London): Tutor in Psychology and Philosophy under the University of London Tutorial Classes Committee and the Workers' Educational Association.

See Robert Crawford, 'T. S. Eliot, A. D. Lindsay and N. M. Tereshchenko', *Balliol College Annual Record* 1983: 'In 1920 Nicholas Mikhailovich Iovetz-Tereshchenko left Russia for Yugoslavia where he became for six years a secondary schoolmaster in schools for Russian refugees. In 1926 he came to Oxford, and two years later graduated B. Litt. in Russian Literature from St Catherine's Society. By 1929 he was lecturing in Oxford in Slavonic subjects. His first and only book, *Friendship-Love in Adolescence* [London, 1936] . . . was the outcome of Iovetz-Tereshchenko's doctoral dissertation in psychology written at London University where he was by that time a tutor in psychology and philosophy under the auspices of the University of London Tutorial Classes Committee, the Workers Educational Association, and the University of Oxford Extension Lectures Committee. One of those thanked in the book's preface for reading the original typescript is T. S. Eliot.

'That Eliot was interested in such a book should not be surprising. As a graduate student of philosophy at Harvard he had taken a laboratory course in experimental psychology, and had been interested in the work of Janet and Ribot. In *Dante*, published in 1929 . . . Eliot discusses in the context of Dante and Beatrice what was to be the subject of the Russian's book:

> In the first place, the type of sexual experience which Dante describes as occurring to him at the age of nine years is by no means impossible or unique. My only doubt (in which I find myself confirmed by a distinguished psychologist) is whether it could have taken place so late in life as the age of nine years. The psychologist agreed with me that it is more likely to occur at about five or six years of age. (*Selected Essays*, 3rd enlarged edn [1951], 273)

'Eliot and Iovetz-Tereshchenko had other interests in common in addition to that dealt with in this passage. Both men were Christians . . . And both, of course, were interested in literature. In 1941 Iovetz-Tereshchenko was lecturing in Oxford on "Some Psychological Theories concerning the Aesthetic Experience, Love, and the Religious Experience".'

**James Joyce** (1882–1941), expatriate Irish novelist, playwright and poet. Having lived in Zurich and Trieste, he moved in 1920 to Paris, where he became a focus for expatriate writers including Pound and Stein. Joyce's *A Portrait of the Artist* was serialised in the *Egoist*, and *Ulysses* in the *Little Review* up to 1920. When *Ulysses* first appeared in book form in 1922, the same year as *The Waste Land*, TSE hailed it as 'the most important expression which the present age has found' – 'a book to which we are all indebted, and from which none of us can escape' ('*Ulysses*, Order and Myth', *Dial* 75, Nov. 1923). TSE said of Joyce, in an interview: 'it has been questioned whether Joyce was influenced by *The Waste Land* or whether he had read my poem or not. The only evidence that James Joyce ever read anything of mine was that one day in Paris he told me he had been (with his children perhaps) to the Jardin des Plantes and had paid his respects to my friend the hippopotamus, one may think that he probably read my poem about the hippopotame after Gautier.' TSE published in the *Criterion* a number of pieces by and about Joyce, and at F&F he was responsible for promoting *Finnegans Wake* (1939). See *The Letters of James Joyce*, ed. Stuart Gilbert and Richard Ellmann (3 vols, 1957, 1966); Richard Ellmann, *James Joyce* (2nd edn, 1982); Kevin Birmingham, *The Most Dangerous Book: The Battle for James Joyce's 'Ulysses'* (2014).

**John Maynard Keynes** (1883–1946), influential economist and theorist of money (expert on macroeconomics); pamphleteer; patron of the arts (begetter and financier of the Arts Theatre, Cambridge); government adviser and negotiator; editor of the *Economic Journal*, 1912–45; columnist for the *Nation and Athenaeum* (of which he was chairman from 1923); intimate of the Bloomsbury circle; trustee of the National Gallery; author of *The Economic Consequences of the Peace* (1919), *A Treatise on Money* (2 vols, 1930), and *The General Theory of Employment, Interest and Money* (1936). He married in 1925 the ballet dancer Lydia Lopokova (1892–1981). See TSE, 'John Maynard Keynes', *New English Weekly*, 16 May 1946, 47–8: 'After the experience of Versailles, and the publication of *The Economic Consequences of the Peace* (the only one of his books which I have ever read: I was at that time occupied, in a humble capacity, with the application of some of the minor financial clauses of that treaty) one rather expected him to retire from public life . . . He foresaw the consequences of bad economics corrupted further by political passion and expediency, and the consequences were realised. Disdainful aloofness would have been the natural resort . . . and certainly, he had at his command a cynical wit which sometimes expressed itself in conversation, when public affairs or economic doctrines were touched upon in private company.'

**James Laughlin** IV (1914–97), scion of a wealthy steel family; poet; publisher of modernist and experimental writers; launched New Directions Publishing Company in 1936 while in his junior year at Harvard (bringing out the first of the annual anthologies *New Directions in Prose and Poetry*, 1936–91). His authors included EP, William Carlos Williams, Elizabeth Bishop, Henry Miller, MM, Wallace Stevens, E. E. Cummings, Lawrence Ferlinghetti, Thomas Merton and Delmore Schwartz. See Ian S. MacNiven, *'Literchoor is my beat': A Life of James Laughlin, publisher of New Directions* (2014).

**Alexis Saint-Léger Léger** (1887–1975) – pen name **Saint-John Perse** – poet and diplomat. Scion of a Bourgignon family, he passed his early years on an island near Guadeloupe in the West Indies, but the family returned to

France in 1899. After studying law at the University of Bordeaux, he joined the Foreign Office as an attaché and worked for six years as Secretary at the French Legation in Peking: his poem *Anabase* is inspired by aspects of his career in China, which included a journey to Outer Mongolia. In 1921, at a conference in Washington, DC, he was recruited by Aristide Briand, Prime Minister of France, as his *chef de cabinet*; and after Briand's death in 1932 he retained high office, serving as *sécretaire générale* of the Foreign Office, 1933–40. Dishonoured by the Vichy government (he was a Grand Officier of the Legion of Honour), he spent the years of WW2 in the USA (serving for a time as a 'consultant' to the Library of Congress); and he went back to France in 1957 (he had closed his diplomatic career in 1950, with the title of *Ambassadeur de France*). His works include *Éloges* (published with help from André Gide, 1911), *Anabase* (1924; trans. TSE as *Anabasis*, 1930); *Exil* (1942), *Pluies* (1943), *Vents* (1946), *Amers* (1957), and *Oiseaux* (1962). In 1924 he published in *Commerce* a translation of the opening section of 'The Hollow Men'. Nobel Laureate in Literature, 1960.

In a copy of *Anabase* (Paris: Librairie Gallimard/ Éditions de La Nouvelle Revue Française, 1925), St-John Perse wrote: '*À T. S. Eliot / dont j'aime et j'admire l'oeuvre / fraternellement / St. J. Perse.*' (TSE Library)

In 1960 TSE recommended St-John Perse for the Nobel Prize. When asked by Uno Willers, secretary of the Svenska Akadamiens Nobel-kommitté, to 'write down a more detailed motivation for your suggestion', TSE responded, 23 Mar. 1960: 'My interest in the work of St-John Perse began many years ago when I translated his *Anabase* into English. This task gave me an intimacy with his style and idiom which I could not have acquired in any other way. It seemed to me then, and it seems to me still, that he had done something highly original – and in a language, the French language, in which such originality is not easily attained. He had invented a form which was different from "free verse" as practiced in France to-day, and different from the "prose-poem" in which some French writers, anxious to escape the limitations of the conventional metrics of their language, take refuge.

'He is the only French poet among my contemporaries, with the solitary exception of [Jules] Supervielle, whose work has continued to interest me. With some of my contemporaries writing in other languages I feel a certain affinity – with [Eugenio] Montale, for example, and with [Giorgios] Seferis so far as I can judge from translations – with Perse, I have felt rather an influence which is visible in some of my poems written after I had translated *Anabase*.'

See also Richard Abel, 'The Influence of St.-John Perse on T. S. Eliot', *Contemporary Literature*, XIV: 2 (Spring 1973), 213–39.

**Louis MacNeice** (1907–63), brought up in Carrickfergus near Belfast, was educated at Marlborough School and Oxford University. In the 1930s he taught Classics at Birmingham University and Bedford College, London; and for twenty years from 1940 he worked for the BBC as writer and producer of radio features and plays. Publications include *Autumn Journal* (1939), *The Burning Perch* (1963); and – in collaboration with WHA – *Letters from Iceland* (1937). TSE was to write of him on 30 May 1941, to the General Establishment Officer of the BBC: 'Mr MacNeice is extremely well-known both as one of the leading poets of his generation and as a prose writer . . . He is, incidentally, a classical scholar of some distinction, and may be regarded as belonging to that rather uncommon type, the well-educated man. He has also a very distinct social charm and likeability.'

TSE in *The Times*, 5 Sept. 1963: 'He had the Irishman's unfailing ear for the music of verse, and he never published a line that is not good reading. I am very proud of having published the first volume he had to offer after coming down from the university. [*Blind Fireworks* (1929), his first book, was published by Victor Gollancz while MacNeice was still an undergraduate.]

'As for the radio plays, no other poet, with the exception of the author of *Under Milk Wood*, has written works as haunting as MacNeice.'

**Philip Mairet** (1886–1975) – who had a Swiss father and English mother – was educated at Hornsey School of Art and worked under the architect C. R. Ashby, 1906–9, before becoming a designer and artificer in stained and painted glass windows for churches. After war service in the British Red Cross and the French Red Cross in France, and having served a term of imprisonment as a conscientious objector, he was a member of the Shakespeare Company at the Old Vic Theatre, London. He then became a journalist, 1926–31, and worked for the formation of the Adler Society (International Society for Individual Psychology) in London: he published *The ABC of Adlerian Psychology* (1926); and in 1932 joined the staff of the *New English Weekly* under its founder A. R. Orage. On Orage's death, Mairet became editor, 1934–49. TSE contributed to *NEW*, and was a member of the editorial board. Mairet convened the group of psychiatrists who wrote the symposium *Christianity and Psychiatry*, and he contributed to the publication under the auspices of the Christian

Frontier Council to the Student Movement Press. He was the dedicatee of TSE's *Notes towards the Definition of Culture* (1948). See Mairet, *A. R. Orage: A Memoir* (1936); Mairet, *Autobiographical and Other Papers*, ed. C. H. Sisson (1981).

**Henry Miller** (1901–1980): expatriate American author (supported for many years by his lover, the diarist Anaïs Nin) of autobiographical novels including *Tropic of Cancer* (1934), *Black Spring* (1936), *Tropic of Capricorn* (1939, and the *Rosy Crucifixion* trilogy (1949–59). Published by the Obelisk Press, Paris, his works were for many years banned in the UK and the USA. Robert Ferguson, *Henry Miller: A Life* (1991), 240, 251: 'He had no interest in people like Pound and Huxley and Eliot whose writing bored him. Pound was "full of shit – the Cantos are the worst crap I ever read. Everything borrowed or stolen. Dry, empty, artificial." Eliot's poetry is described in similar terms in *Tropic of Cancer* – "sterile, hybrid, dry." . . . [O]ther than commercially he did not prize the enthusiasm of Eliot, Pound, Orwell, Connolly *et al.*'

**Paul Elmer More** (1864–1937), critic, scholar, philosopher, grew up in St Louis, Missouri, and attended Washington University before going on to Harvard; at one time he taught French to TSE's brother Henry. Initially a humanist, by the 1930s he had assumed an Anglo-Catholic position not unlike that of TSE (who appreciated the parallels between their spiritual development). See also 'An Anglican Platonist: the Conversion of Paul Elmer More', *TLS*, 30 Oct. 1937, 792. At the outset of his career, More taught classics at Harvard and Bryn Mawr; thereafter he became a journalist, serving as literary editor of the *Independent*, 1901–3, and the *New York Evening Post*, 1903–9, and as editor of *The Nation*, 1909–14, before finally turning to freelance writing and teaching. TSE keenly admired More's many works, in particular *Shelburne Essays* (11 vols, 1904–21), *The Greek Tradition* (5 vols, 1924–31), and *The Demon of the Absolute* (1928); and he took trouble in the 1930s to try to secure a publisher for *Pages from an Oxford Diary* (1937), which More stipulated he would only publish in anonymity.

See further Arthur Hazard Dakin, *Paul Elmer More* (1960) – of which TSE wrote on 29 Mar. 1960: 'What the author says about Paul More and myself seems to me very accurate . . . [W]e did see very nearly eye to eye in theological matters' – and David Huisman, '"A Long Journey Afoot": The Pilgrimages toward Orthodoxy of T. S. Eliot and Paul Elmer More', in *T. S. Eliot and Christian Tradition*, ed. Benjamin G. Lockerd (2014), 251–64.

Frank Vigor Morley (1899–1980), son of a distinguished mathematician – his brothers were the writer Christopher, and Felix (editor of the *Washington Post*) – was brought up in the USA before travelling as a Rhodes Scholar to New College, Oxford, where he earned a doctorate in mathematics. After working for a while at the *Times Literary Supplement*, he became London Manager of the Century Company (Publishers) of New York. In 1929 he became a founding director of Faber & Faber, where he would be a close friend of TSE: for some time they shared an office at Russell Square. Morley would remark that TSE's 'great skill' as a publisher was that he 'had an unerring gift for spotting talent, but he would never fight for people. I used to watch, and know him so well that if he quietly suggested publishing the poetry of Marianne Moore, whom nobody knew, I would take up the cudgels and be the loud hailer' ('The time when Eliot lit the fuse', *Sunday Times*, 8 June 1980).

In 1933 when TSE separated from his wife Vivien, Morley arranged convivial temporary accommodation for him at his farmhouse at Pike's Farm, Lingfield, Surrey. In 1939 Morley moved to the USA, where he became Vice-President of Harcourt Brace and Co. (and during the war he served on the National War Labor Board in Washington, DC). In 1947 he returned with his family to England to take up the post of Director at Eyre & Spottiswoode. A large, learned, ebullient figure, he earned the sobriquet 'Whale' – though not merely on account of corpulence: in his youth he had spent time abroad a whaling ship (he was revolted by the slaughter), and subsequently wrote (with J. S. Hodgson) *Whaling North and South* (1927). His other writings include *Inversive Geometry* (1933), *My One Contribution to Chess* (1947), *The Great North Road* (1961), *The Long Road West: A Journey in History* (1971), and *Literary Britain* (1980); and contributions in verse (along with TSE, GCF and JDH) to *Noctes Binanianae* (privately printed, 1939).

Morley Kennerley told *The Times* (25 Oct. 1980) that 'one of [Morley's] hobbies was to work out complicated problems for his friends, and for those baffled there were amazing practical jokes. Convivial lunches with interesting people were a joy to him ... He found jobs for many and squeezed me into Fabers where he generously put up with my sharing a corner of his room for some years. I was present all day during his interviews, dictation, visitors and often lunch. How he put up with all this I do not know. His correspondence with Ezra Pound was quite something, and I think he out-Pounded Pound.'

In 1939, when Morley was on the point of returning to the USA, GCF wrote of him to the editor of *The Times*: 'Morley is a quite outstanding person . . . [His] first obvious quality is that he is a born "mixer", with an extraordinary range of friends in different walks of life. He is a very good talker, though rather fond – like many Americans – of spinning the yarn out. But he never spins without a purpose. As a negotiator he is in a class by himself. His judgment of men and situations is first rate. He knows the personnel of both the English and American publishing and journalistic worlds.'

On 2 July 1978 Morley told Helen Gardner, of TSE: 'I loved him, as I think you know, near to the side of idolatry.'

**Lady Ottoline Morrell** (1873–1938): daughter of Lieutenant-General Arthur Bentinck and half-sister to the Duke of Portland. In 1902 she married Philip Morrell (1870–1941), Liberal MP for South Oxfordshire 1902–18. A patron of the arts, she entertained a notable literary and artistic circle, first at 44 Bedford Square, then at Garsington Manor, nr. Oxford, where she moved in 1915. She was a lover of Bertrand Russell, who introduced her to TSE, and her numerous other friends included Lytton Strachey, DHL, AH, Siegfried Sassoon, and the Woolfs. Her memoirs (ed. Robert Gathorne-Hardy) appeared as *Ottoline* (1963) and *Ottoline at Garsington* (1974). See Miranda Seymour, *Life on the Grand Scale: Lady Ottoline Morrell* (1992, 1998).

**Edwin Muir** (1887–1959): Scottish poet, novelist, critic; translator (with his wife Willa) of Franz Kafka. TSE to LW, 22 Aug. 1946: 'I am anxious to do anything I can for Muir because I think highly of his best poetry and I think he has not had enough recognition.' To Eleanor Hinkley, 25 Dec. 1955: 'Edwin is a sweet creature . . . [He] is a good poet, and I believe, what is even rarer, a literary man of complete integrity. He is not really Scottish, but Orcadian – in other words, pure Scandinavian.' In a tribute: 'Muir's literary criticism had always seemed to me of the best of our time: after I came to know him, I realised that it owed its excellence not only to his power of intellect and acuteness of sensibility, but to those moral qualities which make us remember him, as you say justly, as "in some ways almost a saintly man". It was more recently that I came to regard his poetry as ranking with the best poetry of our time. As a poet he began late; as a poet he was recognised late; but some of his finest work – perhaps his very finest work – was written when he was already over sixty . . . For this late development we are reminded of the later poetry of Yeats; and Muir had to struggle with bad health also: but in the one case as in the other (and Muir is by no means unworthy to be mentioned together with Yeats) we recognise a triumph of the human spirit' (*The Times*, 7 Jan. 1959).

See too TSE, 'Edwin Muir: 1887–1959: An Appreciation', *Listener*, 28 May 1964, 872. Muir's works include *An Autobiography* (1954); *Selected Poems of Edwin Muir*: preface by TSE (1966); *Selected Letters of Edwin Muir*, ed. P. H. Butter (1974).

**John Middleton Murry** (1889–1957): English writer, critic and editor, founded the magazine *Rhythm*, 1911–13, and worked as a reviewer for the *Westminster Gazette*, 1912–14, and the *Times Literary Supplement*, 1914–18, before becoming editor from 1919 to 1921 of the *Athenaeum*, which he turned into a lively cultural forum – in a letter of 2 July 1919, TSE called it 'the best literary weekly in the Anglo-Saxon world'. In his 'London Letter', *Dial* 72 (May 1921), TSE considered Murry 'genuinely studious to maintain a serious criticism', but he disagreed with his 'particular tastes, as well as his general statements'. After the demise of the *Athenaeum*, Murry went on to edit the *Adelphi*, 1923–48. In 1918, he married Katherine Mansfield (died 1923). He was a friend and biographer of DHL; and as an editor he provided a platform for writers as various as George Santayana, Paul Valéry, DHL, AH, VW, and TSE. His first notable critical work was *Dostoevsky* (1916); his most influential study, *The Problem of Style* (1922). Though as a Romanticist he was an intellectual opponent of the avowedly 'Classicist' Eliot, Murry offered Eliot in 1919 the post of assistant editor on the *Athenaeum* (which Eliot had to decline); in addition, he recommended him to be Clark Lecturer at Cambridge in 1926, and was a steadfast friend to both TSE and his wife Vivien. Eliot wrote in a reference on 9 Sept. 1945 that Murry was 'one of the most distinguished men of letters of this time, and testimony from a contemporary seems superfluous. Several volumes of literary essays of the highest quality are evidence of his eminence as a critic; and even if one took no account of his original contribution, his conduct of the *Athenaeum*, which he edited from 1919 until its absorption into the *Nation*, should be enough to entitle him to the gratitude of his contemporaries and juniors. His direction of the *Adelphi* should also be recognised. Since he has devoted his attention chiefly to social and religious problems, he has written a number of books which no one who is concerned with the same problems, whether in agreement with him or not, can afford to neglect. I am quite sure that no future student of these matters who wishes to understand this age will be able to ignore them, and that no future student of the literary spirit of this age will be able to ignore Mr Murry's criticism.' To Murry's widow, 29 May 1957: 'The friendship between John and myself was of a singular quality, such that it was rather different from any other of my friendships. We did not often meet. We disagreed throughout many years on one point after another. But on the other hand, a very warm affection existed between us in spite of differences of view and infrequency of meetings. This affection was not merely, on my part, a feeling of gratitude for the opportunities he had given me early in my career during his editorship of the *Athenaeum*, but was something solid and permanent. He was one of the strangest and most remarkable men I have known, and no less strange and remarkable was the tie of affection between us.' See F. A. Lea, *The Life of John Middleton Murry* (1959); David Goldie, *A Critical Difference: T. S. Eliot and John Middleton Murry in English Literary Criticism, 1919–1928* (1998).

**Brigid O'Donovan** was TSE's secretary from Jan. 1935 to Dec. 1936.

TSE wrote this reference – addressed to the Clerk of the County Council, Hertford – on 8 Mar. 1940: 'Miss O'Donovan was my secretary here for several years . . . and also assisted me in editing the *Criterion*, a quarterly review. In this capacity she had to interview many visitors, including a good number of people whom I did not wish to see, and always, so far as I know, handled them with both firmness and tact. She made a very good impression upon those who came in contact with her, as several people mentioned to me privately. As she left me, not in order to look for a more highly paid job, but to find one which would give more scope to her energies and initiative, I should certainly suppose that her first motive in applying for any post was that the nature of the work attracted her, though I know that she has to earn her own living . . . I should put her energy decidedly high.

'Miss O'Donovan is decidedly a lady, and I believe her to have a high character, an alert social conscience and even a religious temperament. My relations with her were always most satisfactory and I have pleasure in recommending her for any post that she wishes to obtain.'

See O'Donovan's memoir 'The Love Song of T. S. Eliot', *Confrontation* (Long Island University, NY), Fall/Winter 1975, 3–8 – reported in the *TLS*, 23 Jan. 1976: 'The secretary [. . .] is daughter of Gerald O'Donovan who was Rose Macaulay's beloved friend; Rose introduced Brigid – her god-daughter – to Eliot at Faber and Faber in October 1934, and he gave her the job (he told Rose) on the strength of her big black hat . . .

'The secretaries were responsible for letters rejecting manuscripts from unknown writers; the only rule was that they had to be three paragraphs long. Eliot – at this time working on *Murder in the Cathedral* – was also writing constantly to his friends, and dictated to Miss O'Donovan "quite personal letters" (though of course, as she says, she does not know what letters she did *not* type). Another duty was to cope with Mrs (Vivienne) Eliot, from whom he was separated, and who would turn up at the office to see him without warning:

> I would go down and explain that it was not possible for Mrs Eliot to see her husband, and that he was well. Mrs Eliot, I now understand, suffered from schizophrenia, but at the time I had no idea what was the matter. She was a slight, pathetic, worried figure, badly dressed and very unhappy, her hands screwing up her handkerchief as she wept.
>
> Meanwhile Eliot slipped out of the building, and on return would be on edge for the rest of the day.

'Miss O'Donovan's own relationship with him was always strained, for "from the start I fell in love with him". He kept his distance. But she was made of sterner stuff than Prufrock, and after nearly two years of agonized love she took the opportunity of his absence in America to hand in her notice.'

O'Donovan added in her memoir (p. 6): '[TSE] usually had some amusing and sarcastic comment to make about every incident or individual who came our way, not excluding members of the firm. Nevertheless, he was a warmhearted and affectionate man, and everyone was very fond of him ... When it came to teasing [Geoffrey] Faber it was hard to say whether [Frank] Morley or TSE led the field, but they both gave it considerable thought and preparation.' (Apropos TSE's remark about her 'religious temperament': 'As a let-out from being in love, I took to religion. In a highly embarrassing interview TSE advised me to see Evelyn Underwood, and gave me an introduction to her. For three years I went to her office.')

See too Anne Ridler, 'Confidential Clerk' (letter), *TLS*, 6 Feb. 1976.

**Joseph ('Joe') Oldham** (1874–1969): indefatigable missionary, adviser and organiser for national and international councils and mission boards. Travelling all over the world to confer with educators and colonial administrators, he worked closely with governments and public policy makers. From 1912 to 1927 he was editor of the *International Review of Missions*; and in 1921 became secretary of a new International Missionary Council (IMC). He was also Administrative Director of the International Institute of African Languages and Cultures, 1931–8. From 1934 he was

Chair of the Research Committee for the Universal Christian Council for Life and Work, ably preparing the ground for the establishment in 1948 of the World Council of Churches. In 1939 he launched the fortnightly *Christian News Letter,* to which TSE became a faithful contributor, and he set up too the intellectual discussion group called 'The Moot': a think-tank to which TSE contributed. Writings include *The New Christian Adventure* (1929), *White and Black in Africa* (1930), *Real Life is Meeting* (1941), *New Hope for Africa* (1955). Appointed CBE, 1951. See Kathleen Bliss, 'J. H. Oldham, 1874–1969: from "Edinburgh 1910" to the World Council of Churches', in *Mission Legacies,* ed. G. H. Anderson et al. (1994); K. Clements, *Faith on the Frontier: The Life of J. H. Oldham* (1999); *The Moot Papers: Faith, Freedom and Society, 1938–1947,* ed. K. Clements (2010).

**Ezra Pound** (1885–1972), American poet and critic, was one of the prime impresarios of the modernist movement in London and Paris, and played a major part in launching Eliot as poet and critic – as well as Joyce, Lewis, and many others. TSE called on him at 5 Holland Place Chambers, Kensington, on 22 Sept. 1914, with an introduction from Conrad Aiken. On 30 Sept. 1914, Pound hailed 'Prufrock' as 'the best poem I have yet had or seen from an American'; and on 3 October called Eliot 'the last intelligent man I've found – a young American . . . worth watching – mind "not primitive"' (*Selected Letters of Ezra Pound,* 40–1). Pound was instrumental in arranging for 'Prufrock' to be published in *Poetry* in 1915, and helped to shape *The Waste Land* (1922), which Eliot dedicated to him as 'il miglior fabbro'. The poets remained in loyal correspondence for the rest of their lives. Having initially dismissed Pound's poetry (to CA, 30 Sept. 1914) as 'well-meaning but touchingly incompetent', Eliot went on to champion his work, writing to Gilbert Seldes (27 Dec. 1922): 'I sincerely consider Ezra Pound the most important living poet in the English language.' He wrote an early critical study, *Ezra Pound: His Metric and Poetry* (1917), and went on, as editor of the *Criterion* and publisher at Faber & Faber, to bring out most of Pound's work in the UK, including *Selected Shorter Poems, The Cantos* and *Selected Literary Essays.* After his move to Italy in the 1920s, Pound became increasingly sceptical about the direction of TSE's convictions, but they continued to correspond. TSE told James Laughlin, on the occasion of Pound's seventieth birthday: 'I believe that I have in the past made clear enough my personal debt to Ezra Pound during the years 1915–22. I have also expressed in several ways my opinion of his rank as a poet, as a critic, as impresario of other writers, and as pioneer of metric and poetic language. His 70th birthday is not a moment for qualifying one's praise, but merely for recognition of those services to literature for which he will deserve the gratitude of posterity' (3 Nov. 1955). TSE told Eaghor G. Kostetsky on 6 Jan. 1960 that the Cantos 'is unquestionably the most remarkable long contemporary poem in the English language'. After TSE's death, Pound said of him: 'His was the true Dantescan voice – not honoured enough, and deserving more than I ever gave him.' See *The Selected Letters of Ezra Pound 1907–1941*, ed. D. D. Paige (1950); Humphrey Carpenter, *A Serious Character* (1988); A. David Moody, *Ezra Pound: Poet: A Portrait of the Man and his Work*: I *The Young Genius 1885–1920* (2007), II *The Epic Years 1921–1939* (2014), III *The Tragic Years 1939–1972* (2015).

**Mario Praz** (1896–1982), scholar of English life and literature; author of *La Carne, la Morte e Il Diavolo nella Letteratura Romantica* (1930: *The Romantic Agony*, 1933). Educated in Bologna, Rome and Florence, he came to England in 1923 to study for the title of *libero docente*. He was Senior Lecturer in Italian, Liverpool University, 1924–32; Professor of Italian Studies, Victoria University of Manchester, 1932–4; Professor of English Language and Literature at the University of Rome, 1934–66. In 1952 he was conferred by Queen Elizabeth II with the title of Knight Commander of the British Empire (KBE). In 'An Italian Critic on Donne and Crashaw' (*TLS*, 17 Dec. 1925, 878), TSE hailed Praz's *Secentismo e Marinismo in Inghilterra: John Donne–Richard Crashaw* (1925) as 'indispensable for any student of this period'. In 'A Tribute to Mario Praz', 15 Apr. 1964: 'I immediately recognized these essays – and especially his masterly study of Crashaw – as among the best that I had ever read in that field. His knowledge of the poetry of that period in four languages – English, Italian, Spanish and Latin – was encyclopaedic, and, fortified by his own judgment and good taste, makes that book essential reading for any student of the English "metaphysical poets" . . . I tender these few words in testimony to my gratitude and admiration' (*Friendship's Garland: Essays presented to Mario Praz on His Seventieth Birthday*, ed. V. Gabrieli, 1966). See Praz, 'Dante in Inghilterra', *La Cultura*, Jan. 1930, 65–6; 'T. S. Eliot e Dante', *Letteratura* 15 (July 1937), 12–28; 'T. S. Eliot and Dante', *Southern Review* no. 3 (Winter 1937), 525–48; *The Flaming Heart* (1958).

**Herbert Read** (1893–1968): poet and literary critic, and one of the most influential art critics of the century. Son of a tenant farmer, Read spent his first years in rural Yorkshire; at sixteen, he went to work as a bank clerk, then studied law and economics at Leeds University; later, he joined the Civil Service, working first in the Ministry of Labour and then at the Treasury. During his years of service in WW1, he rose to be a captain in a Yorkshire regiment, the Green Howards (his war poems were published in *Naked Warriors*, 1919); and when on leave to receive the Military Cross in 1917, he dined with TSE at the Monico Restaurant in Piccadilly Circus. This launched a life-long friendship which he was to recall in 'T.S.E. – A Memoir', in *T. S. Eliot: The Man and his Work*, ed. Allen Tate (1966). Within the year, he had also become acquainted with the Sitwells, EP, WL, RA and Ford Madox Ford. He co-founded the journal *Art & Letters*, 1917–20, and wrote essays too for A. R. Orage, editor of the *New Age*. In 1922 he was appointed a curator in the department of ceramics and glass at the Victoria and Albert Museum; and in later years worked for the publishers Routledge & Kegan Paul, and as editor of the *Burlington Magazine*, 1933–9. By 1923 he was writing for the *Criterion*: he was to become one of Eliot's leading contributors and a dependable advisor. In 1924 he edited T. E. Hulme's *Speculations*. Later works include *Art Now* (1933); the introduction to the catalogue of the International Surrealist Exhibition held at the New Burlington Galleries, London, 1936; *Art and Society* (1937) and *Education through Art* (1943). In 1947 he founded (with Roland Penrose) the Institute of Contemporary Art; and in 1953 he was knighted. Eliot, he was to recall (perhaps only half in jest), was 'rather like a gloomy priest presiding over my affections and spontaneity'. According to SS, Eliot said 'of the anarchism of his friend Herbert Read, whom he loved and esteemed very highly: "Sometimes when I read Herbert's inflammatory pamphlets I have the impression that I am reading the pronouncements of an old-fashioned nineteenth-century liberal"' (*The Thirties and After* [1978], 251). Joseph Chiari recalled TSE saying of Read: 'Ah, there is old Herbie, again; he can't resist anything new!' See further Read, 'Eliot, The Leader', *Yorkshire Post*, 5 Jan. 1965; James King, *The Last Modern: A Life of Herbert Read* (1990); *Herbert Read reassessed*, ed. D. Goodway (1998). Jason Harding (*The 'Criterion'*) calculates that Read wrote 68 book reviews, 4 articles, and 5 poems for the *Criterion*.

**Maurice Reckitt** (1888–1980): Anglo-Catholic and Christian socialist writer; editor of *Christendom: A Quarterly Journal of Christian Sociology*, 1931–50; primary organiser of the Oxford Summer School of Sociology. He was an outspoken contributor to Christian policy conferences; at his bidding, numerous thinkers and strategists – including Dorothy L. Sayers and Philip Mairet – participated in the discussion groups he promoted. 'The Christendom group stood for autochthonous thought and activity and was once denounced as "the rudest group in the Church of England"' (*ODNB*). Other works include *Faith and Society* (1932), *Maurice to Temple* (1947), and *Prospect for Christendom* (ed., 1945), to which TSE contributed. See Reckitt, *As It Happened: An Autobiography* (1941); V. A. Demant, *Maurice B. Reckitt: A Record of Vocation and Versatility* (1978); J. S. Peart-Binns, *Maurice B. Reckitt: A Life* (1988).

**Bruce Richmond** (1871–1964), literary editor, was educated at Winchester and New College, Oxford, and called to the Bar in 1897. But he never practised as a barrister; instead, George Buckle, editor of *The Times*, appointed him an assistant editor in 1899, and in 1902 he assumed the editorship of the fledgling *Times Literary Supplement*, which he commanded for thirty-five years. During this period, the 'Lit Sup.' established itself as the premier academic and critical periodical in Britain. He was knighted in 1935. See 'Sir Bruce Richmond' (obit.), *The Times*, 2 Oct. 1964. TSE, who was introduced to Richmond in 1919, enthused to his mother that writing the leading article for the *TLS* was the highest honour 'in the critical world of literature'. In a tribute, he recalled Richmond's 'bird-like alertness of eye, body and mind . . . It was from Bruce Richmond that I learnt editorial standards . . . I learnt from him that it is the business of an editor to know his contributors personally, to keep in touch with them and to make suggestions to them. I tried [at the *Criterion*] to form a nucleus of writers (some of them, indeed, recruited from the *Times Literary Supplement*, and introduced to me by Richmond) on whom I could depend, differing from each other in many things, but not in love of literature and seriousness of purpose . . . It is a final tribute to Richmond's genius as an editor that some of his troupe of regular contributors (I am thinking of myself as well as of others) produced some of their most distinguished critical essays as leaders for the *Literary Supplement* . . . Good literary criticism requires good editors as well as good critics. And Bruce Richmond was a great editor' ('Bruce Lyttelton Richmond', *TLS*, 13 Jan. 1961, 17).

**Michael Roberts** (1902–48), critic, editor, poet, was educated at King's College, London (where he read chemistry), and at Trinity College, Cambridge (mathematics). In the 1930s he worked as a schoolmaster, in London and at the Royal Grammar School, Newcastle upon Tyne. After

WW2, during which he worked for the BBC European Service, he became Principal of the Church of England training college of St Mark and St John, Chelsea, London. He edited the anthologies *New Signatures* (1932) and *New Country* (1933); and *The Faber Book of Modern Verse* (1936). Other works include *The Modern Mind* (1937), *T. E. Hulme* (1938), *The Recovery of the West* (1941). In 1935 he married the critic and biographer Janet Adam Smith. See *A Portrait of Michael Roberts*, ed. T. W. Eason and R. Hamilton (1949); Jason Harding, *'The Criterion': Cultural Politics and Periodical Networks in Inter-War Britain* (2002).

TSE wrote after Roberts's death: 'His scientific bent and training were supplemented and corrected by a philosophic cast of mind; by critical abilities of a very high order; and by an imaginative gift which expressed itself in poetry of a meditative type. Such a combination of powers is unusual; and among men of letters of his generation it was unique. His first notoriety was due to the volume *New Signatures*, a presentation of the poetry which was beginning to attract attention in the late nineteen-twenties; a book which seemed to promise him the place of expositor and interpreter of the poetry of his generation. This book was followed in 1934 by *Critique of Poetry*, a collection of essays ranging between literary criticism, aesthetics and philosophy; then by *The Modern Mind*, a more coherent and profound examination of the age; by a study of T. E. Hulme, which remains the essential piece of bibliography for a man who occupied for his generation something like the place to which Roberts was entitled for his own; and finally, in 1941, by *The Recovery of the West*, an important essay in moral and sociological criticism . . . A little earlier . . . appeared *Orion Marches*, which contains, I think, some of the best of his poems.' Adam Smith to TSE, Good Friday 1949: 'I told Michael, after I had seen you in September, that you had said "I love Michael". He came back to it more than once – "I had not known he had felt that".'

**A. L. Rowse** (1903–97), Cornish historian, was educated at Christ Church, Oxford, and elected a Prize Fellow of All Souls in 1925. He was a lecturer at Merton College, 1927–30, and taught also at the London School of Economics. His books include *Sir Richard Grenville of the Revenge* (1937), *William Shakespeare: A Biography* (1963), *Simon Forman: Sex and Society in Shakespeare's Age* (1974), and *All Souls in My Time* (1993), and poetry gathered up in *A Life* (1981). Though he failed in 1952 to be elected Warden of All Souls, he was elected a Fellow of the British Academy in 1958 and made a Companion of Honour in 1997. See Richard Ollard, *A Man of Contradictions: A Life of A. L. Rowse* (1999), and *The Diaries of A. L. Rowse*, ed. Ollard (2003). TSE, who for a while knew him as 'Al', wrote to Geoffrey Curtis on 1 May 1944: 'Rowse is an old friend of mine, and a very touching person: the suppressed Catholic and the rather less suppressed Tory (with a real respect for Good Families), the miner's son and the All Souls Fellow, the minor poet and the would-be politician, the proletarian myth and the will-to-power, are always at odds in a scholarly retiring mind and a frail body. He is also very patronising, and one likes it.' Rowse for his part saluted Eliot as 'nursing father to us all', and he dedicated *The Expansion of Elizabethan England* (1955) to 'T. S. Eliot who gave me my first introduction to the world of letters'.

**William Saroyan** (1908–81), Armenian-American writer from Fresno, California, was author of *The Daring Young Man on the Flying Trapeze* (1934). Novelist, playwright, screenwriter, essayist, Saroyan became a prolific author: successes included *Inhale and Exhale* (short fictions, 1936), and *The Time of Your Life* (play, 1939), winner of the Pulitzer Prize (declined) and the New York Drama Critics' Circle Award, and adapted for a 1948 movie starring James Cagney.

**Stephen Spender** (1909–95), poet and critic, won a rapid reputation with his first collection *Poems* (F&F, 1933), following an appearance in Michael Roberts's anthology *New Signatures* (1932). He cultivated friendships with some of the foremost younger writers of the period, including WHA, Christopher Isherwood, John Lehmann, and J. R. Ackerley. For a brief while in the 1930s he joined the Communist Party and went to Spain to serve the Republican cause. With Cyril Connolly he set up the magazine *Horizon* in 1940. In the post-war years he was to be a visiting professor at a number of American universities, and he undertook trips on behalf of the British Society for Cultural Freedom, the Congress for Cultural Freedom, and PEN. He served, too, as poetry consultant to the Library of Congress, 1965–6. For fourteen years from 1953 he was co-editor of the magazine *Encounter*, which – as it was ultimately proven – was from the start the beneficiary of funding from the CIA.

Other works include *The Destructive Element* (1935), *Forward from Liberalism* (1937), *World within World* (autobiography, 1951), *Collected Poems* (1955), *The Struggle of the Modern* (1963), *The Thirties and After* (1978), *New Selected Journals 1939–1995*, ed. Lara Feigel and John Sutherland with Natasha Spender (2012), and *The Temple* (novel, 1989). See also John Sutherland, *Stephen Spender: The Authorized Biography* (2004). He was instrumental in setting up *Index on Censorship* in 1971, and was Professor of English at University College, London, 1970–5. He was elected Companion of Literature by the Royal Society of Literature (1977), and knighted in 1983.

**Geoffrey Tandy** (1900–69) – marine biologist specialising in algology – served towards the end of WW1 in the Royal Field Artillery, studied forestry at Oxford, and became Assistant Keeper of Botany at the Natural History Museum, London, 1926–48. After joining the Navy in 1939, he was engaged throughout the war as a code-breaker at Bletchley Park; this was followed by a period at the Foreign Office, 1948–54. In the 1930s he wrote a 'Broadcasting Chronicle' for the *Criterion*; and he also did broadcast readings for the BBC (including the first reading of TSE's *Practical Cats* on Christmas Day 1937: see 'Masters of the Microphone', *Radio Times*, 19 Jan. 1939). Tandy, who was tall, skinny and big-bearded, earned this mention in the Auden–MacNeice 'Last Will and Testament': 'item, a box of talc / To Geoffrey Tandy in case he shaves again'. In 1923 Tandy married Doris (Polly), and they had three children – Richard, Alison, Anthea – and became close friends of TSE, who was chosen as godfather to Anthea (one of the dedicatees of *Old Possum's Book of Practical Cats*). Tandy's second wife was Maire McDermott. See too Miles Geoffrey Thomas Tandy, 'A Life in Translation: Biography and the Life of Geoffrey Tandy' (MA thesis, Institute of Education, Univ. of Warwick, Sept. 1995); and David Collard, 'Old Possum and the limbs of satan' http://davidjcollard.blogspot.co.uk/2013/06/old-possum-and-limbs-of-satan.html.

**Walter Frederick Tomlin** (1914–88): writer and administrator. Educated at Brasenose College, Oxford, he joined the British Council and served in Iraq, Turkey, France and Japan. Anglo-Catholic in religion, he wrote a study of Simone Weil; a book on R. G. Collingwood; and he edited volumes on WL, Arnold Toynbee and Charles Dickens. He was President of the Dickens Fellowship, 1987–8, and served on the executive committee of international PEN. His memoir *T. S. Eliot: A Friendship* appeared in 1988.

**Charles Williams** (1886–1945), novelist, poet, playwright, religious and theological writer; historical biographer; critic; member of the Inklings; went to work for Oxford University Press in 1908 and remained there, in positions of increasing editorial seniority, for the rest of his career. His oeuvre embraces novels – 'spiritual shockers', as he styled them – including

*War in Heaven* (1930), *The Greater Trumps* (1932), *Descent into Hell* (F&F, 1937), and *All Hallows' Eve* (F&F, 1945); and non-fiction and theological writings including *The Descent of the Dove: A Short History of the Holy Spirit in the Church* (1939) – which TSE thought 'one of the most interesting and readable books on any theological subject that I have ever read' – and *The Figure of Beatrice* (1943): 'at once a good introduction to Dante and to the thought of Charles Williams'. See Grevel Lindop, *Charles Williams: The Third Inkling* (2015); Philip Zaleski and Carol Zaleski, *The Fellowship: The Literary Lives of the Inklings: J. R. R. Tolkien, C. S. Lewis, Owen Barfield, Charles Williams* (2015).

**John Dover Wilson** (1881–1969): literary and textual scholar; Professor of Education, King's College, London, 1924–35; Regius Professor of Rhetoric and English Literature, Edinburgh, 1935–45. Renowned as editor of the New Cambridge Shakespeare, 1921–66. His works include *Shakespeare's Hand in the Play of 'Sir Thomas More'* (1923); *The Essential Shakespeare* (1932); *The Fortunes of Falstaff* (1943); and *Shakespeare's Happy Comedies* (1962).

**Virginia Woolf** (1882–1941), novelist, essayist and critic, was author of *Jacob's Room* (1922), *Mrs Dalloway* (1925), and *To the Lighthouse* (1927); *A Room of One's Own* (1928), a classic of feminist criticism; and *The Common Reader* (1925). Daughter of the biographer and editor Leslie Stephen (1832–1904), she married Leonard Woolf in 1912, published her first novel *The Voyage Out* in 1915, and founded the Hogarth Press with her husband in 1917. The Hogarth Press published TSE's *Poems* (1919), *The Waste Land* (1923), and *Homage to John Dryden* (1923). TSE published in the *Criterion* Woolf's essays and talks including 'Kew Gardens', 'Character in Fiction', and 'On Being Ill'. Woolf became a friend and correspondent; her diaries and letters give first-hand accounts of Eliot. Woolf wrote to her sister Vanessa Bell, 22 July 1936: 'I had a visit, long ago, from Tom Eliot, whom I love, or could have loved, had we both been in the prime and not in the sere; how necessary do you think copulation is to friendship? At what point does "love" become sexual?' (*Letters*, vol. 6). Eliot wrote in 1941 that Woolf 'was the centre, not merely of an esoteric group, but of the literary life of London. Her position was due to a concurrence of qualities and circumstances which never happened before, and which I do not think will ever happen again. It maintained the dignified and admirable tradition of Victorian upper middle-class culture – a situation in which the artist was neither the servant of the exalted patron, the parasite of the plutocrat, nor the entertainer of the mob – a situation in which the producer and the consumer of art were on an equal footing, and that neither the highest nor the lowest.' To Enid Faber, 27 Apr. 1941: '[Virginia] was a personal friend who seemed to me (mutatis considerably mutandis) like a member of my own family; and I miss her dreadfully, but I don't see her exactly as her relatives see her, and my admiration for the ideas of her milieu – now rather old-fashioned – is decidedly qualified.' See further Hermione Lee, *Virginia Woolf* (1996).

**William Butler Yeats** (1865–1939): Irish poet and playwright; Nobel Laureate. According to TSE, he was 'one of those few whose history is the history of their own time, who are part of the consciousness of an age' (*On Poetry and Poets*). TSE met Yeats soon after his arrival in London, but despite their mutual admiration of EP, they had little contact until 1922, when TSE told OM that Yeats was 'one of the very small number of people with whom one can talk profitably of poetry'. In his review of *Per Amica Silentia Lunae*, TSE said 'One is never weary of the voice, though the accents are strange' ('A Foreign Mind', *Athenaeum*, 4 July 1919). He was keen to publish Yeats in the *Criterion*: see 'A Biographical Fragment', in *Criterion* 1 (July 1923), 'The Cat and the Moon', 2 (July 1924), 'The Tower', 5 (June 1927). Yeats was instinctively opposed to TSE's work, but he discussed it at length in his introduction to the *Oxford Book of Modern Verse* (1936), and declared after the publication of *The Waste Land* that he found it 'very beautiful' (Jan. 1923). Valerie Eliot told Francis Warner, 21 Sept. 1966: 'There is very little correspondence between the two poets in my files and, curiously enough, in more than fifteen years I only heard my husband speak of Yeats occasionally and he said that no particular meeting remained in his mind. They had, of course, met many times – and there was the vicarious association when Pound was acting as the Irishman's secretary – but it was a formal friendship, due partly, perhaps, to the difference of age.' See further Michael Butler Yeats, 'Eliot and Yeats: A Personal View', in *The Placing of T. S. Eliot,* ed. Jewel Spears Brooker (1991), 169–84; Roy Foster, *Yeats: A Life*: I *The Apprentice Mage* (1997), II *The Arch-Poet* (2003).

# INDEX OF CORRESPONDENTS
# AND RECIPIENTS

Gill, Eic, 481
Gough, Edward P., 331–2
Gough, Lionel, 140
Graham, Gerald, 336–7, 522–3
Granville-Barker, Harley, 681–2
Gregory, Benjamin, 231–2
Gregory, Horace, 237–8
Gregory, Wilma, 705–6, 733–4
Grierson, John, 415
Grieve, C. M. ('Hugh MacDiarmid'), 790–1,
  890, 953–4
Grigson, Geoffrey, 132, 546, 572–3, 956–7,
  991–2
Guggenheim Foundation, The, 293
Guinness, Bryan, 592
Gunn, Daisy, 558–9

Haigh-Wood, Maurice, 74–5, 208–9*, 647,
  786–7, 902–4, 907–8, 928, 930–3, 951–3
Harris, Charles, 94–5
Harrison, G. B., 364–5
Harvey, Evelyn M., 996–7
Hassall, Christopher, 18
Hawkins, A. Desmond, 30–1, 468–9, 480,
  581–2, 614–15, 621–3, 755, 768–70,
  862–3, 929–30, 936–7, 987–8
Hayward, John, 16–17, 63, 66, 71*, 76–7,
  81–2, 89–90, 91–2, 114, 132–4, 154–5,
  227–8, 250, 310–11, 341, 347–8, 361,
  373, 404–5, 453–4, 465, 469–70, 470,
  473, 494, 534, 536, 555, 562, 563, 586–7,
  603–5, 606–7, 610–13, 618–19, 626–7,
  634, 649, 662, 671, 673, 674, 710–11,
  732, 738–9, 799–800, 860, 864–5, 874–5,
  878, 879, 934, 976–7, 1006–7, 1010,
  1019
Hebert, A. G., 41–2, 57–8, 186
Henn, T. R., 98–9, 289–90
Hennecke, Hans, 354–5
Heppenstall, Rayner, 51–2, 60–1, 165,
  182–3, 225–6, 743, 798–9
Hicks, Granville, 88–9
Higginson, G. F., 303–4, 926–7, 928–9,
  934–5, 972–3, 975–6, 986–7
Hindmarsh, L. K., 759–60
Hinkley, Susan, 53–5, 97–8, 889–90
Hodgson, Ralph, 947, 982, 985
Home Office: H. M. Undersecretary of State,
  Aliens' Department, 378
Hood, Frederic, 209–10
Hopkins, Mabel, 1009
Hoskyns, Edwyn, 396–7, 418
Husain, I., 100–1, 984–5
Hutchinson, Mary, 39–40, 742, 821
Huxley, Aldous, 218–19, 294–5, 919–20

Iovetz-Tereshchenko, N. M., 369, 550–1
Iremonger, F. A., 380–1, 439
Isherwood, Christopher, 508

Jackson, H. David, 626
Jolas, Eugene, 663
Jones, Cheslyn, P. M., 299–300
Jones, P. M. Mansell, 403–4
Joyce, James, 55–6, 120–1, 166, 195, 223,
  267, 295, 337, 357–8, 384, 836
Joyce, Lucia, 51*

Kahane, Jack, 47–8
Kallen, Horace, 1004
Kauffer, E. McKnight, 773, 774
Keynes, John Maynard, 591, 990–1
Knights, L. C., 283–4

Lang, Cosmo Gordon, Archbishop of York,
  then of Canterbury, 735–6
Lansdale, Henry Nelson, 899–900
Laughlin, James, 19–20, 104–5, 552, 580–1,
  725
Leadbitter, Nicolette, 75
Leeper, Janet, 95–6
Léger, Alexis St-Léger (St-John Perse), 579–
  80, 634–5, 682–3
Léon, Paul, 265, 601–2, 731–2, 751–3,
  766–7
Levertoff, Denise, 175–6
Lewis, C. McKenzie, Jr, 102–3
Lewis, Wyndham, 289, 746, 873
Lloyds Bank: The Manager, 936

Macaulay, Rose, 449
MacCarthy, Desmond, 92–3, 1011–13
MacCurdy, John T., 244*
MacDonagh, Donagh, 84, 111, 326–7, 974
Macdonald, Angus, 466–7, 530–1
MacIntyre, A. H., 350
MacKenzie, John C., 583
Mackenzie, Kenneth, 333–4, 349
Maclagan, Eric, 860–1
Macmillan & Co., Messrs, 946
Macmurray, John, 734–5
MacNeice, Louis, 43, 207, 228–9, 266, 277,
  323, 386–7, 448, 459–62, 574, 668–9,
  671–2, 676–7, 727, 751, 969–70, 1005
McPherrin, Jeanette, 334–6, 360, 539–40
Madge, Charles, 483–5, 524
Mairet, Philip, 5–6, 280, 313–14, 557–8,
  728, 774–5, 820, 866–8
Manton, Guy, 411
Manwaring, Elizabeth, 48–9, 82–3
Maritain, Jacques, 917, 918–19, 962–3

# GENERAL INDEX

Brancusi, Constantin: *Sculpture for the Blind*, 859n
Brémond, Abbé Henri, 167
Bressey, Sir Charles: Report ('London Traffic Improvement'), 914–15, 920–1
Breton, André: *Position politique du surréalisme*, 5n
Breton, André, 250
Brett, Virginia, 454
Bridges, Robert: *Collected Poems*, 178, 193
Bridie, James (pen name of Osborne Henry Mavor), 557n
Bridson, D. G., 302n; broadcast version of *TWL*, 745n, 747n, 749n, 750n, 760–1, 762n; *Prospero and Ariel*, 761n
Brinton, Henry: sends Church manifesto to TSE, 393
British Broadcasting Corporation (BBC): poetry readings, 326; talks on 'Christian Life and Work' conferences, 380n; TSE's broadcast talks, 431, 439, 441, 445; broadcasts TSE's cat poems, 716–18, 805; broadcasts *TWL*, 747n, 760; fees to TSE for broadcasts of poems, 888n
British Drama League, 897n
British Red Cross Society: fund-raising event, 500n
Britten, Benjamin, 262n, 727n
Broad, A. Moxon (solicitor), 255
Bromage, Bernard W.: on T. E. Lawrence, 162
Bronowski, Jacob, **724n**
Brooke, Rupert, 537
Brooke-Pechell, Sir Augustus, 7th Baronet, 681n
Brooks, Cleanth, **536n**; essay on *TWL*, 536–8
Brown, Harry, **901n**, 992, 1018
Brown, Spencer Curtis, 423n
Browne, E. (Elliott) Martin, **1032**; earnings, 377; in Cambridge with TSE, 470; and medieval religious drama, 550; and SS's *Trial of a Judge*, 653, 680; recommends seeing *Mourning Becomes Electra*, 723; and TSE's revision of *MiC*, 748; TSE sends *FR* to, 800, 802, 804; comments on *FR*, 837–40, 844–7, 864; and John Gielgud's interest in *FR*, 941; and publication of *FR*, 967; dines with TSE and John Gielgud, 976, 978n; and production of *FR*, 978, 979n, 995n; *Babel: A Dramatic Poem*, 128; *The Making of T. S. Eliot's Plays*, 702n, 800n, 844n, 967n, 976n, 978n
Browne, Sir Thomas: *Pseudodoxia Epidemica*, 449n

Browning, Robert, 12, 818
Brunner, Emil, 504, 642n
Buber, Martin: *Die Frage an den Einzelnen*, 396, 418
Buber, Max, 504
Buchner, Georg: *Dantons Tod* (trans. SS and Goronwy Rees), 881
Budapest: production of *MiC*, 377n
Buddha, Gautama, 417n
Bulgakoff, Father Sergius, 181, 186, 443; *The Lamb of God*, 186
Bulwer-Lytton, Victor, 2nd Earl of Lytton: on establishment of National Theatre, 795
Bunting, Basil, 221n, **328**, 1020n, 1021
Burns, Robert, 556
Burns, Tom F., **338n**; sends Ann Bowes Lyon poems to TSE, 485–7; TSE dines with, 604, 622n; and Speaight's *Thomas Becket*, 850, 856
'Burnt Norton', 40n, 76n, 168n, 183n, 201, 291
Burra, Peter, 327n
Burton, Basil, 82
Busson, Abbé, 993n
Bussy, Dorothy, **15n**, 628, 642n
Butchart, Montgomery, **388n**; on Robert Sutherland's novel, 594; TSE writes to, 741; TSE recommends John Reid to, 758; and Ronald Duncan, 825; and Henry Miller's *Plasma and Magma*, 830
Butler, Nicholas Murray, 551
Butts, Mary (Mrs Aitken), 434n, **512–13n**, 533; 'Mappa Mundi' (story), 512–13
Byron, George Gordon, 6th Baron, 123–4, 339, 386, 406, 408, 541

Cadoux, Arthur Temple: *Jesus and Civil Government*, 565, 584
Caetani, Camillo, 716
Caetani, Marguerite, **1008n**; and *Anabase*, 1009
Calder-Marshall, Arthur, 468
Cameron, Alan, 405
Cameron, Allen, 781n
Cameron, Elizabeth, 89
Camoens Prize/Prémio Camões (Portugal), 843–4, 878–9, 884
Campion, Edmund, 856n
Canby, Henry S., 544n
'Cape Ann', 19n
Cape, Jonathan (publisher), 212n, 219n, 240, 572
Carew Hunt, R. W., 534
Carlow, George Lionel Seymour Dawson-Damer, Viscount: publishes part of JJ's

Cyriax, Dr Anna, 931
Czechoslovakia: Germany annexes, 966n

Dalbiez, Roland: *La méthode psycho-analytique et la doctrine Freudienne*, 280, 558n
Dalí, Salvador, 423
Dano-British Association, 660
Dante Alighieri, 185n, 217, 497n, 539
D'Arcy, Martin, 1033–4; and conversions to Catholicism, 13; discussions with de la Bedoyère, 186n; reviews Huxley's *Eyeless in Gaza*, 247–8; and Abdication Crisis, 520
Dark, Sidney: and Leeper's *England and the British*, 96; and Oxford conference on Church, Community and State, 641; alarm at anti-Semitism, 999, 1001n
darts (game), 311
Das, Prafulla, 983n
Davidson, Angus: notifies TSE of Mary Butts's death, 533
Davidson, Donald, 536n
Davies, Hugh Sykes, 91n, 279n, 1078
Davies, Idris: TSE comments on poems, 771; *Gwalia Deserta*, 772n
Davis, Philip, 351
Dawson, Christopher, 85, 215, 267, 478, 1027, 1033; *Christianity and Sex*, 576, 706n; *The Making of Europe*, 998
Dawson, Geoffrey, 562
Dawson, Ian, 979n
Day Lewis, Cecil: TSE criticises writing, 370; suggested for Elizabeth Bowen's short story collection, 391; speaks at fund-raising event, 500n; TSE proposes to write history of literature from Marxist viewpoint, 545; LW declines to release poems for F&F publication, 703
Dazzi, M. T., 688n
de la Bedoyère, Michael, 186n
de la Mare, Richard, 514n; reads Hassall's poem, 18; as director of Faber & Faber, 257n; MacDonagh on, 327n; and JJ's *Work in Progress*, 337, 357, 766; and WHA's *Look Stranger*, 414n; and Medley as prospective illustrator, 452; on WHA's *Ascent of F6*, 462n; on David Jones's *In Parenthesis*, 622n; and Enid Starkie's *Rimbaud*, 714n; and Michael Roberts's *T. E. Hulme*, 747; and publication of SS's *Trial of a Judge*, 793; *Christian Polity*, 127n
de la Mare, Walter: Denise Levertov favours, 175n; and Barnett Freedman's dust jacket

to *Early One Morning*, 263n, 264, 324; in Elizabeth Bowen's anthology of short stories, 390; as judge for Royal Medal for Poetry, 412n; and George Barker, 734; Miss Swan's affection for, 1010n; 'Physic' (story), 455
de Maistre, Roy, 452n
Demant, Vigo Auguste, 1034–5; Every criticises over Social Credit, 113n; in Chandos Group, 136; on peace, 786, 797–8; and JMM's conversion, 831n; report on Oxford Conference, 892–3; proposes rival magazine to *Theology*, 955, 960; (ed.) *Faith that Illuminates*, 126
Dennis, Forbes, 205n
Dent, E. J., 699
Dent, J. M. (publishers), 111
d'Erlanger, Emile Beaumont: translates *MiC* with Cattaui, 352, 361, 375, 377, 613
Desclée de Brouwer (publisher), 962n, 963n, 965, 993
Deutsch, Babette, 327
'Development of Shakespeare's Verse, The: Two Lectures', 670n, 682n
Devlin, Denis, 79, 1012
*Dhammapada*, The: trans. Irving Babbitt, 243, 497n, 617
Dickens, Yvonne S., 908n
Dickinson, Emily, 70
Dickinson, Patric, 233n, 403n
Dillon, Dr Frederick, 931n, 986n
Dismorr, Jessica, 17n
Distributist League, 313
Dix, Dom Gregory, 955–6
Dobrée, Bonamy, 1035–6; returns to England, 5; appointed Professor of English at Leeds, 38, 123; descent from Dermot Macmorragh, 77; speaks well of Susan Hinkley, 97; and TSE's visit to USA, 339; TSE visits in Leeds, 757; disparages Leavis, 862; and Every's idea for education and the Moot, 943n; edits *Troilus and Cressida*, 982; 'English Poetic Drama', 813; 'Notes on Shakespeare's Verse', 756; 'T. S. Eliot: A Personal Reminiscence', 385n
Dobrée, Georgina, 123, 167, 386, 408
Dobrée, Valentine (née Gladys May Brooke-Pechell), 408, 681n
Dodd Mead (music publishers), 698n
Dodds, E. R., 228, 266n
Dollfuss, Engelbert, 450n
Dolphin Books, London, 167n
Donne, John, 64n, 65, 82, 88n, 89n, 100, 468

letter to *Time* magazine on review of *MiC*, 850–2; and VHE's confinement to asylum, 930n; proposes public office for TSE on 50th birthday, 958n

Eliot, Marian Cushing (TSE's sister), 246n, 1017

Eliot, Martha May, 516

Eliot, Mary Caroline, 567n

Eliot, Mather Greenleaf, 311n

Eliot, Minna Charlotte Sessinghaus, 688

Eliot, Samuel, 134n

Eliot, Samuel Ely, 311n

Eliot, Theresa, 382n, 501–2

Eliot, Thomas Dawes, **263n**

Eliot, Thomas Hopkinson (TSE's cousin), 959n

Eliot, Thomas Lamb, **263n**, 559n, 588n

Eliot, (Esmé) Valerie (TSE's second wife): on 'the Heaviside Layer' in *Cats*, 99n; on TSE's visit to Little Gidding, 213n; enquires about Rotha film with TSE, 262n; on TSE's wish to meet Agatha Christie, 430n; conversation with ALR, 669n; on TSE's Shakespeare lectures, 670n; on Léger's *Anabase*, 729n; on WL's portrait of TSE, 874n; confirms TSE not visiting VHE at Northumberland House, 930; on VHE's confinement to asylum, 932n, 934n

Eliot, Vivien (Vivienne; TSE's first wife; née Haigh-Wood), **1038**; treatment of TSE, 10n; sends Christmas cards in TSE's name, 52; enquires of GCF about TSE's health, 205–6; meets TSE, 208; lets flat to music student, 246; visit to USA, 246, 255; joins Eliot's Club, 257nn; TSE encounters and flees from, 305; finances, 315n, 647, 787, 911, 932, 933–5; requests removal of piano, 315; complains of being followed, 407; supposed sale of TSE's books, 586n; retains some of TSE's books, 648; mental disturbance, 909–10; TSE's payments to support, 927–9, 932n, 935–6, 975; as voluntary patient in French sanatorium, 927; TSE authorises final committal to asylum (Northumberland House), 928–35; rental payments, 935n; writes to Janes, 951; attempts to escape from asylum, 972–3, 975n; move to alternative home, 973, 975; official Receiver appointed, 975

Eliot, William Greenleaf: informs TSE of More's death, 559; sends biography of father to TSE, 688

Eliot House, Cambridge, Mass., 204, 419, 420, 434, 525, 541n, 648, 986n

Eliot's Club, London, 257n, 259, 384

Elizabeth (housekeeper), 563, 565, 606–7

*Elizabethan Essays*, 217

'Elldrop and Appleplex', 383

Elliot family (Scotland): character, 133–4, 172, 648

Elliott, R. M., 525n

Elsmith, Dorothy Olcott, **345n**

Elton, Oliver, 464n

Eluard, Paul, 282

Emperor's Gate (No. 11), Kensington, 534n, 536, 563, 577

Empson, William, **194n**; introduction to Kitamura's essay, 81n; co-edits *Experiment*, 108n; TSE recommends for university post in Egypt, 284; spends evening with JDH and TSE, 347n; and Mass Observation, 485n; proposes book on Buddhas, 636; books sent to in China, 906; *The Face of the Buddha*, ed. Rupert Arrowsmith, 637n; 'Villanelle', 488

English Association, 180, 670n, 828

English Church Union, 286–7, 322; Book Committee, 94n, 286, 333–4, 349

*English Review, The* (later *New English Review Magazine*), 95

English Verse Speaking Association, 610

'Epistle, An' (parody), 672

Epstein, Jacob, 747

Erasmus, Desiderius, 206

Ervine, St John, 242n

Esher, Oliver Sylvain Baliol Brett, 3rd Viscount, 500n

*Essays Ancient and Modern*, 77, 102, 126, 129, 183n, 192, 2117

*Essays and Studies* (magazine), 80n

*Europäische Revue*, 570

Evans, Edith, 848n

Evans, Myfanwy (Mrs John Piper): 'A Japanese Tale', 471–2

Every, George, **1038**; as potential author, 42n; contributes to *Christendom*, 130; recommends Cheslyn P. M. Jones to write to TSE, 299n; Festschrift for, 339n; on TSE's confessor, 359n; on Bethell, 479n; produces *MiC*, 511; and Abdication Crisis, 520; TSE comments on poems, 521; reviews Ingram's *Christianity – Right or Left?*, 538, 564; and Fr Kelly's lecture notes, 542; on *The English Renaissance*, 666; sends Norman Nicholson poems to TSE, 667; and JMM's conversion, 830–1; mentors Tomlin, 861; and JMM's report on first Moot, 875; arranges summer lectures at Swanwick, 915; on education and the Moot, 943; and Demant's

Irvine, Harry, 129, 139, 184
Irving, Sir Henry, 792n
Isaacs, Jack, **93n**
Isherwood, Christopher, 508n; collaborates with WHA, 198n, 370n, 391, 414, 508n; considered for Bowen's short story anthology, 391; revisions to *Ascent of F6*, 462n; makes alterations to *Ascent of F6*, 508; on SS's *Trial of a Judge*, 661n; travels to China with WHA, 679n; lecture on behalf of Group Theatre, 762n
Isherwood, Henry, 606

Jackson, H. David: enquires about Chorus in *MiC*, 626
Jackson, Holbrook, 314n
Jacobi, Derek, 489n
James, D. G., 479n
James, Henry, 355, 434, 443; *The Turn of the Screw*, 842n, 869
James VI, King of Scotland: *The Kingis Quair*, 466–7, 520, 530, 544, 608, 628
Janes, W. L.: pension, 189; on practical jokes, 227; size of feet, 449n; in hospital, 711, 973–4, 976, 1018; and VHE's properties, 932; VHE requests help from, 951; ill health, 952
Jaquin, Noel, 788
'Jellicle and Other Cats' (broadcast), 888n
Jenkins, W. B., 257n
Jennings, Humphrey, 485n
Jennings, Richard, 341, 454, 671n
Jenyns, Soame, 1007
Jerrihoppers (Gerry & Mabel Hopkins), 645, 649, 1006, 1010, 1014
Jerrold, Douglas, 95, 799n
Jessop, T. E., 380n
Jews: in Nazi Germany, 419n; and anti-Semitism in Britain, 999–1000
Joachim, H. H., 924
Joad, C. E. M., 915
John, Augustus: resigns from Royal Academy, 874n
John of the Cross, St, 168, 183, 922
Johnson, Lionel, 150n, 196–7
Johnson, Samuel: *Prayers and Meditations*, 872
Johnston, Denis, 593n, 1012
Johnstone, William, 987n
Johst, Hanns, 877n
Jolas, Eugene, 55n, **663n**; sends questionnaire to TSE, 663
Jolas, Maria, 55–6, 67–8, 166
Jones, Alun, 12n
Jones, Caradog, 502n

Jones, Cheslyn P. M., **299n**
Jones, David, 604, 612; *The Anathemata*, 622n; *In Parenthesis*, 621
Jones, Henry Arthur, 766
Jones, P. M. Mansell, **403n**
Jonesport, Maine, 398
Jouhandeau, Marcel: *Véronicana*, 15
Jouve, Pierre-Jean, 483n, 922; 'Grandeur Actuelle de Mozart', 744n
Joyce, James, **1045–6**; TSE defends against Burke Savage, 39; and daughter Lucia's illustrations, 47n; reputation, 152; Petitjean on, 163; and TSE's visit to Paris, 195, 223; Paul Léon meets and works with, 265n; TSE reimburses, 267, 295; Caresse Crosby publishes poems, 275, 572; Niall Montgomery's article on, 327n; in Copenhagen, 357–8; extracts published by Lord Carlow, 602, 616, 731–2, 766, 836n; affinity with David Jones, 622n; analysed, 622n; unpublished parts published by *Criterion*, 763; eyesight problems, 836; and printing of *Work in Progress*, 836; *Time* magazine on, 851n; calls F&F 'Feeler and Fumbler', 1010n; *Anna Livia Plurabella*, 265n; 'Dubliners', 39n; *Finnegans Wake*, 663n; 'From a Banned Writer to a Banned Singer', 357n; *Haveth Childers Everywhere*, 47n, 265n; *Our Exagmination*, 120, 122n, 138n, 160, 166; *Tales Told*, 265n; *Ulysses*, 67n, 120n, 123, 152, 154n, 157, 357, 434, 483, 767n; *Work in Progress*, 55, 67, 163, 223, 295, 337, 384, 475, 601–2, 616, 731–2, 751–2, 766
Joyce, Lucia, 47n, **51n**, 56, 67–8, 267, 345, 368, 616n

Kafka, Franz: *The Trial*, 854n
Kahane, Jack, **47n**; and EP's review of *Tropic of Cancer*, 20n; and Henry Miller's collection of stories and essays, 553n; publishes Anaïs Nin, 599n; and Durrell's *Black Book*, 626n, 653n, 806, 810n, 997n; and Henry Miller's *Max and the White Phagocytes*, 651n
Kallen, Horace Meyer, 526, **1004n**
Kauffer, E. McKnight: illustrates *Marina*, 344n; TSE enquires about job for Barker, 773; birthday, 781n
Keats, John, 91
Kelham: Society of the Sacred Mission, 57n, 287, 299n, 532–3, 564, 604
Kelly, Bernard, 799
Kelly, Gerald, 803

Maury, Pierre, 630n
Max Müller, Friedrich, 274n
Mazower, André, 114
Medley, Robert, 207n, 451, 7727n
Melville, Herman: *Moby-Dick* (broadcast serial), 970
Melville, Robert, **918n**
Menasce, Jean de (Pierre de Menasce), **32n**; and French translation of *MiC*, 32
Mendizábal, Alfred, 880, 919, 962n
Mendonça, Antonio de, **164n**; and Salazar's *Une Révolution dans La Paix*, 639, 686
Menjou, Adolphe, 430
Mensbrugghe, Fr Alexis van der: *Dyad to Triad*, 44n
Mercury Theatre, Notting Hill, 140, 462n, 1018
Merriman, Roger Bigelow ('Frisky'), 988
*Mesures* (magazine), 357
Micklem, Nathaniel, 964
Middleton, Richard, 391
Middleton, Thomas, 283; *The Revenger's Tragedy* (earlier attrib. to Cyril Tourneur), 489
Miles, Hamish, 434
*Milky Way, The* (film), 430
Miller, A. W. R., 566n
Miller, Francis P., 27n
Miller, Gilbert, 850n
Miller, Henry, **1049**; affair with Bachman, 7n; FVM contrasts with Djuna Barnes's *Nightwood*, 142; *Hamlet* correspondence with Fraenkel, 383n, 389n, 425, 1020n; Hawkins on, 480; on D. H. Lawrence, 585, 704, 806, 812, 829n; sends Anaïs Nin works to TSE, 593, 598n, 623; writes on Hans Reichel, 623n; esteems Durrell, 624n; payments from *Criterion*, 651; meets TSE, 654n, 1020n; justifies own persistence, 684n; and Durrell's *Black Book*, 779n, 806; edits Villa Seurat Series, 810n; on speedy judging and liking, 829n; associated with Durrell, 997n; in London, 1019; *Black Spring*, 7, 389, 480n, 553, 668; *Max and the White Phagocytes*, 651, 667, 684; *Scenario*, 652; *Tropic of Cancer*, 20, 668, 806, 1020n
Miller, Dr Reginald, 909–10, 911n, 975
Millin, Sarah Gertrude, 1010
Milton, John, 90, 123, 180, 402–3
miracles: TSE on, 125
Mirfield: College of the Resurrection, 44n, 532, 757, 960
Mirrlees, Emily Lina (née Moncrieff; 'Mappie/Mappy'), **329n**, 494

Mirrlees, Hope, **21n**, 329n, 351, 494, 612
Mirrlees, William Julius, 329n
Moberly, Sir Walter, 380n, 448, 824n
Moe, Henry Allen, 357n, **1020n**, 1021; *Plasma and Magma*, 830n
Moller, Fri., 358
Monk, Geoffrey, 727n
Monnier, Adrienne, 120n, 138n, 229n
Monophysite heresy, 157
Monro, Alida, 271, 311
Monroe, Harriet, 399n
Montgomery, James, 327n
Montgomery, Neil, 820n, 866–8
Montgomery, Niall, 327, **1003n**, 1011; self-description, 1012–13
Moore, Henry, 17n
Moore, Hubert Stuart, 87
Moore, Leonard, 513
Moore, Marianne, 282, 792
Moore, Merrill, **886n**; recommends Robert Lowell to TSE, 954
Moot, the, 823–4, 866n, 876, 943, 953n, 960, 1025
Morand, Paul, 496n
More, Louis T., 231, 302
More, Paul Elmer, **1048–9**; TSE sends copy of *FLA* to, 11; fund in honour of, 101; praises TSE's 'Religion and Literature', 129n; religious beliefs, 137n, 442n; illness, 271, 302, 381, 472, 499n; and TSE's visit to USA, 302, 381; contributes to *American Review*, 442; TSE writes tribute on, 445n, 459, 499; TSE's paper on, 445; death, 559; on proposed anthology of children's verse, 679n; W. G. Eliot on, 688; essay on, 811; *The Greek Tradition*, 445n; *Marginalia*, 500
More, Sir Thomas, 894n
Morgan, Charles, 654n
Morley, Christina McLeod, 8n, 223–4, 229, 645, 803, 863
Morley, Christopher, 9
Morley, Dr Frank (FVM's father), **690n**
Morley, Frank Vigor, **1050–1**; in USA, 67, 804; nickname ('the Whale'), 69n; on *TWL* portrait of TSE, 73n; praises Arthur Wheen, 81n; returns to England (March 1936), 114–15; on Djuna Barnes's *Nightwood*, 141–4, 151, 154n, 159, 179, 191, 239, 320; EP on, 144; in Paris, 160; and Saroyan's *Inhale & Exhale*, 161, 263n; and publication and editing of *Criterion*, 168, 307n, 356; on Edmund Wilson, 174n; interviews Djuna Barnes at Faber office, 197n; and Cape's publishing WHA and SS

appointment with TSE, 826; declines to give talk at Swanwick, 915

*Portfolio: An Intercontinental Review*, 275n

Portland, William John Bentinck, 6th Duke of: *Men Women and Things*, 733, 739

Portmeirion, North Wales, 498n

Portugal, 79, 864–5, 874, 877–9, 881

Potter, Phyllis M., **361n**

Potter, Stephen: *The Muse in Chains*, 16n

Pound, Dorothy (EP's wife), **305n**; TSE on, 355, 782; undergoes surgical operation, 972

Pound, Ezra, **1055–6**; political and economic interests and beliefs, 20, 104; annotates and corrects *TWL*, 86; letter to Pollinger, 103; poems in *Faber Modern Verse*, 137, 145, 191, 207, 234; on Robert Bridges, 178; Connolly on influence on TSE, 193n; on Lionel Johnson, 197; Phyllis Bottome's article on, 205; helps TSE with Italian poets, 217; fascism, 234n; TSE comments on cantos, 355; sends new cantos to TSE for *Criterion*, 398–401, 417, 460, 505; and 'the Old Bitch on the monument', 417, 422; TSE sends cheques to, 471, 489, 505n; disparages Flint, 510n; and TSE's views on Dante, 539; and John Reid, 568–9, 746; works analysed, 622n; GCF urged to write to in Latin, 644; on Leopardi, 689; Durrell dismisses, 704; on TSE's entertaining Olga Rudge, 711n; passes on request for TSE to write on nature of stage plays, 736; fondness for Japanese, 737; TSE on, 782; translates children's book, 806; on music publishing, 807n, 808n, 816, 822, 853; puzzles TSE on music, 807; and *Southern Review* publication of *Symposium* articles, 862n; anthology of French poets, 923; death of mother-in-law, 971–2, 982; in London, 982; *ABC of Reading*, 828n; *Canto XLVI*, 104n; 'D'Artagnan Twenty Years After', 398n; *XI Cantos*, 923; *Fifth Decade of the Cantos*, 505–6; *Guide to Kulchur*, 599n, 689, 828, 853, 859; 'Less Polite Essays', 817n; *Make It New*, 192n, 517; *Money*, 103; *Polite Essays*, 69n, 150n, 192n, 517, 585n, 817n; *The Spirit of Romance*, 217; *Ta Hio*, 145; *30 Cantos*, 59

Power, William, **22n**

Powys, Llewellyn: essay on Thomas Shoel, 236

'Practical Cat, The', 709n

Prather, Elmer, 657n

Praz, Mario, **1056**; 'T. S. Eliot and Dante', 217n, 539

Prewett (churchman), 535

Price, Fran, 370n

Priestley, J. B.: *Time and the Conways*, 66n

Prince, F. T., **482n**; recommends Swart's *The Interpreter* to TSE, 994; at dinner party with Sarah Gertrude Millin, 1010n; 'A Muse for William Maynard' (poem), 482; *Poems*, 482n, 772; 'The Tears for William Maynard', 561

*Princeton Alumni Weekly*, 445n, 459

Pringle, Alan J., 602n, 625n, 667, 871, 996

Prokosch, Frederic, 282, **791n**; *The Carnival*, 898; *The Seven Who Fled*, 898

Propertius, 567

Proust, Marcel, 13, 404

*Prufrock*: Laughlin praises, 19n

Purdon, Louie, 973n

Purohit Swami, Shri, **588n**; translates *Upanishads* with WBY, 274n; and Patanjali's *Aphorisms*, 573, 588

Purves, John: and TSE's lecture on Cowley, 554

Pusey, Edward Bouverie, 922

Pusey House, Oxford, 349

Quennell, Peter, 341n, 774n, 811n, 979n

*Quia Amore Langueo*, 549

Quiller-Couch, Sir Arthur ('Q'), 38, 549n

Racine, Jean, 5

Radcliffe, Philip, 913n

*Radio Times* (magazine), 494

Raine, Kathleen, **259n**; 'The Taurus' (story), 279

Rambert, Dame Marie, **292n**

Randall, Sir Alec, **660n**

Randall, A. W. G.: sends Nicolette Leadbitter's poems to TSE, 75

Randolph, New Hampshire: Mount Crescent Hotel, 271

Random House (publishers), 324n, 325

'Rannoch, by Glencoe', 19n

Ransom, John Crowe, 536n, 560n, 954n

Ras, Daulat, 77

Raven, Charles Earle, 418n

Rawlinson, Captain, 535

Rawlinson, H. G.: *India*, 825n

Ray, Man: portrait of VW, 574n

Rea, Fred, **332n**

Read, Herbert, **1056–7**; TSE criticises, 5–6, 180; discovers Yorkshire cheese, 38; and publication of Heppenstall's book, 51n; on Shelley, 90; TSE invites to translate

Read, Herbert (*cont.*) Hofmannsthal, 121; and James Hanley, 182; on Heppenstall's poems, 225; and Elizabeth Bowen's short story anthology, 391; and surrealism, 469; and Hayward's wheelchair, 619; TSE suggests Henry Miller write to, 624; as prospective candidate for Norton Professorship, 678; TSE recommends to read Laurie Lee's poems, 734; and Tate's dramatisation of *Turn of the Screw*, 869; on *Old Possum's Book of Practical Cats*, 872; commends Robert Payne's translation of Pasternak to TSE, 983n; *Collected Essays in Literary Criticism*, 981n; *In Defence of Shelley and Other Essays*, 72n, 91n; *Poetry and Anarchism*, 819

Rebora, Piero, 1014

Reckitt, Maurice, 96, 136n, 215, 285, 313n, 444, 511, 522, 1057–8

Red Scotland Committee, 954

Redmond, William (Liam), 79, 84n

Reed, Revd D. V., 359n

Reed, John, 88–9

Rees, Goronwy, 622n, 881

Rees, Sir Richard, 106n

Reeve, Diana, 128

Reeves, James, 84

Reform Club, London, 645n

Reichel, Hans, 623n

Reid, Forrest, 327

Reid, John, 741, 746, 758, 807

Reith, John, Baron, 368n, 526

'Religion and Literature', 129

'Religious Drama: Medieval and Modern', 359, 550n, 603, 606n

Renaud-Thévenet, Mme (of Brussels), 621

*Revelation* (ed. John Baillie and Hugh Martin), 362n, 443, 496n, 623

Reynold, Gonzague de, 878, 879n

Rhondda, Margaret Haig Thomas, Viscountess, 1007, 1010

Rhys, Keridrych, 1012

Rice, Elmer: produces *MiC*, 9, 62

Richards, I. A., **291n**; TSE recommends C. M. Lewis to study under, 103; and Empson's application for post in Egypt, 285; praises Miss Lloyd-Thomas, 290; praises 'Burnt Norton', 291; judges poetry for Royal Medals, 412n; and WHA's King's Medal for Poetry, 562; Vincent Swart works under, 994

Richards, P. S.: TSE meets, 130, 181; reviews Babbitt's translation of *Dhammapada*, 243; meets TSE at Worthing, 854n; *On Being Human: New Shelburne Essays*,

382n; 'The Religious Philosophy of Paul Elmer More', 230n, 381n

Richardson, Maurice L., 449

Richmond, Sir Bruce Lyttelton, 1058; and review of *Nightwood*, 159n; TSE visits, 630n, 639; invites TSE to address Friends of Salisbury Cathedral, 818–19, 881

Richmond, Elena, Lady (née Rathbone): entertains TSE, 239; TSE reports to on visit to Wales, 644

Riddle, Donald Wayne, 396

Ridler, Anne, *see* Bradby, Anne Barbara

Ridler, Vivian, 457n, 896n

Ridley, Joyce: translates Lautréamont, 609

Rilke, Rainer Maria, 557

Rimbaud, Arthur, 609n, 714

Rivière, Jacques, 541

Roberts, Andrew D., 654n

Roberts, Evan, 630n

Roberts, Michael, 1058–9; and EP's poems in *Faber Modern Verse*, 137–8, 145, 191, 207, 234; mountaineering, 145; and Djuna Barnes's *Nightwood*, 159n; writes on T. E. Hulme, 233, 240, 278, 290, 655, 701, 730; TSE proposes review by Tomlin, 282; submits essays to TSE, 424; visits TSE, 566; birth of son, 654; sends poems to TSE, 654; and Norman Nicholson's poems, 667; reviews R. A. Wilson's *The Birth of Language*, 701; comments on BBC broadcast of *TWL*, 747, 749n, 762; and *Southern Review* publication of *Symposium* articles, 862n; on Macavity, 908; gives talk at Swanwick, 915; and Hawkins's Authors Guild Editions project, 936; proposes book on criticism, 950n; on Authors Guild committee, 987n; *Critique of Poetry*, 240, 435, 951; *The Modern Mind*, 240n, 278n, 435, 950n; *New Signatures* (ed.), 633n; 'The Poetry of T. S. Eliot', 240n; *T. E. Hulme*, 731n; *see also* Adam Smith, Janet; *Faber Book of Modern Verse*

Roberts, Sydney Castle, **293n**, 522n

Roché, Louis, 674n

Rochefoucauld, Edmée, Duchesse de la (née Frisch), 372, 378

Rochefoucauld, Jean, Duc de la, 372n

Rochester Cathedral, 359

*Rock, The*, 180n, 204n, 353, 420, 590, 900

Roditi, Edouard, 228, 378

Roger-Cornaz, Frédéric, 487–8, 496, 542, 547

*Room Service* (Marx Brothers film), 1007n

Roosevelt, Franklin D., 351, 356–7, 373n

translation of Buchner's *Dantons Tod* with Goronwy Rees, 881; contractual agreement with F&F, 968; *The Burning Cactus*, 167, 968; *Forward from Liberalism*, 296n; *The Still Centre* (poems), 968n, 1008; *The Temple*, 645n; *Trial of a Judge* (play), 296n, 389n, 652, 661, 680, 764n, 794, 852; *Vienna*, 661n

Spens, Sir Will, **287n**, 397, 470, 906n, 989

Spottiswoode, Raymond: *A Grammar of Film*, 415n

Spurr, Barry, 359n

Staempfli, Edward, 475n, 483, 493

Stamp, Sir Josiah (later Baron), 627, 688

Stapledon, Olaf, **502n**

Starch, Daniel: constructs list of world's greatest books, 529n

Starkie, Enid: *Arthur Rimbaud*, 714–16

Stauffer, Thomas, 835n

Stawar, A., 392n

Stead, William Force: and TSE's *A Song for Simeon*, 64; and Robert Sencourt's 'Consecration of Genius', 464, 493; essay on Christopher Smart and Thomas Gray, 725–6; sends Johnson's *Prayers and Meditations* to TSE, 872

Stearns, Major Thomas, 53

Stein, Gertrude, 105, 513n

Stephen, Judith, 664n, 675n

Stern, William, 525

Stevens, Wallace: 'Bantams in Pinewoods', 149n

Stewart, Charles W. ('Goblin'), 71n, **256n**, 367, 753, 812, 985

Stewart, Hugh Fraser, **211n**

Stewart, J. A., 228

Stone, Reynolds, 167

Stonehill, C. A.: acquires copy of Huxley's *Jonah* inscribed to TSE, 222n

Stonier, G. W.: 'The Mystery of Ezra Pound', 755, 769n

Stork, Charles Wharton, 371n

Storrs, Sir Ronald, 565

Strachey, Lytton, 487

Strand Film Company, 262n

Strauss, Bobby, 526

Street, A. G., 356n

Street, G. S., 356

Strickland, A. W., 977

Struve, Gleb, 516n

Stuart, Morna *see* Nicholas (Stuart), Morna

Student Christian Movement, 112n, 287, 332n, 696, 1007; *see also* Swanwick, Derbyshire

Student Movement House, London, 298n, 907

Sudetenland, 966n

Sullivan John, 357

Summers, Montague, **490n**

Suner, Senor, 919

surrealism, 5n, 14, 72n, 214, 469, 609n, 744n

Sutherland, Robert *see* Garioch, Robert

Sutro, Alfred, 766

Swabey, Henry S.: EP on, 144n, 149; criticises Chichester Theological College, 895; 'The English Church and Money', 135n, 476–8

Swan, Ethel, 726, 732, 1010

Swanwick, Derbyshire: SCM Conferences, 112, 287, 298n, 306

Swart, Edward Vincent: *The Interpreter*, 994

'Sweeney Agonistes', 62n, 168n, 180, 383, 900, 1015

Swinburne, Algernon Charles, 31, 870n

Swingler, Randall, 769

Symons, Julian, 738n; (ed.) *Twentieth Century Verse*, 738n, 783

Symons, W. Travers, 136n, 558

Szik, Alexander, 377n

Talcott, Priscilla Stearns, 53

Tallents, Stephen, 811

Talybont, Cardiganshire, 1017

Tandy family: send birthday greetings to TSE, 989n

Tandy, Alison: TSE sends poems to, 3n, 26n, 70, 374, 436, 561, 692, 739–40; TSE's Christmas present for, 729n; TSE unable to attend birthday party, 739, 1024; sends cat drawings to TSE, 827; TSE thanks for Christmas present, 1022

Tandy, Anthea, 723

Tandy, Doris (Polly), **68n**; invites TSE to visit, 507–8, 605, 612; TSE enquires about Christmas presents, 723, 1013; sends gift to TSE, 754–5

Tandy, Geoffrey, **1061**; commentates on film *The Way to the Sea*, 262n; suggested as possible reader for BBC, 321, 326n; TSE proposes introducing to JDH, 453; shows Myfanwy Evans's 'Japanese Tale' to TSE, 471–2; friendship with TSE, 489; drinking with TSE and George Barnes, 494; and Ian Cox's *Desire Provoketh*, 570n; Morleys visit, 645; and broadcasts of TSE cat poems, 717n, 888; TSE enquires about family Christmas presents, 729; and Jaquin's hand-reading, 788n; on *Burnt*